Lecture Notes in Computer Science 12648

Advanced Research in Computing and Software Science

Subline of Lecture Notes in Computer Science

More information about this subseries at http://www.springer.com/series/7407

Nobuko Yoshida (Ed.)

Programming Languages and Systems

30th European Symposium on Programming, ESOP 2021
Held as Part of the European Joint Conferences
on Theory and Practice of Software, ETAPS 2021
Luxembourg City, Luxembourg, March 27 – April 1, 2021
Proceedings

Springer

Editor
Nobuko Yoshida
Imperial College
London, UK

ISSN 0302-9743 ISSN 1611-3349 (electronic)
Lecture Notes in Computer Science
ISBN 978-3-030-72018-6 ISBN 978-3-030-72019-3 (eBook)
https://doi.org/10.1007/978-3-030-72019-3

LNCS Sublibrary: SL1 – Theoretical Computer Science and General Issues

This Springer imprint is published by the registered company Springer Nature Switzerland AG
The registered company address is: Gewerbestrasse 11, 6330 Cham, Switzerland

ETAPS Foreword

Welcome to the 24th ETAPS! ETAPS 2021 was originally planned to take place in Luxembourg in its beautiful capital Luxembourg City. Because of the Covid-19 pandemic, this was changed to an online event.

ETAPS 2021 was the 24th instance of the European Joint Conferences on Theory and Practice of Software. ETAPS is an annual federated conference established in 1998, and consists of four conferences: ESOP, FASE, FoSSaCS, and TACAS. Each conference has its own Program Committee (PC) and its own Steering Committee (SC). The conferences cover various aspects of software systems, ranging from theoretical computer science to foundations of programming languages, analysis tools, and formal approaches to software engineering. Organising these conferences in a coherent, highly synchronised conference programme enables researchers to participate in an exciting event, having the possibility to meet many colleagues working in different directions in the field, and to easily attend talks of different conferences. On the weekend before the main conference, numerous satellite workshops take place that attract many researchers from all over the globe.

ETAPS 2021 received 260 submissions in total, 115 of which were accepted, yielding an overall acceptance rate of 44.2%. I thank all the authors for their interest in ETAPS, all the reviewers for their reviewing efforts, the PC members for their contributions, and in particular the PC (co-)chairs for their hard work in running this entire intensive process. Last but not least, my congratulations to all authors of the accepted papers!

ETAPS 2021 featured the unifying invited speakers Scott Smolka (Stony Brook University) and Jane Hillston (University of Edinburgh) and the conference-specific invited speakers Işil Dillig (University of Texas at Austin) for ESOP and Willem Visser (Stellenbosch University) for FASE. Inivited tutorials were provided by Erika Ábrahám (RWTH Aachen University) on analysis of hybrid systems and Madhusudan Parthasarathy (University of Illinois at Urbana-Champaign) on combining machine learning and formal methods.

ETAPS 2021 was originally supposed to take place in Luxembourg City, Luxembourg organized by the SnT - Interdisciplinary Centre for Security, Reliability and Trust, University of Luxembourg. University of Luxembourg was founded in 2003. The university is one of the best and most international young universities with 6,700 students from 129 countries and 1,331 academics from all over the globe. The local organisation team consisted of Peter Y.A. Ryan (general chair), Peter B. Roenne (organisation chair), Joaquin Garcia-Alfaro (workshop chair), Magali Martin (event manager), David Mestel (publicity chair), and Alfredo Rial (local proceedings chair).

ETAPS 2021 was further supported by the following associations and societies: ETAPS e.V., EATCS (European Association for Theoretical Computer Science), EAPLS (European Association for Programming Languages and Systems), and EASST (European Association of Software Science and Technology).

The ETAPS Steering Committee consists of an Executive Board, and representatives of the individual ETAPS conferences, as well as representatives of EATCS, EAPLS, and EASST. The Executive Board consists of Holger Hermanns (Saarbrücken), Marieke Huisman (Twente, chair), Jan Kofron (Prague), Barbara König (Duisburg), Gerald Lüttgen (Bamberg), Caterina Urban (INRIA), Tarmo Uustalu (Reykjavik and Tallinn), and Lenore Zuck (Chicago).

Other members of the steering committee are: Patricia Bouyer (Paris), Einar Broch Johnsen (Oslo), Dana Fisman (Be'er Sheva), Jan-Friso Groote (Eindhoven), Esther Guerra (Madrid), Reiko Heckel (Leicester), Joost-Pieter Katoen (Aachen and Twente), Stefan Kiefer (Oxford), Fabrice Kordon (Paris), Jan Křetínský (Munich), Kim G. Larsen (Aalborg), Tiziana Margaria (Limerick), Andrew M. Pitts (Cambridge), Grigore Roşu (Illinois), Peter Ryan (Luxembourg), Don Sannella (Edinburgh), Lutz Schröder (Erlangen), Ilya Sergey (Singapore), Mariëlle Stoelinga (Twente), Gabriele Taentzer (Marburg), Christine Tasson (Paris), Peter Thiemann (Freiburg), Jan Vitek (Prague), Anton Wijs (Eindhoven), Manuel Wimmer (Linz), and Nobuko Yoshida (London).

I'd like to take this opportunity to thank all the authors, attendees, organizers of the satellite workshops, and Springer-Verlag GmbH for their support. I hope you all enjoyed ETAPS 2021.

Finally, a big thanks to Peter, Peter, Magali and their local organisation team for all their enormous efforts to make ETAPS a fantastic online event. I hope there will be a next opportunity to host ETAPS in Luxembourg.

February 2021

Marieke Huisman
ETAPS SC Chair
ETAPS e.V. President

Preface

Welcome to the 30th European Symposium on Programming! ESOP 2021 was originally planned to take place in Luxembourg. Because of the COVID-19 pandemic, this was changed to an online event. ESOP is one of the European Joint Conferences on Theory and Practice of Software (ETAPS). It is devoted to fundamental issues in the specification, design, analysis, and implementation of programming languages and systems.

This volume contains 24 papers, which the program committee selected among 79 submissions. Each submission received between three and five reviews. After an author response period, the papers were discussed electronically among the 25 PC members and 98 external reviewers. The nine papers for which the PC chair had a conflict of interest (11% of the total submissions) were kindly handled by Patrick Eugster.

The quality of the submissions for ESOP 2021 was astonishing, and very sadly, we had to reject many strong papers. I would like to thank all the authors who submitted their papers to ESOP 2021.

Finally, I truly thank the members of the program committee. I am very impressed by their insightful and constructive reviews – every PC member has contributed very actively to the online discussions under this difficult COVID-19 situation, and supported Patrick and me. It was a real pleasure to work with all of you! I am also grateful to the nearly 100 external reviewers, who provided their expert opinions.

I would like to thank the ESOP 2020 chair Peter Müller for his instant help and guidance on many occasions. I thank all who contributed to the organisation of ESOP– the ESOP steering committee and its chair Peter Thiemann as well as the ETAPS steering committee and its chair Marieke Huisman, who provided help and guidance. I would also like to thank Alfredo Rial Duran, Barbara König, and Francisco Ferreira for their help with the proceedings.

January 2021 Nobuko Yoshida

In the originally published version of the ESOP 2021 preface, in the last sentence, there was an error in the name of "Barbara König".This has now been corrected.

Preface

Welcome to the 30th European Symposium on Programming! ESOP 2021 was originally planned to take place in Luxembourg. Because of the COVID-19 pandemic, this was changed to an online event. ESOP is one of the European Joint Conferences on Theory and Practice of Software (ETAPS). It is devoted to fundamental issues in the specification, design, analysis, and implementation of programming languages and systems.

This volume contains 24 papers, which the program committee selected among 79 submissions. Each submission received between three and five reviews. After an author response period, the papers were discussed electronically among the 25 PC members and 98 external reviewers. The nine papers for which the PC chair had a conflict of interest (11% of the total submissions) were kindly handled by Patrick Cousot.

The quality of the submissions for ESOP 2021 was astonishing, and very sadly, we had to reject many strong papers. I would like to thank all the authors who submitted their papers to ESOP 2021.

Finally, I truly thank the members of the program committee. I am very impressed by their insightful and constructive reviews – every PC member has contributed very actively to the online discussions under this difficult COVID-19 situation, and supported Patrick and me. It was a real pleasure to work with all of you! I am also grateful to the nearly 100 external reviewers, who provided their expert opinions.

I would like to thank the ESOP 2020 chair Peter Müller for his instant help and guidance on many occasions. I thank all who contributed to the organisation of ESOP – the ESOP steering committee and its chair Peter Thiemann, as well as the ETAPS steering committee and its chair Marieke Huisman, who provided help and guidance. I would also like to thank [illegible], Barbara König, and Francisco Ferreira for their help with the proceedings.

January 2021 Nobuko Yoshida

In the originally published version of the ESOP 2021 preface, in the last sentence, there was an error in the name of "Barbara König". This has now been corrected.

Organization

Program Committee

Stephanie Balzer	CMU
Sandrine Blazy	University of Rennes 1 - IRISA
Viviana Bono	Università di Torino
Brijesh Dongol	University of Surrey
Patrick Eugster	Università della Svizzera italiana (USI)
Marco Gaboardi	Boston University
Dan Ghica	University of Birmingham
Justin Hsu	University of Wisconsin-Madison
Zhenjiang Hu	Peking University
Robbert Krebbers	Radboud University Nijmegen
Hongjin Liang	Nanjing University
Yu David Liu	SUNY Binghamton
Étienne Lozes	I3S, University of Nice & CNRS
Corina Pasareanu	CMU/NASA Ames Research Center
Alex Potanin	Victoria University of Wellington
Guido Salvaneschi	University of St. Gallen
Alan Schmitt	Inria
Taro Sekiyama	National Institute of Informatics
Zhong Shao	Yale University
Sam Staton	University of Oxford
Alexander J. Summers	University of British Columbia
Vasco T. Vasconcelos	University of Lisbon
Tobias Wrigstad	Uppsala University
Nicolas Wu	Imperial College London
Nobuko Yoshida	Imperial College London
Damien Zufferey	MPI-SWS

Additional Reviewers

Adamek, Jiri
Alglave, Jade
Álvarez Picallo, Mario
Ambal, Guillaume
Amtoft, Torben
Ancona, Davide
Atig, Mohamed Faouzi
Avanzini, Martin
Bengtson, Jesper
Besson, Frédéric
Bodin, Martin
Canino, Anthony
Casal, Filipe
Castegren, Elias
Castellan, Simon
Chakraborty, Soham
Charguéraud, Arthur
Chen, Liqian

Chen, Yixuan
Chini, Peter
Chuprikov, Pavel
Cogumbreiro, Tiago
Curzi, Gianluca
Dagnino, Francesco
Dal Lago, Ugo
Damiani, Ferruccio
Derakhshan, Farzaneh
Dexter, Philip
Dezani-Ciancaglini, Mariangiola
Emoto, Kento
Fernandez, Kiko
Fromherz, Aymeric
Frumin, Daniil
Gavazzo, Francesco
Gordillo, Pablo
Gratzer, Daniel
Guéneau, Armaël
Iosif, Radu
Jacobs, Jules
Jiang, Hanru
Jiang, Yanyan
Jongmans, Sung-Shik
Jovanović, Dejan
Kaminski, Benjamin Lucien
Kerjean, Marie
Khayam, Adam
Kokologiannakis, Michalis
Krishna, Siddharth
Laird, James
Laporte, Vincent
Lemay, Mark
Lindley, Sam
Long, Yuheng
Mamouras, Konstantinos
Mangipudi, Shamiek
Maranget, Luc
Martínez, Guido
Mehrotra, Puneet
Miné, Antoine
Mordido, Andreia
Muroya, Koko
Murray, Toby
Møgelberg, Rasmus Ejlers
New, Max
Noizet, Louis
Noller, Yannic
Novotný, Petr
Oliveira Vale, Arthur
Orchard, Dominic
Padovani, Luca
Pagani, Michele
Parthasarathy, Gaurav
Paviotti, Marco
Power, John
Poças, Diogo
Pérez, Jorge A.
Qu, Weihao
Rand, Robert
Rouvoet, Arjen
Sammler, Michael
Sato, Tetsuya
Sterling, Jonathan
Stutz, Felix Matthias
Sutre, Grégoire
Swamy, Nikhil
Takisaka, Toru
Toninho, Bernardo
Toro, Matias
Vene, Varmo
Viering, Malte
Wang, Di
Zufferey, Damien

Contents

The Decidability of Verification under PS 2.0

Parosh Aziz Abdulla[1], Mohamed Faouzi Atig(✉)[1], Adwait Godbole[2], S. Krishna[2], and Viktor Vafeiadis[3]

[1] Uppsala University, Uppsala, Sweden
{parosh,mohamed_faouzi.atig}@it.uu.se
[2] IIT Bombay, Mumbai, India
{adwaitg,krishnas}@cse.iitb.ac.in
[3] MPI-SWS, Kaiserslautern, Germany
viktor@mpi-sws.org

Abstract. We consider the reachability problem for finite-state multi-threaded programs under the *promising semantics* (PS 2.0) of Lee et al., which captures most common program transformations. Since reachability is already known to be undecidable in the fragment of PS 2.0 with only release-acquire accesses (PS 2.0-ra), we consider the fragment with only relaxed accesses and promises (PS 2.0-rlx). We show that reachability under PS 2.0-rlx is undecidable in general and that it becomes decidable, albeit non-primitive recursive, if we bound the number of promises. Given these results, we consider a bounded version of the reachability problem. To this end, we bound both the number of promises and of "*view-switches*", i.e., the number of times the processes may switch their local views of the global memory. We provide a code-to-code translation from an input program under PS 2.0 (with relaxed and release-acquire memory accesses along with promises) to a program under SC, thereby reducing the bounded reachability problem under PS 2.0 to the bounded context-switching problem under SC. We have implemented a tool and tested it on a set of benchmarks, demonstrating that typical bugs in programs can be found with a small bound.

Keywords: Model-Checking · Memory Models · Promising Semantics

1 Introduction

An important long-standing open problem in PL research has been to define a weak memory model that captures the semantics of concurrent memory accesses in languages like Java and C/C++. A model is considered good if it can be implemented efficiently (i.e., if it supports all usual compiler optimizations and its accesses are compiled to plain x86/ARM/Power/RISCV accesses), and is easy to reason about. To address this problem, Kang et al. [16] introduced the *promising semantics*. This was the first model that supported basic invariant reasoning, the DRF guarantee, and even a non-trivial program logic [30].

In the promising semantics, the memory is modeled as a set of timestamped messages, each corresponding to a write made by the program. Each process/thread records its own view of the memory—i.e., the latest timestamp for

N. Yoshida (Ed.): ESOP 2021, LNCS 12648, pp. 1–29, 2021.
https://doi.org/10.1007/978-3-030-72019-3_1

each memory location that it is aware of. A message has the form $(x, v, (f, t], V)$ where x is a location, v a value to be stored for x, $(f, t]$ is the timestamp interval corresponding to the write and V is the local view of the process who made the write to x. When reading from memory, a process can either return the value stored at the timestamp in its view or advance its view to some larger timestamp and read from that message. When a process p writes to memory location x, a new message with a timestamp larger than p's view of x is created, and p's view is advanced to include the new message. In addition, in order to allow load-store reorderings, a process is allowed to *promise* a certain write in the future. A promise is also added as a message in the memory, except that the local view of the process is not updated using the timestamp interval in the message. This is done only when the promise is eventually fulfilled. A *consistency* check is used to ensure that every promised message can be *certified* (i.e., made fulfillable) by executing that process on its own. Furthermore, this should hold from any future memory (i.e., from any extension of the memory with additional messages). The quantification prevents deadlocks (i.e., processes from making promises they are not able to fulfil). However, the unbounded number of future memories, that need to be checked, makes the verification of even simple programs practically infeasible. Moreover, a number of transformations based on global value range analysis as well as register promotion were not supported in [16].

To address these concerns, Lee et al. developed a new version of the promising semantics, PS 2.0 [22] PS 2.0 simplifies the consistency check and instead of checking the promise fulfilment from all future memories, PS 2.0 checks for promise fulfilment only from a specially crafted extension of the current memory called capped memory. PS 2.0 also introduces the notion of reservations, which allows a process to secure a timestamp interval in order to perform a future atomic read-modify-write instruction. The reservation blocks any other message from using that timestamp interval. Because of these changes, PS 2.0 supports register promotion and global value range analysis, while capturing all features (process local optimizations, DRF guarantees, hardware mappings) of the original promising semantics. Although PS 2.0 can be considered a semantic breakthough, it is a very complex model: it supports two memory access modes, relaxed (`rlx`) and release-acquire (`ra`), along with promises, reservations and certifications.

Let PS 2.0-rlx (resp. PS 2.0-`ra`) be the fragment of PS 2.0 allowing only relaxed (`rlx`) (resp. release-acquire (`ra`)) memory accesses. A natural and fundamental question to investigate is the verification of concurrent programs under PS 2.0. Consider the reachability problem, i.e., whether a given configuration of a concurrent finite-state program is reachable. Reachability with only `ra` accesses has already been shown to be undecidable [1], even without promises and reservations. That leaves us only the PS 2.0-rlx fragment, which captures the semantics of concurrent 'relaxed' memory accesses in programming languages such as Java and C/C++. We show that if an unbounded number of promises is allowed, the reachability problem under PS 2.0-rlx is undecidable. Undecidability is obtained with an execution with only 2 processes and 3 context switches, where a context is a computation segment in which only one process is active.

Then, we show that reachability under PS 2.0-rlx becomes decidable if we bound the number of promises at any time (however, the total number of promises made within a run can be unbounded). The proof introduces a new memory model with higher order words LoHoW, which we show equivalent to PS 2.0-rlx in terms of reachable states. Under the bounded promises assumption, we use the decidability of the coverability problem of well structured transition systems (WSTS) [7,13] to show that the reachability problem for LoHoW with bounded number of promises is decidable. Further, PS 2.0-rlx without promises and reservations has a non-primitive recursive lower bound. Our decidability result covers the relaxed fragment of the RC11 model [20,16] (which matches the PS 2.0-rlx fragment with no promises). Given the high complexity for PS 2.0-rlx and the undecidability of PS 2.0-`ra`, we next consider a bounded version of the reachability problem. To this end, we propose a parametric under-approximation in the spirit of *context bounding* [9,33,21,26,24,29,1,3]. The aim of context bounding is to restrict the otherwise unbounded interaction between processes, and has been shown experimentally in the case of SC programs to maintain enough behaviour coverage for bug detection [24,29]. The concept of context bounding has been extended for weak memory models. For instance, for RA, Abdula et al. [1] proposed *view bounding* using the notion of view-switching messages and a translation that keeps track of the causality between different variables. Since PS 2.0 subsumes RA, we propose a bounding notion that extends view bounding.

Using our new bounding notion, we propose a source-to-source translation from programs under PS 2.0 to context-bounded executions of the transformed program under SC. The challenges in our translation differ a lot from that in [1], as we have to provide a procedure that (i) handles different memory accesses `rlx` and `ra`, (ii) guesses the promises and reservations in a non-deterministic manner, and (iii) verifies that promises are fulfilled using the capped memory.

We have implemented this reduction in a tool, PS2SC. Our experimental results demonstrate the effectiveness of our approach. We exhibit cases where hard-to-find bugs are detectable using a small view-bound. Our tool displays resilience to trivial changes in the position of bugs and the order of processes. Further, in our code-to-code translation, the mechanism for making and certifying promises and reservations is isolated in one module, and can easily be changed to cover different variants of the promising semantics.

For lack of space, detailed proofs can be found in [5].

2 Preliminaries

In this section, we introduce the notation that will be used throughout.

Notations. Given two natural numbers $i, j \in \mathbb{N}$ s.t. $i \leq j$, we use $[i, j]$ to denote $\{k \mid i \leq k \leq j\}$. Let A and B be two sets. We use $f : A \to B$ to denote that f is a function from A to B. We define $f[a \mapsto b]$ to be the function f' s.t. $f'(a) = b$ and $f'(a') = f(a')$ for all $a' \neq a$. For a binary relation R, we use $[R]^*$ to denote its reflexive and transitive closure. Given an alphabet Σ, we use Σ^* (resp. Σ^+) to denote the set of possibly empty (resp. non-empty) finite words (also called simple words) over Σ. A higher order word over Σ is an element of $(\Sigma^*)^*$ (i.e., word of words). Let $w = a_1 a_2 \cdots a_n$ be a simple word over Σ, we use $|w|$ to denote the length of w. Given an index i in $[1, |w|]$, we use $w[i]$ to denote the ith letter of w. Given two indices i and j s.t. $1 \leq i \leq j \leq |w|$, we use $w[i, j]$ to denote the word $a_i a_{i+1} \cdots a_j$. Sometimes, we see a word as a function from $[1, |w|]$ to Σ.

Program Syntax. The simple programming language we use is described in Figure 1. A program *Prog* consists of a set Loc of (global) variables or memory locations, and a set $\mathcal{P}$ of processes. Each process p declares a set $\mathsf{Reg}(p)$ of (local) *registers* followed by a sequence of labeled instructions. We assume that these sets of registers are disjoint and we use $\mathsf{Reg} := \cup_p \mathsf{Reg}(p)$ to denote their union. We assume also a (potentially unbounded) data domain Val from which the registers and locations take values. All locations and registers are assumed to be initialized with the special value $0 \in \mathsf{Val}$ (if not mentioned otherwise). An instruction $\mathfrak{i}$ is of the form $\lambda : \mathfrak{s}$ where λ is a unique label and $\mathfrak{s}$ is a statement. We use $\mathbb{L}_p$ to denote the set of all labels of the process p, and $\mathbb{L} = \bigcup_{p \in \mathcal{P}} \mathbb{L}_p$ the set of all labels of all processes. We assume that the execution of the process p starts always with a unique initial instruction labeled by λ^p_{init}.

$$
\begin{array}{l}
\mathit{Prog} ::= \texttt{var}\ x^*(\texttt{proc}\ p || \ldots || \texttt{proc}\ p) \\
\texttt{proc}\ p ::= \mathsf{Reg}(p)\ \mathfrak{i}^* \\
\mathfrak{i} ::= \lambda : \mathfrak{s} \\
\mathfrak{s} \in \mathsf{St} ::= \\
\quad \mathsf{skip} \quad |s; s \quad |\texttt{assume}(x = e) \\
\quad |\texttt{do}\ s^*\ \texttt{while}\ e \quad |\texttt{while}\ e\ \texttt{do}\ s^* \texttt{done} \\
\quad |\texttt{if}\ e\ \texttt{then}\ s\ \texttt{else}\ s \\
\quad |\$r := e \quad |\$r := x^o \quad |x^o := \$r \\
\quad |\$r := \mathbf{FADD}^{o,o}(x, v) \\
\quad |\$r := \mathbf{CAS}^{o,o}(x, v, v) \quad |\mathsf{SC\text{-}fence} \\
o \in \mathsf{Mode} ::= \mathsf{rlx}|\mathsf{ra}
\end{array}
$$

Fig. 1: Syntax of programs.

A write instruction is of the form $x^o = \$r$ assigns the value of register $\$r$ to the location x, and o denotes the access mode. If $o = \mathsf{rlx}$, the write is a *relaxed* write, while if $o = \mathsf{ra}$, it is a *release* write. A read instruction $\$r = x^o$ reads the value of the location x into the local register $\$r$. Again, if the access mode $o = \mathsf{rlx}$, it is a *relaxed* read, and if $o = \mathsf{ra}$, it is an *acquire* read. Atomic updates or RMW instructions are either compare-and-swap ($\mathbf{CAS}^{o_r, o_w}$) or $\mathbf{FADD}^{o_r, o_w}$. Both have a pair of accesses $(o_r, o_w \in \{\mathsf{rel}, \mathsf{acq}, \mathsf{rlx}\})$ to the same location – a read followed by a write. Following [22], $\mathbf{FADD}(x, v)$ stores the value of x into a register $\$r$, and adds v to x, while $\mathbf{CAS}(x, v_1, v_2)$ compares an expected value v_1 to the value in x, and if the values are same, sets the value of x to v_2. The old value of x is then stored in $\$r$. A *local* assignment instruction $\$r = e$ assigns to the register $\$r$ the value of e, where e is an expression over a set of operators, constants as well as the contents of the registers of the current process, but not referring to the set of locations. The fence instruction $\mathsf{SC\text{-}fence}$ is used to enforce sequential consistency if it is placed between two memory access operations. For simplicity, we will write $\texttt{assume}(x = e)$ instead of $\$r = x; \texttt{assume}(\$r = e)$. This notation is extended in the straightforward manner to conditional statements.

3 The Promising Semantics

In this section, we recall the promising semantics [22]. We present here $\mathsf{PS\ 2.0}$ with three memory accesses, *relaxed*, *release writes* (`rel`) and *acquire reads* (`acq`).

Read-modify-writes (RMW) instructions have two access modes - one for read and one for write. We keep aside the release and acquire fences (and subsequent access modes), since they do not affect the results of this paper.

Timestamps. PS 2.0 uses timestamps to maintain a total order over all the writes to the same variable. We assume an infinite set of timestamps Time, densely totally ordered by $\leq$, with 0 being the minimum element. A *view* is a timestamp function $V : \mathsf{Loc} \rightarrow \mathsf{Time}$ that records the largest known timestamp for each location. Let $\mathbb{T}$ be the set containing all the timestamp functions, along with the special symbol $\perp$. Let V_{init} represent the initial view where all locations are mapped to 0. Given two views V and V', we use $V \leq V'$ to denote that $V(x) \leq V'(x)$ for $x \in \mathsf{Loc}$. The merge operation $\sqcup$ between two views V and V' returns the pointwise maximum of V and V', i.e., $(V \sqcup V')(y)$ is the maximum of $V(y)$ and $V'(y)$. Let $\mathcal{I}$ denote the set of all intervals over Time. The timestamp intervals in $\mathcal{I}$ have the form $(f, t]$ where either $f = t = 0$ or $f < t$, with $f, t \in \mathsf{Time}$. Given an interval $I = (f, t] \in \mathcal{I}$, $I.\mathtt{frm}$ and $I.\mathtt{to}$ denote f, t respectively.

Memory. In PS 2.0, the memory is modelled as a set of concrete *messages* (which we just call messages), and *reservations*. Each message represents the effect of a write or a RMW operation and each reservation is a timestamp interval reserved for future use. In more detail, a message m is a tuple $(x, v, (f, t], V)$ where $x \in \mathsf{Loc}$, $v \in \mathsf{Val}$, $(f, t] \in \mathcal{I}$ and $V \in \mathbb{T}$. A reservation r is a tuple $(x, (f, t])$. Note that a reservation, unlike a message, does not commit to any particular value. We use $m.\mathsf{loc}$ ($r.\mathsf{loc}$), $m.\mathtt{val}$, $m.\mathtt{to}$ ($r.\mathtt{to}$), $m.\mathtt{frm}$ ($r.\mathtt{frm}$) and $m.\mathsf{View}$ to denote respectively x, v, t, f and V. Two elements (either messages or reservations) are said to be *disjoint* ($m_1 \# m_2$) if they concern different variables ($m_1.\mathsf{loc} \neq m_2.\mathsf{loc}$) or their intervals do not overlap ($m_1.\mathtt{to} \leq m_2.\mathtt{frm} \vee m_1.\mathtt{frm} \geq m_2.\mathtt{to}$). Two sets of elements M, M' are disjoint, denoted $M \# M'$, if $m \# m'$ for every $m \in M, m' \in M'$. Two elements m_1, m_2 are *adjacent* denoted $\mathsf{Adj}(m_1, m_2)$ if $m_1.\mathsf{loc} = m_2.\mathsf{loc}$ and $m_1.\mathtt{to} = m_2.\mathtt{frm}$. A memory M is a set of pairwise disjoint messages and reservations. Let $\widetilde{M}$ be the subset of M containing only messages (no reservations). For a location x, let $M(x)$ be $\{m \in M \mid m.\mathsf{loc} = x\}$. Given a view V and a memory M, we say $V \in M$ if $V(x) = m.\mathtt{to}$ for some message $m \in \widetilde{M}$ for every $x \in \mathsf{Loc}$. Let $\mathbb{M}$ denote the set of all memories.

Insertion into Memory. Following [22], a memory M can be extended with a *message* (due to the execution of a write/RMW instruction) or a *reservation* m with $m.\mathsf{loc} = x$, $m.\mathtt{frm} = f$ and $m.\mathtt{to} = t$ in a number of ways:

Additive insertion $M \overset{A}{\hookleftarrow} m$ is defined only if (1) $M \# \{m\}$; (2) if m is a message, then no message $m' \in M$ has $m'.\mathsf{loc} = x$ and $m'.\mathtt{frm} = t$; and (3) if m is a reservation, then there exists a message $m' \in \widetilde{M}$ with $m'.\mathsf{loc} = x$ and $m'.\mathtt{to} = f$. The extended memory $M \overset{A}{\hookleftarrow} m$ is then $M \cup \{m\}$.

Splitting insertion $M \overset{S}{\hookleftarrow} m$ is defined if m is a message, and, if there exists a message $m' = (x, v', (f, t'], V)$ with $t < t'$ in M. Then M is updated to $M \overset{S}{\hookleftarrow} m = (M \backslash \{m'\} \cup \{m, (x, v', (t, t'], V)\})$.

Lowering Insertion $M \overset{L}{\hookleftarrow} m$ is only defined if there exists m' in M that is identical to $m = (x, v, (f, t], V)$ except for $m.\mathsf{View} \leq m'.\mathsf{View}$. Then, M is updated to $M \overset{L}{\hookleftarrow} m = M \setminus \{m'\} \cup \{m\}$.

Transition System of a Process. Given a process $p \in \mathcal{P}$, a state σ of p is defined by a pair (λ, R) where $\lambda \in \mathbb{L}$ is the label of the next instruction to be executed by p and $R : \mathsf{Reg} \rightarrow \mathsf{Val}$ maps each register of p to its current value. (Observe that we use the set of all labels $\mathbb{L}$ (resp. registers Reg) instead of $\mathbb{L}_p$ (resp. $\mathsf{Reg}\,(p)$) in the definition of σ just for the sake of simplicity.) Transitions between the states of p are of the form $(\lambda, R) \overset{t}{\underset{p}{\Rightarrow}} (\lambda', R')$ with t is on one of the following forms: ϵ, $\mathtt{rd}(o, x, v)$, $\mathtt{wt}(o, x, v)$, $\mathtt{U}(o_r, o_w, x, v_r, v_w)$, and SC-fence. A transition of the form $(\lambda, R) \xrightarrow[p]{\mathtt{rd}(o,x,v)} (\lambda', R')$ denotes the execution of a read instruction of the form $\$r = x^o$ labeled by λ where (1) λ' is the label of the next instructions that can be executed after the instruction labelled by λ, and (2) R' is the mapping that results from updating the value of the register $\$r$ in R to v. The transition relation $(\lambda, R) \overset{t}{\underset{p}{\Rightarrow}} (\lambda', R')$ is defined in similar manner for the other cases of t where $\mathtt{wt}(o, x, v)$ stands for a write instruction that writes the value v to x, $\mathtt{U}(o_r, o_w, x, v_r, v_w)$ stands for a RMW that reads the value v_r from x and write v_w to it, SC-fence stands for a SC-fence instruction, and ϵ stands for the execution of the other local instructions. Observe that o, o_r, o_w are the access modes which can be $\mathtt{rlx}$ or $\mathtt{ra}$. We use $\mathtt{ra}$ for both release and acquire. Finally, we use $(\lambda, R) \overset{t}{\underset{p}{\rightarrow}} (\lambda', R')$, with $t \neq \epsilon$, to denote that $(\lambda, R) \overset{\epsilon}{\underset{p}{\Rightarrow}} \sigma_1 \overset{\epsilon}{\underset{p}{\Rightarrow}} \cdots \overset{\epsilon}{\underset{p}{\Rightarrow}} \sigma_n \overset{t}{\underset{p}{\Rightarrow}} \sigma_{n+1} \overset{\epsilon}{\underset{p}{\Rightarrow}} \cdots \overset{\epsilon}{\underset{p}{\Rightarrow}} (\lambda', R')$.

Machine States. A machine state $\mathcal{MS}$ is a tuple $((\mathsf{J}, \mathsf{R}), \mathsf{VS}, \mathsf{PS}, M, G)$, where $\mathsf{J} : \mathcal{P} \mapsto \mathbb{L}$ maps each process p to the label of the next instruction to be executed, $\mathsf{R} : \mathsf{Reg} \rightarrow \mathsf{Val}$ maps each register to its current value, $\mathsf{VS} = \mathcal{P} \rightarrow \mathbb{T}$ is the process view map, which maps each process to a view, M is a memory and $PS : \mathcal{P} \mapsto \mathbb{M}$ maps each process to a set of messages (called *promise* set), and $G \in \mathbb{T}$ is the global view (that will be used by SC fences). We use $\mathcal{C}$ to denote the set of all machine states. Given a machine state $\mathcal{MS} = ((\mathsf{J}, \mathsf{R}), \mathsf{VS}, \mathsf{PS}, M, G)$ and a process p, let $\mathcal{MS}{\downarrow}p$ denote $(\sigma, \mathsf{VS}(p), \mathsf{PS}(p), M, G)$, with $\sigma = (\mathsf{J}(p), \mathsf{R}(p))$, (i.e., the projection of the machine state to the process p). We call $\mathcal{MS}{\downarrow}p$ the process configuration. We use $\mathcal{C}_p$ to denote the set of all process configurations.

The initial machine state $\mathcal{MS}_{\text{init}} = ((\mathsf{J}_{\text{init}}, \mathsf{R}_{\text{init}}), \mathsf{VS}_{\text{init}}, \mathsf{PS}_{\text{init}}, M_{\text{init}}, G_{\text{init}})$ is one where: (1) $\mathsf{J}_{\text{init}}(p)$ is the label of the initial instruction of p; (2) $\mathsf{R}_{\text{init}}(\$r) = 0$ for every $\$r \in \mathsf{Reg}$; (3) for each p, $\mathsf{VS}(p) = V_{\text{init}}$ as the initial view (that maps each location to the timestamp 0); (4) for each p, the set of promises $\mathsf{PS}_{\text{init}}(p)$ is empty; (5) the initial memory M_{init} contains exactly one initial message $(x, 0, (0, 0], V_{\text{init}})$ per location x; and (6) the initial global view maps each location to 0.

Transition Relation. We first describe the transition $(\sigma, V, P, M, G) \underset{p}{\rightarrow} (\sigma', V', P', M', G')$ between process configurations in $\mathcal{C}_p$ from which we induce the transition relation between machine states.

Memory Helpers

(MEMORY : NEW)

$$\frac{}{(P,M) \xrightarrow{m} \left(P', M \overset{A}{\hookleftarrow} m\right)}$$

MEMORY FULFIL

$$\frac{\hookleftarrow \in \left\{\overset{S}{\hookleftarrow}, \overset{L}{\hookleftarrow}\right\}, P' = P \hookleftarrow m, M' = M \hookleftarrow m}{(P,M) \xrightarrow{m} (P' \backslash \{m\}, M')}$$

Process Helpers

$$\frac{\begin{array}{c} m = (x, -, (-,t], K) \in M \quad V(x) \leq t \\ o = \texttt{rlx} \Rightarrow V' = V[x \mapsto t] \\ o = \texttt{ra} \Rightarrow V' = V[x \mapsto t] \sqcup K \end{array}}{V \xrightarrow[\text{rd}]{o,m} V'}$$

$$\frac{\begin{array}{c} m = (x, -, (-,t], K) \in M, V(x) < t \\ o = \texttt{rlx} \Rightarrow K = \bot, o = \texttt{ra} \Rightarrow P(x) = \emptyset \wedge K = V' \\ (P,M) \xrightarrow{m} (P', M') \quad V' = V[x \mapsto t] \end{array}}{(V,P,M) \xrightarrow[\text{wt}]{o,m} (V', P', M')}$$

Process Steps

Read

$$\frac{\sigma \xrightarrow[p]{rd(o,x,v)} \sigma' \qquad m = (x, v, (-,-], \ -), \quad V \xrightarrow[\text{rd}]{o,m} V'}{(\sigma, V, P, M, G) \underset{p}{\rightarrow} (\sigma', V', P, M, G)}$$

Write

$$\frac{\sigma \xrightarrow[p]{wt(o,x,v)} \sigma' \qquad m = (x, v, (-,-], -), (V, P, M) \xrightarrow[\text{wt}]{o,m} (V', P', M')}{(\sigma, V, P, M, G) \underset{p}{\rightarrow} (\sigma', V', P', M', G)}$$

SC-fence

$$\frac{\sigma \xrightarrow[p]{\text{SC-fence}} \sigma'}{(\sigma, V, P, M, G) \underset{p}{\rightarrow} (\sigma', V \sqcup G, P, M, G \sqcup V)}$$

Promise

$$\frac{\begin{array}{c} m = (-,-,(-,-], K), \\ M' = M \overset{A}{\hookleftarrow} m, \ K \in M' \end{array}}{(\sigma, V, P, M, G) \underset{p}{\rightarrow} \left(\sigma, V, P \overset{A}{\hookleftarrow} m, M', G\right)}$$

Update

$$\frac{\begin{array}{c} \sigma \xrightarrow[p]{U(o_r, o_w, x, v_r, v_w)} \sigma'', m_r = (x, v_r, (-,t], \ -), \ m_w = (x, v_w, (t,-], -), \\ V \xrightarrow[\text{rd}]{o_r, m_r} V'', \ (V'', P, M) \xrightarrow[\text{wt}]{o_w, m_w} (V', P', M') \end{array}}{(\sigma, V, P, M, G) \underset{p}{\rightarrow} (\sigma', V', P', M', G)}$$

Fig. 2: A subset of PS 2.0 inference rules at the process level.

Process Relation. The formal definition of $\underset{p}{\rightarrow}$ is given in Figure 2. Below, we explain these inference rules. Note that the full set of rules can be found in [5].

Read A process p can read from M by observing a message $m = (x, v, (f, t], K)$ if $V(x) \leq t$ (i.e., p must not be aware of a later message for x). In case of a relaxed read $\texttt{rd}(\texttt{rlx}, x, v)$, the process view of x is updated to t, while for an acquire read $\texttt{rd}(\texttt{ra}, x, v)$, the process view is updated to $V[x \mapsto t] \sqcup K$. The global memory M, the set of promises P, and the global view G remain the same.

Write. A process can add a fresh message to the memory (MEMORY : NEW) or fulfil an outstanding promise (MEMORY : FULFILL). The execution of a write $\texttt{wt}(\texttt{rlx}, x, v)$) results in a message m with location x along with a timestamp interval $(-, t]$. Then, the process view for x is updated to t. In case of a release write $\texttt{wt}(\texttt{ra}, x, v)$) the updated process view is also attached to m, and ensures that the process does not have an outstanding promise on x. (MEMORY : FULFILL) allows to split a promise interval or lower its view before fulfilment.

Update. When a process performs a RMW, it first reads a message $m = (x, v, (f, t], K)$ and then writes an update message with $\texttt{frm}$ timestamp equal to t; that is, a message of the form $m' = (x, v', (t, t'], K')$. This forbids any other write to be placed between m and m'. The access modes of the reads and writes in the update follow what has been described for the read and write above.

Promise, Reservation and Cancellation. A process can non-deterministically *promise* future writes which are not release writes. This is done by adding a message m to the memory M s.t. $m\#M$ and to the set of promises P. Later, a relaxed write instruction can fulfil an existing promise. Recall that the execution of a release write requires that the set of promises to be empty and thus it can not be used to fulfil a promise. In the reserve step, the process reserves a timestamp interval to be used for a later RMW instruction reading from a certain message without fixing the value it will write. A reservation is added both to the memory and the promise set. The process can drop the reservation from both sets using the cancel step in non-deterministic manner.

SC fences. The process view V is merged with the global view G, resulting in $V \sqcup G$ as the updated process view and global view.

Machine Relation. We are ready now to define the induced transition relation between machine states. For machine states $\mathcal{MS} = ((J, R), VS, PS, M, G)$ and $\mathcal{MS}' = ((J', R'), VS', PS', M', G')$, we write $\mathcal{MS} \xrightarrow[p]{} \mathcal{MS}'$ iff (1) $\mathcal{MS}{\downarrow}p \xrightarrow[p]{} \mathcal{MS}{\downarrow}p$ and $(J(p'), VS(p'), PS(p')) = (J'(p'), VS'(p'), PS'(p'))$ for all $p' \neq p$.

Consistency. According to Lee et al. [22], there is one final requirement on machine states called *consistency*, which roughly states that, from every encountered machine state, all the messages promised by a process p can be *certified* (i.e., made fulfillable) by executing p on its own from a certain future memory (called capped memory), i.e., extension of the memory with additional reservation. Before defining consistency, we need to introduce capped memory.

Cap View, Cap Message and Capped Memory. The last element of a memory M with respect to a location x, denoted by $\overline{m}_{M,x}$, is an element from $M(x)$ with the highest timestamp among all elements of $M(x)$ and is defined as $\overline{m}_{M,x} = \max_{m \in M(x)} m.\mathtt{to}$. The *cap view* of a memory M, denoted by $\widehat{V}_M$, is the view which assigns to each location x, the $\mathtt{to}$ timestamp in the message $\overline{m}_{\widetilde{M},x}$. That is, $\widehat{V}_M = \lambda x.\overline{m}_{\widetilde{M},x}.\mathtt{to}$. Recall that $\widetilde{M}$ denote the subset of M containing only messages (no reservations). The *cap message* of a memory M with respect to a location x, is given by $\widehat{m}_{M,x} = (x, \overline{m}_{\widetilde{M},x}.\mathtt{val}, (\overline{m}_{M,x}.\mathtt{to}, \overline{m}_{M,x}.\mathtt{to}+1], \widehat{V}_M)$.

Then, the capped memory of a memory M, wrt. a set of promises P, denoted by $\widehat{M}_P$, is an extension of M, defined as: (1) for every $m_1, m_2 \in M$ with $m_1.\mathsf{loc} = m_2.\mathsf{loc}$, $m_1.\mathtt{to} < m_2.\mathtt{frm}$, and there is no message $m' \in M(m_1.\mathsf{loc})$ such that $m_1.\mathtt{to} < m'.\mathtt{to} < m_2.\mathtt{to}$, we include a reservation $(m_1.\mathsf{loc}, (m_1.\mathtt{to}, m_2.\mathtt{frm}])$ in $\widehat{M}_P$, and (2) we include a cap message $\widehat{m}_{M,x}$ in $\widehat{M}_P$ for every variable x unless $\overline{m}_{M,x}$ is a reservation in P.

Consistency. A machine state $\mathcal{MS} = ((J, R), VS, PS, M, G)$ is *consistent* if every process p can certify/fulfil all its promises from the capped memory $\widehat{M}_{PS(p)}$, i.e., $((J, R), VS, PS, \widehat{M}_{PS(p)}, G) \ [\xrightarrow[p]{}]^* \ ((J', R'), VS', PS', M', G')$ with $PS'(p) = \emptyset$.

The Reachability Problem in PS 2.0. A run of *Prog* is a sequence of the form: $\mathcal{MS}_0 [\xrightarrow[p_{i_1}]{}]^* \mathcal{MS}_1 [\xrightarrow[p_{i_2}]{}]^* \mathcal{MS}_2 [\xrightarrow[p_{i_3}]{}]^* \ldots [\xrightarrow[p_{i_n}]{}]^* \mathcal{MS}_n$ where $\mathcal{MS}_0 = \mathcal{MS}_{\text{init}}$ is the initial machine state and $\mathcal{MS}_1, \ldots, \mathcal{MS}_n$ are consistent machine states. Then, $\mathcal{MS}_0, \ldots, \mathcal{MS}_n$ are said to be reachable from $\mathcal{MS}_{\text{init}}$.

Given an instruction label function $J : \mathcal{P} \to \mathbb{L}$ that maps each process $p \in \mathcal{P}$ to an instruction label in $\mathbb{L}_p$, the *reachability* problem asks whether there exists a machine state of the form $((J, R), V, P, M, G)$ that is reachable from $\mathcal{MS}_{\text{init}}$. A positive answer to this problem means that J is reachable in *Prog* in PS 2.0.

4 Undecidability of Consistent Reachability in PS 2.0

The reachability problem is undecidable for PS 2.0 even for finite-state programs. The proof is by a reduction from Post's Correspondence Problem (PCP) [28]. A PCP instance consists of two sequences $u_1, \ldots, u_n$ and $v_1, \ldots, v_n$ of non-empty words over some alphabet Σ. Checking whether there exists a sequence of indices $j_1, \ldots, j_k \in \{1, \ldots, n\}$ s.t. $u_{j_1} \ldots u_{j_k} = v_{j_1} \ldots v_{j_k}$ is undecidable. Our proof works with the fragment of PS 2.0 having only relaxed (`rlx`) memory accesses and crucially uses unboundedly many promises to ensure that a process cannot skip any writes made by another process. We construct a concurrent program with two processes p_1 and p_2 over a finite data domain. The code of p_1 is split into two modes: a generation mode and a validation mode by a `if` and its `else` branch. The `if` branch is entered when the value of a boolean location *validate* is 0 (its initial value). We show that reaching the instructions annotated by // and // in p_1, p_2 is possible iff the PCP instance has a solution. We give below an overview of the execution steps leading to the annotated instructions.

- Process p_1 promises to write letters of u_i (one by one) to a location x, and the respective indices i to a location *index*. The number of made promises is arbitrary, since it depends on the length of the PCP solution. Observe that the sequence of promises made to the variable *index* corresponds to the guessed solution of the PCP problem.
- Before switching out of context, p_1 certifies its promise using the `if` branch which consists of a loop that non-deterministically chooses an index i and writes i to *index* and u_i to x. The promises of p_1 are as yet not fulfilled; this happens in the `else` branch of p_1, when it writes the promised values.
- p_2 reads from the sequences of promises written to x and *index* and copies them (one by one) to variables y and *index'* respectively. Then, p_2 sets *validate* to 1 and reaches //.
- The `else` branch in p_1 is enabled at this point, where p_1 reads the sequence of indices from *index'*, and each time it reads an index i from *index'*, it checks that it can read the sequence of letters of v_i from y.
- p_1 copies the sequence of observed values from y and *index'* back to x and *index* respectively. To fulfil the promises, it is crucial that the sequence of read values from *index'* (resp. y) is the same as the sequence of promised values to *index* (resp. x). Since y holds a sequence $v_{i_1} \ldots v_{i_k}$, the promises

are fulfilled if and only if this sequence is same as the promised sequence $u_{i_1} \dots u_{i_k}$. This happens only when $i_1, \dots, i_k$ is a PCP solution.
– At the end of promise fulfilment, p_1 reaches $//$.

Our undecidability result is also *tight* in the sense that the reachability problem becomes decidable when we restrict ourselves to machine states where the number of promises is bounded. Further, our proof is robust: it goes through for PS 1.0 [16]. Let us call the fragment of PS 2.0 with only `rlx` memory accesses PS 2.0-rlx.

Theorem 1. *The reachability problem for concurrent programs over a finite data domain is undecidable under PS 2.0-rlx.*

5 Decidable Fragments of PS 2.0

Since keeping `ra` memory accesses renders the reachability problem undecidable [1] and so does having unboundedly many promises when having `rlx` memory accesses (Theorem 1), we address in this section the decidability problem for PS 2.0-rlx with a bounded number of promises in any reachable configuration. Bounding the number of promises in any reachable machine state does not imply that the total number of promises made during that run is bounded. Let bdPS 2.0-rlx represent the restriction of PS 2.0-rlx to boundedly many promises where the number of promises in each reachable machine state is smaller or equal to a given constant. Notice that the fragment bdPS 2.0-rlx subsumes the relaxed fragment of the RC11 model [20,16].We assume here a finite data domain.

To establish the decidability of the reachability of bdPS 2.0-rlx, we introduce an alternate memory model for concurrent programs called LoHoW (for "lossy higher order words"). We present the operational semantics of LoHoW, and show that (1) PS 2.0-rlx is reachability equivalent to LoHoW, (2) under the bounded promise assumption, reachability is decidable in LoHoW (hence, bdPS 2.0-rlx).

Introduction to LoHoW. Given a concurrent program *Prog*, a *state* of LoHoW maintains a collection of higher order words, one per location of *Prog*, along with the states of all processes. The higher order word HW_x corresponding to the location x is a word of simple words, representing the sub memory $M(x)$ in PS 2.0-rlx. Each simple word in HW_x is an ordered sequence of "memory types", that is, messages or promises in $M(x)$, maintained in the order of their `to` timestamps in the memory. The word order between memory types in HW_x represents the order induced by time stamps between memory types in $M(x)$. The key information to encode in each memory type of HW_x is: (1) is it a message (msg) or a promise (`prm`) in $M(x)$, (2) the process (p) which added it to $M(x)$, the value (`val`) it holds, (3) the set S (called pointer set) of processes that have seen this memory type in $M(x)$ and (4) whether the adjacent time interval to the right of this memory type in $M(x)$ has been reserved by some process.

Memory Types. To keep track of (1-4) above, a *memory type* is an element of $\Sigma \cup \Gamma$ with, $\Sigma = \{\mathsf{msg}, \mathtt{prm}\} \times \mathsf{Val} \times \mathcal{P} \times 2^{\mathcal{P}}$ (for 1-3) and $\Gamma = \{\mathsf{msg}, \mathtt{prm}\} \times \mathsf{Val} \times \mathcal{P} \times 2^{\mathcal{P}} \times \mathcal{P}$ (for 4). We write a memory type as $(r, v, p, S, \underline{?})$. Here r represents either msg (message) or prm (promise) in $M(x)$, v is the value, p is the process that added the message/promise, S is a *pointer set* of processes whose local view (on x) agrees with the to timestamp of the message/promise. If the type $\in \Gamma$, the fifth component ($\underline{?}$) is the process id that has reserved the time slot right-adjacent to the message/promise. $\underline{?}$ is a wildcard that may (or not) be matched.

Simple Words. A simple word $\in \Sigma^*\#(\Sigma \cup \Gamma)$, and each HW_x is a word $\in (\Sigma^*\#(\Sigma \cup \Gamma))^+$. # is a special symbol not in $\Sigma \cup \Gamma$, which separates the last symbol from the rest of the simple word. Consecutive symbols of Σ in a simple word in HW_x represent adjacent messages/promises in $M(x)$ and are hence unavailable for a RMW. # does not correspond to any element from the memory, and is used to demarcate the last symbol of the simple word.

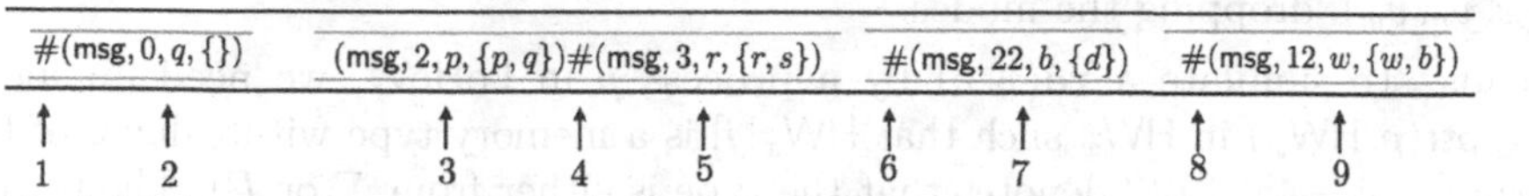

Fig. 3: A higher order word HW (black) with four embedded simple words (pink).

Higher order words. A *higher order word* is a sequence of simple words. Figure 3 depicts a higher order word with four simple words. We use a left to right order in both simple words and higher order words. Furthermore, we extend in the straightforward manner the classical word indexation strategy to higher order words. For example, the symbol at the third position of the higher order word HW in Figure 3 is $\mathsf{HW}[3] = (\mathsf{msg}, 2, p, \{p, q\})$. A higher order word HW is *well-formed* iff for every $p \in \mathcal{P}$, there is a unique position i in HW having p in its pointer set; that is, $\mathsf{HW}[i]$ is of the form $(-, -, -, S, \underline{?}) \in \Sigma \cup \Gamma$ s.t. $p \in S$. The higher order word given in Figure 3 is well-formed. We will use $\mathsf{ptr}(p, \mathsf{HW})$ to denote the unique position i in HW having p in its pointer set. We assume that all the manipulated higher order words are well-formed.

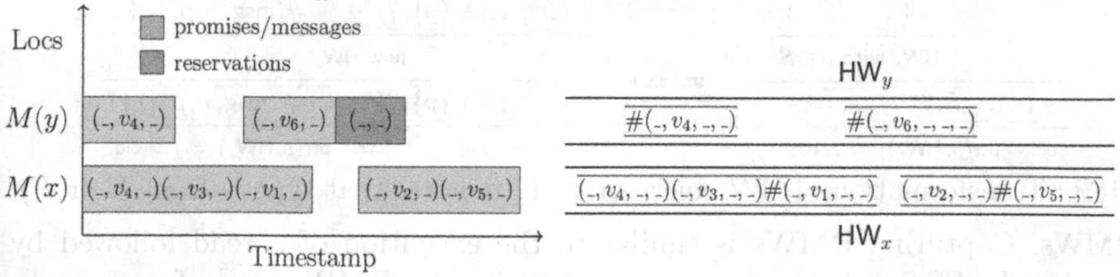

Fig. 4: Map from memories $M(x), M(y)$ to higher order words $\mathsf{HW}_x, \mathsf{HW}_y$.

Each higher order word HW_x represents the entire space $[0, \infty)$ of available timestamps in $M(x)$. Each simple word in HW_x represents a timestamp interval $[f, t]$, while consecutive simple words represent disjoint timestamp intervals (while preserving order). The memory types constituting each simple word take up *adjacent* timestamp intervals, spanning the timestamp interval of the simple word. The adjacency of timestamp intervals within simple words is used in RMW steps and reservations. The last symbol in a simple word denotes a message/promise which, (1) if in Σ, is available for a RMW, while (2) if in Γ, is unavailable for RMW since it is followed by a reservation. Symbols at positions other than the rightmost in a simple word, represent messages/promises which are not available for RMW. Figure 4 presents a mapping from a memory of PS 2.0-rlx to a collection of higher order words (one per location) in LoHoW.

Initializing higher order words. For each location $x \in$ Loc, the initial higher order word $\mathsf{HW}_x^{\mathrm{init}}$ is defined as $\overline{\#(\mathsf{msg}, 0, p_1, \mathcal{P})}$, where $\mathcal{P}$ is the set of all processes and p_1 is some process in $\mathcal{P}$. The set of all higher order words $\mathsf{HW}_x^{\mathrm{init}}$ for all locations x represents the initial memory of PS 2.0-rlx where all locations have value 0, and all processes are aware of the initial message.

Simulating PS 2.0 Memory Operations in LoHoW. In the following, we describe how to handle PS 2.0-rlx instructions in LoHoW. Since we only have the rlx mode, we denote Reads, Writes and RMWs as $\mathsf{wt}(x, v)$, $\mathsf{rd}(x, v)$ and $\mathsf{U}(x, v_r, v_w)$, dropping the modes.

Reads. To simulate a $\mathsf{rd}(x, v)$ by a process p in LoHoW, we need an index $j \geq \mathsf{ptr}(p, \mathsf{HW}_x)$ in HW_x such that $\mathsf{HW}_x[j]$ is a memory type with value v of the form $(-, v, -, S', ?)$ (? denotes that the type is either from Σ or Γ). The read is simulated by adding p to the set S' and removing it from its previous set.

$$\cfrac{\mathsf{ptr}(p, \mathsf{HW}_x) \quad j \geq \mathsf{ptr}(p, \mathsf{HW}_x)}{\underbrace{\cdots\ \overline{(-,-,-,S,?)}\ \cdots\ \overline{(-,v,-,S',?)}\ \cdots}_{\mathsf{HW}_x \text{ with } p \in S}} \xrightarrow{\mathsf{rd}(x,v)} \cfrac{\mathsf{ptr}(p, \mathsf{HW}_x) := j}{\underbrace{\cdots\ \overline{(-,-,-,S\setminus\{p\},?)}\ \cdots\ \overline{(-,v,-,S'\cup\{p\},?)}\ \cdots}_{\text{new } \mathsf{HW}_x}}$$

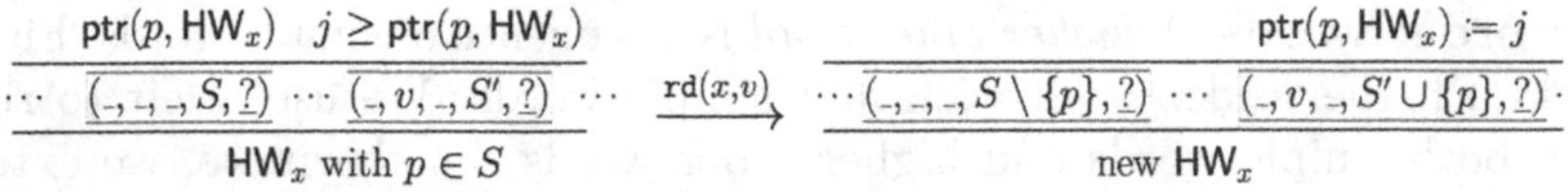

Fig. 5: Transformation of HW_x on a read. (? denotes that type is from Σ or Γ)

Writes. A $\mathsf{wt}(x, v)$ by a process p (writing v to x) is simulated by adding a new msg type in HW_x with a timestamp higher than the view of p for x: (1) add the simple word $(\mathsf{msg}, v, p, \{p\})$ to the right of $\mathsf{ptr}(p, \mathsf{HW}_x)$ or (2) there is $\alpha \in \Sigma$ such that the word $w\#\alpha$ is in HW_x to the right of $\mathsf{ptr}(p, \mathsf{HW}_x)$. Modify $w\#\alpha$ to get $w\alpha\#(\mathsf{msg}, v, p, \{p\})\cdot$. Remove p from its previous pointer set.

$$\cfrac{\mathsf{old} = \mathsf{ptr}(p, \mathsf{HW}_x)}{\underbrace{\cdots\ \overline{(-,-,-,S,?)}\ \cdots}_{\mathsf{HW}_x \text{ with } p \in S}} \xrightarrow[(1)]{\mathsf{wt}(x,v)} \cfrac{\mathsf{old} \qquad \mathsf{ptr}(p, \mathsf{HW}_x) > \mathsf{old}}{\cdots\ \overline{(-,-,-,S\setminus\{p\},?)}\ \cdots\ \overline{\#(\mathsf{msg}, v, p, \{p\})}\ \cdots}_{\text{new } \mathsf{HW}_x}$$

$$\cfrac{\mathsf{old} = \mathsf{ptr}(p, \mathsf{HW}_x) \quad j > \mathsf{old}}{\cdots\ \overline{(-,-,-,S,?)}\ \cdots\ w\#\alpha\ \cdots} \xrightarrow[(2)]{\mathsf{wt}(x,v)} \cfrac{\mathsf{old} \qquad \mathsf{ptr}(p, \mathsf{HW}_x) := j > \mathsf{old}}{\cdots\ \overline{(-,-,-,S\setminus\{p\},?)}\ \cdots\ w\alpha\#(\mathsf{msg}, v, p, \{p\})\ \cdots}$$

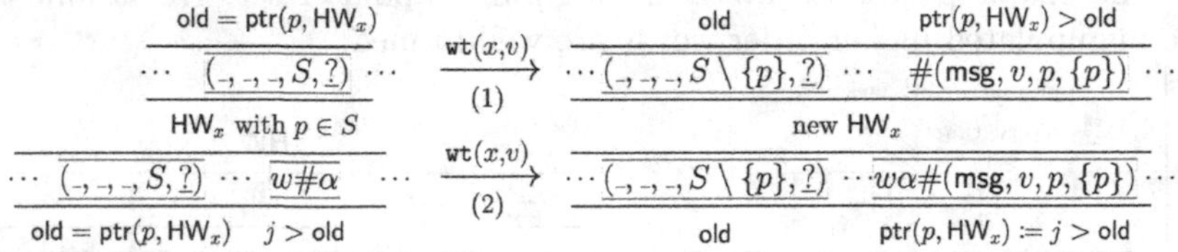

Fig. 6: Transformation of HW_x on a write. (? denotes that type is from Σ or Γ).

RMWs. Capturing RMWs is similar to the execution of a read followed by a write. In PS 2.0-rlx, a process p performing an RMW, reads from a message with a timestamp interval $(, t]$ and adds a message to $M(x)$ with timestamp interval $(t, -]$. Capturing RMWs needs higher order words. Consider a $\mathsf{U}(x, v_r, v_w)$ step by process p. Then, there is a simple word $\overline{\cdots \#(-, v_r, -, S)}$ in HW_x having $(-, v_r, -, S)$ as the last memory type whose position is to the right of $\mathsf{ptr}(p, \mathsf{HW}_x)$. As usual, p is removed from its pointer set, $\#(-, v_r, -, S)$ is replaced with $(-, v_r, -, S\setminus\{p\})\#$ and $(-, v_w, p, \{p\})$ is appended, resulting in extending $\overline{\cdots \#(-, v_r, -, S)}$ to $\overline{\cdots (-, v_r, -, S\setminus\{p\})\#(-, v_w, p, \{p\})}$.

Promises, Reservations and Cancellations. Handling promises made by a process p in PS 2.0-rlx is similar to handling $\mathsf{wt}(x, v)$: we add the simple word $\overline{\#(\mathsf{prm}, v, p, \{\})}$ in HW_x to the right of the position $\mathsf{ptr}(p, \mathsf{HW}_x)$, or append $(\mathsf{prm}, v, p, \{\})$ at the

end of a simple word with a position larger than $\mathsf{ptr}(p, \mathsf{HW}_x)$. The memory type has tag prm (a promise), and the pointer set is empty (since making a promise does not lift the view of the promising process). Splitting the time interval of a promise is simulated in LoHoW by inserting a new memory type right before the corresponding promise memory type $(\mathtt{prm}, -, p, S)$, while fulfilment of a promise by a process p results in replacing $(\mathtt{prm}, v, p, S)$ with $(\mathsf{msg}, v, p, S \cup \{p\})$.

In PS 2.0-rlx, a process p makes a reservation by adding the pair $(x, (f, t])$ to the memory, given that there is a message/promise in the memory with timestamp interval $(-, f]$. In LoHoW this is captured by "tagging" the rightmost memory type (message/promise) in a simple word with the name of the process that makes the reservation. This requires us to consider the memory types from $\Gamma = \{\mathsf{msg}, \mathtt{prm}\} \times \mathsf{Val} \times \mathcal{P} \times 2^{\mathcal{P}} \times \mathcal{P}$ where the last component stores the process which made the reservation. Such a memory type always appears at the end of a simple word, and represents that the next timestamp interval adjacent to it has been reserved. Observe that nothing can be added to the right of a memory type of the form $(\mathsf{msg}, v, p, S, q)$. Thus, reservations are handled as follows.

(Res) Assume the rightmost symbol in a simple word as (msg, v, p, S). To capture the reservation by q, (msg, v, p, S) is replaced with $(\mathsf{msg}, v, p, S, q)$.

(Can) A cancellation is done by removing the last component q from $(\mathsf{msg}, v, p, S, q)$ resulting in (msg, v, p, S).

Certification In PS 2.0-rlx, certification for a process p happens from the capped memory, where intermediate time slots (other than reserved ones) are blocked, and any new message can be added only at the maximal timestamp. This is handled in LoHoW by one of the following: (1) Addition of new memory types is allowed only at the right end of any HW_x, or (2) If the rightmost memory type in HW_x is of form $(-, v, -, -, q)$ with $q \neq p$ (a reservation by q), then the word $\#(\mathsf{msg}, v, q, \{\})$ is appended at end of HW_x.

Memory is altered in PS 2.0-rlx during certification phase to check for promise fulfilment, and at the end of the certification phase, we resume from the memory which was there before. To capture this in LoHoW, we work on a duplicate of $(\mathsf{HW}_x)_{x \in \mathsf{Loc}}$ in the certification phase. Notice that the duplication allows losing non-deterministically, *empty memory types*: these are memory types whose pointer set is empty, as well as *redundant simple words*, which are simple words consisting entirely of empty memory types. This copy of HW_x is then modified during certification, and is discarded once we finish the certification phase.

5.1 Formal Model of LoHoW

In the following, we formally define LoHoW and state the equivalence of the reachability problem in PS 2.0-rlx and LoHoW. For a memory type $m = (r, v, p, S)$ (or $m = (r, v, p, S, q)$), we use $m.value$ to denote v. For a memory type $(r, v, p, S, \underline{?})$ and a process $p' \in \mathcal{P}$, we define the following: $\mathsf{add}(m, p') \equiv (r, v, p, S \cup \{p'\}, \underline{?})$ and $\mathsf{del}(m, p') \equiv (r, v, p, S \setminus \{p'\}, \underline{?})$. This corresponds to the addition/deletion of the process p' to/from the set of pointers of m. Extending the above notation, given a higher order word HW, a position $i \in \{1, \ldots, |\mathsf{HW}|\}$, and $p \in \mathcal{P}$, we define the following: $\mathsf{add}(\mathsf{HW}, p, i) \equiv \mathsf{HW}[1, i-1] \cdot \mathsf{add}(\mathsf{HW}[i], p) \cdot \mathsf{HW}[i+1, |\mathsf{HW}|]$, $\mathsf{add}(\mathsf{HW}, p, i) \equiv \mathsf{HW}[1, i-1] \cdot \mathsf{add}(\mathsf{HW}[i], p) \cdot \mathsf{HW}[i+1, |\mathsf{HW}|]$, and $\mathsf{mov}(\mathsf{HW}, p, i) \equiv \mathsf{add}(\mathsf{del}(\mathsf{HW}, p), p, i)$. This corresponds to the addition/deletion/relocation of the pointer p to/from the word $\mathsf{HW}[i]$.

Insertion into higher order words. A higher order word HW can be extended in position $1 \leq j \leq |\mathsf{HW}|$ with a memory type $m = (r, v, p, \{p\})$ as follows:

• *Insertion as a new simple word* is defined only if $\mathsf{HW}[j-1] = \#$ (i.e., the position j is the end of a simple word). Let $\mathsf{HW}' = \mathsf{del}(\mathsf{HW}, p)$ (i.e., removing p from its previous set of pointers). Then, the insertion of m results in

$$\mathsf{HW} \overset{N}{\underset{j}{\hookleftarrow}} m \equiv \mathsf{HW}'[1, j] \cdot \underbrace{\#(r, v, p, \{p\})}_{\text{new simple word}} \cdot \mathsf{HW}'[j+1, |\mathsf{HW}|]$$

• *Insertion at the end of a simple word* is defined only if $\mathsf{HW}[j-1] = \#$ and $\mathsf{HW}[j] \in \Sigma$ (i.e., the last memory type in the simple word should be free from reservations). Let $\mathsf{HW}' = \mathsf{del}(\mathsf{HW}, p)$. For $\mathsf{HW}' = w_1 \cdot \#m' \cdot w_2$, and $|w_1 \cdot \#m'| = j$ the insertion of m results in

$$\mathsf{HW} \overset{E}{\underset{j}{\hookleftarrow}} m \equiv w_1 \cdot m' \cdot \underbrace{\#(r, v, p, \{p\})}_{m \text{ extends } m'} \cdot w_2$$

• *Splitting a promise* is defined only if $m' = \mathsf{HW}[j]$ has form $(\mathtt{prm}, -, p, -, \underline{?})$ (i.e., the memory type at position j is a promise). Let $\mathsf{HW}' = \mathsf{del}(\mathsf{HW}, p)$. Then,

$$\mathsf{HW} \overset{SP}{\underset{j}{\hookleftarrow}} m \equiv \begin{cases} \mathsf{HW}'[1, j-2] \cdot \underbrace{(r, v, p, \{p\}) \cdot \#m'}_{m \text{ splits } m'} \cdot \mathsf{HW}'[j+1, |\mathsf{HW}|] & \text{if } \mathsf{HW}'[j-1] = \# \\ \mathsf{HW}'[1, j-1] \cdot \underbrace{(r, v, p, \{p\}) \cdot m'}_{m \text{ splits } m'} \cdot \mathsf{HW}'[j+1, |\mathsf{HW}|] & \text{if } \mathsf{HW}'[j-1] \neq \# \end{cases}$$

Observe that in both cases we insert the new type m just before position j.

• *Fulfilment of a promise* is defined only if $m' = \mathsf{HW}[j]$ is of the form $(\mathtt{prm}, v, p, S)$ or $(\mathtt{prm}, v, p, S, q)$. Let $\mathsf{HW}' = \mathsf{del}(\mathsf{HW}, p)$. Then, the extended higher order

$$\mathsf{HW} \overset{FP}{\underset{j}{\hookleftarrow}} m \equiv \mathsf{HW}'[1, j-1] \cdot \underbrace{(\mathsf{msg}, v, p, S \cup \{p\}, \underline{?})}_{m' \text{ is fulfilled by } p} \cdot \mathsf{HW}'[j+1, |\mathsf{HW}'|]$$

where $\underline{?}$ is q if $m' = (\mathtt{prm}, v, p, S, q) \in \Gamma$ and is omitted if $m' = (\mathtt{prm}, v, p, S) \in \Sigma$.

Making/Canceling a reservation. A higher order word HW can also be modified by p by making/cancelling a reservation at a position $1 \leq j \leq |\mathsf{HW}|$. We define the operation $Make(\mathsf{HW}, p, j)$ ($Cancel(\mathsf{HW}, p, j)$) that reserves (cancels) a time slot at j. $Make(\mathsf{HW}, p, j)$ (resp. $Cancel(\mathsf{HW}, p, j)$) is only defined if $\mathsf{HW}[j]$ is of the form (r, v, q, S) (resp. (r, v, q, S, p)) and $\mathsf{HW}[j-1] = \#$. Then, we have $Make(\mathsf{HW}, p, j) \equiv \mathsf{HW}[1, j-1] \cdot (r, v, q, S, p) \cdot \mathsf{HW}[j+1, |\mathsf{HW}|]$ and $Cancel(\mathsf{HW}, p, j) \equiv \mathsf{HW}[1, j-1] \cdot (r, v, q, S) \cdot \mathsf{HW}[j+1, |\mathsf{HW}|]$.

Process configuration in LoHoW. A configuration of $p \in \mathcal{P}$ in LoHoW consists of a pair $(\sigma, \mathbf{HW})$ where (1) σ is the process state maintaining the instruction label and the register values (see Subsection 3), and $\mathbf{HW}$ is a mapping from the set of locations to higher order words. The transition relations $\xrightarrow[p]{\mathtt{std}}$ and $\xrightarrow[p]{\mathtt{cert}}$ between process configurations are given in Figure 7; the transition relation $\xrightarrow[p]{\mathtt{cert}}$ is used only in the certification phase while $\xrightarrow[p]{\mathtt{std}}$ is used to simulate the standard phase of PS 2.0-rlx. A read operation in both phases (standard and certification) is handled by reading a value from a memory type which is on the right of the current pointer of p. A write operation, in the standard phase, can result in the insertion, on the right of the current pointer of p, of a new memory type at the end of a simple word or as a new simple word. The memory type resulting from a write in the certification phase is only allowed to be inserted at the end of the higher order word or at the reserved slots (using the rule splitting a reservation). Write can also be used to fulfil a promise or to split a promise (i.e., partial fulfilment) during the both phases. Making/canceling a reservation will result in tagging/untagging a memory type at the end of a simple word on the right of the current pointer of p. The case of RMW is similar to a read followed by a write operations (whose resulting memory type should be inserted to the right of the read memory type). Finally, a promise can only be made during the standard phase and the resulting memory type will be inserted at the end of a simple word or as a new word on the right of the current pointer of p.

$$\frac{\sigma \xrightarrow[p]{\mathtt{rd}(x,v)} \sigma',\ \ i \geq \mathsf{ptr}(p, \mathbf{HW}(x)),\ \ v = \mathbf{HW}(x)[i].value, \quad \mathbf{HW}' = \mathbf{HW}[x \mapsto \mathsf{mov}(\mathbf{HW}(x), p, i)]}{(\sigma, \mathbf{HW}) \xrightarrow[p]{a} (\sigma', \mathbf{HW}')} \quad \begin{array}{c}\texttt{Read}\\ a \in \{\mathtt{cert}, \mathtt{std}\}\end{array}$$

$$\frac{\sigma \xrightarrow[p]{\mathtt{wt}(x,v)} \sigma',\ \ i \geq \mathsf{ptr}(p, \mathbf{HW}(x)), \quad \mathbf{HW}' = \mathbf{HW}[x \mapsto (\mathbf{HW}(x) \overset{K}{\underset{i}{\hookleftarrow}} (\mathsf{msg}, v, p, \{p\}))]}{(\sigma, \mathbf{HW}) \xrightarrow[p]{\mathtt{std}} (\sigma', \mathbf{HW}')} \quad \begin{array}{c}\texttt{Standard write}\\ K \in \{N, E\}\end{array}$$

$$\frac{i \geq \mathsf{ptr}(p, \mathbf{HW}(x)),\ \ \mathbf{HW}' = \mathbf{HW}[x \mapsto Make(\mathbf{HW}(x), p, i)]}{(\sigma, \mathbf{HW}) \xrightarrow[p]{\mathtt{std}} (\sigma, \mathbf{HW}')} \quad \texttt{Making a reservation}$$

$$\frac{\sigma \xrightarrow[p]{\mathtt{U}(x,v_r,w_r)} \sigma',\ \ i \geq \mathsf{ptr}(p, \mathbf{HW}(x)),\ \ v_r = \mathbf{HW}(x)[i].value, \quad \mathbf{HW}' = \mathbf{HW}[x \mapsto (\mathbf{HW}(x) \overset{E}{\underset{i}{\hookleftarrow}} (\mathsf{msg}, w_r, p, \{p\}))]}{(\sigma, \mathbf{HW}) \xrightarrow[p]{\mathtt{std}} (\sigma', \mathbf{HW}')} \quad \texttt{Standard update}$$

$$\frac{i \geq \mathsf{ptr}(p, \mathbf{HW}(x)),\ \ \mathbf{HW}' = \mathbf{HW}[x \mapsto (\mathbf{HW}(x) \overset{E}{\underset{i}{\hookleftarrow}} (\mathtt{prm}, v, p, \{\}))]}{(\sigma, \mathbf{HW}) \xrightarrow[p]{\mathtt{std}} (\sigma, \mathbf{HW}')} \quad \texttt{Promise}$$

$$\frac{\sigma \xrightarrow[p]{\mathsf{(SC\text{-}fence)}} \sigma',\ \ i_x = max(\mathsf{ptr}(p, \mathbf{HW}(x)), \mathsf{ptr}(g, \mathbf{HW}(x))), \quad \mathbf{HW}' = \mathbf{HW}[x \mapsto \mathsf{mov}(\mathbf{HW}(x), p, i_x)]_{x \in \mathsf{Loc}}[x \mapsto \mathsf{mov}(\mathbf{HW}(x), g, i_x)]_{x \in \mathsf{Loc}}}{(\sigma, \mathbf{HW}) \xrightarrow[p]{a} (\sigma', \mathbf{HW}')} \quad \begin{array}{c}\texttt{SC-fence}\\ a \in \{\mathtt{std}, \mathtt{cert}\}\end{array}$$

Fig. 7: A subset of LoHoW inference rules at the process level.

Losses in LoHoW. Let HW and HW′ be two higher order words in $(\Sigma^* \#(\Sigma \cup \Gamma))^+$. Let us assume that $\mathsf{HW} = u_1 \# a_1 u_2 \# a_2 \ldots u_k \# a_k$ and $\mathsf{HW}' = v_1 \# b_1 v_2 \# b_2 \ldots v_m \# b_m$, with $u_i, v_i \in \Sigma^*$ and $a_i, b_j \in \Sigma \cup \Gamma$. We extend the subword relation $\sqsubseteq$ to higher order word as follows: $\mathsf{HW} \sqsubseteq \mathsf{HW}'$ iff there is a strictly increasing function $f : \{1, \ldots, k\} \to \{1, \ldots, m\}$ s.t. (1) $u_i \sqsubseteq v_{f(i)}$ for all $1 \le i \le k$, (2) $a_i = b_{f(i)}$, and (3) we have the same number of memory types of the form $(\mathtt{prm}, -, -, -)$ or $(\mathtt{prm}, -, -, -, -)$ in HW and HW'. The relation $\sqsubseteq$ corresponds to the loss of some special empty memory types and redundant simple words (as explained earlier). The relation $\sqsubseteq$ is extended to mapping from locations to higher order words as follows: $\mathbf{HW} \sqsubseteq \mathbf{HW}'$ iff $\mathbf{HW}(x) \sqsubseteq \mathbf{HW}'(x)$ for all $x \in \mathsf{Loc}$.

LoHoW states. A LoHoW state $\mathfrak{st}$ is a tuple $((\mathsf{J}, \mathsf{R}), \mathbf{HW})$ where $\mathsf{J} : \mathcal{P} \mapsto \mathbb{L}$ maps each process p to the label of the next instruction to be executed, $\mathsf{R} : \mathsf{Reg} \to \mathsf{Val}$ maps each register to its current value, and $\mathbf{HW}$ is a mapping from locations to higher order words. The initial LoHoW state $\mathfrak{st}_{\mathsf{init}}$ is defined as $((\mathsf{J}_{\mathsf{init}}, \mathsf{R}_{\mathsf{init}}), \mathbf{HW}_{\mathsf{init}})$ where: (1) $\mathsf{J}_{\mathsf{init}}(p)$ is the label of the initial instruction of p; (2) $\mathsf{R}_{\mathsf{init}}(\$r) = 0$ for every $\$r \in \mathsf{Reg}$; and (3) $\mathbf{HW}_{\mathsf{init}}(x) = \mathsf{HW}_x^{\mathsf{init}}$ for all $x \in \mathsf{Loc}$.

For two LoHoW states $\mathfrak{st} = ((\mathsf{J}, \mathsf{R}), \mathbf{HW})$ and $\mathfrak{st}' = ((\mathsf{J}', \mathsf{R}'), \mathbf{HW}')$ and $a \in \{\mathtt{std}, \mathtt{cert}\}$, we write $\mathfrak{st} \xrightarrow[p]{a} \mathfrak{st}'$ iff one of the following cases holds: (1) $((\mathsf{J}(p), \mathsf{R}), \mathbf{HW}) \xrightarrow[p]{a} ((\mathsf{J}'(p), \mathsf{R}'), \mathbf{HW}')$ and $\mathsf{J}(p') = \mathsf{J}'(p')$ for all $p' \neq p$, or (2) $(\mathsf{J}, \mathsf{R}) = (\mathsf{J}', \mathsf{R}')$ and $\mathbf{HW} \sqsubseteq \mathbf{HW}'$.

Two phases LoHoW states. A two-phases state of LoHoW is $\mathcal{S} = (\pi, p, \mathfrak{st}_{\mathtt{std}}, \mathfrak{st}_{\mathtt{cert}})$ where $\pi \in \{\mathtt{cert}, \mathtt{std}\}$ is a flag describing whether the LoHoW is in "standard" phase or "certification" phase, p is the process which evolves in one of these phases, while $\mathfrak{st}_{\mathtt{std}}$, $\mathfrak{st}_{\mathtt{cert}}$ are two LoHoW states (one for each phase). When the LoHoW is in the standard phase, then $\mathfrak{st}_{\mathtt{std}}$ evolves, and when the LoHoW is in certification phase, $\mathfrak{st}_{\mathtt{cert}}$ evolves. A two-phases LoHoW state is said to be initial if it is of the form $(\mathtt{std}, p, \mathfrak{st}_{\mathsf{init}}, \mathfrak{st}_{\mathsf{init}})$, where $p \in \mathcal{P}$ is any process. The transition relation $\to$ between two-phases LoHoW states is defined as follows: Given $\mathcal{S} = (\pi, p, \mathfrak{st}_{\mathtt{std}}, \mathfrak{st}_{\mathtt{cert}})$ and $\mathcal{S}' = (\pi', p', \mathfrak{st}'_{\mathtt{std}}, \mathfrak{st}'_{\mathtt{cert}})$, we have $\mathcal{S} \to \mathcal{S}'$ iff one of the following cases holds:

- **During the standard phase.** $\pi = \pi' = \mathtt{std}$, $p = p'$, $\mathfrak{st}_{\mathtt{cert}} = \mathfrak{st}'_{\mathtt{cert}}$ and $\mathfrak{st}_{\mathtt{std}} \xrightarrow[p]{\mathtt{std}} \mathfrak{st}'_{\mathtt{std}}$. This corresponds to simulating a standard step of process p.
- **During the certification phase.** $\pi = \pi' = \mathtt{cert}$, $p = p'$, $\mathfrak{st}_{\mathtt{std}} = \mathfrak{st}'_{\mathtt{std}}$ and $\mathfrak{st}_{\mathtt{cert}} \xrightarrow[p]{\mathtt{cert}} \mathfrak{st}'_{\mathtt{cert}}$. This simulates a certification step of process p.
- **From the standard phase to the certification phase.** $\pi = \mathtt{std}$, $\pi' = \mathtt{cert}$, $p = p'$, $\mathfrak{st}_{\mathtt{std}} = \mathfrak{st}'_{\mathtt{std}} = ((\mathsf{J}, \mathsf{R}), \mathbf{HW})$, and $\mathfrak{st}'_{\mathtt{cert}}$ is of the form $((\mathsf{J}, \mathsf{R}), \mathbf{HW}')$ where for every $x \in \mathsf{Loc}$, $\mathbf{HW}'(x) = \mathbf{HW}(x)\#(\mathsf{msg}, v, q, \{\})$ if $\mathbf{HW}(x)$ is of the form $w \cdot \#(-, v, -, -, q)$ with $q \neq p$, and $\mathbf{HW}'(x) = \mathbf{HW}(x)$ otherwise. This corresponds to the copying of the standard LoHoW state to the certification LoHoW state in order to check if the set of promises made by the process p can be fulfilled. This transition rule can be implemented by a sequence of transitions which copies one symbol at a time, from $\mathbf{HW}$ to $\mathbf{HW}'$.

– **From the certification phase to standard phase.** $\pi = \texttt{cert}$, $\pi' = \texttt{std}$, $\mathfrak{st}_{\texttt{std}} = \mathfrak{st}'_{\texttt{std}}$, $\mathfrak{st}_{\texttt{cert}} = \mathfrak{st}'_{\texttt{cert}}$, and $\mathfrak{st}_{\texttt{cert}}$ is of the form $((\mathsf{J}, \mathsf{R}), \mathbf{HW})$ with $\mathbf{HW}(x)$ does not contain any memory type of form $(\texttt{prm}, -, p, -, \underline{?})$ for all $x \in \mathsf{Loc}$ (i.e., all promises made by p are fulfilled).

The Reachability Problem in LoHoW. Given an instruction label function $J : \mathcal{P} \rightarrow \mathbb{L}$ that maps each $p \in \mathcal{P}$ to a label in $\mathbb{L}_p$, the *reachability* problem in LoHoW asks whether there exists a two phases LoHoW state $\mathcal{S}$ of the form $(\texttt{std}, -, ((J, R), \mathbf{HW}), ((J', R'), \mathbf{HW}'))$ s.t. (1) $\mathbf{HW}(x)$ and $\mathbf{HW}'(x)$ do not contain any memory type of the form $(\texttt{prm}, -, p, -, \underline{?})$ for all $x \in \mathsf{Loc}$, and (2) $\mathcal{S}$ is reachable in LoHoW (i.e., $\mathcal{S}_0 \, [\rightarrow]^* \, \mathcal{S}'$ where $\mathcal{S}_0$ is an initial two-phases LoHoW states). A positive answer to this problem means J is reachable in *Prog* in LoHoW. The following theorem states the equivalence between LoHoW and PS 2.0-rlx in terms of reachable instruction label functions.

Theorem 2. *An instruction label function J is reachable in a program Prog in* LoHoW *iff J is reachable in Prog in PS 2.0-rlx.*

5.2 Decidability of LoHoW with Bounded Promises

The equivalence of the reachability in LoHoW and PS 2.0-rlx, coupled with Theorem 1 shows that reachability is undecidable in LoHoW. To recover decidability, we look at LoHoW with only bounded number of the promise memory type in any higher order word. Let K-LoHoW denote LoHoW with a number of promises bounded by K. (Observe that K-LoHoW corresponds to bdPS 2.0-rlx.)

Theorem 3. *The reachability problem is decidable for K-*LoHoW.

As a corollary of Theorem 3, the decidability of reachability follows for bdPS 2.0-rlx. The proof makes use of the framework of *Well-Structured Transition Systems* (WSTS) [7,13]. Next, we state that the reachability problem for K-LoHoW (even for $K = 0$) is highly non-trivial (i.e., non-primitive recursive). The proof is done by reduction from the reachability problem for lossy channel systems, in a similar to the case of TSO [8] where we insert SC-fence instructions everywhere in the process that simulates the lossy channel process (in order to ensure that no promises can be made by that process).

Theorem 4. *The reachability problem for K-*LoHoW *is non-primitive recursive.*

6 Source to Source Translation

In this section, we propose an algorithmic approach for state reachability in concurrent programs under PS 2.0. We first recall the notion of view altering reads [1], and that of bounded contexts in SC [29].

View Altering Reads. A read from the memory is view altering if it changes the view of the process reading it. This means that the view in the message being

read from was greater than the process view on some variable. The message which is read from in turn is called a view altering message. A run in which the total number of view altering reads (across all threads) is bounded (by some parameter) is called a view-bounded run. The underapproximate analysis for PS 2.0-ra without promises and reservations [1] considered view bounded runs.
Essential Events. An essential event in a run ρ of a program under PS 2.0 is either a promise, a reservation or a view altering read by some process in the run.
Bounded Context. A context is an uninterrupted sequence of actions by a single process. In a run having K contexts, the execution switches from one process to another $K-1$ times. A K bounded context run is one where the number of context switches are bounded by $K \in \mathbb{N}$. The K bounded context reachability problem in SC checks for the existence of a K bounded context run reaching some chosen instruction. Now we define the notion of bounding for PS 2.0.
The Bounded Consistent Reachability Problem. A run ρ of a concurrent program under PS 2.0, $\mathcal{MS}_0 \, [\underset{p_{i_1}}{\longrightarrow}]^* \, \mathcal{MS}_1 \, [\underset{p_{i_2}}{\longrightarrow}]^* \, \mathcal{MS}_2 \, [\underset{p_{i_3}}{\longrightarrow}]^* \ldots [\underset{p_{i_n}}{\longrightarrow}]^* \, \mathcal{MS}_n$ is called K *bounded* iff the number of essential events in ρ is $\leq K$. The K bounded reachability problem for PS 2.0 checks for the existence of a run ρ of *Prog* which is K-bounded. Assuming *Prog* has n processes, we propose an algorithm that reduces the K bounded reachability problem to a $K+n$ bounded context reachability problem of a program $[\![Prog]\!]$ under SC.
Translation Overview. We now provide a brief overview of the data structures and procedures utilized in our translation; the full details and correctness are in [5]. Let *Prog* be a concurrent program under PS 2.0 with set of processes $\mathcal{P}$ and locations Loc. Our algorithm relies on a source to source translation of *Prog* to a bounded context SC program $[\![Prog]\!]$, as shown in Figure 8 and operates on the same data domain (need not be finite). The translation (i) adds a new process (MAIN) that initializes the global variables of $[\![Prog]\!]$, (2) for each process $p \in \mathcal{P}$ adds local variables, which are initialized by the function INITPROC.

$$
\begin{aligned}
[\![Prog]\!] &:= (\langle\text{global vars}\rangle; \langle\textsc{Main}\rangle; ([\![\texttt{proc } p \texttt{ reg } \$r^* i^*]\!])^* \\
[\![\texttt{proc } p \texttt{ reg } \$r^* \; i^*]\!] &:= \texttt{proc } p \texttt{ reg } \$r^* \\
&\quad \langle\text{local vars}\rangle\langle\textsc{InitProc}\rangle\langle\text{CSO}\rangle^{p,\lambda_0}([\![i]\!]^p)^* \\
[\![\lambda : i]\!]^p &:= \lambda : \langle\text{CSI}\rangle; [\![s]\!]^p; \langle\text{CSO}\rangle^{p,\lambda} \\
[\![\texttt{if } exp \texttt{ then } i^* \texttt{ else } i^*]\!]^p &:= \texttt{if } exp \texttt{ then } ([\![i]\!]^p)^* \texttt{ else}([\![i]\!]^p)^* \\
[\![\texttt{while } exp \texttt{ do } i^*]\!]^p &:= \texttt{while } exp \texttt{ do } ([\![i]\!]^p)^* \\
[\![\texttt{assume}(exp)]\!]^p &:= \texttt{assume}(exp) \\
[\![\$r = exp]\!]^p &:= \$r = exp \\
[\![x = \$r]\!]^p_{o \in \{\texttt{rlx},\texttt{ra}\}} &:= \text{ see write Pseudocode} \\
[\![\$r = x]\!]^p_{o \in \{\texttt{rlx},\texttt{ra}\}} &:= \text{ see read Pseudocode}
\end{aligned}
$$

Fig. 8: Source-to-source translation map

This is followed by the code block $\langle CSO\rangle^{p,\lambda_0}$ (Context Switch Out) that optionally enables the process to switch out of context. For each λ labeled instruction i in p, the map $[\![\lambda : i]\!]^p$ transforms it into a sequence of instructions as follows : the code block $\langle CSI \rangle$ (Context Switch In) checks if the process is active in the current context; then it transforms each statement s of instruction i into a sequence of instructions following the map $[\![s]\!]^p$, and finally executes the code block $\langle CSO \rangle^{p,\lambda}$. $\langle CSO \rangle^{p,\lambda}$ facilitates two things: when the process is at an instruction label λ, (1) allows p to make promises/reservations after λ, s.t. the control is back at λ after certification; (2) it ensures that the machine state is consistent when p switches out of context. Translation of `assume`, `if` and `while` statements keep the same statement. Translation of read and write statements are described later. Translation of RMW statements are omitted for ease of presentation.

The set of promises a process makes has to be constrained with respect to the set of promises that it can certify To address this, in the translation, processes run in two modes : a 'normal' mode and a 'check' (*consistency check*) mode. In the normal mode, a process does not make any promises or reservations. In the check mode, the process may make promises and reservations and subsequently certify them before switching out of context. In any context, a process first enters the normal mode, and then, before exiting the context it enters the check mode. The check mode is used by the process to (1) make new promises/reservations and (2) certify consistency of the machine state. We also add an optional parameter, called *certification depth* (`certDepth`), which constrains the number of steps a process may take in the check mode to certify its promises. Figure 9 shows the structure of a translated run under SC.

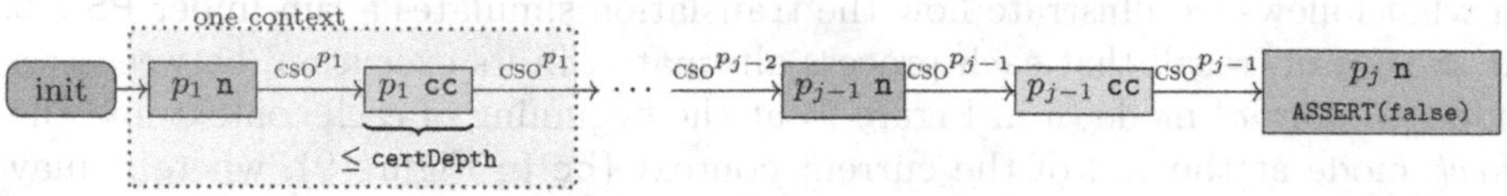

Fig. 9: Control flow: In each context, a process runs first in normal mode `n` and then in consistency check mode `cc`. The transitions between these modes is facilitated by the CSO code block of the respective process. We check assertion failures for $K + n$ context-bounded executions ($j \leq K + n$).

To reduce the PS 2.0 run into a bounded context SC run, we use the bound on the number of essential events. From the run ρ in PS 2.0, we construct a K bounded run ρ' in PS 2.0 where the processes run in the order of generation of essential events. So, the process which generates the first essential event is run first, till that event happens, then the second process which generates the second essential event is run, and so on. This continues till $K + n$ contexts : the K bounds the number of essential events, and the n is to ensure all processes are run to completion. The bound on the number of essential events gives a bound on the number of timestamps that need to be maintained. As observed in [1], each view altering read requires two timestamps; additionally, each promise/reservation requires one timestamp. Since we have K such essential events, $2K$ time stamps suffice. We choose $\mathsf{Time} = \{0, 1, 2, \ldots, 2K\}$ as the set of timestamps. Now we briefly give a high level overview of the translation.

Data Structures. The `message` data structure represents a message generated as a write or a promise and has 4 fields (i) *var*, the address of the memory location written to; (ii) the timestamp t in the view associated with the message; (iii) v, the value written; and (iv) *flag*, that keeps track of whether it is a message or a promise; and, in case of a promise, which process it belongs to. The View data structure stores, for each memory location x, (i) a timestamp $t \in \mathsf{Time}$, (ii) a value v written to x, (iii) a Boolean $l \in \{\texttt{true}, \texttt{false}\}$ representing whether t is an *exact* timestamp (which can be used for essential events) or an *abstract* timestamp (which corresponds to non-essential events).

Global Variables. The `Memory` is an array of size K holding elements of type `message` . This array is populated with the view altering messages, promises and reservations generated by the program. We maintain counters for (1) the number of elements in `Memory` ; (2) the number of context switches that have occurred; and (3) the number of essential events that have occurred.

Local Variables. In addition to its local registers, each process has local variables including (1) a local variable `view` which stores a local instance of the view function (this is of type View), (2) a flag denoting whether the process is running in the current context, and (3) a flag *checkMode* denoting whether the process is in the certification phase. We implement the certification phase as a function call, and hence store the process state and return address, while entering it.

6.1 Translation Maps

In what follows we illustrate how the translation simulates a run under PS 2.0. At the outset, recall that each process alternates, in its execution, between two modes: a *normal* mode (`n` in Figure 9) at the beginning of each context and the *check* mode at the end of the current context (`cc` in Figure 9), where it may make new promises and certify them before switching out of context.

Context Switch Out ($CSO^{p,\lambda}$). We describe the CSO module; Algorithm 1 of Figure 10 provides its pseudocode. $\mathrm{CSO}^{p,\lambda}$ is placed after each instruction λ in the original program and serves as an entry and exit point for the consistency check phase of the process. When in normal mode (`n`) after some instruction λ, CSO non-deterministically guesses whether the process should exit the context at this point, and sets the *checkMode* flag to true and subsequently, saves its local state and the return address (to mark where to resume execution from, in the next context). The process then continues its execution in the consistency check mode (`cc`) from the current instruction label (λ) itself. Now the process may generate new promises (see Algorithm 1 of Figure 10) and certify these as well as earlier made promises. In order to conclude the check mode phase, the process will enter the CSO block at some different instruction label λ'. Now since the *checkMode* flag is true, the process enters the else branch, verifies that there are no outstanding promises of p to be certified. Since the promises are not yet fulfilled, when p switches out of context, it has to mark all its promises uncertified. When the context is back to p again, this will be used to fulfil the promises or to certify them again before the context switches out of p again.

Then it exits the check mode phase, setting *checkMode* to false. Finally it loads the saved state, and returns to the instruction label λ (where it entered check mode) and exits the context. Another process may now resume execution.

Algorithm 1: CSO

```
/* nondeterministically enter
   check mode and exit context      */
if nondet() then
    if ¬checkMode then
        /* enter consistency check
           */
        if not in context then
            enter context
        end
        checkMode ← true
        save localstate
        returnAddr ← λ
    else
        /* consistency check
           successful!              */
        ensure all promises certified
        /* for next context         */
        mark all promises
          uncertified
        checkMode ← false
        load localstate
        goto returnAddr
        exit context
    end
end
```

Algorithm 2: Write

```
update localstate with write
if nondet() then
                /* (i) no fresh timestamp */
    if checkMode then
        /* write is not a promise      */
        certify message with reservation
          or splitting
else if nondet() then /* (ii) new ts */
    generate a view; generate a message
    if checkMode then
        insert message into Memory as
          Promise and certify
    else
        insert message into Memory as
          concrete message
    end
else     /* (iii) fulfill old promise */
    get Promise from Memory
    check variable, value and view match
    if checkMode then
        mark message as certified
    else
        mark message as fulfilled
    end
    replace message into Memory
end
```

Fig. 10: Algorithms for CSO and Write

Write Statements. The translation of a write instruction $[\![x := \$r]\!]_o$, where $o \in \{\texttt{rlx}, \texttt{ra}\}$ of a process p is given in Algorithm 2 of Figure 10. This is the general pseudo code for both kinds of memory accesses, with specific details pertaining to the particular access mode omitted. Let us first consider execution in the normal mode (i.e., *checkMode* is false). First, the process updates its local state with the value that it will write. Then, the process non-deterministically chooses one of three possibilities for the write, it either (i) does not assign a fresh timestamp (non-essential event), (ii) assigns a fresh timestamp and adds it to memory, or (iii) fulfils some outstanding promise.

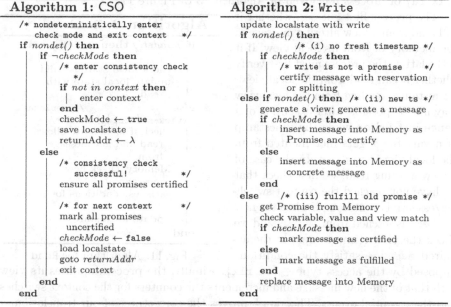

Let us now consider a write executing when *checkMode* is true, and highlight differences with the normal mode. In case (i), non essential events exclude promises and reservations. Then, while in certification phase, since we use a capped memory, the process can make a write if either (1) the write interval can be generated through splitting insertion or (2) the write can be certified with the help of a reservation. Basically the writes we make either split an existing interval (and add this to the left of a promise), or forms a part of a reservation. Thus, the time stamp of a neighbour is used. In case (ii) when a fresh time stamp is used, the write is made as a promise, and then certified before switching out of context. The analogue of case (iii) is the certification of promises for the current context; promise fulfilment happens only in the normal mode. To help a process decide the value of a promise, we use the fact that CBMC allows us to assign a non-deterministic value of a variable. On top of that, we have implemented an optimization that checks the set of possible values to be written in the future.

Read Statements. The translation of a read instruction $[\![\$r := x]\!]_o$, $o \in \{\mathtt{rlx}, \mathtt{ra}\}$ of process p is given in Algorithm 3 of Figure 11.

The process first guesses, whether it will read from a view altering message in the memory of from its local view. If it is the latter, the process must first verify whether it can read from the local view ; for instance, reading from the local view may not be possible after execution of a `fence` instruction when the timestamp of a variable x gets incremented from the local view t to $t' > t$. In the case of a view altering read, we first check that we have not reached the context switching/essential event bound. Then the new message is fetched from Memory and we check the view (timestamps) in the acquired message satisfy the conditions imposed by the access type $\in \{\mathtt{ra}, \mathtt{rlx}\}$. Finally, the process updates its view with that of the new message and increments the counters for the context switches and the essential events. Theorem 5 proves the correctness of our translation.

Algorithm 3: Read

```
if nondet() then /* local read
 */
    check local state is valid
    update local state with
     read
else                  /* nonlocal
 (view-switching) read */
    check if local state allows
     read and get message
     from
    Memory. check new
     message
    satisfies conditions for read

    update local state
end
```

Fig. 11: Algorithm for Read

Theorem 5. *Given a program Prog under PS 2.0, and $K \in \mathbb{N}$, the source to source translation constructs a program $[\![prog]\!]$ whose size is polynomial in Prog and K such that, there is a K-bounded run of Prog under PS 2.0 reaching a set of instruction labels, if and only if there is a $K{+}n$-bounded context run of $[\![prog]\!]$ under SC that reaches the same set of instruction labels.*

7 Implementation and Experimental Results

In order to check the efficiency of the source-to-source translation, we implement a prototype tool, PS2SC which is the first tool to handle PS 2.0. PS2SC takes as input a C program and a bound K and translates it to a program *Prog'* to be run under SC. We use CBMC v5.10 as the backend verifier for *Prog'*. CBMC takes as input L, the loop unrolling parameter for bounded model checking of *Prog'*. If PS2SC returns *unsafe*, then the program has an unsafe execution. Conversely, if it returns *safe* then none of the executions within the subset violate any assertion. K may be iteratively incremented to increase the number of executions explored. PS2SC has a functionality of *partial-promises* allowing subsets of processes to promise, providing an effective under-approximation technique.

We now report the results of experiments we have performed with PS2SC. We have two objectives: (1) studying the performance of PS2SC on thin-air litmus tests and benchmarks utilizing promises, and (2) comparing PS2SC with other model checkers when operating in the promise-free mode. In the first case we show that PS2SC is able to uncover bugs in litmus tests and examples with few reads and writes to the shared memory. When this interaction and subsequent non-determinism of PS 2.0 increases, we also enable *partial promises*. For the second case we compare PS2SC with three model checkers CDSCHECKER [25], GENMC [18] and RCMC [17] that support the promise-free subset of PS 2.0. Our observations highlight the ability to detect hard to find bugs with small K for unsafe benchmarks. We do not consider compilation time for any tool while reporting the results. For PS2SC, the time reported is the time taken by the CBMC backend for analysis. The timeout used is 1hr for all benchmarks. All experiments are conducted on a machine with 3.00 GHz Intel Core i5-3330 CPU and 8GB RAM running an Ubuntu-16 64-bit operating system. We denote timeout by 'TO', and memory limit exceeded by 'MLE'.

Benchmarks Utilizing Promises. In the following, we report the performance of PS2SC on litmus tests and parametrized tests.

Litmus Tests. We test PS2SC on litmus-tests adapted from [16,22,11,23]. These examples are small programs that serve as barebones thin-air tests for the C11 memory model. Consistency tests based on the Java Memory Model are proposed in [23], which were experimented on by [27] with their MRDer tool. Like MRDer, PS2SC is able to verify most of these tests within 1 minute which shows its ability to handle typical programming idioms of PS 2.0 (see Table 1).

testcase	K	PS2SC
ARM_weak	4	0.765s
Upd-Stuck	4	1.252s
split	4	25.737s
LBd	3	1.481s
LBfd	3	1.512s
CYC	5	1.967s
Coh-CYC	5	42.67s
Pugh2	3	13.725s
Pugh3	3	12.920s
Pugh8	3	1.67s
Pugh5	5	4.811s
Pugh10	5	3.868s
Pugh13	5	3.345s

Table 1: Litmus Tests

Parameterized Tests. In Table 2, we consider unsafe examples adapted from the Fibonacci-based benchmarks of SV-COMP 2019 [10]. In these examples a process is required to generate a promise (speculative write) with value as the ith fibonacci number. This promise is certified using *process-local* reads. Thus though the parameter i increases the interaction of the promising process with the memory remains constant. The **CAS** variant requires the process to make use of reservations. We note that PS2SC uncovers the bugs effectively in these cases. In cases where promise-certificate requires reads from external processes, the amount of shared-memory interaction increases with i. In this case, we use *partial promises*.

testcase	K	PS2SC
fib_local_3	4	0.742s
fib_local_4	4	0.761s
fib_local_cas_3	4	1.132s
fib_local_cas_4	4	1.147s

testcase	K	PS2SC[1p]
fib_global_2	4	55.972s
fib_global_3	4	2m4s
fib_global_4	4	4m20s
exp_global_1	4	19m37s
exp_global_2	4	41m12s

Table 2: Above: testcases with local reads, Below: global reads

How to recover tractable analysis? We note that though the above example consists of several processes interacting with the memory, the bug can be uncovered even if only a *single* process is allowed to make promising writes. We run PS2SC in the partial-promises mode. We considered the case where only a single process generates promises, and PS2SC was able to uncover the bug. The results obtained are in Table 2, where PS2SC[1p] denotes that only one process is permitted to perform promises. We then repeat our experiments on other unsafe benchmarks - including `ExponentialBug` from Fig. 2 of [15] - and have similar observations. To summarize, we note that the huge non-determinism of PS 2.0 can be fought by using the modular approach of partial-promises.

Comparing with Other Tools. In this section, we compare performance of PS2SC in promise-free mode with CDSChecker [25], GenMC [18] and Rcmc [17] (which do not support promises). The main objective of this section is to provide evidence for the practicability of the essential-event-bounding technique. The results of this section indicate that the source-to-source translation with K-essential-event bounding is effective at uncovering hard to find bugs in non-trivial programs. Additionally, we observe that in most examples considered, we had $K \leq 10$. We provide here a subset of the experimental results and the remaining in the full version of the paper [5]. In the tables that follow we provide the value of K (for PS2SC) and the value of L (loop-unrolling bound) for all tools.

Parameterized Benchmarks. In Table 3, we experiment on two parametrized benchmarks: `ExponentialBug` (Fig. 2 of [15]) and `Fibonacci` (from SV-COMP 2019). In `ExponentialBug`(N) N is the number writes made to a variable by a process. We note that in `ExponentialBug`(N) the number of executions grows as $N!$, while the processes have to follow a specific interleaving to uncover the hard to find bug. In `Fibonacci`(N), two processes compute the value of the nth fibonacci number in a distributed fashion.

benchmark	L	K	PS2SC	CDSC	GenMC	RCMC
exponential_25_unsafe	25	10	3.532s	7.239s	3.736s	TO
exponential_50_unsafe	50	10	6.128s	36.361s	39.920s	TO
fibonacci_3_unsafe	3	20	9.392s	46m8s	0.462s	0.544s
fibonacci_4_unsafe	4	20	34.019s	TO	12.437s	18.953s

Table 3: Parameterized benchmarks

Concurrent data structures based benchmarks. In Table 4, we consider benchmarks based on concurrent data structures. The first of these is a concurrent locking algorithm originating from [14]. The second, `LinuxLocks(N)` is adapted from evaluations of CDSChecker [25]. We note that if not completely fenced, it is unsafe. We fence all but one lock access. Both these results show the ability of our tool to uncover bugs with a small value of K.

benchmark	L	K	PS2SC	CDSC	GenMC	RCMC
hehner2_unsafe	4	5	7.207s	0.033s	0.094s	0.087s
hehner3_unsafe	4	5	28.345s	0.036s	2m53s	1m13s
linuxlocks2_unsafe	2	4	0.547s	0.032s	0.073s	0.078s
linuxlocks3_unsafe	2	4	1.031s	0.031s	0.083s	0.081s

Table 4: Concurrent data structures

Variations of mutual exclusion protocols. We consider variants of mutual exclusion protocols from SV-COMP 2019. The fully fenced versions of the protocols are *safe*. We modify these protocols by introducing bugs and comparing the performance of PS2SC for bug detection with the other tools. These benchmarks are parameterized by the number of processes. In Table 5, we unfence a single process of the Peterson and Szymanski protocols making them *unsafe*. These are benchmarks `petersonU(i)` and `szymanskiU(i)` where `i` is the number of processes.

In `petersonB(i)`, we keep all processes fenced but introduce a bug into the critical section of a process (write a value to a shared variable and read a different value from it). We note that the other tools do not scale, while PS2SC is able to detect the bug within one minute, showing that essential event-bounding is an effective under-approximation technique for bug-finding.

benchmark	L	K	PS2SC	CDSChecker	GenMC	RCMC
petersonU(4)	1	6	1.408s	0.039s	TO	9.129s
petersonU(8)	1	6	47.786s	TO	TO	TO
szymanskiU(4)	1	2	1.015s	0.043s	MLE	TO
szymanskiU(8)	1	2	6.176s	TO	TO	TO
petersonB(3)	1	2	0.487s	0.053s	0.083s	0.087s
petersonB(5)	1	2	2.713s	TO	TO	TO
petersonB(7)	1	2	11.008s	TO	TO	TO

Table 5: Mutual exclusion benchmarks with a single unfenced process

Remark. Through all these experiments, we observe that SMC tools and our tool try to tackle the same problem by using orthogonal approaches to finding bugs. Hence, through the experiments above we are not trying to pitch one approach against the other, but rather trying to highlight the differences in their features. We have exhibited examples where our tool is able to uncover hard-to-find bugs faster than the others with relatively small values of K.

8 Related Work and Conclusion

Most of the existing verification work for C/C++ concurrency models concern the development of stateless model checking coupled with dynamic partial order reduction (e.g., [6,17,18,26,25]) and do not handle the promising semantics. Context-bounding has been proposed in [29] for programs running under SC. This work has been extended in different directions and has led to efficient and scalable techniques for the analysis of concurrent programs (see e.g., [24,21,33,32,12,34]). In the context of weak memory models, context-bounded analyses have been proposed for TSO/PSO [9,31] and POWER [3].

The decidability of the verification problems for programs running under weak memory models has been addressed for TSO [8], RA [1], SRA [19], and POWER [2]. We believe that our proof techniques can be easily adapted to work with different variants of the promising semantics [16] (see [4]). For instance, in the code-to-code translation, the mechanism for making and certifying promises and reservations is isolated in one module, which can be easily changed to cover different variants of the promising semantics. Furthermore, the undecidability proof still goes through for [16]. Moreover, providing a tool for the verification of (among other things) litmus tests, will provide a valuable environment which can be used in further improvements of the promising semantics. To the best of our knowledge, this the first time that this problem is investigated for PS 2.0-rlx and PS2SC is the first tool for automated verification of programs under PS 2.0. Finally, studying the decidability problem for related models that solve the thin-air problem (e.g., Paviotti et al. [27]) is interesting and kept as future work.

References

1. Abdulla, P.A., Arora, J., Atig, M.F., Krishna, S.N.: Verification of programs under the release-acquire semantics. In: McKinley, K.S., Fisher, K. (eds.) Proceedings of the 40th ACM SIGPLAN Conference on Programming Language Design and Implementation, PLDI 2019, Phoenix, AZ, USA, June 22-26, 2019. pp. 1117–1132. ACM (2019)
2. Abdulla, P.A., Atig, M.F., Bouajjani, A., Derevenetc, E., Leonardsson, C., Meyer, R.: Safety verification under power. In: NETYS 2020. Lecture Notes in Computer Science, Springer (2020), to appear
3. Abdulla, P.A., Atig, M.F., Bouajjani, A., Ngo, T.P.: Context-bounded analysis for POWER. In: Legay, A., Margaria, T. (eds.) Tools and Algorithms for the Construction and Analysis of Systems - 23rd International Conference, TACAS 2017, Held as Part of the European Joint Conferences on Theory and Practice of Software, ETAPS 2017, Uppsala, Sweden, April 22-29, 2017, Proceedings, Part II. Lecture Notes in Computer Science, vol. 10206, pp. 56–74. Springer (2017)
4. Abdulla, P.A., Atig, M.F., Godbole, A., Krishna, S.N., Vafeiadis, V.: Verification of c11 programs with relaxed accesses (2019), `https://www.cse.iitb.ac.in/~krishnas/ps1.pdf`
5. Abdulla, P.A., Atig, M.F., Godbole, A., Krishna, S.N., Vafeiadis, V.: The decidability of verification under promising 2.0. CoRR **abs/2007.09944** (2020), `https://arxiv.org/abs/2007.09944`
6. Abdulla, P.A., Atig, M.F., Jonsson, B., Ngo, T.P.: Optimal stateless model checking under the release-acquire semantics. Proc. ACM Program. Lang. **2**(OOPSLA), 135:1–135:29 (2018)
7. Abdulla, P.A., Jonsson, B.: Verifying programs with unreliable channels. Inf. Comput. **127**(2), 91–101 (1996)
8. Atig, M.F., Bouajjani, A., Burckhardt, S., Musuvathi, M.: On the verification problem for weak memory models. In: Hermenegildo, M.V., Palsberg, J. (eds.) Proceedings of the 37th ACM SIGPLAN-SIGACT Symposium on Principles of Programming Languages, POPL 2010, Madrid, Spain, January 17-23, 2010. pp. 7–18. ACM (2010)
9. Atig, M.F., Bouajjani, A., Parlato, G.: Getting rid of store-buffers in TSO analysis. In: Gopalakrishnan, G., Qadeer, S. (eds.) Computer Aided Verification - 23rd International Conference, CAV 2011, Snowbird, UT, USA, July 14-20, 2011. Proceedings. Lecture Notes in Computer Science, vol. 6806, pp. 99–115. Springer (2011)
10. Beyer, D.: Automatic verification of C and java programs: SV-COMP 2019. In: Beyer, D., Huisman, M., Kordon, F., Steffen, B. (eds.) Tools and Algorithms for the Construction and Analysis of Systems - 25 Years of TACAS: TOOLympics, Held as Part of ETAPS 2019, Prague, Czech Republic, April 6-11, 2019, Proceedings, Part III. Lecture Notes in Computer Science, vol. 11429, pp. 133–155. Springer (2019)
11. Chakraborty, S., Vafeiadis, V.: Grounding thin-air reads with event structures. Proc. ACM Program. Lang. **3**(POPL), 70:1–70:28 (2019)
12. Emmi, M., Qadeer, S., Rakamaric, Z.: Delay-bounded scheduling. In: Ball, T., Sagiv, M. (eds.) Proceedings of the 38th ACM SIGPLAN-SIGACT Symposium on Principles of Programming Languages, POPL 2011, Austin, TX, USA, January 26-28, 2011. pp. 411–422. ACM (2011)
13. Finkel, A., Schnoebelen, P.: Well-structured transition systems everywhere! Theor. Comput. Sci. **256**(1-2), 63–92 (2001)

14. Hehner, E.C.R., Shyamasundar, R.K.: An implementation of P and V. Inf. Process. Lett. **12**(4), 196–198 (1981)
15. Huang, J.: Stateless model checking concurrent programs with maximal causality reduction. In: Grove, D., Blackburn, S. (eds.) Proceedings of the 36th ACM SIGPLAN Conference on Programming Language Design and Implementation, Portland, OR, USA, June 15-17, 2015. pp. 165–174. ACM (2015)
16. Kang, J., Hur, C., Lahav, O., Vafeiadis, V., Dreyer, D.: A promising semantics for relaxed-memory concurrency. In: Castagna, G., Gordon, A.D. (eds.) Proceedings of the 44th ACM SIGPLAN Symposium on Principles of Programming Languages, POPL 2017, Paris, France, January 18-20, 2017. pp. 175–189. ACM (2017)
17. Kokologiannakis, M., Lahav, O., Sagonas, K., Vafeiadis, V.: Effective stateless model checking for C/C++ concurrency. Proc. ACM Program. Lang. **2**(POPL), 17:1–17:32 (2018)
18. Kokologiannakis, M., Raad, A., Vafeiadis, V.: Model checking for weakly consistent libraries. In: McKinley, K.S., Fisher, K. (eds.) Proceedings of the 40th ACM SIGPLAN Conference on Programming Language Design and Implementation, PLDI 2019, Phoenix, AZ, USA, June 22-26, 2019. pp. 96–110. ACM (2019)
19. Lahav, O., Boker, U.: Decidable verification under a causally consistent shared memory. In: Donaldson, A.F., Torlak, E. (eds.) Proceedings of the 41st ACM SIGPLAN International Conference on Programming Language Design and Implementation, PLDI 2020, London, UK, June 15-20, 2020. pp. 211–226. ACM (2020)
20. Lahav, O., Vafeiadis, V., Kang, J., Hur, C., Dreyer, D.: Repairing sequential consistency in C/C++11. In: Cohen, A., Vechev, M.T. (eds.) Proceedings of the 38th ACM SIGPLAN Conference on Programming Language Design and Implementation, PLDI 2017, Barcelona, Spain, June 18-23, 2017. pp. 618–632. ACM (2017)
21. Lal, A., Reps, T.W.: Reducing concurrent analysis under a context bound to sequential analysis. Formal Methods Syst. Des. **35**(1), 73–97 (2009)
22. Lee, S., Cho, M., Podkopaev, A., Chakraborty, S., Hur, C., Lahav, O., Vafeiadis, V.: Promising 2.0: global optimizations in relaxed memory concurrency. In: Donaldson, A.F., Torlak, E. (eds.) Proceedings of the 41st ACM SIGPLAN International Conference on Programming Language Design and Implementation, PLDI 2020, London, UK, June 15-20, 2020. pp. 362–376. ACM (2020)
23. Manson, J., Pugh, W., Adve, S.V.: The java memory model. In: Palsberg, J., Abadi, M. (eds.) Proceedings of the 32nd ACM SIGPLAN-SIGACT Symposium on Principles of Programming Languages, POPL 2005, Long Beach, California, USA, January 12-14, 2005. pp. 378–391. ACM (2005)
24. Musuvathi, M., Qadeer, S.: Iterative context bounding for systematic testing of multithreaded programs. In: Ferrante, J., McKinley, K.S. (eds.) Proceedings of the ACM SIGPLAN 2007 Conference on Programming Language Design and Implementation, San Diego, California, USA, June 10-13, 2007. pp. 446–455. ACM (2007)
25. Norris, B., Demsky, B.: Cdschecker: checking concurrent data structures written with C/C++ atomics. In: Hosking, A.L., Eugster, P.T., Lopes, C.V. (eds.) Proceedings of the 2013 ACM SIGPLAN International Conference on Object Oriented Programming Systems Languages & Applications, OOPSLA 2013, part of SPLASH 2013, Indianapolis, IN, USA, October 26-31, 2013. pp. 131–150. ACM (2013)
26. Norris, B., Demsky, B.: A practical approach for model checking C/C++11 code. ACM Trans. Program. Lang. Syst. **38**(3), 10:1–10:51 (2016)
27. Paviotti, M., Cooksey, S., Paradis, A., Wright, D., Owens, S., Batty, M.: Modular relaxed dependencies in weak memory concurrency. In: Müller, P. (ed.) Programming

Languages and Systems - 29th European Symposium on Programming, ESOP 2020, Held as Part of the European Joint Conferences on Theory and Practice of Software, ETAPS 2020, Dublin, Ireland, April 25-30, 2020, Proceedings. Lecture Notes in Computer Science, vol. 12075, pp. 599–625. Springer (2020)

28. Post, E.L.: A variant of a recursively unsolvable problem. Bull. Amer. Math. Soc. **52**, 264–268 (1946)
29. Qadeer, S., Rehof, J.: Context-bounded model checking of concurrent software. In: Halbwachs, N., Zuck, L.D. (eds.) Tools and Algorithms for the Construction and Analysis of Systems, 11th International Conference, TACAS 2005, Held as Part of the Joint European Conferences on Theory and Practice of Software, ETAPS 2005, Edinburgh, UK, April 4-8, 2005, Proceedings. Lecture Notes in Computer Science, vol. 3440, pp. 93–107. Springer (2005)
30. Svendsen, K., Pichon-Pharabod, J., Doko, M., Lahav, O., Vafeiadis, V.: A separation logic for a promising semantics. In: Ahmed, A. (ed.) Programming Languages and Systems - 27th European Symposium on Programming, ESOP 2018, Held as Part of the European Joint Conferences on Theory and Practice of Software, ETAPS 2018, Thessaloniki, Greece, April 14-20, 2018, Proceedings. Lecture Notes in Computer Science, vol. 10801, pp. 357–384. Springer (2018)
31. Tomasco, E., Nguyen, T.L., Fischer, B., Torre, S.L., Parlato, G.: Using shared memory abstractions to design eager sequentializations for weak memory models. In: Cimatti, A., Sirjani, M. (eds.) Software Engineering and Formal Methods - 15th International Conference, SEFM 2017, Trento, Italy, September 4-8, 2017, Proceedings. Lecture Notes in Computer Science, vol. 10469, pp. 185–202. Springer (2017)
32. Torre, S.L., Madhusudan, P., Parlato, G.: Context-bounded analysis of concurrent queue systems. In: Ramakrishnan, C.R., Rehof, J. (eds.) Tools and Algorithms for the Construction and Analysis of Systems, 14th International Conference, TACAS 2008, Held as Part of the Joint European Conferences on Theory and Practice of Software, ETAPS 2008, Budapest, Hungary, March 29-April 6, 2008. Proceedings. Lecture Notes in Computer Science, vol. 4963, pp. 299–314. Springer (2008)
33. Torre, S.L., Madhusudan, P., Parlato, G.: Reducing context-bounded concurrent reachability to sequential reachability. In: Bouajjani, A., Maler, O. (eds.) Computer Aided Verification, 21st International Conference, CAV 2009, Grenoble, France, June 26 - July 2, 2009. Proceedings. Lecture Notes in Computer Science, vol. 5643, pp. 477–492. Springer (2009)
34. Torre, S.L., Madhusudan, P., Parlato, G.: Model-checking parameterized concurrent programs using linear interfaces. In: Touili, T., Cook, B., Jackson, P.B. (eds.) Computer Aided Verification, 22nd International Conference, CAV 2010, Edinburgh, UK, July 15-19, 2010. Proceedings. Lecture Notes in Computer Science, vol. 6174, pp. 629–644. Springer (2010)

Data Flow Analysis of Asynchronous Systems using Infinite Abstract Domains

Snigdha Athaiya(✉)[1], Raghavan Komondoor[1], and K. Narayan Kumar[2]

[1] Indian Institute of Science, Bengaluru, India
{snigdha,raghavan}@iisc.ac.in
[2] Chennai Mathematical Institute, Chennai, India
kumar@cmi.ac.in

Abstract. Asynchronous message-passing systems are employed frequently to implement distributed mechanisms, protocols, and processes. This paper addresses the problem of precise data flow analysis for such systems. To obtain good precision, data flow analysis needs to somehow skip execution paths that read more messages than the number of messages sent so far in the path, as such paths are infeasible at run time. Existing data flow analysis techniques do elide a subset of such infeasible paths, but have the restriction that they admit only finite abstract analysis domains. In this paper we propose a generalization of these approaches to admit infinite abstract analysis domains, as such domains are commonly used in practice to obtain high precision. We have implemented our approach, and have analyzed its performance on a set of 14 benchmarks. On these benchmarks our tool obtains significantly higher precision compared to a baseline approach that does not elide any infeasible paths and to another baseline that elides infeasible paths but admits only finite abstract domains.

Keywords: Data Flow Analysis · Message-passing systems.

1 Introduction

Distributed software that communicates by asynchronous message passing is a very important software paradigm in today's world. It is employed in varied domains, such as distributed protocols and workflows, event-driven systems, and UI-based systems. Popular languages used in this domain include Go (https://golang.org/), Akka (https://akka.io/), and P (https://github.com/p-org).

Analysis and verification of asynchronous systems is an important problem, and poses a rich set of challenges. The research community has focused historically on a variety of approaches to tackle this overall problem, such as model checking and systematic concurrency testing [25,13], formal verification to check properties such as reachability or coverability of states [41,3,2,21,18,31,19,1], and data flow analysis [29].

Data flow analysis [32,30] is a specific type of verification technique that propagates values from an *abstract domain* while accounting for all paths in a

N. Yoshida (Ed.): ESOP 2021, LNCS 12648, pp. 30–58, 2021.
https://doi.org/10.1007/978-3-030-72019-3_2

program. It can hence be used to check whether a property or assertion always holds. The existing verification and data flow analysis approaches mentioned earlier have a major limitation, which is that they admit only finite abstract domains. This, in general, limits the classes of properties that can be successfully verified. On the other hand, data flow analysis of sequential programs using infinite abstract domains, e.g., *constant propagation* [32], *interval analysis* [12], and *octagons* [44], is a well developed area, and is routinely employed in verification settings. In this paper we seek to bridge this fundamental gap, and develop a precise data flow analysis framework for message-passing asynchronous systems that admits infinite abstract domains.

1.1 Motivating Example: Leader election

```
max := process number; send ⟨1, max⟩
Process is in active mode
while true do
    if process is in passive mode then
        receive a mesg and send this same mesg
    else if message ⟨1, i⟩ arrives then
        if i ≠ max then
            Send message ⟨2, i⟩; left := i
        else
            Declare max as the global maximum
            nr_leaders++; assert(nr_leaders = 1)
    else if message ⟨2, j⟩ arrives then
        if left > j and left > max then
            max := left
            Send message ⟨1, max⟩
        else
            Process enters passive mode
```

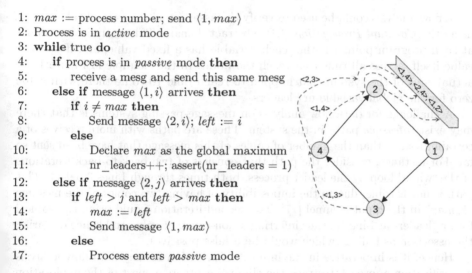

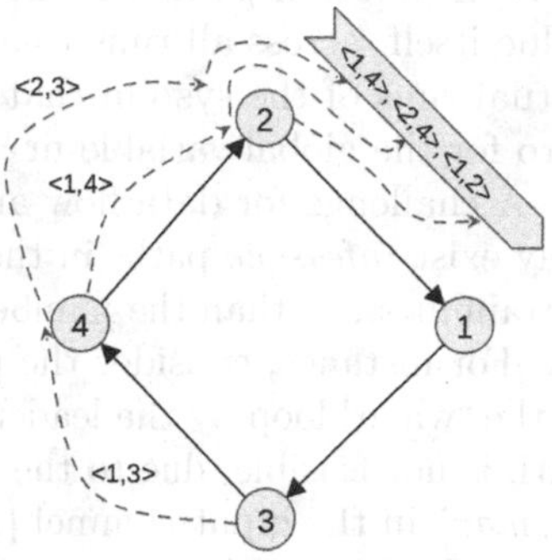

Fig. 1. Pseudo-code of each process in leader election, and a partial run

To motivate our work we use a benchmark program[3] in the *Promela* language [25] that implements a *leader election* protocol [17]. In the protocol there is a ring of processes, and each process has a unique number. The objective is to discover the "leader", which is the process with the maximum number. The pseudo-code of each process in the protocol is shown in the left side of Figure 1. Each process has its own copy of local variables *max* and *left*, whereas nr_leaders is a global variable that is common to all the processes (its initial value is zero). Each process sends messages to the next process in the ring via an unbounded FIFO channel. Each process becomes "ready" whenever a message is available for it to receive, and at any step of the protocol any one ready process (chosen

[3] file **assertion.leader.prm** in www.imm.dtu.dk/~albl/promela-models.zip.

non-deterministically) executes one iteration of its "while" loop. (We formalize these execution rules in a more general fashion in Section 2.1.) The messages are a 2-tuple $\langle x, i \rangle$, where x can be 1 or 2, and $1 \leq i \leq max$. The right side of Figure 1 shows a snapshot at an intermediate point during a run of the protocol. Each dashed arrow between two nodes represents a send of a message and a (completed) receipt of the same message. The block arrow depicts the channel from Process 2 to Process 1, which happens to contain three sent (but still unreceived) messages.

It is notable that in any run of the protocol, Lines 10-11 happen to get executed only by the actual leader process, and that too, exactly once. Hence, the assertion never fails. The argument for this claim is not straightforward, and we refer the reader to the paper [17] for the details.

1.2 Challenges in property checking

Data flow analysis could be used to verify the assertion in the example above, e.g., using the *Constant Propagation* (CP) abstract domain. This analysis determines at each program point whether each variable has a fixed value, and if yes, the value itself, across all runs that reach the point. In the example in Figure 1, all actual runs of the system that happen to reach Line 10 come there with value zero for the global variable nr_leaders.

A challenge for data flow analysis on message-passing systems is that there may exist *infeasible* paths in the system. These are paths with more receives of a certain message than the number of copies of this message that have been sent so far. For instance, consider the path that consists of two back-to-back iterations of the "while" loop by the leader process, both times through Lines 3,6,9-11. This path is not feasible, due to the impossibility of having two copies of the message $\langle 1, max \rangle$ in the input channel [17]. The second iteration would bring the value 1 for nr_leaders at Line 10, thus inferring a non-constant value and hence declaring the assertion as failing (which would be a false positive).

Hence, it is imperative in the interest of precision for any data flow analysis or verification approach to track the channel contents as part of the exploration of the state space. Tracking the contents of unbounded channels precisely is known to be undecidable even when solving problems such as reachability and coverability (which are simpler than data flow analysis). Hence, existing approaches either bound the channels (which in general causes unsoundness), or use sound abstractions such as *unordered channels* (also known as the Petri Net or VASS abstraction) or *lossy channels*. Such abstractions suffice to elide a subset of infeasible paths. In our running example, the unordered channel abstraction happens to suffice to elide infeasible paths that could contribute to a false positive at the point of the assertion. However, the analysis would need to use an abstract domain such as CP to track the values of integer variables. This is an infinite domain (due to the infinite number of integers). The most closely related previous dataflow analysis approach for distributed systems [29] does use the unordered channel abstraction, but does not admit infinite abstract domains, and hence cannot verify assertions such as the one in the example above.

1.3 Our Contributions

This paper is the first one to the best of our knowledge to propose an approach for data flow analysis for asynchronous message-passing systems that (a) admits infinite abstract domains, (b) uses a reasonably precise channel abstraction among the ones known in the literature (namely, the unordered channels abstraction), and (c) computes maximally precise results possible under the selected channel abstraction. Every other approach we are aware of exhibits a strict subset of the three attributes listed above. It is notable that previous approaches do tackle the infinite state space induced by the unbounded channel contents. However, they either do not reason about variable values at all, or only allow variables that are based on finite domains.

Our primary contribution is an approach that we call *Backward DFAS*. This approach is maximally precise, and admits a class of infinite abstract domains. This class includes well-known examples such as Linear Constant Propagation (LCP) [51] and Affine Relationships Analysis (ARA) [46], but does not include the full (CP) analysis. We also propose another approach, which we call *Forward DFAS*, which admits a broader class of abstract domains, but is not guaranteed to be maximally precise on all programs.

We describe a prototype implementation of both our approaches. On a set of 14 real benchmarks, which are small but involve many complex idioms and paths, our tool verifies approximately 50% more assertions than our implementation of the baseline approach [29].

The rest of the paper is structured as follows. Section 2 covers the background and notation that will be assumed throughout the paper. We present the Backward DFAS approach in Section 3, and the Forward DFAS approach in Section 4. Section 5 discusses our implementation and evaluation. Section 6 discusses related work, and Section 7 concludes the paper.

2 Background and Terminology

Vector addition systems with states or VASS [27] are a popular modelling technique for distributed systems. We begin this section by defining an extension to VASS, which we call a *VASS-Control Flow Graph* or *VCFG*.

Definition 1. *A* VASS-Control Flow Graph *or VCFG $\mathcal{G}$ is a graph, and is described by the tuple $\langle Q, \delta, r, q_0, V, \pi, \theta \rangle$, where*
Q is a finite set of nodes, $\delta \subseteq Q \times Q$ is a finite set of edges,
$r \in \mathbb{N}$, q_0 is the start *node, V is a set of variables or memory locations,*
$\pi : \delta \to A$ maps each edge to an action, *where $A \equiv ((V \to \mathbb{Z}) \to (V \to \mathbb{Z}))$,*
$\theta : \delta \to \mathbb{Z}^r$ maps each edge to a vector in $\mathbb{Z}^r$.

For any edge $e = (q_1, q_2) \in \delta$, if $\pi(e) = a$ and $\theta(e) = w$, then a is called the *action* of e and w is called the *queuing vector* of e. This edge is depicted as $q_1 \xrightarrow{a,w} q_2$. The variables and the *actions* are the only additional features of a VCFG over VASS.

A *configuration* of a VCFG is a tuple $\langle q, c, \xi \rangle$, where $q \in Q$, $c \in \mathbb{N}^r$ and $\xi \in (V \rightarrow \mathbb{Z})$. The initial configuration of a VCFG is $\langle q_0, \mathbf{0}, \xi_0 \rangle$, where $\mathbf{0}$ denotes a vector with r zeroes, and ξ_0 is a given initial valuation for the variables. The VCFG can be said to have r *counters*. The vector c in each configuration can be thought of as a valuation to the counters. The transitions between VCFG configurations are according to the rule below:

$$\frac{e = (q_1, q_2),\ e \in \delta,\ \pi(e) = a,\ \theta(e) = w,\ a(\xi_1) = \xi_2,\ c_1 + w = c_2,\ c_2 \geq \mathbf{0}}{\langle q_1, c_1, \xi_1 \rangle \Rightarrow_e \langle q_2, c_2, \xi_2 \rangle}$$

2.1 Modeling of Asynchronous Message Passing Systems as VCFGs

Asynchronous systems are composed of finite number of independently executing processes that communicate with each other by passing messages along FIFO channels. The processes may have local variables, and there may exist shared (or global) variables as well. For simplicity of presentation we assume all variables are global.

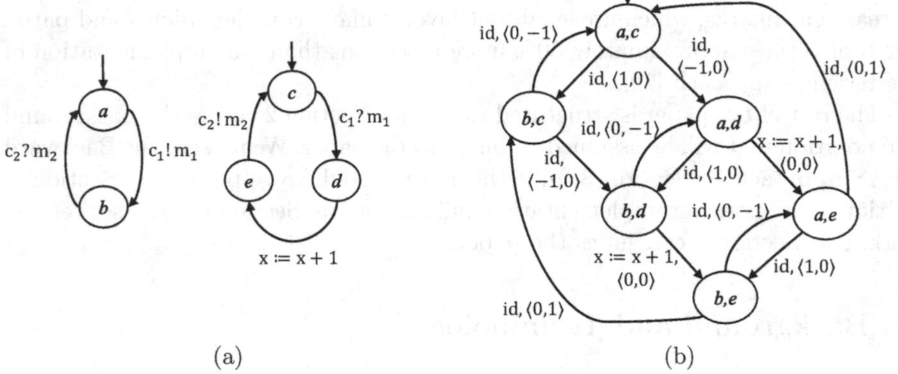

Fig. 2. (a) Asynchronous system with two processes, (b) its VCFG model

Figure 2(a) shows a simple asynchronous system with two processes. In this system there are two channels, c_1 and c_2, and a message alphabet consisting of two elements, m_1 and m_2. The semantics we assume for message-passing systems is the same as what is used by the tool Spin [25]. A configuration of the system consists of the current control states of all the processes, the contents of all the channels, and the values of all the variables. A single transition of the system consists of a transition of one of the processes from its current control-state to a successor control state, accompanied with the corresponding queuing operation or variable-update action. A transition labeled c ! m can be taken unconditionally, and results in 'm' being appended to the tail of the channel 'c'. A transition labeled c ? m can be taken only if an instance of 'm' is available at the head of 'c', and results in this instance getting removed from 'c'. (Note, based on the context, we over-load the term "message" to mean either an element of the message alphabet, or an instance of a message-alphabet element in a channel at run-time.)

Asynchronous systems can be modeled as VCFGs, and our approach performs data flow analysis on VCFGs. We now illustrate how an asynchronous system can be modeled as a VCFG. We assume a fixed number of processes in the system. We do this illustration using the example VCFG in Figure 2(b), which models the system in Figure 2(a). Each node of the VCFG represents a tuple of control-states of the processes, while each edge corresponds to a transition of the system. The action of a VCFG edge is identical to the action that labels the corresponding process transition. ("id" in Figure 2(b) represents the *identity* action) The VCFG will have as many counters as the number of unique pairs $(\mathrm{c_i}, \mathrm{m_j})$ such that the operation $\mathrm{c_i}\,!\,\mathrm{m_j}$ is performed by any process. If an edge e in the VCFG corresponds to a send transition $\mathrm{c_i}\,!\,\mathrm{m_j}$ of the system, then e's queuing vector would have a +1 for the counter corresponding to $(\mathrm{c_i}, \mathrm{m_j})$ and a zero for all the other counters. Analogously, a receive operation gets modeled as -1 in the queuing vector. In Figure 2(b), the first counter is for $(\mathrm{c_1},\mathrm{m_1})$ while the second counter is for $(\mathrm{c_2},\mathrm{m_2})$. Note that the +1 and -1 encoding (which are inherited from VASS's) effectively cause FIFO channels to be treated as unordered channels.

When each process can invoke procedures as part of its execution, such systems can be modeled using *inter-procedural* VCFGs, or iVCFGs. These are extensions of VCFGs just as standard inter-procedural control-flow graphs are extensions of control-flow graphs. Constructing an iVCFG for a given system is straightforward, under a restriction that at most one of the processes in the system can be executing a procedure other than its main procedure at any time. This restriction is also present in other related work [29,5].

2.2 Data flow analysis over iVCFGs

Data flow analysis is based on a given *complete lattice* $\mathcal{L}$, which serves as the abstract domain. As a pre-requisite step before we can perform our data flow analysis on iVCFGs, we first consider each edge $v \xrightarrow{a,w} w$ in each procedure in the iVCFG, and replace the (concrete) action a with an abstract action f, where $f : \mathcal{L} \to \mathcal{L}$ is a given abstract transfer function that *conservatively over-approximates* [12] the behavior of the concrete action a.

Let p be a path in a iVCFG, let p_0 be the first node in the path, and let ξ_i be a valuation to the variables at the beginning of p. The path p is said to be *feasible* if, starting from the configuration $\langle p_0, \mathbf{0}, \xi_i \rangle$, the configuration $\langle q, d, \xi \rangle$ obtained at each successive point in the path is such that $d \geq \mathbf{0}$, with successive configurations along the path being generated as per the rule for transitions among VCFG configurations that was given before Section 2.1. For any path $p = e_1 e_2 \ldots e_k$ of an iVCFG, we define its *path transfer function* $ptf(p)$ as $f_{e_k} \circ f_{e_{k-1}} \cdots \circ f_{e_1}$, where f_e is the abstract action associated with edge e.

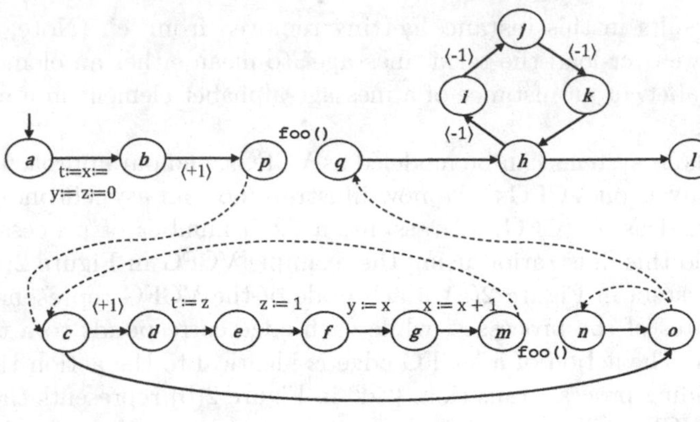

Fig. 3. Example iVCFG

The standard data flow analysis problem for sequential programs is to compute the join-over-all-paths (JOP) solution. Our problem statement is to compute the join-over-all-feasible-paths (JOFP) solution for iVCFGs. Formally stated, if *start* is the entry node of the "main" procedure of the iVCFG, given any node *target* in any procedure of the iVCFG, and an "entry" value $d_0 \in \mathcal{L}$ at *start* such that d_0 conservatively over-approximates ξ_0, we wish to compute the JOFP value at *target* as defined by the following expression:

$$\bigsqcup_{\substack{p \text{ is a feasible and interprocedurally valid} \\ \text{path in the iVCFG from } start \text{ to } target}} (ptf(p))(d_0)$$

Intuitively, due to the unordered channel abstraction, every run of the system corresponds to a feasible path in the iVCFG, but not vice versa. Hence, the JOFP solution above is guaranteed to conservatively over-approximate the JOP solution on the *runs* of the system (which is not computable in general).

3 Backward DFAS Approach

In this section we present our key contribution – the *Backward DFAS* (Data Flow Analysis of Asynchronous Systems) algorithm – an interprocedural algorithm that computes the precise JOFP at any given node of the iVCFG.

We begin by presenting a running example, which is the iVCFG with two procedures depicted in Figure 3. There is only one channel and one message in the message alphabet in this example, and hence the *queuing vectors* associated with the edges are of size 1. The edges without the vectors are implicitly associated with zero vectors. The *actions* associated with edges are represented in the form of assignment statements. The edges without assignment statements next to them have *identity* actions. The upper part of the Figure 3, consisting of nodes

$a, b, p, q, h, i, j, k, l$, is the VCFG of the "main" procedure. The remaining nodes constitute the VCFG of the (tail) recursive procedure `foo`. The solid edges are intra-procedural edges, while dashed edges are inter-procedural edges.

Throughout this section we use *Linear Constant Propagation* (LCP) [51] as our example data flow analysis. LCP, like CP, aims to identify the variables that have constant values at any given location in the system. LCP is based on the same infinite domain as CP; i.e., each abstract domain element is a mapping from variables to (integer) values. The "$\sqsupseteq$" relation for the LCP lattice is also defined in the same way as for CP. The encoding of the transfer functions in LCP is as follows. Each edge (resp. path) maps the outgoing value of each variable to *either* a constant, *or* to a linear expression in the incoming value of at most one variable into the edge (resp. path), *or* to a special symbol $\top$ that indicates an unknown outgoing value. For instance, for the edge $g \rightarrow m$ in Figure 3, its transfer function can be represented symbolically as (t'=t,x'=x+1,y'=y,z'=z), where the primed versions represent outgoing values and unprimed versions represent incoming values.

Say we wish to compute the JOFP at node k. The only feasible paths that reach node k are the ones that attain calling-depth of three or more in the procedure `foo`, and hence encounter at least three *send* operations, which are required to clear the three *receive* operations encountered from node h to node k. All such paths happen to bring the constant values (t = 1, z = 1) to the node k. Hence, (t = 1, z = 1) is the precise JOFP result at node k. However, infeasible paths, if not elided, can introduce imprecision. For instance, the path that directly goes from node c to node o in the outermost call to the Procedure `foo` (this path is of calling-depth zero) brings values of zero for all four variables, and would hence prevent the precise fact (t = 1, z = 1) from being inferred.

3.1 Assumptions and Definitions

The set of all $\mathcal{L} \rightarrow \mathcal{L}$ transfer functions clearly forms a complete lattice based on the following ordering: $f_1 \sqsupseteq f_2$ iff for all $d \in \mathcal{L}$, $f_1(d) \sqsupseteq f_2(d)$. Backward DFAS makes a few assumptions on this lattice of transfer functions. The first is that this lattice be of *finite height*; i.e., all strictly ascending chains of elements in this lattice are finite (although no a priori bound on the sizes of these chains is required). The second is that a representation of transfer functions is available, as are operators to compose, join, and compare transfer functions. Note, the two assumptions above are also made by the classical "functional" inter-procedural approach of Sharir and Pnueli [55]. Thirdly, we need distributivity, as defined below: for any $f_1, f_2, f \in \mathcal{L} \rightarrow \mathcal{L}$, $(f_1 \sqcup f_2) \circ f = (f_1 \circ f) \sqcup (f_2 \circ f)$. The distributivity assumption is required only if the given system contains recursive procedure calls.

Linear Constant Propagation (LCP) [51] and Affine Relationships Analysis (ARA) [46] are well-known examples of analyses based on infinite abstract domains that satisfy all of the assumptions listed above. Note that the CP transfer-functions lattice is not of finite height. Despite the LCP abstract domain being the same as the CP abstract domain, the encoding chosen for LCP transfer functions (which was mentioned above), ensures that LCP uses a strict, finite-height subset of the full CP transfer-functions lattice that is closed under join and function composition operations. The trade-off is that LCP transfer functions for assignment statements whose RHS is not a linear expression and for conditionals are less precise than the corresponding CP transfer functions.

Our final assumption is that procedures other than "main" may send messages, but should not have any "receive" operations. Previous approaches that have addressed data flow analysis or verification problems for asynchronous systems with recursive procedures also have the same restriction [54,29,19].

We now introduce important terminology. The ***demand*** of a given path p in the VCFG is a vector of size r, and is defined as follows:

$$demand(p) = \begin{cases} max(\mathbf{0} - w, \mathbf{0}), & \text{if } p = (v \xrightarrow{f,w} z) \\ max(demand(p') - w, \mathbf{0}), & \text{if } p = (e.p'), \text{where } e \equiv (v \xrightarrow{f,w} z) \end{cases}$$

Intuitively, the demand of a path p is the minimum required vector of counter values in any starting configuration at the entry of the path for there to exist a sequence of transitions among configurations that manages to traverse the entire path (following the rule given before Section 2.1). It is easy to see that a path p is feasible *iff* $demand(p) = \mathbf{0}$.

A set of paths C is said to ***cover*** a path p iff: (a) all paths in C have the same start and end nodes (respectively) as p, (b) for each $p' \in C$, $demand(p') \leq demand(p)$, and (c) $(\sqcup_{p' \in C} ptf(p')) \sqsupseteq ptf(p)$. (Regarding (b), any binary vector operation in this paper is defined as applying the same operation on every pair of corresponding entries, i.e., point-wise.)

A *path template* $(p_1, p_2, \ldots, p_n)$ of any procedure F_i is a sequence of paths in the VCFG of F_i such that: (a) path p_1 begins at the entry node en_{F_i} of F_i and path p_n ends at return node ex_{F_i} of F_i, (b) for all $p_i, 1 \leq i < n$, p_i ends at a call-site node, and (c) for all $p_i, 1 < i \leq n$, p_i begins at a return-site node v_r^i, such that v_r^i corresponds to the call-site node v_c^{i-1} at which p_{i-1} ends.

3.2 Properties of Demand and Covering

At a high level, Backward DFAS works by growing paths in the backward direction by a single edge at a time starting from the target node (node k in our example in Figure 3). Every time this process results in a path reaching the *start* node (node a in our example), and the path is feasible, the approach simply transfers the entry value d_0 via this path to the target node. The main challenge is that due to the presence of cycles and recursion, there are an infinite number of feasible paths in general. In this subsection we present a set of lemmas that embody our intuition on how a finite subset of the set of all paths can be enumerated such that the join of the values brought by these paths is equal to the JOFP. We then present our complete approach in Section 3.3.

Demand Coverage Lemma: *Let p_2 and p_2' be two paths from a node v_i to a node v_j such that $demand(p_2') \leq demand(p_2)$. If p_1 is any path ending at v_i, then $demand(p_1.p_2') \leq demand(p_1.p_2)$.* □

This lemma can be argued using induction on the length of path p_1. A similar observation has been used to solve coverability of lossy channels and well-structured transition systems in general [3,18,2]. An important corollary of this lemma is that for any two paths p_2' and p_2 from v_i to v_j such that $demand(p_2') \leq demand(p_2)$, if there exists a path p_1 ending at v_i such that $p_1.p_2$ is feasible, then $p_1.p_2'$ is also feasible.

Function Coverage Lemma: *Let p_2 be a path from a node v_i to a node v_j, and P_2 be a set of paths from v_i to v_j such that $(\bigsqcup_{p_2' \in P_2} ptf(p_2')) \sqsupseteq ptf(p_2)$. Let p_1 be any path ending at v_i and p_3 be any path beginning at v_j. Under the distributivity assumption stated in Section 3.1, the following property holds: $(\bigsqcup_{p_2' \in P_2} ptf(p_1.p_2'.p_3)) \sqsupseteq ptf(p_1.p_2.p_3)$.* □

The following result follows from the Demand and Function Coverage Lemmas and from monotonicity of the transfer functions:

Corollary 1: *Let p_2 be a path from a node v_i to a node v_j, and P_2 be a set of paths from v_i to v_j such that P_2 covers p_2. Let p_1 be any path ending at v_i. Then, the set of paths $\{p_1.p_2' \mid p_2' \in P_2\}$ covers the path $p_1.p_2$.* □

We now use the running example from Figure 3 to illustrate how we leverage Corollary 1 in our approach. When we grow paths in backward direction from the target node k, two candidate paths that would get enumerated (among others) are $p_i \equiv hijk$ and $p_j \equiv hijkhijk$ (in that order). Now, p_i covers p_j. Therefore, by Corollary 1, any backward extension $p_1.p_j$ of p_j (p_1 is any path prefix) is guaranteed to be covered by the analogous backward extension $p_1.p_i$ of p_i. By definition of covering, it follows that $p_1.p_i$ brings in a data value that conservatively over-approximates the value brought in by $p_1.p_j$. Therefore, our approach discards p_j as soon as it gets enumerated. To summarize, our approach discards any path as soon as it is enumerated if it is covered by some subset of the previously enumerated and retained paths.

Due to the finite height of the transfer functions lattice, and because demand vectors cannot contain negative values, at some point in the algorithm every new path that can be generated by backward extension at that point would be discarded immediately. At this point the approach would terminate, and soundness would be guaranteed by definition of covering.

In the inter-procedural setting the situation is more complex. We first present two lemmas that set the stage. The lemmas both crucially make use of the assumption that recursive procedures are not allowed to have "receive" operations. For any path p_a that contains no receive operations, and for any demand vector d, we first define $supply(p_a, d)$ as $min(s, d)$, where s is the sum of the queuing vectors of the edges of p_a.

Supply Limit Lemma: *Let p_1, p_2 be two paths from v_i to v_j such that there are no receive operations in p_1 and p_2. Let p_b be any path beginning at v_j. If $demand(p_b) = d$, and if $supply(p_1, d) \geq supply(p_2, d)$, then $demand(p_1.p_b) \leq demand(p_2.p_b)$.* □

A set of paths P is said to ***d-supply-cover*** a path p_a iff: (a) all paths in P have the same start node and same end node (respectively) as p_a, (b) $(\bigsqcup_{p' \in P} ptf(p')) \sqsupseteq ptf(p_a)$, and (c) for each $p' \in P$, $supply(p', d) \geq supply(p_a, d)$.

Supply Coverage Lemma: *If $p_a.p_b$ is a path, and demand$(p_b) = d$, and if a set of paths P d-supply-covers p_a, and p_a as well as all paths in P have no receive operations, then the set of paths $\{p'.p_b \mid p' \in P\}$ covers the path $p_a.p_b$.*

Proof argument: Since P d-supply-covers p_a, by the Supply Limit Lemma, we have (a): for all $p' \in P$, $demand(p'.p_b) \leq demand(p_a.p_b)$. Since P d-supply-covers p_a, we also have $(\sqcup_{p' \in P} ptf(p')) \sqsupseteq ptf(p_a)$. From this, we use the Function Coverage lemma to infer that (b): $(\sqcup_{p' \in P} ptf(p'.p_b)) \sqsupseteq ptf(p_a.p_b)$. The result now follows from (a) and (b). □

Consider path *hijk* in our example, which gets enumerated and retained (as discussed earlier). This path gets extended back as *qhijk*; let us denote this path as p'. Let d be the demand of p' (i.e., is equal to 3). Our plan now is to extend this path in the backward direction all the way up to node p, by prepending interprocedurally valid and complete (i.e., IVC) paths of procedure `foo` in front of p'. An IVC path is one that begins at the entry node of `foo`, ends at the return node of `foo`, is of arbitrary calling depth, has balanced calls and returns, and has no pending returns when it completes [50]. First, we enumerate the IVC path(s) with calling-depth zero (i.e., path *co* in the example), and prepend them in front of p'. We then produce deeper IVC paths, in phases. In each phase i, $i > 0$, we inline IVC paths of calling-depth $i - 1$ that have been enumerated and retained so far into the path templates of the procedure to generate IVC paths of calling-depth i, and prepend these IVC paths in front of p'. We terminate when each IVC path that is generated in a particular phase j is d-supply-covered by some subset P of IVC paths generated in previous phases.

The soundness of discarding the IVC paths of phase j follows from the Supply Coverage lemma (p' would take the place of p_b in the lemma's statement, while the path generated in phase j would take the place of p_a in the lemma statement). The termination condition is guaranteed to be reached eventually, because: (a) the supplies of all IVC paths generated are limited to d, and (b) the lattice of transfer functions is of finite height. Intuitively, we could devise a sound termination condition even though deeper and deeper IVC paths can increment counters more and more, because a deeper IVC path that increments the counters beyond the demand of p' does not really result in lower overall demand when prepended before p' than a shallower IVC path that also happens to meet the demand of p' (Supply Limit lemma formalizes this).

In our running example, for the path *qhijk*, whose demand is equal to three, prefix generation for it happens to terminate in the fifth phase. The IVC paths that get generated in the five phases are, respectively, $p_0 = co$, $p_1 = cdefgmcono$, $p_2 = (cdefgm)^2 co(no)^2$, $p_3 = (cdefgm)^3 co(no)^3$, $p_4 = (cdefgm)^4 co(no)^4$, and $p_5 = (cdefgm)^5 co(no)^5$. $supply(p_3, 3) = supply(p_4, 3) = supply(p_5, 3) = 3$. The LCP transfer functions of the paths are as follows. $ptf(p_3)$ is (t'=1, x'=x+3, y'=x+2, z'=1), $ptf(p_4)$ is (t'=1, x'=x+4, y'=x+3, z'=1), while $ptf(p_5)$ is (t'=1, x'=x+5, y'=x+4, z'=1). $\{p_3, p_4\}$ 3-supply-covers p_5.

We also need a result that when the IVC paths in the jth phase are d-supply-covered by paths generated in preceding phases, then the IVC paths that would be generated in the $(j+1)th$ would also be d-supply-covered by paths generated

---

Algorithm 1 Backward DFAS algorithm

1: **procedure** COMPUTEJOFP(*target*)
        ▷ Returns JOFP from *start* $\in$ *Nodes* to *target* $\in$ *Nodes*, entry value $d_0 \in \mathcal{L}$.
2:    **for all** $v \in$ *Nodes* **do**   ▷ *Nodes* is the set of all nodes in the VCFG
3:       $sPaths(v) = \emptyset$
4:    For each intra-proc VCFG edge $v \to target$, add this edge to *workList* and to *sPaths(v)*
5:    **repeat**
6:       Remove any path p from *workList*.
7:       Let v_1 be the start node of p.
8:       **if** v_1 is a return-site node, with incoming return edge from func. F_1 **then**
9:          Let v_3 be the call-site node corresponding to v_1, e_1 be the call-site-to-entry edge from v_3 to en_{F_1}, and r_1 be the exit-to-return-site edge from ex_{F_1} to v_1.
10:          **for all** $p_1 \in$ COMPUTEENDTOEND(F_1, *demand(p)*) **do**
11:             $p_2 = e_1.p_1.r_1.p$
12:             **if** COVERED(p_2, $sPaths(v_3)$) returns *false* **then**
13:                Add p_2 to $sPaths(v_3)$ and to *workList*.
14:       **else if** v_1 is the entry node of a func. F_1 **then**
15:          **for all** $v_3 \in$ *call-sites* (F_1) **do**
16:             Let e_1 be the call edge from v_3 to v_1.
17:             $p_2 = e_1.p.$
18:             **if** COVERED(p_2, $sPaths(v_3)$) returns *false* **then**
19:                Add p_2 to $sPaths(v_3)$ and to *workList*.
20:       **else**
21:          **for all** intra-procedural edges $e = v_3 \xrightarrow{f,w} v_1$ in the VCFG **do**
22:             **if** COVERED($e.p$, $sPaths(v_3)$) returns *false* **then**
23:                Add the path $(e.p)$ to $sPaths(v_3)$ and to *workList*.
24:    **until** *workList* is empty
25:    $P = \{p \mid p \in sPaths(start), demand(p) = \overline{0}\}$
26:    **return** $\bigsqcup_{p \in P} (ptf(p))(d_0)$

---

in phases that preceded j. This can be shown using a variant of the Supply Coverage Lemma, which we omit in the interest of space. Once this is shown, it then follows inductively that none of the phases after phase j are required, which would imply that it would be safe to terminate.

The arguments presented above were in a restricted setting, namely, that there is only one call in each procedure, and that only recursive calls are allowed. These restrictions were assumed only for simplicity, and are not actually assumed in the algorithm to be presented below.

3.3   Data Flow Analysis Algorithm

Our approach is summarized in Algorithm 1. COMPUTEJOFP is the main routine. The algorithm works on a given iVCFG (which is an implicit parameter to the algorithm), and is given a *target* node at which the JOFP is to be computed.

Algorithm 2 Routines invoked for inter-procedural processing in Backward DFAS algorithm

procedure COMPUTEENDTOEND(F, d)
  ▷ Returns a set of paths that d-supply-covers each IVC path of the procedure F.
  for all $F_i \in$ *Funcs* **do**
    Place all 0-depth paths from F_i in *sIVCPaths*(F_i, d)
  repeat
    pathsAdded = *false*
    for all path template $(p_1, p_2, \ldots, p_n)$ in any function $F_i \in$ *Funcs* **do**
      Let F_1 be the procedure called from the call-site at which p_1 ends, F_2 be the procedure called from the call-site at which p_2 ends, and so on.
      for all $p'_1 \in$ *sIVCPaths*(F_1, d), $p'_2 \in$ *sIVCPaths*(F_2, d), ... **do**
        Let $p' = p_1.e_1.p'_1.r_1.p_2.e_2.p'_2.r_2.\ldots.p_n$, where each e_i is the call-edge that leaves the call-site node at which p_i ends and r_i is the return edge corresponding to e_i.
        if DSCOVERED(p', d, *sIVCPaths*(F_i, d)) returns *false* **then**
          Add the path p' to *sIVCPaths*(F_i, d). pathsAdded = *true*.
  until pathsAdded is *false*
  return *sIVCPaths*(F, d)

A key data structure in the algorithm is *sPaths*; for any node v, *sPaths*(v) is the set of all paths that start from v and end at *target* that the algorithm has generated and retained so far. The *workList* at any point stores a subset of the paths in *sPaths*, and these are the paths of the iVCFG that need to be extended backward.

To begin with, all edges incident onto *target* are generated and added to the sets *sPaths* and *workList* (Line 4 in Algorithm 1). In each step the algorithm picks up a path p from *workList* (Line 6), and extends this path in the backward direction. The backward extension has three cases based on the start node of the path p. The simplest case is the intra-procedural case, wherein the path is extended backwards in all possible ways by a single edge (Lines 21-23). The routine COVERED, whose definition is not shown in the algorithm, checks if its first argument (a path) is covered by its second argument (a set of paths). Note, covered paths are not retained.

When the start node of p is the entry node of a procedure F_1 (Lines 14-19), the path is extended backwards via all possible call-site-to-entry edges for procedure F_1.

If the starting node of path p is a return-site node v_1 (Lines 8-13) in a calling procedure, we invoke a routine COMPUTEENDTOEND (in line 10 of Algorithm 1). This routine, which we explain later, returns a set IVC paths of the called procedure such that *every* IVC path of the called procedure is d-supply-covered by some subset of paths in the returned set, where d denotes $demand(p)$. These returned IVC paths are prepended before p (Line 11), with the call-edge e_1 and return edge r_1 appropriately inserted.

The final result returned by the algorithm (see Lines 25 and 26 in Algorithm 1) is the join of the values transferred by the zero-demand paths (i.e., feasible paths) starting from the given entry value $d_0 \in \mathcal{L}$.

Routine ComputeEndToEnd: This routine is specified in Algorithm 2, and is basically a generalization of the approach that we described in Section 3.2, now handling multiple call-sites in each procedure, mutual recursion, calls to non-recursive procedures, etc. We do assume for simplicity of presentation that there are no cycles (i.e., loops) in the procedures, as this results in a fixed number of path templates in each procedure. There is no loss of generality here because we allow recursion. The routine incrementally populates a group of sets – there is a set named $sIVCPaths(F_i, d)$ for each procedure F_i in the system. The idea is that when the routine completes, $sIVCPaths(F_i, d)$ will contain a set of IVC paths of F_i that d-supply-cover all IVC paths of F_i. Note that we simultaneously populate covering sets for all the procedures in the system in order to handle mutual recursion.

The routine ComputeEndToEnd first enumerates and saves all zero-depth paths in all procedures (see Line 3 in Algorithm 2). The routine then iteratively takes a path template at a time, and fills in the "holes" between corresponding (call-site, return-site) pairs of the form v_c^{i-1}, v_r^i in the path template with IVC paths of the procedure that is called from this pair of nodes, thus generating a deeper IVC path (see the loop in lines 6-11). A newly generated IVC path p' is retained only if it is not d-supply-covered by other IVC paths already generated for the current procedure F_i (Lines 10-11). The routine terminates when no more IVC paths that can be retained are generated, and returns the set $sIVCPaths(F, d)$.

3.4 Illustration

We now illustrate our approach using the example in Figure 3. Algorithm 1 would start from the target node k, and would grow paths one edge at a time. After four steps the path *hijk* would be added to *sPaths*(h) (the intermediate steps would add suffixes of this path to *sPaths*(i), *sPaths*(j), and *sPaths*(k)). Next, path *khijk* would be generated and discarded, because it is covered by the "root" path k. Hence, further iterations of the cycle are avoided. On the other hand, the path *hijk* would get extended back to node q, resulting in path *qhijk* being retained in *sPaths*(q). This path would trigger a call to routine ComputeEndToEnd. As discussed in Section 3.2, this routine would return the following set of paths: $p_0 = co$, and $p_i = (cdefgm)^i co(no)^i$ for each $1 \leq i \leq 4$. (Recall, as discussed in Section 3.2, that $(cdefgm)^5 co(no)^5$ and deeper IVC paths are 3-supply-covered by the paths $\{p_3, p_4\}$.)

Each of the paths returned above by the routine ComputeEndToEnd would be prepended in front of *qhijk*, with the corresponding call and return edges inserted appropriately. These paths would then be extended back to node a. Hence, the final set of paths in *sPaths*(a) would be *abpcoqhijk*, *abpcdefgmconoqhijk*, $abp(cdefgm)^2 co(no)^2$, $abp(cdefgm)^3 co(no)^3$, and $abp(cdefgm)^4 co(no)^4$. Of these paths, the first two are ignored, as they are not feasible. The initial data-flow value (in which all variables are non-constant) is sent via the remaining three paths. In all these three paths the final values of variables 't' and 'z' are one. Hence, these two constants are inferred at node k.

3.5 Properties of the algorithm

We provide argument sketches here about the key properties of Backward DFAS. Detailed proofs are available in the appendix that accompanies this paper [4].

Termination. The argument is by contradiction. For the algorithm to not terminate, one of the following two scenarios must happen. The first is that an infinite sequence of paths gets added to some set *sPaths*(v). By Higman's lemma it follows that embedded within this infinite sequence there is an infinite sequence $p_1, p_2, \ldots$, such that for all i, $\mathit{demand}(p_i) \leq \mathit{demand}(p_{i+1})$. Because the algorithm never adds covered paths, it follows that for all i: $\bigsqcup_{1 \leq k \leq i+1} \mathit{ptf}(p_k) \sqsupset \bigsqcup_{1 \leq k \leq i} \mathit{ptf}(p_k)$. However, this contradicts the assumption that the lattice of transfer functions is of finite height. The second scenario is that an infinite sequence of IVC paths gets added to some set *sIVCPaths*(F, d) for some procedure F and some demand vector d in some call to routine ComputeEndToEnd. Because the "supply" values of the IVC paths are bounded by d, it follows that embedded within the infinite sequence just mentioned there must exist an infinite sequence of paths $p_1, p_2, \ldots$, such that for all i, $\mathit{supply}(p_i, d) \geq \mathit{supply}(p_{i+1}, d)$. However, since d-supply-covered paths are never added, it follows that for all i: $\bigsqcup_{1 \leq k \leq i+1} \mathit{ptf}(p_k) \sqsupset \bigsqcup_{1 \leq k \leq i} \mathit{ptf}(p_k)$. However, this contradicts the assumption that the lattice of transfer functions is of finite height.

Soundness and Precision. We already argued informally in Section 3.2 that the algorithm explores all feasible paths in the system, omitting only paths that are covered by other already-retained paths. By definition of covering, this is sufficient to guarantee over-approximation of the JOFP. The converse direction, namely, under-approximation, is obvious to see as every path along which the data flow value d_0 is sent at the end of the algorithm is a feasible path. Together, these two results imply that the algorithm is guaranteed to compute the precise JOFP.

Complexity. We show the complexity of our approach in the single-procedure setting. Our analysis follows along the lines of the analysis of the backwards algorithm for coverability in VASS [6]. The overall idea, is to use the technique of Rackoff [48] to derive a bound on the length of the paths that need to be considered. We derive a complexity bound of $O(\Delta . h^2 . \mathbf{L}^{2r+1} . r . log(\mathbf{L}))$, where Δ is the total number of transitions in the VCFG, Q is the number of VCFG nodes, h is the height of lattice of $\mathcal{L} \to \mathcal{L}$ functions, and $\mathbf{L} = (Q.(h+1).2)^{(3r)!+1}$.

4 Forward DFAS Approach

The Backward DFAS approach, though precise, requires the transfer function lattice to be of finite height. Due to this restriction, infinite-height abstract domains like Octagons [44], which need *widening* [12], are not accommodated by Backward DFAS. To address this, we present the Forward DFAS approach, which admits *any* complete lattice as an abstract domain (if the lattice is of infinite height then a widening operator should also be provided). The trade-off is precision. Forward DFAS elides only some of the infeasible paths in the VCFG, and hence, in general, computes a conservative *over-approximation* of the JOFP. Forward DFAS is conceptually not as sophisticated as Backward DFAS, but is still a novel proposal from the perspective of the literature.

The Forward DFAS approach is structured as an instantiation of Kildall's data flow analysis framework [32]. This framework needs a given complete lattice, the elements of which will be propagated around the VCFG as part of the fix point computation. Let $\mathcal{L}$ be the given underlying finite or infinite complete lattice. $\mathcal{L}$ either needs to not have any infinite *ascending chains* (e.g., Constant Propagation), or $\mathcal{L}$ needs to have an associated widening operator "$\nabla_{\mathcal{L}}$". The complete lattice D that we use in our instantiation of Kildall's framework is defined as $D \equiv D_{r,\kappa} \to \mathcal{L}$, where $\kappa \geq 0$ is a user-given non-negative integer, and $D_{r,\kappa}$ is the set of all vectors of size r (where r is the number of counters in the VCFG) such that all entries of the vectors are integers in the range $[0, \kappa]$. The ordering on this lattice is as follows: $(d_1 \in D) \sqsubseteq (d_2 \in D)$ iff $\forall c \in D_{r,\kappa}.\ d_1(c) \sqsubseteq_{\mathcal{L}} d_2(c)$. If a widening operator $\nabla_{\mathcal{L}}$ has been provided for $\mathcal{L}$, we define a widening operator ∇ for D as follows: $d_1 \nabla d_2 \ \equiv\ \lambda c \in D_{r,\kappa}.\ d_1(c)\ \nabla_{\mathcal{L}}\ d_2(c)$.

We now need to define the abstract transfer functions with signature $D \to D$ for the VCFG edges, to be used within the data flow analysis. As an intermediate step to this end, we define a ternary relation *boundedMove1* as follows. Any triple of integers $(p, q, s) \in$ *boundedMove1* iff

$$
\begin{array}{lr}
(0 \leq p \leq \kappa) \wedge & \\
((q \geq 0 \wedge p + q \leq \kappa \wedge s = p + q) \vee & (a) \\
\ (q \geq 0 \wedge p + q > \kappa \wedge s = \kappa) \vee & (b) \\
\ (q < 0 \wedge p = \kappa \wedge 0 \leq s \leq \kappa \wedge \kappa - s \leq -1 * q) \vee & (c) \\
\ (q < 0 \wedge p < \kappa \wedge p + q \geq 0 \wedge s = p + q)) & (d)
\end{array}
$$

We now define a ternary relation *boundedMove* on vectors. A triple of vectors (c_1, c_2, c_3) belongs to relation *boundedMove* iff all three vectors are of the same size, and for each index i, $(c_1[i], c_2[i], c_3[i]) \in$ *boundedMove1*.

We now define the $D \to D$ transfer function for the VCFG edge $q_1 \xrightarrow{f,w} q_2$ as follows:

$$
fun(l \in D) \ \equiv\ \lambda c_2 \in D_{r,\kappa}. \left(\bigsqcup_{c_1 \text{ such that } (c_1, w, c_2) \in boundedMove} f(l(c_1)) \right)
$$

Finally, let l_0 denote following function: $\lambda c \in D_{r,\kappa}.$ if c is $\mathbf{0}$ then d_0 else $\bot$, where $d_0 \in \mathcal{L}$. We can now invoke Kildall's algorithm using the *fun* transfer functions defined above at all VCFG edges, using l_0 as the fact at the "entry" to the "main" procedure. After Kildall's algorithm has finished computing the fix point solution, if $l_v^D \in D$ is the fix point solution at any node v, we return the value $(\sqcup_{c \in D_{r,\kappa}} l_v^D(c))$ as the final result at v.

The intuition behind the approach above is as follows. If v is a vector in the set $D_{r,\kappa}$, and if (c, m) is a channel-message pair, then the value in the (c, m)th slot of v encodes the number of instances of message m in channel c currently. An important note is that if this value is κ, it actually indicates that there are κ or more instances of message m in channel c, whereas if the value is less than κ it represents itself. Hence, we can refer to vectors in $D_{r,\kappa}$ as *bounded queue configurations.* If $d \in D$ is a data flow fact that holds at a node of the VCFG after data flow analysis terminates, then for any $v \in D_{r,\kappa}$ if $d(v) = l$, it indicates that l is a (conservative over-approximation) of the join of the data flow facts brought by all feasible paths that reach the node such that the counter values at the ends of these paths are as indicated by v (the notion of what counter values are indicated by a vector $v \in D_{r,\kappa}$ was described earlier in this paragraph).

The relation *boundedMove* is responsible for blocking the propagation along some of the infeasible paths. The intuition behind it is as follows. Let us consider a VCFG edge $q_1 \xrightarrow{f:\mathcal{L}\to\mathcal{L},w} q_2$. If c_1 is a bounded queue configuration at node q_1, then, c_1 upon propagation via this edge will become a bounded queue configuration c_2 at q_2 iff $(c_1, w, c_2) \in$ *boundedMove*. Lines (a) and (b) in the definition of *boundedMove1* correspond to sending a message; line (b) basically throws away the precise count when the number of messages in the channel goes above κ. Line (c) corresponds to receiving a message when all we know is that the number of messages currently in the channel is greater than or equal to κ. Line (d) is key for precision when the channel has less than κ messages, as it allows a receive operation to proceed only if the requisite number of messages are present in the channel.

The formulation above extends naturally to inter-procedural VCFGs using generic inter-procedural frameworks such as the *call strings* approach [55]. We omit the details of this in the interest of space.

Properties of the approach: Since Forward DFAS is an instantiation of Kildall's algorithm, it derives its properties from the same. As the set $D_{r,k}$ is a finite set, it is easy to see that the fix-point algorithm will terminate.

To argue the soundness of the algorithm, we consider the *concrete lattice* $D_c \equiv D_r \to \mathcal{L}$, and the following "concrete" transfer function for the VCFG edge $q_1 \xrightarrow{f,w} q_2$: $\mathit{fun\_conc}(l \in D_c) \equiv \lambda c_2 \in D_r.\ \left(\bigsqcup_{c_1 \in D_r \text{ such that } c_1 + w = c_2} f(l(c_1))\right)$, where D_r is the set of all vectors of size r of natural numbers. We then argue that the abstract transfer function *fun* defined earlier is a *consistent abstraction* [12] of *fun*_*conc*. This soundness argument is given in detail in the appendix that accompanies this paper [4].

If we restrict our discussion to single-procedure systems, the complexity of our approach is just the complexity of applying Kildall's algorithm. This works out to $O(Q^2 \kappa^r h)$, where Q is the number of VCFG nodes, and h is either the height of the lattice $\mathcal{L}$ or the maximum increasing sequence of values from $\mathcal{L}$

that is obtainable at any point using the lattice $\mathcal{L}$ in conjunction with Kildall's algorithm, using the given widening operation $\nabla_{\mathcal{L}}$.

c	t	x	y	z
1	0	0	0	0

(1)

m	t	x	y	z
2	0	1	0	1

(2)

c	t	x	y	z
1	0	0	0	0
2	0	1	0	1

(3)

m	t	x	y	z
2	0	1	0	1
3	1	2	1	1

(4)

c	t	x	y	z
1	0	0	0	0
2	0	1	0	1
3	1	2	1	1

(5)

m	t	x	y	z
2	0	1	0	1
3	1	$\top$	$\top$	1

(6)

o	t	x	y	z
1	0	0	0	0
2	0	1	0	1
3	1	$\top$	$\top$	1

(7)

k	t	x	y	z
1	1	$\top$	$\top$	1
2	1	$\top$	$\top$	1
3	1	$\top$	$\top$	1

(8)

Fig. 4. Data flow facts over a run of the algorithm

Illustration: We illustrate Forward DFAS using the example in Figure 3. Figure 4 depicts the data flow values at four selected nodes as they get updated over eight selected points of time during the run of the algorithm. In this illustration we assume a context insensitive analysis for simplicity (it so happens that context sensitivity does not matter in this specific example). We use the value $\kappa = 3$. Each small table is a data flow fact, i.e., an element of $D \equiv D_{r,\kappa} \to \mathcal{L}$. The top-left cell in the table shows the node at which the fact arises. In each row the first column shows the counter value, while the remaining columns depict the known constant value of the variables ($\top$ indicates unknown). Here are some interesting things to note. When any tuple of constant values transfers along the path from node c to node m, the constant values get updated due to the assignment statements encountered, *and* this tuple shifts from counter i to counter $i + 1$ (if i is not already equal to κ) due to the "send" operation encountered. When we transition from Step (5) to Step (6) in the figure, we get $\top$'s, as counter values 2 and 3 in Step (5) both map to counter value 3 in Step (6) due to κ being 3 (hence, the constant values get *joined*). The value at node o (in Step (7)) is the join of values from Steps (5) and (6). Finally, when the value at node o propagates to node k, the tuple of constants associated with counter value 3 end up getting mapped to all lower values as well due to the receive operations encountered.

Note, the precision of our approach in general increases with the value of κ (the running time increases as well). For instance, if κ is set to 2 (rather than 3) in the example, some more infeasible paths would be traversed. Only z = 1 would be inferred at node k, instead of (t = 1, z = 1).

5 Implementation and Evaluation

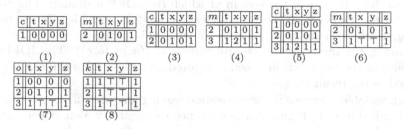

We have implemented prototypes of both the Forward DFAS and Backward DFAS approaches, in Java. Both the implementations have been parallelized, using the ThreadPool library. With Backward DFAS the iterations of the outer "repeat" loop in Algorithm 1 run in parallel, while with Forward DFAS propagations of values from different nodes to their respective successors happen in parallel. Our implementations currently target systems without procedure calls, as none of our benchmarks had recursive procedure calls.

Our implementations accept a given system, and a "target" control state q in one of the processes of the system at which the JOFP is desired. They then construct the VCFG from the system (see Section 2.1), and identify the *target set* of q, which is the set of VCFG nodes in which q is a constituent. For instance, in Figure 2, the target set for control state e is $\{(a, e), (b, e)\}$. The JOFPs at the nodes in the target set are then computed, and the join of these JOFPs is returned as the result for q.

Each variable reference in any transition leaving any control state is called a "use". For instance, in Figure 2, the reference to variable x along the outgoing transition from state d is one use. In all our experiments, the objective is to find the uses that are definitely constants by computing the JOFP at all uses. This is a common objective in many research papers, as finding constants enables optimizations such as constant folding, and also checking assertions in the code. We instantiate Forward DFAS with the Constant Propagation (CP) analysis, and Backward DFAS with the LCP analysis (for the reason discussed in Section 3.1). We use the bound $\kappa = 2$ in all runs of Forward DFAS, except with two benchmarks which are too large to scale to this bound. We discuss this later in this section. All the experiments were run on a machine with 128GB RAM and four AMD Opteron 6386 SE processors (64 cores total).

5.1 Benchmarks and modeling

Table 1. Information about the benchmarks. Abbreviations used: (a) prtcl = protocol, (b) comm = communication, (c) app = application

Benchmark (1)	**Description (2)**	**#Proc (3)**	**#Var (4)**	r **(5)**	**#VCFG nodes (6)**
mutex	mutual exclusion example	3	1	6	4536
bartlett	Bartlett's alternating-bit prtcl	3	3	7	17864
leader	leader election prtcl	2	11	12	16002
lynch	distorted channel comm prtcl	3	5	27	168912
peterson	Peterson's mutual exclusion prtcl	3	4	4	6864
boundedAsync	illustrative example	3	5	10	14375
receive1	illustrative example	2	5	13	1160
server	actor-based client server app	3	3	6	1232
chameneos	Chameneos concurrency game	3	9	10	45584
replicatingStorage	replicating storage system	4	4	8	47952
event_bus_test	publish-subscribe system	2	2	5	160
jobqueue_test	concurrent job queue system	4	1	10	28800
bookCollectionStore	REST app	2	2	12	2162
nursery_test	structured concurrency app	3	2	4	1260

We use 14 benchmarks for our evaluations. These are described in the first two columns of Table 1. Four benchmarks – bartlett, leader, lynch, and peterson – are Promela models for the Spin model-checker. Three benchmarks – boundedAsync, receive1, and replicatingStorage – are from the P language repository (www.github.com/p-org). Two benchmarks – server and chameneos – are from the Basset repository (www.github.com/SoftwareEngineeringToolDemos/FSE-2010-Basset). Four benchmarks – event_bus_test, jobqueue_test, nursery_test, and bookCollectionStore – are real world Go programs. There is one toy example "mutex", for ensuring mutual exclusion, via blocking receive messages, that we have made ourselves. We provide precise links to the benchmarks in the appendix [4].

Our DFAS implementations expect the asynchronous system to be specified in an XML format. We have developed a custom XML schema for this, closely based on the Promela modeling language used in Spin [26]. We followed this direction in order to be able to evaluate our approach on examples from different languages. We manually translated each benchmark into an XML file, which we call a *model*. As the input XML schema is close to Promela, the Spin models were easily translated. Other benchmarks had to be translated to our XML schema by understanding their semantics.

Note that both our approaches are expensive in the worst-case (exponential or worse in the number of counters r). Therefore, we have chosen benchmarks that are moderate in their complexity metrics. Still, these benchmarks are real and contain complex logic (e.g., the leader election example from Promela, which was discussed in detail in Section 1.1). We have also performed some manual simplifications to the benchmarks to aid scalability (discussed below). Our evaluation is aimed towards understanding the impact on precision due to infeasible paths in real benchmarks, and not necessarily to evaluate applicability of our approach to large systems.

We now list some of the simplifications referred to above. Language-specific idioms that were irrelevant to the core logic of the benchmark were removed. The number of instances of identical processes in some of the models were reduced in a behavior-preserving manner according to our best judgment. In many of the benchmarks, messages carry *payload*. Usually the payload is one byte. We would have needed 256 counters just to encode the payload of one 1-byte message. Therefore, in the interest of keeping the analysis time manageable, the payload size was reduced to 1 bit or 2 bits. The reduction was done while preserving key behavioral aspects according to our best judgment. Finally, procedure calls were inlined (there was no use of recursion in the benchmarks).

In the rest of this section, whenever we say "benchmark", we actually mean the model we created corresponding to the benchmark. Table 1 also shows various metrics of our benchmarks (based on the XML models). Column 3-6 depict, respectively, the number of processes, the total number of variables, the number of "counters" r, and the total number of nodes in the VCFG. We provide our XML models of all our benchmarks, as well as full output files from the runs of our approach, as a downloadable folder (https://drive.google.com/drive/folders/81DloNfm6_UHFyz7qni8rZjwCp-a8oCV).

5.2 Data flow analysis results

Table 2. Data flow analysis results

Benchmark (1)	#Var. uses (2)	#Asserts (3)	DFAS Approach #Consts. (4)		DFAS Approach #Verified (5)		Baseline Approaches #Consts. (6)		Baseline Approaches #Verified (7)	
			Forw.	Back.	Forw.	Back.	JOP	CCP	JOP	CCP
mutex	6	2	6	6	2	2	0	0	0	0
bartlett	9	1	0	0	0	0	0	0	0	0
leader	54	4	20	6	4	0	6	6	2	0
lynch	6	2	4	3	0	0	4	3	0	0
peterson	14	2	0	0	0	0	0	0	0	0
boundedAsync	24	8	8	8	0	0	8	8	0	0
receive1	9	5	8	8	4	4	2	8	2	4
server	4	1	0	0	0	0	0	0	0	0
chameneos	35	2	2	2	0	0	2	2	0	0
replicatingStorage	8	1	2	0	1	0	0	0	0	0
event_bus_test	5	3	3	3	3	3	0	2	0	2
jobqueue_test	3	1	0	1	0	1	0	0	0	0
bookCollectionStore	10	8	8	10	6	8	0	8	0	6
nursery_test	2	2	2	2	2	2	0	2	0	2
Total	189	42	63	49	22	20	22	39	4	14

We structure our evaluation as a set of research questions (RQs) below. Table 2 summarizes results for the first three RQs, while Table 3 summarizes results for RQ 4.

RQ 1: *How many constants are identified by the Forward and Backward DFAS approaches?* Column (2) in Table 2 shows the number of *uses* in each benchmark. Columns (4)-Forw and (4)-Back show the number of uses identified as constants by the Forward and Backward DFAS approaches, respectively. In total across all benchmarks Forward DFAS identifies 63 constants whereas Backward DFAS identifies 49 constants.

Although in aggregate Backward DFAS appears weaker than Forward DFAS, Backward DFAS infers more constants than Forward DFAS in two benchmarks – jobqueue_test and bookCollectionStore. Therefore, the two approaches are actually incomparable. The advantage of Forward DFAS is that it can use relatively more precise analyses like CP that do not satisfy the assumptions of Backward DFAS, while the advantage of Backward DFAS is that it always computes the precise JOFP.

RQ 2: *How many assertions are verified by the approaches?* Verifying assertions that occur in code is a useful activity as it gives confidence to developers. All but one of our benchmarks had assertions (in the original code itself, before modeling).

We carried over these assertions into our models. For instance, for the benchmark *leader*, the assertion appears in Line 11 in Figure 1. In some benchmarks, like jobqueue_test, the assertions were part of test cases. It makes sense to verify these assertions as well, as unlike in testing, our technique considers all possible interleavings of the processes. As "bookCollectionStore" did not come with any assertions, a graduate student who was unfamiliar with our work studied the benchmark and suggested assertions.

Column (3) in Table 2 shows the number of assertions present in each benchmark. Columns (5)-Forw and (5)-Back in Table 2 show the number of assertions declared as safe (i.e., verified) by the Forward and Backward DFAS approaches, respectively. An assertion is considered verified iff constants (as opposed to "$\top$") are inferred for all the variables used in the assertion, and if these constants satisfy the assertion. As can be seen from the last row in Table 2, both approaches verify a substantial percentage of all the assertions – 52% by Forward DFAS and 48% by Backward DFAS. We believe these results are surprisingly useful, given that our technique needs no loop invariants or usage of theorem provers.

RQ 3: *Are the DFAS approaches more precise than baseline approaches?* We compare the DFAS results with two baseline approaches. The first baseline is a Join-Over-all-Paths (JOP) analysis, which basically performs CP analysis on the VCFG without eliding any infeasible paths. Columns (6)-JOP and (7)-JOP in Table 2 show the number of constants inferred and the number of assertions verified by the JOP baseline. It can be seen that Backward DFAS identifies 2.2 times the number of constants as JOP, while Forward DFAS identifies 2.9 times the number of constants as JOP (see columns (4)-Forw, (4)-Back, and (6)-JOP in the **Total** row in Table 2). In terms of assertions, each of them verifies almost 5 times as many assertions as JOP (see columns (5)-Forw, (5)-Back, and (7)-JOP in **Total** row in Table 2.) It is clear from the results that eliding infeasible paths is extremely important for precision.

The second baseline is Copy Constant Propagation (CCP) [50]. This is another variant of constant propagation that is even less precise than LCP. However, it is based on a finite lattice, specifically, an IFDS [50] lattice. Hence this baseline represents the capability of the closest related work to ours [29], which elides infeasible paths but supports only IFDS lattices, which are a sub-class of finite lattices. (Their implementation also used a finite lattice of predicates, but we are not aware of a predicate-identification tool that would work on our benchmarks out of the box.) We implemented the CCP baseline within our Backward DFAS framework. This baseline hence computes the JOFP using CCP (i.e., it elides infeasible paths).

Columns (6)-CCP and (7)-CCP in Table 2 show the number of constants inferred and the number of assertions verified by the CCP baseline. From the **Total** row in Table 2 it can be seen that Forward DFAS finds 62% more constants than CCP, while Backward DFAS finds 26% more constants than CCP. With respect to number of assertions verified, the respective gains are 57% and 43%. In other words, infinite domains such as CP or LCP can give significantly more precision than closely related finite domains such as CCP.

Table 3. Execution time in seconds

	mut.	bar.	lea.	lyn.	pet.	bou.	rec.	ser.	cha.	rep.	eve.	job.	boo.	nur.
Forw	1.2	14.0	1.3	8.0	1.2	21.0	1.2	1.2	18.0	2.4	1.2	1.2	1.2	1.2
Back	5.0	11.0	284.0	118.0	13.0	21.0	8.0	3.0	220.0	21.0	3.0	140.0	16.0	1.0
JOP	1.2	1.3	1.6	8.0	1.2	1.4	1.3	1.2	3.1	3.0	1.1	1.4	1.2	1.2
CCP	5.0	12.0	226.0	116.0	12.0	14.0	8.0	3.0	156.0	24.0	3.0	51.0	30.0	1.0

RQ 4: *How does the execution cost of DFAS approaches compare to the cost of the JOP baseline?* The columns in Table 3 correspond to the benchmarks (only first three letters of each benchmark's name are shown in the interest of space). The rows show the running times for Forward DFAS, Backward DFAS, JOP baseline, and CCP baseline, respectively.

The JOP baseline was quite fast on almost all benchmarks (except lynch). This is because it maintains just a single data flow fact per VCFG node, in contrast to our approaches. Forward DFAS was generally quite efficient, except on chameneos and lynch. On these two benchmarks, it scaled only with $\kappa = 1$ and $\kappa = 0$, respectively, encountering memory-related crashes at higher values of κ (we used $\kappa = 2$ for all other benchmarks). These two benchmarks have large number of nodes and a high value of r, which increases the size of the data flow facts.

The running time of Backward DFAS is substantially higher than the JOP baseline. One reason for this is that being a demand-driven approach, the approach is invoked separately for each *use* (Table 2, Col. 2), and the cumulative time across all these invocations is reported in the table. In fact, the mean time per query for Backward DFAS is less than the total time for Forward DFAS on 9 out of 14 benchmarks, in some cases by a factor of 20x. Also, unlike Forward DFAS, Backward DFAS visits a small portion of the VCFG in each invocation. Therefore, Backward DFAS is more memory efficient and scales to all our benchmarks. Every invocation of Backward DFAS consumed less than 32GB of memory, whereas with Forward DFAS, three benchmarks (leader, replicatingStorage, and jobqueue_test) required more than 32GB, and two (lynch and chameneos) needed more than the 128 GB that was available in the machine. On the whole, the time requirement of Backward DFAS is still acceptable considering the large precision gain over the JOP baseline.

5.3 Limitations and Threats to Validity

The results of the evaluation using our prototype implementation are very encouraging, in terms of both usefulness and efficiency. The evaluation does however pose some threats to the validity of our results. The benchmark set, though extracted from a wide set of sources, may not be exhaustive in its idioms. Also, while modeling, we had to simplify some of the features of the benchmarks in order to let the approaches scale. Therefore, applicability of our approach directly on real systems with all their language-level complexities, use of libraries, etc., is not yet established, and would be a very interesting line of future work.

6 Related Work

The modeling and analysis of *parallel systems*, which include asynchronous systems, multi-threaded systems, distributed systems, event-driven systems, etc., has been the focus of a large body of work, for a very long time. We discuss some of the more closely related previous work, by dividing the work into four broad categories.

Data Flow Analysis: The work of Jhala et al. [29] is the closest work that addresses similar challenges as our work. They combine the Expand, Enlarge and Check (EEC) algorithm [21] that answers control state reachability in WSTS [18], with the unordered channel abstraction, and the IFDS [50] algorithm for data flow analysis, to compute the JOFP solution for all nodes. They admit only IDFS abstract domains, which are finite by definition. Some recent work has extended this approach for analyzing JavaScript [60] and Android [45] programs. Both our approaches are dissimilar to theirs, and we admit infinite lattices (like CP and LCP). On the other hand, their approach is able to handle parameter passing between procedures, which we do not.

Bronevetsky et al. [8] address generalized data flow analysis of a very restricted class of systems, where any receive operation must receive messages from a specific process, and channel contents are not allowed to cause non-determinism in control flow. Other work has addressed analysis of asynchrony in web applications [28,42]. These approaches are efficient, but over-approximate the JOFP by eliding only certain specific types of infeasible paths.

Formal Modeling and Verification: Verification of asynchronous systems has received a lot of attention over a long time. VASS [31] and Petri nets [49] (which both support unordered channel abstraction) have been used widely to model parallel and asynchronous processes [31,38,54,29,19,5]. Different analysis problems based on these models have been studied, such as reachability of configurations [7,43,34,35], coverability and boundedness [31,3,2,18,21,6], and coverability in the presence of stacks or other data structures [57,5,9,10,40].

The *coverability* problem mentioned above is considered equivalent to control state reachability, and has received wide attention [1,14,29,19,54,20,33,5,56]. Abdulla et al. [3] were the first to provide a backward algorithm to answer coverability. Our Backward DFAS approach is structurally similar to their approach, but is a strict generalization, as we incorporate data flow analysis using infinite abstract domains. (It is noteworthy that when the abstract domain is finite, then data flow analysis can be reduced to coverability.) One difference is that we use the unordered channel abstraction, while they use the lossy channel abstraction. It is possible to modify our approach to use lossy channels as well (when there are no procedure calls, which they also do not allow); we omit the formalization of this due to lack of space.

Bouajjani and Emmi [5] generalize over previous coverability results by solving the coverability problem for a class of multi-procedure systems called recursively parallel programs. Their class of systems is somewhat broader than ours, as they allow a caller to receive the messages sent by its callees. Our ComputeEndToEnd routine in Algorithm 2 is structurally similar to their approach. They admit finite abstract domains only. It would be interesting future work to extend the Backward DFAS approach to their class of systems.

Our approaches explore all interleavings between the processes, following the Spin semantics. Whereas, the closest previous approaches [29,5] only address "event-based" systems, wherein a set of processes execute sequentially without interleaving at the statement level, but over an unbounded schedule (i.e., each process executes from start to finish whenever it is scheduled).

Other forms of verification: Proof-based techniques have been explored for verifying asynchronous and distributed systems [24,58,47,22]. These techniques need inductive variants and are not as user-friendly as data flow analysis techniques. Behavioral types have been used to tackle specific analysis problems such as deadlock detection and correct usage of channels [36,37,52].

Testing and Model Checking: Languages and tools such as Spin and Promela [26], P [15], P# [13], and JPF-Actor [39] have been used widely to model-check asynchronous systems. A lot of work has been done in testing of asynchronous systems [16,13,53,23,59] as well. Such techniques are bounded in nature and cannot provide the strong verification guarantees that data flow analysis provides.

7 Conclusions and Future Work

In spite of the substantial body of work on analysis and verification of distributed systems, there is no existing approach that performs precise data flow analysis of such systems using infinite abstract domains, which are otherwise very commonly used with sequential programs. We propose two data flow analysis approaches that solve this problem – one computes the precise JOFP solution always, while the other one admits a fully general class of infinite abstract domains. We have implemented our approaches, analyzed 14 benchmarks using the implementation, and have observed substantially higher precision from our approach over two different baseline approaches.

Our approach can be extended in many ways. One interesting extension would be to make Backward DFAS work with infinite height lattices, using widening. Another possible extension could be the handling of parameters in procedure calls. There is significant scope for improving the scalability using better engineering, especially for Forward DFAS. One could explore the integration of partial-order reduction [11] into both our approaches. Finally, we would like to build tools based on our approach that apply directly to programs written in commonly-used languages for distributed programming.

References

1. Abdulla, P.A., Bouajjani, A., Jonsson, B.: On-the-fly analysis of systems with unbounded, lossy fifo channels. In: International Conference on Computer Aided Verification. pp. 305–318. Springer (1998)
2. Abdulla, P.A., Cerans, K., Jonsson, B., Tsay, Y.K.: General decidability theorems for infinite-state systems. In: Proceedings 11th Annual IEEE Symposium on Logic in Computer Science. pp. 313–321. IEEE (1996)
3. Abdulla, P.A., Jonsson, B.: Verifying programs with unreliable channels. information and computation **127**(2), 91–101 (1996)
4. Athaiya, S., Komondoor, R., Kumar, K.N.: Data flow analysis of asynchronous systems using infinite abstract domains (2021), https://arxiv.org/abs/2101.10233
5. Bouajjani, A., Emmi, M.: Analysis of recursively parallel programs. In: ACM Sigplan Notices. vol. 47, pp. 203–214. ACM (2012)
6. Bozzelli, L., Ganty, P.: Complexity analysis of the backward coverability algorithm for vass. In: Int. Workshop on Reachability Problems. pp. 96–109. Springer (2011)
7. Brand, D., Zafiropulo, P.: On communicating finite-state machines. Journal of the ACM (JACM) **30**, 323–342 (1983)
8. Bronevetsky, G.: Communication-sensitive static dataflow for parallel message passing applications. In: 2009 International Symposium on Code Generation and Optimization. pp. 1–12. IEEE (2009)
9. Cai, X., Ogawa, M.: Well-structured pushdown systems. In: International Conference on Concurrency Theory. pp. 121–136. Springer (2013)
10. Chadha, R., Viswanathan, M.: Decidability results for well-structured transition systems with auxiliary storage. In: International Conference on Concurrency Theory. pp. 136–150. Springer (2007)
11. Clarke, E.M., Grumberg, O., Minea, M., Peled, D.: State space reduction using partial order techniques. International Journal on Software Tools for Technology Transfer **2**(3), 279–287 (1999)
12. Cousot, P., Cousot, R.: Abstract interpretation: a unified lattice model for static analysis of programs by construction or approximation of fixpoints. In: Proceedings of the 4th ACM SIGACT-SIGPLAN symposium on Principles of programming languages. pp. 238–252 (1977)
13. Deligiannis, P., Donaldson, A.F., Ketema, J., Lal, A., Thomson, P.: Asynchronous programming, analysis and testing with state machines. In: Proceedings of the 36th ACM SIGPLAN Conference on Programming Language Design and Implementation. pp. 154–164 (2015)
14. Delzanno, G., Raskin, J.F., Van Begin, L.: Towards the automated verification of multithreaded java programs. In: International Conference on Tools and Algorithms for the Construction and Analysis of Systems. pp. 173–187. Springer (2002)
15. Desai, A., Gupta, V., Jackson, E., Qadeer, S., Rajamani, S., Zufferey, D.: P: safe asynchronous event-driven programming. ACM SIGPLAN Notices **48**, 321–332 (2013)
16. Desai, A., Qadeer, S., Seshia, S.A.: Systematic testing of asynchronous reactive systems. In: Proceedings of the 2015 10th Joint Meeting on Foundations of Software Engineering. pp. 73–83 (2015)
17. Dolev, D., Klawe, M., Rodeh, M.: An o (n log n) unidirectional distributed algorithm for extrema finding in a circle. Journal of Algorithms **3**(3), 245–260 (1982)
18. Finkel, A., Schnoebelen, P.: Well-structured transition systems everywhere! Theoretical Computer Science **256**(1-2), 63–92 (2001)

19. Ganty, P., Majumdar, R., Rybalchenko, A.: Verifying liveness for asynchronous programs. In: ACM SIGPLAN Notices. vol. 44, pp. 102–113. ACM (2009)
20. Geeraerts, G., Heußner, A., Raskin, J.F.: On the verification of concurrent, asynchronous programs with waiting queues. ACM Transactions on Embedded Computing Systems (TECS) **14**, 58 (2015)
21. Geeraerts, G., Raskin, J.F., Van Begin, L.: Expand, enlarge and check: New algorithms for the coverability problem of wsts. Journal of Computer and system Sciences **72**(1), 180–203 (2006)
22. v. Gleissenthall, K., Kıcı, R.G., Bakst, A., Stefan, D., Jhala, R.: Pretend synchrony: synchronous verification of asynchronous distributed programs. Proceedings of the ACM on Programming Languages **3**(POPL), 1–30 (2019)
23. Guo, H., Wu, M., Zhou, L., Hu, G., Yang, J., Zhang, L.: Practical software model checking via dynamic interface reduction. In: Proceedings of the Twenty-Third ACM Symposium on Operating Systems Principles. pp. 265–278 (2011)
24. Hawblitzel, C., Howell, J., Kapritsos, M., Lorch, J.R., Parno, B., Roberts, M.L., Setty, S., Zill, B.: Ironfleet: proving practical distributed systems correct. In: Proceedings of the 25th Symposium on Operating Systems Principles. pp. 1–17 (2015)
25. Holzmann, G.J.: The model checker spin. IEEE Transactions on software engineering **23**(5), 279–295 (1997)
26. Holzmann, G.J.: The SPIN model checker: Primer and reference manual, vol. 1003. Addison-Wesley Reading (2004)
27. Hopcroft, J., Pansiot, J.J.: On the reachability problem for 5-dimensional vector addition systems. Theoretical Computer Science **8**, 135–159 (1979)
28. Jensen, S.H., Madsen, M., Møller, A.: Modeling the html dom and browser api in static analysis of javascript web applications. In: Proceedings of the 19th ACM SIGSOFT symposium and the 13th European conference on Foundations of software engineering. pp. 59–69. ACM (2011)
29. Jhala, R., Majumdar, R.: Interprocedural analysis of asynchronous programs. In: ACM SIGPLAN Notices. vol. 42, pp. 339–350. ACM (2007)
30. Kam, J.B., Ullman, J.D.: Monotone data flow analysis frameworks. Acta informatica **7**, 305–317 (1977)
31. Karp, R.M., Miller, R.E.: Parallel program schemata. Journal of Computer and system Sciences **3**, 147–195 (1969)
32. Kildall, G.A.: A unified approach to global program optimization. In: Proceedings of the 1st annual ACM SIGACT-SIGPLAN symposium on Principles of programming languages. pp. 194–206. ACM (1973)
33. Kochems, J., Ong, C.H.L.: Safety verification of asynchronous pushdown systems with shaped stacks. In: International Conference on Concurrency Theory. pp. 288–302. Springer (2013)
34. Kosaraju, S.R.: Decidability of reachability in vector addition systems. In: STOC. vol. 82, pp. 267–281. ACM (1982)
35. Lambert, J.L.: A structure to decide reachability in petri nets. Theoretical Computer Science **99**, 79–104 (1992)
36. Lange, J., Ng, N., Toninho, B., Yoshida, N.: Fencing off go: Liveness and safety for channel-based programming. ACM SIGPLAN Notices **52**(1), 748–761 (2017)
37. Lange, J., Ng, N., Toninho, B., Yoshida, N.: A static verification framework for message passing in go using behavioural types. In: Proceedings of the 40th International Conference on Software Engineering. pp. 1137–1148 (2018)
38. Lautenbach, K., Schmid, H.: Use of petri nets for proving correctness of concurrent process systems. Proceedings of IFIP Congress pp. 187–191 (1974)

39. Lauterburg, S., Karmani, R.K., Marinov, D., Agha, G.: Basset: A tool for systematic testing of actor programs (Jul 2019), https://github.com/SoftwareEngineeringToolDemos/FSE-2010-Basset
40. Leroux, J., Praveen, M., Sutre, G.: Hyper-ackermannian bounds for pushdown vector addition systems. In: Proceedings of the Joint Meeting of the Twenty-Third EACSL Annual Conference on Computer Science Logic (CSL) and the Twenty-Ninth Annual ACM/IEEE Symposium on Logic in Computer Science (LICS). p. 63. ACM (2014)
41. Lynch, N.A.: Distributed algorithms. Elsevier (1996)
42. Madsen, M., Tip, F., Lhoták, O.: Static analysis of event-driven node. js javascript applications. In: ACM SIGPLAN Notices. vol. 50, pp. 505–519. ACM (2015)
43. Mayr, E.W., Meyer, A.R.: The complexity of the finite containment problem for petri nets. Journal of the ACM (JACM) **28**, 561–576 (1981)
44. Miné, A.: The octagon abstract domain. Higher-order and symbolic computation **19**, 31–100 (2006)
45. Mishra, A., Kanade, A., Srikant, Y.: Asynchrony-aware static analysis of android applications. In: 2016 ACM/IEEE International Conference on Formal Methods and Models for System Design (MEMOCODE). pp. 163–172. IEEE (2016)
46. Müller-Olm, M., Seidl, H.: Precise interprocedural analysis through linear algebra. In: ACM SIGPLAN Notices. vol. 39, pp. 330–341. ACM (2004)
47. Padon, O., McMillan, K.L., Panda, A., Sagiv, M., Shoham, S.: Ivy: safety verification by interactive generalization. In: Proceedings of the 37th ACM SIGPLAN Conference on Programming Language Design and Implementation. pp. 614–630 (2016)
48. Rackoff, C.: The covering and boundedness problems for vector addition systems. Theoretical Computer Science **6**, 223–231 (1978)
49. Reisig, W.: Petri nets: an introduction, vol. 4. Springer Science & Business Media (2012)
50. Reps, T., Horwitz, S., Sagiv, M.: Precise interprocedural dataflow analysis via graph reachability. In: Proceedings of the 22nd ACM SIGPLAN-SIGACT symposium on Principles of programming languages. pp. 49–61. ACM (1995)
51. Sagiv, M., Reps, T., Horwitz, S.: Precise interprocedural dataflow analysis with applications to constant propagation. Theoretical Computer Science **167**, 131–170 (1996)
52. Scalas, A., Yoshida, N., Benussi, E.: Verifying message-passing programs with dependent behavioural types. In: Proceedings of the 40th ACM SIGPLAN Conference on Programming Language Design and Implementation. pp. 502–516 (2019)
53. Sen, K., Agha, G.: Automated systematic testing of open distributed programs. In: International Conference on Fundamental Approaches to Software Engineering. pp. 339–356. Springer (2006)
54. Sen, K., Viswanathan, M.: Model checking multithreaded programs with asynchronous atomic methods. In: International Conference on Computer Aided Verification. pp. 300–314. Springer (2006)
55. Sharir, M., Pnueli, A.: Two approaches to interprocedural data flow analysis. In: Muchnick, S.S., Jones, N.D. (eds.) Program Flow Analysis: Theory and Application. Prentice Hall Professional Technical Reference (1981)
56. Stiévenart, Q., Nicolay, J., De Meuter, W., De Roover, C.: Mailbox abstractions for static analysis of actor programs. In: 31st European Conference on Object-Oriented Programming (ECOOP 2017). Schloss Dagstuhl-Leibniz-Zentrum fuer Informatik (2017)

57. Torre, S.L., Madhusudan, P., Parlato, G.: Context-bounded analysis of concurrent queue systems. In: TACAS (2008)
58. Wilcox, J.R., Woos, D., Panchekha, P., Tatlock, Z., Wang, X., Ernst, M.D., Anderson, T.: Verdi: a framework for implementing and formally verifying distributed systems. In: Proceedings of the 36th ACM SIGPLAN Conference on Programming Language Design and Implementation. pp. 357–368 (2015)
59. Yang, J., Chen, T., Wu, M., Xu, Z., Liu, X., Lin, H., Yang, M., Long, F., Zhang, L., Zhou, L.: Modist: Transparent model checking of unmodified distributed systems. Proceedings of the Symposium on Networked Systems Design and Implementation (2009)
60. Yee, M.H., Badouraly, A., Lhoták, O., Tip, F., Vitek, J.: Precise dataflow analysis of event-driven applications. arXiv preprint arXiv:1910.12935 (2019)

Types for Complexity of Parallel Computation in Pi-Calculus

Patrick Baillot[1] and Alexis Ghyselen[1] ✉

Univ Lyon, CNRS, ENS de Lyon, Universite Claude-Bernard Lyon 1, LIP, F-69342, Lyon Cedex 07, France

✉alexis.ghyselen@ens-lyon.fr

Abstract. Type systems as a technique to analyse or control programs have been extensively studied for functional programming languages. In particular some systems allow to extract from a typing derivation a complexity bound on the program. We explore how to extend such results to parallel complexity in the setting of the pi-calculus, considered as a communication-based model for parallel computation. Two notions of time complexity are given: the total computation time without parallelism (the work) and the computation time under maximal parallelism (the span). We define operational semantics to capture those two notions, and present two type systems from which one can extract a complexity bound on a process. The type systems are inspired both by size types and by input/output types, with additional temporal information about communications.

Keywords: Type Systems · Pi-calculus · Process Calculi · Complexity Analysis · Implicit Computational Complexity · Size Types

1 Introduction

The problem of certifying time complexity bounds for programs is a challenging question, related to the problem of statically inferring time complexity, and it has been extensively studied in the setting of sequential programming languages. One particular approach to these questions is that of type systems, which offers the advantage of providing an analysis which is formally-grounded, compositional and modular. In the functional framework several rich type systems have been proposed, such that if a program can be assigned a type, then one can extract from the type derivation a complexity bound for its execution on any input (see e.g. [21,25,22,20,6,4]). The type system itself thus provides a complexity certification procedure, and if a type inference algorithm is also provided one obtains a complexity inference procedure. This research area is also related to implicit computational complexity, which aims at providing type systems or static criteria to characterize some complexity classes within a programming language (see e.g. [24,13,33,18,15]), and which have sometimes in a second step inspired a complexity certification or inference procedure.

However, while the topic of complexity certification has been thoroughly investigated for sequential programs both for space and time bounds, there only

N. Yoshida (Ed.): ESOP 2021, LNCS 12648, pp. 59–86, 2021.
https://doi.org/10.1007/978-3-030-72019-3_3

have been a few contributions in the settings of parallel programs and distributed systems. In these contexts, several notions of cost can be of interest to abstract the computation time. First one can wish to know what is during a program execution the total cumulated computation time on all processors. This is called the *work* of the program. Second, one can wonder if an infinite number of processors were available, what would be the execution time of the program when it is maximally parallelized. This is called the *span* or *depth* of the program.

The paper [23] has addressed the problem of analysing the time complexity of programs written in a parallel first-order functional language. In this language one can spawn computations in parallel and use the resulting values in the body of the program. This allows to express a large bunch of classical parallel algorithms. Their approach is based on amortized complexity and builds on a line of work in the setting of sequential languages to define type systems, which allow to derive bounds on the work and the span of the program. However, the language they are investigating does not allow communication between those computations in parallel. Our goal is to provide an approach to analyse the time complexity of programs written in a rich language for communication-based parallel computation, allowing the representation of several synchronization features. We use for that π-calculus, a process calculus which provides process creation, channel name creation and name-passing in communication. An alternative approach could be to use a language described with session types, as in [9,10]. We will discuss the expressivity for both languages in Section 4.2.

We want to propose methods that, given a parallel program written in π-calculus, allow to derive upper bounds on its work and span. Let us mention that these notions are not only of theoretical interest. Some classical results provide upper bounds, expressed by means of the work (w) and span (s), on the evaluation time of a parallel program on a given number p of processors. For instance such a program can be evaluated on a shared-multiprocessor system (SMP) with p processors in time $O(\max(w/p, s))$ (see e.g. [19]).

Our goal in this paper is essentially fundamental and methodological, in the sense that we aim at proposing type systems which are general enough, well-behaved and provide good complexity properties. We do not focus yet at this stage on the design and efficiency of type inference algorithms.

We want to be able to derive complexity bounds which are parametric in the size of inputs, for instance which depend on the length of a list. For that it will be useful to have a language of types that can carry information about sizes, and for this reason we take inspiration from size types [26,6]. So data-types will be annotated with an index which will provide some information on the size of values. Our approach then follows the standard approach to typing in the π-calculus, namely typing a channel by providing the types of the messages that can be sent or received through it. Actually a second ingredient will be necessary for us, input/output types. In this setting a channel is given a set of capabilities: it can be an input, an output, or have both input/output capabilities.

Contributions. We consider a π-calculus with an explicit `tick` construction; this allows to specify several cost models, instead of only counting the number of reduction steps. Two semantics of this π-calculus are proposed to define formally the work and the span of a process. We then design two type systems for the π-calculus, one for the work and one for the span, and establish for both a soundness theorem: if a process is well-typed in the first (resp. second) type system, then its type provides an expression which, for its execution on any input, bounds the work (resp. span). This approach by type system is generic: the soundness proof relies on subject reduction, and it gives a compositional and flexible result that could be adapted to extensions of the base language.

Discussion. Note that even though one of the main usages of π-calculus is to specify and analyse concurrent systems, the present paper does not aim at analysing the complexity of arbitrary π-calculus concurrent programs. Indeed, some typical examples of concurrent systems like semaphores will simply not be typable in the system for span (see Sect. 4.2), because of linearity conditions. As explained above, our interest here is instead focused on parallel computation expressed in the π-calculus, which can include some form of cooperative concurrency. We believe the analysis of complexity bounds for concurrent π-calculus is another challenging question, which we want to address in future work.

A comparison with related works will be done in Sect. 6.

2 The Pi-calculus with Semantics for Work and Span

In this work, we consider the π-calculus as a model of parallelism. The main points of π-calculus are that processes can be composed in parallel, communication between processes happens with the use of channels, and channel names can be created dynamically.

2.1 Syntax, Congruence and Standard Semantics for π-Calculus

We present here a classical syntax for the asynchronous π-calculus. More details about π-calculus and variants of the syntax can be found in [34]. We define the sets of *variables*, *expressions* and *processes* by the following grammar.

$$v := x, y, z \mid a, b, c \qquad e := v \mid 0 \mid \mathtt{s}(e) \mid [] \mid e :: e'$$

$$P, Q := 0 \mid (P \mid Q) \mid !a(\tilde{v}).P \mid a(\tilde{v}).P \mid \overline{a}\langle\tilde{e}\rangle \mid (\nu a)P \mid \mathtt{tick}.P$$

$$\mid \mathtt{match}(e)\ \{0 \mapsto P;;\ \mathtt{s}(x) \mapsto Q\} \mid \mathtt{match}(e)\ \{[] \mapsto P;;\ x :: y \mapsto Q\}$$

Variables x, y, z denote *base type variables*, they represent integers or lists. Variables a, b, c denote *channel names*. The notation $\tilde{v}$ stands for a sequence of variables $v_1, v_2, \dots, v_k$. In the same way, $\tilde{e}$ is a sequence of expressions. We work up to α-renaming, and we write $P[\tilde{v} := \tilde{e}]$ to denote the substitution of the free variables $\tilde{v}$ in P by $\tilde{e}$. For the sake of simplicity, we consider only integers and lists as base types in the following, but the results can be generalized to other algebraic data-types.

Intuitively, $P \mid Q$ stands for the parallel composition of P and Q, $a(\tilde{v}).P$ represents an input: it stands for the reception on the channel a of a tuple of values identified by the variables $\tilde{v}$ in the continuation P. The process $!a(\tilde{v}).P$ is a replicated version of $a(\tilde{v}).P$, it behaves like an infinite number of $a(\tilde{v}).P$ in parallel. The process $\overline{a}\langle\tilde{e}\rangle$ represents an output: it sends a sequence of expressions on the channel a. A process $(\nu a)P$ dynamically creates a new channel name a and then proceeds as P. We also have classical pattern matching on data types, and finally, in $\mathtt{tick}.P$, the tick incurs an additional cost of one. This constructor is the source of time complexity in a program. It can represent different cost models and it is more general than only counting the number of reduction steps. For example, by adding a `tick` after each input, we can count the number of communications in a process. By adding it after each replicated input on a channel a, we can count the number of calls to a. And if we want to count the number of reduction steps, we can add a `tick` after each input and pattern matching.

We can now describe the classical semantics for this calculus. We first define on those processes a congruence relation $\equiv$: this is the least congruence relation closed under:

$$P \mid 0 \equiv P \qquad P \mid Q \equiv Q \mid P \qquad P \mid (Q \mid R) \equiv (P \mid Q) \mid R$$

$$(\nu a)(\nu b)P \equiv (\nu b)(\nu a)P \qquad (\nu a)(P \mid Q) \equiv (\nu a)P \mid Q \text{ (when } a \text{ is not free in } Q)$$

Note that the last rule can always be applied from right to left by α-renaming. Also, one can see that contrary to usual congruence relation for the π-calculus, we do not consider the rule for replicated input ($!P \equiv \;!P \mid P$) as it will be captured by the semantics, and α-conversion is not taken as an explicit rule in the congruence. By associativity, we will often write parallel composition for any number of processes and not only two. Another way to see this congruence relation is that, up to congruence, a process is entirely described by a set of channel names and a multiset of processes. Formally, we can give the following definition.

Definition 1 (Guarded Processes and Canonical Form). *A process G is* guarded *if it has one of the following shapes:*

$$G := !a(\tilde{v}).P \;\Big|\; a(\tilde{v}).P \;\Big|\; \overline{a}\langle\tilde{e}\rangle \;\Big|\; \mathtt{tick}.P \;\Big|$$

$$\mathtt{match}(e)\ \{\mathtt{0} \mapsto P;;\ \mathtt{s}(x) \mapsto Q\} \;\Big|\; \mathtt{match}(e)\ \{[] \mapsto P;;\ x :: y \mapsto Q\}$$

We say that a process is in canonical form *if it has the form $(\nu\tilde{a})(G_1 \mid \cdots \mid G_n)$ with $G_1, \ldots, G_n$ guarded processes.*

The properties of this canonical form can be found in the technical report [5], here we only use it to give an intuition of how one could understand a process. Thus, it is enough to consider that for each process P, there is a process in canonical form congruent to P. Moreover, this canonical form is unique up to the ordering of names and processes, and up to congruence inside guarded processes.

We can now define the usual reduction relation for the π-calculus, that we denote $P \to Q$. It is defined by the rules given in Figure 1. The rules for integers are not detailed as they can be deduced from the ones for lists. Remark that substitution should be well-defined in order to do some reduction steps: channel names must be substituted by other channel names and base type variables can be substituted by any expression except channel names. However, when we will consider typed processes, this will always yield well-defined substitutions.

$$\frac{}{!a(\tilde{v}).P \mid \overline{a}\langle\tilde{e}\rangle \to !a(\tilde{v}).P \mid P[\tilde{v} := \tilde{e}]} \qquad \frac{}{a(\tilde{v}).P \mid \overline{a}\langle\tilde{e}\rangle \to P[\tilde{v} := \tilde{e}]}$$

$$\frac{}{\texttt{match}([])\ \{[] \mapsto P;;\ x :: y \mapsto Q\} \to P}$$

$$\frac{}{\texttt{match}(e :: e')\ \{[] \mapsto P;;\ x :: y \mapsto Q\} \to Q[x, y := e, e']}$$

$$\frac{P \to Q}{P \mid R \to Q \mid R} \qquad \frac{P \to Q}{(\nu a)P \to (\nu a)Q} \qquad \frac{P \equiv P' \quad P' \to Q' \quad Q' \equiv Q}{P \to Q}$$

Fig. 1. Standard Reduction Rules

For now, this relation cannot reduce a process of the form $\texttt{tick}.P$. So, we need to introduce a reduction rule for $\texttt{tick}$. From this semantics, we will define a reduction corresponding to total complexity (*work*). Then, we will define parallel complexity (*span*) by taking an expansion of the standard reduction.

2.2 Semantics and Complexity

Work. We first describe a semantics for the work, that is to say the total number of ticks during a reduction without parallelism. The time reduction $\to_1$ is defined in Figure 2. Intuitively, this reduction removes exactly one tick at the top-level.

$$\frac{}{\texttt{tick}.P \to_1 P}$$

$$\frac{P \to_1 P'}{P \mid Q \to_1 P' \mid Q} \qquad \frac{Q \to_1 Q'}{P \mid Q \to_1 P \mid Q'} \qquad \frac{P \to_1 P'}{(\nu a)P \to_1 (\nu a)P'}$$

Fig. 2. Simple Tick Reduction Rules

Then from any process P, a sequence of reduction steps to Q is just a sequence of one-step reductions with $\to$ or $\to_1$, and the work complexity of this sequence is the number of $\to_1$ steps. In this paper, we always consider the worst-case complexity so the work of a process is defined as the maximal complexity over all such sequences of reduction steps from this process.

Notice that with this semantics for work, adding `tick` in a process does not change its behaviour: we do not create nor erase reduction paths.

Span. A more interesting notion of complexity in this calculus is the parallel one. Before presenting the semantics, we present with some simple examples what kind of properties we want for this parallel complexity.

First, we want a parallel complexity that works as if we had an infinite number of processors. So, on the process $\mathtt{tick}.0 \mid \mathtt{tick}.0 \mid \mathtt{tick}.0 \mid \cdots \mid \mathtt{tick}.0$ we want the complexity to be 1, whatever the number of `tick` in parallel.

Moreover, reductions with a zero-cost complexity (in our setting, this should mean all reductions except when we reduce a `tick`) should not harm this maximal parallelism. For example $a().\mathtt{tick}.0 \mid \overline{a}\langle\rangle \mid \mathtt{tick}.0$ should also have complexity one, because intuitively this synchronization between the input and the output can be done independently of the `tick` on the right, and then the `tick` on the left can be reduced in parallel with the `tick` on the right.

Finally, as before for the work, adding a `tick` should not change the behaviour of a process. For instance, consider the process $\mathtt{tick}.a().P_0 \mid a().\mathtt{tick}.P_1 \mid \overline{a}\langle\rangle$, where a is not used in P_0 and P_1. This process should have the complexity $max(1 + C_0, 1 + C_1)$, where C_i is the cost of P_i. Indeed, there are two possible reductions, either we reduce the tick, and then we synchronize the left input with the output, and continue with P_0, or we first do the synchronization with the right input and the output, we then reduces the ticks and finally we continue as P_1.

A possible way to define such a parallel complexity would be to take causal complexity [13,12,11], however we believe there is a simpler presentation for our case. In the technical report [5], we prove the equivalence between causal complexity and the notion presented here. The idea has been proposed by Naoki Kobayashi (private communication). It consists in introducing a new construction for processes, $m : P$, where m is an integer. A process using this constructor will be called an *annotated process*. Intuitively, this annotated process has the meaning *P with m ticks before*. We can then enrich the congruence relation $\equiv$ with the following rules:

$$m : (P \mid Q) \equiv (m : P) \mid (m : Q) \qquad m : (\nu a)P \equiv (\nu a)(m : P)$$

$$m : (n : P) \equiv (m + n) : P \qquad 0 : P \equiv P$$

This intuitively means that the ticks can be distributed over parallel composition, name creation can be done before or after ticks without changing the semantics, ticks can be grouped together, and finally zero tick is equivalent to nothing.

With this congruence relation and this new constructor, we can give a new shape to the canonical form presented in Definition 1.

Definition 2 (Canonical Form for Annotated Processes). *An annotated process is in canonical form if it has the shape:*

$$(\nu\tilde{a})(n_1 : G_1 \mid \cdots \mid n_m : G_m)$$

with $G_1, \dots, G_m$ guarded annotated processes.

Remark that the congruence relation above allows to obtain this canonical form from any annotated processes. With this intuition in mind, we can then define a reduction relation $\Rightarrow_p$ for annotated processes. The rules are given in Figure 3. We do not detail the rules for integers as they are deducible from the ones for lists. Intuitively, this semantics works as the usual semantics for pi-calculus, but when doing a synchronization, we keep the maximal annotation, and ticks are memorized in the annotations.

$$\frac{}{(n : a(\tilde{v}).P) \mid (m : \overline{a}\langle\tilde{e}\rangle) \Rightarrow_p (max(m,n) : P[\tilde{v} := \tilde{e}])} \qquad \frac{}{\mathtt{tick}.P \Rightarrow_p 1 : P}$$

$$\frac{}{(n : !a(\tilde{v}).P) \mid (m : \overline{a}\langle\tilde{e}\rangle) \Rightarrow_p (n : !a(\tilde{v}).P) \mid (max(m,n) : P[\tilde{v} := \tilde{e}])}$$

$$\frac{}{\mathtt{match}([])\ \{[] \mapsto P;;\ x :: y \mapsto Q\} \Rightarrow_p P}$$

$$\frac{}{\mathtt{match}(e :: e')\ \{[] \mapsto P;;\ x :: y \mapsto Q\} \Rightarrow_p Q[x, y := e, e']}$$

$$\frac{P \Rightarrow_p Q}{P \mid R \Rightarrow_p Q \mid R} \qquad \frac{P \Rightarrow_p Q}{(\nu a)P \Rightarrow_p (\nu a)Q} \qquad \frac{P \Rightarrow_p Q}{(n : P) \Rightarrow_p (n : Q)}$$

$$\frac{P \equiv P' \qquad P' \Rightarrow_p Q' \qquad Q' \equiv Q}{P \Rightarrow_p Q}$$

Fig. 3. Reduction Rules

We can then define the parallel complexity of an annotated process.

Definition 3 (Parallel Complexity). *Let P be an annotated process. We define its* local complexity *$\mathcal{C}_\ell(P)$ by:*

$$\mathcal{C}_\ell(n : P) = n + \mathcal{C}_\ell(P) \qquad \mathcal{C}_\ell(P \mid Q) = \max(\mathcal{C}_\ell(P), \mathcal{C}_\ell(Q))$$

$$\mathcal{C}_\ell((\nu a)P) = \mathcal{C}_\ell(P) \qquad \mathcal{C}_\ell(G) = 0 \textit{ if } G \textit{ is a guarded process}$$

Equivalently, $\mathcal{C}_\ell(P)$ is the maximal integer that appears in the canonical form of P. Then, for an annotated process P, its global parallel complexity *is given by $max\{n \mid P \Rightarrow_p^* Q \wedge \mathcal{C}_\ell(Q) = n\}$ where $\Rightarrow_p^*$ is the reflexive and transitive closure of $\Rightarrow_p$.*

To show that this parallel complexity is well-behaved, we give the following lemma.

Lemma 1 (Reduction and Local Complexity). *Let P, P' be annotated processes such that $P \Rightarrow_p P'$. Then, we have $\mathcal{C}_\ell(P') \geq \mathcal{C}_\ell(P)$.*

This lemma is proved by induction. The main point is that guarded processes have a local complexity equal to zero, so doing a reduction will always increase this local complexity. Thus, in order to bound the complexity of an annotated process, we need to reduce it with $\Rightarrow_p$, and then we have to take the maximum local complexity over all normal forms. Moreover, this semantics respects the conditions given in the beginning of this section.

2.3 An Example Process

As an example, we show a way to encode a usual functional program in π-calculus. In order to do this, we use replicated input to encode functions, and we use a return channel for the output. So, given a channel f representing a function F such that $\overline{f}\langle y,a\rangle$ returns $F(y)$ on the channel a, we can write the "map" function in our calculus as described in Figure 4. The main idea for this kind of encoding is to use the dynamic creation of names ν to create the return channel before calling a function, and then to use this channel to obtain back the result of this call. Note that we chose here as cost model the number of calls to f, and we can see the versatility of a `tick` constructor instead of a complexity that relies only on the number of reduction steps.

With this process, on a list of length n, the work is n. However, as all calls to f could be done in parallel, the span is 1 for any non-empty list as input.

$$
\begin{array}{l}
!\mathrm{map}(x,f,a).\ \mathtt{match}(x)\ \{\\
\quad [\,]\mapsto\ \overline{a}\langle x\rangle\ \ ;;\\
\quad y::x_1\mapsto\ (\nu b)(\nu c)(\mathtt{tick}.\overline{f}\langle y,b\rangle\ \mid\ \overline{\mathrm{map}}\langle x_1,f,c\rangle\ \mid\ b(z).c(x_2).\overline{a}\langle z::x_2\rangle)\\
\}
\end{array}
$$

Fig. 4. The Map Function

3 Size Types for the Work

We now define a type system to bound the work of a process. The goal is to obtain a soundness result: if a process P is typable then we can derive an integer expression K such that the work of P is bounded by K.

3.1 Size Input/Output Types

Our type system relies on the definition of indices to keep track of the size of values in a process. Those indices were for example used in [6] and are greatly inspired by [26]. The main idea of those types in a sequential setting is to control recursive calls by ensuring a decreasing in the sizes.

Definition 4. *The set of* indices *for natural numbers is given by the following grammar.*

$$I, J, K := i, j, k \mid f(I_1, \ldots, I_n)$$

The variables i, j, k are called index variables. The set of index variables is denoted $\mathcal{V}$. The symbol f is an element of a given set of function symbols containing addition and multiplication. We also assume that we have the subtraction as a function symbol, with $n - m = 0$ when $m \geq n$. Each function symbol f of arity $\mathtt{ar}(f)$ *comes with an interpretation $[\![f]\!] : \mathbb{N}^{\mathtt{ar}(f)} \to \mathbb{N}$.*

Given an index valuation $\rho : \mathcal{V} \to \mathbb{N}$, we extend the interpretation of function symbols to indices, noted $[\![I]\!]_\rho$ in the natural way. In an index I, the substitution of the occurrences of i in I by J is denoted $I\{J/i\}$.

Definition 5 (Constraints on Indices). *Let $\phi \subset \mathcal{V}$ be a set of index variables.* A constraint *C on ϕ is an expression with the shape $I \bowtie J$ where I and J are indices with free variables in ϕ and $\bowtie$ denotes a binary relation on integers. Usually, we take $\bowtie \in \{\leq, <, =, \neq\}$. Finite set of constraints are denoted Φ.*

For a set $\phi \subset \mathcal{V}$, we say that a valuation $\rho : \phi \to \mathbb{N}$ *satisfies* a constraint $I \bowtie J$ on ϕ, noted $\rho \vDash I \bowtie J$ when $[\![I]\!]_\rho \bowtie [\![J]\!]_\rho$ holds. Similarly, $\rho \vDash \Phi$ holds when $\rho \vDash C$ for all $C \in \Phi$. Likewise, we note $\phi; \Phi \vDash C$ when for all valuations ρ on ϕ such that $\rho \vDash \Phi$ we have $\rho \vDash C$. Remark that the order $\leq$ in a context $\phi; \Phi$ is not total in general, for example $(i, j); \cdot \nvDash i \leq ij$ and $(i, j); \cdot \nvDash ij \leq i$.

Definition 6. *The set of* base types *is given by the following grammar.*

$$\mathcal{B} := \mathsf{Nat}[I, J] \mid \mathsf{List}[I, J](\mathcal{B})$$

Intuitively, an integer n of type $\mathsf{Nat}[I, J]$ must be such that $I \leq n \leq J$. Likewise, a list of type $\mathsf{List}[I, J](\mathcal{B})$ must have a length between I and J. With those types comes a notion of subtyping, in order to have some flexibility on bounds. This is described by the rules of Figure 5. In a subtyping judgement $\phi; \Phi \vdash T \sqsubseteq T'$ the free index variables of T, T', Φ should be included in ϕ.

$$\frac{\phi; \Phi \vDash I' \leq I \qquad \phi; \Phi \vDash J \leq J'}{\phi; \Phi \vdash \mathsf{Nat}[I, J] \sqsubseteq \mathsf{Nat}[I', J']}$$

$$\frac{\phi; \Phi \vDash I' \leq I \qquad \phi; \Phi \vDash J \leq J' \qquad \phi; \Phi \vdash \mathcal{B} \sqsubseteq \mathcal{B}'}{\phi; \Phi \vdash \mathsf{List}[I, J](\mathcal{B}) \sqsubseteq \mathsf{List}[I', J'](\mathcal{B}')}$$

Fig. 5. Subtyping Rules for Base Size Types

Then, after base types, we have to give a type to channel names in a process. As we want to generalize subtyping for channel types, we will use input/output types [34]. Intuitively, in such a type, in addition to the types that can be sent and received for a channel, a channel is given a set of capabilities: either it is both an input and output channel, or it has only one of those capabilities. This is useful in order to use subtyping, as an input channel and an output channel do not behave in the same way with regards to subtyping. Indeed, an input/output channel is invariant for subtyping, an input channel is covariant and an output channel is contravariant. Unlike in usual input/output types, in this work we also distinguish two kinds of channels : the *simple channels* (that we will often call channels), and replicated channels (called *servers*).

Definition 7. *The set of types is given by the following grammar.*

$$T := \mathcal{B} \mid \mathsf{ch}(\tilde{T}) \mid \mathsf{in}(\tilde{T}) \mid \mathsf{out}(\tilde{T}) \mid \forall \tilde{i}.\mathsf{serv}^K(\tilde{T}) \mid \forall \tilde{i}.\mathsf{iserv}^K(\tilde{T}) \mid \forall \tilde{i}.\mathsf{oserv}^K(\tilde{T})$$

The three different types for channels and servers correspond to the three different sets of capabilities. We note serv when the server have both capabilities, iserv when it has only input and oserv when it has only output. Then, for servers, we have additional information: there is a quantification over index variables, and the index K stands for the *complexity* of the process spawned by this server. A typical example could be a server taking as input a list and a channel, and sending to this channel the sorted list, in time $k \cdot n$ where n is the size of the list : $P = \, !a(x,b).\cdots \overline{b}\langle e \rangle$ where e represents at the end of the process the list x sorted. Such a server name a could be given the type $\forall i.\mathsf{serv}^{k \cdot i}(\mathsf{List}[0,i](\mathcal{B}), \mathsf{out}(\mathsf{List}[0,i](\mathcal{B})))$. This type means that for all integers i, if given a list of size at most i and an output channel waiting for a list of size at most i, the process spawned by this server will stop at time at most $k \cdot i$. Those bounded index variables $\tilde{i}$ are very useful especially for replicated input. As a replicated input is made to be used several times with different values, it is useful to allow this kind of polymorphism on indices. Moreover, if a replicated input is used to encode a recursion, with this polymorphism we can take into account the different recursive calls with different values and different complexities.

$$\frac{(\phi,\tilde{i});\Phi \vdash \tilde{T} \sqsubseteq \tilde{U} \qquad (\phi,\tilde{i});\Phi \vdash \tilde{U} \sqsubseteq \tilde{T} \qquad (\phi,\tilde{i});\Phi \vDash K = K'}{\phi;\Phi \vdash \forall \tilde{i}.\mathsf{serv}^K(\tilde{T}) \sqsubseteq \forall \tilde{i}.\mathsf{serv}^{K'}(\tilde{U})}$$

$$\frac{}{\phi;\Phi \vdash \forall \tilde{i}.\mathsf{serv}^K(\tilde{T}) \sqsubseteq \forall \tilde{i}.\mathsf{iserv}^K(\tilde{T})} \qquad \frac{}{\phi;\Phi \vdash \forall \tilde{i}.\mathsf{serv}^K(\tilde{T}) \sqsubseteq \forall \tilde{i}.\mathsf{oserv}^K(\tilde{T})}$$

$$\frac{(\phi,\tilde{i});\Phi \vdash \tilde{T} \sqsubseteq \tilde{U} \quad (\phi,\tilde{i});\Phi \vDash K' \leq K}{\phi;\Phi \vdash \forall \tilde{i}.\mathsf{iserv}^K(\tilde{T}) \sqsubseteq \forall \tilde{i}.\mathsf{iserv}^{K'}(\tilde{U})} \qquad \frac{(\phi,\tilde{i});\Phi \vdash \tilde{U} \sqsubseteq \tilde{T} \quad (\phi,\tilde{i});\Phi \vDash K \leq K'}{\phi;\Phi \vdash \forall \tilde{i}.\mathsf{oserv}^K(\tilde{T}) \sqsubseteq \forall \tilde{i}.\mathsf{oserv}^{K'}(\tilde{U})}$$

$$\frac{\phi;\Phi \vdash T \sqsubseteq T' \qquad \phi;\Phi \vdash T' \sqsubseteq T''}{\phi;\Phi \vdash T \sqsubseteq T''}$$

Fig. 6. Subtyping Rules for Server Types

Then, we describe subtyping for servers in Figure 6. As explained previously, capabilities modify the variance of types, and a channel can lose capabilities by subtyping. Subtyping for channel types can be deduced from the rules for servers. Note that the transitivity rule is not necessary and the subtyping relation could be exhaustively described. However, in order to reduce the number of rules, we present subtyping with a transitivity rule. Finally, subtyping can be extended to contexts, and we write $\Gamma \sqsubseteq \Delta$ when Γ and Δ have the same domain and for each variable $v : T \in \Gamma$ and $v : T' \in \Delta$, we have $T \sqsubseteq T'$.

$$\frac{v : T \in \Gamma}{\phi; \Phi; \Gamma \vdash v : T} \qquad \frac{}{\phi; \Phi; \Gamma \vdash 0 : \mathsf{Nat}[0,0]} \qquad \frac{}{\phi; \Phi; \Gamma \vdash [] : \mathsf{List}[0,0](\mathcal{B})}$$

$$\frac{\phi; \Phi; \Gamma \vdash e : \mathsf{Nat}[I,J]}{\phi; \Phi; \Gamma \vdash \mathsf{s}(e) : \mathsf{Nat}[I+1, J+1]}$$

$$\frac{\phi; \Phi; \Gamma \vdash e : \mathcal{B} \qquad \phi; \Phi; \Gamma \vdash e' : \mathsf{List}[I,J](\mathcal{B})}{\phi; \Phi; \Gamma \vdash e :: e' : \mathsf{List}[I+1, J+1](\mathcal{B})}$$

$$\frac{\phi; \Phi; \Delta \vdash e : U \qquad \phi; \Phi \vdash \Gamma \sqsubseteq \Delta \qquad \phi; \Phi \vdash U \sqsubseteq T}{\phi; \Phi; \Gamma \vdash e : T}$$

Fig. 7. Typing Rules for Expressions

We can now present the type system. Rules for expressions are given in Figure 7. The typing for expressions $\phi; \Phi; \Gamma \vdash e : T$ means that under the constraints Φ, in the context Γ, the expression e can be given the type T. We use the notation $\phi; \Phi; \Gamma \vdash \tilde{e} : \tilde{T}$ for a sequence of typing judgements for expressions in the tuple $\tilde{e}$.

Then, rules for processes are described in Figure 8 and Figure 9. Figure 9 describes rules specific to work, whereas rules in Figure 8 will be reused for span. A typing judgement $\phi; \Phi; \Gamma \vdash P \triangleleft K$ intuitively means that under the constraints Φ, in a context Γ, a process P is typable and its work complexity is bounded by K.

The rules can be seen as a combination of input/output typing rules with rules found in a size type system. The main differences are that because of the two kinds of channels, we need two rules for an output. And, for servers, quantification over index variables should be taken in account. Note that a replicated input has complexity zero, and it is a call to this server that generates complexity in the type system. This is because once defined, a replicated input stays during all the reduction, so we do not want them to generate complexity. Note also that the pattern matching rules are the only ones which add constraints in the hypothesis, which provide information on the size in the typing. This is particularly useful for recursion. Finally, there is an explicit rule for subtyping, and in this rule we can arbitrarily increase the index corresponding to the complexity.

$$\frac{}{\phi;\Phi;\Gamma \vdash 0 \lhd 0} \qquad \frac{\phi;\Phi;\Gamma, a:T \vdash P \lhd K}{\phi;\Phi;\Gamma \vdash (\nu a)P \lhd K}$$

$$\frac{\phi;\Phi;\Gamma \vdash e : \mathsf{Nat}[I,J] \qquad \phi;(\Phi, I \leq 0);\Gamma \vdash P \lhd K \qquad \phi;(\Phi, J \geq 1);\Gamma, x : \mathsf{Nat}[I-1, J-1] \vdash Q \lhd K}{\phi;\Phi;\Gamma \vdash \mathtt{match}(e)\ \{0 \mapsto P;;\ \mathtt{s}(x) \mapsto Q\} \lhd K}$$

$$\frac{\phi;\Phi;\Gamma \vdash e : \mathsf{List}[I,J](\mathcal{B}) \qquad \phi;(\Phi, I \leq 0);\Gamma \vdash P \lhd K \qquad \phi;(\Phi, J \geq 1);\Gamma, x : \mathcal{B}, y : \mathsf{List}[I-1, J-1](\mathcal{B}) \vdash Q \lhd K}{\phi;\Phi;\Gamma \vdash \mathtt{match}(e)\ \{[] \mapsto P;;\ x :: y \mapsto Q\} \lhd K}$$

$$\frac{\phi;\Phi;\Delta \vdash P \lhd K \qquad \phi;\Phi \vdash \Gamma \sqsubseteq \Delta \qquad \phi;\Phi \vDash K \leq K'}{\phi;\Phi;\Gamma \vdash P \lhd K'}$$

Fig. 8. Common Typing Rules for Processes

$$\frac{\phi;\Phi;\Gamma \vdash P \lhd K \qquad \phi;\Phi;\Gamma \vdash Q \lhd K'}{\phi;\Phi;\Gamma \vdash P \mid Q \lhd K + K'} \qquad \frac{\phi;\Phi;\Gamma \vdash P \lhd K}{\phi;\Phi;\Gamma \vdash \mathtt{tick}.P \lhd K + 1}$$

$$\frac{\phi;\Phi;\Gamma \vdash a : \forall \tilde{i}.\mathsf{iserv}^K(\tilde{T}) \qquad (\phi, \tilde{i});\Phi;\Gamma, \tilde{v} : \tilde{T} \vdash P \lhd K}{\phi;\Phi;\Gamma \vdash !a(\tilde{v}).P \lhd 0}$$

$$\frac{\phi;\Phi;\Gamma \vdash a : \mathsf{in}(\tilde{T}) \qquad \phi;\Phi;\Gamma, \tilde{v} : \tilde{T} \vdash P \lhd K}{\phi;\Phi;\Gamma \vdash a(\tilde{v}).P \lhd K}$$

$$\frac{\phi;\Phi;\Gamma \vdash a : \mathsf{out}(\tilde{T}) \qquad \phi;\Phi;\Gamma \vdash \tilde{e} : \tilde{T}}{\phi;\Phi;\Gamma \vdash \overline{a}\langle \tilde{e} \rangle \lhd 0}$$

$$\frac{\phi;\Phi;\Gamma \vdash a : \forall \tilde{i}.\mathsf{oserv}^K(\tilde{T}) \qquad \phi;\Phi;\Gamma \vdash \tilde{e} : \tilde{T}\{\tilde{J}/\tilde{i}\}}{\phi;\Phi;\Gamma \vdash \overline{a}\langle \tilde{e} \rangle \lhd K\{\tilde{J}/\tilde{i}\}}$$

Fig. 9. Work Typing Rules for Processes

3.2 Subject Reduction

We now state the properties of this typing system. We do not detail the proofs as we will be more precise in the following sections with the type system for span. In the type system for work, we can easily obtain some properties such as weakening and strengthening and that index variables can be substituted by any index in a typing derivation. Finally, we have that substitution in processes preserves typing. With those properties, we obtain the usual subject reduction.

Theorem 1 (Subject Reduction). *If* $\phi;\Phi;\Gamma \vdash P \lhd K$ *and* $P \to Q$ *then* $\phi;\Phi;\Gamma \vdash Q \lhd K$.

Then, we also obtain the following theorem.

Theorem 2 (Quantitative Subject Reduction). *If* $P \to_1 Q$ *and* $\phi;\Phi;\Gamma \vdash P \lhd K$ *then we have* $\phi;\Phi;\Gamma \vdash Q \lhd K'$ *with* $\phi;\Phi \vDash K' + 1 \leq K$.

So, as a consequence we almost immediately obtain that K is indeed a bound on the work of P if we have $\phi; \Phi; \Gamma \vdash P \triangleleft K$.

Note that this soundness result is easily adaptable to similar type systems for work. As stated before, we can enrich the type system with other algebraic data-types and the proof can easily be adapted. Moreover, we can get rid of the distinction between channels and servers and take a similar typing for both, and we still get the soundness. We decided here to present this version as an introduction for the type system for span, but the work in itself can be of interest.

For example, an interesting consequence of this soundness theorem is that it immediately gives soundness for any subsystem. In particular, we detail in the technical report [5] a (slightly) weaker typing system where the shape of types are restricted in order to have an inference procedure close to the one in [4].

4 Types for Parallel Complexity

We present here a type system for span, so we want as previously a type system such that typing a process gives us a bound on its span. Formally, we will prove the following theorem:

Theorem 3 (Typing and Complexity). *Let P be a process and m be its global parallel complexity. If we have $\phi; \Phi; \Gamma \vdash P \triangleleft K$, then $\phi; \Phi \vDash K \geq m$.*

Remark that this theorem talks about open processes. However, our notion of complexity does not behave well with open processes. For example the process $\mathtt{match}(v)\ \{0 \mapsto P;;\ \mathtt{s}(x) \mapsto Q\}$ is in normal form for a variable v, so this process has global complexity 0. Still, we will also obtain the following corollary:

Corollary 1 (Complexity and Open Processes).

- *If $\phi; \Phi; \Gamma, \tilde{v} : \tilde{T} \vdash P \triangleleft K$, then for any sequence of expressions $\tilde{e}$ such that $\phi; \Phi; \Gamma \vdash \tilde{e} : \tilde{T}$, K is a bound on the global complexity of $P[\tilde{v} := \tilde{e}]$*
- *If $\phi; \Phi; \Gamma \vdash P \triangleleft K$, then for any other annotated process Q such that $\phi; \Phi; \Gamma \vdash Q \triangleleft K'$, $max(K, K')$ is a bound on the global complexity of $P \mid Q$.*

So, when we give a typing $\phi; \Phi; \Gamma \vdash P \triangleleft K$ for an open process, we should not see K as a bound on the actual complexity on P, but we should see it as a bound on the complexity of this particular process in an environment respecting the type of Γ. So, in $\phi; \Phi; v : \mathsf{Nat}[2, 10] \vdash \mathtt{match}(v)\ \{0 \mapsto P;;\ \mathtt{s}(x) \mapsto Q\} \triangleleft K$, K is a bound on the complexity of this pattern matching under the assumption that the environment gives to v an integer value between 2 and 10.

4.1 Size Types with Time

The type system is an extension of the previous one. In order to take into account parallelism, we need a way to synchronize the time between processes in parallel, thus we will add some time information in types, as in [27] or [9].

Definition 8. *The set of types and* base types *are given by the grammar:*

$$\mathcal{B} := \mathsf{Nat}[I,J] \mid \mathsf{List}[I,J](\mathcal{B})$$

$$T := \mathcal{B} \mid \mathsf{ch}_I(\tilde{T}) \mid \mathsf{in}_I(\tilde{T}) \mid \mathsf{out}_I(\tilde{T}) \mid \forall_I \tilde{i}.\mathsf{serv}^K(\tilde{T}) \mid \forall_I \tilde{i}.\mathsf{iserv}^K(\tilde{T}) \mid \forall_I \tilde{i}.\mathsf{oserv}^K(\tilde{T})$$

As before, we have channel types, server types, and input/output capabilities in those types. For a channel type or a server type, the index I is called the *time* of this type. Giving a channel name the type $\mathsf{ch}_I(\tilde{T})$ ensures that communication on this channel should happen within time I. For example, a channel name of type $\mathsf{ch}_0(\tilde{T})$ should be used to communicate before any tick occurs. With this information, we can know when the continuation of an input will be available. Likewise, a server name of type $\forall_I \tilde{i}.\mathsf{iserv}^K(\tilde{T})$ should be used in a replicated input, and this replicated input should be ready to receive for any time greater than I. Typically, a process $\mathtt{tick}.!a(\tilde{v}).P$ enforces that the type of a is $\forall_I \tilde{i}.\mathsf{iserv}^K(\tilde{T})$ with I greater than one, as the replicated input is not ready to receive at time zero.

As before, we define a notion of subtyping on those types. The rules are essentially the same as the ones in Figures 5 and 6. The only difference is that we force the time of a type to be invariant in subtyping.

In order to write the typing rules, we need some other definitions to work with time in types. The first thing we need is a way to advance time.

Definition 9 (Advancing Time in Types). *Given a set of index variables ϕ, a set of constraints Φ, a type T and an index I, we define T after I time units, denoted $\langle T \rangle_{-I}^{\phi;\Phi}$ by:*

- $\langle \mathcal{B} \rangle_{-I}^{\phi;\Phi} = \mathcal{B}$
- $\langle \mathsf{ch}_J(\tilde{T}) \rangle_{-I}^{\phi;\Phi} = \mathsf{ch}_{(J-I)}(\tilde{T})$ *if* $\phi;\Phi \vDash J \geq I$. *It is undefined otherwise.*
  Other channel types follow exactly the same pattern.
- $\langle \forall_J \tilde{i}.\mathsf{serv}^K(\tilde{T}) \rangle_{-I}^{\phi;\Phi} = \forall_{(J-I)} \tilde{i}.\mathsf{serv}^K(\tilde{T})$ *if* $\phi;\Phi \vDash J \geq I$.
  Otherwise, $\langle \forall_J \tilde{i}.\mathsf{serv}^K(\tilde{T}) \rangle_{-I}^{\phi;\Phi} = \forall_{(J-I)} \tilde{i}.\mathsf{oserv}^K(\tilde{T})$
- $\langle \forall_J \tilde{i}.\mathsf{iserv}^K(\tilde{T}) \rangle_{-I}^{\phi;\Phi} = \forall_{(J-I)} \tilde{i}.\mathsf{iserv}^K(\tilde{T})$ *if* $\phi;\Phi \vDash J \geq I$.
  It is undefined otherwise.
- $\langle \forall_J \tilde{i}.\mathsf{oserv}^K(\tilde{T}) \rangle_{-I}^{\phi;\Phi} = \forall_{(J-I)} \tilde{i}.\mathsf{oserv}^K(\tilde{T})$.

This definition can be extended to contexts, with $\langle v : T, \Gamma \rangle_{-I}^{\phi;\Phi} = v : \langle T \rangle_{-I}^{\phi;\Phi}, \langle \Gamma \rangle_{-I}^{\phi;\Phi}$ *if* $\langle T \rangle_{-I}^{\phi;\Phi}$ *is defined. Otherwise,* $\langle v : T, \Gamma \rangle_{-I} = \langle \Gamma \rangle_{-I}^{\phi;\Phi}$. *We will often omit the* $\phi;\Phi$ *in the notation when it is clear from the context.*

Recall that as the order $\leq$ *on indexes is not total,* $\phi;\Phi \nvDash J \geq I$ *does not mean that* $\phi;\Phi \vDash J < I$.

Let us explain a bit the definition here. For base types, there is no time indication thus nothing happens. Then, one can wonder what happens when the time of T is not greater than I. For non-server channel types, we consider that their time is over, thus we erase them from the context. For servers this is a bit more complicated. Indeed, when a server is defined, it must stay available until the end. Thus, an output to a server should always be possible, no matter the time. Still, the input capability of a server should not be available eternally, as the time I is supposed to mean the time for which a replicated input is effectively defined. So, when this time has passed, we should not be able to define a replicated input any more.

Definition 10 (Time Invariant Context). *Given a set of index variables ϕ and a set of constraints Φ, a context Γ is said to be* time invariant *when it only contains base type variables or output server types $\forall_I \tilde{i}.\mathsf{oserv}^K(\tilde{T})$ with $\phi; \Phi \vDash I = 0$.*

Such a context is thus invariant by the operator $\langle\cdot\rangle_{-I}$ for any I. This is typically the kind of context that we need to define a server, as a server should not be dependent on the time it is called. We can now present the type system. Typing rules for expressions and some processes do not change, they can be found in Figure 7 and Figure 8. In Figure 10, we present the remaining rules in this type system that differ from the ones in Figure 9. As before, a typing judgement $\phi; \Phi; \Gamma \vdash P \triangleleft K$ intuitively means that under the constraints Φ, in a context Γ, a process P is typable and its span complexity is bounded by K.

$$\frac{\phi; \Phi; \Gamma \vdash P \triangleleft K \qquad \phi; \Phi; \Gamma \vdash Q \triangleleft K}{\phi; \Phi; \Gamma \vdash P \mid Q \triangleleft K} \qquad \frac{\phi; \Phi; \langle\Gamma\rangle_{-1} \vdash P \triangleleft K}{\phi; \Phi; \Gamma \vdash \mathtt{tick}.P \triangleleft K + 1}$$

$$\frac{\phi; \Phi; \Gamma, \Delta \vdash a : \forall_I \tilde{i}.\mathsf{iserv}^K(\tilde{T}) \qquad \begin{array}{c}\phi; \Phi \vdash \langle\Gamma\rangle_{-I}^{\phi;\Phi} \sqsubseteq \Gamma' \text{ and } \Gamma' \text{ time invariant} \\ \phi, \tilde{i}; \Phi; \Gamma', \tilde{v} : \tilde{T} \vdash P \triangleleft K\end{array}}{\phi; \Phi; \Gamma, \Delta \vdash !a(\tilde{v}).P \triangleleft I}$$

$$\frac{\phi; \Phi; \Gamma \vdash a : \mathsf{in}_I(\tilde{T}) \qquad \phi; \Phi; \langle\Gamma\rangle_{-I}, \tilde{v} : \tilde{T} \vdash P \triangleleft K}{\phi; \Phi; \Gamma \vdash a(\tilde{v}).P \triangleleft K + I}$$

$$\frac{\phi; \Phi; \Gamma \vdash a : \mathsf{out}_I(\tilde{T}) \qquad \phi; \Phi; \langle\Gamma\rangle_{-I} \vdash \tilde{e} : \tilde{T}}{\phi; \Phi; \Gamma \vdash \overline{a}\langle\tilde{e}\rangle \triangleleft I}$$

$$\frac{\phi; \Phi; \Gamma \vdash a : \forall_I \tilde{i}.\mathsf{oserv}^K(\tilde{T}) \qquad \phi; \Phi; \langle\Gamma\rangle_{-I} \vdash \tilde{e} : \tilde{T}\{\tilde{J}/\tilde{i}\}}{\phi; \Phi; \Gamma \vdash \overline{a}\langle\tilde{e}\rangle \triangleleft K\{\tilde{J}/\tilde{i}\} + I}$$

Fig. 10. Span Typing Rules for Processes

The rule for parallel composition shows that we consider parallel complexity as we take the maximum between the two processes instead of the sum. In practice, we ask for the same complexity K in both branches of parallel composition, but with the subtyping rule, it corresponds indeed to the maximum. For input server, we integrate some weakening on context (Δ), and we want a time invariant context to type the server, as a server should not depend on time. Weakening is important since some types are not time invariant, such as channels. So, we need to separate time invariant types that can be used in the continuation P from other types.

Some rules make the time advance in their continuation, for example the tick rule or input rule. This is expressed by the advance time operator on contexts, and because time advances, the complexity also increases. Also, remark that because of the advance of time, some channels name could disappear, thus there is a kind of "time uniqueness" for channels, contrary to the previous section. This will be detailed later. Also, note that in the rule for replicated input, there is an explicit subtyping in the premises. This is because $\langle \Gamma \rangle_{-I}^{\phi;\Phi}$ is not time invariant, since the type of a is at least $\forall_0 \tilde{i}.\mathsf{iserv}^K(\tilde{T})$ in this case. However, if this server had both input and output capabilities, we can give a time invariant type for a (or other servers) just by removing the input capability, which can be done by subtyping.

Looking back at Corollary 1, we can for example understand the rule for input by taking the judgement $\phi; \Phi; a : \mathsf{ch}_3() \vdash a().\mathtt{tick}.0 \triangleleft 4$. This expresses that with an environment providing a message on a within 3 times units, this process terminates in 4 time units.

Finally, we can see that if we remove all size annotations and merge server types and channel types together, we get back the classical input/output types, and all the rules described here are admissible in the classical input/output type system for the π-calculus.

4.2 Examples

An Example to Justify the Use of Time. In order to justify the use of time in types for span, and to show how we could find the time of a channel, we present here three examples of recursive calls with different behaviour. We do not detail here a typing derivation, a more detailed example will be described later, in Section 5. Usually, type inference for a size system reduces to satisfying a set of constraints on indices. We believe that even with time indexes on channels, type inference is still reducible to satisfying such a set of constraints. So, for the sake of simplicity, we will describe this example with constraints.

We define three processes P_1, P_2 and P_3 by:

$$P_l \equiv !a(n,r).\mathtt{tick}.\mathtt{match}(n)\ \{0 \mapsto \overline{r}\langle\rangle;;\ \mathtt{s}(m) \mapsto (\nu r')(\nu r'')(Q_l)\}$$

for the following definition of Q_i:

$$Q_1 \equiv \overline{a}\langle m, r'\rangle \mid \overline{a}\langle m, r''\rangle \mid r'().r''().\overline{r}\langle\rangle$$
$$Q_2 \equiv \overline{a}\langle m, r'\rangle \mid r'().\overline{a}\langle m, r''\rangle \mid r''().\overline{r}\langle\rangle$$
$$Q_3 \equiv \overline{a}\langle m, r'\rangle \mid r'().(\overline{a}\langle m, r''\rangle \mid \overline{r}\langle\rangle) \mid r''().0$$

So intuitively, for P_1 the two recursive calls are done after one unit of time in parallel, and the return signal on r is done when both processes have done their return signal on r' and r''. So, this is total parallelism for the two recursive calls (the span is linear in n). For P_2, a first recursive call is done, and then the process waits for the return signal on r', and when it receives it, the second recursive call begins. So, this is totally sequential (the span is exponential in n). Finally, for P_3 we have an intermediate situation between totally parallel and totally sequential. The process starts with a recursive call. Then, it waits for the return signal on r'. When this signal arrives, it immediately starts the second recursive call and immediately does the return signal on r. So, intuitively, the second recursive call starts when all the "left" calls have been done. Note that those three servers have the same work, which is exponential in n.

So, let us type the three examples with the type system for span. For the sake of simplicity, we omit the typing of expressions, we only consider the difficult branch for the match constructors, and we focus on complexity and time. We consider the following context that is used for the three processes:

$$\Gamma \equiv a : \forall_0 i.\mathsf{oserv}^{f(i)}(\mathsf{Nat}[0,i], \mathsf{ch}_{g(i)}()), n : \mathsf{Nat}[0,i], r : \mathsf{ch}_{g(i)}$$

We have two unknown function symbols: f, that represents the complexity of the server, and g, the time for the return channel. We also use this second context:

$$\Delta \equiv \langle\Gamma\rangle_{-1}, m : \mathsf{Nat}[0, i{-}1], r' : \mathsf{ch}_{g'(i)}, r'' : \mathsf{ch}_{g''(i)}$$

This gives two more unknown functions, g' and g'' corresponding respectively to the time of r' and r'' when defined. The three processes start with the same typing. We use a double line to express that we do not use a real typing rule, so we can omit some premises or do simultaneously several typing rules.

$$\dfrac{\dfrac{\dfrac{i; i \geq 1; \Delta \vdash Q_l \lhd f(i){-}1}{i; \cdot; \langle\Gamma\rangle_{-1} \vdash \mathtt{match}(n)\ \{0 \mapsto \overline{r}\langle\rangle;;\ \mathtt{s}(m) \mapsto (\nu r')(\nu r'')(Q_i)\} \lhd f(i){-}1}}{i; \cdot; \Gamma \vdash \mathtt{tick.match}(n)\ \{0 \mapsto \overline{r}\langle\rangle;;\ \mathtt{s}(m) \mapsto (\nu r')(\nu r'')(Q_l)\} \lhd f(i)}}{\cdot; \cdot; a : \forall_0 i.\mathsf{oserv}^{f(i)}(\mathsf{Nat}[0,i], \mathsf{ch}_{g(i)}()) \vdash P_l \lhd 0}$$

The first thing to remark is that the typing does a `tick` typing rule. In this rule for `tick`, the complexity on the bottom should have the shape $K+1$ for some K, so here we obtain immediately that $f(i) \geq 1$. In the same way, r should still be defined in $\langle\Gamma\rangle_{-1}$, so by definition of time advance, it means that $g(i) \geq 1$.

Then, for the three processes, the typing gives the following conditions on the indices, for $i \geq 1$. For Q_1:

$$f(i){-}1 \geq f(i{-}1) \qquad g'(i) = g(i{-}1) \qquad g''(i) = g(i{-}1)$$

$$g''(i) \geq g'(i) \qquad g(i){-}1 \geq g''(i) \qquad f(i){-}1 \geq g(i){-}1$$

The first constraint is because the total complexity $f(i){-}1$ must be greater than the complexity of the two recursive calls $f(i{-}1)$. Then, r' and r'' must have a time equal to $g(i{-}1)$ in order to correspond to the type of a in the outputs $\overline{a}\langle m, r'\rangle$ and $\overline{a}\langle m, r''\rangle$. Finally, as r'' waits for input after r', the time of r'' must be greater than the time of r'. Similarly, the time of r (which is equal to $g(i){-}1$) must be greater than the time of r'', and the total complexity $f[i]{-}1$ must be greater than the complexity of $r'().r''().\overline{r}\langle\rangle$ which is equal to the time of r. So, we can satisfy the conditions with the following choice:

$$f(i) \equiv i+1 \qquad g(i) \equiv i+1 \qquad g'(i) \equiv g''(i) \equiv i$$

So, as expected, the span, represented by the function f, is indeed linear.

Then, for Q_2, the second call is delayed of $g'(i)$ time units because we need to wait for r'. Thus, we obtain the following constraints.

$$f(i)-1 \geq f(i-1) \qquad g'(i) = g(i-1) \qquad f(i)-1 \geq g'(i) + f(i-1)$$
$$g''(i)-g'(i) = g(i-1) \qquad g(i)-1 \geq g''(i) \qquad f(i)-1 \geq g(i)-1$$

This delay of $g'(i)$ time units can be seen in the third and fourth constraints. Again, the third constraint is because the complexity should be greater that the complexity of the second call, and the type of r'' should correspond to the type in a. Thus, we can take

$$f(i) \equiv 2^{i+1}-1 \qquad g(i) \equiv 2^{i+1}-1$$

So, we indeed obtain the exponential complexity.

However, with those two examples, the time of the channel r is always equal to the complexity of the server a, so we cannot really see the usefulness of time. Still, with the next example we obtain something more interesting. So, for Q_3, this time the fifth constraint on $g(i)$ (depending on when the output to r is done) is different, and we obtain:

$$f(i)-1 \geq f(i-1) \qquad g'(i) = g(i-1) \qquad f(i)-1 \geq g'(i) + f(i-1)$$
$$g''(i)-g'(i) = g(i-1) \qquad g(i)-1 \geq g'(i) \qquad f(i)-1 \geq g(i)-1 \qquad f(i)-1 \geq g''(i)$$

The last constraint is because, again, the complexity should be greater that the complexity of calling r''. So, using the equalities, and by removing redundant inequalities, we obtain for f and g:

$$f(i) \geq 1 + g(i-1) + f(i-1) \qquad g(i) \geq 1 + g(i-1) \qquad f(i) \geq 1 + 2 \cdot g(i-1)$$

Thus, we can take:

$$g(i) \equiv i+1 \qquad f(i) \equiv \frac{(i+1)(i+2)}{2}$$

The complexity is quadratic in n. Note that for this example, the complexity f depends directly on g, and g is given by a recursive equation independent of f. So in a sense, to find the complexity, we need to find first the delay of the second recursive call. Without time indications on channel, it would not be possible to track and obtain this recurrence relation on g and thus we could not deduce the complexity.

Note that the two first examples used channels as a return signal for a parallel computation, whereas for the last example, channels are used as a synchronization point in the middle of a computation. We believe that this flexibility of channels justifies the use of π-calculus to reason about parallel computation. Moreover, this work is a step to a more expressive type system inspired by [27], taking in account concurrent behaviour. Indeed, as we will show, the current type system fails to capture some simple concurrency.

Limitations of the Type System. Our current type system enforces some kind of time uniqueness in channels. Indeed, take the process $a().\mathtt{tick}.\overline{a}\langle\rangle$. When trying to type this process, we obtain:

$$\dfrac{\dfrac{\cdot;\cdot \vdash \mathsf{ch}_I() \sqsubseteq \mathsf{in}_I()}{\cdot;\cdot;a:\mathsf{ch}_I() \vdash a:\mathsf{in}_I()} \quad \dfrac{\dfrac{\text{Error}}{\cdot;\cdot;\langle a:\mathsf{ch}_0()\rangle_{-1} \vdash \overline{a}\langle\rangle \lhd 0}}{\cdot;\cdot;a:\mathsf{ch}_0() \vdash \mathtt{tick}.\overline{a}\langle\rangle \lhd 1}}{\cdot;\cdot;a:\mathsf{ch}_I() \vdash a().\mathtt{tick}.\overline{a}\langle\rangle \lhd I+1}$$

As by definition $\langle a:\mathsf{ch}_0()\rangle_{-1}$ is $\emptyset$, we cannot type the output on a. So, channels have strong constraints on the time they can be used. This is true especially when channels are not used linearly. Still, note that we can type a process of the shape $a().0 \mid \overline{a}\langle\rangle \mid \mathtt{tick}.\overline{a}\langle\rangle$, so it is better than plain linearity on channels. This restriction limits examples of concurrent behaviours. For example, take two processes P_1 and P_2 that should be executed but not simultaneously. In order to do that in a concurrent setting, we can use semaphores. In π-calculus, we could consider the process $(\nu a)(a().P_1' \mid a().P_2' \mid \overline{a}\langle\rangle)$, where P_1' is P_1 with an output $\overline{a}\langle\rangle$ at the end, likewise for P_2'. This is a way to simulate semaphore in π-calculus. Now, we can see that this example has the same problem as the example given above if for example P_1 contains a $\mathtt{tick}$, thus we cannot type this kind of processes.

Still, we believe that for parallel computation, our type system should be quite expressive in practice. Indeed, as stated above, the restriction appears especially when channels are not used linearly. However, it is known that linear π-calculus in itself is expressive for parallel computation [31]. For example, classical encodings of functional programs in a parallel setting rely on the use of linear return signals, as we will see in the example for bitonic sort in Sect. 5. Moreover, session types can also be encoded in linear π-calculus in the presence of variant types [28,8]. Note that in order to encode a calculus as the one in [9], we would also need recursive types. Our calculus and its proof of soundness could be extended to variant types, but not straightforwardly to recursive types. However, we believe the results on the linear π-calculus we cited suggest that the restriction given above should not be too harmful for parallel computation.

4.3 Complexity Results

In this section, we show how to prove that our type system indeed gives a bound on the number of time reduction steps of a process following the maximal progress assumption. We only give in this section intuitions about the proofs. The detailed proofs can be found in the technical report [5].

In the following section, as we will work with the reduction $\Rightarrow_p$, we need to consider annotated processes instead of simple processes. So, we need to enrich our type system with a rule for the constructor $n : P$.

$$\frac{\phi;\Phi;\langle\Gamma\rangle_{-n} \vdash P \lhd K}{\phi;\Phi;\Gamma \vdash n : P \lhd K+n}$$

As the intuition suggested, this rule is equivalent to n times the typing rule for `tick`. We can now work on the properties of our type system on annotated processes.

The procedure to prove the subject reduction for $\Rightarrow_p$ in this type system is intrinsically more difficult than the one for Theorem 1. So, from the proof of subject reduction for span, one could deduce the proof of subject reduction for work, just by forgetting the consideration with time and the constructor $n : P$ in the following proof. Thus, in the technical report, only the proof for span is detailed.

Again, we have both weakening and strengthening in this type system. We also have a property specific to size type systems, expressing that an index variable can be substituted by any index. We also need a lemma specific to the notion of time.

Definition 11 (Delaying). *Given a type T and an index I, we define the* delaying *of T by I units of time, denoted T_{+I}:*

$$\mathcal{B}_{+I} = \mathcal{B} \qquad (\mathsf{ch}_J(\tilde{T}))_{+I} = \mathsf{ch}_{J+I}(\tilde{T})$$

and for other channel and server types, the definition is in correspondence with the one on the right above. This definition can be extended to contexts.

Lemma 2 (Delaying). *If $\phi; \Phi; \Gamma \vdash P \triangleleft K$ then $\phi; \Phi; \Gamma_{+I} \vdash P \triangleleft K + I$.*

With this lemma, we can see that if we add a delay of I time units in the contexts for all channels, it increases the complexity by I time units, thus we see the link between time in types and the complexity. Then, we can show the usual substitution lemma.

Lemma 3 (Substitution).

1. *If $\phi; \Phi; \Gamma, v : T \vdash e' : U$ and $\phi; \Phi; \Gamma \vdash e : T$ then $\phi; \Phi; \Gamma \vdash e'[v := e] : U$.*
2. *If $\phi; \Phi; \Gamma, v : T \vdash P \triangleleft K$ and $\phi; \Phi; \Gamma \vdash e : T$ then $\phi; \Phi; \Gamma \vdash P[v := e] \triangleleft K$.*

Finally, we can show that typing behaves well with congruence.

Lemma 4 (Congruence and Typing). *Let P and Q be annotated processes such that $P \equiv Q$. Then, $\phi; \Phi; \Gamma \vdash P \triangleleft K$ if and only if $\phi; \Phi; \Gamma \vdash Q \triangleleft K$.*

And with all this, we obtain the subject reduction.

Theorem 4 (Subject Reduction). *If $\phi; \Phi; \Gamma \vdash P \triangleleft K$ and $P \Rightarrow_p Q$ then $\phi; \Phi; \Gamma \vdash Q \triangleleft K$.*

The proof is done by induction on $P \Rightarrow_p Q$. The proof can be rather tedious because of subtyping and input/output types that generate a lot of cases for subtyping, and, as expected, the most difficult cases are for communications.

Now that we have the subject reduction for $\Rightarrow_p$, we can easily deduce a more generic form of Theorem 3.

Theorem 5. *Let P be an annotated process and let m be its global parallel complexity. Then, for a typing $\phi; \Phi; \Gamma \vdash P \lhd K$, we have $\phi; \Phi \vDash K \geq m$.*

Corollary 1 is then obtained with the substitution lemma and the rule for parallel composition.

5 An Example: Bitonic Sort

As an example for this type system, we show how to obtain the bound on a common parallel algorithm: bitonic sort [1]. The particularity of this sorting algorithm is that it admits a parallel complexity in $\mathcal{O}(log(n)^2)$. We will show here that our type system allows to derive this bound for the algorithm, just as the paper-and-pen analysis. Actually we consider here a version for lists, which is not optimal for the number of operations, but we obtain the usual number of comparisons. For the sake of simplicity, we present here the algorithm for lists of size a power of 2. Let us briefly sketch the ideas of this algorithm. For a formal description see [1].

- A *bitonic sequence* is either a sequence composed of an increasing sequence followed by a decreasing sequence (e.g. [2, 7, 23, 19, 8, 5]), or a cyclic rotation of such a sequence (e.g. [8, 5, 2, 7, 23, 19]).
- The algorithm uses 2 main functions, `bmerge` and `bsort`.
- `bmerge` takes a bitonic sequence and recursively sorts it, as follows:
  Assume $s = [a_0, \ldots, a_{n-1}]$ is a bitonic sequence such that $[a_0, \ldots, a_{n/2-1}]$ is increasing and $[a_{n/2} \ldots, a_{n-1}]$ is decreasing, then we consider:
  $s_1 = [\min(a_0, a_{n/2}), \min(a_1, a_{n/2+1}) \ldots, \min(a_{n/2-1}, a_{n-1})]$
  $s_2 = [\max(a_0, a_{n/2}), \max(a_1, a_{n/2+1}) \ldots, \max(a_{n/2-1}, a_{n-1})]$
  Then we have: s_1 and s_2 are bitonic and satisfy: $\forall x \in s_1, \forall y \in s_2, x \leq y$.
  `bmerge` then applies recursively to s_1 and s_2 to produce a sorted sequence.
- `bsort` takes a sequence and recursively sorts it. It starts by separating the sequence in two. Then, it recursively sorts the first sequence in increasing order, and the second sequence in decreasing order. With this, we obtain a bitonic sequence that can be sorted with `bmerge`.

We will encode this algorithm in π-calculus with a boolean type. As expressed before, our results can easily be extended to support boolean with a conditional constructor.

First, we suppose that a server for comparison `lessthan` is already implemented. We start with `bcompare` such that given two lists of same length, it creates the list of maximum and the list of minimum. This is described in Figure 11.

We present here intuitively the typing. To begin with, we suppose that `lessthan` is given the server type $_0\mathsf{oserv}^0(\mathcal{B}, \mathcal{B}, \mathsf{ch}_0(\mathsf{Bool}))$, saying that this is a server ready to be called, and it takes in input a channel that is used to return the boolean value. With this, we can give to `bcompare` the following server type:

$$\forall_0 i.\mathsf{serv}^1(\mathsf{List}[0,i](\mathcal{B}), \mathsf{List}[0,i](\mathcal{B}), \mathsf{out}_1(\mathsf{List}[0,i](\mathcal{B}), \mathsf{List}[0,i](\mathcal{B})))$$

```
!bcompare(l1,l2,a). match(l1) {
  [] ↦ ā⟨l1,l2⟩ ;;
  x::l1' ↦ match(l2) {
    [] ↦ ā⟨l1,l2⟩ ;;
    y::l2' ↦ (νb)(νc)(
      bcompare‾⟨l1',l2',b⟩ | tick.lessthan‾⟨x,y,c⟩
      | b(lm,lM).c(z).if z then ā⟨x::lm,y::lM⟩ else ā⟨y::lm,x::lM⟩
    )
  }
}
!bmerge(up,l,a). match(l) {
  [] ↦ ā⟨l⟩ ;;
  [y] ↦ ā⟨l⟩ ;;
  _ ↦ let (l1,l2) = partition(l) in (νb)(νc)(νd)(
    bcompare‾⟨l1,l2,b⟩ | b(p1,p2).(bmerge‾⟨up,p1,c⟩ | bmerge‾⟨up,p2,d⟩)
    | c(q1).d(q2). if up then let l' = q1 @ q2 in ā⟨l'⟩
                         else let l' = q2 @ q1 in ā⟨l'⟩
  )
}
!bsort(up,l,a). match(l) {
  [] ↦ ā⟨l⟩ ;;
  [y]↦ ā⟨l⟩ ;;
  _ ↦ let (l1,l2) = partition(l) in (νb)(νc)(νd)(
    bsort‾⟨tt,l1,b⟩ | bsort‾⟨ff,l2,c⟩
    | b(q1).c(q2).let q = q1 @ q2 in bmerge‾⟨up,q,d⟩ | d(p).ā⟨p⟩
  )
}
```

Fig. 11. Bitonic Sort

The important things to notice is that this server has complexity 1, and the channel taken in input has a time 1. In order to verify that this type is correct, we would first need to apply the rule for replicated input. Let us denote by Γ the hypothesis on those two servers names, and Γ' be as Γ except that for `bcompare` we only have the output capability. Then, Γ' is indeed time invariant, and we have $\vdash \langle \Gamma \rangle_{-0} \sqsubseteq \Gamma'$, so we can continue the typing with this context Γ'. Then, we need to show that the process after the replicated input indeed has complexity 1. In the cases of empty list, this can be done easily. In the non-empty case, for the ν constructor, we must give a type to the channels b and c. We use:

$$b : \mathsf{ch}_1(\mathsf{List}[0, i{-}1](\mathcal{B}), \mathsf{List}[0, i{-}1](\mathcal{B})) \qquad c : \mathsf{ch}_1(\mathsf{Bool})$$

And we can then type the different processes in parallel.

- For the call to `bcompare`, the arguments have the expected type, and this call has complexity 1 because of the type of `bcompare`.

- For the process $\mathtt{tick}.\overline{\mathtt{lessthan}}\langle x, y, c\rangle$, the tick enforces a decreasing of time 1 in the context. This modifies in particular the time of c, that becomes 0. Thus, we can do the call to `lessthan` as everything is well-typed.
- Finally, for the last process, because b has a time equal to 1, the first input has complexity 1 and it enforces again a decreasing of 1 time unit. In particular, the times of c and a become 0. Then, as there is no more `tick` and all channels have time 0, the typing proceeds without difficulties.

So, we can indeed give this server type to `bcompare`, and thus we can call this server and it generates a complexity of 1.

Then, to present the process for bitonic sort, let us use the macro $\mathtt{let}\ \tilde{v} = f(\tilde{e})\ \mathtt{in}\ P$ to represent $(\nu a)(\overline{f}\langle\tilde{e}, a\rangle \mid a(\tilde{v}).P)$, and let us also use a generalized pattern matching. We also assume that we have a function for concatenation of lists and a function `partition` taking a list of size $2n$, and giving two lists corresponding to the first n elements and the last n elements. Then, the process for bitonic sort is given in Figure 11.

Without going into details, the main point in the typing of those relations is to find a solution to a recurrence relation for the complexity of server types. In the typing of `bmerge`, we suppose given a list of size smaller than 2^i and we choose both the complexity of this type and the time of the channel a equal to a certain index K (with i free in K). So, it means we chose for `bmerge` the type:

$$\forall_0 i.\mathsf{serv}^K(\mathsf{Bool}, \mathsf{List}[0, 2^i](\mathcal{B}), \mathsf{out}_K(\mathsf{List}[0, 2^i](\mathcal{B})))$$

Then, the typing gives us the following condition.

$$i \geq 1 \text{ implies } K \geq 1 + K\{i\text{-}1/i\}$$

Indeed, the two recursive calls to `bmerge` are done after one unit of time (because the input $b(p_1, p_2)$ takes one unit of time, as expressed by the type of `bcompare`), and with a list of size 2^{i-1}. And then, the continuation after those recursive calls (the process after $c(q_1).d(q_2)$) does not generate any complexity. So, we can take $K = i$, and thus `bmerge` has logarithmic complexity. Then, in the same way we obtain a recurrence relation for the complexity K' of `bsort` on an input list of size smaller than 2^i.

$$i \geq 1 \text{ implies } K' \geq K'\{i\text{-}1/i\} + i$$

Again, the two recursive calls are done on lists of size 2^{i-1}. This time, the delay of i in the recurrence relation is given by the continuation, because of the call to `bmerge` that generates a complexity of i. Thus, we can take a K' in $\mathcal{O}(i^2)$, and we obtain in the end that bitonic sort is indeed in $\mathcal{O}(log(n)^2)$ on a list of size n.

Remark that in this example, the type system gives recurrence relations corresponding to the usual recurrence relations we would obtain with a complexity analysis by hand. Here, the recurrence relation is only on K because channel names are only used as return channels, so their time is always equal to the complexity of the server that uses them. In general this is not the case as we saw before, so we obtain in general mutually recurrent relations when defining a server.

6 Related Work

An analysis of the complexity of parallel functional programs based on types has been carried out in [23]. Their system can analyse the work and the span (called depth in this paper), and makes use of amortized complexity analysis, which allows to obtain sharp bounds. However, the kind of parallelism they analyse is limited to parallel composition. So on the one hand we are considering a more general model of parallelism, and on the other hand we are not taking advantage of amortized analysis as they do. The paper [17] proposes a complexity analysis of parallel functional programs written in interaction nets, a graph-based language derived from linear logic. Their analysis is based on size types. However, their model is also quite different from ours as interaction nets do not provide name-passing.

Other works like [2] tackle the problem of analysing the parallel complexity of a distributed system by building a distributed flow graph and searching for a path of maximal cost in this graph. Another approach to analyse loops with concurrency in an actor-based language is done by *rely-guarantee reasoning* [3]. Those approaches give interesting results on some classes of systems, but they cannot be directly applied to the π-calculus language we are considering, with dynamic creation of processes and channels. Moreover, they do not offer the same compositionality as analysis based on type systems. The paper [16] studies distributed systems that are comparable to those of [2], and analyses their complexity by means of a behaviour type system. In a second step the types are used to run an analysis that returns complexity bounds. So this approach is more compositional than that of [2], but still does not apply to our π-calculus language.

Let us now turn to related works in the setting of π-calculus or process calculi. To our knowledge, the first work to study parallel complexity in π-calculus by types was given by Kobayashi [27], as another application of his type system for deadlock freedom, further developed in other papers [30]. In his setting, channels are typed with *usages*, which are simple CCS-like processes to describe the behaviour of a channel. In order to carry out complexity analysis, those usages are annotated by two time informations, *obligation* and *capability*. The obligation level is the time at which a channel is ready to perform an action, and the capability level is the time at which it successfully finds a communication partner. We believe that when they are not infinite, the sum of those levels is related to our own time annotation of channels. The definition of parallel complexity in this work differs from ours, as it loses some non-deterministic paths and the extension with dependent types is suggested but not detailed. It is not clear to us if everything can be adapted to reason only about our parallel complexity, but we plan to study it in future work. More recently Das et al. in [9,10] proposed a type system with temporal session types to capture several parallel cost models with the use of a *tick* constructor. Our usage of time was inspired by their types with the usual *next* modality of temporal logic, but in this paper they also use the *always* and *eventually* modalities to gain expressivity. We believe that because our usage of time is more permissive, those modalities would not be useful in our calculus. Because of session-types, they have linearity for the use of data-types such as lists, but they obtain deadlock-freedom contrary to our calculus. Moreover, they provide decidable operations to simplify the use of their types, such as subtyping, but they do not define dependent types nor size types that are useful to treat data-types. Still, they provide a significant number of examples to show the expressivity of their type system.

The methodology of our work is inspired by implicit computational complexity, which aims at characterizing complexity classes by means of dedicated programming languages, mainly in the sequential setting, for instance by providing languages for FPTIME functions. Some results have been adapted to the concurrent case, but mainly for the work complexity or for other languages than the π-calculus, e.g. [32,14,7] (the latter reference is for a higher-order π-calculus). The paper [13] is closer to our setting as it defines a notion of causal complexity in π-calculus and gives a type system characterizing processes with polynomial complexity. However, contrarily to those works we do not restrict to a particular complexity class (like FPTIME) and we handle the case of the span.

Technically, the types we use are inspired from linear dependent types [6]. Those are one of the many variants of size types, which were introduced in [26].

7 Perspectives

We see several possible future directions to this work:

- Type inference: we plan to investigate how type inference could be automatized or partially automatized for the span type system. We will study typing by constraint generation and explore whether existing off-the-shelf solvers or new procedures could allow to solve these constraints. Preliminary results (see [5]) show that the case of work is manageable, and it generates a set of constraints close to the one in [4]. However, the case of span could require more sophisticated reasoning because of the strong distinction between servers and channels with the advancing of time.
- We have mentioned that our type system for span is not adapted to analyse some concurrent systems such as the simple example of the semaphore (Sect. 4.2). However, we believe that a type system based on an adaptation of usages [27,30,29] could be promising for this purpose.
- It would be challenging to examine whether similar type systems could be developed to account for some other complexity properties, for instance to extract the number of parallel processes needed to achieve the span.

Acknowledgements We are grateful to Naoki Kobayashi for suggesting the definition of annotated processes and their reduction that we use in this paper.

This work was supported by the LABEX MILYON (ANR-10-LABX-0070) of Universite de Lyon.

References

1. Akl, S.G.: Encyclopedia of Parallel Computing, chap. Bitonic Sort, pp. 139–146. Springer US, Boston, MA (2011)
2. Albert, E., Correas, J., Johnsen, E.B., Román-Díez, G.: Parallel cost analysis of distributed systems. In: Static Analysis - 22nd International Symposium, SAS 2015, Saint-Malo, France, September 9-11, 2015, Proceedings. Lecture Notes in Computer Science, vol. 9291, pp. 275–292. Springer (2015)
3. Albert, E., Flores-Montoya, A., Genaim, S., Martin-Martin, E.: Rely-guarantee termination and cost analyses of loops with concurrent interleavings. Journal of Automated Reasoning **59**(1), 47–85 (2017)
4. Avanzini, M., Dal Lago, U.: Automating sized-type inference for complexity analysis. Proceedings of the ACM on Programming Languages **1**(ICFP), 43 (2017)
5. Baillot, P., Ghyselen, A.: Types for Complexity of Parallel Computation in Pi-calculus (Technical Report) (Oct 2020), `https://hal.archives-ouvertes.fr/hal-02961427`, working paper or preprint
6. Dal Lago, U., Gaboardi, M.: Linear dependent types and relative completeness. In: Logic in Computer Science (LICS), 2011 26th Annual IEEE Symposium on. pp. 133–142. IEEE (2011)
7. Dal Lago, U., Martini, S., Sangiorgi, D.: Light logics and higher-order processes. Mathematical Structures in Computer Science **26**(6), 969–992 (2016)
8. Dardha, O., Giachino, E., Sangiorgi, D.: Session types revisited. Information and Computation **256**, 253 – 286 (2017)
9. Das, A., Hoffmann, J., Pfenning, F.: Parallel complexity analysis with temporal session types. Proc. ACM Program. Lang. **2**(ICFP), 91:1–91:30 (2018)
10. Das, A., Hoffmann, J., Pfenning, F.: Work analysis with resource-aware session types. In: Proceedings of the 33rd Annual ACM/IEEE Symposium on Logic in Computer Science, LICS 2018, Oxford, UK, July 09-12, 2018. pp. 305–314. ACM (2018)
11. Degano, P., Gadducci, F., Priami, C.: Causality and replication in concurrent processes. In: Perspectives of System Informatics. pp. 307–318. Springer Berlin Heidelberg (2003)
12. Degano, P., Priami, C.: Causality for mobile processes. In: Automata, Languages and Programming. pp. 660–671. Springer Berlin Heidelberg (1995)
13. Demangeon, R., Yoshida, N.: Causal computational complexity of distributed processes. In: Proceedings of the 33rd Annual ACM/IEEE Symposium on Logic in Computer Science. pp. 344–353. LICS '18, ACM (2018)
14. Di Giamberardino, P., Dal Lago, U.: On session types and polynomial time. Mathematical Structures in Computer Science **-1** (2015)
15. Gaboardi, M., Marion, J., Rocca, S.R.D.: A logical account of pspace. In: Proceedings of the 35th ACM SIGPLAN-SIGACT Symposium on Principles of Programming Languages, POPL 2008, San Francisco, California, USA, January 7-12, 2008. pp. 121–131. ACM (2008)
16. Giachino, E., Johnsen, E.B., Laneve, C., Pun, K.I.: Time complexity of concurrent programs - - A technique based on behavioural types -. In: Formal Aspects of Component Software - 12th International Conference, FACS 2015, Niterói, Brazil, October 14-16, 2015, Revised Selected Papers. Lecture Notes in Computer Science, vol. 9539, pp. 199–216. Springer (2016)
17. Gimenez, S., Moser, G.: The complexity of interaction. In: Proceedings of the 43rd Annual ACM SIGPLAN-SIGACT Symposium on Principles of Programming

Languages, POPL 2016, St. Petersburg, FL, USA, January 20 - 22, 2016. pp. 243–255 (2016)
18. Hainry, E., Marion, J.Y., Péchoux, R.: Type-based complexity analysis for fork processes. In: Foundations of Software Science and Computation Structures - 16th International Conference, FOSSACS 2013, Held as Part of the European Joint Conferences on Theory and Practice of Software, ETAPS 2013, Rome, Italy, March 16-24, 2013. Proceedings. Lecture Notes in Computer Science, vol. 7794, pp. 305–320. Springer (2013)
19. Harper, R.: Practical Foundations for Programming Languages. Cambridge University Press (2012)
20. Hoffmann, J., Aehlig, K., Hofmann, M.: Multivariate amortized resource analysis. ACM Trans. Program. Lang. Syst. **34**(3), 14:1–14:62 (2012)
21. Hoffmann, J., Aehlig, K., Hofmann, M.: Resource aware ML. In: Computer Aided Verification - 24th International Conference, CAV 2012, Berkeley, CA, USA, July 7-13, 2012 Proceedings. Lecture Notes in Computer Science, vol. 7358, pp. 781–786. Springer (2012)
22. Hoffmann, J., Hofmann, M.: Amortized resource analysis with polynomial potential. In: Programming Languages and Systems, 19th European Symposium on Programming, ESOP 2010, Held as Part of the Joint European Conferences on Theory and Practice of Software, ETAPS 2010, Paphos, Cyprus, March 20-28, 2010. Proceedings. Lecture Notes in Computer Science, vol. 6012, pp. 287–306. Springer (2010)
23. Hoffmann, J., Shao, Z.: Automatic static cost analysis for parallel programs. In: Vitek, J. (ed.) Programming Languages and Systems. pp. 132–157. Springer Berlin Heidelberg, Berlin, Heidelberg (2015)
24. Hofmann, M.: Linear types and non-size-increasing polynomial time computation. Information and Computation **183**(1), 57–85 (2003)
25. Hofmann, M., Jost, S.: Static prediction of heap space usage for first-order functional programs. In: Conference Record of POPL 2003: The 30th SIGPLAN-SIGACT Symposium on Principles of Programming Languages, New Orleans, Louisisana, USA, January 15-17, 2003. pp. 185–197. ACM (2003)
26. Hughes, J., Pareto, L., Sabry, A.: Proving the correctness of reactive systems using sized types. In: Proceedings of the 23rd ACM SIGPLAN-SIGACT symposium on Principles of programming languages. pp. 410–423. ACM (1996)
27. Kobayashi, N.: A type system for lock-free processes. Information and Computation **177**(2), 122 – 159 (2002)
28. Kobayashi, N.: Type systems for concurrent programs. In: Formal Methods at the Crossroads. From Panacea to Foundational Support, pp. 439–453. Springer (2003)
29. Kobayashi, N.: Type-based information flow analysis for the π-calculus. Acta Informatica **42**(4-5), 291–347 (2005)
30. Kobayashi, N.: A new type system for deadlock-free processes. In: International Conference on Concurrency Theory. pp. 233–247. Springer (2006)
31. Kobayashi, N., Pierce, B.C., Turner, D.N.: Linearity and the pi-calculus. ACM Trans. Program. Lang. Syst. **21**(5), 914–947 (sep 1999)
32. Madet, A., Amadio, R.M.: An elementary affine λ-calculus with multithreading and side effects. In: Typed Lambda Calculi and Applications - 10th International Conference, TLCA 2011, Novi Sad, Serbia, June 1-3, 2011. Proceedings. Lecture Notes in Computer Science, vol. 6690, pp. 138–152. Springer (2011)
33. Marion, J.Y.: A type system for complexity flow analysis. In: Proceedings of the 26th Annual IEEE Symposium on Logic in Computer Science, LICS 2011, June 21-24, 2011, Toronto, Ontario, Canada. pp. 123–132. IEEE Computer Society (2011)

34. Sangiorgi, D., Walker, D.: The pi-calculus: a Theory of Mobile Processes. Cambridge university press (2003)

Checking Robustness Between Weak Transactional Consistency Models*

Sidi Mohamed Beillahi(✉), Ahmed Bouajjani, and Constantin Enea

Université de Paris, IRIF, CNRS, Paris, France, {beillahi,abou,cenea}@irif.fr

Abstract. Concurrent accesses to databases are typically encapsulated in transactions in order to enable isolation from other concurrent computations and resilience to failures. Modern databases provide transactions with various semantics corresponding to different trade-offs between consistency and availability. Since a weaker consistency model provides better performance, an important issue is investigating the weakest level of consistency needed by a given program (to satisfy its specification). As a way of dealing with this issue, we investigate the problem of checking whether a given program has the same set of behaviors when replacing a consistency model with a weaker one. This property known as *robustness* generally implies that any specification of the program is preserved when weakening the consistency. We focus on the robustness problem for consistency models which are weaker than standard serializability, namely, causal consistency, prefix consistency, and snapshot isolation. We show that checking robustness between these models is polynomial time reducible to a state reachability problem under serializability. We use this reduction to also derive a pragmatic proof technique based on Lipton's reduction theory that allows to prove programs robust. We have applied our techniques to several challenging applications drawn from the literature of distributed systems and databases.

Keywords: Transactional databases · Weak consistency · Program verification

1 Introduction

Concurrent accesses to databases are typically encapsulated in transactions in order to enable isolation from other concurrent computations and resilience to failures. Modern databases provide transactions with various semantics corresponding to different tradeoffs between consistency and availability. The strongest consistency level is achieved with *serializable* transactions [42] whose outcome in concurrent executions is the same as if the transactions were executed atomically in some order. Since serializability (SER) carries a significant penalty on availability, modern databases often provide weaker consistency models, e.g.,

* This work is supported in part by the European Research Council (ERC) under the European Union's Horizon 2020 research and innovation programme (grant agreement No 678177).

T. Yoshida (Ed.): ESOP 2021, LNCS 12648, pp. 87–117, 2021.
https://doi.org/10.1007/978-3-030-72019-3_4

causal consistency (CC) [38], prefix consistency (PC) [22, 25], and snapshot isolation (SI) [12]. Causal consistency requires that if a transaction t_1 "affects" another transaction t_2, e.g., t_1 executes before t_2 in the same session or t_2 reads a value written by t_1, then the updates in these two transactions are observed by any other transaction in this order. Concurrent transactions, which are not causally related to each other, can be observed in different orders, leading to behaviors that are not possible under SER. Prefix consistency requires that there is a total commit order between all the transactions such that each transaction observes all the updates in a prefix of this sequence (PC is stronger than CC). Two transactions can observe the *same* prefix, which leads to behaviors that are not admitted by SER. Snapshot isolation further requires that two different transactions observe different prefixes if they both write to a common variable.

Since a weaker consistency model provides better performance, an important issue is identifying the *weakest* level of consistency needed by a program (to satisfy its specification). One way to tackle this issue is checking whether a program P designed under a consistency model S has the same behaviors when run under a weaker consistency model W. This property of a program is generally known as *robustness* against substituting S with W. It implies that any specification of P is preserved when weakening the consistency model (from S to W). Preserving any specification is convenient since specifications are rarely present in practice.

The problem of checking robustness for a given program has been investigated in several recent works, but only when the stronger model (S) is SER, e.g., [9, 10, 19, 26, 13, 40], or sequential consistency in the non-transactional case, e.g. [36, 15, 29]. However, there is a large class of specifications that can be implemented even in the presence of "anomalies", i.e., behaviors which are not admitted under SER (see [46] for a discussion). In this context, an important question is whether a certain implementation (program) is robust against substituting a weak consistency model, e.g., SI, with a weaker one, e.g., CC.

In this paper, we consider the sequence of increasingly strong consistency models mentioned above, CC, PC, and SI, and investigate the problem of checking robustness for a given program against weakening the consistency model to one in this range. We study the asymptotic complexity of this problem and propose effective techniques for establishing robustness based on abstraction. There are two important cases to consider: robustness against substituting SI with PC and PC with CC, respectively. Robustness against substituting SI with CC can be obtained as the conjunction of these two cases.

In the first case (SI vs PC), checking robustness for a program P is reduced to a reachability (assertion checking) problem in a composition of P under PC with a monitor that checks whether a PC behavior is an "anomaly", i.e., admitted by P under PC, but not under SI. This approach raises two non-trivial challenges: (1) defining a monitor for detecting PC vs SI anomalies that uses a minimal amount of auxiliary memory (to remember past events), and (2) determining the complexity of checking if the composition of P with the monitor reaches a specific control location[1] under the (weaker) model PC. Interestingly enough,

[1] We assume that the monitor goes to an error location when detecting an anomaly.

we address these two challenges by studying the relationship between these two weak consistency models, PC and SI, and *serializability*. The construction of the monitor is based on the fact that the PC vs SI anomalies can be defined as roughly, the difference between the PC vs SER and SI vs SER anomalies (investigated in previous work [13]), and we show that the reachability problem under PC can be reduced to a reachability problem under SER. These results lead to a polynomial-time reduction of this robustness problem (for arbitrary programs) to a reachability problem under SER, which is important from a practical point of view since the SER semantics (as opposed to the PC or SI semantics) can be encoded easily in existing verification tools (using locks to guard the isolation of transactions). These results also enable a precise characterization of the complexity class of this problem.

Checking robustness against substituting PC with CC is reduced to the problem of checking robustness against substituting SER with CC. The latter has been shown to be polynomial-time reducible to reachability under SER in [10]. This surprising result relies on the reduction from PC reachability to SER reachability mentioned above. This reduction shows that a given program P reaches a certain control location under PC iff a transformed program P', where essentially, each transaction is split in two parts, one part containing all the reads, and one part containing all the writes, reaches the same control location under SER. Since this reduction preserves the structure of the program, CC vs PC anomalies of a program P correspond to CC vs SER anomalies of the transformed program P'.

Beyond enabling these reductions, the characterization of classes of anomalies or the reduction from the PC semantics to the SER semantics are also important for a better understanding of these weak consistency models and the differences between them. We believe that these results can find applications beyond robustness checking, e.g., verifying conformance to given specifications.

As a more pragmatic approach for establishing robustness, which avoids a non-reachability proof under SER, we have introduced a proof methodology that builds on Lipton's reduction theory [39] and the concept of commutativity dependency graph introduced in [9], which represents mover type dependencies between the transactions in a program. We give sufficient conditions for robustness in all the cases mentioned above, which characterize the commutativity dependency graph associated to a given program.

We tested the applicability of these verification techniques on a benchmark containing seven challenging applications extracted from previous work [30, 34, 19]. These techniques are precise enough for proving or disproving the robustness of all these applications, for all combinations of the consistency models.

Complete proofs and more details can be found in [11].

2 Overview

We give an overview of the robustness problems investigated in this paper, discussing first the case PC vs. CC, and then SI vs PC. We end with an example that illustrates the robustness checking technique based on commutativity arguments.

```
Process 1                        Process 2

CreateEvent(v, e1, 3):           CreateEvent(v, e2, 3):
[ Tickets[v][e1] := 3 ]          [ Tickets[v][e2] := 3 ]

CountTickets(v):                 CountTickets(v):
[ r := ∑_e Tickets[v][e] ]       [ r := ∑_e Tickets[v][e] ]
```

(a) FusionTicket.

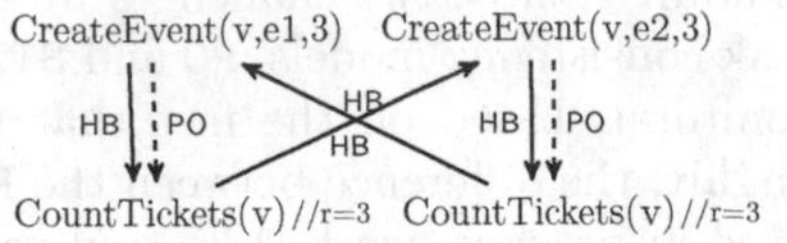

(b) A CC trace of FusionTicket.

```
Process 1                        Process 2

Register(u, p1):                 Register(u, p2):
[ r := RegisteredUsers[u]        [ r := RegisteredUsers[u]
  assume r == 0                    assume r == 0
  RegisteredUsers[u] := 1          RegisteredUsers[u] := 1
  Password[u] := p1 ]              Password[u] := p2 ]
```

(c) Twitter.

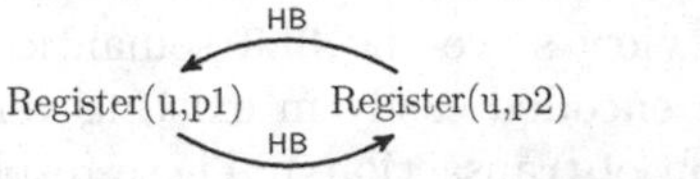

(d) A CC and PC trace of Twitter.

```
Process 1                        Process 2

RegisterRd(u, p1):               RegisterRd(u, p2):
[ r := RegisteredUsers[u]        [ r := RegisteredUsers[u]
  assume r == 0 ]                  assume r == 0 ]

RegisterWr(u, p1):               RegisterWr(u, p2):
[ RegisteredUsers[u] := 1        [ RegisteredUsers[u] := 1
  Password[u] := p1 ]              Password[u] := p2 ]
```

(e) Transformed Twitter.

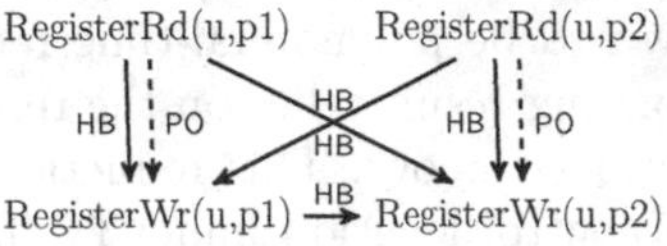

(f) A CC and SER trace of transformed Twitter.

```
Process 1                   Process 2                   Process 3

PlaceBet(1,2):              PlaceBet(2,3):              SettleBet():
[ assume time < TIMEOUT     [ assume time < TIMEOUT     [Bets' := Bets
    Bets[1] := 2 ]              Bets[2] := 3 ]           n := Bets'.Length
                                                         assume time > TIMEOUT & n > 0
                                                         select i s.t. Bets'[i] ≠ ⊥
                                                         return := Bets'[i] ]
```

(g) Betting.

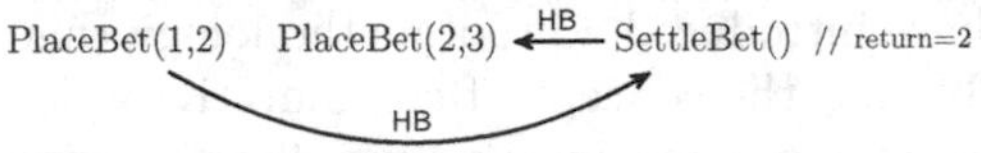

(h) A PC and SI trace of Betting.

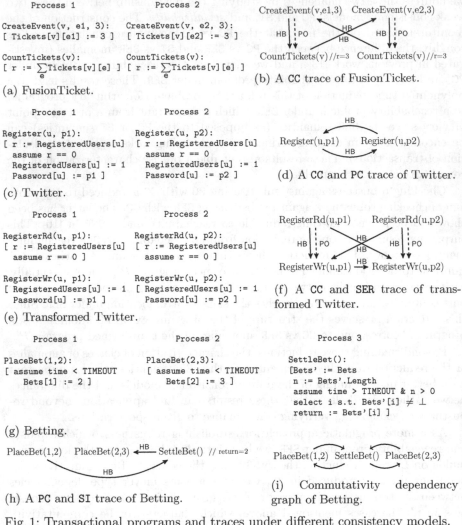

(i) Commutativity dependency graph of Betting.

Fig. 1: Transactional programs and traces under different consistency models.

Robustness PC vs CC. We illustrate the robustness against substituting PC with CC using the FusionTicket and the Twitter programs in Figure 1a and Figure 1c, respectively. FusionTicket manages tickets for a number of events, each event being associated with a venue. Its state consists of a two-dimensional map that stores the number of tickets for an event in a given venue (r is a local variable, and the assignment in `CountTickets` is interpreted as a read of the shared state). The program has two processes and each process contains two transactions. The first transaction creates an event e in a venue v with a number of tickets n, and the second transaction computes the total number of tickets for all the events in a venue v. A possible candidate for a specification of this program is that the values computed in `CountTickets` are monotonically increasing since each such value is computed after creating a new event. Twitter provides a transaction for registering a new user with a given username and password, which is executed by two parallel processes. Its state contains two maps that record whether a given username has been registered (0 and 1 stand for non-registered and registered, respectively) and the password for a given username. Each transaction first checks whether a given username is free (see the `assume` statement). The intended specification is that the user must be registered with the given password when the registration transaction succeeds.

A program is robust against substituting PC with CC if its set of behaviors under the two models coincide. We model behaviors of a given program as *traces*, which record standard control-flow and data-flow dependencies between transactions, e.g., the order between transactions in the same session and whether a transaction reads the value written by another (read-from). The transitive closure of the union of all these dependency relations is called *happens-before*. Figure 1b pictures a trace of FusionTicket where the concrete values which are read in a transaction are written under comments. In this trace, each process registers a different event but in the same venue and with the same number of tickets, and it ignores the event created by the other process when computing the sum of tickets in the venue.

Figure 1b pictures a trace of FusionTicket under CC, which is a witness that FusionTicket is *not* robust against substituting PC with CC. This trace is also a violation of the intended specification since the number of tickets is not increasing (the sum of tickets is 3 in both processes). The happens-before dependencies (pictured with HB labeled edges) include the program-order PO (the order between transactions in the same process), and read-write dependencies, since an instance of CountTickets(v) does not observe the value written by the CreateEvent transaction in the other process (the latter overwrites some value that the former reads). This trace is allowed under CC because the transaction CreateEvent(v, e1, 3) executes concurrently with the transaction CountTickets(v) in the other process, and similarly for CreateEvent(v, e2, 3). However, it is not allowed under PC since it is impossible to define a total commit order between CreateEvent(v, e1, 3) and CreateEvent(v, e2, 3) that justifies the reads of both CountTickets(v) transactions (these reads should correspond to the updates in a prefix of this order). For instance, assuming that CreateEvent(v, e1, 3) commits before CreateEvent(v, e2, 3), CountTickets(v) in the second process must observe the effect of CreateEvent(v, e1, 3) as well since it observes the effect of CreateEvent(v, e2, 3). However, this contradicts the fact that CountTickets(v) computes the sum of tickets as being 3.

On the other hand, Twitter is robust against substituting PC with CC. For instance, Figure 1d pictures a trace of Twitter under CC, where the `assume` in both transactions pass. In this trace, the transactions Register(u,p1) and Register(u,p2) execute concurrently and are unaware of each other's writes (they are not causally related). The HB dependencies include write-write dependencies since both transactions write on the same location (we consider the transaction in Process 2 to be the last one writing to the `Password` map), and read-write dependencies since each transaction reads `RegisteredUsers` that is written by the other. This trace is also allowed under `PC` since the commit order can be defined such that Register(u,p1) is ordered before Register(u,p2), and then both transactions read from the initial state (the empty prefix). Note that this trace has a cyclic happens-before which means that it is not allowed under serializability.

Checking robustness `PC` vs `CC`. We reduce the problem of checking robustness against substituting `PC` with `CC` to the robustness problem against substituting `SER` with `CC` (the latter reduces to a reachability problem under `SER` [10]). This reduction relies on a syntactic program transformation that rewrites `PC` behaviors of a given program P to `SER` behaviors of another program P'. The program P' is obtained by splitting each transaction t of P into two transactions: the first transaction performs all the reads in t and the second performs all the writes in t (the two are related by program order). Figure 1e shows this transformation applied on Twitter. The trace in Figure 1f is a serializable execution of the transformed Twitter which is "observationally" equivalent to the trace in Figure 1d of the original Twitter, i.e., each read of the shared state returns the same value and the writes on the shared state are applied in the same order (the acyclicity of the happens-before shows that this is a serializable trace). The transformed FusionTicket coincides with the original version because it contains no transaction that both reads and writes on the shared state.

We show that `PC` behaviors and `SER` behaviors of the original and transformed program, respectively, are related by a bijection. In particular, we show that any `PC` vs. `CC` robustness violation of the original program manifests as a `SER` vs. `CC` robustness violation of the transformed program, and vice-versa. For instance, the `CC` trace of the original Twitter in Figure 1d corresponds to the `CC` trace of the transformed Twitter in Figure 1f, and the acyclicity of the latter (the fact that it is admitted by `SER`) implies that the former is admitted by the original Twitter under `PC`. On the other hand, the trace in Figure 1b is also a `CC` of the transformed FusionTicket and its cyclicity implies that it is not admitted by FusionTicket under `PC`, and thus, it represents a robustness violation.

Robustness `SI` vs `PC`. We illustrate the robustness against substituting `SI` with `PC` using Twitter and the Betting program in Figure 1g. Twitter is *not* robust against substituting `SI` with `PC`, the trace in Figure 1d being a witness violation. This trace is also a violation of the intended specification since one of the users registers a password that is overwritten in a concurrent transaction. This `PC` trace is not possible under `SI` because Register(u,p1) and Register(u,p2) observe the same prefix of the commit order (i.e., an empty prefix), but they write to a common memory location Password[u] which is not allowed under `SI`.

On the other hand, the Betting program in Figure 1g, which manages a set of bets, is robust against substituting `SI` with `PC`. The first two processes execute one transaction that places a bet of a value v with a unique bet identifier id, assuming that the bet expiration time is not yet reached (bets are recorded in the map `Bets`). The third process contains a single transaction that settles the betting assuming that the bet expiration time was reached and at least one bet has been placed. This transaction starts by taking a snapshot of the `Bets` map into a local variable `Bets'`, and then selects a random non-null value (different from $\bot$) in the map to correspond to the winning bet. The intended specification of this program is that the winning bet corresponds to a genuine bet that was placed. Figure 1g pictures a PC trace of Betting where SettleBet observes only the bet of the first process PlaceBet(1,2). The HB dependency towards the second process denotes a read-write dependency (SettleBet reads a cell of the map `Bets` which is overwritten by the second process). This trace is allowed under SI because no two transactions write to the same location.

Checking robustness SI vs PC. We reduce robustness against substituting PC with CC to a reachability problem under SER. This reduction is based on a characterization of happens-before cycles[2] that are possible under PC but not SI, and the transformation described above that allows to simulate the PC semantics of a program on top of SER. The former is used to define an instrumentation (monitor) for the transformed program that reaches an error state iff the original program is not robust. Therefore, we show that the happens-before cycles in PC traces that are not admitted by SI must contain a transaction that (1) overwrites a value written by another transaction in the cycle and (2) reads a value overwritten by another transaction in the cycle. For instance, the trace of Twitter in Figure 1d is not allowed under SI because Register(u,p2) overwrites a value written by Register(u,p1) (the password) and reads a value overwritten by Register(u,p1) (checking whether the username u is registered). The trace of Betting in Figure 1g is allowed under SI because its happens-before is acyclic.

Checking robustness using commutativity arguments. Based on the reductions above, we propose an approximated method for proving robustness based on the concept of mover in Lipton's reduction theory [39]. A transaction is a left (resp., right) mover if it commutes to the left (resp., right) of another transaction (by a different process) while preserving the computation. We use the notion of mover to characterize the data-flow dependencies in the happens-before. Roughly, there exists a data-flow dependency between two transactions in some execution if one doesn't commute to the left/right of the other one.

We define a commutativity dependency graph which summarizes the happens-before dependencies in all executions of a transformed program (obtained by splitting the transactions of the original program as explained above), and derive a proof method for robustness which inspects paths in this graph. Two transactions t_1 and t_2 are linked by a directed edge iff t_1 *cannot* move to the right of t_2 (or t_2 cannot move to the left of t_1), or if they are related by the program order. Moreover, two transactions t_1 and t_2 are linked by an undirected edge iff they are the result of splitting the same transaction.

A program is robust against substituting PC with CC if roughly, its commutativity dependency graph does *not* contain a *simple* cycle of directed edges with two distinct transactions t_1 and t_2, such that t_1 does not commute left because of another transaction t_3 in the cycle that reads a variable that t_1 writes to,

[2] Traces with an acyclic happens-before are not robustness violations because they are admitted under serializability, which implies that they are admitted under the weaker model SI as well.

```
⟨prog⟩      ::= program ⟨process⟩*
⟨process⟩   ::= process ⟨pid⟩ regs ⟨reg⟩* ⟨txn⟩*
⟨txn⟩       ::= begin ⟨read⟩* ⟨test⟩* ⟨write⟩* commit
⟨read⟩      ::= ⟨label⟩: ⟨reg⟩ := ⟨var⟩; goto ⟨label⟩;
⟨test⟩      ::= ⟨label⟩: assume ⟨bexpr⟩; goto ⟨label⟩;
⟨write⟩     ::= ⟨label⟩: ⟨var⟩ := ⟨reg-expr⟩; goto ⟨label⟩;
```

Fig. 2: The syntax of our programming language. a^* indicates zero or more occurrences of a. ⟨*pid*⟩, ⟨*reg*⟩, ⟨*label*⟩, and ⟨*var*⟩ represent a process identifier, a register, a label, and a shared variable, respectively. ⟨*reg-expr*⟩ is an expression over registers while ⟨*bexpr*⟩ is a Boolean expression over registers, or the non-deterministic choice $*$.

and t_2 does not commute right because of another transaction t_4 in the cycle (t_3 and t_4 can coincide) that writes to a variable that t_2 either reads from or writes to[3]. For instance, Figure 1i shows the commutativity dependency graph of the transformed Betting program, which coincides with the original Betting because PlaceBet(1,2) and PlaceBet(2,3) are write-only transactions and SettleBet() is a read-only transaction. Both simple cycles in Figure 1i contain just two transactions and therefore do not meet the criterion above which requires at least 3 transactions. Therefore, Betting is robust against substituting `PC` with `CC`.

A program is robust against substituting `SI` with `PC`, if roughly, its commutativity dependency graph does *not* contain a *simple* cycle with two successive transactions t_1 and t_2 that are linked by an undirected edge, such that t_1 does not commute left because of another transaction t_3 in the cycle that writes to a variable that t_1 writes to, and t_2 does not commute right because of another transaction t_4 in the cycle (t_3 and t_4 can coincide) that writes to a variable that t_2 reads from[4]. Betting is also robust against substituting `SI` with `PC` for the same reason (simple cycles of size 2).

3 Consistency Models

Syntax. We present our results in the context of the simple programming language, defined in Figure 2, where a program is a parallel composition of *processes* distinguished using a set of identifiers $\mathbb{P}$. A process is a sequence of *transactions* and each transaction is a sequence of *labeled instructions.* A transaction starts with a `begin` instruction and finishes with a `commit` instruction. Instructions include assignments to a process-local *register* from a set $\mathbb{R}$ or to a *shared variable* from a set $\mathbb{V}$, or an `assume`. The assignments use values from a data domain

[3] The transactions t_1, t_2, t_3, and t_4 correspond to t_1, t_i, t_n, and t_{i+1}, respectively, in Theorem 6.

[4] The transactions t_1, t_2, t_3, and t_4 correspond to t_1, t_2, t_n, and t_3, respectively, in Theorem 7.

$\mathbb{D}$. An assignment to a register $\langle reg \rangle := \langle var \rangle$ is called a *read* of the shared-variable $\langle var \rangle$ and an assignment to a shared variable $\langle var \rangle := \langle reg \rangle$ is called a *write* to the shared-variable $\langle var \rangle$. The `assume` $\langle bexpr \rangle$ blocks the process if the Boolean expression $\langle bexpr \rangle$ over registers is false. It can be used to model conditionals. The `goto` statement transfers the control to the program location (instruction) specified by a given label. Since multiple instructions can have the same label, `goto` statements can be used to mimic imperative constructs like loops and conditionals inside transactions.

We assume w.l.o.g. that every transaction is written as a sequence of reads or `assume` statements followed by a sequence of writes (a single `goto` statement from the sequence of read/`assume` instructions transfers the control to the sequence of writes). In the context of the consistency models we study in this paper, every program can be equivalently rewritten as a set of transactions of this form.

To simplify the technical exposition, programs contain a bounded number of processes and each process executes a bounded number of transactions. A transaction may execute an unbounded number of instructions but these instructions concern a bounded number of variables, which makes it impossible to model SQL (select/update) queries that may access tables with a statically unknown number of rows. Our results can be extended beyond these restrictions as explained in Remark 1 and Remark 2.

Semantics. We describe the semantics of a program under four consistency models, i.e., causal consistency[5] (CC), prefix consistency (PC), snapshot isolation (SI), and serializability (SER).

In the semantics of a program under CC, shared variables are replicated across each process, each process maintaining its own local valuation of these variables. During the execution of a transaction in a process, its writes are stored in a *transaction log* that can be accessed only by the process executing the transaction and that is broadcasted to all the other processes at the end of the transaction. To read a shared variable x, a process p first accesses its transaction log and takes the last written value on x, if any, and then its own valuation of the shared variable, if x was not written during the current transaction. Transaction logs are delivered to every process in an order consistent with the *causal* relation between transactions, i.e., the transitive closure of the union of the *program order* (the order in which transactions are executed by a process), and the *read-from* relation (a transaction t_1 reads-from a transaction t_2 iff t_1 reads a value that was written by t_2). When a process receives a transaction log, it immediately applies it on its shared-variable valuation.

In the semantics of a program under PC and SI, shared variables are stored in a central memory and each process keeps a local valuation of these variables. When a process starts a new transaction, it fetches a consistent snapshot of the shared variables from the central memory and stores it in its local valuation of these variables. During the execution of a transaction in a process, writes to shared variables are stored in the local valuation of these variables, and in a transaction log. To read a shared variable, a process takes its own valuation of the

[5] We consider a variation known as causal convergence [20, 16]

shared variable. A process commits a transaction by applying the updates in the transaction log on the central memory in an atomic way (to make them visible to all processes). Under SI, when a process applies the writes in a transaction log on the central memory, it must ensure that there were no concurrent writes that occurred after the last fetch from the central memory to a shared variable that was written during the current transaction. Otherwise, the transaction is aborted and its effects discarded.

In the semantics of a program under SER, we adopt a simple operational model where we keep a single shared-variable valuation in a central memory (accessed by all processes) with the standard interpretation of read and write statements. Transactions execute serially, one after another.

We use a standard model of executions of a program called *trace*. A trace represents the order between transactions in the same process, and the data-flow in an execution using standard happens-before relations between transactions. We assume that each transaction in a program is identified uniquely using a transaction identifier from a set $\mathbb{T}$. Also, $f : \mathbb{T} \to 2^{\mathbb{S}}$ is a mapping that associates each transaction in $\mathbb{T}$ with a sequence of read and write events from the set

$$\mathbb{S} = \{\mathsf{re}(t, x, v), \mathsf{we}(t, x, v) : t \in \mathbb{T}, x \in \mathbb{V}, v \in \mathbb{D}\}$$

where $\mathsf{re}(t, x, v)$ is a read of x returning v, and $\mathsf{we}(t, x, v)$ is a write of v to x.

Definition 1. *A* trace *is a tuple* $\tau = (\rho, f, \mathsf{TO}, \mathsf{PO}, \mathsf{WR}, \mathsf{WW}, \mathsf{RW})$ *where* $\rho \subseteq \mathbb{T}$ *is a set of transaction identifiers, and*

- TO *is a mapping giving the order between events in each transaction, i.e., it associates each transaction* t *in* ρ *with a total order* $\mathsf{TO}(t)$ *on* $f(t) \times f(t)$.
- PO *is the program order relation, a strict partial order on* $\rho \times \rho$ *that orders every two transactions issued by the same process.*
- WR *is the read-from relation between distinct transactions* $(t1, t2) \in \rho \times \rho$ *representing the fact that* $t2$ *reads a value written by* $t1$.
- WW *is the store order relation on* $\rho \times \rho$ *between distinct transactions that write to the same shared variable.*
- RW *is the conflict order relation between distinct transactions, defined by* $\mathsf{RW} = \mathsf{WR}^{-1}; \mathsf{WW}$ *(; denotes the sequential composition of two relations).*

For simplicity, for a trace $\tau = (\rho, f, \mathsf{TO}, \mathsf{PO}, \mathsf{WR}, \mathsf{WW}, \mathsf{RW})$, we write $t \in \tau$ instead of $t \in \rho$. We also assume that each trace contains a fictitious transaction that writes the initial values of all shared variables, and which is ordered before any other transaction in program order. Also, $\mathbb{T}\mathsf{r}_{\mathsf{X}}(\mathcal{P})$ is the set of traces representing executions of program $\mathcal{P}$ under a consistency model X.

For each $\mathsf{X} \in \{\mathtt{CC}, \mathtt{PC}, \mathtt{SI}, \mathtt{SER}\}$, the set of traces $\mathbb{T}\mathsf{r}_{\mathsf{X}}(\mathcal{P})$ can be described using the set of properties in Table 1. A trace τ is possible under causal consistency iff there exist two relations CO a partial order (causal order) and ARB a total order (arbitration order) that includes CO, such that the properties $\mathsf{AxCausal}$, AxArb, and $\mathsf{AxRetVal}$ hold [27, 16]. $\mathsf{AxCausal}$ guarantees that the program order and the read-from relation are included in the causal order, and AxArb guarantees

AxCausal	$\mathsf{CO}_0^+ \subseteq \mathsf{CO}$
AxArb	$ARB_0^+ \subseteq ARB$
AxCC	AxRetVal $\wedge$ AxCausal $\wedge$ AxArb
AxPrefix	$ARB; \mathsf{CO} \subseteq \mathsf{CO}$
AxPC	AxPrefix $\wedge$ AxCC
AxConflict	$\mathsf{WW} \subseteq \mathsf{CO}$
AxSI	AxConflict $\wedge$ AxPC
AxSer	AxRetVal $\wedge$ AxCausal $\wedge$ AxArb $\wedge$ $\mathsf{CO} = ARB$

where

$\mathsf{CO}_0 = \mathsf{PO} \cup \mathsf{WR}$ and $ARB_0 = \mathsf{PO} \cup \mathsf{WR} \cup \mathsf{WW}$

AxRetVal $= \forall\, t \in \tau.\ \forall\, \mathsf{re}(t, x, v) \in f(t)$ we have that

- there exist a transaction $t_0 = Max_{ARB}(\{t' \in \tau \mid (t', t) \in \mathsf{CO} \wedge \exists\, \mathsf{we}(t', x, \cdot) \in f(t')\})$ and an event $\mathsf{we}(t_0, x, v) = Max_{\mathsf{TO}(t_0)}(\{\mathsf{we}(t_0, x, \cdot) \in f(t_0)\})$.

Table 1: Declarative definitions of consistency models. For an order relation $\leq$, $a = Max_{\leq}(A)$ iff $a \in A \wedge \forall\, b \in A.\ b \leq a$.

that the causal order and the store order are included in the arbitration order. AxRetVal guarantees that a read returns the value written by the last write in the last transaction that contains a write to the same variable and that is ordered by CO before the read's transaction. We use AxCC to denote the conjunction of these three properties. A trace τ is possible under prefix consistency iff there exist a causal order CO and an arbitration order ARB such that AxCC holds and the property AxPrefix holds as well [27]. AxPrefix guarantees that every transaction observes a prefix of transactions that are ordered by ARB before it. We use AxPC to denote the conjunction of AxCC and AxPrefix. A trace τ is possible under snapshot isolation iff there exist a causal order CO and an arbitration order ARB such that AxPC holds and the property AxConflict holds [27]. AxConflict guarantees that if two transactions write to the same variable then one of them must observe the other. We use AxSI to denote the conjunction of AxPC and AxConflict. A trace τ is serializable iff there exist a causal order CO and an arbitration order ARB such that the property AxSer holds which implies that the two relations CO and ARB coincide. Note that for any given program $\mathcal{P}$, $\mathbb{T}\mathrm{r}_{\mathtt{SER}}(\mathcal{P}) \subseteq \mathbb{T}\mathrm{r}_{\mathtt{SI}}(\mathcal{P}) \subseteq \mathbb{T}\mathrm{r}_{\mathsf{PC}}(\mathcal{P}) \subseteq \mathbb{T}\mathrm{r}_{\mathsf{CC}}(\mathcal{P})$. Also, the four consistency models we consider disallow anomalies such as dirty and phantom reads.

For a given trace $\tau = (\rho, f, \mathsf{TO}, \mathsf{PO}, \mathsf{WR}, \mathsf{WW}, \mathsf{RW})$, the happens before order is the transitive closure of the union of all the relations in the trace, i.e., $\mathsf{HB} = (\mathsf{PO} \cup \mathsf{WR} \cup \mathsf{WW} \cup \mathsf{RW})^+$. A classic result states that a trace τ is serializable iff HB is acyclic [2, 47]. Note that HB is acyclic implies that WW is a total order between transactions that write to the same variable, and $(\mathsf{PO} \cup \mathsf{WR})^+$ and $(\mathsf{PO} \cup \mathsf{WR} \cup \mathsf{WW})^+$ are acyclic.

3.1 Robustness

In this work, we investigate the problem of checking whether a program $\mathcal{P}$ under a semantics $\mathsf{Y} \in \{\mathtt{PC}, \mathtt{SI}\}$ produces the same set of traces as under a weaker semantics $\mathsf{X} \in \{\mathtt{CC}, \mathtt{PC}\}$. When this holds, we say that $\mathcal{P}$ is *robust* against X relative to Y.

Definition 2. *A program $\mathcal{P}$ is called* robust *against a semantics* $\mathsf{X} \in \{\texttt{CC}, \texttt{PC}, \texttt{SI}\}$ *relative to a semantics* $\mathsf{Y} \in \{\texttt{PC}, \texttt{SI}, \texttt{SER}\}$ *such that* Y *is stronger than* X *iff* $\mathbb{T}r_{\mathsf{X}}(\mathcal{P}) = \mathbb{T}r_{\mathsf{Y}}(\mathcal{P})$.

If $\mathcal{P}$ is not robust against X relative to Y then there must exist a trace $\tau \in \mathbb{T}r_{\mathsf{X}}(\mathcal{P}) \setminus \mathbb{T}r_{\mathsf{Y}}(\mathcal{P})$. We say that τ is a robustness violation trace.

We illustrate the notion of robustness on the programs in Figure 3, which are commonly used in the literature. In all programs, transactions of the same process are aligned vertically and ordered from top to bottom. Each read instruction is commented with the value it reads in some execution.

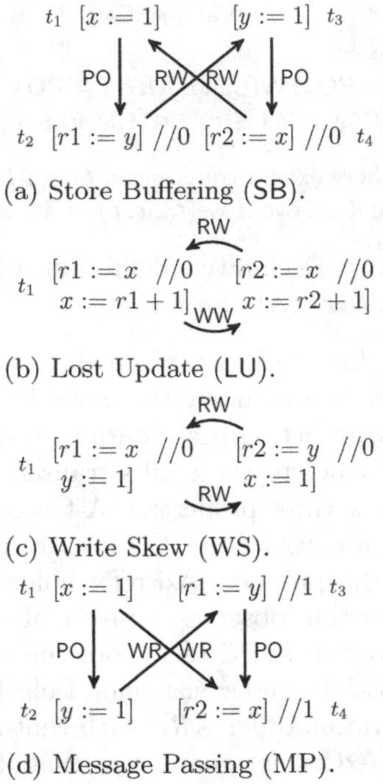

Fig. 3: Litmus programs

The store buffering (SB) program in Figure 3a contains four transactions that are issued by two distinct processes. We emphasize an execution where t_2 reads 0 from y and t_4 reads 0 from x. This execution is allowed under CC since the two writes by t_1 and t_3 are not causally dependent. Thus, t_2 and t_4 are executed without seeing the writes from t_3 and t_1, respectively. However, this execution is not feasible under PC (which implies that it is not feasible under both SI and SER). In particular, we cannot have neither $(t_1, t_3) \in ARB$ nor $(t_3, t_1) \in ARB$ which contradicts the fact that ARB is total order. For example, if $(t_1, t_3) \in ARB$, then $(t_1, t_4) \in \mathsf{CO}$ (since $ARB; \mathsf{CO} \subset \mathsf{CO}$) which contradicts the fact that t_4 does not see t_1. Similarly, $(t_3, t_1) \in ARB$ implies that $(t_3, t_2) \in \mathsf{CO}$ which contradicts the fact that t_2 does not see t_3. Thus, SB is not robust against CC relative to PC.

The lost update (LU) program in Figure 3b has two transactions that are issued by two distinct processes. We highlight an execution where both transactions read 0 from x. This execution is allowed under PC since both transactions are not causally dependent and can be executed in parallel by the two processes. However, it is not allowed under SI since both transactions write to a common variable (i.e., x). Thus, they cannot be executed in parallel and one of them must see the write of the other. Thus, SB is not robust against PC relative to SI.

The write skew (WS) program in Figure 3c has two transactions that are issued by two distinct processes. We highlight an execution where t_1 reads 0 from x and t_2 reads 0 from y. This execution is allowed under SI since both transactions are not causally dependent, do not write to a common variable, and can be executed in parallel by the two processes. However, this execution is not allowed under SER since one of the two transactions must see the write of the other. Thus, WS is not robust against SI relative to SER.

The message passing (MP) program in Figure 3d has four transactions issued by two processes. Because t_1 and t_2 are causally dependent, under any semantics $\mathsf{X} \in \{\mathtt{CC}, \mathtt{PC}, \mathtt{SI}, \mathtt{SER}\}$ we only have three possible executions of MP, which correspond to either t_3 and t_4 not observing the writes of t_1 and t_2, or t_3 and t_4 observe the writes of both t_1 and t_2, or t_4 observes the write of t_1 (we highlight the values read in the second case in Figure 3d). Therefore, the executions of this program under the four consistency models coincide. Thus, MP is robust against CC relative to any other model.

4 Robustness Against CC Relative to PC

We show that checking robustness against CC relative to PC can be reduced to checking robustness against CC relative to SER. The crux of this reduction is a program transformation that allows to simulate the PC semantics of a program $\mathcal{P}$ using the SER semantics of a program $\mathcal{P}_\clubsuit$. Checking robustness against CC relative to SER can be reduced in polynomial time to reachability under SER [10].

Given a program $\mathcal{P}$ with a set of transactions $\mathsf{Tr}(\mathcal{P})$, we define a program $\mathcal{P}_\clubsuit$ such that every transaction $t \in \mathsf{Tr}(\mathcal{P})$ is split into a transaction $t[r]$ that contains all the read/`assume` statements in t (in the same order) and another transaction $t[w]$ that contains all the write statements in t (in the same order). In the following, we establish the following result:

Theorem 1. *A program $\mathcal{P}$ is robust against* CC *relative to* PC *iff $\mathcal{P}_\clubsuit$ is robust against* CC *relative to* SER.

Intuitively, under PC, processes can execute concurrent transactions that fetch the same consistent snapshot of the shared variables from the central memory and subsequently commit their writes. Decoupling the read part of a transaction from the write part allows to simulate such behaviors even under SER.

The proof of this theorem relies on several intermediate results concerning the relationship between traces of $\mathcal{P}$ and $\mathcal{P}_\clubsuit$. Let $\tau = (\rho, \mathsf{PO}, \mathsf{WR}, \mathsf{WW}, \mathsf{RW}) \in \mathbb{T}\mathsf{r}_\mathsf{X}(\mathcal{P})$ be a trace of a program $\mathcal{P}$ under a semantics X. We define the trace $\tau_\clubsuit = (\rho_\clubsuit, \mathsf{PO}_\clubsuit, \mathsf{WR}_\clubsuit, \mathsf{WW}_\clubsuit, \mathsf{RW}_\clubsuit)$ where every transaction $t \in \tau$ is split into two transactions $t[r] \in \tau_\clubsuit$ and $t[w] \in \tau_\clubsuit$, and the dependency relations are straightforward adaptations, i.e.,

- $\mathsf{PO}_\clubsuit$ is the smallest transitive relation that includes $(t[r], t[w])$ for every t, and $(t[w], t'[r])$ if $(t, t') \in \mathsf{PO}$,
- $(t'[w], t[r]) \in \mathsf{WR}_\clubsuit$, $(t'[w], t[w]) \in \mathsf{WW}_\clubsuit$, and $(t'[r], t[w]) \in \mathsf{RW}_\clubsuit$ if $(t', t) \in \mathsf{WR}$, $(t', t) \in \mathsf{WW}$, and $(t', t) \in \mathsf{RW}$, respectively.

For instance, Figure 4 pictures the trace $\tau_\clubsuit$ for the LU trace τ given in Figure 3b. For traces τ of programs that contain singleton transactions, e.g., SB in Figure 3a, $\tau_\clubsuit$ coincides with τ.

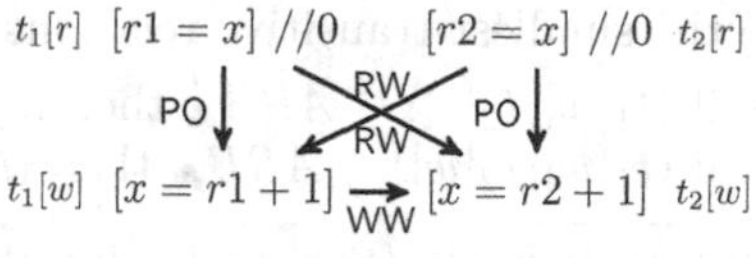

Fig. 4: A trace of the transformed LU program ($\mathsf{LU}_\clubsuit$).

Conversely, for a given trace $\tau_\clubsuit = (\rho_\clubsuit, \mathsf{PO}_\clubsuit, \mathsf{WR}_\clubsuit, \mathsf{WW}_\clubsuit, \mathsf{RW}_\clubsuit) \in \mathbb{T}\mathsf{r}_\mathsf{X}(\mathcal{P}_\clubsuit)$

of a program $\mathcal{P}_\clubsuit$ under a semantics X, we define the trace $\tau = (\rho, \mathsf{PO}, \mathsf{WR}, \mathsf{WW}, \mathsf{RW})$ where every two components $t[r]$ and $t[w]$ are merged into a transaction $t \in \tau$. The dependency relations are defined in a straightforward way, e.g., if $(t'[w], t[w]) \in \mathsf{WW}_\clubsuit$ then $(t', t) \in \mathsf{WW}$.

The following lemma shows that for any semantics $\mathsf{X} \in \{\mathtt{CC}, \mathtt{PC}, \mathtt{SI}\}$, if $\tau \in \mathbb{T}\mathsf{r}_\mathsf{X}(\mathcal{P})$ for a program $\mathcal{P}$, then $\tau_\clubsuit$ is a valid trace of $\mathcal{P}_\clubsuit$ under X, i.e., $\tau_\clubsuit \in \mathbb{T}\mathsf{r}_\mathsf{X}(\mathcal{P}_\clubsuit)$. Intuitively, this lemma shows that splitting transactions in a trace and defining dependency relations appropriately cannot introduce cycles in these relations and preserves the validity of the different consistency axioms.

The proof of this lemma relies on constructing a causal order $\mathsf{CO}_\clubsuit$ and an arbitration order $ARB_\clubsuit$ for the trace $\tau_\clubsuit$ starting from the analogous relations in τ. In the case of CC, these are the smallest transitive relations such that:

- $\mathsf{PO}_\clubsuit \subseteq \mathsf{CO}_\clubsuit \subseteq ARB_\clubsuit$, and
- if $(t_1, t_2) \in \mathsf{CO}$ then $(t_1[w], t_2[r]) \in \mathsf{CO}_\clubsuit$, and if $(t_1, t_2) \in ARB$ then $(t_1[w], t_2[r]) \in ARB_\clubsuit$.

For PC and SI, $\mathsf{CO}_\clubsuit$ must additionally satisfy: if $(t_1, t_2) \in ARB$, then $(t_1[w], t_2[w]) \in \mathsf{CO}_\clubsuit$. This is required in order to satisfy the axiom AxPrefix, i.e., $ARB_\clubsuit; \mathsf{CO}_\clubsuit \subset \mathsf{CO}_\clubsuit$, when $(t_1[w], t_2[r]) \in ARB_\clubsuit$ and $(t_2[r], t_2[w]) \in \mathsf{CO}_\clubsuit$.

This construction ensures that $\mathsf{CO}_\clubsuit$ is a partial order and $ARB_\clubsuit$ is a total order because CO is a partial order and ARB is a total order. Also, based on the above rules, we have that: if $(t_1[w], t_2[r]) \in \mathsf{CO}_\clubsuit$ then $(t_1, t_2) \in \mathsf{CO}$, and similarly, if $(t_1[w], t_2[r]) \in ARB_\clubsuit$ then $(t_1, t_2) \in ARB$.

Lemma 1. *If $\tau \in \mathbb{T}r_X(\mathcal{P})$, then $\tau_\clubsuit \in \mathbb{T}r_X(\mathcal{P}_\clubsuit)$.*

Before presenting a strengthening of Lemma 1 when X is CC, we give an important characterization of CC traces. This characterization is stated in terms of acyclicity properties.

Lemma 2. *τ is a trace under* CC *iff ARB_0^+ and $\mathsf{CO}_0^+; \mathsf{RW}$ are acyclic (ARB_0 and CO_0 are defined in Table 1).*

Next we show that a trace τ of a program $\mathcal{P}$ is CC iff the corresponding trace $\tau_\clubsuit$ of $\mathcal{P}_\clubsuit$ is CC as well. This result is based on the observation that cycles in ARB_0^+ or $\mathsf{CO}_0^+; \mathsf{RW}$ cannot be broken by splitting transactions.

Lemma 3. *A trace τ of $\mathcal{P}$ is* CC *iff the corresponding trace $\tau_\clubsuit$ of $\mathcal{P}_\clubsuit$ is* CC.

The following lemma shows that a trace τ is PC iff the corresponding trace $\tau_\clubsuit$ is SER. The if direction in the proof is based on constructing a causal order CO and an arbitration order ARB for the trace τ from the arbitration order $ARB_\clubsuit$ in $\tau_\clubsuit$ (since $\tau_\clubsuit$ is a trace under serializability $\mathsf{CO}_\clubsuit$ and $ARB_\clubsuit$ coincide). These are the smallest transitive relations such that:

- if $(t_1[w], t_2[r]) \in ARB_\clubsuit$ then $(t_1, t_2) \in \mathsf{CO}$,
- if $(t_1[w], t_2[w]) \in ARB_\clubsuit$ then $(t_1, t_2) \in ARB$[6].

[6] If $t_1[w]$ is empty (t_1 is read-only), then we set $(t_1, t_2) \in ARB$ if $(t_1[r], t_2[w]) \in \mathsf{CO}_\clubsuit$. If $t_2[w]$ is empty, then $(t_1, t_2) \in ARB$ if $(t_1[w], t_2[r]) \in \mathsf{CO}_\clubsuit$. If both $t_1[w]$ and $t_2[w]$ are empty, then $(t_1, t_2) \in ARB$ if $(t_1[r], t_2[r]) \in \mathsf{CO}_\clubsuit$.

The only-if direction is based on the fact that any cycle in the dependency relations of τ that is admitted under PC (characterized in Lemma 7) is "broken" by splitting transactions. Also, splitting transactions cannot introduce new cycles that do not originate in τ.

Lemma 4. *A trace* τ *is* PC *iff* $\tau_\clubsuit$ *is* SER

The lemmas above are used to prove Theorem 1 as follows:

PROOF of Theorem 1: For the if direction, assume by contradiction that $\mathcal{P}$ is not robust against CC relative to PC. Then, there must exist a trace $\tau \in \mathbb{T}\mathrm{r}_{\mathrm{CC}}(\mathcal{P}) \setminus \mathbb{T}\mathrm{r}_{\mathrm{PC}}(\mathcal{P})$. Lemmas 3 and 4 imply that the corresponding trace $\tau_\clubsuit$ of $\mathcal{P}_\clubsuit$ is CC and not SER. Thus, $\mathcal{P}_\clubsuit$ is not robust against CC relative to SER. The only-if direction is proved similarly. □

Robustness against CC relative to SER has been shown to be reducible in polynomial time to the reachability problem under SER [10]. Given a program $\mathcal{P}$ and a control location ℓ, the reachability problem under SER asks whether there exists an execution of $\mathcal{P}$ under SER that reaches ℓ. Therefore, as a corollary of Theorem 1, we obtain the following:

Corollary 1. *Checking robustness against* CC *relative to* PC *is reducible to the reachability problem under* SER *in polynomial time.*

In the following we discuss the complexity of this problem in the case of finite-state programs (bounded data domain). The upper bound follows from Corollary 1 and standard results about the complexity of the reachability problem under sequential consistency, which extend to SER, with a bounded [35] or parametric number of processes [45]. For the lower bound, given an instance $(\mathcal{P}, \ell)$ of the reachability problem under sequential consistency, we construct a program $\mathcal{P}'$ where each statement s of $\mathcal{P}$ is executed in a different transaction that guards[7] the execution of s using a global lock (the lock can be implemented in our programming language as usual, e.g., using a busy wait loop for locking), and where reaching the location ℓ enables the execution of a "gadget" that corresponds to the SB program in Figure 3a. Executing each statement under a global lock ensures that every execution of $\mathcal{P}'$ under CC is serializable, and faithfully represents an execution of $\mathcal{P}$ under sequential consistency. Moreover, $\mathcal{P}$ reaches ℓ iff $\mathcal{P}'$ contains a robustness violation, which is due to the SB execution.

Corollary 2. *Checking robustness of a program with a fixed number of variables and bounded data domain against* CC *relative to* PC *is PSPACE-complete when the number of processes is bounded and EXPSPACE-complete, otherwise.*

5 Robustness Against PC Relative to SI

In this section, we show that checking robustness against PC relative to SI can be reduced in polynomial time to a reachability problem under the SER semantics. We reuse the program transformation from the previous section that allows to simulate PC behaviors on top of SER, and additionally, we provide a characterization of traces that distinguish the PC semantics from SI. We use this

[7] That is, the transaction is of the form [lock; s; unlock]

characterization to define an instrumentation (monitor) that is able to detect if a program under PC admits such traces.

We show that the happens-before cycles in a robustness violation (against PC relative to SI) must contain a WW dependency followed by a RW dependency, and they should not contain two successive RW dependencies. This follows from the fact that every happens-before cycle in a PC trace must contain either two successive RW dependencies, or a WW dependency followed by a RW dependency. Otherwise, the happens-before cycle would imply a cycle in the arbitration order. Then, any trace under PC where all its simple happens-before cycles contain two successive RW dependencies is possible under SI. For instance, the trace of the non-robust LU execution in Figure 3b contains WW dependency followed by a RW dependency and does not contain two successive RW dependencies which is disallowed SI, while the trace of the robust WS execution in Figure 3c contains two successive RW dependencies. As a first step, we prove the following theorem characterizing traces that are allowed under both PC and SI.

Theorem 2. *A program $\mathcal{P}$ is robust against* PC *relative to* SI *iff every happens-before cycle in a trace of $\mathcal{P}$ under* PC *contains two successive* RW *dependencies.*

Before giving the proof of the above theorem, we state several intermediate results that characterize cycles in PC or SI traces. First, we show that every PC trace in which all simple happens-before cycles contain two successive RW is also a SI trace.

Lemma 5. *If a trace τ is* PC *and all happens-before cycles in τ contain two successive* RW *dependencies, then τ is* SI.

The proof of Theorem 2 also relies on the following lemma that characterizes happens-before cycles permissible under SI.

Lemma 6. *[23, 13] If a trace τ is* SI*, then all its happens-before cycles must contain two successive* RW *dependencies.*

Proof of Theorem 2: For the only-if direction, if $\mathcal{P}$ is robust against PC relative to SI then every trace τ of $\mathcal{P}$ under PC is SI as well. Therefore, by Lemma 6, all cycles in τ contain two successive RW which concludes the proof of this direction. For the reverse, let τ be a trace of $\mathcal{P}$ under PC such that all its happens-before cycles contain two successive RW. Then, by Lemma 5, we have that τ is SI. Thus, every trace τ of $\mathcal{P}$ under PC is SI. □

Next, we present an important lemma that characterizes happens before cycles possible under the PC semantics. This is a strengthening of a result in [13] which shows that all happens before cycles under PC must have two successive dependencies in {RW, WW} and at least one RW. We show that the two successive dependencies cannot be RW followed WW, or two successive WW.

Lemma 7. *If a trace τ is* PC *then all happens-before cycles in τ must contain either two successive* RW *dependencies or a* WW *dependency followed by a* RW *dependency.*

Combining the results of Theorem 2 and Lemmas 4 and 7, we obtain the following characterization of traces which violate robustness against PC relative to SI.

Theorem 3. *A program $\mathcal{P}$ is not robust against* PC *relative to* SI *iff there exists a trace $\tau_\clubsuit$ of $\mathcal{P}_\clubsuit$ under* SER *such that the trace τ obtained by merging*[8] *read and write transactions in $\tau_\clubsuit$ contains a happens-before cycle that does not contain two successive* RW *dependencies, and it contains a* WW *dependency followed by a* RW *dependency.*

The results above enable a reduction from checking robustness against PC relative to SI to a reachability problem under the SER semantics. For a program $\mathcal{P}$, we define an instrumentation denoted by $[\![\mathcal{P}]\!]$, such that $\mathcal{P}$ is not robust against PC relative to SI iff $[\![\mathcal{P}]\!]$ violates an assertion under SER. The instrumentation consists in rewriting every transaction of $\mathcal{P}$ as shown in Figure 6.

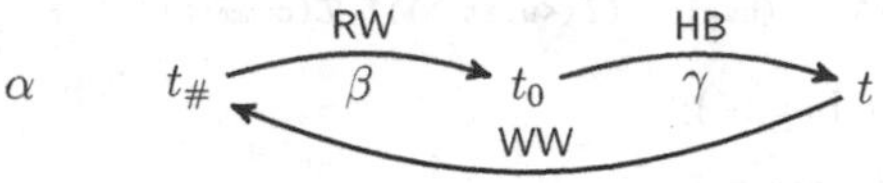

Fig. 5: Execution simulating a violation to robustness against PC relative to SI.

The instrumentation $[\![\mathcal{P}]\!]$ running under SER simulates the PC semantics of $\mathcal{P}$ using the same idea of decoupling the execution of the read part of a transaction from the write part. It violates an assertion when it simulates a PC trace containing a happens-before cycle as in Theorem 3. The execution corresponding to this trace has the shape given in Figure 5, where $t_\#$ is the transaction that occurs between the WW and the RW dependencies, and every transaction executed after $t_\#$ (this can be a full transaction in $\mathcal{P}$, or only the read or write part of a transaction in $\mathcal{P}$) is related by a happens-before path to $t_\#$ (otherwise, the execution of this transaction can be reordered to occur before $t_\#$). A transaction in $\mathcal{P}$ can have its read part included in α and the write part included in β or γ. Also, β and γ may contain transactions in $\mathcal{P}$ that executed only their read part. It is possible that $t_0 = t$, $\beta = \gamma = \epsilon$, and $\alpha = \epsilon$ (the LU program shown in Figure 3b is an example where this can happen). The instrumentation uses auxiliary variables to track happens-before dependencies, which are explained below.

The instrumentation executes (incomplete) transactions without affecting the auxiliary variables (without tracking happens-before dependencies) (lines 3 and 5) until a non-deterministically chosen point in time when it declares the current transaction as the candidate for $t_\#$ (line 9). Only one candidate for $t_\#$ can be chosen during the execution. This transaction executes only its reads and it chooses non-deterministically a variable that it could write as a witness for the WW dependency (see lines 16-22). The name of this variable is stored in a global variable `varW` (see the definition of $\mathcal{I}_\#($ x := e $)$). The writes are *not* applied on the shared memory. Intuitively, $t_\#$ should be thought as a transaction whose writes are delayed for later, after transaction t in Figure 5 executed. The instrumentation checks that $t_\#$ and t can be connected by some happens-before path that includes the RW and WW dependencies, and that does not contain two consecutive RW dependencies. If it is the case, it violates an assertion at the commit point of t. Since the write part of $t_\#$ is intuitively delayed to execute after t, the process executing $t_\#$ is disabled all along the execution (see the `assume false`).

[8] This transformation has been defined at the beginning of Section 4.

Transaction "**begin** ⟨read⟩* ⟨test⟩* ⟨write⟩* **commit**" is rewritten to:

```
1 if ( !done# )
2  if ( * )
3   begin <read>* <test>* commit
4   if ( !done# )
5    begin <write>* commit
6   else
7    I(begin) (I(<write>))* I(commit)
8  else
9   begin (I#(<read>))* <test>* (I#(<write>))* I#(commit)
10  assume false;
11 else if ( * )
12  rdSet' := ∅;
13  wrSet' := ∅;
14  I(begin) (I(<read>))* <test>* I(commit)
15  I(begin) (I(<write>))* I(commit)
```

$\mathcal{I}_{\#}$(r := x):

```
16 r := x;
17 hbR['x'] := 0;
18 rdSet := rdSet ∪ { 'x' };
```

$\mathcal{I}_{\#}$(x := e):

```
19 if ( varW == ⊥ and * )
20   varW := 'x';
```

$\mathcal{I}_{\#}$(commit):

```
21 assume ( varW != ⊥ )
22 done# := true
```

$\mathcal{I}$(begin):

```
23 begin
24 hb := ⊥
25 if ( hbP != ⊥ and hbP < 2 )
26   hb := 0;
27 else if ( hbP = 2 )
28   hb := 2;
```

$\mathcal{I}$(commit):

```
29 assume ( hb != ⊥ )
30 assert ( hb == 2 or varW ∉ wrSet' );
31 if ( hbP == ⊥ or hbP > hb )
32   hbP = hb;
33 for each 'x' ∈ wrSet'
34   if ( hbW['x'] == ⊥ or hbW['x'] > hb )
35     hbW['x'] = hb;
36 for each 'x' ∈ rdSet'
37   if ( hbR['x'] == ⊥ or hbR['x'] > hb )
38     hbR['x'] = hb;
39 rdSet := rdSet ∪ rdSet';
40 wrSet := wrSet ∪ wrSet';
41 commit
```

$\mathcal{I}$(r := x):

```
42 r := x;
43 rdSet' := rdSet' ∪ { 'x' };
44 if ( 'x' ∈ wrSet )
45   if ( hbW['x'] != 2 )
46     hb := 0
47   else if ( hb == ⊥ )
48     hb := hbW['x']
```

$\mathcal{I}$(x := e):

```
49 x := e;
50 wrSet' := wrSet' ∪ { 'x' };
51 if ( 'x' ∈ wrSet )
52   if ( hbW['x'] != 2 )
53     hb := 0
54   else if ( hb == ⊥ )
55     hb := hbW['x']
56 if ( 'x' ∈ rdSet )
57   if ( hb = ⊥ or hb > hbR['x'] + 1 )
58     hb := min(hbR['x'] + 1,2)
```

Fig. 6: A program instrumentation for checking robustness against PC relative to SI. The auxiliary variables used by the instrumentation are shared variables, except for `hbP`, `rdSet'`, and `wrSet'`, which are process-local variables, and they are initially set to ⊥. This instrumentation uses program constructs which can be defined as syntactic sugar from the syntax presented in Section 3, e.g., if-then-else statements (outside transactions).

After choosing the candidate for $t_{\#}$, the instrumentation uses the auxiliary variables for tracking happens-before dependencies. Therefore, `rdSet` and `wrSet` record variables read and written, respectively, by transactions that are connected by a happens-before path to $t_{\#}$ (in a trace of $\mathcal{P}$). This is ensured by the assume at line 29. During the execution, the variables read or written by a transaction[9] that writes a variable in `rdSet` (see line 56), or reads or writes a variable in `wrSet` (see lines 44 and 51), will be added to these sets (see lines 39

[9] These are stored in the local variables `rdSet'` and `wrSet'` while the transaction is running.

and 40). Since the variables that $t_{\#}$ writes in $\mathcal{P}$ are not recorded in `wrSet`, these happens-before paths must necessarily start with a RW dependency (from $t_{\#}$). When the assertion fails (line 30), the condition `varW` $\in$ `wrSet`' ensures that the current transaction has a WW dependency towards the write part of $t_{\#}$ (the current transaction plays the role of t in Figure 5).

The rest of the instrumentation checks that there exists a happens-before path from $t_{\#}$ to t that does not include two consecutive RW dependencies, called a $\texttt{SI}_\neg$ path. This check is based on the auxiliary variables whose name is prefixed by `hb` and which take values in the domain $\{\bot, 0, 1, 2\}$ ($\bot$ represents the initial value). Therefore,

- `hbR['x']` (resp., `hbW['x']`) is 0 iff there exists a transaction t' that reads `x` (resp., writes to `x`), such that there exists a $\texttt{SI}_\neg$ path from $t_{\#}$ to t' that ends with a dependency which is *not* RW,
- `hbR['x']` (resp., `hbW['x']`) is 1 iff there exists a transaction t' that reads `x` (resp., writes to `x`) that is connected to $t_{\#}$ by a $\texttt{SI}_\neg$ path, and *every* $\texttt{SI}_\neg$ path from $t_{\#}$ to a transaction t'' that reads `x` (resp., writes to `x`) ends with an RW dependency,
- `hbR['x']` (resp., `hbW['x']`) is 2 iff there exists no $\texttt{SI}_\neg$ path from $t_{\#}$ to a transaction t' that reads `x` (resp., writes to `x`).

The local variable `hbP` has the same interpretation, except that t' and t'' are instantiated over transactions in the same process (that already executed) instead of transactions that read or write a certain variable. Similarly, the variable `hb` is a particular case where t' and t'' are instantiated to the current transaction. The violation of the assertion at line 30 implies that `hb` is 0 or 1, which means that there exists a $\texttt{SI}_\neg$ path from $t_{\#}$ to t.

During each transaction that executes after $t_{\#}$, the variable `hb` characterizing happens-before paths that end in this transaction is updated every time a new happens-before dependency is witnessed (using the values of the other variables). For instance, when witnessing a WR dependency (line 44), if there exists a $\texttt{SI}_\neg$ path to a transaction that writes to `x`, then the path that continues with the WR dependency towards the current transaction is also a $\texttt{SI}_\neg$ path, and the last dependency of this path is not RW. Therefore, `hb` is set to 0 (see line 46). Otherwise, if every path to a transaction that writes to `x` is not a $\texttt{SI}_\neg$ path, then every path that continues to the current transaction (by taking the WR dependency) remains a non $\texttt{SI}_\neg$ path, and `hb` is set to the value of `hbW['x']`, which is 2 in this case (see line 48). Before ending a transaction, the value of `hb` can be used to modify the `hbR`, `hbW`, and `hbP` variables, but only if those variables contain bigger values (see lines 31–38).

The correctness of the instrumentation is stated in the following theorem.

Theorem 4. *A program $\mathcal{P}$ is robust against* PC *relative to* SI *iff the instrumentation in Figure 6 does not violate an assertion when executed under* SER.

Theorem 4 implies the following complexity result for finite-state programs. The lower bound is proved similarly to the case CC vs PC.

Corollary 3. *Checking robustness of a program with a fixed number of variables and bounded data domain against* PC *relative to* SI *is PSPACE-complete when the number of processes is bounded and EXPSPACE-complete, otherwise.*

Checking robustness against CC relative to SI can be also shown to be reducible (in polynomial time) to a reachability problem under SER by combining the results of checking robustness against CC relative to PC and PC relative to SI.

Theorem 5. *A program* $\mathcal{P}$ *is robust against* CC *relative to* SI *iff* $\mathcal{P}$ *is robust against* CC *relative to* PC *and* $\mathcal{P}$ *is robust against* PC *relative to* SI.

Remark 1. Our reductions of robustness checking to reachability apply to an extension of our programming language where the number of processes is unbounded and each process can execute an arbitrary number of times a statically known set of transactions. This holds because the instrumentation in Figure 6 and the one in [10] (for the case CC vs. SER) consist in adding a set of instructions that manipulate a fixed set of process-local or shared variables, which do not store process or transaction identifiers. These reductions extend also to SQL queries that access unbounded size tables. Rows in a table can be interpreted as memory locations (identified by primary keys in unbounded domains, e.g., integers), and SQL queries can be interpreted as instructions that read/write a set of locations in one shot. These possibly unbounded sets of locations can be represented symbolically using the conditions in the SQL queries (e.g., the condition in the WHERE part of a SELECT). The instrumentation in Figure 6 needs to be adapted so that read and write sets are updated by adding sets of locations for a given instruction (represented symbolically as mentioned above).

6 Proving Robustness Using Commutativity Dependency Graphs

We describe an approximated technique for proving robustness, which leverages the concept of left/right mover in Lipton's reduction theory [39]. This technique reasons on the *commutativity dependency graph* [9] associated to the transformation $\mathcal{P}_\clubsuit$ of an input program $\mathcal{P}$ that allows to simulate the PC semantics under serializability (we use a slight variation of the original definition of this class of graphs). We characterize robustness against CC relative to PC and PC relative to SI in terms of certain properties that (simple) cycles in this graph must satisfy.

We recall the concept of movers and the definition of commutativity dependency graphs. Given a program $\mathcal{P}$ and a trace $\tau = t_1 \cdot \ldots \cdot t_n \in \mathbb{T}\mathsf{r}_{\mathtt{SER}}(\mathcal{P})$ of $\mathcal{P}$ under serializability, we say that $t_i \in \tau$ *moves right (resp., left)* in τ if $t_1 \cdot \ldots \cdot t_{i-1} \cdot t_{i+1} \cdot t_i \cdot t_{i+2} \cdot \ldots \cdot t_n$ (resp., $t_1 \cdot \ldots \cdot t_{i-2} \cdot t_i \cdot t_{i-1} \cdot t_{i+1} \cdot \ldots \cdot t_n$) is also a valid execution of $\mathcal{P}$, t_i and t_{i+1} (resp., t_{i-1}) are executed by distinct processes, and both traces reach the same end state. A transaction $t \in \mathsf{Tr}(\mathcal{P})$ is not a right (resp., left) mover iff there exists a trace $\tau \in \mathbb{T}\mathsf{r}_{\mathtt{SER}}(\mathcal{P})$ such that $t \in \tau$ and t doesn't move right (resp., left) in τ. Thus, when a transaction t is *not* a right mover then there must exist another transaction $t' \in \tau$ which caused t to not be permutable to the right (while preserving the end state). Since t and t' do not commute, then this must be because of either a write-read, write-write, or a read-write dependency relation between the two transactions. We say that t is not a right mover because of t' and a dependency relation that is either write-read, write-write, or read-write. Notice that when t is not a right mover because of t' then t' is not a left mover because of t.

We define $\mathsf{M_{WR}}$ as a binary relation between transactions such that $(t, t') \in \mathsf{M_{WR}}$ when t is *not* a right mover because of t' and a write-read dependency (t' reads some value written by t). We define the relations $\mathsf{M_{WW}}$ and $\mathsf{M_{RW}}$ corresponding to write-write and read-write dependencies in a similar way. We call $\mathsf{M_{WR}}$, $\mathsf{M_{WW}}$, and $\mathsf{M_{RW}}$, *non-mover* relations.

The *commutativity dependency graph* of a program $\mathcal{P}$ is a graph where vertices represent transactions in $\mathcal{P}$. Two vertices are linked by a program order edge if the two transactions are executed by the same process. The other edges in this graph represent the "non-mover" relations $\mathsf{M_{WR}}$, $\mathsf{M_{WW}}$, and $\mathsf{M_{RW}}$. Two vertices that represent the two components $t[w]$ and $t[r]$ of the same transaction t (already linked by PO edge) are also linked by an undirected edge labeled by STO (same-transaction relation).

Our results about the robustness of a program $\mathcal{P}$ are stated over a slight variation of the commutativity dependency graph of $\mathcal{P}_\clubsuit$ (where a transaction is either read-only or write-only). This graph contains additional undirected edges that link every pair of transactions $t[r]$ and $t[w]$ of $\mathcal{P}_\clubsuit$ that were originally components of the same transaction t in $\mathcal{P}$. Given such a commutativity dependency graph, the robustness of $\mathcal{P}$ is implied by the absence of cycles of specific shapes. These cycles can be seen as an abstraction of potential robustness violations for the respective semantics (see Theorem 6 and Theorem 7). Figure 7 pictures the commutativity dependency graph for the MP program. Since every transaction in MP is singleton, the two programs MP and $\mathsf{MP}_\clubsuit$ coincide.

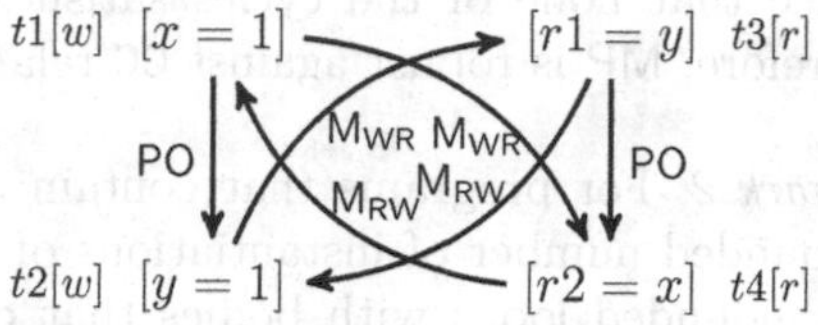

Fig. 7: The commutativity dependency graph of the $\mathsf{MP}_\clubsuit$ program.

Using the characterization of robustness violations against CC relative to SER from [10] and the reduction in Theorem 1, we obtain the following result concerning the robustness against CC relative to PC.

Theorem 6. *Given a program $\mathcal{P}$, if the commutativity dependency graph of the program $\mathcal{P}_\clubsuit$ does not contain a simple cycle formed by $t_1 \cdots t_i \cdots t_n$ such that:*

- $(t_n, t_1) \in \mathsf{M_{RW}}$;
- $(t_j, t_{j+1}) \in (\mathsf{PO} \cup \mathsf{WR})^*$, *for* $j \in [1, i-1]$;
- $(t_i, t_{i+1}) \in (\mathsf{M_{RW}} \cup \mathsf{M_{WW}})$;
- $(t_j, t_{j+1}) \in (\mathsf{M_{RW}} \cup \mathsf{M_{WW}} \cup \mathsf{M_{WR}} \cup \mathsf{PO})$, *for* $j \in [i+1, n-1]$.

Then $\mathcal{P}$ is robust against CC *relative to* PC.

Next we give the characterization of commutativity dependency graphs required for proving robustness against PC relative to SI.

Theorem 7. *Given a program $\mathcal{P}$, if the commutativity dependency graph of the program $\mathcal{P}_{\clubsuit}$ does not contain a simple cycle formed by $t_1 \cdots t_n$ such that:*

- $(t_n, t_1) \in \mathsf{M_{WW}}$, $(t_1, t_2) \in \mathsf{STO}$, *and* $(t_2, t_3) \in \mathsf{M_{RW}}$;
- $(t_j, t_{j+1}) \in (\mathsf{M_{RW}} \cup \mathsf{M_{WW}} \cup \mathsf{M_{WR}} \cup \mathsf{PO} \cup \mathsf{STO})^*$, *for* $j \in [3, n-1]$;
- $\forall\, j \in [2, n-2]$.
  - *if* $(t_j, t_{j+1}) \in \mathsf{M_{RW}}$ *then* $(t_{j+1}, t_{j+2}) \in (\mathsf{M_{WR}} \cup \mathsf{PO} \cup \mathsf{M_{WW}})$;
  - *if* $(t_{j+1}, t_{j+2}) \in \mathsf{M_{RW}}$ *then* $(t_j, t_{j+1}) \in (\mathsf{M_{WR}} \cup \mathsf{PO})$.
- $\forall\, j \in [3, n-3]$. *if* $(t_{j+1}, t_{j+2}) \in \mathsf{STO}$ *and* $(t_{j+2}, t_{j+3}) \in \mathsf{M_{RW}}$ *then* $(t_j, t_{j+1}) \in \mathsf{M_{WW}}$.

then $\mathcal{P}$ *is robust against* PC *relative to* SI.

In Figure 7, we have three simple cycles in the graph:

- $(t1[w], t4[r]) \in \mathsf{M_{WR}}$ and $(t4[r], t1[w]) \in \mathsf{M_{RW}}$,
- $(t2[w], t3[r]) \in \mathsf{M_{WR}}$ and $(t3[r], t2[w]) \in \mathsf{M_{RW}}$,
- $(t1[w], t2[w]) \in \mathsf{PO}$, $(t2[w], t3[r]) \in \mathsf{M_{WR}}$, $(t3[r], t4[r]) \in \mathsf{PO}$, and $(t4[r], t1[w]) \in \mathsf{M_{RW}}$.

Notice that none of the cycles satisfies the properties in Theorems 6 and 7. Therefore, MP is robust against CC relative to PC and against PC relative to SI.

Remark 2. For programs that contain an unbounded number of processes, an unbounded number of instantiations of a fixed number of process "templates", or unbounded loops with bodies that contain entire transactions, a sound robustness check consists in applying Theorem 6 and Theorem 7 to (bounded) programs that contain two copies of each process template, and where each loop is unfolded exactly two times. This holds because the mover relations are "static", they do not depend on the context in which the transactions execute, and each cycle requiring more than two process instances or more than two loop iterations can be short-circuited to a cycle that exists also in the bounded program. Every outgoing edge from a third instance/iteration can also be taken from the second instance/iteration. Two copies/iterations are necessary in order to discover cycles between instances of the same transaction (the cycles in Theorem 6 and Theorem 7 are simple and cannot contain the same transaction twice). These results extend easily to SQL queries as well because the notion of mover is independent of particular classes of programs or instructions.

7 Experimental Evaluation

We evaluated our approach for checking robustness on 7 applications extracted from the literature on databases and distributed systems, and an application Betting designed by ourselves. Two applications were extracted from the OLTP-Bench benchmark [30]: a vote recording application (Vote) and a consumer review application (Epinions). Three applications were obtained from Github projects (used also in [9, 19]): a distributed lock application for the Cassandra database (CassandraLock [24]), an application for recording trade activities

(SimpleCurrencyExchange [48]), and a micro social media application (Twitter [49]). The last two applications are a movie ticketing application (FusionTicket) [34], and a user subscription application inspired by the Twitter application (Subscription). Each application consists of a set of SQL transactions that can be called an arbitrary number of times from an arbitrary number of processes. For instance, Subscription provides an AddUser transaction for adding a new user with a given username and password, and a RemoveUser transaction for removing an existing user. (The examples in Figure 1 are particular variations of FusionTicket, Twitter, and Betting.) We considered five variations of the robustness problem: the three robustness problems we studied in this paper along with robustness against SI relative to SER and against CC relative to SER. The artifacts are available in a GitHub repository [31].

Table 2: Results of the experiments. The columns titled X-Y stand for the result of applications robustness against X relative to Y.

Application	Transactions	Robustness				
		CC-PC	PC-SI	CC-SI	SI-SER	CC-SER
Betting	2	yes	yes	yes	yes	yes
CassandraLock	3	yes	yes	yes	yes	yes
Epinions	8	no	yes	no	yes	no
FusionTicket	3	no	no	no	yes	no
SimpleCurrencyExchange	4	yes	yes	yes	yes	yes
Subscription	2	yes	no	no	yes	no
Twitter	3	no	no	no	yes	no
Vote	1	yes	yes	yes	no	no

In the first part of the experiments, we check for robustness violations in bounded-size executions of a given application. For each application, we have constructed a client program with a fixed number of processes (2) and a fixed number of transactions of the corresponding application (at most 2 transactions per process). For each program and pair of consistency models, we check for robustness violations using the reductions to reachability under SER presented in Section 4 and Section 5 in the case of pairs of weak consistency models, and the reductions in [9, 10] when checking for robustness relative to SER.

We check for reachability (assertion violations) using the Boogie program verifier [8]. We model tables as unbounded maps in Boogie and SQL queries as first-order formulas over these maps (that may contain existential or universal quantifiers). To model the uniqueness of primary keys we use Boogie linear types.

Table 2 reports the results of this experiment (cells filled with "no")[10]. Five applications are not robust against at least one of the semantics relative to some other stronger semantics. The runtimes (wall-clock times) for the robustness checks are all under one second, and the memory consumption is around 50 Megabytes. Concerning scalability, the reductions to reachability presented in Section 4 and Section 5 show that checking robustness is as hard as checking

[10] The Twitter client in Table 2, which is not PC vs CC robust, is different from the one described in Section 2. This client program consists of two processes, each executing FollowUser and AddTweet.

reachability (the size of the instrumented program is only linear in the size of the original program). Therefore, checking robustness will also suffer from the classic state explosion problem when increasing the number of processes. On the other hand, increasing the number of transactions in a process does not seem to introduce a large overhead. Increasing the number of transactions per process in the clients of Epinions, FusionTicket, and SimpleCurrencyExchange from 2 to 5 introduces a running time overhead of at most 25%.

All the robustness violations we report correspond to violations of the intended specifications. For instance: (1) the robustness violation of Epinions against `CC` relative to `PC` allows two users to update their ratings for a given product and then when each user queries the overall rating of this product they do not observe the latest rating that was given by the other user, (2) the robustness violation of Subscription against `PC` relative to `SI` allows two users to register new accounts with the same identifier, and (3) the robustness violation of Vote against `SI` relative to `SER` allows the same user to vote twice. The specification violation in Twitter was reported in [19]. However, it was reported as violation of a different robustness property (`CC` relative to `SER`) while our work shows that the violation persists when replacing a weak consistency model (e.g., `SI`) with a weaker one (e.g. `CC`). This implies that this specification violation is not present under `SI` (since it appears in the difference between `CC` and `SI` behaviors), which cannot be deduced from previous work.

In the second part of the experiments, we used the technique described in Section 6, based on commutativity dependency graphs, to prove robustness. For each application (set of transactions) we considered a program that for each ordered pair of (possibly identical) transactions in the application, contains two processes executing that pair of transactions. Following Remark 2, the robustness of such a program implies the robustness of a *most general client* of the application that executes each transaction an arbitrary number of times and from an arbitrary number of processes. We focused on the cases where we could not find robustness violations in the first part. To build the "non-mover" relations M_{WR}, M_{WW}, and M_{RW} for the commutativity dependency graph, we use the left/right mover check provided by the CIVL verifier [33]. The results are reported in Table 2, the cells filled with "yes". We showed that the three applications Betting, CassandraLock and SimpleCurrencyExchange are robust against any semantics relative to some other stronger semantics. As mentioned earlier, all these robustness results are established for arbitrarily large executions and clients with an arbitrary number of processes. For instance, the robustness of SimpleCurrencyExchange ensures that when the exchange market owner observes a trade registered by a user, they observe also all the other trades that were done by this user in the past.

In conclusion, our experiments show that the robustness checking techniques we present are effective in proving or disproving robustness of concrete applications. Moreover, it shows that the robustness property for different combinations of consistency models is a relevant design principle, that can help in choosing the right consistency model for realistic applications, i.e., navigating the trade-off between consistency and performance (in general, weakening the consistency leads to better performance).

8 Related Work

The consistency models in this paper were studied in several recent works [21, 20, 25, 43, 16, 44, 14]. Most of them focused on their operational and axiomatic formalizations. The formal definitions we use in this paper are based on those given in [25, 16]. Biswas and Enea [14] shows that checking whether an execution is CC is polynomial time while checking whether it is PC or SI is NP-complete.

The robustness problem we study in this paper has been investigated in the context of weak memory models, but only relative to sequential consistency, against Release/Aquire (RA), TSO and Power [36, 17, 15, 29]. Checking robustness against CC and SI relative to SER has been investigated in [9, 10]. In this work, we study the robustness problem between two weak consistency models, which poses different non-trivial challenges. In particular, previous work proposed reductions to reachability under sequential consistency (or SER) that relied on a concept of minimal robustness violations (w.r.t. an operational semantics), which does not apply in our case. The relationship between PC and SER is similar in spirit to the one given by Biswas and Enea [14] in the context of checking whether an execution is PC. However, that relationship was proven in the context of a "weaker" notion of trace (containing only program order and read-from), and it does not extend to our notion of trace. For instance, that result does not imply preserving WW dependencies which is crucial in our case.

Some works describe various over- or under-approximate analyses for checking robustness relative to SER. The works in [13, 18, 19, 26, 40] propose static analysis techniques based on computing an abstraction of the set of computations, which is used for proving robustness. In particular, [19, 40] encode program executions under the weak consistency model using FOL formulas to describe the dependency relations between actions in the executions. These approaches may return false alarms due to the abstractions they consider in their encoding. Note that in this paper, we prove a strengthening of the results of [13] with regard to the shape of happens before cycles allowed under PC.

An alternative to *trace-based* robustness, is *state-based* robustness which requires that a program is robust if the sets of reachable states under two semantics coincide. While state-robustness is the necessary and sufficient concept for preserving state-invariants, its verification, which amounts in computing the set of reachable states under the weak semantics models is in general a hard problem. The decidability and the complexity of this problem has been investigated in the context of relaxed memory models such as TSO and Power, and it has been shown that it is either decidable but highly complex (non-primitive recursive), or undecidable [5, 6]. Automatic procedures for approximate reachability/invariant checking have been proposed using either abstractions or bounded analyses, e.g., [7, 4, 28, 1]. Proof methods have also been developed for verifying invariants in the context of weakly consistent models such as [37, 32, 41, 3]. These methods, however, do not provide decision procedures.

References

1. Abdulla, P.A., Atig, M.F., Bouajjani, A., Ngo, T.P.: Context-bounded analysis for POWER. In: Legay, A., Margaria, T. (eds.) Tools and Algorithms for the Construction and Analysis of Systems - 23rd International Conference, TACAS 2017, Held as Part of the European Joint Conferences on Theory and Practice of Software, ETAPS 2017, Uppsala, Sweden, April 22-29, 2017, Proceedings, Part II. Lecture Notes in Computer Science, vol. 10206, pp. 56–74 (2017). https://doi.org/10.1007/978-3-662-54580-5_4, https://doi.org/10.1007/978-3-662-54580-5_4
2. Adya, A.: Weak consistency: A generalized theory and optimistic implementations for distributed transactions. Ph.D. thesis (1999)
3. Alglave, J., Cousot, P.: Ogre and pythia: an invariance proof method for weak consistency models. In: Castagna, G., Gordon, A.D. (eds.) Proceedings of the 44th ACM SIGPLAN Symposium on Principles of Programming Languages, POPL 2017, Paris, France, January 18-20, 2017. pp. 3–18. ACM (2017), http://dl.acm.org/citation.cfm?id=3009883
4. Alglave, J., Kroening, D., Tautschnig, M.: Partial orders for efficient bounded model checking of concurrent software. In: Sharygina, N., Veith, H. (eds.) Computer Aided Verification - 25th International Conference, CAV 2013, Saint Petersburg, Russia, July 13-19, 2013. Proceedings. Lecture Notes in Computer Science, vol. 8044, pp. 141–157. Springer (2013). https://doi.org/10.1007/978-3-642-39799-8_9, https://doi.org/10.1007/978-3-642-39799-8_9
5. Atig, M.F., Bouajjani, A., Burckhardt, S., Musuvathi, M.: On the verification problem for weak memory models. In: Hermenegildo, M.V., Palsberg, J. (eds.) Proceedings of the 37th ACM SIGPLAN-SIGACT Symposium on Principles of Programming Languages, POPL 2010, Madrid, Spain, January 17-23, 2010. pp. 7–18. ACM (2010). https://doi.org/10.1145/1706299.1706303, https://doi.org/10.1145/1706299.1706303
6. Atig, M.F., Bouajjani, A., Burckhardt, S., Musuvathi, M.: What's decidable about weak memory models? In: Seidl, H. (ed.) Programming Languages and Systems - 21st European Symposium on Programming, ESOP 2012, Held as Part of the European Joint Conferences on Theory and Practice of Software, ETAPS 2012, Tallinn, Estonia, March 24 - April 1, 2012. Proceedings. Lecture Notes in Computer Science, vol. 7211, pp. 26–46. Springer (2012). https://doi.org/10.1007/978-3-642-28869-2_2, https://doi.org/10.1007/978-3-642-28869-2_2
7. Atig, M.F., Bouajjani, A., Parlato, G.: Getting rid of store-buffers in TSO analysis. In: Gopalakrishnan, G., Qadeer, S. (eds.) Computer Aided Verification - 23rd International Conference, CAV 2011, Snowbird, UT, USA, July 14-20, 2011. Proceedings. Lecture Notes in Computer Science, vol. 6806, pp. 99–115. Springer (2011). https://doi.org/10.1007/978-3-642-22110-1_9, https://doi.org/10.1007/978-3-642-22110-1_9
8. Barnett, M., Chang, B.E., DeLine, R., Jacobs, B., Leino, K.R.M.: Boogie: A modular reusable verifier for object-oriented programs. In: de Boer, F.S., Bonsangue, M.M., Graf, S., de Roever, W.P. (eds.) Formal Methods for Components and Objects, 4th International Symposium, FMCO 2005, Amsterdam, The Netherlands, November 1-4, 2005, Revised Lectures. Lecture Notes in Computer Science, vol. 4111, pp. 364–387. Springer (2005). https://doi.org/10.1007/11804192_17, https://doi.org/10.1007/11804192_17

9. Beillahi, S.M., Bouajjani, A., Enea, C.: Checking robustness against snapshot isolation. In: Dillig, I., Tasiran, S. (eds.) Computer Aided Verification - 31st International Conference, CAV 2019, New York City, NY, USA, July 15-18, 2019, Proceedings, Part II. Lecture Notes in Computer Science, vol. 11562, pp. 286–304. Springer (2019). https://doi.org/10.1007/978-3-030-25543-5_17, https://doi.org/10.1007/978-3-030-25543-5_17
10. Beillahi, S.M., Bouajjani, A., Enea, C.: Robustness against transactional causal consistency. In: Fokkink, W.J., van Glabbeek, R. (eds.) 30th International Conference on Concurrency Theory, CONCUR 2019, August 27-30, 2019, Amsterdam, the Netherlands. LIPIcs, vol. 140, pp. 30:1–30:18. Schloss Dagstuhl - Leibniz-Zentrum für Informatik (2019). https://doi.org/10.4230/LIPIcs.CONCUR.2019.30, https://doi.org/10.4230/LIPIcs.CONCUR.2019.30
11. Beillahi, S.M., Bouajjani, A., Enea, C.: Checking robustness between weak transactional consistency models. CoRR **abs/2101.09032** (2021), http://arxiv.org/abs/2101.09032
12. Berenson, H., Bernstein, P.A., Gray, J., Melton, J., O'Neil, E.J., O'Neil, P.E.: A critique of ANSI SQL isolation levels. In: Carey, M.J., Schneider, D.A. (eds.) Proceedings of the 1995 ACM SIGMOD International Conference on Management of Data, San Jose, California, USA, May 22-25, 1995. pp. 1–10. ACM Press (1995). https://doi.org/10.1145/223784.223785, https://doi.org/10.1145/223784.223785
13. Bernardi, G., Gotsman, A.: Robustness against consistency models with atomic visibility. In: Desharnais, J., Jagadeesan, R. (eds.) 27th International Conference on Concurrency Theory, CONCUR 2016, August 23-26, 2016, Québec City, Canada. LIPIcs, vol. 59, pp. 7:1–7:15. Schloss Dagstuhl - Leibniz-Zentrum für Informatik (2016). https://doi.org/10.4230/LIPIcs.CONCUR.2016.7, https://doi.org/10.4230/LIPIcs.CONCUR.2016.7
14. Biswas, R., Enea, C.: On the complexity of checking transactional consistency. Proc. ACM Program. Lang. **3**(OOPSLA), 165:1–165:28 (2019). https://doi.org/10.1145/3360591, https://doi.org/10.1145/3360591
15. Bouajjani, A., Derevenetc, E., Meyer, R.: Checking and enforcing robustness against TSO. In: Felleisen, M., Gardner, P. (eds.) Programming Languages and Systems - 22nd European Symposium on Programming, ESOP 2013, Held as Part of the European Joint Conferences on Theory and Practice of Software, ETAPS 2013, Rome, Italy, March 16-24, 2013. Proceedings. Lecture Notes in Computer Science, vol. 7792, pp. 533–553. Springer (2013). https://doi.org/10.1007/978-3-642-37036-6_29, https://doi.org/10.1007/978-3-642-37036-6_29
16. Bouajjani, A., Enea, C., Guerraoui, R., Hamza, J.: On verifying causal consistency. In: Castagna, G., Gordon, A.D. (eds.) Proceedings of the 44th ACM SIGPLAN Symposium on Principles of Programming Languages, POPL 2017, Paris, France, January 18-20, 2017. pp. 626–638. ACM (2017), http://dl.acm.org/citation.cfm?id=3009888
17. Bouajjani, A., Meyer, R., Möhlmann, E.: Deciding robustness against total store ordering. In: Aceto, L., Henzinger, M., Sgall, J. (eds.) Automata, Languages and Programming - 38th International Colloquium, ICALP 2011, Zurich, Switzerland, July 4-8, 2011, Proceedings, Part II. Lecture Notes in Computer Science, vol. 6756, pp. 428–440. Springer (2011). https://doi.org/10.1007/978-3-642-22012-8_34, https://doi.org/10.1007/978-3-642-22012-8_34
8. Brutschy, L., Dimitrov, D., Müller, P., Vechev, M.T.: Serializability for eventual consistency: criterion, analysis, and applications. In: Castagna, G., Gordon, A.D. (eds.) Proceedings of the 44th ACM SIGPLAN Symposium on Principles of Pro-

gramming Languages, POPL 2017, Paris, France, January 18-20, 2017. pp. 458–472. ACM (2017), http://dl.acm.org/citation.cfm?id=3009895
19. Brutschy, L., Dimitrov, D., Müller, P., Vechev, M.T.: Static serializability analysis for causal consistency. In: Foster, J.S., Grossman, D. (eds.) Proceedings of the 39th ACM SIGPLAN Conference on Programming Language Design and Implementation, PLDI 2018, Philadelphia, PA, USA, June 18-22, 2018. pp. 90–104. ACM (2018). https://doi.org/10.1145/3192366.3192415, https://doi.org/10.1145/3192366.3192415
20. Burckhardt, S.: Principles of eventual consistency. Found. Trends Program. Lang. **1**(1-2), 1–150 (2014). https://doi.org/10.1561/2500000011, https://doi.org/10.1561/2500000011
21. Burckhardt, S., Gotsman, A., Yang, H., Zawirski, M.: Replicated data types: specification, verification, optimality. In: Jagannathan, S., Sewell, P. (eds.) The 41st Annual ACM SIGPLAN-SIGACT Symposium on Principles of Programming Languages, POPL '14, San Diego, CA, USA, January 20-21, 2014. pp. 271–284. ACM (2014). https://doi.org/10.1145/2535838.2535848, https://doi.org/10.1145/2535838.2535848
22. Burckhardt, S., Leijen, D., Protzenko, J., Fähndrich, M.: Global sequence protocol: A robust abstraction for replicated shared state. In: Boyland, J.T. (ed.) 29th European Conference on Object-Oriented Programming, ECOOP 2015, July 5-10, 2015, Prague, Czech Republic. LIPIcs, vol. 37, pp. 568–590. Schloss Dagstuhl - Leibniz-Zentrum für Informatik (2015). https://doi.org/10.4230/LIPIcs.ECOOP.2015.568, https://doi.org/10.4230/LIPIcs.ECOOP.2015.568
23. Cahill, M.J., Röhm, U., Fekete, A.D.: Serializable isolation for snapshot databases. ACM Trans. Database Syst. **34**(4), 20:1–20:42 (2009). https://doi.org/10.1145/1620585.1620587, https://doi.org/10.1145/1620585.1620587
24. Cassandra-lock: https://github.com/dekses/cassandra-lock
25. Cerone, A., Bernardi, G., Gotsman, A.: A framework for transactional consistency models with atomic visibility. In: Aceto, L., de Frutos-Escrig, D. (eds.) 26th International Conference on Concurrency Theory, CONCUR 2015, Madrid, Spain, September 1.4, 2015. LIPIcs, vol. 42, pp. 58–71. Schloss Dagstuhl - Leibniz-Zentrum für Informatik (2015). https://doi.org/10.4230/LIPIcs.CONCUR.2015.58, https://doi.org/10.4230/LIPIcs.CONCUR.2015.58
26. Cerone, A., Gotsman, A.: Analysing snapshot isolation. J. ACM **65**(2), 11:1–11:41 (2018). https://doi.org/10.1145/3152396, https://doi.org/10.1145/3152396
27. Cerone, A., Gotsman, A., Yang, H.: Algebraic laws for weak consistency. In: Meyer, R., Nestmann, U. (eds.) 28th International Conference on Concurrency Theory, CONCUR 2017, September 5-8, 2017, Berlin, Germany. LIPIcs, vol. 85, pp. 26:1–26:18. Schloss Dagstuhl - Leibniz-Zentrum für Informatik (2017). https://doi.org/10.4230/LIPIcs.CONCUR.2017.26, https://doi.org/10.4230/LIPIcs.CONCUR.2017.26
28. Dan, A.M., Meshman, Y., Vechev, M.T., Yahav, E.: Effective abstractions for verification under relaxed memory models. Comput. Lang. Syst. Struct. **47**, 62–76 (2017). https://doi.org/10.1016/j.cl.2016.02.003, https://doi.org/10.1016/j.cl.2016.02.003
29. Derevenetc, E., Meyer, R.: Robustness against power is pspace-complete. In: Esparza, J., Fraigniaud, P., Husfeldt, T., Koutsoupias, E. (eds.) Automata, Languages, and Programming - 41st International Colloquium, ICALP 2014, Copenhagen, Denmark, July 8-11, 2014, Proceedings, Part II. Lecture Notes in Computer

Science, vol. 8573, pp. 158–170. Springer (2014). https://doi.org/10.1007/978-3-662-43951-7_14, https://doi.org/10.1007/978-3-662-43951-7_14
30. Difallah, D.E., Pavlo, A., Curino, C., Cudré-Mauroux, P.: Oltp-bench: An extensible testbed for benchmarking relational databases. Proc. VLDB Endow. **7**(4), 277–288 (2013). https://doi.org/10.14778/2732240.2732246, http://www.vldb.org/pvldb/vol7/p277-difallah.pdf
31. Experiments: https://github.com/relative-robustness/artifact
32. Gotsman, A., Yang, H., Ferreira, C., Najafzadeh, M., Shapiro, M.: 'cause i'm strong enough: reasoning about consistency choices in distributed systems. In: Bodík, R., Majumdar, R. (eds.) Proceedings of the 43rd Annual ACM SIGPLAN-SIGACT Symposium on Principles of Programming Languages, POPL 2016, St. Petersburg, FL, USA, January 20 - 22, 2016. pp. 371–384. ACM (2016). https://doi.org/10.1145/2837614.2837625, https://doi.org/10.1145/2837614.2837625
33. Hawblitzel, C., Petrank, E., Qadeer, S., Tasiran, S.: Automated and modular refinement reasoning for concurrent programs. In: Kroening, D., Pasareanu, C.S. (eds.) Computer Aided Verification - 27th International Conference, CAV 2015, San Francisco, CA, USA, July 18-24, 2015, Proceedings, Part II. Lecture Notes in Computer Science, vol. 9207, pp. 449–465. Springer (2015). https://doi.org/10.1007/978-3-319-21668-3_26, https://doi.org/10.1007/978-3-319-21668-3_26
34. Holt, B., Bornholt, J., Zhang, I., Ports, D.R.K., Oskin, M., Ceze, L.: Disciplined inconsistency with consistency types. In: Aguilera, M.K., Cooper, B., Diao, Y. (eds.) Proceedings of the Seventh ACM Symposium on Cloud Computing, Santa Clara, CA, USA, October 5-7, 2016. pp. 279–293. ACM (2016). https://doi.org/10.1145/2987550.2987559, https://doi.org/10.1145/2987550.2987559
35. Kozen, D.: Lower bounds for natural proof systems. In: 18th Annual Symposium on Foundations of Computer Science, Providence, Rhode Island, USA, 31 October - 1 November 1977. pp. 254–266. IEEE Computer Society (1977). https://doi.org/10.1109/SFCS.1977.16, https://doi.org/10.1109/SFCS.1977.16
36. Lahav, O., Margalit, R.: Robustness against release/acquire semantics. In: McKinley, K.S., Fisher, K. (eds.) Proceedings of the 40th ACM SIGPLAN Conference on Programming Language Design and Implementation, PLDI 2019, Phoenix, AZ, USA, June 22-26, 2019. pp. 126–141. ACM (2019). https://doi.org/10.1145/3314221.3314604, https://doi.org/10.1145/3314221.3314604
37. Lahav, O., Vafeiadis, V.: Owicki-gries reasoning for weak memory models. In: Halldórsson, M.M., Iwama, K., Kobayashi, N., Speckmann, B. (eds.) Automata, Languages, and Programming - 42nd International Colloquium, ICALP 2015, Kyoto, Japan, July 6-10, 2015, Proceedings, Part II. Lecture Notes in Computer Science, vol. 9135, pp. 311–323. Springer (2015). https://doi.org/10.1007/978-3-662-47666-6_25, https://doi.org/10.1007/978-3-662-47666-6_25
38. Lamport, L.: Time, clocks, and the ordering of events in a distributed system. Commun. ACM **21**(7), 558–565 (1978). https://doi.org/10.1145/359545.359563, https://doi.org/10.1145/359545.359563
39. Lipton, R.J.: Reduction: A method of proving properties of parallel programs. Commun. ACM **18**(12), 717–721 (1975). https://doi.org/10.1145/361227.361234, https://doi.org/10.1145/361227.361234
40. Nagar, K., Jagannathan, S.: Automated detection of serializability violations under weak consistency. In: Schewe, S., Zhang, L. (eds.) 29th International Conference on Concurrency Theory, CONCUR 2018, September 4-7, 2018, Beijing,

China. LIPIcs, vol. 118, pp. 41:1–41:18. Schloss Dagstuhl - Leibniz-Zentrum für Informatik (2018). https://doi.org/10.4230/LIPIcs.CONCUR.2018.41, https://doi.org/10.4230/LIPIcs.CONCUR.2018.41

41. Najafzadeh, M., Gotsman, A., Yang, H., Ferreira, C., Shapiro, M.: The CISE tool: proving weakly-consistent applications correct. In: Alvaro, P., Bessani, A. (eds.) Proceedings of the 2nd Workshop on the Principles and Practice of Consistency for Distributed Data, PaPoC@EuroSys 2016, London, United Kingdom, April 18, 2016. pp. 2:1–2:3. ACM (2016). https://doi.org/10.1145/2911151.2911160, https://doi.org/10.1145/2911151.2911160

42. Papadimitriou, C.H.: The serializability of concurrent database updates. J. ACM **26**(4), 631–653 (1979). https://doi.org/10.1145/322154.322158, https://doi.org/10.1145/322154.322158

43. Perrin, M., Mostéfaoui, A., Jard, C.: Causal consistency: beyond memory. In: Asenjo, R., Harris, T. (eds.) Proceedings of the 21st ACM SIGPLAN Symposium on Principles and Practice of Parallel Programming, PPoPP 2016, Barcelona, Spain, March 12-16, 2016. pp. 26:1–26:12. ACM (2016). https://doi.org/10.1145/2851141.2851170, https://doi.org/10.1145/2851141.2851170

44. Raad, A., Lahav, O., Vafeiadis, V.: On the semantics of snapshot isolation. In: Enea, C., Piskac, R. (eds.) Verification, Model Checking, and Abstract Interpretation - 20th International Conference, VMCAI 2019, Cascais, Portugal, January 13-15, 2019, Proceedings. Lecture Notes in Computer Science, vol. 11388, pp. 1–23. Springer (2019). https://doi.org/10.1007/978-3-030-11245-5_1, https://doi.org/10.1007/978-3-030-11245-5_1

45. Rackoff, C.: The covering and boundedness problems for vector addition systems. Theor. Comput. Sci. **6**, 223–231 (1978). https://doi.org/10.1016/0304-3975(78)90036-1, https://doi.org/10.1016/0304-3975(78)90036-1

46. Shapiro, M., Ardekani, M.S., Petri, G.: Consistency in 3d. In: Desharnais, J., Jagadeesan, R. (eds.) 27th International Conference on Concurrency Theory, CONCUR 2016, August 23-26, 2016, Québec City, Canada. LIPIcs, vol. 59, pp. 3:1–3:14. Schloss Dagstuhl - Leibniz-Zentrum für Informatik (2016). https://doi.org/10.4230/LIPIcs.CONCUR.2016.3, https://doi.org/10.4230/LIPIcs.CONCUR.2016.3

47. Shasha, D.E., Snir, M.: Efficient and correct execution of parallel programs that share memory. ACM Trans. Program. Lang. Syst. **10**(2), 282–312 (1988). https://doi.org/10.1145/42190.42277, https://doi.org/10.1145/42190.42277

48. Trade: https://github.com/Haiyan2/Trade

49. Twitter: https://github.com/edmundophie/cassandra-twitter

Verified Software Units

Lennart Beringer

Princeton University, Princeton NJ 08544, USA
eberinge@cs.princeton.edu

Abstract. Modularity - the partitioning of software into units of functionality that interact with each other via interfaces - has been the mainstay of software development for half a century. In case of the C language, the main mechanism for modularity is the compilation unit / header file abstraction. This paper complements programmatic modularity for C with modularity idioms for specification and verification in the context of Verifiable C, an expressive separation logic for CompCert Clight. Technical innovations include (i) *abstract predicate declarations* – existential packages that combine Parkinson & Bierman's abstract predicates with their client-visible reasoning principles; (ii) *residual* predicates, which help enforcing data abstraction in callback-rich code; and (iii) an application to pure (Smalltalk-style) objects that connects code verification to model-level reasoning about features such as subtyping, *self*, inheritance, and late binding. We introduce our techniques using concrete example modules that have all been verified using the Coq proof assistant and combine to fully linked verified programs using a novel, abstraction-respecting component composition rule for Verifiable C.

Keywords: Verified Software Unit · Abstract Predicate Declaration · Residual Predicate · Positive Subtyping · Verified Software Toolchain.

1 Introduction

Separation logic [61,53] constitutes a powerful framework for verifying functional correctness of imperative programs. Foundational implementations in interactive proof assistants such as Coq exploit the expressiveness of modern type theory to construct semantic models that feature higher-order impredicative quantification, step-indexing, and advanced notions of ghost state [4,36]. On the basis of proof rules that are justified w.r.t. the operational semantics of the programming language in question, these systems perform symbolic execution and employ multiple layers of tactical or computational proof automation to assist the engineer in the construction of concrete verification scripts. Perhaps most importantly, these implementations integrate software verification and model-level validation, by embedding assertions shallowly in the proof assistant's ambient logic; this permits specifications to refer to executable model programs or domain-specific constructions that are then amenable to code-independent analysis in Coq.

To realize the potential of separation logic, such implementations must be provided for mainstream languages and compatible with modern software engineering principles and programming styles. This paper addresses this challenge

N. Yoshida (Ed.): ESOP 2021, LNCS 12648, pp. 118–147, 2021.
https://doi.org/10.1007/978-3-030-72019-3_5

for Verifiable C, the program logic of the Verified Software Toolchain (VST [4]). We advance Verifiable C's methodology as follows.

1. We provide general infrastructure for *modular verification of modular programs* by extending Beringer and Appel's recent theory of function specification subsumption and intersection specifications [15] to a formal calculus for composing *verified software units* (VSUs) at their specification interface. Each VSU equips a compilation unit's header file with VST specifications of its API-exposed functions. Composition of VSUs matches the respective import and export interfaces, applying subsumption as necessary. Crucially, a compilation unit's private functions remain hidden and only need to be specified locally. Composition is compatible with source-level linking for CompCert Clight and supports repeated import of library modules (§3).
2. Utilizing existential abstraction [46] and parametricity, we extend work on abstract predicates [56] to provide clients with specification interfaces that differ in the degree to which module-internal representation details are revealed. This flexibility is achieved by codifying how the reasoning principles associated with a predicate can be selectively communicated to clients, using a device we call *(existentially) abstract predicate declarations* (APDs) (§4).
3. To investigate specification modularity in the presence of callbacks, we study variants of the subject-observer design pattern; we demonstrate that by complementing a module's *primary* predicate with *residual* predicates, representation hiding can be respected even at transient interaction points, where an invocation of a module's operation is interrupted, the module's invariant may be violated, and yet its internal state must remain unmodified and unexposed until the operation is resumed (§5).
4. We present a novel approach to foundational reasoning about object principles that modularly separates C code verification from model-level behavior. Exploiting the theory of positive subtyping [30], we cover subtyping, interfaces with multiple implementations, dynamic dispatch, *self*, and late binding, for a simple Smalltalk-style object model with static typing (§6).

This paper is accompanied by a development in Coq [14] that conservatively extends VST with the VSU infrastructure and contains several case studies. In addition to the examples detailed in the paper, the Coq code treats (i) the running example ("piles") of Beringer and Appel's development [15]; we retain their ability to substitute representation-altering but specification-preserving implementations; (ii) a variant of Barnett and Naumann's Master-Clock example [12], as another example of tightly coupled program units; and (iii) an implementation of the Composite design pattern, obtained by transcribing a development from the Verifast code base [35]. In addition, a VSU interface that unifies the APIs of B^+-trees and tries was recently developed by Kravchuk-Kirilyuk [40].

To see how APDs build on Parkinson and Bierman's work, consider a *concrete* representation predicate in the style of Reynolds [61]: list x α p specifies that address p represents a monotone list α of numbers greater than x:

$$\text{list x nil p} \stackrel{\text{def}}{=} (\text{p=null}) \ \& \ \mathsf{emp} \qquad \text{list x } (\text{a::}\alpha) \text{ p} \stackrel{\text{def}}{=} \exists \text{ q. a} > \text{x} \ \& \ \text{p} \mapsto \text{a, q} * \text{list a } \alpha \text{ q.}$$

Being defined in terms of $\mapsto$, this definition assumes a specific data layout (a two-field **struct**). Representation-specific predicates enable verification of concrete implementations of operations such as *reverse*. But a client-facing specification of the entire list module should only expose the predicate in its folded form – a simple case of an abstract predicate. Indeed, while VST fully supports API exposure of **struct**s (incl. stack allocation), all examples in this paper employ an essentially "dataless" programming discipline [8,60,37] in which **struct**s are at most exposed as forward declarations. Clearly, such programmatic encapsulation should not be compromised through the use of concrete predicate definitions.

To regulate whether a predicate is available in its abstract or unfolded form at a particular program point, Parkinson and Bierman employ a notion of scope: predicates are available in their unfolded form when in scope and are treated symbolically elsewhere. This separation can naturally align with the partitioning into compilation units, but is all-or-nothing. But even in the absence of specifications, *different clients need different interfaces*: C developments routinely provide multiple header files for a single code unit, differing in the amount to which representational information is exposed. Mundane examples include special-purpose interfaces for internal performance monitoring or debugging. Extending this observation to specifications means supporting multiple public invariants. Indeed, several levels of visibility are already conceivable for our simple list predicate:

- no (un)folding, no exposed reasoning principles: properties that follow from the predicate's definition cannot be exploited during client-side verification;
- no (un)folding, but reasoning principles are selectively exposed; for example, one may expose the model-level property that α is strictly increasing, or the fact that the head pointer is null exactly if α is empty;
- the set of exposed reasoning principles includes fold/unfold lemmas (perhaps with the least-fixed-point property inherent in the inductive definition of the predicate), but the internal representation of nodes is encapsulated using a further predicate; hence, implementations are free to select a different **struct** layout, for example by swapping the order of fields;
- the predicate definition is fully exposed, including the internal data layout.

APDs support such flexibility by combining zero or more abstract predicate *declarations* (no definitions, to maintain implementation-independence) with axioms that selectively expose the predicates' reasoning principles. In parallel to programmatic forward declarations, an APD is exported in the specification interface of an API and is substantiated – in implementation-dependent fashion – in the VST proof of the corresponding compilation unit. This substantiation includes the validation of the exposed axioms. When specifying the API of a module, the engineer may not only refer to any APDs introduced by the module in question, but may also assume APDs for data structures provided by other modules (whose header files are typically **#include**d in the API in question). Matching the APD assumptions and provisions of different modules occurs naturally during the application of our component linking rule, ensuring that fully linked programs contain no unresolved APD assumptions.

Before going into technical details, we first summarize key aspects of VST.

2 Program verification using VST

Verification using VST happens exclusively inside the Coq proof environment, and operates directly on abstract syntax trees of CompCert Clight. Typically, these ASTs result from feeding a C source file through CompCert's frontend, clightgen, but they may also originate from code synthesis. Either way, verification applies to the same code that is then manipulated by CompCert's optimization and backend phases. This eliminates the assurance gap that emerges when a compiler's (intermediate) representation diverges syntactically or semantically from a verification tool's representation. The absence of such gaps is the gist of VST's machine-checked soundness proof: verified programs are safe w.r.t. the operational semantics of Clight; this guarantee includes memory safety (absence of null-pointer dereferences, out-of-bounds array accesses, use-after-frees,...) but also absence of unintended numeric overflows or race conditions. As Clight code is still legal C code (although slightly simplified, and with evaluation order determinized), verification happens at a level the programmer can easily grasp.

In contrast to other verification tools, VST does not require source code to be annotated with specifications. Instead, the verification engineer writes specifications in a separate Coq file. By not mixing specifications (let alone aspects of proof, such as loop invariants) with source code, VST easily supports associating multiple specifications with a function and constructing multiple proofs for a given code/specification pair.

We write function specifications ϕ in the form $\{P\} \leadsto \{v.\ Q\}$ where v denotes the (sometimes existentially quantified) return value and P and Q are separation logic assertions. To shield details of its semantic model, VST exposes heap assertions using the type **mpred** rather than as direct Coq-level predicates. On top of **mpred**, assertions are essentially embedded shallowly, giving the user access to the logical and programmatic features of Coq when defining specifications.

VST's top-level notion asserting that a (closed) program p – which must include main, with a standard specification – has been verified in Coq is $\vdash p : G$ ("**semax_prog**"). Here, G – of type **funspecs**, i.e. associating specifications ϕ to function identifiers f – constitutes a witnessing proof context that contains specifications for all functions in p and must itself be justified: for each $(f, \phi_f) \in G$, the user must exhibit a Coq proof of $G \vdash f : \phi_f$ ("**semax_body**"), expressing that f satisfies ϕ_f under hypotheses in G. VST's step-indexed model ensures logical consistency in case of (mutual) recursion.

We exploit Beringer and Appel [15]'s theory of specification *subsumption* $\phi <: \psi$ which extends parameter adaptation [38,50,48] to step-indexed separation logics for C and allows a function verified w.r.t ϕ to be used by clients expecting specification ψ. This theory includes a notion of specification *intersection* $\wedge$ which – similar to, e.g. the `also` combinator of the Java Modelling Language (JML, [19])– allows functions to have multiple specifications. Noticeably, subsumption and intersection are related in formally the same manner as intersection types and subtyping are in type theory: in particular, they satisfy the laws $\phi_1 \wedge \phi_2 <: \phi_i$ (for $i \in \{1, 2\}$) and $\dfrac{\psi <: \phi_1 \quad \psi <: \phi_2}{\psi <: \phi_1 \wedge \phi_2}$ (cf. [58], page 206).

3 VSU calculus

As described above, VST verification amounts to exhibiting a G with $\vdash p : G$. In contrast to VST's previous linking regime, VSU ensures existence of G during component linking without actually constructing G, maintaining representation hiding and non-exposure of private functions. Indeed, the modules' specification interfaces (specs of imported and exported functions) suffice for proving that a suitable G exists, as long as each module's individual justification includes the verification of its private functions.

3.1 Components and soundness

VSU extends CompCert's distinction between internal functions (those equipped locally with a function body) and external functions (functions defined in other compilation units, incl. system functions). Given a Clight compilation unit p, we denote these (disjoint) sets by $\mathit{IntFuns}(p)$ and $\mathit{ExtFuns}(p)$, respectively. VSU further distinguishes between system functions (typically provided by the OS) and ordinary external functions: the former ones are not expected to be verified using VST even in a fully linked program, so VSU merely records their use.

VSU's main judgment is $\vdash_P^{\mathcal{S}} [\mathcal{I}]\, p\, [\mathcal{E}]$, to be read as *using specified imports* $\mathcal{I}$ *and system functions* $\mathcal{S}$*,* p *provides/ exports functions (with specifications)* $\mathcal{E}$*, using internal memory satisfying (initially)* P. The entities $\mathcal{S}$, $\mathcal{I}$, and $\mathcal{E}$ are all **funspecs**, while P specifies the memory holding p's global variables; P's formal type is **globals** $\rightarrow$ **mpred** where **globals** refers to a map from global identifiers to CompCert values.

The judgment $\vdash_P^{\mathcal{S}} [\mathcal{I}]\, p\, [\mathcal{E}]$ is formally introduced as an existential abstraction (in Coq: a **Record** type) over a proof context G, which is again of type **funspecs**:

$$\vdash_P^{\mathcal{S}} [\mathcal{I}]\, p\, [\mathcal{E}] \stackrel{\text{def}}{=} \exists G.\, G \vdash_P^{\mathcal{S}} [\mathcal{I}]\, p\, [\mathcal{E}].$$

The role of G is to serve as the witness justifying the specification interface; as such it associates specifications also to p's private functions; existentially hiding it shields implementation details.

The formation of the lower-level judgment $G \vdash_P^{\mathcal{S}} [\mathcal{I}]\, p\, [\mathcal{E}]$ is subject to the following constraints:

Definition 1. *Proof context G justifies a component (specification) for Clight compilation unit p with respect to system calls $\mathcal{S}$, imports $\mathcal{I}$, exports $\mathcal{E}$, and predicate P, notation $G \vdash_P^{\mathcal{S}} [\mathcal{I}]\, p\, [\mathcal{E}]$, if*

1. $\mathit{dom}\,\mathcal{I} \cap \mathit{dom}\,\mathcal{S} = \emptyset$ *and* $\mathit{dom}\,\mathcal{I} \cup \mathit{dom}\,\mathcal{S} \subseteq \mathit{ExtFuns}(p)$,
2. $\mathit{dom}\,G = \mathit{IntFuns}(p) \cup \mathit{dom}\,\mathcal{S}$, *with* $G(i) = \mathcal{S}(i)$ *whenever* $i \in \mathit{dom}\,\mathcal{S}$,
3. $\mathit{dom}\,\mathcal{E} \subseteq \mathit{dom}\,G$, *with* $G(i) <: \mathcal{E}(i)$ *for all* $i \in \mathit{dom}\,\mathcal{E}$,
4. $\mathcal{I} \cup G \vdash_{\mathsf{func}} \mathit{funs}_p : G$,
5. $\forall\, g, \mathsf{InitGPred}(\mathsf{Vardefs}(p))\, g \vdash P\, g$

The first three clauses are largely administrative; they express, respectively, that (1) system functions and imported functions are disjoint sets of external functions, (2) G contains specifications for exactly the system functions and the internal functions, and (3) all exported specifications are abstractions of entries in G, in the sense of specification subsumption $<:$.

Clause (4) constitutes the main proof obligation and refers to a slight refactoring of VST's function-verification judgment $G_1 \vdash_{\mathsf{func}} \mathit{funs} : G_2$ (**semax-func**), where *funs* associates CompCert function definitions with identifiers. The instantiation $\mathcal{I} \cup G \vdash_{\mathsf{func}} \mathit{funs}_p : G$ hence requires that imports $\mathcal{I}$ suffice for justifying all entries in G: each system function specification in G must be valid, and each specification of an internal function must be justified by a VST proof the corresponding function body in *funs*; calls to internal and system functions inside the body are resolved by reference to G, and calls to external functions are resolved by the import specifications, $\mathcal{I}$.

Finally, clause (5) requires p's global variables to collectively satisfy P (after initialization) but avoids referring to these variables by name.

We point out two further aspects of Definition 1. First, we note that system functions may be exported (we do not require $\mathit{dom}\,\mathcal{S} \cap \mathit{dom}\,\mathcal{E} = \emptyset$), and that imports and exports are distinct ($\mathit{dom}\,\mathcal{I} \cap \mathit{dom}\,\mathcal{E} = \emptyset$ follows). Second, we note that for $\mathcal{I} = \emptyset$, clause (4) yields $G \vdash_{\mathsf{func}} \mathit{funs}_p : G$, i.e. the heart of VST's soundness condition **semax_prog** for programs comprised of a single compilation unit. Hence, the goal of VSU verification is to exhaustively apply VSU's combination rule (presented in the next subsection) until all imports have been resolved.

Once a component has been verified and is exposed as $\vdash_P^{\mathcal{S}} [\mathcal{I}]\, p\, [\mathcal{E}]$, the specifications of p's private functions are hidden inside the existentially quantified context G and hence inaccessible.

3.2 Derived rules

It is easy to derive a rule of consequence from Definition 1 that strengthens imports and relaxes exports:

$$\frac{\mathcal{I}' <: \mathcal{I} \qquad \vdash_P^{\mathcal{S}} [\mathcal{I}]\, p\, [\mathcal{E}] \qquad \mathcal{E} \sqsubseteq \mathcal{E}' \qquad \forall g, P\, g \vdash P'\, g}{\vdash_{P'}^{\mathcal{S}} [\mathcal{I}']\, p\, [\mathcal{E}']}\ \text{VSUCONSEQ}$$

For imported functions, we require pointwise subsumption, by defining $\mathcal{I}' <: \mathcal{I}$ to hold if $\mathit{dom}\,\mathcal{I} = \mathit{dom}\,\mathcal{I}'$ and $\mathcal{I}'(i) <: \mathcal{I}(i)$ for all $i \in \mathit{dom}\,\mathcal{I}$. On the export side, we allow hiding of entries, by defining $\mathcal{E} \sqsubseteq \mathcal{E}'$ to hold if $\mathit{dom}\,\mathcal{E}' \subseteq \mathit{dom}\,\mathcal{E}$ and $\mathcal{E}(i) <: \mathcal{E}'(i)$ for all $i \in \mathit{dom}\,\mathcal{E}'$. The calculus is invariant in the specifications of system functions, but allows weakening of the initialization predicate. The derivation of this rule instantiates the context witnessing the concluding judgment by the (abstract) witness obtained from unfolding the hypothetical judgment.

VSU's workhorse is the composition rule, VSULINK, shown in Figure 1. The side conditions treat the components symmetrically and are motivated as follows. The rule constructs a component specification for a linked program p that retains the internal functions of p_1 and p_2, and also any unresolved external functions, as

$$
\begin{array}{ll}
(a) & \vdash^{\mathcal{S}_1}_{P_1} [\mathcal{I}_1]\, p_1\, [\mathcal{E}_1] \qquad \vdash^{\mathcal{S}_2}_{P_2} [\mathcal{I}_2]\, p_2\, [\mathcal{E}_2] \\[1ex]
(b) & \begin{array}{c} \forall i \in \mathit{IntFuns}(p_1) \cup (\mathit{ExtFuns}(p_1) \setminus \mathit{IntFuns}(p_2)), p(i) = p_1(i) \\ \forall i \in \mathit{IntFuns}(p_2) \cup (\mathit{ExtFuns}(p_2) \setminus \mathit{IntFuns}(p_1)), p(i) = p_2(i) \\ \mathit{dom}\, p = \mathit{dom}\, p_1 \cup \mathit{dom}\, p_2 \end{array} \\[1ex]
(c) & \begin{array}{c} \forall i \in (\mathit{IntFuns}(p_1) \cap \mathit{IntFuns}(p_2)) \cup (\mathit{ExtFuns}(p_1) \cap \mathit{ExtFuns}(p_2)),\ p_1(i) = p_2(i) \\ \forall i \in \mathit{IntFuns}(p_1) \cap \mathit{ExtFuns}(p_2),\ \mathit{sig}(p_1(i)) = \mathit{sig}(p_2(i)) \wedge i \in \mathit{dom}\, \mathcal{I}_2 \\ \forall i \in \mathit{IntFuns}(p_2) \cap \mathit{ExtFuns}(p_1),\ \mathit{sig}(p_2(i)) = \mathit{sig}(p_1(i)) \wedge i \in \mathit{dom}\, \mathcal{I}_1 \end{array} \\[1ex]
(d) & \mathit{dom}\, \mathcal{S}_1 \cap \mathit{IntFuns}(p_2) = \emptyset \qquad \mathit{dom}\, \mathcal{S}_2 \cap \mathit{IntFuns}(p_1) = \emptyset \\[1ex]
(e) & \begin{array}{c} \forall i \in \mathit{dom}\, \mathcal{I}_2 \cap (\mathit{dom}\, \mathcal{S}_1 \cup \mathit{IntFuns}(p_1)),\ i \in \mathit{dom}\, \mathcal{E}_1 \wedge \mathcal{E}_1(i) <: \mathcal{I}_2(i) \\ \forall i \in \mathit{dom}\, \mathcal{I}_1 \cap (\mathit{dom}\, \mathcal{S}_2 \cup \mathit{IntFuns}(p_2)),\ i \in \mathit{dom}\, \mathcal{E}_2 \wedge \mathcal{E}_2(i) <: \mathcal{I}_1(i) \end{array} \\[1ex]
(f) & \forall i \in \mathit{dom}\, \mathcal{I}_1 \cap \mathit{dom}\, \mathcal{I}_2,\ \mathcal{I}_1(i) = \mathcal{I}_2(i) \\[1ex]
(g) & \mathcal{I} = \mathcal{I}_1 \setminus (\mathit{dom}\, \mathcal{S}_2 \cup \mathit{IntFuns}(p_2)) \cup \mathcal{I}_2 \setminus (\mathit{dom}\, \mathcal{S}_1 \cup \mathit{IntFuns}(p_1)) \\[1ex]
(h) & \mathsf{Vardefs}(p_1) \cap \mathsf{Vardefs}(p_2) = \emptyset \quad \mathsf{Vardefs}(p_1) \cup \mathsf{Vardefs}(p_2) = \mathsf{Vardefs}(p) \\ \hline
 & \vdash^{\mathcal{S}_1 \curlywedge \mathcal{S}_2}_{P_1 * P_2} [\mathcal{I}]\, p\, [\mathcal{E}_1 \curlywedge \mathcal{E}_2]
\end{array}
$$

Fig. 1. VSU's rule of component composition, VSULink.

detailed in side conditions (b). Condition (c) requires functions classified identically by p_1 and p_2 to have identical definitions, and requires differently classified functions to have identical type signatures and be in the import set of the compilation unit not providing the implementation. Condition (d) formalizes that system functions are not locally defined in either unit. Condition (e) expresses that a function imported by one module and programmatically provided by the other module must be exported by the provider; this condition ensures that the export contract cannot be bypassed. Condition (f) expresses that functions imported by both units must be imported identically - if necessary, this can be achieved using the consequence rule. Condition (g) calculates the remaining import specifications by combining the constituent imports, removing entries for the resolved functions, and ensuring the absence of duplicates. The final condition, (h), mandates that global variables from p_1 and p_2 be distinct (hence initialization predicates have disjoint footprints) and propagated to p.

The most interesting aspect of the rule is the duplicate use of the intersection operator, $C_1 \curlywedge C_2$, for constructing the concluding specifications of exported functions and system functions. The general definition of this operator is

$$
C_1 \curlywedge C_2 := \lambda i. \begin{cases} C_1(i) \wedge C_2(i) & \text{if } i \in \mathit{dom}\, C_1 \cap \mathit{dom}\, C_2 \\ C_1(i) & \text{if } i \in \mathit{dom}\, C_1 \setminus \mathit{dom}\, C_2 \\ C_2(i) & \text{if } i \in \mathit{dom}\, C_2 \setminus \mathit{dom}\, C_1 \end{cases}
$$

where $\wedge$ denotes the specification intersection operator mentioned in Section 2. Thus, exporting $\mathcal{E}_1 \mathbin{\wedge\!\!\!\wedge} \mathcal{E}_2$ effectively exports both $\mathcal{E}_1$ and $\mathcal{E}_2$, and similarly for $\mathcal{S}_1 \mathbin{\wedge\!\!\!\wedge} \mathcal{S}_2$. Indeed, the individual export specifications can be reestablished using the consequence rule, as the properties of intersection specifications mentioned in Section 2 lift to (export specification) contexts: we have $C_1 \mathbin{\wedge\!\!\!\wedge} C_2 \sqsubseteq C_i$ for $i \in \{1,2\}$ and $\dfrac{X \sqsubseteq C_1 \quad X \sqsubseteq C_2}{X \sqsubseteq C_1 \mathbin{\wedge\!\!\!\wedge} C_2}$ for any X.

By permitting functions f that are internal to both p_1 and p_2, VSU supports diamond-shaped composition patterns in which a sub-component, e.g. a library, is imported multiple times. Conditions (*b*) and (*c*) ensure that all copies of a repeatedly imported function f have the same body (i.e. CompCert AST), and that this body is retained in p. However, the library's export specification may have been imported differently by the different units, hence G_1 and G_2 may well associate different (and formally incompatible) specifications with f. As G_1 and G_2 are existentially hidden, we cannot inspect these specifications: adding a side condition to the rule that mentions the specifications $G_1(f)$ and $G_2(f)$ would violate the abstraction principle. Nevertheless, the proof of the composition rule still requires us to attach *some* specification to the shared function, when constructing the witnessing context of the concluding judgment, G. Our solution is to use intersection $\mathbin{\wedge\!\!\!\wedge}$, i.e. to instantiate the witness G with $G_1 \mathbin{\wedge\!\!\!\wedge} G_2$ in the Coq proof of VSULINK. By terminating the Coq proof script with **Qed** rather than **Defined**, this instantiation is opaque to clients: applications of VSULINK during program verification merely see that *some* G exists.

Most side conditions of the rule are computational; in our applications of the rule in Sections 4.5 and 5, Coq's tactical engine solves the majority of them.

4 APDs and specification interfaces

We now turn to the organization of predicates and function specifications. Our organization reflects typical realizations of abstraction principles in C, where heap data structures are introduced using forward declarations and referred to via pointers in header files, while the selection of a concrete representation (perhaps using private static variables) is private to an implementation. We illustrate our approach using Parkinson and Bierman's connection pool example [56],

```
typedef struct database *Database;
typedef struct connection *Connection;
Connection consConn (Database d);
Database newDB (int DBidentifier);
```

```
#include "Connection.h"
typedef struct pool *Pool;
Pool consPool (Database d);
Connection getConn (Pool p);
void freeConn (Pool p, Connection c);
```

Fig. 2. Connection pools in C: Connection.h (left) and Connectionpool.h (right).

ported to C as an implementation of the APIs in Figure 2. Using forward declarations, the header files reveal only minimal information about the implementation. Connection.h allows clients to create a database entity (the parameter denotes a unique identifier; Parkinson and Bierman omit this constructor and do not model the type database explicitly) and to create connections to a database using the constructor consConn. Connectionpool.h models a collection of (dormant) connections associated with a database; clients construct a pool using consPool, request connections using getConn, and return them using freeConn.

4.1 Abstract predicate declarations (APDs)

Figure 3 introduces abstract predicate declarations for the three data structures. Each APD declares zero or more spatial predicates, i.e. **mpreds** relating a CompCert (pointer) value to suitable semantic information. Semantic information for the database is a DBindex (effectively a mathematical integer); connection and pool structures maintain pointers to the database; connections have additional internal state represented by the (abstract) type ConnTP.

```
Record DatabaseAPD := {
  DB: DBIndex → val → mpred;
  DB_ptrnull: ∀ db s, DB db s ⊢
     !!(is_pointer_or_null s) }.
Record PoolAPD := {
  CPool: val → val → mpred;
  CPool_ptrnull: ∀ d p, CPool d p ⊢
     !!(is_pointer_or_null p) }.

Record ConnectionAPD := {
  ConnTP:Type;
  Conn: (val * ConnTP) → val → mpred;
  NextConn: ConnTP → globals → mpred;
  Conn_isptr: ∀ C c, Conn C c ⊢ !!(isptr c);
  Conn_validptr: ∀ C c, Conn C c ⊢
                        valid_pointer c }.
```

Fig. 3. APDs for the connection pool example. val is CompCert's type of values.

Specifically, DatabaseAPD corresponds to the Database type declaration in Connection.h and asserts existence of a predicate DB, together with an axiom that enables clients to store a reference to a database in their own data structure. Operator !! injects a Coq proposition into VST's assertion language.

In similar style, ConnectionAPD and PoolAPD declare predicates Conn and CPool for the **struct** declarations connection and pool. In contrast to Parkinson and Bierman, we model that the connection module maintains state using the predicate NextConn. There is no need to reveal the concrete static variable used by our implementation though: **globals** denotes the collection of all such variables in VST. We assert that the head values of Conn and CPool are provably nonnull pointers and that a Conn's head pointer is furthermore valid.

All APDs are introduced as (dependent) **Record** types in Coq. We will construct values of these types in Section 4.3, i.e. implementation-dependent concrete predicate definitions and lemmas validating the axioms. But first, we use the APD types abstractly to introduce specifications for the two modules.

4.2 Abstract specification interfaces (ASIs)

Abstract specification interfaces (ASIs) consist of VST specifications for the API-exposed functions, parametric in all relevant APDs. In addition to the APDs introduced above, our example uses a third APD, denoted M, that declares an abstract predicate $\mathsf{Mem_M}\ \mathsf{gv}$ and represents the malloc/free library.

Figure 4 shows the ASI of Connection.h. We use subscripts to refer to the APD parameters: for example, $\mathsf{DB_D}\ i\ p$ is the **mpred** obtained by applying the DB component of a database APD D to index i and pointer value p.

Function	Spec
newDB(i; gv)	$\{\mathsf{Mem_M}\ \mathsf{gv}\} \rightsquigarrow \{p.\ \mathsf{DB_D}\ i\ p * \mathsf{Mem_M}\ \mathsf{gv}\}$
consConn(d; gv)	$\{\mathsf{DB_D}\ i\ d * \mathsf{NextConn_C}\ c\ \mathsf{gv} * \mathsf{Mem_M}\ \mathsf{gv}\} \rightsquigarrow$ $\left\{p.\begin{array}{l}\text{if } p = \text{null then } \mathsf{NextConn_C}\ c\ \mathsf{gv} * \mathsf{DB_D}\ i\ d * \mathsf{Mem_M}\ \mathsf{gv}\\ \text{else } \exists c'.\ \mathsf{NextConn_C}\ c'\ \mathsf{gv} * \mathsf{Conn_C}\ (d,c)\ p * \mathsf{DB_D}\ i\ d * \mathsf{Mem_M}\ \mathsf{gv}\end{array}\right\}$

Fig. 4. ASI for Connection.h, parametric in databases (D), connections (C), and memory systems (M). $\mathsf{Mem_M}\ \mathsf{gv}$ represents M's abstract predicate for a memory manager that is accessed by malloc and free.

A specification $\mathrm{F}(\vec{x};\mathsf{gv}) : \{Pre\} \rightsquigarrow \{v.\ Post\}$ is to be understood in safety-guaranteeing partial-correctness style, where $\vec{x}$ denotes a list of actual arguments (of type val), gv refers to (if present) the global environment, v (again of type val) represents the return value (if present), and other items are implicitly universally quantified. Callers of such a function select instantiations for the universally quantified entities ("witnesses") and must then establish *Pre*.

Thus, the specification of newDB asserts that a new database entity satisfying $\mathsf{DB_D}\ i\ p$ is allocated at the return value p, for the database with index i (an input argument). The allocation draws upon the abstract predicate $\mathsf{Mem_M}\ \mathsf{gv}$ which is "located" at some global variable that is private to the malloc/free library.

The specification of constructor consConn refers to $\mathsf{Mem_M}\ \mathsf{gv}$ in similar fashion and advances the module's connection counter from c to some c' upon success; in contrast to Parkinson and Bierman, we also support unsuccessful requests.

The ASI for Connectionpool.h in Figure 5 is additionally parametric in an PoolAPD, P. Our specifications are again slightly more precise than the ones given by Parkinson and Bierman. As a consequence, the precondition of a sequence such as $p :=$ `consPool`$(s); c :=$ `getConn`$(s);$ `freeConn`(p, c) is $\mathsf{DB_D}\ i\ d * \mathsf{Mem_M}\ \mathsf{gv} * \mathsf{NextConn_C}\ s\ \mathsf{gv}$ rather then **emp**, hence exposing the reliance on the memory manager etc..Prefixing the instruction $d :=$ `newDB`(i) establishes $\mathsf{DB_D}\ i\ d$; we will explain how the latter two conjuncts are provided in Section 4.5.

4.3 Verification of ASI-specified compilation units

Substantiating the ASI of a header file, means to give – for a concrete implementation – concrete definitions for the predicates in the newly introduced APDs,

Function	Spec
$\mathsf{consPool}(d;\mathsf{gv})$	$\{\mathsf{Mem_M\ gv}\} \rightsquigarrow \{p.\ \mathsf{CPool_P}\ d\ p * \mathsf{Mem_M\ gv}\}$
$\mathsf{getConn}(p;\mathsf{gv})$	$\{\mathsf{CPool_P}\ d\ p * \mathsf{DB_D}\ i\ d * \mathsf{NextConn_C}\ c\ \mathsf{gv} * \mathsf{Mem_M\ gv}\} \rightsquigarrow \left\{ n. \begin{array}{l} \mathsf{CPool_P}\ d\ p * \mathsf{DB_D}\ i\ d * \mathsf{Mem_M\ gv} * \\ \text{if } n = \text{null then } \mathsf{NextConn_C}\ c\ \mathsf{gv} \\ \text{else } \exists c'\ c''.\ \mathsf{NextConn_C}\ c'\ \mathsf{gv} * \mathsf{Conn_C}\ (d,c'')\ n \end{array} \right\}$
$\mathsf{freeConn}(p,i;\mathsf{gv})$	$\{\mathsf{CPool_P}\ d\ p * \mathsf{Conn_C}\ (d,c)\ i * \mathsf{Mem_M\ gv}\} \rightsquigarrow \{\mathsf{CPool_P}\ d\ p * \mathsf{Mem_M\ gv}\}$

Fig. 5. The ASI for Connectionpool.h is parametric in a database APD (D), a connection APD (C), a connection pool APD (P), and a memory manager APD (M). As consPool takes a formal parameter d, the reader may have expected the specification $\{\mathsf{DB_D}\ i\ d * \mathsf{Mem_M\ gv}\} \rightsquigarrow \{p.\ \mathsf{CPool_P}\ d\ p * \mathsf{DB_D}\ i\ d * \mathsf{Mem_M\ gv}\}$ which is indeed derivable from the one given using VST's frame rule.

show that these definitions validate the associated axioms, and finally construct a VSU that has the ASI's specifications as the export interface $\mathcal{E}$. All these constructions are parametric in the APDs provided by other modules.

We refer the reader to our source code [14] for the C implementation, the (concrete) predicate definitions, and the proofs of the APD-supporting axioms. In case of Connection.c, these proofs reveal the instantiation of the APD's ConnTP to Coq's type of integers, Z, corresponding to the existence of a global integer variable in the C code that maintains a connection counter; the corresponding $. \mapsto .$ predicate then furnishes the abstract predicate NextConn.

The substantiations of a unit's APDs are subsequently used to instantiate its ASI and the specifications of its imported function, yielding (together with specifications of private functions) a proof context G that the unit's local function bodies are then verified against. APDs provided by other compilation units are left abstract, so expose only their axioms. Specifically, the substantiation for Connection.c yields values c and d of types ConnectionAPD and DatabaseAPD, respectively, the predicate $N = \mathsf{NextConn}\ c\ 0$, and a VSU

$$\mathsf{VSU_{Conn}} \stackrel{\text{def}}{=} \vdash^{\emptyset}_{N} [\mathcal{I}_{\mathtt{Conn}}]\ \mathit{Connection.prog}\ [\mathcal{E}_{\mathtt{Conn}}]$$

where $\mathcal{E}_{\mathtt{Conn}}$ is the partial specialization of the specifications in Figure 4 to C $= c$ and D $= d$, *Connection.prog* is CompCert's AST for Connection.c, and $\mathcal{I}_{\mathtt{Conn}}$ contains a specification for surelymalloc. For ConnectionPool.c, we similarly obtain a value p of type ConnectionpoolAPD and a VSU

$$\mathsf{VSU_{Pool}} \stackrel{\text{def}}{=} \vdash^{\emptyset}_{\mathtt{emp}} [\mathcal{I}_{\mathtt{Pool}}]\ \mathit{Connectionpool.prog}\ [\mathcal{E}_{\mathtt{Pool}}],$$

where $\mathcal{I}_{\mathtt{Pool}}$ is comprised of the (abstract) specification of consConn and specifications for free and surelymalloc, and $\mathcal{E}_{\mathtt{Pool}}$ is the partial specialization of Figure 5 to P $= p$. Both VSUs are parametric in M, but $\mathsf{VSU_{Pool}}$'s additional parameters D and C are instantiated when $\mathsf{VSU_{Conn}}$ and $\mathsf{VSU_{Pool}}$ are combined using rule VSULink. The result, $\mathsf{VSU_{CP}}$, is still parametric in M but has resolved the imports of consConn, leaving only imports for free and surelymalloc.

4.4 A VSU for a malloc-free library

A recent application of VST is Appel and Naumann's verification of a malloc/free library [5]. Internally maintaining a fixed number of freelists – for entities of different size – this library exposes four functions in its API: malloc, free, pre_fill, try_pre_fill. When porting this development to the VSU framework, these give rise to two ASIs. The first one contains specifications for all four functions and is suitable for resource-aware clients. It employs the APD MallocFree_R_APD:

Record MallocTokenAPD := {
  malloc_token': share → Z → val → mpred;
  malloc_token'_valid_pointer: ∀ sh sz p, malloc_token' sh sz p ⊢ valid_pointer p;
  malloc_token'_facts: ∀ sh sz p, malloc_token' sh sz p ⊢ !! malloc_compatible sz p }.
Record MallocFree_R_APD :=
  { MF_Tok_R :> MallocTokenAPD; mem_mgr_R: resvec → globals → mpred }.

mem_mgr_R models the freelists as a resource vector that indicates the length of each freelist. The predicate malloc token' refers to the piece of memory that is typically located at a small negative offset of a malloc'ed entity and holds administrative information of the library, but conceptually, it also constitutes a token that enables clients to share malloc'ed entities among different threads without loosing the ability to safely free entities. The second ASI only exposes malloc and free, and employs the more abstract APD

Record MallocFreeAPD :=
  { MF_Tok :> MallocTokenAPD; mem_mgr: globals → mpred }.

MF_Tok still presents a malloc token but mem_mgr now hides the existence of freelists - indeed, constructing a MallocFreeAPD from a MallocFree_R_APD simply quantifies existentially over a resource vector. Our proofs first refactor the prior verification as a VSU that exports a resource-aware ASI and then use VSUCONSEQ (and export restriction ⊑ from Section 3.2) to weaken the resulting VSU to a VSU that only exports a resource-ignorant ASI. We denote the latter as $\mathsf{VSU}_{\mathtt{MF}}$; the predicate $\mathsf{Mem}_{\mathsf{M}}$ gv is now revealed to be a shorthand for mem_mgr gv, parametric in a MallocFreeAPD M, and we use $\mathsf{Mem}_{\mathtt{MF}}$ gv below to refer to its instantiation for $\mathsf{VSU}_{\mathtt{MF}}$.

4.5 Putting it all together

Using VSULINK again, we link $\mathsf{VSU}_{\mathtt{CP}}$ with a library VSU (reducing surelymalloc to malloc and the system function exit) and then with $\mathsf{VSU}_{\mathtt{MF}}$, obtaining

$$\mathsf{VSU}_{\mathtt{AppLib}} \stackrel{\text{def}}{=} \vdash^{\mathcal{S}_{\mathtt{Core}}}_{\mathsf{Mem}_{\mathtt{MF}} * N} [\,]\ \mathit{coreprog}\ [\mathcal{E}_{\mathtt{Core}}].$$

Here, *coreprog* contains all code (application plus library) with the exception of main. Note that $\mathsf{VSU}_{\mathtt{AppLib}}$'s set of imports is empty; $\mathcal{S}_{\mathtt{Core}}$ contains axiomatic specifications of OS functions such as exit and mmap.

Independent from the construction of $\mathsf{VSU}_{\mathtt{AppLib}}$ we verify main, i.e. an exemplary client or unit test, as a **semax_body** statement w.r.t. a not yet instantiated copy of $\mathcal{E}_{\mathsf{Core}}$. The specification that main is verified against a <: specialization of VST's general main_spec but is still abstract in the APDs of the application's code modules – see [14] for details.

Finally, we connect $\mathsf{VSU}_{\mathtt{AppLib}}$ with the verification of main to obtain a proof of VST's **semax_prog** statement. It is in this last proof that the satisfaction of the abstract initialization predicates for the global variables, $\mathsf{Mem}_{\mathsf{MF}}$ and N, is established from VST's internal initialization predicates.

5 Modular verification of the Subject/Observer pattern

Programs in imperative or object-oriented languages often contain callbacks: chains of function calls $A.m() \to B.n() \to A.l()$ between modules A and B in which m's invocation of n (and hence the return of control to A in the call to l) happens when A's state is *invalid*, i.e. does not satisfy A's invariant. Clearly, mandating satisfaction of the invariant in l's precondition – a typical requirement of API-level specifications – then prevents the verification of n.

A typical example is the chain update $\to$ notify $\to$ get in the subject-observer pattern, a widely used design pattern [23] that has served as a litmus test for modular specification of callback-rich programming in the literature. Figures 6 and 7 contain excerpts of a transcription of Parkinson's [55] code into[1] C. Each Subject maintains a list of subscribers – a list of observers that will be notified whenever the Subject's state is updated and then synchronize their internal state accordingly using get. The intended invariants express that each Subject's observers are in sync – a property that is violated during update's traversal of its observer list, when not-yet-notified observers are out of sync but (precisely in order to get back in sync) nevertheless invoke get.

The dominant technique for dealing with such situations in SMT-based tools employs ghost fields that track validity and unfolding of invariants and are supported by further (ghost) infrastructure that controls ownership (see e.g. [47,11]). However, this does not necessarily achieve comprehensive representation hiding: for example, the permission to violate Subject's invariant in get's precondition propagates to the precondition of notify, allowing the latter function to access the field[2] Subject.value. Furthermore, the invariant-regulating techniques typically require that SMT solving be carried out on a whole-program basis.

The flexibility of APDs to introduce multiple predicates enables an alternative in which callbacks are specified using special-purpose predicates that – similar to typestates [62] – emphasize protocol-style behavior, do not reveal the

---

[1] Our implementation [14] contains two further callbacks, newObs $\to$ registr $\to$ notify and registr $\to$ notify $\to$ get; the former one commences in the constructor, before any invariant has been established.

[2] For example, one may insert abstraction-violating get/putfield instructions in the subject-observer code at http://comcom.csail.mit.edu/e4pubs/{#}observer. This tool implements an advanced variant of invariance regulation using ghost instructions, semantic collaboration [59], for Eiffel. Fields are not private, and the methodology does not prevent representation exposure between such closely coupled classes.

```
/* SubjectObserver.h */
typedef struct subject *Subject;
typedef struct observer *Observer;

/* Subject.h*/
#include "SubjectObserver.h"
Subject newSubject (void);
void registr (Subject s, Observer o);
void update (Subject s, int n);
int get (Subject s);
int freeSubject(Subject s);
Observer detachfirst(Subject s);

/*Observer.h */
#include "SubjectObserver.h"
Observer newObs (Subject s);
void notify (Observer o);
int val (Observer o);
void freeObserver (Observer o);
```

```
/* Subject_rep.h */
#include "SubjectObserver.h"
typedef struct node *Node;
struct node {
  Observer obs;
  struct node * next;
};
struct subject {
  Node obs;
  unsigned value;
};

/*Observer_rep.h*/
#include "SubjectObserver.h"
struct observer {
  Subject sub;
  int cache;
};
```

Fig. 6. Subject/Observer: header files. The left column shows the public APIs; Subject_rep.h and Observer_rep.h are private to their respective module implementations.

```
/* Subject c */
#include "surelyMalloc.h"
#include "Observer.h"
#include "Subject.h"
#include "Subject_rep.h"

int get (Subject s) { return (s→ value); };
void update (Subject s, int v) {
  s→ value = v; Node n = s →obs;
  while (n) { notify(n→ obs); n = n →next; } }
```

```
/* Observer.c */
#include "surelyMalloc.h"
#include "Observer.h"
#include "Subject.h"
#include "Observer_rep.h"

void notify (Observer o) {
  o →cache = get(o →sub);
  return; }
```

Fig. 7. Excerpts from Subject.c and Observer.c for the callback update → notify → get.

validity of module invariants, and maintain representational hiding by being just as abstract as a module's main predicate.

Concretely, our approach employs semantic subjects that are comprised of a list of observer references and a (current) value, while observers are represented as a subject pointer and the cache:

Definition SubjRep:= (list val) ∗ Z. **Definition** ObsRep := val ∗ Z.

Next, our APDs complement the predicates relevant for API calls by external clients, Srep and Orep, by (residual) predicates for calling the Subject functions registr, update, and get, and the Observer functions notify and val; we also introduce a predicate for the postcondition of get, GetPost:

Record SubjectAPD := {
Srep, RegPre, UpdPre, GetPre, GetPost: SubjRep → val → mpred;
SubjRegister: ∀ S s, Srep S s ⊢ RegPre S s;
SubjUpdate: ∀ S s, Srep S s ⊢ UpdPre S s;
SubjGetPrePost: ∀ S s, Srep S s ⊢ GetPre S s ∗ (GetPost S s -∗ Srep S s);
GetPre_ptrnull: ∀ S s, GetPre S s ⊢ !!(is_pointer_or_null s) }

Record ObserverAPD := { Orep, NtfPre, ValPre: ObsRep → val → mpred;
ObsNtfy: ∀ O o, Orep O o ⊢ NtfPre O o; ObsVal: ∀ O o, Orep O o ⊢ ValPre O o;
NtfPre_isptr: ∀ O o, NtfyPre O o ⊢ !!(isptr o) }

Entailment axioms such as SubjUpdate permit external clients to invoke callback functions directly but may be omitted for functions that should *only* be invoked via callbacks. The residual predicates sanction indirect invocations via callbacks without revealing the satisfaction status of module-internal invariants.

Axiom SubjGetPrePost splits Srep into a token that can (only) be used to invoke get, plus a token for reestablishing Srep from GetPost. The latter is a separating implication −∗ rather than an entailment: it represents the requirement that an observer yields back control to its subject after completing a callback to get – the subject had retained part of its state prior to invoking notify.

To enforce these behaviors, we employ the specifications in Figures 8 and 9; again, the ASIs are parametric in all APDs mentioned, notwithstanding the mutual dependence of the modules. Using axiom SubjGetPrePost, one may show

Function	Spec
update(s, v)	$\{\mathsf{UpdPre}_{\mathsf{SP}}\ (l, z)\ s * \mathsf{Observers}\ \mathsf{NtfPre}_{\mathsf{OP}}\ s\ \mathit{vals}\ l\}$ $\leadsto \{\mathsf{Srep}_{\mathsf{SP}}\ (l, v)\ s * \mathsf{Observers}\ \mathsf{Orep}_{\mathsf{OP}}\ s\ v^{\lvert l \rvert}\ l\}$
get(s)	$\{\mathsf{GetPre}_{\mathsf{SP}}\ S\ s\} \leadsto \{p.\ !!(p = \mathit{snd}(S))\ \&\&\ \mathsf{GetPost}_{\mathsf{SP}}\ S\ s\}$

Fig. 8. ASI of Subject (excerpt), parametric in a SubjectAPD (SP), an ObserverAPD (OP), and a MemoryAPD (M).

that the specifications for get and notify are in subsumption relationship with large-footprint counterparts that permit invocations by external clients:

$$\{\mathsf{Srep}_{\mathsf{SP}}\ S\ s\} \leadsto \{p.\ !!(p = \mathit{snd}\ S)\ \&\&\ \mathsf{Srep}_{\mathsf{SP}}\ S\ s\}$$
$$\{\mathsf{NtfPre}_{\mathsf{OP}}\ (s, c)\ o * \mathsf{Srep}_{\mathsf{SP}}\ S\ s\} \leadsto \{\mathsf{Orep}_{\mathsf{OP}}\ (s, \mathit{snd}\ S)\ o * \mathsf{Srep}_{\mathsf{SP}}\ S\ s\}$$

The specification of update makes reference to an auxiliary Coq function that represents the "big" separating conjunction $*_{(v,o) \in combine(vals,l)} P\,(s, v)\, o$,

Observers (P:ObsRep → val → mpred) (s:val) (*vals*: list Z) (l: list val): mpred.

The substantiation of these interfaces relative to our C implementations defines the main predicates as

Definition Srep $(l, v)\ s := \exists o.$ listrep $l\ o * s \overset{\mathsf{Ews}}{\longmapsto}_{\mathsf{STP}} (o, v * \mathsf{Mtok}(\mathsf{Ews}, \mathsf{STP}, s)$.

Definition Orep $O\ o := o \overset{\mathsf{Ews}}{\longmapsto}_{\mathsf{OTP}} O * \mathsf{Mtok}(\mathsf{Ews}, \mathsf{OTP}, o)$.

Function	Spec
newObs(s; gv)	$\{\mathsf{RegPre}_{\mathsf{SP}}\ S\ s * \mathsf{Mem}_{\mathsf{M}}\ \mathsf{gv}\} \leadsto$ $\{p.\ \mathsf{Orep}_{\mathsf{OP}}\ (s, \mathit{snd}\ S)\ p * \mathsf{Srep}_{\mathsf{SP}}(p :: \mathit{fst}\ S, \mathit{snd}\ S)\ s * \mathsf{Mem}_{\mathsf{M}}\ \mathsf{gv}\}$
notify(o)	$\{\mathsf{NtfPre}_{\mathsf{OP}}(s, c)\ o * \mathsf{GetPre}_{\mathsf{SP}}\ S\ s\} \leadsto$ $\{\mathsf{Orep}_{\mathsf{OP}}(s, \mathit{snd}\ S)\ o * \mathsf{GetPost}_{\mathsf{SP}}\ S\ s\}$
val(o)	$\{\mathsf{ValPre}_{\mathsf{OP}}\ (s, c)\ o\} \leadsto \{c.\ \mathsf{Orep}_{\mathsf{OP}}\ (s, c)\ o\}$
freeObserver(o; gv)	$\{\mathsf{Orep}_{\mathsf{OP}}\ O\ o * \mathsf{Mem}_{\mathsf{M}}\ \mathsf{gv}\} \leadsto \{\mathsf{Mem}_{\mathsf{M}}\ \mathsf{gv}\}$

Fig. 9. ASI of Observer, parametric in APDs SP, OP, and M.

Here, listrep is a typical list representation predicate over Node items, modeling the observers associated with a Subject. STP and OTP are shorthands for Clight's representation of the struct definitions Subject and Observer, Ews represents an exclusive writable share in VST, and Mtok(.,.,.) is a variant of predicate malloc_token' from Section 4.4.

Some residual predicates are minor variants of Srep and Orep. For example,

Definition NtfyPre $O\ o := \mathsf{Mtok}(\mathsf{Ews}, \mathsf{OTP}, o) * \exists v.\ o \overset{\mathsf{Ews}}{\longmapsto}_{\mathsf{OTP}} (\mathit{fst}\ O, v)$.

existentially abstracts over $\mathit{snd}\ O$ but is otherwise identical to Orep. This makes validating axiom ObsNtfy trivial. As NtfyPre does not depend on a subject's value, no modification of the latter can affect the former's. Other residual predicates – like RegPre – are even definitionally equal to the main predicates, but the APD mechanism ensures that this fact is not exposed to clients.

Our C implementation permits GetPre and GetPost to actually be defined identically (indeed, getters typically don't alter data structures...):

Definition GetPrePost $(l, v)\ s := s.\mathsf{value} \overset{\mathsf{Ews}}{\longmapsto}_{\mathsf{STP}} v * \mathsf{Mtok}(\mathsf{Ews}, \mathsf{STP}, s)$.

Here, the $p.\pi \overset{sh}{\longmapsto}_t v$ is a variant of $p \overset{sh}{\longmapsto}_t v$ that specifies the content at $p.\pi$, where path π is a list of field names and array subscripts. Thus, GetPrePost only specifies the content of s.value; the remaining portion of s is exactly what is retained when SubjGetPrePost splits off GetPre from a Subject. The motivation for this handling is that the invariant of the loop in update (which contains the callback to get via notify) only traverses the node list. Specifically, an invariant involving the full Srep would not ensure that the spine of the list remains unchanged, as the definition of Srep quantifies existentially over the node list. This aspect illustrates the danger of predicates that are too abstract to be useful.

Constructing VSUs for `Subject` and `Observer` proceeds straight-forwardly; we exercise VSU's support for shared libraries by first combining surelyMalloc with each of these VSUs separately, before linking the resulting VSUs with each other, with $\mathsf{VSU}_{\mathsf{MF}}$, and with a main client as described in Section 4.5.

5.1 Specification and proof reuse

To evaluate specification modularity and proof reuse, we verified several variations of our implementation. First, to evaluate robustness under representational change, we have Subject internally maintain a freelist of Observer nodes:

```
struct subject { Node fl; Node obs; unsigned value; };
```

The freelist is drawn upon in registr (we only invoke surely_malloc if fl is null) and replenished in detachfirst. Constructor newSubject creates an empty freelist, and freeSubject frees the entire list.

The code modification triggers new Clight ASTs, but the majority of Coq files can then simply be reprocessed: the model-level definitions, APDs, and ASIs of Subject and Observer remain unchanged, and so do the files associated with verifying Observer, linking, and main. The *only* modifications are in the implementation-dependent validation of Subject, namely in the definitions of the representation predicates and in the VST proofs of the individual functions.

Second, we verified a variant in which notify's invocation of get is replaced by a function pointer. The key code modifications are

```
/*Addition in SubjectObserver.h*/          /*Modification in Observer.h*/
typedef int (*callback)(Subject s);        void notify (Observer o, callback f);

/*Modification in Observer.c*/
void notify (Observer o, callback f) { o→cache = f(o→sub); return; };
```

The calls to notify in update and registr obtain the additional argument &get, and the specification of get can be removed from the imports of the Observer VSU. The small specification of notify becomes

$$\mathsf{notify}(o,g):\ \begin{array}{l}\{\mathsf{NtfPre}\ (s,c)\ o * \mathsf{GetPre_{SP}}\ S\ s * \mathsf{funcptr'}\ \phi_{\mathsf{get}}\ g\}\\ \rightsquigarrow\ \{\mathsf{Orep_{OP}}(s, \mathit{snd}\ S)\ o * \mathsf{GetPost_{SP}}\ S\ s\}\end{array}$$

where $\mathsf{funcptr'}\ \phi\ g$ expresses that value g is a pointer to some function satisfying specification ϕ, and ϕ_{get} is the entry for get from Fig. 8. notify's large specification is adapted similarly. Repairing the proofs incurs changes in < 10 lines of Coq.

A third modification exploits VST's support for impredicative quantification to abstract over $\mathsf{GetPre_{SP}}$ and $\mathsf{GetPre_{SP}}$ in the definition of ϕ, such that notify's specification is effectively parametric in suitable GetPre/GetPost pairs. Adapting the verification involves step-indexed aspects of VST and hence requires a little more work; details are included in the Coq development [14].

Finally, we verified a variation in which observers register with two subjects, as an example of a more complex interaction pattern. As this affects model-level functionality, modifications are not confined to module-internal predicate definitions but affect APDs declarations and ASI definitions. However, neither the encapsulation of representation nor the modularity of verification were compromised; supporting more than two subjects per observer would likely be similar.

5.2 Pattern-level specification

An alternative specification of subject-observer was proposed by Parkinson [55], who sidesteps the conflict between callbacks, modularity, and abstraction. Giving up on specifying the two classes independently, this approach defines a single abstract predicate, SubObs, that ties a subject to all its observers and yields aggregate-level function specifications. We can recover such an aggregate interface by proving that the specifications involving SubObs are abstractions (in the sense of . <: .) of the exports of the SubjectObserver VSU, generically in APDs SP and OP. Indeed, Parkinson's formulation amounts to a two-predicate APD:

Record AggAPD :=
{ Sub: val → list val → Z → mpred; Obs: val → val → Z → mpred }.

with specifications shown in Figure 10, using the derived notions

Definition SubObs $s\ O\ v$:= Sub $s\ O\ v * *_{o \in O}$Obs $o\ s\ v$.
Definition Obs$_{_}$ $o\ s$:= $\exists v$. Obs $o\ s\ v$. *(* Obs$_{_}$ is related to Obs as $\mapsto_{\_}$ is to $\mapsto$. *)*
Definition SubObs$_{_}$ $s\ O$:= $\exists v$. SubObs $s\ O\ v$.

Function	Spec
newSubject(gv)	{Mem$_M$ gv} ⇝ {s. SubObs$_{_A}$ s nil $*$ Mem$_M$ gv}
registr(s, o; gv)	{Sub$_A$ $s\ O\ v *$ Obs$_{_A}$ $o\ s *$ Mem$_M$ gv} ⇝ {Sub$_A$ $s\ (o :: O)\ v *$ Obs$_A$ $o\ s\ v *$ Mem$_M$ gv}
update(s, v)	{SubObs$_{_A}$ $s\ O$} ⇝ {SubObs$_A$ $s\ O\ v$}
get(s)	{Sub$_A$ $s\ O\ v$} ⇝ {v. Sub$_A$ $s\ O\ v$}
newObs(s; gv)	{SubObs$_A$ $s\ O\ v *$ Mem$_M$ gv} ⇝ {p. SubObs$_A$ $s\ (p :: O)\ v *$ Mem$_M$ gv}
notify(o)	{Sub$_A$ $s\ O\ v *$ Obs$_{_A}$ $o\ s$} ⇝ {Sub$_A$ $s\ O\ v *$ Obs$_A$ $o\ s\ v$}
val(o)	{SubObs$_A$ $s\ O\ v$} ⇝ {v. SubObs$_A$ $s\ O\ v$}

Fig. 10. Selected aggregate specifications, parametric in an AggAPD A. Except for the occurrence of Mem$_M$ gv, the specifications coincide with Parkinson [55]'s specifications.

Constructing an AggAPD A from a SP/OP pair is trivial: take Sub to be Srep$_{SP}$ and Obs to be Orep$_{OP}$; proving the . <: . lemmas is then straight-forward.

SubObs constitutes a *pattern invariant*, or the pattern's primary predicate, with residuals Sub and Obs. From the aggregate's point of view, update → notify → get is not a callback but an internal nesting of invocations, so the small-footprint specifications typically don't pose a problem for existing methodologies; client-visible specifications with large footprints can be derived using the frame rule. In this sense, the pattern reestablishes "sequential atomicity" of operations. Exploring whether other design patterns can be similarly derived from the ASIs of their constituent classes is a topic for future research: *are typical design patterns the abstraction units at which sequential atomicity is reestablished, callbacks at most occur in valid states, and residual predicates are avoided?*

An aggregate specification for the function pointer implementation from Section 5.1 can be obtained using a modified AggAPD, with residual predicates GetPre etc.. But a better option is to remove the pattern-internal functions notify, registr, and perhaps even get from the aggregate ASI. In fact, notify's new signature reveals the use of function pointers, hence even an aggregate-level specification would have to include funcptr′ $\phi\ g$ terms. Thus, we instead employ the notion ⊑ from Section 3.2 to lift the VSU for SubjectObserver with function pointers from Section 5.1 to a VSU for the aggregate but narrowed ASI and then reverify main w.r.t the latter.

6 Verification of object principles

This section considers features that – together with state encapsulation and modularity – are cornerstones of object orientation: the ability for (instances of) multiple implementations of an interface to dynamically coexist and interact, dynamic dispatch, subtyping, *self*, and inheritance. To maintain the dataless discipline, we employ a uniform but simple object encoding that is typical for industrial and open-source C developments: dynamic dispatch is implemented using function pointers that are bundled into separate **struct**s (method tables) that are accessible as the first element of the object representations. Subtyping – providing additional methods – and representation inheritance are modeled by extending these **struct**s, respectively, but are orthogonal to each other, and only the former one is exposed in APIs. In the second half of this section, we hide the dynamic dispatch mechanism behind a wrapper interface. We specify objects by reference to a semantic (Coq-level) object model, thus comprehensively separating object reasoning from C-level reasoning: constructors establish, and methods maintain, abstract object predicates that clients need not (and cannot) unfold.

We again proceed in stages, using the widely used running example of points located on a one-dimensional axis (see e.g. [18]). Figure 11 shows a preliminary API for basic, bumpable, and colored points, organized in a simple subtyping relationship. We provide multiple implementations for each interface (using different data representations), each exposing its set of constructors in a separate header file - Figure 12 shows implementation **I1**. Clients select an implementation during object creation but cannot otherwise distinguish between them: method dispatch selects the appropriate function from the method table, as in

```
typedef struct point *Point;
struct methods {
  int (*get) (Point);
  void (*set) (Point, int); };
typedef struct methods * Methods;

typedef struct bpoint *BPoint;
struct bmethods {
  int (*get) (Point);
  void (*set) (Point, int);
  void (*bump) (BPoint); };
typedef struct bmethods * BMethods;

typedef struct bmethods * BMethods;

typedef struct cpoint *CPoint;
struct cmethods {
  int (*get) (Point);
  void (*set) (Point, int);
  void (*bump) (BPoint);
  int (*getC) (CPoint); };
typedef struct cmethods * CMethods;
struct point { Methods mtable; };
struct bpoint { BMethods mtable; };
struct cpoint { CMethods mtable; };
```

Fig. 11. PointInterface.h, containing three interfaces for one-dimensional points

```
BPoint bp = makeBPoint_I1(4); int i = ((BMethods)(bp→mtable))→get((Point)bp)).
```

```
struct point_I1 {          struct bpoint_I1 {          struct cpoint_I1 {
  Methods mtable;            BMethods mtable;            CMethods mtable;
  int value; };              int value; };               int value; int color; };

int get_I1 (Point p) { return (((struct point_I1 *)p)→ value); }
void set_I1 (Point p, int i) { ((struct point_I1 *)p)→ value = i; return; }
void bump_I1 (BPoint p) { ((struct bpoint_I1 *)p)→ value++; return; }
int getC_I1 (CPoint p) { return (((struct cpoint_I1 *)p)→ color); }
BPoint makeBPoint_I1 (int i) {
  struct bpoint_I1 *p = (struct bpoint_I1 *)surely_malloc(sizeof *p);
  BMethods m = (BMethods)surely_malloc(sizeof *m);
  m → get = &get_I1; m → set = &set_I1; m → bump = &bump_I1;
  p → value = i; p → mtable = m; return ((BPoint)p); }
```

Fig. 12. Implementation **I1**. Constructors makePoint_I1 and makeCPoint_I1 omitted. A second implementation **I2** employs representations point_I2 etc. and exposes constructors makeBPoint_I2 etc.

The basis of object specifications is a general method table predicate:

$$\mathsf{MTable}(\mathcal{T}, k, \mathit{names}, m, \mathit{specs}, \mathcal{I}) \mathrel{\widehat{=}} \mathsf{Mtok}(\mathsf{Ews}, k, m) * \\ \exists\, \pi.!!(\mathsf{readable}(\pi)) \;\&\&\; *_{(\mu,\phi)\in \mathit{names}\times \mathit{specs}}\, \exists\, v.\mathsf{funcptr}(\phi\,\mathcal{I}, v) * m.\mu \mapsto_k^{\pi} v.$$

It asserts that the **struct** m (of shape k) contains at field names *names* pointers to functions satisfying *specs*, where $\mathcal{I}$ is of Coq-type $\mathsf{Pred(T)} \mathrel{\widehat{=}} (\mathsf{T{*}val}) \to \mathsf{mpred}$ and *specs* has type list $(\mathsf{Pred(T)} \to \mathsf{funspec})$. A generic object layout predicate

$$\mathcal{N}\; T\; \mathit{tbl}\; (\sigma\; k : \mathsf{type})\; \mathit{names}\; \mathit{specs}\; (x : T * \mathit{val}) : \mathsf{mpred} = \\ \exists\, \delta\, \mathcal{I}.\; \mathcal{I}\, x * \mathsf{Mtok}(\mathsf{Ews}, \delta, \mathit{snd}\; x) * \\ \exists\, m.\, (\mathit{snd}\; x).\mathit{tbl} \mapsto_{\sigma}^{\mathsf{Ews}} m \;*\; \mathsf{MTable}(T, k, \mathit{names}, m, \mathit{specs}, \mathcal{I})$$

then combines a specified method table (located at field *tbl*) with the requirement that the (memory identified by the) object pointer satisfy $\mathcal{I}$. C types σ and δ represent the object's static and dynamic types. The joint use of $\mathcal{I}$ in MTable and $\mathcal{N}$ ensures that an object's methods agree with its data component on what representation predicate should be maintained. The existential abstraction over $\mathcal{I}$ ensures representation hiding: external clients merely see a invariant of (Coq) type T. Thus, different C implementations of an object interface may employ different representations but still satisfy the same external specification.

Specifically, we introduce Coq-level object interface types in the style of Hofmann and Pierce's object model [30]:

```
Record PointM (X:Type):Type := { get : X → Z; set : X → Z → X; }
Record BPointM (X:Type):Type :=
  { PointM_of_BPointM :> PointM X; bump : X → X; bumpable : X → Prop; }.
Inductive Color:Type := blue | red | green.
Record CPointM (X:Type):Type :=
  { BPointM_of_CPointM :> BPointM X; getC: X → Color; color_code: Color → Z; }.
```

The parameters X represent *semantic* object representations. On the one hand, we may instantiate these and define Coq-level behaviors, like m1, bm1, cm1:

Record PointRep := { value : Z }.
Record CPointRep := { pointRep :> PointRep; color : Color }.
Definition m1: PointM PointRep :=
{| get := fun s ⇒ value s; set := fun s i ⇒ {| value := i |} |}.
Definition bm1: BPointM PointRep :=
{| PointM_of_BPointM := m1; bump := fun s ⇒ {| value := value s + 1 |};
bumpable := fun s ⇒ min_signed ≤ value s < max_signed |}.
Definition cm1: CPointM CPointRep := {| ... *(*details omitted*)* |}

But the interface types also enable specifications for $\mathsf{get}(p)$ and $\mathsf{set}(p, j)$:

$$\mathsf{get\_spec}\ T\ (P : \mathsf{PointM}\ T) \mathrel{\widehat{=}} \lambda \mathcal{I} : \mathsf{Pred}\, T.\ \{\mathcal{I}(t,p)\} \rightsquigarrow \{\mathsf{get}\ T\ P\ t.\ \mathcal{I}(t,p)\}$$
$$\mathsf{set\_spec}\ T\ (P : \mathsf{PointM}\ T) \mathrel{\widehat{=}} \lambda \mathcal{I} : \mathsf{Pred}\, T.$$
$$\{\mathsf{min\_signed} \le j \le \mathsf{max\_signed}\ \&\ \mathcal{I}(t,p)\} \rightsquigarrow \{\mathcal{I}(\mathsf{set}\ T\ P\ t\ j, p)\}$$

Thus, each method has a Coq-level counterpart that is parametric in (semantic) representations and behaviors. To specify the constructors, we first define specializations of $\mathcal{N}$ for the three interfaces by instantiating with the appropriate method specifications and syntactic elements:

$$\begin{array}{l} \mathcal{P}\ T\ (P : \mathsf{PointM}\ T) : \mathsf{Pred}\, T \mathrel{\widehat{=}} \\ \quad \mathcal{N}\ T\ \mathtt{mtable}\ \mathtt{point}\ \mathtt{methods}\ [\mathtt{get};\mathtt{set}]\ [\mathsf{get\_spec}\ T\ P; \mathsf{set\_spec}\ T\ P] \\ \mathcal{B}\ T\ (B : \mathsf{BPointM}\ T) : \mathsf{Pred}\, T \mathrel{\widehat{=}} \\ \quad \mathcal{N}\ T\ \mathtt{mtable}\ \mathtt{bpoint}\ \mathtt{bmethods}\ [\mathtt{get};\mathtt{set};\mathtt{bump}] \\ \qquad [\mathsf{get\_spec}\ T\ B; \mathsf{set\_spec}\ T\ B; \mathsf{bump\_spec}\ T\ B] \\ \mathcal{C}\ T\ (C : \mathsf{CPointM}\ T) : \mathsf{Pred}\, T \mathrel{\widehat{=}} \\ \quad \mathcal{N}\ T\ \mathtt{mtable}\ \mathtt{cpoint}\ \mathtt{cmethods}\ [\mathtt{get};\mathtt{set};\mathtt{bump};\mathtt{getC}] \\ \qquad [\mathsf{get\_spec}\ T\ C; \mathsf{set\_spec}\ T\ C; \mathsf{bump\_spec}\ T\ C; \mathsf{getC\_spec}\ T\ C] \end{array}.$$

Here, `point`, `bpoint`, `cpoint` and `methods`, `bmethods`, `cmethods` are the **struct**s defined in the header file (Figure 11) and `mtable`, `get`, …, `getC` are the field names in these **struct**s. The exemplary spec for base point constructors is then

$$\mathsf{makePoint}(i; \mathsf{gv}) : \{\mathsf{min\_signed} \le i \le \mathsf{max\_signed}\ \&\ \mathsf{Mem_M}\ \mathsf{gv}\}$$
$$\rightsquigarrow \{p.\ \mathsf{Mem_M}\ \mathsf{gv} * \mathcal{P}\ T\ P\ (\mathsf{Init\_Point}(i), p)\}.$$

Verifying **I1** and **I2** then yields VSUs whose export interfaces tie makePoint_I1 makePoint_I2 to the specialization of this constructor to $P :=$ m1, and similarly for the other constructors. The resulting objects behave indistinguishably; the existential quantification over $\mathcal{I}$ in the definition of $\mathcal{N}$ carries over to $\mathcal{P}$, $\mathcal{B}$, and $\mathcal{C}$, ensuring that the representational differences between **I1** and **I2** are hidden from clients: when verifying a method call, clients unroll $\mathcal{P}$ etc., but each time receive a "fresh" symbolic representation predicate $\mathcal{I}$.

Wrapper-based verification The unrolling of object predicates corresponds to the exposure of the method table in our API. Programmatically, better encapsulation is provided by wrappers that hide the function pointer mechanism, like

```
int GET (Point p) { Methods m = p→mtable; return (m→get(p)); }
```

The header file for these wrappers resembles the API of an ADT, but merely disguises object-orientation: we still support multiple implementations (using the same constructors as above), and operations are still invoked using dynamic dispatch. On the specification side, wrappers can be modeled as an APD

Record WrapperAPD := { Wr_Pt: ∀ T, PointM T → Pred T;
Wr_BPt: ∀ T, BPointM T → Pred T; Wr_CPt: ∀ T, CPointM T → Pred T }.

with one constructor per interface, in resemblance to the use of class names to index predicate families [56]. The VSU for the wrapper then encapsulates the object predicates $\mathcal{P}$ etc., exporting an ASI with specifications such as

$$\mathsf{GET}(p) : \begin{array}{l} \{\mathsf{Wr\_Pt}\ W\ T\ P\ (t,p)\} \leadsto \{\mathsf{get}\ T\ P\ t. \mathsf{Wr\_Pt}\ W\ T\ P\ (t,p)\} \wedge \\ \{\mathsf{Wr\_BPt}\ W\ T\ P\ (t,p)\} \leadsto \{\mathsf{get}\ T\ P\ t.\ \mathsf{Wr\_BPt}\ W\ T\ P\ (t,p)\} \wedge \\ \{\mathsf{Wr\_CPt}\ W\ T\ P\ (t,p)\} \leadsto \{\mathsf{get}\ T\ P\ t.\ \mathsf{Wr\_CPt}\ W\ T\ P\ (t,p)\} \end{array}$$

We can further improve client-side usability by replacing these intersection specifications by a deep embedding of the three interface alternatives; this eliminates a corresponding case distinction in client-side proofs, when symbolic execution reaches the invocation of a wrapper function. As an example, we verified a linked list module that permits insertion of basic, bumpable, or colored points and provides map operations that apply SET, BUMP, ... to all elements. Each element may internally employ **I1** or **I2**. Of course, the precondition of mapping BUMP requires all elements to be of dynamic type (at least) BPoint and have a bumpable coordinate; however, this condition emerges as a constraint on semantic objects and can be discharged without unfolding object representation predicates.

Self and late binding Verification using the above constructions fails for methods whose body contains virtual calls on *self*: the definition of $\mathcal{N}$ effectively separates the object's data region from the method table upon method entry, making only the former accessible inside the body. To overcome this limitation, we define a variant of $\mathcal{N}$ using the higher-order recursive functor

$$\begin{array}{l} \mathcal{F}\ (\mathcal{I}\ X : \mathsf{Pred}\,T) : \mathsf{Pred}\,T \mathrel{\widehat{=}} \\ \quad \lambda(x : T * val).\ \exists\,\delta\,m.\ \mathcal{I}\ x * \mathsf{Mtok}(\mathsf{Ews}, \delta, snd\ x) * (snd\ x).tbl \mapsto_{\sigma}^{\mathsf{Ews}} m \\ \qquad\qquad\qquad\qquad\qquad * \rhd \mathsf{MTable}(T, k, names, m, specs, X) \end{array}$$

in which $\mathcal{I}$ is now a parameter (we eschew the parameters $T, \ldots, specs$ for readability) and X plays the role of $\mathcal{N}$. Recursion via X is protected by VST's [4] modality $\rhd$; indeed, any access to a method table inside a method happens at least one step *later* than the method's own invocation. Contractiveness of $\mathcal{F}$ (proven in VST) ensures the existence of a fixed point $\widehat{\mathcal{F}}(\mathcal{I}) := HORec(\mathcal{F}(\mathcal{I}))$. Recovering the quantification over $\mathcal{I}$, we then replace $\mathcal{N}$ with $\mathcal{N}^* := \exists \mathcal{I}.\ \widehat{\mathcal{F}}(\mathcal{I})$. With this modification in place, one may verify virtual calls on *self*, like a variant of **I1** that implements bump using get and set (still w.r.t. m1, bm1, and cm1).

An important application of *self* is (observably behavior-altering) method overriding. At the semantic level, Hofmann and Pierce explicate how positive subtyping supports both early and late binding variants of overriding; these differ in whether the observable behavior of bump (when implemented in terms of get and set) is affected when a subclass subsequently overrides set to, say, reset the coordinate to 0. Furthermore, method overriding may affect how functions defined in a superclass act on subclass-introduced state components. For example, one may impose that updating the coordinate turns a point's color blue. Semantically, all these variations yield novel behaviors m2, bm2, and cm2, etc. that can be compared to the earlier behaviors using Hofmann and Pierce's theory. As a consequence of our two-level reasoning, and the choice to parameterise constructor/method specifications by behaviors, we can leverage their techniques: implementations **I3**, **I4**... that realize the overriding variants can be verified as further VSUs for our earlier export interface, by (now) specializing the constructor specifications to m2, etc.. Afterwards, the modified behaviors propagate through dynamic dispatch and wrappers as expected, permitting clients of e.g. the list module to map bump over elements with different behavior. Side conditions during symbolic method calls refer exclusively to semantic objects and behaviors, do not necessitate the unrolling of representation predicates, and can often just be discharged using simplification.

7 Discussion

Related and future work Certified Abstraction Layers (CAL, [24,26]) are used in the CertiKOS project [25] to verify feature-rich operating system kernels and hypervisors in Coq. CAL permits horizontal and vertical composition of components, and establishes full abstraction between the imports and exports. CAL's methodology was recently rephrased as a synthesis from a systems-oriented DSL, DeepSEA, to C, with a CompCert backend [64]. However, "(T)here is no use of C pointers and no built-in support of dynamic memory allocation (every DeepSEA object is realized as a set of static variables), so programs that need dynamic allocation will have to implement it themselves" ([64], page 10). While this fragment remarkably suffices for the intended application area, it is unlikely to satisfy general-purpose programmers or compiler writers for other systems languages.

Ironclad Apps and Ironfleet [29,28] are systems based on Dafny and TLA+ for verifying safety and liveness of distributed systems, and app security. By connecting model-level, concurrency-aware reasoning, state-machine refinement, and Floyd-Hoare verification, their approach provides abstraction-bridging functionality similar to that of proof-assistant-based reasoning, trading off TCB size and foundational integration in an logical framework against automation and developer productivity. Ironclad Apps compile to verified assembly; Ironfleet employs a formally unverified route via Dafny and the .NET compiler for C#.

Überspark [67] is a system based on Frama-C and SMT for compositionally verifying commodity system software written in C and assembly. Überspark's primary applications are hypervisor components and OS kernels, but it currently addresses only safety and security properties (memory separation, control-flow integrity, information flow) rather than functional correctness. The same limitation applies to proof-carrying code systems [49,3,6,13,27], at (virtual) machine or assembly level. Several PCC systems proposed hierarchies of formalisms that connect operational semantics, a general-purpose program logic, and tactical checkers or algorithmic inference systems for higher-level type systems, abstract interpretation, or program analyses [16,2,17,1]. VST's tactical automation is optimized for symbolic execution and functional correctness, but the underlying proof rules could equally well be used to prove soundness of static analyses or code synthesizers; we expect our structuring principles for separate compilation will be just as useful in these scenarios as they are for functional correctness.

McKinna and Burstall [45] pioneered the use of existential abstraction to formally tie programs to their specifications and proofs in a modern proof assistant. VSU realizes aspects of their vision of deliverables for a mainstream language but is at this point not endowed with similarly rigorous categorical underpinnings.

Representation hiding in separation logic can also be obtained using hypothetical frame rules [54,10], but no such rule is provided by VST at present. Pragmatically, the two approaches appear complementary: modules that expose interesting state (e.g. a list ADT, the point objects,...) favor existential abstraction/APDs, as clients can access associated reasoning principles on demand, at specific program points. In contrast, modules like the resource-unaware memory manager might benefit from hypothetical framing: the predicate $\mathsf{Mem_M}\ \mathsf{gv}$ carries no client-relevant information but still needs to be carried around in many function specifications in our treatment.

VST's specification subsumption resembles behavioral subtyping [44,42], a notion commonly used in verification tools for Java-like languages for relating specifications across a class hierarchy. Exploring the relationship between our use of positive subtyping, other notions of subtyping and inheritance, and Liskov's Substitution Principle [43] constitutes future work.

By supporting field update, Hofmann and Pierce's theory addresses shortcomings of purely functional object models, but its support for object aggregates or complex ownership structures appears limited and not much studied. A two-level encoding could likely also be developed for concurrency-inspired object models [33,32,31], perhaps by adapting the theory of interaction trees [68,39]. However, VST's partial-correctness interpretation of triples limits the end-to-end usefulness of coinductive reasoning. A recent proposal for integrating statically typed Smalltalk-inspired objects into a functional calculus is Wyvern [52].

In the context of SMT-based verification tools, Parkinson and Bierman [57] highlight examples that go beyond behavioral subtyping, and Summers et al. [66] identify a catalog of advanced uses of class invariants. We intend to apply VST to the former soon; a better understanding of the latter could perhaps commence by recasting Drossopoulou et al.'s general framework for object invariants [22] in separation logic. However, some aspects of class/object invariants may not immediately transfer from Java-like to Smalltalk-style object models.

In Java, an object's representation remains constant over its lifetime. By separately quantifying over $\mathcal{I}$, our pre- and postconditions may support dynamic representation change a la Fickle [21] (with suitable updates to the method table), as long as both representations fit into an object's top-level **struct**.

Krishnaswami et al. [41] verify subject-observer and other patterns (iterators, flyweight, factory) by equipping a functional language, Idealized ML, with effectful specifications based on higher-order separation logic. Their verification was partially formalized in a predicative Hoare Type Theory/Ynot and employs abstract module definitions that combine code and specification. Their use of separating implication can likely be transferred to our setting, but their implementation does not separate the functionality of subjects and observers to same extent and thus does not raise the same specification challenges. Considerate reasoning [65], object propositions [51], and multi-object languages such as Rumer [9] are alternatives in the design space spanned by invariant techniques, aliasing/separation and ownership; all validate variants of Composite pattern.

Extrapolating from our exploration of the Composite pattern, it appears feasible to generate VST specifications, loop invariants, and APD declarations from Verifast [34]; synthesizing full proofs will be more challenging.

Object encodings in the Linux kernel, GTK/GObject, or the SQLite database engine deviate from the Smalltalk tradition and expose APIs that are not fully dataless. We suspect these systems also differ from standard language-level object disciplines in their need for deeply layered ownership control or model-level object aggregates. Like Schreiner's encoding [63], these systems thus provide interesting opportunities for future case studies.

Conclusion The ability of type theory to capture modularity and abstraction is well-established. But while, e.g. Mitchell and Plotkin's insight has been highly influential in the world of functional programming, it has not yet made its way into verification tools for mainstream languages. Taking inspiration from their work, we introduced Verified Software Units as a general component calculus for VST, and developed an infrastructure for separating the declarations of abstract predicates from concrete predicate definitions. We showed that residual predicates support callbacks which violate operation atomicity, as is the case in the subject-observer pattern. Finally, we introduced a two-level approach to specifying object principles, yielding a simple logic for Smalltalk-style objects in C. Together, these innovations substantially advance VST's capability to verify modular C developments that employ diverse programming styles.

Acknowledgments: This work was funded by the National Science Foundation under the awards 1005849 (*Verified High Performance Data Structure Implementations*, Beringer) and 1521602 *Expedition in Computing: The Science of Deep Specification*, Appel). The author is grateful to the members of both projects for their feedback and greatly appreciates the reviewers' comments and suggestions.

References

1. Ahmed, A., Appel, A.W., Richards, C.D., Swadi, K.N., Tan, G., Wang, D.C.: Semantic foundations for typed assembly languages. ACM Trans. Program. Lang.

Syst. **32**(3), 7:1–7:67 (2010), https://doi.org/10.1145/1709093.1709094

2. Albert, E., Puebla, G., Hermenegildo, M.V.: Abstraction-carrying code. In: Baader and Voronkov [7], pp. 380–397, https://doi.org/10.1007/978-3-540-32275-7_25
3. Appel, A.W.: Foundational proof-carrying code. In: LICS'01: 16th Annual IEEE Symposium on Logic in Computer Science, Proceedings. pp. 247–256. IEEE Computer Society (2001), https://doi.org/10.1109/LICS.2001.932501
4. Appel, A.W., Dockins, R., Hobor, A., Beringer, L., Dodds, J., Stewart, G., Blazy, S., Leroy, X.: Program Logics for Certified Compilers. Cambridge (2014)
5. Appel, A.W., Naumann, D.A.: Verified sequential malloc/free. In: Ding, C., Maas, M. (eds.) ISMM'20: 2020 ACM SIGPLAN International Symposium on Memory Management. pp. 48–59. ACM (2020), https://doi.org/10.1145/3381898.3397211
6. Aspinall, D., Gilmore, S., Hofmann, M., Sannella, D., Stark, I.: Mobile resource guarantees for smart devices. In: Barthe, G., Burdy, L., Huisman, M., Lanet, J., Muntean, T. (eds.) CASSIS'04: International Workshop on Construction and Analysis of Safe, Secure, and Interoperable Smart Devices, Revised Selected Papers. LNCS, vol. 3362, pp. 1–26. Springer (2004), https://doi.org/10.1007/978-3-540-30569-9_1
7. Baader, F., Voronkov, A. (eds.): LPAR'04: Logic for Programming, Artificial Intelligence, and Reasoning, 11th International Conference, Proceedings, LNCS, vol. 3452. Springer (2005), https://doi.org/10.1007/b106931
8. Balzer, R.M.: Dataless programming. In: American Federation of Information Processing Societies: Proceedings of the AFIPS '67 Fall Joint Computer Conference. AFIPS Conference Proceedings, vol. 31, pp. 535–544. AFIPS / ACM / Thomson Book Company, Washington D.C. (1967), https://doi.org/10.1145/1465611.1465683
9. Balzer, S.: Rumer: A programming language and modular verification technique based on relationships. Ph.D. thesis, ETH Zürich (2011)
10. Banerjee, A., Naumann, D.A.: Local reasoning for global invariants, part II: dynamic boundaries. J. ACM **60**(3), 19:1–19:73 (2013), http:/doi.acm.org/10.1145/2485981
11. Barnett, M., DeLine, R., Fähndrich, M., Leino, K.R.M., Schulte, W.: Verification of object-oriented programs with invariants. Journal of Object Technology **3**(6), 27–56 (2004), https://doi.org/10.5381/jot.2004.3.6.a2
12. Barnett, M., Naumann, D.A.: Friends need a bit more: Maintaining invariants over shared state. In: Kozen, D., Shankland, C. (eds.) Mathematics of Program Construction, 7th International Conference, MPC 2004, Proceedings. LNCS, vol. 3125, pp. 54–84. Springer (2004), https://doi.org/10.1007/978-3-540-27764-4_5
13. Barthe, G., Crégut, P., Grégoire, B., Jensen, T.P., Pichardie, D.: The MOBIUS proof carrying code infrastructure. In: de Boer, F.S., Bonsangue, M.M., Graf, S., de Roever, W.P. (eds.) FMCO'07: Formal Methods for Components and Objects, 6th International Symposium, Revised Lectures. LNCS, vol. 5382, pp. 1–24. Springer (2007), https://doi.org/10.1007/978-3-540-92188-2_1
14. Beringer, L.: Verified Software Units – Coq development (2021), https://www.cs.princeton.edu/~eberinge/VSU_Esop21.tar.gz
15. Beringer, L., Appel, A.W.: Abstraction and subsumption in modular verification of C programs. In: ter Beek, M.H., McIver, A., Oliveira, J.N. (eds.) Formal Methods - The Next 30 Years - Third World Congress, FM 2019, Proceedings. LNCS, vol. 11800, pp. 573–590. Springer (2019), https://doi.org/10.1007/978-3-030-30942-8_34

16. Beringer, L., Hofmann, M., Momigliano, A., Shkaravska, O.: Automatic certification of heap consumption. In: Baader and Voronkov [7], pp. 347–362, https://doi.org/10.1007/978-3-540-32275-7_23
17. Besson, F., Jensen, T.P., Pichardie, D.: Proof-carrying code from certified abstract interpretation and fixpoint compression. Theor. Comput. Sci. **364**(3), 273–291 (2006), https://doi.org/10.1016/j.tcs.2006.08.012
18. Bruce, K.B., Cardelli, L., Pierce, B.C.: Comparing object encodings. Inf. Comput. **155**(1-2), 108–133 (1999), https://doi.org/10.1006/inco.1999.2829
19. Chalin, P., Kiniry, J.R., Leavens, G.T., Poll, E.: Beyond assertions: Advanced specification and verification with JML and ESC/Java2. In: de Boer, F.S., Bonsangue, M.M., Graf, S., de Roever, W.P. (eds.) Formal Methods for Components and Objects, 4th International Symposium, FMCO 2005, Revised Lectures. LNCS, vol. 4111, pp. 342–363. Springer (2005), https://doi.org/10.1007/11804192_16
20. Clarke, D., Drossopoulou, S., Noble, J., Wrigstad, T.: Aliasing, confinement, and ownership in object-oriented programming. In: Cebulla, M. (ed.) Object-Oriented Technology. ECOOP 2007 Workshop Reader, Final Reports. LNCS, vol. 4906, pp. 40–49. Springer (2007), https://doi.org/10.1007/978-3-540-78195-0_5
21. Drossopoulou, S., Damiani, F., Dezani-Ciancaglini, M., Giannini, P.: Fickle : Dynamic object re-classification. In: Knudsen, J.L. (ed.) ECOOP 2001 - Object-Oriented Programming, 15th European Conference, Proceedings. LNCS, vol. 2072, pp. 130–149. Springer (2001), https://doi.org/10.1007/3-540-45337-7_8
22. Drossopoulou, S., Francalanza, A., Müller, P., Summers, A.J.: A unified framework for verification techniques for object invariants. In: Vitek, J. (ed.) ECOOP 2008 - Object-Oriented Programming, 22nd European Conference, Proceedings. LNCS, vol. 5142, pp. 412–437. Springer (2008), https://doi.org/10.1007/978-3-540-70592-5_18
23. Gamma, E., Helm, R., Johnson, R., Vlissides, J.: Design Patterns: Elements of Reusable Object-Oriented Software. Addison-Wesley Longman Publishing Co., Inc., USA (1995)
24. Gu, R., Koenig, J., Ramananandro, T., Shao, Z., Wu, X.N., Weng, S., Zhang, H., Guo, Y.: Deep specifications and certified abstraction layers. In: Rajamani, S.K., Walker, D. (eds.) Proceedings of the 42nd Annual ACM SIGPLAN-SIGACT Symposium on Principles of Programming Languages, POPL 2015. pp. 595–608. ACM (2015), https://doi.org/10.1145/2676726.2676975
25. Gu, R., Shao, Z., Chen, H., Kim, J., Koenig, J., Wu, X.N., Sjöberg, V., Costanzo, D.: Building certified concurrent OS kernels. Commun. ACM **62**(10), 89–99 (2019), https://doi.org/10.1145/3356903
26. Gu, R., Shao, Z., Kim, J., Wu, X.N., Koenig, J., Sjöberg, V., Chen, H., Costanzo, D., Ramananandro, T.: Certified concurrent abstraction layers. In: Foster, J.S., Grossman, D. (eds.) Proceedings of the 39th ACM SIGPLAN Conference on Programming Language Design and Implementation, PLDI 2018. pp. 646–661. ACM (2018), https://doi.org/10.1145/3192366.3192381
27. Hamid, N.A., Shao, Z., Trifonov, V., Monnier, S., Ni, Z.: A syntactic approach to foundational proof-carrying code. J. Autom. Reasoning **31**(3-4), 191–229 (2003), https://doi.org/10.1023/B:JARS.0000021012.97318.e9
28. Hawblitzel, C., Howell, J., Kapritsos, M., Lorch, J.R., Parno, B., Roberts, M.L., Setty, S.T.V., Zill, B.: Ironfleet: proving safety and liveness of practical distributed systems. Commun. ACM **60**(7), 83–92 (2017), https://doi.org/10.1145/3068608
29. Hawblitzel, C., Howell, J., Lorch, J.R., Narayan, A., Parno, B., Zhang, D., Zill, B.: Ironclad apps: End-to-end security via automated full-system verification. In:

Flinn, J., Levy, H. (eds.) 11th USENIX Symposium on Operating Systems Design and Implementation, OSDI '14. pp. 165–181. USENIX Association (2014), https://www.usenix.org/conference/osdi14/technical-sessions/presentation/hawblitzel
30. Hofmann, M., Pierce, B.C.: Positive subtyping. Inf. Comput. **126**(1), 11–33 (1996), https://doi.org/10.1006/inco.1996.0031
31. Honsell, F., Lenisa, M., Redamalla, R.: Coalgebraic semantics and observational equivalences of an imperative class-based OO-language. Electron. Notes Theor. Comput. Sci. **104**, 163–180 (2004), https://doi.org/10.1016/j.entcs.2004.08.024
32. Huisman, M., Jacobs, B.: Inheritance in higher order logic: Modeling and reasoning. In: Theorem Proving in Higher Order Logics. LNCS, vol. 1869, pp. 301–319. Springer (2000)
33. Jacobs, B.: Objects and classes, co-algebraically. In: Freitag, B., Jones, C.B., Lengauer, C., Schek, H. (eds.) Object Orientation with Parallelism and Persistence. pp. 83–103. Kluwer Academic Publishers (1995)
34. Jacobs, B., Smans, J., Philippaerts, P., Vogels, F., Penninckx, W., Piessens, F.: Verifast: A powerful, sound, predictable, fast verifier for C and java. In: Bobaru, M.G., Havelund, K., Holzmann, G.J., Joshi, R. (eds.) NASA Formal Methods - Third International Symposium, NFM 2011. Proceedings. LNCS, vol. 6617, pp. 41–55. Springer (2011), https://doi.org/10.1007/978-3-642-20398-5_4
35. Jacobs, B., Smans, J., Piessens, F.: Verifying the composite pattern using separation logic. In: Specification and verification of component-based systems – Workshop at ACM SIGSOFT/FSE 16 (2008), available at https://people.cs.kuleuven.be/~bart.jacobs/verifast
36. Jung, R., Krebbers, R., Jourdan, J.H., Bizjak, A., Birkedal, L., Dreyer, D.: Iris from the ground up: A modular foundation for higher-order concurrent separation logic. Journal of Functional Programming **28** (2018)
37. Kay, A.C.: The early history of Smalltalk. In: Lee, J.A.N., Sammet, J.E. (eds.) History of Programming Languages Conference (HOPL-II), Preprints. pp. 69–95. ACM (1993), https://doi.org/10.1145/154766.155364
38. Kleymann, T.: Hoare logic and auxiliary variables. Formal Asp. Comput. **11**(5), 541–566 (1999), https://doi.org/10.1007/s001650050057
39. Koh, N., Li, Y., Li, Y., Xia, L., Beringer, L., Honoré, W., Mansky, W., Pierce, B.C., Zdancewic, S.: From C to interaction trees: specifying, verifying, and testing a networked server. In: Mahboubi, A., Myreen, M.O. (eds.) Proceedings of the 8th ACM SIGPLAN International Conference on Certified Programs and Proofs, (CPP'19). pp. 234–248. ACM (2019), https://doi.org/10.1145/3293880.3294106
40. Kravchuk-Kirilyuk, A.Y.: The B^+-tree Index as a Verified Software Unit. Master's thesis, Department of Computer Science, Princeton University (2020)
41. Krishnaswami, N.R., Aldrich, J., Birkedal, L., Svendsen, K., Buisse, A.: Design patterns in separation logic. In: Kennedy, A., Ahmed, A. (eds.) Proceedings of TLDI'09: 2009 ACM SIGPLAN International Workshop on Types in Languages Design and Implementation. pp. 105–116. ACM (2009), https://doi.org/10.1145/1481861.1481874
42. Leavens, G.T., Naumann, D.A.: Behavioral subtyping, specification inheritance, and modular reasoning. ACM Trans. on Programming Languages and Systems **37**(4), 13:1–13:88 (2015), https://doi.org/10.1145/2766446
43. Liskov, B.: Keynote address - data abstraction and hierarchy. SIGPLAN Not. **23**(5), 17–34 (Jan 1987), https://doi.org/10.1145/62139.62141
44. Liskov, B., Wing, J.M.: A behavioral notion of subtyping. ACM Trans. Program. Lang. Syst. **16**(6), 1811–1841 (1994), https://doi.org/10.1145/197320.197383

45. McKinna, J., Burstall, R.M.: Deliverables: A categorial approach to program development in type theory. In: Borzyszkowski, A.M., Sokolowski, S. (eds.) Mathematical Foundations of Computer Science 1993, 18th International Symposium, MFCS'93. Lecture Notes in Computer Science, vol. 711, pp. 32–67. Springer (1993), https://doi.org/10.1007/3-540-57182-5_3
46. Mitchell, J.C., Plotkin, G.D.: Abstract types have existential type. ACM Trans. on Programming Languages and Systems **10**(3), 470–502 (Jul 1988)
47. Müller, P., Poetzsch-Heffter, A., Leavens, G.T.: Modular invariants for layered object structures. Sci. Comput. Program. **62**(3), 253–286 (2006), https://doi.org/10.1016/j.scico.2006.03.001
48. Naumann, D.A.: Deriving sharp rules of adaptation for Hoare logics. Tech. Rep. 9906, Department of Computer Science, Stevens Institute of Technology (1999)
49. Necula, G.C.: Proof-carrying code. In: Lee, P., Henglein, F., Jones, N.D. (eds.) Conference Record of POPL'97: The 24th ACM SIGPLAN-SIGACT Symposium on Principles of Programming Languages. pp. 106–119. ACM Press (1997), https://doi.org/10.1145/263699.263712
50. Nipkow, T.: Hoare logics for recursive procedures and unbounded nondeterminism. In: Bradfield, J.C. (ed.) Computer Science Logic, 16th International Workshop, CSL 2002, 11th Annual Conference of the EACSL, Proceedings. Lecture Notes in Computer Science, vol. 2471, pp. 103–119. Springer (2002), http://dx.doi.org/10.1007/3-540-45793-3_8
51. Nistor, L., Aldrich, J., Balzer, S., Mehnert, H.: Object propositions. In: Jones, C.B., Pihlajasaari, P., Sun, J. (eds.) FM 2014: Formal Methods - 19th International Symposium, Singapore, May 12-16, 2014. Proceedings. LNCS, vol. 8442, pp. 497–513. Springer (2014), https://doi.org/10.1007/978-3-319-06410-9_34
52. Nistor, L., Kurilova, D., Balzer, S., Chung, B., Potanin, A., Aldrich, J.: Wyvern: A simple, typed, and pure object-oriented language. In: Proceedings of the 5th Workshop on MechAnisms for SPEcialization, Generalization and InHerItance. pp. 9–16. MASPEGHI '13, Association for Computing Machinery, New York, NY, USA (2013), https://doi.org/10.1145/2489828.2489830
53. O'Hearn, P.W.: Separation logic. Commun. ACM **62**(2), 86–95 (2019), https://doi.org/10.1145/3211968
54. O'Hearn, P.W., Yang, H., Reynolds, J.C.: Separation and information hiding. ACM Trans. Program. Lang. Syst. **31**(3), 11:1–11:50 (2009), https://doi.org/10.1145/1498926.1498929
55. Parkinson, M.: Class invariants: the end of the road? (2007), contained in [20]. Also available at https://people.dsv.su.se/~tobias/iwaco/p3-parkinson.pdf
56. Parkinson, M.J., Bierman, G.M.: Separation logic and abstraction. In: Palsberg, J., Abadi, M. (eds.) Proceedings of the 32nd ACM SIGPLAN-SIGACT Symposium on Principles of Programming Languages, POPL 2005. pp. 247–258. ACM (2005), https://doi.org/10.1145/1040305.1040326
57. Parkinson, M.J., Bierman, G.M.: Separation logic, abstraction and inheritance. In: Necula, G.C., Wadler, P. (eds.) Proceedings of the 35th ACM SIGPLAN-SIGACT Symposium on Principles of Programming Languages, POPL 2008. pp. 75–86. ACM (2008), https://doi.org/10.1145/1328438.1328451
58. Pierce, B.C.: Types and Programming Languages. MIT Press, Cambridge, Mass. (2002)
59. Polikarpova, N., Tschannen, J., Furia, C.A., Meyer, B.: Flexible invariants through semantic collaboration. In: Jones, C.B., Pihlajasaari, P., Sun, J. (eds.) FM 2014:

Formal Methods - 19th International Symposium. LNCS, vol. 8442, pp. 514–530. Springer (2014), https://doi.org/10.1007/978-3-319-06410-9_35
60. Reynolds, J.C.: GEDANKEN - a simple typeless language based on the principle of completeness and the reference concept. Commun. ACM **13**(5), 308–319 (1970), https://doi.org/10.1145/362349.362364
61. Reynolds, J.C.: Separation logic: A logic for shared mutable data structures. In: 17th IEEE Symposium on Logic in Computer Science (LICS 2002), Proceedings. pp. 55–74. IEEE Computer Society (2002), https://doi.org/10.1109/LICS.2002.1029817
62. Saini, D., Sunshine, J., Aldrich, J.: A theory of typestate-oriented programming. In: Proceedings of the 12th Workshop on Formal Techniques for Java-Like Programs, FTFJP 2010, Maribor, Slovenia, June 22, 2010. pp. 9:1–9:7. ACM (2010), https://doi.org/10.1145/1924520.1924529
63. Schreiner, A.T.: Objektorientierte Programmierung mit ANSI-C. Hanser (1994), https://www.cs.rit.edu/~ats
64. Sjöberg, V., Sang, Y., Weng, S.c., Shao, Z.: DeepSEA: A language for certified system software. Proc. ACM Program. Lang. **3**(OOPSLA), 136:1–136:27 (Oct 2019), http://doi.acm.org/10.1145/3360562
65. Summers, A.J., Drossopoulou, S.: Considerate reasoning and the composite design pattern. In: Barthe, G., Hermenegildo, M.V. (eds.) Verification, Model Checking, and Abstract Interpretation, 11th International Conference, VMCAI 2010, Proceedings. LNCS, vol. 5944, pp. 328–344. Springer (2010), https://doi.org/10.1007/978-3-642-11319-2_24
66. Summers, A.J., Drossopoulou, S., Müller, P.: The need for flexible object invariants. In: International Workshop on Aliasing, Confinement and Ownership in Object-Oriented Programming (IWACO'09). ACM (2009), https://doi.org/10.1145/1562154.1562160
67. Vasudevan, A., Chaki, S., Maniatis, P., Jia, L., Datta, A.: überspark: Enforcing verifiable object abstractions for automated compositional security analysis of a hypervisor. In: Holz, T., Savage, S. (eds.) 25th USENIX Security Symposium, USENIX Security 16. pp. 87–104. USENIX Association (2016), https://www.usenix.org/conference/usenixsecurity16/technical-sessions/presentation/vasudevan
68. Xia, L., Zakowski, Y., He, P., Hur, C., Malecha, G., Pierce, B.C., Zdancewic, S.: Interaction trees: representing recursive and impure programs in Coq. Proc. ACM Program. Lang. **4**(POPL), 51:1–51:32 (2020), https://doi.org/10.1145/3371119

An Automated Deductive Verification Framework for Circuit-building Quantum Programs

Christophe Chareton[1,2,✉], Sébastien Bardin[2], François Bobot[2], Valentin Perrelle[2], and Benoît Valiron[1]

[1] LMF, CentraleSupélec, Université Paris-Saclay, Gif-sur-Yvette, France
firstname.lastname@lri.fr

[2] CEA, LIST, Université Paris-Saclay, Palaiseau, France
firstname.lastname@cea.fr

Abstract. While recent progress in quantum hardware open the door for significant speedup in certain key areas, quantum algorithms are still hard to implement right, and the validation of such quantum programs is a challenge. In this paper we propose QBRICKS, a formal verification environment for circuit-building quantum programs, featuring both parametric specifications *and* a high degree of proof automation. We propose a logical framework based on first-order logic, and develop the main tool we rely upon for achieving the automation of proofs of quantum specification: PPS, a parametric extension of the recently developed path sum semantics. To back-up our claims, we implement and verify parametric versions of several famous and non-trivial quantum algorithms, including the quantum parts of *Shor's integer factoring*, quantum phase estimation (QPE) and Grover's search.

Keywords: deductive verification, quantum programming, quantum circuits

1 Introduction

1.1 Quantum computing. Quantum programming is seen as a potential revolution for many computing applications: cryptography [61], deep learning [7], optimization [23,22], solving linear systems [33], etc. In all of these domains, current quantum algorithms beat the best known classical algorithms by either quadratic or even exponential factors. In parallel to the rise of quantum algorithms, the design of quantum hardware has moved from lab-benches [14] to programmable, 50-qubits machines designed by industrial actors [4,38] reaching the point where quantum computers beat classical computers for specific tasks [4]. This has stirred a shift from a theoretical standpoint on quantum algorithms to a more programming-oriented view with the question of their concrete coding and implementation [66,65,55].

In this context, an important problem is the adequacy between the mathematical description of an algorithm and its concrete implementation as a program.

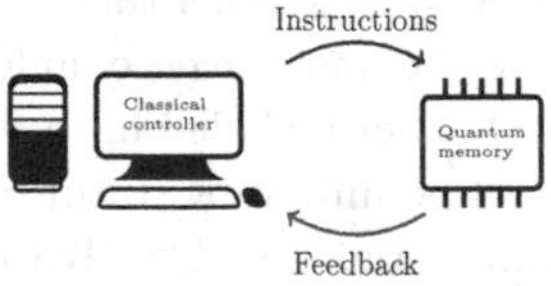

Fig. 1: The hybrid model

N. Yoshida (Ed.): ESOP 2021, LNCS 12648, pp. 148–177, 2021.
https://doi.org/10.1007/978-3-030-72019-3_6

1.2 The hybrid model. The vast majority of quantum algorithms are described within the *quantum co-processor model* [42], i.e. a hybrid model where a *classical* computer controls a *quantum* co-processor holding a quantum memory (cf. Figure 1). The co-processor is able to apply a fixed set of elementary operations (buffered as *quantum circuits*) to update and query (*measure*) the quantum memory. Importantly, while measurement allows one to retrieve classical (probabilistic) information from the quantum memory, it also modifies it (*destructive effect*). The quantum memory state is represented by a linear combination of possible concrete values, generalizing the classical notion of probabilities to the complex case, and the core of a quantum algorithm consists in successfully setting the memory in a specific *quantum state.*

Major *quantum programming languages* such as Quipper [30], Liqui|⟩ [67], Q# [64], ProjectQ [63], Silq [8], and the rich ecosystem of existing quantum programming frameworks [55] follow this hybrid model. Such *circuit-building quantum languages* are the current consensus for high-level executable quantum programming languages.

1.3 The problem with quantum algorithms. Starting from an initial state, a quantum algorithm typically describes a series of high-level operations which, once composed, realize the desired state. Each high-level operation may itself be described in a similar way, until one reaches elementary operations (*quantum gates*). Describing an algorithm therefore requires both to list these elementary operations, or *quantum circuit*, and to specify the circuit's behavior.

A major issue is then to verify that the quantum circuit generated by the code written as an implementation of a given algorithm is indeed a run of this algorithm, and that the circuit has indeed the specified characteristics of shape (for instance: a polynomial size).

While testing and debugging are the common verification practice in classical programming, they become extremely complicated in the quantum case: debugging and assertion checking are problematic due to the destructive aspect of quantum measurement, the probabilistic nature of quantum algorithms seriously impedes system-level quantum testing, and classical emulation of quantum algorithms is (strongly believed to be) intractable. On the other hand, nothing prevents *a priori* the formal verification [15] of quantum programs.

1.4 Goal and challenges. *Our goal is to provide an automated formal verification framework for circuit-building quantum programs.* Such a framework should satisfy the following principles: (1) *Parametricity:* it should allow parametric (i.e. scale-invariant) specifications and proofs, so as to enable the generic specification and verification of parametrized implementations. This is crucial as quantum algorithms always describe *parametrized families* of circuits; (2) *Proof automation:* it should, as far as possible, provide automatic proof means in order to ease adoption.

Prior works on quantum formal verification do not fully reach these goals together, as they are either not parametric, or not automated. Model-checking methods [27,70] are fully automatic but not parametric – moreover they are highly scale-sensitive. Recently, Amy [1,2] developed a powerful framework for reasoning over quantum circuits, the *path-sums symbolic representation*. Thanks to their good compositional properties, reasoning with path-sums is well automated and can scale up to large problem instances (up to 100 qubits). Yet, the method is not parametric and only addresses fixed-size circuits. On the other side of the spectrum, several approaches deal with parametricity but sacrifice automation as they generate proof obligations in higher-order logic, supported with proof assistants such as Coq or Isabelle/HOL. One can cite the approach of Boender et al. [10], Qwire [53,58], SQIR [35,34] or QHL [68,71,46,69,45]. Combined with the use of the standard *matrix semantics* for quantum circuits — that we show in Section 8 cumbersome for automation — only very few realistic quantum programs have been verified in a parametric way [45,35,34].

1.5 Proposal. We propose QBRICKS, an automated formal verification framework for circuit-building quantum programs, featuring parametric specification *together* with a high degree of proof automation.

We bring two key innovations along the road: **(Key 1)** we propose the new *parametrized path-sums (PPS)* symbolic representation of families of quantum circuits, extending path-sums [1] to the parametric case while keeping good compositional properties. PPS prove extremely useful both as a specification mechanism and as an automation mechanism; (**Key 2**) we carefully tune together our programming language (QBRICKS-DSL) and specification logic (QBRICKS-SPEC) so that the corresponding verification problem remains automatable in practice — first-order proof obligations — while the framework is still expressive enough to write, specify and verify realistic quantum programs (Shor order finding — Shor-OF [61], QPE [41,16], Grover [31]).

1.6 Contributions. We bring the following contributions.

- A flexible symbolic representation for reasoning about quantum states, building upon the recent path-sum symbolic representation [1,2]. Our representation, called *parametrized path-sums (PPS)*, retains the compositional and closure properties of regular path-sums while allowing *genericity* and *parametricity* of both specifications and proofs. Especially, first-order logic together with PPS provide a unified and powerful way to reason about many essential quantum concepts (Section 5.2) and fit well with the standard way of describing quantum algorithms. We are the first to highlight this connection and make PPS a "first-class" concept, where prior works are limited to standard path sums, or rely on the standard matrix semantics;
- A programming and verification framework, that is: on one hand, a core domain-specific language (QBRICKS-DSL, Section 4) for describing families of quantum circuits, with enough expressive power to describe parametric circuits from non-trivial quantum algorithms; and on the other hand, a *first-order* logical (domain-specific) specification language (QBRICKS-SPEC, Section 5), tightly integrated with PPS and QBRICKS-DSL to specify properties of parametrized programs representing families of quantum circuits. The careful interplay between these two components yields first-order proof obligations, and thus is a key aspect of proof automation;

- A dedicated proof engine: we introduce the Hybrid Quantum Hoare Logic (HQHL) deduction system for deductive verification over circuit-building quantum programs. It is tightly coupled with PPS and produces proof obligations in the QBRICKS-SPEC logic (Section 6);
- This framework is embedded in the Why3 deductive verification tool [9,24] as a DSL (Section 7), and provides proof automation mechanisms dedicated to the quantum case. This material is grounded in standard mathematics theories (linear algebra, arithmetic, complex numbers, binary operations, *etc.*) with 450+ definitions and 1,000+ lemmas. *All lemmas have been proved in Why3*, and the whole framework is publicly available;
- We present in Section 8 *the first ever verified parametric implementation of the quantum part of Shor's factoring algorithm* [61] (Order Finding, including the polynomial complexity of the circuits produced by our implementation and probability requirements), as well as verified parametric implementations of other major quantum algorithms: Quantum Phase Estimation (QPE) [41,16][3], Grover's (search) algorithm [31] and Quantum Fourier Transform (QFT) [18]. Our method achieves a high level of proof automation (96% on Shor-OF), significantly reducing proof effort (factor 13.6x vs. QHL on Grover, factors 7.7x and 6.4x vs. SQIR on resp. QPE and Grover).

Additional technical material can be found in the online extended versione [13]. Implementation and benchmarks are available online[54].

1.7 Discussion. The scope of this paper is limited to proving properties of circuit-building quantum programs. We do not claim to support right now the interactions between classical data and quantum data (referred to as "classical control" in the literature), nor the probabilistic side-effect resulting from the measurement. Still, we are already able to target realistic implementations of famous quantum algorithms, and thanks to equational theories for complex and real number we can automatically *reason* on the probabilistic outcome of a measurement. Also, we do not claim any novelty in the proofs for Shor-OF, QPE or Grover by themselves, but rather the first *highly-automated* parametric correctness proofs of the circuits produced by programs implementing them, and the first parametric correctness proofs of an implementation of Shor-OF.

2 Background: Quantum Algorithms and Programs

While in classical computing, the state of a bit is either 0 or 1, in quantum computing [50] the state of a *quantum bit* (or *qubit*) is described by *amplitudes* over the two elementary values 0 and 1 (denoted in the Dirac notation with $|0\rangle$ and $|1\rangle$), i.e. linear combinations $\alpha_0|0\rangle + \alpha_1|1\rangle$ where α_0 and α_1 are any *complex values* satisfying $|\alpha_0|^2 + |\alpha_1|^2 = 1$. In a sense, amplitudes are *generalization of probabilities*. More generally, the state of a *qubit register* of n qubits

[3] QPE is a major quantum building block, at the heart of, e.g., HHL [33] logarithmic linear system solving algorithm or quantum simulation [28].

("qubit-vector") is any *superposition* of the 2^n elementary bit-vectors ("basis element", where a bit-vector $k \in \{0..2^n-1\}$ is denoted $|k\rangle_n$), that is any $|u\rangle_n = \sum_{k=0}^{2^n-1} \alpha_k |k\rangle_n$ such that $\sum_{k=0}^{2^n-1} |\alpha_k|^2 = 1$. For example, in the case of two qubits, the basis is $|00\rangle$, $|01\rangle$, $|10\rangle$ and $|11\rangle$ (also abbreviated $|0\rangle_2$, $|1\rangle_2$, $|2\rangle_2$ and $|3\rangle_2$). Such a (*quantum state*) vector $|k\rangle_n$ is called a *ket* of length n (and dimension 2^n).

Technically speaking, we say that the quantum state of a register of n qubits is represented by a normalized vector in a Hilbert space of finite dimension 2^n (a.k.a. finite-dimensional Hilbert space), whose basis is generated by the Kronecker product (a.k.a. tensor product, denoted $\otimes$) over the elementary bit-vectors. For instance, for $n = 2$: $|0\rangle \otimes |0\rangle$, $|0\rangle \otimes |1\rangle$, $|1\rangle \otimes |0\rangle$ and $|1\rangle \otimes |1\rangle$ act as definitions for $|00\rangle$, $|01\rangle$, $|10\rangle$ and $|11\rangle$.

2.1 Quantum data manipulation. The core of a quantum algorithm consists in manipulating a qubit register through two main classes of operations. (1) *Quantum gate.* Local operation on a fixed number of qubits, whose action consists in the application of a *unitary map* to the corresponding quantum state vector i.e. a linear and bijective operation preserving norm and orthogonality. The fact that unitary maps are bijective ensures that every unitary gate admits an *inverse*. Unitary maps over n qubits are usually represented as $2^n \times 2^n$ *matrices*. (2) *Measurement.* The retrieval of classical information out of the quantum memory. This operation is probabilistic and modifies the state of a quantum register: measuring the n-qubit system $\sum_{k=0}^{2^n-1} \alpha_k |k\rangle_n$ returns the bit-vector k of length n with probability $|\alpha_k|^2$. Quantum gates might be applied in *sequence* or in *parallel*: sequence application corresponds to *map composition* (or, equivalently, matrix multiplication), while parallel application corresponds to the *Kronecker product*, or tensor product, of the original maps — or, equivalently, the Kronecker product of their matrix representations.[4]

2.2 Quantum circuits. In a way similar to classical Boolean functions, the application of quantum gates can be written in a diagrammatic notation: *quantum circuits.* Qubits are represented with horizontal wires and gates with boxes. Circuits are built *compositionally,* from a given set of *atomic gates* and by a small set of *circuit*

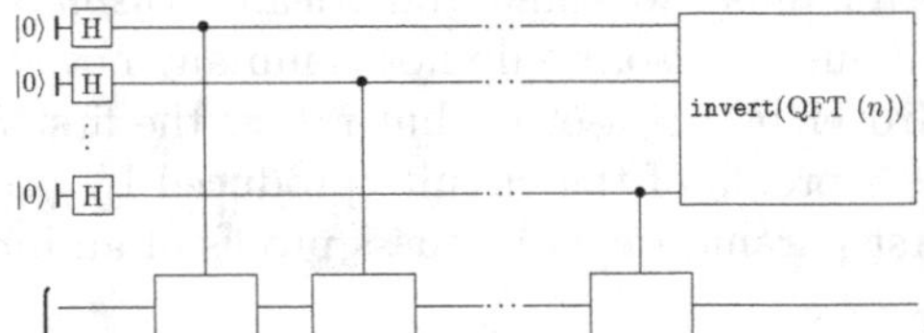

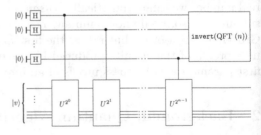

Fig. 2: The circuit for QPE

[4] Given two matrices A (with r rows and c columns) and B, their Kronecker product is the matrix $A \otimes B = \begin{pmatrix} a_{11}B & \dots a_c B \\ \vdots & \ddots & \vdots \\ a_{r1}B & \dots a_{rc}B \end{pmatrix}$. This operation is central in quantum information representation. It enjoys a number of useful algebraic properties such as associativity, bilinearity or the equality $(A \otimes B) \cdot (C \otimes D) = (A \cdot C) \otimes (B \cdot D)$, where $\cdot$ denotes matrix multiplication.

combinators, including: parallel and sequential compositions, circuit inverting, controlling, iteration, ancilla creation, etc. As an example of a quantum circuit, we show in Figure 2 the bird's-eye view of the circuit for QPE, the (quantum) phase estimation algorithm, a standard primitive in many quantum algorithms. QPE is *parametrized* by n (a number of wires) and U (a unitary *oracle*) and is built as follows. First, a register of n qubits is initialized in state $|0\rangle$, while another one is initialized in state $|v\rangle_n$. Then comes the circuit itself: a structured sequence of quantum gates, using the unary Hadamard gate H, the circuits U^{2^i} (realizing U to the power 2^i) and the reversed Quantum Fourier Transform `inverse`(QFT (n)) . Sub-circuits U^{2^i} and `inverse`(QFT (n)) are both defined in a similar way.

Here, one should simply note two things: (1) the circuit is made of parallel compositions of Hadamard gates and of sequential compositions of controlled U^{2^i} (the controlled operation is depicted with vertical lines and symbol $\bullet$); (2) the circuit is *parametrized* by n and by U. This is very common: in general, a quantum algorithm constructs a circuit whose size and shape depend on the parameters of the problem. It describes a *family of quantum circuits.*

2.3 Reasoning on circuits and the matrix semantics. Quantum circuits essentially describe unitary operators [50] acting on Hilbert spaces. In finite dimension, unitary matrices faithfully represent unitary operators: it has been the original mathematical formalism for circuits – coined here as the *matrix semantics.* If this representation is well-adapted for representing simple high-level circuit combinators such as the action of control or inversion, it is not well-suited for specifying the behavior of many complex circuits coming from the literature. Because of this cumbersomeness, textbook descriptions of circuits make use of an informal representation: operators are described by their action on a basis vector (see, for example the description of Shor-OF in [50, p. 232]). This is however understood as a shortcut notation for matrices which remains the main medium for reasoning on circuits. Formal approaches to quantum computation [35,34,53,58,68,71,46,69,45] witness this prevalence of matrices as circuit representation.

2.4 Path-sum representation. Path sums [1,2] are a recent symbolic representation. Its strength is to formalize the notation used in quantum algorithm literature (eg, [50]). A unitary operator U is written as $U : |x\rangle \mapsto PS(x)$ where x is a bit vector and $PS(x)$ is defined with the syntax of Fig. 3. In the Figure, addition and multiplication over real are denoted rescpectively with $+$ and $\cdot$, and $x_{[i]}$ is the ith projection of bit vector x. The term n is an integer index, characterizing the *range* of the path-sum. Then each term $k \in [\![0, 2^n[\![$ in the path-sum is defined through:

1. the *phase polynomial* $P_k(x)$ – a real value building complex scalar $e^{2\cdot\pi\cdot i\cdot P_k(x)}$;
2. the *basis-ket* function $\phi_k(x)$, defining the ket-vector $|\phi_k(x)\rangle$ this scalar value applies to.

This representation is closed under functional composition and Kronecker product. For instance, if U is defined as in Fig. 3 and if V sends y to $PS'(y)$ defined

$$
\begin{aligned}
PS(x) &::= \frac{1}{\sqrt{2}^n} \sum_{k=0}^{2^n-1} e^{2\cdot\pi\cdot i\cdot P_k(x)} |\phi_k(x)\rangle \\
P(x) &::= \frac{x_{[j]}}{2^k} \mid P(x)\cdot P(x) \mid P(x)+P(x) \\
|\phi(x)\rangle &::= |b_{[1]}(x)\rangle \otimes \ldots \otimes |b_{[n]}(x)\rangle \\
b_{[j]}(x) &::= x_{[j']} \mid \neg b_{[j']}(x) \mid b_{[j']}(x) \wedge b_{[j'']}(x) \mid b_{[j']}(x)\ \texttt{XOR}\ b_{[j'']}(x) \mid \texttt{tt} \mid \texttt{ff}
\end{aligned}
$$

Fig. 3: Syntax for regular path-sums [2,1]

as $\frac{1}{\sqrt{2}^{n'}} \sum_{k=0}^{2^{n'}-1} e^{2\cdot\pi\cdot i\cdot P'_k(y)} |\phi'_k(y)\rangle$, then $U \otimes V$ sends $|x\rangle \otimes |y\rangle$ to

$$
\frac{1}{\sqrt{2}^{n+n'}} \sum_{j=0}^{2^{n+n'}-1} e^{2\cdot\pi\cdot i(P_{j/2^n}(x)+P'_{j\%2^n}(y))} |\phi_{j/2^n}(x)\rangle \otimes |\phi'_{j\%2^n}(y)\rangle \quad (1)
$$

which is in the form shown in Figure 3. The compositionality of this semantics is used by Amy [2] to prove the equivalence of large circuit instances. Nonetheless, its main limitation stands in the fact that path-sums only address fixed-size circuits. Albeit a compositional tool, useful to automate proofs, it cannot be used for proving properties of parametrized circuit-building quantum programs.

This paper proposes an extension of path-sum semantics to address the parametric verification of quantum programs.

3 Introducing PPS

In this section, we introduce the main logical apparatus of our framework: parametrized path-sums. We first present a motivating example and then discuss the construction.

A circuit C_n defined as

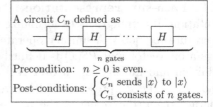

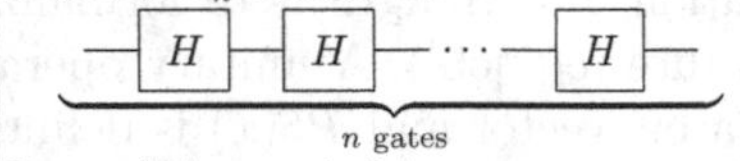

Precondition: $n \geq 0$ is even.

Post-conditions: $\begin{cases} C_n \text{ sends } |x\rangle \text{ to } |x\rangle \\ C_n \text{ consists of } n \text{ gates.} \end{cases}$

Fig. 4: Motivating Example

3.1 Motivating example. Let us consider the n-indexed family of circuits consisting of n Hadamard gates, in sequence, as shown in Figure 4. Sequencing two Hadamard gates can easily be shown equivalent to the identity operation. In other word, when fed with $|0\rangle$, if n is even the circuit outputs $|0\rangle$. Albeit small, this circuit family together with its simple specification exemplifies the typical framework we aim at in the context of certification of quantum programs.

- The description of the circuit family is parametrized by a classical parameter (here, the non-negative integer n);

- The pre-condition imposes both constraints (here, the evenness of n) and soundness conditions (here, the non-negativeness of n) on the parameters;
- The post-condition can both refer to the semantics of the circuit result and to its form and shape (here, its size).

The circuit family presented in Figure 4 will be used in the rest of the paper as a running, toy example for QBRICKS. In particular, we show in Example 1 how to code it in our framework and how to express the specification in Example 4. Its parametrized implementation in QBRICKS is three lines of code long and its specifications takes six lines. It is proved by recurrence over the parameter n, the induction step requiring two calls for lemmas (depending on the evenness of parameter n).

3.2 Parametrizing path-sums. In order to formalize the semantics of the example of Fig. 4, we aim at generalizing path-sums.

Illustration. For a fixed n, the circuit C_n implements either the identity (when n is even), in which case the path-sum is $PS_{Id}(x) = \frac{1}{\sqrt{2}^0}\sum_{k=0}^{2^0-1} e^{2i\pi\cdot 0}|x\rangle$ or the Hadamard gate (when n is odd), in which case the path sum is $PS_H(x) = \frac{1}{\sqrt{2}^1}\sum_{k=0}^{2^1-1} e^{2i\pi\frac{k\cdot x}{2}}|k\rangle$ A candidate parametric path-sum for the family of circuits $\{C_n\}_n$ from Figure 4 could then be written in factorized form as

$$PS_n(x) = \frac{1}{\sqrt{2}^{n\%2}} \sum_{k=0}^{2^{n\%2}-1} e^{2i\pi\frac{(n\%2)\cdot k\cdot x}{2}} |\mathtt{if\ even}(n)\ \mathtt{then}\ x\ \mathtt{else}\ k\rangle. \quad (2)$$

Generalization. In general, parametrized Path Sums (PPS) are defined over a language of typed terms with possibly free (typed) variables. At the very minimum the language has to be equipped with Boolean values (to handle the values of the ket-vector) and integers (for instance to handle the range).

Given such a language, a PPS is a path-sum where the range, the phase polynomial and the basis-ket can in general be explicit, open terms referring to external parameters. Formally, a pps is defined as a function inputting a set of parameters $\overline{p}$ and outputting:

- a parametrized integer $\mathtt{pps\_width}(h,\overline{p})$, featuring the number of qubits the target circuit is acting on — its *width*;
- another parametrized integer $\mathtt{pps\_range}(h,\overline{p})$, abbreviated as $\mathtt{r}(h,\overline{p})$. It indicates the *range* of the sum (defined as the set $\mathrm{BV}_{\mathtt{r}(h,\overline{p})}$ of bit vectors of length $\mathtt{r}(h,\overline{p})$);
- a *basis ket function* $\mathtt{pps\_ket}(h,\overline{p})$, generalizing term ϕ from Table 3. For any pair (x,y), of a bit vector x of length $\mathtt{pps\_width}(h,\overline{p})$ (standing for an input basis vector) and a bit vector of length $\mathtt{r}(h,\overline{p})$, it returns a bit vector of length $\mathtt{pps\_width}(h,\overline{p})$ (standing for an output basis vector);
- a parametrized *angle function* $\mathtt{pps\_angle}(h,\overline{p})(x,y)$, generalizing the phase polynomial P from Table 3. For any pair (x,y) such as above, it returns a real value θ.

Then, the behaviour of a parametrized quantum circuit $C(\overline{p})$ is described as the *i*/*o* function inputting a basis ket $|x(\overline{p})\rangle$ of length the width of $C(\overline{p})$ and outputting the parametrized sum term:

$$\texttt{pps\_apply}(h,\overline{p})(|x(\overline{p})\rangle) = \frac{1}{\sqrt{2}^{\texttt{r}(h,\overline{p})}} \sum_{y \in \mathrm{BV}_{\texttt{r}(h,\overline{p})}} e^{2i\pi * \texttt{pps\_angle}(h,\overline{p})(x,y)} |\texttt{pps\_ket}(h,\overline{p})(x,y)\rangle$$

For sake of readability, we often ommit the explicit mention of the parameters. For instance, the PPS P induced by (2) is parametrized by the integer n. It is such that for any `int` n, $\texttt{pps\_width}(P,n) = 1$ and $\texttt{pps\_range}(P,n) = n\%2$. Furthermore for any bit vectors x, y of lengths 1 and $n\%2$, $\texttt{pps\_ket}(P,n)(x,y)$ is equal to x if n is even and to y otherwise, and $\texttt{pps\_angle}(P,n)(x,y) = n\%2 \cdot x_{[0]} \cdot y_{[0]}$. One then gets expression (2) by applying $\texttt{pps\_apply}(P,\overline{p})$.

Hence, the term language needed for describing PPS of otherwise sophisticated families of quantum circuits can afford to be minimal: first-order typed terms equipped with an equational theory are enough. We also find out that first-order, predicate logic is suitable for specifying the properties of quantum programs: there is no need for higher-order logic such as the ones of Coq or Isabelle/HOL. This is the key to automation.

4 Qbricks-DSL

Qbricks-DSL is the (domain-specific) language of our framework. It is designed as a first-order, functional language aimed at *circuit description*. Measurement is out of the scope of the language, and all Qbricks-DSL expressions are terminating. We follow a very simple strategy for circuit building: we use a regular inductive datatype for circuits, where the data constructors are elementary gates, sequential and parallel composition, and ancilla creation. In particular, unlike Quipper [30] or Qwire [53], a quantum circuit is not a function acting on qubits: it is a simple, static object. Nonetheless, as illustrated by our experimentations (Section 8), this does impede neither expressiveness nor parametricity.

Furthermore, even if the language does not feature measurement, it is nonetheless possible to *reason* on probabilistic outputs of circuits, if we were to measure the result of a circuit. Indeed, this can be expressed in a regular theory of real and complex numbers (See Section 6.5).

4.1 Syntax of Qbricks-DSL. Qbricks-DSL is a small first-order functional, call-by-value language with a special datatype `circ` as the medium to build and manipulate circuits. The core of Qbricks-DSL can be presented as the simply-typed calculus presented in Figure 6. The basic data constructors for `circ` are `CNOT`, `SWAP`, `ID`, the Hadamard superposition gate `H`, phase shift gate $\texttt{Ph}(e)$ and the parametrized rotation $\texttt{R}_z(e)$. The constructors for high-level circuit operations are sequential composition `SEQ`, parallel composition `PAR` and ancilla creation/termination `ANC` (see Figure 5 for details).

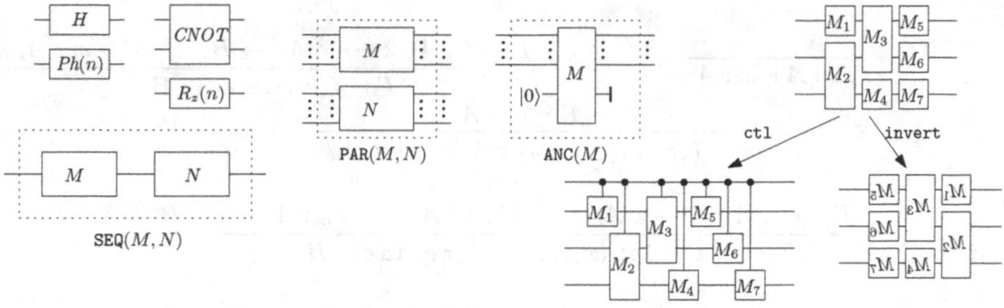

Fig. 5: Circuit combinators

Expression	e	$::= x \mid c \mid f(e_1,\dots,e_n) \mid \mathtt{let}\,\langle x_1,\dots,x_n\rangle = e\,\mathtt{in}\,e' \mid$ $\mathtt{if}\,e_1\,\mathtt{then}\,e_2\,\mathtt{else}\,e_3 \mid \mathtt{iter}\ f\ e_1\ e_2$
Data Constructor	c	$::= \underline{n} \mid \mathtt{tt} \mid \mathtt{ff} \mid \langle e_1,\dots,e_n\rangle \mid \mathtt{CNOT} \mid \mathtt{SWAP} \mid \mathtt{ID} \mid \mathtt{H} \mid \mathtt{Ph}(e) \mid \mathtt{R}_z(e) \mid$ $\mathtt{ANC}(e) \mid \mathtt{SEQ}(e_1,e_2) \mid \mathtt{PAR}(e_1,e_2)$
Function	f	$::= f_{\mathrm{d}} \mid f_{\mathrm{c}}$
Declaration	d	$::= \mathtt{let}\ f_{\mathrm{d}}(x_1,\dots,x_n) = e$
Type	A	$::= \mathtt{bool} \mid \mathtt{int} \mid \top \mid A_1 \times \cdots \times A_n \mid \mathtt{circ}.$
Value	v	$::= x \mid \underline{n} \mid \mathtt{tt} \mid \mathtt{ff} \mid \langle v_1,\dots,v_n\rangle \mid$ $\mathtt{CNOT} \mid \mathtt{SWAP} \mid \mathtt{ID} \mid \mathtt{H} \mid \mathtt{Ph}(\underline{n}) \mid \mathtt{R}_z(\underline{n}) \mid \mathtt{ANC}(v) \mid \mathtt{SEQ}(v_1,v_2) \mid \mathtt{PAR}(v_1,v_2)$
Context	$C[-]$	$::= [-] \mid f(v_1,\dots v_{i-1}, C[-], e_{i+1},\dots,e_n) \mid$ $\mathtt{let}\,\langle x_1,\dots,x_n\rangle = C[-]\,\mathtt{in}\,e' \mid \mathtt{if}\,C[-]\,\mathtt{then}\,e_2\,\mathtt{else}\,e_3 \mid$ $\mathtt{iter}\ f\ C[-]\ e \mid \mathtt{iter}\ f\ v\ C[-] \mid \langle v_1,\dots v_{i-1}, C[-], e_{i+1},\dots,e_n\rangle \mid$ $\mathtt{CNOT} \mid \mathtt{ID} \mid \mathtt{H} \mid \mathtt{Ph}(C[-]) \mid \mathtt{R}_z(C[-]) \mid \mathtt{ANC}(C[-]) \mid$ $\mathtt{SEQ}(C[-], e) \mid \mathtt{SEQ}(v, C[-]) \mid \mathtt{PAR}(C[-], e) \mid \mathtt{PAR}(v, C[-])$

Fig. 6: Syntax for QBRICKS-DSL

On top of `circ`, the type system of QBRICKS-DSL features the type of integers `int` (with constructors $\underline{n}$, one for each integer n), the type of Booleans `bool` (with constructors `tt` and `ff`) and the type of n-ary products (with constructor $\langle e_1,\dots,e_n\rangle$). This type system is not meant to be exhaustive and it can be extended with usual constructs such as floats, lists and other user-defined inductive datatypes — its embedding into WhyML makes it easy to use such types. The term constructs are limited to function calls, `let`-style composition, test with `if-then-else` and simple iteration: `iter` $f\ n\ a$ stands for $f(f(\cdots f(a)\cdots))$, with n calls to f. We again stress that this could easily be extended — we just do not need it.

The language is first-order: this is reflected by the types A of expressions. The type of a function is given by the types of its arguments and the type of its output. The type of a function with inputs of types A_i and output of type B is written $A_1 \times \cdots \times A_n \to B$.

A function f is either a function f_{d} defined with a declaration d or a constant function f_{c}. The functions defined by declarations must not be mutually recursive: this small, restricted language only features iteration. Constant functions consist in integer operators ($+$, $*$, $-$, *etc*), Boolean operators ($\wedge$, $\vee$, $\neg$, $\rightarrow$, *etc*),

$$\frac{}{\Gamma, x : A \vdash x : A} \qquad \frac{\Gamma \vdash f : A_1 \times \cdots \times A_n \to B \qquad \Gamma \vdash e_i : A_i}{\Gamma \vdash f(e_1, \ldots, e_n) : B}$$

$$\frac{\Gamma \vdash e_i : A_i}{\Gamma \vdash \langle e_1, \ldots, e_n \rangle : A_1 \times \cdots \times A_n}$$

$$\frac{\Gamma \vdash e_1 : A_1 \times \cdots \times A_n \qquad \Gamma, x_1 : A_1, \ldots, x_n : A_n \vdash e_2 : B}{\Gamma \vdash \texttt{let}\, \langle x_1, \ldots, x_n \rangle = e_1\, \texttt{in}\, e_2 : B}$$

$$\frac{\Gamma \vdash e_1 : \texttt{bool} \quad \Gamma \vdash e_2 : A \quad \Gamma \vdash e_3 : A}{\Gamma \vdash \texttt{if}\, e_1\, \texttt{then}\, e_2\, \texttt{else}\, e_3 : A} \qquad \frac{f : A \to A \quad \Gamma \vdash e_1 : \texttt{int} \quad \Gamma \vdash e_2 : A}{\Gamma \vdash \texttt{iter}\ f\ e_1\ e_2 : A}$$

Fig. 7: Typing rules for QBRICKS-DSL

comparison operators ($<, \leq, \geq, >, =, \neq : \texttt{int} \times \texttt{int} \to \texttt{bool}$) and high-level circuit operators: `ctl`, `invert` : `circ` $\to$ `circ` for controlling and inverting circuits, and `width`, `size` : `circ` $\to$ `int` for counting the number of input and output wires, and the number of gates (not counting `ID` nor `SWAP`) in the circuit C. See Figure 5 for the intuitive definition of circuit combinators.

The typing rules are the usual ones, summarized for convenience in Table 7.

4.2 Operational semantics. As any other regular functional programming language, QBRICKS-DSL is equipped with an operational semantics based on beta-reduction and substitution. We define a notion of value and applicative context as in Fig. 6. We then define a rewriting strategy as the relation defined with $C[e] \to C[e']$ whenever $e \to e'$ is one of the rule of Table 8. The table is split into the rules for the language constructs and the rules defining the behavior of the constant functions. We only give a subset of the latter rules. For instance, the arithmetic operations are defined in a canonical manner, and the Boolean and comparison operators are defined in a similar manner on values of type `int` and `bool`. The rules for the constant functions acting on circuits are also for the most part straightforward: the size of a sequence is the sum of the sizes of the compounds for instance. The rules which we do not provide are the ones for the control operation `ctl`: the intuition behind their definition can be found in [13]. For the elementary gates, any definition can be used (see e.g. [50]), as long as it can be written with the chosen set of gates. One just has to adjust the lemmas referring to `ctl` in QBRICKS-SPEC. Similarly, the inverse of elementary gates are not given: we can choose the usual ones from the literature —and this definition is then parametrized by the choice of gates.

4.3 Properties. The targeted low-level representation for an expression of type `circ` is a value made of the circuit data constructors presented in Table 6: a value v of type `circ` is made out of the grammar $\texttt{SEQ}(v_1, v_2) \mid \texttt{ANC}(v) \mid \texttt{PAR}(v_1, v_2) \mid \texttt{CNOT} \mid \texttt{SWAP} \mid \texttt{ID} \mid \texttt{H} \mid \texttt{Ph}(\underline{n}) \mid \texttt{R}_z(\underline{n})$. Since recursions are reduced to finite iterations, we can derive the following lemma through a simple inductive reasoning:

Language constructs	
Assuming that there is a declaration $f(x_1, \dots, x_n) \triangleq e$.	
$f(v_1, \dots, v_n) \to e[x_1 := v_1, \dots, x_n := v_n]$	
$\texttt{let}\ \langle x_1, \dots, x_n\rangle = \langle v_1, \dots, v_n\rangle\ \texttt{in}\ e \to e[x_1 := v_1, \dots, x_n := v_n]$	
$\texttt{if tt then}\ e_1\ \texttt{else}\ e_2 \to e_1$	
$\texttt{if ff then}\ e_1\ \texttt{else}\ e_2 \to e_2$	
when $n \leq 0$: $\texttt{iter}\ f\ \underline{n}\ a \to a$	
when $n > 0$: $\texttt{iter}\ f\ \underline{n}\ a \to f(\texttt{iter}\ f\ \underline{n-1}\ a)$	
Constant functions (subset of the rules)	
$\underline{n} + \underline{m} \to \underline{n+m}$	$\texttt{width(CNOT)} \to 2$
$\underline{n} - \underline{m} \to \underline{n-m}$	$\texttt{width(SWAP)} \to 2$
$\underline{n} * \underline{m} \to \underline{n*m}$	$\texttt{width}(g) \to 1$ (g other gate)
$\texttt{size(ID)} \to 0$	$\texttt{width}(\texttt{SEQ}(v_1, v_2)) \to \texttt{width}(v_1)$
$\texttt{size(SWAP)} \to 0$	$\texttt{width}(\texttt{PAR}(v_1, v_2)) \to \texttt{width}(v_1) + \texttt{width}(v_2)$
$\texttt{size}(g) \to 1$ (g other gate)	$\texttt{width}(\texttt{ANC}(v)) \to \texttt{width}(v) - 1$
$\texttt{size}(\texttt{SEQ}(v_1, v_2)) \to \texttt{size}(v_1) + \texttt{size}(v_2)$	$\texttt{invert}(\texttt{SEQ}(v_1, v_2)) \to \texttt{SEQ}(\texttt{invert}(v_2), \texttt{invert}(v_1))$
$\texttt{size}(\texttt{PAR}(v_1, v_2)) \to \texttt{size}(v_1) + \texttt{size}(v_2)$	$\texttt{invert}(\texttt{PAR}(v_1, v_2)) \to \texttt{PAR}(\texttt{invert}(v_1), \texttt{invert}(v_2))$
$\texttt{size}(\texttt{ANC}(v)) \to \texttt{size}(v)$	$\texttt{invert}(\texttt{ANC}(v)) \to \texttt{ANC}(\texttt{invert}(v))$

Table 8: Operational semantics for QBRICKS-DSL

Lemma 1 (Safety properties and normalization). *Provided that $\vdash e : A$ is a closed expression, and provided that all the functions in e recursively admit (external) definitions, then either e is a value or it reduces. If $\Gamma \vdash e : A$ and $e \to e'$, then $\Gamma \vdash e' : A$. Finally, the reduction strategy ($\to$) is normalizing: there does not exist an infinite reduction sequence $e_1 \to e_2 \to \dots$* □

Example 1. The example of Section 3.1 can be written in QBRICKS-DSL as

$$\texttt{let aux}(x) = \texttt{SEQ}(x, \texttt{H})$$
$$\texttt{let main}(n) = \texttt{iter aux}\ n\ \texttt{ID}$$

The function **aux** inputs a circuit and appends a Hadamard gate at the end. The function **main** then inputs an integer parameter **n** and iterates the function **aux** to obtain **n** Hadamard in sequence. In particular, one can show that for instance

$$\texttt{main}\ \underline{4} \to^* \texttt{SEQ(SEQ(SEQ(SEQ(ID,H),H),H),H)},$$

that is, a sequence of 4 Hadamard gates.

4.4 Universality and usability of the chosen circuit constructs.

A *universal* (resp. *pseudo-universal*) set of elementary gates is such that they can be composed thanks to sequence or parallelism so as to perform (resp. approach arbitrarily close) any unitary matrix. In QBRICKS-DSL, we chose the small pseudo-universal elementary set $\{\texttt{CNOT}, \texttt{SWAP}, \texttt{ID}, \texttt{H}\} \cup \bigcup_{n \in \mathbb{N}} \{\texttt{Ph}(\underline{n}), \texttt{R}_z(\underline{n}), \}$. Other gates can then be defined as macros on top of them. If one aims at using QBRICKS inside a verification compilation tool-chain, these macros can for instance be the gates of the targeted architecture.

4.5 Validity of circuits. A circuit is represented as a rigid rectangular shape with a fixed number of input and output wires. In particular, there is a notion of validity: a `circ` object only makes sense provided two constraints:

- in $\texttt{SEQ}(C_1, C_2)$, the two circuits C_1 and C_2 should have the same width. For instance, $\texttt{SEQ}(\texttt{CNOT}, \texttt{H})$ is not valid. This is a simple *syntactic* constraint;
- in $\texttt{ANC}(C)$, the circuit C should have $n+1$ wires. Moreover, if given as input a vector where the last qubit is in state $|0\rangle$, its output should also leave this qubit in state $|0\rangle$. This condition is, on the other hand, a *semantic* constraint.

Note that even these syntactic constraints cannot be checked by a simple typing procedure, because of the higher-order reasoning involved here: the constraints must hold for any value of the parameters. All these constraints apply on parametrized circuits. They translate into constraints for the parameters of their related PPS and are expressed in our domain-specific logical specification language, QBRICKS-SPEC. They are meant to be sent as proof obligations to a proof engine.

Example 2. Note how the circuit generated by `main` in Example 1 is not necessarily a valid circuit (although in this case it is). This is one of the constraints that can be handled by QBRICKS-SPEC, as shown in Example 4.

4.6 Denotational semantics. As all expressions in QBRICKS-DSL are terminating, one can use regular sets as denotational semantics for the language. In order to be able to handle the definitions coming up in Section 5, we include in the denotation of each type an "error" element $\perp$ We therefore define the denotation of basic types as the set of their values: $[\![\texttt{bool}]\!] = \{\mathtt{tt}, \mathtt{ff}, \perp\}$, $[\![\texttt{int}]\!] = \mathbb{Z} \cup \{\perp\}$ and $[\![\texttt{circ}]\!] = \{v \mid\ \vdash v : \texttt{circ}\} \cup \{\perp\}$. Product types are defined as the set-product: $[\![A_1 \times \cdots \times A_n]\!] = ([\![A_1]\!] \times \cdots \times [\![A_n]\!]) \cup \{\perp\}$ and $[\![\top]\!] = \{\star, \perp\}$, the singleton set. Finally, functions are defined as set-functions from the input set to the output set. The denotation of the language constructs are the usual one in a semantics based on sets ; for the constant functions, the definitions are the canonical ones: arithmetic operations maps to arithmetic operations for instance. In QBRICKS-DSL, everything is well-defined and $\perp$ is only attainable from $\perp$. For instance, $\perp + x = \perp$.

Note that in the denotational semantics one can build non-valid circuits. For instance, the circuit $\texttt{SEQ}(\texttt{CNOT}, \texttt{H})$ is a member of $[\![\texttt{circ}]\!]$. This is to be expected as we have the following property:

Lemma 2 (Soundness). *Provided that* $\vdash e : A$, *we have* $[\![e]\!] \in [\![A]\!] \setminus \{\perp\}$. *Moreover, provided that* $e \to e'$ *then we have* $[\![e]\!] = [\![e']\!]$. □

It is however possible to formalize the notion of syntactically valid circuits as a subset of $[\![\texttt{circ}]\!]$.

Definition 1. We define the (syntactic) unary relation $\mathcal{V}_{\text{syntax}}$ on $[\![\texttt{circ}]\!]$ as follows: Each one of the gates belongs to $\mathcal{V}_{\text{syntax}}$; if C_1 and C_2 belongs to $\mathcal{V}_{\text{syntax}}$ then so does $\texttt{PAR}(C_1, C_2)$; if moreover $2 \leq [\![\texttt{width}]\!](C_1)$ then $\texttt{ANC}(C_1)$ belongs to $\mathcal{V}_{\text{syntax}}$ and if $[\![\texttt{width}]\!](C_1) = [\![\texttt{width}]\!](C_2)$ then $\texttt{SEQ}(C_1, C_2)$ belongs to $\mathcal{V}_{\text{syntax}}$.

5 QBRICKS-SPEC

The language QBRICKS-DSL is only aimed at manipulating circuits. The reasoning features of QBRICKS —and the PPS introduced in Section 3— are defined in the logic and the specification tools offered within QBRICKS-SPEC.

5.1 Syntax of QBRICKS-SPEC. We define QBRICKS-SPEC as a first-order, predicate logic with the following syntax.

$$\begin{array}{rll} \text{Formula} & \phi, \psi ::= & \phi \vee \psi \mid \phi \wedge \psi \mid \neg\phi \mid \phi \rightarrow \psi \mid \\ & & R(\hat{e}_1, \ldots, \hat{e}_n) \mid \hat{e}_1 = \hat{e}_2 \\ \text{First-order expression} & \hat{e} \quad ::= & x \mid c(\hat{e}_1, \ldots, \hat{e}_n) \mid f(\hat{e}_1, \ldots, \hat{e}_n) \mid f_\ell(\hat{e}_1, \ldots, \hat{e}_n). \end{array}$$

The first-order expressions $\hat{e}$ form a subset of QBRICKS-DSL: they are restricted to variables and (formal) function calls to other first-order expressions. Unlike regular, general expressions —meant to be computational vehicles— these first-order expressions only aim at being reasoned upon. The function names are then expanded with counterpart *logical functions* f_ℓ. Among these new functions, we introduce one function $\texttt{iter}_f : \texttt{int} \times A \rightarrow A$ for each function $f : A \rightarrow A$, standing for the equational counterpart of the iteration[5]. The logic functions are defined equationally in the logic: see Section 6.4 for details. The relation R ranges over a list of constant relations over first-order expressions. In QBRICKS-SPEC, we identify relations and functions of return type `bool`. A special relation is the equality: we explicitly introduce it in the syntax to emphasize the fact that QBRICKS-SPEC is meant to deal with equational theories.

The type system of QBRICKS-SPEC is extended with opaque types, equipped with constant functions and relations to reason upon them. They come with no computational content: the aim is purely to be able to *express and prove specification properties* of programs. This is why we do not incorporate them in QBRICKS-DSL's type system.

The opaque types we consider in QBRICKS-SPEC are `complex`, `real`, `pps`, `ket` and `bitvector`. The operators and relations for these new types are given in Table 9. Note that in the rest of the paper we will omit the cast operations `i_to_r` and `r_to_c`. We will also use a declared exponentiation function $[-]^{[-]}$ overloaded with types `complex` $\times$ `int` $\rightarrow$ `complex` and `real` $\times$ `int` $\rightarrow$ `real`. For any integer n and boolean b, constructor `bv_cst` buildsthe bit vector of length n and constant value b. Other functions for types `complex`, `real` and `bitvector` are standard. Types `pps` and `ket` are novel and form the main reasoning vehicle in QBRICKS-SPEC.

5.2 The types pps and ket. In short, the type `pps` encodes our *parametrized path sum* (PPS) representation for expressions of type `circ` in QBRICKS-DSL, while `ket` encodes the notion of ket-vector. As these types are pure reasoning apparatuses, we only need them in QBRICKS-SPEC and they are defined uniquely through an equational theory.

[5] This is required to stay within the grammar of terms of QBRICKS-SPEC.

complex and real	pps
i, π : complex	pps_width : pps → int
i_to_r : int → real	pps_range : pps → int
r_to_c : real → complex	pps_angle : pps × bitvector × bitvector → real
Re, Im, abs : complex → real	pps_ket : pps × bitvector × bitvector → bitvector
$e^{[]}$: complex → complex	pps_apply : pps × ket → ket
$-_c, +_c, *_c, /_c$: complex × complex → complex	pps_equiv : pps × pps → bool
$-_r, +_r, *_r, /_r$: real × real → real	circ_to_pps : circ → pps
$\sqrt{-}$: real → real	**ket**
bitvector	ket_length : ket → int
bv_length : bitvector → int	ket_get : ket × bitvector → complex
bv_cst : int × bool → bitvector	bv_to_ket : bitvector → ket
bv_get : bitvector × int → bool	$+_k, -_k, \otimes_k$: ket × ket → ket
bv_set : bitvector × int × bool → bitvector	$*_k$: complex × ket → ket

Table 9: Primary operators for QBRICKS-SPEC

The type pps is equipped with four opaque accessors: pps_width, pps_width, pps_width, pps_ket and pps_angle acting on pps from Section 3.2 and with the function circ_apply. If path-sums compose nicely, a given linear map does not have a unique representative path-sum (partly due to the fact that phase polynomials are equal modulo 2π). To capture this equivalence, we introduce the constant relation pps_equiv. In order to relate circuits and PPS, we introduce the constant function circ_to_pps: it returns *one possible* PPS that *represents* the input circuit. The chosen PPS is built in a constructive manner on the structure of the circuit. A useful relation is $(- \triangleright -)$ relating a circuit and a PPS: it is defined as $(c \triangleright h) \triangleq$ pps_equiv(circ_to_pps(c), h). Another useful macro is function circ_apply : circ × ket → ket, defined as

$$\texttt{circ\_apply}(C, k) \triangleq \texttt{pps\_apply}(\texttt{circ\_to\_pps}(C), k)$$

The type ket is equipped with standard operations for manipulating ket-vectors (Table 9). bv_to_ket turns a bit vector into a basis ket-vector ; ket_length returns the number of qubits in the ket ; ket_get returns the amplitude of the corresponding basis ket-vector. The other operations are the usual operations on vectors: addition, subtraction, tensors, scalar multiplication.

5.3 Denotational semantics of the new types. The denotational semantics of real and complex are respectively the sets $\mathbb{R} \cup \{\bot\}$ and $\mathbb{C} \cup \{\bot\}$, and the denotation of the operators are the canonical ones. As for Section 4.6, $\bot$ maps to $\bot$, so for instance $\bot +_r x = \bot$. The denotation of bitvector is defined as the set of all bit-vectors, together with the "error" element $\bot$. The constant functions are mapped to their natural candidate definition, using $\bot$ as the default result when they should not be defined. So for instance, $[\![\texttt{bv\_cst}]\!](-1, \texttt{tt}) = \bot$. An element of ket is meant to be a ket-vector: we defined $[\![\texttt{ket}]\!]$ as the set of *all* possible ket-vectors $\sum_{i=0}^{2^n} \alpha_n |b_n\rangle_m$, for all possible $m, n \in \mathbb{N}$, $\alpha_n \in \mathbb{C}$ and bit-vectors b_n of size m, together with the error element $\bot$. Finally, pps is defined as the set of formal path-sums, as defined in Section 3.2, together with the error element $\bot$. The denotation of the constant functions are defined as discussed in Section 5.2. As an example, $[\![\texttt{pps\_range}]\!]$ returns the range of the corresponding PPS. The map `circ_to_pps` builds a valid PPS out of the input circuit, or $\perp$ if the circuit is not valid.

The defined PPS follows the structure of the circuit. For instance, as shown in Eq. (1) on Page 154 the PPS $\mathtt{circ\_to\_pps}(\mathtt{SEQ}(C_1, C_2))$ is the sequential composition of the two PPS $\mathtt{circ\_to\_pps}(C_1)$ and $\mathtt{circ\_to\_pps}(C_2)$. This kind of compositionality is what helps with automation.

5.4 Regular sequents in QBRICKS-SPEC. Formulas in QBRICKS-SPEC are typed objects —and, as mentioned in Section 5.1 one can identify them with first-order expressions of type `bool`. Due to this correspondence, we shall only say that logic judgments in QBRICKS-SPEC are well-formed judgments of the form $\Delta \vdash \phi$ where the well-formedness means that $\Delta \vdash \phi : \mathtt{bool}$ is a valid typing judgment in QBRICKS-DSL. That being said, a well-formed judgment $\Delta \vdash \phi$ is valid whenever it holds in the denotational semantics: for every instantiation σ sending $x : A$ in Δ to $[\![A]\!]$, the denotation $[\![\phi]\!]_\sigma$ is valid. In particular, the (free) variables of ϕ can be regarded as universally quantified by the context Δ.

5.5 Parametricity of PPS. A regular path-sum is not parametric: it represents *one* fixed functional. So why did we chose $[\![\mathtt{pps}]\!]$ to be a set of path-sums? Let us consider an example.

Example 3. Consider the motivating example of Section 3.1 and its instantiation in Example 1 on page 159. The function `main` describes a family of circuits indexed by an integer parameter n. Now, consider the typing judgment

$$h : \mathtt{pps}, n : \mathtt{int} \vdash (\mathtt{main}(n) \rhd h) : \mathtt{bool}.$$

It can be regarded as a relation between PPS h and integers n, valid whenever h represents $\mathtt{main}(n)$. Technically, this relation is not quite the graph of a function (since several PPS might match the circuit $\mathtt{main}(n)$).

5.6 Standard matrix semantics and correctness of PPS semantics. Similarly to the type `pps`, QBRICKS is endowed with a (logical) type `matrix` to handle the matrix interpretation of circuits, together with various functions and relations to reason on it. In particular, QBRICKS features a function $\mathtt{mat\_get} : \mathtt{matrix} \times \mathtt{int} \times \mathtt{int} \to \mathtt{complex}$, formalizing the access to a matrix element, and a function $\mathtt{circ\_to\_mat} : \mathtt{circ} \to \mathtt{matrix}$ realizing the matrix corresponding to a circuit. We then formally show, within our framework (proven in Why3), that for any valid circuit C and ket k of length $\mathtt{width}(C)$, applying $\mathtt{circ\_to\_pps}(C)$ on k is equivalent to multiplying it by $\mathtt{circ\_to\_mat}(C)$:

Theorem 1 (Soundness of PPS wrt matrix semantics).

$$C : \mathtt{circ}, k : \mathtt{ket} \vdash \mathtt{ket\_length}(k) = \mathtt{width}(C) \land \mathtt{valid}(C) \to \mathtt{apply\_mat}(\mathtt{circ\_to\_mat}\, C, k) = \mathtt{pps\_apply}(\mathtt{circ\_to\_pps}\, C, k)$$

6 Reasoning on Quantum Programs

Thanks to the logic presented in Section 5.4, it is possible to write QBRICKS-SPEC formulas and to express properties of terms of the restricted syntax of Section 5.1. Provided that the regular sequents are *simple enough*, these can automatically be handled with the use of SMT solvers.

In this section, we define a specific Hoare logic, *Hybrid Hoare Logic (HQHL)*, to express pre- and post-conditions for arbitrary QBRICKS-DSL terms. We then discuss the validity of such judgments and explain how to decompose them into elementary, regular sequents (proof obligations). The claim —backed up by our experiments in Section 8— is that the obtained sequents are in practice *simple enough* to be dealt with automatically.

We do not present all HQHL rules here, but simply aim to give an intuition of how and why one can rely on an automated deductive system to derive QBRICKS-SPEC judgments. The complete set of HQHL rules is presented in [13].

6.1 HQHL judgments. In order to be able to express program specifications with pre- and post-conditions, we introduce Hybrid Quantum Hoare Logic (HQHL) sequents of the form $\Delta \Vdash \{\phi\}e\{\psi\} : A$ (we omit the type A when irrelevant or clear). The formula ψ can make use of a reserved free variable `result` of type A. Such a sequent is then well-formed provided that $\Delta \vdash \phi : \texttt{bool}$, $\Delta, \texttt{result} : A \vdash \psi : \texttt{bool}$ and $\Delta \vdash e : A$ are valid typing judgments. Note how the reserved free variable `result` is being added to Δ for typing ψ. For convenience, as syntactic sugar we allow indexed variables $\texttt{result}_i$ to stand for the ith projection of a tuple.

The validity of an HQHL sequent can be defined semantically, similarly to what was done in Section 5.4: $\Delta \Vdash \{\phi\}e\{\psi\} : A$ is valid whenever it is both well-formed and when for every instantiation σ sending $x : A$ in Δ to $[\![A]\!]$ and sending `result` to $[\![e]\!]$, the denotation $[\![\phi \to \psi]\!]_\sigma$ is valid.

In the following sections, we describe the deduction rules that we rely on in QBRICKS. They are designed to be used in a bottom-up strategy to break down judgments into pieces reasoning on smaller terms. Along the way, there is the need for introducing invariants and assertions. As usual, some of these assertions can be derived by computing the weakest-preconditions: we do not necessarily have to introduce every single one. When attaining a term of the restricted grammar of QBRICKS-SPEC that cannot be further decomposed, one can rely on the rule

$$\frac{\Gamma \vdash \phi \to \psi[\texttt{result} := \hat{e}]}{\Gamma \Vdash \{\phi\}\ \hat{e}\ \{\psi\} : A}\ (\texttt{f-o})$$

to generate a proof obligation as a regular sequent in QBRICKS-SPEC.

6.2 Deduction rules for term constructs. Figure 10 presents the deduction rules for the term constructs of QBRICKS-DSL carrying a computational content: iteration, tests, function evaluation, etc. We also present a standard weakening rule (`weaken`) and an example of rule for rewriting: The deduction rule (`eq`) states that whenever two expressions are equal one can substitute one

$$\frac{\Gamma, x \Vdash \{\phi \wedge x \leq 0\}\ e_2\ \{P[x, \texttt{result}]\} \quad \Gamma, x, y \Vdash \{\phi \wedge P[x, y]\}\ f(y)\ \{P[x+1, \texttt{result}]\}}{\Gamma \Vdash \{\phi\}\ \texttt{iter}\ f\ \hat{e}_1\ e_2\ \{P[\hat{e}_1, \texttt{result}]\}}\ (\texttt{iter})$$

$$\frac{\Gamma \Vdash \{P\}e_1\{Q[x_i := \texttt{result}_i\} \quad \Gamma, x_1, \ldots, x_n \Vdash \{Q\}e_2\{R\}}{\Gamma \Vdash \{P\}\texttt{let}\, x_1, \ldots, x_n = e_1\ \texttt{in}\, e_2\{R\}}\ (\texttt{let})$$

$$\frac{\Gamma \Vdash \{P\}e_1\{Q[x := \texttt{result}\} \quad \Gamma, x \Vdash \{Q \wedge x\}e_2\{R\} \quad \Gamma, x \Vdash \{Q \wedge \neg x\}e_3\{R\}}{\Gamma \Vdash \{P\}\texttt{if}\ e_1\ \texttt{then}\ e_2[x := e_1]\ \texttt{else}\ e_3[x := e_1]\{R\}}\ (\texttt{if})$$

$$\frac{\forall i, \Gamma \Vdash \{P\}e_i\{R_i[\texttt{result}]\}}{\Gamma \Vdash \{P\}\langle e_1, \ldots, e_2\rangle\{R_1[\texttt{result}_1] \wedge \cdots \wedge R_n[\texttt{result}_n]\}}\ (\texttt{tuple})$$

$$\frac{f(x_1, \ldots, x_n) \triangleq e \quad \Gamma \Vdash \{P\}e[x_1 := e_1, \ldots, x_n := e_n]\{R\}}{\Gamma \Vdash \{P\}f(e_1, \ldots, e_n)\{R\}}\ (\texttt{decl})$$

$$\frac{\Gamma \vdash P \to P' \quad \Gamma \Vdash \{P'\}\ e\ \{Q'\} : A \quad \Gamma, \texttt{result} : A \vdash Q' \to Q}{\Gamma \Vdash \{P\}e\{Q\} : A}\ (\texttt{weaken})$$

$$\frac{\Gamma \vdash e_1 = e_2 : A \quad \Gamma \Vdash \{P[e_1]\}\ e[e_1]\ \{Q[e_1]\} : A}{\Gamma \Vdash \{P[e_2]\}\ e[e_2]\ \{Q[e_2]\} : A}\ (\texttt{eq})$$

Fig. 10: Deduction rules for QBRICKS: HQHL rules for term constructs

for the other inside a HQHL judgment. Finally, we can derive from the semantics the usual substitution rules. For instance, provided that $\Gamma, x : A \vdash \psi$ and $\Gamma \vdash \hat{e} : A$ then $\Gamma \vdash \psi[x := \hat{e}]$. Note that in the rules, the first-order expressions of the form $\hat{e}$ are from the restricted grammar of terms of QBRICKS-SPEC.

6.3 Deduction rules for pps. The main tools to relate circuits and PPS are the constant function `circ_to_pps`, its relational counterpart $(- \triangleright -)$, and the declared function `circ_apply`. They can be specified inductively on the structure of the input circuit. The complete set of rules for `circ_to_pps` and $(- \triangleright -)$ can be found in [13].

***Compositionality of* SEQ.** For instance, one can derive the deduction rules for `circ_apply` applied to `SEQ` from Table 11. These rules can be used in a bottom-up manner to derive composable, elementary properties of circuits out of sub-circuits. In the table, we abbreviate `pps_acc(circ_to_pps(−))` with $C_{\texttt{acc}}$, for `acc` $\in$ {`width, range, ket,angle`} and, given two bit vectors x and y, $x \cdot y$ denotes their concatenation.

***Example of deduction rule for* HAD.** Using the notations from above, we define the following axiom for function `circ_to_pps` applied to the gate `HAD`:

$$\dfrac{\texttt{Prec-SEQ} \triangleq \begin{array}{l} \Gamma \Vdash \{\phi\}C_1\{\texttt{C\_width(result},\{p\}) = w\} \\ \Gamma \Vdash \{\phi\}C_1\{\texttt{C\_width(result},\{p\}) = w\} \end{array}}{\Gamma \Vdash \{\phi\}\texttt{SEQ}(C_1, C_2)\{\texttt{C\_width(result},\{p\}) = w\}}\ \texttt{SEQ}_w$$

$$\dfrac{\{\texttt{Prec-SEQ}\} \quad \begin{array}{l} \Gamma \Vdash \{\phi_1\}C_1\{\texttt{C\_range(result},\{p\}) = r_1(\{p\})\} \\ \Gamma \Vdash \{\phi_2\}C_2\{\texttt{C\_range(result},\{p\}) = r_2(\{p\})\} \end{array}}{\Gamma \Vdash \{\phi_1 \ \wedge \ \phi_2\}\texttt{SEQ}(C_1, C_2)\{\texttt{C\_range(result},\{p\}) = r_1(\{p\}) + r_2(\{p\})\}}\ \texttt{SEQ}_r$$

$$\dfrac{\{\texttt{Prec-SEQ}\} \quad \begin{array}{l} \Gamma \Vdash \{\phi_1\}C_1\{\texttt{C\_angle(result},\{p\})(x, y_1) = a_1(\{p\}, x, y_1)\} \\ \Gamma \Vdash \{\phi_1\}C_1\{\texttt{C\_ket(result},\{p\})(x, y_1) = k_1(\{p\}, x, y_1)\} \\ \Gamma \Vdash \{\phi_2\}C_2\{\texttt{C\_angle(result},\{p\})(k_1(\{p\}, x, y_1), y_2) \\ \quad = a_2(\{p\}, x, y_1, y_2)\} \end{array}}{\begin{array}{l}\Gamma \Vdash \{\phi_1 \ \wedge \ \phi_2\}\texttt{SEQ}(C_1, C_2)\{\texttt{C\_angle(result},\{p\})(x, y_1 \cdot y_2) \\ \quad = a_1(\{p\}, x, y_1) + a_2(\{p\}, x, y_1, y_2)\}\end{array}}\ \texttt{SEQ}_a$$

$$\dfrac{\{\texttt{Prec-SEQ}\} \quad \begin{array}{l} \Gamma \Vdash \{\phi_1\}C_1\{\texttt{C\_ket(result},\{p\})(x, y_1) = k_1(\{p\}, x, y_1)\} \\ \Gamma \Vdash \{\phi_2\}C_2\{\texttt{C\_ket(result},\{p\})(k_1(\{p\}, x, y_1), y_2) \\ \quad = k_2(\{p\}, x, y_1 \cdot y_2)\} \end{array}}{\Gamma \Vdash \{\phi_1 \ \wedge \ \phi_2\}\texttt{SEQ}(C_1, C_2)\{\texttt{C\_ket(result},\{p\})(x, y_1 \cdot y_2) = k_2(\{p\}, x, y_1 \cdot y_2)\}}\ \texttt{SEQ}_k$$

Fig. 11: Deduction rules for `circ_apply` on sequence of circuits

$$\Gamma, x, y : \texttt{bitvector} \Vdash$$
$$\left\{ \begin{array}{l} \texttt{bv\_length}(x) = 1 \\ \texttt{bv\_length}(y) = 1 \end{array} \right\} \texttt{HAD} \left\{ \begin{array}{c} \texttt{C\_width(result)} = 1, \\ \texttt{C\_range(result)} = 1, \\ \texttt{C\_angle(result},x,y) = x_{[0]} * y_{[0]}, \\ \texttt{C\_ket(result},x,y) = y \end{array} \right\}$$

Example 4. Consider the motivating example of Section 3.1 and its instantiation in Example 1. We can now give a specification to the function `main`, as follows:

$$n : \texttt{int}, m : \texttt{int}, x : \texttt{ket} \Vdash \quad \begin{array}{c} \{n \geq 0 \wedge \texttt{ket\_length}(x) = 1 \wedge n = 2 * m\} \\ \texttt{main}(n) \\ \{\texttt{circ\_apply(result},x) = x\}\,. \end{array}$$

The fact that `circ_apply` is well-defined implies that C is valid.

6.4 Equational reasoning. The SMT solvers we aim at using to discharge proof obligations require equational theories describing how to reason on the constant functions that were introduced. Some of these equational theories, such as bit-vectors and algebraic fields, are standard and well-known in verification. Together with a few properties on square-root, exponentiation, real and imaginary parts, the latter is all we need for `real` and `complex`: in quantum computation, the manipulations of real and complex numbers turn out to be quite limited – we do not need anything related to real or complex analysis.

The main difficulty in the design of QBRICKS has been to lay out equational theories and lemmas for `circ`, `pps` and `ket` that can efficiently help in automatically discharging proof obligations. Many of these equations and lemmas are quite straightforward. For instance, we turn the rewriting rules of Table 8 into equations, such as $(x, y : \texttt{circ}) \vdash \texttt{width}(\texttt{PAR}(x, y)) = \texttt{width}(x) + \texttt{width}(y)$, or $a : A, n : \texttt{int} \vdash \texttt{iter}_f(a, n+1) = f(\texttt{iter}_f(a, n))$. These equations maps the (syntactic) computational behavior of expressions into the logic.

Other equations express purely semantic properties. For instance,

$$\Gamma, k : \texttt{ket} \vdash \texttt{circ\_apply}(\texttt{SEQ}(C_1, C_2), k) = \texttt{circ\_apply}(C_1, \texttt{circ\_apply}(C_2, k)) \quad (3)$$

(together with a few hypotheses ensuring correct widths) can be derived from Table 11 and is part of the equational theory.

6.5 Additional deductive rules. QBRICKS provides additional reasoning rules, that we do not have space enough to detail here. Upon them are:

Circuit complexity. Certifying the complexity of quantum implementations (e.g., polynomial number of gates in the size of the input) is of primary importance as in mid-term, implementations will have to deal with limited hardware capacities, hence the need for tight circuit constructions. We stress that, while raised by several programming [30] or compilation works [48], this aspect of certification is not addressed by existing formal verification approaches [35,45,1].

Probabilities. The probability of obtaining a result by a measurement is correlated with the amplitudes of the corresponding ket-basis vectors in the quantum state of the memory. In QBRICKS-SPEC we define $\texttt{proba\_partial\_measure} : \texttt{circ} \times \texttt{ket} \times \texttt{bitvector} \rightarrow \texttt{real}$ meaning that when the input circuit is applied to the input ket, if we were to measure the result the probability of obtaining the given vector would be the result of the function.

Wire identification. In some situation, to add a gate in a circuit it is easier to give the number (identifier) of the wire on which the gate applies (such as "apply `HAD` on wire n") instead of sequencing the circuit with $\texttt{Id}^{\otimes n-1} \otimes \texttt{HAD}$. This is for instance the design chosen in QASM or SQIR [35].

In QBRICKS it is possible to define such a macro with the use of a derived constructor $\texttt{PLACE}(C, k, n)$. For any circuit C and any integers k, n, if $0 \leq k \leq n - \texttt{width}(C)$, $\texttt{PLACE}(C, k, n)$ applies C on wires k to $k + \texttt{width}(C) - 1$. It is defined as $\texttt{ID}^{\otimes k} \otimes C \otimes \texttt{ID}^{\otimes n-k-\texttt{C\_width}(C)}$, where for any $0 < i$, $\texttt{ID}^i \triangleq \texttt{iter par-ID}\ (i-1)\ \texttt{ID}$ and $\texttt{par-ID}(C) \triangleq \texttt{PAR}(C, \texttt{ID})$. Similarly, QBRICKS also provides constructor $\texttt{CONT}(C, c, k, n)$ with additional index c in $[\![0, n[\![$ and not in $[\![k, k + \texttt{width}(c)[\![$. Using adequate qubit permutation, through combinations of `PLACE` and `SWAP`, it applies $\texttt{PLACE}(C, k, n)$ with control c.

7 Implementation

The framework described so far is implemented as a DSL embedded inside the Why3 deductive verification platform [9,25], written in the WhyML programming language. This allows us to benefit from several strengths of Why3, such as efficient code extraction toward Ocaml, generation of proof obligations (to implement the HQHL mechanism) and access to several proof means: SMT solvers, interactive proof commands or export to proof assistants (Coq, Isabelle/HOL) —although we do not use this latter option in our case-studies.

The development itself counts 17,000+ lines of code, including 400+ definitions and 1700+ lemmas, all proved within Why3. Most of the development concerns the (verified) mathematical libraries. They cover the mathematical structures at stake in quantum computing (complex numbers, Kronecker product, bit-vectors, etc.), together with a *formally verified collection* of mathematical results. Only two theorems are assumed (for any real x: if $0 \leq x \leq 1$ then $\texttt{sin}(\pi x) \leq \pi x$, and $x \leq \texttt{sin}(\pi \frac{x}{2})$). Proving them requires function derivation material, not available in Why3 so far. Hence we chose to assume these standard results.

8 Case studies and experimental evaluation

We develop and prove parametric implementations of Grover's search, the Quantum Fourier Transform (QFT), the Quantum Phase Estimation (QPE) and the first ever verified implementation of the quantum part of Shor's algorithm (Shor-OF). We also implemented Deutsch-Jozsa (DJ) for comparison.

8.1 Examples of formal specifications. Let us first introduce some of the formal specifications we proved. The specification for QPE [41,16] is shown in Figure 12(a). The procedure inputs a unitary operator U and an eigenvector $|v\rangle$ of U and finds the ghost ([26]) eigenvalue $e^{2\pi i \Phi_v}$ associated with $|v\rangle$. The specification for Shor-OF [61] is shown in Figure 12(b). We developed a certified *concrete* implementation following the implementation proposed in [5] —a reference in term of complexity.[6] The specification for Grover [31] is shown in Figure 12(c). Given a predicate with k true value in $[\![0, 2^n[\![$, Grover's algorithm outputs one of these true values with good probability.

Each of these specifications makes use of specific functions that we do not have the space to detail here (see [13] for details). We however want to note two things. First, these specifications describe results of measurement (with the dedicated functions `proba_partial_measure_x`). As discussed in Section 6.5, if QBRICKS-DSL is not able to handle measurement we are still able with QBRICKS-SPEC to reason on the *result* of a measurement, as this is a simple function over complex amplitudes. Another thing to note is that, for Shor-OF and Grover, our specification discuss the *polynomial size* of the produced circuit.

[6] A further refinement is possible [5], using a hybrid version of the Quantum Fourier Transform, but it would require adding effective measure operation and classical control to QBRICKS.

$$\begin{array}{c}\Gamma, (f:\texttt{pps}), (C:\texttt{circ}), (|v\rangle:\texttt{ket}), (k,n:\texttt{int}), (\texttt{ghost}\ \theta:\texttt{real}), (j:\texttt{ghost int}) \Vdash \\ \left((C \rhd f) \wedge \texttt{width}(C) = n \wedge 0 < k \wedge \texttt{Eigen}(f, |v\rangle, e^{2\pi i * \theta})\right) \\ \texttt{QPE}(C,k,n) \\ \left(\begin{array}{c}\texttt{proba\_partial\_measure\_p}(\texttt{result}, k|v\rangle, \texttt{error} < \frac{1}{2^{k+1}}) \geq \frac{4}{\pi^2} \wedge \\ \theta = \frac{j}{2^k} \rightarrow \texttt{proba\_partial\_measure}(\texttt{result}, |v\rangle, |j\rangle_k) = 1\end{array}\right)\end{array}$$

(a) Specification for our implementation of Quantum Phase estimation

$$\begin{array}{c}\Gamma(a,b,n:\texttt{int}), (j:\texttt{ghost int}) \Vdash \\ \left(\texttt{co\_prime}(a,b) \wedge 1 \leq b < 2^n \wedge 1 \leq j < b \wedge a^j \% b = 1\right) \\ \texttt{Shor-circ}(a,r,n) \\ \left(\begin{array}{c}\texttt{proba\_partial\_measure\_p}(|1\rangle_n, \texttt{error}_1 \leq \frac{1}{2*2^{n*2}}) \geq \frac{4}{\pi^2} \wedge \\ \texttt{proba\_partial\_measure\_p}(|1\rangle_n, \texttt{error}_2 \leq \frac{1}{2*2^{n*2}}) \geq \frac{\phi(r)}{r} \times \frac{4}{\pi^2} \wedge \\ \texttt{size}(\texttt{result}) = \texttt{Shor-poly}(n) \wedge \\ \texttt{ancillas}(\texttt{result}) = n+2 \wedge \texttt{width}(\texttt{result}) = 3*n\end{array}\right)\end{array}$$

(b) Specification for our implementation of Shor-OF algorithm

$$\begin{array}{c}\Gamma, (C:\texttt{circ}), (f:\texttt{int} \rightarrow \texttt{bool}), (n,i,k:\texttt{int}) \Vdash \\ \left(\begin{array}{c}\texttt{implements}(C,f) \wedge 1 < n \wedge 1 \leq k < 2^n - 1 \wedge 1 \leq i \\ \wedge\ \texttt{Card}(\{j \mid 0 \leq j < 2^n \wedge f(j) = \texttt{true}\}) = k\end{array}\right) \\ \texttt{Grover}(C,k,n) \\ \left(\begin{array}{c}\texttt{proba\_partial\_measure}_f(\texttt{result}, \texttt{bv\_cst}\ (n,0), f) = \sin^2\left(\arcsin\left(\sqrt{\frac{k}{2^n}}\right)(1+2i)\right) \wedge \\ \texttt{size}(\texttt{result}) = i * (\texttt{size}(C) * \mathcal{O}(n)) \wedge \\ \texttt{width}(\texttt{result}) = n \wedge \texttt{ancillas}(\texttt{result}) = 1\end{array}\right)\end{array}$$

(c) Specification for our implementation of Grover's algorithm

Fig. 12: Specifications of the main implementations

8.2 Experimental evaluation. Different metrics about our formal developments are reported in Table 13[7]: lines of decorated code, number of lemmas, proof obligations (PO), automatically proven PO (within time limit 5 seconds) and their percentage among POs, interactive commands we entered to discharge them and time required for the automatic verification of these proofs.

Note that metrics for each implementation strictly concern the code that is *proper* to it (eg., QPE contains calls to QFT but QPE line in Table 13 does not include the QFT implementation. The whole Shor-OF development is reported in the "Shor-OF full".

Result. *QBRICKS did allow us to implement and verify in a parametric manner the Shor-OF, QPE and Grover algorithms, at a rather smooth cost and with high proof automation (95% on average, 95% for full Shor-OF).*

8.3 Prior verification efforts. Before comparing our approach to prior attempts (Table 14), we first introduce these cases.

[7] Experiments were run on Linux, on a PC equipped with an Intel(R) Core(TM) i7-7820HQ 2.90GHz and 15 GB RAM. We used Why3 version 1.2.0 with solvers Alt-Ergo-2.2.0, CVC 3-2.4.1, CVC4-1.0, Z3-4.4.1.

	#LoC + Spec	#Extr.	#Def.	#Lem.	#POs	Automation # Aut.	% Aut.	#Cmd	Verif. time
DJ	57	11	2	1	72	61	>84%	39	1m19s
Grover	193	39	6	8	505	479	>94%	125	4m43s
QFT	65	18	3	0	62	53	>85%	37	1m11s
QPE	175	24	3	8	282	262	>92%	94	4m35s
Shor-OF	923	132	28	14	2473	2386	>96%	421	<18m
Shor-OF (full)	1163	174	34	22	2817	2701	>95%	552	<23m
Total	1423	224	42	31	3394	3241	>95%	716	<29m

#LoC + Spec.: lines of decorated code — # Extr.: lines of extracted code (OCaml)
#Aut.: automatically proven POs — #Cmd: interactive commands
#Verif. time: automated proof verification time

Table 13: Implementation & verification for case studies with QBRICKS

Regular path-sums. [2,1] uses path sums for the verification of several circuits of complexity similar to that of QFT (QFT, Hidden shift, generalized Toffoli, etc). Yet, these experiments consider fixed circuits (up to 100 qubits) and the technique cannot be applied to parametric families of circuits or circuit-building languages.

QHL. Liu et al. [45] report about the parametric verification of Grover search algorithm, on a *restricted case* [8] and in the *high-level* algorithm description formalism of QHL – especially QHL has no notion of circuit. So for instance one cannot reason upon the size of a circuit within QHL.

SQIR. Finally, Hietala et al. [35] have presented a parametric (circuit-building) implementation of the Deutsch-Jozsa algorithm in Coq, with two independent full correctness proofs. Recently (Oct. 2020), the authors also presented parametrized versions of QFT, QPE and Grover algorithms [34].

8.4 Evaluation: benefits of PPS and QBRICKS. So as to evaluate the proof effort gain of using pps instead of matrices, Table 14 shows some comparison between our case studies implementations and equivalent proved implementations from the literature: the Grover algorithm implementation from [45] in Isabelle/HOL and the implementations [35,34] using SQIR and Coq. As supplementary comparison terms, we implemented QBRICKS versions of both QFT and Deutsch-Jozsa using exclusively matrices.

For example the QBRICKS implementation of QFT with pps is 18 lines long, with 47 lines of specifications and intermediary lemmas, and its proof required 37 additional interactive commands, hence Spec + Cmd = 84. In comparison, the corresponding SQIR development uses 287 interactive commands (7.7x more).

Conclusion. Relying on PPS semantics and first-order logic instead of matrices and higher-order logics strongly eases the proof effort. In term of command

[8] The case in [45, p. 232] concerns cases where the number k of seeked values is equal to 2^j for a given integer j.

	Qbricks pps				Qbricks Matrix			
	LoC	Spec	Cmd	Spec+Cmd	LoC	Spec	Cmd	Spec+Cmd
DJ	11	46	39	85	11	129	131(>3.3x)	260(>3x)
QFT	18	47	37	84	18	172	106(>2.8x)	278 (>3.3x)
Grover	39	154	125	279				
QPE	23	152	94	246				
	SQIR				QHL			
	LoC	Spec	Cmd	Spec+Cmd	LoC	Spec	Cmd	Spec+Cmd
DJ	10	39	222(>5.6x)	261(>3x)				
QFT	10	44	287(>7.7x)	331(>3.9x)				
Grover	15	121	805(>6.4x)	926(>3.3x)	90	1263	1712(>13.6x)	2975 (>10.6x)
QPE	40	86	726(>7.7x)	812(>3.3x)				

#LoC.: lines of code – # Spec.: lines of spec. and lemmas – #Cmd: proof commands

Table 14: Compared implementations of case studies, using matrices and pps

lines, proofs are consistently at least 5.6x shorter than non Qbricks examples, up to 13.6x for the case of Grover in QHL and 7.7x for QPE and QFT in SQIR.[9]

9 Related works

Formal verification of quantum circuits. Prior efforts regarding quantum circuit verification [27,45,70,53,56,1,2,35,34] have been described throughout the paper, especially in Sections 1, 3.1 and 8. Our technique is more automated than those based on interactive proving [35,34,45], borrows and extends the path sum representation [2] to the parametric case, and do consider a circuit-building language rather than a high-level algorithm description language [45].

Quantum Languages and Deductive Verification. Liu *et al.* [45] introduce Quantum Hoare Logic for high-level description of quantum algorithms. QHL and our own HQHL are different, as the underlying formalisms have different focus. While QHL deals with measurement and classical control, it does not allow reasoning on the structure of the circuit. On the other hand, Qbricks does not handle classical control, but it brings better proof automation and deduction rules for reasoning on circuits. Combining the two approaches is an exciting research direction.

Verified Circuit Optimizations. Formal methods and other program analysis techniques are also used in quantum compilation for verifying circuit *optimization* techniques [52,6,32,3,62,57,35]. Epecially, the ZX-calculus [17] represents

[9] The difference with SQIR in the column "Spec+Cmd" is less stringent. By the way, it turns out that SQIR syntax for specifications is often more succint, as eg, Qbricks writes each precondition in a separated line, where Coq writes the same as a single-line conjunction.

quantum circuits by diagrams amenable to automatic simplification through dedicated rewriting rules. This framework leads to a graphical proof assistant [40] geared at certifying the semantic equivalence between circuit diagrams, with application to circuit equivalence checking and certified circuit compilation and optimization [21,20,39]. Yet, formal tools based on ZX-calculus are restricted to fixed circuits, and parametrized approaches are so far limited to pen-and-paper proofs [12].

Other quantum applications of formal methods. Huang *et al.* [36,37] proposes a "runtime-monitoring like" verification method for quantum circuits, with an annotation language restricted to structural properties of interest (e.g., superposition or entanglement). Similarly, [44] describes a projection based assertion language for quantum programs. Verification of these assertions is led by statistical testing instead of formal proofs. The recent Silq language [8] also represents an advance in the way toward automation in quantum programming. It automatizes uncomputation operations, enabling the programmer to abstract from low level implementation details. Also specialized type systems for quantum programming languages, based on linear logic [60,59,43] and dependent types [51,53], have been developed to tackle the non-duplicability of qubits and structural circuit constraints. Finally, formal methods are also at stake for the verification of quantum cryptography protocols [49,29,11,47,19].

10 Conclusion

We address the problem of automating correctness proofs of quantum programs. While relying on the general framework of deductive verification, we finely tune our domain-specific circuit-building language QBRICKS-DSL together with its new logical specification language QBRICKS-SPEC in order to keep correctness reasoning over relevant quantum programs within first-order theory. Also, we introduce and intensively build upon *parametrized path sums* (PPS), a symbolic representation for quantum circuits represented as functions transforming quantum data registers. We develop verified parametric implementations of the Shor-OF algorithm (first verified implementation) and other famous non-trivial quantum algorithms (including QPE and Grover search), showing significant improvement over prior attempts – when available.

Acknowledgments. This work was supported in part by the French National Research Agency (ANR) under the research project SoftQPRO ANR17-CE25-0009-02, and by the DGE of the French Ministry of Industry under the research project PIA-GDN/QuantEx P163746- 484124.

References

1. M. Amy. *Formal Methods in Quantum Circuit Design.* PhD thesis, University of Waterloo, Ontario, Canada, 2019.
2. M. Amy. Towards large-scale functional verification of universal quantum circuits. In P. Selinger and G. Chiribella, editors, *Proceedings 15th International Conference on Quantum Physics and Logic, QPL 2018*, volume 287 of *Electronic Proceedings in Theoretical Computer Science*, pages 1–21, Halifax, Canada, 2019. EPTCS.
3. M. Amy, M. Roetteler, and K. M. Svore. Verified compilation of space-efficient reversible circuits. In R. Majumdar and V. Kuncak, editors, *Proceedings of the 29th International Conference on Computer Aided Verification (CAV 2017), Part II*, volume 10427 of *Lecture Notes in Computer Science*, pages 3–21, Heidelberg, Germany, 2017. Springer.
4. F. Arute, K. Arya, R. Babbush, D. Bacon, J. C. Bardin, R. Barends, R. Biswas, S. Boixo, F. G. S. L. Brandao, D. A. Buell, et al. Quantum supremacy using a programmable superconducting processor. *Nature*, 574(7779):505–510, 2019.
5. S. Beauregard. Circuit for shor's algorithm using 2n+ 3 qubits. *arXiv preprint quant-ph/0205095*, 2002.
6. D. Bhattacharjee, M. Soeken, S. Dutta, A. Chattopadhyay, and G. D. Micheli. Reversible pebble games for reducing qubits in hierarchical quantum circuit synthesis. In *Proceedings of the 49th IEEE International Symposium on Multiple-Valued Logic (ISMVL 2019)*, pages 102–107, Fredericton, NB, Canada, 2019. IEEE.
7. J. Biamonte, P. Wittek, N. Pancotti, P. Rebentrost, N. Wiebe, and S. Lloyd. Quantum machine learning. *Nature*, 549(7671):195, 2017.
8. B. Bichsel, M. Baader, T. Gehr, and M. T. Vechev. Silq: a high-level quantum language with safe uncomputation and intuitive semantics. In A. F. Donaldson and E. Torlak, editors, *Proceedings of the 41st ACM SIGPLAN International Conference on Programming Language Design and Implementation, PLDI 2020, London, UK, June 15-20, 2020*, pages 286–300. ACM, 2020.
9. F. Bobot, J.-C. Filliâtre, C. Marché, and A. Paskevich. Why3: Shepherd Your Herd of Provers. In *Proceedings of Boogie 2011: First International Workshop on Intermediate Verification Languages*, Wroclaw, Poland, 53–64, 2011. Available online as `hal-00790310`.
10. J. Boender, F. Kammüller, and R. Nagarajan. Formalization of quantum protocols using coq. In C. Heunen, P. Selinger, and J. Vicary, editors, *Proceedings of the 12th International Workshop on Quantum Physics and Logic (QPL 2015)*, volume 195 of *Electronic Proceedings in Theoretical Computer Science*, pages 71–83, Oxford, UK, 2015. EPTCS.
11. A. Broadbent. How to verify a quantum computation. *Theory of Computing*, 14(1):1–37, 2018.
12. T. Carette, D. Horsman, and S. Perdrix. SZX-calculus: Scalable graphical quantum reasoning. In P. Rossmanith, P. Heggernes, and J. Katoen, editors, *44th International Symposium on Mathematical Foundations of Computer Science, MFCS 2019, August 26-30, 2019, Aachen, Germany*, volume 138 of *LIPIcs*, pages 55:1–55:15. Schloss Dagstuhl - Leibniz-Zentrum für Informatik, 2019.
13. C. Chareton, S. Bardin, F. Bobot, V. Perrelle, and B. Valiron. Toward certified quantum programming. *arXiv preprint arXiv:2003.05841*, 2020.
14. I. L. Chuang, N. Gershenfeld, and M. Kubinec. Experimental implementation of fast quantum searching. *Physical review letters*, 80(15):3408, 1998.

15. E. M. Clarke and J. M. Wing. Formal methods: State of the art and future directions. *ACM Computing Surveys (CSUR)*, 28(4):626–643, 1996.
16. R. Cleve, A. Ekert, C. Macchiavello, and M. Mosca. Quantum algorithms revisited. *Proceedings of the Royal Society of London. Series A: Mathematical, Physical and Engineering Sciences*, 454(1969):339–354, 1998.
17. B. Coecke and A. Kissinger. *Picturing quantum processes*. Cambridge University Press, Cambridge, United Kingdom, 2017.
18. D. Coppersmith. An approximate fourier transform useful in quantum factoring. *arXiv preprint quant-ph/0201067*, 1994.
19. T. A. Davidson. *Formal verification techniques using quantum process calculus*. PhD thesis, University of Warwick, 2012.
20. N. de Beaudrap, R. Duncan, D. Horsman, and S. Perdrix. Pauli fusion: a computational model to realise quantum transformations from ZX terms. Available online as arXiv:1904.12817, 2019.
21. A. Fagan and R. Duncan. Optimising Clifford circuits with Quantomatic. In P. Selinger and G. Chiribella, editors, *Proceedings of the 15th International Conference on Quantum Physics and Logic (QPL 2018)*, volume 287 of *Electronic Notes In Theoretical Computer Science*, pages 85–105, Halifax, Canada, 2018. EPTCS.
22. E. Farhi, J. Goldstone, and S. Gutmann. A quantum approximate optimization algorithm. Available online as `arXiv:1411.4028`, 2014.
23. E. Farhi, J. Goldstone, S. Gutmann, J. Lapan, A. Lundgren, and D. Preda. A quantum adiabatic evolution algorithm applied to random instances of an np-complete problem. *Science*, 292(5516):472–475, 2001.
24. J. Filliâtre and C. Marché. The Why/Krakatoa/Caduceus platform for deductive program verification. In W. Damm and H. Hermanns, editors, *Proceedings of the 19th International Conference on Computer Aided Verification (CAV 2007)*, volume 4590 of *Lecture Notes in Computer Science*, pages 173–177, Berlin, Germany, 2007. Springer.
25. J. Filliâtre and A. Paskevich. Why3 - where programs meet provers. In M. Felleisen and P. Gardner, editors, *Proceedings of the 22nd European Symposium on Programming Languages and Systems (ESOP 2013), Held as Part of the European Joint Conferences on Theory and Practice of Software (ETAPS 2013)*, volume 7792 of *Lecture Notes in Computer Science*, pages 125–128, Rome, Italy, 2013. Springer.
26. J.-C. Filliâtre, L. Gondelman, and A. Paskevich. The spirit of ghost code. *Formal Methods in System Design*, 48(3):152–174, 2016.
27. S. J. Gay, R. Nagarajan, and N. Papanikolaou. QMC: a model checker for quantum systems. In A. Gupta and S. Malik, editors, *Proceeding of the 20th International Conference on Computer Aided Verification (CAV 2008)*, volume 5123 of *Lecture Notes in Computer Science*, pages 543–547, Princeton, NJ, USA, 2008. Springer.
28. I. M. Georgescu, S. Ashhab, and F. Nori. Quantum simulation. *Reviews of Modern Physics*, 86(1):153, 2014.
29. A. Gheorghiu, T. Kapourniotis, and E. Kashefi. Verification of quantum computation: An overview of existing approaches. *Theory of Computing Systems*, 63(4):715–808, 2019.
30. A. S. Green, P. L. Lumsdaine, N. J. Ross, P. Selinger, and B. Valiron. Quipper: A scalable quantum programming language. In H.-J. Boehm and C. Flanagan, editors, *Proceedings of the ACM SIGPLAN Conference on Programming Language Design and Implementation, (PLDI'13)*, pages 333–342, Seattle, WA, USA, 2013. ACM.

31. L. K. Grover. A fast quantum mechanical algorithm for database search. In G. L. Miller, editor, *Proceedings of the Twenty-Eighth Annual ACM Symposium on the Theory of Computing (STOC)*, pages 212–219, Philadelphia, Pennsylvania, USA, 1996. ACM.
32. W. Haaswijk, M. Soeken, A. Mishchenko, and G. De Micheli. SAT-based exact synthesis: Encodings, topology families, and parallelism. To apprear in *IEEE Transactions on Computer-Aided Design of Integrated Circuits and Systems*, https://doi,org/10.1109/TCAD.2019.2897703, 2019.
33. A. W. Harrow, A. Hassidim, and S. Lloyd. Quantum algorithm for linear systems of equations. *Physical Review Letters*, 103:150502, Oct 2009.
34. K. Hietala, R. Rand, S.-H. Hung, L. Li, and M. Hicks. Proving quantum programs correct. *arXiv preprint arXiv:2010.01240*, 2020.
35. K. Hietala, R. Rand, S.-H. Hung, X. Wu, and M. Hicks. A verified optimizer for quantum circuits. *Proceedings of the ACM on Programming Languages*, 5(POPL):1–29, 2021.
36. Y. Huang and M. Martonosi. QDB: from quantum algorithms towards correct quantum programs. In T. Barik, J. Sunshine, and S. Chasins, editors, *Proceedings of the 9th Workshop on Evaluation and Usability of Programming Languages and Tools (PLATEAU@SPLASH 2018)*, volume 67 of *OpenAccess Series in Informatics (OASIcs)*, pages 4:1–4:14, Boston, Massachusetts, USA, 2018. Schloss Dagstuhl - Leibniz-Zentrum fuer Informatik.
37. Y. Huang and M. Martonosi. Statistical assertions for validating patterns and finding bugs in quantum programs. In S. B. Manne, H. C. Hunter, and E. R. Altman, editors, *Proceedings of the 46th International Symposium on Computer Architecture (ISCA 2019)*, pages 541–553, Phoenix, AZ, USA, 2019. ACM.
38. IBM Blog. On quantum supremacy. Blog Article[10], 2019.
39. A. Kissinger and J. van de Wetering. Reducing t-count with the ZX-calculus. Available online as arXiv:1903.10477, 2019.
40. A. Kissinger and V. Zamdzhiev. Quantomatic: A proof assistant for diagrammatic reasoning. In A. P. Felty and A. Middeldorp, editors, *Proceedings for the 25th International Conference on Automated Deduction (CADE-25)*, volume 9195 of *Lecture Notes in Computer Science*, pages 326–336, Berlin, Germany, 2015. Springer.
41. A. Y. Kitaev. Quantum measurements and the abelian stabilizer problem. Available online as `arXiv:quant-ph/9511026`, 1995.
42. E. Knill. Conventions for quantum pseudocode. Technical report, Los Alamos National Lab., NM (United States), 1996.
43. U. D. Lago, A. Masini, and M. Zorzi. Quantum implicit computational complexity. *Theoretical Computer Science*, 411(2):377–409, 2010.
44. G. Li, L. Zhou, N. Yu, Y. Ding, M. Ying, and Y. Xie. Projection-based runtime assertions for testing and debugging quantum programs. *Proc. ACM Program. Lang.*, 4(OOPSLA):150:1–150:29, 2020.
45. J. Liu, B. Zhan, S. Wang, S. Ying, T. Liu, Y. Li, M. Ying, and N. Zhan. Formal verification of quantum algorithms using quantum hoare logic. In I. Dillig and S. Tasiran, editors, *Computer Aided Verification*, pages 187–207, Cham, 2019. Springer International Publishing.
46. T. Liu, Y. Li, S. Wang, M. Ying, and N. Zhan. A theorem prover for quantum hoare logic and its applications. Available as `arXiv:1601.03835`, 2016.

[10] https://www.ibm.com/blogs/research/2019/10/on-quantum-supremacy/

47. U. Mahadev. Classical verification of quantum computations. In M. Thorup, editor, *Proceedings of the 59th IEEE Annual Symposium on Foundations of Computer Science (FOCS 2018)*, pages 259–267, Paris, France, 2018. IEEE Computer Society.
48. G. Meuli, M. Soeken, M. Roetteler, and T. Häner. Enabling accuracy-aware quantum compilers using symbolic resource estimation. *Proc. ACM Program. Lang.*, 4(OOPSLA), 2020.
49. R. Nagarajan and S. Gay. Formal verification of quantum protocols. Available online as `arXiv:quant-ph/0203086`, 2002.
50. M. A. Nielsen and I. Chuang. *Quantum computation and quantum information.* Cambridge University Press, Cambridge, United Kingdom, 2002.
51. L. Paolini, M. Piccolo, and M. Zorzi. qPCF: Higher-order languages and quantum circuits. *Journal of Automated Reasoning*, 63(4):941–966, Dec 2019.
52. A. Parent, M. Roetteler, and K. M. Svore. REVS: a tool for space-optimized reversible circuit synthesis. In I. Phillips and H. Rahaman, editors, *Proceedings of the 9th International Conference on Reversible Computation (RC 2017)*, volume 10301 of *Lecture Notes in Computer Science*, pages 90–101, Kolkata, India, 2017. Springer.
53. J. Paykin, R. Rand, and S. Zdancewic. QWIRE: a core language for quantum circuits. In G. Castagna and A. D. Gordon, editors, *Proceedings of the 44th ACM SIGPLAN Symposium on Principles of Programming Languages (POPL'17)*, pages 846–858, Paris, France, 2017. ACM.
54. Qbricks repository. `https://cchareton.github.io/Qbricks`.
55. Quantum Computing Report. List of tools. Available online[11], 2019.
56. R. Rand. *Formally Verified Quantum Programming.* PhD thesis, University of Pennsylvania, 2018.
57. R. Rand, J. Paykin, D. Lee, and S. Zdancewic. ReQWIRE: Reasoning about reversible quantum circuits. In P. Selinger and G. Chiribella, editors, *Proceedings 15th International Conference on Quantum Physics and Logic (QPL 2018)*, volume 287 of *Electronic Proceedings in Theoretical Computer Science*, pages 299–312, Halifax, Canada, 2018. EPTCS.
58. R. Rand, J. Paykin, and S. Zdancewic. QWIRE practice: Formal verification of quantum circuits in coq. In B. Coecke and A. Kissinger, editors, *Proceedings 14th International Conference on Quantum Physics and Logic (QPL 2017)*, volume 266 of *Electronic Proceedings in Theoretical Computer Science*, pages 119–132, Nijmegen, The Netherlands, 2017. EPTCS.
59. N. J. Ross. *Algebraic and Logical Methods in Quantum Computation.* PhD thesis, Dalhousie University, 2015.
60. P. Selinger and B. Valiron. A lambda calculus for quantum computation with classical control. *Mathematical Structures in Computer Science*, 16:527–552, 2006.
61. P. W. Shor. Algorithms for quantum computation: Discrete log and factoring. In *Proceedings of the 35th Annual Symposium on Foundations of Computer Science (FOCS'94)*, pages 124–134, Santa Fe, New Mexico, US., 1994. IEEE, IEEE Computer Society Press.
62. M. Soeken, T. Häner, and M. Roetteler. Programming quantum computers using design automation. Available online as `arXiv:1803.01022`, 2018.
63. D. S. Steiger, T. Häner, and M. Troyer. ProjectQ: an open source software framework for quantum computing. *Quantum*, 2:49, Jan. 2018.

[11] `https://quantumcomputingreport.com/resources/tools/`

64. K. M. Svore, A. Geller, M. Troyer, J. Azariah, C. Granade, B. Heim, V. Kliuchnikov, M. Mykhailova, A. Paz, and M. Roetteler. Q#: Enabling scalable quantum computing and development with a high-level domain-specific language. Available online as `arXiv:1803.00652`, 2018.
65. K. M. Svore and M. Troyer. The quantum future of computation. *IEEE Computer*, 49(9):21–030, 2016.
66. B. Valiron, N. J. Ross, P. Selinger, D. S. Alexander, and J. M. Smith. Programming the quantum future. *Communications of the ACM*, 58(8):52–61, 2015.
67. D. Wecker and K. M. Svore. LIQUi|⟩: A software design architecture and domain-specific language for quantum computing. Available online as `arXiv:1402.4467`, 2014.
68. M. Ying. Floyd-hoare logic for quantum programs. *ACM Transactions on Programming Languages and Systems (TOPLAS)*, 33(6):19:1–19:49, 2011.
69. M. Ying. Toward automatic verification of quantum programs. *Formal Aspects of Computing*, 31(1):3–25, 2019.
70. M. Ying, Y. Li, N. Yu, and Y. Feng. Model-checking linear-time properties of quantum systems. *ACM Transactions on Computational Logic*, 15(3):22:1–22:31, 2014.
71. M. Ying, S. Ying, and X. Wu. Invariants of quantum programs: characterisations and generation. In *Proceedings of the 44th ACM SIGPLAN Symposium on Principles of Programming Languages (POPL 2017)*, pages 818–832, Paris, France, 2017. ACM.

Nested Session Types

(✉) Ankush Das[1], Henry DeYoung[1], Andreia Mordido[2], and Frank Pfenning[1]

[1] Carnegie Mellon University, Pittsburgh, PA, USA
{ankushd,hdeyoung,fp}@cs.cmu.edu
[2] LASIGE, Faculdade de Ciências, Universidade de Lisboa, Lisbon, Portugal
afmordido@ciencias.ulisboa.pt

Abstract. Session types statically describe communication protocols between concurrent message-passing processes. Unfortunately, parametric polymorphism even in its restricted prenex form is not fully understood in the context of session types. In this paper, we present the metatheory of session types extended with prenex polymorphism and, as a result, nested recursive datatypes. Remarkably, we prove that type equality is decidable by exhibiting a reduction to trace equivalence of deterministic first-order grammars. Recognizing the high theoretical complexity of the latter, we also propose a novel type equality algorithm and prove its soundness. We observe that the algorithm is surprisingly efficient and, despite its incompleteness, sufficient for all our examples. We have implemented our ideas by extending the Rast programming language with nested session types. We conclude with several examples illustrating the expressivity of our enhanced type system.

1 Introduction

Session types express and enforce interaction protocols in message-passing systems [29,44]. In this work, we focus on *binary session types* that describe bilateral protocols between two endpoint processes performing dual actions. Binary session types obtained a firm logical foundation since they were shown to be in a Curry-Howard correspondence with linear logic propositions [7,8,47]. This allows us to rely on properties of cut reduction to derive type safety properties such as *progress (deadlock freedom)* and *preservation (session fidelity)*, which continue to hold even when extended to recursive types and processes [17].

However, the theory of session types is still missing a crucial piece: a general understanding of prenex (or ML-style) parametric polymorphism, encompassing recursively defined types, polymorphic type constructors, and nested types. We abbreviate the sum of these features simply as *nested types* [3]. Prior work has restricted itself to parametric polymorphism either: in prenex form without nested types [26,45]; with explicit higher-rank quantifiers [6,38] (including bounded ones [24]) but without general recursion; or in specialized form for iteration at the type level [46]. None of these allow a free, *nested* use of polymorphic type constructors combined with prenex polymorphism.

N. Yoshida (Ed.): ESOP 2021, LNCS 12648, pp. 178–206, 2021.
https://doi.org/10.1007/978-3-030-72019-3_7

In this paper, we develop the metatheory of this rich language of nested session types. Nested types are reasonably well understood in the context of functional languages [3,32] and have a number of interesting applications [10,28,37]. One difficult point is the interaction of nested types with polymorphic recursion and type inference [36]. By adopting bidirectional type-checking we avoid this particular set of problems altogether, at the cost of some additional verbosity. However, we have a new problem namely how to handle type equality ($\equiv$) given that session type definitions are generally *equirecursive* and *not generative*. This means that even before we consider nesting, with the definitions

$$\mathsf{list}[\alpha] = \oplus\{\mathbf{nil} : \mathbf{1}, \mathbf{cons} : \alpha \otimes \mathsf{list}[\alpha]\} \qquad \mathsf{list}'[\alpha] = \oplus\{\mathbf{nil} : \mathbf{1}, \mathbf{cons} : \alpha \otimes \mathsf{list}'[\alpha]\}$$

we have $\mathsf{list}[A] \equiv \mathsf{list}'[B]$ and also $\mathsf{list}[\mathsf{list}'[A]] \equiv \mathsf{list}'[\mathsf{list}[B]]$ provided $A \equiv B$. The reason is that both types specify the same communication behavior—only their name (which is irrelevant) is different. As the second of these equalities shows, deciding the equality of nested occurrences of type constructors is inescapable: allowing type constructors (which are necessary in many practical examples) means we also have to solve type equality for nested types. For example, the types $\mathsf{Tree}[\alpha]$ and $\mathsf{STree}[\alpha][\kappa]$ represent binary trees and their faithfully (and efficiently) serialized form respectively.

$$\mathsf{Tree}[\alpha] = \oplus\{\mathbf{node} : \mathsf{Tree}[\alpha] \otimes \alpha \otimes \mathsf{Tree}[\alpha], \mathbf{leaf} : \mathbf{1}\}$$

$$\mathsf{STree}[\alpha, \kappa] = \oplus\{\mathbf{nd} : \mathsf{STree}[\alpha, \alpha \otimes \mathsf{STree}[\alpha, \kappa]], \mathbf{lf} : \kappa\}$$

We have that $\mathsf{Tree}[\alpha] \otimes \kappa$ is isomorphic to $\mathsf{STree}[\alpha, \kappa]$ and that the processes witnessing the isomorphism can be easily implemented (see Section 9).

At the core of type checking lies *type equality*. We show that we can translate type equality for nested session types to the trace equivalence problem for deterministic first-order grammars, shown to be decidable by Jančar, albeit with doubly-exponential complexity [31]. Solomon [42] already proved a related connection between *inductive* type equality for nested types and language equality for deterministic pushdown automata (DPDA). The difference is that the standard session type equality is defined coinductively, as a bisimulation, rather than via language equivalence [23]. This is because session types capture communication behavior rather than the structure of closed values so a type such as $\mathsf{R} = \oplus\{\mathbf{a} : \mathsf{R}\}$ is not equal to the empty type $\mathsf{E} = \oplus\{\}$. The reason is that the former type can send infinitely many $\mathbf{a}$'s while the latter cannot, and hence their communication behavior is different, implying that the types must be different. Interestingly, if we imagine a lazy functional language such as Haskell with non-generative recursive types, then R and E would also be different. In fact, nothing in our analysis of equirecursive nested types depends on linearity, just on the coinductive interpretation of types. Our key results, namely decidability of type equality and a practical algorithm for it, apply to lazy functional languages!

The decision procedure for deterministic first-order grammars does not appear to be directly suitable for implementation, in part due to its doubly-exponential complexity bound. Instead we develop an algorithm combining loop detection [23] with instantiation [18] and a special treatment of reflexivity. The algorithm is sound, but incomplete, and reports success, a counterexample, or an inconclusive outcome (which counts as failure). In our experience, the algorithm is surprisingly efficient and sufficient for all our examples.

We have implemented nested session types and integrated them with the Rast language that is based on session types [17,18,19]. We have evaluated our prototype on several examples such as the Dyck language [21], an expression server [45] and serializing binary trees, and standard polymorphic data structures such as lists, stacks and queues.

Most closely related to our work is context-free session types (CFSTs) [45]. CFSTs also enhance the expressive power of binary session types by extending types with a notion of sequential composition of types. In connection with CFSTs, we identified a proper fragment of nested session types closed under sequential composition and therefore nested session types are strictly more expressive than CFSTs.

The main technical contributions of our work are:

- A uniform language of session types supporting prenex polymorphism, type constructors, and nested types and its type safety proof (Sections 3, 6).
- A proof of decidability of type equality (Section 4).
- A practical algorithm for type equality and its soundness proof (Section 5).
- A proper fragment of nested session types that is closed under sequential composition, the main feature of context-free session types (Section 7).
- An implementation and integration with the Rast language (Section 8).

2 Overview of Nested Session Types

The main motivation for studying nested types is quite practical and generally applicable to programming languages with structural type systems. We start by applying parametric type constructors for a standard polymorphic queue data structure. We also demonstrate how the types can be made more precise using nesting. A natural consequence of having nested types is the ability to capture (communication) patterns characterized by context-free languages. As an illustration, we express the Dyck language of balanced parentheses and show how nested types are connected to DPDAs also.

Queues A standard application of parameterized types is the definition of polymorphic data structures such as lists, stacks, or queues. As a simple example, consider the nested type:

$$\mathsf{queue}[\alpha] \triangleq \&\{\mathbf{ins} : \alpha \multimap \mathsf{queue}[\alpha], \mathbf{del} : \oplus\{\mathbf{none} : \mathbf{1}, \mathbf{some} : \alpha \otimes \mathsf{queue}[\alpha]\}\}$$

The type queue, parameterized by α, represents a queue with values of type α. A process providing this type offers an *external choice* ($\&$) enabling the client to either *insert* a value of type α in the queue (label **ins**), or to *delete* a value from the queue (label **del**). After receiving label **ins**, the provider expects to receive a value of type α (the $\multimap$ operator) and then proceeds to offer $\mathsf{queue}[\alpha]$. Upon reception of the label **del**, the provider queue is either empty, in which case it sends the label **none** and terminates the session (as prescribed by type **1**), or is non-empty, in which case it sends a value of type α (the $\otimes$ operator) and recurses with $\mathsf{queue}[\alpha]$.

Although parameterized type definitions are sufficient to express the standard interface to polymorphic data structures, we propose *nested session types* which are considerably more expressive. For instance, we can use type parameters to track the number of elements in the queue in its type!

$$\mathsf{queue}[\alpha, x] \triangleq \&\{\mathbf{ins} : \alpha \multimap \mathsf{queue}[\alpha, \mathsf{Some}[\alpha, x]], \mathbf{del} : x\}$$

$$\mathsf{Some}[\alpha, x] \triangleq \oplus\{\mathbf{some} : \alpha \otimes \mathsf{queue}[\alpha, x]\} \qquad \mathsf{None} \triangleq \oplus\{\mathbf{none} : \mathbf{1}\}$$

The second type parameter x tracks the number of elements. This parameter can be understood as a *symbol stack*. On inserting an element, we recurse to $\mathsf{queue}[\alpha, \mathsf{Some}[\alpha, x]]$ denoting the *push* of Some symbol on stack x. We initiate the empty queue with the type $\mathsf{queue}[\alpha, \mathsf{None}]$ where the second parameter denotes *an empty symbol stack*. Thus, a queue with n elements would have the type $\mathsf{queue}[\alpha, \mathsf{Some}^n[\alpha, \mathsf{None}]]$. On receipt of the del label, the type transitions to x which can either be None (if the queue is empty) or $\mathsf{Some}[\alpha, x]$ (if the queue is non-empty). In the latter case, the type sends label **some** followed by an element, and transitions to $\mathsf{queue}[\alpha, x]$ denoting a *pop* from the symbol stack. In the former case, the type sends the label none and terminates. Both these behaviors are reflected in the definitions of types Some and None.

Context-Free Languages Recursive session types capture the class of regular languages [45]. However, in practice, many useful languages are beyond regular. As an illustration, suppose we would like to express a balanced parentheses language, also known as the Dyck language [21] with the end-marker \$. We use **L** to denote an opening symbol, and **R** to denote a closing symbol (in a session-typed mindset, **L** can represent client request and **R** is server response). We need to enforce that each **L** has a corresponding closing **R** and they are properly nested. To express this, we need to track the number of **L**'s in the output with the session type. However, this notion of *memory* is beyond the expressive power of regular languages, so mere recursive session types will not suffice.

We utilize the expressive power of nested types to express this behavior.

$$T[x] \triangleq \oplus\{\mathbf{L} : T[T[x]], \mathbf{R} : x\} \qquad D \triangleq \oplus\{\mathbf{L} : T[D], \$: \mathbf{1}\}$$

The nested type $T[x]$ takes x as a type parameter and either outputs **L** and continues with $T[T[x]]$, or outputs **R** and continues with x. The type D either outputs **L** and continues with $T[D]$, or outputs \$ and terminates. The type D expresses a Dyck word with end-marker \$ [34].

The key idea here is that the number of T's in the type of a word tracks the number of unmatched **L**'s in it. Whenever the type $T[x]$ outputs **L**, it recurses with $T[T[x]]$ incrementing the number of T's in the type by 1. Dually, whenever the type outputs **R**, it recurses with x decrementing the number of T's in the type by 1. The type D denotes a balanced word with no unmatched **L**'s. Moreover, since we can only output \$ (or **L**) at the type D and *not* **R**, we obtain the invariant that any word of type D must be balanced. If we imagine the parameter x as the symbol stack, outputting an **L** pushes T on the stack, while outputting **R** pops T from the stack. The definition of D ensures that once an **L** is outputted, the symbol stack is initialized with $T[D]$ indicating one unmatched **L**.

Nested session types do not restrict communication so that the words represented *have to be balanced*. To this end, the type D' can model the *cropped Dyck language*, where *unbalanced* words can be captured.

$$T'[x] \triangleq \oplus\{\mathbf{L} : T'[T'[x]], \mathbf{R} : x, \$: \mathbf{1}\} \qquad D' \triangleq \oplus\{\mathbf{L} : T'[D'], \$: \mathbf{1}\}$$

The only difference between types $T[x]$ and $T'[x]$ is that $T'[x]$ allows us to terminate at any point using the \$ label which immediately transitions to type **1**. Nested session types can not only capture the class of deterministic context-free languages recognized by DPDAs that *accept by empty stack* (balanced words), but also the class of deterministic context-free languages recognized by DPDAs that *accept by final state* (cropped words).

Multiple Kinds of Parentheses We can use nested types to express more general words with different kinds of parentheses. Let **L** and **L**$'$ denote two kinds of opening symbols, while **R** and **R**$'$ denote their corresponding closing symbols respectively. We define the session types

$$\begin{aligned} S[x] &\triangleq \oplus\{\mathbf{L} : S[S[x]], \mathbf{L}' : S'[S[x]], \mathbf{R} : x\} \\ S'[x] &\triangleq \oplus\{\mathbf{L} : S[S'[x]], \mathbf{L}' : S'[S'[x]], \mathbf{R}' : x\} \\ E &\triangleq \oplus\{\mathbf{L} : S[E], \mathbf{L}' : S'[E], \$: \mathbf{1}\} \end{aligned}$$

We *push* symbols S and S' to the stack on outputting **L** and **L**$'$ respectively. Dually, we *pop* S and S' from the stack on outputting **R** and **R**$'$ respectively. Then, the type E defines an *empty stack*, thereby representing a balanced Dyck word. This technique can be generalized to any number of kinds of brackets.

Multiple States as Multiple Parameters Using defined type names with *multiple* type parameters, we enable types to capture the language of DPDAs with several states. Consider the language $L_3 = \{\mathbf{L}^n \mathbf{a}\, \mathbf{R}^n \mathbf{a} \cup \mathbf{L}^n \mathbf{b}\, \mathbf{R}^n \mathbf{b} \mid n > 0\}$, proposed by Korenjak and Hopcroft [34]. A word in this language starts with a sequence of opening symbols **L**, followed by an *intermediate symbol*, either **a** or **b**. Then, the word contains as many closing symbols **R** as there were **L**s and terminates with the symbol **a** or **b** *matching* the intermediate symbol.

$$U \triangleq \oplus\{\mathbf{L} : O[C[A], C[B]]\} \qquad O[x, y] \triangleq \oplus\{\mathbf{L} : O[C[x], C[y]], \mathbf{a} : x, \mathbf{b} : y\}$$

$$C[x] \triangleq \oplus\{\mathbf{R} : x\} \qquad A \triangleq \oplus\{\mathbf{a} : \mathbf{1}\} \qquad B \triangleq \oplus\{\mathbf{b} : \mathbf{1}\}$$

The L_3 language is characterized by session type U. Since the type U is unaware of which intermediate symbol among **a** or **b** would eventually be chosen, it cleverly maintains *two symbol stacks* in the two type parameters x and y of O. We initiate type U with outputting $\mathbf{L}$ and transitioning to $O[C[A], C[B]]$ where the symbol C tracks that we have outputted *one* $\mathbf{L}$. The types A and B represent the intermediate symbols that might be used in the future. The type $O[x, y]$ can either output an $\mathbf{L}$ and transition to $O[C[x], C[y]]$ *pushing* the symbol C onto *both* stacks; or it can output $\mathbf{a}$ (or $\mathbf{b}$) and transition to the first (resp. second) type parameter x (resp. y). Intuitively, the type parameter x would have the form $C^n[A]$ for $n > 0$ (resp. y would be $C^n[B]$). Then, the type $C[x]$ would output an $\mathbf{R}$ and *pop* the symbol C from the stack by transitioning to x. Once all the closing symbols have been outputted (note that you cannot terminate pre-emptively), we transition to type A or B depending on the intermediate symbol chosen. Type A outputs $\mathbf{a}$ and terminates, and similarly, type B outputs $\mathbf{b}$ and terminates. Thus, we simulate the L_3 language (not possible with context-free session types [45]) using two type parameters.

More broadly, nested types can neatly capture *complex server-client interactions*. For instance, client requests can be captured using labels $\mathbf{L}, \mathbf{L}'$ while server responses can be captured using labels $\mathbf{R}, \mathbf{R}'$ expressing *multiple kinds* of requests. Balanced words will then represent that all requests have been handled. The types can also guarantee that responses do not exceed requests.

3 Description of Types

The underlying base system of session types is derived from a Curry-Howard interpretation [7,8] of intuitionistic linear logic [25]. Below we describe the session types, their operational interpretation and the continuation type.

A, B, C	$::=$	$\oplus\{\ell : A_\ell\}_{\ell \in L}$	send label $k \in L$	continue at type A_k
	$\mid$	$\&\{\ell : A_\ell\}_{\ell \in L}$	receive label $k \in L$	continue at type A_k
	$\mid$	$A \otimes B$	send channel $a : A$	continue at type B
	$\mid$	$A \multimap B$	receive channel $a : A$	continue at type B
	$\mid$	$\mathbf{1}$	send close message	no continuation
	$\mid$	α	type variable	
	$\mid$	$V[\overline{B}]$	defined type name	

The basic type operators have the usual interpretation: the *internal choice* operator $\oplus\{\ell : A_\ell\}_{\ell \in L}$ selects a branch with label $k \in L$ with corresponding continuation type A_k; the *external choice* operator $\&\{\ell : A_\ell\}_{\ell \in L}$ offers a choice with labels $\ell \in L$ with corresponding continuation types A_ℓ; the *tensor* operator $A \otimes B$ represents the channel passing type that consists of sending a channel of type A and proceeding with type B; dually, the *lolli* operator $A \multimap B$ consists of receiving a channel of type A and continuing with type B; the *terminated session* $\mathbf{1}$ is the operator that closes the session.

We also support *type constructors* to define new *type names*. A type name V is defined according to a *type definition* $V[\overline{\alpha}] = A$ that is parameterized by a sequence of *distinct type variables* $\overline{\alpha}$ that the type A can refer to. We can use type names in a type expression using $V[\overline{B}]$. Type expressions can also refer to parameter α available in scope. The *free variables* in type A refer to the set of type variables that occur freely in A. Types without any free variables are called *closed types.* We call any type not of the form $V[\overline{B}]$ to be *structural.*

All type definitions are stored in a finite global *signature* Σ defined as

$$\text{Signature } \Sigma ::= \cdot \mid \Sigma, V[\overline{\alpha}] = A$$

In a *valid signature*, all definitions $V[\overline{\alpha}] = A$ are contractive, meaning that A is *structural*, i.e. not itself a type name. This allows us to take an *equirecursive* view of type definitions, which means that unfolding a type definition does not require communication. More concretely, the type $V[\overline{B}]$ is considered equivalent to its unfolding $A[\overline{B}/\overline{\alpha}]$. We can easily adapt our definitions to an *isorecursive* view [35,20] with explicit unfold messages. All type names V occurring in a valid signature must be defined, and all type variables defined in a valid definition must be distinct. Furthermore, for a valid definition $V[\overline{\alpha}] = A$, the free variables occurring in A must be contained in $\overline{\alpha}$. This top-level scoping of all type variables is what we call the *prenex form of polymorphism.*

4 Type Equality

Central to any practical type checking algorithm is type equality. In our system, it is necessary for the rule of identity (forwarding) and process spawn, as well as the channel-passing constructs for types $A \otimes B$ and $A \multimap B$. However, with nested polymorphic recursion, checking equality becomes challenging. We first develop the underlying theory of equality providing its definition, and then establish its reduction to checking trace equivalence of deterministic first-order grammars.

4.1 Type Equality Definition

Intuitively, two types are equal if they permit exactly the *same* communication behavior. Formally, type equality is captured using a coinductive definition following seminal work by Gay and Hole [23].

Definition 1. *We first define* $\mathsf{unfold}_\Sigma(A)$ *as*

$$\frac{V[\overline{\alpha}] = A \in \Sigma}{\mathsf{unfold}_\Sigma(V[\overline{B}]) = A[\overline{B}/\overline{\alpha}]}\ \mathsf{def} \qquad\qquad \frac{A \neq V[\overline{B}]}{\mathsf{unfold}_\Sigma(A) = A}\ \mathsf{str}$$

Unfolding a structural type simply returns A. Since type definitions are *contractive* [23], the result of unfolding is never a type name application and it always terminates in one step.

Definition 2. *Let Type be the set of closed type expressions (no free variables). A relation $\mathcal{R} \subseteq$ Type $\times$ Type is a type bisimulation if $(A, B) \in \mathcal{R}$ implies:*

- *If* $\mathsf{unfold}_\Sigma(A) = \oplus\{\ell : A_\ell\}_{\ell \in L}$, *then* $\mathsf{unfold}_\Sigma(B) = \oplus\{\ell : B_\ell\}_{\ell \in L}$ *and also* $(A_\ell, B_\ell) \in \mathcal{R}$ *for all* $\ell \in L$.

– *If* $\mathsf{unfold}_\Sigma(A) = \&\{\ell : A_\ell\}_{\ell \in L}$*, then* $\mathsf{unfold}_\Sigma(B) = \&\{\ell : B_\ell\}_{\ell \in L}$ *and also* $(A_\ell, B_\ell) \in \mathcal{R}$ *for all* $\ell \in L$*.*
– *If* $\mathsf{unfold}_\Sigma(A) = A_1 \otimes A_2$*, then* $\mathsf{unfold}_\Sigma(B) = B_1 \otimes B_2$ *and* $(A_1, B_1) \in \mathcal{R}$ *and* $(A_2, B_2) \in \mathcal{R}$*.*
– *If* $\mathsf{unfold}_\Sigma(A) = A_1 \multimap A_2$*, then* $\mathsf{unfold}_\Sigma(B) = B_1 \multimap B_2$ *and* $(A_1, B_1) \in \mathcal{R}$ *and* $(A_2, B_2) \in \mathcal{R}$*.*
– *If* $\mathsf{unfold}_\Sigma(A) = \mathbf{1}$*, then* $\mathsf{unfold}_\Sigma(B) = \mathbf{1}$*.*

Definition 3. *Two closed types* A *and* B *are equal* ($A \equiv B$) *iff there exists a type bisimulation* $\mathcal{R}$ *such that* $(A, B) \in \mathcal{R}$*.*

When the signature Σ is not clear from context we add a subscript, $A \equiv_\Sigma B$. This definition only applies to types with no free type variables. Since we allow parameters in type definitions, we need to define equality in the presence of free type variables. To this end, we define the notation $\forall \mathcal{V}.\, A \equiv B$ where $\mathcal{V}$ is a collection of type variables and A and B are valid types w.r.t. $\mathcal{V}$ (i.e., free variables in A and B are contained in $\mathcal{V}$).

Definition 4. *We define* $\forall \mathcal{V}.\, A \equiv B$ *iff for all closed type substitutions* $\sigma : \mathcal{V}$*, we have* $A[\sigma] \equiv B[\sigma]$*.*

4.2 Decidability of Type Equality

Solomon [42] proved that types defined using parametric type definitions with an *inductive interpretation* can be translated to DPDAs, thus reducing type equality to language equality on DPDAs. However, our type definitions have a *coinductive interpretation.* As an example, consider the types $A = \oplus\{\mathbf{a} : A\}$ and $B = \oplus\{\mathbf{b} : B\}$. With an *inductive* interpretation, types A and B are empty (because they do not have terminating symbols) and, thus, are equal. However, with a *coinductive* interpretation, type A will send an infinite number of **a**'s, and B will send an infinite number of **b**'s, and are thus not equal. Our reduction needs to account for this coinductive behavior.

We show that type equality of nested session types is decidable via a reduction to the trace equivalence problem of deterministic first-order grammars [30]. A *first-order grammar* is a structure $(\mathcal{N}, \mathcal{A}, \mathcal{S})$ where $\mathcal{N}$ is a set of non-terminals, $\mathcal{A}$ is a finite set of *actions*, and $\mathcal{S}$ is a finite set of *production rules.* The arity of non-terminal $X \in \mathcal{N}$ is written as $\mathsf{arity}(X) \in \mathbb{N}$. Production rules rely on a countable set of *variables* $\mathcal{V}$, and on the set $\mathcal{T}_\mathcal{N}$ of *regular terms* over $\mathcal{N} \cup \mathcal{V}$. A term is *regular* if the set of subterms is finite (see [30]).

Each production rule has the form $X\overline{\alpha} \xrightarrow{a} E$ where $X \in \mathcal{N}$ is a non-terminal, $a \in \mathcal{A}$ is an action, and $\overline{\alpha} \in \mathcal{V}^*$ are variables that the term $E \in \mathcal{T}_\mathcal{N}$ can refer to. A grammar is *deterministic* if for each pair of $X \in \mathcal{N}$ and $a \in \mathcal{A}$, there is at most one rule of the form $X\overline{\alpha} \xrightarrow{a} E$ in $\mathcal{S}$. The substitution of terms $\overline{B}$ for variables $\overline{\alpha}$ in a rule $X\overline{\alpha} \xrightarrow{a} E$, denoted by $X\overline{B} \xrightarrow{a} E[\overline{B}/\overline{\alpha}]$, is the rule $(X\overline{\alpha} \xrightarrow{a} E)[\overline{B}/\overline{\alpha}]$. Given a set of rules $\mathcal{S}$, the trace of a term T is defined as $\mathsf{traces}_\mathcal{S}(T) = \{\overline{a} \in \mathcal{A}^* \mid (T \xrightarrow{\overline{a}} T') \in \mathcal{S},$ for some $T' \in \mathcal{T}_\mathcal{N}\}$. Two terms are *trace equivalent*, written as $T \sim_\mathcal{S} T'$, if $\mathsf{traces}_\mathcal{S}(T) = \mathsf{traces}_\mathcal{S}(T')$.

The crux of the reduction lies in the observation that session types can be translated to terms and type definitions can be translated to production rules of a first-order grammar. We start the translation of nested session types to grammars by first making an initial pass over the signature and introducing fresh *internal names* such that the new type definitions alternate between structural (except $\mathbf{1}$ and α) and non-structural types. These internal names are parameterized over their free type variables, and their definitions are added to the signature. This *internal renaming* simplifies the next step where we translate this extended signature to grammar production rules.

Example 1. As a running example, consider the queue type from Section 2:

$$Q[\alpha] = \&\{\mathbf{ins} : \alpha \multimap Q[\alpha], \mathbf{del} : \oplus\{\mathbf{none} : \mathbf{1}, \mathbf{some} : \alpha \otimes Q[\alpha]\}\}$$

After performing internal renaming for this type, we obtain the following signature:

$$Q[\alpha] = \&\{\mathbf{ins} : X_0[\alpha], \mathbf{del} : X_1[\alpha]\} \qquad X_1[\alpha] = \oplus\{\mathbf{none} : \mathbf{1}, \mathbf{some} : X_2[\alpha]\}$$
$$X_0[\alpha] = \alpha \multimap Q[\alpha] \qquad X_2[\alpha] = \alpha \otimes Q[\alpha]$$

We introduce the fresh internal names X_0, X_1 and X_2 (parameterized with free variable α) to represent the continuation type in each case. Note the alternation between structural and non-structural types (of the form $V[\overline{B}]$).

Next, we translate this extended signature to the grammar $\mathcal{G} = (\mathcal{N}, \mathcal{A}, \mathcal{S})$ aimed at reproducing the behavior prescribed by the types as grammar actions.

$$\begin{aligned}
\mathcal{N} &= \{Q, X_0, X_1, X_2, \bot\} \\
\mathcal{A} &= \{\&\mathbf{ins}, \&\mathbf{del}, \multimap_1, \multimap_2 \oplus\mathbf{none}, \oplus\mathbf{some}, \otimes_1, \otimes_2, \} \\
\mathcal{S} &= \{Q\alpha \xrightarrow{\&\mathbf{ins}} X_0\alpha,\ Q\alpha \xrightarrow{\&\mathbf{del}} X_1\alpha,\ X_0\alpha \xrightarrow{\multimap_1} \alpha,\ X_0\alpha \xrightarrow{\multimap_2} Q\alpha, \\
&\quad X_1\alpha \xrightarrow{\oplus\mathbf{none}} \bot,\ X_1\alpha \xrightarrow{\oplus\mathbf{some}} X_2\alpha,\ X_2\alpha \xrightarrow{\otimes_1} \alpha,\ X_2\alpha \xrightarrow{\otimes_2} Q\alpha\}
\end{aligned}$$

Essentially, each defined type name is translated to a fresh non-terminal. Each type definition then corresponds a sequence of rules: one for each possible continuation type with the appropriate label that leads to that continuation. For instance, the type $Q[\alpha]$ has two possible continuations: transition to $X_0[\alpha]$ with action $\&\mathbf{ins}$ or to $X_1[\alpha]$ with action $\&\mathbf{del}$. The rules for all other type names is analogous. When the continuation is $\mathbf{1}$, we transition to the nullary non-terminal $\bot$ disabling any further action. When the continuation is α, we transition to α. Since each type name is defined once, the produced grammar is deterministic.

Formally, the translation from an (extended) signature to a grammar is handled by two simultaneous tasks: translating type definitions into production rules (function τ below), and converting type names, variables and the terminated session into grammar terms (function $(\!|\cdot|\!)$). The function $(\!|\cdot|\!) : \mathit{OType} \to \mathcal{T}_{\mathcal{N}}$ from open session types to grammar terms is defined by:

$$\begin{aligned}
(\!|\mathbf{1}|\!) &= \bot && \text{type } \mathbf{1} \text{ translates to } \bot \\
(\!|\alpha|\!) &= \alpha && \text{type variables translate to themselves} \\
(\!|V[B_1, \ldots, B_n]|\!) &= V(\!|B_1|\!) \cdots (\!|B_n|\!) && \text{type names translate to first-order terms}
\end{aligned}$$

Due to this mapping, throughout this section we will use type names indistinctly as type names or as non-terminal first-order symbols.

The function τ converts a type definition $V[\overline{\alpha}] = A$ into a set of production rules and is defined according to the structure of A as follows:

$$\begin{aligned}
\tau(V[\overline{\alpha}] = \oplus\{\ell\colon A_\ell\}_{\ell\in L}) &= \{(\!|V[\overline{\alpha}]|\!) \xrightarrow{\oplus\ell} (\!|A_\ell|\!) \mid \ell \in L\}\\
\tau(V[\overline{\alpha}] = \&\{\ell\colon A_\ell\}_{\ell\in L}) &= \{(\!|V[\overline{\alpha}]|\!) \xrightarrow{\&\ell} (\!|A_\ell|\!) \mid \ell \in L\}\\
\tau(V[\overline{\alpha}] = A_1 \otimes A_2) &= \{(\!|V[\overline{\alpha}]|\!) \xrightarrow{\otimes_i} (\!|A_i|\!) \mid i = 1,2\}\\
\tau(V[\overline{\alpha}] = A_1 \multimap A_2) &= \{(\!|V[\overline{\alpha}]|\!) \xrightarrow{\multimap_i} (\!|A_i|\!) \mid i = 1,2\}
\end{aligned}$$

The function τ identifies the actions and continuation types corresponding to A and translates them to grammar rules. Internal and external choices lead to actions $\oplus\ell$ and $\&\ell$, for each $\ell \in L$, with A_ℓ as the continuation type. The type $A_1 \otimes A_2$ enables two possible actions, $\otimes_1$ and $\otimes_2$, with continuation A_1 and A_2 respectively. Similarly $A_1 \multimap A_2$ produces the actions $\multimap_1$ and $\multimap_2$ with A_1 and A_2 as respective continuations. Contractiveness ensures that there are no definitions of the form $V[\overline{\alpha}] = V'[\overline{B}]$. Our internal renaming ensures that we do not encounter cases of the form $V[\overline{\alpha}] = \mathbf{1}$ or $V[\overline{\alpha}] = \alpha$ because we do not generate internal names for them. For the same reason, the $(\!|\cdot|\!)$ function is only defined on the complement types $\mathbf{1}$, α and $V[\overline{B}]$.

The τ function is extended to translate a signature by being applied pointwise. Formally, $\tau(\Sigma) = \bigcup_{(V[\overline{\alpha}]=A)\in\Sigma} \tau(V[\overline{\alpha}] = A)$. Connecting all pieces, we define the fog function that translates a signature to a grammar as:

$$\begin{aligned}
&\mathsf{fog}(\Sigma) = (\mathcal{N}, \mathcal{A}, \mathcal{S}), \text{ where:} && \mathcal{S} = \tau(\Sigma)\\
&\mathcal{N} = \{X \mid (X\overline{\alpha} \xrightarrow{a} E) \in \tau(\Sigma)\} && \mathcal{A} = \{a \mid (X\overline{\alpha} \xrightarrow{a} E) \in \tau(\Sigma)\}
\end{aligned}$$

The grammar is constructed by first computing $\tau(\Sigma)$ to obtain all the production rules. $\mathcal{N}$ and $\mathcal{A}$ are constructed by collecting the set of non-terminals and actions from these rules. The finite representation of session types and uniqueness of definitions ensure that $\mathsf{fog}(\Sigma)$ is a deterministic first-order grammar.

Checking equality of types A and B given signature Σ finally reduces to (i) internal renaming of Σ to produce Σ', and (ii) checking trace-equivalence of terms $(\!|A|\!)$ and $(\!|B|\!)$ given grammar $\mathsf{fog}(\Sigma')$. If A and B are themselves structural, we generate internal names for them also during the internal renaming process. Since we assume an *equirecursive* and *non-generative* view of types, it is easy to show that internal renaming does not alter the communication behavior of types and preserves type equality. Formally, $A \equiv_\Sigma B$ iff $A \equiv_{\Sigma'} B$.

Theorem 1. *$A \equiv_\Sigma B$ if and only if $(\!|A|\!) \sim_\mathcal{S} (\!|B|\!)$, where $(\mathcal{N}, \mathcal{A}, \mathcal{S}) = \mathsf{fog}(\Sigma')$ and Σ' is the extended signature for Σ.*

Proof. For the direct implication, assume that $(\!|A|\!) \not\sim_\mathcal{S} (\!|B|\!)$. Pick a sequence of actions in the difference of the traces and let w_0 be its greatest prefix occurring in both traces. Either w_0 is a maximal trace for one of the terms, or we have $(\!|A|\!) \xrightarrow{w_0} (\!|A'|\!)$ and $(\!|B|\!) \xrightarrow{w_0} (\!|B'|\!)$, with $(\!|A'|\!) \xrightarrow{a_1} (\!|A''|\!)$ and $(\!|B'|\!) \xrightarrow{a_2} (\!|B''|\!)$, where

$a_1 \neq a_2$. In both cases, with a simple case analysis on the definition of the translation τ, we conclude that $A' \not\equiv B'$ and so $A \not\equiv B$. For the reciprocal implication, assume that $(\!|A|\!) \sim_{\mathcal{S}} (\!|B|\!)$. Consider the relation

$$\mathcal{R} = \{(A_0, B_0) \mid \mathsf{traces}_{\mathcal{S}}((\!|A_0|\!)) = \mathsf{traces}_{\mathcal{S}}((\!|B_0|\!))\} \subseteq \mathit{Type} \times \mathit{Type}.$$

Obviously, $(A, B) \in \mathcal{R}$. To prove that $\mathcal{R}$ is a type bisimulation, let $(A_0, B_0) \in \mathcal{R}$ and proceed by case analysis on A_0 and B_0. For the case $\mathsf{unfold}_{\Sigma}(A_0) = \oplus\{\ell\colon A_\ell\}_{\ell \in L}$, we have $(\!|A_0|\!) \xrightarrow{\oplus\ell} (\!|A_\ell|\!)$. Since, by hypothesis, the traces coincide, $\mathsf{traces}_{\mathcal{S}}((\!|A_0|\!)) = \mathsf{traces}_{\mathcal{S}}((\!|B_0|\!))$, we have $(\!|B_0|\!) \xrightarrow{\oplus\ell} (\!|B_\ell|\!)$ and, thus, $\mathsf{unfold}_{\Sigma}(B_0) = \oplus\{\ell\colon B_\ell\}_{\ell \in L}$. Moreover, Jančar [30] proves that $\mathsf{traces}_{\mathcal{S}}((\!|A_\ell|\!)) = \mathsf{traces}_{\mathcal{S}}((\!|B_\ell|\!))$. Hence, $(A_\ell, B_\ell) \in \mathcal{R}$. The other cases and a detailed proof can be found in [14].

However, type equality is not only restricted to closed types (see Definition 4). To decide equality for open types, i.e. $\forall \mathcal{V}.\, A \equiv B$ given signature Σ, we introduce a fresh label ℓ_α and type A_α for each $\alpha \in \mathcal{V}$. We extend the signature with type definitions: $\Sigma^* = \Sigma \cup_{\alpha \in \mathcal{V}} \{A_\alpha = \oplus\{\ell_\alpha\colon A_\alpha\}\}$. We then replace all occurrences of α in A and B with A_α and check their equality with signature Σ^*. We prove that this substitution preserves equality.

Theorem 2. *$\forall \mathcal{V}.\, A \equiv_\Sigma B$ iff $A[\sigma^*] \equiv_{\Sigma^*} B[\sigma^*]$ where $\sigma^*(\alpha) = A_\alpha$ for all $\alpha \in \mathcal{V}$.*

Proof (Sketch). The direct implication is trivial since σ^* is a closed substitution. Reciprocally, we assume that $\forall \mathcal{V}.\, A \not\equiv_\Sigma B$. Then there must exist some substitution σ' such that $A[\sigma'] \not\equiv_\Sigma B[\sigma']$. We use this constraint to and prove that $A[\sigma^*] \not\equiv_{\Sigma^*} B[\sigma^*]$. The exact details can be found in our tech report [14].

Theorem 3. *Checking $\forall \mathcal{V}.\, A \equiv B$ is decidable.*

Proof. Theorem 2 reduces equality of open types to equality of closed types. Theorem 1 reduces equality of closed nested session types to trace equivalence of first-order grammars. Jančar [30] proved that trace equivalence for first-order grammars is decidable, hence establishing the decidability of equality for nested session types.

5 Practical Algorithm for Type Equality

Although type equality can be reduced to trace equivalence for first-order grammars (Theorem 1 and Theorem 2), the latter problem has a very high theoretical complexity with no known practical algorithm [30]. In response, we have designed a coinductive algorithm for approximating type equality. Taking inspiration from Gay and Hole [23], we attempt to construct a bisimulation. Our proposed algorithm is sound but incomplete and can terminate in three states: *(i)* types are proved equal by constructing a bisimulation, *(ii)* counterexample detected by identifying a position where types differ, or *(iii)* terminated without a conclusive answer due to incompleteness. We interpret both *(ii)* and *(iii)* as a failure of type-checking (but there is a recourse; see Section 5.1). The algorithm

$$\frac{\mathcal{V} \,;\, \Gamma \vdash A_\ell \equiv B_\ell \quad (\forall \ell \in L)}{\mathcal{V} \,;\, \Gamma \vdash \oplus\{\ell : A_\ell\}_{\ell \in L} \equiv \oplus\{\ell : B_\ell\}_{\ell \in L}} \oplus \qquad \frac{\mathcal{V} \,;\, \Gamma \vdash A_\ell \equiv B_\ell \quad (\forall \ell \in L)}{\mathcal{V} \,;\, \Gamma \vdash \&\{\ell : A_\ell\}_{\ell \in L} \equiv \&\{\ell : B_\ell\}_{\ell \in L}} \&$$

$$\frac{\mathcal{V} \,;\, \Gamma \vdash A_1 \equiv B_1 \quad \mathcal{V} \,;\, \Gamma \vdash A_2 \equiv B_2}{\mathcal{V} \,;\, \Gamma \vdash A_1 \otimes A_2 \equiv B_1 \otimes B_2} \otimes \qquad \frac{\mathcal{V} \,;\, \Gamma \vdash A_1 \equiv B_1 \quad \mathcal{V} \,;\, \Gamma \vdash A_2 \equiv B_2}{\mathcal{V} \,;\, \Gamma \vdash A_1 \multimap A_2 \equiv B_1 \multimap B_2} \multimap$$

$$\frac{}{\mathcal{V} \,;\, \Gamma \vdash \mathbf{1} \equiv \mathbf{1}}\ \mathbf{1} \qquad \frac{\alpha \in \mathcal{V}}{\mathcal{V} \,;\, \Gamma \vdash \alpha \equiv \alpha}\ \mathsf{var} \qquad \frac{\mathcal{V} \,;\, \Gamma \vdash \overline{A} \equiv \overline{A'}}{\mathcal{V} \,;\, \Gamma \vdash V[\overline{A}] \equiv V[\overline{A'}]}\ \mathsf{refl}$$

$$\frac{\begin{array}{c} V_1[\overline{\alpha_1}] = A \in \Sigma \qquad V_2[\overline{\alpha_2}] = B \in \Sigma \qquad \mathcal{C} = \langle \mathcal{V} \,;\, V_1[\overline{A_1}] \equiv V_2[\overline{A_2}] \rangle \\ \mathcal{V} \,;\, \Gamma, \mathcal{C} \vdash_\Sigma A[\overline{A_1}/\overline{\alpha_1}] \equiv B[\overline{A_2}/\overline{\alpha_2}] \end{array}}{\mathcal{V} \,;\, \Gamma \vdash_\Sigma V_1[\overline{A_1}] \equiv V_2[\overline{A_2}]}\ \mathsf{expd}$$

$$\frac{\begin{array}{c} \langle \mathcal{V}' \,;\, V_1[\overline{A_1'}] \equiv V_2[\overline{A_2'}] \rangle \in \Gamma \\ \exists \sigma' : \mathcal{V}'.\ \left(\mathcal{V} \,;\, \Gamma \Vdash V_1[\overline{A_1'[\sigma']}] \equiv V_1[\overline{A_1}] \wedge \mathcal{V} \,;\, \Gamma \Vdash V_2[\overline{A_2'[\sigma']}] \equiv V_2[\overline{A_2}]\right) \end{array}}{\mathcal{V} \,;\, \Gamma \vdash V_1[\overline{A_1}] \equiv V_2[\overline{A_2}]}\ \mathsf{def}$$

Fig. 1. Algorithmic Rules for Type Equality

is deterministic (no backtracking) and the implementation is quite efficient in practice. For all our examples, type checking is instantaneous (see Section 8).

The fundamental operation in the equality algorithm is *loop detection* where we determine if we have already added an equation $A \equiv B$ to the bisimulation we are constructing. Due to the presence of *open types* with free type variables, determining if we have considered an equation already becomes a difficult operation. To that purpose, we make an initial pass over the given types and introduce fresh internal names as described in Example 1 (but also for $\mathbf{1}$ and α for simplicity). In the resulting signature defined type names and structural types alternate and we can perform loop detection entirely on defined type names (whether internal or external). The formal rules for this internal renaming are described in the technical report [14].

Based on the invariants established by internal names, the algorithm only needs to alternately compare two type names or two *structural types*. The rules are shown in Figure 1. The judgment has the form $\mathcal{V} \,;\, \Gamma \vdash_\Sigma A \equiv B$ where $\mathcal{V}$ contains the free type variables in the types A and B, Σ is a fixed *valid* signature containing type definitions of the form $V[\overline{\alpha}] = C$, and Γ is a collection of *closures* $\langle \mathcal{V} \,;\, V_1[\overline{A_1}] \equiv V_2[\overline{A_2}] \rangle$. If a derivation can be constructed, all *closed instances* of all closures are included in the resulting bisimulation (see the proof of Theorem 4). A closed instance of closure $\langle \mathcal{V} \,;\, V_1[\overline{A_1}] \equiv V_2[\overline{A_2}] \rangle$ is obtained by applying a closed substitution σ over variables in $\mathcal{V}$, i.e., $V_1[\overline{A_1[\sigma]}] \equiv V_2[\overline{A_2[\sigma]}]$ such that the types $V_1[\overline{A_1[\sigma]}]$ and $V_2[\overline{A_2[\sigma]}]$ have no free type variables. Because the signature Σ is fixed, we elide it from the rules in Figure 1.

In the type equality algorithm, the rules for type operators simply compare the components. If the type constructors (or the label sets in the $\oplus$ and $\&$ rules) do not match, then type equality fails having constructed a counterexample to bisimulation. Similarly, two type variables are considered equal iff they have the same name, as exemplified by the var rule.

The rule of reflexivity is needed explicitly here (but not in the version of Gay and Hole) due to the incompleteness of the algorithm: we may otherwise fail to recognize type names parameterized with equal types as equal. Note that the refl rule checks a sequence of types in the premise.

Now we come to the key rules, expd and def. In the expd rule we expand the definitions of $V_1[\overline{A_1}]$ and $V_2[\overline{A_2}]$, and add the closure $\langle \mathcal{V} ; V_1[\overline{A_1}] \equiv V_2[\overline{A_2}] \rangle$ to Γ. Since the equality of $V_1[\overline{A_1}]$ and $V_2[\overline{A_2}]$ must hold for all its closed instances, the extension of Γ with the corresponding closure remembers exactly that.

The def rule only applies when there already exists a closure in Γ with the same type names V_1 and V_2. In that case, we try to find a substitution σ' over $\mathcal{V}'$ such that $V_1[\overline{A_1}]$ is equal to $V_1[\overline{A'_1[\sigma']}]$ and $V_2[\overline{A_2}]$ is equal to $V_2[\overline{A'_2[\sigma']}]$. Immediately after, the refl rule applies and recursively calls the equality algorithm on both type parameters. The substitution σ' is computed by a standard matching algorithm on first-order terms (which is linear-time), applied on the syntactic structure of the types. Existence of such a substitution ensures that any closed instance of $\langle \mathcal{V} ; V_1[\overline{A_1}] \equiv V_2[\overline{A_2}] \rangle$ is also a closed instance of $\langle \mathcal{V}' ; V_1[\overline{A'_1}] \equiv V_2[\overline{A'_2}] \rangle$, which are already present in the constructed type bisimulation, and we can terminate our equality check, having successfully *detected a loop*.

The algorithm so far is sound, but potentially non-terminating. There are two points of non-termination: *(i)* when encountering name/name equations, we can use the expd rule indefinitely, and *(ii)* we call the type equality recursively in the def rule. To ensure termination in the former case, we restrict the expd rule so that for any pair of type names V_1 and V_2 there is an upper bound on the number of closures of the form $\langle - ; V_1[-] \equiv V_2[-] \rangle$ allowed in Γ. We define this upper bound as the *depth bound* of the algorithm and allow the programmer to specify this depth bound. Surprisingly, a depth bound of 1 suffices for all of our examples. In the latter case, instead of calling the general type equality algorithm, we introduce the notion of *rigid equality*, denoted by $\mathcal{V} ; \Gamma \Vdash A \equiv B$. The only difference between general and rigid equality is that we cannot employ the expd rule for rigid equality. Since the size of the types reduce in all equality rules except for expd, this algorithm terminates. When comparing two instantiated type names, our algorithm first tries reflexivity, then tries to close a loop with def, and only if neither of these is applicable or fails do we expand the definitions with the expd rule. Note that if type names have no parameters, our algorithm specializes to Gay and Hole's (with the small optimizations of reflexivity and internal naming), which means our algorithm is sound and complete on monomorphic types.

Soundness. We establish the soundness of the equality algorithm by constructing a type bisimulation from a derivation of $\mathcal{V} ; \Gamma \vdash A \equiv B$ by *(i)* collecting the conclusions of all the sequents, and *(ii)* forming all closed instances from them.

Definition 5. *Given a derivation $\mathcal{D}$ of $\mathcal{V}$; $\Gamma \vdash A \equiv B$, we define the set $\mathcal{S}(\mathcal{D})$ of closures. For each sequent (regular or rigid) of the form $\mathcal{V}$; $\Gamma \vdash A \equiv B$ in $\mathcal{D}$, we include the closure $\langle \mathcal{V} \; ; \; A \equiv B \rangle$ in $\mathcal{S}(\mathcal{D})$.*

Theorem 4 (Soundness). *If $\mathcal{V}$; $\cdot \vdash A \equiv B$, then $\forall \mathcal{V}. A \equiv B$. Consequently, if $\mathcal{V}$ is empty, we get $A \equiv B$.*

Proof. Given a derivation $\mathcal{D}_0$ of $\mathcal{V}_0$; $\cdot \vdash A_0 \equiv B_0$, construct $\mathcal{S}(\mathcal{D}_0)$ and define relation $\mathcal{R}_0$ as follows:

$$\mathcal{R}_0 = \{(A[\sigma], B[\sigma]) \mid \langle \mathcal{V} \; ; \; A \equiv B \rangle \in \mathcal{S}(\mathcal{D}_0) \text{ and } \sigma \text{ over } \mathcal{V}\}$$

Then, construct $\mathcal{R}_i$ $(i \geq 1)$ as follows:

$$\mathcal{R}_i = \{(V[\overline{A}], V[\overline{B}]) \mid V[\overline{\alpha}] = C \in \Sigma \text{ and } (A^j, B^j) \in \mathcal{R}_{i-1} \; \forall j \in 1..|\overline{\alpha}|\}$$

Consider $\mathcal{R}$ to be the *reflexive transitive closure* of $\bigcup_{i \geq 0} \mathcal{R}_i$. Note that extending a relation by its reflexive transitive closure preserves its bisimulation properties since the bisimulation is strong. If $\mathcal{R}$ is a type bisimulation, then our theorem follows since the closure $\langle \mathcal{V}_0 \; ; \; A_0 \equiv B_0 \rangle \in \mathcal{S}(\mathcal{D}_0)$, and hence, for any closed substitution σ, $(A_0[\sigma], B_0[\sigma]) \in \mathcal{R}$.

All that remains is to prove that $\mathcal{R}$ is a type bisimulation. We achive this via a case analysis on the rule that added a pair (A, B) to $\mathcal{R}$. The complete proof is described in the technical report [14].

5.1 Type Equality Declarations

One of the primary sources of incompleteness in our algorithm is its inability to *generalize the coinductive hypothesis.* As an illustration, consider the following two types D and D', which only differ in the names, but have the same structure.

$$T[x] \triangleq \oplus\{\mathbf{L} : T[T[x]], \mathbf{R} : x\} \qquad D \triangleq \oplus\{\mathbf{L} : T[D], \$: \mathbf{1}\}$$

$$T'[x] \triangleq \oplus\{\mathbf{L} : T'[T'[x]], \mathbf{R} : x\} \qquad D' \triangleq \oplus\{\mathbf{L} : T'[D'], \$: \mathbf{1}\}$$

To establish $D \equiv D'$, our algorithm explores the $\mathbf{L}$ branch and checks $T[D] \equiv T'[D']$. A corresponding closure $\langle \cdot \; ; \; T[D] \equiv T'[D'] \rangle$ is added to Γ, and our algorithm then checks $T[T[D]] \equiv T'[T'[D']]$. This process repeats until it exceeds the depth bound and terminates with an inconclusive answer. What the algorithm never realizes is that $T[x] \equiv T'[x]$ for all $x \in$ *Type*; it fails to generalize to this hypothesis and is always inserting closed equality constraints to Γ.

To allow a recourse, we permit the programmer to declare (concrete syntax)

```
eqtype T[x] = T'[x]
```

an equality constraint easily verified by our algorithm. We then *seed* the Γ in the equality algorithm with the corresponding closure from the eqtype constraint which can then be used to establish $D \equiv D'$

$$\cdot \; ; \; \langle x \; ; \; T[x] \equiv T'[x] \rangle \vdash D \equiv D'$$

which, upon exploring the **L** branch reduces to

$$\cdot \; ; \; \langle x \; ; \; T[x] \equiv T'[x] \rangle, \langle \cdot \; ; \; D \equiv D' \rangle \vdash T[D] \equiv T'[D']$$

which holds under the substitution $[D/x]$ as required by the def rule.

In the implementation, we first collect all the eqtype declarations in the program into a global set of closures Γ_0. We then validate every eqtype declaration by checking $\mathcal{V} \; ; \; \Gamma_0 \vdash A \equiv B$ for every pair (A, B) (with free variables $\mathcal{V}$) in the eqtype declarations. Essentially, this ensures that all equality declarations are valid w.r.t. each other. Finally, all equality checks are then performed under this more general Γ_0. The soundness of this approach can be proved with the following more general theorem.

Theorem 5 (Seeded Soundness). *For a valid set of* eqtype *declarations* Γ_0, *if* $\mathcal{V} \; ; \; \Gamma_0 \vdash A \equiv B$, *then* $\forall \mathcal{V}. A \equiv B$.

Our soundness proof can easily be modified to accommodate this requirement. Intuitively, since Γ_0 is valid, all closed instances of Γ_0 are already proven to be bisimilar. Thus, all properties of a type bisimulation are still preserved if all closed instances of Γ_0 are added to it.

One final note on the rule of reflexivity: a type name may *not* actually depend on its parameter. As a simple example, we have $V[\alpha] = \mathbf{1}$; a more complicated one would be $V[\alpha] = \oplus\{a : V[V[\alpha]], b : \mathbf{1}\}$. When applying reflexivity, we would like to conclude that $V[A] \equiv V[B]$ regardless of A and B. This could be easily established with an equality type declaration eqtype $V[\alpha] = V[\beta]$. In order to avoid this syntactic overhead for the programmer, we determine for each parameter α of each type name V whether its definition is nonvariant in α. This information is recorded in the signature and used when applying the reflexivity rule by ignoring nonvariant arguments.

6 Formal Language Description

In this section, we present the program constructs we have designed to realize nested polymorphism which have also been integrated with the Rast language [17,18,19] to support general-purpose programming. The underlying base system of session types is derived from a Curry-Howard interpretation [7,8] of intuitionistic linear logic [25]. The key idea is that an intuitionistic linear sequent $A_1 \; A_2 \; \ldots \; A_n \vdash A$ is interpreted as the interface to a process P. We label each of the antecedents with a channel name x_i and the succedent with channel name z. The x_i's are *channels used by* P and z is the *channel provided by* P.

$$(x_1 : A_1) \; (x_2 : A_2) \ldots (x_n : A_n) \vdash P :: (z : C)$$

The resulting judgment formally states that process P provides a service of session type C along channel z, while using the services of session types $A_1, \ldots, A_n$ provided along channels $x_1, \ldots, x_n$ respectively. All these channels must be distinct. We abbreviate the antecedent of the sequent by Δ.

Due to the presence of type variables, the formal typing judgment is extended with $\mathcal{V}$ and written as

Type	Cont.	Process Term	Cont.	Description
$c : \oplus\{\ell : A_\ell\}_{\ell \in L}$	$c : A_k$	$c.k \; ; \; P$	P	send label k on c
		$\mathsf{case}\; c\; (\ell \Rightarrow Q_\ell)_{\ell \in L}$	Q_k	receive label k on c
$c : \&\{\ell : A_\ell\}_{\ell \in L}$	$c : A_k$	$\mathsf{case}\; c\; (\ell \Rightarrow P_\ell)_{\ell \in L}$	P_k	receive label k on c
		$c.k \; ; \; Q$	Q	send label k on c
$c : A \otimes B$	$c : B$	$\mathsf{send}\; c\; w \; ; \; P$	P	send channel $w : A$ on c
		$y \leftarrow \mathsf{recv}\; c \; ; \; Q_y$	$Q_y[w/y]$	receive channel $w : A$ on c
$c : A \multimap B$	$c : B$	$y \leftarrow \mathsf{recv}\; c \; ; \; P_y$	$P_y[w/y]$	receive channel $w : A$ on c
		$\mathsf{send}\; c\; w \; ; \; Q$	Q	send channel $w : A$ on c
$c : \mathbf{1}$	—	$\mathsf{close}\; c$	—	send *close* on c
		$\mathsf{wait}\; c \; ; \; Q$	Q	receive *close* on c

Table 1. Session types with operational description

$$\mathcal{V} \; ; \; \Delta \vdash_{\Sigma} P :: (x : A)$$

where $\mathcal{V}$ stores the type variables α, Δ represents the linear antecedents $x_i : A_i$, P is the process expression and $x : A$ is the linear succedent. We propose and maintain that all free type variables in Δ, P, and A are contained in $\mathcal{V}$. Finally, Σ is a fixed valid signature containing type and process definitions. Table 1 overviews the session types, their associated process terms, their continuation (both in types and terms) and operational description. For each type, the first line describes the provider's viewpoint, while the second line describes the client's matching but dual viewpoint.

We formalize the operational semantics as a system of *multiset rewriting rules* [9]. We introduce semantic objects $\mathsf{proc}(c, P)$ and $\mathsf{msg}(c, M)$ which mean that process P or message M provide along channel c. A process configuration is a multiset of such objects, where any two provided channels are distinct.

6.1 Basic Session Types

We briefly review the structural types already existing in the Rast language. The *internal choice* type constructor $\oplus\{\ell : A_\ell\}_{\ell \in L}$ is an n-ary labeled generalization of the additive disjunction $A \oplus B$. Operationally, it requires the provider of $x : \oplus\{\ell : A_\ell\}_{\ell \in L}$ to send a label label $k \in L$ on channel x and continue to provide type A_k. The corresponding process term is written as $(x.k \; ; \; P)$ where the continuation P provides type $x : A_k$. Dually, the client must branch based on the label received on x using the process term $\mathsf{case}\; x\; (\ell \Rightarrow Q_\ell)_{\ell \in L}$ where Q_ℓ is the continuation in the ℓ-th branch.

$$\frac{(k \in L) \quad \mathcal{V} \; ; \; \Delta \vdash P :: (x : A_k)}{\mathcal{V} \; ; \; \Delta \vdash (x.k \; ; \; P) :: (x : \oplus\{\ell : A_\ell\}_{\ell \in L})} \oplus R$$

$$\frac{(\forall \ell \in L) \quad \mathcal{V} \; ; \; \Delta, (x : A_\ell) \vdash Q_\ell :: (z : C)}{\mathcal{V} \; ; \; \Delta, (x : \oplus\{\ell : A_\ell\}_{\ell \in L}) \vdash \mathsf{case}\; x\; (\ell \Rightarrow Q_\ell)_{\ell \in L} :: (z : C)} \oplus L$$

Communication is asynchronous, so that the client $(c.k\ ;\ Q)$ sends a message k along c and continues as Q without waiting for it to be received. As a technical device to ensure that consecutive messages on a channel arrive in order, the sender also creates a fresh continuation channel c' so that the message k is actually represented as $(c.k\ ;\ c \leftrightarrow c')$ (read: send k along c and continue along c'). When the message k is received along c, we select branch k and also substitute the continuation channel c' for c.

$$(\oplus S) : \mathsf{proc}(c, c.k\ ;\ P) \ \mapsto\ \mathsf{proc}(c', P[c'/c]), \mathsf{msg}(c, c.k\ ;\ c \leftrightarrow c')$$
$$(\oplus C) : \mathsf{msg}(c, c.k\ ;\ c \leftrightarrow c'), \mathsf{proc}(d, \mathsf{case}\ c\ (\ell \Rightarrow Q_\ell)_{\ell \in L}) \ \mapsto\ \mathsf{proc}(d, Q_k[c'/c])$$

The *external choice* constructor $\&\{\ell : A_\ell\}_{\ell \in L}$ generalizes additive conjunction and is the *dual* of internal choice reversing the role of the provider and client. The corresponding rules for statics and dynamics are skipped for brevity and presented in the technical report [14].

The *tensor* operator $A \otimes B$ prescribes that the provider of $x : A \otimes B$ sends a channel, say w of type A and continues to provide type B. The corresponding process term is $\mathsf{send}\ x\ w\ ;\ P$ where P is the continuation. Correspondingly, its client must receive a channel on x using the term $y \leftarrow \mathsf{recv}\ x\ ;\ Q$, binding it to variable y and continuing to execute Q.

$$\frac{\mathcal{V}\ ;\ \Delta \vdash P :: (x : B)}{\mathcal{V}\ ;\ \Delta, (y : A) \vdash (\mathsf{send}\ x\ y\ ;\ P) :: (x : A \otimes B)}\ \otimes R$$

$$\frac{\mathcal{V}\ ;\ \Delta, (y : A), (x : B) \vdash Q :: (z : C)}{\mathcal{V}\ ;\ \Delta, (x : A \otimes B) \vdash (y \leftarrow \mathsf{recv}\ x\ ;\ Q) :: (z : C)}\ \otimes L$$

Operationally, the provider $(\mathsf{send}\ c\ d\ ;\ P)$ sends the channel d and the continuation channel c' along c as a message and continues with executing P. The client receives channel d and continuation channel c' appropriately substituting them.

$$(\otimes S) : \mathsf{proc}(c, \mathsf{send}\ c\ d\ ;\ P) \mapsto \mathsf{proc}(c', P[c'/c]), \mathsf{msg}(c, \mathsf{send}\ c\ d\ ;\ c \leftrightarrow c')$$
$$(\otimes C) : \mathsf{msg}(c, \mathsf{send}\ c\ d\ ;\ c \leftrightarrow c'), \mathsf{proc}(e, x \leftarrow \mathsf{recv}\ c\ ;\ Q) \ \mapsto\ \mathsf{proc}(e, Q[c', d/c, x])$$

The dual operator $A \multimap B$ allows the provider to receive a channel of type A and continue to provide type B. The client of $A \multimap B$, on the other hand, sends the channel of type A and continues to use B using dual process terms as $\otimes$.

The type $\mathbf{1}$ indicates *termination* requiring that the provider of $x : \mathbf{1}$ send a *close* message, formally written as $\mathsf{close}\ x$ followed by terminating the communication. Correspondingly, the client of $x : \mathbf{1}$ uses the term $\mathsf{wait}\ x\ ;\ Q$ to wait for x to terminate before continuing with executing Q.

A forwarding process $x \leftrightarrow y$ identifies the channels x and y so that any further communication along either x or y will be along the unified channel. Its typing rule corresponds to the logical rule of identity.

$$\frac{}{\mathcal{V}\ ;\ y : A \vdash (x \leftrightarrow y) :: (x : A)}\ \mathsf{id}$$

Operationally, a process $c \leftrightarrow d$ *forwards* any message M that arrives on d to c and vice-versa. Since channels are used linearly, the forwarding process can then terminate, ensuring proper renaming, as exemplified in the rules below.

$(\mathsf{id}^+C) : \mathsf{msg}(d', M), \mathsf{proc}(c, c \leftrightarrow d) \;\mapsto\; \mathsf{msg}(c, M[c/d])$
$(\mathsf{id}^-C) : \mathsf{proc}(c, c \leftrightarrow d), \mathsf{msg}(e, M(c)) \;\mapsto\; \mathsf{msg}(e, M(c)[d/c])$

We write $M(c)$ to indicate that c must occur in message M ensuring that M is the sole client of c.

Process Definitions Process definitions have the form $\Delta \vdash f[\overline{\alpha}] = P :: (x : A)$ where f is the name of the process and P its definition, with Δ being the channels used by f and $x : A$ being the offered channel. In addition, $\overline{\alpha}$ is a sequence of type variables that Δ, P and A can refer to. These type variables are implicitly universally quantified at the outermost level and represent prenex polymorphism. All definitions are collected in the fixed global signature Σ. For a *valid signature*, we require that $\overline{\alpha}\ ;\ \Delta \vdash P :: (x : A)$ for every definition, thereby allowing definitions to be mutually recursive. A new instance of a defined process f can be spawned with the expression $x \leftarrow f[\overline{A}]\ \overline{y}\ ;\ Q$ where $\overline{y}$ is a sequence of channels matching the antecedents Δ and $\overline{A}$ is a sequence of types matching the type variables $\overline{\alpha}$. The newly spawned process will use all variables in $\overline{y}$ and provide x to the continuation Q.

$$\frac{\overline{y' : B'} \vdash f[\overline{\alpha}] = P_f :: (x' : B) \in \Sigma \qquad \Delta' = \overline{(y : B')[\overline{A}/\overline{\alpha}]} \quad \mathcal{V}\ ;\ \Delta, (x : B[\overline{A}/\overline{\alpha}]) \vdash Q :: (z : C)}{\mathcal{V}\ ;\ \Delta, \Delta' \vdash (x \leftarrow f[\overline{A}]\ \overline{y}\ ;\ Q) :: (z : C)}\ \mathsf{def}$$

The declaration of f is looked up in the signature Σ (first premise), and $\overline{A}$ is substituted for $\overline{\alpha}$ while matching the types in Δ' and $\overline{y}$ (second premise). Similarly, the freshly created channel x has type A from the signature with $\overline{A}$ substituted for $\overline{\alpha}$.

The complete set of rules for the type system and the operational semantics for our language are presented in [14].

.2 Type Safety

The extension of session types with nested polymorphism is proved type safe by the standard theorems of *preservation* and *progress*, also known as *session fidelity* and *deadlock freedom*. At runtime, a program is represented using a multiset of semantic objects denoting processes and messages defined as a *configuration*.

$$\mathcal{S} \ ::= \ \cdot \mid \mathcal{S}, \mathcal{S}' \mid \mathsf{proc}(c, P) \mid \mathsf{msg}(c, M)$$

We say that $\mathsf{proc}(c, P)$ (or $\mathsf{msg}(c, M)$) provide channel c. We stipulate that no two distinct semantic objects in a configuration provide the same channel.

Type Preservation The key to preservation is defining the rules to *type a configuration*. We define a well-typed configuration using the judgment $\Delta_1 \vDash_\Sigma \mathcal{S} :: \Delta_2$ denoting that configuration $\mathcal{S}$ uses channels Δ_1 and provides channels Δ_2. A configuration is always typed w.r.t. a valid signature Σ. Since the signature Σ is fixed, we elide it from the presentation.

$$\frac{}{\Delta \vDash (\cdot) :: \Delta}\ \mathsf{emp} \qquad \frac{\Delta_1 \vDash \mathcal{S}_1 :: \Delta_2 \qquad \Delta_2 \vDash \mathcal{S}_2 :: \Delta_3}{\Delta_1 \vDash (\mathcal{S}_1, \mathcal{S}_2) :: \Delta_3}\ \mathsf{comp}$$

$$\frac{\cdot\,;\ \Delta \vdash P :: (x : A)}{\Delta \vDash \mathsf{proc}(x, P) :: (x : A)}\ \mathsf{proc} \qquad \frac{\cdot\,;\ \Delta \vdash M :: (x : A)}{\Delta \vDash \mathsf{msg}(x, M) :: (x : A)}\ \mathsf{msg}$$

Fig. 2. Typing rules for a configuration

The rules for typing a configuration are defined in Figure 2. The emp rule states that an empty configuration does not consume any channels provides all channels it uses. The comp rule composes two configurations $\mathcal{S}_1$ and $\mathcal{S}_2$; $\mathcal{S}_1$ provides channels Δ_2 while $\mathcal{S}_2$ uses channels Δ_2. The rule proc creates a singleton configuration out of a process. Since configurations are runtime objects, they do not refer to any free variables and $\mathcal{V}$ is empty. The msg rule is analogous.

Global Progress To state progress, we need to define a *poised process* [39]. A process $\mathsf{proc}(c, P)$ is poised if it is trying to receive a message on c. Dually, a message $\mathsf{msg}(c, M)$ is poised if it is sending along c. A configuration is poised if every message or process in the configuration is poised. Intuitively, this represents that the configuration is trying to communicate *externally* along one of the channels it uses or provides.

Theorem 6 (Type Safety). *For a well-typed configuration* $\Delta_1 \vDash_\Sigma \mathcal{S} :: \Delta_2$,

(i) (Preservation) If $\mathcal{S} \mapsto \mathcal{S}'$*, then* $\Delta_1 \vDash_\Sigma \mathcal{S}' :: \Delta_2$
(ii) (Progress) Either $\mathcal{S}$ *is poised, or* $\mathcal{S} \mapsto \mathcal{S}'$.

Proof. Preservation is proved by case analysis on the rules of operational semantics. First, we invert the derivation of the current configuration $\mathcal{S}$ and use the premises to assemble a new derivation for $\mathcal{S}'$. Progress is proved by induction on the right-to-left typing of $\mathcal{S}$ so that either $\mathcal{S}$ is empty (and therefore poised) or $\mathcal{S} = (\mathcal{D}, \mathsf{proc}(c, P))$ or $\mathcal{S} = (\mathcal{D}, \mathsf{msg}(c, M))$. By the induction hypothesis, either $\mathcal{D} \mapsto \mathcal{D}'$ or $\mathcal{D}$ is poised. In the former case, $\mathcal{S}$ takes a step (since $\mathcal{D}$ does). In the latter case, we analyze the cases for P and M, applying multiple steps of inversion to show that in each case either $\mathcal{S}$ can take a step or is poised.

7 Relationship to Context-Free Session Types

As ordinarily formulated, session types express communication protocols that can be described by regular languages [45]. In particular, the type structure is necessarily tail recursive. Context-free session types (CFSTs) were introduced by Thiemann and Vascoconcelos [45] as a way to express a class of communication protocols that are not limited to tail recursion. CFSTs express protocols that can be described by single-state, real-time DPDAs that use the empty stack acceptance criterion [1,34].

Despite their name, the essence of CFSTs is not their connection to a particular subset of the (deterministic) context-free languages. Rather, the essence of CFSTs is that session types are enriched to admit a notion of sequential composition. Nested session types are strictly more expressive than CFSTs, in the sense that there exists a proper fragment of nested session types that is closed under a notion of sequential composition. (In keeping with process algebras like ACP [2], we define a sequential composition to be an operation that satisfies the laws of a right-distributive monoid.)

Consider (up to α,β,η-equivalence) the linear, tail functions from types to types with unary type constructors only:

$$S,T ::= \hat{\lambda}\alpha.\,\alpha \mid \hat{\lambda}\alpha.\,V[S\,\alpha] \mid \hat{\lambda}\alpha.\oplus\{\ell : S_\ell\,\alpha\}_{\ell\in L} \mid \hat{\lambda}\alpha.\,\&\{\ell : S_\ell\,\alpha\}_{\ell\in L} \\ \mid \hat{\lambda}\alpha.\,A \otimes (S\,\alpha) \mid \hat{\lambda}\alpha.\,A \multimap (S\,\alpha)$$

The linear, tail nature of these functions allows the type α to be thought of as a continuation type for the session. The functions S are closed under function composition, and the identity function, $\hat{\lambda}\alpha.\,\alpha$, is included in this class of functions. Moreover, because these functions are tail functions, composition right-distributes over the various logical connectives in the following sense:

$$\begin{aligned}(\hat{\lambda}\alpha.\,V[S\,\alpha]) \circ T &= \hat{\lambda}\alpha.\,V[(S \circ T)\,\alpha] \\ (\hat{\lambda}\alpha.\oplus\{\ell : S_\ell\,\alpha\}_{\ell\in L}) \circ T &= \hat{\lambda}\alpha.\oplus\{\ell : (S_\ell \circ T)\,\alpha\}_{\ell\in L} \\ (\hat{\lambda}\alpha.\,A \otimes (S\,\alpha)) \circ T &= \hat{\lambda}\alpha.\,A \otimes ((S \circ T)\,\alpha)\end{aligned}$$

and similarly for $\&$ and $\multimap$. Together with the monoid laws of function composition, these distributive properties justify defining sequential composition as $S; T = S \circ T$.

This suggests that although many details distinguish our work from CFSTs, nested session types cover the essence of sequential composition underlying context-free session types. However, even stating a theorem that every CFST process can be translated into a well-typed process in our system of nested session types is difficult because the two type systems differ in many details: we include $\otimes$ and $\multimap$ as session types, but CFSTs do not; CFSTs use a complex kinding system to incorporate unrestricted session types and combine session types with ordinary function types; the CFST system uses classical typing for session types and a procedure of type normalization, whereas our types are intuitionistic and do not rely on normalization; and the CFST typing rules are based on natural deduction, rather than the sequent calculus. With all of these differences, a formal translation, theorem, and proof would not be very illuminating beyond the essence already described here. Empirically, we can also give analogues of the published examples for CFSTs (see, e.g., the first two examples of Section 9).

Finally, nested session types are strictly *more* expressive than CFSTs. Recall from Section 2 the language $L_3 = \{\mathbf{L}^n\mathbf{a}\,\mathbf{R}^n\mathbf{a} \cup \mathbf{L}^n\mathbf{b}\,\mathbf{R}^n\mathbf{b} \mid n > 0\}$, which can be expressed using nested session types with *two* type parameters used in an essential way. Moreover, Korenjak and Hopcroft [34] observe that this language cannot be recognized by a single-state, real-time DPDA that uses empty stack acceptance, and thus, CFSTs cannot express the language L_3. More broadly, nested types allow for finitely many states and acceptance by empty stack or final state, while CFSTs only allow a single state and empty stack acceptance.

8 Implementation

We have implemented a prototype for nested session types and integrated it with the open-source Rast system [17]. Rast (Resource-aware session types) is a programming language which implements the intuitionistic version of session types [7] with support for arithmetic refinements [18], ergometric [16] and temporal [15] types for complexity analysis. Our prototype extension is implemented in Standard ML (8011 lines of code) containing a lexer and parser (1214 lines), a type checker (3001 lines) and an interpreter (201 lines) and is well-documented. The prototype is available in the Rast repository [13].

Syntax A program contains a series of mutually recursive type and process declarations and definitions, concretely written as

```
type V[x1]...[xk] = A
decl f[x1]...[xk] : (c1 : A1) ... (cn : An) |- (c : A)
proc c <- f[x] c1 ... cn = P
```

Type $V[\overline{x}]$ is represented in concrete syntax as `V[x1]...[xk]`. The first line is a *type definition*, where V is the type name parameterized by type variables $x_1, \ldots, x_k$ and A is its definition. The second line is a *process declaration*, where f is the process name (parameterized by type variables $x_1, \ldots, x_k$), $(c_1 : A_1) \ldots (c_n : A_n)$ are the used channels and corresponding types, while the offered channel is c of type A. Finally, the last line is a *process definition* for the same process f defined using the process expression P. We use a hand-written lexer and shift-reduce parser to read an input file and generate the corresponding abstract syntax tree of the program. The reason to use a hand-written parser instead of a parser generator is to anticipate the most common syntax errors that programmers make and respond with the best possible error messages.

Once the program is parsed and its abstract syntax tree is extracted, we perform a *validity check* on it. This includes checking that type definitions, and process declarations and definitions are closed w.r.t. the type variables in scope. To simplify and improve the efficiency of the type equality algorithm, we also assign internal names to type subexpressions parameterized over their free index variables. These internal names are not visible to the programmer.

Type Checking and Error Messages The implementation is carefully designed to produce precise error messages. To that end, we store the extent (source location) information with the abstract syntax tree, and use it to highlight the source of the error. We also follow a bi-directional type checking [40] algorithm reconstructing intermediate types starting with the initial types provided in the declaration. This helps us precisely identify the source of the error. Another particularly helpful technique has been *type compression*. Whenever the type checker expands a type $V[\overline{A}]$ defined as $V[\overline{\alpha}] = B$ to $B[\overline{A}/\overline{\alpha}]$ we record a reverse mapping from $B[\overline{A}/\overline{\alpha}]$ to $V[\overline{\alpha}]$. When printing types for error messages this mapping is consulted, and complex types may be compressed to much simpler forms, greatly aiding readability of error messages.

9 More Examples

Expression Server We adapt the example of an arithmetic expression from prior work on context-free session types [45]. The type of the server is defined as

```
type bin = +{ b0 : bin, b1 : bin, $ : 1 }
type tm[K] = +{ const : bin * K,
                add : tm[tm[K]],
                double : tm[K] }
```

The type `bin` represents a constant binary natural number. A process *providing* a binary number sends a stream of bits, `b0` and `b1`, starting with the least significant bit and eventually terminated by `$`.

An arithmetic term, parameterized by continuation type `K` can have one of three forms: a constant, the sum of two terms, or the double of a term. Consequently, the type `tm[K]` ensures that a process providing `tm[K]` is a *well-formed term*: it either sends the `const` label followed by sending a constant binary number of type `bin` and continues with type `K`; or it sends the `add` label and continues with `tm[tm[K]]`, where the two terms denote the two summands; or it sends the `double` label and continues with `tm[K]`. In particular, the continuation type `tm[tm[K]]` in the `add` branch enforces that the process must send exactly two summands for sums.

As a first illustration, consider two binary constants a and b, and suppose that we want to create the expression $a + 2b$. We can issue commands to the expression server in a *prefix notation* to obtain $a+2b$, as shown in the following `exp[K]` process, which is parameterized by a continuation type `K`.

```
decl exp[K] : (a : bin) (b : bin) (k : K) |- (e : tm[K])
proc e <- exp[K] a b k =
  e.add ; e.const ; send e a ; % (b:bin) (k:K) |- (e : tm[K])
  e.double ; e.const ; send e b ; % (k:K) |- (e : K)
  e <-> k
```

In prefix notation, $a+2b$ would be written $+\ (a)\ (2\ b)$, which is exactly the form followed by the `exp` process: The process sends `add`, followed by `const` and the number `a`, followed by `double`, `const`, and `b`. Finally, the process continues at type `K` by forwarding `k` to `e` (intermediate typing contexts on the right).

To evaluate a term, we can define an `eval` process, parameterized by type `K`:

```
decl eval[K] : (t : tm[K]) |- (v : bin * K)
```

The `eval` process uses channel `t : tm[K]` as argument, and offers `v : bin * K`. The process evaluates term `t` and sends its binary value along `v`. The technical report contains the full implementation [14].

Serializing binary trees Another example from [45] is serializing binary trees. Here we adapt that example to our system. Binary trees can be described by:

```
type Tree[a] = +{ node : Tree[a] * a * Tree[a] , leaf : 1 }
```

These trees are polymorphic in the type of data stored at each internal node. A tree is either an internal node or a leaf, with the internal nodes storing channels that emit the left subtree, data, and right subtree. Owing to the multiple channels stored at each node, these trees do not exist in a serial form.

We can, however, use a different type to represent serialized trees:

```
type STree[a][K] = +{ nd : STree[a][a * STree[K]] , lf : K }
```

A serialized tree is a stream of node and leaf labels, `nd` and `lf`, parameterized by a continuation type `K`. Like `add` in the expression server, the label `nd` continues with type `STree[a][a * STree[K]]`: the label `nd` is followed by the serialized left subtree, which itself continues by sending the data stored at the internal node and then the serialized right subtree, which continues with type `K`.[3]

Using these types, it is relatively straightforward to implement processes that serialize and deserialize such trees. The process `serialize` can be declared with:

```
decl serialize[a][K] : (t : Tree[a]) (k : K) |- (s : STree[a][K])
```

This process uses channels `t` and `k` that hold the tree and continuation, and offers that tree's serialization along channel `s`. If the tree is only a leaf, then the process forwards to the continuation. Otherwise, if the tree begins with a node, then the serialization begins with `nd`. A recursive call to `serialize` serves to serialize the right subtree with the given continuation. A subsequent recursive call serializes the left subtree with the data together with the right subtree's serialization as the new continuation.

It is also possible to implement a process for deserializing trees, but because of space limitations, we will not describe `deserialize` here.

```
decl deserialize[a][K] : (s : STree[a][K]) |- (tk : Tree[a] * K)
```

Generalized tries for binary trees Using nested types in Haskell, prior work [28] describes an implementation of generalized tries that represent mappings on binary trees. Our type system is expressive enough to represent such generalized tries. We can reuse the type `Tree[a]` of binary trees given above. The type `Trie[a][b]` describes tries that represent mappings from `Tree[a]` to type `b`:

---

[3] The presence of `a *` means that this is not a true serialization because it sends a separate channel along which the data of type `a` is emitted. But there is no uniform mechanism for serializing polymorphic data, so this is as close to a true serialization as possible. Concrete instances of type `Tree` with, say, data of base type `int` could be given a true serialization by "inlining" the data of type `int` in the serialization.

```
type Trie[a][b] = &{ lookup_leaf : b ,
                     lookup_node : Trie[a][a -o Trie[a][b]] }
```

A process for looking up a tree in such tries can be declared by:

```
decl lookup_tree[a][b] : (m : Trie[a][b]) (t : Tree[a]) |- (v : b)
```

To lookup a tree in a trie, first determine whether that tree is a `leaf` or a `node`. If the tree is a `leaf`, then sending `lookup_leaf` to the trie will return the value of type `b` associated with that tree in the trie.

Otherwise, if the tree is a `node`, then sending `lookup_node` to the trie results in a trie of type `Trie[a][a -o Trie[a][b]]` that represents a mapping from left subtrees to type `a -o Trie[a][b]`. We then lookup the left subtree in this trie, resulting in a process of type `a -o Trie[a][b]` to which we send the data stored at our original tree's root. That results in a trie of type `Trie[a][b]` that represents a mapping from right subtrees to type `b`. Therefore, we finally lookup the right subtree in this new trie and obtain a result of type `b`, as desired.

We can define a process that constructs a trie from a function on trees:

```
decl build_trie[a][b] : (f : Tree[a] -o b) |- (m : Trie[a][b])
```

Both `lookup_tree` and `build_trie` can be seen as analogues to `deserialize` and `serialize`, respectively, converting a lower-level representation to a higher-level representation and vice versa. These types and declarations mean that tries represent total mappings; partial mappings are also possible, at the expense of some additional complexity.

All our examples have been implemented and type checked in the open-source Rast repository [13]. We have also further implemented the standard polymorphic data structures such as lists, stacks and queues.

10 Further Related Work

To our knowledge, our work is the first proposal of polymorphic recursion using nested type definitions in session types. Thiemann and Vasconcelos [45] use polymorphic recursion to update the channel between successive recursive calls but do not allow type constructors or nested types. An algorithm to check type equivalence for the non-polymorphic fragment of context-free session types has been proposed by Almeida et al. [1].

Other forms of polymorphic session types have also been considered in the literature. Gay [24] studies bounded polymorphism associated with branch and choice types in the presence of subtyping. He mentions recursive types (which are used in some examples) as future work, but does not mention parametric type definitions or nested types. Bono and Padovani [4,5] propose (bounded) polymorphism to type the endpoints in copyless message-passing programs inspired by session types, but they do not have nested types. Following Kobayashi's approach [33], Dardha et al. [12] provide an encoding of session types relying on linear and variant types and present an extension to enable parametric and bounded polymorphism (to which recursive types were added separately [11]) but not parametric type definitions nor nested types. Caires et al. [6] and Perez et al. [38] provide behavioral polymorphism and a relational parametricity principle for session types, but without recursive types or type constructors.

Nested session types bear important similarities with first-order cyclic terms, as observed by Jančar. Jančar [30] proves that the trace equivalence problem of first-order grammars is decidable, following the original ideas by Stirling for the language equality problem in deterministic pushdown automata [43]. These ideas were also reformulated by Sénizergues [41]. Henry and Sénizergues [27] proposed the only practical algorithm to decide the language equivalence problem on deterministic pushdown automata that we are aware of. Preliminary experiments show that such a generic implementation, even if complete in theory, is a poor match for the demands made by our type checker.

11 Conclusion

Nested session types extend binary session types with parameterized type definitions. This extension enables us to express polymorphic data structures just as naturally as in functional languages. The proposed types are able to capture sequences of communication actions described by deterministic context-free languages recognized by deterministic pushdown automata with several states, that accept by empty stack or by final state. In this setting, we show that type equality is decidable. To offset the complexity of type equality, we give a practical type equality algorithm that is sound, efficient, but incomplete.

In the future, we are planning to explore subtyping for nested types. In particular, since the language inclusion problem for simple languages [22] is undecidable, we believe subtyping can be reduced to inclusion and would also be undecidable. Despite this negative result, it would be interesting to design an algorithm to approximate subtyping. That would significantly increase the programs that can be type checked in the system. In another direction, since Rast [17] supports arithmetic refinements for lightweight verification, it would be interesting to explore how refinements interact with polymorphic type parameters, namely in the presence of subtyping. We would also like to explore examples where the current type equality is not adequate. Finally, protocols in distributed algorithms such as consensus or leader election (Raft, Paxos, etc.) depend on unbounded memory and cannot usually be expressed with finite control structure. In future work, we would like to see if these protocols can be expressed with nested session types.

Acknowledgements. Support for this research was provided by the Fundação para a Ciência e a Tecnologia (Portuguese Foundation for Science and Technology) through the Carnegie Mellon Portugal Program – Visiting Faculty Program and through the LASIGE Research Unit, ref. UIDB/00408/2020, and by the National Science Foundation under SaTC Award 1801369, CAREER Award 1845514 and Grant No. 1718276.

References

1. Almeida, B., Mordido, A., Vasconcelos, V.T.: Deciding the bisimilarity of context-free session types. In: Biere, A., Parker, D. (eds.) Tools and Algorithms for the Construction and Analysis of Systems - 26th International Conference, TACAS 2020, Held as Part of the European Joint Conferences on Theory and Practice of Software, ETAPS 2020, Dublin, Ireland, April 25-30, 2020, Proceedings, Part II. Lecture Notes in Computer Science, vol. 12079, pp. 39–56. Springer (2020). https://doi.org/10.1007/978-3-030-45237-7_3, `https://doi.org/10.1007/978-3-030-45237-7`
2. Bergstra, J.A., Klop, J.W.: Acpτ a universal axiom system for process specification. In: Wirsing, M., Bergstra, J.A. (eds.) Algebraic Methods: Theory, Tools and Applications. pp. 445–463. Springer Berlin Heidelberg, Berlin, Heidelberg (1989)
3. Bird, R.S., Meertens, L.G.L.T.: Nested datatypes. In: Jeuring, J. (ed.) Mathematics of Program Construction, MPC'98, Marstrand, Sweden, June 15-17, 1998, Proceedings. Lecture Notes in Computer Science, vol. 1422, pp. 52–67. Springer (1998). https://doi.org/10.1007/BFb0054285
4. Bono, V., Padovani, L.: Polymorphic endpoint types for copyless message passing. In: Silva, A., Bliudze, S., Bruni, R., Carbone, M. (eds.) Proceedings Fourth Interaction and Concurrency Experience, ICE 2011, Reykjavik, Iceland, 9th June 2011. EPTCS, vol. 59, pp. 52–67 (2011). https://doi.org/10.4204/EPTCS.59.5
5. Bono, V., Padovani, L.: Typing copyless message passing. Log. Methods Comput. Sci. **8**(1) (2012). https://doi.org/10.2168/LMCS-8(1:17)2012
6. Caires, L., Pérez, J.A., Pfenning, F., Toninho, B.: Behavioral polymorphism and parametricity in session-based communication. In: Felleisen, M., Gardner, P. (eds.) Programming Languages and Systems. pp. 330–349. Springer Berlin Heidelberg, Berlin, Heidelberg (2013)
7. Caires, L., Pfenning, F.: Session types as intuitionistic linear propositions. In: P.Gastin, F.Laroussinie (eds.) Proceedings of the 21st International Conference on Concurrency Theory (CONCUR 2010). pp. 222–236. Springer LNCS 6269, Paris, France (Aug 2010)
8. Caires, L., Pfenning, F., Toninho, B.: Linear logic propositions as session types. Mathematical Structures in Computer Science **760** (11 2014)
9. Cervesato, I., Scedrov, A.: Relating state-based and process-based concurrency through linear logic (full-version). Information and Computation **207**(10), 1044 – 1077 (2009). https://doi.org/10.1016/j.ic.2008.11.006, special issue: 13th Workshop on Logic, Language, Information and Computation (WoLLIC 2006)
10. Connelly, R.H., Morris, F.L.: A generalisation of the trie data structure. Mathematical Structures in Computer Science **5**(3), 381–418 (1995)
11. Dardha, O.: Recursive session types revisited. In: Carbone, M. (ed.) Third Workshop on Behavioural Types (BEAT 2014). pp. 27–34. EPTCS 162 (Sep 2014)
12. Dardha, O., Giachino, E., Sangiorgi, D.: Session types revisited. Inf. Comput. **256**, 253–286 (2017). https://doi.org/10.1016/j.ic.2017.06.002
13. Das, A., Derakhshan, F., Pfenning, F.: Rast implementation. `https://bitbucket.org/fpfenning/rast/src/master/` (2019), accessed: 2019-11-11
14. Das, A., DeYoung, H., Mordido, A., Pfenning, F.: Nested polymorphic session types (2020), `https://arxiv.org/abs/2010.06482`
15. Das, A., Hoffmann, J., Pfenning, F.: Parallel complexity analysis with temporal session types. Proc. ACM Program. Lang. **2**(ICFP), 91:1–91:30 (Jul 2018). https://doi.org/10.1145/3236786

16. Das, A., Hoffmann, J., Pfenning, F.: Work analysis with resource-aware session types. In: Proceedings of the 33rd Annual ACM/IEEE Symposium on Logic in Computer Science. pp. 305–314. LICS '18, ACM, New York, NY, USA (2018). https://doi.org/10.1145/3209108.3209146
17. Das, A., Pfenning, F.: Rast: Resource-Aware Session Types with Arithmetic Refinements (System Description). In: Ariola, Z.M. (ed.) 5th International Conference on Formal Structures for Computation and Deduction (FSCD 2020). Leibniz International Proceedings in Informatics (LIPIcs), vol. 167, pp. 33:1–33:17. Schloss Dagstuhl–Leibniz-Zentrum für Informatik, Dagstuhl, Germany (2020). https://doi.org/10.4230/LIPIcs.FSCD.2020.33
18. Das, A., Pfenning, F.: Session Types with Arithmetic Refinements. In: Konnov, I., Kovács, L. (eds.) 31st International Conference on Concurrency Theory (CONCUR 2020). Leibniz International Proceedings in Informatics (LIPIcs), vol. 171, pp. 13:1–13:18. Schloss Dagstuhl–Leibniz-Zentrum für Informatik, Dagstuhl, Germany (2020). https://doi.org/10.4230/LIPIcs.CONCUR.2020.13
19. Das, A., Pfenning, F.: Verified linear session-typed concurrent programming. In: 22nd International Symposium on Principles and Practice of Declarative Programming. PPDP '20, Association for Computing Machinery, New York, NY, USA (2020). https://doi.org/10.1145/3414080.3414087
20. Derakhshan, F., Pfenning, F.: Circular Proofs as Session-Typed Processes: A Local Validity Condition. arXiv e-prints arXiv:1908.01909 (Aug 2019)
21. Dyck: Gruppentheoretische studien. (mit drei lithographirten tafeln.). Mathematische Annalen **20**, 1–44 (1882), `http://eudml.org/doc/157013`
22. Friedman, E.P.: The inclusion problem for simple languages. Theor. Comput. Sci. **1**(4), 297–316 (1976). https://doi.org/10.1016/0304-3975(76)90074-8
23. Gay, S., Hole, M.: Subtyping for session types in the pi calculus. Acta Informatica **42**(2), 191–225 (Nov 2005). https://doi.org/10.1007/s00236-005-0177-z
24. Gay, S.J.: Bounded polymorphism in session types. Math. Struct. Comput. Sci. **18**(5), 895–930 (2008). https://doi.org/10.1017/S0960129508006944
25. Girard, J.Y., Lafont, Y.: Linear logic and lazy computation. In: Ehrig, H., Kowalski, R., Levi, G., Montanari, U. (eds.) TAPSOFT '87. pp. 52–66. Springer Berlin Heidelberg, Berlin, Heidelberg (1987)
26. Griffith, D.: Polarized Substructural Session Types. Ph.D. thesis, University of Illinois at Urbana-Champaign (Apr 2016)
27. Henry, P., Sénizergues, G.: Lalblc a program testing the equivalence of dpda's. In: International Conference on Implementation and Application of Automata. pp. 169–180. Springer (2013)
28. Hinze, R.: Generalizing generalized tries. Journal of Functional Pogramming **10**(4), 327–351 (Jul 2010)
29. Honda, K.: Types for dyadic interaction. In: Best, E. (ed.) CONCUR'93. pp. 509–523. Springer Berlin Heidelberg, Berlin, Heidelberg (1993)
30. Jančar, P.: Short decidability proof for DPDA language equivalence via 1st order grammar bisimilarity. CoRR **abs/1010.4760** (2010), `http://arxiv.org/abs/1010.4760`
31. Jancar, P.: Bisimilarity on basic process algebra is in 2-exptime (an explicit proof). arXiv preprint arXiv:1207.2479 (2012)
32. Johann, P., Ghani, N.: Haskell programming with nested types: A principled approach. Higher-Order and Symbolic Computation **22**(2), 155–189 (Jun 2009)
33. Kobayashi, N.: Type systems for concurrent programs. In: Aichernig, B.K., Maibaum, T.S.E. (eds.) Formal Methods at the Crossroads. From Panacea to Foundational Support, 10th Anniversary Colloquium of UNU/IIST, the International

Institute for Software Technology of The United Nations University, Lisbon, Portugal, March 18-20, 2002, Revised Papers. Lecture Notes in Computer Science, vol. 2757, pp. 439–453. Springer (2002). https://doi.org/10.1007/978-3-540-40007-3_26
34. Korenjak, A.J., Hopcroft, J.E.: Simple deterministic languages. In: 7th Annual Symposium on Switching and Automata Theory (swat 1966). pp. 36–46. IEEE (1966)
35. Lindley, S., Morris, J.G.: Talking bananas: Structural recursion for session types. In: Proceedings of the 21st ACM SIGPLAN International Conference on Functional Programming. p. 434–447. ICFP 2016, Association for Computing Machinery, New York, NY, USA (2016). https://doi.org/10.1145/2951913.2951921
36. Mycroft, A.: Polymorphic type schemes and recursive definitions. In: Paul, M., Robinet, B. (eds.) International Symposium on Programming. pp. 217–228. Springer Berlin Heidelberg, Berlin, Heidelberg (1984)
37. Okasaki, C.: Purely Functional Data Structures. Ph.D. thesis, Department of Computer Science, Carnegie Mellon University (1996)
38. Pérez, J.A., Caires, L., Pfenning, F., Toninho, B.: Linear logical relations and observational equivalences for session-based concurrency. Information and Computation **239**, 254–302 (2014)
39. Pfenning, F., Griffith, D.: Polarized substructural session types. In: Pitts, A. (ed.) Foundations of Software Science and Computation Structures. pp. 3–22. Springer Berlin Heidelberg, Berlin, Heidelberg (2015)
40. Pierce, B.C., Turner, D.N.: Local type inference. ACM Trans. Program. Lang. Syst. **22**(1), 1–44 (Jan 2000). https://doi.org/10.1145/345099.345100
41. Sénizergues, G.: L(a)=l(b)? A simplified decidability proof. Theor. Comput. Sci. **281**(1-2), 555–608 (2002). https://doi.org/10.1016/S0304-3975(02)00027-0
42. Solomon, M.H.: Type definitions with parameters. In: Aho, A.V., Zilles, S.N., Szymanski, T.G. (eds.) Conference Record of the Fifth Annual ACM Symposium on Principles of Programming Languages, Tucson, Arizona, USA, January 1978. pp. 31–38. ACM Press (1978). https://doi.org/10.1145/512760.512765
43. Stirling, C.: Decidability of DPDA equivalence. Theor. Comput. Sci. **255**(1-2), 1–31 (2001). https://doi.org/10.1016/S0304-3975(00)00389-3
44. Takeuchi, K., Honda, K., Kubo, M.: An interaction-based language and its typing system. In: Halatsis, C., Maritsas, D.G., Philokyprou, G., Theodoridis, S. (eds.) PARLE '94: Parallel Architectures and Languages Europe, 6th International PARLE Conference, Athens, Greece, July 4-8, 1994, Proceedings. Lecture Notes in Computer Science, vol. 817, pp. 398–413. Springer (1994). https://doi.org/10.1007/3-540-58184-7_118
45. Thiemann, P., Vasconcelos, V.T.: Context-free session types. In: Garrigue, J., Keller, G., Sumii, E. (eds.) Proceedings of the 21st ACM SIGPLAN International Conference on Functional Programming, ICFP 2016, Japan. pp. 462–475. ACM (2016). https://doi.org/10.1145/2951913.2951926, `https://doi.org/10.1145/2951913`
46. Thiemann, P., Vasconcelos, V.T.: Label-dependent session types. Proceedings of the ACM on Programming Languages **4**(POPL), 67:1–67:29 (2020). https://doi.org/10.1145/3371135
47. Wadler, P.: Propositions as sessions. In: Thiemann, P., Findler, R.B. (eds.) ACM SIGPLAN International Conference on Functional Programming, ICFP'12, Copenhagen, Denmark, September 9-15, 2012. pp. 273–286. ACM (2012). https://doi.org/10.1145/2364527.2364568, `https://doi.org/10.1145/2364527.2364568`

Coupled Relational Symbolic Execution for Differential Privacy

Gian Pietro Farina[1], Stephen Chong[2], and Marco Gaboardi(✉)[3]

[1] University at Buffalo SUNY, Buffalo, USA, gianpiet@buffalo.edu
[2] Harvard University, Cambridge, USA, chong@seas.harvard.edu
[3] Boston University, Boston, USA, gaboardi@bu.edu

Abstract. Differential privacy is a de facto standard in data privacy with applications in the private and public sectors. Most of the techniques that achieve differential privacy are based on a judicious use of randomness. However, reasoning about randomized programs is difficult and error prone. For this reason, several techniques have been recently proposed to support designer in proving programs differentially private or in finding violations to it.

In this work we propose a technique based on symbolic execution for reasoning about differential privacy. Symbolic execution is a classic technique used for testing, counterexample generation and to prove absence of bugs. Here we use symbolic execution to support these tasks specifically for differential privacy. To achieve this goal, we design a relational symbolic execution technique which supports reasoning about probabilistic coupling, a formal notion that has been shown useful to structure proofs of differential privacy. We show how our technique can be used to both verify and find violations to differential privacy.

1 Introduction

Differential Privacy [8] has become a de facto gold standard definition of privacy for statistical analysis. This success is mostly due to the generality of the definition, its robustness and compositionality. However, getting differential privacy right in practice is a hard task. Even privacy experts have released fragile code subject to attacks [13, 17] and published incorrect algorithms [16]. This challenge has motivated the development of techniques to support programmers to show their algorithms differentially private. Among the techniques that have been proposed there are type systems [12,18,20,24,26], methods based on model checking and program analysis [2,15,22,23], and program logics [3,4,21]. Several works have also focused on developing techniques to find violations to differential privacy [2, 5, 6, 23, 27]. Most of these works focus only on either verifying a program differentially private or finding violations. Exceptions are the recent works by Barthe et al. [2] and Wang et al. [23] (developed concurrently to our work) which propose method that can instead address both.

Motivated by this picture, we propose a new technique named Coupled Relational Symbolic Execution (CRSE), which supports proving and finding violation

N. Yoshida (Ed.): ESOP 2021, LNCS 12648, pp. 207–233, 2021.
https://doi.org/10.1007/978-3-030-72019-3_8

to differential privacy. Our technique is based on two essential ingredients: relational symbolic execution [10] and approximate probabilistic couplings [3].

Relational Symbolic Execution. Symbolic execution is a classic technique used for bug finding, testing and proving. In symbolic execution an evaluator executes the program which consumes symbolic inputs instead of concrete ones. The evaluator follows, potentially, all the execution paths the program could take and collects constraints over the symbolic values, corresponding to these paths. Similarly, in relational symbolic execution [10] (RSE) one is concerned with bug finding, testing, or proving for *relational properties*. These are properties about two executions of two potentially different programs. RSE executes two potentially different programs in a symbolic fashion and exploits relational assumptions about the inputs or the programs in order to reduce the number of states to analyze. This is effective when the codes of the two programs share some similarities, and when the property under consideration is relational in nature, as in the case of differential privacy.

Approximate Probabilistic Couplings. Probabilistic coupling is a proof technique useful to lift a relation over the support of a joint distribution to a relation over the two probability marginals of the joint. This allows one to reason about relations between probability distributions by reasoning about relations on their support, which can be usually done in a symbolic way. In this approach the actual probabilistic reasoning is confined to the soundness of the verification system, rather than being spread everywhere in the verification effort. A relaxation of the notion of coupling, called *approximate probabilistic coupling* [3, 4], has been designed to reason about differential privacy. This can be seen as a regular probabilistic coupling with some additional parameters describing how close the two probability distribution are.

In this work, we combine these two approaches in a framework called Coupled Relational Symbolic Execution. In this framework, a program is executed in a relational and symbolic way. When some probabilistic primitive is executed, CRSE introduces constraints corresponding to the existence of an approximate probabilistic coupling on the output. These constraints are combined with the constraints on the execution traces generated by symbolically and relationally executing other non-probabilistic commands. These combined constraints can be exploited to reduce the number of states to analyze. When the execution is concluded CRSE checks whether there is a coupling between the two outputs, or whether there is some violation to the coupling. We show the soundness of this approach for both proving and refuting differential privacy. However, for finding violations, one cannot reason only symbolically, and since checking a coupling directly can be computationally expensive, we devise several heuristics which can be used to facilitate this task. Using these techniques, CRSE allows one to verify differential privacy for an interesting class of programs, including programs working on countable input and output domains, and to find violations to programs that are not differentially private.

CRSE is not a replacement for other techniques that have been proposed for the same task, it should be seen as an additional method to put in the set of tools of the privacy developer which provides a high level of generality. Indeed, by being a totally symbolic technique, it can leverage a plethora of current technologies such as SMT solvers, algebraic solvers, and numeric solvers.

Summarizing, the contribution of our work are:

- We combine relational symbolic execution and approximate probabilistic coupling in a new technique: Coupled Relational Symbolic Execution.
- We show CRSE sound for proving programs differentially private
- We devise a set of heuristic - one of them sound, and the others useful - that can help a programmer in finding violations to differential privacy.
- We show how CRSE can help in proving and refuting differential privacy for an interesting class of programs

Most of the proofs are omitted here, more details can be found in [9,11].

2 CRSE Informally

We will introduce CRSE through three examples of programs showing potential errors in implementations of differentially private algorithms. Informally, a randomized function A over a set of databases $\mathcal{D}$ is ϵ-differential privacy (ϵ-DP) if it maps two databases D_1 and D_2 that differ for the data of one single individual (denoted $D_1 \sim D_2$) to output distributions that are indistinguishable up to some value ϵ - usually referred to as the privacy budget. This is formalized by requiring that for every $D_1 \sim D_2$ and for every u: $\Pr[\mathcal{A}(D_1) = u] \leq e^{\epsilon} \Pr[\mathcal{A}(D_2) = u]$. The smaller the ϵ, the more privacy is guaranteed.

Algorithm 1
A bad use of Randomized Response

Input: $\epsilon \in \mathcal{R}^+, x_1, x_2 \in \{true, false\}$
Precondtion: $x_1 \neq x_2$
Postcondition: $o_1 = o_2 \wedge \epsilon_c \leq \epsilon$

1: $o \leftarrow RR_\epsilon(x)$
2: **return** o

Fig. 1: Algorithm 1 is not ϵ-DP.

Randomized response with wrong noise. A standard primitive to achieve differential privacy when the data is a single boolean is randomized response [25]. We will use this (simplified) primitive to give an idea of how CRSE works. This primitive can be actually reduced to the primitives that CRSE uses and so it won't be included in later sections. The primitive $RR_p(b)$ takes in input $p \in (\frac{1}{2}, 1)$ and a boolean b and it outputs b with probability p, and $\bar{b}$ with probability $1 - p$. By unfolding the definition of differential privacy it is easy to see that this primitive is $log[-p/(p-1)]$-DP. This is internalized in CRSE thanks to the the existence of an $log[-p/(p-1)]$-approximate lifting (Definition 2) of the equality relation $=$ between the distributions $RR_p(b)$ and $RR_p(\bar{b})$. When CRSE executes line 1, it assumes that $o_1 = o_2$ and it sets a counter ϵ_c, representing the privacy budget required by the primitive, to $\log[-\frac{\epsilon}{\epsilon-1}]$. In order to check whether this program is actually ϵ-DP it will then try to check whether this set of conditions implies the postcondition $\Psi \equiv o_1 = o_2 \wedge \epsilon_c \leq \epsilon$. This implication will fail. Indeed, there are value of ϵ, say $\epsilon = 0.7$, which give a value of ϵ_c which is actually greater than ϵ. This shows that the user may have confused the ϵ parameter with the parameter p that the randomized response primitive takes in input. If the user substituted line 1 with the following $p \leftarrow \frac{e^\epsilon}{1+e^\epsilon}; o \xleftarrow{\$} RR_p(x)$, then CRSE would have considered the following conditions instead: $o_1 = o_2$ and $\epsilon_c = \log[-\frac{p}{p-1}] \wedge p = \frac{e^\epsilon}{1+e^\epsilon}$. These conditions would then imply the postcondition Ψ proving the correcteness of the program.

The intuition behind this proof is that everytime CRSE executes a random assignment of the form $o \xleftarrow{\$} RR_p(x)$, it is allowed to assume that $o_1 = o_2$ as long as it spends a certain amount of privacy budget, i.e. $log[-\frac{p}{p-1}]$. These assumptions are recorded in a set of constraints which is then used to see if it implies the condition that two output variables are equal and the budget spent does not exceed ϵ. As a consequence of the definition of approximate lifting, this implies differential privacy (Lemma 2). If this fails, CRSE will provide a counterexample in the form of values for the inputs x_1, x_2, ϵ, p. Such counterexamples to the postcondition do not necessarily denote a counterxampled to the privacy of the algorithm (as we will see later the logic of couplings which CRSE is based on is not complete w.r.t the differential privacy notion) but only potential candidates, and hence need to be further checked.

Algorithm 2 A buggy Above Threshold

Input: $t, \epsilon \in \mathbb{R}, D \in \mathcal{D}, q[i] : \mathcal{D} \rightarrow \mathbb{N}$
Output: $o : [\perp^i, z, \perp^{n-i-1}]$
Precondition: $D_1 \sim D_2 \Rightarrow |q[i](D_1) - q[i](D_2)| \leq 1$
Postcondition: $o_1 = o_2 \wedge \epsilon_c \leq \epsilon$

$o \leftarrow \perp^n; r \leftarrow n+1$
$\hat{t} \xleftarrow{\$} lap_{\frac{\epsilon}{2}}(t)$
for $(i$ **in** $1{:}n)$ **do**
  $\hat{s} \xleftarrow{\$} lap_{\frac{\epsilon}{4}}(q[i](D))$
  if $\hat{s} > \hat{t} \wedge r = n+1$ **then**
    $o[i] \leftarrow \hat{s}; r \leftarrow i$
return o

Algorithm 3 Another buggy Above Threshold

Input: $t, \epsilon \in \mathbb{R}, D \in \mathcal{D}, q[i] : \mathcal{D} \rightarrow \mathbb{N}$
Output: $o \in \{\perp, \top\}^n$
Precondition: $D_1 \sim D_2 \Rightarrow |q[i](D_1) - q[i](D_2)| \leq 1$
Postcondition: $o_1 = o_2 \wedge \epsilon_c \leq \epsilon$

$\hat{t} \xleftarrow{\$} lap_{\frac{\epsilon}{2}}(t)$
for $(i$ **in** $1{:}n)$ **do**
  if $q[i](D) \geq \hat{t}$ **then**
    $o[i] \leftarrow \top$
  else
    $o[i] \leftarrow \perp$
return o

Two buggy Sparse Vector implementations. The next two examples are variations of the algorithm *above threshold*, a component of the *sparse vector* technique, a classical technique which is still subject of studies for improvement [7,14]. Given a numeric threshold, an array of numeric queries of length n, and a dataset, this algorithm returns the index of the first query whose result exceeds the threshold - and potentially it should also return the value of that query. This should be done in a way that preserves differential privacy. To do this in the right way, a program should add noise to the threshold, even if it is not sensitive data, add noise to each query, compare the values, and return the index of the first query for which this comparison succeed. The noise that is usually added is sampled from the Laplace distribution, one of the main primitive in differential privacy. The analysis of this algorithm is rather complex: it uses the noise on the threshold as a way to pay only once for all the queries that are below the threshold, and the noise on the queries to pay for the first and only query that is above the threshold, if any. Due to this complex analysis [16], this algorithm has been a benchmark for tools for reasoning about differential privacy [2,3,26].

Algorithm 2 has a bug making the (whole) program not differentially private, for values of n greater than 4. The program initializes an array of outputs o to all bottom values, and a variable r to $n+1$ which will be used as guard in the main loop. It then adds noise to the threshold, and iterates over all the queries adding noise to their results. If one of the noised-results is above the noisy threshold it saves the value in the array of outputs and updates the value of the guard variable, causing it to exit the main loop. Otherwise it keeps iterating. The bug is returning the value of the noisy query that is above the threshold and not only its index, as done by the instruction in red in line 6 - this is indeed not enough for guaranteeing differential privacy. For $n < 5$ this program can be shown ϵ-differentially private by using the composition property of differential privacy that says that the k-fold composition of ϵ-DP programs is $k\epsilon$-differentially private (Section 3). However, for $n \geq 5$ the more sophisticated analysis we described above fails. The proof principle CRSE will use to try to show this program ϵ-differentially private is to prove the assertion $o_1 = \iota \implies o_2 = \iota \wedge \epsilon_c \leq \epsilon$, for every $\iota \leq n$ - the soundness of this principle has been proved in [3]. That is, CRSE will try to prove the following assertions (which would prove the program ϵ-differentially private):

- $o_1 = [\hat{s}_1, \bot, \ldots, \bot] \implies o_2 = [\hat{s}_1, \bot, \ldots, \bot] \wedge \epsilon_c \leq \epsilon$
- $o_1 = [\bot, \hat{s}_1, \ldots, \bot] \implies o_2 = [\bot, \hat{s}_1, \ldots, \bot] \wedge \epsilon_c \leq \epsilon$

...

- $o_1 = [\bot, \ldots, \hat{s}_1] \implies o_2 = [\bot, \ldots, \hat{s}_1] \wedge \epsilon_c \leq \epsilon$

While proving the first assertion, CRSE will first couple at line 3 the threshold as $\hat{t}_1 + k_0 = \hat{t}_2$, for $k_0 > 1$ where 1 is the sensitivity of the queries, which is needed to guarantee that all the query results below the threshold in one run stay below the threshold in the other run, then, it will increase appropriately the privacy budget by $k_0\frac{\epsilon}{2}$. As a second step it will couple $\hat{s}_1 + k_1 = \hat{s}_2$ in line 4. Now, the only way for the assertion $o_1 = [\hat{s}_1, \bot, \bot] \implies o_2 = [\hat{s}_1, \bot, \bot]$ to hold, is guaranteeing that both $\hat{s_1} = \hat{s}_2$ and $\hat{s}_1 \geq t_1 \implies \hat{s_2} \geq t_2$ hold. But these two assertions are not consistent with each other because $k_0 \geq 1$. That is, the only way, using these coupling rules, to guarantee that the run on the right follows the same branches of the run on the left (this being necessary for proving the postcondition) is to couple the samples $\hat{s}_1$ and $\hat{s}_2$ so that they are different, this necessarily implying the negation of the postcondition. This would not be the case if we were returning only the index of the query, since we can have that both the queries are above the threshold but return different values. Indeed, by substituting line 7 with $o[i] \xleftarrow{\$} \top$ the program can be proven ϵ-differentially private. So the *refuting* principle CRSE will use here is the one that finds a trace on the left run such that the only way the right run can be forced to follow it is by making the output variables different.

A second example with bug of the above threshold algorithm is shown in Figure 3. In this example, in the body of the loop, the test is performed between the noisy threshold and the actual value of the query on the database - that is, we don't add noise to the query. CRSE will use for this example another *refuting* principle based on reachability. In particular, it will vacuously couple the two thresholds at line 1. That is it will not introduce any relation between $\hat{t}_1$, and $\hat{t}_2$. CRSE will then search for a trace which is satisfiable in the first run but not in the second one. This translates in an output event which has positive probability on the first run but 0 probability in the second one leading to an unbounded privacy loss, and making the algorithm not ϵ-differentially private for all finite ϵ. Interestingly this unbounded privacy loss can be achieved with just 2 iterations.

3 Preliminaries

Let A be a denumerable set, a *subdistribution* over A is a function $\mu : A \to [0, 1]$ with weight $\sum_{a \in A} \mu(a)$ less or equal than 1. We denote the set of subdistributions over A as $\mathbf{sdistr}(A)$. When a subdistribution has weight equal to 1, then we call it a *distribution*. We denote the set of distributions over A by $\mathbf{distr}(A)$. The *null* subdistribution $\mu_0 : A \to [0, 1]$ assigns to every element of A mass 0. The Dirac's distribution $\mathbf{unit}(a) : A \to [0, 1]$, defined for $a \in A$ as $\mathbf{unit}(a)(x) \equiv 1$ if $x = a$, and $\mathbf{unit}(a)(x) \equiv 0$, otherwise. The set of subprobability distributions can be given the structure of a *monad*, with unit the function **unit**. We have also a function $\mathbf{bind} \equiv \lambda\mu.\lambda f.\lambda a. \sum_{b \in \mathcal{O}'} \mu(b) \cdot f(b)(a)$ allowing us to compose subdistributions (as we compose monads). We will use the notion of ϵ-divergence $\Delta_\epsilon(\mu_1, \mu_2)$ between two subdistributions $\mu_1, \mu_2 \in \mathbf{sdistr}(A)$ to define approximate coupling, this is defined as: $\Delta_\epsilon(\mu_1, \mu_2) \equiv \sup_{E \subseteq O} \big(\mu_1(E) - \exp(\epsilon) \cdot \mu_2(E)\big)$.

Formally, differential privacy is a property of a probabilistic program:

Definition 1 (Differential Privacy [8]). *Let $\epsilon \geq 0$ and $\sim \subseteq \mathcal{D} \times \mathcal{D}$. A program $\mathcal{A} : \mathcal{D} \to \mathbf{distr}(\mathcal{O})$ is ϵ-differentially private with respect to $\sim$ iif $\forall D \sim D'. \forall u \in \mathcal{O}$:*

$$\Pr[\mathcal{A}(D) = u] \leq e^\epsilon \Pr[\mathcal{A}(D') = u]$$

The adjacency relation $\sim$ over the set of databases $\mathcal{D}$ models which pairs of input databases should be indistinguishable to an adversary. In its most classical definition, $\sim$ relates databases that differ in one record in terms of hamming distance. Differentially private programs can be composed [8]: given programs A_1 and A_2, respectively ϵ_1 and ϵ_2 differentially private, their sequential composition $A(D) \equiv A_2(\langle A_1(D), D\rangle)$ is $\epsilon_1 + \epsilon_2$-differentially private. We say that a function $f : \mathcal{D} \to \mathbb{Z}$ is k *sensitive* if $|f(x) - f(y)| \leq k$, for all $x \sim y$. Functions with bounded sensitivity can be made differentially private by adding Laplace noise:

Lemma 1 (Laplace Mechanism [8]). *Let $\epsilon > 0$, and assume that $f : \mathcal{D} \mapsto \mathbb{Z}$ is a k sensitive function with respect to $\sim \subseteq \mathcal{D} \times \mathcal{D}$. Then the randomized algorithm mapping d to $f(D) + \nu$, where ν is sampled from a discrete version of the Laplace distribution with scale $\frac{1}{\epsilon}$, is $k\epsilon$-differentially private w.r.t to $\sim$.*

The notion of approximate probabilistic coupling is internalized by the notion of approximate lifting [3].

Definition 2. *Given $\mu_1 \in \mathbf{distr}(A), \mu_2 \in \mathbf{distr}(B)$, a relation $\Psi \subseteq A \times B$, and $\epsilon \in \mathbb{R}$, we say that μ_1, μ_2 are related by the ϵ approximate lifting of Ψ, denoted $\mu_1(\Psi)^\epsilon\mu_2$, iff there exists $\mu_L, \mu_R \in \mathbf{distr}(A \times B)$ such that: 1) $\lambda a. \sum_b \mu_L(a,b) = \mu_1$ and $\lambda b. \sum_a \mu_R(a,b) = \mu_2$, 2) $\{(a,b) | \mu_L(a,b) > 0 \vee \mu_R(a,b) > 0\} \subseteq \Psi$, 3) $\Delta_\epsilon(\mu_L, \mu_R) \leq 0$.*

Approximate lifting satisfies the following fundamental property [3]:

Lemma 2. *Let $\mu_1, \mu_2 \in \mathbf{distr}(A), \epsilon \geq 0$. Then $\Delta_\epsilon(\mu_1, \mu_2) \leq 0$ iff $\mu_1(=)^\epsilon\mu_2$.*

From Lemma 2 we have that an algorithm A is ϵ-differentially private w.r.t to $\sim$ iff $A(D_1)(=)^\epsilon A(D_2)$ for all $D_1 \sim D_2$. The next lemma [3], finally, casts the Laplace mechanisms in terms of couplings:

Lemma 3. *Let $L_{v_1,b}, L_{v_2,b}$ two Laplace random variables with mean v_1, and v_2 respectively, and scale b. Then*

$$L_{v_1,b}\,\{(z_1,z_2) \mid z_1 + k = z_2 \in \mathbb{Z} \times \mathbb{Z}\}^{|k+v_1-v_2|\epsilon}\, L_{v_2,b},$$

for all $k \in \mathbb{Z}, \epsilon \geq 0$.

4 Concrete languages

In this section we sketch the two CRSE concrete languages, the unary one PFOR and the relational one RPFOR. These will be the basis on which we will design our *symbolic* languages in the next section.

4.1 PFOR

PFOR is a basic FOR-like language with arrays, to represent databases and other data structures, and probabilistic sampling from the Laplace distribution. The full syntax is pretty standard and we fully present it in the extended version [11]. In the following we have a simplified syntax:

$$\mathcal{C} \ni c ::= \texttt{skip} \mid c;c \mid x \leftarrow e \mid x \xleftarrow{\$} lap_e(e) \mid \texttt{if } e \texttt{ then } c \texttt{ else } c \mid \ldots$$

The set of commands $\mathcal{C}$ includes assignments, the `skip` command, sequencing, branching, and (not showed) array assignments and looping construct. Finally, we also include a primitive instruction $x \xleftarrow{\$} lap_{e_2}(e_1)$ to model random sampling from the Laplace distribution. Arithmetic expressions $e \in \mathcal{E}$ are built out of integers, array accesses and lengths, and elements in $\mathcal{X}_p$. The set $\mathcal{X}_p$ contains values denoting random expressions, that is values coming from a random assignment or arithmetic expressions involving such values. We will use capital letters such as $X, Y, \ldots$ to range over $\mathcal{X}_p$. The set of values is $\mathcal{V} \equiv \mathbb{Z} \cup \mathcal{X}_p$. In Figure 2, we introduce a grammar of constraints for random expressions, where X ranges over $\mathcal{X}_p$ and $n, n_1, n_2 \in \mathbb{Z}$. The simple constraints in the syntactic categories ra and re record that a random value is either associated with a specific distribution, or that the computation is conditioned on some random expression being greater than 0 or less than or equal than 0. The former constraints, as we will see, come from branching instructions. We treat constraint lists p, p', in Figure 2 as lists of simple constraints and hence, from now on, we will use the infix operators :: and @, respectively, for appending a simple constraint to a constraint and for concatenating two constraints. The symbol [] denotes the empty list of probabilistic constraints. Environments in the set $\mathcal{M}$, or probabilistic memories, map program variables to values in $\mathcal{V}$, and array names to elements in $\mathbf{Array} \equiv \bigcup_i \mathcal{V}^i$, so the type of a memory $m \in \mathcal{M}$ is $\mathbb{V} \to \mathcal{V} \cup \mathbb{A} \to \mathbf{Array}$. We will distinguish between probabilistic concrete memories in $\mathcal{M}$ and concrete memories in the set $\mathcal{M}_c \equiv \mathbb{V} \to \mathbb{Z} \cup \mathbb{A} \to \bigcup_i \mathbb{Z}^i$. Probabilistic concrete memories are meant to denote subdistributions over the set of concrete memories $\mathcal{M}_c$.

$$
\begin{aligned}
ra &::= X \xleftarrow{\$} lap_{n_2}(n_1) \\
re &::= n \mid X \mid re \oplus re \\
P \ni p &::= X = re \mid re > 0 \mid \\
&\quad re \leq 0 \mid ra \mid p :: P \mid []
\end{aligned}
$$

Fig. 2: Probabilistic constraints

Expressions in PFOR are given meaning through a big-step evaluation semantics specified by a judgment of the form: $\langle m, e, p \rangle \downarrow_c \langle v, p' \rangle$, where $m \in \mathcal{M}, e \in \mathcal{E}, p, p' \in P, v \in \mathcal{V}$. The judgments reads as: expression e reduces to the value v and probabilistic constraints p' in an environment m with probabilistic concrete constraints p. We omit the rules for this judgment here, but we will present similar rules for the symbolic languages in the next section. Commands are given

$$
\textbf{if-false}\ \frac{\langle m, e, p \rangle \downarrow_c \langle v, p' \rangle \qquad v \in \mathbb{Z} \qquad v \leq 0}{\langle m, \mathtt{if}\ e\ \mathtt{then}\ c_1\ \mathtt{else}\ c_2, p \rangle \to_c \langle m, c_2, p' \rangle}
$$

$$
\textbf{if-true-prob}\ \frac{\langle m, e, p \rangle \downarrow_c \langle v, p' \rangle \qquad v \in \mathcal{X}_p \qquad p'' \equiv p'@v > 0}{\langle m, \mathtt{if}\ e\ \mathtt{then}\ c_1\ \mathtt{else}\ c_2, p \rangle \to_c \langle m, c_1, p'' \rangle}
$$

$$
\textbf{lap-ass}\ \frac{\begin{array}{c}\langle m, e_1, p \rangle \downarrow_c \langle n_1, p_1 \rangle \qquad \langle m, e_2, p_1 \rangle \downarrow_c \langle n_2, p_2 \rangle \qquad n_2 > 0 \\ X\ \mathbf{fresh}(\mathcal{X}_p) \qquad p' \equiv p_1@X = lap_{n_2}(n_1)\end{array}}{\langle m, x \xleftarrow{\$} lap_{e_2}(e_1), p \rangle \to_c \langle m[x \mapsto X], \mathtt{skip}, p' \rangle}
$$

Fig. 3: PFOR selected rules

meaning through a small-step evaluation semantics specified by a judgment of the form: $\langle m, c, p\rangle \rightarrow_{\mathrm{c}} \langle m', c', p'\rangle$, where $m, m' \in \mathcal{M}, c, c' \in \mathcal{C}, p, p' \in P$. The judgment reads as: the probabilistic concrete configuration $\langle m, c, p\rangle$ steps in to the probabilistic concrete configuration $\langle m', c', p'\rangle$. Figure (3) shows a selection of the rules defining this judgment. Most of the rules are self-explanatory so we only describe the ones which are non standard. Rule **lap-ass** handles the random assignment. It evaluates the mean e_1 and the scale e_2 of the distribution and checks that e_2 actually denotes a positive number. The semantic predicate **fresh** asserts that the first argument is drawn nondeterministically from the second argument and that it was never used before in the computation. Notice that if one of these two expressions reduces to a probabilistic symbolic value the computation halts. Rule **if-true-prob** (and **if-false-prob**) reduces the guard of a branching instruction to a value. If the value is a probabilistic symbolic constraint then it will nondeterministically choose one of the two branches recording the choice made in the list of probabilistic constraints. If instead the value of the guard is a numerical constant it will choose the right branch deterministically using the rules **if-false** and **if-true** (not showed).

We call a probabilistic concrete configuration of the form $\langle m, \mathtt{skip}, p\rangle$ final. A set of concrete configurations $\mathscr{D}$ is called final and we denote it by $\mathbf{Final}(\mathscr{D})$ if all its concrete configurations are final. We will use this predicate even for sets of sets of concrete configurations with the obvious lifted meaning. As clear from the rules a run of a PFOR program can generate many different final concrete configurations. A different judgment of the form $\mathscr{D} \Rightarrow_{\mathrm{c}} \mathscr{D}'$, where $\mathscr{D}, \mathscr{D}' \in \mathcal{P}(\mathcal{M} \times \mathcal{C} \times P)$, and in particular its transitive and reflexive closure ($\Rightarrow_{\mathrm{c}}^{*}$), will help us in collecting all the possible final configurations stemming from a computation. We have only one rule that defines this judgment:

Sub-distr-step

$$\frac{\langle m, c, p\rangle \in \mathscr{D} \quad \mathscr{D}' \equiv (\mathscr{D} \setminus \{\langle m, c, p\rangle\}) \cup \{\langle m', c', p'\rangle \mid \langle m, c, p\rangle \rightarrow_{\mathrm{c}} \langle m', c', p'\rangle\}}{\mathscr{D} \Rightarrow_{\mathrm{c}} \mathscr{D}'}$$

Rule **Sub-distr-step** nondeterministically selects a configuration $s = \langle m, c, p\rangle$ from $\mathscr{D}$, removes s from it, and adds to $\mathscr{D}'$ all the configurations s' that are reachable from s.

In section 3 we defined the notions of lifting, coupling and differential privacy using subdistributions in the form of functions from a set of atomic events to the interval $[0, 1]$. The semantics of the languages proposed so far though only deal with subdistributions represented as set of concrete probabilistic configurations. We now show how to map the latter to the former. In Figure 4 we define a translation function ($[\![\cdot;\cdot]\!]^{\mathbf{mp}}$) and, auxiliary functions as well, between a single probabilistic concrete configuration and a subdistribution defined using the $\mathbf{unit}(\cdot)/\mathbf{bind}(\cdot,\cdot)$ constructs. We make use of the constant subdistribution μ_0 which maps every element to mass 0, and is usually referred to as the *null* subdistribution, also by $lap_{n_2}(n_1)(z)$ we denote the mass of (discrete version of) the Laplace distribution centered in n_1 with scale n_2 at the point z.

The idea of the translation is that we can transform a probabilistic concrete memory $m_s \in \mathcal{M}$ into a distribution over fully concrete memories in $\mathcal{M}_c$ by

$$
\begin{aligned}
[\![m_s;p]\!]^{\mathbf{mp}} &= \mathbf{bind}([\![p]\!]^{\mathbf{p}}, (\lambda s_o.\mathbf{unit}(s_o(m_s))))\\
[\![[]]\!]^{\mathbf{p}} &= \mathbf{unit}([])\\
[\![X = re :: p']\!]^{\mathbf{p}} &= \mathbf{bind}([\![p']\!]^{\mathbf{p}}, \lambda s_o.\mathbf{bind}([\![re]\!]^{\mathbf{re}}_{s_o}, \lambda z_o.\mathbf{unit}(X = z_o :: s_o)))\\
[\![re > 0 :: p']\!]^{\mathbf{p}} &= \mathbf{bind}([\![p']\!]^{\mathbf{p}}, \lambda s_o.\mathbf{bind}([\![re]\!]^{\mathbf{re}}_{s_o}, \lambda z_o.\text{if } (z_o > 0) \text{ then } \mathbf{unit}(z_o) \text{ else } \mu_0))\\
[\![re \leq 0 :: p']\!]^{\mathbf{p}} &= \mathbf{bind}([\![p']\!]^{\mathbf{p}}, \lambda s_o.\mathbf{bind}([\![re]\!]^{\mathbf{re}}_{s_o}, \lambda z_o.\text{if } (z_o \leq 0) \text{ then } \mathbf{unit}(z_o) \text{ else } \mu_0))\\
[\![lap_{n_2}(n_1)]\!]^{\mathbf{re}}_s &= \lambda z.lap_{n_2}(n_1)(z)\\
[\![n]\!]^{\mathbf{re}}_s &= \mathbf{unit}(n)\\
[\![X]\!]^{\mathbf{re}}_s &= \mathbf{unit}(s(X))\\
[\![re_1 \oplus re_2]\!]^{\mathbf{re}}_s &= \mathbf{bind}([\![re_1]\!]^{\mathbf{re}}_s, \lambda v_1.\mathbf{bind}([\![re_2]\!]^{\mathbf{re}}_s, \lambda v_2.\mathbf{unit}(v_1 \oplus v_2)))
\end{aligned}
$$

Fig. 4: Translation from configurations to subdistributions.

sampling from the distributions of the probabilistic variables defined in m_s in the order they were declared which is specified by the probabilistic path constraints. To do this we first build a substitution for the probabilistic variable which maps them into integers and then we perform the substitution on m_s. Given a set of probabilistic concrete memories we can then turn them in a subdistribution by summing up all the translations of the single probabilistic configurations. Indeed, given two subdistributions μ_1, μ_2 defined over the same set we can always define the subdistribution $\mu_1 + \mu_2$ by the mapping $(\mu_1 + \mu_2)(a) = \mu_1(a) + \mu_2(a)$.

The following Lemma states an equivalence between these two representations of probability subdistributions. The hypothesis of the theorem involve a well-formedness judgment, $m \vdash p$, which has not been specified for lack of space but can be found in the extended version [11], it deals with well-formedness of the probabilistic path constraint p with respect to the concrete probabilistic memory m.

Lemma 4. *If* $m \vdash p$ *and* $\{\langle m, c, p\rangle\} \Rightarrow^*_{\mathrm{c}} \{\langle m_1, \mathtt{skip}, p_1\rangle, \ldots, \langle m_n, \mathtt{skip}, p_n\rangle\}$ *then* $\mathbf{bind}([\![m;p]\!]^{mp}, [\![c]\!]_C) = \sum_{i=1}^{n} [\![m_i;p_i]\!]^{mp}$

This lemma justifies the following definition for the semantics of a program.

Definition 3. *The semantics of a program c executed on memory m and probability path constraint* p_0 *is* $[\![c]\!]_C(m_0, p_0) \equiv \sum_{(m,\mathtt{skip},p)\in\mathcal{D}} [\![m;p]\!]^{mp}$, *when* $\{\langle m, c, p\rangle\} \Rightarrow^*_{\mathrm{c}} \mathcal{D}$, ***Final***$(\mathcal{D})$, *and* $m_0 \vdash p_0$. *If* $p_0 = []$ *we write* $[\![c]\!]_C(m_0)$.

4.2 RPFOR

In order to be able to reason about differential privacy we will build on top of PFOR a relational language called RPFOR with a relational semantics dealing with pair of traces. Intuitively, an execution of a single RPFOR program represents the execution of two PFOR programs. Inspired by the approach of [19], we extend the grammar of PFOR with a pair constructor $\langle\cdot|\cdot\rangle$ which can be used at the level of values $\langle v_1|v_2\rangle$, expressions $\langle e_1|e_2\rangle$, or commands $\langle c_1|c_2\rangle$, where c_i, e_i, v_i for $i \in \{1, 2\}$ are commands, expressions, and values in PFOR. This entails that pairs cannot be nested. This syntactic invariant is preserved by the rules handling the branching instruction. Pair constructs are used to indicate where commands, values, or expressions might be different in the two unary executions represented by a single RPFOR execution. The set of expressions and commands in RPFOR, $\mathcal{E}_\text{r}, \mathcal{C}_\text{r}$ are generated by the grammars:

$$\mathcal{E}_\text{r} \ni e_r ::= v \mid e \mid \langle e_1 | e_2 \rangle \qquad \mathcal{C}_\text{r} \ni c_r ::= x \leftarrow e_r \mid x \xleftarrow{\$} lap_{e_r}(e_r) \mid c \mid \langle c_1 | c_2 \rangle$$

where $v \in \mathcal{V}_\text{r}, e, e_1, e_2 \in \mathcal{E}, c, c_1, c_2 \in \mathcal{C}$. Values can now be also pairs of unary values, that is $\mathcal{V}_\text{r} \equiv \mathcal{V} \cup \mathcal{V}^2$.

To define the semantics for RPFOR, we first extend memories to allow program variables to map to pairs of integers, and array variables to map to pairs of arrays. In the following we will use the following projection functions $\lfloor \cdot \rfloor_i$ for $i \in \{1, 2\}$, which project, respectively, the first (left) and second (right) elements of a pair construct (i.e., $\lfloor \langle c_1 | c_2 \rangle \rfloor_i = c_i$, $\lfloor \langle e_1 | e_2 \rangle \rfloor_i = e_i$ with $\lfloor v \rfloor_i = v$ when $v \in \mathcal{V}$), and are homomorphic for other constructs.

The semantics of expressions in RPFOR is specified through the following judgment $\langle m_1, m_2, e, p_1, p_2 \rangle \downarrow_\text{rc} \langle v, p_1', p_2' \rangle$, where $m_1, m_2 \in \mathcal{M}, p_1, p_2, p_1', p_2' \in P, e \in \mathcal{E}_\text{r}, v \in \mathcal{V}_\text{r}$. Similarly, for commands, we have the following judgment $\langle m_1, m_2, c, p_1, p_2 \rangle \rightarrow_\text{rc} \langle m_1', m_2', c', p_1', p_2' \rangle$. Again, we use the predicate $\textbf{Final}(\cdot)$ for configurations $\langle m_1, m_2, c, p_1, p_2 \rangle$ such that $c = \texttt{skip}$, and lift the predicate to sets of configurations as well. Intuitively a relational probabilistic concrete configuration $\langle m_1, m_2, c, p_1, p_2 \rangle$ denotes a pair of probabilistic concrete states, that is a pair of subdistributions over the space of concrete memories. In Figure 5 a selection of the rules defining the judgments is presented. Most of the rules are quite natural. Notice how branching instructions combine both probabilistic and relational nondeterminism.

r-if-conc-conc-true-false

$$\frac{\langle m_1, m_2, e, p_1, p_2 \rangle \downarrow_\text{rc} \langle v, p_1', p_2' \rangle \qquad \lfloor v \rfloor_1, \lfloor v \rfloor_2 \in \mathbb{Z} \qquad \lfloor v \rfloor_1 > 0 \qquad \lfloor v \rfloor_2 \leq 0}{\langle m_1, m_2, \texttt{if } e \texttt{ then } c_1 \texttt{ else } c_2, p_1, p_2 \rangle \rightarrow_\text{rc} \langle m_1, m_2, \langle \lfloor c_1 \rfloor_1 | \lfloor c_2 \rfloor_2 \rangle, p_1', p_2' \rangle}$$

r-if-prob-prob-true-false

$$\frac{\langle m_1, m_2, e, p_1, p_2 \rangle \downarrow_\text{rc} \langle v, p_1', p_2' \rangle \qquad \lfloor v \rfloor_1, \lfloor v \rfloor_2 \in \mathcal{X}_p}{\begin{array}{c}\langle m_1, m_2, \texttt{if } e \texttt{ then } c_1 \texttt{ else } c_2, p_1, p_2 \rangle \rightarrow_\text{rc} \\ \langle m_1, m_2, \langle \lfloor c_1 \rfloor_1 | \lfloor c_2 \rfloor_2 \rangle, \lfloor v \rfloor_1 > 0 @ p_1', \lfloor v \rfloor_2 \leq 0 @ p_2' \rangle\end{array}}$$

r-pair-step

$$\frac{\begin{array}{cc}\{i, j\} = \{1, 2\} & \langle \lfloor m \rfloor_i, c_i, p_i \rangle \rightarrow_\text{c} \langle m_i', c_i', p_i' \rangle \\ c_j' = c_j \quad\quad p_j' = p_j & m_j' = \lfloor m \rfloor_j\end{array}}{\langle m_1, m_2, \langle c_1 | c_2 \rangle, p_1, p_2 \rangle \rightarrow_\text{rc} \langle m_1', m_2', \langle c_1' | c_2' \rangle, p_1', p_2' \rangle}$$

Fig. 5: RPFOR selected rules

So, as in the case of PFOR, we collect sets of relational configurations using the judgment $\mathscr{R} \Rightarrow_{\mathrm{rc}} \mathscr{R}'$ with $\mathscr{R}, \mathscr{R}' \in \mathcal{P}(\mathcal{M} \times \mathcal{M} \times \mathcal{C}_{\mathrm{r}} \times P \ \times P)$, defined by only one rule:

SUB-PDISTR-STEP

$$\frac{\begin{array}{c}\langle m_1, m_2, c, p_1, p_2\rangle \in \mathscr{R} \\ \mathscr{R}_t \equiv \{\langle m_1', m_2', c', p_1', p_2'\rangle \mid \langle m_1, m_2, c, p_1, p_2\rangle \rightarrow_{\mathrm{rc}} \langle m_1', m_2', c', p_1', p_2'\rangle\} \\ \mathscr{R}' \equiv \left(\mathscr{R} \setminus \{\langle m_1, m_2, c, p_1, p_2\rangle\}\right) \cup \mathscr{R}_t\end{array}}{\mathscr{R} \Rightarrow_{\mathrm{rc}} \mathscr{R}'}$$

This rule picks and remove non deterministically one relational configuration from a set and adds to it all those configurations that are reachable from it. As mentioned before a run of a program in RPFOR corresponds to the execution of two runs the program in PFOR. Before making this precise we extend projection functions to relational configurations in the following way: $\lfloor\langle m_1, m_2, c, p_1, p_2\rangle\rfloor_i = \langle m_i, c, p_i\rangle$, for $i \in \{1, 2\}$. Projection functions extend in the obvious way also to sets of relational configurations. We are now ready to state the following lemma relating the execution in RPFOR to the one in PFOR:

Lemma 5. *Let $i \in \{1, 2\}$ then $\mathscr{R} \Rightarrow_{\mathrm{rc}}^{*} \mathscr{R}'$ iff $\lfloor\mathscr{R}\rfloor_i \Rightarrow_{\mathrm{c}}^{*} \lfloor\mathscr{R}'\rfloor_i$.*

5 Symbolic languages

In this section we lift the concrete languages, presented in the previous section, to their symbolic versions (respectively, SPFOR and SRPFOR) by extending them with symbolic values $X \in \mathcal{X}$. We use intentionally the same metavariables for symbolic values in $\mathcal{X}$ and $\mathcal{X}_p$ since they both represent symbolic values of some sort. However, we assume $\mathcal{X}_p \cap \mathcal{X} = \emptyset$ - this is because we want symbolic values in $\mathcal{X}$ to denote only unknown sets of integers, rather than sets of probability distributions. So, the meaning of X should then be clear from the context.

5.1 SPFOR

SPFOR expressions extend PFOR expressions with symbolic values $X \in \mathcal{X}$ Commands in SPFOR are the same as in PFOR but now symbolic values can appear in expressions.

In order to collect constraints on symbolic values we extend configurations with set of constraints over integer values, drawn from the set $\mathcal{S}$ (Figure 6a), not to be confused with probabilistic path constraints (Figure 6b). The former express constraints over integer values, for instance parameters of the distributions. In particular constraint expressions include standard arithmetic expressions with values being symbolic or integer constants, and array selection. Probabilistic path constraints now can also contain symbolic integer values. Hence,

$$\mathcal{S}_e \ni e ::= n \mid X \mid i \mid e \oplus e \mid |e| \mid \mathbf{store}(e,e,e) \mid \mathbf{select}(e,e)$$
$$\mathcal{S} \ni s ::= \top \mid e \circ e \mid s \wedge s \mid \neg s \mid \forall i.s$$

(a) Symbolic constraints. $X \in \mathcal{X}, n \in \mathbf{V}$.

$$sra ::= Y \overset{\$}{\leftarrow} lap_{c_e}(c_e)$$
$$sre ::= n \mid X \mid Y \mid re \oplus re$$
$$SP ::= Y = re \mid re > 0 \mid re \leq 0 \mid ra$$

(b) Prob. constraints. $c_e \in \mathcal{S}, X \in \mathcal{X}, Y \in \mathcal{X}_p$

Fig. 6: Grammar of constraints

probabilistic path constraints now can be symbolic. This is needed to address examples branching on probabilistic values, such as the Above Threshold algorithm we discussed in Section 2.

Memories can now contain symbolic values and we represent arrays in memory as pairs (X, v), where v is a (concrete or symbolic) integer value representing the length of the array, and X is a symbolic value representing the array content. The content of the arrays is kept and refined in the set of constraints by means of the $\mathbf{select}(\cdot,\cdot)$ and $\mathbf{store}(\cdot,\cdot,\cdot)$ operations. The semantics of expressions is captured by the judgment $(m, e, p, s) \downarrow_{\text{SP}} (v, p', s')$ including now a set of constraints over integers. The rules of the judgment are fully described in the extended version [11]. We briefly describe a selection of the rules. Rule **S-P-Op-2** applies when an arithmetic operation has both of its operands that reduce respectively to elements in $\mathcal{X}_p$. Appropriately it updates the set of probabilistic constraints. Rules **S-P-Op-5** instead fires when one of them is an integer and the other is a symbolic value. In this case only the list of symbolic constraints needs to be updated. Finally, in rule **S-P-Op-6** one of the operands reduces to an element in $\mathcal{X}_p$ and the other to an element in $\mathcal{X}$. We only update the list of probabilistic constraints appropriately, as integer constraints cannot contain symbols in $\mathcal{X}_p$.

The semantics of commands of SPFOR is described by small step semantics judgments of the form: $(m, c, p, s) \rightarrow_{\text{SP}} (m', c', p', s')$, including a set of constraints over integers. We provide a selection of the rules in Figure 7. Rule **S-P-If-sym-true** fires when a branching instruction is to be executed and the guard is reduced to either an integer or a value in $\mathcal{X}$, denoted by the set $\mathbf{V}_{\text{is}}$. In this case we can proceed with the true branch recording in the set of integer constraints the fact that the guard is greater than 0. Rule **S-P-If-prob-false** handles a branching instruction which has a guard reducing to a value in $\mathcal{X}_p$. In this case we can proceed in both branches, even though here we only show one of the two rules, by recording the conditioning fact on the list of probabilistic constraints. Finally, rule **S-P-Lap-Ass** handles probabilistic assignment. After having reduced both the expression for the mean and the expression for the scale to values we check that those are both either integers or symbolic integers, if that's the case we make sure that the scale is greater than 0 and we add a probabilistic constraints recording the fact that the modified variable now points to a probabilistic symbolic value related to a Laplace distribution.

The semantics of SPFOR has two sources of nondeterminism, from guards which reduce to symbolic values, and from guards which reduce to a probabilistic symbolic value. The collecting semantics of SPFOR, specified by judgments as

$$\textbf{S-P-If-sym-true}\quad \frac{(m,e,p,s) \downarrow_{\mathrm{SP}} (v,p',s') \qquad v \in \mathbf{V}_{\mathrm{is}}}{(m, \mathtt{if}\ e\ \mathtt{then}\ c_{tt}\ \mathtt{else}\ c_{ff}, p, s) \rightarrow_{\mathrm{SP}} (m, c_{tt}, p', s' \cup \{v > 0\})}$$

$$\textbf{S-P-If-prob-false}\quad \frac{(m,e,p,s) \downarrow_{\mathrm{SP}} (v,p',s') \qquad v \in \mathcal{X}_p}{(m, \mathtt{if}\ e\ \mathtt{then}\ c_{tt}\ \mathtt{else}\ c_{ff}, p, s) \rightarrow_{\mathrm{SP}} (m, c_{ff}, p'@[v \leq 0], s')}$$

$$\textbf{S-P-Lap-Ass}\quad \frac{\begin{array}{c}(m,e_a,p,s) \downarrow_{\mathrm{SP}} (v_a,p',s') \qquad (m,e_b,p',s') \downarrow_{\mathrm{SP}} (v_b,p'',s'') \qquad X\,\mathbf{fresh}(\mathcal{X}_p)\\ v_a, v_b \in \mathbf{V}_{\mathrm{is}} \qquad s''' = s'' \cup \{v_b > 0\} \qquad p''' = p''@[X \xleftarrow{\$} lap_{v_b}(v_a)]\end{array}}{(m, x \xleftarrow{\$} lap_{e_b}(e_a), p, s) \rightarrow_{\mathrm{SP}} (m[x \mapsto X], \mathtt{skip}, p''', s''')}$$

Fig. 7: SPFOR: Semantics of commands (selected rules)

$\mathscr{H} \Rightarrow_{\mathrm{sp}} \mathscr{H}'$ (for sets of configurations $\mathscr{H}$ and $\mathscr{H}'$) takes care of both of them. The rule for this judgment form is:

$$\textbf{s-p-collect}\quad \frac{\begin{array}{c}\mathscr{D}_{[s]} \subseteq \mathscr{H} \qquad \mathscr{H}' \equiv \{(m',c',p',s') \mid \exists (m,c,p,s) \in \mathscr{D}_{[s]} \text{ s.t.}\\ (m,c,p,s) \rightarrow_{\mathrm{SP}} (m',c',p',s') \wedge \mathbf{SAT}(s')\}\end{array}}{\mathscr{H} \Rightarrow_{\mathrm{sp}} (\mathscr{H} \setminus \mathscr{D}_{[s]}) \cup \mathscr{H}'}$$

Unlike in the deterministic case of the rule **Set-Step**, where only one configuration was chosen nondeterministically from the initial set, here we select nondeterministically a (maximal) set of configurations all sharing the same symbolic constraints. The notation $\mathscr{D}_{[s]} \subseteq \mathscr{H}$ means that $\mathscr{D}$ is the maximal subset of configuration in $\mathscr{H}$ which have s as set of constraints. We use $\mathscr{H} \overset{\mathscr{D}_{[s]}}{\underset{\mathrm{sp}}{\Longrightarrow}} \mathscr{H}'$ when we want to make explicit the set of symbolic configurations, $\mathscr{D}_{[s]}$, that we are using to make the step. Intuitively, **s-p-collect** starts from a set of configurations and reaches all of those that are reachable from it - all the configurations that have a satisfiable set of constraints and are reachable from one of the original configurations with only one step of the symbolic semantics. Notice that in a set of constraints we can have constraints involving probabilistic symbols, e.g. if the i-th element of an array is associated with a random expression. Nevertheless, the predicate $\mathbf{SAT}(\cdot)$ does not need to take into consideration relations involving probabilistic symbolic constraints but only relations involving symbolic values denoting integers. The following lemma of coverage connects PFOR with SPFOR ensuring that a concrete execution is covered by a symbolic one.

Lemma 6 (Probabilistic Unary Coverage). *If* $\mathscr{H} \overset{\mathscr{D}_{[s]}}{\underset{\mathrm{sp}}{\Longrightarrow}} \mathscr{H}'$ *and* $\sigma \models_{\mathcal{I}} \mathscr{D}_{[s]}$ *then* $\exists \sigma', \mathscr{D}_{[s']} \subseteq \mathscr{H}'$ *such that* $\sigma' \models_{\mathcal{I}} \mathscr{D}_{[s']}$, *and* $\sigma(\mathscr{D}_{[s]}) \Rightarrow^*_{\mathrm{p}} \sigma'(\mathscr{D}_{[s']})$.

5.2 SRPFOR

The language presented in this section is the the symbolic extension of the concrete language RPFOR. It can also be seen as the relational extension of SPFOR.

The key part of this language's semantics will be the handling of the probabilistic assignment. For that construct we will provide 2 rules instead of one. The first one is the obvious one which carries on a standard symbolic probabilistic assignment. The second one will implement a coupling semantics. The syntax of the SRPFOR, presented in Figure 8, extends the syntax of RPFOR by adding symbolic values. The main change is in the grammar of expressions, while the syntax for commands is almost identical to that of RPFOR.

$$\mathcal{E}_{\mathrm{rs}} \ni e_{sr} ::= e_s \mid \langle e_s | e_s \rangle \mid e_{sr} \oplus e_{sr} \mid a[e_{sr}]$$
$$\mathcal{C}_{\mathrm{rs}} \ni c_{sr} ::= c_s \mid \langle c_s | c_s \rangle \mid c_{sr};c_{sr} \mid x \leftarrow e_{sr} \mid a[e_{sr}] \leftarrow e_{sr} \mid x \xleftarrow{\$} lap_{e_s}(e_{sr}) \mid \texttt{if } e_{sr} \texttt{ then } c_{sr} \texttt{ else } c_{sr} \mid \texttt{for } (x \texttt{ in } e_{sr}{:}e_{sr}) \texttt{ do } c_{sr} \texttt{ od}$$

Fig. 8: SRPFOR syntax. $e_s \in \mathcal{E}_{\mathrm{s}}, c_s \in \mathcal{C}_{\mathrm{s}}$.

As in the case of RPFOR, only unary symbolic expressions and commands are admitted in the pairing construct. This invariant is maintained by the semantics rules. As for the other languages, we provide a big-step evaluation semantics for expressions whose judgments are of the form $(m_1, m_2, e, p_1, p_2, s) \downarrow_{\text{SRP}} (v, p_1', p_2', s')$. The only rule defining the judgment $\downarrow_{\text{SRP}}$ is **S-R-P-Lift** and it is presented in the extended version [11]. The rule projects the symbolic relational expression first on the left and evaluates it to a unary symbolic value, potentially updating the probabilistic symbolic constraints and the symbolic constraints. It then does the same projecting the expression on the right but starting from the potentially previously updated constraints. Now, the only case when the value returned is unary is when both the previous evaluation returned equal integers, in all the other cases a pair of values is returned. So, the relational symbolic semantics leverages the unary semantics. For the semantics of commands we use the following evaluation contexts to simplify the exposition:

$$\mathcal{CTX} ::= [\,\cdot\,] \mid \mathcal{CTX};c$$
$$\mathcal{P} ::= \langle \cdot;c|\cdot \rangle \mid \langle \cdot| \cdot ;c \rangle \mid \langle \cdot|\cdot \rangle \mid \langle \cdot;c| \cdot ;c \rangle$$

Notice how $\mathcal{P}$ gets saturated by pairs of commands. Moreover, we separate commands in two classes. We call *synchronizing* all the commands in $\mathcal{C}_{\mathrm{rs}}$ with the following shapes $x \xleftarrow{\$} lap_{e_2}(e_1)$, $\langle x \xleftarrow{\$} lap_{e_2}(e_1) | x' \xleftarrow{\$} lap_{e_2'}(e_1') \rangle$, since they allow synchronization of two runs using coupling rules. We call non synchronizing all the other commands.

Semantics of non synchronizing commands We consider judgments of the form $(m_1, m_2, c, p_1, p_2, s) \rightarrow_{\text{SRP}} (m_1', m_2', c', p_1', p_2', s')$ and a selection of the rules is given in Figure 9. An explanation of the rules follows. Rule **s-r-if-prob-prob-true-false** fires when evaluating a branching instruction. In particular, it fires when the guard evaluates on both side to a probabilistic symbolic value. In this case the semantics can continue with the true branch on the left run and

s-r-if-prob-prob-true-false

$$\frac{\begin{array}{c}(m_1, m_2, e, p_1, p_2, s) \downarrow_{\mathrm{SRP}} (v, p_1', p_2', s') \qquad \lfloor v \rfloor_1, \lfloor v \rfloor_2 \in \mathcal{X}_p \\ p_1'' \equiv p_1'@[\lfloor v \rfloor_1 > 0] \qquad p_2'' \equiv p_2'@[\lfloor v \rfloor_2 \leq 0]\end{array}}{(m_1, m_2, \texttt{if } e \texttt{ then } c_{tt} \texttt{ else } c_{ff}, p_1, p_2, s) \to_{\mathrm{SRP}} (m_1, m_2, \langle \lfloor c_{tt} \rfloor_1 | \lfloor c_{ff} \rfloor_2 \rangle, p_1'', p_2'', s')}$$

s-r-if-prob-sym-true-false

$$\frac{\begin{array}{c}(m_1, m_2, e, p_1, p_2, s) \downarrow_{\mathrm{SRP}} (v, p_1', p_2', s') \\ \lfloor v \rfloor_1 \in \mathcal{X}_p \; \lfloor v \rfloor_2 \in \mathcal{X} \qquad p_1'' \equiv p_1'@[\lfloor v \rfloor_1 > 0] \qquad s''' \equiv s'' \cup \{\lfloor v \rfloor_2 \leq 0\}\end{array}}{(m_1, m_2, \texttt{if } e \texttt{ then } c_{tt} \texttt{ else } c_{ff}, p_1, p_2, s) \to_{\mathrm{SRP}} (m_1, m_2, c_{tt}, p_1'', p_2', s''')}$$

s-r-pair-lap-skip

$$\frac{(m_1, x \xleftarrow{\$} lap_{e_b}(e_a), p_1, s) \to_{\mathrm{SP}} (m_1', \texttt{skip}, p_1', s')}{(m_1, m_2, \langle x \xleftarrow{\$} lap_{e_b}(e_a) | \texttt{skip} \rangle, p_1, p_2, s) \to_{\mathrm{SRP}} (m_1', m_2, \langle \texttt{skip} | \texttt{skip} \rangle, p_1', p_2, s')}$$

s-r-pair-lapleft-sync

$$\frac{c \not\equiv x \xleftarrow{\$} lap_{e_b'}(e_a') \qquad \mathcal{P} \equiv \langle \cdot | \cdot \rangle \qquad (m_2, c, p_2, s) \to_{\mathrm{SP}} (m_2', c', p_2', s')}{(m_1, m_2, \mathcal{P}(x \xleftarrow{\$} lap_{e_b}(e_a), c), p_1, p_2, s) \to_{\mathrm{SRP}} (m_1, m_2', \langle x \xleftarrow{\$} lap_{e_b}(e_a) | c' \rangle, p_1, p_2', s')}$$

s-r-pair-ctxt-1

$$\frac{\begin{array}{c}x \xleftarrow{\$} lap_{e_b}(e_a) \notin \{c_1, c_2\} \qquad |\{c_1, c_2\}| = 2 \qquad \{1, 2\} = \{i, j\} \\ c_i' \equiv c_i \qquad p_i' \equiv p_i \\ m_i' \equiv m_i \qquad (m_j, c_j, p_j, s) \to_{\mathrm{SP}} (m_j', c_j', p_j', s')\end{array}}{(m_1, m_2, \mathcal{P}(c_1, c_2), p_1, p_2, s) \to_{\mathrm{SRP}} (m_1', m_2', \mathcal{P}(c_1', c_2'), p_1', p_2', s')}$$

s-r-pair-ctxt-2

$$\frac{\mathcal{P} \not\equiv \langle \cdot | \cdot \rangle \qquad (m_1, m_2, \langle c_1 | c_2 \rangle, p_1, p_2, s) \to_{\mathrm{SRP}} (m_1', m_2', \langle c_1' | c_2' \rangle, p_1', p_2', s')}{(m_1, m_2, \mathcal{P}(c_1, c_2), p_1, p_2, s) \to_{\mathrm{SRP}} (m_1', m_2', \mathcal{P}(c_1', c_2'), p_1', p_2', s')}$$

Fig. 9: SRPFOR: Semantics of non synchronizing commands. Selected rules.

with the false branch on the right one. Notice that commands are projected to avoid pairing commands appearing in a nested form. Rule **s-r-if-prob-sym-true-false** applies when the guard of a branching instruction evaluates to a probabilistic symbolic value on the left run and a symbolic integer value on the right one. The rule allows to continue on the true branch on the left run and on the false branch on the right one. Notice that in one case the probabilistic list of constraints is updated, while on the other the symbolic set of constraints.

Rule **s-r-pair-lap-skip** handles the pairing command where on the left hand side we have a probabilistic assignment and on the right a skip instruction. In this case, there is no *hope for synchronization* between the two runs and hence we can just perform the left probabilistic assignment relying on the unary symbolic semantics. Rule **s-r-pair-lapleft-sync** instead applies when on the left we have a probabilistic assignment and on the right we have another arbitrary command. In this case we can hope to reach a situation where on the right run another probabilistic assignment appears. Hence, it makes sense to continue the computation in a unary way on the right side. Again $\rightarrow_{\text{SRP}}$ is a nondeterministic semantics. The nondeterminism comes from the use of probabilistic symbols and symbolic values as guards, and by the relational approach. So, in order to collect all the possible traces stemming from such nondeterminism we define a collecting semantics relating set of configurations to set of configurations.

The semantics is specified through a judgment of the form: $\mathscr{SR} \Rightarrow_{\text{srp}} \mathscr{SR}'$, with $\mathscr{SR}, \mathscr{SR}' \in \mathcal{P}(\boldsymbol{\mathcal{M}}_{\text{SP}} \times \boldsymbol{\mathcal{M}}_{\text{SP}} \times \mathcal{C}_{\text{rs}} \times SP \times SP \times \mathcal{S})$. The only rule defining the judgment is the following natural lifting of the one for the unary semantics.

s-r-p-collect

$$\frac{\begin{array}{c}\mathscr{R}_{[s]} \subseteq \mathscr{SR} \qquad \mathscr{SR}' \equiv \{(m_1', m_2', c', p_1', p_2', s') \mid \\ \exists (m_1, m_2, c, p_1, p_2, s) \in \mathscr{R}_{[s]} \text{ s.t. } (m_1, m_2, c, p_1, p_2, s) \rightarrow_{\text{SRP}} (m_1', m_2', c', p_1', p_2', s') \\ \wedge \mathbf{SAT}(s')\}\end{array}}{\mathscr{SR} \Rightarrow_{\text{srp}} \left(\mathscr{SR} \setminus \mathscr{R}_{[s]}\right) \cup \mathscr{SR}'}$$

The rule, and the auxiliary notation $\mathscr{R}_{[s]}$, is pretty similar to that of SPFOR, the only difference is that here sets of symbolic relational probabilistic configurations are considered instead of symbolic (unary) probabilistic configurations.

Semantics of synchronizing commands We define a new judgment with form $\mathscr{G} \rightsquigarrow \mathscr{G}'$, with $\mathscr{G}, \mathscr{G}' \in \mathcal{P}(\mathcal{P}(\boldsymbol{\mathcal{M}}_{\text{SP}} \times \boldsymbol{\mathcal{M}}_{\text{SP}} \times \mathcal{C}_{\text{rs}} \times SP \times SP \times \mathcal{S}))$. In Figure 10, we give a selection of the rules. Rule **Proof-Step-No-Sync** applies when no synchronizing commands are involved, and hence there is no possible coupling rule to be applied. In the other rules, we use the variable ϵ_c to symbolically count the privacy budget in the current relational execution. The variable gets increased when the rule **Proof-Step-Lap-Gen** fires. This symbolic counter variable is useful when trying to prove equality of certain variables without spending more than a specific budget. This rule is the one we can use in most cases when we need to reason about couplings on the Laplace distributions. In the set of sets of configurations $\mathscr{G}$, a set of configurations, $\mathscr{SR}$, is nondeterministically chosen. Among elements in $\mathscr{SR}$ a configuration is also nondeterministically chosen. Using contexts we check that in the selected configuration the next command to execute is the probabilistic assignment. After reducing to values both the mean and scale expression, and verified (that is, assumed in the set of constraints) that in the two runs the scales have the same value, the rule adds to the set of constraints a new element, that is, $E'' = E' + |\lfloor v_a \rfloor_1 - \lfloor v_a \rfloor_2| \cdot K'$, where K, K', E'' are fresh symbols denoting integers and E' is the symbolic integer to which the budget variable ϵ_c maps to. Notice that ϵ_c needs to point to the same symbol in both memories. This is because it is a shared variable tracking the privacy budget spent so far in both runs. This new constraint increases the budget spent. The other constraint added is the real coupling relation, that is $X_1 + K = X_2$. Where X_1, X_2 are fresh in $\mathcal{X}$. Later, K will be existentially quantified in order to search for a proof of ϵ-indistinguishability.

Rule **Proof-Step-Avoc** does not use any coupling rule but treats the samples in a purely symbolic manner. It intuitively asserts that the two samples are

Proof-Step-No-Sync

$$\frac{\mathcal{SR} \in \mathcal{G} \qquad \mathcal{SR} \Rightarrow_{\text{srp}} \mathcal{SR}' \qquad \mathcal{G}' \equiv (\mathcal{G} \setminus \{\mathcal{SR}\}) \cup \{\mathcal{SR}'\}}{\mathcal{G} \rightsquigarrow \mathcal{G}'}$$

Proof-Step-No-Coup

$$\frac{\begin{array}{c}(m_1, m_2, \mathcal{CTX}[x \xleftarrow{\$} lap_{e_b}(e_a)], p_1, p_2, s) \in \mathcal{SR} \in \mathcal{G} \\ (m_1, m_2, e_a, p_1, p_2, s) \quad \downarrow_{\text{SRP}} (v_a, p_1', p_2', s_a) \\ (m_1, m_2, e_b, p_1', p_2', s_a) \quad \downarrow_{\text{SRP}} (v_b, p_1'', p_2'', s_b) \\ X_1, X_2\, \mathbf{fresh}(\mathcal{X}_p) \qquad m_1' \equiv m_1[x \mapsto X_1] \qquad m_2' \equiv m_2[x \mapsto X_2] \\ p_1''' \equiv p_1''@[X_1 \xleftarrow{\$} lap_{\lfloor v_b \rfloor_1}(\lfloor v_a \rfloor_1)] \qquad p_2''' \equiv p_2''@[X_2 \xleftarrow{\$} lap_{\lfloor v_b \rfloor_2}(\lfloor v_a \rfloor_2)] \\ \mathcal{SR}' \equiv \left(\mathcal{SR} \setminus \{(m_1, m_2, \mathcal{CTX}[x \xleftarrow{\$} lap_{e_b}(e_a)], p_1, p_2, s)\}\right) \cup \\ \{(m_1', m_2', \mathcal{CTX}[\mathtt{skip}], p_1''', p_2''', s'')\} \qquad \mathcal{G}' \equiv \left(\mathcal{G} \setminus \{\mathcal{SR}\}\right) \cup \{\mathcal{SR}'\}\end{array}}{\mathcal{G} \rightsquigarrow \mathcal{G}'}$$

Proof-Step-Avoc

$$\frac{\begin{array}{c}(m_1, m_2, \mathcal{CTX}[x \xleftarrow{\$} lap_{e_b}(e_a)], p_1, p_2, s) \in \mathcal{SR} \in \mathcal{G} \\ (m_1, m_2, e_a, p_1, p_2, s) \downarrow_{\text{SRP}} (v_a, p_1', p_2', s_a) \\ (m_1, m_2, e_b, p_1', p_2', s_a) \downarrow_{\text{SRP}} (v_b, p_1'', p_2'', s_b) \\ X_1, X_2\, \mathbf{fresh}(\mathcal{X}) \qquad m_1' \equiv m_1[x \mapsto X_1] \qquad m_2' \equiv m_2[x \mapsto X_2] \\ \mathcal{G}' \equiv (\mathcal{G} \setminus \{\mathcal{SR}\}) \cup \{\mathcal{SR}'\} \\ \mathcal{SR}' \equiv (\mathcal{SR} \setminus \{(m_1, m_2, \mathcal{CTX}[x \xleftarrow{\$} lap_{e_b}(e_a)], p_1, p_2, s)\}) \\ \cup \{(m_1', m_2', \mathcal{CTX}[\mathtt{skip}], p_1'', p_2'', s'')\}\end{array}}{\mathcal{G} \rightsquigarrow \mathcal{G}'}$$

Proof-Step-Lap-Gen

$$\frac{\begin{array}{c}(m_1, m_2, \mathcal{CTX}[x \xleftarrow{\$} lap_{e_b}(e_a)], p_1, p_2, s) \in \mathcal{SR} \in \mathcal{G} \\ (m_1, m_2, e_a, p_1, p_2, s) \downarrow_{\text{SRP}} (v_a, p_1', p_2', s_a) \\ (m_1, m_2, e_b, p_1', p_2', s_a) \downarrow_{\text{SRP}} (v_b, p_1'', p_2'', s_b) \\ s' \equiv s_b \cup \{\lfloor v_b \rfloor_1 = \lfloor v_b \rfloor_2, \lfloor v_b \rfloor_1 > 0\} \qquad m_1(\epsilon_c) = E' = m_2'(\epsilon_c) \\ E'', X_1, X_2, K, K'\, \mathbf{fresh}(\mathcal{X}) \qquad m_1' \equiv m_1[x \mapsto X_1][\epsilon_c \mapsto E''] \\ m_2' = m_2[x \mapsto X_2][\epsilon_c \mapsto E''] \qquad m(\epsilon) = E \\ s'' \equiv s' \cup \{X_1 + K = X_2, K \leq K', K' \cdot E = \lfloor v_b \rfloor_1, \\ E'' = E' + |\lfloor v_a \rfloor_1 - \lfloor v_a \rfloor_2| \cdot K'\} \\ p_1''' \equiv p_1''@[X_1 \xleftarrow{\$} lap_{\lfloor v_b \rfloor_1}(\lfloor v_a \rfloor_1)] \qquad p_2''' \equiv p_2''@[X_2 \xleftarrow{\$} lap_{\lfloor v_b \rfloor_2}(\lfloor v_a \rfloor_2)] \\ \mathcal{G}' \equiv (\mathcal{G} \setminus \{\mathcal{SR}\}) \cup \{\mathcal{SR}'\} \\ \mathcal{SR}' \equiv (\mathcal{SR} \setminus \{(m_1, m_2, \mathcal{CTX}[x \xleftarrow{\$} lap_{e_b}(e_a)], p_1, p_2, s)\}) \\ \cup \{(m_1', m_2', \mathcal{CTX}[\mathtt{skip}], p_1''', p_2''', s'')\}\end{array}}{\mathcal{G} \rightsquigarrow \mathcal{G}'}$$

Fig. 10: SRPFOR: Proof collecting semantics, selected rules

drawn from the distributions and assigns to them arbitrary integers free to vary on the all domain of the Laplace distribution.

Finally, rule **Proof-Step-No-Coup** applies to synchronizing commands as well. It does not add any relational constraints to the samples. This rules intuitively means that we are not correlating in any way the two samples. Notice that since we are not using any coupling rule we don't need to check that the scale value is the same in the two runs as it is requested in the previous rule. We could think of this as a way to encode the relational semantics of the program in an expression which later can be fed in input to other tools.

The main difference with the previous rule is that here we treat the sampling instruction symbolically and that is why the fresh symbols are in $\mathcal{X}_p$, denoting subdistributions, rather than in $\mathcal{X}$, denoting sampled integers. When the program involves a synchronizing command we basically fork the execution when it is time to execute it. The set of configurations allow us to explore different paths, one for every rule applicable.

6 Metatheory

The coverage lemma can be extended also to the relational setting.

Lemma 7 (Probabilistic Relational Coverage). *If* $\mathcal{SR} \xrightarrow[\text{srp}]{\mathcal{R}_{[s]}} \mathcal{SR}'$ *and* $\sigma \models_{\mathcal{I}} \mathcal{R}_{[s]}$ *then* $\exists \sigma', \mathcal{R}_{[s']} \in \mathcal{SR}'$ *such that* $\mathcal{R}_{[s']} \subseteq \mathcal{SR}', \sigma' \models_{\mathcal{I}} \mathcal{R}_{[s']}$, *and* $\sigma(\mathcal{R}_{[s]}) \Rightarrow^*_{\text{rp}} \sigma'(\mathcal{R}_{[s']})$.

This can also be extended to $\rightsquigarrow$ if we consider only the fragment that only uses the rules **Proof-Step-No-Sync**, and **Proof-Step-No-Coupl**.

The language of relational assertions $\Phi, \Psi \ldots$ is defined using first order predicate logic formulas involving relational program expressions and logical variables in LogVar. The interpretation of a relational assertions is naturally defined as a subset of $\mathcal{M}_c \times \mathcal{M}_c$, the set of pairs of memories modeling the assertion. We will denote by $[\![\cdot]\!]$. the substitution function mapping the variables in an assertion to the values they have in a memory (unary or relational). More details are in [10].

Definition 4. *Let* Φ, Ψ *be relational assertions,* $c \in \mathcal{C}_r$, $\mathcal{I} : \mathsf{LogVar} \rightarrow \mathbb{R}$ *be an interpretation defined on* ϵ. *We say that,* Φ *yields* Ψ *through* c *within* ϵ *under* $\mathcal{I}$ *(and we write* $\mathcal{I} \vdash c : \Phi \xrightarrow{\epsilon} \Psi$*) iff*

1. $\{\{\{\langle m_{I_1}, m_{I_2}, c, [], [], [\![\Phi]\!]_{m_I} \rangle\}\}\} \rightsquigarrow^* \mathcal{G}$
2. $\exists \mathcal{H}_{\text{sr}} = \{\mathcal{H}s_1, \ldots, \mathcal{H}s_t\} \in \mathcal{G}$ *such that* ***Final***$(\mathcal{H}_{\text{sr}})$ *and* $\forall \langle m_1, m_2, \texttt{skip}, p_1, p_2, s \rangle \in \bigcup_{\mathcal{D} \in \mathcal{H}_{\text{sr}}} \mathcal{D}.\ \exists \vec{k}.\ s \implies [\![\Psi \wedge \epsilon_c \leq \epsilon]\!]_{\langle m_1 | m_2 \rangle}$ *where* $m_I \equiv \langle m_{I_1} | m_{I_2} \rangle = \langle m'_{I_1}[\epsilon_c \mapsto 0] | m'_{I_2}[\epsilon_c \mapsto 0] \rangle$, m'_{I_1}, *and* m'_{I_2} *are fully symbolic memories, and* $\vec{k} = k_1, k_2, \ldots$ *are the symbols generated by the rules for synchronizing commands.*

The idea of this definition is to make the proof search automated. When proving differential privacy we will usually consider Ψ as being equality of the output variables in the two runs and Φ as being our preconditions. We can now prove the soundness of our approach.

Lemma 8 (Soundness). *Let $c \in \mathcal{C}_r$. If $\mathcal{I} \vdash c : D_1 \sim D_2 \xrightarrow{\epsilon} o_1 = o_2$ then c is ϵ-differentially private.*

We can also prove the soundness of refutations obtained by the semantics.

Lemma 9 (Soundness for refutation). *Suppose that we have a reduction $\{\{\{\langle m_1, m_2, c, [], [], [\![\Phi]\!]_{\langle m_1|m_2\rangle}\rangle\}\}\} \rightsquigarrow \mathcal{G}$, and $\mathcal{H}s \in \mathcal{H} \in \mathcal{G}$ and, $\exists\sigma \models_{\mathbb{Z}} s$ such that $\Delta_\epsilon([\![\lfloor c\rfloor_1]\!]_{\mathcal{C}}(\sigma(m_1)), [\![\lfloor c\rfloor_2]\!]_{\mathcal{C}}(\sigma(m_2))) > 0$ then c is not differentially private.*

7 Strategies for counterexample finding

Lemma 9 is hard to use to find counterexamples in practice. For this reasons we will now describe three strategies that can help in reducing the effort in counterexample finding. These strategies help in isolating traces that could potentially lead to violations. For this we need first some notation. Given a set of constraints s we define the triple $\Omega = \langle \Omega_1, \Omega_2, C(\vec{k})\rangle \equiv \langle \lfloor s\rfloor_1, \lfloor s\rfloor_2, s \setminus (\lfloor s\rfloor_1 \cup \lfloor s\rfloor_2)\rangle$. We sometimes abuse notation and consider Ω also as a set of constraints given by the union of its first, second and third projection, and we will also consider a set of constraints as a single proposition given by the conjunction of its elements. The set $C(\vec{k})$ contains relational constraints coming from either preconditions or invariants or, from the rule **Proof-Step-Lap-Gen**. The potentially empty vector $\vec{k} = K_1, \ldots K_n$ is the set of fresh symbols K generated by that rule. In the rest of the paper we will assume the following simplifying assumption.

Assumption 1 *Consider $c \in \mathcal{C}_r$ with output variable o, then c is such that $\{\{\{\langle m_1, m_2, c, [], [], s\rangle\}\}\} \rightsquigarrow^* \mathcal{G}$ and $\forall \mathcal{H}\langle \Omega_1, C(\vec{k}), \Omega_2\rangle \in \mathcal{H} \in \mathcal{G}.\mathbf{Final}(\mathcal{H}) \wedge o_1 = o_2 \implies \Omega_1 \Leftrightarrow \Omega_2$.*

This assumption allow us to consider only programs for which it is necessary for the output variable on both runs to assume the same value, that the two runs follow the same branches. That is, if the two output differ then the two executions must have, at some point, taken different branches.

The following definition will be used to distinguish relational traces which are reachable on one run but not on the other. We call these traces *orthogonal.*

Definition 5. *A final relational symbolic trace is orthogonal when its set of constraints is such that $\exists\sigma.\sigma \not\models \Omega_2$ and $\sigma \models \Omega_1 \wedge C(\vec{k})$. That is a trace for which $\neg(\Omega_1 \wedge C(\vec{k}) \implies \Omega_2)$ is satisfiable.*

The next definition, instead, will be used to isolate relational traces for which it is not possible that the left one is executed but the right one is not. We call these traces *specular.*

Definition 6. *A final relational symbolic trace is specular if $\exists\vec{k}.\Omega_1 \wedge C(\vec{k}) \implies \Omega_2$.*

The constraint $\Omega_1 \wedge C(\vec{k})$ includes all the constraints coming from the left projection's branching of the symbolic execution and all the relational assumptions such as the adjacency condition, and all constraints added by the potentially fired **Proof-Step-Lap-Gen** rule. A specular trace is such that its left projection constraints plus the relational assumptions imply the right projection constraints. We will now describe our three strategies.

Strategy A In this strategy CRSE uses only the rule **Proof-Step-Avoc** for sampling instructions, also this strategy searches for orthogonal relational traces. Under assumption 1, if this happens for a program then it must be the case that the program can output one value on one run with some probability but the same value has 0 probability of being output on the second run. This implies that for some input the program has an unbounded privacy loss. To implement this strategy CRSE looks for orthogonal relational traces $\langle m_1, m_2, \texttt{skip}, p_1, p_2, \Omega\rangle$ such that: $\exists\sigma.\sigma \models \Omega_1 \wedge C(\vec{k})$ but $\sigma \not\models \Omega_2$. Notice that using this strategy $\vec{k}$ will always be empty, as the rule used for samplings does not introduce any coupling between the two samples.

Strategy B This strategy symbolically executes the program in order to find a specular trace for which no matter how we relate, within the budget, the various pairs of samples X_1^i, X_2^i in the two runs - using the relational schema $X_1^i + K_i = X_2^i$ - the postcondition is always false. That is CRSE looks for specular relational traces $\langle m_1, m_2, \texttt{skip}, p_1, p_2, \Omega\rangle$ such that: $\forall\vec{k}.[(\Omega_1 \wedge C(\vec{k}) \implies \Omega_2) \wedge [\![\epsilon_c \leq \epsilon)]\!]_{\langle m_1|m_2\rangle}] \implies [\![o_1 \neq o_2]\!]_{\langle m_1|m_2\rangle}$.

Strategy C This strategy looks for relational traces for which the output variable takes the same value on the two runs but too much of the budget was spent. That is CRSE looks for traces $\langle m_1, m_2, \texttt{skip}, p_1, p_2, \Omega\rangle$ such that: $\forall\vec{k}.[\Omega_1 \wedge C(\vec{k}) \wedge \Omega_2 \implies [\![o_1 = o_2]\!]_{\langle m_1|m_2\rangle}] \implies [\![\epsilon_c > \epsilon]\!]_{\langle m_1|m_2\rangle}$.

Of the presented strategies only strategy A is sound with respect to counterexample finding, while the other two apply when the algorithm cannot be proven differentially private by any combination of the rules. In this second case though, CRSE provides counterexamples which agree with other refutation oriented results in literature. This strategies are hence termed *useful* because they amount to heuristics that can be applied in some situations.

8 Examples

In this section we will review the examples presented in Section 2 and variations thereof to show how CRSE works.

Unsafe Laplace mechanism: Algorithm 4. This algorithm is not ϵ-d.p because the noise is a constant and it is not calibrated to the sensitivity r of the query q. This translates in any attempt based on coupling rules to use too much of the budget. This program has only one possible final relational trace:

$\langle m_1, m_2, \texttt{skip}, p_1, p_2, \langle \Omega_1, C(\vec{k}, \Omega_2)\rangle\rangle$. Since there are no branching instructions $\Omega_1 = \{\lfloor 2E \rfloor_1 > 0\}$ and $\Omega_2 = \emptyset$, where $m_1(\epsilon) = m_2(\epsilon) = E$. Since there is one sampling instruction $C(\vec{k})$ will include $\{|Q_{d1} - Q_{d2}| \leq R, \mathrm{P}_1 + K = \mathrm{P}_2, E_c =| K | \cdot K' \cdot E, O_1 = \mathrm{P}_1 + Q_{d1}, O_2 = \mathrm{P}_2 + Q_{d2}\}$, with $m_1(o) = O_1, m_2(o) = O_2, m_1(\epsilon_c) = m_2(\epsilon_c) = E_c, m_i(\rho_i) = \mathrm{P}_i$. Intuitively, given this set of constraints, if it has to be the case that $O_1 = O_2$ then, $Q_{d1} - Q_{d_2} = K$. But $Q_{d1} - Q_{d_2}$ can be R and hence, E_c is at least R. So, if we want to equate the two output we need to spend r times the budget. Any relational input satisfying the precondition will give us a counterexample, provided the two projections are different.

Algorithm 4
A buggy Laplace mechanism

Input: q: $\mathcal{D} \to \mathbb{Z}$, $D : \mathcal{D}, \epsilon : \mathcal{R}^+$
Output: $o : \{true, false\}$
Precondition
$D_1 \sim D_2 \Rightarrow |q(D_1) - q(D_2)| \leq r$
Postcondition $o_1 = o_2$

1: $v \leftarrow q(D)$
2: $\rho \xleftarrow{\$} lap_\epsilon(0)$
3: $o \leftarrow v + \rho$
4: **return** o

A safe Laplace mechanism. By substituting line 2 in Algorithm 4 with $\rho \xleftarrow{\$} lap_{r*\epsilon}(0)$ we get an ϵ-DP algorithm. Indeed when executing that line CRSE would generate the following constraint $\mathrm{P}_1 + K_0 = \mathrm{P}_2 \wedge | K_0 + 0 - 0 | \leq K_1 \wedge O_1 = V_1 + \mathrm{P}_1 \wedge O_2 = V_2 + \mathrm{P}_2$. Which by instantiating $K = 0, K_1 = V_2 - V_1$ implies $O_1 = O_2 \wedge E_c \leq E$.

Unsafe sparse vector implementation: Algorithm 2. We already discussed why this algorithm is not ϵ-differentially private. Algorithm 2 satisfies Assumption 1 because it outputs the whole array o which takes values of the form $\perp^i, t$ or $\perp^n$ for $1 \leq i \leq n$ and $t \in \mathbb{R}$. The array, hence, encodes the whole trace. So if two runs of the algorithm output the same value it must be the case that they followed the same branching instructions. Let's first notice that the algorithm is trivially ϵ differentially private, for any ϵ, when the number of iterations n is less than or equal to 4.

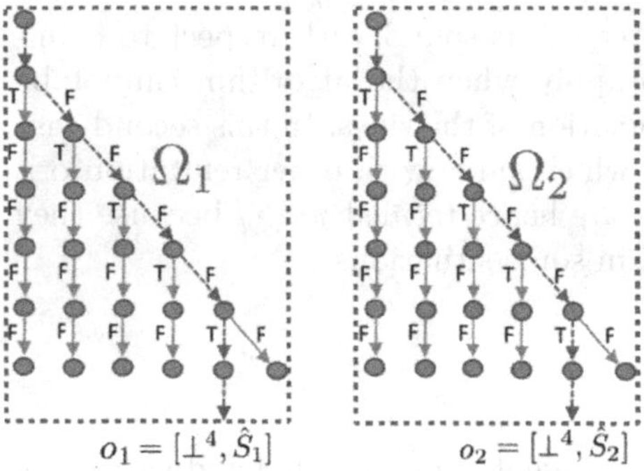

Fig. 11: Two runs of Alg. 2.

Indeed it is enough to apply the sequential composition theorem and get the obvious bound $\frac{\epsilon}{4} \cdot n$.

CRSE can prove this by applying the rule **Proof-Step-Lap-Gen** n times, and then choosing $K_1, \ldots, K_n$ all equal to 0. This would imply the statement of equality of the output variables spending less than ϵ. A potential counterexample can be found in 5 iterations. If we apply strategy B to this algorithm and follow the relational symbolic trace that applies the rule **Proof-Step-Lap-Gen** for all the samplings we can isolate the relational specular trace shown in Figure 11, which corresponds to the left execution following the false branch for the first four iterations and then following the true branch and setting the fifth element of the array to the sampled value. Let's denote the respective final relational configuration by $\langle m_1, m_2, \mathtt{skip}, p_1, p_2, s\rangle$. The set of constraints is as follows: $s = \langle \Omega_1, C(\vec{k}), \Omega_2\rangle = \langle\{T_1 > S_1^1, T_1 > S_1^2, T_1 > S_1^3, T_1 > S_1^4, T_1 \leq S_1^5\}, \{T_1 + k_0 = T_2, S_1^1 + k_1 = S_2^1, S_1^2 + k_2 = S_2^2, S_1^3 + k_3 = S_2^3, S_1^4 + k_4 = S_2^4, S_1^5 + k_5 = S_2^5, E_6 = k_0\frac{\epsilon}{2} + \frac{\epsilon}{4}\sum_{i=1}^{4} k_i \dots\}, \{T_2 > S_2^1, T_2 > S_2^2, T_2 > S_2^3, T_2 > S_2^4, T_2 \leq S_2^5\}\rangle$ with $m_1(\epsilon_c) = m_2(\epsilon_c) = E_6, m_1(o) = [S_1^1, \dots, S_1^5], m_2(o) = [S_2^1, \dots, S_2^5], m_1(t) = T_1, m_2(t) = T_2$.

We can see that strategy B applies, because we have $\models \forall\vec{k}.[(\Omega_1 \wedge C(\vec{k}) \implies \Omega_2) \wedge [\![\epsilon_c \leq \epsilon)]\!]_{\langle m_1|m_2\rangle}] \implies [\![o_1 \neq o_2]\!]_{\langle m_1|m_2\rangle}$. Computing the probability associated with these two traces we can verify that we have a counterexample. This pair of traces is, in fact, the same that has been found in [16] for a slightly more general version of Algorithm (2). Strategy B selects this relational trace since in order to make sure that the traces follow the same branches, the coupling rules enforce necessarily that the two samples released are different, preventing CRSE to prove equality of the output variables in the two runs.

Unsafe sparse vector implementation: Algorithm 3. Also this algorithm satisfies Assumption 1. The algorithm is ϵ-differentially private for one iteration. This is because, intuitively, adding noise to the threshold protects the result of the query as well at the branching instruction, but only for one iteration. The algorithm is not ϵ-differentially private, for any finite ϵ already at the second iteration, and a witness for this can be found using CRSE. We can see this using strategy B. Thanks to this strategy we will isolate a relational orthogonal trace, similarly to what has been found in [16] for the same algorithm. CRSE will unfold the loop twice, and it will scan all relational traces to see if there is an orthogonal trace. In particular, the relational trace that corresponds to the output $o_1 = o_2 = [\bot, \top]$, that is the the trace with set of constraints $\langle \Omega_1, C(\vec{k}), \Omega_2\rangle = \langle\{T_1 > q_{1d1}, T_1 \leq q_{2d1}\}, \{|q_{1d1} - q_{1d2}| \leq 1, |q_{2d1} - q_{2d2}| \leq 1\}\{T_2 > q_{1d2}, T_2 \leq q_{2d2}\}\rangle$. Since the vector $\vec{k}$ is empty we can omit it and just write C. It is easy to see now that the following sigma: $\sigma \equiv [q_{1d1} \mapsto 0, q_{2d1} \mapsto 1, q_{1d2} \mapsto 1, q_{2d2} \mapsto 0]$, proves that this relational trace is orthogonal: that is $\sigma \models \Omega_1 \wedge C$, but $\sigma \not\models \Omega_2$.

Indeed if we consider two inputs D_1, D_2 and two queries q_1, q_2 such that: $q_1(D_1) = q_2(D_2) = 0, q_2(D_1) = q_1(D_2) = 1$ we get that the probability of outputting the value $o = [\bot, \top]$ is positive in the first run, but it is 0 on the second. Hence, the algorithm can only be proven to be ∞-differentially private.

A safe sparse vector implementation. Algorithm 2 can be proven ϵ-d.p if we replace $o[i]\leftarrow\top$ to line 7. Let us consider a proof of this statement for $n = 5$. CRSE will try to prove the following postconditions: $o_1 = [\top, \bot, \dots, \bot] \implies o_2 = [\top, \bot, \dots, \bot] \wedge \epsilon_c \leq \epsilon, \dots, o_1 = [\bot, \dots, \bot, \top] \implies o_2 = [\bot, \dots, \bot, \top] \wedge \epsilon_c \leq \epsilon$. The only interesting iteration will be the i-th one, in all the others the postcondition will be vacuously true. Also, the budget spent will be $k_0\frac{\epsilon}{2}$, the one spent for the threshold. For all the other sampling instruction we can spend 0 by just setting $k_j = q[j](D_2) - q[j](D_1)$ for $j \neq i$, that is by coupling $\hat{s}_1 + k_j = \hat{s}_2$, with $k_j = q[j](D_2) - q[j](D_1)$, spending $|k_j + q[j](D_2) - q[j](D_1)| = 0$. So, at the i-th iteration the samples are coupled $\hat{s}_1 + k_i = \hat{s}_2$, with $k_i = 1$. So if $\hat{s}_1 \geq \hat{t}_1$ then also $\hat{s}_2 \geq \hat{t}_2$, and also, if $\hat{s}_1 < \hat{t}_1$ then also $\hat{s}_2 < \hat{t}_2$. This implies that at th i-th iteration we enter on the right run the true branch iff we enter the true branch on the left one. This by spending $|k_i + q[i](D_2) - q[i](D_1)|\frac{\epsilon}{4} \leq 2\frac{\epsilon}{4}$. The total privacy budget spent will then be equal to ϵ.

9 Related Works

There is now a wide array of formal techniques for reasoning about differential privacy, e.g. [1–6, 12, 15, 18, 20–23, 23, 24, 26, 27]. We will discuss here the techniques that are closest to our work. In [1] the authors devised a synthesis framework to automatically discover proofs of privacy using coupling rules similar to ours. However, their approach is not based on relational symbolic execution but on synthesis technique. Moreover, their framework cannot be directly used to find violations of differential privacy. In [2] the authors devise a decision logic for differential privacy which can soundly prove or disprove differential privacy. The programs considered there do not allow assignments to real and integer variables inside the body of while loops. While their technique is different from our, their logic could be potentially integrated in our framework as a decision procedure. In the recent concurrent work [23], the authors propose an automated technique for proving or finding violations to differential privacy based on program analysis, standard symbolic execution and on the notion of *randomness alignment*, which in their approach plays the role that approximate coupling plays for us here. Their approach focuses on efficiency and scalability, while we focus here more on the fundational aspects of our technique.

Another recent concurrent work [27] combines testing based on (unary) symbolic execution with approximate coupling for proving and finding violations to differential privacy. Their symbolic execution engine is similar to our SPFOR, and is used to reduce the numbers of tests that need to be generated, and for building privacy proofs from concrete executions. Their approach relies more directly on testing, providing an approximate notion of privacy. As discussed in their paper this could be potentially mitigated by using a relational symbolic execution engine as the one we propose here, at the cost of using more complex constraints. Another related work is [15], proposing model checking for finding counterexamples to differential privacy. The main difference with our work is in the basic technique and in the fact that model checking reason about a model of the code, rather than the code itself. They also consider the above threshold example and they are able to handle only a finite number of iterations.

Other work has studied how to find violations to differential privacy through testing [5, 6]. The approaches proposed in [5, 6] differ from ours in two ways: first, they use a statistical approach; second, they look at concrete values of the data and the privacy parameters. By using symbolic execution we are able to reason about symbolic values, and so consider ϵ-differential privacy for any finite ϵ. Moreover, our technique does not need sampling - although we still need to compute distributions to confirm a violation. Our work can be seen as a probabilistic extension of the framework presented in [10], where sampling instructions in the relational symbolic semantics are handled through rules inspired by the logic apRHL$^+$ [3]. This logic can be used to prove differential privacy but does not directly help in finding counterexamples when the program is not private.

10 Conclusion

We presented CRSE: a symbolic execution engine framework integrating relational reasoning and probabilistic couplings. The framework allows both proving and refuting differential privacy. When proving CRSE can be seen as strong postcondition calculus. When refuting CRSE uses several strategies to isolate potentially *dangerous* traces. Future work includes interfacing more efficiently CRSE with numeric solvers to find maximums of ratios of probabilities of traces.

Acknowledgements We warmly thank the reviewers for helping us improving the paper. This work was supported by the National Science Foundation under Grant No. 1565365, 1565387 and 2040215.

References

1. Albarghouthi, A., Hsu, J.: Synthesizing coupling proofs of differential privacy. Proc. ACM Program. Lang. **2**(POPL), 58:1–58:30 (Dec 2017)
2. Barthe, G., Chadha, R., Jagannath, V., Sistla, A.P., Viswanathan, M.: Deciding differential privacy for programs with finite inputs and outputs. In: LICS '20. pp. 141–154. ACM (2020)
3. Barthe, G., Gaboardi, M., Grégoire, B., Hsu, J., Strub, P.Y.: Proving differential privacy via probabilistic couplings. In: LICS '16. pp. 749–758. ACM, New York, NY, USA (2016)
4. Barthe, G., Köpf, B., Olmedo, F., Zanella Beguelin, S.: Probabilistic relational reasoning for differential privacy. ACM SIGPLAN Notices **47**(1), 97–110 (2012)
5. Bichsel, B., Gehr, T., Drachsler-Cohen, D., Tsankov, P., Vechev, M.: Dp-finder: Finding differential privacy violations by sampling and optimization. In: CCS '18. pp. 508–524 (2018)
6. Ding, Z., Wang, Y., Wang, G., Zhang, D., Kifer, D.: Detecting violations of differential privacy. In: CCS 2018. pp. 475–489 (2018)
7. Ding, Z., Wang, Y., Zhang, D., Kifer, D.: Free gap information from the differentially private sparse vector and noisy max mechanisms. Proc. VLDB Endow. **13**(3), 293–306 (2019). https://doi.org/10.14778/3368289.3368295, `http://www.vldb.org/pvldb/vol13/p293-ding.pdf`
8. Dwork, C., McSherry, F., Nissim, K., Smith, A.D.: Calibrating noise to sensitivity in private data analysis. In: TCC. LNCS, vol. 3876, pp. 265–284. Springer (2006)
9. Farina, G.P.: Coupled Relational Symbolic Execution. Ph.D. thesis, University at Buffalo, SUNY (2020), `https://search.proquest.com/pqdtglobal/docview/2385305218/`
10. Farina, G.P., Chong, S., Gaboardi, M.: Relational symbolic execution. In: PPDP '19. pp. 10:1–10:14. ACM, New York, NY, USA (2019)

11. Farina, G.P., Chong, S., Gaboardi, M.: Coupled relational symbolic execution for differential privacy. CoRR **abs/2007.12987** (2020), https://arxiv.org/abs/2007.12987
12. Gaboardi, M., Haeberlen, A., Hsu, J., Narayan, A., Pierce, B.C.: Linear dependent types for differential privacy. In: POPL. pp. 357–370 (2013)
13. Haeberlen, A., Pierce, B.C., Narayan, A.: Differential privacy under fire. In: Proceedings of the 20th USENIX Security Symposium (Aug 2011)
14. Kaplan, H., Mansour, Y., Stemmer, U.: The sparse vector technique, revisited. In: Advances in Neural Information Processing Systems 33: Annual Conference on Neural Information Processing Systems, NeurIPS 2020 (2020), https://arxiv.org/abs/2010.00917, to appear
15. Liu, D., Wang, B., Zhang, L.: Model checking differentially private properties. In: APLAS 2018. pp. 394–414 (2018)
16. Lyu, M., Su, D., Li, N.: Understanding the sparse vector technique for differential privacy. Proc. VLDB Endow. **10**(6), 637–648 (Feb 2017)
17. Mironov, I.: On significance of the least significant bits for differential privacy. In: CCS 2012. pp. 650–661 (2012)
18. Near, J.P., Darais, D., Abuah, C., Stevens, T., Gaddamadugu, P., Wang, L., Somani, N., Zhang, M., Sharma, N., Shan, A., Song, D.: Duet: an expressive higher-order language and linear type system for statically enforcing differential privacy. Proc. ACM Program. Lang. **3**(OOPSLA), 172:1–172:30 (2019)
19. Pottier, F., Simonet, V.: Information flow inference for ml. In: ACM SIGPLAN Notices. vol. 37, pp. 319–330. ACM (2002)
20. Reed, J., Pierce, B.C.: Distance makes the types grow stronger: a calculus for differential privacy. In: ICFP 2010. pp. 157–168. ACM (2010)
21. Sato, T., Barthe, G., Gaboardi, M., Hsu, J., Katsumata, S.: Approximate span liftings: Compositional semantics for relaxations of differential privacy. In: LICS 2019. pp. 1–14. IEEE (2019)
22. Tschantz, M.C., Kaynar, D.K., Datta, A.: Formal verification of differential privacy for interactive systems (extended abstract). In: MFPS 2011. ENTCS (2011)
23. Wang, Y., Ding, Z., Kifer, D., Zhang, D.: Checkdp: An automated and integrated approach for proving differential privacy or finding precise counterexamples. In: Proceedings of the 2020 ACM SIGSAC Conference on Computer and Communications Security (2020), to appear
24. Wang, Y., Ding, Z., Wang, G., Kifer, D., Zhang, D.: Proving differential privacy with shadow execution. In: PLDI 2019. pp. 655–669. ACM (2019)
25. Warner, S.L.: Randomized response: A survey technique for eliminating evasive answer bias. Journal of the American Statistical Association **60**(309), 63–69 (1965)
26. Zhang, D., Kifer, D.: Lightdp: towards automating differential privacy proofs. In: POPL 2017. pp. 888–901. ACM (2017)
27. Zhang, H., Roth, E., Haeberlen, A., Pierce, B.C., Roth, A.: Testing differential privacy with dual interpreters. Proc. ACM Program. Lang. (OOPSLA) (2020), to appear

Graded Hoare Logic and its Categorical Semantics

Marco Gaboardi[1(✉)], Shin-ya Katsumata[2], Dominic Orchard[3], and Tetsuya Sato[4]

[1] Boston University, Boston, USA gaboardi@bu.edu
[2] National Institute of Informatics, Tokyo, Japan s-katsumata@nii.ac.jp
[3] University of Kent, Canterbury, United Kingdom d.a.orchard@kent.ac.uk
[4] Tokyo Institute of Technology, Tokyo, Japan tsato@c.titech.ac.jp

Abstract. Deductive verification techniques based on program logics (i.e., the family of Floyd-Hoare logics) are a powerful approach for program reasoning. Recently, there has been a trend of increasing the expressive power of such logics by augmenting their rules with additional information to reason about program side-effects. For example, general program logics have been augmented with cost analyses, logics for probabilistic computations have been augmented with estimate measures, and logics for differential privacy with indistinguishability bounds. In this work, we unify these various approaches via the paradigm of *grading*, adapted from the world of functional calculi and semantics. We propose *Graded Hoare Logic* (GHL), a parameterisable framework for augmenting program logics with a preordered monoidal analysis. We develop a semantic framework for modelling GHL such that grading, logical assertions (pre- and post-conditions) and the underlying effectful semantics of an imperative language can be integrated together. Central to our framework is the notion of a *graded category* which we extend here, introducing *graded Freyd categories* which provide a semantics that can interpret many examples of augmented program logics from the literature. We leverage coherent fibrations to model the base assertion language, and thus the overall setting is also fibrational.

1 Introduction

The paradigm of *grading* is an emerging approach for augmenting language semantics and type systems with fine-grained information [40]. For example, a *graded monad* provides a mechanism for embedding side-effects into a pure language, exactly as in the approach of monads, but where the types are augmented ("graded") with information about what effects may occur, akin to a type-and-effect system [24,42]. As another example, *graded comonadic* type operators in linear type systems can capture non-linear dataflow and properties of data use [7,16,44]. In general, graded types augment a type system with some algebraic structure which serves to give a parameterisable fine-grained program analysis capturing the underlying structure of a type theory or semantics.

N. Yoshida (Ed.): ESOP 2021, LNCS 12648, pp. 234–263, 2021.
https://doi.org/10.1007/978-3-030-72019-3_9

Much of the work in graded types has arisen in conjunction with categorical semantics, in which graded modal type operators are modelled via graded monads [13,17,25,36,33], graded comonads (often with additional graded monoidal structure) [7,16,25,43,44], graded 'joinads' [36], graded distributive laws between graded (co)monads [15], and graded Lawvere theories [27].

So far grading has mainly been employed to reason about functional languages and calculi, thus the structure of the λ-calculus has dictated the structure of categorical models (although some recent work connects graded monads with classical dataflow analyses on CFGs [21]). We investigate here the paradigm of grading instead applied to *imperative* languages. As it happens, there is already a healthy thread of work in the literature augmenting program logics (in the family of Floyd-Hoare logics) with analyses that resemble notions of grading seen more recently in the functional world. The general approach is to extend the power of deductive verification by augmenting program logic rules with an analysis of side effects, tracked by composing rules. For example, work in the late 1980s and early 1990s augmented program logics with an analysis of computation time, accumulating a cost measure [37,38], with more recent fine-grained resource analysis based on multivariate analysis associated to program variables [8]. As another example, the Union Bound Logic of Barthe et al. [5] defines a Hoare-logic-style system for reasoning about probabilistic computations with judgments $\vdash_\beta c : \phi \Rightarrow \psi$ for a program c annotated by the maximum probability β (the union bound) that ψ does not hold. The inference rules of Union Bound Logic track and compute the union bound alongside the standard rules of Floyd-Hoare logic. As a last example, Approximate Relational Hoare Logic [2,6,39,48] augments a program logic with measures of the ϵ-δ bounds for reasoning about differential privacy.

In this work, we show how these disparate approaches can be unified by adapting the notion of grading to an imperative program-logic setting, for which we propose *Graded Hoare Logic* (GHL): a parameterisable program logic and reasoning framework graded by a preordered monoidal analysis. Our core contribution is GHL's underlying semantic framework which integrates grading, logical assertions (pre- and post-conditions) and the effectful semantics of an imperative language. This framework allows us to model, in a uniform way, the different augmented program logics discussed above.

Graded models of functional calculi tend to adopt either a graded monadic or graded comonadic model, depending on the direction of information flow in the analysis. We use the opportunity of an imperative setting (where the λ-calculus' asymmetrical 'many-inputs-to-one-output' model is avoided) to consider a more flexible semantic basis of *graded categories*. Graded categories generalise graded (co)monadic approaches, providing a notion of graded denotation without imposing on the placement (or 'polarity') of grading.

Outline Section 2 begins with an overview of the approach, focusing on the example of Union Bound Logic and highlighting the main components of our semantic framework. The next three sections then provide the central contributions:

- Section 3 defines GHL and its associated assertion logic which provides a flexible, parameterisable program logic for integrating different notions of side-effect reasoning, parameterised by a preordered monoidal analysis. We instantiate the program logic to various examples.
- Section 4 explores graded categories, an idea that has not been explored much in the literature, and for which there exists various related but not-quite-overlapping definitions. We show that graded categories can abstract graded monadic and graded comonadic semantics. We then extend graded categories to Freyd categories (generally used as a more flexible model of effects than monads), introducing the novel structure of *graded Freyd categories.*
- Section 5 develops the semantic framework for GHL, based on graded Freyd categories in a fibrational setting (where *coherent fibrations* [22] model the assertion logic) integrated with the graded Freyd layer. We instantiate the semantic model to capture the examples presented in Section 3 and others drawn from the literature mentioned above.

An extended version of this paper provides appendices which include further examples and proof details [14].

2 Overview of GHL and Prospectus of its Model

As discussed in the introduction, several works explore Hoare logics combined with some form of implicit or explicit grading for program analysis. Our aim is to study these in a uniform way. We informally introduce of our approach here.

We start with an example which can be derived in Union Bound Logic [5]:

$$\vdash_{0.05} \{\top\}\ \mathtt{do}\, v_1 \leftarrow \mathtt{Gauss}(0,1); \mathtt{do}\, v_2 \leftarrow \mathtt{Gauss}(0,1); v := \mathtt{max}(v_1, v_2)\ \{v \leq 2\}$$

This judgment has several important components. First, we have primitives for *procedures with side-effects* such as $\mathtt{do}\, v_1 \leftarrow \mathtt{Gauss}(0,1)$. This procedure samples a random value from the standard normal distribution with mean 0 and variance 1 and stores the result in the variable v_1. This kind of procedure with side effects differs from a regular assignment such as $v := \mathtt{max}(v_1, v_2)$, which is instead considered to be pure (wrt. probabilities) in our approach.

The judgment has grade '0.05' which expresses a bound on the probability that the postcondition is false, under the assumption of the precondition, after executing the program; we can think of it as the probability of failing to guarantee the postcondition. In our example (call it program P), since the precondition is true, this can be expressed as: $\Pr_{[\![P]\!](m)}[v > 2] \leq 0.05$ where $[\![P]\!](m)$ is the probability distribution generated in executing the program. The grade of P in this logic is derived using three components. First, sequential composition:

$$\frac{\vdash_{\beta} \{\psi\}\, P_1\, \{\psi_1\} \quad \vdash_{\beta'} \{\psi_1\}\, P_2\, \{\phi\}}{\vdash_{\beta+\beta'} \{\psi\}\, P_1; P_2\, \{\phi\}}$$

which sums the failure probabilities. Second, an axiom for Gaussian distribution:

$$\vdash_{0.025} \{\top\}\ \mathtt{do}\, v \leftarrow \mathtt{Gauss}(0,1)\ \{v \leq 2\}$$

with a basic constant 0.025 which comes from the property of the Gaussian distribution we are considering. Third, by the following judgment which is derivable by the assignment and the consequence rules, which are the ones from Hoare Logic with a trivial grading 0 which is the unit of addition:

$$\vdash_0 \{v_1 \leq 2 \vee v_2 \leq 2\}\, v := \mathtt{max}(v_1, v_2)\, \{v \leq 2\}$$

Judgments for more complex examples can be derived using the rules for conditional and loops. These rules also consider grading, and the grading can depend on properties of the program. For example the rule for conditionals is:

$$\frac{\vdash_\beta \{\psi \wedge e_b = \mathtt{tt}\}\, P_1\, \{\phi\} \qquad \vdash_\beta \{\psi \wedge e_b = \mathtt{ff}\}\, P_2\, \{\phi\}}{\vdash_\beta \{\psi\}\, \mathtt{if}\, e_b\, \mathtt{then}\, P_1\, \mathtt{else}\, P_2\, \{\phi\}}$$

This allows one to reason also about the grading in a conditional way, through the two assumptions $\psi \wedge e_b = \mathtt{tt}$ and $\psi \wedge e_b = \mathtt{ff}$. We give more examples later.

Other logics share a similar structure as that described above for the Union Bound logic, for example the relational logic apRHL [2], and its variants [48,49], for reasoning about differential privacy. Others again use a similar structure implicitly, for example the Hoare Logic to reason about asymptotic execution cost by Nielson [37], Quantitative Hoare Logic [8], or the relational logic for reasoning about program counter security presented by Barthe [3].

To study the semantics of these logics in a uniform way, we first abstract the logic itself. We design a program logic, which we call Graded Hoare Logic (GHL), containing all the components discussed above. In particular, the language is a standard imperative language with conditional and loops. Since our main focus is studying the semantics of grading, for simplicity we avoid using a 'while' loop, using instead a bounded 'loop' operation ($\mathtt{loop}\, e\, \mathtt{do}\, P$). This allow us to focus on the grading structures for total functions, leaving the study of the interaction between grading and partiality to future work. The language is parametric in the operations that are supported in expressions—common in several treatments of Hoare Logic—and in a set of procedures and commands with side effects, which are the main focus of our work. GHL is built over this language and an *assertion logic* which is parametric in the basic predicates that can be used to reason about programs. GHL is also parametric in a preordered monoid of grades, and in the axioms associated with basic procedures and commands with side effects. This generality is needed in order to capture the different logics we mentioned before.

GHL gives us a unified syntax, but our real focus is the semantics. To be as general as possible we turn to the language of category theory. We give a categorical framework which can capture different computational models and side effects, with denotations that are refined by predicates and grades describing program behaviours. Our framework relates different categories (modelling different aspects of GHL) as summarized by the following informal diagram (1).

$$\begin{array}{ccc} \mathbb{P} & \xrightarrow{\dot{I}} & \mathbb{E} \\ {\scriptstyle p}\downarrow & & \downarrow{\scriptstyle q} \\ \mathbb{V} & \xrightarrow{I} & \mathbb{C} \end{array} \qquad (1)$$

This diagram should not be understood as a commutative diagram in **CAT** as $\mathbb{E}$ is a graded category and hence not an object of **CAT**.

The category $\mathbb{V}$ models values and pure computations, the category $\mathbb{C}$ models impure computations, $\mathbb{P}$ is a category of predicates, and $\mathbb{E}$ is a *graded category* whose hom-sets are indexed by *grades*—elements of a preordered monoid. The presentation of graded categories is new here, but has some relation to other structures of the same name (discussed in Section 4).

This diagram echos the principle of *refinement as functors* proposed by Melliès and Zeilberger [32]. The lower part of the diagram offers an interpretation of the language, while the upper part offers a logical refinement of programs with grading. However, our focus is to introduce a new *graded refinement* view. The ideas we use to achieve this are to interpret the base imperative language using a *Freyd category* $I : \mathbb{V} \to \mathbb{C}$ (traditionally used to model effects) with countable coproducts, to interpret the assertion logic with a *coherent fibration* $p : \mathbb{P} \to \mathbb{V}$, and to interpret GHL as a *graded Freyd category* $\dot{I} : \mathbb{P} \to \mathbb{E}$ with homogeneous coproducts. In addition, the graded category $\mathbb{E}$ has a functor[5] q into $\mathbb{C}$ which erases assertions and grades and extracts the denotation of effectful programs, in the spirit of refinements. The benefit of using a Freyd category as a building block is that they are more flexible than other structures (e.g., monads) for constructing models of computational effects [47,51]. For instance, in the category **Meas** of measurable spaces and measurable functions, we cannot define state monads since there are no exponential objects. However, we can still have a model of first-order effectful computations using Freyd categories [46].

Graded Freyd categories are a new categorical structure that we designed for interpreting GHL judgments (Section 4.2). The major difference from an ordinary Freyd category is that the 'target' category is now a *graded category* ($\mathbb{E}$ in the diagram (1)). The additional structure provides what we need in order to interpret judgments including grading.

To show the generality of this structure, we present several approaches to instantiating the categorical framework of GHL's semantics, showing constructions via graded monads and graded comonads preserving coproducts.

Part of the challenge in designing a categorical semantics for GHL is to carve out and implement the implicit assumptions and structures used in the semantics of the various Hoare logics. A representative example of this challenge is the interpretation of the rule for conditionals in Union Bound Logic that we introduced above. We interpret the assertion logic in (a variant of) coherent fibrations $p : \mathbb{P} \to \mathbb{V}$, which model the $\wedge\vee\exists$=-fragment of first-order predicate logic [22]. In this abstract setup, the rule for conditionals may become *unsound* as it is built on the implicit assumption that the type Bool, which is interpreted as $1+1$, consists only of two elements, but this may fail in general $\mathbb{V}$. For example, a suitable coherent fibration for relational Hoare logic would take $\mathbf{Set}^2$ as the base category, but we have $\mathbf{Set}^2(1, 1+1) \cong 4$, meaning that there are four global elements in the interpretation of Bool. We resolve this problem by introducing

[5] More precisely, this is not quite a functor because $\mathbb{E}$ is a graded category; see Definition 9 for the precise meaning.

a side condition to guarantee the decidability of the boolean expression:

$$\frac{\vdash_m \{\psi \wedge e_b = \mathtt{tt}\}\, P_1\, \{\phi\} \quad \vdash_m \{\psi \wedge e_b = \mathtt{ff}\}\, P_2\, \{\phi\} \quad \psi \vdash e_b = \mathtt{tt} \vee e_b = \mathtt{ff}}{\vdash_m \{\psi\}\, \mathtt{if}\, e_b\, \mathtt{then}\, P_1\, \mathtt{else}\, P_2\, \{\phi\}}$$

This is related to the synchronization condition appearing in the relational Hoare logic rule for conditional commands (e.g., [6]).

Another challenge in the design of the GHL is how to assign a grade to the loop command $\mathtt{loop}\, e\, \mathtt{do}\, P$. We may naïvely give it the grade $m_l \triangleq \bigvee_{i \in \mathbb{N}} m^i$, where m is the grade of P, because P is repeatedly executed some finite number of times. However, the grade m_l is a very loose over-approximation of the grade of $\mathtt{loop}\, e\, \mathtt{do}\, P$. Even if we obtain some knowledge about the iteration count e in the assertion logic, this cannot be reflected in the grade. To overcome this problem, we introduce a Hoare logic rule that can estimate a more precise grade of $\mathtt{loop}\, e\, \mathtt{do}\, P$, provided that the value of e is determined:

$$\frac{\forall 0 \leq z < N.\ \vdash_m \{\psi_{z+1}\}\, P\, \{\psi_z\} \quad \psi_N \vdash e_n = \lceil N \rceil}{\vdash_{m^N} \{\psi_N\}\, \mathtt{loop}\, e_n\, \mathtt{do}\, P\, \{\psi_0\}}$$

This rule brings together the assertion language and grading, creating a dependency from the former to the latter, and giving us the structure needed for a categorical model. The right premise is a judgment of the assertion logic (under program variables Γ_{M} and pre-condition ψ_N) requiring that e is statically determinable as N. This premise makes the rule difficult to use in practical applications where e is dynamic. We expect a more "dependent" version of this rule is possible with a more complex semantics internalizing some form of data-dependency. Nevertheless, the above is enough to study the semantics of grading and its interaction with the Hoare Logic structure, which is our main goal here.

3 Loop Language and Graded Hoare Logic

After introducing some notation and basic concepts used throughout, we outline a core imperative loop language, parametric in its set of basic commands and procedures (Section 3.2). We then define a template of an assertion logic (Section 3.3), which is the basis of Graded Hoare Logic (Section 3.4).

3.1 Preliminaries

Throughout, we fix an infinite set **Var** of variables which are employed in the loop language (as the names of mutable program variables) and in logic (to reason about these program variables).

A *many-sorted signature* Σ is a tuple (S, O, ar) where S, O are sets of sorts and operators, and $ar : O \to S^+$ assigns argument sorts and a return value sort to operators (where S^+ is a non-empty sequence of sorts, i.e., an operator o with signature $(s_1 \times \ldots \times s_n) \to s$ is summarized as $ar(o) = \langle s_1, \ldots, s_n, s\rangle \in S^+$). We say that another many-sorted signature $\Sigma' = (S', O', ar')$ is an *extension* of Σ if $S \subseteq S'$ and $O \subseteq O'$ and $ar(o) = ar'(o)$ for all $o \in O$.

Let $\Sigma = (S, \cdots)$ be a many-sorted signature. A *context* for Σ is a (possibly empty) sequence of pairs $\Gamma \in (\mathbf{Var} \times S)^*$ such that all variables in Γ are distinct. We regard Γ as a partial mapping from **Var** to S. The set of contexts for Σ is denoted $\mathbf{Ctx}_\Sigma$. For $s \in S$ and $\Gamma \in \mathbf{Ctx}_\Sigma$, we denote by $\mathbf{Exp}_\Sigma(\Gamma, s)$ the set of Σ-expressions of sort s under the context Γ. When Σ, Γ are obvious, we simply write $e : s$ to mean $e \in \mathbf{Exp}_\Sigma(\Gamma, s)$. This set is inductively defined as usual.

An *interpretation* of a many-sorted signature $\Sigma = (S, O, ar)$ in a cartesian category $(\mathbb{V}, 1, \times)$ consists of an assignment of an object $[\![s]\!] \in \mathbb{V}$ for each sort $s \in S$ and an assignment of a morphism $[\![o]\!] \in \mathbb{V}([\![s_1]\!] \times \cdots \times [\![s_n]\!], [\![s]\!])$ for each $o \in O$ such that $ar(o) = \langle s_1, \ldots, s_n, s \rangle$. Once such an interpretation is given, we extend it to Σ-expressions in the standard way (see, e.g. [9,45]). First, for a context $\Gamma = x_1 : s_1, \cdots, x_n : s_n \in \mathbf{Ctx}_\Sigma$, by $[\![\Gamma]\!]$ we mean the product $[\![s_1]\!] \times \cdots \times [\![s_n]\!]$. Then we inductively define the interpretation of $e \in \mathbf{Exp}_\Sigma(\Gamma, s)$ as a morphism $[\![e]\!] \in \mathbb{V}([\![\Gamma]\!], [\![s]\!])$.

Throughout, we write bullet-pointed lists marked with $\star$ for the mathematical data that are parameters to Graded Hoare Logic (introduced in Section 3.4).

3.2 The Loop Language

We introduce an imperative language called the loop language, with a finite looping construct. The language is parameterised by the following data:

- $\star$ a many-sorted signature $\Sigma = (S, O, ar)$ extending a base signature (S_0, O_0, ar_0) of sort $S_0 = \{\texttt{bool}, \texttt{nat}\}$ with essential constants as base operators O_0, shown here with their signatures for brevity rather than defining ar_0 directly:

  $$O_0 = \{\texttt{tt} : \texttt{bool}, \texttt{ff} : \texttt{bool}\} \cup \{\lceil k \rceil : \texttt{nat} \mid k \in \mathbb{N}\}$$

  where `bool` is used for branching control-flow and `nat` is used for controlling loops, whose syntactic constructs are given below. We write $\lceil k \rceil$ to mean the embedding of semantic natural numbers into the syntax.
- $\star$ a set **CExp** of *command names* (ranged over by c) and a set $\mathbf{PExp}_s$ of *procedure names of sort* s (ranged over by p) for each sort $s \in S$.

When giving a program, we first fix a context Γ_M for the program variables. We define the set of *programs* (under a context Γ_M) by the following grammar:

$$P ::= P\,;P \mid \texttt{skip} \mid v := e \mid \texttt{do}\,c \mid \texttt{do}\,v \leftarrow p \mid \texttt{if}\,e_b\,\texttt{then}\,P\,\texttt{else}\,P \mid \texttt{loop}\,e_n\,\texttt{do}\,P$$

where $v \in \Gamma_\mathsf{M}$, e_b, e_n are well-typed Σ-expressions of sort `bool` and `nat` under Γ_M, and $c \in \mathbf{CExp}$. In assignment commands, $e \in \mathbf{Exp}_\Sigma(\Gamma_\mathsf{M}, \Gamma(v))$. In procedure call commands, $p \in \mathbf{PExp}_{\Gamma(v)}$. Each program must be well-typed under Γ_M. The typing rules are routine so we omit them.

Thus, programs can be sequentially composed via ; with `skip` as the trivial program which acts as a unit to sequencing. An assignment $v := e$ assigns expressions to a program variable v. Commands can be executed through the instruction $\texttt{do}\,c$ which yields some side effects but does not return any value.

Procedures can be executed through a similar instruction $\mathtt{do}\, v \leftarrow p$ which yields some side effect but also returns a value which is used to update v. Finally, conditionals are guarded by a boolean expression e_b and the iterations of a looping construct are given by a natural number expression e_n (which is evaluated once at the beginning of the loop to determine the number of iterations).

This language is rather standard, except for the treatment of commands and procedures of which we give some examples here.

Example 1. Cost Information: a simple example of a command is `tick`, which yields as a side effect the recording of one 'step' of computation.

Control-Flow Information: two other simple example of commands are `cfTT` and `cfFF`, which yield as side effects the recording of either true or false to a log. A program can be augmented with these commands in its branches to give an account of a program's control flow. We will use these commands to reason about control-flow security in Example 3.

Probability Distributions: a simple example of a procedure is $\mathtt{Gauss}(x, y)$, which yields as a side effect the introduction of new randomness in the program, and which returns a random sample from the Gaussian distribution with mean and variance specified by $x, y \in \Gamma_{\mathsf{M}}$. We will see how to use this procedure to reason about probability of failure in Example 4.

Concrete instances of the loop language typically include conversion functions between the sorts in Σ, e.g., so that programs can dynamically change control flow depending on values of program variables. In other instances, we may have a language manipulating richer data types, e.g., reals or lists, and also procedures capturing higher-complexity computations, such as Ackermann functions.

3.3 Assertion Logic

We use an assertion logic to reason about properties of basic expressions. We regard this reasoning as a meta-level activity, thus the logic can have more sorts and operators than the loop language. Thus, over the data specifying the loop language, we build formulas of the assertion logic by the following data:

- ⋆ a many-sorted signature $\Sigma_l = (S_l, O_l, ar_l)$ extending Σ.
- ⋆ a set P_l of atomic propositions and a function $par_l : P_l \to S_l^*$ assigning input sorts to them. We then inductively define the set $\mathbf{Fml}_{\Sigma_l}(\Gamma)$ of formulas under $\Gamma \in \mathbf{Ctx}_{\Sigma_l}$ as in Figure 1 (over the page), ranged over by ψ and ϕ.
- ⋆ a $\mathbf{Ctx}_{\Sigma_l}$-indexed family of subsets $\mathbf{Axiom}(\Gamma) \subseteq \mathbf{Fml}_{\Sigma_l}(\Gamma) \times \mathbf{Fml}_{\Sigma_l}(\Gamma)$.

The assertion logic is a fragment of the many-sorted first-order logic over Σ_l-terms admitting: 1) finite conjunctions, 2) countable disjunctions, 3) existential quantification, and 4) equality predicates. Judgements in the assertion logic have the form $\Gamma \mid \psi_1, \cdots, \psi_n \vdash \phi$ (read as $\psi_1 \wedge \cdots \wedge \psi_n$ implies ϕ), where $\Gamma \in \mathbf{Ctx}_{\Sigma_l}$ is a context giving types to variables in the formulas $\psi_1, \cdots, \psi_n, \phi \in \mathbf{Fml}_{\Sigma_l}(\Gamma)$. The logic has the axiom rule deriving $\Gamma \mid \psi \vdash \phi$ for each pair (ψ, ϕ) of formulas in $\mathbf{Axiom}(\Gamma)$. The rest of inference rules of this logic are fairly standard and so we omit them (see e.g. [22, Section 3.2 and Section 4.1]).

The set $\mathbf{Fml}_{\Sigma_l}(\Gamma)$ of formulas under $\Gamma \in \mathbf{Ctx}_{\Sigma_l}$ is inductively defined as follows:

1. For all $p \in P_l$ and $par_l(p) = s_1 \cdots s_n$ and $t_i : \mathbf{Exp}_{\Sigma_l}(\Gamma, s_i)$ $(1 \leq i \leq n)$ implies $p(t_1, \cdots, t_n) \in \mathbf{Fml}_{\Sigma_l}(\Gamma)$
2. For all $s \in S_l$ and $t, u \in \mathbf{Exp}_{\Sigma_l}(\Gamma, s)$, $t = u \in \mathbf{Fml}_{\Sigma_l}(\Gamma)$.
3. For all finite families $\{\phi_i \in \mathbf{Fml}_{\Sigma_l}(\Gamma)\}_{i \in \Lambda}$, we have $\bigwedge \phi_i \in \mathbf{Fml}_{\Sigma_l}(\Gamma)$.
4. For all countable families $\{\phi_i \in \mathbf{Fml}_{\Sigma_l}(\Gamma)\}_{i \in \Lambda}$, we have $\bigvee \phi_i \in \mathbf{Fml}_{\Sigma_l}(\Gamma)$.
5. For all $\phi \in \mathbf{Fml}_{\Sigma_l}(\Gamma, x : s)$, we have $(\exists x : s \;.\; \phi) \in \mathbf{Fml}_{\Sigma_l}(\Gamma)$.

Fig. 1. Formula formation rules

In some of our examples we will use the assertion logic to reason about programs in a relational way, i.e., to reason about two executions of a program (we call them *left* and *right* executions). This requires basic predicates to manage expressions representing pairs of values in our assertion logic. As an example, we could have two predicates $\mathsf{eqv}_{\langle 1 \rangle}$, $\mathsf{eqv}_{\langle 2 \rangle}$, that can assert the equality of the left and right executions of an expression to some value, respectively. That is, the formula $\mathsf{eqv}_{\langle 1 \rangle}(e_b, \mathsf{true})$, which we will write using infix notation $e_b\langle 1 \rangle = \mathsf{true}$, asserts that the left execution of the boolean expression e_b is equal to true.

3.4 Graded Hoare Logic

We now introduce Graded Hoare Logic (GHL), specified by the following data:

- ⋆ a preordered monoid $(M, \leq, 1, \cdot)$ (*pomonoid* for short) (where $\cdot$ is monotonic with respect to $\leq$) for the purposes of program analysis, where we refer to the elements $m \in M$ as *grades*;
- ⋆ two functions which define the grades and pre- and post-conditions of commands **CExp** and procedures **PExp**:

$$C_{\mathsf{c}} : \mathbf{Fml}_{\Sigma_l}(\Gamma_{\mathsf{M}}) \times M \to 2^{\mathbf{CExp}}$$
$$C^s_{\mathsf{p}} : \mathbf{Fml}_{\Sigma_l}(\Gamma_{\mathsf{M}}) \times M \times \mathbf{Fml}_{\Sigma_l}(r : s) \to 2^{\mathbf{PExp}_s} \quad (s \in S \wedge r \notin \mathsf{dom}(\Gamma_{\mathsf{M}}))$$

The function C_{c} takes a pre-condition and a grade, returning a set of command symbols satisfying these specifications. A command c may appear in $C_{\mathsf{c}}(\phi, m)$ for different pairs (ϕ, m), enabling pre-condition-dependent grades to be assigned to c. Similarly, the function C^s_{p} takes a pre-condition, a grade, and a postcondition for return values, and returns a set of procedure names of sort s satisfying these specifications. Note, r is a distinguished variable (for return values) not in Γ_{M}. The shape of C_{c} and C_{c} as predicates over commands and procedures, indexed by assertions and grades, provides a way to link grades and assertions for the effectful operations of GHL. Section 3.5 gives examples exploiting this.

From this structure we define a *graded Hoare logic* by judgments of the form: $\vdash_m \{\phi\}\ P\ \{\psi\}$ denoting a program P with pre-condition $\phi \in \mathbf{Fml}_{\Sigma_l}(\Gamma_{\mathsf{M}})$, post-condition $\psi \in \mathbf{Fml}_{\Sigma_l}(\Gamma_{\mathsf{M}})$ and analysis $m \in M$. Graded judgments are defined inductively via the inference rules given in Table 1. Ignoring grading, many of the rules are fairly standard for a Floyd-Hoare program logic. The rule for `skip` is standard but includes grading by the unit 1 of the monoid. Similarly, assignment

$$\frac{}{\vdash_1 \{\psi\}\, \texttt{skip}\, \{\psi\}} \qquad \frac{\vdash_m \{\psi\}\, P_1\, \{\psi_1\} \quad \vdash_{m'} \{\psi_1\}\, P_2\, \{\phi\}}{\vdash_{m \cdot m'} \{\psi\}\, P_1; P_2\, \{\phi\}} \qquad \frac{}{\vdash_1 \{\psi[e/v]\}\, v := e\, \{\psi\}}$$

$$\frac{f \in C_{\mathsf{c}}(\psi, m)}{\vdash_m \{\psi\}\, \texttt{do}\, c\, \{\psi\}} \qquad \frac{p \in C_{\mathsf{p}}^{\Gamma_{\mathsf{M}}(v)}(\psi, m, \phi)}{\vdash_m \{\psi\}\, \texttt{do}\, v \leftarrow p\, \{(\exists v : \Gamma_{\mathsf{M}}(v)\ .\ \psi) \wedge \phi[v/r]\}}$$

$$\frac{\Gamma_{\mathsf{M}} \mid \psi' \vdash \psi \quad m \leq m' \quad \Gamma_{\mathsf{M}} \mid \phi \vdash \phi' \quad \vdash_m \{\psi\}\, P\, \{\phi\}}{\vdash_{m'} \{\psi'\}\, P\, \{\phi'\}}$$

$$\frac{\forall 0 \leq z < N.\ \vdash_m \{\psi_{z+1}\}\, P\, \{\psi_z\} \quad \Gamma_{\mathsf{M}} \mid \psi_N \vdash e_n = \lceil N \rceil}{\vdash_{m^N} \{\psi_N\}\, \texttt{loop}\, e_n\, \texttt{do}\, P\, \{\psi_0\}}$$

$$\frac{\vdash_m \{\psi \wedge e_b = \texttt{tt}\}\, P_1\, \{\phi\} \quad \vdash_m \{\psi \wedge e_b = \texttt{ff}\}\, P_2\, \{\phi\} \quad \Gamma_{\mathsf{M}} \mid \psi \vdash e_b = \texttt{tt} \vee e_b = \texttt{ff}}{\vdash_m \{\psi\}\, \texttt{if}\, e_b\, \texttt{then}\, P_1\, \texttt{else}\, P_2\, \{\phi\}}$$

Table 1. Graded Hoare Logic Inference Rules

is standard, but graded with 1 since we do not treat it specially in GHL. Sequential composition takes the monoid multiplication of the grades of the subterms. The rules for commands and procedures use the functions C_{c} and C_{p} introduced above. Notice that the rule for commands uses as the pre-condition as its post-condition, since commands have only side effects and they do not return any value. The rule for procedures combines the pre- and post-conditions given by C_{p} following the style of Floyd's assignment rule [12].

The non-syntax-directed consequence rule is similar to the usual consequence rule, and in addition allows the assumption on the grade to be weakened (*approximated*) according to the ordering of the monoid.

The shape of the loop rule is slightly different from the usual one. It uses the assertion-logic judgment $\Gamma_{\mathsf{M}} \mid \psi_N \vdash e_n = \lceil N \rceil$ to express the assumption that e_n evaluates to $\lceil N \rceil$. Under this assumption it uses a family of assertions ψ_z indexed by the natural numbers $z \in \{0, 1, \ldots, N-1\}$ to conclude the post-condition ψ_0. This family of assertions plays the role of the classical invariant in the Floyd-Hoare logic rule for 'while'. Assuming that the grade of the loop body is m, the grade of the loop command is then m^N, where $m^0 = 1$ and $m^{k+1} = m \cdot m^k$. By instantiating this rule with $\psi_z = (\theta \wedge e_n = \lceil z \rceil)$, the loop rule also supports the following derived rule which is often preferable in examples:

$$\frac{\forall 0 \leq z < N.\ \vdash_m \{\theta \wedge e_n = \lceil z+1 \rceil\}\, P\, \{\theta \wedge e_n = \lceil z \rceil\}}{\vdash_{m^N} \{\theta \wedge e_n = \lceil N \rceil\}\, \texttt{loop}\, e_n\, \texttt{do}\, P\, \{\theta \wedge e_n = \lceil 0 \rceil\}}$$

The rule for the conditional is standard except for the condition $\Gamma_{\mathsf{M}} \mid \psi \vdash e_b = \texttt{tt} \vee e_b = \texttt{ff}$. While this condition may seem obvious, it is actually important to make GHL sound in various semantics (mentioned in Section 2). As an example, suppose that a semantics $[\![-]\!]$ of expressions is given in the product category $\mathbf{Set}^2$, which corresponds to two semantics $[\![-]\!]_1, [\![-]\!]_2$ of expressions in **Set**. Then the side condition for the conditional is to guarantee that for any boolean expression e_b, and pair of memories (ρ_1, ρ_2) satisfying the precondition ψ, the pair $([\![e_b]\!]_1(\rho_1), [\![e_b]\!]_2(\rho_2))$ is either $[\![\texttt{tt}]\!] = (\mathsf{tt}, \mathsf{tt})$ or $[\![\texttt{ff}]\!] = (\mathsf{ff}, \mathsf{ff})$. We note that other relational logics such as apRHL [6] employ an equivalent syntactic side condition in their rule for conditionals.

3.5 Example Instantiations of GHL

Example 2 (Simple cost analysis). We can use the `tick` command discussed in Example 1 to instrument programs with *cost* annotations. We can then use GHL to perform cost analysis by instantiating GHL with the additive natural number monoid $(\mathbb{N}, \leq, 0, +)$ and $\texttt{tick} \in C_{\mathsf{c}}(\phi, 1)$. Thus, we can form judgments $\vdash_1 \{\phi\}\, \mathbf{do}\, \texttt{tick}\, \{\phi\}$ which account for cost via the judgment's grade. Sequential composition accumulates cost and terms like `skip` and assignment have 0 cost.

Let us use this example to illustrate how C_{c} can assign multiple pre-condition-grade pairs to a command. Suppose that we modify the semantics of `tick` so that it reports unit cost 1 when variable x is 0, otherwise cost 2. We can then define C_{c} so that $\texttt{tick} \in C_{\mathsf{c}}(x = \lceil 0 \rceil, 1)$ and also $\texttt{tick} \in C_{\mathsf{c}}(x \neq \lceil 0 \rceil, 2)$. In this way, we can give different grades to programs depending on their pre-conditions.

Example 3 (Program Counter Security). We can use the commands `cfTT` and `cfFF` discussed in Example 1 to instrument programs with *control flow* annotations, recording to an external log. GHL can then be used to reason about program counter security [35][3, Section 7.2] of instrumented programs. This is a relational security property similar to non-interference (requiring that private values do not influence public outputs) but where only programs with the same control flow are considered.

Firstly, any conditional statement $\mathbf{if}\, e_b\, \mathbf{then}\, P_t\, \mathbf{else}\, P_f$ in a program is elaborated to a statement $\mathbf{if}\, e_b\, \mathbf{then}\, (\texttt{cfTT}; P_t)\, \mathbf{else}\, (\texttt{cfFF}; P_f)$. We then instantiate GHL with a monoid of words over $\{\texttt{tt}, \texttt{ff}\}$ with prefix order: $2^* \triangleq (\{\texttt{tt}, \texttt{ff}\}^*, \leq, \epsilon, \cdot)$ and we consider $\texttt{cfTT} \in C_{\mathsf{c}}(\phi, \texttt{tt})$ and $\texttt{cfTT} \in C_{\mathsf{c}}(\phi, \texttt{ff})$. We can thus form judgments of the shape $\vdash_{\texttt{tt}} \{\phi\}\, \mathbf{do}\, \texttt{cfTT}\, \{\phi\}$ and $\vdash_{\texttt{ff}} \{\phi\}\, \mathbf{do}\, \texttt{cfFF}\, \{\phi\}$ which account for control-flow information (forming paths) via the judgment's grade. Sequential composition concatenates control-flow paths and terms like `skip` and assignment do not provide any control-flow information, i.e. ϵ.

We then instantiate the assertion logic to support relational reasoning, i.e., where the expressions of the language are interpreted as pair of values. For an expression e, interpreted as a pair (v_1, v_2) then we write $e\langle 1 \rangle = v_1$ to say that the first component (left execution) equals v_1 and $e\langle 2 \rangle = v_2$ to say that the second component (right execution) equals v_2. In the assertion logic, we can then describe public values which need to be equal, following the tradition in reasoning about non-interference, by the predicate $e\langle 1 \rangle = e\langle 2 \rangle$. Private data are instead interpreted as a pair of arbitrary values. (Section 3.3 suggested the notation $\mathsf{eqv}_{\langle i \rangle}(e, b)$ for $e\langle i \rangle = b$, but we use the latter for compactness here).

As an example, one can prove the following judgment where x is a public variable and y is a private one, and $b \in \{\texttt{tt}, \texttt{ff}\}$:

$$\vdash_b \{x\langle 1\rangle{=}x\langle 2\rangle \wedge x\langle 1\rangle{=}b\}\,\texttt{if}\;x\;\texttt{then}\,(\texttt{cfTT};x{=}1;y{=}1)\;\texttt{else}\,(\texttt{cfFF};x{=}2;y{=}2)\{x\langle 1\rangle{=}x\langle 2\rangle\}$$

This judgment shows the program is non-interferent, since the value of x is independent from the value of the private variable y, and secure in the program counter model, since the control flow does not depend on the value of y. Conversely, the following judgment is not derivable for both $b = \texttt{tt}$ and $b = \texttt{ff}$:

$$\vdash_b \{x\langle 1\rangle{=}x\langle 2\rangle \wedge y\langle 1\rangle{=}b\}\,\texttt{if}\;y\;\texttt{then}\,(\texttt{cfTT};x{=}1;y{=}1)\;\texttt{else}\,(\texttt{cfFF};x{=}1;y{=}2)\{x\langle 1\rangle{=}x\langle 2\rangle\}$$

This program is non-interferent but is not secure in the program counter model because the control flow leaks information about y which is a private variable.

Example 4 (Union Bound Logic). Section 1 discussed the Union Bound logic by Barthe et al. [5]. This logic embeds smoothly into GHL by using the pomonoid $(\mathbb{R}_{\geq 0}, \leq, 0, +)$ and procedures of the form $\texttt{sample}_{\mu,e}$ as samplings from a probabilistic distribution μ parametrised over the syntax of GHL expressions e. Following Barthe et al. [5], we consider a semantically defined set for C_p:

$$C_p(\phi, \beta, \psi) = \{\texttt{sample}_{\mu,e} \mid \forall s.s \in [\![\phi]\!] \Longrightarrow \Pr_{s' \leftarrow [\![\texttt{sample}_{\mu,e}]\!](s)}[s' \in [\![\neg\psi]\!] \leq \beta)\}$$

This definition captures that, assuming the pre-condition holds for an input memory state s, then for output value s' from sampling $\texttt{sample}_{\mu,e}$, the probability that the post-condition is false is bounded above by β. This allow us to consider different properties of the distribution μ with parameter e.

4 Graded Categories

Now that we have introduced GHL and key examples, we turn to the core of its categorical semantics: *graded categories.*

Graded monads provide a notion of sequential composition for morphisms of the form $I \to T_m J$, i.e., with structure on the target/output capturing some information by the grade m drawn from a pomonoid [24]; dually, graded comonads provide composition for $D_m I \to J$, i.e. with structure on the source/input with grade m [43]. We avoid the choice of whether to associate grading with the input or output by instead introducing *graded categories*, which are agnostic about the polarity (or position) of any structure and grading. Throughout this section, we fix a pomonoid $(M, \leq, 1, \cdot)$ (with $\cdot$ monotonic wrt. $\leq$).

Definition 1. An *M-graded category* $\mathbb{C}$ consists of the following data:

- A class $\mathbf{Obj}(\mathbb{C})$ of objects. $I \in \mathbb{C}$ denotes $I \in \mathbf{Obj}(\mathbb{C})$.
- A homset $\mathbb{C}(I, J)(m)$ for all objects $I, J \in \mathbb{C}$ and $m \in M$. We often write $f : I \to_m J$ to mean $f \in \mathbb{C}(I, J)(m)$, and call m the *grade* of f;
- An upcast functions $\uparrow^n_m : \mathbb{C}(I, J)(m) \to \mathbb{C}(I, J)(n)$ for all grades $m \leq n$;
- Identity morphisms $\mathrm{id}_I \in \mathbb{C}(I, I)(1)$ for all $I \in \mathbb{C}$;
- Composition $\circ : \mathbb{C}(J, K)(n) \times \mathbb{C}(I, J)(m) \to \mathbb{C}(I, K)(m \cdot n)$.

Graded categories satisfy the usual categorical laws of identity and associativity, and also the commutativity of upcast and composition: $\uparrow^{n'}_n g \circ \uparrow^{m'}_m f = \uparrow^{m' \cdot n'}_{m \cdot n} (g \circ f)$, corresponding to monotonicity of $(\cdot)$ with respect to $\leq$.

An intuitive meaning of a graded category's morphisms is: $f \in \mathbb{C}(A,B)(m)$ if the *value* or the *price* of a morphism $f : A \to B$ is *at most* m with respect to the ordering $\leq$ on M. We do not yet give a polarity or direction to this price, i.e., whether the price is *consumed* or *produced* by the computation. Thus, graded categories give a non-biased view; we need not specify whether grading relates to the source or target of a morphism.

Graded categories were first introduced by Wood [54, Section 1] (under the name 'large V-categories'), and Levy connected them with models of call-by-push-value [28]. Therefore we do not claim the novelty of Definition 1.

Example 5. A major source of graded categories is via graded (co)monads. Let $(M, \leq, 1, \cdot)$ be a pomonoid, regarded as a monoidal category. A *graded monad* [50,24] on a category $\mathbb{C}$ (or more precisely an *M-graded monad*) is a lax monoidal functor $(T, \eta, \mu) : (M, \leq, 1, \cdot) \to ([\mathbb{C}, \mathbb{C}], \mathrm{Id}, \circ)$. Concretely, this specifies:

- a functor $T : (M, \leq) \to [\mathbb{C}, \mathbb{C}]$ from the preordered set $(M, \leq)$ to the endofunctor category over $\mathbb{C}$. For an ordered pair $m \leq m'$ in M then $T(m \leq m') : Tm \to Tm'$ is a natural transformation;
- a unit $\eta : \mathrm{Id} \to T1$ and a multiplication $\mu_{m,m'} : Tm \circ Tm' \to T(m \cdot m')$, natural in $m, m' \in M$.

They satisfy the graded versions of the usual monad axioms:

$$\begin{array}{ccc} TmJ & \xrightarrow{Tm\eta_J} & Tm(T1J) \\ {\scriptstyle \eta_{TmJ}}\downarrow & \searrow\!\!\!\searrow & \downarrow{\scriptstyle \mu_{m,1,J}} \\ T1(TmJ) & \xrightarrow{\mu_{1,m,J}} & TmJ \end{array} \qquad \begin{array}{ccc} Tm(Tm'(Tm''J)) & \xrightarrow{\mu_{m,m',Tm''J}} & T(m \cdot m')(Tm''J) \\ {\scriptstyle Tm\mu_{m',m'',J}}\downarrow & & \downarrow{\scriptstyle \mu_{mm',m'',J}} \\ Tm(T(m' \cdot m'')J) & \xrightarrow{\mu_{m,m'm'',J}} & T(m \cdot m' \cdot m'')J \end{array}$$

Graded comonads are dually defined (i.e., as a graded monad on $\mathbb{C}^{op}$).

By mimicking the construction of Kleisli categories, we can construct an M-graded category $\mathbb{C}_T$ (we call it the Kleisli M-graded category of T) from a category $\mathbb{C}$ with an M-graded monad T on $\mathbb{C}$.[6]

- $\mathbf{Obj}(\mathbb{C}_T) \triangleq \mathbf{Obj}(\mathbb{C})$ and $\mathbb{C}_T(X,Y)(m) \triangleq \mathbb{C}(X, TmY)$.
- For $f : X \to_m Y$ and n such that $m \leq n$, we define $\uparrow_m^n f \triangleq T(m \leq n)_Y \circ f$.
- Identity and composition are defined by: $\mathrm{id}_X \triangleq \eta_X : X \to_1 X$ and $g \circ f \triangleq \mu_{m,n,Z} \circ Tm\, g \circ f$ for $f : X \to_m Y$ and $g : Y \to_n Z$.

The dual construction is possible. Let D be an M^{op}-graded comonad on a category $\mathbb{C}$. We then define $\mathbb{C}_D$ by $\mathbb{C}_D(X,Y)(m) = \mathbb{C}(DmX, Y)$; the rest of data is similar to the case of graded monads. This yields an M-graded category $\mathbb{C}_D$.

Remark 1. As an aside (included for completeness but not needed in the rest of the paper), graded categories are an instance of *enriched categories*. For the enriching category, we take the presheaf category $[M, \mathbf{Set}]$, together with *Day's convolution product* [10].

[6] Not to be confused with the Kleisli category of graded monads by Fujii et al. [13].

4.1 Homogeneous Coproducts in Graded Categories

We model boolean values and natural numbers by the binary coproduct $1+1$ and the countable coproduct $\coprod_{i \in \mathbb{N}} 1$. We thus define what it means for a graded category to have coproducts. The following definition of binary coproducts easily extends to coproducts of families of objects.

Definition 2. Let $\mathbb{C}$ be an M-graded category. A *homogeneous binary coproduct* of $X_1, X_2 \in \mathbb{C}$ consists of an object $Z \in \mathbb{C}$ together with injections $\iota_1 \in \mathbb{C}(X_1, Z)(1)$ and $\iota_2 \in \mathbb{C}(X_2, Z)(1)$ such that, for any $m \in M$ and $Y \in \mathbb{C}$, the function $\lambda f \,.\, (f \circ \iota_1, f \circ \iota_2)$ of type $\mathbb{C}(Z, Y)(m) \to \mathbb{C}(X_1, Y)(m) \times \mathbb{C}(X_2, Y)(m)$ is invertible. The inverse is called the *cotupling* and denoted by $[-,-]$. It satisfies the usual law of coproducts ($i = 1, 2$):

$$[f_1, f_2] \circ \iota_i = f_i, \qquad [\iota_1, \iota_2] = \mathrm{id}_Z,$$
$$g \circ [f_1, f_2] = [g \circ f_1, g \circ f_2], \qquad [\uparrow^n_m f_1, \uparrow^n_m f_2] = \uparrow^n_m [f_1, f_2].$$

When homogeneous binary coproducts of any combination of $X_1, X_2 \in \mathbb{C}$ exists, we say that $\mathbb{C}$ has homogeneous binary coproducts.

The difference between homogeneous coproducts and coproducts in ordinary category theory is that the cotupling is restricted to take morphisms with the same grade. A similar constraint is seen in some effect systems, where the typing rule of conditional expressions require each branch to have the same effect.

Proposition 1. *Let $\{\iota_i \in \mathbb{C}(X_i, Z)\}_{i \in I}$ be a coproduct of $\{X_i\}_{i \in I}$ in an ordinary category $\mathbb{C}$.*

1. *Suppose that T is an M-graded monad on $\mathbb{C}$. Then $\{\eta_Z \circ \iota_i \in \mathbb{C}_T(X_i, Z)(1)\}_{i \in I}$ is a homogeneous coproduct in $\mathbb{C}_T$.*
2. *Suppose that (D, ε, δ) is an M^{op}-graded comonad on $\mathbb{C}$ such that each $Dm : \mathbb{C} \to \mathbb{C}$ preserves the coproduct $\{\iota_i\}_{i \in I}$. Then $\{\iota_i \circ \varepsilon_I \in \mathbb{C}_D(X_i, Z)(1)\}_{i \in I}$ is a homogeneous coproduct in $\mathbb{C}_D$.*

4.2 Graded Freyd Categories with Countable Coproducts

We now introduce the central categorical structure of the loop language and GHL semantics: *graded Freyd categories* with homogeneous countable coproducts.

Definition 3. An M-graded Freyd category with homogeneous countable coproducts consists of the following data:

1. A cartesian monoidal category $(\mathbb{V}, 1, \times, l, r, a)$ with countable coproducts such that for all $V \in \mathbb{V}$, the functor $V \times (-) : \mathbb{V} \to \mathbb{V}$ preserves coproducts.
2. An M-graded category $\mathbb{C}$ such that $\mathbf{Obj}(\mathbb{C}) = \mathbf{Obj}(\mathbb{V})$ and $\mathbb{C}$ has homogeneous countable coproducts.
3. A function $I_{V,W} : \mathbb{V}(V, W) \to \mathbb{C}(V, W)(1)$ for each $V, W \in \mathbb{C}$. Below we may omit writing subscripts of I. The role of this function is to inject pure computations into effectful computations.

4. A function $(*)_{V,X,W,Y} : \mathbb{V}(V,W) \times \mathbb{C}(X,Y)(m) \to \mathbb{C}(V \times X, W \times Y)(m)$ for each $V, W, X, Y \in \mathbb{C}$ and $m \in M$. Below we use it as an infix operator and sometimes omit its subscripts. The role of this function is to combine pure computations and effectful computations in parallel.

The function I and $(*)$ satisfy the following equations:

$$I(\mathrm{id}_X) = \mathrm{id}_X \quad I(g \circ f) = Ig \circ If \quad I(f \times g) = f * Ig \quad \mathrm{id}_V * \mathrm{id}_X = \mathrm{id}_{V*X},$$
$$(g \circ f) * (i \circ j) = (g * i) \circ (f * j) \quad f * \uparrow^n_m g = \uparrow^n_m (f * g)$$
$$f \circ I(l_X) = I(l_X) \circ (\mathrm{id}_1 * f) \quad I(a_{X',Y',Z'}) \circ ((f \times g) * h) = (f * (g * h)) \circ I(a_{X,Y,Z})$$

These are analogous to the usual Freyd categories axioms. We also require that:

1. For any countable coproduct $\{\iota_i \in \mathbb{V}(X_i, Y)\}_{i \in A}$, $\{I(\iota_i) \in \mathbb{C}(X_i, Y)(1)\}_{i \in A}$ is a homogeneous countable coproduct.
2. For any homogeneous countable coproduct $\{\iota_i \in \mathbb{C}(X_i, Y)(1)\}_{i \in A}$ and $V \in \mathbb{V}$, $\{\mathrm{id}_V * \iota_i \in \mathbb{C}(V \times X_i, V \times Y)(1)\}_{i \in A}$ is a homogeneous countable coproduct.

We denote an M-graded Freyd category with countable coproducts by the tuple $(\mathbb{V}, 1, \times, \mathbb{C}, I, (*))$ capturing the main details of the cartesian monoidal structure of $\mathbb{V}$, the base category $\mathbb{C}$, the lifting function I and the action $(*)$.

If the grading pomonoid M is trivial, $\mathbb{C}$ becomes an ordinary category with countable coproducts. We therefore simply call it a Freyd category with countable coproducts. This is the same as a *distributive Freyd category* in the sense introduced by Power [46] and Staton [51]. We will use non-graded Freyd categories to give a semantics of the loop language in Section 4.3. An advantage of Freyd categories is that they encompasses a broad class of models of computations, not limited to those arising from monads. A recent such example is Staton's category of *s-finite kernels* [52][7].

We could give an alternative abstract definition of M-graded Freyd category using 2-categorical language: a graded Freyd category is an equivariant morphism in the category of actions from a cartesian category to M-graded categories. The full detail of this formulation will be discussed elsewhere.

A Freyd category typically arises from a strong monad on a cartesian category [47]. We give here a graded analogue of this fact. First, we recall the notion of *strength* for graded monads [24, Definition 2.5]. Let $(\mathbb{C}, 1, \times)$ be a cartesian monoidal category. A *strong* M-graded monad is a pair of an M-graded monad (T, η, μ) and a natural transformation $\mathrm{st}_{I,J,m} \in \mathbb{C}(I \times TmJ, Tm(I \times J))$ satisfying graded versions of the four coherence laws in [34, Definition 3.2]. We dually define a *costrong* M-graded comonad $(D, \varepsilon, \delta, \mathrm{cs})$ to be the M-graded comonad equipped with the *costrength* $\mathrm{cs}_{I,J,m} \in \mathbb{C}(Dm(I \times J), I \times DmJ)$.

Proposition 2. *Let* $(\mathbb{C}, 1, \times)$ *be a cartesian monoidal category.*

1. *Let* $(T, \eta, \mu, \mathrm{st})$ *be a strong* M*-graded monad on* $\mathbb{C}$*. The Kleisli* M*-graded category* $\mathbb{C}_T$*, together with* $If = \eta_W \circ f$ *and* $f * g = \mathrm{st}_{W,Y} \circ (f \times g)$ *forms an* M*-graded Freyd category with homogeneous countable coproducts.*

[7] It is not known whether the category of s-finite kernels is a Kleisli category.

2. *Let* $(D, \varepsilon, \delta, \mathrm{cs})$ *be a costrong* M^{op}*-graded comonad on* $\mathbb{C}$ *such that each* Dm *preserves countable coproducts. Then the coKleisli* M*-graded category* $\mathbb{C}_D$ *together with* $If = f \circ \varepsilon_V$ *and* $f * g = (f \times g) \circ \mathrm{cs}_{V,X}$ *forms an* M*-graded Freyd category with homogeneous countable coproducts.*

We often use the following 'ext' operation to structure interpretations of programs and GHL derivations. Let $\delta_X \in \mathbb{V}(X, X \times X)$ be the diagonal morphism. Then $\mathsf{ext} : \mathbb{C}(X,Y)(m) \to \mathbb{C}(X, X \times Y)(m)$ is defined as $\mathsf{ext}(f) = (X * f) \circ I\delta_X$. When viewing X as a set of environments, $\mathsf{ext}(f)$ may be seen as executing an effectful procedure f under an environment, then extending the environment with the return value of f. In a non-graded setting, the definition of ext is analogous.

4.3 Semantics of The Loop Language in Freyd Categories

Towards the semantics of GHL, we first give a more standard, non-graded categorical semantics of the loop language. We first prepare the following data.

- ⋆ A Freyd category $(\mathbb{V}, 1, \times, \mathbb{C}, I, *)$ with countable coproducts.
- ⋆ A coproduct $\{\mathsf{tt}, \mathsf{ff} \in \mathbb{V}(1, \mathsf{Bool})\}$ of 1 and 1 in $\mathbb{V}$.
- ⋆ A coproduct $\{\lfloor k \rfloor \in \mathbb{V}(1, \mathsf{Nat})\}_{k \in \mathbb{N}}$ of $\mathbb{N}$-many 1s in $\mathbb{V}$.
- ⋆ An interpretation $[\![-]\!]$ of Σ in $\mathbb{V}$ such that

$$[\![\mathtt{bool}]\!] = \mathsf{Bool} \qquad [\![\mathtt{tt}]\!] = \mathsf{tt} \in \mathbb{V}(1, \mathsf{Bool}) \qquad [\![\mathtt{ff}]\!] = \mathsf{ff} \in \mathbb{V}(1, \mathsf{Bool})$$
$$[\![\mathtt{nat}]\!] = \mathsf{Nat} \qquad [\![\lceil k \rceil]\!] = \lfloor k \rfloor \in \mathbb{V}(1, \mathsf{Nat}).$$

For convenience, we let $\mathsf{M} \triangleq [\![\Gamma_{\mathsf{M}}]\!]$ (Section 3.1), i.e., all relevant (mutable) program variables are in scope, and write $\pi_v \in \mathbb{V}(\mathsf{M}, [\![\Gamma_{\mathsf{M}}(v)]\!])$ for the projection morphism associated to a program variable $v \in \Gamma_{\mathsf{M}}$.

Pure expressions are interpreted as $\mathbb{V}$-morphisms and impure commands and procedures are interpreted as $\mathbb{C}$-morphisms, of the form:

- ⋆ (expressions) A morphism $[\![e]\!] \in \mathbb{V}(\mathsf{M}, [\![s]\!])$ for all $e \in \mathbf{Exp}_\Sigma(\Gamma_{\mathsf{M}}, s)$; see Section 3.1.
- ⋆ (commands) A morphism $[\![c]\!] \in \mathbb{C}(\mathsf{M}, 1)$ for each $c \in \mathbf{CExp}$.
- ⋆ (procedures) A morphism $[\![p]\!] \in \mathbb{C}(\mathsf{M}, [\![s]\!])$ for each $s \in S$ and $p \in \mathbf{PExp}_s$.

For the interpretation of programs, we first define some auxiliary morphisms. For all $v \in \Gamma_{\mathsf{M}}$, let $\mathsf{upd}_v \in \mathbb{V}(\mathsf{M} \times [\![\Gamma_{\mathsf{M}}(v)]\!], \mathsf{M})$ to be the unique morphism (capturing memory updates) satisfying $\pi_v \circ \mathsf{upd}_v = \pi_2$ and $\pi_w \circ \mathsf{upd}_v = \pi_w \circ \pi_1$ for any $w \in \Gamma_{\mathsf{M}}$ such that $v \neq w$. We define $\mathsf{sub}(v, e) \in \mathbb{V}(\mathsf{M}, \mathsf{M})$ by $\mathsf{sub}(v, e) \triangleq \mathsf{upd}_v \circ \langle \mathsf{id}_{\mathsf{M}}, [\![e]\!] \rangle$, which updates the memory configuration at variable v with the value of e.

For the interpretation of conditional and loop commands, we need coproducts over M. Since $\mathbb{V}$ is distributive, we can form a binary coproduct $\mathsf{M} \times \mathsf{Bool}$ and a countable coproduct $\mathsf{M} \times \mathsf{Nat}$ with injections respectively defined as ($\forall k \in \mathbb{N}$):

$$\mathsf{tm} \triangleq \langle \mathsf{id}_{\mathsf{M}}, \mathsf{tt} \circ !_{\mathsf{M}} \rangle \in \mathbb{V}(\mathsf{M}, \mathsf{M} \times \mathsf{Bool}) \qquad [k] \triangleq \langle \mathsf{id}_{\mathsf{M}}, \lfloor k \rfloor \circ !_{\mathsf{M}} \rangle \in \mathbb{V}(\mathsf{M}, \mathsf{M} \times \mathsf{Nat})$$
$$\mathsf{fm} \triangleq \langle \mathsf{id}_{\mathsf{M}}, \mathsf{ff} \circ !_{\mathsf{M}} \rangle \in \mathbb{V}(\mathsf{M}, \mathsf{M} \times \mathsf{Bool})$$

By Condition 1 of Definition 3, these coproducts are mapped to coproducts in $\mathbb{C}$ with injections:

$$\{I(\mathsf{tm}), I(\mathsf{fm}) \in \mathbb{C}(\mathsf{M}, \mathsf{M} \times \mathsf{Bool})\}, \qquad \{I([k]) \in \mathbb{C}(\mathsf{M}, \mathsf{M} \times \mathsf{Nat}) \mid k \in \mathbb{N}\}.$$

The cotuplings of these coproducts (written $[f, g]$ and $[f^{(k)}]_{k\in\mathbb{N}}$ respectively) are used next to interpret conditionals and loops.
We interpret a program P of the loop language as a morphism $[\![P]\!] \in \mathbb{C}(\mathsf{M}, \mathsf{M})$:

$$\begin{aligned}
[\![P; P']\!] &= [\![P']\!] \circ [\![P]\!] & [\![\mathtt{skip}]\!] &= \mathrm{id}_{\mathsf{M}}\\
[\![\mathsf{do}\, v \leftarrow p]\!] &= I(\mathsf{upd}_v) \circ \mathsf{ext}[\![p]\!] & [\![\mathsf{do}\, c]\!] &= I(\pi_1) \circ \mathsf{ext}[\![c]\!]\\
[\![v := e]\!] &= I(\mathsf{sub}(v, e))\\
[\![\mathtt{if}\; e_b\; \mathtt{then}\; P\; \mathtt{else}\; P']\!] &= [\, [\![P]\!], [\![P']\!] \,] \circ \mathsf{ext}(I[\![e_b]\!])\\
[\![\mathtt{loop}\; e_n\; \mathtt{do}\; P]\!] &= [\, [\![P]\!]^{(k)} \,]_{k\in\mathbb{N}} \circ \mathsf{ext}(I[\![e_n]\!])
\end{aligned}$$

Thus, the semantics of $\mathtt{loop}\, e_n\, \mathtt{do}\, P$ is such that, if the expression e_n evaluates to some natural number $\lceil k \rceil$ then $\mathtt{loop}\, e_n\, \mathtt{do}\, P$ is equivalent to the k-times sequential composition of P.

5 Modelling Graded Hoare Logic

We now define the categorical model of GHL, building on the non-graded Freyd semantics of Section 4.3. Section 5.1 first models the base assertion logic, for which we use fibrations, giving an overview of the necessary mathematical machinery for completeness. Section 5.2 then defines the semantics of GHL and Section 5.3 instantiates it for the examples discussed previously in Section 3.

5.1 Interpretation of the Assertion Logic using Fibrations

Our assertion logic (Section 3) has logical connectives of finite conjunctions, countable disjunctions, existential quantification and an equality predicate. A suitable categorical model for this fragment of first-order logic is offered by a *coherent fibration* [22, Def. 4.2.1], extended with countable joins in each fibre. We recap various key definitions and terminology due to Jacobs' textbook [22].

In the following, let $\mathbb{P}$ and $\mathbb{V}$ be categories and $p : \mathbb{P} \to \mathbb{V}$ a functor.

We can regard functor p as attaching *predicates* to each object in $\mathbb{V}$. When $p\psi = X$, we regard $\psi \in \mathbb{P}$ as a predicate over $X \in \mathbb{V}$. When $f \in \mathbb{P}(\psi, \phi)$ is a morphism, we regard this as saying that pf maps elements satisfying ψ to those satisfying ϕ in $\mathbb{V}$. Parallel to this view of functors assigning predicates is the notion that entities in $\mathbb{P}$ are 'above' those in $\mathbb{V}$ when they are mapped to by p.

Definition 4 ('Aboveness'). An object $\psi \in \mathbb{P}$ is said to be *above* an object $X \in \mathbb{V}$ if $p\psi = X$. Similarly, a morphism[8] $\dot{f} \in \mathbb{P}(\psi, \phi)$ is said to be *above* a morphism f in $\mathbb{V}$ if $p\dot{f} = f \in \mathbb{V}(p\psi, p\phi)$. A morphism in $\mathbb{P}$ is *vertical* if it is above an identity morphism. Given $\psi, \phi \in \mathbb{P}$ and $f \in \mathbb{V}(p\psi, p\phi)$, then we denote the *set of all morphisms in* $\mathbb{P}$ *above* f as $\mathbb{P}_f(\psi, \phi) = \{\dot{f} \in \mathbb{P}(\psi, \phi) \mid p\dot{f} = f\}$.

[8] The dot notation here introduces a new name and should not be understood as applying some mathematical operator on f.

Definition 5 (Fibre category). A *fibre category* over $X \in \mathbb{V}$ is a subcategory of $\mathbb{P}$ consisting of objects above X and morphisms above id_X. This subcategory is denoted by $\mathbb{P}_X$, and thus the homsets of $\mathbb{P}_X$ are $\mathbb{P}_X(\psi, \phi) = \mathbb{P}_{\mathrm{id}_X}(\psi, \phi)$.

We are ready to recall the central concept in fibrations: *cartesian morphisms.*

Definition 6 (Cartesian morphism). A morphism $\dot{f} \in \mathbb{P}(\psi, \phi)$ is *cartesian* if for any $\alpha \in \mathbb{P}$ and $g \in \mathbb{V}(p\alpha, p\psi)$, the post-composition of $\dot{f}$ in $\mathbb{P}$, regarded as a function of type $\dot{f} \circ - : \mathbb{P}_g(\alpha, \psi) \to \mathbb{P}_{g \circ p\dot{f}}(\alpha, \phi)$, is a bijection. This amounts to the following *universal property* of cartesian morphism: for any $\dot{h} \in \mathbb{P}(\alpha, \phi)$ above $g \circ p\dot{f}$, there exists a unique morphism $\dot{g} \in \mathbb{P}(\alpha, \psi)$ above g such that $\dot{h} = \dot{f} \circ \dot{g}$. Intuitively, $\dot{f}$ represents the situation where ψ is a *pullback* or *inverse image* of ϕ along $p\dot{f}$, and the universal property corresponds to that of pullback.

Definition 7 (Fibration). Finally, a functor $p : \mathbb{P} \to \mathbb{V}$ is a *fibration* if for any $\psi \in \mathbb{P}$, $X \in \mathbb{V}$, and $f \in \mathbb{V}(X, p\psi)$, there exists an object $\phi \in \mathbb{P}$ and a cartesian morphism $\dot{f} \in \mathbb{P}(\phi, \psi)$ above f, called the *cartesian lifting* of f with ψ. We say that a fibration $p : \mathbb{P} \to \mathbb{V}$ is *posetal* if each $\mathbb{P}_X$ is a poset, corresponding to the implicational order between predicates. When $\psi \le \phi$ holds in $\mathbb{P}_X$, we denote the corresponding vertical morphism in $\mathbb{P}$ as $\psi \nearrow \phi$.

Posetal fibrations are always faithful. The cartesian lifting of $f \in \mathbb{V}(X, p\psi)$ with ψ uniquely exists. We thus write it by $\overline{f}\psi$, and its domain by $f^*\psi$. It can be easily shown that for any morphism $f \in \mathbb{V}(X, Y)$ in $\mathbb{V}$, the assignment $\psi \in \mathbb{P}_Y \mapsto f^*\psi \in \mathbb{P}_X$ extends to a monotone function $f^* : \mathbb{P}_Y \to \mathbb{P}_X$. We call it the *reindexing function* (along f). Furthermore, the assignment $f \mapsto f^*$ satisfies the (contravariant) functoriality: $\mathrm{id}_X^* = \mathrm{id}_{\mathbb{P}_X}$ and $(g \circ f)^* = f^* \circ g^*$. A fibration is a *bifibration* if each reindexing function $f^* : \mathbb{P}_Y \to \mathbb{P}_X$ for $f \in \mathbb{V}(X, Y)$ has a left adjoint, denoted by $f_* : \mathbb{P}_X \to \mathbb{P}_Y$. $f_*\psi$ is always associated with a morphism $\underline{f}\psi : f_*\psi \to \psi$ above f, and this is called the *opcartesian lifting* of f with ψ. For the universal property of the opcartesian lifting, see Jacobs [22, Def. 9.1.1].

Fibrations for our Assertion Logic It is widely known that *coherent fibrations* are suitable for interpreting the $\wedge, \vee, \exists, =$-fragment of first-order logic (see [22, Chapter 4, Def. 4.2.1]). Based on this fact, we introduce a class of fibrations that are suitable for our assertion logic—due to the countable joins of the assertion logic we modify the definition of coherent fibration accordingly.

Definition 8. A *fibration for assertion logic* over $\mathbb{V}$ is a posetal fibration $p : \mathbb{P} \to \mathbb{V}$ for cartesian $\mathbb{V}$ with distributive countable coproducts, such that:

1. Each fibre poset $\mathbb{P}_X$ is a distributive lattice with finite meets $\top_X, \wedge$ and countable joins $\bot_X, \vee$.
2. Each reindexing function f^* preserves finite meets and countable joins.
3. The reindexing function $c_{X,Y}^*$ along the contraction $c_{X,Y} \triangleq \langle \pi_1, \pi_2, \pi_2 \rangle \in \mathbb{V}(X \times Y, X \times Y \times Y)$ has a left adjoint $\mathrm{Eq}_{X,Y} \dashv c_{X,Y}^*$. This satisfies *Beck-Chevalley condition* and *Frobenius property*; we refer to [22, Definition 3.4.1].

4. The reindexing function $w^*_{X,Y}$ along the weakening $w_{X,Y} \triangleq \pi_1 \in \mathbb{V}(X \times Y, X)$ has a left adjoint $\exists_{X,Y} \dashv w^*_{X,Y}$. This satisfies *Beck-Chevalley condition* and *Frobenius property*; we refer [22, Definition 1.9.1, 1.9.12].

This is almost the same as the definition of coherent fibrations [22, Definition 4.2.1]; the difference is that 1) the base category $\mathbb{V}$ has countable coproducts 2) we require each fibre to be a poset; this makes object equalities hold on-the-nose, and 3) we require each fibre to have countable joins. They will be combined with countable coproducts of $\mathbb{V}$ to equip $\mathbb{P}$ with a countable coproduct [22].

Example 6. A typical example of a fibration for assertion logic is the subobject fibration $p^{\mathbf{Set}} : \mathbf{Pred} \to \mathbf{Set}$; the category **Pred** has objects pairs (X, ψ) of sets such that $\psi \subseteq X$, and morphisms of type $(X, \psi) \to (Y, \phi)$ as functions $f : X \to Y$ such that $f(\psi) \subseteq \phi$. The functor p sends (X, ψ) to X and f to itself. More examples can be found in the work of Jacobs [22, Section 4].

For a parallel pair of morphisms $f, g \in \mathbb{V}(X, Y)$, we define the equality predicate $\mathrm{Eq}(f, g)$ above X to be $\langle \mathrm{id}_X, f, g\rangle^* \mathrm{Eq}_{X,Y}(\top_{X \times Y})$ [22, Notation 3.4.2]. Intuitively, $\mathrm{Eq}(f, g)$ corresponds to the predicate $\{x \in X \mid f(x) = g(x)\}$. In this paper, we will use some facts about the equality predicate shown by Jacobs [22, Proposition 3.4.6, Lemma 3.4.5, Notation 3.4.2, Example 4.3.7].

The Semantics of Assertion Logic We move to the semantics of our assertion logic in a fibration $p : \mathbb{P} \to \mathbb{V}$ for assertion logic. The basic idea is to interpret a formula $\psi \in \mathbf{Fml}_{\Sigma_l}(\Gamma)$ as an object in $\mathbb{P}_{[\![\Gamma]\!]}$, and an entailment $\Gamma \mid \psi \vdash \phi$ as the order relation $[\![\psi]\!] \leq [\![\phi]\!]$ in $\mathbb{P}_{[\![\Gamma]\!]}$. The semantics is given by the following interpretation of the data specifying the assertion logic (given in Section 3.3):

- ⋆ A fibration $p : \mathbb{P} \to \mathbb{V}$ for assertion logic.
- ⋆ An interpretation $[\![-]\!]$ of Σ_l in $\mathbb{P}$ that coincides with the one $[\![-]\!]$ of Σ in $\mathbb{V}$.
- ⋆ An object $[\![P]\!] \in \mathbb{P}_{[\![par(P)]\!]}$ for each atomic proposition $P \in P_l$ (recall *par* assigns input sorts to atomic propositions in P_l, parameterising the logic).
- ⋆ We require that for any $\Gamma \in \mathbf{Ctx}_{\Sigma_l}$ and $(\psi, \phi) \in \mathbf{Axiom}(\Gamma)$, $[\![\psi]\!] \leq [\![\phi]\!]$ holds in $\mathbb{P}_{[\![\Gamma]\!]}$. This expresses an implicational axiom in the coherent logic.

The interpretation $[\![\psi]\!]$ of $\psi \in \mathbf{Fml}_{\Sigma_l}(\Gamma)$ is inductively defined as a $\mathbb{P}_{[\![\Gamma]\!]}$-object:

$$[\![P(t_1, \cdots, t_n)]\!] = \langle [\![t_1]\!], \cdots, [\![t_n]\!]\rangle^* [\![P]\!] \qquad [\![t = u]\!] = \mathrm{Eq}([\![t]\!], [\![u]\!])$$
$$[\![\bigwedge \psi_i]\!] = \bigwedge [\![\psi_i]\!] \qquad [\![\bigvee \psi_i]\!] = \bigvee [\![\psi_i]\!] \qquad [\![\exists x : s \,.\, \psi]\!] = \exists_{[\![\Gamma]\!],[\![s]\!]} [\![\psi]\!]$$

5.2 Interpretation of Graded Hoare Logic

We finally introduce the semantics of Graded Hoare logic. This semantics interprets derivations of GHL judgements $\vdash_m \{\psi\}\ P\ \{\phi\}$ as m-graded morphisms in a graded category. Moreover, it is built *above* the interpretation $[\![P]\!] \in \mathbb{C}(\mathsf{M}, \mathsf{M})$ of the program P in the non-graded semantics introduced in Section 4.3. The underlying structure is given as a combination of a fibration for the assertion logic and a graded category over $\mathbb{C}$, as depicted in (1) (Section 2, p. 237).

Definition 9. A *GHL structure* over a Freyd category $(\mathbb{V}, 1, \times, \mathbb{C}, I, *)$ with countable coproducts and a fibration $p : \mathbb{P} \to \mathbb{V}$ for assertion logic comprises:

1. An M-graded Freyd category $(\mathbb{P}, \dot{1}, \dot{\times}, \mathbb{E}, \dot{I}, \circledast)$ with homogeneous countable coproducts.
2. A function $q_{\psi,\phi,m} : \mathbb{E}(\psi, \phi)(m) \to \mathbb{C}(p\psi, p\phi)$ (subscripts may be omitted), which maps to the base denotational model, erasing assertions and grades.

The above data satisfy the following properties:

1. That q behaves 'functorialy' preserving structure from $\mathbb{E}$ to $\mathbb{V}$:

$$q(\mathrm{id}_\phi) = \mathrm{id}_{p\phi}, \quad q(g \circ f) = qg \circ qf, \quad q_{\psi,\phi,n}(\uparrow_m^n f) = q_{\psi,\phi,m} f$$
$$q(\dot{I}f) = I(pf), \quad q(f \circledast g) = pf * qg$$

2. For any homogeneous countable coproduct $\{\iota_i \in \mathbb{E}(\psi_i, \phi)(1)\}_{i \in \Lambda}$, $\{q\iota_i \in \mathbb{C}(p\psi_i, p\phi)\}_{i \in \Lambda}$ is a countable coproduct.
3. (Ex falso quodlibet) $q_{\perp_X,\phi,m} : \mathbb{E}(\perp_X, \phi)(m) \to \mathbb{C}(X, p\phi)$ is a bijection.

The last statement asserts that if the precondition is the least element $\perp_X$ in the fibre over $X \in \mathbb{V}$, which represents the false assertion, we trivially conclude any postcondition ϕ and grading m for any morphisms of type $X \to p\phi$ in $\mathbb{C}$.

The semantics of GHL then requires a graded Freyd category with countable coproducts, and morphisms in the graded category guaranteeing a sound model of the effectful primitives (commands/procedures), captured by the data:

- ⋆ A GHL structure $(\mathbb{P}, \dot{1}, \dot{\times}, \mathbb{E}, \dot{I}, \circledast, q)$ over the Freyd category $(\mathbb{V}, 1, \times, \mathbb{C}, I, *)$ with countable coproducts and the fibration $p : \mathbb{P} \to \mathbb{V}$ for assertion logic.
- ⋆ For each $c \in C_{\mathsf{c}}(\psi, m)$ a morphism $\langle c \rangle \in \mathbb{E}(\llbracket \psi \rrbracket, \dot{1})(m)$ such that $q\langle c \rangle = \llbracket c \rrbracket$.
- ⋆ For each $p \in C^s_{\mathsf{p}}(\psi, m, \phi)$ a morphism $\langle p \rangle \in \mathbb{E}(\llbracket \psi \rrbracket, \llbracket \phi \rrbracket)(m)$ such that $q\langle p \rangle = \llbracket p \rrbracket$.

where $\llbracket c \rrbracket$, $\llbracket p \rrbracket$ and later $\llbracket e \rrbracket$ are from the underlying non-graded model (Sec. 4.3).

We interpret a derivation of GHL judgement $\vdash_m \{\phi\}\, P\, \{\psi\}$ as a morphism

$$\llbracket \vdash_m \{\phi\}\, P\, \{\psi\} \rrbracket \in \mathbb{E}(\llbracket \phi \rrbracket, \llbracket \psi \rrbracket)(m) \quad \text{such that} \quad q_{\llbracket \phi \rrbracket, \llbracket \psi \rrbracket, m} \llbracket \vdash_m \{\phi\}\, P\, \{\psi\} \rrbracket = \llbracket P \rrbracket.$$

The constraint on the right is guaranteed by the soundness of the interpretation (Theorem 1). From the functor-as-refinement viewpoint [32], the interpretation $\llbracket \vdash_m \{\phi\}\, P\, \{\psi\} \rrbracket$ witnesses that $\llbracket P \rrbracket$ respects refinements ϕ and ψ of M, and additionally it witnesses the grade of $\llbracket P \rrbracket$ being m. We first cover the simpler cases of the interpretation of GHL derivations:

$$\llbracket \vdash_1 \{\psi\}\, \mathtt{skip}\, \{\psi\} \rrbracket = \mathrm{id}_{\llbracket \psi \rrbracket}$$
$$\llbracket \vdash_{m_1 \cdot m_2} \{\psi\}\, P_1 \,;\, P_2\, \{\theta\} \rrbracket = \llbracket \vdash_{m_2} \{\psi_1\}\, P_2\, \{\theta\} \rrbracket \circ \llbracket \vdash_{m_1} \{\psi\}\, P_1\, \{\psi_1\} \rrbracket$$
$$\llbracket \vdash_1 \{\psi[e/v]\}\, v := e\, \{\psi\} \rrbracket = \dot{I}(\overline{\mathsf{sub}(v, e)}\llbracket \psi \rrbracket)$$
$$\llbracket \vdash_m \{\psi\}\, \mathsf{do}\, c\, \{\psi\} \rrbracket = \dot{I}(\pi_1) \circ \mathsf{ext}\langle c \rangle$$
$$\llbracket \vdash_m \{\psi\}\, \mathsf{do}\, v \leftarrow p\, \{(\exists v \,.\, \psi) \wedge \phi\} \rrbracket = \dot{I}(\underline{\mathsf{upd}_v}(\llbracket \psi \rrbracket \mathbin{\dot{\times}} \llbracket \phi \rrbracket)) \circ \mathsf{ext}\langle p \rangle$$
$$\llbracket \vdash_{m'} \{\psi'\}\, P\, \{\phi'\} \rrbracket = \dot{I}(\llbracket \phi \rrbracket \nearrow \llbracket \phi' \rrbracket) \circ \uparrow_m^{m'} \llbracket \vdash_m \{\psi\}\, P\, \{\phi\} \rrbracket \circ \dot{I}(\llbracket \psi' \rrbracket \nearrow \llbracket \psi \rrbracket)$$

The morphisms with upper and lower lines are cartesian liftings and op-cartesian liftings in the fibration $p : \mathbb{P} \to \mathbb{V}$ of the assertion logic. The codomain of the interpretation of the procedure call $\mathtt{do}\, v \leftarrow p$ is equal to $[\![(\exists v \,.\, \psi) \wedge \phi]\!]$.

The above interpretations largely follow the form of the underlying model of Section 4.3, with the additional information and underlying categorical machinery for grades and assertions here; we now map to $\mathbb{E}$. The interpretation of conditional and loop commands requires some more reasoning.

Conditionals Let p_1, p_2 be the interpretations of each branch of the conditional command:

$$p_1 = [\![\vdash_m \{\psi \wedge e_b = \mathtt{tt}\}\, P_1\, \{\phi\}]\!] \in \mathbb{E}([\![\psi \wedge e_b = \mathtt{tt}]\!], [\![\phi]\!])(m)$$
$$p_2 = [\![\vdash_m \{\psi \wedge e_b = \mathtt{ff}\}\, P_2\, \{\phi\}]\!] \in \mathbb{E}([\![\psi \wedge e_b = \mathtt{ff}]\!], [\![\phi]\!])(m)$$

We consider the cocartesian lifting $\underline{\langle \mathsf{id}_\mathsf{M}, [\![e_b]\!]\rangle}[\![\psi]\!] : [\![\psi]\!] \to \langle \mathsf{id}_\mathsf{M}, [\![e_b]\!]\rangle_* [\![\psi]\!]$. We name its codomain Im. Next, cartesian morphisms $\overline{\mathsf{tm}}(\mathsf{Im}) : \mathsf{tm}^*\mathsf{Im} \to \mathsf{Im}$ and $\overline{\mathsf{fm}}(\mathsf{Im}) : \mathsf{fm}^*\mathsf{Im} \to \mathsf{Im}$ in $\mathbb{P}$ are above the coproduct $(\mathsf{M} \times \mathsf{Bool}, \mathsf{tm}, \mathsf{fm})$ in $\mathbb{V}$. Then the interpretations of the preconditions of P_1, P_2 are inverse images of Im along $\mathsf{tm}, \mathsf{fm} : \mathsf{M} \to \mathsf{M} \times \mathsf{Bool}$:

Lemma 1. $[\![\psi \wedge e_b = \mathtt{tt}]\!] = \mathsf{tm}^*\mathsf{Im}$ *and* $[\![\psi \wedge e_b = \mathtt{ff}]\!] = \mathsf{fm}^*\mathsf{Im}$.

The side condition of the conditional rule ensures that $(\mathsf{Im}, \overline{\mathsf{tm}}(\mathsf{Im}), \overline{\mathsf{fm}}(\mathsf{Im}))$ is a coproduct in $\mathbb{P}$:

Lemma 2. $\Gamma_\mathsf{M} \mid \psi \vdash e_b = \mathtt{tt} \vee e_b = \mathtt{ff}$ *implies* $\mathsf{Im} = \mathsf{tm}_*\mathsf{tm}^*\mathsf{Im} \vee \mathsf{fm}_*\mathsf{fm}^*\mathsf{Im}$.

Therefore the image of the coproduct $(\mathsf{Im}, \overline{\mathsf{tm}}(\mathsf{Im}), \overline{\mathsf{fm}}(\mathsf{Im}))$ by $\dot{I}$ yields a homogeneous coproduct in $\mathbb{E}$. We take the cotupling $[p_1, p_2] \in \mathbb{E}(\mathsf{Im}, [\![\phi]\!])(m)$ with respect to this homogeneous coproduct. We finally define the interpretation of the conditional rule to be the following composite:

$$[\![\vdash_m \{\psi\}\mathtt{if}\, e_b\, \mathtt{then}\, P_1\, \mathtt{else}\, P_2\{\phi\}]\!] = [p_1, p_2] \circ \dot{I}(\underline{\langle \mathsf{id}_\mathsf{M}, [\![e_b]\!]\rangle}[\![\psi]\!]) \in \mathbb{E}([\![\psi]\!], [\![\phi]\!])(m).$$

Loops Fix $N \in \mathbb{N}$, and suppose that $\vdash_m \{\psi_{i+1}\}\, P\, \{\psi_i\}$ is derivable in the graded Hoare logic for each $0 \le i < N$. Let $p_i \in \mathbb{E}([\![\psi_{i+1}]\!], [\![\psi_i]\!])(m)$ be the interpretation $[\![\vdash_m \{\psi_{i+1}\}\, P_i\, \{\psi_i\}]\!]$. We then define a countable family of morphisms (we use here ex falso quodlibet):

$$b_i = \begin{cases} q^{-1}_{\perp_\mathsf{M}, [\![\psi_0]\!], m^N}([\![P]\!]^{(i)}) \in \mathbb{E}(\perp_\mathsf{M}, [\![\psi_0]\!])(m^N) & (i \neq N) \\ p_0 \circ \cdots \circ p_N \qquad\qquad \in \mathbb{E}([\![\psi_N]\!], [\![\psi_0]\!])(m^N) & (i = N) \end{cases}$$

Let $\theta_i \triangleq \mathrm{cod}(b_i)$. Then $\coprod_{i \in \mathbb{N}} \theta_i = \bigvee_{i \in \mathbb{N}} [i]_* \theta_i = [N]_* [\![\psi_N]\!]$ because $[i]_*\theta_i$ is either $\perp_{\mathsf{M} \times \mathsf{Nat}}$ or $[N]_*[\![\psi_N]\!]$. We then send the coproduct $\theta_i \to \coprod_{i \in \mathbb{N}} \theta_i$ by $\dot{I}$ and obtain a homogeneous coproduct in $\mathbb{E}$. By taking the cotupling of all b_i with this homogeneous coproduct, we obtain a morphism $[b_i]_{i \in \mathbb{N}} \in \mathbb{E}([N]_*[\![\psi_N]\!], [\![\psi_0]\!])(m^N)$.

Lemma 3. $\Gamma_\mathsf{M} \mid \psi_N \vdash e_n = \lceil N \rceil$ *implies* $\langle \mathsf{id}_\mathsf{M}, [\![e_N]\!]\rangle_* [\![\psi_N]\!] = [N]_* [\![\psi_N]\!]$.

We then define $[\![\vdash_{m^N} \{\psi_N\}\,\mathtt{loop}\,e_n\,\mathtt{do}\,P\,\{\psi_0\}]\!] = [b_i]_{i\in\mathbb{N}} \circ \dot{I}(\underline{\langle \mathrm{id}_{\mathsf{M}}, [\![e_n]\!]\rangle}[\![\psi_N]\!])$.

Theorem 1 (Soundness of GHL). *For any derivation of a GHL judgement* $\vdash_m \{\phi\}\,P\,\{\psi\}$, *we have* $q_{[\![\phi]\!],[\![\psi]\!],m}[\![\vdash_m \{\phi\}\,P\,\{\psi\}]\!] = [\![P]\!]$.

5.3 Instances of Graded Hoare Logic

We first present a construction of GHL structures from graded monad liftings, which are a graded version of the concept of *monad lifting* [11,19,26].

Definition 10. [Graded Liftings of Monads] Consider two cartesian categories $\mathbb{E}$ and $\mathbb{C}$ and a functor $q\colon \mathbb{E} \to \mathbb{C}$ strictly preserving finite products. We say that a strong M-graded monad $(\dot{T}, \dot{\eta}, \dot{\mu}_{m,m'}, \mathrm{st}_m)$ on $\mathbb{E}$ is an *M-graded lifting* of a strong monad $(T, \eta^T, \mu, \mathrm{st})$ on $\mathbb{C}$ along q if $q \circ \dot{T}m = T \circ q$, $q(\dot{\eta}_\psi) = \eta_{q\psi}$, $q(\dot{\mu}_{m,m',\psi}) = \mu_{q\psi}$, $q(\dot{T}(m_1 \leq m_2)_\psi) = \mathrm{id}$, $q(\dot{\mathrm{st}}_{\psi,\phi,m}) = \mathrm{st}_{q\psi,q\phi}$.

Theorem 2. *Let $\mathbb{V}$ be cartesian category with distributive countable coproducts, and let $p\colon \mathbb{P} \to \mathbb{V}$ be a fibration for assertion logic. Let T be a strong monad on $\mathbb{V}$ and $\dot{T}$ be an M-graded lifting of T along p. Then the M-graded Freyd category $(\mathbb{P}, 1, \dot{\times}, \mathbb{P}_{\dot{T}}, J, \circledast)$ with homogeneous countable coproducts, together with the function $q_{\psi,\phi,m}\colon \mathbb{P}_{\dot{T}}(\psi,\phi)(m) \to \mathbb{V}_T(p\psi, p\phi)$ defined by $q_{\psi,\phi,m}(f) = pf$ is a GHL structure over $(\mathbb{V}, 1, \times, \mathbb{V}_T, I, *)$ and p.*

Before seeing examples, we introduce a notation and fibrations for the assertion logic. Let $p : \mathbb{P} \to \mathbb{V}$ be a fibration for the assertion logic. Below we use the following notation: for $f \in \mathbb{V}(I,J)$ and $\psi \in \mathbb{P}_I$ and $\phi \in \mathbb{P}_J$, by $f : \psi \dot{\to} \phi$ we mean the statement "there exists a morphism $\dot{f} \in \mathbb{P}(\psi,\phi)$ such that $p\dot{f} = f$". Such $\dot{f}$ is unique due to the faithfulness of $p : \mathbb{P} \to \mathbb{V}$.

Example 7 (Example 4: Union Bound Logic). To derive the GHL structure suitable for the semantics of the Union Bound Logic discussed in Example 4, we invoke Theorem 2 by letting p be $p^{\mathbf{Set}} : \mathbf{Pred} \to \mathbf{Set}$ (Example 6), T be the subdistribution monad $\mathcal{D}$ and $\dot{T}$ be the strong $(\mathbb{R}_{\geq 0}, \leq, 0, +)$-graded lifting $\mathcal{U}$ of $\mathcal{D}$ defined by $\mathcal{U}(\delta)(X,P) \triangleq (\mathcal{D}(X), \{d \mid d(X \setminus P) \leq \delta\})$. The induced GHL structure is suitable for the semantics of GHL for Union Bound Logic in Example 4. The soundness of inference rules follow from the GHL structure as we have showed in Section 5.2. To complete the semantics of GHL for the Union Bound Logic, we give the semantics $\langle p \rangle$ of procedures $p \in C^s_{\mathsf{p}}$. Example 4 already gave a semantic condition for these operators:

$$\begin{aligned}
&C^s_{\mathsf{p}}(\phi,\beta,\psi)\\
&= \{\mathtt{sample}_{\mu,e} \mid \forall s. s \in [\![\phi]\!] \implies \Pr_{s' \leftarrow [\![\mathtt{sample}_{\mu,e}]\!](s)}[s' \in [\![\neg\psi]\!] \leq \beta)\}\\
&= \{\mathtt{sample}_{\mu,e} \mid [\![\mathtt{sample}_{\mu,e}]\!] \in \mathbf{Pred}_{\mathcal{U}}([\![\phi]\!],[\![\psi]\!])(\beta)\}
\end{aligned}$$

For any $\mathtt{sample}_{\mu,e} \in C_p(\phi,\beta,\psi)$, the interpretation $\langle \mathtt{sample}_{\mu,e} \rangle$ is $[\![\mathtt{sample}_{\mu,e}]\!]$.

Example 8 (Example 3: Program Counter Security). To derive the GHL structure suitable for GHL with program counter security, we invoke Theorem 2 with:

- The category **ERel** of endorelations defined as follows: an object (X, R) is a pair of $X \in \mathbf{Set}$ and $R \subseteq X \times X$ (i.e. an endorelation R on X) and an arrow $f: (X, R) \to (Y, S)$ is a function $f: X \to Y$ such that $(f \times f)(R) \subseteq S$.
- The fibration for the assertion logic $e : \mathbf{ERel} \to \mathbf{Set}$ given by $(X, R) \mapsto X$ and $f \mapsto f$.
- The writer monad $W_s X = X \times \{\mathtt{tt}, \mathtt{ff}\}^*$ on **Set** with the monoid of bit strings.
- The strong 2^*-graded lifting of W_s along $e : \mathbf{ERel} \to \mathbf{Set}$, given by $\dot{W}_s\sigma(X, R) = (W_s X, \{((x, \sigma'), (y, \sigma')) \mid (x, y) \in R \wedge \sigma' \leq \sigma\})$.

The derived GHL structure is suitable for the semantics of GHL in Example 3. To complete the structure of the logic, we need to interpret two commands $\mathtt{cfTT}, \mathtt{cfFF} \in \mathbf{CExp}$ and set the axioms of commands C_c.

First $[\![\mathtt{cfTT}]\!], [\![\mathtt{cfFF}]\!]: [\![\mathsf{M}]\!] \to 1$ in $\mathbf{ERel}_{\dot{W}}$ are defined by $[\![\mathtt{cfTT}]\!] \equiv (*, \mathtt{tt})$ and $[\![\mathtt{cfFF}]\!] \equiv (*, \mathtt{ff})$. Finally, we define C_c by (recall $\leq$ is prefix ordering of strings):

$$C_\mathsf{c}(\psi, \sigma) = \{\mathtt{cfTT} \mid \mathtt{tt} \leq \sigma\} \cup \{\mathtt{cfFF} \mid \mathtt{ff} \leq \sigma\}.$$

Note, the graded lifting $\dot{W}_s\sigma$ relates only the pair of (x, σ') and (y, σ') with common strings of control flow. Hence, the derivation of proof tree of this logic forces the target program to have the same control flow under the precondition.

Example 9 (GHL Structure from the product comonad). In the category **Set**, the functor $CX \triangleq X \times \mathbb{N}$ forms a coproduct-preserving comonad called the *product comonad.* The right adjoint $I: \mathbf{Set} \to \mathbf{Set}_C$ of the coKleisli resolution of C yields a Freyd category with countable coproducts. We next introduce a $(\mathbb{N}, \leq, 0\max)$-graded lifting $\dot{C}$ of the comonad C along the fibration $p^{\mathbf{Set}}: \mathbf{Pred} \to \mathbf{Set}$. It is defined by $\dot{C}n(X, P) \triangleq (CX, \{(x, m) \in X \times \mathbb{N} \mid x \in P, m \geq n\})$. Similarly, we give an $(\mathbb{N}, \leq, 0\max)$-graded Freyd category $(J, \circledast)$ induced by the graded lifting $\dot{C}$. In this way we obtain a GHL structure.

By instantiating GHL with the above GHL structure, we obtain a program logic useful for reasoning about security levels. For example, when program P_1 requires security level 3 and P_2 requires security level 7, the sequential composition $P_1; P_2$ requires the higher security level 7 ($= \max(3, 7)$).

We give a simple structure for verifying security levels determined by memory access. Fix a function $\mathsf{VarLV}: \mathrm{dom}(\Gamma_\mathsf{M}) \to \mathbb{N}$ assigning security levels to variables. For any expression e, we define its required security level $\mathtt{SecLV}(e) = \sup\{\mathsf{VarLV}(x) \mid x \in \mathrm{FV}(e)\}$. Using this, for each expression e of sort $s \in S$ we introduce a procedure $\mathtt{secr}_e \in \mathbf{PExp}_s$ called *secured expression.* It returns the value of e if the level is high enough, otherwise it returns a meaningless contant:

$$[\![\mathtt{secr}_e]\!](n, \xi) = \text{if } n \geq \mathtt{SecLV}(e) \text{ then } [\![e]\!](\xi) \text{ else a fixed constant } c_s.$$

Secured expressions can be introduced through the following C_p:

$$C^s_\mathsf{p}(\phi, l, \psi) = \{\mathtt{secr}_e \mid e : s, [\![\mathtt{secr}_e]\!] \in \mathbf{Pred}_C([\![\phi]\!], [\![\psi]\!])(l), \mathsf{SecLV}(e) \leq l\}.$$

The pomonoid $(\mathbb{N}, \leq, 0, \max)$ in the above can also be replaced with a join semilattice with a least element $(Q, \leq, \perp, \vee)$. Thus, GHL can be instantiated to a graded comonadic model of security and its associated reasoning.

6 Related Work

Several works have studied abstract semantics of Hoare Logic. Martin et al. [31] give a categorical framework based on traced symmetric monoidal closed categories. They also show that their framework can handle extensions such as separation logic. However their framework does not directly model effects and it cannot accommodate grading as is. Goncharov and Shröder [18] study a Hoare Logic to reason in a generic way about programs with side effects. Their logic and underlying semantics is based on an order-enriched monad and they show a relative completeness result. Similarly, Hasuo [20] studies an abstract weakest precondition semantics based on order-enriched monad. A similar categorical model has also been used by Jacobs [23] to study the Dijkstra monad and the Hoare monad. In the logic by Goncharov and Shröder [18] effects are encapsulated in monadic types, while the weakest precondition semantics by Hasuo [20] and the semantics by Jacobs [23] have no underlying calculus. Moreover, none of them is graded. Maillard et al. [29] study a semantics framework based on the Dijkstra monad for program verification. Their framework enables reasoning about different side effects and it separates specification from computation. Their Dijkstra monad has a flavor of grading but the structure they use is more complex than a pomonoid. Maillard et al. [30] focus on relational program logics for effectful computations. They show how these logics can be derived in a relational dependent type theory, but their logics are not graded.

As we discussed in the introduction, several works have used *grading* structures similar to the one we study in this paper, although often with different names. Katsumata studied monads graded by a pomonoid as a semantic model for effects system [24]. A similar approach has also been studied elsewhere [36,42]. Formal categorical properties of graded monads are pursued by Fujii et al. [13]. Zhang defines a notion of *graded category*, but it differs to ours, and is instead closer to a definition of a graded monad [55]. As we showed in Section 4, graded categories can be constructed both by monads and comonads graded by a pomonoid, and it can also capture graded structures that do not arise from either of them. Milius et al. [33] also studied monads graded by a pomonoid in the context of trace semantics where the grading represents a notion of depth corresponding to trace length. Exploring whether there is a generalization of our work to traces is an interesting future work.

Various works study comonads graded with a semiring structure as a semantic model of contextual computations captured by means of type systems [7,16,44]. In contrast, our graded comonads are graded by a pomonoid. The additive structure of the semiring in those works is needed to merge the gradings of different instances of the same variable. This is natural for the λ-calculus where the context represent multiple inputs, but there is only one conclusion (output). Here instead, we focus on an imperative language. So, we have only one input, the starting memory, and one output, the updated memory. Therefore, it is natural to have just the multiplicative structure of the semiring as a pomonoid. The categorical axiomatics of semiring-graded comonads are studied by Katsumata from the double-category theoretic perspective [25].

Apart from graded monads, several generalizations of monads has been proposed. Atkey introduces *parameterized monads* and corresponding *parameterized Freyd categories* [1], demonstrating that parameterized monads naturally model effectful computations with preconditions and postconditions. Tate defines *productors* with composability of effectful computations controlled by a relational 'effector' structure [53]. Orchard et al. define *category-graded monads*, generalizing graded and parameterised monads via lax functors and sketch a model of Union Bound Logic in this setting (but predicates and graded-predicate interaction are not modelled, as they are here) [41]. Interesting future work is to combine these general models of computational effects with Hoare logic.

7 Conclusion

We have presented a Graded Hoare Logic as a parameterisable framework for reasoning about programs and their side effects, and studied its categorical semantics. The key guiding idea is that grading can be seen as a refinement of effectful computations. This has brought us naturally to graded categories but to fully internalize this refinement idea we further introduced the new notion of graded Freyd categories. To show the generality of our framework we have shown how different examples are naturally captured by it.

We conclude with some reflections on possible future work.

Future work Carbonneaux et al. present a quantitative verification approach for amortized cost analysis via a Hoare logic augmented with multivariate quantities associated to program variables [8]. Judgments $\vdash \{\Gamma; Q\} S \{\Gamma'; Q'\}$ have pre- and post-conditions Γ and Γ' and potential functions Q and Q'. Their approach can be mapped to GHL with a grading monoid representing how the potential functions change. However, the multivariate nature of the analysis requires a more fine-grained connection between the structure of the memory and the structure of grades, which have not been developed yet. We leave this for future work.

GHL allows us to capture the dependencies between assertions and grading that graded program logics usually use. However, some graded systems (e.g. [4]) use more explicit dependencies by allowing grade variables—which are also used for grading polymorphism. We plan to explore this direction in future work.

The setting of graded categories in this work subsumes both graded monads and graded comonads and allows flexibility in the model. However, most of our examples in Section 5.3 are related to graded monads. The literature contains various graded comonad models of data-flow properties: like liveness analysis [44], sensitivities [7], timing and scheduling [16], and information-flow control [40]. Future work is to investigate how these structures could be adopted to GHL for reasoning about programs.

Acknowledgements Katsumata and Sato carried out this research supported by ERATO HASUO Metamathematics for Systems Design Project (No. JPMJER1603), JST. Orchard is supported by EPSRC grant EP/T013516/1. Gaboard is supported by the National Science Foundation under Grant No. 2040222.

References

1. Atkey, R.: Parameterised notions of computation. J. Funct. Program. **19**(3-4), 335–376 (2009). https://doi.org/10.1017/S095679680900728X
2. Barthe, G., Gaboardi, M., Grégoire, B., Hsu, J., Strub, P.: Proving differential privacy via probabilistic couplings. In: 2016 31st Annual ACM/IEEE Symposium on Logic in Computer Science (LICS). pp. 1–10 (2016). https://doi.org/10.1145/2933575.2934554
3. Barthe, G.: An introduction to relational program verification (2020), http://software.imdea.org/~gbarthe/__introrelver.pdf, working Draft
4. Barthe, G., Gaboardi, M., Arias, E.J.G., Hsu, J., Roth, A., Strub, P.: Higher-order approximate relational refinement types for mechanism design and differential privacy. In: Rajamani, S.K., Walker, D. (eds.) Proceedings of the 42nd Annual ACM SIGPLAN-SIGACT Symposium on Principles of Programming Languages, POPL 2015, Mumbai, India, January 15-17, 2015. pp. 55–68. ACM (2015). https://doi.org/10.1145/2676726.2677000
5. Barthe, G., Gaboardi, M., Grégoire, B., Hsu, J., Strub, P.: A Program Logic for Union Bounds. In: 43rd International Colloquium on Automata, Languages, and Programming, ICALP 2016, July 11-15, 2016, Rome, Italy. pp. 107:1–107:15 (2016). https://doi.org/10.4230/LIPIcs.ICALP.2016.107
6. Barthe, G., Köpf, B., Olmedo, F., Zanella-Béguelin, S.: Probabilistic relational reasoning for differential privacy. ACM Trans. Progr. Lang. Syst. **35**(3), 9:1–9:49 (Nov 2013). https://doi.org/10.1145/2492061
7. Brunel, A., Gaboardi, M., Mazza, D., Zdancewic, S.: A core quantitative coeffect calculus. In: Shao, Z. (ed.) Programming Languages and Systems - 23rd European Symposium on Programming, ESOP 2014, ETAPS 2014, Grenoble, France, April 5-13, 2014, Proceedings. Lecture Notes in Computer Science, vol. 8410, pp. 351–370. Springer (2014). https://doi.org/10.1007/978-3-642-54833-8_19
8. Carbonneaux, Q., Hoffmann, J., Shao, Z.: Compositional certified resource bounds. In: Proceedings of the 36th ACM SIGPLAN Conference on Programming Language Design and Implementation, Portland, OR, USA, June 15-17, 2015. pp. 467–478 (2015). https://doi.org/10.1145/2737924.2737955
9. Crole, R.L.: Categories for types. Cambridge University Press (1993)
10. Day, B.: Construction of Biclosed Categories. Ph.D. thesis, School of Mathematics of the University of New South Wales (1970)
11. Filinski, A.: Controlling Effects. Ph.D. thesis, Carnegie Mellon University (1996)
12. Floyd, R.W.: Assigning meanings to programs. Proceedings of Symposium on Applied Mathematics **19**, 19–32 (1967). https://doi.org/10.1007/978-94-011-1793-7_4
13. Fujii, S., Katsumata, S.y., Mellies, P.A.: Towards a formal theory of graded monads. In: International Conference on Foundations of Software Science and Computation Structures. pp. 513–530. Springer (2016). https://doi.org/10.1007/978-3-662-49630-5_30
14. Gaboardi, M., Katsumata, S., Orchard, D., Sato, T.: Graded Hoare Logic and its Categorical Semantics. CoRR **abs/2007.11235** (2020), https://arxiv.org/abs/2007.11235
15. Gaboardi, M., Katsumata, S., Orchard, D.A., Breuvart, F., Uustalu, T.: Combining effects and coeffects via grading. In: Garrigue, J., Keller, G., Sumii, E. (eds.) Proceedings of the 21st ACM SIGPLAN International Conference on Functional Programming, ICFP 2016, Nara, Japan, September 18-22, 2016. pp. 476–489. ACM (2016). https://doi.org/10.1145/2951913.2951939

16. Ghica, D.R., Smith, A.I.: Bounded linear types in a resource semiring. In: Shao, Z. (ed.) Programming Languages and Systems - 23rd European Symposium on Programming, ESOP 2014, Held as Part of the European Joint Conferences on Theory and Practice of Software, ETAPS 2014, Grenoble, France, April 5-13, 2014, Proceedings. Lecture Notes in Computer Science, vol. 8410, pp. 331–350. Springer (2014). https://doi.org/10.1007/978-3-642-54833-8_18
17. Gibbons, J.: Comprehending ringads - for phil wadler, on the occasion of his 60th birthday. In: Lindley, S., McBride, C., Trinder, P.W., Sannella, D. (eds.) A List of Successes That Can Change the World - Essays Dedicated to Philip Wadler on the Occasion of His 60th Birthday. Lecture Notes in Computer Science, vol. 9600, pp. 132–151. Springer (2016). https://doi.org/10.1007/978-3-319-30936-1_7
18. Goncharov, S., Schröder, L.: A Relatively Complete Generic Hoare Logic for Order-Enriched Effects. In: 28th Annual ACM/IEEE Symposium on Logic in Computer Science, LICS 2013, New Orleans, LA, USA, June 25-28, 2013. pp. 273–282. IEEE Computer Society (2013). https://doi.org/10.1109/LICS.2013.33
19. Goubault-Larrecq, J., Lasota, S., Nowak, D.: Logical relations for monadic types. Mathematical Structures in Computer Science **18**(6), 1169–1217 (2008). https://doi.org/10.1017/S0960129508007172
20. Hasuo, I.: Generic weakest precondition semantics from monads enriched with order. Theoretical Computer Science **604**, 2 – 29 (2015). https://doi.org/https://doi.org/10.1016/j.tcs.2015.03.047, coalgebraic Methods in Computer Science
21. Ivašković, A., Mycroft, A., Orchard, D.: Data-Flow Analyses as Effects and Graded Monads. In: Ariola, Z.M. (ed.) 5th International Conference on Formal Structures for Computation and Deduction (FSCD 2020). Leibniz International Proceedings in Informatics (LIPIcs), vol. 167, pp. 15:1–15:23. Schloss Dagstuhl–Leibniz-Zentrum für Informatik, Dagstuhl, Germany (2020). https://doi.org/10.4230/LIPIcs.FSCD.2020.15
22. Jacobs, B.: Categorical Logic and Type Theory. Elsevier (1999)
23. Jacobs, B.: Dijkstra and Hoare monads in monadic computation. Theor. Comput. Sci. **604**, 30–45 (2015). https://doi.org/10.1016/j.tcs.2015.03.020
24. Katsumata, S.: Parametric effect monads and semantics of effect systems. In: Jagannathan, S., Sewell, P. (eds.) The 41st Annual ACM SIGPLAN-SIGACT Symposium on Principles of Programming Languages, POPL '14, San Diego, CA, USA, January 20-21, 2014. pp. 633–646. ACM (2014). https://doi.org/10.1145/2535838.2535846
25. Katsumata, S.: A Double Category Theoretic Analysis of Graded Linear Exponential Comonads. In: Baier, C., Lago, U.D. (eds.) Foundations of Software Science and Computation Structures - 21st International Conference, FOSSACS 2018, ETAPS 2018, Thessaloniki, Greece, April 14-20, 2018, Proceedings. Lecture Notes in Computer Science, vol. 10803, pp. 110–127. Springer (2018). https://doi.org/10.1007/978-3-319-89366-2_6
26. Katsumata, S., Sato, T., Uustalu, T.: Codensity lifting of monads and its dual. Logical Methods in Computer Science **14**(4) (2018). https://doi.org/10.23638/LMCS-14(4:6)2018
27. Kura, S.: Graded Algebraic Theories. In: International Conference on Foundations of Software Science and Computation Structures. pp. 401–421. Springer (2020). https://doi.org/10.1007/978-3-030-45231-5_21
28. Levy, P.B.: Locally graded categories. Slides available at http://www.cs.bham.ac.uk/~pbl/papers/locgrade.pdf (2019)

29. Maillard, K., Ahman, D., Atkey, R., Martínez, G., Hritcu, C., Rivas, E., Tanter, É.: Dijkstra monads for all. Proc. ACM Program. Lang. **3**(ICFP), 104:1–104:29 (2019). https://doi.org/10.1145/3341708
30. Maillard, K., Hritcu, C., Rivas, E., Muylder, A.V.: The next 700 relational program logics. Proc. ACM Program. Lang. **4**(POPL), 4:1–4:33 (2020). https://doi.org/10.1145/3371072
31. Martin, U., Mathiesen, E.A., Oliva, P.: Hoare Logic in the Abstract. In: Ésik, Z. (ed.) Computer Science Logic. pp. 501–515. Springer Berlin Heidelberg, Berlin, Heidelberg (2006). https://doi.org/10.1007/11874683_33
32. Melliès, P., Zeilberger, N.: Functors are Type Refinement Systems. In: Rajamani, S.K., Walker, D. (eds.) Proceedings of the 42nd Annual ACM SIGPLAN-SIGACT Symposium on Principles of Programming Languages, POPL 2015, Mumbai, India, January 15-17, 2015. pp. 3–16. ACM (2015). https://doi.org/10.1145/2676726.2676970
33. Milius, S., Pattinson, D., Schröder, L.: Generic Trace Semantics and Graded Monads. In: Moss, L.S., Sobocinski, P. (eds.) 6th Conference on Algebra and Coalgebra in Computer Science (CALCO 2015). Leibniz International Proceedings in Informatics (LIPIcs), vol. 35, pp. 253–269. Schloss Dagstuhl–Leibniz-Zentrum fuer Informatik (2015). https://doi.org/10.4230/LIPIcs.CALCO.2015.253
34. Moggi, E.: Notions of computation and monads. Inf. Comput. **93**(1), 55–92 (1991). https://doi.org/10.1016/0890-5401(91)90052-4
35. Molnar, D., Piotrowski, M., Schultz, D., Wagner, D.A.: The program counter security model: Automatic detection and removal of control-flow side channel attacks. In: Won, D., Kim, S. (eds.) Information Security and Cryptology - ICISC 2005, 8th International Conference, Seoul, Korea, December 1-2, 2005, Revised Selected Papers. Lecture Notes in Computer Science, vol. 3935, pp. 156–168. Springer (2005). https://doi.org/10.1007/11734727_14
36. Mycroft, A., Orchard, D.A., Petricek, T.: Effect Systems Revisited - Control-Flow Algebra and Semantics. In: Probst, C.W., Hankin, C., Hansen, R.R. (eds.) Semantics, Logics, and Calculi - Essays Dedicated to Hanne Riis Nielson and Flemming Nielson on the Occasion of Their 60th Birthdays. Lecture Notes in Computer Science, vol. 9560, pp. 1–32. Springer (2016). https://doi.org/10.1007/978-3-319-27810-0_1
37. Nielson, H.R.: A Hoare-like proof system for analysing the computation time of programs. Science of Computer Programming **9**(2), 107–136 (1987). https://doi.org/10.1016/0167-6423(87)90029-3
38. Nielson, H.R., Nielson, F.: Semantics with applications, vol. 104. Springer (1992)
39. Olmedo, F.: Approximate Relational Reasoning for Probabilistic Programs. Ph.D. thesis, Technical University of Madrid (2014)
40. Orchard, D., Liepelt, V., III, H.E.: Quantitative program reasoning with graded modal types. Proc. ACM Program. Lang. **3**(ICFP), 110:1–110:30 (2019). https://doi.org/10.1145/3341714
41. Orchard, D., Wadler, P., III, H.E.: Unifying graded and parameterised monads. In: New, M.S., Lindley, S. (eds.) Proceedings Eighth Workshop on Mathematically Structured Functional Programming, MSFP@ETAPS 2020, Dublin, Ireland, 25th April 2020. EPTCS, vol. 317, pp. 18–38 (2020). https://doi.org/10.4204/EPTCS.317.2
42. Orchard, D.A., Petricek, T., Mycroft, A.: The semantic marriage of monads and effects. CoRR **abs/1401.5391** (2014), http://arxiv.org/abs/1401.5391

43. Petricek, T., Orchard, D.A., Mycroft, A.: Coeffects: Unified static analysis of context-dependence. In: Fomin, F.V., Freivalds, R., Kwiatkowska, M.Z., Peleg, D. (eds.) Automata, Languages, and Programming - 40th International Colloquium, ICALP 2013, Riga, Latvia, July 8-12, 2013, Proceedings, Part II. Lecture Notes in Computer Science, vol. 7966, pp. 385–397. Springer (2013). https://doi.org/10.1007/978-3-642-39212-2_35
44. Petricek, T., Orchard, D.A., Mycroft, A.: Coeffects: a calculus of context-dependent computation. In: Jeuring, J., Chakravarty, M.M.T. (eds.) Proceedings of the 19th ACM SIGPLAN international conference on Functional programming, Gothenburg, Sweden, September 1-3, 2014. pp. 123–135. ACM (2014). https://doi.org/10.1145/2628136.2628160
45. Pitts, A.M.: Categorical logic. Tech. rep., University of Cambridge, Computer Laboratory (1995)
46. Power, J.: Generic models for computational effects. Theoretical Computer Science **364**(2), 254–269 (2006). https://doi.org/10.1016/j.tcs.2006.08.006
47. Power, J., Thielecke, H.: Environments, continuation semantics and indexed categories. In: Abadi, M., Ito, T. (eds.) Theoretical Aspects of Computer Software. pp. 391–414. Springer Berlin Heidelberg, Berlin, Heidelberg (1997)
48. Sato, T.: Approximate Relational Hoare Logic for Continuous Random Samplings. In: Birkedal, L. (ed.) The Thirty-second Conference on the Mathematical Foundations of Programming Semantics, MFPS 2016, Carnegie Mellon University, Pittsburgh, PA, USA, May 23-26, 2016. Electronic Notes in Theoretical Computer Science, vol. 325, pp. 277–298. Elsevier (2016). https://doi.org/10.1016/j.entcs.2016.09.043
49. Sato, T., Barthe, G., Gaboardi, M., Hsu, J., Katsumata, S.: Approximate Span Liftings: Compositional Semantics for Relaxations of Differential Privacy. In: 34th Annual ACM/IEEE Symposium on Logic in Computer Science, LICS 2019, Vancouver, BC, Canada, June 24-27, 2019. pp. 1–14 (2019). https://doi.org/10.1109/LICS.2019.8785668
50. Smirnov, A.: Graded monads and rings of polynomials. J. Math. Sci. **151**(3), 3032–3051 (2008). https://doi.org/10.1007/s10958-008-9013-7
51. Staton, S.: Freyd categories are Enriched Lawvere Theories. Electronic Notes in Theoretical Computer Science **303**, 197 – 206 (2014). https://doi.org/https://doi.org/10.1016/j.entcs.2014.02.010, proceedings of the Workshop on Algebra, Coalgebra and Topology (WACT 2013)
52. Staton, S.: Commutative semantics for probabilistic programming. In: Yang, H. (ed.) Programming Languages and Systems - 26th European Symposium on Programming, ESOP 2017, ETAPS 2017, Uppsala, Sweden, April 22-29, 2017, Proceedings. Lecture Notes in Computer Science, vol. 10201, pp. 855–879. Springer (2017). https://doi.org/10.1007/978-3-662-54434-1_32
53. Tate, R.: The sequential semantics of producer effect systems. In: Giacobazzi, R., Cousot, R. (eds.) The 40th Annual ACM SIGPLAN-SIGACT Symposium on Principles of Programming Languages, POPL '13, Rome, Italy - January 23 - 25, 2013. pp. 15–26. ACM (2013). https://doi.org/10.1145/2429069.2429074
54. Wood, R.J.: V-indexed categories, chap. 2, pp. 126–140. No. 661 in Lecture Notes in Mathematics, Springer (1978). https://doi.org/10.1007/BFb0061362
55. Zhang, J.J.: Twisted graded algebras and equivalences of graded categories. Proceedings of the London Mathematical Society **3**(2), 281–311 (1996). https://doi.org/10.1112/plms/s3-72.2.281

Do Judge a Test by its Cover
Combining Combinatorial and Property-Based Testing *

Harrison Goldstein(✉)[1], John Hughes[2], Leonidas Lampropoulos[3], and Benjamin C. Pierce[1]

[1] University of Pennsylvania, Philadelphia PA 19104, USA
[2] Chalmers University of Technology and Quviq AB, 412 96 Gothenburg, Sweden
[3] University of Maryland, College Park MD 20742, USA

Abstract. *Property-based testing* uses randomly generated inputs to validate high-level program specifications. It can be shockingly effective at finding bugs, but it often requires generating a very large number of inputs to do so. In this paper, we apply ideas from *combinatorial testing*, a powerful and widely studied testing methodology, to modify the distributions of our random generators so as to find bugs with fewer tests. The key concept is *combinatorial coverage*, which measures the degree to which a given set of tests exercises every possible choice of values for every small combination of input features.

In its "classical" form, combinatorial coverage only applies to programs whose inputs have a very particular shape—essentially, a Cartesian product of finite sets. We generalize combinatorial coverage to the richer world of algebraic data types by formalizing a class of *sparse test descriptions* based on regular tree expressions. This new definition of coverage inspires a novel *combinatorial thinning* algorithm for improving the coverage of random test generators, requiring many fewer tests to catch bugs. We evaluate this algorithm on two case studies, a typed evaluator for System F terms and a Haskell compiler, showing significant improvements in both.

Keywords: Combinatorial testing, Combinatorial coverage, QuickCheck, Property-based testing, Regular tree expressions, Algebraic data types

1 Introduction

Property-based testing, popularized by tools like *QuickCheck* [7], is a principled way of testing software that focuses on functional specifications rather than suites of input-output examples. A property is a formula like

$$\forall x.\ P(x,\ f(x)),$$

* For the full version, including all appendices, visit `https://harrisongoldste.in/papers/quick-cover.pdf`.

✉ `hgo@seas.upenn.edu`

N. Yoshida (Ed.): ESOP 2021, LNCS 12648, pp. 264–291, 2021.
https://doi.org/10.1007/978-3-030-72019-3_10

where f is the function under test and P is some executable logical relationship between an input x and the output $f(x)$. The test harness generates random values for x, hoping to either uncover a counterexample—an x for which $\neg P(x, f(x)))$, indicating a bug—or else provide confidence that f is correct with respect to P.

With a well-designed random test case generator, property-based testing has a non-zero probability of generating *every* valid test case (up to a given size limit); property-based testing is thus guaranteed to find any bug that can be provoked by an input below the size limit... eventually. Unfortunately, since each input is generated independently, random testing may end up repeating the same or similar tests many times before happening across the specific input which provokes a bug. This poses a particular problem in settings like *continuous integration*, where feedback is needed quickly—it would be nice to have an automatic way to guide the generator to a more interesting and diverse set of inputs, "thinning" the distribution to find bugs with fewer tests.

Combinatorial testing, an elegant approach to testing from the software engineering literature [2,16,17], offers an attractive metric for judging which tests are most interesting. In its classical presentation, combinatorial testing advocates choosing tests to maximize *t-way coverage* of a program's input space—i.e., to exercise all possible choices of concrete values for every combination of t input parameters. For example, suppose a program p takes Boolean parameters `w`, `x`, `y`, and `z`, and suppose we want to test that p behaves well for every choice of values for every pair of these four parameters. If we choose carefully, we can check all such choices—all 2*-way interactions*—with just five test cases:

```
1.  w = False   x = False   y = False   z = False
2.  w = False   x = True    y = True    z = True
3.  w = True    x = False   y = True    z = True
4.  w = True    x = True    y = False   z = True
5.  w = True    x = True    y = True    z = False
```

You can check for yourself: for any two parameters, every combination of values for these parameters is covered by some test. For example, "`w = False` and `x = False`" is covered by #1, while both "`w = True` and `x = True`" and "`w = True` and `y = True`" are covered by #5. Any other test case we could come up with would check a redundant set of 2-way interactions. Thus, we get 100% pairwise coverage with just five out of the $2^4 = 16$ possible inputs. This advantage improves exponentially with the number of parameters.

Why is this interesting? Because surveys of real-world systems have shown that bugs are often provoked by specific choices of just a few parameters [16]. Indeed, one study involving a distributed database at NASA found that, out of 100 known failures, 93 were caused by 2-way parameter interactions; the remaining 7 failures were each caused by no more than 6 parameters interacting together [14]. This suggests that combinatorial testing is an effective way to choose test cases for real systems.

If combinatorial coverage can be used to concentrate bug-finding power into small sets of tests, it is natural to wonder whether it could also be used to thin the distribution of a random generator. So far, combinatorial testing has mostly been applied in settings where the input to a program is just a vector of parameters, each drawn from a small finite set. Could we take it further? In particular, could we transfer ideas from combinatorial testing to the richer setting addressed by *QuickCheck*—i.e., functional programs whose inputs are drawn from structured, potentially infinite data types like lists and trees?

Our first contribution is showing how to generalize the definition of combinatorial coverage to work with *regular tree expressions*, which themselves generalize the algebraic data types found in most functional languages. Instead of covering combinations of parameter choices, we measure coverage of *test descriptions*—concise representations of sets of tests, encoding potentially interesting interactions between data constructors. For example, the test description cons(true, ◇false) describes the set of Boolean lists that have true as their first element, followed by at least one false somewhere in the tail.

Our second contribution is a method for enhancing property-based testing using combinatorial coverage. We propose an algorithm that uses combinatorial coverage information to thin an existing random generator, leading it to more interesting test suites that find bugs more often. A concrete realization of this algorithm in a tool called *QuickCover* was able, in our experiments, to guide random generation to find bugs using an average of 10× fewer tests than *QuickCheck*. While *generating* test suites is (considerably) slower, *running* the tests can be much faster. As such, *QuickCover* excels in settings where tests are particularly costly to run, as well as in situations like continuous-integration, when the cost of test generation is amortized over many runs of the test suite.

In summary, we offer these contributions:

- We generalize the notion of combinatorial coverage to work over a set of *test descriptions* and show how this new definition generalizes to algebraic data types with the help of regular tree expressions (Section 3). Section 4 describes the technical details behind the specific way we choose to represent these descriptions.
- We propose a process for guiding the test distribution of an existing random generator based on our generalized notion of combinatorial coverage (Section 5).
- Finally, we demonstrate, with two case studies, that *QuickCover* can find bugs using significantly fewer tests (Section 6) than pure random testing.

We conclude with an overview of related work (Section 7), and ideas for future work (Section 8).

2 Classical Combinatorial Testing

To set the stage, we begin with a brief review of "classical" combinatorial testing.

Combinatorial testing measures the "combinatorial coverage" of test suites, aiming to find more bugs with fewer tests. Standard presentations [16] are phrased in terms of a number of separate input parameters. Here, for notational consistency with the rest of the paper, we will instead assume that a program takes a single input consisting of a tuple of values.

Assume we are given some finite set $\mathcal{C}$ of *constructors*, and consider the set of n-tuples over $\mathcal{C}$:

$$\{\mathsf{tuple}_n(C_1,\ \ldots,\ C_n) \mid C_1,\ \ldots,\ C_n \in \mathcal{C}\}$$

(The "constructor" tuple_k is not strictly needed in this section, but it makes the generalization to constructor trees and tree regular expressions in Section 3 smoother.) We can use these tuples to represent test inputs to systems. For example a web application might be tested under configurations

$$\mathsf{tuple}_4(\mathsf{Safari},\ \mathsf{MySQL},\ \mathsf{Admin},\ \mathsf{English})$$

in order to verify some end-to-end property of the system.

A *specification* of a set of tuples is written informally using notation like:

$$\mathsf{tuple}_4(\mathsf{Safari}{+}\mathsf{Chrome},\ \mathsf{Postgres}{+}\mathsf{MySQL},\ \mathsf{Admin}{+}\mathsf{User},\ \mathsf{French}{+}\mathsf{English})$$

This specification restricts the set of valid tests to those that have valid browsers in the first position, valid databases in the second, and so on. Specifications are thus a lot like types—they pick out a set of valid tests from some larger set. We define this notation precisely in Section 3.

To define combinatorial coverage, we introduce the notion of *partial* tuples—i.e., tuples where some elements are left indeterminate (written $\top$). For example:

$$\mathsf{tuple}_4(\mathsf{Chrome},\ \top,\ \mathsf{Admin},\ \top).$$

A description is *compatible* with a specification if its concrete (non-$\top$) constructors are valid in the positions where they appear. Thus, the description above is compatible with our web-app configuration specification, while this one is not:

$$\mathsf{tuple}_4(\mathsf{MySQL},\ \mathsf{MySQL},\ \mathsf{French},\ \top)$$

We say a test *covers* a description—which, conversely, *describes* the test—when the tuple matches the description in every position that does not contain $\top$. For example, the description

$$\mathsf{tuple}_4(\mathsf{Chrome},\ \top,\ \mathsf{Admin},\ \top)$$

describes these tests:

$$\mathsf{tuple}_4(\mathsf{Chrome},\ \mathsf{MySQL},\ \mathsf{Admin},\ \mathsf{English})$$
$$\mathsf{tuple}_4(\mathsf{Chrome},\ \mathsf{MySQL},\ \mathsf{Admin},\ \mathsf{French})$$
$$\mathsf{tuple}_4(\mathsf{Chrome},\ \mathsf{Postgres},\ \mathsf{Admin},\ \mathsf{English})$$
$$\mathsf{tuple}_4(\mathsf{Chrome},\ \mathsf{Postgres},\ \mathsf{Admin},\ \mathsf{French})$$

Finally, we call a description *t-way* if it fixes exactly t constructors, leaving the rest as $\top$.

Now, suppose a system under test takes a tuple of configuration values as input. Given some correctness property (e.g., the system does not crash), a test for the system is simply a particular tuple, while a test *suite* is a set of tuples. We can then define *combinatorial coverage* as follows:

Definition 1. *The t-way* combinatorial coverage *of a test suite is the proportion of t-way descriptions, compatible with a given specification, that are covered by some test in the suite.*

We say that t is the *strength* of the coverage.

A test suite with 100% 2-way coverage for the present example can be quite small. For example,

$$\begin{aligned}&\mathsf{tuple}_4(\mathsf{Chrome},\ \mathsf{Postgres},\ \mathsf{Admin},\ \mathsf{English})\\&\mathsf{tuple}_4(\mathsf{Chrome},\ \mathsf{MySQL},\ \mathsf{User},\ \mathsf{French})\\&\mathsf{tuple}_4(\mathsf{Safari},\ \mathsf{Postgres},\ \mathsf{User},\ \mathsf{French})\\&\mathsf{tuple}_4(\mathsf{Safari},\ \mathsf{MySQL},\ \mathsf{Admin},\ \mathsf{French})\\&\mathsf{tuple}_4(\mathsf{Safari},\ \mathsf{MySQL},\ \mathsf{User},\ \mathsf{English})\end{aligned}$$

achieves 100% coverage with just five tests. The fact that a single test covers many different descriptions is what makes combinatorial testing work: while the number of descriptions that must be covered is combinatorially large, a single test can cover combinatorially many descriptions. In general, for a tuple of size n, the number of descriptions is given by $\binom{n}{t}$ ways to choose t parameters multiplied by the number of distinct values each parameter can take on.

3 Generalizing Coverage

Of course, inputs to programs are often more complex than just tuples of enumerated values, especially in the world of functional programming. To apply the ideas of combinatorial coverage in this richer world, we generalize tuples to *constructor trees* and tuple specifications to *regular tree expressions*. We can then give a generalized definition of test descriptions that makes sense for algebraic data types, setting up for a more powerful definition of combinatorial coverage.

A *ranked alphabet* Σ is a finite set of atomic *data constructors*, each with a specified *arity*. For example, the ranked alphabet

$$\Sigma_{\mathsf{list(bool)}} \triangleq \{(\mathsf{cons},\ 2),\ (\mathsf{nil},\ 0),\ (\mathsf{true},\ 0),\ (\mathsf{false},\ 0)\}$$

defines the constructors needed to represent lists of Booleans. Given a ranked alphabet Σ, the set of *trees* over Σ is the least set $\mathcal{T}_\Sigma$ that satisfies the equation

$$\mathcal{T}_\Sigma = \{C(t_1,\ \ldots,\ t_n) \mid (C,\ n) \in \Sigma \wedge t_1,\ \ldots,\ t_n \in \mathcal{T}_\Sigma\}.$$

Regular tree expressions are a compact and powerful tool for specifying sets of trees [9,10]. They are generated by the following syntax:

$$\begin{aligned} e \triangleq\ & \top \\ |\ & e_1 + e_2 \\ |\ & \mu X.\ e \\ |\ & X \\ |\ & C(e_1,\ \ldots,\ e_n) \text{ for } (C,\ n) \in \Sigma \end{aligned}$$

Each of these operations has an analog in standard regular expressions over strings: + corresponds to disjunction of regular expressions, μ corresponds to iteration, and the parent-child relationship corresponds to concatenation. These expressions give us a rich language for describing tree structures.

The *denotation* function $[\![\cdot]\!]$ mapping regular tree expressions to sets of trees is the least function satisfying the equations:

$$\begin{aligned} [\![\top]\!] &= \mathcal{T}_\Sigma \\ [\![C(e_1,\ \ldots,\ e_n)]\!] &= \{C(t_1,\ \ldots,\ t_n) \mid t_i \in [\![e_i]\!]\} \\ [\![e_1 + e_2]\!] &= [\![e_1]\!] \cup [\![e_2]\!] \\ [\![\mu X.\ e]\!] &= [\![e[\mu X.\ e/X]]\!] \end{aligned}$$

Regular tree expressions subsume standard first-order algebraic data type definitions. For example, the Haskell definition

```
data BoolList = Cons Bool BoolList | Nil
```

is equivalent to the regular tree expression

$$\mu X.\ \mathsf{cons}(\mathsf{true} + \mathsf{false},\ X) + \mathsf{nil}.$$

Crucially for our purposes, regular tree expressions can also be used to define sets of trees that cannot be described with plain ADTs. For example, the expression

$$\mathsf{cons}(\mathsf{true} + \mathsf{false},\ \mathsf{nil})$$

denotes all single-element Boolean lists, while

$$\mu X.\ \mathsf{cons}(\mathsf{true},\ X) + \mathsf{nil}$$

describes the set of lists that only contain true. Regular tree expressions can even express constraints like "true appears at some point in the list":

$$\mu X.\ \mathsf{cons}(\top,\ X) + \mathsf{cons}(\mathsf{true},\ \mu Y.\ \mathsf{cons}(\top,\ Y) + \mathsf{nil})$$

This machinery smoothly generalizes the structures we saw in Section 3. Tuples are just a special form of trees, while specifications and test descriptions can be written as regular tree expressions. This gives us most of what we need to define algebraic data types.

Recall the definition of t-way combinatorial coverage: "the proportion of (1) t-way descriptions, (2) compatible with a given specification, that (3) are covered by some test in the suite." What does this mean in the context of regular tree expressions and trees?

Condition (3) is easy: a test (i.e., a tree) t covers a test description (a regular tree expression) d if $t \in [\![d]\!]$.

For (2), consider some regular tree expression τ representing an algebraic data type that we would like to cover. We say that a description d is compatible with τ if $[\![\tau]\!] \cap [\![d]\!] \neq \varnothing$. As with string regular expressions, this can be checked efficiently.

The only remaining question is (1): which set of t-way descriptions to use. We argue in the next section that the set of *all* regular tree expressions is too broad, and we offer a simple and natural alternative.

4 Sparse Test Descriptions

A naïve way to generalize the definition of t-way descriptions to regular tree expressions would be to first define the *size* of a regular tree expression as the number of operators (constructors, $+$, or μ) in it and then define a t-way description to be any regular tree expression of size t. However, this approach does not specialize nicely to the classical case; for example the description

$$\mathsf{tuple}_4(\mathsf{Safari} + \mathsf{Chrome},\ \top,\ \top,\ \top)$$

would be counted as "4-way" (3 constructors and 1 "+" operator), even though it is covered by *every* well-formed test. Worse, "interesting" descriptions are often quite large. For example, the smallest possible description of lists in which true is followed by false,

$$\mu X.\ \mathsf{cons}(\top,\ X) + \mathsf{cons}(\mathsf{true},\ \mu Y.\ \mathsf{cons}(\top,\ Y) + \mathsf{cons}(\mathsf{false},\ \mu Z.\ \mathsf{cons}(\top,\ Z) + \mathsf{nil}))$$

has size $t = 14$. We want a representation that packs as much information as possible into small descriptions, making t-way coverage meaningful for small values of t and increasing the complexity of the interactions captured by our definition of coverage.

In sum, we want a definition of coverage that straightforwardly specializes to the tuples-of-constructors case and that captures interesting structure with small descriptions.

Our proposed solution, described next, takes inspiration from temporal logic. We first encode an "eventually" ($\diamond$) operator that allows us to write the expression from above much more compactly as $\diamond\mathsf{cons}(\mathsf{true},\ \diamond\mathsf{false})$. This can be read as "somewhere in the tree, there is a cons node with a true node to its left and a false node somewhere in the tree to its right." Then we define a restricted form of *sparse test descriptions* using just $\diamond$, $\top$, and constructors.

4.1 Encoding "Eventually"

The "eventually" operator can actually be encoded using the regular tree expression operators we have already defined—i.e., we can add it without adding any formal power. First, define the set of *templates* for the ranked alphabet Σ:

$$\mathbb{T} \triangleq \{C(\top_1, \ldots, \top_{i-1}, [\,], \top_{i+1} \ldots, \top_n) \mid (C, n) \in \Sigma, 1 \le i \le n\}$$

That is, for each constructor C in Σ, the set of templates $\mathbb{T}$ contains $C([\,], \top, \ldots, \top)$, $C(\top, [\,], \top, \ldots, \top)$, etc., all the way to $C(\top, \ldots, \top, [\,])$, enumerating every way to place one hole in the constructor and fill every other argument slot with $\top$. (Nullary constructors are ignored.) Then we define "next" ($\circ e$) and "eventually" ($\diamond e$) as

$$\circ e \triangleq \sum_{T \in \mathbb{T}} T[e]$$

$$\diamond e \triangleq \mu X.\ e + \circ X$$

where $T[e]$ is the replacement of $[\,]$ in T with e.[3] Intuitively, $\circ e$ describes any tree $C(t_1, \ldots, t_n)$ in which e describes some direct child (i.e., t_1, t_2, and so on), while $\diamond e$ describes anything described by e, plus (unrolling the μ) anything described by $\circ e$, $\circ\circ e$, and so on.

This is not the only way to design a compact, expressive subset of regular tree expressions, but our evaluation shows that this has useful properties. In addition, the $\diamond$ notation gives an elegant way to write descriptions like the one from the previous section ($\diamond$cons(true, $\diamond$false),), neatly capturing "somewhere in the tree" constraints that would require many more symbols in the bare language of regular tree expressions.

4.2 Defining Coverage

Even in the language with just $\diamond$, $\top$, and constructors, there is still a fair amount of freedom in how we define the set of t-way descriptions. In this section we present one possibility that we have found to be useful in practice; in Section 8 we discuss another interesting option.

The set of *sparse test descriptions* for a given Σ is the trees generated by

$$\begin{aligned} d \triangleq\ & \top \\ & \mid \diamond C(d_1, \ldots, d_n) \text{ for } (C, n) \in \Sigma, \end{aligned}$$

that is, trees consisting of constructors prefixed by $\diamond$ and $\top$. We call these descriptions "sparse" because they match specific ancestor-descendant arrangements of

[3] This construction is why we choose to deal with finite ranked alphabets: if Σ were infinite, $\mathbb{T}$ would be infinite, and $\circ e$ would be an infinite term that is not expressible as a standard regular tree expression.

constructors but place no restriction on the constructors in between, due to the "eventually" before each constructor.

Sparse test descriptions are designed to be compact, useful in practice, and compatible with the classical definition of coverage. For that reason we aim to keep them as information-dense as possible. First, we do not include the μ operator directly, instead relying on $\diamond$: indeed, $\diamond$ captures a pattern of recursion that is general enough to express interesting non-local constraints while keeping description complexity low. Similarly, we do not need to include the + operator: any test that covers any test that covers either $C(d_1, \ldots, d_n)$ or $D(d_1, \ldots, d_m)$ will also necessarily cover $C(d_1, \ldots, d_n) + D(d_1, \ldots, d_m)$.

Removing explicit uses of μ and + does limit the expressive power of sparse test descriptions a little—for example it rules out complex mutually recursive definitions. However, we do not intend to use descriptions to specify entire languages, only fragments of languages that we hope to cover with testing. Naturally, there are many other possible formats for test descriptions that would be interesting to explore—we leave that for future work. In this paper, we chose to make descriptions very compact while preserving most of their expressive power, and the case studies in Section 6 demonstrate that such a choice works well in at least two challenging domains that are relevant to programming languages as a whole.

Finally, we define the size of a description based on the number of constructors it contains. Intuitively, a t-way description is one with t constructors; however, in order to be consistent with the classical definition, we omit constructors whose types permit no alternatives. For example, all of the tuple constructors (e.g. tuple_4 in our running example) are left out of the size calculation. This makes t-way sparse test description coverage specialize to exactly classical t-way parameter interaction coverage for the case of tuples of sums of nullary constructors.

Sparse descriptions work as expected for types like

$$\mathsf{tuple}_4(\mathsf{Safari}{+}\mathsf{Chrome},\ \mathsf{Postgres}{+}\mathsf{MySQL},\ \mathsf{Admin}{+}\mathsf{User},\ \mathsf{French}{+}\mathsf{English}).$$

Despite some stray occurrences of $\diamond$, as in

$$\diamond\mathsf{tuple}_4(\diamond\mathsf{Chrome},\ \diamond\mathsf{MySQL},\ \top,\ \top),$$

the descriptions still describe the same sets of tests as the standard tuple descriptions without the uses of $\diamond$. Thus, our new definition of combinatorial coverage generalizes the classical one.

These descriptions capture a rich set of test constraints in a compact form. The real proof of this is in our evaluation results—see Section 6 for those—but a few more examples may help illustrate.

Boolean Lists As a first example, consider the type of Boolean lists:

$$\tau_{\mathsf{list(bool)}} \triangleq \mu X.\ \mathsf{cons}(\mathsf{true} + \mathsf{false},\ X) + \mathsf{nil}.$$

The set of all 2-way descriptions that are compatible with $\tau_{\mathsf{list(bool)}}$ is:

$$\diamond\mathsf{cons}(\diamond\mathsf{true},\ \top) \quad \diamond\mathsf{cons}(\diamond\mathsf{false},\ \top) \quad \diamond\mathsf{cons}(\top,\ \diamond\mathsf{nil})$$
$$\diamond\mathsf{cons}(\top,\ \diamond\mathsf{cons}(\top,\ \top)) \quad \diamond\mathsf{cons}(\top,\ \diamond\mathsf{true}) \quad \diamond\mathsf{cons}(\top,\ \diamond\mathsf{false})$$

Unpacking the notation, $\diamond\mathsf{cons}(\diamond\mathsf{true},\ \top)$ describes the set of trees where "at some point in the tree there is a cons node with a true node somewhere in its left child."

Arithmetic Expressions Consider the type of simple arithmetic expressions over the constants 0, 1, and 2:

$$\tau_{\mathsf{expr}} \triangleq \mu X.\ \mathsf{add}(X,\ X) + \mathsf{mul}(X,\ X) + \mathsf{0} + \mathsf{1} + \mathsf{2}.$$

This type has 2-way descriptions like

$$\diamond\mathsf{add}(\diamond\mathsf{mul}(\top,\ \top),\ \top) \text{ and } \diamond\mathsf{mul}(\top,\ \diamond\mathsf{add}(\top,\ \top)),$$

which capture different nestings of addition and multiplication.

System F For a more involved example, let's look at some 2-way sparse descriptions for a much more complex data structure: terms of the polymorphic lambda calculus, System F.

$$\tau \triangleq \mathcal{U} \mid \tau_1 \to \tau_2 \mid n \mid \forall.\tau$$
$$e \triangleq () \mid n \mid \lambda\tau.\ e \mid (e_1\ e_2) \mid \Lambda.e \mid (e\ \tau)$$

(We use de Bruijn indices for variable binding, meaning that each variable occurrence in the syntax tree is represented by a natural number indicating which enclosing abstraction it was bound by.)

System F syntax can be represented using a regular tree expression like

$$\mu X.\ \mathsf{unit} + \mathsf{var}(\textsc{Var}) + \mathsf{abs}(\textsc{Type},\ X) + \mathsf{app}(X,\ X) + \mathsf{tabs}(X) + \mathsf{tapp}(X,\ \textsc{Type}),$$

where TYPE is defined in a similar way and VAR represents natural-number de Bruijn indices.

This already admits useful 2-way descriptions like

$$\diamond\mathsf{app}(\diamond\mathsf{abs}(\top,\ \top),\ \top) \text{ and } \diamond\mathsf{app}(\diamond\mathsf{app}(\top,\ \top),\ \top),$$

which capture relationships between lambda abstractions and applications. In Section 6.1, we use descriptions like these to find bugs in an evaluator for System F expressions; they ensure that our test suite adequately covers different nestings of abstractions and applications that might provoke bugs.

With a little domain-specific knowledge, we can make the descriptions capture even more. When setting up our case study in Section 6.2, which searches for bugs in GHC's strictness analyzer, we found that it was often useful to track coverage of the *seq* function, which takes two functions as arguments, executes the first for any side-effects (e.g., exceptions), and then executes the second. Modifying our regular expression type to include *seq* as a first-class constructor results in 2-way descriptions now include interactions like

$$\diamond\mathsf{seq}(\diamond\mathsf{app}(\top,\ \top),\ \top)$$

that encode interactions of *seq* with other System F constructors. These interactions are crucial for finding bugs in a strictness analyzer, since *seq* gives fine-grained control over the evaluation order within a Haskell expression.

5 Thinning Generators with QuickCover

Having generalized the definition of combinatorial coverage to structured data types, the next step is to explore ways of using coverage to improve property-based testing.

When we first approached this problem, we planned to follow the conventional combinatorial testing methodology of generating *covering arrays* [38], i.e., test suites with 100% t-way coverage for a given t. Rather than use an unbounded stream of random tests—the standard methodology in property-based testing—we would test properties using just the tests in some pre-generated covering array. However, we encountered two major problems with this approach. First, as t grows, covering arrays become frighteningly expensive to generate. While there are efficient methods for generating covering arrays in special cases like 2-way coverage [8], general algorithms for generating compact covering arrays are complex and often slow [23]. Second, we found that covering arrays for sets of test descriptors in the format described above did not do particularly well at finding bugs! In a series of preliminary experiments with one of our case studies, we found that with 4-way coverage (the highest we could generate in reasonable time), our covering arrays did not reliably catch all of the bugs in our test system. Fortunately, after some more head scratching and experimenting, we discovered an alternate approach that works quite well. The trick is to embrace the randomness that makes property-based testing so effective.

In the remainder of this section, we first present an algorithm that uses combinatorial coverage to "thin" a random generator, guiding it to more interesting inputs. Rather than generating a fixed set of tests in the style of covering arrays, this approach produces an unbounded stream of interesting test inputs. Then we discuss some concrete details behind *QuickCover*, the Haskell implementation of our algorithm that we used to obtain the experimental results in Section 6.

5.1 Online Generator Thinning

The core of our algorithm is *QuickCheck*'s standard generate-and-test loop. Given a test generator `gen` and a property `p`, *QuickCheck* generates inputs repeatedly until either (1) the property fails, or (2) a time limit is reached.

```
QuickCheck(gen, p):
  repeat LIMIT times:
    # Generate 1 new input
    x = gen()
    # Check the property
    if !p(x), return False
  return True
```

LIMIT is chosen based on the user's specific *testing budget*, and it can vary significantly in practice. In the experiments below, we know *a priori* that a bug exists in the program, so we set LIMIT to infinity and just run tests until the property fails.

Our algorithm modifies this basic one to use combinatorial coverage information when choosing the next test to run.

```
QuickCover(strength, fanout, gen, p):
  coverage = initCoverage()
  repeat LIMIT times:
    # Generate fanout potential inputs
    xs = listOf(gen(), fanout)
    # Find the input with the best improved coverage
    x = argmax[x in xs](
      coverageImprovement(x, coverage, strength) )
    # Check the property
    if !p(x), return False
    # Update the coverage information
    coverage = updateCoverage(x, coverage, strength)
  return True
```

The key idea is that, instead of generating a single input at each iteration, we generate several (controlled by the parameter fanout) and select the one that increases combinatorial coverage the most. We test the property on that input and, if it does not fail, update the coverage information based on the test we ran and keep going.

This algorithm is generic with respect to the representation for coverage information, but the particular choice of data structure and interpretation makes a significant difference in both efficiency and effectiveness. In our implementation, coverage information is represented by a multi-set of descriptions:

```
initCoverage():
  return emptyMultiset()

coverageImprovement(x, coverage, strength):
  ds = descriptions(x, strength)
  return sum([ 1 / (count(d, coverage) + 1)
               for d in ds ])

updateCoverage(x, coverage, strength):
  return union(descriptions(x, strength), coverage)
```

At the beginning, the multi-set is empty; as testing progresses, each test is evaluated based on `coverageImprovement`. If a description d had previously been covered n times, it contributes $\frac{1}{n+1}$ to the score. For example, if a test input covers d_1 and d_2, where previously d_1 was not covered and d_2 was covered 3 times, the total score for the test input would be $1 + 0.25 = 1.25$.

At first glance, one might think of a simpler approach based on sets instead of multi-sets. Indeed, this was the first thing we tried, but it turned out to perform substantially worse than the multiset-based one in our experiments. The reason is that just covering each description once turns out not to be sufficient to find all bugs, and, once most descriptions have been covered, this approach essentially degenerates to normal random testing. By contrast, the multi-set representation continues to be useful over time; after each description has been covered once, the algorithm begins to favor inputs that cover descriptions a second time, then a third time, and so on. This allows *QuickCover* to generate arbitrarily large test suites that continue to benefit from combinatorial coverage.

Keeping track of coverage information like this does create some overhead.[4] For each test that *QuickCover* considers (including those that are never run), it needs to analyze which descriptions the test covers and check those against the current multi-set. This overhead means that *QuickCover* is often much slower than *QuickCheck* with respect to to generating tests. In the next section, we explore use cases for *QuickCover* that overcome this overhead by running fewer tests.

6 Evaluation

Since *QuickCover* adds some overhead to generating tests, one might expect that it will be particularly well suited to situations where each test may be run many times. The primary goal of our experimental evaluation was to test this hypothesis.

[4] The overhead introduced is highly variable and based largely on the exact implementation of the underlying test generator. Appendix A goes into slightly more detail on the asymptotics, but broadly speaking the time it *QuickCover* to generate a test is linear in the fan-out and exponential in the coverage strength.

Of course, running the same test repeatedly *on the same code* is pointless: if it were ever going to fail, it would do so on the first run (ignoring the thorny possibility of "flaky tests" due to nondeterminism [25]). However, running the same test on *successive versions of the code* is not only useful; it is standard practice in two common settings: *regression testing*, i.e., checking that code is still working after changes, and especially *continuous integration*, where regression tests are run automatically every time a developer checks in a new version of the code. In these settings, the overhead introduced by generating many tests and discarding some without running them can be amortized, since the same tests may be reused very many times, so that the cost of generating the test suite becomes less important than the cost of running it.

In order to validate this theory, we designed two experiments using *QuickCover*. The primary goal of these experiments was to answer the question: Does *QuickCover* actually reduce the number of tests needed to find bugs in a real system?

Both case studies answer this question in the affirmative. The first case study, in particular, demonstrates a situation where *QuickCover* needs an average 10× fewer tests to find bugs, compared to pure random testing. We choose an evaluator for System F terms as our example because it allows us to test how *QuickCover* behaves in a small but realistic scenario that requires a fairly complex random testing setup. Our second case study expands on results from Pałka et al. [32], scaling up and applying *QuickCover* to find bugs in the Glasgow Haskell Compiler (GHC) [27].

A secondary goal of our evaluation was to understand whether the generator thinning overhead is *always* too high to make *QuickCover* useful for real-time property-based testing, or if there are any cases where using *QuickCover* would yield a wall-clock improvement even if tests are only run once. Our second case study answers this question in the affirmative.

6.1 Case Study: Normalization Bugs in System F

Our first case study uses combinatorial coverage to thin a highly tuned and optimized test generator for System F [12, 35] terms. The generator produces well-typed System F terms by construction (no mean feat on its own) and is tuned to produce a highly varied distribution of different terms. Despite all the care put into the base generator, we found that modifying the test distribution using *QuickCover* results in a test suite that finds bugs with many fewer inputs.

Generating "interesting" programs (for finding compiler bugs, for example) is an active research area. For instance, a generator for well-typed simply typed lambda-terms has been used to reveal bugs in GHC [6, 20, 32], while a generator for C programs that avoid "undefined behaviors" has been used to find many bugs in production compilers [24, 34, 41] The cited studies are all examples of *differential testing*, where different compilers (or different versions of the same compiler) were run against each other on the same inputs to reveal discrepancies. Similarly, for the present case study we tested different evaluation strategies for System F, comparing the behavior of various buggy versions to a reference implementation.

Recall the definition of System F from Section 4.2. Let $e[v/n]$ stand for substituting v for variable n in e, and $e \uparrow_n$ for "lifting"—incrementing the indices of all variables above n in e. Then, for example, the standard rule for substituting a type τ for variable n inside a type abstraction $\Lambda. e$ requires lifting τ and incrementing the de Bruijn index of the variable being substituted by one:

$$(\Lambda. e)[\tau/n] = \Lambda. e[\tau \uparrow_0 /n + 1]$$

Here are two ways to get this wrong: forget to lift the variables, or forget to increment the index. Those bugs would lead to the following erroneous definitions (the missing operation is shown in red):

$$(\Lambda. e)[\tau/n] = \Lambda. e[\tau \uparrow_0 /n + 1] \quad \text{and} \quad (\Lambda. e)[\tau/n] = \Lambda. e[\tau \uparrow_0 /n + 1].$$

Inspired by errors like these (specifically in the substitution and variable lifting functions), we inserted bugs by hand to create 19 "mutated" versions of two different evaluation relations. (The bugs are described in detail in Appendix C.) The two evaluation relations simplify terms in slightly different ways: the first implements standard big-step evaluation (`eval`), and the second uses a parallel evaluation relation to fully normalize terms (`peval`). (We chose to check both evaluation orders, since some mutations only cause a bug in one implementation or the other.) Since we were interested in bugs in either evaluation order, we tested a joint property:

```
eval e == eval_mutated e && peval e == peval_mutated e
```

Starting with a highly tuned generator for System F terms as our baseline, we used both *QuickCheck* and *QuickCover* to generate a stream of test values for `e` and measured the average number of tests required to find a bug (i.e., Mean-Tests-To-Failure, or MTTF) for each approach.

Surprisingly, we found little or no difference in MTTF between 2-way, 3-way, and 4-way testing, but changing the fan-out did make a large impact. Figure 1 shows both absolute MTTF for various choices of fan-out ($\log_{10}$ scale) and the performance improvement as a ratio of un-thinned MTTF to thinned MTTF. All choices of fan-out produced better MTTF results than the baseline, but higher values of fan-out tended to be more effective on average. In our best experiment, a fan-out of 30 found a bug in an average of 15× fewer tests than the baseline; the overall average was about 10× better. Figure 2 shows the total MTTF improvement across 19 bugs, compared to the maximum theoretical improvement. If our algorithm were able to perfectly pick the best test input every time, the improvement would be proportional to the fan-out (i.e., it is impossible for our algorithm be more than 10× better with a fan-out of 10). On the other hand, if combinatorial coverage were irrelevant to test failure, then we would expect the *QuickCover* test suites to have the *same* MTTF as *QuickCheck*. It is clear from the figure that *QuickCover* is really quite effective in this setting: for small

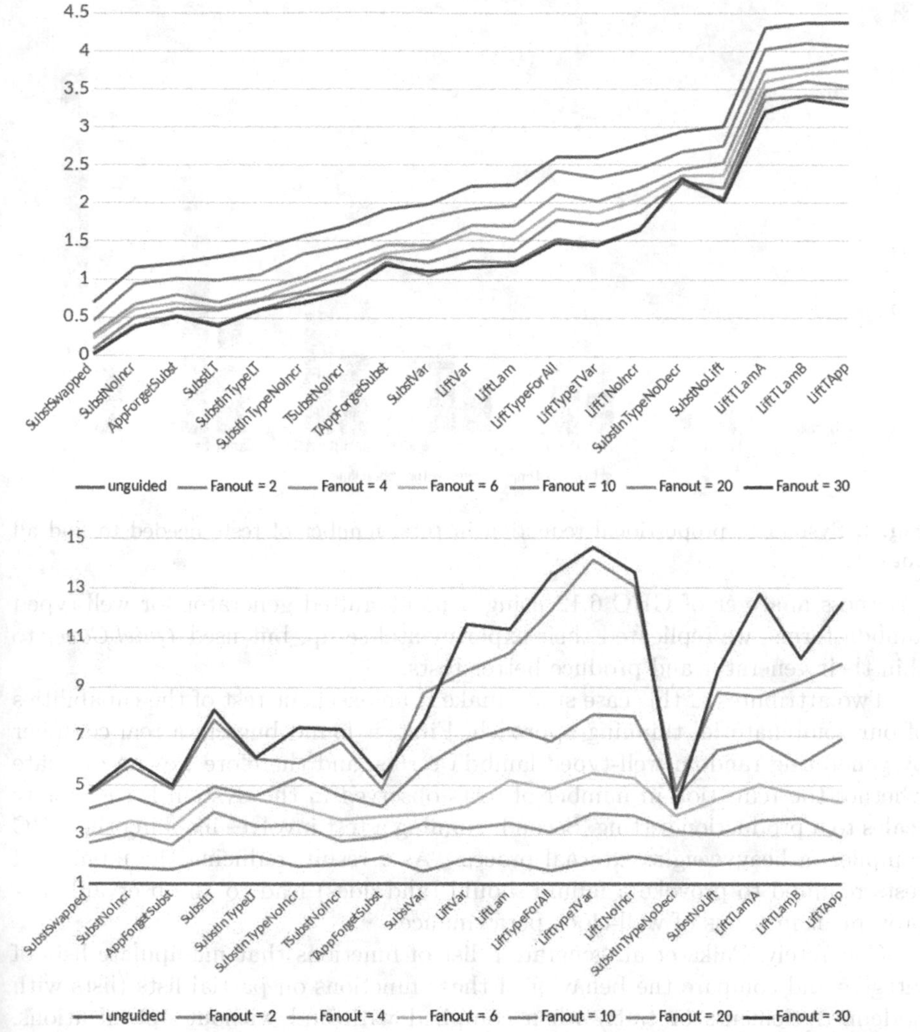

Fig. 1. Top: System F MTTF, $\log_{10}$ scale, plotted in order of MTTF for un-thinned random tests, $t = 2$. Bottom: System F MTTF ratio of MTTF for un-thinned random tests to MTTF for *QuickCover*, $t = 2$.

fan-outs, it is very close to the theoretical optimum, and with a fan-out of 30 it achieves about $\frac{1}{3}$ of the potential improvement—that is, three *QuickCover* test cases are more likely to provoke a bug than thirty *QuickCheck* ones.

6.2 Case Study: Strictness Analysis Bugs in GHC

To evaluate how our approach scales, and to investigate whether *QuickCover* can be used not only to reduce the number of tests required but also to speed up bug-finding, we replicated the case study of Pałka et al. [32], which found bugs in the

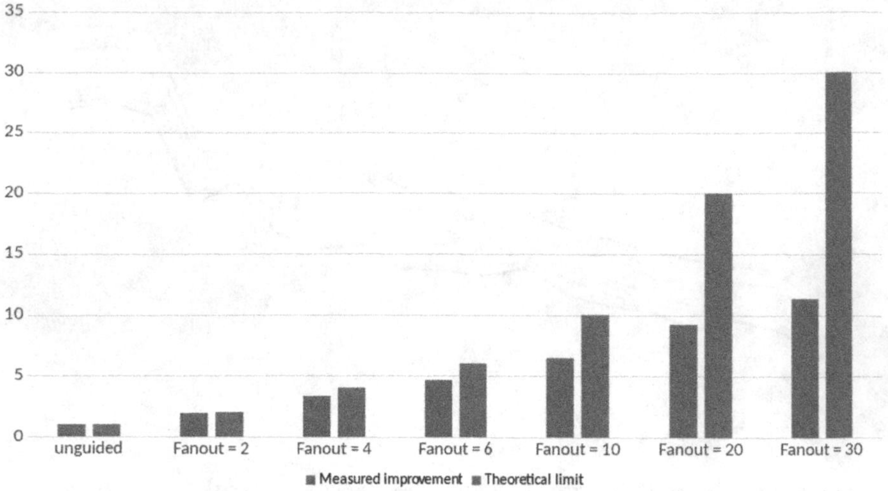

Fig. 2. System F, proportional reduction in total number of tests needed to find all bugs.

strictness analyzer of GHC 6.12 using a hand-crafted generator for well-typed lambda terms; we replicated their experimental setup, but used *QuickCover* to thin their generator and produce better tests.

Two attributes of this case study make it an excellent test of the capabilities of our combinatorial thinning approach. First, it found bugs in a real compiler by generating random well-typed lambda terms, and therefore we can evaluate whether the reduction in number of tests observed in the System F case study scales to a production setting. Second, running a test involves invoking the GHC compiler, a heavyweight external process. As a result, reducing the number of tests required to provoke a failure should (and does) lead to an observable improvement in terms of wall-clock performance.

Concretely, Pałka et al. generate a list of functions that manipulate lists of integers and compare the behavior of these functions on partial lists (lists with undefined elements or tails) when compiled with and without optimizations, another example of differential testing. They uncover errors in the strictness analyzer component of GHC's optimizer that lead to inconsistencies where the un-optimized version of the compiled code correctly fails with an error while the optimized version prints something to the screen before failing:

Input	$-O0$ Output	$-O2$ Output
`[undefined]`	`Exception`	`[Exception]`
`[1,undefined]`	`Exception`	`[1,Exception]`
`[1,2,undefined]`	`Exception`	`[1,2,Exception]`

Finally, to balance the costly compiler invocation with the similarly costly smart generation process, Pałka et al. group 1000 generated functions together in a single module to be compiled; this number was chosen to strike a precise 50-50 balance between generation time and compilation/execution time for each generated module. Since our thinning approach itself introduces approximately a 25% overhead in generation time, we increased the number of tests per module to 1250 to maintain the same balance and make a fair comparison.

We ran our experiments in a Virtual Box running Ubuntu 12.04 (a version old enough to allow for executing GHC 6.12.1), with 4GB RAM in a host machine running i7-8700 @ 3.2GHz. We performed 100 runs of the original case study and 100 runs of our variant that adds combinatorial thinning, using a fan-out of 2 and a strength of 2. We found that our approach reduces the mean number of *tests* required from 21268 ± 1349 to 14895 ± 1056, a 42% improvement, and reduces the mean *time* to failure from 193 ± 13 seconds to 149 ± 12, a 30% improvement.

7 Related Work

A detailed survey of the (vast) combinatorial testing literature can be found in [30]. Here we discuss just the most closely related work, in particular, other attempts to generalize combinatorial testing to structured and infinite domains. We also discuss other approaches to property based testing with similar goals to to ours, such as adaptive random testing and coverage-guided fuzzing.

7.1 Generalizations of Combinatorial Testing

Salecker and Glesner [37] extend combinatorial testing to sets of terms generated by a context-free grammar. Their approach cleverly maps context-free grammar derivations up to some depth k to sets of parameter choices; then it uses standard full-coverage test suite generation algorithms to pick a subset of derivations to test. The main limitation of this approach is the parameter k. By limiting the derivation depth, this approach only defines coverage over a finite subset of the input type. By contrast, our definition of coverage works over infinite types by exploiting the recursive nature of the $\diamond$ operator. We focus on description size rather than term size, which provides more flexibility for "packing" multiple descriptions into a single test.

Another approach to combinatorial testing of context-free inputs is due to Lämmel and Schulte [19]. Their system also uses a depth bound, but it provides the user finer-grained control. At each node in the grammar, the user is free to limit the coverage requirements and prune unnecessary tests. This is an elegant solution for situations where the desired interactions are known *a priori*. Unfortunately, this approach needs to be re-tuned manually to every specific type and use-case, so it is not the general solution we were after.

Finally, Kuhn et al. [15] present a notion of *sequence covering arrays* to describe combinatorial coverage of sequences of events. We believe that t-way sequence covering arrays in their system are equivalent to $(2t-1)$-way full-coverage test suites of the appropriate list type in ours. They also have a reasonably efficient algorithm for generating covering arrays in this specialized case.

Our idea to use regular tree expressions for coverage is partly inspired by Usaola et al. [40] and Mariani et al. [26]. Rather than generate a set of terms to cover an ADT, these works generate strings to cover (i.e. match in every possible way) a particular regular expression. This turns out to be quite a different problem, but these explorations led us to consider coverage in context of of formal languages.

7.2 Comparison with Enumerative Property-Based Testing

Another approach to property-based testing research is based on enumeration of small test cases, rather than random generation. Tools like *SmallCheck* [36] offer guarantees that there is no counterexample smaller than a certain limit, and moreover always report the smallest counterexample when it exists. To compare our approach with this type of tool, we repeated our System F evaluation with a variety of enumerative testing tools.

We first tried SmallCheck, which enumerates all test cases up to a given *depth*. Unfortunately, the number of System F terms rises very rapidly with the depth: SmallCheck quickly enumerated 708 terms of depth up to three, but could not enumerate all terms of depth four within 20 minutes of CPU time.[5] Only one of the 19 bugs we planted was provoked by any of those 708 terms.

However, SmallCheck wastes effort generating syntactically correct terms that are not type correct; only 140 of the 708 were well-typed. *Lazy SmallCheck* [36] exploits laziness in property preconditions to discard many test cases in a group—in this case, all those terms that fail a type-check in the same way are discarded together. Because well-typedness is such a strong precondition, Lazy SmallCheck is able to dramatically reduce the number of terms needed at each depth, enabling us to increase the depth limit to 4, and generate over five million terms. The result was a much more comprehensive test suite than normal SmallCheck, but it still only found 8 out of our 19 bugs.

The problem here is that the smallest counterexamples we are searching for are quite small terms, but may nevertheless have a few fairly deep nodes in their syntax trees. More recent enumerative tools, such as LeanCheck [3], enumerate test cases in *size* order, instead of in *depth* order, thus reaching terms with just a few deeper nodes much earlier in the enumeration. For this example, LeanCheck runs out of memory after about 11 million tests. but this was enough to find all but four of the planted bugs.

However, LeanCheck does not use the Lazy SmallCheck optimization, and so is mostly testing ill-typed terms, for which our property holds vacuously. *SciFe* [18] enumerates in size order *and* uses the Lazy SmallCheck optimization, with good results. It is hard to apply SciFe, which is designed to test Scala, to our Haskell code, so instead we created a Lazy SmallCheck variant that enumerates in size order. With this variant, we could find all of the planted bugs, with counterexample sizes varying from 5 to 14. Lazy SmallCheck does not report the number of tests needed to find a counterexample, just the size at which it was found, together with the number of test cases of each size. We can therefore only

[5] Compiled with ghc -O2, on an Intel i7-6700k with 32GB of RAM under Windows 10.

give a lower bound for the number of tests needed to find each bug. Figure 3 plots this lower bound against the average number of tests needed by QuickCheck and by QuickCover. For these bugs, it is clear that the enumerative approach is not competitive with QuickCheck, let alone with QuickCover. The improvement in the numbers of tests needed ranges from 1.7 to 5.5 *orders of magnitude*, with a mean across all the bugs of 3.3 orders of magnitude.

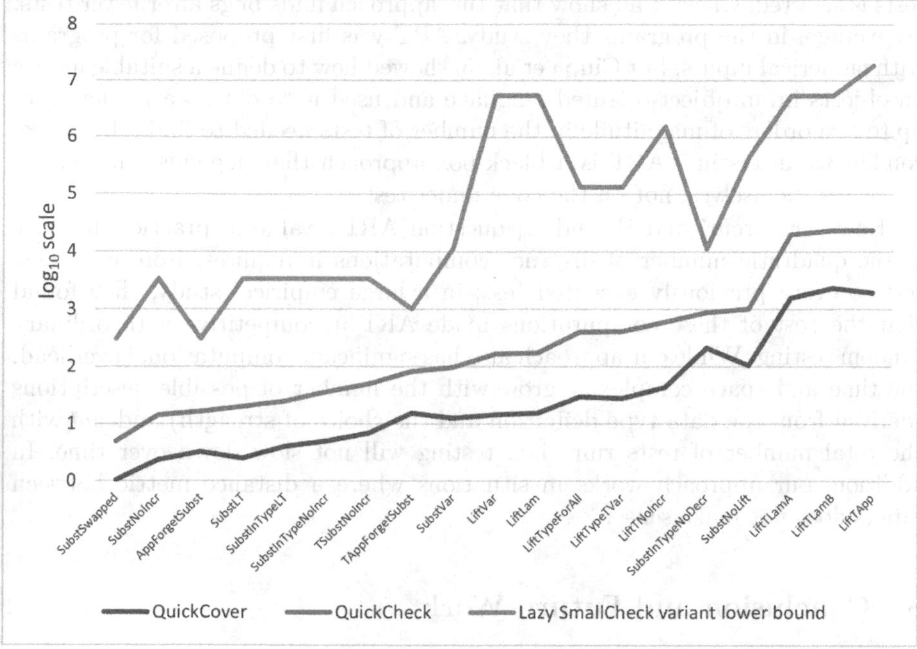

Fig. 3. System F MTTF for QuickCheck and QuickCover, and the *lower bound* on the number of tests run by our Lazy SmallCheck variant, $\log_{10}$ scale.

7.3 Comparison with Fuzzing Techniques

Coverage-guided fuzzing tools like AFL [22] can be viewed as a way of using a different form of feedback (branch instead of combinatorial coverage) to improve the generation of random inputs by finding more "interesting" tests. Fuzzing is a huge topic [43] that has exploded in popularity recently, with researchers evaluating the benefits of using more forms of feedback [13, 31], incorporating learning [28,33] or symbolic [39,42] techniques, and bringing the benefits of these methods to functional programming [11, 21]. One fundamental difference, however, is that all of these techniques are *online* and *grey-box*: they instrument and execute the program on various inputs in order to obtain feedback. In contrast, combinatorial coverage can be computed without any knowledge of the code itself, therefore providing a convenient black-box alternative that can be valuable when the same test suite is to be used for many versions of the code (such as in regression testing) or when executing the code is costly (such as when testing production compilers).

Chen et al.'s *adaptive random testing* (ART) [4] uses an algorithm that, like *QuickCover*'s, generates a set of random tests and selects the most interesting to run. Rather than using combinatorial coverage, ART requires a *distance metric* on test cases—at each step, the candidate which is farthest from the already-run tests is selected. Chen et al. show that this approach finds bugs after fewer tests, on average, in the programs they study. ART was first proposed for programs with numerical inputs, but Ciupa et al. [5] showed how to define a suitable metric on objects in an object-oriented language and used it to obtain a reduction of up to two orders of magnitude in the number of tests needed to find a bug. Like combinatorial testing, ART is a black-box approach that depends only on the test cases themselves, not on the code under test.

However, Arcuri and Briand [1] question ART's value in practice, because of the quadratic number of distance computations it requires, from each new test to every previously executed test; in a large empirical study, they found that the cost of these computations made ART uncompetitive with ordinary random testing. While our approach also has significant computational overhead, the time and space complexity grow with the number of possible descriptions (derived from the data type definition and the choice of strength) and *not* with the total number of tests run—i.e., testing will not slow down over time. In addition, our approach works in situations where a distance metric between inputs does not make sense.

8 Conclusion and Future Work

We have presented a generalized definition of combinatorial coverage and an effective way to use that definition for property-based testing, generalizing the definition of combinatorial coverage to work in the realm of algebraic data types with the help of regular tree expressions. Our sparse test descriptions provide a robust way to look at combinatorial testing, which specializes to the classical approach. We use these sparse descriptions as a basis for *QuickCover*—a tool that thins a random generator to increase combinatorial coverage. Two case studies show that *QuickCover* is useful in practice, finding bugs using an average of 10× fewer tests.

The rest of this section sketches a number of potential directions for further research.

8.1 Variations

Our experiments show that sparse test descriptions are a good way to define combinatorial coverage for algebraic data types, but they are certainly not the the only way. Here we discuss some variations and why they might be interesting to explore.

Representative Samples of Large Types Perhaps it is possible to do combinatorial testing with ADTs by having humans decide exactly which trees to cover. This approach is already widely used in combinatorial testing to deal with types like machine integers that, though technically finite, are much too large for testing to efficiently cover all their "constructors." For example, if a human tester knows (by reading the code, or because they wrote it) that it contains an if-statement guarded by `x < 5`, they might choose to cover

$$\mathtt{x} \in \{-2147483648,\ 0,\ 4,\ 5,\ 6,\ 2147483647\}.$$

The tester might choose values around 5 because those are important to the specific use case and boundary values and 0 to check for common edge-cases. Concretely, this practice means that instead of trying to cover $\mathsf{tuple}_3(\textsc{Int},\ \mathsf{true}+\mathsf{false},\ \mathsf{true}+\mathsf{false})$, the tester covers the specification

$$\mathsf{tuple}_3(-2147483648 + 0 + 4 + 5 + 6 + 2147483647,\ \mathsf{true}+\mathsf{false},\ \mathsf{true}+\mathsf{false}).$$

In our setting, this might mean choosing a representative set of *constructor trees* to cover, and then treating them like a finite set. In much the same way as with integers, rather than cover

$$\mathsf{tuple}_3(\tau_{\mathsf{list(bool)}},\ \mathsf{true}+\mathsf{false},\ \mathsf{true}+\mathsf{false}),$$

we could treat a selection of lists as atomic constructors, and cover the specification

$$\mathsf{tuple}_3(\boxed{[]} + \boxed{[\mathsf{true},\ \mathsf{false}]} + \boxed{[\mathsf{false},\ \mathsf{false},\ \mathsf{false}]},\ \mathsf{true}+\mathsf{false},\ \mathsf{true}+\mathsf{false})$$

which has 2-way descriptions like

$$\mathsf{tuple}_3(\boxed{[]},\ \top,\ \mathsf{false}) \quad \text{and} \quad \mathsf{tuple}_3(\boxed{[\mathsf{true},\ \mathsf{false}]},\ \mathsf{true},\ \top).$$

Just as testers choose representative sets of integers, they could choose sets of trees that they think are interesting and only cover those trees. Of course, the set of all trees for a type is usually much larger and more complex than the set of integers, so this approach may not be as practical for structured types as for integers. Still, it is possible that small amounts of human intervention could help guide the choice of descriptions to cover.

Type-Tagged Constructors Another variation to our approach would change the way that ADTs are translated into constructor trees. In Appendix B we show a simple example of a `Translation` for lists of Booleans, but an interesting problem arises if we consider *lists of* lists of Booleans. The most basic approach would be to use the same constructors (`LCNil` and `LCCons`) for both "levels" of list. For example, `[[True]]` would become (with a small abuse of notation)

```
LCCons (LCCons LCTrue LCNil) LCNil.
```

Depending on the application, it might actually make more sense to use different constructors for the different list types (`[Bool]` vs. `[[Bool]]`). For example, `[[True]]` could instead be translated as

```
LCOuterCons (LCInnerCons LCTrue LCInnerNil) LCInnerNil
```

(with a slight abuse of notation), allowing for a broader range of potential test descriptions. This observation can be generalized to any polymorphic ADT: any time a single constructor is used at multiple types, it is likely beneficial to differentiate between them by translating to constructor tree nodes tagged with a monomorphized type.

Pattern Descriptions A third potential variation is a modification to make test descriptions a bit less sparse. Recall that sparse test descriptions are defined as

$$d \triangleq \top \mid \diamond C(d_1, \ \ldots, \ d_n).$$

What if we chose this instead?

$$d \triangleq \diamond d'$$
$$d' \triangleq C(d'_1, \ \ldots, \ d'_n)$$

In the former case, every relationship is "eventual": there is never a requirement that a particular constructor appear *directly* beneath another. In the latter case, the descriptions enforce a direct parent-child relationship, and we simply allow the expression to match anywhere in the term. We might call this class "pattern" test descriptions.

We chose sparse descriptions for this work because putting $\diamond$ before every constructor leaves more opportunities for nodes matching different descriptions to be "interleaved" within a term, leading to smaller test suites in general. In some small experiments, this alternative proposal seemed to perform similarly across the board but worse in a few cases. Even so, experimenting with the use of eventually in descriptions might lead to interesting new ideas.

8.2 Combinatorial Coverage of More Types

Our sparse tree description definition of combinatorial coverage is focused on inductive algebraic types. While these encompass a wide range of the types that functional programmers use, it is far from everything. One interesting extension would generalize descriptions to co-inductive types. We actually think that the current definition might almost suffice—regular tree expressions can denote infinite structures, so this generalization would likely only affect our algorithms and the implementation of *QuickCover*. We also should be able to include Generalized Algebraic Data Types (GADTs) without too much hassle. The biggest unknown is function types, which seem to require something more powerful than regular tree expressions to describe; indeed, it is not clear that combinatorial testing even makes sense for higher-order values.

8.3 Regular Tree Expressions for Directed Generation

As we have shown, regular tree expressions are a powerful language for picking out subsets of types. In this paper, we mostly focused on automatically generating small descriptions, but it might be possible to apply this idea more broadly for specifying sets of tests. One straightforward extension would be to use the same machinery that we use for *QuickCover* but, instead of covering an automatically generated set of descriptions, ensure that, at a minimum, some manually specified set of expressions is covered. For example, we could use a modified version of our algorithm to generate a test set where

$$\mathsf{nil},\ \mathsf{cons}(\top,\ \mathsf{nil}),\ \text{and}\ \mu X.\ \mathsf{cons}(\mathsf{true},\ X) + \mathsf{nil}$$

are all covered. (Concretely, this would be a test suite containing, at a minimum, the empty list, a singleton list, and a list containing only true.) This might be useful for cases where the testers know *a priori* that certain shapes of inputs are important to test, but they still want to explore random inputs with those shapes.

A different approach would be to create a tool that synthesizes *QuickCheck* generators that only generate terms matching a particular regular tree expression. This idea, related to work on adapting *branching processes* to control test distributions [29], would make it easy to write highly customized generators and meticulously control the generated test suites.

Acknowledgments

Thank you to Calvin Beck, Filip Niksic, and Irene Yoon for help with the early development of these ideas. Thanks to Kostis Sagonas, Alexandra Silva, and Andrew Hirsch for feedback along the way. This work was supported by NSF awards #1421243, *Random Testing for Language Design* and #1521523, *Expeditions in Computing: The Science of Deep Specification*, by the Defense Advanced Research Projects Agency (DARPA) under Contract No. HR0011-18-C-0011, by the United States Air Force and DARPA under Contract No FA8750-16-C-0022 (any opinions, findings and conclusions or recommendations expressed in this material are those of the authors and do not necessarily reflect the views of Vetenskapsrådet, the NSF, the United States Air Force, or DARPA), and by Vetenskapsrådet in Sweden for funding under the SyTeC project (grant number 2016-06204).

References

1. Arcuri, A., Briand, L.C.: Adaptive random testing: an illusion of effectiveness? In: Dwyer, M.B., Tip, F. (eds.) Proceedings of the 20th International Symposium on Software Testing and Analysis, ISSTA 2011, Toronto, ON, Canada, July 17-21, 2011. pp. 265–275. ACM (2011). https://doi.org/10.1145/2001420.2001452, `https://doi.org/10.1145/2001420.2001452`

2. Bell, K.Z., Vouk, M.A.: On effectiveness of pairwise methodology for testing network-centric software. In: 2005 International Conference on Information and Communication Technology. pp. 221–235. IEEE (2005)
3. Braquehais, R.M.: Tools for discovery, refinement and generalization of functional properties by enumerative testing (October 2017), http://etheses.whiterose.ac.uk/19178/
4. Chen, T.Y., Leung, H., Mak, I.K.: Adaptive random testing. In: Maher, M.J. (ed.) Advances in Computer Science - ASIAN 2004, Higher-Level Decision Making, 9th Asian Computing Science Conference, Dedicated to Jean-Louis Lassez on the Occasion of His 5th Cycle Birthday, Chiang Mai, Thailand, December 8-10, 2004, Proceedings. Lecture Notes in Computer Science, vol. 3321, pp. 320–329. Springer (2004). https://doi.org/10.1007/978-3-540-30502-6_23, https://doi.org/10.1007/978-3-540-30502-6_23
5. Ciupa, I., Leitner, A., Oriol, M., Meyer, B.: ARTOO: adaptive random testing for object-oriented software. In: Schäfer, W., Dwyer, M.B., Gruhn, V. (eds.) 30th International Conference on Software Engineering (ICSE 2008), Leipzig, Germany, May 10-18, 2008. pp. 71–80. ACM (2008). https://doi.org/10.1145/1368088.1368099, https://doi.org/10.1145/1368088.1368099
6. Claessen, K., Duregård, J., Palka, M.H.: Generating constrained random data with uniform distribution. J. Funct. Program. **25** (2015). https://doi.org/10.1017/S0956796815000143, http://dx.doi.org/10.1017/S0956796815000143
7. Claessen, K., Hughes, J.: Quickcheck: a lightweight tool for random testing of haskell programs. In: Odersky, M., Wadler, P. (eds.) Proceedings of the Fifth ACM SIGPLAN International Conference on Functional Programming (ICFP '00), Montreal, Canada, September 18-21, 2000. pp. 268–279. ACM (2000). https://doi.org/10.1145/351240.351266, https://doi.org/10.1145/351240.351266
8. Colbourn, C.J., Cohen, M.B., Turban, R.: A deterministic density algorithm for pairwise interaction coverage. In: Hamza, M.H. (ed.) IASTED International Conference on Software Engineering, part of the 22nd Multi-Conference on Applied Informatics, Innsbruck, Austria, February 17-19, 2004. pp. 345–352. IASTED/ACTA Press (2004)
9. Comon, H., Dauchet, M., Gilleron, R., Löding, C., Jacquemard, F., Lugiez, D., Tison, S., Tommasi, M.: Tree automata techniques and applications. Available on: http://www.grappa.univ-lille3.fr/tata (2007), release October, 12th 2007
10. Courcelle, B.: Fundamental properties of infinite trees. Theor. Comput. Sci. **25**, 95–169 (1983). https://doi.org/10.1016/0304-3975(83)90059-2, https://doi.org/10.1016/0304-3975(83)90059-2
11. Gill, A., Runciman, C.: Haskell program coverage. In: Keller, G. (ed.) Proceedings of the ACM SIGPLAN Workshop on Haskell, Haskell 2007, Freiburg, Germany, September 30, 2007. pp. 1–12. ACM (2007). https://doi.org/10.1145/1291201.1291203, https://doi.org/10.1145/1291201.1291203
12. Girard, J.Y.: Interprétation fonctionnelle et élimination des coupures de l'arithmétique d'ordre supérieur. Ph.D. thesis, Éditeur inconnu (1972)
13. Havrikov, N., Zeller, A.: Systematically covering input structure. In: 34th IEEE/ACM International Conference on Automated Software Engineering, ASE 2019, San Diego, CA, USA, November 11-15, 2019. pp. 189–199. IEEE (2019). https://doi.org/10.1109/ASE.2019.00027, https://doi.org/10.1109/ASE.2019.00027

14. Kuhn, D.R., Wallace, D.R., Gallo, A.M.: Software fault interactions and implications for software testing. IEEE Transactions on Software Engineering **30**(6), 418–421 (2004). https://doi.org/10.1109/TSE.2004.24
15. Kuhn, D.R., Higdon, J.M., Lawrence, J., Kacker, R., Lei, Y.: Combinatorial methods for event sequence testing. In: Antoniol, G., Bertolino, A., Labiche, Y. (eds.) Fifth IEEE International Conference on Software Testing, Verification and Validation, ICST 2012, Montreal, QC, Canada, April 17-21, 2012. pp. 601–609. IEEE Computer Society (2012). https://doi.org/10.1109/ICST.2012.147, `https://doi.org/10.1109/ICST.2012.147`
16. Kuhn, D.R., Kacker, R.N., Lei, Y.: Practical combinatorial testing. NIST special Publication **800**(142), 142 (2010)
17. Kuhn, D.R., Wallace, D.R., Gallo, A.M.: Software fault interactions and implications for software testing. IEEE transactions on software engineering **30**(6), 418–421 (2004)
18. Kuraj, I., Kuncak, V., Jackson, D.: Programming with enumerable sets of structures. In: Aldrich, J., Eugster, P. (eds.) Proceedings of the 2015 ACM SIGPLAN International Conference on Object-Oriented Programming, Systems, Languages, and Applications, OOPSLA 2015, part of SPLASH 2015, Pittsburgh, PA, USA, October 25-30, 2015. pp. 37–56. ACM (2015). https://doi.org/10.1145/2814270.2814323, `https://doi.org/10.1145/2814270.2814323`
19. Lämmel, R., Schulte, W.: Controllable combinatorial coverage in grammar-based testing. In: Uyar, M.Ü., Duale, A.Y., Fecko, M.A. (eds.) Testing of Communicating Systems, 18th IFIP TC6/WG6.1 International Conference, TestCom 2006, New York, NY, USA, May 16-18, 2006, Proceedings. Lecture Notes in Computer Science, vol. 3964, pp. 19–38. Springer (2006). https://doi.org/10.1007/11754008_2, `https://doi.org/10.1007/11754008_2`
20. Lampropoulos, L., Gallois-Wong, D., Hritcu, C., Hughes, J., Pierce, B.C., Xia, L.: Beginner's Luck: a language for property-based generators. In: Proceedings of the 44th ACM SIGPLAN Symposium on Principles of Programming Languages, POPL 2017, Paris, France, January 18-20, 2017. pp. 114–129 (2017), `http://dl.acm.org/citation.cfm?id=3009868`
21. Lampropoulos, L., Hicks, M., Pierce, B.C.: Coverage guided, property based testing. PACMPL **3**(OOPSLA), 181:1–181:29 (2019). https://doi.org/10.1145/3360607, `https://doi.org/10.1145/3360607`
22. lcamtuf: AFL quick start guide. `http://lcamtuf.coredump.cx/afl/QuickStartGuide.txt` (Apr 2018)
23. Lei, Y., Kacker, R., Kuhn, D.R., Okun, V., Lawrence, J.: Ipog: A general strategy for t-way software testing. In: 14th Annual IEEE International Conference and Workshops on the Engineering of Computer-Based Systems (ECBS'07). pp. 549–556. IEEE (2007)
24. Livinskii, V., Babokin, D., Regehr, J.: Random testing for c and c++ compilers with yarpgen. Proceedings of the ACM on Programming Languages **4**(OOPSLA), 1–25 (2020)
25. Luo, Q., Hariri, F., Eloussi, L., Marinov, D.: An empirical analysis of flaky tests. In: Proceedings of the 22nd ACM SIGSOFT International Symposium on Foundations of Software Engineering. pp. 643–653 (2014)
26. Mariani, L., Pezzè, M., Willmor, D.: Generation of integration tests for self-testing components. In: Núñez, M., Maamar, Z., Pelayo, F.L., Pousttchi, K., Rubio, F. (eds.) Applying Formal Methods: Testing, Performance and M/ECommerce, FORTE 2004 Workshops The FormEMC, EPEW, ITM, Toledo, Spain,

October 1-2, 2004. Lecture Notes in Computer Science, vol. 3236, pp. 337–350. Springer (2004). https://doi.org/10.1007/978-3-540-30233-9_25, https://doi.org/10.1007/978-3-540-30233-9_25

27. Marlow, S., Peyton-Jones, S.: The Glasgow Haskell Compiler. In: Brown, A., Wilson, G. (eds.) The Architecture of Open Source Applications, vol. II. Available online under the Creative Commons Attribution 3.0 Unported license (March 2012), http://www.aosabook.org/en/ghc.html
28. Mathis, B., Gopinath, R., Zeller, A.: Learning input tokens for effective fuzzing. In: Khurshid, S., Pasareanu, C.S. (eds.) ISSTA '20: 29th ACM SIGSOFT International Symposium on Software Testing and Analysis, Virtual Event, USA, July 18-22, 2020. pp. 27–37. ACM (2020). https://doi.org/10.1145/3395363.3397348, https://doi.org/10.1145/3395363.3397348
29. Mista, A., Russo, A., Hughes, J.: Branching processes for quickcheck generators. In: Wu, N. (ed.) Proceedings of the 11th ACM SIGPLAN International Symposium on Haskell, Haskell@ICFP 2018, St. Louis, MO, USA, September 27-17, 2018. pp. 1–13. ACM (2018). https://doi.org/10.1145/3242744.3242747, https://doi.org/10.1145/3242744.3242747
30. Nie, C., Leung, H.: A survey of combinatorial testing. ACM Comput. Surv. **43**(2) (Feb 2011). https://doi.org/10.1145/1883612.1883618, https://doi.org/10.1145/1883612.1883618
31. Padhye, R., Lemieux, C., Sen, K., Simon, L., Vijayakumar, H.: Fuzzfactory: domain-specific fuzzing with waypoints. Proc. ACM Program. Lang. **3**(OOPSLA), 174:1–174:29 (2019). https://doi.org/10.1145/3360600, https://doi.org/10.1145/3360600
32. Pałka, M.H., Claessen, K., Russo, A., Hughes, J.: Testing an optimising compiler by generating random lambda terms. In: Proceedings of the 6th International Workshop on Automation of Software Test. pp. 91–97. AST '11, ACM, New York, NY, USA (2011). https://doi.org/10.1145/1982595.1982615, http://doi.acm.org/10.1145/1982595.1982615
33. Reddy, S., Lemieux, C., Padhye, R., Sen, K.: Quickly generating diverse valid test inputs with reinforcement learning. In: Rothermel, G., Bae, D. (eds.) ICSE '20: 42nd International Conference on Software Engineering, Seoul, South Korea, 27 June - 19 July, 2020. pp. 1410–1421. ACM (2020). https://doi.org/10.1145/3377811.3380399, https://doi.org/10.1145/3377811.3380399
34. Regehr, J., Chen, Y., Cuoq, P., Eide, E., Ellison, C., Yang, X.: Test-case reduction for C compiler bugs. In: ACM SIGPLAN Conference on Programming Language Design and Implementation, PLDI '12, Beijing, China - June 11 - 16, 2012. pp. 335–346 (2012). https://doi.org/10.1145/2254064.2254104, http://www.cs.utah.edu/~regehr/papers/pldi12-preprint.pdf
35. Reynolds, J.C.: Towards a theory of type structure. In: Robinet, B. (ed.) Programming Symposium, Proceedings Colloque sur la Programmation, Paris, France, April 9-11, 1974. Lecture Notes in Computer Science, vol. 19, pp. 408–423. Springer (1974). https://doi.org/10.1007/3-540-06859-7_148, https://doi.org/10.1007/3-540-06859-7_148
36. Runciman, C., Naylor, M., Lindblad, F.: Smallcheck and lazy smallcheck: automatic exhaustive testing for small values. In: Gill, A. (ed.) Proceedings of the 1st ACM SIGPLAN Symposium on Haskell, Haskell 2008, Victoria, BC, Canada, 25 September 2008. pp. 37–48. ACM (2008).

https://doi.org/10.1145/1411286.1411292, `https://doi.org/10.1145/1411286.1411292`
37. Salecker, E., Glesner, S.: Combinatorial interaction testing for test selection in grammar-based testing. In: Antoniol, G., Bertolino, A., Labiche, Y. (eds.) Fifth IEEE International Conference on Software Testing, Verification and Validation, ICST 2012, Montreal, QC, Canada, April 17-21, 2012. pp. 610–619. IEEE Computer Society (2012). https://doi.org/10.1109/ICST.2012.148, `https://doi.org/10.1109/ICST.2012.148`
38. Sarkar, K., Colbourn, C.J.: Upper bounds on the size of covering arrays. SIAM J. Discrete Math. **31**(2), 1277–1293 (2017). https://doi.org/10.1137/16M1067767, `https://doi.org/10.1137/16M1067767`
39. Stephens, N., Grosen, J., Salls, C., Dutcher, A., Wang, R., Corbetta, J., Shoshitaishvili, Y., Kruegel, C., Vigna, G.: Driller: Augmenting fuzzing through selective symbolic execution. In: Network and Distributed System Security Symposium (NDSS) (2016)
40. Usaola, M.P., Romero, F.R., Aranda, R.R., de Guzmán, I.G.R.: Test case generation with regular expressions and combinatorial techniques. In: 2017 IEEE International Conference on Software Testing, Verification and Validation Workshops, ICST Workshops 2017, Tokyo, Japan, March 13-17, 2017. pp. 189–198. IEEE Computer Society (2017). https://doi.org/10.1109/ICSTW.2017.38, `https://doi.org/10.1109/ICSTW.2017.38`
41. Yang, X., Chen, Y., Eide, E., Regehr, J.: Finding and understanding bugs in C compilers. In: Proceedings of the 32nd ACM SIGPLAN Conference on Programming Language Design and Implementation, PLDI 2011, San Jose, CA, USA, June 4-8, 2011. pp. 283–294 (2011). https://doi.org/10.1145/1993498.1993532, `http://www.cs.utah.edu/~regehr/papers/pldi11-preprint.pdf`
42. Yun, I., Lee, S., Xu, M., Jang, Y., Kim, T.: QSYM : A practical concolic execution engine tailored for hybrid fuzzing. In: 27th USENIX Security Symposium (USENIX Security 18). pp. 745–761. USENIX Association, Baltimore, MD (2018), `https://www.usenix.org/conference/usenixsecurity18/presentation/yun`
43. Zeller, A., Gopinath, R., Böhme, M., Fraser, G., Holler, C.: The fuzzing book. In: The Fuzzing Book. Saarland University (2019), `https://www.fuzzingbook.org/`, retrieved 2019-09-09 16:42:54+02:00

For a Few Dollars More

Verified Fine-Grained Algorithm Analysis Down to LLVM

Maximilian P. L. Haslbeck[1] (✉)
and Peter Lammich[2]

[1] Technische Universität München, München, Germany
haslbema@in.tum.de
[2] The University of Manchester, Manchester, England
peter.lammich@manchester.ac.uk

Abstract. We present a framework to verify both, functional correctness and worst-case complexity of practically efficient algorithms. We implemented a stepwise refinement approach, using the novel concept of *resource currencies* to naturally structure the resource analysis along the refinement chain, and allow a fine-grained analysis of operation counts. Our framework targets the LLVM intermediate representation. We extend its semantics from earlier work with a cost model. As case study, we verify the correctness and $O(n \log n)$ worst-case complexity of an implementation of the introsort algorithm, whose performance is on par with the state-of-the-art implementation found in the GNU C++ Library.

Keywords: Algorithm Analysis · Program Verification · Refinement

1 Introduction

In general, not only correctness, but also the complexity of algorithms is important. While it is obvious that the performance *observed* during experiments is essential to solve practical problems efficiently, also the *theoretical* worst-case complexity of algorithms is crucial: a good worst-case complexity avoids timing regressions when hitting worst-case input, and, even more important, prevents denial of service attacks that intentionally produce worst-case scenarios to overload critical computing infrastructure.

For example, the C++ standard requires implementations of *std::sort* to have worst-case complexity $O(n \log n)$ [7]. Note that this rules out quicksort [12], which is very fast in practice, but has quadratic worst-case complexity. Nevertheless, some standard libraries, most prominently LLVM's *libc++* [20], still use sorting algorithms with quadratic worst-case complexity.[3]

A practically efficient sorting algorithm with $O(n \log n)$ worst-case complexity is Musser's introsort [22]. It combines quicksort with the $O(n \log n)$ heapsort algorithm, which is used as fallback when the quicksort recursion depth

[3] See, e.g., `https://bugs.llvm.org/show_bug.cgi?id=20837`.

N. Yoshida (Ed.): ESOP 2021, LNCS 12648, pp. 292–319, 2021.
https://doi.org/10.1007/978-3-030-72019-3_11

exceeds a certain threshold. It allows to implement standard-compliant, practically efficient sorting algorithms. Introsort is implemented by, e.g., the GNU C++ Library (*libstdc++*) [8].

In this paper, we present techniques to formally verify both, correctness and worst-case complexity of practically efficient implementations. We build on two previous lines of research by the authors.

On one hand, we have the Isabelle Refinement Framework [19], which allows for a modular top-down verification approach. It utilizes stepwise refinement to separate the different aspects of an efficient implementation, such as algorithmic idea and low-level optimizations. It provides a nondeterminism monad to formalize programs and refinements, and the Sepref tool to automate canonical data refinement steps. Its recent LLVM back end [15] allows to verify algorithms with competitive performance compared to (unverified) highly optimized C/C++ implementations. The Refinement Framework has been used to verify the functional correctness of an implementation of introsort that performs on par with *libstdc++*'s implementation [17].

On the other hand, we already have extended the Refinement Framework to reason about complexity [11]. However, this only supports the Imperative/HOL back end [16]. It generates implementations in functional languages, which are inherently less efficient than highly optimized C/C++ implementations. This paper combines and extends these two approaches. Our main contributions are.

- We present a generalized nondeterminism monad with resource cost, apply it to resource functions to model fine-grained currencies (Section 2) and show how they can be used to naturally structure refinement.
- We extend the LLVM back end [15] with a cost model, and amend its basic reasoning infrastructure (Section 3).
- We extend the Sepref tool (Section 4) to synthesize executable imperative code in LLVM, together with a proof of correctness and complexity. Our approach seamlessly supports imperative and amortized data structures.
- We extend the verification of introsort to also show a worst-case complexity of $O(n \log n)$, thus meeting the C++11 *stdlib* specification [7] (Section 5). The performance of our implementation is still on par with *libstdc++*. We believe that this is the first time that both, correctness and complexity of a sorting algorithm have been formally verified down to a competitive implementation.

Our formalization is available at `https://www21.in.tum.de/~haslbema/llvm-time`.

2 Specification of Algorithms With Resources

We use the formalism of monads [24] to elegantly specify programs with resource usage. We first describe a framework that works for a very generic notion of *resource*, and then instantiate it with *resource functions*, which model resources of different *currencies*. We then describe a refinement calculus and show how currencies can be used to structure stepwise refinement proofs. Finally, we report on automation and give some examples.

2.1 Nondeterministic Computations With Resources

Let us examine the features we require for our computation model.

First, we want to specify programs by their desired properties, without having to fix a concrete implementation. In general, those programs have more than one correct result for the same input. Consider, e.g., sorting a list of pairs of numbers by the first element. For the input $[(1,2),(2,2),(1,3)]$, both $[(1,2),(1,3),(2,2)]$ and $[(1,3),(1,2),(2,2)]$ are valid results. Formally, this is modelled as a *set* of possible results. When we later fix an implementation, the set of possible results may shrink. For example, the (stable) insertion sort algorithm always returns the list $[(1,2),(1,3),(2,2)]$. We say that insertion sort *refines* our specification of sorting.

Second, we want to define recursion by a standard fixed-point construction over a flat lattice. The bottom of this lattice must be a dedicated element, which we call `fail`. It represents a computation that may not terminate.

Finally, we want to model the resources required by a computation. For nondeterministic programs, these may vary depending on the nondeterministic choices made during the computation. As we model computations by their possible results, rather than by the exact path in the program that leads to the result, we also associate resource cost with possible results. When more than one computation path leads to the same result, we take the supremum of the used resources. The notion of refinement is now extended to a subset of results that are computed using less resources.

We now formalize the above intuition: The type

(α,γ) *NREST* = `fail` | `res` $(\alpha \rightarrow \gamma$ *option*$)$

models a nondeterministic computation with results of type α and resources of type γ.[4] That is, a computation is either `fail`, or `res` M, where M is a partial function from possible results to resources.

We define `spec` Φ T as a computation of any result r that satisfies Φ r using $T\ r$ resources: `spec` Φ T = `res` $(\lambda r.$ `if` $\Phi\ r$ `then` *Some* $(T\ r)$ `else` *None*$)$. By abuse of notation, we write `spec` x T for `spec` $(\lambda r.\ r{=}x)$ $(\lambda\_.\ T)$.

Based on an ordering on the resources γ, we define the *refinement ordering* on NREST, by first lifting the ordering to *option* with *None* as the bottom element, then pointwise to functions and finally to (α,γ) *NREST*, setting `fail` as the top element. This matches the intuition of refinement: $m \leq m'$ reads as *m refines m′*, i.e., m has less possible results than m', computed with less resources.

We require the resources γ to have a complete lattice structure, such that we can form suprema over the (possibly infinitely many) paths that lead to the same result. Moreover, when sequentially composing computations, we need to add up the resources. This naturally leads to a monoid structure $(\gamma, 0, +)$, where 0, intuitively, stands for no resources.

We call such types γ *resource types*, if they have a complete lattice and monoid structure. Note that, in an earlier iteration of this work [11], the resource type

[4] The name NREST abbreviates **N**ondeterministic **RES**ult with **T**ime, and has been inherited from our earlier formalizations.

was fixed to extended natural numbers ($enat = \mathbb{N} \cup \{\infty\}$), measuring the resource consumption with a single number. Also note that $(\alpha, unit)$ *NREST* is isomorphic to our original nondeterministic result monad without resources [19].

If γ is a resource type, so is $\eta \rightarrow \gamma$. Intuitively, such resources consist of coins of different *resource currencies* η, the amount of coins being measured by γ.

Example 1. In the following we use the resource type $ecost = string \rightarrow enat$, i.e., we have currencies described by a string, whose amount is measured by extended natural numbers, where ∞ models arbitrary resource usage. Note that, while the resource type $string \rightarrow enat$ guides intuition, most of our theory works for general resource types of the form $\eta \rightarrow \gamma$ or even just γ.

We define the function $\$_s\ n$ to be the resource function that uses $n :: enat$ coins of the currency $s :: string$, and write $\$_s$ as shortcut for $\$_s\ 1$.

A program that sorts a list in $O(n^2)$ can be specified by:

$$sort_{spec}\ xs = \texttt{spec}\ (\lambda xs'.\ sorted\ xs' \wedge mset\ xs' = mset\ xs)\ (\$_q\ |xs|^2 + \$_c)$$

that is, a list xs can result in any sorted list xs' with the same elements, and the computation takes (at most) quadratically many q coins in the list length, and one c coin, independently of the list length. Intuitively, the q and c coins represent the constant factors of an algorithm that implements that specification and are later elaborated by exchanging them into several coins of more fine-grained currencies, corresponding to the concrete operations in the algorithm, e.g., comparisons and memory accesses. Abstract currencies like q and c only *"have value"* if they can be exchanged to meaningful other currencies, and finally pay for the resource costs of a concrete implementation.

2.2 Atomic Operations and Control Flow

In order to conveniently model actual computations, we define some combinators. The `elapse` $m\ t$ combinator adds the (constant) resources t to all results of m:

$$\begin{aligned}
&\texttt{elapse} :: (\alpha,\gamma)\ NREST \rightarrow \gamma \rightarrow (\alpha,\gamma)\ NREST\\
&\texttt{elapse fail}\ t = \texttt{fail}\\
&\texttt{elapse (res}\ M)\ t = \texttt{res}\ (\lambda x.\ \texttt{case}\ M\ x\ \texttt{of}\ None \Rightarrow None\\
&\qquad\qquad\qquad\qquad\qquad\qquad\qquad\quad \mid Some\ t' \Rightarrow Some\ (t + t'))
\end{aligned}$$

The program[5] `return` x computes the single result x without using any resources:

$$\begin{aligned}
&\texttt{return} :: \alpha \rightarrow (\alpha,\gamma)\ NREST\\
&\texttt{return}\ x = \texttt{res}\ [\ x \mapsto 0\ ]
\end{aligned}$$

The combinator `bind` $m\ f$ models the sequential composition of computations m and f, where f may depend on the result of m:

[5] Note that our shallow embedding makes no formal distinction between syntax and semantics. Nevertheless, we refer to an entity of type *NREST*, as *program* to emphasize the syntactic aspect, and as *computation* to emphasize the semantic aspect.

$$\texttt{bind} :: (\alpha,\gamma)\ \mathit{NREST} \rightarrow (\alpha \rightarrow (\beta,\gamma)\ \mathit{NREST}) \rightarrow (\beta,\gamma)\ \mathit{NREST}$$
$$\texttt{bind fail}\ f = \texttt{fail}$$
$$\texttt{bind (res}\ M)\ f = \mathit{Sup}\ \{\ \texttt{elapse}\ (f\ x)\ t\ |x\ t.\ M\ x = \mathit{Some}\ t\ \}$$

If the first computation m fails, then also the sequential composition fails. Otherwise, we consider all possible results x with resources t of m, invoke $f\ x$, and add the cost t for computing x to the results of $f\ x$. The supremum aggregates the cases where f yields the same result, via different intermediate results of m, and also makes the whole expression fail if one of the $f\ x$ fails.

Example 2. We now illustrate an effect that stems from our decision to aggregate the resource usage of different computation paths that lead to the same result. Consider the program

$$\texttt{res}\ (\lambda n{::}\mathit{nat}.\ \mathit{Some}\ (\$_c\ n));\ \texttt{return}\ \mathit{0}$$

It first chooses an arbitrary natural number n consuming n coins of currency c, and then returns the result *0*. That is, there are arbitrarily many paths that lead to the result 0, consuming arbitrarily many c coins. The supremum of this is ∞, such that the above program is equal to $\texttt{elapse (return}\ \mathit{0})\ (\$_c\ \infty)$. Note that none of the computation paths actually attains the aggregated resource usage. We will come back to this in Section 4.4.

Finally, we use Isabelle/HOL's *if-then-else* and define a recursion combinator `rec` via a fixed-point construction [13], to get a complete set of basic combinators. As these combinators also incur cost in the target LLVM, we define resource aware variants. Furthermore we also derive a while combinator:

$$\texttt{if}_c\ b\ \texttt{then}\ c_1\ \texttt{else}\ c_2 = \texttt{elapse}\ (r \leftarrow b;\ \texttt{if}\ r\ \texttt{then}\ c_1\ \texttt{else}\ c_2)\ \$_{if}$$
$$\texttt{rec}_c\ F\ x = \texttt{elapse}\ (\texttt{rec}\ (\lambda D\ x.\ F\ (\lambda x.\ \texttt{elapse}\ (D\ x)\ \$_{call})\ x)\ x)\ \$_{call}$$
$$\texttt{while}_c\ b\ f\ s = \texttt{rec}_c\ (\lambda D\ s.\ \texttt{if}_c\ b\ s\ \texttt{then}\ s \leftarrow f\ s;\ D\ s\ \texttt{else return}\ s)\ s$$

Here, the guard of $\texttt{if}_c$ is a computation itself, and we consume an additional *if* coin to account for the conditional branching in the target model. Similarly, every recursive call consumes an additional *call* coin.

Assertions fail if their condition is not met, and return *unit* otherwise:

$$\texttt{assert}\ P = \texttt{if}\ P\ \texttt{then return ()}\ \texttt{else fail}$$

They are used to express preconditions of a program. A Hoare-triple for program m, with precondition P, postcondition Q and resource usage t is written as a refinement condition: $m \leq \texttt{assert}\ P;\ \texttt{spec}\ Q\ (\lambda\_.\ t)$

Example 3. Comparison of two list elements at a cost of t can be specified by:

$$\mathit{idxs\_cmp}_{spec}\ xs\ i\ j\ (t) = \texttt{assert}\ (i{<}|xs| \wedge j{<}|xs|);\ \texttt{spec}\ (xs!i < xs!j)\ (\lambda\_.\ t)$$

where $xs!i$ is the ith element of list xs. Instead of fixing the cost for specifications, we pass them as parameter t. This allows us to refine different instances of abstract data types (here lists) by different concrete data structures with different costs. To make bigger programs more readable, we note the cost parameter in parenthesis at the end of the line, as, e.g., in Example 4.

2.3 Refinement on NREST

We have used the refinement ordering to express Hoare triples. Two other applications of refinement are data refinement and currency refinement.

Data Refinement A typical use-case of refinement is to implement an *abstract* data type by a *concrete* data type. For example, we could implement (finite) sets of numbers by sorted lists. We define a *refinement relation* R between sorted lists and sets. A concrete computation $m_\dagger$ that yields sorted lists then refines an abstract computation m that yields sets, if every possible concrete result is related to a possible abstract result. Formally, $m_\dagger \le \Downarrow_D R\ m$, where the operator $\Downarrow_D$ is defined, for arguments R and m, by the following two rules.

$$\Downarrow_D R\ (\texttt{res}\ M) = \texttt{res}\ (\lambda c.\ \mathit{Sup}\ \{M\ a \mid a.\ (c,a) \in R\}) \qquad \Downarrow_D R\ \texttt{fail} = \texttt{fail}$$

Again, we use the supremum to aggregate the costs of all abstract results that are related to a concrete result. As in Example 2, this leads to the possibility that the supremum cost is not attained, which we discuss in Section 4.4.

Currency Refinement Consider we want to refine Example 3 into a program that first accesses the elements and then compares them.

Example 4. We refine $\mathit{idxs\_cmp}_{spec}$ $(\$_{idxs\_cmp})$ from Example 3 as follows:

$$\begin{array}{ll}
\multicolumn{2}{l}{\mathit{idxs_cmp}\ xs\ i\ j =}\\
\quad \texttt{assert}\ (i{<}|xs| \wedge j{<}|xs|); & \\
\quad xsi \leftarrow \mathit{list_get}_{spec}\ xs\ i; & (\$_{lookup})\\
\quad xsj \leftarrow \mathit{list_get}_{spec}\ xs\ j; & (\$_{lookup})\\
\quad \texttt{return}\ (xsi < xsj) & (\$_{less})
\end{array}$$

where $\mathit{list\_get}_{spec}\ xs\ i\ (T) = \texttt{assert}\ (i < |xs|);\ \texttt{spec}\ (xs!i)\ T$ and $\texttt{return}\ x\ (T)$ returns the result x incurring cost T.

Note that *idxs_cmp* and $\mathit{idxs\_cmp}_{spec}$ use different, incompatible currency systems. To compare them, we need to exchange coins: one *idxs_cmp* coin will be traded for two *lookup* coins and one *less* coin.

To make that happen we introduce the currency refinement $\Downarrow_C E\ m$. Here, the *exchange rate* $E :: \eta_a \to \eta_c \to \gamma$ specifies for each abstract currency $c_a :: \eta_a$ how many of the coins of the concrete currency $c_c :: \eta_c$ are needed. Note that, in general, one abstract coin may be exchanged into multiple coins of different currencies. For a resource type γ that provides a multiplication operation $(*)$ we define the operator $\Downarrow_C$ with the following two rules.

$$\begin{aligned}
\Downarrow_C E\ (\texttt{res}\ M) &= \texttt{res}\ (\lambda\ r.\ \texttt{case}\ M\ r\ \texttt{of}\ \mathit{None} \Rightarrow \mathit{None} \mid \\
&\qquad \mathit{Some}\ t \Rightarrow \mathit{Some}\ (\lambda c_c.\ \textstyle\sum_{c_a} t\ c_a * E\ c_a\ c_c))\\
\Downarrow_C E\ \texttt{fail} &= \texttt{fail}
\end{aligned}$$

The refined computation has the same results as the original. To get the amount of a concrete coin c_c for some result r with resource function t, we sum, over all abstract coins c_a, the amount of abstract coins needed in the original computation ($t\ c_a$) weighted by the exchange rate ($E\ c_a\ c_c$).

For the sum to make sense, there must be only finitely many abstract coins c_a with $t\ c_a * E\ c_a\ c_c \neq 0$. This can be ensured by restricting the resource functions t of the computation to use finitely many different coins, or by restricting the exchange rate E accordingly. The latter can be checked syntactically in practice.

Example 5. For refining the specification $idxs\_cmp_{spec}$ we can use the exchange rate $E_1 = 0(idxs\_cmp{:=}\ \$_{lookup}\ 2 + \$_{less})$, which does the correct exchange for *idxs_cmp* and is zero everywhere else. Here, + and 0 are lifted to functions in a pointwise manner, and $f(\cdot{:=}\cdot)$ denotes a function update. We can now prove:

$$idxs\_cmp\ xs\ i\ j \leq \Downarrow_C E_1\ (idxs\_cmp_{spec}\ xs\ i\ j\ (\$_{idxs\_cmp}))$$

2.4 Refinement Patterns

In practice, we encounter certain recurring patterns of refinement, which we describe in this section.

Refinement of Specifications Instead of only asking *whether* a program m satisfies a specification **res** M, we also ask *how much* it satisfies the specification, i.e. what is the difference of the resources specified and actually used, denoted by $gwp\ m\ M$.[6] We have the following equality: $m \leq \texttt{res}\ M \Leftrightarrow Some\ 0 \leq gwp\ m\ M$.

To get some intuition let us fix the resource to be time. Then, $gwp\ m\ M$ is the *latest* feasible time at which we can start m to still match the deadline M. If there is no feasible starting time ($gwp\ m\ M = None$), m does not fulfill the specification M. If it has some value t, this is the latest feasible starting time of all computation paths in m.

Using *gwp*, we can implement a syntax driven verification condition generator, as already described in [11].

Lockstep Refinement We often refine a compound program by refining some of its components. Let A and C be two structurally equal programs (i.e., they have the same structure of combinators $\texttt{if}_c$, $\texttt{rec}_c$, **bind**, etc.), and let A_i and C_i be the pairs of corresponding basic components, for $i \in \{0, \ldots, n\}$. Provided with refinement lemmas $\Phi_i\ x \wedge (x_\dagger, x) \in R'_i \implies C_i\ x_\dagger \leq \Downarrow_D R_i\ (\Downarrow_C E\ (A_i\ x))$ for each of those pairs,[7] an automatic procedure walks through the program and establishes a refinement $C \leq \Downarrow_D R_n\ (\Downarrow_C E\ A)$. This process generates verification conditions for ensuring the preconditions Φ_i, which can be discharged automatically or, if required, via interactive proof.

[6] The definition of *gwp* requires γ to provide a difference operator, dual to its + operator. It is a straightforward generalization of the concept defined in [11], and thus omitted here. We only note that the resource types *unit*, *enat*, and *ecost* provide a suitable difference operator.

[7] The refinement relations R'_i and R_i relate the parameters and respectively the result of those components.

Note that, while the data refinements R_i can be different for each component i, the exchange rate E must be the same for all components. Currently, we align the exchange rates by manually deriving specialized versions of the component refinement lemmas. However, we believe that this can be automated in many practical cases, by collecting constraints on the exchange rate during the lockstep refinement, which are solved afterwards to obtain a unified exchange rate. We leave the implementation of this idea to future work.

Separating Analysis of Resource Usage and Correctness We can disregard resource usage and only focus on refinement of functional correctness, and then add resource usage analysis later. This is useful to separate the concerns of functional correctness and resource usage proof. We will describe a practical example later (Section 5.5), and only present an alternative way to prove the refinement in Example 4 here:

First, for functional correctness, we use the specification $\mathit{idxs\_cmp}_{\mathit{spec}}\ (\infty)$ and a program $\mathit{idxs\_cmp}_{\infty}$ similar to $\mathit{idxs\_cmp}$ but with all the costs replaced by ∞. Proving the refinement $\mathit{idxs\_cmp}_{\infty}\ \mathit{xs}\ i\ j \leq \mathit{idxs\_cmp}_{\mathit{spec}}\ \mathit{xs}\ i\ j\ (\infty)$ only requires showing verification conditions that correspond to functional properties and termination. In particular, assertions and annotated invariants in the concrete program have to be proved. Proof obligations on resource usage, however, collapse into the trivial $t \leq \infty$. For the same reason, we get $\mathit{idxs\_cmp}\ \mathit{xs}\ i\ j \leq \mathit{idxs\_cmp}_{\infty}\ \mathit{xs}\ i\ j$, and by transitivity obtain

$$\mathit{idxs\_cmp}\ \mathit{xs}\ i\ j \leq \mathit{idxs\_cmp}_{\mathit{spec}}\ \mathit{xs}\ i\ j\ (\infty)$$

Next, we prove $\mathit{idxs\_cmp}\ \mathit{xs}\ i\ j \leq_n \texttt{spec}\ (\lambda\_.\ \mathit{True})\ (\$_{\mathit{lookup}}\ 2 + \$_{\mathit{less}})$. Here, the refinement relation $m \leq_n m' = m \neq \texttt{fail} \implies m \leq m'$ assumes that the concrete program does *not* fail. This has the effect that, during the refinement proof, assertions and annotated invariants in the concrete program can be assumed to hold, and we can focus on the resource usage proof.

Finally, the two refinements can be combined to obtain

$$\mathit{idxs\_cmp}\ \mathit{xs}\ i\ j \leq \mathit{idxs\_cmp}_{\mathit{spec}}\ \mathit{xs}\ i\ j\ (\$_{\mathit{lookup}}\ 2 + \$_{\mathit{less}})$$

3 LLVM With Cost Semantics

The NREST-monad allows to specify programs with their resource usage in abstract currencies. Those currencies only have a meaning when they finally can be exchanged for the costs of concrete computations. In the following we present such a concrete computation model, namely a shallow embedding of the LLVM semantics into Isabelle/HOL. The embedding is an extension of our earlier work [15] to also account for costs. In Section 4 we then report on linking the LLVM back end with the NREST front end.

3.1 Basic Monad

At the basis of our LLVM formalization is a monad that provides the notions of non-termination, failure, state, and execution costs.

α *mres* = *NTERM* | *FAIL* | *SUCC* α *cost state*
α *M* = *state* $\rightarrow$ α *mres*

Here, *cost* is a type for execution costs, which forms a monoid with operation + and neutral element 0, and *state* is an arbitrary type.[8]

The type α *M* describes a program that, when executed on a state, either does not terminate (*NTERM*), fails (*FAIL*), or returns a result of type α, its execution costs, and a new state (*SUCC*).

It is straightforward to define the monad operations `return` and `bind`, as well as a recursion combinator `rec` over *M*. Thanks to the shallow embedding, we can also use Isabelle HOL's *if-then-else* to get a complete set of basic operations. As an example, we show the definition of the `bind` operation, in the case that both arguments successfully compute a result:

Assume $m\ s = SUCC\ x\ c_1\ s_1$ and $f\ x\ s_1 = SUCC\ r\ c_2\ s_2$
then we have `bind` $m\ f\ s = SUCC\ r\ (c_1{+}c_2)\ s_2$

That is, the result x and state s_1 after the first operation m is passed into the second operation *f*, and the result and state after the `bind` is what emerges from *f*. The cost for the `bind` is the sum of the costs for both operations.

The basic monad operations do not cost anything. To account for execution costs, we define an explicit operation `consume` $c\ s = SUCC\ ()\ c\ s$.[9]

3.2 Shallowly Embedded LLVM Semantics

The formalization of the LLVM semantics is organized in layers. At the bottom, there is a memory model that stores deeply embedded values, and comes with basic operations for allocation/deallocation, loading, storing, and pointer manipulation. Also the basic arithmetic operations are defined on deeply embedded integers. These operations are phrased in the basic monad, but consume no costs. This way, we could take them unchanged from our original LLVM formalization without cost [15]. For example, the low-level load operation has the signature *raw_load* :: *raw_ptr* $\rightarrow$ *val M*. Here, *raw_ptr* is the pointer type of our memory model, consisting of a block address and an offset, and *val* is our value type, which can be an integer, a pointer, or a pair of values.

On top of the basic layer, we define operations that correspond to the actual LLVM instructions. Here, we map from deeply embedded values to shallowly embedded values, and add the execution costs.

For example, the semantics of LLVM's load instruction is defined as follows:

8 Note that this differs from the NREST monad in Section 2.1: it is deterministic, and provides a state. Because of determinism, we never need to form a supremum, and thus can base our cost model on natural numbers rather than enats. We leave a unification of the two monads to future work.

9 For NREST, we defined a *higher-order* operation `elapse`, while we use the *first-order* operation `consume` here. This is for historical reasons. Note that `elapse` can be defined in terms of `consume`, and vice versa.

$$
\begin{aligned}
&\mathit{ll\_load} :: \alpha\ \mathit{ptr} \rightarrow \alpha\ M\\
&\mathit{ll\_load}\ p =\\
&\quad \mathtt{consume}\ \$_{load};\\
&\quad r \leftarrow \mathit{raw\_load}\ (\mathit{the\_raw\_ptr}\ p);\\
&\quad \mathit{checked\_from\_val}\ r
\end{aligned}
$$

It consumes the cost[10] for the operation, and then forwards to the *raw_load* operation of the lower layer, where *the_raw_ptr* and *checked_from_val* convert between the shallow and deep embedding of values.

Like in the original formalization[11], an LLVM program is represented by a set of monomorphic constant definitions of the shape *def*, defined as follows:

$$
\begin{aligned}
&\mathit{def} = \mathit{proc\_name}\ \mathit{var}^* \equiv \mathit{block}\\
&\mathit{block} = \mathit{var} \leftarrow \mathit{cmd};\ \mathit{block} \mid \mathtt{return}\ \mathit{var}\\
&\mathit{cmd} = \mathit{ll\_{<}opcode{>}}\ \mathit{arg}^* \mid \mathit{ll\_call}\ \mathit{proc\_name}\ \mathit{arg}^* \mid \mathit{llc\_if}\ \mathit{arg}\ \mathit{block}\ \mathit{block}\\
&\qquad \mid \mathit{llc\_while}\ \mathit{block}\ \mathit{block}\\
&\mathit{arg} = \mathit{var} \mid \mathit{number} \mid \mathit{null} \mid \mathit{init}
\end{aligned}
$$

The code generator checks that the set of definitions is complete and adheres to the required shape. It then translates them into LLVM code, which merely amounts to pretty printing and translating the structured control flow by `if` and `while`[12] statements to the unstructured control flow of LLVM. A powerful preprocessor can convert a more general class of terms to the restricted shape required by the code generator. This conversion is done inside the logic, i.e., the processed program is proved to be equal to the original. Preprocessing steps include monomorphization of polymorphic constants, extraction of fixed-point combinators to recursive function definitions, and conversion of tuple constructors and destructors to LLVM's *insertvalue* and *extractvalue* instructions.

In summary, the layered architecture of our LLVM formalization allowed for a smooth integration of the cost aspect, reusing most of the existing formalization nearly unchanged. Note that we opted to integrate the cost aspect into the existing top layer, which converts between deep and shallow embedding. Alternatively, we could have added another layer on top of the shallow embedding. While the latter would have been the cleaner design, we opted for the former approach to avoid the boilerplate of adding a new layer. This was feasible as the original top layer was quite thin, such that adding another aspect there did not result in excessive complexity.

---

[10] See Section 3.3 for an explanation of our cost model.

[11] Actually, the only change to the original formalization is the introduction of the *ll_call* instruction, to make the costs of a function call visible.

[12] Primitive while loops are not strictly required, as they can always be replaced by tail recursion. Indeed, our code generator can be configured to not accept while loops, and our preprocessor can automatically convert while loops to tail-recursive functions. However, the efficiency of the generated code then relies on LLVM's optimization pass to detect the tail recursion and transform it to a loop again.

3.3 Cost Model

As a cost model for running time, we chose to count how often each instruction is executed. That is, we set *cost* = *string* ⇀ *nat*, where the string encodes the name of an instruction. It is straightforward to define *0* and *+* such that (*cost*,*0*,*+*) forms a monoid. It is thus a valid cost model for our monad.

But how realistic is our cost model, counting LLVM instructions? During compilation, LLVM text will be transformed by LLVM's optimizer, and finally, the LLVM's back end will translate LLVM instructions to machine instructions. Moreover, the actual running time of a machine program does not only depend on the number of executed instructions, but effects like pipeline flushes and cache misses also play an important role. Thus, without factoring in the details of the optimization passes and the target machine architecture, our cost model can, at best, be a rough approximation of the actual running time.

However, we can sensibly assume that a single instruction in the original LLVM text will result in at most a (small) constant number of machine instructions, and that each machine instruction has a constant worst-case execution time. Thus, the steps counted by our model linearly correlate to an upper bound of the actual execution time, though the exact correlation depends on the actual program, optimizer passes, and target architecture. Hence, while our cost model cannot be used for precise statements about execution time, it can be used to prove worst-case complexity. That is, a program that we have proved efficient will be compiled to an efficient machine program. Moreover, we can hope that the constant factors in the proved complexity are related to the actual constant factors in the machine program, i.e., an LLVM program with small constant factors will compile to a machine program with small constant factors.

The above discussion justifies the following design choices: The *insertvalue* and *extractvalue* instructions, which are used to construct and destruct tuple values, have no associated costs. The main reason for this design is to enable transparent use of tupled values, e.g., to encode the state of a while loop. We expect LLVM to translate the members of the tuple to separate registers anyway, such that no real costs are associated with tupling/untupling.

We define the *malloc* instruction to take cost proportional to the number of allocated elements. Note that LLVM itself does not provide memory management, and our code generator forwards memory management instructions to the *libc* implementation of the target platform. We use the *calloc* function here, which is supposed to initialize the allocated memory with zeros. While the exact costs of that are implementation dependent, they certainly will depend on the size of the allocated block.

Charguéraud and Pottier [6, §2.7] discuss the adequacy of abstract cost models in a functional setting. In their classification, our abstraction is on Level 2.

3.4 Reasoning Setup

Once we have defined the semantics, we need to set up some basic reasoning infrastructure. The original Isabelle-LLVM already comes with a quite generic separation logic and verification condition generation framework. Here, we report on our extensions to resources using time credits.

Separation Logic with Time Credits Our reasoning infrastructure is based on separation logic with time credits [1,6,10]. We follow the algebraic approach of Calcagno *et al.* [3], using an earlier extension [15] of Klein *et al.* [18].

A separation algebra on type α induces a *separation logic* on assertions that are predicates over α. To guide intuition, elements of α are called *heaps* here. We use the following separation logic operators: The assertion $\uparrow\Phi$ holds for an empty heap if Φ holds, $\square{=}\uparrow \mathit{True}$ describes the empty heap, and $\exists_A$ is the existential quantifier lifted to assertions. The *separating conjunction* $P \star Q$ describes a heap comprised from two disjoint parts, one described by P and the other described by Q, and entailment $P \vdash Q$ states that Q holds for every heap described by P.

Separation algebras naturally extend over product and function types, i.e., for separation algebras α, β, and any type γ, also $\alpha \times \beta$ and $\gamma \to \alpha$ are separation algebras, where the operations are lifted pointwise.

Note that *enat* forms a separation algebra, where elements, i.e. time credits, are always disjoint. Hence, also $\mathit{ecost} = \mathit{string} \to \mathit{enat}$, and $\mathit{amemory} \times \mathit{ecost}$ are separation algebras, where *amemory* is the separation algebra that we already used in [15] to describe the abstract memory of LLVM. Thus, $\mathit{amemory} \times \mathit{ecost}$ induces a separation logic with time credits that match our cost model. The *time credit assertion* $\$\,c = (\lambda a.\ a{=}(\mathit{0},c))$ describes an empty memory ($\mathit{0}$) and precisely the time c. The primitive assertions on *amemory* are lifted analogously to describe no time credits.

Weakest Precondition and Hoare Triples We start by defining a concrete state *cstate* that describes the memory content and the available resources:

$$\mathit{cstate} = \mathit{memory} \times \mathit{ecost}$$

where *memory* is the memory type from our original LLVM formalization. Based on this, we define the weakest precondition predicate:

$$\mathit{wp} :: \alpha\ M \to (\alpha \to \mathit{cstate} \to \mathit{bool}) \to \mathit{cstate} \to \mathit{bool}$$
$$\mathit{wp}\ m\ Q\ (s,\mathit{cc}) = (\exists r\ c\ s'.\ m\ s = \mathit{SUCC}\ r\ c\ s' \wedge c \leq \mathit{cc} \wedge Q\ r\ (s', \mathit{cc}-c)).$$

Intuitively, the costs *cc* stored in the state is the *credit* available to the program. The weakest precondition holds if the program runs with real costs c that are within the available credit, and Q holds for the result r, the new memory s', and the new credit, $\mathit{cc}-c$, which is the old credit reduced by the actually required costs. Note that actual costs have type $\mathit{cost} = \mathit{string} \to \mathit{nat}$, i.e., are always finite, while the credits have type $\mathit{ecost} = \mathit{string} \to \mathit{enat}$, i.e., there can be infinite credits. Setting the credit to be infinite for all instruction types yields the classical weakest precondition that requires termination, but enforces no time limit.

Our concrete state type, in particular the memory, does not form a separation algebra, as the natural memory model of LLVM has no natural notion of partial memories. Thus, we define an abstraction function that maps a concrete state to an abstract state *astate*, which forms a separation algebra:

$$astate = amemory \times ecost \qquad abs\ (m,\ c) = (abs_m\ m,\ c)$$

Again, *amemory* and abs_m is the abstract state and abstraction function from the original LLVM formalization. The costs already form a separation algebra, so we do not abstract them further.

With this, we can instantiate a generic VCG infrastructure: let *cstate* be concrete states, $wp :: \alpha\ M \to (\alpha \to cstate \to bool) \to cstate \to bool$ be a weakest precondition predicate, and *astate* an abstract state, linked to concrete states via an abstraction function $abs :: cstate \to astate$. Further, assume that *wp* distributes over conjunctions, i.e.,

$$wp\ c\ Q_1\ s \wedge wp\ c\ Q_2\ s \implies wp\ c\ (\lambda r\ s'.\ Q_1\ r\ s' \wedge Q_2\ r\ s')\ s$$

Finally, let $\top$ be an *affine top* [5], i.e., an assertion with $\square \vdash \top$ and $\top \star \top = \top$, which captures resources that can be safely discarded. We define the *Hoare triple* $\{P\}\ c\ \{Q\}$ to hold iff:

$$\forall F\ s.\ (P \star F)\ (abs\ s) \implies wp\ c\ (\lambda r\ s'.\ (Q\ r \star \top \star F)\ (abs\ s'))\ s$$

Intuitively, $\{P\}\ c\ \{Q\}$ holds if, for all states that contain a part described by assertion P, command c terminates with result r and a state where that part is replaced by a part described by $Q\ r \star \top$, and the rest of the state has not changed. Here, $Q\ r$ is the postcondition of the Hoare triple, and $\top$ describes resources that may be left over and can be discarded.

In our case, we set $\top$ to describe the empty memory and any amount of time credits. This matches the intuition that a program must free all its memory, but may run faster than estimated, i.e., leave over some time credits. Note that our *wp* distributes over conjunctions.

The generic VCG infrastructure now provides us with a syntax driven VCG with a simple frame inference heuristics.

3.5 Primitive Setup

Once we have defined the basic reasoning infrastructure, we have to prove Hoare triples for the basic LLVM instructions and control flow combinators. As we have added the cost aspect only at the top level of our semantics, we can reuse most of the material from our original LLVM formalization without time. Technically, we instantiate our reasoning infrastructure with a weakest precondition predicate *wpn*, which only holds for programs that consume no costs. We define:

$$wpn\ m\ Q\ s = wp\ m\ (FST \circ Q)\ (s,0)\ \textbf{where}\ FST\ P = \lambda(s,c).\ P\ s \wedge c{=}0$$

The resulting reasoning infrastructure is identical with the one of our original formalization, most of which could be reused. Only for the topmost level, i.e., for those functions that correspond to the functional semantics of the actual LLVM instructions, we lift the Hoare triples over *wpn* to Hoare triples over *wp*:

$$\{P\}\ c\ \{Q\}_{wpn} = \{FST\ P\}\ c\ \{FST \circ Q\}$$

Example 6. Recall the low-level *raw_load* and the high-level *ll_load* instruction from Section 3.2. The *raw_load* instruction consumes no costs, and our original LLVM formalization provides the following Hoare triple:

$$\{raw\_pto\ p\ x\}\ raw\_load\ p\ \{\lambda r.\ \uparrow(r{=}x) \star raw\_pto\ p\ x\}_{wpn}$$

This can be transferred to a Hoare triple over *wp*:

$$\{FST\ (raw\_pto\ p\ x)\}\ raw\_load\ p\ \{\lambda r.\ \uparrow(r{=}x) \star FST\ (raw\_pto\ p\ x)\}$$

which is then used to prove the Hoare triple for the program *ll_load*

$$\{\$\ \$_{load} \star pto\ p\ x\}\ ll\_load\ p\ \{\lambda r.\ \uparrow(r{=}x) \star pto\ p\ x\}$$

where $pto\ p\ x = FST\ (raw\_pto\ (the\_raw\_ptr\ p)\ (to\_val\ x))$.

Using the VCG and the Hoare triples for the LLVM instructions, we can now define and prove correct data structures and algorithms. While this works smoothly for simple data structures like arrays, it does not scale to more complex developments. In contrast, NREST *does* scale, but lacks support for the low-level pointer reasoning required for basic data structures. In the next section, we show how to combine both approaches, with the LLVM level providing basic data structures and the NREST level using them as building blocks for larger algorithms.

4 Automatic Refinement

In this section we describe a tool to synthesize a concrete program in the LLVM-monad from an abstract algorithm in the NREST-monad. It can automatically refine abstract functional data structures to imperative heap-based ones. We will describe the synthesis predicate *hnr* that connects the two monads, the synthesis tool, and a way to extract Hoare triples from *hnr* predicates. Finally, we will discuss an effect that prevents combining *hnr* with data refinements in the NREST-monad in the general case.

4.1 Heap nondeterminism refinement

The *heap nondeterminism refinement* predicate $hnr\ \Gamma\ m_\dagger\ \Gamma'\ R\ m$ intuitively expresses that the concrete program $m_\dagger$ computes a concrete result that relates, via the *refinement assertion* R, to a result in the abstract program m, using at most the resources specified by m for that result. A refinement assertion describes how an abstract variable is refined by a concrete value on the heap. It can also contain time credits. The assertions Γ and Γ' constitute the heaps before and after the computation and typically are a separating conjunction of refinement assertions for the respective parameters of $m_\dagger$ and m. Formally, we define:

$$\begin{array}{l} hnr\ \Gamma\ m_\dagger\ \Gamma'\ R\ m = m \neq \texttt{fail} \implies \\ \quad (\forall F\ s\ c.\ (\Gamma \star F)\ (abs_m\ s{,}c) \implies \\ \qquad (\exists r_a\ c_a.\ \texttt{elapse}\ (\texttt{return}\ r_a)\ c_a \leq m \\ \qquad\quad \wedge\ wp\ m_\dagger\ (\lambda r\ (s'{,}c').\ (\Gamma' \star R\ r\ r_a \star F \star \mathbb{T})\ (abs_m\ s'{,}c'))\ (s,\ c{+}c_a))) \end{array}$$

The predicate holds if either the abstract program fails or if, for all heaps and resources (s,c) that satisfy the pre-assertion Γ with some frame F, there exists an abstract result and cost (r_a,c_a) that refine m, and $m_\dagger$ terminates with concrete result r in a state s' where Γ' with the frame holds, and r relates to the abstract result via assertion R. The execution costs of $m_\dagger$ and the time credits c' required by the post-assertion Γ' are paid for by the specified cost c_a and the time credits c described by the pre-assertion Γ. Thus, the real costs are paid by a combination of the advertised costs in the abstract program and the potential difference of Γ' and Γ, allowing to seamlessly model amortized computation costs.

Using the affine top $\top$, it is possible for the program to throw away portions of the heap. Note that our $\top$ can only discard time credits. Memory must be explicitly freed by the concrete program $m_\dagger$.

Also note that *hnr* is not tied to the LLVM semantics specifically. It actually is a general pattern for combining the NREST-monad with any other program semantics that provides a weakest precondition and a separation algebra for data and resources.

4.2 The Sepref Tool

The Sepref tool [14,15] automatically synthesizes a concrete program in the LLVM-monad from an abstract algorithm in the NREST-monad. It symbolically executes the abstract program while maintaining refinements for the abstract variables to a concrete representation and generates a concrete program as well as a valid *hnr* predicate. Proof obligations[13] that occur during this process are discharged automatically, guided by user-provided hints where necessary.

The synthesis requires rules for all abstract combinators. For example, `bind` is processed by the following rule:

1 $\quad [\![\ \mathit{hnr}\ \Gamma\ m_\dagger\ \Gamma'\ R_x\ m;$

2 $\quad\ (\forall x\ x_\dagger.\ \mathit{hnr}\ (R_x\ x_\dagger\ x \star \Gamma')\ (f_\dagger\ x_\dagger)\ (R'_x\ x_\dagger\ x \star \Gamma'')\ R_y\ (f\ x));$

3 $\quad\ \mathit{MK\_FREE}\ R'_x\ \mathit{free}\ ]\!]\ \Longrightarrow$

4 $\quad \mathit{hnr}\ \Gamma\ (x_\dagger \leftarrow m_\dagger;\ r_\dagger \leftarrow f_\dagger\ x_\dagger;\ \mathit{free}\ x_\dagger;\ \texttt{return}\ r_\dagger)\ \Gamma''\ R_y\ (x \leftarrow m;\ f\ x)$

To refine $x \leftarrow m; f\,x$, we first execute m, synthesizing the concrete program $m_\dagger$ (line 1). The state after m is $R_x\ x_\dagger\ x \star \Gamma'$, where x is the result created by m. From this state, we execute $f\,x$ and synthesize $f_\dagger\ x_\dagger$ (line 2). The new state is $R'_x\ x_\dagger\ x \star \Gamma'' \star R_y\ y_\dagger\ y$, where y is the result of $f\,x$. Now, the intermediate variable x goes out of scope and has to be deallocated. The predicate *MK_FREE* R'_x *free* (line 3) states that *free* is a deallocator for data structures implemented by refinement assertion R'_x. Note that *free* can only use time credits that are stored in R'_x. Typically, these are payed for during creation of the data structure. This way amortization can be used effectively to hide the necessary *free* operation and its costs in the abstract program.

All other combinators ($\texttt{rec}_c$, $\texttt{if}_c$, $\texttt{while}_c$, etc.) have similar rules that are used to decompose an abstract program into parts, synthesize corresponding con-

[13] E.g. from implementing mathematical integers with fixed-bit machine words.

crete parts recursively and combine them afterwards with the respective combinators from LLVM. At the leaves of this decomposition, atomic operations need to be provided with suitable synthesis predicates.

An example is a list lookup that is implemented by an array:

$$\begin{aligned}&hnr\ (array_A\ p\ xs \star snat_A\ i_\dagger\ i)\\&\quad(array\_nth\ p\ i_\dagger)\\&\quad(array_A\ p\ xs \star snat_A\ i_\dagger\ i)\ id_A\ (list\_get_{spec}\ xs\ i\ (\lambda\_.\ array\_get_{cost}))\end{aligned}$$

where $array_A$, $snat_A$ and id_A relate a list with an array, an unbounded natural number with a bounded signed word and identical elements respectively. With an array at address p holding the list xs and an index $i_\dagger$ that is a bounded signed word representing an unbounded natural number i, $array\_nth$ leaves the parameters unchanged and extracts the element specified by $list\_get_{spec}$ incurring costs $array\_get_{cost}{=}\$_{ofs\_ptr} + \$_{load}$.

Ideally, each operation has its own currency (e.g. *list_get*). However, as our definition of *hnr* does not support currency refinement, the basic operations must use the currencies of the LLVM cost model. To still obtain modular *hnr* rules, we encapsulate specifications for data structures with their cost, e.g. by defining $array\_get_{spec}{=}list\_get_{spec}\ (\lambda\_.\ array\_get_{cost})$. These can easily be introduced in an additional refinement step. Automating this process, and possibly integrating currency refinement into *hnr* is left to future work.

4.3 Extracting Hoare Triples

Note that *hnr* predicates cannot always be expressed as Hoare triples, as the running time bound of the abstract program may depend on the result, which we cannot refer to in the precondition of a Hoare triple, where we have to express the allowed running time as time credits. However, if the running time bound does not depend on the result, we can write *hnr* as a Hoare triple:

$$hnr\ \Gamma\ m_\dagger\ \Gamma'\ R\ (\mathtt{spec}\ \Phi\ (\lambda\_.\ T)) = \{\$T{\star}\Gamma\}m_\dagger\{\lambda r.\ \Gamma'{\star}\exists_A r_a.\ R\ r\ r_a \star \uparrow(\Phi\ r_a)\}$$

While intermediate components might not be of this form, final algorithms typically are. At the end of a development, this rule allows to extract a Hoare triple in the underlying LLVM semantics, cutting out the NREST-monad. For validating the correctness claim of an algorithm, only the final Hoare triple needs to be inspected, which only uses concepts of the underlying semantics.

Note that the above rule is an equivalence. Thus, it can also be used to obtain synthesis rules from Hoare triples provided by the basic VCG infrastructure.

4.4 Attain Supremum

We comment on a problem that arises when composing *hnr* predicates and data refinement in the NREST monad. Consider the following programs and relations:

$$\begin{aligned}m' &= \mathtt{res}\ [x \mapsto \$_a,\ y \mapsto \$_b] && R_R = \{(z,a),(z,b)\}\\ m &= \mathtt{res}\ [z \mapsto \$_a + \$_b] && R_A = id_A\\ m_\dagger &= \mathtt{consume}\ (\$_a + \$_b);\ \mathtt{return}\ z\end{aligned}$$

Data refinement defines the resource bound for a concrete result (here z) as the supremum over all bounds of related results (here x, y). Thus, we have $m \leq \Downarrow_C R_R\ m'$. Moreover, we trivially have $hnr \ \Box\ m_\dagger\ \Box\ R_A\ m$. Intuitively, we want to compose these two refinements, to obtain $hnr\ \Box\ m_\dagger\ \Box\ (R_A \circ R_R)\ m'$. However, as our definition of *hnr* does not form a supremum, this would require $\$_a + \$_b \leq \$_a$ or $\$_a + \$_b \leq \$_b$, which obviously does not hold.

We have not yet found a way to define *hnr* or $\Downarrow_D$ in a form that does not exhibit this effect. Instead, we explicitly require that the supremum of the data refinement has a witness. The predicate *attains_sup* $m\ m'\ R_R$ characterizes that situation: it holds, if for all results r of m the supremum of the set of all abstractions $(r,r') \in R_R$ applied to m' is in that set. This trivially holds if R_R is *single-valued*, i.e. any concrete value is related with at most one abstract value, or if m' is *one-time*, i.e. assigns the same resource bound to all its results.

In practice we *do* encounter non-single-valued relations[14], but they only occur as intermediate results where the composition with an *hnr* predicate is not necessary. Also, collapsing synthesis predicates and refinements in the NREST-monad typically is performed for the final algorithm whose running time does not depend on the result, thus is *one-time*, and ultimately *attains_sup*.

5 Case Study: Introsort

In this section, we apply our framework to the introsort algorithm [22]. We build upon the verification of its functional correctness [17] to verify its running time analysis and synthesize competitive efficient LLVM code for it. Following the "top-down" mantra, we use several intermediate steps to refine a specification down to an implementation.

5.1 Specification of Sorting

We start with the specification of sorting a slice of a list:

$$\begin{array}{l} \textit{slice\_sort}_{spec}\ xs_0\ l\ h\ (T) = \\ \quad \texttt{assert}\ (l \leq h \wedge h \leq \textit{length}\ xs_0); \\ \quad \texttt{spec}\ (\lambda xs.\ \textit{slice\_sort\_aux}\ xs_0\ l\ h\ xs)\ (\lambda\_.\ T) \end{array}$$

where *slice_sort_aux* $xs_0\ l\ h\ xs$ states that xs is a permutation of xs_0, xs is sorted between l and h and equal to xs_0 anywhere else.

5.2 Introsort's Idea

The introsort algorithm is based on quicksort. Like quicksort, it finds a pivot element, partitions the list around the pivot, and recursively sorts the two partitions. Unlike quicksort, however, it keeps track of the recursion depth, and if it

[14] The relation *oarr*, described in earlier work [17, 4.2] by one of the authors, is used to model ownership of parts of a list on an abstract level and is an example for a relation that is not single-valued.

exceeds a certain value (typically $\lfloor 2 \log n \rfloor$), it falls back to heapsort to sort the current partition. Intuitively, quicksort's worst-case behaviour can only occur when unbalanced partitioning causes a high recursion depth, and the introsort algorithm limits the recursion depth, falling back to the $O(n \log n)$ heapsort algorithm. This combines the good practical performance of quicksort with the good worst-case complexity of heapsort.

Our implementation of introsort follows the implementation of *libstdc++*, which includes a second optimization: a first phase executes quicksort (with fallback to heapsort), but stops the recursion when the partition size falls below a certain threshold τ. Then, a second phase sorts the whole list with one final pass of insertion sort. This exploits the fact that insertion sort is actually faster than quicksort for *almost-sorted* lists, i.e., lists where any element is less than τ positions away from its final position in the sorted list. While the optimal threshold τ needs to be determined empirically, it does not influence the worst-case complexity of the final insertion sort, which is $O(\tau n) = O(n)$ for constant τ. The threshold τ will be an implicit parameter from now on.

While this seems like a quite concrete optimization, the two phases are already visible in the abstract algorithm, which is defined as follows in NREST:

$$
\begin{array}{ll}
\mathit{introsort}\ \mathit{xs}\ l\ h = & \\
\quad \mathbf{assert}(l \le h); & \\
\quad n \leftarrow \mathbf{return}\ h{-}l; & (\$_{sub}) \\
\quad \mathbf{if}_c\ n > 1\ \mathbf{then} & (\$_{lt}) \\
\quad\quad \mathit{xs} \leftarrow \mathit{almost\_sort}_{spec}\ \mathit{xs}\ l\ h; & (\$_{almost\_sort}) \\
\quad\quad \mathit{xs} \leftarrow \mathit{final\_sort}_{spec}\ \mathit{xs}\ l\ h & (\$_{final\_sort}) \\
\quad\quad \mathbf{return}\ \mathit{xs} & \\
\quad \mathbf{else\ return}\ \mathit{xs} &
\end{array}
$$

where $\mathit{almost\_sort}_{spec}\ (T)$ specifies an algorithm that almost-sorts a list, consuming at most T resources and $\mathit{final\_sort}_{spec}\ (T)$ specifies an algorithm that sorts an almost-sorted list, consuming at most T resources.

The program *introsort* leaves trivial lists unchanged and otherwise executes the first and second phase. Its resource usage is bounded by the sum of the first and second phase and some overhead for the subtraction, comparison, and *if-then-else*. Using the verification condition generator we prove that *introsort* is correct, i.e., refines the specification of sorting a slice:

$$\mathit{introsort}\ \mathit{xs}\ l\ h \le \Downarrow_C E_{is}\ (\mathit{slice\_sort}_{spec}\ \mathit{xs}\ l\ h\ (\$_{sort}))$$

where $E_{is} = 0(\mathit{sort}{:=}\mathit{introsort}_{cost})$ is the exchange rate used at this step and $\mathit{introsort}_{cost} = \$_{sub} + \$_{if} + \$_{lt} + \$_{almost\_sort} + \$_{final\_sort}$ is the total allotted cost for introsort.

5.3 Quicksort Scheme

The first phase can be implemented in the following way:

$$\mathit{introsort\_aux}\ \mu\ \mathit{xs}\ l\ h =$$

```
2      d ← depth_spec l h;                        ($_depth)
3      rec_c (λintrosort_rec (xs,l,h,d).
4        assert (l ≤ h);
5        n ← h−l;                                 ($_sub)
6        if_c n > τ then                          ($_lt)
7          if_c d = 0 then                        ($_eq)
8            slice_sort_spec xs l h               ($_sort_c (μ (h-l)))
9          else
10           (xs,m) ← partition_spec xs l h;      ($_partition_c (h-l))
11           d' ← d − 1;                          ($_sub)
12           xs ← introsort_rec (xs,l,m,d');
13           xs ← introsort_rec (xs,m,h,d');
14           return xs
15       else return xs
16     ) (xs,l,h,d)
```

where $partition_{spec}$ partitions a slice into two non-empty partitions, returning the start index m of the second partition, and $depth_{spec}$ specifies $\lfloor 2 \log(h - l) \rfloor$.

Let us first analyze the recursive part: if the slice is shorter than the threshold τ, it is simply returned (line 15). Unless the recursion depth limit is reached, the slice is partitioned using $h - l$ $partition_c$ coins, and the procedure is called recursively for both partitions (lines 10-14). Otherwise, the slice is sorted at a price of $\mu\ (h{-}l)$ $sort_c$ coins (line 8). The function μ here represents the leading term in the asymptotic costs of the used sorting algorithm, and the $sort_c$ coin can be seen as the constant factor. This currency will later be exchanged into the respective currencies that are used by the sorting algorithm. Note that we use currency $sort_c$ to describe costs per comparison of a sorting algorithm, while currency *sort* describes the cost for a whole sorting algorithm.

Showing that the procedure results in an almost-sorted list is straightforward. The running time analysis, however, is a bit more involved. We presume a function μ that maps the length of a slice to an upper bound on the abstract steps required for sorting the slice. We will later use heapsort with $\mu_{nlogn}\ n = n \log n$.

Consider the recursion tree of a call in *introsort_rec*: We pessimistically assume that for every leaf in the recursion tree we need to call the fallback sorting algorithm. Furthermore, we have to partition at every inner node. This has cost linear in the length of the current slice. For each following inner level the lengths of the slices add up to the current one's, and so do the incurred costs. Finally we have some overhead at every level including the final one. The cost of the recursive part of *introsort_aux* is:

$$\begin{aligned} &introsort\_rec_{cost}\ \mu\ (n,d) = \$_{sort_c}\ (\mu\ n) + \$_{partition_c}\ d * n \\ &\quad + ((d{+}1){*}n){*}(\$_{if}\ 2 + \$_{call}\ 2 + \$_{eq} + \$_{lt} + \$_{sub}\ 2) \end{aligned}$$

The correctness of the running time bound is proved by induction over the recursion of *introsort_rec*. If the recursion limit is reached ($d{=}0$), the first summand pays for the fallback sorting algorithm. If $d{>}0$, part of the second summand pays for the partitioning of the current slice, then the list is split into two and the recursive costs are payed for by parts of all three summands. To bound the costs for the fallback sorting algorithm, μ needs to be *superadditive*: $\mu\ a + \mu\ b \leq \mu\ (a{+}b)$. In both cases, the third summand pays for the overhead in the current call.

For $d{=}\lfloor 2 \log n \rfloor$ and an $O(n \log n)$ fallback sorting algorithm ($\mu{=}\mu_{nlogn}$), $introsort\_rec_{cost}\ \mu_{nlogn}$ is in $O(n \log n)$.[15] In fact, any $d{\in}O(\log n)$ would do.

Before executing the recursive method, *introsort_aux* calculates the depth limit d. The correctness theorem then reads:

$$introsort\_aux\ \mu_{nlogn}\ xs\ l\ h \leq \Downarrow_C (E_{isa} (h{-}l)) (almost\_sort_{spec}\ xs\ l\ h\ \$_{almost\_sort})$$

with $E_{isa}\ n\ =\ 0(almost\_sort{:=}\ \$_{depth}\ +\ introsort\_rec_{cost}\ \mu_{nlogn}\ (n,\ \lfloor 2 \log n \rfloor))$.

Note that specifications typically use a single coin of a specific currency for their abstract operation, which is then exchanged for the actual costs, usually depending on the parameters.

This concludes the interesting part of the running time analysis of the first phase. It is now left to plug in an $O(n \log n)$ fallback sorting algorithm, and a linear partitioning algorithm.

Heapsort Independently of introsort, we have proved correctness and worst-case complexity of heapsort, yielding the following refinement lemma:

$$heapsort\ xs\ l\ h \leq \Downarrow_C (E_{hs}\ (h{-}l))\ (slice\_sort_{spec}\ xs\ l\ h\ (\$_{sort}))$$

where $E_{hs}\ n\ =\ 0(sort{:=}\ c_1\ +\ log\ n * c_2\ +\ n * c_3\ +\ (n * log\ n) * c_4)$ for some constants c_i :: *ecost*.

Assuming that $n \geq 2$,[16] we can estimate $E_{hs}\ n\ sort \leq \mu_{nlogn}\ n * c$, for $c = c_1 + c_2 + c_3 + c_4$, and thus get, for $E_{hs'}\ =\ 0(sort_c\ :=\ c)$:

$$\begin{aligned}&\Downarrow_C (E_{hs}\ (h{-}l))\ (slice\_sort_{spec}\ xs\ l\ h\ (\$_{sort}))\\ &\leq \Downarrow_C E_{hs'}\ (slice\_sort_{spec}\ xs\ l\ h\ (\$_{sort_c}\ (\mu_{nlogn}\ (h{-}l))))\end{aligned}$$

and, by, transitivity

$$heapsort\ xs\ l\ h \leq \Downarrow_C E_{hs'}\ (slice\_sort_{spec}\ xs\ l\ h\ (\$_{sort_c}\ (\mu_{nlogn}\ (h{-}l))))$$

Note that our framework allowed us to easily convert the abstract currency from a single operation-specific *sort* coin to a $sort_c$ coin for each comparison operation.

Partition and Depth Computation We implement partitioning with the Hoare partitioning scheme using the median-of-3 as the pivot element. Moreover, we implement the computation of the depth limit $(2\lfloor \log(h-l) \rfloor)$ by a loop that counts how often we can divide by two until zero is reached. This yields the following refinement lemmas:

$$\begin{aligned}&pivot\_partition\ xs\ l\ h \leq \Downarrow_C E_{pp}\ (partition_{spec}\ xs\ l\ h\ (\$_{partition_c}\ (h{-}l)))\\ &calc\_depth\ l\ h \leq \Downarrow_C (E_{cd}\ (h{-}l))\ (depth_{spec}\ l\ h\ (\$_{depth}))\end{aligned}$$

---

[15] More precisely, the sum over all (finitely many) currencies is in $O(n \log n)$.

[16] Note that this is a valid assumption, as heapsort will never be called for trivial slices.

Combining the Refinements We replace $\mathit{slice\_sort}_{spec}$, $\mathit{partition}_{spec}$ and depth_{spec} by their implementations *heapsort*, *pivot_partition* and *calc_depth*. We call the resulting implementation $\mathit{introsort\_aux}_2$, and prove

$$\mathit{introsort\_aux}_2\ xs\ l\ h \leq \Downarrow_C(E_{aux}\ (h-l))\ (\mathit{introsort\_aux}\ \mu_{nlogn}\ xs\ l\ h)$$

where the exchange rate E_{aux} combines the exchange rates $E_{hs'}$, E_{pp} and E_{cd} for the component refinements.

Transitive combination with the correctness lemma for *introsort_aux* then yields the correctness lemma for $\mathit{introsort\_aux}_2$:

$$\mathit{introsort\_aux}_2\ xs\ l\ h \leq \Downarrow_C(E_{isa2}\ (h-l))\ (\mathit{almost\_sort}_{spec}\ xs\ l\ h\ (\$_{almost\_sort}))$$

where $E_{isa2}\ n = \mathit{0}(\mathit{almost\_sort}{:=}\downarrow_C(E_{aux}\ n)\ (\mathit{introsort\_aux}_{cost}\ n))$ and the operation $\downarrow_C E\ t$ applies an exchange rate to a resource function.

Refining Resources The stepwise refinement approach allows to structure an algorithm verification in a way that correctness arguments can be conducted on a high level and implementation details can be added later. Resource currencies permit the same for the resource analysis of algorithms: they summarize compound costs, allow reasoning on a higher level of abstraction and can later be refined into fine-grained costs. For example, in the resource analysis of *introsort_aux* the currencies sort_c and $\mathit{partition}_c$ abstract the cost of the respective subroutines. The abstract resource argument is independent from their implementation details, which are only added in a subsequent refinement step, via the exchange rate E_{aux}.

5.4 Final Insertion Sort

The second phase is implemented by insertion sort, repeatedly calling the subroutine *insert*. The specification of *insert* for an index i captures the intuition that it goes from a slice that is sorted up to index $i-1$ to one that is sorted up to index i. Insertion is implemented by moving the last element to the left, as long as the element left of it is greater (or the start of the list has been reached). Moving an element to its correct position takes at most τ steps, as after the first phase the list is almost sorted, i.e., any element is less than τ positions away from its final position in the sorted list. Moreover, elements originally at positions greater τ will never reach the beginning of the list, which allows for the *unguarded* optimization. It omits the bounds check for those elements, saving one index comparison in the innermost loop. Formalizing these arguments yields the implementation *final_insertion_sort* that satisfies

$$\mathit{final\_insertion\_sort}\ xs\ l\ h \leq \Downarrow_C(E_{fis}(h-l))\ (\mathit{final\_sort}_{spec}\ xs\ l\ h\ (\$_{final\_sort}))$$

where $E_{fis}\ n = \mathit{0}(\mathit{final\_sort}{:=}\mathit{final\_insertion}_{cost}\ n)$, and $\mathit{final\_insertion}_{cost}\ n$ is linear in n.

Note that *final_insertion_sort* and $\mathit{introsort\_aux}_2$ use the same currency system. Plugging both refinements into *introsort* yields $\mathit{introsort}_2$ and the lemma

$$\mathit{introsort}_2\ xs\ l\ h \leq \Downarrow_C(E_{is2}(h-l))\ (\mathit{introsort}\ xs\ l\ h)$$

where the exchange rate E_{is2} combines the rates E_{isa2} and E_{fis}.

5.5 Separating Correctness and Complexity Proofs

A crucial function in heapsort is *sift_down*, which restores the heap property by moving the top element down in the heap. To implement this function, we first prove correct a version $sift\_down_1$, which uses swap operations to move the element. In a next step, we refine this to $sift\_down_2$, which saves the top element, then executes upward moves instead of swaps, and, after the last step, moves the saved top element to its final position. This optimization spares half of the memory accesses, exploiting the fact that the next swap operation will overwrite an element just written by the previous swap operation.

However, this refinement is not structural: it replaces swap operations by move operations, and adds an additional move operation at the end. At this point, we chose to separate the functional correctness and resource aspect, to avoid the complexity of a combined non-structural functional and currency refinement. It turns out that proving the complexity of the optimized version $sift\_down_2$ directly is straightforward. Thus, as sketched in Section 2.4, we first prove[17] $sift\_down_2 \leq sift\_down_1 \leq sift\_down_{spec}\ (\infty)$, ignoring the resource aspect. Separately, we prove $sift\_down_2 \leq_n \mathtt{spec}\ (\lambda\_.\ True)\ sift\_down_{cost}$, and combine the two statements to get $sift\_down_2 \leq sift\_down_{spec}\ sift\_down_{cost}$.

5.6 Refining to LLVM

The above abstract programs implicitly come with a fixed type and comparison operator for the elements of the list to be sorted. Those programs use abstract operations and currencies for arithmetic operations on indexes, control flow, comparisons and read/write of a random-access iterator (abstracted by lists with update and lookup operations).

When we further assume an LLVM program that refines the comparison operator in LLVM, and specify how the random-access data structure should be implemented — we choose arrays — we can automatically synthesize an LLVM program *introsort_impl* that refines $introsort_2$, i.e., satisfies the theorem:

$$\begin{array}{l} hnr\ (array_A\ p\ xs \star snat_A\ l_\dagger\ l \star snat_A\ h_\dagger\ h) \\ \quad (introsort\_impl\ p\ l_\dagger\ h_\dagger) \\ \quad (snat_A\ l_\dagger\ l \star snat_A\ h_\dagger\ h)\ array_A\ (introsort_2\ xs\ l\ h) \end{array}$$

Combination with the refinement lemmas for $introsort_2$ and *introsort*, followed by conversion to a Hoare triple, yields our final correctness statement:

$$\begin{array}{l} l \leq h \wedge h < length\ xs_0 \implies \\ \{\$(introsort\_impl_{cost}\ (h{-}l)) \star array_A\ p\ xs_0 \star snat_A\ l_\dagger\ l \star snat_A\ h_\dagger\ h\} \\ \quad introsort\_impl\ p\ l_\dagger\ h_\dagger \\ \{\lambda r.\ \exists_A xs.\ array_A\ r\ xs \star \uparrow(slice\_sort\_aux\ xs_0\ l\ h\ xs) \star snat_A\ l_\dagger\ l \star snat_A\ h_\dagger\ h\} \end{array}$$

where $introsort\_impl_{cost} :: nat \rightarrow ecost$ is the cost bound obtained from applying the exchange rates E_{is} and then E_{is2} to $\$_{sort}$.

[17] Note that we have omitted the function parameters for better readability.

Note that this statement is independent of the Refinement Framework. Thus, to believe in its meaningfulness, one has to only check the formalization of Hoare triples, separation logic, and the LLVM semantics.

To formally prove the statement "*introsort_impl has complexity* $O(n \log n)$", we observe that $introsort\_impl_{cost}$ uses only finitely many currencies, and only finitely many coins of each currency. We define the overall number of coins as

$$introsort\_impl_{allcost}\ n = \Sigma c.\ introsort\_impl_{cost}\ n\ c$$

which expands to

$$introsort\_impl_{allcost}\ n = 4693 + 5 * \ log\ n + 231 * n + 455 * (n * log\ n)$$

which, in turn, is routinely proved to be in $O(n \log n)$.

As a last step, we instantiate the element type to 64-bit unsigned integers and the comparison operation to LLVM's *icmp_ult* instruction, to obtain a program that sorts integers in ascending order. Our code generator can export this to actual LLVM text and a corresponding header file for interfacing our sorting algorithm from C or C++.

As LLVM does not support generics, we cannot implement a replacement for C++'s generic *std::sort<T>*. However, by repeating the last step for different types and compare operators, we can implement a replacement for any fixed *T*.

5.7 Benchmarks

In this section we present benchmarks comparing the code extracted from our formalization with the real world implementation of introsort from the GNU C++ Library (*libstdc++*). Also, as a regression test, we compare with the code extracted from an earlier formalization of introsort [17] that did not verify the running time complexity and used an earlier iteration of the Sepref framework and LLVM semantics without time.

The results are shown in Figure 1. As expected, all three implementations have similar running times. Note that the small differences are well within the noise of the measurements. We conclude that adding the complexity proof to our introsort formalization, and the time aspect to our refinement process has not introduced any timing regressions in the generated code. Note, however, that the code generated by our current formalization is not identical to what the original formalization generated. This is mainly due to small changes in the formalization introduced when adding the timing aspect.

6 Conclusions

We have presented a refinement framework for the simultaneous verification of functional correctness and complexity of algorithm implementations with competitive practical performance.

We use stepwise refinement to separate high-level algorithmic ideas from low-level optimizations, enabling convenient verification of highly optimized algorithms. The novel concept of resource currencies also allows structuring of the

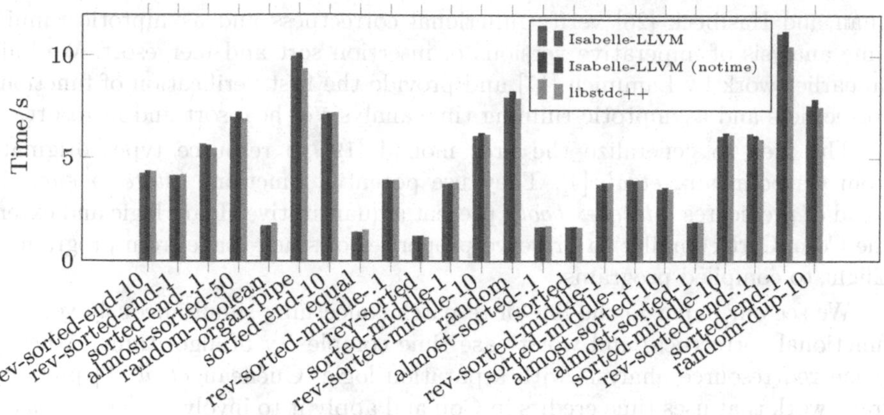

Fig. 1. Comparison of the running time measured for the code generated by the formalization described in this paper (Isabelle-LLVM), the original formalization from [17] (notime), and the *libstdc++* implementation. Arrays with 10^8 *uint64*s with various distributions were sorted, and we display the smallest time of 10 runs. The programs were compiled with *clang-10 -O3*, and run on an Intel XEON E5-2699 with 128GiB RAM and 256K/55M L2/L3 cache. See [17] for details of the benchmarking method.

complexity proofs along the refinement chain. Our framework refines down to the LLVM intermediate representation, such that we can use a state-of-the-art compiler to generate performant programs.

As a case-study, we have proved the functional correctness and complexity of the introsort sorting algorithm. Our verified implementation performs on par with the (unverified) state-of-the-art implementation from the GNU C++ Library. It also provably meets the C++11 standard library [7] specification for *std::sort*, which in particular requires a worst-case time complexity of $O(n \log n)$. We are not aware of any other verified real-world implementations of sorting algorithms that come with a complexity analysis.

Our work is a combination and substantial extension of an earlier refinement framework for functional correctness [15] which also comes with a verification of introsort [17], and a refinement framework for a single *enat*-valued currency [11]. In particular, we have generalized the refinement framework to arbitrary resources, introduced currencies that help organizing refinement proofs, extended the LLVM semantics and reasoning infrastructure with a cost model, connected it to the refinement framework via a new version of the Sepref tool, and, finally, added the complexity analysis for introsort.

6.1 Related Work

Nipkow *et al.* [23, §4.1] collect verification efforts concerning sorting algorithms. We add a few instances verifying running time: Wang *et al.* use TiML [25] to verify correctness and asymptotic time complexity of mergesort automatically.

Zhan and Haslbeck [26] verify functional correctness and asymptotic running time analysis of imperative versions of insertion sort and mergesort. We build on earlier work by Lammich [17] and provide the first verification of functional correctness and asymptotic running time analysis of heapsort and introsort.

The idea to generalize the nres monad [19] to resource types originates from Carbonneaux *et al.* [4]. They use potential functions ($state \to enat$) instead of predicates ($state \to bool$), present a quantitative Hoare logic and extend the CompCert compiler to preserve properties of stack-usage from programs in Clight to compiled programs.

We see our paper in the line of research concerning simultaneously verifying functional correctness and worst-case time complexity of algorithms. Atkey [1] pioneered resource analysis with separation logic, Guéneau *et al.* [9] present a framework that uses time credits in Coq and apply it to involved algorithms and data structures [10,6]. We further develop their work in three ways: First, while time credits usually are natural numbers [1,9,26,21,6] or integers [10], we generalize to an abstract resource type and specifically use resource currencies for a fine-grained analysis. Second, we use stepwise refinement to structure the verification and make the resource analysis of larger use-cases manageable. Third, we provide facilities to automatically extract efficient competitive code from the verification. The following are the most complex algorithms and data structures with verified running time analysis using time credits and separation logic we are aware of: a linear time selection algorithm [26], an incremental cycle detection algorithm [10], Union-Find [6], Edmonds-Karp and Kruskal's algorithm [11].

6.2 Future Work

A verified compiler down to machine code would further reduce the trusted code base of our approach. While that is not expected to be available soon for LLVM in Isabelle, the NREST-monad and the Sepref tool are general enough to connect to a different back end. Formalizing one of the CompCert C semantics [2] in Isabelle, connecting it to the NREST-monad and then processing synthesized C code with CompCert's verified compiler would be a way to go.

In this paper we apply our framework to verify an involved algorithm that only uses basic data structures, i.e. arrays. A next step is to verify more involved data structures, e.g. by porting existing verifications of the Imperative Collections Framework [16] to LLVM. We do not yet see how to reason about the running time of data structures like hash maps, where worst-case analysis would be possible but not useful. In general, extending the framework to average-case analysis and probabilistic programs are exciting roads to take.

We plan to implement more automation, saving the user from writing boilerplate code when handling resource currencies and exchange rates.

Neither the LLVM nor the NREST level of our framework is tied to running time. Applying it to other resources like maximum heap space consumption might be a next step.

References

1. Atkey, R.: Amortised resource analysis with separation logic. In: Gordon, A.D. (ed.) European Symposium on Programming, ESOP 2010. Lecture Notes in Computer Science, vol. 6012, pp. 85–103. Springer (2010). https://doi.org/10.1007/978-3-642-11957-6_6, https://doi.org/10.1007/978-3-642-11957-6_6
2. Blazy, S., Leroy, X.: Mechanized semantics for the Clight subset of the C language. J. Autom. Reason. **43**(3), 263–288 (2009). https://doi.org/10.1007/s10817-009-9148-3, https://doi.org/10.1007/s10817-009-9148-3
3. Calcagno, C., O'Hearn, P.W., Yang, H.: Local action and abstract separation logic. In: Symposium on Logic in Computer Science (LICS 2007). pp. 366–378. IEEE Computer Society (2007). https://doi.org/10.1109/LICS.2007.30, https://doi.org/10.1109/LICS.2007.30
4. Carbonneaux, Q., Hoffmann, J., Ramananandro, T., Shao, Z.: End-to-end verification of stack-space bounds for C programs. In: O'Boyle, M.F.P., Pingali, K. (eds.) ACM SIGPLAN Conference on Programming Language Design and Implementation, PLDI '14, Edinburgh, United Kingdom - June 09 - 11, 2014. pp. 270–281. ACM (2014). https://doi.org/10.1145/2594291.2594301, https://doi.org/10.1145/2594291.2594301
5. Charguéraud, A.: Separation logic for sequential programs (functional pearl). Proc. ACM Program. Lang. **4**(ICFP), 116:1–116:34 (2020). https://doi.org/10.1145/3408998, https://doi.org/10.1145/3408998
6. Charguéraud, A., Pottier, F.: Verifying the correctness and amortized complexity of a union-find implementation in separation logic with time credits. J. Autom. Reason. **62**(3), 331–365 (2019). https://doi.org/10.1007/s10817-017-9431-7, https://doi.org/10.1007/s10817-017-9431-7
7. cppreference: C++ standard library specification of sort. https://en.cppreference.com/w/cpp/algorithm/sort, accessed: 2020-10-12
8. The GNU C++ library, https://gcc.gnu.org/onlinedocs/libstdc++/, version 7.4.0
9. Guéneau, A., Charguéraud, A., Pottier, F.: A fistful of dollars: Formalizing asymptotic complexity claims via deductive program verification. In: Ahmed, A. (ed.) Programming Languages and Systems - 27th European Symposium on Programming, ESOP 2018. Lecture Notes in Computer Science, vol. 10801, pp. 533–560. Springer (2018). https://doi.org/10.1007/978-3-319-89884-1_19, https://doi.org/10.1007/978-3-319-89884-1_19
10. Guéneau, A., Jourdan, J., Charguéraud, A., Pottier, F.: Formal proof and analysis of an incremental cycle detection algorithm. In: Harrison, J., O'Leary, J., Tolmach, A. (eds.) 10th International Conference on Interactive Theorem Proving, ITP 2019. LIPIcs, vol. 141, pp. 18:1–18:20. Schloss Dagstuhl - Leibniz-Zentrum für Informatik (2019). https://doi.org/10.4230/LIPIcs.ITP.2019.18, https://doi.org/10.4230/LIPIcs.ITP.2019.18
11. Haslbeck, M.P.L., Lammich, P.: Refinement with time - refining the run-time of algorithms in Isabelle/HOL. In: Harrison, J., O'Leary, J., Tolmach, A. (eds.) 10th International Conference on Interactive Theorem Proving, ITP 2019. LIPIcs, vol. 141, pp. 20:1–20:18. Schloss Dagstuhl - Leibniz-Zentrum für Informatik (2019). https://doi.org/10.4230/LIPIcs.ITP.2019.20, https://doi.org/10.4230/LIPIcs.ITP.2019.20
12. Hoare, C.A.R.: Algorithm 64: Quicksort. Commun. ACM **4**(7), 321– (Jul 1961). https://doi.org/10.1145/366622.366644, http://doi.acm.org/10.1145/366622.366644

13. Krauss, A.: Recursive definitions of monadic functions. In: Bove, A., Komendantskaya, E., Niqui, M. (eds.) Proceedings Workshop on Partiality and Recursion in Interactive Theorem Provers, PAR 2010, Edinburgh, UK, 15th July 2010. EPTCS, vol. 43, pp. 1–13 (2010). https://doi.org/10.4204/EPTCS.43.1, https://doi.org/10.4204/EPTCS.43.1
14. Lammich, P.: Refinement to Imperative/HOL. In: Urban, C., Zhang, X. (eds.) Interactive Theorem Proving - 6th International Conference, ITP 2015. Lecture Notes in Computer Science, vol. 9236, pp. 253–269. Springer (2015). https://doi.org/10.1007/978-3-319-22102-1_17, https://doi.org/10.1007/978-3-319-22102-1_17
15. Lammich, P.: Generating verified LLVM from Isabelle/HOL. In: Harrison, J., O'Leary, J., Tolmach, A. (eds.) 10th International Conference on Interactive Theorem Proving, ITP 2019. LIPIcs, vol. 141, pp. 22:1–22:19. Schloss Dagstuhl - Leibniz-Zentrum für Informatik (2019). https://doi.org/10.4230/LIPIcs.ITP.2019.22, https://doi.org/10.4230/LIPIcs.ITP.2019.22
16. Lammich, P.: Refinement to Imperative HOL. J. Autom. Reason. **62**(4), 481–503 (2019). https://doi.org/10.1007/s10817-017-9437-1, https://doi.org/10.1007/s10817-017-9437-1
17. Lammich, P.: Efficient verified implementation of introsort and pdqsort. In: Peltier, N., Sofronie-Stokkermans, V. (eds.) IJCAR 2020. Lecture Notes in Computer Science, vol. 12167, pp. 307–323. Springer (2020). https://doi.org/10.1007/978-3-030-51054-1_18, https://doi.org/10.1007/978-3-030-51054-1_18
18. Lammich, P., Meis, R.: A Separation Logic Framework for Imperative HOL. Archive of Formal Proofs (Nov 2012), http://isa-afp.org/entries/Separation_Logic_Imperative_HOL.html, Formal proof development
19. Lammich, P., Tuerk, T.: Applying data refinement for monadic programs to Hopcroft's algorithm. In: Beringer, L., Felty, A.P. (eds.) Interactive Theorem Proving - Third International Conference, ITP 2012. Lecture Notes in Computer Science, vol. 7406, pp. 166–182. Springer (2012). https://doi.org/10.1007/978-3-642-32347-8_12, https://doi.org/10.1007/978-3-642-32347-8_12
20. "libc++" c++ standard library, https://libcxx.llvm.org/
21. Mével, G., Jourdan, J., Pottier, F.: Time credits and time receipts in Iris. In: Caires, L. (ed.) Programming Languages and Systems - 28th European Symposium on Programming, ESOP 2019. Lecture Notes in Computer Science, vol. 11423, pp. 3–29. Springer (2019). https://doi.org/10.1007/978-3-030-17184-1_1, https://doi.org/10.1007/978-3-030-17184-1_1
22. Musser, D.R.: Introspective sorting and selection algorithms. Softw. Pract. Exp. **27**(8), 983–993 (1997)
23. Nipkow, T., Eberl, M., Haslbeck, M.P.L.: Verified textbook algorithms - A biased survey. In: Hung, D.V., Sokolsky, O. (eds.) Automated Technology for Verification and Analysis - 18th International Symposium, ATVA 2020. Lecture Notes in Computer Science, vol. 12302, pp. 25–53. Springer (2020). https://doi.org/10.1007/978-3-030-59152-6_2, https://doi.org/10.1007/978-3-030-59152-6_2
24. Wadler, P.: Comprehending monads. In: Proceedings of the 1990 ACM Conference on LISP and Functional Programming. p. 61–78. LFP '90, Association for Computing Machinery, New York, NY, USA (1990). https://doi.org/10.1145/91556.91592, https://doi-org.manchester.idm.oclc.org/10.1145/91556.91592
25. Wang, P., Wang, D., Chlipala, A.: TiML: a functional language for practical complexity analysis with invariants. Proc. ACM Program. Lang. **1**(OOPSLA), 79:1–79:26 (2017). https://doi.org/10.1145/3133903, https://doi.org/10.1145/3133903

26. Zhan, B., Haslbeck, M.P.L.: Verifying asymptotic time complexity of imperative programs in Isabelle. In: Galmiche, D., Schulz, S., Sebastiani, R. (eds.) Automated Reasoning - 9th International Joint Conference, IJCAR 2018. Lecture Notes in Computer Science, vol. 10900, pp. 532–548. Springer (2018). https://doi.org/10.1007/978-3-319-94205-6_35, https://doi.org/10.1007/978-3-319-94205-6_35

Run-time Complexity Bounds Using Squeezers

Oren Ish-Shalom[1]✉, Shachar Itzhaky[2], Noam Rinetzky[1], and Sharon Shoham[1]

[1] Tel Aviv University, Tel Aviv, Israel
tuna.is.good.for.you@gmail.com
[2] Technion, Haifa, Israel

Abstract. Determining upper bounds on the time complexity of a program is a fundamental problem with a variety of applications, such as performance debugging, resource certification, and compile-time optimizations. Automated techniques for cost analysis excel at bounding the resource complexity of programs that use integer values and linear arithmetic. Unfortunately, they fall short when execution traces become more involved, esp. when data dependencies may affect the termination conditions of loops. In such cases, state-of-the-art analyzers have shown to produce loose bounds, or even no bound at all.

We propose a novel technique that generalizes the common notion of recurrence relations based on ranking functions. Existing methods usually unfold one loop iteration, and examine the resulting relations between variables. These relations assist in establishing a recurrence that bounds the number of loop iterations. We propose a different approach, where we derive recurrences by comparing *whole traces* with *whole traces* of a lower rank, avoiding the need to analyze the complexity of intermediate states. We offer a set of global properties, defined with respect to whole traces, that facilitate such a comparison, and show that these properties can be checked efficiently using a handful of local conditions. To this end, we adapt *state squeezers*, an induction mechanism previously used for verifying safety properties. We demonstrate that this technique encompasses the reasoning power of bounded unfolding, and more. We present some seemingly innocuous, yet intricate, examples where previous tools based on *cost relations* and control flow analysis fail to solve, and that our squeezer-powered approach succeeds.

1 Introduction

Cost analysis is the problem of estimating the resource usage of a given program, over all of its possible executions. It complements functional verification—of safety and liveness properties—and is an important task in formal software certification. When used in combination with functional verification, cost analysis ensures that a program is not only correct, but completes its processing in a reasonable amount of time, uses a reasonable amount of memory, communication bandwidth, etc. In this work we focus on run-time complexity analysis. While the area has been studied extensively, e.g., [19], [28], [3], [14], [6], [16], [21], [12], [9], the general problem of constraining the number of iterations in programs containing loops with arbitrary termination conditions remains hard.

A prominent approach to computing upper bounds on the time complexity of a program identifies a well-founded numerical measure over program states that decreases in

N. Yoshida (Ed.): ESOP 2021, LNCS 12648, pp. 320–347, 2021.
https://doi.org/10.1007/978-3-030-72019-3_12

```
void binary_counter(unsigned int n) {
  unsigned int c[n];
  memset(c,0,n*sizeof(unsigned int));
  int i=0;
  while (i < n) {
    if (c[i] == 1) /*scan 1-prefix*/{c[i] = 0; i++;           }
    else           /*increment*/    {c[i] = 1; i=0; print(c);}
  }}
```

Fig. 1. A program that produces all combinations of n bits.

every step of the program, also called a *ranking function*. In this case, an upper bound on the measure of the initial states comprises an upper bound on the program's time complexity. Finding such measures manually is often extremely difficult. The *cost relations* approach, dating back to [28], attempts to automate this process by using the control flow graph of the program to extract recurrence formulas that characterize this measure. Roughly speaking, the recurrences relate the measures (costs) of adjacent nodes in the graph, taking into account the cost of the step between them. In this way, the cost relations track the evolution of the measure between *every* pair of consecutive states along the executions of the program.

One limitation of cost relations is the need to capture the number of steps remaining for execution in *every* state, that is, all intermediate states along all executions. If the structure of the state is complex, this may require higher order expressions, e.g., summing over an unbounded number of elements. As an example, consider the program in Fig. 1 that implements a binary counter represented by an array of bits.

In this case, a ranking function that decreases between every two consecutive iterations of the loop, or even between two iterations that print the value of the counter, depends on the *entire* content of the array. Attempting to express a ranking function over the scalar variables of this program is analogous to abstracting the loop as a finite-state system that ignores the content of the array, and as such contains transition cycles (e.g. the abstract state $\langle n \mapsto n_0, i \mapsto 0\rangle$, obtained by projecting the state to the scalar variables only, repeats multiple times in any trace)—meaning that no strictly decreasing function can be defined in this way. Similarly, any attempt to consider a bounded number of bits will encounter the same difficulty.

In this paper, we propose a novel approach for extracting recurrence relations capturing the time complexity of an imperative program, modeled as a transition system, by relating whole traces instead of individual states. The key idea is to relate a trace to (one or more) shorter traces. This allows to formulate a recurrence that resolves to the length of the trace and recurs over the values at the initial states only. We sidestep the need to take into account the more complex parts of the state that change along the trace (e.g., in the case of the binary counter, the array is initialized with zeros).

Our approach relies on the notion of *state squeezers* [22], previously used exclusively for the verification of safety properties. We present a novel aspect where the same squeezers can be used to determine complexity bounds, by replacing the safety property check with trace length judgements.

Squeezers provide a means to perform induction on the "size" of (initial) states to prove that all reachable states adhere to a given specification. This is accomplished by attaching *ranks* from a well-founded set to states, and defining a *squeezer function* that maps states to states of a lower rank. Note that the notion of a rank used in our work is distinct from that of a ranking function, and the two should not be confused; in particular, a rank is not required to decrease on execution steps. Previously, squeezers were utilized for safety verification: the ability to establish safety is achieved by having the squeezer map states in a way that forms a (relaxed form of) a *simulation relation*, ensuring that the traces of the lower-rank states simulate the traces of the higher rank states. Due to the simulation property, which is verified locally, safety over states with a *base* rank, carries over (by induction over the rank) to states of any higher rank.

In this work, we use the construction of well-founded ranks and squeezers to define a *recurrence formula* representing (an upper bound on) the time complexity of the procedure being analyzed. We do so by expressing the complexity (length) of traces in terms of the complexity of lower-rank traces. This new setting raises additional challenges: it is no longer sufficient to relate traces to lower-rank traces; we also need to *quantify the discrepancy* between the lengths of the traces, as well as between their ranks. This is achieved by a certain form of simulation that is parameterized by *stuttering shapes* (for the lengths) and by means of a *rank bounding function* (for the ranks). Furthermore, while [22] limits each trace to relate to a *single* lower-rank trace, we have found that it is sometimes beneficial to employ a *decomposition* of the original trace into *several* consecutive *trace segments*, so that each segment corresponds to *some* (possibly different) lower-rank trace.The segmentation simplifies the analysis of the length of the entire trace, since it creates sub-analyses that are easier to carry out, and the sum of which gives the desired recurrence formula. This also enables a richer set of recurrences to be constructed automatically, namely non-single recurrences (meaning that the recursive reference may appear more than once on the right hand side of the equation).

The base case of the recurrence is obtained by computing an upper bound on the time complexity of base-rank states. This is typically a simpler problem that may be addressed, e.g., by symbolic execution due to the bounded nature of the base. The solution to the recurrence formula with the respective base case soundly overapproximates the time complexity of the procedure.

We show that, conceptually, the classical approach for generating recurrences based on ranking functions can be viewed as a special case of our approach where the squeezer maps a state to its immediate successor. The real power of our approach is in the freedom to define other squeezers, producing simpler recursions, and avoiding the need for complex ranking functions.

Our use of squeezers for extracting recurrences that bound the complexity of imperative programs is related to the way analyses for functional programs (e.g. [20]) use the term(s) in recursive function calls to extract recurrences. The functional programming style coincidentally provides such candidate terms. The novelty of our approach is in introducing the concept of a squeezer explicitly, leading to a more flexible analysis as it does not restrict the squeezer to follow specific terms in the program. In particular, this allows reasoning over space in imperative programs as well.

The main results of this paper can be summarized as follows:

- We propose a novel technique for run-time complexity analysis of imperative programs based on state squeezers. Squeezers, together with rank-bounding functions, are used for extracting recurrence relations whose solutions overapproximate the length of executions of the input program.
- We formalize the notions of *state squeezers*, *partitioned simulation* and *rank bounding functions* that underlie the approach, and establish conditions that ensure soundness of the recurrence relations.
- We demonstrate that squeezers and rank bounding functions can be efficiently synthesized and verified, due to their compactness, especially relative to explicit ranking functions.
- We implemented our approach and applied it successfully to several small but intricate programs, some of which could not have been handled by existing techniques.

2 Overview

In this section we give a high level description of our technique for complexity analysis using the binary counter example in Fig. 1.

Example: Binary counter The procedure in Fig. 1 receives as an input a number n of bits and iterates over all their possible values in the range $0...2^n - 1$. The "current" value is maintained in an array c which is initialized to zero and whose length is n. $c[0]$ represents the least significant bit. The loop scans the array from the least significant bit forward looking for the leftmost 0 and zeroing the prefix of 1s. As soon as it encounters a 0, it sets it to 1 and starts the scan from the beginning. The program terminates when it reaches the end of the array ($i = n$), all array entries are zeros, and the last value was $111\ldots$; at this point all the values have been enumerated.

Existing analyses All recent methods that we are aware of (such as [16,4,20]) fail to analyze the complexity of this procedure (in fact, most methods will fail to realize that the loop terminates at all). One reason for that is the need to model the contents of the array whose size in unknown at compile time. However, even if data *were* modeled somehow and taken into account, finding a ranking function, which underlies existing approaches, is hard since this function is required to decrease between *any* two consecutive iterations along *any* execution. Here for instance, to the best of our knowledge, such a function would depend on an unbounded number of elements of the array; it would need to extract the current value as an integer, along the lines of $\sum_{j=0}^{n-1} c[j] \cdot 2^j$.

The use of a ranking function for complexity analysis is somewhat analogous to the use of inductive invariants in safety verification. Both are based on induction over time along an execution. This paper is inspired by previous work [22] showing that verification can also be done when the induction is performed on the size (*rank*) of the state rather than on the number of iterations, where the size of the state may correspond, e.g., to the size of an unbounded data structure. We argue that similar concepts can be applied in a framework for complexity classification. That is, we try to infer a recurrence relation that is *based on the rank* of the state and correlates the lengths of *complete* executions—executions that start from an initial state—of different ranks. This sidesteps the need to express the length of *partial* executions, which start from intermediate states. While the approach applies to bounded-state systems as well, its benefits become most apparent when the program contains a-priori unbounded stores, such as arrays.

Our approach. Roughly speaking, our approach for computing recurrence formulas that provide an upper bound on the complexity of a procedure is based on the following ingredients:

– A *rank* function $r : init \to X$ that maps initial states to ranks from a well founded set $(X, \prec)$ with base B. Intuitively, the rank of the initial state governs the time complexity of the entire trace, and we also consider it to be the rank of the trace. As we shall soon see, this rank can be significantly simpler than a ranking function.
– A *squeezer* $\curlyvee : \Sigma \to \Sigma$ that maintains (some variant of) a simulation relation, thus ensuring a bona fide correspondence between higher-rank traces and lower-rank traces through correspondence between states.
– A *trace partition* $p_d : \Sigma \to [1..d]$ that maps each state to a segment-identifier $i \in [1..d]$, and induces a decomposition of a trace into *segments*, allowing $\curlyvee$ to map each of them to a separate, lower-rank *mini-trace*.
– A *rank-bounding* function $\hat{\curlyvee} : X \times [1..d] \to X$ that provides an upper bound on the rank of the initial states of the d mini-traces based on the rank of the higher-rank trace. (The rank is *not* required to be uniform across mini-traces).

All of these ingredients are synthesized automatically, as we discuss in Section 4. Next, we elaborate on each of these ingredients, and illustrate them using the binary counter example. We further demonstrate how we use these ingredients to find recurrence formulas describing (an upper bound on) the complexity of the program.

Some notations We adopt a standard encoding of a program as a transition system over a state space Σ, with a set of initial states $init \subseteq \Sigma$ and transition function $tr : \Sigma \to \Sigma$, where a transition corresponds to a loop iteration. We use $reach \subseteq \Sigma$ to denote the set of reachable states, $reach = \{\sigma \mid \exists \sigma_0, k.\ tr^k(\sigma_0) = \sigma \wedge \sigma_0 \in init\}$.

Defining the rank of a state Ranks are taken from a well founded set $(X, \prec)$ with a basis $B \subseteq X$ that contains all the minimal elements of X. The rank function, $r : init \to X$, aims to abstract away irrelevant data from the (initial) state that does *not* effect the execution time, and only uses state "features" that do. When proper ranks are used, the rank of an initial state is all that is needed to provide a tight bound on its trace length. Since ranks are taken from a well founded set, they can be recursed over. In the binary counter example, the chosen rank is n, namely, the rank function maps each state to the size of the array. (Notice that the rank does not depend on the contents of the array; in contrast, bounding the trace length from any intermediate state, and not just initial states, would have required considering the content of the array).

Given the rank function, our analysis extracts a recurrence formula for the complexity function $comp_x : X \to \mathbb{N} \cup \{\infty\}$ that provides an upper bound on the number of iterations of tr based on the rank of the *initial states*. In our exposition, we sometimes

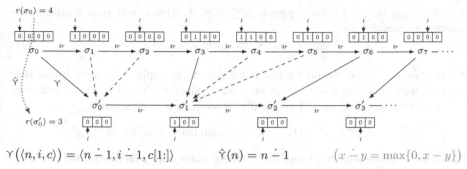

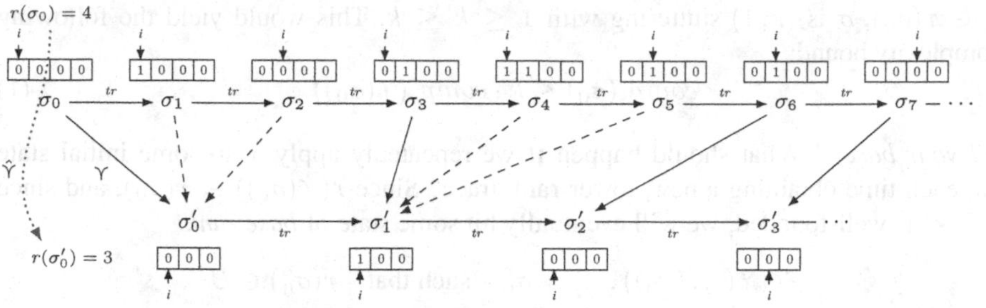

$$\Upsilon(\langle n, i, c\rangle) = \langle n \dot{-} 1, i \dot{-} 1, c[1:]\rangle \qquad \hat{\Upsilon}(n) = n \dot{-} 1 \qquad (x \dot{-} y = \max\{0, x - y\})$$

Fig. 2. Correspondence between two traces of the binary counter program. Squeezer removes the leftmost array entry, that represents the least significant bit. The rank is the array size, i.e., four on the upper trace and three on the lower one. The simulation includes only 1-,2- and 3-steps, so the length of the upper trace is at most three times that of the lower trace, yielding an overall complexity bound of $O(3^n)$.

also refer to a time complexity function over states, $comp_s : init \to \mathbb{N} \cup \{\infty\}$, which is defined directly on the (initial) states, as the number of iterations in an execution that starts with some $\sigma_0 \in init$.

Defining a squeezer The squeezer $\Upsilon : \Sigma \to \Sigma$ is a function that maps states to states of lower-rank traces (where the rank of a trace is determined by the rank of its initial state), down to the base ranks B. Its importance is in defining a correspondence between higher-rank traces and lower-rank ones that can be verified locally, by examining individual states rather than full traces. The kind of correspondence that the squeezer is required to ensure affects the flexibility of the approach and the kind of recurrence formulas that it may yield. To start off, consider a rather naive squeezer that satisfies the following local properties:

- rank decrease of non-base initial states: $\sigma_0 \in init \wedge r(\sigma_0) \notin B \Rightarrow r(\Upsilon(\sigma_0)) \prec r(\sigma_0)$, and
- simulation
  - initial anchor: $\sigma_0 \in init \Rightarrow \Upsilon(\sigma_0) \in init$,
  - k-step: $\sigma \in reach \Rightarrow \exists k.\ tr(\Upsilon(\sigma)) = \Upsilon(tr^k(\sigma))$.

As an example, the squeezer we consider for the binary counter program is rather intuitive: it removes the least significant bit ($c[0]$), and adjusts the index i accordingly. Doing so yields a state with rank $r(\Upsilon(\sigma_0)) = r(\sigma_0) - 1$. Fig. 2 shows the correspondence between a 4-bit binary counter, and a 3-bit one. The figure illustrates the simulation k-step property for $k = 1, 2, 3$: σ_0 and σ_3 are $(3, 1)$-stuttering, σ_1 and σ_4 are $(2, 1)$-stuttering, and σ_2, σ_5 and σ_6 are $(1, 1)$-stuttering.

The simulation property induces a correlation between a higher rank trace τ and a lower rank one τ', such that every step of τ' is matched by k steps in τ. Whenever a state σ satisfies the k-step property, we will refer to it as being $(k, 1)$-*stuttering*. (We usually only care about the smallest k that satisfies the property for a given σ.) Now suppose that there exists some $\widehat{k} \in \mathbb{N}^+$ such that for every trace $\tau(\sigma_0)$ and every state

$\sigma \in \tau(\sigma_0)$, σ is $(k, 1)$-stuttering with $1 \leq k \leq \widehat{k}$. This would yield the following complexity bound:

$$comp_s(\sigma_0) \leq \widehat{k} \cdot comp_s(\curlyvee(\sigma_0)). \tag{1}$$

All your base [3] What should happen if we repeatedly apply $\curlyvee$ to some initial state σ_0, each time obtaining a new, lower-rank trace? Since $r(\curlyvee(\sigma_0)) \prec r(\sigma_0)$, and since $(X, \prec)$ is well-founded, we will eventually hit some state of *base rank*:

$$\curlyvee(\curlyvee(\ldots(\sigma_0))\ldots) = \sigma_0^\circ \quad \text{such that} \quad r(\sigma_0^\circ) \in B$$

Hence, if we know the complexity of the initial states with a base rank, we can apply Eq. (1) iteratively to compute an upper bound of the complexity of *any* initial state.

How many steps will be needed to get from an arbitrary initial state σ_0 to σ_0°? Clearly, this depends on the rank, and the way in which $\curlyvee$ decreases it.

Consider the binary counter program again, with the rank $r(\sigma) = n$. $(\mathbb{N}, <)$ is well-founded, with a single minimum 0. If we define, e.g., $B = \{0, 1\}$, we know that the length of any trace with $n \in B$ is bounded by a constant, 2. (Bounding the length of traces starting from an initial state σ_0 where $r(\sigma_0) \in B$ can be done with known methods, e.g., symbolic execution). Since the rank decreases by 1 on each "squeeze", we get the following exponential bound:

$$comp_s(\sigma_0) \leq 2 \cdot 3^{n-1} = O(3^n) \tag{2}$$

The last logical step, going from (1) to (2), is, in fact, highly involved: since Eq. (1) is a mapping of *states*, solving such a recurrence for arbitrary $\curlyvee$ cannot be carried out using known automated methods. Instead, we implicitly used the rank of the state, n, to extract a recurrence over scalar values and obtain a closed-form expression. Let us make this reasoning explicit by first expressing Eq. (1) in terms of $comp_x$ instead of $comp_s$:

$$comp_x(n) \leq \widehat{k} \cdot comp_x(n-1)$$

Here, $n - 1$ denotes the rank obtained when squeezing an initial state of rank n. Unlike Eq. (1), this is a recurrence formula over $(\mathbb{N}, <)$ that may be solved algorithmically, leading to the solution $comp_x(n) = O(3^n)$.

Surplus analysis Assuming the worst k for all the states in the trace can be too conservative; in particular, if there are only a few states that satisfy the $\widehat{k}$-step property, and all the others satisfy the 1-step property. In the latter case, if we know that at most b states in any one trace have $k > 1$, we can formulate the tighter bound:

$$comp_s(\sigma_0) \leq comp_s(\curlyvee(\sigma_0)) + \widehat{k} \cdot b \tag{3}$$

Incidentally, in the current setting of the binary counter program, the number of $\widehat{k}$-steps (3-steps) is *not* bounded. So we cannot apply the inequality (3) repeatedly on any trace, as the number of 3-steps depends on the initial state. However, we can improve the analysis by partitioning the trace to two parts, as we explain next.

[3] https://knowyourmeme.com/memes/all-your-base-are-belong-to-us

Segments and mini-traces Note that both (1) and (3) "suffer" from an inherent restriction that the right hand side contains *exactly* one recursive reference. As such, they are limited in expressing certain kinds of complexity classes.

In order to get more diverse recurrences, including non-single recurrences, we propose an extension of the simulation property that allows more than one lower-rank trace:

- *partitioned* simulation
  - initial anchor: $\sigma_0 \in init \Rightarrow \curlyvee(\sigma_0) \in init$ *(same as before)*,
  - k-step: $\sigma \in reach \Rightarrow \exists k.\, tr\big(\curlyvee(\sigma)\big) = \curlyvee\big(tr^k(\sigma)\big)$ *(same as before)* or $\curlyvee\big(tr(\sigma)\big) \in init$ *(switch)*

This definition allows a new mini-trace to start at any point along a higher-rank trace τ, thus marking the beginning of a new segment of τ. When this occurs, we call $tr(\sigma)$ a *switch state*. For the sake of uniformity, we also refer to all initial states $\sigma_0 \in init$ as switch states. Hence, each segment of τ starts with a switch state, and the mini-traces are the lower-level traces that correspond to the segments (these are the traces that start from $\curlyvee(\sigma_s)$, where σ_s is a switch state). The length of τ can now be expressed as the *sum* of lower-level mini-traces.

However, there are two problems remaining. First, we need to extend the "rank decrease of non-base initial states" requirement to any switch state in order to ensure that the ranks of all mini-traces are indeed lower. Namely, we need to require that if σ_s is any switch state in a trace from σ_0, then $r\big(\curlyvee(\sigma_s)\big) \prec r(\sigma_0)$. Second, even if we extend the rank decrease requirement, this definition does not suggest a way to bound the number of correlated mini-traces and their respective ranks, and therefore suggests no effective way to produce an equation for $comp_s$ as before.

To sidestep the problem of a potentially unbounded number of mini-traces, we augment the definition of simulation with a *trace partition* function; to address the challenge of the rank decrease we use a *rank-bounding* function, which is responsible both for ensuring that the rank of the mini-traces decreases and for bounding their ranks.

Defining a partition We define a function $p_d : \Sigma \to \{1, \ldots, d\}$, parameterized by a constant d, called a *partition function*, that is weakly monotone along any trace ($p_d(\sigma) \leq p_d(tr(\sigma))$). This function induces a partition of any trace τ into (at most) d segments by grouping states based on the value of $p_d(\sigma)$. To ensure the segments and mini-traces are aligned, we require that switch states only occur at segment boundaries.

- *d-partitioned* simulation:
  - initial anchor: $\sigma_0 \in init \Rightarrow \curlyvee(\sigma_0) \in init$ *(same as before)*,
  - k-step: $\sigma \in reach \Rightarrow \exists k.\, tr\big(\curlyvee(\sigma)\big) = \curlyvee\big(tr^k(\sigma)\big)$ *(same as before)* or $\curlyvee\big(tr(\sigma)\big) \in init \wedge p_d(\sigma) < p_d\big(tr(\sigma)\big)$ *(segment switch)*

In our running example, let us change $\curlyvee$ so that it shrinks the state by removing the *most* significant bit instead of the least. This leads to a partition of the execution trace for $r(\sigma_0) = n$ into two segments, as shown in Fig. 3. The partition function is $p_d = (i \geq n \,||\, c[n-1])\ ?\ 2\ :\ 1$ (essentially, $c[n-1] + 1$, except that the final state is slightly different). As can be seen from the figure, each segment simulates a mini-trace

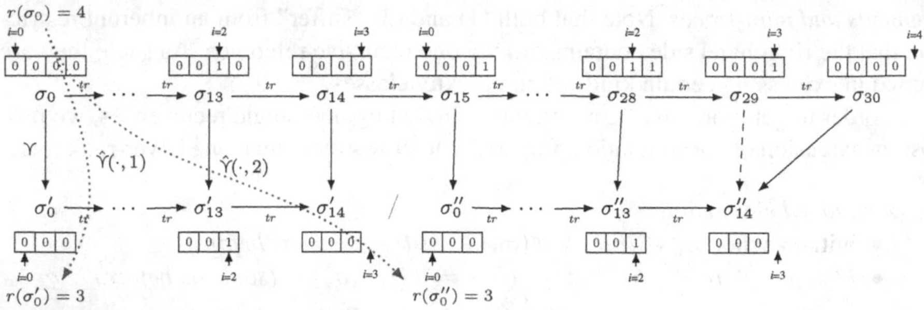

$\Upsilon(\langle n, i, c\rangle) = \langle n \dot{-} 1, (i < n)\ ?\ i : i{-}1, c[:n{-}1]\rangle \qquad \hat{\Upsilon}(n, 1) = n \dot{-} 1$

Fig. 3. An execution trace of the binary counter program that corresponds to two mini-traces of lower rank.

of rank $n-1$, with $k=1$ for all the steps except for the last step (at σ_{28}) where $k=2$. In this case, it would be folly to use the recurrence (1) with $\widehat{k}=2$, since all the steps are 1:1 except one. Instead, we can formulate a tighter bound:

$$comp_s(\sigma_0) \leq comp_s(\sigma_0') + comp_s(\sigma_0'') + 2$$

Where: $comp_s(\sigma_0')$, $comp_s(\sigma_0'')$ are the lengths of the mini-traces, and 2 is the surplus from the switch transition $\sigma_{14} \rightarrow \sigma_{15}$ plus the 2-step at σ_{28}. In the case of this program, we know that $r(\sigma_0') = r(\sigma_0'') = r(\sigma_0) - 1$, for any initial state σ_0, therefore, turning to $comp_x$, we can derive and solve the recurrence $comp_x(n) = 2 \cdot comp_x(n-1) + 2$, which together with the base yields the bound:

$$comp_x(n) = 2^{n+1} - 2$$

Clearly, a general condition is required in order to identify the ranks of the corresponding initial states of the (lower-rank) mini-traces (and at the same time, ensure that they decrease).

Bounding the ranks of squeezed switch states This is not a trivial task, since as previously noted, the squeezed ranks could be different, and may depend on properties present in the corresponding switch states. To achieve this goal, once a partition function p_d is defined, we also define a rank-bounding function $\hat{\Upsilon} : X \times \{1, \ldots, d\} \rightarrow X$, where for any $\sigma_0 \in init$ and switch state σ_s, $\hat{\Upsilon}$ provides a bound for the rank of $\Upsilon(\sigma_s)$ based on that of σ_0:

$$r(\Upsilon(\sigma_s)) \preceq \hat{\Upsilon}\big(r(\sigma_0), p_d(\sigma_s)\big) \prec r(\sigma_0) \tag{4}$$

The rightmost inequality ensures that a mini-trace that starts from $\Upsilon(\sigma_s)$ is of lower-rank than σ_0, and as such extends the "rank decrease" requirement to all mini-traces. Based on this restriction, we can formulate a recurrence for $comp_x$ based on the initial rank $\rho = r(\sigma_0)$, as follows:

$$comp_x(\rho) \leq \sum_{i=1}^{d} comp_x\big(\hat{\Upsilon}(\rho, i)\big) \; + \; (d-1) \; + \; \widehat{k} \cdot b \tag{5}$$

Where b, as before, is the number of k-steps for which $k > 1$, and $\widehat{k}$ is the bound on k ($k \leq \widehat{k}$). The expression $(d-1)$ represents the transitions between segments, and $\widehat{k} \cdot b$ represents the surplus of the ρ-rank trace over the total lengths of the mini-traces.

It should be clear from the definition above, that $\hat{\curlyvee}$ is quite intricate. How would we compute it effectively? The rank decrease of the initial states and the simulation properties were *local* by nature, and thus amenable to validation with an SMT solver. The $\hat{\curlyvee}$ function is inherently *global*, defined w.r.t. an entire trace. This makes the property (4) challenging for verification methods based on SMT. To render this check more feasible with first-order reasoning, we introduce two special cases where the problem of checking (4) becomes easier: rank preservation and a single segment, explained next.

Taming $\hat{\curlyvee}$ with rank preservation To obtain rank preservation, we extend the rank function to all states (instead of just the initial states), and require that the rank is preserved along transitions. This is appropriate in some of the scenarios we encountered. For example, the binary counter illustration satisfies the property that along any execution $\{\sigma_i\}_{i=0}^{\infty}$, the rank is preserved: $r(\sigma_i) = r(\sigma_{i+1})$. Rank preservation means that given a switch state σ_s of an arbitrary segment i, we know that $r(\sigma_s) = r(\sigma_0)$. Once this is set, $\hat{\curlyvee}$ only needs to overapproximate the rank of $\curlyvee(\sigma_s)$ in terms of the rank of the same state σ.

Taming $\hat{\curlyvee}$ with a single segment In this case, checking (4) reduces to a single check of the initial state, which is the only switch state. It turns out that the restriction to a single segment is still expressive enough to handle many loop types.

Putting it all together Theoretically, r, $\curlyvee$, p_d, and $\hat{\curlyvee}$ can be manually written by the user. However, this is a rather tedious task, that is straightforward enough to be automated. We observed that all the aforementioned functions are simple enough entities, that can be expressed through a strict syntax using first order logic. Similar to [22], we apply a generate-and-test synthesis procedure to enumerate a space of possible expressions representing them. This process is explained in Section 4.

3 Complexity Analysis based on Squeezers

In this section we develop the formal foundations of our approach for extracting recurrence relations describing the time complexity of an imperative program based on state squeezers. We present the ingredients that underly the approach, the conditions they are required to satisfy, and the recurrence relations they induce. In the next section, we explain how to extract the recurrences automatically. Given the recurrence relation, a dedicated (external) tool may be applied to end up with a closed formula, similar to [3].

We use *transition systems* to capture the semantics of a program.

Definition 1 (Transition Systems). *A transition system is a tuple $(\Sigma, init, tr)$, where Σ is a set of* states, *$init \subseteq \Sigma$ is a set of* initial states *and $tr : \Sigma \to \Sigma$ is a* transition function *(rather than a transition relation, since only deterministic procedures are* *considered). The set of* terminal states $F \subseteq \Sigma$ *is implicitly defined by* $tr(\sigma) = \sigma$. *An* execution trace *(or a* trace *in short) is a finite or infinite sequence of states* $\tau = \sigma_0, \sigma_1, \ldots$ *such that* $\sigma_{i+1} = tr(\sigma_i)$ *for every* $0 \leq i < |\tau|$. *A state* $\sigma \in \Sigma$ *defines an execution trace* $\tau(\sigma) = \{tr^i(\sigma)\}_{i \in \mathbb{N}}$. *Whenever there exists an index* $0 \leq k \leq |\tau|$ *s.t.* $\sigma_k \in F$, *we truncate* $\tau(\sigma)$ *into a finite trace* $\{tr^i(\sigma)\}_{i=0}^{k}$, *where* k *is the minimal such index. The trace is* initial *if it starts from an initial state, i.e.,* $\sigma \in init$. *Unless explicitly stated otherwise, all traces we consider are initial. The set of* reachable states *is* $reach = \{\sigma \in \Sigma \mid \exists \sigma_0 \in init \,.\, \sigma \in \tau(\sigma_0)\}$.

Roughly, to represent a program by a transition system, we translate it into a single loop program, where *init* consists of the states encountered when entering the loop, and transitions correspond to iterations of the loop.

In the sequel, we fix a transition system $(\Sigma, init, tr)$ with a set F of terminal states and a set *reach* of reachable states.

Definition 2 (Complexity over states). *For a state* $\sigma \in \Sigma$, *we denote by* $comp_s(\sigma)$ *the number of transitions from* σ *to a terminal state along* $\tau(\sigma)$ *(the trace that starts from* σ*). Formally, if* $\tau(\sigma)$ *does not include a terminal state, i.e., the procedure does* not *terminate from* σ, *then* $comp_s(\sigma) = \infty$. *Otherwise:*

$$comp_s(\sigma) = \min\{k \in \mathbb{N} \mid tr^k(\sigma) \in F\}.$$

The complexity function of the program maps each initial state $\sigma_0 \in init$ *to its time complexity* $comp_s(\sigma_0) \in \mathbb{N} \cup \{\infty\}$.

Our complexity analysis derives a recurrence relation for the complexity function by expressing the length of a trace in terms of the lengths of traces that start from lower rank states. This is achieved by (i) attaching to each initial state a *rank* from a well-founded set that we use as the argument of the complexity function and that we recur over, and (ii) defining a *squeezer* that maps each state from the original trace to a state in a lower-rank trace; the mapping forms a *partitioned simulation* according to a *partition function* that decomposes a trace to segments; each segment is simulated by a (separate) lower-rank trace, allowing to express the length of the former in terms of the latter, and finally, (iii) defining a *rank bounding function* that expresses (an upper bound on) the ranks of the lower-rank traces in terms of the rank of the higher-rank trace. We elaborate on these components next.

3.1 Time complexity as a function of rank

We start by defining a rank function that allows us to express the time complexity of an initial state by means of its rank.

Definition 3 (Rank). *Let* X *be a set, and* $\prec$ *be a well-founded partial order over* X. *Let* $B \supseteq \min(X)$ *be a* base *for* X, *where* $\min(X)$ *is the set of all the minimal elements of* X *w.r.t.* $\prec$. *A* rank function $r : init \to X$ *maps each initial state to a rank in* X. *We extend the notion of a rank to initial traces as follows. Given an initial trace* $\tau = \tau(\sigma_0)$, *we define its rank to be the rank of* σ_0. *We refer to states* σ_0 *such that* $r(\sigma_0) \in B$ *as the* base states. *Similarly, (initial) traces whose ranks are in* B *are called* base traces.

In our analysis, ranks range over $X = \mathbb{N}^m$ (for some $m \in \mathbb{N}^+$), with $\prec$ defined by the lexicographic order. Ranks let us abstract away data inside the initial execution states which does *not* affect the worst-case bound on the trace length. For example, the length of traces of the binary counter program (Fig. 1) is completely agnostic to the actual content of the array at the initial state. The only parameter that affects its trace length is the array size, and not which integers are stored inside it. Hence, a suitable rank function in this example maps an initial state to its array length. This is despite the fact that the execution does depend on the content of the array, and, in particular, the number of remaining iterations from an intermediate state within the execution depends on it. The partial order $\prec$ and the base set B will be used to define the recurrence formula as we explain in the sequel.

We will assume from now on that $(X, \prec, B)$, as well as the rank function, are fixed, and can be understood from context. The rank function r induces a complexity function $comp_x : X \to \mathbb{N} \cup \{\infty\}$ over ranks, defined as follows.

Definition 4 (Complexity over ranks). *The complexity function over ranks, $comp_x$: $X \to \mathbb{N} \cup \{\infty\}$, is defined by:*

$$comp_x(\rho) = \max\{comp_s(\sigma_0) \mid r(\sigma_0) \preceq \rho \wedge \sigma_0 \in init\}$$

The definition ensures that for every initial state $\sigma_0 \in init$, we can compute (an upper bound on) its time complexity based on its rank, as follows: $comp_s(\sigma_0) \leq comp_x(r(\sigma_0))$. The complexity of ρ takes into account all states with $r(\sigma) \preceq \rho$ and not only those with rank exactly ρ, to ensure monotonicity of $comp_x$ in the rank (i.e., if $\rho_1 \preceq \rho_2$ then $comp_x(\rho_1) \leq comp_x(\rho_2)$). Our approach is targeted at extracting a recurrence relation for $comp_x$.

3.2 Complexity decomposition by partitioned simulation

In order to express the length of a trace in terms of the lengths of traces of lower ranks, we use a *squeezer* that maps states from the original trace to states of lower-rank traces and (implicitly) induces a correspondence between the original trace and the lower-rank trace(s). For now, we do not require the squeezer to decrease the rank of the trace; this requirement will be added later. The squeezer is accompanied by a partition function to form a *partitioned simulation* that allows a single higher-rank trace to be matched to multiple lower-rank traces such that their lengths may be correlated.

Definition 5 (Squeezer, $\curlyvee$). *A squeezer is a function $\curlyvee : \Sigma \to \Sigma$.*

Definition 6. *A function $p_d : \Sigma \to \{1, \ldots, d\}$, where $d \in \mathbb{N}^+$ is called a d-*partition function *if for* every *trace $\tau = \sigma_0, \sigma_1, \ldots$ it holds that $p_d(\sigma_{i+1}) \geq p_d(\sigma_i)$ for every $0 \leq i < |\tau|$.*

The partition function partitions a trace into a bounded number of *segments*, where each segment consists of states with the same value of p_d. We refer to the first state of a segment as a *switch state*, and to the last state of a finite segment as a *last state* (note that if τ is infinite, its last segment has no last state). In particular, this means that the initial state of a trace is a switch state. (Note that a state may be a switch state in one trace but not in another, while a last state is a last state in any trace, as long as the same partition function is considered.)

Our complexity analysis requires the squeezer to form a partitioned simulation with respect to p_d. Roughly, this means that the squeezer maps each segment of a trace to a (lower-rank) trace that "simulates" it. To this end, we require *all* the states σ within a segment of a trace to be (h, ℓ)-"stuttering", for some $h \geq \ell \geq 1$. Stuttering lets h consecutive transitions of σ be matched to ℓ consecutive transitions of its squeezed counterpart. If $h = \ell$, the state σ contributes to the complexity the same number of steps as the squeezed state. Otherwise, σ contributes $h - \ell$ additional steps, resulting in a longer trace. Recall that terminal states also have outgoing transitions (to themselves), however these transitions do not capture actual steps; they do not contribute to the complexity. Hence, stuttering also requires that "real" transitions of σ are matched to "real" transitions of its squeezed counterpart, namely, if the latter encounter a terminal state, so must the former. For the last states of segments the requirement is slightly different as the simulation ends at the last state, and a new simulation begins in the next segment. In order to account for the transition from the last state of one segment to the first (switch) state of the next segment, last states are considered $(2, 1)$-stuttering if they are squeezed into terminal states, unless they are terminal themselves[4]. In any other case, they are considered $(1, 1)$-stuttering. The formal definitions follow.

Definition 7 (Stuttering States). *A non-last state $\sigma \in \Sigma$ is called a* (h, ℓ)-stuttering *state, for $h \geq \ell \geq 1$, if: (i) $tr^{\ell}(\curlyvee(\sigma)) = \curlyvee(tr^{h}(\sigma))$; (ii) for every $i < \ell$, $tr^{i}(\curlyvee(\sigma)) \notin F$; (iii) $tr^{\ell}(\curlyvee(\sigma)) \in F$ implies that $\curlyvee(tr^{h}(\sigma)) \in F$. A last state $\sigma \in \Sigma$ is* $(1, 1)$-stuttering *if $\sigma \in F$ or $\curlyvee(\sigma) \notin F$. Otherwise, it is* $(2, 1)$-stuttering.

To obtain a partitioned simulation, switch states (along any trace), which start new segments, are further required to be squeezed into initial states (since our complexity analysis only applies to initial states). We denote by $\mathbb{S}_{p_d}(\tau)$ the switch states of trace τ according to partition p_d and by $\mathbb{S}_{p_d}$ the switch states of *all* traces according to the partition p_d. Namely, $\mathbb{S}_{p_d} = init \cup \{tr(\sigma) \mid \sigma \in reach \wedge p_d(\sigma) < p_d(tr(\sigma))\}$.

Definition 8 (Partitioned Simulation). *We say that a squeezer $\curlyvee : \Sigma \to \Sigma$ forms a* $\{(h_i, \ell_i)\}_{i=1}^{n}$-partitioned simulation *according to p_d, denoted $\curlyvee \sim \mathbb{PS}_{p_d}(\{(h_i, \ell_i)\}_{i=1}^{n})$ if for every reachable state σ we have that:*

- *σ is (h_i, ℓ_i)-stuttering for some $1 \leq i \leq n$, and*
- *$\sigma \in \mathbb{S}_{p_d} \Rightarrow \curlyvee(\sigma) \in init$.*

Note that Definition 7 implies that a non-terminal state may only be squeezed into a terminal state if it is the last state in its segments. When $\{(h_i, \ell_i)\}_{i=1}^{n}$ is irrelevant or clear from the context, we omit it from the notation and simply write $\curlyvee \sim \mathbb{PS}_{p_d}$.

[4] Considering a non-terminal last state that is squeezed into a terminal state as $(1, 0)$-stuttering may have been more intuitive than $(2, 1)$-stuttering, but both properly capture the discrepancy between the number of transitions in the higher and lower rank traces, and $(2, 1)$ better fits the rest of the technical development, which assumes that $h_i, \ell_i \geq 1$.

A trace squeezed by $\curlyvee \sim \mathbb{PS}_{pd}\left(\{(h_i,\ell_i)\}_{i=1}^n\right)$ may have an unbounded number of (h_i,ℓ_i)-stuttering states, which hinders the ability to define a recurrence relation based on the simulation. To overcome this, our complexity decomposition may use $\widehat{k} \geq 1$ to capture a common multiplicative factor of *all* the stuttering pairs, with the target of leaving only a *bounded* number of states whose stuttering exceeds $\widehat{k}$ and needs to be added separately. This will become important in Theorem 1.

Observation 1 (Complexity decomposition) *Let* $\curlyvee \sim \mathbb{PS}_{pd}\left(\{(h_i,\ell_i)\}_{i=1}^n\right)$*, and* $\widehat{k} \geq 1$*. Let* $\mathbb{E}_{\widehat{k}} \subseteq \{1,\ldots,n\}$ *be the set of indices such that* $\frac{h_i}{\ell_i} > \widehat{k}$*. Then for every* $\sigma_0 \in init$ *we have that*

$$comp_s(\sigma_0) \leq \sum_{\sigma \in \mathbb{S}_{p_d}(\tau(\sigma_0))} \widehat{k} \cdot comp_s(\curlyvee(\sigma)) + \sum_{i \in \mathbb{E}_{\widehat{k}}} \sum_{\sigma \in \mathbb{K}_i(\tau(\sigma_0))} h_i - \ell_i \cdot \widehat{k}$$

where $\mathbb{K}_i(\tau(\sigma_0))$ *is the multiset of* (h_i,ℓ_i)*-stuttering states in* $\tau(\sigma_0)$*.*

In the observation, the first addend summarizes the complexity contributed by all the lower-rank traces, while using $\widehat{k}$ as an upper bound on the "inflation" of the traces. However, the states that are (h_i,ℓ_i)-stuttering with $\frac{h_i}{\ell_i}$ that exceeds $\widehat{k}$ contribute additional $h_i - (\ell_i \cdot \widehat{k})$ steps to the complexity, and as a result, need to be taken into account separately. This is handled by the second addend, which adds the steps that were not accounted for by the first addend. While we use the same inflation factor $\widehat{k}$ across the entire trace, a simple extension of the decomposition property may consider a different factor $\widehat{k}$ in each segment. Note that the first addend always sums over a finite number of elements since the number of switch states is at most d – the number of segments. If $\tau(\sigma_0)$ is finite, the second addend also sums over a finite number of elements.

Observation 1 considers the complexity function over states, and is oblivious to the rank. In particular, it does not rely on the squeezer decreasing the rank of states. Next, we use this observation as the basis for extracting a recurrence relation for the complexity function over ranks, in which case, decreasing the rank becomes important.

3.3 Extraction of recurrence relations over ranks

Based on the complexity decomposition, we define recurrence relations that capture $comp_x$ — the time complexity of the initial states as a function of their ranks. To go from the complexity as a function of the actual states (as in Observation 1) to the complexity as a function of their ranks, we need to express the rank of $\curlyvee(\sigma_s)$ for a switch state σ_s as a function of the rank of σ_0. To this end, we define $\hat{\curlyvee}$:

Definition 9. *Given* r*,* $\curlyvee$ *and* p_d *such that* $\curlyvee \sim \mathbb{PS}_{p_d}$*, a function* $\hat{\curlyvee} : X \times \{1,\ldots,d\} \to X$ *is a* rank bounding function *if for every* $\rho \in X - B$ *and* $1 \leq i \leq d$*, if* $\tau(\sigma_0)$ *is an initial trace such that* $r(\sigma_0) = \rho$*, and* $\sigma_s \in \mathbb{S}_{p_d}(\tau(\sigma_0))$ *is a switch state such that* $p_d(\sigma_s) = i$*, the following holds:*

$$\textit{(i) upper bound: } r\left(\curlyvee(\sigma_s)\right) \preceq \hat{\curlyvee}(\rho, i) \quad \textit{and} \quad \textit{(ii) rank decrease: } \hat{\curlyvee}(\rho, i) \prec \rho$$

In other words, Definition 9 requires that for every non-base initial state $\sigma_0 \in init$ and switch state σ_s at segment i of $\tau(\sigma_0)$, we have that $r(\Upsilon(\sigma_s)) \preceq \hat{\Upsilon}(r(\sigma_0), i) \prec r(\sigma_0)$. Recall that $r(\Upsilon(\sigma_s))$ is well defined since $\Upsilon(\sigma_s)$ is required to be an initial state. The definition states that $\hat{\Upsilon}(\rho, i)$ provides an upper bound on the rank of squeezed switch states in a non-base trace of rank ρ. $comp_x(r(\Upsilon(\sigma))) \leq comp_x(\hat{\Upsilon}(\rho, i))$ is ensured by the monotonicity of $comp_x$. This definition also requires the rank of non-base traces to strictly decrease when they are squeezed, as captured by the "rank decrease" inequality.

Obtaining a rank bounding function, or even verifying that a given $\hat{\Upsilon}$ satisfies this requirement, is a challenging task. We return to this question later in this section.

These conditions allow to substitute the states for ranks in the first addend of Observation 1, and hence obtain recurrence relations for $comp_x$ over the (decreasing) ranks. To handle the second addend, we also need to bound the number of states whose stuttering, $\frac{h_i}{\ell_i}$, exceeds $\widehat{k}$. This is summarized by the following theorem:

Theorem 1. *Let $r : init \to X$ be a rank function, $\Upsilon : \Sigma \to \Sigma$ a squeezer and $p_d : \Sigma \to \{1, \dots, d\}$ a partition function such that $\Upsilon \sim \mathbb{PS}_{p_d}(\{(h_i, \ell_i)\}_{i=1}^n)$. Let $\hat{\Upsilon} : X \times \{1, \dots, d\} \to X$ be a rank bounding function w.r.t. r, Υ and p_d. If, for some $\widehat{k} \geq 1$, the number of (h_i, ℓ_i)-stuttering states that appear along* any *non-base initial trace is bounded by a constant $b_i \in \mathbb{N}$ whenever $i \in \mathbb{E}_{\widehat{k}}$, then*

$$comp_x(\rho) \leq \sum_{i=1}^{d} \widehat{k} \cdot comp_x(\hat{\Upsilon}(\rho, i)) + \sum_{i \in \mathbb{E}_{\widehat{k}}} b_i \cdot (h_i - \ell_i \cdot \widehat{k}). \tag{6}$$

Note that a state may be (h_i, ℓ_i)-stuttering for several i's, in which case, it is sound to count it towards any of the b_i's; in particular, we choose the one that minimizes $h_i - \ell_i \cdot \widehat{k}$.

Corollary 1. *Under the premises of Theorem 1, if $f : X \to \mathbb{N} \cup \{\infty\}$ satisfies $f(\rho) = \sum_{i=1}^{d} \widehat{k} \cdot f(\hat{\Upsilon}(\rho, i)) + \sum_{i \in \mathbb{E}_{\widehat{k}}} b_i \cdot (h_i - \ell_i \cdot \widehat{k})$ for every $\rho \in X - B$, and $comp_x(\rho) \leq f(\rho)$ for every $\rho \in B$, then $comp_x(\rho) \leq f(\rho)$ for every $\rho \in X$. We conclude that $comp_s(\sigma_0) \leq f(r(\sigma_0))$ for every $\sigma_0 \in init$.*

Base-case complexity In order to apply Cor. 1, we need to accompany Eq. (6) with a bound on $comp_x(\rho)$ for the base ranks, $\rho \in B$. Fortunately, this is usually a significantly easier task. In particular, the running time of the base cases is often constant, because intuitively, the following are correlated: (a) the rank, (b) the size of the underlying data structure, and (c) the number of iterations. In this case, symbolic execution may be used to obtain bounds for base cases (as we do in our work). In essence, any method that can yield a closed-form expression for the complexity of the base cases is viable. In particular, we can apply our technique on the base case as a subproblem.

3.4 Establishing the requirements of the recurrence relations extraction

Theorem 1 defines a recurrence relation from which an upper bound on the complexity function, $comp_x$, can be computed (Cor. 1). However, to ensure correctness, the premises of Theorem 1 must be verified. The requirement that $\curlyvee \sim \mathbb{PS}_{p_d}(\{(h_i, \ell_i)\}_{i=1}^n)$ (see Definition 8) may be verified *locally* by examining individual (reachable) states: for any (reachable) state σ, the check for (h_i, ℓ_i)-stuttering and switch states can, and should, be done in tandem, and require only observing at most $\max_i h_i$ transition steps from σ and $\max_i \ell_i$ from $\curlyvee(\sigma)$. In contrast, the property required of $\hat{\curlyvee}$ is *global*: it requires $\hat{\curlyvee}(\rho, i)$ to provide an upper bound on the rank of *any* squeezed switch state that may occur in *any* position along *any* non-base initial trace whose initial state has rank ρ. Similarly, the property required of the bounds b_i is also *global*: that the number of (h_i, ℓ_i)-stuttering states along *any* non-base initial trace is at most b_i. It is therefore not clear how these requirements may be verified in general. We overcome this difficulty by imposing additional restrictions, as we discuss next.

Establishing bounds on the number of occurrences of stuttering states Bounds on the number of occurrences *per trace* that are sound *for every trace* are difficult to obtain in general. While clever analysis methods exist that can do this kind of accounting, we found that a stronger, simpler condition applies in many cases:

– For every $\sigma \in \mathit{reach}$, either:
  - σ is (h_i, ℓ_i)-stuttering with $\frac{h_i}{\ell_i} \leq \widehat{k}$; <u>or</u>
  - σ is (h_i, ℓ_i)-stuttering (with $\frac{h_i}{\ell_i} > \widehat{k}$), *and* either σ is a <u>switch state</u> or $tr^{h_i}(\sigma)$ is a <u>last state</u>.

This restricts these cases to occur only at the beginnings and ends of segments. It implies a total bound of $2d\cdot \max_i(h_i - \ell_i \cdot \widehat{k})$ on the "surplus" of any trace, therefore, we substitute this expression for the rightmost sum in Eq. (6).

Validating a rank bounding function The definition of a rank bounding function (Definition 9) encapsulates two parts. Part (ii) ensures that the rank decreases: $\hat{\curlyvee}(\rho, i) \prec \rho$ for every $\rho \in X - B$. Verifying that this requirement holds does not involve any reasoning about the states, nor traces, of the transition system. Part (i) ensures that $\hat{\curlyvee}$ provides an upper bound on the rank of squeezed switch states. Formally, it requires that $r(\curlyvee(\sigma_s)) \preceq \hat{\curlyvee}(r(\sigma_0), i)$ for every switch state σ_s in segment $i \in \{1, \ldots, d\}$ along a trace that starts from a non-base initial state σ_0. Namely, it relates the rank of the squeezed switch state, $\curlyvee(\sigma_s)$, to the rank of the initial state, σ_0, where no bound on the length of the trace between the initial state σ_0 and the switch state σ_s is known a priori. As such, it involves global reasoning about traces. We identify two cases in which such reasoning may be avoided: (i) The partition p_d consists of a single segment (i.e., $d = 1$); or (ii) The rank function extends to *any* state (and not just the initial states), while being preserved by tr. In both of these cases, we are able to verify the correctness of $\hat{\curlyvee}$ locally.

A single segment. In this case, the only switch state along a trace is the initial state, and hence the upper-bound requirement of $\hat{\curlyvee}$ boils down to the requirement that for every $\sigma_0 \in \mathit{init}$ such that $r(\sigma_0) \in X - B$, we have that $r(\curlyvee(\sigma_0)) \preceq \hat{\curlyvee}(r(\sigma_0), 1)$.

Lemma 1. *Let r, $\curlyvee$ and $p_1 : \Sigma \to \{1\}$ such that $\curlyvee \sim \mathbb{PS}_{p_1}$. Then $\hat{\curlyvee} : X \times \{1\} \to X$ satisfies the upper-bound requirement of a rank bounding function if and only if $r(\curlyvee(\sigma_0)) \preceq \hat{\curlyvee}(r(\sigma_0), 1)$ for every $\sigma_0 \in \mathit{init}$ such that $r(\sigma_0) \in X - B$.*

Rank preservation. Another case in which the upper-bound property of $\hat{\Upsilon}$ may be verified locally is when the r can be extended to *all* states while being preserved by tr:

Definition 10. *A function* $\hat{r} : \Sigma \to X$ extends *the rank function* $r : init \to \Sigma$ *if* $\hat{r}$ *agrees with* r *on the initial states, i.e.,* $\hat{r}(\sigma_0) = r(\sigma_0)$ *for every initial state* $\sigma_0 \in init$. *The extended rank function* $\hat{r}$ *is* preserved by tr, *if for every reachable state* σ, *we have that* $\hat{r}(tr(\sigma)) = \hat{r}(\sigma)$.

Preservation of $\hat{r}$ by tr ensures that all states along a (reachable) trace share the same rank. In particular, for a reachable switch state σ_s that lies along $\tau(\sigma_0)$, rank preservation ensures that $\hat{r}(\sigma_s) = \hat{r}(\sigma_0) = r(\sigma_0)$ (the last equality is due to the extension property), allowing us to recover the rank of σ_0 from the rank of σ_s. Therefore, the upper-bound requirement of $\hat{\Upsilon}$ simplifies into the *local* requirement that for every reachable switch state σ_s such that $\hat{r}(\sigma_s) \in X - B$, we have that $\hat{r}(\Upsilon(\sigma_s)) \preceq \hat{\Upsilon}(\hat{r}(\sigma_s), i)$, for every $i \in \{1, \ldots, d\}$.

Lemma 2. *Let* r, Υ *and* $p_d : \Sigma \to \{1, \ldots, d\}$ *such that* $\Upsilon \sim \mathbb{PS}_{p_d}$. *Suppose that* $\hat{r} : \Sigma \to X$ *extends* r *and is preserved by* tr. *Then* $\hat{\Upsilon} : X \times \{1, \ldots, d\} \to X$ *satisfies the upper-bound requirement of a rank bounding function if and only if* $\hat{r}(\Upsilon(\sigma_s)) \preceq \hat{\Upsilon}(\hat{r}(\sigma_s), i)$ *for every reachable switch state* σ_s *such that* $\hat{r}(\sigma_s) \in X - B$ *and for every* $i \in \{1, \ldots, d\}$.

Remark 1. The notion of a partitioned simulation requires a switch state σ_s to be squeezed into an initial state. This requirement may be relaxed into the requirement that σ_s is squeezed into a *reachable* state $\Upsilon(\sigma_s)$, provided that we are able to still ensure that the rank of (some) *initial* state σ_0' leading to $\Upsilon(\sigma_s)$ is smaller than the rank of the trace on which σ_s lies, and that the rank of σ_0' is properly captured by $\hat{\Upsilon}$. One case in which this is possible, is when r is extended to $\hat{r}$ that is preserved by tr, as in this case $\hat{r}(\Upsilon(\sigma_s)) = \hat{r}(\sigma_0') = r(\sigma_0')$.

This subsection described *local* properties that ensure that a given program satisfies the requirements of Theorem 1. The locality of the properties facilitates the use of SMT solvers to perform these checks automatically. This is a key step for effective application of the method.

3.5 Trace-length vs. state-size recurrences with squeezers

A plethora of work exists for analyzing the complexity of programs (see Section 6 for a discussion of related works). Most existing techniques for automatic complexity analysis aim to find a recurrence relation on the length of the execution trace, relating the length of a trace from some state to the length of the remaining trace starting at its successor. These are recurrences on *time*, if you will, whereas our approach generates recurrences on the state *size* (captured by the rank). Is our approach completely orthogonal to preceding methods? Not quite. It turns out that from a conceptual point of view, our approach can formulate a recurrence on time as well, as we demonstrate in this section.

Obtaining trace-length recurrences based on state squeezers The key idea is to use tr itself as a squeezer that squeezes each state into its immediate successor. Putting aside the initial-anchor requirement momentarily, such a squeezer forms a partitioned simulation with a single segment (i.e., $p_d \equiv 1$), in which all the states along a trace are $(1,1)$-stuttering, except for the last one (if the trace is finite), which is $(2,1)$-stuttering. Recall that squeezers must also preserve initial states (see Definition 8), a property that may be violated when $\curlyvee = tr$, as the successor of an initial state is not necessarily an initial state. We restore the initial-anchor property by setting $\widehat{init} = \Sigma$, i.e., every state is considered an initial state[5].

A consequence of this definition is that $comp_x$ will now provide an upper bound on the time complexity of *every* state and not only of the initial states, in terms of a rank that needs to be defined. If we further define a rank-bounding function $\hat{\curlyvee}$ we may extract a recurrence relation of the form

$$comp_x(\rho) = comp_x(\hat{\curlyvee}(\rho)) + 1$$

(we use $\hat{\curlyvee}(\rho)$ as an abbreviation of $\hat{\curlyvee}(\rho, 1)$, since this is a special case where $d = 1$).

Defining the rank and the rank bounding function Recall that the rank $r : \Sigma \to X$ captures the features of the (initial) states that determine the complexity. To allow maximal precision, especially since *all* states are now initial, we set X to be the set of *states* Σ, and define r to be the identity function, $r(\sigma) = \sigma$. With this definition, $comp_x$ and $comp_s$ become one. Next, we need to define $\prec$ and B, while ensuring that $\curlyvee$ squeezes the (non-base) initial states, which are now *all* the states, into states of a lower rank according to $\prec$. Since squeezers act like transitions now, having that $\curlyvee = tr$, they have the effect of decreasing the number of transitions remaining to reach a terminal state (provided that the trace is finite). We use this observation to define $\prec \subseteq \Sigma \times \Sigma$. Care is needed to ensure that $(\Sigma, \prec)$ is well-founded, i.e., every descending chain is finite, even though the program may *not* terminate. Here is the definition that achieves this goal:

$$\sigma_1 \prec \sigma_2 \Leftrightarrow comp_s(\sigma_1) < comp_s(\sigma_2) \tag{7}$$

Since $\curlyvee = tr$ does not decrease $comp_s$ for states that belong to infinite (non-terminating) traces ($comp_s(\curlyvee(\sigma)) = comp_s(\sigma) = \infty$, hence $\curlyvee(\sigma) \nprec \sigma$), they must be included in B, together with the terminal states, which are minimal w.r.t. $\prec$. Namely, $B = F \cup \{\sigma \mid comp_s(\sigma) = \infty\}$. Technically, this means that the base of the recurrence needs to define $comp_x$ for these states.

The final piece in the puzzle is setting $\hat{\curlyvee} = tr$. Since $\curlyvee \sim \mathbb{PS}_{p_d}(\{(1,1),(2,1)\})$ (when $\widehat{init} = \Sigma$), where the number of $(2,1)$-stuttering states that appear along any non-base initial trace is bounded by 1, we may use Theorem 1, setting $\hat{k} = 1$, to derive the following recurrence relation, which reflects induction over time:

$$comp_x(\sigma) = comp_x(tr(\sigma)) + 1.$$

[5] In fact, it suffices to consider $\widehat{init} = reach$, in which case we may be able to take advantage of information from static analyses

The formulation above represents a degenerate, naïve, choice of ingredients for the sake of a theoretical construction, whose purpose is to lay the foundation for a general framework that takes its strengths from both induction over time and induction over rank. This construction does not exploit the full flexibility of our framework. In particular, ranking functions obtained from termination proofs, as used in [5], may be used to augment the rank in this setting. Further, invariants inferred from static analysis can be used to refine the recurrences.

4 Synthesis

So far we have assumed that the rank function r, partition function p_d, squeezer $\curlyvee$ and a rank bounding function $\hat{\curlyvee}$ are all readily available. Clearly, they are specific to a given program. It would be too tedious for a programmer to provide these functions for the analysis of the underlying complexity. In this section we show how to automate the process of obtaining $(r, p_d, \curlyvee, \hat{\curlyvee})$ for a class of typical looping programs. We take advantage of the fact that these components are much more compact than other kinds of auxiliary functions commonly used for resource analysis, such as monotonically decreasing measures used as ranking functions. For example, a ranking function for the binary counter program shown in Fig. 1 is:

$$m(n, i, c) = \left(n \cdot \sum_{j=0}^{n-1} 2^j \cdot c[j] \right) + (2^i - 1) + (n - i)$$

whereas the rank, partition, $\curlyvee$ and $\hat{\curlyvee}$ are

$$r(n, i, c) = n \qquad \curlyvee(n, i, c) = \big(n - 1, (i \geq n)\ ?\ i - 1 : i, c[:n-1]\big)$$
$$\hat{\curlyvee}(\rho) = \rho - 1 \qquad p_d(n, i, c) = (i \geq n \,||\, c[n-1])\ ?\ 2 : 1$$

This enables the use of a relatively naïve enumerative approach of multi-phase generate-and-test, employing some early pruning to discard obviously non-qualifying candidates.

4.1 SyGuS

The generation step of the synthesis loop applies syntax guided synthesis (SyGuS [7]). Like any other SyGuS method, defining the underlying grammars is more art than science. It should be expressive enough to capture the desired terms, but strict enough to effectively bound the search space.

Ranks are taken from $\mathbb{N}^m$ where $m \in \{1, 2, 3\}$ and $\prec$ is the usual lexicographic order. The rank function r comprises of one expression for each coordinate, constructed by adding / subtracting integer variables and array sizes. Boolean variables are not used in rank expressions.

Partition functions p_d. Our implementation currently supports a maximum number of two segments. This means that the partition function only assigns the values 1 and 2, and we synthesize it by generating a condition over the program's variables, *cond*, that selects between them: $p_d(\sigma) = cond(\sigma)\ ?\ 2 : 1$. Handling up to two segments is *not* an inherent limitation, but we found that for typically occurring programs, two segments are sufficient.

Squeezers $\curlyvee$ are the only ingredient that requires substantial synthesis effort. We represent squeezers as small loop-free imperative programs, which are natural for representing state transformations. We use a rather standard syntax with 'if-then-else' and assignments, plus a `remove-adjust` operation that removes array entries and adjusts indices relating to them accordingly. .

Rank bounding functions $\hat{\curlyvee}$. With a well-chosen squeezer $\curlyvee$, it suffices to consider quite simple rank bounds for the mini-traces. Hence, the rank-bounds defined by $\hat{\curlyvee}$ are obtained by adding, subtracting and multiplying variables with small constants (for each coordinate of the rank). Similar to the choice of ranks, targeting simple expressions for $\hat{\curlyvee}$ helps reduce the complexity of the final recurrence that is generated from the process.

4.2 Verification

For the sake of verifying the synthesized ingredients, we fix a set $\{h_i, \ell_i\}$ of stuttering shapes, and check the requirements of Theorem 1 as discussed in Section 3.4. In particular, we check that p_d is weakly monotone, i.e., that *cond* cannot change from true to false in any step of tr. Note that some of the properties may be used to discriminate some of the ingredients independent of the others. For example, the simulation requirement only depends on $\curlyvee$ and p_d.

Unbounded verification Once candidates pass a preliminary screening phase, they are verified by encoding the program and all the components $r, p_d, \curlyvee, \hat{\curlyvee}$ as first-order logic expressions, and using an SMT solver (Z3 [13]) to verify that the requirements are fulfilled for all traces of the program.
As mentioned in Section 3.4, all the checks are local and require observing a bounded set of steps starting from a given σ. The only facet of the criteria that is difficult to encode is the fact they are required of the reachable states (and not any state). Of course, if we are able to ascertain that these are met for *all* $\sigma \in \Sigma$, including unreachable states, then the result is sound. However, for some programs and squeezers, the required properties (esp., simulation) do not hold universally, but are violated by unreachable states. To cope with this situation without having to manually provide invariants that capture properties of the reachable states, we use a CHC solver, Spacer [23], which is part of Z3, to check whether all the reachable states in the unbounded-state system induced by the input program satisfy these properties. This can be seen as a reduction from the problem of verifying the premises of Theorem 1 to that of verifying a safety property.

5 Empirical Evaluation

We implemented our complexity analyzer as a publicly available tool, SqzComp, that receives a program in a subset of C and produces recurrence relations. SqzComp is written in C++, using the Z3 C++ API [13], and using Spacer [23] via its SMTLIB2-compatible interface. Since our squeezers may remove elements from arrays, we initially encoded arrays as SMT sequences. However, we found that it is beneficial to

Description	Real complexity	Inferred bound CoFloCo	Inferred bound SqzComp	SqzComp Time	SqzComp d
array: max value	$O(\|A\|)$	$O(\|A\|)$	$O(\|A\|)$	< 1 sec	1
array: min value	$O(\|A\|)$	$O(\|A\|)$	$O(\|A\|)$	< 1 sec	1
array: find first	$O(\|A\|)$	$O(\|A\|)$	$O(\|A\|)$	< 1 sec	1
array: find last	$O(\|A\|)$	$O(\|A\|)$	$O(\|A\|)$	< 1 sec	1
array: is-sorted	$O(\|A\|)$	$O(\|A\|)$	$O(\|A\|)$	< 1 sec	1
array: longest asc. prefix	$O(\|A\|)$	$O(\|A\|)$	$O(\|A\|)$	< 1 sec	1
array: binary search	$O(\log(\|A\|))$	$O(\log(\|A\|))$	$O(\log(\|A\|))$	< 1 sec	1
gcd	$\max(x, y)$	$O(x + y)$	$O(x + y)$	< 1 sec	1
two-phase loop 1	$O(2n - 2x + y)$	$O(2n - 2x + y)$	$O(2n + 2y)$	< 1 sec	1
two-phase loop 2	$O(n - x + m - y)$	$O(n - x + m - y)$	$O(n - x + m - y)$	< 1 sec	1
two-phase loop 3	$O(n)$	$O(n)$	$O(n)$	< 1 sec	1
two-phase loop 4	$O(2n - x - z)$	$O(2n - x - z)$	$O(2n)$	< 1 sec	1
multi-path loop 1	$O(n)$	$O(3n)$	$O(n)$	< 1 sec	1
multi-path loop 2	$O(n)$	$O(n)$	$O(n)$	< 1 sec	1
multi-path loop 3	$O(n)$	$O(n)$	$O(n)$	< 1 sec	1
tricky init loop	$O(z)$	$O(z)$	$O(z)$	4 min	1
nested loop 1	$O(\|x - y\|)$	$O(\|x - y\|)$	$O(x + y)$	< 1 sec	1
nested loop 2	$O(a^2)$	$O(a^2)$	$O(a^2)$	16 min	1
context sensitive loop	$O(\max(n - m, m))$	$O(\max(n - m, m))$	$O(n)$	7 min	1
binary counter	$O(2^{n+1})$	∞	$O(2^{n+1})$	34 min	2
subsets	$O(\binom{n-m}{k})$	∞	$O(\binom{n-m}{k})$	50 min	2
monotone sequences	$O(\binom{n}{k})$	∞	$O(\binom{n}{k})$	50 min	2

Table 1. Experimental results. In array programs, A denotes an array. x, y, z, n, m, k, a are integer variables.

restrict squeezers to only remove the first or last elements of an array, resulting in a more efficient encoding with the theory of arrays. For the base case of generated recurrences, we use the symbolic execution engine KLEE [11] to bound the total number of iterations by a constant.

5.1 Experiments

We evaluated our tool, SqzComp, on a variety of benchmark programs taken from [16], as well as three additional programs: the binary counter example from Section 2, a subsets example, described in Section 5.2, and an example computing monotone sequences. These examples exhibit intricate time complexities. From the benchmark suite of [16] we filtered out non-deterministic programs, as well as programs that failed syntactic constraints that our frontend cannot currently handle. We compared SqzComp to CoFloCo [16]—the state of the art tool for complexity analysis of imperative programs.

Table 1 summarizes the results of our experiments. The first column presents the name of the program, which describes its characteristics (each of the "two-phase loop" programs consists of a loop with an if statement, where the branch executed changes starting from some iteration). The second column specifies the real complexity, while the following two columns present the bounds inferred by SqzComp and by CoFloCo, respectively. (For SqzComp, the reported bounds are the solutions of the recurrences

```
1 void subsets(uint n, uint k, uint m) {
2   uint I[k]; int j = 0; bool f = true;
3   while (j >= 0) {
4     if (j >= k)    /*start left scan*/{f=false; j--;}
5     else if (j==0 && f)       /*init*/{f=true;I[0]=m;j++;}
6     else if (f)         /*right fill*/{f=true;I[j]=I[j-1]+1;j++;}
7     else if (I[j]>=n-k+j)/*left scan*/{f=false; j--;}
8     else          /*start right fill*/{f=true; I[j]=I[j]+1;j++;}
9  }}
```

```
squeezer(uint I[], uint n, uint k, uint m, int j, bool f) {
  if      (I[0]==m  &&  j>0) { m++; remove I[0]; k--; j--; }
  else if (I[0]==m)          { m++; remove I[0]; k--;      }
  else                       { m++;                        }
}
```

Fig. 4. An example program that produces all subsets of $\{m, \ldots, n-1\}$ of size k; below is the synthesized squeezer.

output by the tool.) The fourth and fifth columns present the analysis running time, respectively the number of segments used in the analysis, of SqzComp.

CoFloCo's analysis time is always in the order of magnitude of 0.1 second, whether it succeeds to find a complexity bound or not. Our analysis is considerably slower, mostly due to the naïve implementation of the synthesizer. When both CoFloCo and SqzComp succeed, the bounds inferred by CoFloCo are sometimes tighter.

However, SqzComp manages to find tight complexity bounds for the new examples, which are not solved by CoFloCo, and to the best of our knowledge, are beyond reach of existing tools. (We also encoded the new examples as OCaml programs and ran the tool of [20] on them, and it failed to infer bounds.)

5.2 Case study: Subsets example

This subsection presents one challenging example from our benchmarks, the subsets example, and the details of its complexity analysis. Notably, our method is able to infer a binomial bound, which is asymptotically tight.

The code, shown in Fig. 4, iterates over all the subsets of `{m,...,n-1}` of size `k`. The "current" subset is maintained in an array `I` whose length is `k`, and which is always sorted, thus avoiding generating the same set more than once. The first k iterations of the loop fill the array with values `{m,m+1,...,m+k-1}`, which represent the first subset generated. This is taken care of by the branches at lines 5, 6 that perform a "right fill" phase, filling in the array with an ascending sequence starting from `m` at `I[0]`. Once the first k iterations are done, `j` reaches the end of the array (`j=k`) and so the next iteration will execute line 4, turning off the flag `f`, signifying that the array should now be scanned leftwards. In each successive iteration, `j` is decreased, looking for the rightmost element that can be incremented. For example, if $n = 8$, $I = [2, 6, 7]$, this rightmost element is $I[0] = 2$. After that element is incremented, the flag `f` is turned on again, completing the "left scan" phase and starting a "right fill" phase.

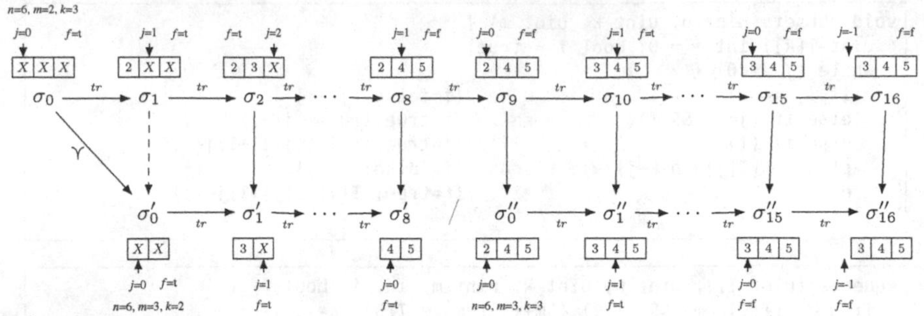

Fig. 5. An illustration of the 2-partitioned simulation for the subsets example. In the univariate case, the rank of the upper trace is $n - m$ and that of the lower traces is $n - m - 1$. In the multivariate case, the upper trace is of rank $(n-m, k)$, lower traces of ranks $(n-m-1, k-1)$, $(n - m - 1, k)$.

A univariate recurrence Consider the rank function $r(I, n, k, m, j, f) = n - m$, defined with respect to $(\mathbb{N}, <)$, and the squeezer shown below the program in Fig. 4. The squeezer observes the first element of the array: if it is equal to m (the lower bound of the range), it removes it from the array, shrinking its size (k) by one. It then adjusts the index j to keep pointing to the same element; unless $j = 0$, in which case that element is removed. This squeezer forms a 2-partitioned simulation, as illustrated by the traces in Fig. 5. All states are $(1,1)$-stuttering, except for σ_0, which is $(2,1)$-stuttering, as caused by the removal of $I[0]$ when $j = 0$. The rank bounding function is $\hat{\Upsilon}(i, \rho) = \rho - 1$ for $i \in \{1, 2\}$. We therefore obtain the following recurrence relation:

$$comp_x(\rho) \leq 1 + comp_x(\rho - 1) + comp_x(\rho - 1).$$

The base of the recurrence is $comp_x(0) = 1$, leading to the solution $comp_x(\rho) \leq 2^{\rho+1} - 1$. This means that for an initial state, $comp_s(I, n, k, m, 0, \mathsf{true}) \leq comp_x(n - m) \leq 2^{n-m+1} - 1$.

A multivariate recurrence Consider an alternative rank definition $r(I, n, k, m, j, f) = (n - m, k)$ defined with respect to $(\mathbb{N} \times \mathbb{N}, <)$, where '$<$' denotes the lexicographic order, together with the same squeezer and partition as before. The rank bounding function is now $\hat{\Upsilon}((\rho_1, \rho_2), i) = \begin{cases} (\rho_1 - 1, \rho_2 - 1) & i = 1 \\ (\rho_1 - 1, \rho_2) & i = 2 \end{cases}$. The corresponding recurrence relation is:

$$comp_x(\rho_1, \rho_2) \leq 1 + comp_x(\rho_1 - 1, \rho_2 - 1) + comp_x(\rho_1 - 1, \rho_2)$$

with base $comp_x(0, \_) = 1$, resulting in the solution $comp_x(\rho_1, \rho_2) \leq \binom{\rho_1+2}{\rho_2}$. That is, for an initial state, $comp_s(I, n, k, m, 0, \mathsf{true}) \leq comp_x(n - m, k) \leq \binom{n-m+2}{k}$.

Interestingly, this example demonstrates that the same squeezer may yield different recurrences, when different ranks (and rank bounding functions) are considered. It also demonstrates a case where different segments of a trace are mapped to mini-traces of a different rank.

6 Related Work

This section focuses on exploring existing methods for *static* complexity analysis of *imperative* programs. Dynamic profiling and analysis [26] are a separate research area, more related to testing, and generally do not provide formal guarantees. We further focus on works that determine *asymptotic* complexity bounds, and use the number of iterations executed as their cost model; we refrain from thoroughly covering previous techniques that analyze complexity at the instruction level.

Static cost analysis The seminal work of [28] defined a two steps meta-framework where recurrence relations are extracted from the underlying program, and then analyzed to provide closed-form upper bounds. Broadly speaking, cost relations are a generalized framework that captures the essence of most of the works mentioned in this section.

[4] and [16] infer cost relations of imperative programs written in Java and C respectively. Cost relations resemble somewhat limited C procedures: They are capable of recursive calls to other cost relations, and they can handle non-determinism that arises either as a consequence of direct `nondet()` in the program, or as a result of inherent imprecision of static analysis. They define for every basic block of the program its own cost relation function, and then form chains according to the control flow graph of the program. They use numerical abstract domains to support a context sensitive analysis of whether a chain of visits to specific basic blocks is feasible or not. Once all infeasible chains are removed, disjunctive analysis determines an overall approximation of the heaviest chain, representing the max number of iterations.

[19] uses multiple counter instrumentation that are automatically inserted in various points in the code, initialized and incremented. These ghost counters enable to infer an overall complexity bound by applying appropriate abstract interpretation handling numeric domains. [18] and [17] apply code transformations to represent multi-path loops and nested loops in a canonical way. Then, paths connecting pairs of "interesting" code points π_1, π_2 (loop headers etc.) are identified, in a way that satisfies some properties. For instance, π_1 is reached twice *without* reaching π_2. The path property induces progress invariants, which are then analyzed to infer the overall complexity bound.

[24] define an abstraction of the program to a *size-change-graph*, where transition edges of the control flow graph are annotated to capture sound over-approximation relations between integer variables. The graph is then searched for infinitely decreasing sequences, represented as words in an ω-regular language. This representation concisely characterizes program termination. [29] then harnesses the size-change abstraction from [24] to analyze the complexity of imperative programs. First, they apply standard program transformations like pathwise analysis to summarize inner nested loops. Then, they heuristically define a set of scalar rank functions they call norms. These norms are somewhat similar to our rank function in the sense that they help to abstract away program parts that do not effect its complexity. The program is then represented as a size-change graph, and multi-path contextualization [25] prunes subsequent transitions which are infeasible.

[8] introduces *difference constraints* in the context of termination, to bound variables x' in current iteration with some y in previous iteration plus some constant c:

$x' \leq y + c$. [27] extends difference constraints to complexity analysis. Indeed, it is quite often the case that ideas from the area of program termination are assimilated in the context of complexity analysis and vice versa. They exploit the observation that typical operations on loop counters like increment, decrement and resets are essentially expressible as difference constraints. They design an abstraction based on the domain of difference constraints, and obtain relevant invariants which are then used in determining upper bounds. [10] is very similar, only that it represents a program as an integer transition system and allows nonlinear numerical constraints and ranking functions. As we mentioned earlier, all of these approaches are based on identifying the progress of executions over time, characterizing the progress between two given points in the program. In contrast, our approach allows to reason over state size and compares whole executions.

Squeezers. The notion of squeezers was introduced by [22] for the sake of safety verification. As discussed in Section 1, the challenges in complexity analysis are different, and require additional ingredients beyond squeezers. [15,1,2] introduce *well structured transition systems*, where a well-quasi order (wqo) on the set of states induces a simulation relation. This property ensures decidability of safety verification of such systems (via a backward reachability algorithm). Our use of squeezers that decrease the rank of a state and induce a sort of a simulation relation may resemble the wqo of a well structured transition system. However, there are several key differences: we do not require the order (which is defined on ranks) to be a wqo. Further, we do not require a simulation relation between *any* states whose ranks are ordered, only between a state and its squeezed counterpart. Notably, our work considers complexity analysis rather than safety verification.

7 Conclusion

This work introduces a novel framework for run-time complexity analysis. The framework supports derivation of recurrence relations based on inductive reasoning, where the form of induction depends on the choice of a squeezer (and rank bounding function). The new approach thus offers more flexibility than the classical methods where induction is coupled with the time dimension. For example, when the rank captures the "state size", the approach mimics induction over the space dimension, reasoning about whole traces, and alleviating the need to describe the intricate development of states over time. We demonstrate that such squeezers and rank bounding functions, which we manage to synthesize automatically, facilitate complexity analysis for programs that are beyond reach for existing methods. Thanks to the simplicity and compactness of these ingredients, even a rather naïve enumeration was able to find them efficiently.

Acknowledgements. The research leading to these results has received funding from the European Research Council under the European Union's Horizon 2020 research and innovation programme (grant agreement No [759102-SVIS]). This research was partially supported by the United States-Israel Binational Science Foundation (BSF) grant No. 2016260 and 2018675, the Israeli Science Foundation (ISF) grants No. 1996/18, 1810/18, 243/19 and 2740/19, and the Pazy Foundation.

References

1. Abdulla, P.A., Cerans, K., Jonsson, B., Tsay, Y.: General decidability theorems for infinite-state systems. In: Proceedings, 11th Annual IEEE Symposium on Logic in Computer Science, New Brunswick, New Jersey, USA, July 27-30, 1996. pp. 313–321. IEEE Computer Society (1996)
2. Abdulla, P.A., Cerans, K., Jonsson, B., Tsay, Y.: Algorithmic analysis of programs with well quasi-ordered domains. Inf. Comput. **160**(1-2), 109–127 (2000)
3. Albert, E., Arenas, P., Genaim, S., Puebla, G.: Automatic inference of upper bounds for recurrence relations in cost analysis. In: Alpuente, M., Vidal, G. (eds.) Static Analysis. pp. 221–237. Springer Berlin Heidelberg, Berlin, Heidelberg (2008)
4. Albert, E., Arenas, P., Genaim, S., Puebla, G., Zanardini, D.: COSTA: design and implementation of a cost and termination analyzer for java bytecode. In: Formal Methods for Components and Objects, 6th International Symposium, FMCO 2007, Amsterdam, The Netherlands, October 24-26, 2007, Revised Lectures. pp. 113–132 (2007)
5. Albert, E., Bofill, M., Borralleras, C., Martin-Martin, E., Rubio, A.: Resource analysis driven by (conditional) termination proofs. Theory Pract. Log. Program. **19**(5-6), 722–739 (2019). https://doi.org/10.1017/S1471068419000152, `https://doi.org/10.1017/S1471068419000152`
6. Alonso-Blas, D.E., Genaim, S.: On the limits of the classical approach to cost analysis. In: Miné, A., Schmidt, D. (eds.) Static Analysis. pp. 405–421. Springer Berlin Heidelberg, Berlin, Heidelberg (2012)
7. Alur, R., Bodík, R., Dallal, E., Fisman, D., Garg, P., Juniwal, G., Kress-Gazit, H., Madhusudan, P., Martin, M.M.K., Raghothaman, M., Saha, S., Seshia, S.A., Singh, R., Solar-Lezama, A., Torlak, E., Udupa, A.: Syntax-guided synthesis. In: Irlbeck, M., Peled, D.A., Pretschner, A. (eds.) Dependable Software Systems Engineering, NATO Science for Peace and Security Series, D: Information and Communication Security, vol. 40, pp. 1–25. IOS Press (2015)
8. Ben-Amram, A.M.: Size-change termination with difference constraints. ACM Trans. Program. Lang. Syst. **30**(3) (May 2008)
9. Breck, J., Cyphert, J., Kincaid, Z., Reps, T.: Templates and recurrences: Better together. In: Proceedings of the 41st ACM SIGPLAN Conference on Programming Language Design and Implementation. p. 688–702. PLDI 2020, Association for Computing Machinery, New York, NY, USA (2020)
10. Brockschmidt, M., Emmes, F., Falke, S., Fuhs, C., Giesl, J.: Alternating runtime and size complexity analysis of integer programs. In: Ábrahám, E., Havelund, K. (eds.) Tools and Algorithms for the Construction and Analysis of Systems - 20th International Conference, TACAS 2014, Held as Part of the European Joint Conferences on Theory and Practice of Software, ETAPS 2014, Grenoble, France, April 5-13, 2014. Proceedings. Lecture Notes in Computer Science, vol. 8413, pp. 140–155. Springer (2014)
11. Cadar, C., Dunbar, D., Engler, D.: Klee: Unassisted and automatic generation of high-coverage tests for complex systems programs. In: Proceedings of the 8th USENIX Conference on Operating Systems Design and Implementation. pp. 209–224. OSDI'08, USENIX Association, Berkeley, CA, USA (2008), `http://dl.acm.org/citation.cfm?id=1855741.1855756`
12. Cousot, P., Halbwachs, N.: Automatic discovery of linear restraints among variables of a program. In: Proceedings of the 5th ACM SIGACT-SIGPLAN Symposium on Principles of Programming Languages. p. 84–96. POPL '78, Association for Computing Machinery, New York, NY, USA (1978)
13. De Moura, L., Bjørner, N.: Z3: An efficient SMT solver. In: Proceedings of the Theory and Practice of Software, 14th International Conference on Tools and Algorithms for the Con-

struction and Analysis of Systems. pp. 337–340. TACAS'08/ETAPS'08, Springer-Verlag, Berlin, Heidelberg (2008)
14. Debray, S.K., Lin, N.W.: Cost analysis of logic programs. ACM Trans. Program. Lang. Syst. **15**(5), 826–875 (Nov 1993)
15. Finkel, A., Schnoebelen, P.: Well-structured transition systems everywhere! THEORETICAL COMPUTER SCIENCE **256**(1), 2001 (1998)
16. Flores-Montoya, A.: Upper and lower amortized cost bounds of programs expressed as cost relations. vol. 9995, pp. 254–273 (11 2016)
17. Gulwani, S.: The reachability-bound problem. Tech. Rep. MSR-TR-2009-146 (October 2009), https://www.microsoft.com/en-us/research/publication/the-reachability-bound-problem/
18. Gulwani, S., Jain, S., Koskinen, E.: Control-flow refinement and progress invariants for bound analysis. In: Proceedings of the 30th ACM SIGPLAN Conference on Programming Language Design and Implementation. p. 375–385. PLDI '09, Association for Computing Machinery, New York, NY, USA (2009)
19. Gulwani, S., Mehra, K.K., Chilimbi, T.M.: Speed: precise and efficient static estimation of program computational complexity. In: Shao, Z., Pierce, B.C. (eds.) POPL. pp. 127–139. ACM (2009), http://dblp.uni-trier.de/db/conf/popl/popl2009.html#GulwaniMC09
20. Hoffmann, J., Aehlig, K., Hofmann, M.: Resource aware ML. In: Madhusudan, P., Seshia, S.A. (eds.) Computer Aided Verification - 24th International Conference, CAV 2012, Berkeley, CA, USA, July 7-13, 2012 Proceedings. Lecture Notes in Computer Science, vol. 7358, pp. 781–786. Springer (2012)
21. Hoffmann, J., Hofmann, M.: Amortized resource analysis with polynomial potential: A static inference of polynomial bounds for functional programs (extended version) (03 2010)
22. Ish-Shalom, O., Itzhaky, S., Rinetzky, N., Shoham, S.: Putting the squeeze on array programs: Loop verification via inductive rank reduction. In: Beyer, D., Zufferey, D. (eds.) Verification, Model Checking, and Abstract Interpretation - 21st International Conference, VMCAI 2020, New Orleans, LA, USA, January 16-21, 2020, Proceedings. Lecture Notes in Computer Science, vol. 11990, pp. 112–135. Springer (2020)
23. Komuravelli, A., Gurfinkel, A., Chaki, S.: Smt-based model checking for recursive programs. CoRR **abs/1405.4028** (2014), http://arxiv.org/abs/1405.4028
24. Lee, C.S., Jones, N.D., Ben-Amram, A.M.: The size-change principle for program termination. In: Proceedings of the 28th ACM SIGPLAN-SIGACT Symposium on Principles of Programming Languages. p. 81–92. POPL '01, Association for Computing Machinery, New York, NY, USA (2001)
25. Manolios, P., Vroon, D.: Termination analysis with calling context graphs. In: Ball, T., Jones, R.B. (eds.) Computer Aided Verification. pp. 401–414. Springer Berlin Heidelberg, Berlin, Heidelberg (2006)
26. Mera, E., López-García, P., Puebla, G., Carro, M., Hermenegildo, M.V.: Combining static analysis and profiling for estimating execution times. In: International Symposium on Practical Aspects of Declarative Languages. pp. 140–154. Springer (2007)
27. Sinn, M., Zuleger, F., Veith, H.: Complexity and resource bound analysis of imperative programs using difference constraints. J. Autom. Reasoning **59**(1), 3–45 (2017)
28. Wegbreit, B.: Mechanical program analysis. Commun. ACM **18**(9), 528–539 (Sep 1975)
29. Zuleger, F., Gulwani, S., Sinn, M., Veith, H.: Bound analysis of imperative programs with the size-change abstraction. In: Yahav, E. (ed.) Static Analysis. pp. 280–297. Springer Berlin Heidelberg, Berlin, Heidelberg (2011)

Complete trace models of state and control*

Guilhem Jaber[1] (✉) and Andrzej S. Murawski[2] (✉)

[1] Université de Nantes, LS2N CNRS, Inria, Nantes, France
guilhem.jaber@univ-nantes.fr
[2] University of Oxford, Oxford, UK
andrzej.murawski@cs.ox.ac.uk

Abstract. We consider a hierarchy of four typed call-by-value languages with either higher-order or ground-type references and with either call/cc or no control operator.

Our first result is a fully abstract trace model for the most expressive setting, featuring both higher-order references and call/cc, constructed in the spirit of operational game semantics. Next we examine the impact of suppressing higher-order references and callcc in contexts and provide an operational explanation for the game-semantic conditions known as visibility and bracketing respectively. This allows us to refine the original model to provide fully abstract trace models of interaction with contexts that need not use higher-order references or call/cc. Along the way, we discuss the relationship between error- and termination-based contextual testing in each case, and relate the two to trace and complete trace equivalence respectively.

Overall, the paper provides a systematic development of operational game semantics for all four cases, which represent the state-based face of the so-called semantic cube.

Keywords: contextual equivalence, operational game semantics, higher-order references, control operators

1 Introduction

Research into contextual equivalence has a long tradition in programming language theory, due to its fundamental nature and applicability to numerous verification tasks, such as the correctness of compiler optimisations. Capturing contextual equivalence mathematically, i.e. the *full abstraction* problem [26], has been an important driving force in denotational semantics, which led, among others, to the development of game semantics [2,12]. Game semantics models computation through sequences of question- and answer-moves by two players, traditionally called O and P, who play the role of the context and the program respectively. Because of its interactive nature, it has often been referred to as a middle ground between denotational and operational semantics.

* The full version is available at https://hal.archives-ouvertes.fr/hal-03116698.

N. Yoshida (Ed.): ESOP 2021, LNCS 12648, pp. 348–374, 2021.
https://doi.org/10.1007/978-3-030-72019-3_13

Over the last three decades the game-semantic approach has led to numerous fully abstract models for a whole spectrum of programming paradigms. Most papers in this strand follow a rather abstract pattern when presenting the models, emphasing structure and compositionality, often developing a correspondence with a categorical framework along the way to facilitate proofs. The operational intuitions behind the games are somewhat obscured in this presentation, and left to be discovered through a deeper exploration of proofs.

In contrast, *operational game semantics* aims to define models in which the interaction between the term and the environment is described through a carefully instrumented labelled transition system (LTS), built using the syntax and operational semantics of the relevant language. Here, the derived trace semantics can be shown to be fully abstract. In this line of work, the dynamics is described more directly and provides operational intuitions about the meaning of moves, while not immediately giving structural insights about the structure of the traces.

In this paper, we follow the operational approach and present a whole hierarchy of trace models for higher-order languages with varying access to higher-order state and control. As a vehicle for our study, we use HOSC, a call-by-value higher-order language equipped with general references and continuations. We also consider its sublanguages GOSC, HOS and GOS, obtained respectively by restricting storage to ground values, by removing continuations, and by imposing both restrictions. We study contextual testing of a class of HOSC terms using contexts from each of the languages $\mathbf{x} \in \{\mathrm{HOSC}, \mathrm{GOSC}, \mathrm{HOS}, \mathrm{GOS}\}$; we write $\mathbf{x}$ to refer to each case. Our working notion of convergence will be error reachability, where an error is represented by a free variable. Accordingly, at the technical level, we will study a family of equivalence relations $\cong^{\mathbf{x}}_{err}$, each corresponding to contextual testing with contexts from $\mathbf{x}$, where contexts have the extra power to abort the computation.

Our main results are trace models $\mathbf{Tr}_{\mathbf{x}}(\Gamma \vdash M)$ for each $\mathbf{x} \in \{\mathrm{HOSC}, \mathrm{GOSC}, \mathrm{HOS}, \mathrm{GOS}\}$, which capture $\cong^{\mathbf{x}}_{err}$ through trace equivalence:

$$\Gamma \vdash M_1 \cong^{\mathbf{x}}_{err} M_2 \text{ if and only if } \mathbf{Tr}_{\mathbf{x}}(\Gamma \vdash M_1) = \mathbf{Tr}_{\mathbf{x}}(\Gamma \vdash M_2).$$

It turns out that, for contexts with control (i.e. $\mathbf{x} \in \{\mathrm{HOSC}, \mathrm{GOSC}\}$), $\cong^{\mathbf{x}}_{err}$ coincides with the standard notion of contextual equivalence based on termination, written $\cong^{\mathbf{x}}_{ter}$. However, in the other two cases, the former is strictly more discriminating than the latter. We explain how to account for this difference in the trace-based setting, using *complete* traces.

A common theme that has emerged in game semantics is the comparative study of the power of contexts, as it turned out possible to identify combinatorial conditions, namely *visibility* [3] and *bracketing* [22], that correspond to contextual testing in the absence of general references and control constructs respectively. In brief, visibility states that not all moves can be played, but only those that are enabled by a "visible part" of the interaction, which could be thought of as functions currently in scope. Bracketing in turn imposes a discipline on answers, requiring that the topmost question be answered first. In the paper, we provide an operational reconstruction of both conditions.

$$
\begin{array}{lll}
\sigma,\tau & \triangleq & \mathrm{Unit} \mid \mathrm{Int} \mid \mathrm{Bool} \mid \mathrm{ref}\tau \mid \tau\times\sigma \mid \tau\to\sigma \mid \mathrm{cont}\ \tau \\
U,V & \triangleq & () \mid \mathbf{tt} \mid \mathbf{ff} \mid \widehat{n} \mid x \mid \ell \mid \langle U,V\rangle \mid \lambda x^{\tau}.M \mid \mathbf{rec}\ y(x^{\tau}).M \mid \mathrm{cont}_{\tau}\ K \\
M,N & \triangleq & V \mid \langle M,N\rangle \mid \pi_i M \mid MN \mid \mathrm{ref}_{\tau}\ M \mid !M \mid M := N \mid \mathrm{if}\ M_1\ M_2\ M_3 \mid M\oplus N \\
 & & \mid M \boxdot N \mid M = N \mid \mathrm{call/cc}_{\tau}(x.M) \mid \mathrm{throw}_{\tau}\ \mathrm{M\ to}\ N \\
K & \triangleq & \bullet \mid \langle V,K\rangle \mid \langle K,M\rangle \mid \pi_i K \mid VK \mid KM \mid \mathrm{ref}_{\tau}\ K \mid !K \mid V := K \mid K := M \\
 & & \mid \mathrm{if}\ K\ M\ N \mid K\oplus M \mid V\oplus K \mid K\boxdot M \mid V\boxdot K \mid K = M \mid V = K \\
 & & \mid \mathrm{throw}_{\tau}\ \mathrm{V\ to}\ K \mid \mathrm{throw}_{\tau}\ \mathrm{K\ to}\ M \\
C & \triangleq & \bullet \mid \langle M,C\rangle \mid \langle C,M\rangle \mid \pi_i C \mid \lambda x^{\tau}.C \mid \mathbf{rec}\ y(x^{\tau}).C \mid MC \mid CM \mid \mathrm{ref}_{\tau}\ C \mid !C \\
 & & \mid C := M \mid M := C \mid \mathrm{if}\ C\ M\ N \mid \mathrm{if}\ M\ C\ N \mid \mathrm{if}\ M\ N\ C \mid C\oplus M \mid M\oplus C \\
 & & \mid C\boxdot M \mid M\boxdot C \mid C = M \mid M = C \mid \mathrm{call/cc}_{\tau}(x.C) \mid \mathrm{throw}_{\tau}\ \mathrm{C\ to}\ M \\
 & & \mid \mathrm{throw}_{\tau}\ \mathrm{M\ to}\ C
\end{array}
$$

Notational conventions: $x, y \in \mathbf{Var}$, $\ell \in \mathbf{Loc}$, $n \in \mathbb{Z}$, $i \in \{1,2\}$, $\oplus \in \{+,-,*\}$, $\boxdot \in \{=,<\}$
Syntactic sugar: let $x = M$ in N stands for $(\lambda x.N)M$ (if x does not occur in N we also write $M;N$)

Fig. 1. HOSC syntax

Overall, we propose a unifying framework for studying higher-order languages with state and control, which we hope will make the techniques of (operational) game semantics clearer to the wider community. The construction of the fully abstract LTSs is by no means automatic, as there is no general methodology for extracting trace semantics from game models. Some attempts in that direction have been reported in [25], but the type discipline discussed there is far too weak to be applied to the languages we study. As the most immediate precursor to our work, we see the trace model of contextual interactions between HOS contexts and HOS terms from [23]. In comparison, the models developed in this paper are more general, as they consider the interaction between HOSC terms and contexts drawn from any of the four languages ranged over by **x**.

In the 1990s, Abramsky proposed a research programme, originally called the *semantic cube* [1], which concerned investigating extensions of the purely functional programming language PCF along various axes. From this angle, the present paper is an operational study of a *semantic diamond* of languages with state, with GOS at the bottom, extending towards HOSC at the top, either via GOSC or HOS.

2 HOSC

The main objects of our study will be the language HOSC along with its fragments GOSC, HOS and GOS. HOSC is a higher-order programming language equipped with general references and continuations.

Syntax HOSC syntax is given in Figure 1. Assuming countably infinite sets **Loc** (locations) and **Var** (variables), HOSC typing judgments take the form

$(K[(\lambda x^{\sigma}.M)V],h) \to (K[M\{V/x\}],h)$	$(K[!\ell],h) \to (K[h(\ell)],h)$
$(K[\pi_i\langle V_1,V_2\rangle],h) \to (K[V_i],h)$	$(K[\mathrm{ref}\,V],h) \to (K[\ell],h\cdot[\ell\mapsto V])$
$(K[\mathrm{if}\ \mathbf{tt}\ M_1\ M_2],h) \to (K[M_1],h)$	$(K[\ell := V],h) \to (K[()],h[\ell\mapsto V])$
$(K[\mathrm{if}\ \mathbf{ff}\ M_1\ M_2],h) \to (K[M_2],h)$	$(K[\ell = \ell'],h) \to (K[b],h)$
$(K[\hat{n}\oplus\hat{m}],h) \to (K[\widehat{n\oplus m}],h)$	with $b = \mathbf{tt}$ if $\ell = \ell'$, otherwise $b = \mathbf{ff}$
$(K[\hat{n}\boxdot\hat{m}],h) \to (K[b],h)$	$(K[\underbrace{(\mathbf{rec}\ y(x^{\sigma}).M)}_{U}V],h) \to (K[M\{V/x,U/y\}],h)$
with $b = \mathbf{tt}$ if $n\boxdot m$, otherwise $b = \mathbf{ff}$	
$(K[\mathrm{call/cc}(x.M)],h) \to (K[M\{\mathrm{cont}\,K/x\}],h)$	$(K[\mathrm{throw}\ V\ \mathrm{to}\ \mathrm{cont}\,K'],h) \to (K'[V],h)$

Fig. 2. Operational reduction for HOSC

$\Sigma;\Gamma \vdash M : \tau$, where Σ and Γ are finite partial functions that assign types to locations and variables respectively. In typing judgements, we often write Σ as shorthand for $\Sigma;\emptyset$ (closed) and Γ as shorthand for $\emptyset;\Gamma$ (location-free). Similarly, $\vdash M : \tau$ means $\emptyset;\emptyset \vdash M : \tau$.

Operational semantics A heap h is a finite type-respecting map from **Loc** to values. We write $h : (\Sigma;\Gamma)$, if $\mathrm{dom}(\Sigma) \subseteq \mathrm{dom}(h)$ and $\Sigma;\Gamma \vdash h(\ell) : \sigma$ for $(\ell,\sigma) \in \Sigma$, The operational semantics of HOSC reduces pairs (M,h), where $\Sigma;\Gamma \vdash M : \tau$ and $h : (\Sigma;\Gamma)$. The rules are given in Figure 2, where $\{\cdot\}$ denotes (capture-avoiding) substitution. We write $(M,h) \Downarrow_{ter}$ if there exist V, h' such that $(M,h) \to^{*} (V,h')$ and V is a value.

We distinguish the following fragments of HOSC.

Definition 1. – GOSC *types are* HOSC *types except that reference types are restricted to* $\mathrm{ref}\,\iota$, *where* ι *is given by the grammar* $\iota \triangleq \mathrm{Unit} \mid \mathrm{Int} \mid \mathrm{Bool} \mid \mathrm{ref}\,\iota$. GOSC *terms are* HOSC *terms whose typing derivations (i.e. not only the final typing judgments) rely on* GOSC *types only.* GOSC *is a superset of* FOSC *[8] (*GOSC *also includes references to references - the* $\mathrm{ref}\,\iota$ *case above).*

– HOS *types are* HOSC *types that do not feature the* cont *constructor.* HOS *terms are* HOSC *terms whose typing derivations rely on* HOS *types only. Consequently,* HOS *terms never have subterms of the form* $\mathrm{call/cc}_{\tau}(x.M)$, throw_{τ} M to N *or* $\mathrm{cont}_{\tau}\,K$.

– GOS *is the intersection of* HOS *and* GOSC, *both for types and terms, i.e. there are no continuations and storage is restricted to values of type* ι, *defined above.*

Definition 2. *Given a* HOSC *term* $\Gamma \vdash M : \tau$, *we refer to types in* Γ *and* τ *as* **boundary types**. *Let* $\mathbf{x} \in \{\mathrm{HOSC}, \mathrm{GOSC}, \mathrm{HOS}, \mathrm{GOS}\}$. *We say that a* HOSC *term* $\Gamma \vdash M : \tau$ *has an* $\mathbf{x}$ *boundary if all of its boundary types are from* $\mathbf{x}$.

Remark 1. Note that typing derivations of HOSC terms with an $\mathbf{x}$ boundary may contain arbitrary HOSC types as long as the final typing judgment uses types from $\mathbf{x}$ only. Consequently, if $\mathbf{x} \neq$ HOSC, HOSC terms with an $\mathbf{x}$ boundary form a strict superset of $\mathbf{x}$.

Next we introduce several notions of contextual testing for HOSC-terms, using various kinds of contexts. For a start, we introduce the classic notion of contextual approximation based on observing termination. The notions are parameterized by $\mathbf{x}$, indicating which language is used to build the testing contexts. We write $\Gamma \vdash C : \tau \to \tau'$ if $\Gamma, x : \tau \vdash C[x] : \tau'$, and $\Gamma \vdash C \div \tau$ if $\Gamma \vdash C : \tau \to \tau'$ for some τ'.

Definition 3 (Contextual Approximation). *Let* $\mathbf{x} \in \{\text{HOSC}, \text{GOSC}, \text{HOS}, \text{GOS}\}$. *Given* HOSC *terms* $\Gamma \vdash M_1, M_2 : \tau$ *with an* $\mathbf{x}$ *boundary, we define* $\Gamma \vdash M_1 \lesssim^{\mathbf{x}}_{ter} M_2$ *to hold, when for all contexts* $\vdash C \div \tau$ *built from the syntax of* $\mathbf{x}$, *if* $(C[M_1], \epsilon) \Downarrow_{ter}$ *then* $(C[M_2], \epsilon) \Downarrow_{ter}$.

We also consider another way of testing, based on observing whether a program can reach a breakpoint (error point) inside a context. Technically, the breakpoints are represented as occurrences of a special free error variable err : Unit $\to$ Unit. Reaching a breakpoint then corresponds to convergence to a stuck configuration of the form $(K[err()], h)$: we write $(M, h) \Downarrow_{err}$ if there exist K, h' such that $(M, h) \to^* (K[err()], h')$.

Definition 4 (Contextual Approximation through Error). *Suppose* $\mathbf{x} \in \{\text{HOSC}, \text{FOSC}, \text{HOS}, \text{GOS}\}$. *Given* HOSC *terms* $\Gamma \vdash M_1, M_2 : \tau$ *with an* $\mathbf{x}$ *boundary and* $err \notin \text{dom}(\Gamma)$, *we define* $\Gamma \vdash M_1 \lesssim^{\mathbf{x}}_{err} M_2$ *to hold, when for all contexts* err : Unit $\to$ Unit $\vdash C \div \tau$ *built from* $\mathbf{x}$*-syntax, if* $(C[M_1], \epsilon) \Downarrow_{err}$ *then* $(C[M_2], \epsilon) \Downarrow_{err}$.

For the languages in question, it will turn out that $\lesssim^{\mathbf{x}}_{err}$ is at least as discriminating as $\lesssim^{\mathbf{x}}_{ter}$ for each $\mathbf{x} \in \{\text{HOSC}, \text{GOSC}, \text{HOS}, \text{GOS}\}$, and that they coincide for $\mathbf{x} \in \{\text{HOSC}, \text{GOSC}\}$. We will write $\cong^{\mathbf{x}}_{err}$ and $\cong^{\mathbf{x}}_{ter}$ for the associated equivalence relations.

For higher-order languages with state and control, it is well known that contextual testing can be restricted to evaluation contexts after instantiating the free variables of terms to closed values (the so-called *closed instances of use*, CIU). Let us write $\Sigma, \Gamma' \vdash \gamma : \Gamma$ for substitutions γ such that, for any $(x, \sigma_x) \in \Gamma$, the term $\gamma(x)$ is a value satisfying $\Sigma; \Gamma' \vdash \gamma(x) : \sigma_x$. Then $M\{\gamma\}$ stands for the outcome of applying γ to M.

Definition 5 (CIU Approximation). *Let* $\mathbf{x} \in \{\text{HOSC}, \text{GOSC}, \text{HOS}, \text{GOS}\}$ *and let* $\Gamma \vdash M_1, M_2 : \tau$ *be* HOSC *terms with an* $\mathbf{x}$ *boundary.*

- $\Gamma \vdash M_1 \lesssim^{\mathbf{x}(ciu)}_{ter} M_2 : \tau$, *when for all* Σ, h, K, γ, *all built from* $\mathbf{x}$ *syntax, such that* $h : \Sigma$, $\Sigma \vdash K \div \tau$, *and* $\Sigma \vdash \gamma : \Gamma$, *we have* $(K[M_1\{\gamma\}], h) \Downarrow_{ter}$ *implies* $(K[M_2\{\gamma\}], h) \Downarrow_{ter}$.
- *We write* $\Gamma \vdash M_1 \lesssim^{\mathbf{x}(ciu)}_{err} M_2 : \tau$, *when for all* Σ, h, K, γ, *all built from* $\mathbf{x}$ *syntax, such that* $h : \Sigma; \widehat{err}$, $\Sigma; \widehat{err} \vdash K \div \tau$, *and* $\Sigma; \widehat{err} \vdash \gamma : \Gamma$, *we have* $(K[M_1\{\gamma\}], h) \Downarrow_{err}$ *implies* $(K[M_2\{\gamma\}], h) \Downarrow_{err}$, *where* $err \notin \text{dom}(\Gamma)$ *and* $\widehat{err}$ *stands for* err : Unit $\to$ Unit.

Results stating that "CIU tests suffice" are referred to as CIU lemmas. A general framework for obtaining such results for higher-order languages with effects was developed in [10,33]. The results stated therein are for termination-based testing, i.e. $\Downarrow_{ter}$, but adapting them to $\Downarrow_{err}$ is not problematic.

Lemma 1 (CIU Lemma). *Let* $\mathbf{x} \in \{\text{HOSC}, \text{GOSC}, \text{HOS}, \text{GOS}\}$ *and* $\mathbf{y} \in \{ter, err\}$. *Then we have* $\Gamma \vdash M_1 \lesssim^{\mathbf{x}}_{\mathbf{y}} M_2$ *iff* $\Gamma \vdash M_1 \lesssim^{\mathbf{x}(ciu)}_{\mathbf{y}} M_2$.

The preorders $\lesssim^{\mathbf{x}}_{err}$ will be the central object of study in the paper. Among others, we shall provide their alternative characterizations using trace semantics.The characterizations will apply to a class of terms that we call *cr-free.*

Definition 6. *A* HOSC *term* $\Gamma \vdash M : \tau$ *is* **cr-free** *if it does not contain occurrences of* $\text{cont}_\sigma\, K$ *and locations, and its boundary types are* cont- *and* ref*-free.*

We stress that the boundary restriction applies to Γ and τ only, and subterms of M may well contain arbitrary HOSC types and occurrences of ref_σ, call/cc_σ, throw_σ for any σ. The majority of HOSC/GOSC/HOS/GOS examples studied in the literature, e.g. [28,4,8], are actually cr-free. We will revisit some of them as Examples 6, 7, 10. The fact that cr-free terms may not contain subterms $\text{cont}_\tau\, K$ or ℓ is not really a restriction, as $\text{cont}_\tau\, K$ and ℓ being more of a run-time construct than a feature meant to be used directly by programmers. Finally, we note that the boundary of a cr-free term is an $\mathbf{x}$ boundary for any $\mathbf{x} \in \{\text{HOSC}, \text{GOSC}, \text{HOS}, \text{GOS}\}$. Thus, we can consider approximation between cr-terms for any $\mathbf{x}$ from the range, i.e. the notions $\lesssim^{\mathbf{x}}_{err}$, $\lesssim^{\mathbf{x}}_{ter}$ are all applicable. Consequently, cr-free terms provide a common setting in which the discriminating power of HOSC, GOSC, HOS and GOS contexts can be compared. We discuss the scope for extending our results outside of the cr-free fragment, and for richer type systems, in Section 7.

3 HOSC[HOSC]

Recall that $\lesssim^{\text{HOSC}}_{err}$ concerns testing HOSC terms with HOSC contexts. Accordingly, we call this case HOSC[HOSC]. For $\text{cont}_\sigma(K)$-free terms, we show that $\lesssim^{\text{HOSC}}_{err}$ and $\lesssim^{\text{HOSC}}_{ter}$ coincide, which follows from the lemma below.

Lemma 2. *Let* $\Gamma \vdash M_1, M_2$ *be* HOSC *terms not containing any occurrences of* $\text{cont}_\tau(K)$.

1. $\Gamma \vdash M_1 \lesssim^{\mathbf{x}}_{err} M_2$ *implies* $\Gamma \vdash M_1 \lesssim^{\mathbf{x}}_{ter} M_2$, *for* $\mathbf{x} \in \{$HOSC, GOSC, HOS, GOS$\}$.
2. $\Gamma \vdash M_1 \lesssim^{\mathbf{x}}_{ter} M_2$ *implies* $\Gamma \vdash M_1 \lesssim^{\mathbf{x}}_{err} M_2$, *for* $\mathbf{x} \in \{\text{HOSC}, \text{GOSC}\}$.

In what follows, after introducing several preliminary notions, we shall design a labelled transition system (LTS) whose traces will turn out to capture contextual interactions involved in testing cr-free terms according to $\lesssim^{\text{HOSC}}_{err}$. This will enable us to capture $\lesssim^{\text{HOSC}}_{err}$ via trace inclusion. Actions of the LTS will refer to functions and continuations in a symbolic way, using typed names.

3.1 Names and abstract values

Definition 7. *Let* $\text{FNames} = \biguplus_{\sigma,\sigma'} \text{FNames}_{\sigma\to\sigma'}$ *be the set of* **function names,** *partitioned into mutually disjoint countably infinite sets* $\text{FNames}_{\sigma\to\sigma'}$. *We will use* f, g *to range over* FNames *and write* $f : \sigma \to \sigma'$ *for* $f \in \text{FNames}_{\sigma\to\sigma'}$.

Analogously, let CNames $= \biguplus_\sigma$ CNames$_\sigma$ *be the set of* **continuation names.** *We will use* c, d *to range over* CNames, *and write* $c : \sigma$ *for* $c \in$ CNames$_\sigma$. *Note that the constants represent continuations, so the "real" type of* c *is* cont σ, *but we write* $c : \sigma$ *for the sake of brevity. We assume that* CNames, FNames *are disjoint and let* Names = FNames $\uplus$ CNames. *Elements of* Names *will be weaved into various constructions in the paper, e.g. terms, heaps, etc. We will then write* $\nu(X)$ *to refer to the set of names used in some entity* X.

Because of the shape of boundary types in cr-free terms and, in particular, the presence of product types, the values that will be exchanged between the context and the program take the form of tuples consisting of (), integers, booleans and functions. To describe such scenarios, we introduce the notion of ***abstract values***, which are patterns that match such values. Abstract values are generated by the grammar

$$A, B \triangleq () \mid \mathbf{tt} \mid \mathbf{ff} \mid \widehat{n} \mid f \mid \langle A, B\rangle$$

with the proviso that, in any abstract value, a name may occur at most once. As function names are intrinsically typed, we can assign types to abstract values in the obvious way, writing $A : \tau$.

3.2 Actions and traces

Our LTS will be based on four kinds of actions, listed below. Each action will be equipped with a ***polarity***, which is either Player (P) or Opponent (O). P-actions describing interaction steps made by a tested term, while O-actions involve the context.

- ***Player Answer*** (PA) $\bar{c}(A)$, where $c : \sigma$ and $A : \sigma$. This action corresponds to the term sending an abstract value A through a continuation name c.
- ***Player Question*** (PQ) $\bar{f}(A, c)$, where $f : \sigma \to \sigma'$, $A : \sigma$ and $c : \sigma'$. Here, an abstract value A and a continuation name c are sent by the term through a function name f.
- ***Opponent Answer*** (OA) $c(A)$, $c : \sigma$ then $A : \sigma$. In this case, an abstract value A is received from the environment via the continuation name c.
- ***Opponent Question*** (OQ) $f(A, c)$, where $f : \sigma \to \sigma'$, $A : \sigma$ and $c : \sigma'$. Finally, this action corresponds to receiving an abstract value A and a continuation name c from the environment through a function name f.

In what follows, $\mathbf{a}$ is used to range over actions. We will say that a name is ***introduced*** by an action $\mathbf{a}$ if it is sent or received in $\mathbf{a}$. If $\mathbf{a}$ is an O-action (resp. P-action), we say that the name was introduced by O (resp. P). An action $\mathbf{a}$ is ***justified*** by another action $\mathbf{a}'$ if the name that $\mathbf{a}$ uses to communicate, i.e. f in questions ($\bar{f}(A, c)$, $f(A, c)$) and c in answers ($\bar{c}(A)$, $c(A)$), has been introduced by $\mathbf{a}'$.

We will work with sequences of actions of a very special shape, specified below. The definition assumes two given sets of names, N_P and N_O, which represent names that have already been introduced by P and O respectively.

Definition 8. *Let $N_O, N_P \subseteq$ Names. An (N_O, N_P)-**trace** is a sequence t of actions such that:*

- *the actions alternate between Player and Opponent actions;*
- *no name is introduced twice;*
- *names from N_O, N_P need no introduction;*
- *if an action $\mathbf{a}$ uses a name to communicate then*
  - $\mathbf{a} = \bar{f}(A, c)$ *($f \in N_O$) or* $\mathbf{a} = \bar{c}(A)$ *($c \in N_O$) or* $\mathbf{a} = f(A, c)$ *($f \in N_P$) or* $\mathbf{a} = c(A)$ *($c \in N_P$) or*
  - *the name has been introduced by an earlier action $\mathbf{a}'$ of opposite polarity.*

Note that, due to the shape of actions, a continuation name can only be introduced/justified by a question. Moreover, because names are never introduced twice, if $\mathbf{a}'$ justifies $\mathbf{a}$ then $\mathbf{a}'$ is uniquely determined in a given trace. Readers familiar with game semantics will recognize that traces are very similar to alternating justified sequences except that traces need not be started by O.

Example 1. Let $(N_O, N_P) = (\{c\}, \emptyset)$ where $c : \tau = ((\mathrm{Unit} \to \mathrm{Unit}) \to \mathrm{Unit}) \times (\mathrm{Unit} \to \mathrm{Int})$. Then the following sequence is an (N_O, N_P)-trace:

$$\mathbf{t}_1 = \bar{c}(\langle g_1, g_2 \rangle)\ g_1(f_1, c_1)\ \bar{f_1}((), c_2)\ c_2(())\ \bar{c_1}(())\ c_2(())\ \bar{c_1}(())\ g_2((), c_3)\ \bar{c_3}(2)$$

where $g_1 : (\mathrm{Unit} \to \mathrm{Unit}) \to \mathrm{Unit}$, $g_2 : \mathrm{Unit} \to \mathrm{Int}$, $f_1 : \mathrm{Unit} \to \mathrm{Unit}$, $c_1, c_2 : \mathrm{Unit}$, $c_3 : \mathrm{Int}$.

3.3 Extended syntax and reduction

We extend the definition of HOSC presented in Figure 2 to take into account these names. We refine the operational reduction using continuation names to keep track of the toplevel continuation. We list all the changes below.

- Function names are added to the syntax as *constants*. Since they are meant to represent values, they are also considered to be syntactic values in the extended language.

$$\frac{f \in \mathrm{FNames}_{\sigma \to \sigma'}}{\Sigma; \Gamma \vdash f : \sigma \to \sigma'}$$

- Continuation names are *not* terms on their own. Instead, they are built into the syntax via a new construct $\mathrm{cont}_\sigma\,(K, c)$, subject to the following typing rule.

$$\frac{\Sigma; \Gamma \vdash K : \sigma \to \sigma' \quad c \in \mathrm{CNames}_{\sigma'}}{\Sigma; \Gamma \vdash \mathrm{cont}_\sigma\,(K, c) : \mathrm{cont}\ \sigma}$$

  $\mathrm{cont}_\sigma\,(K, c)$ is a staged continuation that first evaluates terms inside K and, if this produces a value, the value is passed to c. This operational meaning will be implemented through a suitable reduction rule, to be discussed next. $\mathrm{cont}_\sigma\,(K, c)$ is also regarded as a value. Note that we remove the old construct $\mathrm{cont}_\sigma\,K$ from the extended syntax.

- The operational semantics $\rightarrow$ underpinning the LTS is based on triples (M, c, h) such that $\Sigma; \Gamma \vdash M : \sigma$, $c \in \mathrm{CNames}_\sigma$ and $h : \Sigma$. The continuation name c is used to represent the surrounding context, which is left abstract. The previous operational rules $\rightarrow$ are embedded into the new reduction $\rightarrow$ using the rule below.
$$\frac{(M, h) \rightarrow (M', h')}{(M, c, h) \rightarrow (M', c, h')}$$
The two reduction rules related to continuations, previously used to define $\rightarrow$, are *not* included. Instead we use the following rules, which take advantage of the extended syntax.
$$(K[\mathrm{call/cc}_\tau(x.M)], c, h) \rightarrow (K[M\{\mathrm{cont}_\tau(K, c)/x\}], c, h)$$
$$(K[\mathrm{throw}_\tau\ V \text{ to } \mathrm{cont}_\tau(K', c')], c, h) \rightarrow (K'[V], c', h)$$

3.4 Configurations

We write Vals for the extended set of syntactic values, i.e. FNames $\subseteq$ Vals. Let ECtxs stand for the set of extended evaluation contexts, defined as K in Figure 1 taking the extended definition of values into account. Before defining the transition relation of our LTS, we discuss the shape of configurations, providing intuitions behind each component.

Passive configurations take the form $\langle \gamma, \xi, \phi, h \rangle$ and are meant to represent stages at which the environment is to make a move.

- $\gamma : (\mathrm{FNames} \rightharpoonup \mathrm{Vals}) \uplus (\mathrm{CNames} \rightharpoonup \mathrm{ECtxs})$ is a finite map. It will play the role of an environment that relates function names communicated to the environment (i.e. those introduced by P) to syntactic values, and continuation names introduced by P to evaluation contexts.
- $\xi : (\mathrm{CNames} \rightharpoonup \mathrm{CNames})$ is a finite map. It complements the role of γ for continuation names and indicates the continuation to which the outcome of applying $\gamma(c)$ should be passed.
- $\phi \subseteq$ Names. The set ϕ will be used to collect all the names used in the interaction, regardless of which participant introduced them. Following our description above, those introduced by O will correspond to $\phi \setminus \mathrm{dom}(\gamma)$.

The components satisfy healthiness conditions, implied by their role in the system. Let $\Sigma = \mathrm{dom}(h)$.

- If $f : \mathrm{dom}(\gamma) \cap \mathrm{FNames}_{\sigma \rightarrow \sigma'}$ then $\gamma(f)$ is a value such that $\Sigma \vdash \gamma(f) : \sigma \rightarrow \sigma'$.
- $\mathrm{dom}(\xi) = \mathrm{dom}(\gamma) \cap \mathrm{CNames}$.
- If $c : \mathrm{dom}(\gamma) \cap \mathrm{CNames}_\sigma$ and $\Sigma \vdash \gamma(c) : \sigma \rightarrow \sigma'$ then $\xi(c) \in \mathrm{CNames}_{\sigma'}$.
- Finally, names introduced by the environment and communicated to the program may end up in the environments and the heap: $\nu(\mathrm{img}(\gamma)), \nu(\mathrm{img}(\xi)), \nu(\mathrm{img}(h)) \subseteq \phi \setminus \mathrm{dom}(\gamma)$.

Active configurations take the form $\langle M, c, \gamma, \xi, \phi, h \rangle$ and represent interaction steps of the term. The γ, ξ, ϕ, h components have already been described above. For M and c, given $\Sigma = \mathrm{dom}(h)$, we will have $\Sigma; \emptyset \vdash M : \sigma$, $c \in \mathrm{CNames}_\sigma$ and $\nu(M) \cup \{c\} \subseteq \phi \setminus \mathrm{dom}(\gamma)$.

3.5 Transitions

Observe that any closed value V of a cont- and ref-free type σ can be decomposed into an abstract value A (pattern) and the corresponding substitution γ (matching). The set of all such decompositions, written $\mathbf{AVal}_\sigma(V)$, is defined below. Given a value V of a (cr-free) type σ, $\mathbf{AVal}_\sigma(V)$ contains all pairs (A,γ) such that A is an abstract value and $\gamma : \nu(A) \to \text{Vals}$ is a substitution such that $A\{\gamma\} = V$. More concretely,

$$\begin{array}{ll}\mathbf{AVal}_\sigma(V) & \triangleq \{(V,\emptyset)\} \quad \text{for } \sigma \in \{\text{Unit}, \text{Bool}, \text{Int}\}\\ \mathbf{AVal}_{\sigma\to\sigma'}(V) & \triangleq \{(f,[f\mapsto V]) \mid f \in \text{FNames}_{\sigma\to\sigma'}\}\\ \mathbf{AVal}_{\sigma\times\sigma'}(\langle U,V\rangle) & \triangleq \{(\langle A_1,A_2\rangle,\gamma_1\cdot\gamma_2) \mid \\ & \qquad\qquad (A_1,\gamma_1)\in\mathbf{AVal}_\sigma(U),\, (A_2,\gamma_2)\in\mathbf{AVal}_{\sigma'}(V)\}\end{array}$$

Note that, by writing $\cdot$, we mean to implicitly require that the function domains be disjoint. Similarly, when writing $\uplus$, we stipulate that the argument sets be disjoint.

Example 2. Let $\sigma = (\text{Int}\to\text{Bool})\times(\text{Int}\times(\text{Unit}\to\text{Int}))$ and $V \equiv \langle\lambda x^{\text{Int}}.x \neq 1, \langle 2, \lambda x^{\text{Unit}}.3\rangle\rangle$. Then $\mathbf{AVal}_\sigma(V)$ equals

$$\{(\langle f,\langle 2,g\rangle\rangle, [f\mapsto(\lambda x^{\text{Int}}.x\neq 1)]\cdot[g\mapsto(\lambda x^{\text{Unit}}.3)]) \mid \\ f\in\text{FNames}_{\text{Int}\to\text{Unit}},\, g\in\text{FNames}_{\text{Unit}\to\text{Int}}\}.$$

Finally, we present the transitions of what we call the HOSC[HOSC] LTS in Figure 3.

Example 3. Below we analyse the (PQ) rule in more detail.

$$\langle K[fV],c,\gamma,\xi,\phi,h\rangle \xrightarrow{\bar{f}(A,c')} \langle\gamma\cdot\gamma'\cdot[c'\mapsto K],\xi\cdot[c'\mapsto c],\phi\uplus\nu(A)\uplus\{c'\},h\rangle \\ \text{when } f:\sigma\to\sigma',\ (A,\gamma')\in\mathbf{AVal}_\sigma(V) \text{ and } c':\sigma'$$

The use of $\uplus$ in $\phi\uplus\nu(A)\uplus\{c'\}$ is meant to highlight the requirement that the names introduced in $\bar{f}(A,c')$, i.e. $\nu(A)\cup\{c'\}$, should be fresh and disjoint from ϕ. Moreover, note how γ and ξ are updated. In general, γ,ξ,h are updated during P-actions.

Definition 9. *Given two configurations* $\mathbf{C},\mathbf{C}'$, *we write* $\mathbf{C} \stackrel{\mathtt{a}}{\Rightarrow} \mathbf{C}'$ *if* $\mathbf{C} \xrightarrow{\tau}{}^* \mathbf{C}'' \xrightarrow{\mathtt{a}} \mathbf{C}'$, *with* $\xrightarrow{\tau}{}^*$ *representing multiple (possibly none)* τ*-actions. This notation is extended to sequences of actions: given* $\mathtt{t} = \mathtt{a}_1\ldots\mathtt{a}_n$, *we write* $\mathbf{C} \stackrel{\mathtt{t}}{\Rightarrow} \mathbf{C}'$, *if there exist* $\mathbf{C}_1,\ldots,\mathbf{C}_{n-1}$ *such that* $\mathbf{C} \stackrel{\mathtt{a}_1}{\Longrightarrow} \mathbf{C}_1\cdots\mathbf{C}_{n-1} \stackrel{\mathtt{a}_n}{\Longrightarrow} \mathbf{C}'$. *We define* $\mathbf{Tr}_{\text{HOSC}}(\mathbf{C}) = \{\mathtt{t} \mid$ *there exists* $\mathbf{C}'$ *such that* $\mathbf{C} \stackrel{\mathtt{t}}{\Rightarrow} \mathbf{C}'\}$.

Lemma 3. *Suppose* $\mathbf{C} = \langle\gamma,\xi,\phi,h\rangle$ *or* $\mathbf{C} = \langle M,c,\gamma,\xi,\phi,h\rangle$ *are configurations. Then elements of* $\mathbf{Tr}_{\text{HOSC}}(\mathbf{C})$ *are* $(\phi\setminus\text{dom}(\gamma),\text{dom}(\gamma))$*-traces.*

$$
\begin{array}{l|lcl}
(P\tau) & \langle M,c,\gamma,\xi,\phi,h\rangle & \xrightarrow{\tau} & \langle N,c',\gamma,\xi,\phi,h'\rangle \\
& \text{when } (M,c,h) \to (N,c',h') & & \\
(PA) & \langle V,c,\gamma,\xi,\phi,h\rangle & \xrightarrow{\bar{c}(A)} & \langle \gamma\cdot\gamma',\xi,\phi \uplus \nu(A),h\rangle \\
& \text{when } c:\sigma,\ (A,\gamma') \in \mathbf{AVal}_\sigma(V) & & \\
(PQ) & \langle K[fV],c,\gamma,\xi,\phi,h\rangle & \xrightarrow{\bar{f}(A,c')} & \langle \gamma\cdot\gamma'\cdot[c'\mapsto K],\xi\cdot[c'\mapsto c],\phi\uplus\nu(A)\uplus\{c'\},h\rangle \\
& \text{when } f:\sigma\to\sigma',\ (A,\gamma')\in\mathbf{AVal}_\sigma(V),\ c':\sigma' & & \\
(OA) & \langle \gamma,\xi,\phi,h\rangle & \xrightarrow{c(A)} & \langle K[A],c',\gamma,\xi,\phi\uplus\nu(A),h\rangle \\
& \text{when } c:\sigma,\ A:\sigma,\ \gamma(c)=K,\ \xi(c)=c' & & \\
(OQ) & \langle \gamma,\xi,\phi,h\rangle & \xrightarrow{f(A,c)} & \langle VA,c,\gamma,\xi,\phi\uplus\nu(A)\uplus\{c\},h\rangle \\
& \text{when } f:\sigma\to\sigma',\ A:\sigma,\ c:\sigma',\ \gamma(f)=V & &
\end{array}
$$

NB $c:\sigma$ stands for $c \in \text{CNames}_\sigma$.

Fig. 3. HOSC[HOSC] LTS

M_1^{cwl} : let x = ref 0 in let b = ref **ff** in ⟨λf. if ¬(!b) then b := **tt**; f(); x :=!x + 1; b := **ff**; else (), λ_ : Unit.!x⟩	M_2^{cwl} : let x = ref 0 in let b = ref **ff** in ⟨λf. if ¬(!b) then b := **tt**; let n =!x in f(); x := n + 1; b := **ff**; else () , λ_ : Unit.!x⟩

Fig. 4. Callback-with-lock Example [4]

Example 4. In Figure 5, we show that the trace from Example 1 is generated by the configuration $\mathbf{C} \triangleq \langle M_1^{cwl}, c, \emptyset, \emptyset, \{c\}, \emptyset\rangle$, where M_1^{cwl} is given in Figure 4. We write inc $\triangleq \lambda f.\text{if } \neg(!\ell_b)\ (\ell_b := \mathbf{tt}; f(); \ell_x :=!\ell_x + 1; \ell_b := \mathbf{ff})\ ()$, get $\triangleq \lambda\_.!\ell_x$ and $c : ((\text{Unit} \to \text{Unit}) \to \text{Unit}) \times (\text{Unit} \to \text{Int})$. It is interesting to notice that in this interaction, Opponent uses the continuation N twice, incrementing the counter x by two. The second time, it does it without having to call inc again, but rather by using the continuation name c_2.

Remark 2. Due to the freedom of name choice, note that $\mathbf{Tr}_{\text{HOSC}}(\mathbf{C})$ is closed under type-preserving renamings that preserve names from $\mathbf{C}$.

3.6 Correctness and full abstraction

We define two kinds of special configurations that will play an important role in spelling out correctness results for the HOSC[HOSC] LTS. Let $\Gamma = \{x_1 : \sigma_1, \cdots, x_k : \sigma_k\}$. A map ρ from $\{x_1, \cdots, x_k\}$ to the set of abstract values will be called a ***Γ-assignment*** provided, for all $1 \le i \ne j \le k$, we have $\rho(x_i) : \sigma_i$ and $\nu(\rho(x_i)) \cap \nu(\rho(x_j)) = \emptyset$.

$$
\begin{array}{lll}
& \mathbf{C} = \langle M_1^{cwl}, c, \emptyset, \emptyset, \{c\}, \emptyset\rangle & \\
\xrightarrow{\tau^*} & \langle\langle \mathrm{inc}, \mathrm{get}\rangle, c, \emptyset, \emptyset, \{c\}, [\ell_b \mapsto \mathbf{ff}, \ell_x \mapsto 0]\rangle & \\
\xrightarrow{\bar{c}(\langle g_1, g_2\rangle)} & \langle\gamma_1, \emptyset, \{c, g_1, g_2\}, [\ell_b \mapsto \mathbf{ff}, \ell_x \mapsto 0]\rangle & \text{with } \gamma_1 = [g_1 \mapsto \mathrm{inc}, g_2 \mapsto \mathrm{get}], \\
\xrightarrow{g_1(f_1, c_1)} & \langle \mathrm{inc} f_1, c_1, \gamma_1, \emptyset, \phi_2, [\ell_b \mapsto \mathbf{ff}, \ell_x \mapsto 0]\rangle & \text{with } \phi_2 = \{c, g_1, g_2, f_1, c_1\} \\
\xrightarrow{\tau^*} & \langle f_1(); N, c_1, \gamma_1, \emptyset, \phi_2, [\ell_b \mapsto \mathbf{tt}, \ell_x \mapsto 0]\rangle & \text{with } N = \ell_x := !\ell_x + 1; \ell_b := \mathbf{ff} \\
\xrightarrow{\bar{f_1}((), c_2)} & \langle\gamma_2, \xi, \phi_3, [\ell_b \mapsto \mathbf{tt}, \ell_x \mapsto 0]\rangle & \text{with } \gamma_2 = \gamma_1 \cdot [c_2 \mapsto \bullet; N], \\
\xrightarrow{c_2(())} & \langle (); N, c_1, \gamma_2, \xi, \phi_3, [\ell_b \mapsto \mathbf{tt}, \ell_x \mapsto 0]\rangle & \quad \xi = [c_2 \mapsto c_1] \text{ and } \phi_3 = \phi_2 \uplus \{c_2\} \\
\xrightarrow{\tau^*} & \langle (), c_1, \gamma_2, \xi, \phi_3, [\ell_b \mapsto \mathbf{ff}, \ell_x \mapsto 1]\rangle & \\
\xrightarrow{\bar{c_1}(())} & \langle\gamma_2, \xi, \phi_3, [\ell_b \mapsto \mathbf{ff}, \ell_x \mapsto 1]\rangle & \\
\xrightarrow{c_2(())} & \langle (); N, c_1, \gamma_2, \xi, \phi_3, [\ell_b \mapsto \mathbf{ff}, \ell_x \mapsto 1]\rangle & \\
\xrightarrow{\tau^*} & \langle (), c_1, \gamma_2, \xi, \phi_3, [\ell_b \mapsto \mathbf{ff}, \ell_x \mapsto 2]\rangle & \\
\xrightarrow{\bar{c_1}(())} & \langle\gamma_2, \xi, \phi_3, [\ell_b \mapsto \mathbf{ff}, \ell_x \mapsto 2]\rangle & \\
\xrightarrow{g_2((), c_3)} & \langle \mathrm{get}(), c_3, \gamma_2, \xi, \phi_4, [\ell_b \mapsto \mathbf{ff}, \ell_x \mapsto 2]\rangle & \text{with } \phi_4 = \phi_3 \uplus \{c_3\} \\
\xrightarrow{\tau^*} & \langle 2, c_3, \gamma_2, \xi, \phi_4, [\ell_b \mapsto \mathbf{ff}, \ell_x \mapsto 2]\rangle & \\
\xrightarrow{\bar{c_3}(2)} & \langle\gamma_2, \xi, \phi_4, [\ell_b \mapsto \mathbf{ff}, \ell_x \mapsto 2]\rangle &
\end{array}
$$

Fig. 5. Trace derivation in the HOSC[HOSC] LTS

Definition 10 (Program configuration). *Given a Γ-assignment ρ, a cr-free HOSC term $\Gamma \vdash M : \tau$ and $c : \tau$, we define the active configuration $\mathsf{C}_M^{\rho,c}$ by $\mathsf{C}_M^{\rho,c} = \langle M\{\rho\}, c, \emptyset, \emptyset, \nu(\rho) \cup \{c\}, \emptyset\rangle$.*

Note that traces from $\mathbf{Tr}_{\mathrm{HOSC}}(\mathsf{C}_M^{\rho,c})$ will be $(\nu(\rho) \cup \{c\}, \emptyset)$-traces.

Definition 11. *The* HOSC[HOSC] **trace semantics** *of a cr-free HOSC term $\Gamma \vdash M : \tau$ is defined to be*

$$\mathbf{Tr}_{\mathrm{HOSC}}(\Gamma \vdash M : \tau) = \{((\rho, c), t) \mid \rho \textit{ is a } \Gamma\textit{-assignment}, c : \tau, t \in \mathbf{Tr}_{\mathrm{HOSC}}(\mathsf{C}_M^{\rho,c})\}.$$

Example 5. Recall the term $\vdash M_1^{cwl} : \tau$ from Example 4, the trace $\mathtt{t}_1$ and the configuration $\mathbf{C}$ such that $\mathtt{t}_1 \in \mathbf{Tr}_{\mathrm{HOSC}}(\mathbf{C})$. Because M_1^{cwl} is closed ($\Gamma = \emptyset$), the only Γ-assignment is the empty map $\emptyset$. Thus, $\mathbf{C} = \mathsf{C}_{M_1^{cwl}}^{\emptyset,c}$, so $((\emptyset, c), \mathtt{t}_1) \in \mathbf{Tr}_{\mathrm{HOSC}}(\vdash M_1^{cwl} : \tau)$.

Having defined active configurations associated with terms, we now define passive configurations associated with contexts. Let us fix $\diamond \in \mathrm{FNames}_{\mathrm{Unit} \to \mathrm{Unit}}$ and, for each σ, a continuation name $\circ_\sigma \in \mathrm{CNames}_\sigma$. Let $\circ = \bigcup_\sigma \{\circ_\sigma\}$. Intuitively, the names $\diamond$ will correspond to $\Downarrow_{err}$ and $\circ_\sigma$ to $\Downarrow_{ter}$.

Recall that $\widehat{err}$ stands for err : Unit $\to$ Unit. Given a heap $h : \Sigma; \widehat{err}$, an evaluation context $\Sigma; \widehat{err} \vdash K : \tau \to \tau'$ and a substitution $\Sigma; \widehat{err} \vdash \gamma : \Gamma$ (as in the definition of $\lesssim_{err}^{\mathrm{HOSC}(ciu)}$), let us replace every occurrence of $\mathrm{cont}_\sigma\, K'$ inside h, K, γ with $\mathrm{cont}_\sigma(K', \circ_{\sigma'})$, if K' has type $\sigma \to \sigma'$. Moreover, let us replace every occurrence of the variable err with the function name $\diamond$. This is done to adjust h, K, γ to the extended syntax of the LTS: the upgraded versions are called $h_\circ, \gamma_\circ, K_\circ$.

Next we define the set $\mathbf{AVal}_\Gamma(\gamma)$ of all disjoint decompositions of values from $\gamma_\circ$ into abstract values and the corresponding matchings. Recall that $\Gamma = \{x_1 : \sigma_1, \cdots, x_k : \sigma_k\}$. Below $\vec{A_i}$ stands for $(A_1, \cdots, A_k)$, and $\vec{\gamma_i}$ for $(\gamma_1, \cdots, \gamma_k)$.

$$\mathbf{AVal}_\Gamma(\gamma) = \{ \quad (\vec{A_i}, \vec{\gamma_i}) \mid (A_i, \gamma_i) \in \mathbf{AVal}_{\sigma_i}(\gamma_\circ(x_i)),\ i = 1, \cdots, k; \\ \nu(A_1), \cdots, \nu(A_k) \text{ mutually disjoint and without } \diamond \quad \}$$

Definition 12 (Context configuration). *Given Σ, $h : \Sigma; \hat{err}$, $\Sigma; \hat{err} \vdash K : \tau \to \tau'$, $\Sigma; \hat{err} \vdash \gamma : \Gamma$, $(\vec{A_i}, \vec{\gamma_i}) \in \mathbf{AVal}_\Gamma(\gamma)$ and $c : \tau$ ($c \notin \circ$), the corresponding configuration $\mathsf{C}^{\vec{\gamma_i}, c}_{h,K,\gamma}$ is defined by*

$$\mathsf{C}^{\vec{\gamma_i}, c}_{h,K,\gamma} = \langle \biguplus_{i=1}^{k} \gamma_i \uplus \{c \mapsto K_\circ\}, \{c \mapsto \circ_{\tau'}\}, \biguplus_{i=1}^{k} \nu(A_i) \uplus \{c\} \uplus \circ \uplus \{\diamond\}, h_\circ \rangle.$$

Intuitively, the names $\nu(A_i)$ correspond to calling function values extracted from γ, whereas c corresponds to K. Note that traces in $\mathbf{Tr}_{\mathrm{HOSC}}(\mathsf{C}^{\vec{\gamma_i}, c}_{h,K,\gamma})$ will be $(\circ \uplus \{\diamond\}, \biguplus_{i=1}^{k} \nu(A_i) \uplus \{c\})$-traces.

In preparation for the next result, we introduce the following shorthands.

- Given a (N_O, N_P)-trace t, we write $t^\perp$ for the (N_P, N_O)-trace obtained by changing the polarity of each name: $f(A, c')$ becomes $\bar{f}(A, c')$ (and vice versa) and $c(A)$ becomes $\bar{c}(A)$ (and vice versa).
- Given $(\vec{A_i}, \vec{\gamma_i}) \in \mathbf{AVal}_\Gamma(\gamma)$, we define a Γ-assignment $\rho_{\vec{A_i}}$ by $\rho_{\vec{A_i}}(x_i) = A_i$. Note that $\nu(\rho_{\vec{A_i}}) = \biguplus_{i=1}^{k} \mathrm{dom}(\gamma_i)$.

Lemma 4 (Correctness). *Let $\Gamma \vdash M : \tau$ be a cr-free* HOSC *term, let Σ, h, K, γ be as above, $(\vec{A_i}, \vec{\gamma_i}) \in \mathbf{AVal}_\Gamma(\gamma)$, and $c : \tau$ ($c \notin \circ$). Then*

- *$(K[M\{\gamma\}], h) \Downarrow_{err}$ iff there exist t, c' such that $t \in \mathbf{Tr}_{\mathrm{HOSC}}(\mathsf{C}^{\rho_{\vec{A_i}}, c}_{M})$ and $t^\perp\, \bar{\diamond}((), c') \in \mathbf{Tr}_{\mathrm{HOSC}}(\mathsf{C}^{\vec{\gamma_i}, c}_{h,K,\gamma})$.*
- *$(K[M\{\gamma\}], h) \Downarrow_{ter}$ iff there exist t, A, σ such that $t \in \mathbf{Tr}_{\mathrm{HOSC}}(\mathsf{C}^{\rho_{\vec{A_i}}, c}_{M})$ and $t^\perp\, \bar{\circ}_\sigma(A) \in \mathbf{Tr}_{\mathrm{HOSC}}(\mathsf{C}^{\vec{\gamma_i}, c}_{h,K,\gamma})$.*

Moreover, t satisfies $\nu(t) \cap (\circ \cup \{\diamond\}) = \emptyset$.

Intuitively, the lemma above confirms that the potential of a term to converge is determined by its traces. Accordingly, we have:

Theorem 1 (Soundness). *For any cr-free* HOSC *terms $\Gamma \vdash M_1, M_2$, if $\mathbf{Tr}_{\mathrm{HOSC}}(\Gamma \vdash M_1) \subseteq \mathbf{Tr}_{\mathrm{HOSC}}(\Gamma \vdash M_2)$ then $\Gamma \vdash M_1 \lesssim^{\mathrm{HOSC}(ciu)}_{err} M_2$.*

To prove the converse, we need to know that every odd-length trace generated by a term actually participates in a contextual interaction. This will follow from the lemma below. Note that $\Downarrow_{err}$ relies on even-length traces from the context (Lemma 4).

Lemma 5 (Definability). *Suppose $\phi \uplus \{\diamond\} \subseteq$ FNames and t is an even-length $(\circ \uplus \{\diamond\}, \phi \uplus \{c\})$-trace starting with an O-action. There exists a passive configuration* $\mathbf{C}$ *such that the even-length traces* $\mathbf{Tr}_{\text{HOSC}}(\mathbf{C})$ *are exactly the even-length prefixes of t (along with all renamings that preserve types and $\phi \uplus \{c\} \uplus \circ \uplus \{\diamond\}$, cf. Remark 2). Moreover,* $\mathbf{C} = \langle \gamma_\circ \cdot [c \mapsto K_\circ], \{c \mapsto \circ_{\tau'}\}, \phi \uplus \{c\} \uplus \circ \uplus \{\diamond\}, h_\circ\rangle$, *where h, K, γ are built from* HOSC *syntax.*

Proof (Sketch). The basic idea is to use references in order to record all continuation and function names introduced by the environment. For continuations, the use of call/cc$_\tau$ is essential. Once stored in the heap, the names can be accessed by terms when needed in P-actions. The availability of throw and references to all O-continuations means that arbitrary answer actions can be scheduled when needed.

Theorem 2 (Completeness). *For any cr-free* HOSC *terms* $\Gamma \vdash M_1, M_2$, $\Gamma \vdash M_1 \lesssim_{err}^{\text{HOSC}(ciu)} M_2$ *implies* $\mathbf{Tr}_{\text{HOSC}}(\Gamma \vdash M_1) \subseteq \mathbf{Tr}_{\text{HOSC}}(\Gamma \vdash M_2)$.

Theorems 1, 2 (along with Lemmas 1, 2) imply the following full abstraction results.

Corollary 1 (HOSC Full Abstraction). *Suppose $\Gamma \vdash M_1, M_2$ are cr-free* HOSC *terms. Then* $\mathbf{Tr}_{\text{HOSC}}(\Gamma \vdash M_1) \subseteq \mathbf{Tr}_{\text{HOSC}}(\Gamma \vdash M_2)$ *iff* $\Gamma \vdash M_1 \lesssim_{err}^{\text{HOSC}} M_2$ *iff* $\Gamma \vdash M_1 \lesssim_{ter}^{\text{HOSC}} M_2$.

Example 6 (Callback with lock [4]). Recall the term $\vdash M_1^{cwl} : ((\text{Unit} \to \text{Unit}) \to \text{Unit}) \times (\text{Unit} \to \text{Int})$ from Example 4, given in Figure 4. We had $\mathtt{t}_1 = \bar{c}(\langle g_1, g_2\rangle)$ $g_1(f_1, c_1)$ $\bar{f_1}((), c_2)$ $c_2(())$ $\bar{c_1}(())$ $c_2(())$ $\bar{c_1}(())$ $g_2((), c_3)$ $\bar{c_3}(2) \in \mathbf{Tr}_{\text{HOSC}}(\mathsf{C}^{\emptyset,c}_{M_1^{cwl}})$.

Define $\mathtt{t}_2$ to be $\mathtt{t}_1$ except that its last action $\bar{c_3}(2)$ is replaced with $\bar{c_3}(1)$. Observe that $\mathtt{t}_1 \in \mathbf{Tr}_{\text{HOSC}}(\mathsf{C}^{\emptyset,c}_{M_1^{cwl}}) \setminus \mathbf{Tr}_{\text{HOSC}}(\mathsf{C}^{\emptyset,c}_{M_2^{cwl}})$ and $\mathtt{t}_2 \in \mathbf{Tr}_{\text{HOSC}}(\mathsf{C}^{\emptyset,c}_{M_2^{cwl}}) \setminus \mathbf{Tr}_{\text{HOSC}}(\mathsf{C}^{\emptyset,c}_{M_1^{cwl}})$, i.e. by the Corollary above the terms are incomparable wrt $\lesssim_{err}^{\text{HOSC}}$. However, they are equivalent wrt $\lesssim_{err}^{\mathbf{x}}$ for $\mathbf{x} \in \{\text{GOSC}, \text{HOS}, \text{GOS}\}$ [8].

The above Corollary also provides a handle to reason about equivalence via trace equivalence. Sometimes this can be done directly on the LTS, especially when γ can be kept bounded.

Example 7 (Counter [28]). For $i \in \{1, 2\}$, consider the terms $\vdash M_i : (\text{Unit} \to \text{Unit}) \times (\text{Unit} \to \text{Int})$ given by $M_i \equiv \text{let}\, x = \text{ref}\, 0 \,\text{in}\, \langle \mathsf{inc}_i, \mathsf{get}_i\rangle$, where $\mathsf{inc}_1 \equiv (\lambda y.x :=!x+1)$, $\mathsf{inc}_2 \equiv (\lambda y.x :=!x-1)$, $\mathsf{get}_1 \equiv \lambda z.!x$, $\mathsf{get}_2 \equiv \lambda z.-!x$. In this case, $\mathbf{Tr}_{\text{HOSC}}(\mathsf{C}^{\emptyset,c}_{M_i})$ contains (prefixes of) traces of the form $\bar{c}(\langle g, h\rangle)\, t$, where t is built from segments of two kinds: either $g((), c_i)$ $\bar{c_i}(())$ or $h((), c_i')$ $\bar{c}_i'(n)$, where the c_is and c_i's are pairwise different. Moreover, in the latter case, n must be equal to the number of preceding actions of the form $g((), c_i)$. For this example, trace equality could be established by induction on the length of trace. Consequently, $M_1 \cong_{err}^{\text{HOSC}} M_2$.

4 GOSC[HOSC]

Recall that GOSC is the fragment of HOSC in which general storage is restricted to values of *ground* type, i.e. arithmetic/boolean constants, the associated reference names, references to those names and so on. In what follows, we are going to provide characterizations of $\lesssim_{err}^{\mathrm{GOSC}}$ via trace inclusion. Recall that, by Lemma 2, $\lesssim_{err}^{\mathrm{GOSC}} = \lesssim_{ter}^{\mathrm{GOSC}}$. Note that we work in an asymmetric setting with terms belonging to HOSC being more powerful than contexts.

We start off by identifying several technical consequences of the restriction to GOSC syntax. First we observe that GOSC internal reductions never contribute extra names.

Lemma 6. *Suppose* $(M, c, h) \to (M', c', h')$, *where* M *is a* GOSC *term and* h *is a* GOSC *heap. Then* $\nu(M) \cup \{c\} \supseteq \nu(M') \cup \{c'\}$.

Proof. By case analysis. All defining rules for $\to$, with the exception of the $(K[!\ell], h) \to (K[h(\ell)], h)$ rule, are easily seen to satisfy the Lemma (no function or continuation names are added). However, if the heap is restricted to storing elements of type ι (as in GOSC) then $h(\ell)$ will never contain a name, so the Lemma follows.

The lemma has interesting consequences for the shape of traces generated by the context configurations $\mathsf{C}_{h,K,\gamma}^{\vec{\gamma_i},c}$ if they are built from GOSC syntax. Recall that P-actions have the form $\bar{f}(A, c')$ or $\bar{c}(A)$, where f, c are names introduced by O. It turns out that when h, K, γ are restricted to GOSC, more can be said about the origin of the names in traces generated by $\mathsf{C}_{h,K,\gamma}^{\vec{\gamma_i},c}$: they will turn out to come from a restricted set of names introduced by O, which we identify below. The definition below is based on following the justification structure of a trace – recall that one action is said to justify another if the former introduces a name that is used for communication in the latter.

Definition 13. *Suppose* $\phi \uplus \{\diamond\} \subseteq$ FNames *and* $c \in$ CNames. *Let* t *be an odd-length* $(\circ \uplus \{\diamond\}, \phi \uplus \{c\})$*-trace starting with an O-action. The set* $\mathsf{Vis}_P(t)$ *of P-visible names of* t *is defined as follows.*

$$
\begin{array}{rcll}
\mathsf{Vis}_P(t\ c'(A')) &=& \{\diamond\} \cup \circ \cup \nu(A') & c' = c \\
\mathsf{Vis}_P(t\ \bar{f}''(A'', c')\ t'\ c'(A')) &=& \mathsf{Vis}_P(t) \cup \nu(A') & c' \neq c \\
\mathsf{Vis}_P(t\ f'(A', c')) &=& \{\diamond\} \cup \circ \cup \nu(A') \cup \{c'\} & f' \in \phi \\
\mathsf{Vis}_P(t\ \bar{f}''(A'', c'')\ t'\ f'(A', c')) &=& \mathsf{Vis}_P(t) \cup \nu(A') \cup \{c'\} & f' \in \nu(A'') \\
\mathsf{Vis}_P(t\ \bar{c}''(A'')\ t'\ f'(A', c')) &=& \mathsf{Vis}_P(t) \cup \nu(A') \cup \{c'\} & f' \in \nu(A'')
\end{array}
$$

Note that, in the inductive cases, the definition follows links between names introduced by P and the point of their introduction, names introduced in-between are ignored. Here readers familiar with game semantics will notice similarity to the notion of P-view [12].

Next we specify a property of traces that will turn out to be satisfied by configurations corresponding to GOSC contexts.

Definition 14. *Suppose* $\phi \uplus \{\diamond\} \subseteq$ FNames *and* $c \in$ CNames. *Let* t *be a* $(\circ \uplus \{\diamond\}, \phi \uplus \{c\})$*-trace starting with an O-action.* t *is called* **P-visible** *if*

- *for any even-length prefix* $t'\, \bar{f}(A,c)$ *of* t, *we have* $f \in \mathsf{Vis}_P(t')$,
- *for any even-length prefix* $t'\, \bar{c}(A)$ *of* t, *we have* $c \in \mathsf{Vis}_P(t')$.

Lemma 7. *Consider* $\mathbf{C} = \mathsf{C}_{h,K,\gamma}^{\vec{\gamma_i},c}$, *where* h, K, γ *are from* GOSC *and* $(\vec{A_i}, \vec{\gamma_i}) \in \mathbf{AVal}_\Gamma(\gamma)$. *Then all traces in* $\mathbf{Tr}_{\mathrm{HOSC}}(\mathbf{C})$ *are P-visible.*

The Lemma above shows that contextual interactions with GOSC contexts rely on restricted traces. We shall now modify the HOSC[HOSC] LTS to capture the restriction. Note that, from the perspective of the term, the above constraint is a constraint on the use of names by O (context), so we need to talk about O-available names instead. This dual notion is defined below.

Definition 15. *Suppose* $\phi \subseteq$ FNames *and* $c \in$ CNames. *Let* t *be a* $(\phi \uplus \{c\}, \emptyset)$*-trace of odd length. The set* $\mathsf{Vis}_O(t)$ *of* **O-visible names** *of* t *is defined as follows.*

$$
\begin{array}{rll}
\mathsf{Vis}_O(t\ \bar{c'}(A')) = \nu(A') & & c' = c \\
\mathsf{Vis}_O(t\ f''(A'',c')\ t'\ \bar{c'}(A')) = \mathsf{Vis}_O(t) \cup \nu(A') & & c' \neq c \\
\mathsf{Vis}_O(t\ \bar{f'}(A',c')) = \nu(A') \cup \{c'\} & & f' \in \phi \\
\mathsf{Vis}_O(t\ f''(A'',c'')\ t'\ \bar{f'}(A',c')) = \mathsf{Vis}_O(t) \cup \nu(A') \cup \{c'\} & & f' \in \nu(A'') \\
\mathsf{Vis}_O(t\ c''(A'')\ t'\ \bar{f'}(A',c')) = \mathsf{Vis}_O(t) \cup \nu(A') \cup \{c'\} & & f' \in \nu(A'')
\end{array}
$$

Analogously, a $(\phi \uplus \{c\}, \emptyset)$*-trace* t *is* **O-visible** *if, for any even-length prefix* $t'\, f(A,c)$ *of* t, *we have* $f \in \mathsf{Vis}_O(t')$ *and, for any even-length prefix* $t'\, c(A)$ *of* t, *we have* $c \in \mathsf{Vis}_O(t')$.

Example 8. Recall the trace

$$\mathtt{t}_1 = \bar{c}(\langle g_1, g_2\rangle)\ g_1(f_1, c_1)\ \bar{f_1}((), c_2)\ c_2(())\ \bar{c_1}(())\ c_2(())\ \bar{c_1}(())\ g_2((), c_3)\ \bar{c_3}(2)$$

from previous examples. Observe that

$$
\begin{array}{r}
\mathsf{Vis}_O(\bar{c}(\langle g_1, g_2\rangle)\ g_1(f_1, c_1)\ \bar{f_1}((), c_2)) = \{g_1, g_2, c_2\} \\
\mathsf{Vis}_O(\bar{c}(\langle g_1, g_2\rangle)\ g_1(f_1, c_1)\ \bar{f_1}((), c_2)\ c_2(())\ \bar{c_1}(())) = \{g_1, g_2\}
\end{array}
$$

Consequently, the first use of $c_2(())$ in $\mathtt{t}_1$ does not violate O-visibility, but the second one does.

In Figure 6, we present a new LTS, called the GOSC[HOSC] LTS, which will turn out to capture $\lesssim_{err}^{\mathrm{GOSC}}$ through trace inclusion. It is obtained from the HOSC[HOSC] LTS by restricting O-actions to those that rely on O-visible names. Technically, this is done by enriching configurations with an additional component $\mathcal{F}$, which maintains historical information about O-available names immediately before each O-action. After each P-action, $\mathcal{F}$ is accessed to calculate the current set $\mathcal{V}$ of O-available names according to the definition of O-availability and only O-actions compatible with O-availability are allowed to proceed (due

$$
\begin{array}{l|lll}
(P\tau) & \langle M, c, \gamma, \xi, \phi, h, \mathcal{F}\rangle & \xrightarrow{\tau} & \langle N, c', \gamma, \xi, \phi, h', \mathcal{F}\rangle \\
& \text{when } (M, c, h) \to (N, c', h') & & \\
(PA) & \langle V, c, \gamma, \xi, \phi, h, \mathcal{F}\rangle & \xrightarrow{\bar{c}(A)} & \langle \gamma \cdot \gamma', \xi, \phi \uplus \nu(A), h, \mathcal{F}, \mathcal{F}(c) \uplus \nu(A)\rangle \\
& \text{when } c : \sigma \text{ and } (A, \gamma') \in \mathbf{AVal}_\sigma(V) & & \\
(PQ) & \langle K[fV], c, \gamma, \xi, \phi, h, \mathcal{F}\rangle \xrightarrow{\bar{f}(A,c')} & & \\
& & & \langle \gamma \cdot \gamma' \cdot [c' \mapsto K], \xi \cdot [c' \mapsto c], \phi \uplus \phi', h, \mathcal{F}, \mathcal{F}(f) \uplus \phi'\rangle \\
& \text{when } f : \sigma \to \sigma',\ (A, \gamma') \in \mathbf{AVal}_\sigma(V),\ c' : \sigma' \text{ and } \phi' = \nu(A) \uplus \{c'\} & & \\
(OA) & \langle \gamma, \xi, \phi, h, \mathcal{F}, \mathcal{V}\rangle & \xrightarrow{c(A)} & \langle K[A], c', \gamma, \xi, \phi \uplus \nu(A), h, \mathcal{F} \cdot [\nu(A) \mapsto \mathcal{V}]\rangle \\
& \text{when } c \in \mathcal{V},\ c : \sigma,\ A : \sigma,\ \gamma(c) = K,\ \xi(c) = c' & & \\
(OQ) & \langle \gamma, \xi, \phi, h, \mathcal{F}, \mathcal{V}\rangle & \xrightarrow{f(A,c)} & \langle VA, c, \gamma, \xi, \phi \uplus \phi', h, \mathcal{F} \cdot [\phi' \mapsto \mathcal{V}]\rangle \\
& \text{when } f \in \mathcal{V},\ f : \sigma \to \sigma',\ A : \sigma,\ c : \sigma',\ \gamma(f) = V \text{ and } \phi' = \nu(A) \uplus \{c\} & &
\end{array}
$$

Given $N \subseteq$ Names, $[N \mapsto \mathcal{V}]$ stands for the map $[n \mapsto \mathcal{V} \mid n \in N]$.

Fig. 6. GOSC[HOSC] LTS

to the $f \in \mathcal{V}$, $c \in \mathcal{V}$ side conditions). We write $\mathbf{Tr}_{\text{GOSC}}(\mathbf{C})$ for the set of traces generated from $\mathbf{C}$ in the GOSC[HOSC] LTS.

Recall that, given a Γ-assignment ρ, term $\Gamma \vdash M : \tau$ and $c \in \text{CNames}_\tau$, the active configuration $\mathsf{C}_M^{\rho,c}$ was defined by $\mathsf{C}_M^{\rho,c} = \langle M\{\rho\}, c, \emptyset, \emptyset, \nu(\rho) \cup \{c\}, \emptyset\rangle$. We need to upgrade it to the LTS by initializing the new component to the empty map: $\mathsf{C}_{M,vis}^{\rho,c} = \langle M\{\rho\}, c, \emptyset, \emptyset, \nu(\rho) \cup \{c\}, \emptyset, \emptyset\rangle$.

Definition 16. *The* GOSC[HOSC] **trace semantics** *of a cr-free HOSC term* $\Gamma \vdash M : \tau$ *is defined by* $\mathbf{Tr}_{\text{GOSC}}(\Gamma \vdash M : \tau) = \{((\rho, c), t) \mid \rho$ *is a* Γ*-assignment,* $c : \tau$, $t \in \mathbf{Tr}_{\text{GOSC}}(\mathsf{C}_{M,vis}^{\rho,c})\}$.

By construction, it follows that

Lemma 8. $t \in \mathbf{Tr}_{\text{GOSC}}(\mathsf{C}_{M,vis}^{\rho,c})$ *iff* $t \in \mathbf{Tr}_{\text{HOSC}}(\mathsf{C}_M^{\rho,c})$ *and* t *is O-visible.*

Noting that the witness trace t from Lemma 4 is O-visible iff $t^\perp\, \bar{\circ}((), c')$ is P-visible, we can conclude that, for GOSC, the traces relevant to $\Downarrow_{err}$ are O-visible, which yields:

Theorem 3 (Soundness). *For any cr-free* HOSC *terms* $\Gamma \vdash M_1,\ M_2$*, if* $\mathbf{Tr}_{\text{GOSC}}(\Gamma \vdash M_1) \subseteq \mathbf{Tr}_{\text{GOSC}}(\Gamma \vdash M_2)$ *then* $\Gamma \vdash M_1 \lesssim_{err}^{\text{GOSC}(ciu)} M_2$.

To prove the converse, we need a new definability result. This time we are only allowed to use GOSC syntax, but the target is also more modest: we are only aiming to capture P-visible traces.

Lemma 9 (Definability). *Suppose* $\phi \uplus \{\diamond\} \subseteq$ FNames *and* t *is an even-length* P-visible $(\circ \uplus \{\diamond\}, \phi \uplus \{c\})$*-trace starting with an O-action. There exists a passive configuration* $\mathbf{C}$ *such that the even-length traces in* $\mathbf{Tr}_{\text{HOSC}}(\mathbf{C})$ *are exactly the even-length prefixes of* t *(along with all renamings that preserve types and* $\phi \uplus \{c\} \uplus \circ \uplus \{\diamond\}$*). Moreover,* $\mathbf{C} = \langle \gamma_\circ \cdot [c \mapsto K_\circ], \{c \mapsto \circ_{\tau'}\}, \phi \uplus \{c\} \uplus \circ \uplus \{\diamond\}, h_\circ\rangle$*, where* h, K, γ *are built from* GOSC *syntax.*

Proof (Sketch). This time we cannot rely on references to recall on demand all continuation and function names introduced by the environment. However, because t is P-visible, it turns the uses of the names can be captured through variable bindings ($\lambda x. \cdots$ for function and $\mathrm{call/cc}_\tau(x. \dots)$ for continuation names). Using throw, we can then force an arbitrary answer action, as long as it uses a P-available name. To select the right action at each step, we branch on the value of a single global reference of type ref Int that keeps track of the number of steps simulated so far.

Completeness now follows because, for a potential O-visible witness t from Lemma 4, one can create a corresponding context by invoking the Definability result for $t^{\perp}\,\bar{\diamond}((), c')$. It is crucial that the addition of $\bar{\diamond}((), c')$ does not break P-visibility ($\diamond$ is P-visible).

Theorem 4 (Completeness). *For any cr-free* HOSC *terms* $\Gamma \vdash M_1, M_2$*, if* $\Gamma \vdash M_1 \lesssim_{err}^{\mathrm{GOSC}(ciu)} M_2$ *then* $\mathbf{Tr}_{\mathrm{GOSC}}(\Gamma \vdash M_1) \subseteq \mathbf{Tr}_{\mathrm{GOSC}}(\Gamma \vdash M_2)$.

Altogether, Theorems 3, 4 (along with Lemma 1) imply the following result.

Corollary 2 (GOSC Full Abstraction). *Suppose* $\Gamma \vdash M_1, M_2$ *are cr-free* HOSC *terms.* $\mathbf{Tr}_{\mathrm{GOSC}}(\Gamma \vdash M_1) \subseteq \mathbf{Tr}_{\mathrm{GOSC}}(\Gamma \vdash M_2)$ *iff* $\Gamma \vdash M_1 \lesssim_{err}^{\mathrm{GOSC}(ciu)} M_2$ *iff* $\Gamma \vdash M_1 \lesssim_{err}^{\mathrm{GOSC}} M_2$.

Example 9. In the *Callback with lock* example (Example 6), we exhibited traces $\mathtt{t}_1, \mathtt{t}_2$ that separated M_1^{cwl} and M_2^{cwl} with respect to $\lesssim_{err}^{\mathrm{HOSC}}$. Example 8 shows that neither trace is O-visible, i.e. they do not belong to $\mathbf{Tr}_{\mathrm{GOSC}}(\Gamma \vdash M_1)$ or $\mathbf{Tr}_{\mathrm{GOSC}}(\Gamma \vdash M_2)$. Thus, the two traces cannot be used to separate M_1^{cwl}, M_2^{cwl} with respect to $\lesssim_{err}^{\mathrm{GOSC}}$. As already mentioned, this is in fact impossible: we have $\vdash M_1^{cwl} \cong_{err}^{\mathrm{GOSC}} M_2^{cwl}$.

Example 10 (Well-bracketed state change [4]). Consider the following two terms

$$M_1^{wbsc} \triangleq \mathrm{let}\, x = \mathrm{ref}\, 0 \,\mathrm{in}\, \lambda f.(x := 0; f(); x := 1; f(); !x)$$
$$M_2^{wbsc} \triangleq \lambda f.(f(); f(); 1).$$

of type $\tau = (\mathrm{Unit} \to \mathrm{Unit}) \to \mathrm{Int}$, let

$$\mathtt{t}_3 = \bar{c}(g)\;\; g(f_1, c_1)\;\; \bar{f}_1((), c_2)\;\; c_2(())\;\; \bar{f}_1((), c_3)\;\; g(f_2, c_4)\;\; \bar{f}_2((), c_5)\;\; c_3(())\;\; \bar{c}_1(0)$$

and let $\mathtt{t}_4$ be obtained from $\mathtt{t}_3$ by changing 0 in the last action to 1. One can check that both traces are O-visible: in particular, the action $c_3(())$ is not a violation because

$$\mathsf{Vis}_O(\bar{c}(g)\;\; g(f_1, c_1)\;\; \bar{f}_1((), c_2)\;\; c_2(())\;\; \bar{f}_1((), c_3)\;\; g(f_2, c_4)\;\; \bar{f}_2((), c_5)) = \{g, c_3, c_5\}.$$

Moreover, $\mathtt{t}_3 \in \mathbf{Tr}_{\mathrm{GOSC}}(\mathsf{C}^{\emptyset,c}_{M_1^{wbsc}}) \setminus \mathbf{Tr}_{\mathrm{GOSC}}(\mathsf{C}^{\emptyset,c}_{M_2^{wbsc}})$ and $\mathtt{t}_4 \in \mathbf{Tr}_{\mathrm{GOSC}}(\mathsf{C}^{\emptyset,c}_{M_2^{wbsc}}) \setminus \mathbf{Tr}_{\mathrm{GOSC}}(\mathsf{C}^{\emptyset,c}_{M_1^{wbsc}})$. By the Corollary above, we can conclude that M_1^{wbsc}, M_2^{wbsc} are incomparable wrt $\lesssim_{err}^{\mathrm{GOSC}}$. However, they turn out to be $\cong_{err}^{\mathrm{HOS}}$- and $\cong_{err}^{\mathrm{GOS}}$-equivalent.

5 HOS[HOSC]

Recall that HOS is the fragment of HOSC that does not feature continuation types and the associated syntax. In what follows we are going to provide alternative characterisations of $\lesssim_{err}^{\mathrm{HOS}}$ and $\lesssim_{ter}^{\mathrm{HOS}}$ in terms of trace inclusion and complete trace inclusion respectively.

We start off by identifying several technical consequences of the restriction to HOS syntax. First we observe that HOS internal reductions never change the associated continuation name.

Lemma 10. *If* $(M, c, h) \to (M', c', h')$, M *is a* HOS *term and* h *is a* HOS *heap then* $c = c'$.

Proof. The only rule that could change c is the rule for throw, but it is not part of HOS.

The lemma has a bearing on the shape of traces generated by the (passive) configurations $\mathsf{C}_{h,K,\gamma}^{\vec{\gamma_i},c}$ corresponding to HOS contexts. In the presence of throw and storage for continuations, it was possible for P to play answers involving arbitrary continuation names introduced by O. By Lemma 10, in HOS this will be restricted to the continuation name of the current configuration, which will restrict the shape of possible traces. Below we identify the continuation name $top_P(t)$ that becomes the relevant name after trace t. If the last move was an O-question then the continuation name introduced by that move will become that name. Otherwise, we track a chain of answers and questions, similarly to the definition of P-visibility.

Observe that, because h, K, γ are from HOS, $\mathsf{C}_{h,K,\gamma}^{\vec{\gamma_i},c}$ will generate $(\{\circ_{\tau'}, \diamond\}, \phi \uplus \{c\})$-traces, where τ' is the result type of K, because $h_\circ = h, K_\circ = K, \gamma_\circ = \gamma$.

Definition 17. *Suppose* $\phi \uplus \{\diamond\} \subseteq$ FNames *and* $c \in$ CNames. *Let* t *be a* $(\{\circ_{\tau'}, \diamond\}, \phi \uplus \{c\})$*-trace of odd length starting with an O-action. The continuation name* $top_P(t)$ *is defined as follows.*

$$\begin{aligned} top_P(t\ c(A)) &= \circ_{\tau'} \\ top_P(t_1\ \bar{f}(A'', c')\ t_2\ c'(A')) &= top_P(t_1) \\ top_P(t\ f(A', c')) &= c' \end{aligned}$$

We say that a $(\{\circ_{\tau'} \cup \{\diamond\}, \phi \uplus \{c\})$*-trace* t *starting with an O-action is* **P-bracketed** *if, for any prefix* $t'\ \bar{c'}(A)$ *of* t *(i.e. any prefix ending with a P-answer), we have* $c' = top_P(t')$.

Lemma 11. *Consider* $\mathbf{C} = \mathsf{C}_{h,K,\gamma}^{\vec{\gamma_i},c}$, *where* h, K, γ *are from* HOS *and* $(\vec{A_i}, \vec{\gamma_i}) \in$ $\mathbf{AVal}_\Gamma(\gamma)$. *Then all traces in* $\mathbf{Tr}_{\mathrm{HOSC}}(\mathbf{C})$ *are P-bracketed.*

The Lemma above characterizes the restrictive nature of contextual interactions with HOS contexts. Next we shall constrain the HOSC[HOSC] LTS accordingly to capture the restriction. Note that, from the point of view of the term, the above-mentioned constraint concerns the use of continuation names by O (the context), so we need to talk about O-bracketing instead. This dual notion of "a top name for O" is specified below.

$$
\begin{array}{l|lll}
(P\tau) & \langle M, c, \gamma, \xi, \phi, h\rangle & \xrightarrow{\tau} & \langle N, c', \gamma, \xi, \phi, h'\rangle \\
& \text{when } (M, c, h) \rightarrow (N, c', h') & & \\
(PA) & \langle V, c, \gamma, \xi, \phi, h\rangle & \xrightarrow{\bar{c}(A)} & \langle \gamma \cdot \gamma', \xi, \phi \uplus \nu(A), h, c'\rangle \\
& \text{when } c : \sigma,\ (A, \gamma') \in \mathbf{AVal}_\sigma(V),\ \xi(c) = c' & & \\
(PQ) & \langle K[fV], c, \gamma, \xi, \phi, h\rangle & \xrightarrow{\bar{f}(A,c')} & \langle \gamma \cdot \gamma' \cdot [c' \mapsto K], \xi \cdot [c' \mapsto c], \phi \uplus \nu(A) \uplus \{c'\}, h, c'\rangle \\
& \text{when } f : \sigma \rightarrow \sigma',\ (A, \gamma') \in \mathbf{AVal}_\sigma(V),\ c' : \sigma' & & \\
(OA) & \langle \gamma, \xi, \phi, h, c''\rangle & \xrightarrow{c(A)} & \langle K[A], c', \gamma, \xi, \phi \uplus \nu(A), h\rangle \\
& \text{when } c = c'',\ c : \sigma,\ A : \sigma,\ \gamma(c) = K,\ \xi(c) = c' & & \\
(OQ) & \langle \gamma, \xi, \phi, h, c''\rangle & \xrightarrow{f(A,c)} & \langle VA, c, \gamma, \xi \cdot [c \mapsto c''], \phi \uplus \nu(A) \uplus \{c\}, h\rangle \\
& \text{when } f : \sigma \rightarrow \sigma',\ A : \sigma,\ c : \sigma',\ \gamma(f) = V & &
\end{array}
$$

Fig. 7. HOS[HOSC] LTS

Definition 18. *Suppose* $\phi \subseteq \text{FNames}$ *and* $c \in \text{CNames}$. *Let* t *be a* $(\phi \uplus \{c\}, \emptyset)$*-trace of odd length. The continuation name* $top_O(t)$ *is defined as follows. In the first case, the value is* $\bot$ *(representing "none"), because* c *is the top continuation passed by the environment to the term (if it gets answered there is nothing left to answer).*

$$
\begin{aligned}
top_O(t\ \bar{c}(A)) &= \bot \\
top_O(t_1\ f(A'', c')\ t_2\ \bar{c'}(A')) &= top_O(t_1) \\
top_O(t\ \bar{f}(A', c')) &= c'
\end{aligned}
$$

We say that a $(\phi \uplus \{c\}, \emptyset)$*-trace* t *is* **O-bracketed** *if, for any prefix* $t'\ c'(A)$ *of* t *(i.e. any prefix ending with an O-answer), we have* $c' = top_O(t')$.

In Figure 7, we present a new LTS, called the HOS[HOSC] LTS, which will turn out to capture $\lesssim_{err}^{\mathrm{HOS}}$. It is obtained from the HOSC[HOSC] LTS by restricting O-actions to those that satisfy O-bracketing. Technically, this is done by enriching passive configurations with a component for storing the current value of $top_O(t)$. In order to maintain this information, we need to know which continuation will become the top one if P plays an answer. This can be done with a map that maps continuations introduced by O to other continuations. Because its flavour is similar to ξ (which is a map from continuations introduced by P) we integrate this information into ξ. The $c = c''$ side condition then enforces O-bracketing. We shall write $\mathbf{Tr}_{\mathrm{HOS}}(\mathbf{C})$ for the set of traces generated from $\mathbf{C}$ in the HOS[HOSC] LTS.

Recall that, given a Γ-assignment ρ, term $\Gamma \vdash M : \tau$ and $c : \tau$, the active configuration $\mathsf{C}_M^{\rho,c}$ was defined by $\mathsf{C}_M^{\rho,c} = \langle M\{\rho\}, c, \emptyset, \emptyset, \nu(\rho) \cup \{c\}, \emptyset\rangle$. We upgrade it to the new LTS by setting $\mathsf{C}_{M,bra}^{\rho,c} = \langle M\{\rho\}, c, \emptyset, [c \mapsto \bot], \nu(\rho) \cup \{c\}, \emptyset, \emptyset\rangle$. This initializes ξ in such a way that, after $\bar{c}(A)$ is played, the extra component will be set to $\bot$, where $\bot$ is a special element not in CNames.

Definition 19. *The* HOS[HOSC] **trace semantics** *of a cr-free HOSC term* $\Gamma \vdash M : \tau$ *is defined to be* $\mathbf{Tr}_{\mathrm{HOS}}(\Gamma \vdash M : \tau) = \{((\rho, c), t) \mid \rho$ *is a* Γ*-assignment,* $c : \tau$, $t \in \mathbf{Tr}_{\mathrm{HOS}}(\mathsf{C}^{\rho,c}_{M,bra})\}$.

By construction, it follows that

Lemma 12. $t \in \mathbf{Tr}_{\mathrm{HOS}}(\mathsf{C}^{\rho,c}_{M,bra})$ *iff* $t \in \mathbf{Tr}_{\mathrm{HOSC}}(\mathsf{C}^{\rho,c}_{M})$ *and* t *is O-bracketed.*

Noting that the witness trace t from Lemma 4 is O-bracketed iff $t^{\perp}\,\bar{\diamond}((), c')$ is P-bracketed, we can conclude that, for HOS, the traces relevant to $\Downarrow_{err}$ are O-bracketed, which yields:

Theorem 5 (Soundness). *For any cr-free* HOSC *terms* $\Gamma \vdash M_1, M_2$*, if* $\mathbf{Tr}_{\mathrm{HOS}}(\Gamma \vdash M_1) \subseteq \mathbf{Tr}_{\mathrm{HOS}}(\Gamma \vdash M_2)$ *then* $\Gamma \vdash M_1 \lesssim^{\mathrm{HOS}(ciu)}_{err} M_2$.

For the converse, we establish another definability result, this time for a P-bracketed trace.

Lemma 13 (Definability). *Suppose* $\phi \uplus \{\diamond\} \subseteq$ FNames *and* t *is an even-length* P-bracketed $(\{\circ_{\tau'}, \diamond\}, \phi \uplus \{c\})$*-trace starting with an O-action. There exists a passive configuration* $\mathbf{C}$ *such that the even-length traces* $\mathbf{Tr}_{\mathrm{HOSC}}(\mathbf{C})$ *are exactly the even-length prefixes of* t *(along with all renamings that preserve types and* $\phi \uplus \{c, \circ_{\tau'}, \diamond\}$*). Moreover,* $\mathbf{C} = \langle \gamma \cdot [c \mapsto K], \{c \mapsto \circ_{\tau'}\}, \phi \uplus \{c, \circ_{\tau'}, \diamond\}, h\rangle$*, where* h, K, γ *are built from* HOS *syntax.*

Proof (Sketch). Our argument for HOSC is structured in such a way that, for a P-bracketed trace, there is no need for continuations (throwing and continuation capture are not necessary).

Completeness now follows because, for a potential witness trace t from Lemma 4, one can create a corresponding context by invoking the Definability result for $t^{\perp}\,\bar{\diamond}((), c')$. It is crucial that the addition of $\bar{\diamond}((), c')$ does not break P-bracketing (it does not, because the action is a question).

Theorem 6 (Completeness). *For any cr-free* HOSC *terms* $\Gamma \vdash M_1, M_2$*, if* $\Gamma \vdash M_1 \lesssim^{\mathrm{HOS}(ciu)}_{err} M_2$ *then* $\mathbf{Tr}_{\mathrm{HOS}}(\Gamma \vdash M_1) \subseteq \mathbf{Tr}_{\mathrm{HOS}}(\Gamma \vdash M_2)$.

Altogether, Theorems 5, 6 (along with Lemma 1) imply the following result.

Corollary 3 (HOS **Full Abstraction).** *Suppose* $\Gamma \vdash M_1, M_2$ *are cr-free* HOSC *terms. Then* $\mathbf{Tr}_{\mathrm{HOS}}(\Gamma \vdash M_1) \subseteq \mathbf{Tr}_{\mathrm{HOS}}(\Gamma \vdash M_2)$ *iff* $\Gamma \vdash M_1 \lesssim^{\mathrm{HOS}(ciu)}_{err} M_2$ *iff* $\Gamma \vdash M_1 \lesssim^{\mathrm{HOS}}_{err} M_2$.

Example 11 (Assignment/callback commutation [27]). For $i \in \{1, 2\}$, let $f :$ Unit $\to$ Unit $\vdash M_i :$ Unit $\to$ Unit be defined by:

$$M_1 \triangleq \mathrm{let}\, n = \mathrm{ref}\,(0)\, \mathrm{in}\, \lambda y^{\mathrm{Unit}}.\mathrm{if}\ (!n > 0)\ ()\ (n := 1; f()),$$
$$M_2 \triangleq \mathrm{let}\, n = \mathrm{ref}\,(0)\, \mathrm{in}\, \lambda y^{\mathrm{Unit}}.\mathrm{if}\ (!n > 0)\ ()\ (f(); n := 1).$$

Operationally, one can see that $f \vdash M_1 \not\lesssim^{\text{HOS}}_{err} M_2$ due to the following HOS context: let r = ref $(\lambda y.y)$ in (let $f = \lambda y.(!r)()$ in $(r := \bullet; (!r)()))$; *err*. In our framework, this is confirmed by the trace

$$\mathsf{t}_5 \;=\; \bar{c}(g)\;\; g((),c_1)\;\; \bar{f}((),c_2)\;\; g((),c_2)\;\; \bar{c_2}(()),$$

which is in $\mathbf{Tr}_{\text{HOS}}(\mathsf{C}^{\rho,c}_{M_1}) \setminus \mathbf{Tr}_{\text{HOS}}(\mathsf{C}^{\rho,c}_{M_2})$. On the other hand,

$$\mathsf{t}_6 \;=\; \bar{c}(g)\;\; g((),c_1)\;\; \bar{f}((),c_2)\;\; g((),c_2)\;\; \bar{f}((),c_3)$$

is in $\mathbf{Tr}_{\text{HOS}}(\mathsf{C}^{\rho,c}_{M_2}) \setminus \mathbf{Tr}_{\text{HOS}}(\mathsf{C}^{\rho,c}_{M_1})$, so the terms are incomparable. Note, however, that both traces break O-visibility: specifically, we have

$$\mathsf{Vis}_O(\bar{c}(g)\; g((),c_1)\; \bar{f}((),c_2)) = \{c_2\},$$

so the $g((),c_2)$ action violates the condition. Consequently, the traces do not preclude $f \vdash M_1 \cong^{\mathbf{x}}_{err} M_2$ for $\mathbf{x} \in \{\text{GOSC}, \text{GOS}\}$.

For $\mathbf{x} \in \{\text{HOSC}, \text{GOSC}\}$, $\lesssim^{\mathbf{x}}_{err}$ and $\lesssim^{\mathbf{x}}_{ter}$ coincide. Intuitively, this is because the presence of continuations in the context makes it possible to make an escape at any point. In contrast, for HOS, the context must run to completion in order to terminate.

At the technical level, one can appreciate the difference when trying to transfer our results for $\lesssim^{\text{HOS}(ciu)}_{err}$ to $\lesssim^{\text{HOS}(ciu)}_{ter}$. Recall that, according to Lemma 4, $\Downarrow_{ter}$ relies on a witness trace t such that the context configuration generates $t^{\perp}\; \bar{\circ}_{\mathcal{T}'}()$. In HOS, the latter must satisfy P-bracketing, so we need $top_P(t^{\perp}) = \circ_{\mathcal{T}'}$. Note that this is equivalent to $top_O(t) = \perp$. Consequently, only such traces are relevant to observing $\Downarrow_{ter}$.

We shall call an odd-length O-bracketed $(\phi \uplus \{c\}, \emptyset)$-trace t ***complete*** if $top_O(t) = \perp$. Let us write $\mathbf{Tr}_{\text{HOS}}(\Gamma \vdash M_1) \subseteq_c \mathbf{Tr}_{\text{HOS}}(\Gamma \vdash M_2)$ if we have $((\rho,c),t) \in \mathbf{Tr}_{\text{HOS}}(\Gamma \vdash M_2)$ whenever $((\rho,c),t) \in \mathbf{Tr}_{\text{HOS}}(\Gamma \vdash M_1)$ and t is complete. Following our methodology, one can then show:

Theorem 7 (**HOS Full Abstraction for** $\lesssim^{\text{HOS}}_{ter}$**).** *Suppose* $\Gamma \vdash M_1, M_2$ *are cr-free* HOSC *terms.* $\mathbf{Tr}_{\text{HOS}}(\Gamma \vdash M_1) \subseteq_c \mathbf{Tr}_{\text{HOS}}(\Gamma \vdash M_2)$ *iff* $\Gamma \vdash M_1 \lesssim^{\text{HOS}(ciu)}_{ter} M_2$ *iff* $\Gamma \vdash M_1 \lesssim^{\text{HOS}}_{ter} M_2$.

Example 12. Let $M_1 \equiv \lambda f^{\text{Unit}\to\text{Unit}}.f(); \Omega_{\text{Unit}}$ and $M_2 \equiv \lambda f^{\text{Unit}\to\text{Unit}}.\Omega_{\text{Unit}}$. We will see that $\vdash M_1 \not\lesssim^{\text{HOS}}_{err} M_2$ but $\vdash M_1 \lesssim^{\text{HOS}}_{ter} M_2$. To see this, note that $\mathbf{Tr}_{\text{HOS}}(\mathsf{C}^{\rho,c}_{M_1})$ contains prefixes of $\bar{c}(g)\; g(f,c_1)\; \bar{f}((),c_2)\; c_2(())$, while $\mathbf{Tr}_{\text{HOS}}(\mathsf{C}^{\rho,c}_{M_2})$ only those of $\bar{c}(g)\; g(f,c_1)$. Observe that the only complete trace among them is $\bar{c}(g)$. The trace $t = \bar{c}(g)\; g(f,c_1)\; \bar{f}((),c_2)$ is not complete, because $top_O(t) = c_2$. Consequently, $\mathbf{Tr}_{\text{HOS}}(\Gamma \vdash M_1) \not\subseteq \mathbf{Tr}_{\text{HOS}}(\Gamma \vdash M_2)$ but $\mathbf{Tr}_{\text{HOS}}(\Gamma \vdash M_1) \subseteq_c \mathbf{Tr}_{\text{HOS}}(\Gamma \vdash M_2)$.

The theorem above generalizes the characterisation of contextual equivalence between HOS terms with respect to HOS contexts [23], where trace completeness means both O- and P-bracketing and "all questions must be answered". Our definition of completeness is weaker (O-bracketing + "the top question must be answered"), because it also covers HOSC terms. However, in the presence of both O- and P-bracketing, i.e. for HOS terms, they will coincide.

6 GOS[HOSC]

Recall that GOS features ground state only and, technically, is the intersection of GOSC and HOS. Consequently, it follows from the previous sections that GOS contexts yield configurations that satisfy both P-visibility and P-bracketing. For such traces, the definability result for GOSC yields a GOS context. Thus, in a similar fashion to the previous sections, we can conclude that O-visible and O-bracketed traces underpin $\lesssim_{err}^{\mathrm{GOS}}$. To define the GOS LTS we simply combine the restrictions imposed in the previous sections, and define $\mathbf{Tr}_{\mathrm{GOS}}(\Gamma \vdash M)$ analogously. The results on $\lesssim_{ter}^{\mathrm{GOS}}$ from the previous section also carry over to GOS.

Theorem 8 (GOS **Full Abstraction**). *Suppose* $\Gamma \vdash M_1, M_2$ *are cr-free* HOSC *terms. Then:*

- $\mathbf{Tr}_{\mathrm{GOS}}(\Gamma \vdash M_1) \subseteq \mathbf{Tr}_{\mathrm{GOS}}(\Gamma \vdash M_2)$ *iff* $\Gamma \vdash M_1 \lesssim_{err}^{\mathrm{GOS}(ciu)} M_2$ *iff* $\Gamma \vdash M_1 \lesssim_{err}^{\mathrm{GOS}} M_2$.
- $\mathbf{Tr}_{\mathrm{GOS}}(\Gamma \vdash M_1) \subseteq_c \mathbf{Tr}_{\mathrm{GOS}}(\Gamma \vdash M_2)$ *iff* $\Gamma \vdash M_1 \lesssim_{ter}^{\mathrm{GOS}(ciu)} M_2$ *iff* $\Gamma \vdash M_1 \lesssim_{ter}^{\mathrm{GOS}} M_2$.

7 Concluding remarks

Asymmetry Our framework is able to deal with asymmetric scenarios, where programs are taken from HOSC, but are tested with contexts from weaker fragments. For example, we can compare the following two HOSC programs, where $f : ((\mathrm{Unit} \to \mathrm{Unit}) \to \mathrm{Unit}) \to \mathrm{Unit}$ is a free identifier.

let b = ref **ff** in callcc(y.
    f(λg.b := **tt**; g(); throw() to y);
    if !b then () else div)
	callcc(y.
	    f(λg.g(); throw() to y);
	    div)

with div representing divergence. The terms happen to be $\cong_{err}^{\mathrm{HOS}}$-equivalent, but not $\cong_{err}^{\mathrm{HOSC}}$-equivalent.

To see this at the intuitive level, we make the following observations.

- Firstly, we observe that, to distinguish the terms, f should use its argument. Otherwise, the value of b will remain equal to **ff**, and the only subterm that distinguishes the terms ('if !b then () else div') will play the same role as div in the second term.
- Secondly, if f does use its argument, then b will be set to **tt** in the first program, raising the possibility of distinguishing the terms. However, if we allow HOS contexts only then, since the argument to f was used, it will have to run to completion, before 'if !b then () else div' is reached. Consequently, we will encounter 'throw () to *y*' earlier and never reach 'if !b then () else div'. This is represented by the trace

$$\bar{f}(h, c_1) \qquad h(g, c_2) \qquad \bar{g}((), c_3) \qquad c_3(()) \qquad \bar{c}(())$$

This trace is O-bracketed, but not P-bracketed since Player uses throw to answer directly to the initial continuation c rather than c_2.

– Finally, if HOSC contexts are allowed, it is possible to reach the subterm 'if !b then () else div' with b set to **tt**. This is represented by the trace

$$\bar{f}(h, c_1) \quad h(g, c_2) \quad \bar{g}((), c_3) \quad c_1(()) \quad \bar{c}(())$$

This trace is not O-bracketed, because c_1 is answered rather than c_3, like above. Consequently, the trace witnesses termination of the first term, but the second term would diverge during interaction with the same context.

We plan to explore the opportunities presented by this setting in the future, especially with respect to fully abstract translations, for example, from HOSC to GOS.

Richer Types Recall that our full abstraction results are stated for cr-free terms, terms with cont- and ref-free types at the boundary. Here we first discuss how to extend them to more complicated types.

To deal with reference type at the boundary, i.e. location exchange, one needs to generalize the notion of traces, so that they can carry, for each action, a heap representing the values stored in the disclosed part of the heap, as in [23,27]. The extension to sum, recursive and empty types seems conceptually straightforward, by simply extending the definition of abstract values for these types, following the similar notion of ultimate pattern in [24]. The same idea should apply to allow continuation types at the boundary. Operational game semantics for an extension of HOS with polymorphism has been explored in [15].

Innocence On the other hand, all of the languages we considered were stateful. In the presence of state, all of the actions that are represented by labels (and their order and frequency) can be observed, because they could generate a side-effect. A natural question to ask whether the techniques could also be used to provide analogous theorems for purely functional computation, i.e. contexts taken from the language PCF. Here, the situation is different. For example, the terms $f : \mathrm{Int} \to \mathrm{Int} \vdash f(0)$ and $f : \mathrm{Int} \to \mathrm{Int} \vdash$ if $f(0)\ f(0)\ f(0)$ should be equivalent, even though the sets of their traces are incomparable.

It is known [12] that PCF strategies satisfy a uniformity condition called innocence. Unfortunately, restricting our traces to "O-innocent ones" (like we did with O-visibility and O-bracketing) would not deliver the required characterization. Technically, this is due to the fact that, in our arguments, given a single trace (with suitable properties), we can produce a context that induces the given trace and no other traces (except those implied by the definition of a trace). For innocence, this would not be possible due to the uniformity requirement. It will imply that, although we can find a functional context that generates an innocent trace, it might also generate other traces, which then have to be taken into account when considering contextual testing. This branching property makes it difficult to capture equivalence with respect to functional contexts explicitly, e.g. through traces, which is illustrated by the use of the so-called intrinsic quotient in game models of PCF [2,12].

8 Related Work

We have presented four operational game models for HOSC, which capture term interaction with contexts built from any of the four sublanguages $\mathbf{x} \in \{\text{HOSC}, \text{GOSC}, \text{HOS}, \text{GOS}\}$ respectively. The most direct precursor to this work is Laird's trace model for HOS[HOS] [23]. Other frameworks in this spirit include models for objects [18], aspects [16] and system-level code [9]. In [13], Laird's model has been related formally to the denotational game model from [27]. However, in general, it is not yet clear how one can move systematically between the operational and denotational game-based approaches, despite some promising steps reported in [25]. Below we mention other operational techniques for reasoning about contextual equivalence.

In [31], fully abstract Eager-Normal-Form (enf) Bisimulations are presented for an untyped λ-calculus with store and control, similar to HOSC (but with control represented using the $\lambda\mu$-calculus). The bisimulations are parameterised by worlds to model the evolution of store, and bisimulations on contexts are used to deal with control. Like our approach, they are based on symbolic evaluation of open terms. Typed enf-bisimulations, for a language without store and in control-passing style, have been introduced in [24]. Fully-abstract enf-bisimulations are presented in [7] for a language with state only, corresponding to an untyped version of HOS. Earlier works in this strand include [17,29].

Environmental Bisimulations [19,30,32] have also been introduced for languages with store. They work on closed terms, computing the arguments that contexts can provide to terms using an environment similar to our component γ. They have also been extended to languages with call/cc [34] and delimited control operators [5,6].

Kripke Logical Relations [28,4,8] have been introduced for languages with state and control. In [8], a characterization of contextual equivalence for each case $\mathbf{x}[\mathbf{x}]$ ($\mathbf{x} \in \{\text{HOSC}, \text{GOSC}, \text{HOS}, \text{GOS}\}$) is given, using techniques called backtracking and public transitions, which exploit the absence of higher-order store and that of control constructs respectively. Importing these techniques in the setting of Kripke Open Bisimulations [14] should allow one to build a bridge between the game-semantics characterizations and Kripke Logical Relations.

Parametric bisimulations [11] have been introduced as an operational technique, merging ideas from Kripke Logical Relations and Environmental Bisimulations. They do not represent functional values coming from the environment using names, but instead use a notion of global and local knowledge to compute these values, reminiscent of the work on environmental bisimulations. The notion of global knowledge depends itself on a notion of evolving world. To our knowledge, no fully abstract Parametric Bisimulations have been presented.

A general theory of applicative [21] and normal-form bisimulations [20] has been developed, with the goal of being modular with respect to the effects considered. While the goal is similar to our work, the papers consider monadic and algebraic presentation of effects, trying particularly to design a general theory for proving soundness and completeness of such bisimulations. These works complement ours, and we would like to explore possible connections.

References

1. Abramsky, S.: Games in the semantics of programming languages. In: Proceedings of the 11th Amsterdam Colloquium. pp. 1–6. ILLC, Dept. of Philosophy, University of Amsterdam (1997)
2. Abramsky, S., Jagadeesan, R., Malacaria, P.: Full abstraction for PCF. Information and Computation **163**, 409–470 (2000)
3. Abramsky, S., McCusker, G.: Call-by-value games. In: Proceedings of CSL. Lecture Notes in Computer Science, vol. 1414, pp. 1–17. Springer-Verlag (1997)
4. Ahmed, A., Dreyer, D., Rossberg, A.: State-dependent representation independence. In: Proceedings of POPL. pp. 340–353. ACM (2009)
5. Aristizabal, A., Biernacki, D., Lenglet, S., Polesiuk, P.: Environmental Bisimulations for Delimited-Control Operators with Dynamic Prompt Generation. Logical Methods in Computer Science **13**(3) (2017)
6. Biernacki, D., Lenglet, S.: Environmental bisimulations for delimited-control operators. In: Proceedings of APLAS. Lecture Notes in Computer Science, vol. 8301, pp. 333–348. Springer (2013)
7. Biernacki, D., Lenglet, S., Polesiuk, P.: A complete normal-form bisimilarity for state. In: Proceedings of FOSSACS. Lecture Notes in Computer Science, vol. 11425, pp. 98–114. Springer (2019)
8. Dreyer, D., Neis, G., Birkedal, L.: The impact of higher-order state and control effects on local relational reasoning. J. Funct. Program. **22**(4-5), 477–528 (2012)
9. Ghica, D.R., Tzevelekos, N.: A system-level game semantics. Electr. Notes Theor. Comput. Sci. **286**, 191–211 (2012)
10. Honsell, F., Mason, I.A., Smith, S.F., Talcott, C.L.: A variable typed logic of effects. Inf. Comput. **119**(1), 55–90 (1995)
11. Hur, C.K., Dreyer, D., Neis, G., Vafeiadis, V.: The marriage of bisimulations and kripke logical relations. In: Proceedings of POPL. pp. 59–72. ACM (2012)
12. Hyland, J.M.E., Ong, C.H.L.: On Full Abstraction for PCF: I. Models, observables and the full abstraction problem, II. Dialogue games and innocent strategies, III. A fully abstract and universal game model. Information and Computation **163(2)**, 285–408 (2000)
13. Jaber, G.: Operational nominal game semantics. In: Proceedings of FOSSACS. Lecture Notes in Computer Science, vol. 9034, pp. 264–278 (2015)
14. Jaber, G., Tabareau, N.: Kripke open bisimulation - A marriage of game semantics and operational techniques. In: Proceedings of APLAS. Lecture Notes in Computer Science, vol. 9458, pp. 271–291 (2015)
15. Jaber, G., Tzevelekos, N.: Trace semantics for polymorphic references. In: Proceedings of LICS. pp. 585–594. ACM (2016)
16. Jagadeesan, R., Pitcher, C., Riely, J.: Open bisimulation for aspects. In: Proceedings of AOSD. ACM International Conference Proceeding Series, vol. 208, pp. 107–120 (2007)
17. Jeffrey, A., Rathke, J.: Towards a theory of bisimulation for local names. In: Proceedings of LICS. pp. 56–66 (1999)
18. Jeffrey, A., Rathke, J.: A fully abstract may testing semantics for concurrent objects. Theor. Comput. Sci. **338**(1-3), 17–63 (2005)
19. Koutavas, V., Wand, M.: Small bisimulations for reasoning about higher-order imperative programs. In: Proceedings of POPL. pp. 141–152. ACM (2006)
20. Lago, U.D., Gavazzo, F.: Effectful normal form bisimulation. In: Proceedings of ESOP. Lecture Notes in Computer Science, vol. 11423, pp. 263–292. Springer (2019)

21. Lago, U.D., Gavazzo, F., Levy, P.B.: Effectful applicative bisimilarity: Monads, relators, and howe's method. In: Proceedings of LICS. IEEE Press (2017)
22. Laird, J.: Full abstraction for functional languages with control. In: Proceedings of 12th IEEE Symposium on Logic in Computer Science. pp. 58–67 (1997)
23. Laird, J.: A fully abstract trace semantics for general references. In: Proceedings of ICALP, Lecture Notes in Computer Science, vol. 4596, pp. 667–679. Springer (2007)
24. Lassen, S.B., Levy, P.B.: Typed normal form bisimulation. In: Proceedings of CSL, Lecture Notes in Computer Science, vol. 4646, pp. 283–297. Springer (2007)
25. Levy, P.B., Staton, S.: Transition systems over games. In: Proceedings of CSL-LICS. pp. 64:1–64:10 (2014)
26. Milner, R.: Fully abstract models of typed lambda-calculi. Theoretical Computer Science **4**(1), 1–22 (1977)
27. Murawski, A.S., Tzevelekos, N.: Game semantics for good general references. In: Proceedings of LICS. pp. 75–84. IEEE Computer Society Press (2011)
28. Pitts, A.M., Stark, I.D.B.: Operational reasoning for functions with local state. In: Gordon, A.D., Pitts, A.M. (eds.) Higher-Order Operational Techniques in Semantics, pp. 227–273. Cambridge University Press (1998)
29. Sangiorgi, D.: Expressing mobility in process algebras: First-order and higher-order paradigms. Tech. Rep. CST-99-93, University of Edinburgh (1993), PhD thesis
30. Sangiorgi, D., Kobayashi, N., Sumii, E.: Environmental bisimulations for higher-order languages. ACM Trans. Program. Lang. Syst. **33**(1), 5 (2011)
31. Støvring, K., Lassen, S.B.: A complete, co-inductive syntactic theory of sequential control and state. In: POPL. pp. 161–172. ACM (2007)
32. Sumii, E.: A complete characterization of observational equivalence in polymorphic *lambda*-calculus with general references. In: Proceedings of CSL. Lecture Notes in Computer Science, vol. 5771, pp. 455–469. Springer (2009)
33. Talcott, C.L.: Reasoning about functions with effects. In: Gordon, A.D., Pitts, A.M. (eds.) Higher-Order Operational Techniques in Semantics, pp. 347–390. Cambridge University Press (1998)
34. Yachi, T., Sumii, E.: A sound and complete bisimulation for contextual equivalence in λ-calculus with call/cc. In: Proceedings of APLAS. pp. 171–186. Springer (2016)

Session Coalgebras: A Coalgebraic View on Session Types and Communication Protocols

Alex C. Keizer[1], Henning Basold[2] ✉, and Jorge A. Pérez[3,4]

[1] Master of Logic, ILLC, University of Amsterdam, Amsterdam, The Netherlands
[2] LIACS – Leiden University, Leiden, The Netherlands
h.basold@liacs.leidenuniv.nl
[3] University of Groningen, Groningen, The Netherlands
[4] CWI, Amsterdam, The Netherlands
j.a.perez@rug.nl

Abstract Compositional methods are central to the development and verification of software systems. They allow breaking down large systems into smaller components, while enabling reasoning about the behaviour of the composed system. For concurrent and communicating systems, compositional techniques based on *behavioural type systems* have received much attention. By abstracting communication protocols as types, these type systems can statically check that programs interact with channels according to a certain protocol, whether the intended messages are exchanged in a certain order. In this paper, we put on our coalgebraic spectacles to investigate *session types*, a widely studied class of behavioural type systems. We provide a syntax-free description of session-based concurrency as states of coalgebras. As a result, we rediscover type equivalence, duality, and subtyping relations in terms of canonical coinductive presentations. In turn, this coinductive presentation makes it possible to elegantly derive a decidable type system with subtyping for π-calculus processes, in which the states of a coalgebra will serve as channel protocols. Going full circle, we exhibit a coalgebra structure on an existing session type system, and show that the relations and type system resulting from our coalgebraic perspective agree with the existing ones.

Keywords: Session types · Coalgebra · Process calculi · Coinduction.

1 Introduction

Communication protocols enable interactions between humans and computers alike, yet different scientific communities rely on different descriptions of protocols: one community may use textual descriptions, another uses diagrams, and yet another may use types. There is then a mismatch, which is fruitful and hindering at the same time. Fruitful, because different views on protocols lead to different insights and technologies. But hindering, because exactly those insights and technologies cannot be easily exchanged. With this paper, we wish to provide a view of protocols that opens up new links between communities and that, at the same time, contributes new insights into the nature of communication protocols.

N. Yoshida (Ed.): ESOP 2021, LNCS 12648, pp. 375–403, 2021.
https://doi.org/10.1007/978-3-030-72019-3_14

What would such a view of communication protocols be? Software systems typically consist of concurrent, interacting processes that pass messages over channels. Protocols are then a description of the possible exchanges on channels, without ever referring to the exact structure of the processes that use the channels. Since we may, for example, expect to get an answer only after sending a question, it is clear that such exchanges have to happen in an appropriate order. Therefore, protocols have to be a *state-based abstraction of communication behaviour* on channels. Because *coalgebras* provide an abstraction of general state-based behaviour, our proposed view of communication protocols becomes: model the states of a protocol as states of a coalgebra and let the coalgebra govern the exchanges that may happen at each state of the protocol.

The above view of protocols allows us to model protocols as coalgebras. However, protocols are usually not studied for the sake of their description but to achieve certain goals: ensuring correct composition of processes, comparing communication behaviour, or refining and abstracting protocols. *Session types* [19,20] are an approach to communication correctness for processes that pass messages along channels. The idea is simple: describe a protocol as a syntactic object (a type), and use a type system to statically verify that processes adhere to the protocol. This syntactic approach allows the automatic and efficient verification of many correctness properties. However, the syntactic approach depends on choosing *one particular representation of protocols* and *one particular representation of processes*. We show in this paper that our coalgebraic view of protocols can guarantee correct process composition, and allows us to reason about key notions in the world of session types, *type equivalence*, *duality* and *subtyping*, while being completely independent of protocol and process representations.

Our coalgebraic view is best understood by following the distillation process of ideas on a concrete session type system by Vasconcelos [37]. Consider the session type $S = ?\texttt{int}.\,!\texttt{bool}.\,\text{end}$, which specifies the protocol on one endpoint of a channel that receives an integer, then outputs a Boolean, and finally terminates the interaction. Note that the protocol S specifies three different states: an input state, an output state, and a final state. Moreover, we note that S specifies only how the channel is seen from one endpoint; the other endpoint needs to use the channel with the *dual* protocol $!\texttt{int}.\,?\texttt{bool}.\,\text{end}$. Thus, session type systems ensure that the states of S are enabled only in the specified order and that the two channel endpoints implement dual protocols.

A state-based reading of session types is intuitive and is already present in programming concepts such as typestates [15,32,33], theories of behavioural contracts [4,6,7,13], and connections between session types and communicating automata [10,25]. The novelty and insight of the coalgebraic view is that 1. it describes the state-based behaviour of protocols underlying session types, supporting unrestricted types and delegation, without adhering to any specific syntax or target programming model; 2. it offers a general framework in which key notions such as type equivalence, duality, and subtyping arise as instances of well-known coinductive constructions; and 3. it allows us to derive type systems for specific process languages, like the π-calculus.

Session Coalgebras at Work How does this coalgebraic view of protocols work for general session types? Consider a "mathematical server" that offers three operations to clients: integer multiplication, Boolean negation and quitting. The following session type T specifies a protocol to communicate with this server.

$$T = \mu X.\ \& \begin{cases} mul: & ?\texttt{int}.\ ?\texttt{int}.\ !\texttt{int}.\ X \\ neg: & ?\texttt{bool}.\ !\texttt{bool}.\ X \\ quit: & \text{end} \end{cases}$$

T is a recursive protocol, as indicated by "$\mu X.$", which can be repeated. A client can choose, as indicated by &, between the three operations (*mul*, *neg*, and *quit*) and the protocol then continues with the corresponding actions. For instance, after choosing *mul*, the server requests two integers and, once received, promises to send an integer over the channel. We can see states of the protocol T emerging, and it remains to provide a coalgebraic view on the actions of the protocol to obtain what we will call *session coalgebras.*

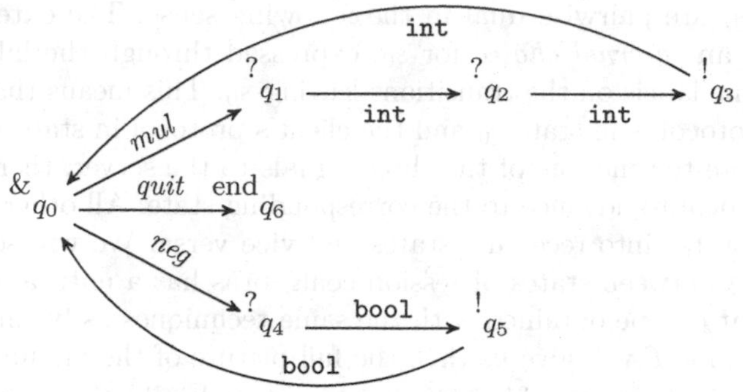

Figure 1. Protocol of the mathematical server as a session coalgebra

Fig. 1 depicts a session coalgebra that describes protocol T. It consists of states $q_0, \ldots, q_6$, each representing a different state of T, and transitions between these states to model the evolution of T. Meaning is given to the different states and transitions through the labels on the states and transitions. The state *labels*, written in purple at top-left of the state name, indicate the branching type of that state. Depending on the branching type, the labels of the transitions bear different meanings. For instance, q_0 is labelled with "&", which indicates that this state initiates an external choice. The labels on the three outgoing transitions for q_0 (*mul*, *neg*, *quit*) correspond then to the possible kinds of message for selecting one of the branches. Continuing, states $q_1, \ldots, q_5$ are labelled with a request for data (label ?) or the sending of data (label !), and the outgoing transition labels indicate the type of the exchanged values (e.g., `bool`). Finally, state q_6 decrees the end of the protocol. Note that the cyclic character of T occurs as transitions back to q_0; there is no need for an explicit operator to capture recursion.

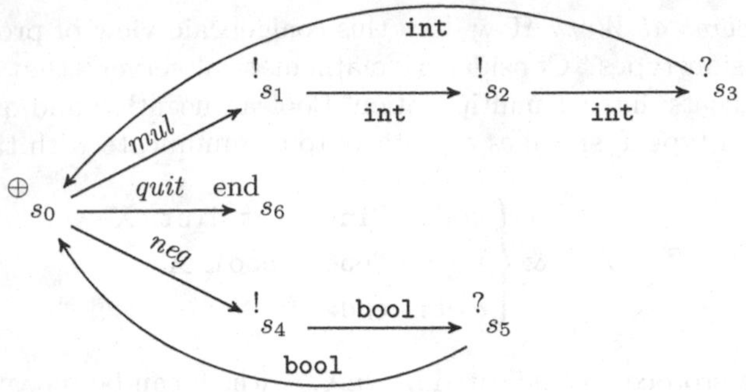

Figure 2. Session coalgebra for the client view protocol the of mathematical server

A session coalgebra models the view on one channel endpoint, but to correctly execute a protocol we also need to consider the *dual* session coalgebra that models the other endpoint's view. In our example, the dual of Fig. 1 is given by the diagram in Fig. 2, which concerns states $s_0, \ldots, s_6$. More precisely, the *states* q_i and s_i are pairwise dual in the following sense. The external choice of q_0 becomes an *internal choice* for s_0, expressed through the label $\oplus$, with exactly the same labels on the transitions leaving s_0. This means that whenever the server's protocol is in state q_0 and the client's protocol in state s_0, then the client can choose to send one of the three signals to the server, thereby forcing the server protocol to advance to the corresponding state. All other states turn from sending states into receiving states and vice versa. We will see that this *duality relation* between states of session coalgebras has a natural coinductive description that can be obtained with the same techniques as bisimilarity. The duality relation for T will give us then the full picture of the intended protocol.

Suppose a client who would only want to use multiplication once but could also handle real numbers as inputs. Such a client had to follow the protocol given by the session coalgebra in Fig. 3, with states $r_0, \ldots, r_5$.

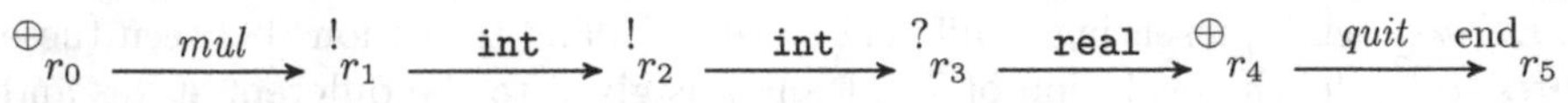

Figure 3. Session coalgebra that uses only part of a mathematical server

In theories of session types, the protocol of Fig. 2 would be a *subtype* of this one (cf. [17,16]). Concretely, this new client can also follow the subtype protocol, and can thus communicate with a server following the protocol of Fig. 1. For session coalgebras, we recover the same notion of subtyping by using specific *simulation* relations that allow us to prove that the behaviour of r_0 can be simulated by s_0. Together, simulations and duality provide the foundation of typical session type systems.

We have used thus far session types and coalgebras for protocols with simple control and with exchanges of simple data values. In contrast, rich session type systems can regulate *session delegation*, the dynamic allocation and exchange of channels by processes. Imagine a process that creates a channel, which should adhere to some protocol T. From an abstract perspective, the process holds both endpoints of the new channel, and has to send one of them to the process it wishes to communicate with. To ensure statically that the receiving process respects the protocol of this new channel, we need to announce this communication as a transmission of the session type T (via an existing channel) and use T to verify the receiving process. Session delegation adds expressiveness and flexibility, but may cause problems in the characterisation of a correct notion of duality [18]. Remarkably, our coalgebraic view of session types makes this characterisation completely natural.

As an example, consider the type $T = \mu X.\ ?X.\ X$, which models a channel endpoint that infinitely often receives channel ends of its own type T. To obtain the dual of T, we may naïvely try to replace the receive with a send, which results in the type $\mu X.\ !X.\ X$. The problem is that the two channel endpoints would not agree on the type they are sending or receiving, as any dual type of T needs to send messages of type T. Thus, the correct dual of T would be the type $U = \mu X.\ !T.\ X$. Both T and U specify the transmission of non-basic types, either the recursion variable X or T, in contrast to the mathematical server that merely stipulated the transmission of basic data values (integers or Booleans).

In our session coalgebras for the mathematical server it sufficed to have simple data types and branching labels on transitions. However, to represent T and U we will need another mechanism to express session delegation. We observe that a transmission in session types consists of the transmitted data and the session type that the protocol must continue with afterwards. Thus, a transition out of a transmitting state in a session coalgebra encompasses both a *data transition* and a *continuation transition*. In diagrams of session coalgebras, we indicate the data transition by a coloured arrow $\longrightarrow$ and an arrow $\dashrightarrow$ connecting the data to the continuation transition. Using the combined transitions, Fig. 4 redraws the multiplication part of the mathematical server in Fig. 1.

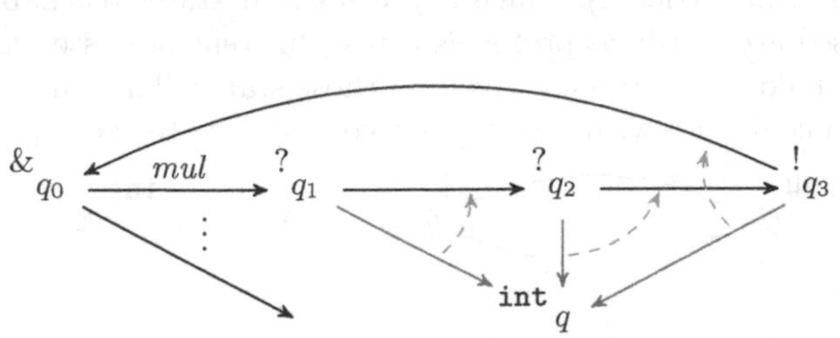

Figure 4. Protocol of mathematical server as session coalgebra

This way, the transition $q_1 \xrightarrow{\texttt{int}} q_2$ has been replaced by *both* a data transition into a new state q *and* a continuation transition into q_2. Moreover, q has been declared as a *data state* that expects an integer to be exchanged (label `int`).

Having added these transitions to our toolbox, we can present the two types T and U as session coalgebras. The diagram in Fig. 5 shows such a session coalgebra, in which we name the states suggestively T and U.

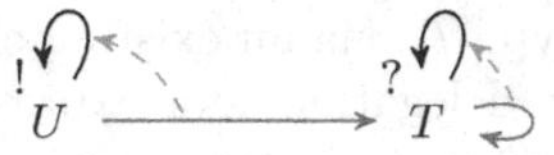

Figure 5. Session coalgebra for a recursive type T and its dual U

Using this presentation as session coalgebras, it is now straightforward to *coinductively* prove that the states T and U are dual: 1. the states have opposite actions; 2. their data transitions point to equal types; and 3. their continuations are dual by coinduction. Clearly, the last step needs some justification but it will turn out that we can appeal to a standard definition of coinduction in terms of greatest fixed points. This demonstrates that our coalgebraic view on session types makes the definition of duality truly natural and straightforward.

Up to here, we have discussed session types and coalgebras that are *linear*, i.e., they enforce that protocols complete exactly once. In many situations, one also needs *unrestricted* types, which enable sharing of channels between processes that access these channels concurrently. This is the case of a process that offers a service for other processes, for instance a web server. Session delegation allows us to create dynamically channels and check their protocols, but the shared channel for *initiating a session* [17] has to offer its protocol to an arbitrary number of clients. Unrestricted types enable us to specify these kind of service offers.

As an example, consider a process that provides a channel for communicating integers to anyone asking, like a town hall official handing out citizen numbers. The type $U' = \mu X.\ \texttt{un}\,!\texttt{int}.\ X$ represents the corresponding protocol, where "un" qualifies the type $!\texttt{int}.\ X$ as unrestricted. This allows the process holding the end of a channel with type U' to transmit an integer to any process that is connected to the shared channel, without any restriction on their number. It is now surprisingly simple to express U' in our coalgebraic view: we introduce a new state label "un" (unrestricted), which expresses that states reachable from this state can be used arbitrarily as protocols across different processes connecting to a channel that follow the protocol given by those states. The following diagram shows a session coalgebra with a state that corresponds to the type U'.

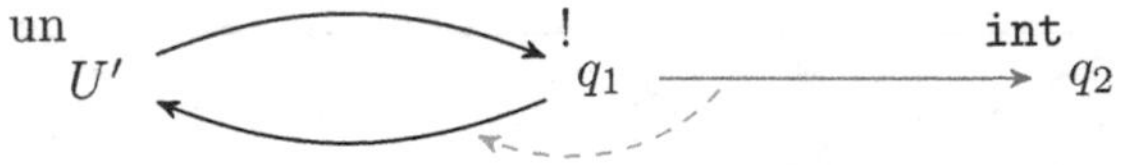

Contributions and Related Work. In this paper, we introduce the notion of *session coalgebra*, which justifies the state-based behaviour of session types from a coalgebraic perspective. This perspective is novel, although specific state-based description of protocols have been considered before [4,6,7,9,10,13,15,25,32,33]. Using coalgebra as a unifying framework for session types has two advantages: 1. session coalgebras can be defined and studied independently from specific syntactic formulations, while keeping the operational behaviour of session types; and 2. we can uncover the innate *coinductive* nature of key notions in session types, such as duality, subtyping, and type equivalence through standard coalgebraic techniques. In particular, although communicating automata can also provide syntax-independent characterisations of session types [10,11], such characterisations do not support delegation, an expressive feature which is cleanly justified in our coalgebraic approach. Coinduction already has been exploited in the definition of type equivalence [35], subtyping [17,16] and, especially, duality for systems with recursive types [3,18,24]. Unlike ours, these previous definitions are language-dependent, as they are tailored to specific process languages and/or syntactic variants of the type discipline. Session coalgebras enable thus the generalisation of insights and technologies from specific languages to any protocol specification that fits under the umbrella of state-based sessions.

To enable the verification of processes against protocols described by session coalgebras, we also contribute a *type system* for π-calculus processes, in which channel types are given by states of an *arbitrary session coalgebra*. Our type system revisits the one by Vasconcelos [37] from our coalgebraic perspective, while extending it with subtyping. Moreover, we provide a *type checking algorithm* for that system, provided that the underlying session coalgebra fulfils two intuitive conditions. In doing so, we show how a specific type syntax can be equipped with a session coalgebra structure and how the two decidability conditions are reflected in the type system. This is in contrast to starting with a specific type syntax and then employing category theoretical ideas [36], where coinductive session types are encoded in a session type system with parametric polymorphism [5]. Instead, we show how a session type system can be derived in general from coalgebras.

Organisation Throughout the remaining paper we will turn the sketched ideas into a coalgebraic framework. We introduce in Sec. 2 a concrete session type syntax that we will use as illustration of our framework. In Sec. 3, we will define session coalgebras as coalgebras for an appropriate functor and show that the type system from Sec. 2 can be equipped with a coalgebraic structure. The promised coinductive view on type equivalence, duality, subtyping, etc. will be provided in Sec. 4. Moreover, we will show that these notions are decidable under certain conditions that hold for any reasonable session type syntax, including the one from Sec. 2. Up to that point, the session coalgebras only had intrinsic meaning and were not associated to any process representation. Section 5 sets forth a type system for π-calculus, in which channels are assigned states of a session coalgebra as types. The resulting type system features subtyping and algorithmic type checking, presented in Sec. 6. Some final thoughts are gathered in Sec. 7. An extended version, available online, collects additional material [22].

$$
\begin{array}{llll}
p ::= & ?T.\,T & T ::= & d \in D \\
| & !T.\,T & | & \mathsf{end} \\
| & \&\{l_i : T_i\}_{i\in I} & | & q\,p \\
| & \oplus\{l_i : T_i\}_{i\in I} & | & X \in \mathsf{Var} \\
 & & | & \mu X.T \\
q ::= & \mathsf{lin} \mid \mathsf{un} & &
\end{array}
$$

Figure 6. Session types over sets of basic data types D and of variables Var

2 Session Types

To motivate the development of session coalgebras, we recall in this section the concrete syntax of an existing session type system by Vasconcelos [37]. After building up our intuition, we introduce session coalgebras in Sec. 3 to show they can represent this concrete type system.

The types of the system that we will be using are generated by the grammar in Fig. 6, relative to a set of basic data types D and a countable set of type variables Var. This grammar has three syntactic categories: pretypes p, qualifiers q, and session types T. A pretype p is simply a communication action: send (!), receive (?), external choice (&), and internal choice ($\oplus$) indexed by a finite sets I of labels, followed by one or multiple session types. The simplest session types are basic data types in D and the completed, or terminated, protocol represented by end. A pretype and qualifier also form a session type, written as $q\ p$. The "lin" qualifier enforces that the communication action p has to be carried out exactly once, while the "un" qualifier allows arbitrary use of p. Finally, we can form recursive session types with the the fixed point operator μ and the use of type variables. We use the usual notion of α-equivalence, (capture-avoiding) substitution, and free and bound types variables for session types.

The grammar allows arbitrary recursive types. We let Type be the set of all T in which recursive types are *contractive* and *closed*, which means that they contain no substrings of the form $\mu X_1.\mu X_2 \ldots \mu X_n.X_i$ and no free type variables.

To lighten up notation, we will usually omit the qualifier lin and assume every type to finalise with end. With these conventions, we write, e.g., `?int.` instead of lin `?int.` end and un `?int.` for a single unrestricted read.

We assume there is some decidable subtyping preorder $\leq_D$ over the basic types. A type is a subtype of another if the subtype can be used anywhere where the supertype was accepted. In examples, we use the basic types `int`, `real` and `bool`, and we assume that `int` is a subtype of `real`, as usual.

An important notion is the *unfolding* of a session type, which we define next:

Definition 1 (Unfolding). *The unfolding of a recursive type $\mu X.T$ is defined recursively*

$$unfold(\mu X.T) = unfold(T[\mu X.T/X])$$

For all other T in Type, *unfold is the identity: $unfold(T) = T$.*

Because we assume that types are contractive, *unfold*(T) terminates for all T. Also, because all types are required to be closed, *unfold*(T) can never be a variable X. Any such variable would have to be bound somewhere before use, meaning it would have been substituted. Furthermore, unfolding a closed type always yields another closed type, as each removed binder always causes a substitution of the bound variable.

3 Session Coalgebra

Here we will discuss *session coalgebras*, the main contribution of this paper. The idea is that session coalgebras will be coalgebras for a specific functor F, which will capture the state labels and the various kinds of transitions that we discussed in Sec. 1. An important feature of coalgebras in general, and session coalgebras in particular, is that the states can be given by an arbitrary set. We will leverage this to define a session coalgebra on the set of types Type introduced in Sec. 2.

Before coming to the definition, let us briefly recall some minimal notions of category theory. We will not require a lot of category theoretical terminology; in fact, we will only use the category **Set** of sets and functions. Moreover, we will be dealing with *functors* $F\colon \mathbf{Set} \to \mathbf{Set}$ on the category **Set**. Such a functor allows us to map a set X to a set $F(X)$, and functions $f : X \to Y$ to functions $F(f) : F(X) \to F(Y)$. To be meaningful, a functor must preserve identity and compositions. That is, F maps the identity function $\mathrm{id}_X : X \to X$ on X to the identity on $F(X)$: $F(\mathrm{id}_X) = \mathrm{id}_{F(X)}$; and, given functions $f\colon X \to Y$ and $g\colon Y \to Z$, we must have $F(g \circ f) = F(g) \circ F(f)$.

A central notion is that of the *coalgebras* for a functor F. A coalgebra is given by a pair (X, c) of a set X and a function $c\colon X \to F(X)$. For simplicity, we often leave out X and refer to c as the coalgebra. The general idea is that the set X is the set of *states* and that c assigns to every state its one-step behaviour. In the case of session coalgebras this will be the state labels and outgoing transitions. Given two coalgebras $c\colon X \to F(X)$ and $d\colon Y \to F(Y)$, we say that $h\colon X \to Y$ is a *homomorphism*, if $d \circ h = F(h) \circ c$. Coalgebras and their homomorphisms form a category, with the same identity maps and composition as in **Set**.

We will have to analyse subsets of coalgebras that are closed under transitions. Given a coalgebra $c\colon X \to F(X)$, we say that $d\colon Y \to F(Y)$ with $Y \subseteq X$ is a *subcoalgebra* of c if the inclusion map $Y \to X$ is a coalgebra homomorphism. Note that in this case $c(Y) \subseteq F(Y)$ and thus d is the restriction of c to Y. Hence, we also refer to Y as subcoalgebra. The subcoalgebra *generated by* $x \in X$ *in* c, denoted by $\langle x \rangle_c$, is the least subset of X that contains x and is a subcoalgebra of c. Intuitively, it is the set of x and all states that are reachable from x.

Coming to the concrete case of session coalgebras, we now construct a functor that allows us to capture the state labels and the different kinds of transitions. Keeping in mind that states of a session coalgebra correspond to states of a protocol, we need to be able to label the states with enabled operations.

Definition 2 (Operations and Polarities). *The* operation *of a state describes the action it represents:* com *marks the transmission (sending or receiving) of a* *value;* branch *marks an (internal or external) choice;* end *marks the completed protocol;* bsc *marks a basic data type; and* un *marks an unrestricted type. States that transmit data (labelled with* com*) or allow for choice (labelled with* branch*) also have a* polarity, *which can be either* in *(a receiving action or external choice) or* out *(a sending action or internal choice). We let O be the set of all operations $O = \{\text{com}, \text{branch}, \text{end}, \text{bsc}, \text{un}\}$ and P the set of polarities $P = \{\text{in}, \text{out}\}$.*

Note that pairs in $\{\text{com}, \text{branch}\} \times P$ directly correspond to the actions of a session type: $? = (\text{com}, \text{in})$, $! = (\text{com}, \text{out})$, $\& = (\text{branch}, \text{in})$ and $\oplus = (\text{branch}, \text{out})$. We will be using these markers to abbreviate the pairs.

Now that we have the possible operations of a protocol, we need to define the transitions that may follow each operation. Recall that the transition at a choice state has to be labelled with messages that resolve that choice. We therefore assume to be given a set $\mathbb{L}$ of possible choice labels. The variable l will be used to refer to an element of $\mathbb{L}$. $\mathcal{P}^+_{<\aleph_0}(\mathbb{L})$ is the set of all finite, non-empty, subsets of $\mathbb{L}$. Variables $L, L_1, L_2, \ldots$ refer to these finite, non-empty subsets of $\mathbb{L}$.

Our goal is to define a *polynomial functor* [14] that captures the states labels and transitions. This requires some further formal language. First, we let $*$ and d be some fixed, distinct, objects. Second, given sets X and Y, we denote by X^Y the set of all (total) functions from Y to X. Finally, given a family of sets $\{X_i\}_{i \in I}$ indexed by some set I, their *coproduct* is the set $\coprod_{i \in I} X_i = \{(i, x) \mid i \in I, x \in X_i\}$.

We are now ready to define session coalgebras:

Definition 3 (Session Coalgebras). *Let A and B be sets defined as follows, where we recall that D is the set of all basic data types.*

$$
\begin{aligned}
A = \;& \{\text{com}\} \times P & B_{\text{com},p} &= \{*, d\} \\
& \cup \{\text{branch}\} \times P \times \mathcal{P}^+_{<\aleph_0}(\mathbb{L}) & B_{\text{branch},p,L} &= L \\
& \cup \{\text{end}\} & B_{\text{end}} &= \emptyset \\
& \cup \{\text{bsc}\} \times D & B_{\text{bsc},d} &= \emptyset \\
& \cup \{\text{un}\} & B_{\text{un}} &= \{*\}
\end{aligned}
$$

The polynomial functor $F : \mathbf{Set} \to \mathbf{Set}$ is defined by

$$F(X) = \coprod_{a \in A} X^{B_a}$$

$$F(f)(a, g) = (a, f \circ g)$$

A coalgebra (X, c) for the functor F is called a session coalgebra.

Let us unfold this definition. Given a session coalgebra $c \colon X \to F(X)$ and a state $x \in X$, we find in $c(x) \in F(X)$ the information of x encoded as a tuple (a, f) with $a \in A$ and $f \colon B_a \to X$. From a, we get directly the operation, and the polarity for com states, the type of values communicated for bsc states or the message labels of branch states. The function f encodes the transitions out of x. The domain of f is exactly the set of labels that have a transition, and is dependent on the kind of state declared by a.

It is convenient to partition the domain of the transition map f into data and continuations. Notice how only com states have data transitions, for other states, all transitions are continuations. As usual, we write $\text{dom}(f)$ for the domain of f.

Definition 4 (Domains). *Suppose* $c(x) = (\mathrm{com}, p, f)$, *then the* data domain *of* f *is* $dom_D(f) = \{d\}$ *and the* continuation domain *is* $dom_C(f) = \{*\}$. *In all other cases,* $dom_D(f) = \emptyset$ *and* $dom_C(f) = dom(f)$.

3.1 Alternative Presentation of Session Coalgebras

Session coalgebras (X, c) are rather complex. We show how to build up c as the combination of two simpler functions, denoted σ and δ, so that $c(x) = (\sigma(x), \delta(x))$ with $\sigma\colon X \to A$ and $\delta(x)\colon B_{\sigma(x)} \to X$. Observe that every state gets an operation in O assigned, thus we may assume that there is a map $\mathrm{op}\colon X \to O$. Depending on the operation given by $\mathrm{op}(x)$, the label on x will then have different other ingredients that are captured in the following proposition.

To formulate the proposition, we need some notation. Suppose $f\colon X \to I$ is a map and $i \in I$. We define the *fibre* X_i^f of f over i to be $X_i^f = \{x \in X \mid f(x) = i\}$. Moreover, we let the *pairing of functions* f and g be $\langle f, g\rangle(x) = (f(x), g(x))$.

Proposition 1. *A session coalgebra* (X, c) *can equivalently be expressed by providing the following maps:*

$op : X \to O$	*maps each state to an operation*
$pol : X_{\mathrm{com}}^{op} + X_{\mathrm{branch}}^{op} \to P$	*maps* com *and* branch *states to a polarity*
$la : X_{\mathrm{branch}}^{op} \to \mathcal{P}_{<\aleph_0}^{+}(\mathbb{L})$	*maps* branch *states to a set of labels*
$da : X_{\mathrm{bsc}}^{op} \to D$	*maps* bsc *states to their basic type*
$\delta_a : X_a^{\sigma} \to X^{B_a}$	*maps each state to a transition function,*

where

$$\sigma(x) = \begin{cases} \langle op, pol\rangle(x) & \text{if } op(x) = \mathrm{com} \\ \langle op, pol, la\rangle(x) & \text{if } op(x) = \mathrm{branch} \\ \langle op, da\rangle(x) & \text{if } op(x) = \mathrm{bsc} \\ op(x) & \text{if } op(x) = \mathrm{end} \text{ or } op(x) = \mathrm{un} \end{cases}$$

We specified δ_a as a family of transition functions to preserve each specific signature. We can define a single global transition function as $\delta(x) = \delta_{\sigma(x)}(x)$. This is how the coalgebra finally becomes $c(x) = (\sigma(x), \delta(x))$. As long as the provided maps fit their signatures, this derived function will conform to $c : X \to F(X)$.

The procedure also works backwards: given any session coalgebra, we can derive functions $\mathrm{op}(x)$, $\mathrm{pol}(x)$, etc. from $c(x)$. We will often use $\mathrm{op}(x)$, $\sigma(x)$, and $\delta(x)$ to refer to those specific parts of an arbitrary session coalgebra.

3.2 Coalgebra of Session Types

In Sec. 1, we informally explained how session types can be represented as states of a session coalgebra. We will now justify this claim by showing that session types are, in fact, states of a specific session coalgebra $(\mathsf{Type}, c_{\mathsf{Type}})$.

We define the functions op, pol, δ, and la (see Prop. 1) on Type. Using Prop. 1, we can then derive $c_{\mathsf{Type}} : \mathsf{Type} \to F(\mathsf{Type})$. Let us begin with the linear types.

T	$c_{\mathsf{Type}}(T)$			
	op(T)	pol(T)	$\delta(T)$	la(T)
$\mathsf{lin}\, ?T.\, T'$	com	*in*	$\delta(T)(*) = T'$ $\delta(T)(d) = T$	
$\mathsf{lin}\, !T.\, T'$		*out*		
$\mathsf{lin}\&\{l_i : T_i\}_{i\in I}$	branch	*in*	$\delta(T)(l_i) = T_i$	$\{l_i \mid i \in I\}$
$\mathsf{lin}\oplus\{l_i : T_i\}_{i\in I}$		*out*		

Under this definition, la(T) is indeed finite, by virtue of an expression being a finite string. The completed protocol end and basic types d are straightforward: $c(\text{end}) = (\text{end})$ and $c(d) = (\text{bsc}, d)$ for any $d \in D$. Recursive types are handled according to their unfolding, $c(\mu X.\, T) = c(\mathit{unfold}(\mu X.\, T))$. Recall that contractivity ensures that *unfold* always terminates. As our types are closed, all recursion variables are substituted during the unfolding of their binder. Consequently, we do not need to define c on these variables. Also note that this definition results in an *equi-recursive* interpretation of recursive types.

Session types can also be unrestricted, and consist of a pretype p with a qualifier un. Session coalgebras have un states to mark unrestricted types; the continuation describes what the actual interaction is. Thus, we define op$(\mathsf{un}\ p)$ = un and $\delta(\mathsf{un}\ p)(*) = \mathsf{lin}\ p$.

Remark 1 (Alternative Syntaxes and their Functors). The unrestricted session types that we have adopted are fairly standard, but they are not the only ones in the literature. Most notably, Gay and Hole [17] defined a type $\urcorner[T_1, \ldots, T_n]$ that allows infinite reading *and* writing. To allow for such behaviour in session coalgebra, we can change B_{un} to a set of two elements, such a $\{*_1, *_2\}$. Like internal choice, the two transitions describe an option of which behaviour to follow, but without sending synchronisation signals. One transition could go to a read, and the other to a write, both recursively continuing as the original type $\urcorner[T_1, \ldots, T_n]$.

It is possible, although not entirely trivial, to change the further definitions appropriately and get a decidable type checking algorithm encompassing both the syntax presented in this work, and Gay and Hole's syntax. We choose not to, so to keep the presentation simpler.

4 Type Equivalence, Duality and Subtyping

Up to here, we have represented session types as session coalgebras, but we have not yet given a precise semantics to them. As a first step, we will define three relations on states: *bisimulation*, *duality*, and *simulation*. Bisimulation is also called behavioural equivalence for types; we will show that bisimilar types are indeed equivalent. Duality specifies complementary types: it tells us which types can form a correct interaction. Simulation will provide a notion of subtyping: it tells us when a type can be used where another type was expected. Besides relations on session coalgebras, we also introduce the *parallelizability* of states that allows us to rule out certain troubling unrestricted types. Finally, we will obtain conditions on coalgebras to ensure the decidability of the three relations and therefore the type system that we derive in Sec. 5.

In the following, we will denote by Rel_X the poset $\mathcal{P}(X \times X)$ of all relations on X ordered by inclusion. Recall that a post-fixpoint of a monotone map $g\colon \mathrm{Rel}_X \to \mathrm{Rel}_X$ is a relation $R \in \mathrm{Rel}_X$ with $R \subseteq g(R)$. Note that Rel_X is a complete lattice and that therefore any monotone map has a greatest post-fixpoint by the Knaster-Tarski Theorem [34]. We will define bisimulation, simulation, and duality as the greatest (post-)fixpoint of monotone functions, which we will therefore call *coinductive definitions*. This definition turns out to be intuitively what we would expect and the interaction of infinite behaviour with other type features is automatically correct. The coinductive definitions also give us immediately proof techniques for equivalence, duality and subtyping: to show that two states are, say, dual we only have to establish a relation that contains both states and show that the relation is a post-fixpoint. This technique can then be improved in various ways [30] and we will show that it is decidable for reasonable session coalgebras.

4.1 Bisimulation

Two states of a coalgebra are said to be *bisimilar* if they exhibit equivalent behaviour. We abstract away from the precise structure of a coalgebra and only consider its observable behaviour. Two states are bisimilar if their labels are equal and if the states at the end of matching transitions are again bisimilar. There is one exception to the equality of labels: basic types can be related via their pre-order, which does not have to coincide with equality.

Fix some coalgebra (X, c) and let $c^* : \mathrm{Rel}_{F(X)} \to \mathrm{Rel}_X$ be the binary preimage of c defined as

$$c^*(R) = \{(x, y) \mid (c(x), c(y)) \in R\}\,.$$

Definition 5. *We define the function* $f_\sim : \mathrm{Rel}_X \to \mathrm{Rel}_{F(X)}$ *as*

$$\begin{aligned} f_\sim(R) = &\{\ ((a, f), (a, f')) \mid (\forall \alpha \in \mathit{dom}(f)) \quad f(\alpha)\ R\ f'(\alpha)\} \\ &\cup \{\ ((\mathrm{bsc}, d, f_\emptyset), (\mathrm{bsc}, d', f_\emptyset)) \mid d \leq_D d' \wedge d' \leq_D d\ \} \end{aligned}$$

where $f_\emptyset\colon \emptyset \to X$ *is the empty function.*

It can be easily checked that, both, c^* and $f_\sim$ are monotone maps and thus also their composition. Thus, the greatest fixpoint in the following definition exists.

Definition 6. *A relation R is called a bisimulation if it is a post-fixpoint of* $c^* \circ f_\sim$. *We call the greatest fixpoint* bisimilarity *and denote it by* $\sim$.

4.2 Duality

Duality describes exactly opposite types in terms of their polarity. That is, the dual of input is output and the dual of output is input: $\overline{in} = out$ and $\overline{out} = in$. We can extend this to tuples a in A, see Def. 3, with the exception of basic types because they do not describe channels:

$$\overline{(\mathrm{com}, p)} = (\mathrm{com}, \overline{p}) \qquad \overline{(\mathrm{end})} = (\mathrm{end})$$
$$\overline{(\mathrm{branch}, p, L)} = (\mathrm{branch}, \overline{p}, L) \qquad \overline{(\mathrm{un})} = (\mathrm{un})$$
$$\overline{(\mathrm{bsc}, d)} \text{ is undefined}$$

The next step is to compare transitions. Continuations of $dom_C(f)$ need to be dual. The data types that are sent or received need to be equivalent, hence transitions of $dom_D(f)$ need to go to bisimilar states. We capture this idea with the monotone map $f_\perp : \mathrm{Rel}_X \to \mathrm{Rel}_{F(X)}$ defined as follows.

$$f_\perp(R) = \left\{ ((a, f), (\overline{a}, f')) \;\middle|\; \begin{matrix} (\forall \alpha \in dom_C(f)) & f(\alpha)\, R\, f'(\alpha) \text{ and} \\ (\forall \beta \in dom_D(f)) & f(\beta) \sim f'(\beta) \end{matrix} \right\}$$

Definition 7. *A relation R is called a* duality relation *if it is a post-fixpoint of $c^* \circ f_\perp$. We call the greatest fixpoint* duality *and denote it by $\perp$.*

It is useful to have a function mapping any $x \in X$ to their dual $\overline{x}$, as long as duality is defined on x. However, even if duality is defined on x, the dual state might not be in X. Thus, we define the *dual closure* of X as the set $X^\perp = X \cup \{\overline{x} \mid \overline{\sigma(x)} \text{ is defined}\}$, where $\overline{x}$ is understood to be an arbitrary state not in X and distinct from $\overline{y}$ for any states $y \in X$ with $x \neq y$. For any of the original states, $c^\perp(x) = c(x)$, but for the new states we define $\sigma^\perp(\overline{x}) = \overline{\sigma(x)}$ and

$$\delta^\perp(\overline{x})(\alpha) = \overline{\delta(x)(\alpha)} \quad \text{for all } \alpha \in dom_C(f), \text{ and}$$
$$\delta^\perp(\overline{x})(\beta) = \delta(x)(\beta) \quad \text{for all } \beta \in dom_D(f)$$

Thus, the dual closure is a coalgebra such that $x \perp \overline{x}$ for any $\overline{x}$. Notice that taking a dual twice always yields a bisimilar type, so we can define the duality function as an involution, $\overline{\overline{x}} = x$, rather than adding more variables. Clearly, the dual closure of a finite set is finite.

Proposition 2. *$x \perp \overline{x}$ for every state x such that $\overline{x}$ is defined.*

4.3 Parallelizability

Unlike a linear endpoint, a channel endpoint with an unrestricted type may be shared between different parallel processes; each of them uses it independently, without informing the others. Furthermore, there is no way to coordinate which process receives which message. If the unrestricted endpoint sends a message, it could be read by a process that just started using the channel, or by a process that is almost done using the channel, or by a process that is anywhere in between.

In practice, this means an unrestricted channel can only perform one kind of communication action. However, session coalgebras allow us to define arbitrarily complex unrestricted types. For example, $\mu X.\ \mathsf{un}\,?\mathtt{int}.\ \mathsf{un}\,?\mathtt{bool}.\ X$ is an element of Type, but we know that sending both `int` and `bool` over the same unrestricted channel causes problems.

Definition 8. *Given a coalgebra (X, c), some subset $Y \subseteq X$ is* parallelizable, *written par(Y), if for every x and y in Y one of the following holds: $x \sim y$, $\sigma(x) = \text{un}$, or $\sigma(y) = \text{un}$.*

We know that un states do not represent communications; any other states, though, have to represent the same kind of action. We make this slightly stronger by requiring they are pairwise bisimilar.

Often we are interested in the parallelizability only of a specific state. Recall that $\langle x \rangle_c$ denotes the subcoalgebra generated by $x \in X$ in c.

Definition 9. *Let $\langle x \rangle_c^{\gg}$ be the smallest subset of $\langle x \rangle_c$ that contains x and is closed under continuation transitions:*

$$\langle x \rangle_c^{\gg} = \bigcap \{ Y \subseteq X \mid x \in Y \text{ and } \delta(y)(\alpha) \in Y \text{ for all } y \in Y \text{ and } \alpha \in dom_C(\delta(y)) \ \}$$

A state x is parallelizable, written par(x), if $\langle x \rangle_c^{\gg}$ is parallelizable.

4.4 Simulation and Subtyping

Intuitively, a coalgebra simulates another if the behaviour of the latter "is contained in" the former. Subtyping, originally defined on session types by Gay and Hole [17], is a notion of substitutability of types [16]. We will define our notion of simulation such that it coincides with subtyping, just like bisimulation provides a notion of type equivalence [17].

Consider a process that expects a channel of type $T = ?\mathtt{real}$. The process reads a value, and expects it to be a real number and treat it as such. We defined `int` as a subtype of `real`, so the process can operate correctly if it receives an integer instead; that is, $?\mathtt{int}$ is a subtype of T. Now consider a process that expects a channel of type `!int`, on which it can send any integer. In this case we cannot restrict the channel to a subtype: as all integers are valid where real numbers are expected, we can generalise the channel type to `!real`.

Now, in the input case the session types are related (in the subtyping relation) in the same order as the data types; this is called *covariance*. For output, the order is reversed; this is called *contravariance*. The same idea holds for labelled choices: the subtype of an external choice can have a subset of choices, while the subtype of an internal choice can add more options. For all types, it holds that states reached through transitions are covariant, i.e., if T is a subtype of U, continuations of T must be subtypes of continuations (of the same label) of U. The monotone map $h_{\sqsubseteq}$ in Fig. 7 captures these ideas formally.

Definition 10. *A relation R is called a* simulation *if it is a post-fixpoint of $c^* \circ h_{\sqsubseteq}$. We call the greatest fixpoint* similarity *and denote it by $\sqsubseteq$.*

$$\begin{aligned}
h_{\sqsubseteq}(R) = {} & \{ ((\mathrm{com}, in, f), (\mathrm{com}, in, g)) \mid f(*)\ R\ g(*) \text{ and } f(d)\ R\ g(d) \} \\
& \cup \{ ((\mathrm{com}, out, f), (\mathrm{com}, out, g)) \mid f(*)\ R\ g(*) \text{ and } g(d)\ R\ f(d) \} \\
& \cup \{ ((\mathrm{branch}, in, L_1, f), \\
& \qquad (\mathrm{branch}, in, L_2, g)) \mid L_1 \subseteq L_2 \text{ and } \forall l \in L_1 .\ f(l)\ R\ g(l) \} \\
& \cup \{ ((\mathrm{branch}, out, L_1, f), \\
& \qquad (\mathrm{branch}, out, L_2, g)) \mid L_2 \subseteq L_1 \text{ and } \forall l \in L_2 .\ f(l)\ R\ g(l) \} \\
& \cup \{ ((\mathrm{bsc}, d, f_{\emptyset}), (\mathrm{bsc}, d', f_{\emptyset})) \mid d \leq_D d' \} \\
& \cup \{ ((\mathrm{end}, f_{\emptyset}), (\mathrm{end}, f_{\emptyset})) \} \\
& \cup \{ ((\mathrm{un}, f), (\mathrm{un}, g)) \mid f(*)\ R\ g(*), \text{ and } \mathrm{par}(f(*)) \text{ iff } \mathrm{par}(g(*)) \}
\end{aligned}$$

Figure 7. Monotone map $h_{\sqsubseteq} \colon \mathrm{Rel}_X \to \mathrm{Rel}_{F(X)}$ that defines simulations

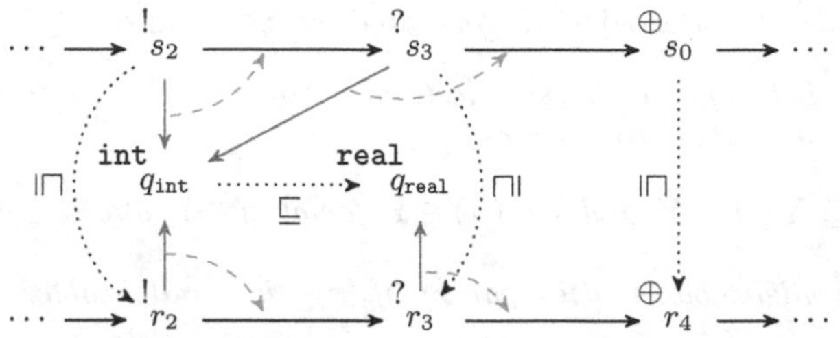

Figure 8. Simulation for two mathematical server clients (indicated by dotted arrows)

Let us illustrate similarity by means of an example.

Example 1. Recall the two client protocols for our mathematical server in Figs. 2 and 3. We can now prove our claim that the latter can also connect to the server because it is a supertype of the client protocol in Fig. 2. To do that, we have to establish a simulation relation between the states of both client protocols. In Fig. 8, we display a part of both session coalgebras side-by-side and indicate with dotted arrows the pairs that have to be related by a simulation relation to show that these states are similar, that is, related by $\sqsubseteq$. It should be noted that we simulate states from the second coalgebra by that of the first, that is, we show $s_k \sqsubseteq r_k$ for the shown states. There is one exception to this, namely $q_{\mathtt{int}} \sqsubseteq q_{\mathtt{real}}$.

The following proposition records some properties of and tight connections between the relations that we introduced.

Proposition 3. *Bisimilarity $\sim$ is an equivalence relation, duality $\perp$ is symmetric, and similarity $\sqsubseteq$ is a preorder. Moreover, for all states x, y, and z of a session coalgebra, we have that*

1. *$x \sim y$ iff $x \sqsubseteq y$ and $y \sqsubseteq x$;*
2. *$x \perp y$ and $x \perp z$ implies $y \sim z$; and*
3. *$x \perp y$ and $y \sim z$ implies $x \perp z$.*

4.5 Decidability

In a practical type checker, we need an algorithm to decide the relations defined above. In this subsection we show an algorithm that computes the answer in finite time for a certain class of types.

Definition 11. *A coalgebra* c *is* finitely generated *if* $\langle x \rangle_c$ *is finite for all* x.

This restriction is not problematic for types, as the following lemma shows.

Lemma 1. *The coalgebra of types* $(\mathsf{Type}, c_{\mathsf{Type}})$ *is finitely generated.*

To determine whether two states x and y are bisimilar, we need to determine if there exists a bisimulation R with $x \mathrel{R} y$. We start with the simplest relation $R = \{(x, y)\}$, and ask if this is a bisimulation.

First, we check that for all $(u, w) \in R$, $\sigma(u) = \sigma(w)$, or in the case of bsc states that $\mathrm{da}(u) \leq_D \mathrm{da}(w)$ and $\mathrm{da}(w) \leq_D \mathrm{da}(u)$. If $\sigma(u) \neq \sigma(w)$ for any pair in R we know that no superset of R is a bisimulation, and the algorithm rejects.

Second, we check the matching transitions. For every $(u, w) \in R$ and $\alpha \in dom(\delta(u))$ we check whether $(\delta(u)(\alpha), \delta(w)(\alpha)) \in R$. If we encounter a missing pair, we add it to R and ask whether this new relation is a bisimulation, i.e., return to the first step. If all destinations for matching transitions are present in R, then R is, by construction, a bisimulation containing (x, y). Hence, $x \sim y$.

This algorithm tries to construct the smallest possible bisimulation containing (x, y), by only adding strictly necessary pairs. If the algorithm rejects, there is no such bisimulation; hence, $x \not\sim y$. Additionally, the algorithm only examines pairs in $\langle x \rangle_c \times \langle y \rangle_c$. If there are finitely many of such pairs, the algorithm will terminate in finite time

The above described algorithm can be suitably adapted to similarity and duality, which gives us the following result.

Theorem 1. *Bisimilarity, similarity, and duality of any states* x *and* y *are decidable if* $\langle x \rangle_c$ *and* $\langle y \rangle_c$ *are finite. Parallelizability of any state* x *is decidable if* $\langle x \rangle_c^{\gtrdot}$ *(Definition 9) is finite.*

Corollary 1. *Bisimilarity, similarity, and duality are decidable for* c_{Type}.

5 Typing Rules

Session types are meant to discipline the behaviour of the channels of an interacting process, so as to ensure that prescribed protocols are executed as intended. Up to here, we have focused on session types (i.e., their representation as session coalgebras and coinductively-defined relations on them) without committing to a specific syntax for processes. This choice is on purpose: our goal is to provide a truly syntax-independent justification for session types. In this section, we introduce a syntactic notion of processes and rely on session coalgebras to define the typing rules for a session type system.

$P, Q ::= \overline{x}\langle y\rangle.P$		output y on channel x
$\mid$	$x(y).P$	bind input from channel x to variable y
$\mid$	$x \triangleright \{l_i : P_i\}_{i\in I}$	offer choices $l_1, l_2, \ldots$
$\mid$	$x \triangleleft l.P$	make choice l
$\mid$	$P \mid Q$	composition
$\mid$	$!P$	replication
$\mid$	$\mathbf{0}$	finished process
$\mid$	$(\nu xy)P$	channel creation

Figure 9. Process syntax

5.1 A Session π-calculus

The π-calculus is a formal model of interactive computation in which processes exchange messages along channels (or names) [26,31]. As such, it is an abstract framework in which key features such as name mobility, (message-passing) concurrency, non-determinism, synchronous communication, and infinite behaviour have rigorous syntactic representations and precise operational meaning. We consider a *session* π-calculus based on [37,17], i.e., a variant of the π-calculus whose operators are tailored to the protocols expressed by session types.

We assume base sets of *variables* $(x, y, z, \ldots)$ and *values* $(v, v', \ldots)$, which can be variables or the Boolean constants (true and false). There is also a set of *labels* $\mathbb{L}$, ranged over by $l, l', \ldots$. The syntax of processes $(P, Q, \ldots)$ is given by the grammar in Fig. 9. We discuss the salient aspects of the syntax. A process $\overline{x}\langle y\rangle.P$ denotes the output of channel y along channel x, which precedes the execution of P. Dually, a process $x(y).P$ denotes the input of a value v along channel x, which precedes the execution of process $P[v/y]$, i.e., the process P in which all free occurrences of y have been substituted by v. Processes $x \triangleright \{l_i : P_i\}_{i\in I}$ and $x \triangleleft l.P$ implement a labelled choice mechanism. Given a finite index set I, process $x \triangleright \{l_i : P_i\}_{i\in I}$, known as branching, denotes an external choice: the reception of a label l_j (with $j \in I$) along channel x precedes the execution of the continuation P_j. Process $x \triangleleft l.P$, known as selection, denotes an internal choice; it is meant to interact with a complementary branching. Given processes P and Q, process $P \mid Q$ denotes their parallel composition, which enables their simultaneous execution. The process $!P$, the replication of P, denotes the composition of infinite copies of P running in parallel, i.e., $P \mid P \mid \cdots$. Process $\mathbf{0}$ denotes inaction. Finally, process $(\nu xy)P$ is arguably the main difference with respect to usual presentations of the π-calculus, and denotes a restriction operator that declares x and y as *covariables*, i.e., as complementary endpoints of the same channel, with scope P.

The operational semantics for processes is defined as a *reduction relation* denoted $\longrightarrow$, by relying on a notion of *structural congruence* on processes, denoted $\equiv$. Figure 10 defines these two notions. Intuitively, two processes are structurally congruent if they are identical in behaviour, but not necessarily in structure. It is the smallest congruence relation satisfying the axioms in Fig. 10 (bottom). We say a process P reduces to Q, written $P \longrightarrow Q$, when there is a single execution step yielding Q from P. We comment on the rules in Fig. 10 (top). R-COM formalizes

Reduction

$$(\nu xy)(\overline{x}\langle v\rangle.P \mid y(z).Q \mid R) \longrightarrow (\nu xy)(P \mid Q[v/z] | R) \qquad \text{[R-COM]}$$

$$(\nu xy)(x \triangleleft l_j.P \mid y \triangleright \{l_i : Q_i\}_{i\in I} \mid R) \longrightarrow (\nu xy)(P \mid Q_j \mid R) \quad (j \in I) \qquad \text{[R-SYNC]}$$

$$\frac{P \longrightarrow Q}{(\nu xy)P \longrightarrow (\nu xy)Q} \qquad \frac{P \longrightarrow Q}{P \mid R \longrightarrow Q \mid R} \qquad \text{[R-RES][R-PAR]}$$

$$\frac{P \equiv P' \quad P \longrightarrow Q \quad Q \equiv Q'}{P' \longrightarrow Q'} \qquad \text{[R-CONG]}$$

Structural congruence

Parallel composition:

$$P \mid Q \equiv Q \mid P \qquad (P \mid Q) \mid R \equiv P \mid (Q \mid R) \qquad P \mid \mathbf{0} \equiv P \qquad !P \equiv P \mid !P$$

Scope restriction:

$$(\nu xy)(\nu vw)P \equiv (\nu vw)(\nu xy)P \qquad (\nu xy)\mathbf{0} \equiv \mathbf{0} \qquad (\nu xy)P \equiv (\nu yx)P$$

$$(\nu xy)(P \mid Q) \equiv ((\nu xy)P) \mid Q \qquad \text{if } x \text{ and } y \text{ not free in } Q$$

Figure 10. Reduction semantics

the exchange a value over a channel formed by two covariables. Similarly, R-SYNC formalises the synchronisation between a branching and a selection that realises the labelled choice. Rules R-RES and R-PAR are contextual rules, which allow reduction to proceed under restriction and parallel composition. Finally, Rule R-CONG says that reduction is closed under structurally congruence: we can use $\equiv$ to promote interactions that match the structure of the rules above.

5.2 Typing Rules

Based on the above, variables P, Q will refer to processes, x, y, z will range over channels and T, U, V are states of some fixed, but arbitrary, session coalgebra (X, c). Variables are associated with these states in a *context* Γ, as described by $\Gamma ::= \emptyset \mid \Gamma, x : T$. A context is an unordered, finite set of pairs, that may have at most one pair (x, T) for each variable x. A context is thus isomorphic to a (partial) function from a finite set of variables to their types. We use Γ to denote this isomorphic function as well: $\Gamma(x) = T$ if $(x, T) \in \Gamma$. The domain of a context is defined accordingly.

We know 'un' types are unrestricted, but they are not the only ones.

Definition 12. *A type is* unrestricted, *written un*(T), *if its operation is* un, end *or* bsc. *A context is unrestricted, written un*(Γ), *if all types in* Γ *are unrestricted, i.e., if* $(x, T) \in \Gamma$ *implies un*(T). *A type is* linear, *written lin*(T), *if it is not unrestricted. A context is linear, if all its types are linear.*

A context Γ may be split into two parts Γ_1 and Γ_2, such that the linear types are strictly divided between Γ_1 and Γ_2, but unrestricted types can be copied. Context split is a ternary relation, defined by the axioms in Fig. 11. We may write $\Gamma_1 \circ \Gamma_2$ to refer to a context Γ for which $\Gamma = \Gamma_1 \circ \Gamma_2$ is in the context split relation. Such a context is not necessarily defined for any given contexts;

$$\emptyset = \emptyset \circ \emptyset \qquad \frac{\Gamma = \Gamma_1 \circ \Gamma_2 \qquad \text{un}(T)}{\Gamma, x : T = (\Gamma_1, x : T) \circ (\Gamma_2, x : T)}$$

$$\frac{\Gamma = \Gamma_1 \circ \Gamma_2}{\Gamma, x : T = (\Gamma_1, x : T) \circ \Gamma_2} \qquad \frac{\Gamma = \Gamma_1 \circ \Gamma_2}{\Gamma, x : T = \Gamma_1 \circ (\Gamma_2, x : T)}$$

Figure 11. Context Split

$$\frac{\text{un}(\Gamma)}{\Gamma \vdash \mathbf{0}} \qquad \frac{\Gamma, x : T, y : U \vdash P \qquad T \perp U}{\Gamma \vdash (\nu xy)P} \qquad \text{[T-INACT][T-RES]}$$

$$\frac{\Gamma_1 \vdash P \qquad \Gamma_2 \vdash Q}{\Gamma_1 \circ \Gamma_2 \vdash P \mid Q} \qquad \frac{\Gamma \vdash P \qquad \text{un}(\Gamma)}{\Gamma \vdash !P} \qquad \text{[T-PAR][T-REP]}$$

$$\frac{c(T) = (?, f) \qquad \Gamma, y : U, x : f(*) \vdash P \qquad f(d) \sqsubseteq U}{\Gamma, x : T \vdash x(y).P} \qquad \text{[T-IN]}$$

$$\frac{c(T) = (!, f) \qquad \Gamma, x : f(*) \vdash P \qquad U \sqsubseteq f(d)}{\Gamma, x : T, y : U \vdash \overline{x}\langle y \rangle.P} \qquad \text{[T-OUT]}$$

$$\frac{c(T) = (\&, L_1, f) \qquad L_1 \subseteq L_2 \qquad \Gamma, x : f(l) \vdash P_l \qquad \forall l \in L_1}{\Gamma, x : T \vdash x \triangleright \{l : P_l\}_{l \in L_2}} \qquad \text{[T-BRANCH]}$$

$$\frac{c(T) = (\oplus, L, f) \qquad \Gamma, x : f(l) \vdash P_l \qquad l \in L}{\Gamma, x : T \vdash x \triangleleft l.P_l} \qquad \text{[T-SEL]}$$

$$\frac{c(T) = (\text{un}, f) \qquad \text{par}(T) \qquad \Gamma, x : f(*) \vdash P}{\Gamma, x : T \vdash P} \qquad \text{[T-UNPACK]}$$

Figure 12. Declarative Typing Rules

we implicitly assume its existence when writing $\Gamma_1 \circ \Gamma_2$. Notice that the use of $\Gamma, x : T$ in the third rule of Fig. 11 carries the assumption that x not in Γ. Otherwise, $\Gamma, x : T$ would have two pairs with x, which is not allowed.

The type system is defined by the rules in Fig. 12. A process P is *well-formed*, under a context Γ, if there is some inference tree whose root is $\Gamma \vdash P$ and whose nodes are all valid instantiations of these type rules. As T-INACT is the only rule that does not depend on the correctness of another process, it forms the leaves of such trees. For well-formed processes, the type system guarantees that:

- If the process terminates, then all linear sessions were completed.
- If a process reads a value from a channel, the value has the type specified by the channel's session type. If a process receives a label, it is one of the labels specified by the channel's session type.

We discuss the typing rules, which can be conveniently read keeping in mind the notations introduced in Def. 3 and Prop. 1. T-INACT ensures that all linear channels in the context are interacted with until the type becomes unrestricted. If our context contains a variable x of type `?int`, then the process is required to read an `int` from it. Thus, $x : ?\texttt{int}. \nvdash \mathbf{0}$. In contrast, process $x(z).\mathbf{0}$ is well-formed for the same context, using T-INACT and T-IN:

$$\dfrac{\dfrac{}{x : \text{end}, z : \texttt{int} \vdash \mathbf{0}}}{x : ?\texttt{int} \vdash x(z).\mathbf{0}}$$

T-RES creates a channel by binding together two covariables x and y, of dual type. T-PAR causes unrestricted channels to be copied and linear channels to get split between composite processes, ensuring the latter occur in only a single process. Recall that replication $!P$ is an infinite composition of a single process P, hence, a replicated process can only use unrestricted channels. Together, T-PAR and T-RES allow us to introduce new covariables, with new types, and distribute them. But, only unrestricted types may be copied. Notice that a process does not specify which types to give the newly bound variables.

$$\begin{array}{rcl} v : \texttt{int} & \vdash & (\nu xy)\, x(z).\mathbf{0} \mid \overline{y}\langle v\rangle.\mathbf{0} \\ x : un?\texttt{int} & \vdash & x(z).\mathbf{0} \mid x(z).\mathbf{0} \\ x :?\texttt{int} & \nvdash & x(z).\mathbf{0} \mid x(z).\mathbf{0} \end{array}$$

Each action on a channel has its own rule: T-IN handles input, binding the channel x to the continuation type and y to some supertype of the received type. T-OUT handles output, which requires the sent variable to have a subtype of whatever type the channel expects to send. T-BRANCH handles external choice, where the process needs to offer at least all choices the type describes, coupled with processes that are correctly typed under the respective continuation types. T-SEL only checks whether the single label that was chosen by the process was a valid option, and if the rest of the process is correct under the continuation type.

These rules are only specified for linear states; T-UNPACK allows a un state to be used as if it was the underlying type, as long as it is parallelizable (Def. 8).

We can actually create structures with un that do not have a syntactical equivalent. For example, let T_{end} be a state with $\sigma(T_{\text{end}}) = \text{un}$ and $\delta(T_{\text{end}})(*) = T_{\text{end}}$. Just like regular end, T_{end} allows no interactions on the channel, but it does not cause a "un" type to be unparallelizable.

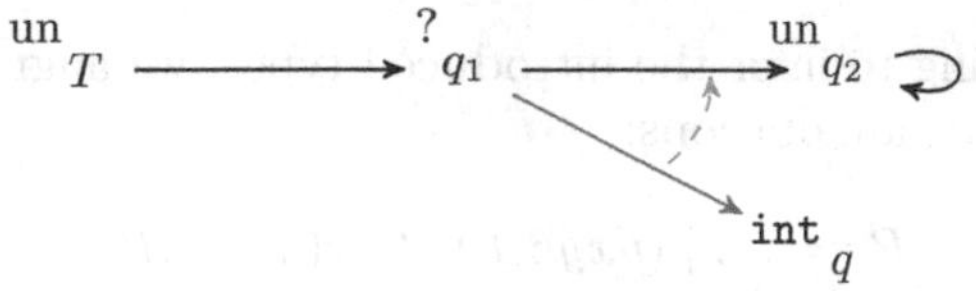

Figure 13. Session coalgebra using an alternative completed protocol

The diagram in Fig. 13 describes a parallelizable unrestricted state T such that each copy of a channel in state T can only do a single receive. However, because it is unrestricted, we can still copy the channel across threads and read a value per copy. We can even read infinitely many values through replication.

$$\begin{array}{lcl} x : T & \nvdash & x(y_1).x(y_2).x(y_3).\mathbf{0} \\ x : T & \vdash & x(y_1).\mathbf{0} \mid x(y_2).\mathbf{0} \mid x(y_3).\mathbf{0} \\ x : T & \vdash & !(x(y).\mathbf{0}) \end{array}$$

Such a type might be interesting in combination with session delegation. A linear session could be established by receiving a channel from an unrestricted channel. By using a structure like T, each thread is guaranteed to establish at most one private session, but there can be many of such sessions in parallel threads.

In Sec. 4, we defined simulation through the intuition of subtyping as substitutability in one direction. We see that substitution is indeed allowed for simulated types.

Theorem 2. *The following, more common, rule is admissible from the rules in Fig. 12.*

$$\frac{\Gamma, x : T \vdash P \qquad U \sqsubseteq T}{\Gamma, x : U \vdash P}$$

That is, we could add the rule as an axiom, without changing the set of typable processes. As a corollary, bisimulation of states implies the states are equivalent with respect to the type system.

Corollary 2. *For all bisimilar types $T \sim U$, contexts Γ and processes P, it holds that $\Gamma, x : T \vdash P$ if and only if $\Gamma, x : U \vdash P$.*

6 Algorithmic Type Checking

The type rules describe what well-formed processes look like, but do not directly allow us to decide whether an arbitrary process is well-formed or not. This is because, beforehand, we do not know:

1. Which type to introduce in reading (T-In) or scope restriction (T-Res), or
2. How to split the context in composite processes (T-Par).

Rather than trying to infer the introduced types, we augment the language of processes with type annotations:

$$P ::= \ldots \mid (\nu xy : T)\, P \mid x(y : T).P$$

We only need to annotate one type for scope restrictions, as we can create the other with the duality function. Other productions are kept unchanged.

When checking a process $P \mid Q$, we pass along the entire context to P, keeping track of all linear variables used, and remove those from the context given to Q. To do this we add an *output* to the algorithm: in an execution $\Gamma_1 \vdash P \,;\, \Gamma_2$, output Γ_2 is the subset of Γ_1 containing only those variables of the input which

$$\Gamma \div \emptyset = \Gamma \qquad \frac{\Gamma_1 \div F = \Gamma_2, x : T \quad \mathrm{un}(T)}{\Gamma_1 \div (F, x) = \Gamma_2} \qquad \frac{\Gamma_1 \div F = \Gamma_2 \quad x \notin dom(\Gamma_2)}{\Gamma_1 \div (F, x) = \Gamma_2}$$

Figure 14. Context Difference

$$\Gamma \vdash \mathbf{0}; \Gamma \qquad \frac{\Gamma_1 \vdash P; \Gamma_2 \quad \Gamma_1 = \Gamma_2}{\Gamma_1 \vdash\, !P; \Gamma_2} \qquad \text{[A-INACT][A-REP]}$$

$$\frac{\Gamma_1 \vdash P \,;\, \Gamma_2 \quad \Gamma_2 \vdash Q \,;\, \Gamma_3}{\Gamma_1 \vdash P \mid Q \,;\, \Gamma_3} \qquad \frac{\Gamma_1, x : T, y : \overline{T} \vdash P; \Gamma_2}{\Gamma_1 \vdash (\nu xy : T)P \,;\, \Gamma_2 \div \{x, y\}} \qquad \text{[A-PAR][A-RES]}$$

$$\frac{c(T) = (?, f) \quad f(d) \sqsubseteq U \quad \Gamma_1, y : U, x : f(*) \vdash P \,;\, \Gamma_2}{\Gamma_1, x : T \vdash x(y : U).P \,;\, \Gamma_2 \div \{x, y\}} \qquad \text{[A-IN]}$$

$$\frac{c(T) = (!, f) \quad U \sqsubseteq f(d) \quad \Gamma_1, x : f(*) \vdash P \,;\, \Gamma_2}{\Gamma_1, x : T, y : U \vdash \overline{x}\langle y \rangle.P \,;\, \Gamma_2 \div \{x\}} \qquad \text{[A-OUT]}$$

$$\frac{c(T) = (\&, L_1, f) \quad L_1 \subseteq L_2 \quad \Gamma_1, x : f(l) \vdash P_l \,;\, \Gamma_l \quad \Gamma_2 = \Gamma_l \div \{x\} \quad \forall l \in L_2}{\Gamma_1, x : T \vdash x \rhd \{l : P_l\}_{l \in L_2} \,;\, \Gamma_2} \qquad \text{[A-BRANCH]}$$

$$\frac{c(T) = (\oplus, L, f) \quad \Gamma_1, x : f(l) \vdash P_l \,;\, \Gamma_2 \quad l \in L}{\Gamma_1, x : T \vdash x \lhd l.P_l \,;\, \Gamma_2 \div \{x\}} \qquad \text{[A-SEL]}$$

$$\frac{c(T) = (\mathrm{un}, f) \quad \mathrm{par}(T) \quad \Gamma_1, x : f(*) \vdash P; \Gamma_2}{\Gamma_1, x : T \vdash P \,;\, (\Gamma_2 \div \{x\}), x : T} \qquad \text{[A-UNPACK]}$$

Figure 15. Algorithmic Type Checking Rules

had unrestricted types or were not used in P. We say subset because we want these variables, if present, to have the same type in Γ_2 as in Γ_1.

Figure 15 lists the algorithmic versions of the type rules. A-PAR, for example, checks parallel processes as described. By construction, Γ_2 is one part of the context split required to instantiate T-PAR. The linear variables of the other part is exactly those which are present in Γ_1 but not in Γ_2. This change in A-PAR requires adjusting the other rules. Firstly, we need the algorithm to accept even when we do not fully complete all sessions of Γ_1 in P. We do this by unconditionally accepting the terminated process. Note that acceptance of the algorithm now only implies well-formedness if the returned context is unrestricted.

Secondly, the algorithm needs to remove linear variables from the output as we use them. We do not, however, want to remove any variable that has a linear type, as that would allow us to accept processes which do not complete all linear sessions. Thus, we introduce the context difference operator $\div$ in Fig. 14. $\Gamma \div \{x\}$ is the context of all variable/type pairs in Γ minus a potential pair including x, but is only defined if $(x, T) \in \Gamma$ implies that T is unrestricted.

We elaborate on A-BRANCH; the algorithm is called once for every branch, yielding a context Γ_l each time. Excluding x, each branch must use the exact same set of linear variables. Thus, we require that all these contexts are equal up to a potential (x, U_l) pair. Specifically, there is some Γ_2 such that $\Gamma_2 = \Gamma_l \div \{x\}$ for any $l \in L_2$, this Γ_2 is the output context.

To motivate this, consider a type $T = \&\{a : T_{un},\, b : \text{end}\}$, where T_{un} is some unrestricted type distinct from end, and some process $P = x \triangleright \{a : \mathbf{0},\, b : \mathbf{0}\}$. Let Γ be some unrestricted context, $\mathbf{0}$ is well-formed for both $\Gamma, x : T_{un}$ and $\Gamma, x : \text{end}$; the algorithm agrees.

$$\Gamma, x : T_{un} \vdash \mathbf{0}\ ;\ (\Gamma, x : T_{un})$$
$$\Gamma, x : \text{end} \vdash \mathbf{0}\ ;\ (\Gamma, x : \text{end})$$

The resulting contexts are not equal. P is well-formed for Γ, so we have to allow x to have different types in the output of different branches in a complete algorithm. A-IN, A-OUT, and A-SEL do not have multiple branches to check, but the ideas are similar. When introducing a new variable, either through a read or scope restriction, the new variable is also removed from the output. A-UNPACK only unpacks unrestricted types. We want those to have the same type in the input as in the output, so we remove the variable and add a pair with the original type.

Take, for example, the process

$$x : \texttt{?int},\ y : \texttt{?int} \quad \vdash \quad x(z_1).\mathbf{0} \mid y(z_2).\mathbf{0}$$

The variables are split correctly, and both split contexts are unrestricted when the process is completed, thus it is well-formed.

If, on the other hand, the left process did not complete the linear session, then the context difference would not have been defined. Take one such process:

$$x : \texttt{?int.?int},\ y : \texttt{?int} \quad \nvdash \quad x(z_1).\mathbf{0} \mid y(z_2).\mathbf{0}$$

We succeed in checking the terminated process of the left part.

$$x : \texttt{?int},\ y : \texttt{?int} \quad \vdash \quad \mathbf{0}\ ; \quad (x : \texttt{?int}, y : \texttt{?int})$$

But x has a linear type in the output. $(x : \texttt{?int}, y : \texttt{?int}) \div \{x\}$ is undefined, so the algorithm rejects this input entirely. The process was indeed not well-formed, and no further parallel processes could fix it; the rejection is expected.

For each process and context there is at most one applicable algorithmic rule: which one is directed by the process syntax and unrestrictedness of a channel being interacted with.

Under the same assumptions as before (i.e., the session coalgebra describing the types is finitely generated), this induced type checking algorithm is decidable, sound, and complete with respect to the type rules defined in Sec. 5.

Theorem 3 (Decidability). *The type checking algorithm terminates in finite time for every input, assuming a finitely generated session coalgebra.*

Having defined algorithmic typechecking, we can go back to the language that we used to define our typing rules by erasing type annotations in input and restriction operators. Let $erase(\cdot)$ denote a function on processes defined as

$$erase((\nu xy : T).Q) = (\nu xy).erase(Q)$$
$$erase(x(y : T).Q) = x(y).erase(Q)$$

and as an homomorphism on the remaining process constructs. We have:

Theorem 4 (Correctness). *For any context Γ and annotated process P, $\Gamma_1 \vdash erase(P)$ iff $\Gamma_1 \vdash P; \Gamma_2$ and $un(\Gamma_2)$.*

7 Concluding Remarks

We have developed a new, language-independent foundation for session types by relying on coalgebras. We introduced session coalgebras, which elegantly capture all communication structures of session types, both linear and unrestricted, without committing to a specific syntactic formulation for processes and types. Session coalgebras allow us to rediscover language-independent coinductive definitions for duality, subtyping, and type equivalence. A key idea is to assimilate channel types to the states of a session coalgebra; we demonstrated this insight by deriving a session type system for the π-calculus, which revisits and extends that by Vasconcelos [37], unlocking decidability results and algorithmic type checking.

Interesting strands for future work include extending our coalgebraic toolbox so as to give a language-independent justification to advanced session type systems, such as context-free session types [35] and multiparty session types [21]. Another line concerns extending our coalgebraic view to include *language-dependent* issues and properties that require a global analysis on session behaviours. Salient examples are *liveness* properties such as (dead)lock-freedom and progress: advanced type systems [23,29,28,8] typically couple (session) types with advanced mechanisms (such as priority-based annotations and strict partial orders), which provide a global insight to rule out the circular dependencies between sessions that are at the heart of stuck processes. Lastly, the whole area of coalgebra now becomes available to explore session types. One possible direction is to make use of final coalgebras and modal logic, which would allow us to analyse the behaviour of session coalgebras. This would be particularly powerful in combination with composition operations for session coalgebras to break down protocols and type checking. Another direction is to use session coalgebras to verify other coalgebras that take on the role of the syntactic π-calculus [12,27] and thereby allowing also for the exploration of other semantics like manifest sharing [1,2] without resorting to a specific syntax.

Acknowledgements We are grateful to the anonymous reviewers for their useful remarks and suggestions. Pérez has been partially supported by the Dutch Research Council (NWO) under project No. 016.Vidi.189.046 (Unifying Correctness for Communicating Software).

References

1. Balzer, S., Pfenning, F.: Manifest sharing with session types. Proc. ACM Program. Lang. **1**(ICFP), 37:1–37:29 (2017). https://doi.org/10.1145/3110281
2. Balzer, S., Toninho, B., Pfenning, F.: Manifest Deadlock-Freedom for Shared Session Types. In: Proc. 28th European Symposium on Programming, ESOP 2019. pp. 611–639 (2019). https://doi.org/10.1007/978-3-030-17184-1_22
3. Bernardi, G., Hennessy, M.: Using higher-order contracts to model session types. Log. Methods Comput. Sci. **12**(2) (2016). https://doi.org/10.2168/LMCS-12(2:10)2016
4. Bravetti, M., Zavattaro, G.: Towards a unifying theory for choreography conformance and contract compliance. In: Lumpe, M., Vanderperren, W. (eds.) Software Composition - 6th International Symposium, SC@ETAPS 2007, Braga, Portugal, March 24-25, 2007, Revised Selected Papers. Lecture Notes in Computer Science, vol. 4829, pp. 34–50. Springer (2007). https://doi.org/10.1007/978-3-540-77351-1_4
5. Caires, L., Pérez, J.A., Pfenning, F., Toninho, B.: Behavioral polymorphism and parametricity in session-based communication. In: Felleisen, M., Gardner, P. (eds.) Programming Languages and Systems - 22nd European Symposium on Programming, ESOP 2013, Held as Part of the European Joint Conferences on Theory and Practice of Software, ETAPS 2013, Rome, Italy, March 16-24, 2013. Proceedings. Lecture Notes in Computer Science, vol. 7792, pp. 330–349. Springer (2013). https://doi.org/10.1007/978-3-642-37036-6_19
6. Carpineti, S., Castagna, G., Laneve, C., Padovani, L.: A formal account of contracts for web services. In: Bravetti, M., Núñez, M., Zavattaro, G. (eds.) Web Services and Formal Methods, Third International Workshop, WS-FM 2006 Vienna, Austria, September 8-9, 2006, Proceedings. Lecture Notes in Computer Science, vol. 4184, pp. 148–162. Springer (2006). https://doi.org/10.1007/11841197_10
7. Castagna, G., Gesbert, N., Padovani, L.: A theory of contracts for web services. ACM Trans. Program. Lang. Syst. **31**(5), 19:1–19:61 (2009). https://doi.org/10.1145/1538917.1538920
8. Coppo, M., Dezani-Ciancaglini, M., Yoshida, N., Padovani, L.: Global progress for dynamically interleaved multiparty sessions. Math. Struct. Comput. Sci. **26**(2), 238–302 (2016). https://doi.org/10.1017/S0960129514000188
9. de Alfaro, L., Henzinger, T.A.: Interface automata. In: Tjoa, A.M., Gruhn, V. (eds.) FSE'01. pp. 109–120. ACM (2001). https://doi.org/10.1145/503209.503226
10. Deniélou, P., Yoshida, N.: Multiparty session types meet communicating automata. In: Seidl, H. (ed.) Programming Languages and Systems - 21st European Symposium on Programming, ESOP 2012, Held as Part of the European Joint Conferences on Theory and Practice of Software, ETAPS 2012, Tallinn, Estonia, March 24 - April 1, 2012. Proceedings. Lecture Notes in Computer Science, vol. 7211, pp. 194–213. Springer (2012). https://doi.org/10.1007/978-3-642-28869-2_10
11. Deniélou, P., Yoshida, N.: Multiparty compatibility in communicating automata: Characterisation and synthesis of global session types. In: Fomin, F.V., Freivalds, R., Kwiatkowska, M.Z., Peleg, D. (eds.) Automata, Languages, and Programming - 40th International Colloquium, ICALP 2013, Riga, Latvia, July 8-12, 2013, Proceedings, Part II. Lecture Notes in Computer Science, vol. 7966, pp. 174–186. Springer (2013). https://doi.org/10.1007/978-3-642-39212-2_18
12. Eberhart, C., Hirschowitz, T., Seiller, T.: An Intensionally Fully-abstract Sheaf Model for pi. In: CALCO'15. pp. 86–100 (2015). https://doi.org/10.4230/LIPIcs.CALCO.2015.86

13. Fournet, C., Hoare, C.A.R., Rajamani, S.K., Rehof, J.: Stuck-free conformance. In: Alur, R., Peled, D.A. (eds.) Computer Aided Verification, 16th International Conference, CAV 2004, Boston, MA, USA, July 13-17, 2004, Proceedings. Lecture Notes in Computer Science, vol. 3114, pp. 242–254. Springer (2004). https://doi.org/10.1007/978-3-540-27813-9_19
14. Gambino, N., Kock, J.: Polynomial functors and polynomial monads. Mathematical Proceedings of the Cambridge Philosophical Society **154** (06 2009). https://doi.org/10.1017/S0305004112000394
15. Garcia, R., Tanter, É., Wolff, R., Aldrich, J.: Foundations of typestate-oriented programming. ACM Trans. Program. Lang. Syst. **36**(4), 12:1–12:44 (2014). https://doi.org/10.1145/2629609
16. Gay, S.J.: Subtyping supports safe session substitution. In: Lindley, S., McBride, C., Trinder, P.W., Sannella, D. (eds.) A List of Successes That Can Change the World - Essays Dedicated to Philip Wadler on the Occasion of His 60th Birthday. Lecture Notes in Computer Science, vol. 9600, pp. 95–108. Springer (2016). https://doi.org/10.1007/978-3-319-30936-1_5
17. Gay, S.J., Hole, M.: Subtyping for session types in the pi calculus. Acta Informatica **42**(2-3), 191–225 (2005). https://doi.org/10.1007/s00236-005-0177-z
18. Gay, S.J., Thiemann, P., Vasconcelos, V.T.: Duality of session types: The final cut. Electronic Proceedings in Theoretical Computer Science **314**, 23–33 (Apr 2020). https://doi.org/10.4204/eptcs.314.3
19. Honda, K.: Types for dyadic interaction. In: Best, E. (ed.) CONCUR '93, 4th International Conference on Concurrency Theory, Hildesheim, Germany, August 23-26, 1993, Proceedings. Lecture Notes in Computer Science, vol. 715, pp. 509–523. Springer (1993). https://doi.org/10.1007/3-540-57208-2_35
20. Honda, K., Vasconcelos, V.T., Kubo, M.: Language Primitives and Type Discipline for Structured Communication-Based Programming. In: Hankin, C. (ed.) ESOP'98. LNCS, vol. 1381, pp. 122–138. Springer (1998). https://doi.org/10.1007/BFb0053567
21. Honda, K., Yoshida, N., Carbone, M.: Multiparty asynchronous session types. In: Necula, G.C., Wadler, P. (eds.) Proceedings of the 35th ACM SIGPLAN-SIGACT Symposium on Principles of Programming Languages, POPL 2008, San Francisco, California, USA, January 7-12, 2008. pp. 273–284. ACM (2008). https://doi.org/10.1145/1328438.1328472
22. Keizer, A.C., Basold, H., Pérez, J.A.: Session coalgebras: A coalgebraic view on session types and communication protocols. CoRR **abs/2011.05712** (2020), https://arxiv.org/abs/2011.05712
23. Kobayashi, N.: A new type system for deadlock-free processes. In: Baier, C., Hermanns, H. (eds.) CONCUR 2006 - Concurrency Theory, 17th International Conference, CONCUR 2006, Bonn, Germany, August 27-30, 2006, Proceedings. Lecture Notes in Computer Science, vol. 4137, pp. 233–247. Springer (2006). https://doi.org/10.1007/11817949_16
24. Lindley, S., Morris, J.G.: Talking bananas: structural recursion for session types. In: Garrigue, J., Keller, G., Sumii, E. (eds.) Proceedings of the 21st ACM SIGPLAN International Conference on Functional Programming, ICFP 2016, Nara, Japan, September 18-22, 2016. pp. 434–447. ACM (2016). https://doi.org/10.1145/2951913.2951921
25. Lozes, É., Villard, J.: Reliable contracts for unreliable half-duplex communications. In: Carbone, M., Petit, J. (eds.) Web Services and Formal Methods - 8th International Workshop, WS-FM 2011, Clermont-Ferrand, France, September 1-2, 2011,

Revised Selected Papers. Lecture Notes in Computer Science, vol. 7176, pp. 2–16. Springer (2011). https://doi.org/10.1007/978-3-642-29834-9_2

26. Milner, R., Parrow, J., Walker, D.: A calculus of mobile processes, I. Inf. Comput. **100**(1), 1–40 (1992). https://doi.org/10.1016/0890-5401(92)90008-4
27. Montanari, U., Pistore, M.: Structured coalgebras and minimal HD-automata for the pi-calculus. Theor. Comput. Sci. **340**(3), 539–576 (2005). https://doi.org/10.1016/j.tcs.2005.03.014
28. Padovani, L.: Deadlock and lock freedom in the linear π-calculus. In: Henzinger, T.A., Miller, D. (eds.) Joint Meeting of the Twenty-Third EACSL Annual Conference on Computer Science Logic (CSL) and the Twenty-Ninth Annual ACM/IEEE Symposium on Logic in Computer Science (LICS), CSL-LICS '14, Vienna, Austria, July 14 - 18, 2014. pp. 72:1–72:10. ACM (2014). https://doi.org/10.1145/2603088.2603116
29. Padovani, L., Vasconcelos, V.T., Vieira, H.T.: Typing liveness in multiparty communicating systems. In: eva Kühn, Pugliese, R. (eds.) Coordination Models and Languages - 16th IFIP WG 6.1 International Conference, COORDINATION 2014, Held as Part of the 9th International Federated Conferences on Distributed Computing Techniques, DisCoTec 2014, Berlin, Germany, June 3-5, 2014, Proceedings. Lecture Notes in Computer Science, vol. 8459, pp. 147–162. Springer (2014). https://doi.org/10.1007/978-3-662-43376-8_10
30. Pous, D.: Complete Lattices and Up-To Techniques. In: Shao, Z. (ed.) APLAS'07. LNCS, vol. 4807, pp. 351–366. Springer (2007). https://doi.org/10.1007/978-3-540-76637-7_24
31. Sangiorgi, D., Walker, D.: The Pi-Calculus - a theory of mobile processes. Cambridge University Press (2001)
32. Strom, R.E., Yemini, S.: Typestate: A programming language concept for enhancing software reliability. IEEE Trans. Software Eng. **12**(1), 157–171 (1986). https://doi.org/10.1109/TSE.1986.6312929
33. Sunshine, J., Naden, K., Stork, S., Aldrich, J., Tanter, É.: First-class state change in Plaid. In: Lopes, C.V., Fisher, K. (eds.) Proceedings of the 26th Annual ACM SIGPLAN Conference on Object-Oriented Programming, Systems, Languages, and Applications, OOPSLA 2011, part of SPLASH 2011, Portland, OR, USA, October 22 - 27, 2011. pp. 713–732. ACM (2011). https://doi.org/10.1145/2048066.2048122
34. Tarski, A.: A lattice-theoretical fixpoint theorem and its applications. Pacific J. Math. **5**(2), 285–309 (1955), https://projecteuclid.org:443/euclid.pjm/1103044538
35. Thiemann, P., Vasconcelos, V.T.: Context-free session types. In: Garrigue, J., Keller, G., Sumii, E. (eds.) Proceedings of the 21st ACM SIGPLAN International Conference on Functional Programming, ICFP 2016, Nara, Japan, September 18-22, 2016. pp. 462–475. ACM (2016). https://doi.org/10.1145/2951913.2951926
36. Toninho, B., Yoshida, N.: Polymorphic session processes as morphisms. In: Alvim, M.S., Chatzikokolakis, K., Olarte, C., Valencia, F. (eds.) The Art of Modelling Computational Systems: A Journey from Logic and Concurrency to Security and Privacy - Essays Dedicated to Catuscia Palamidessi on the Occasion of Her 60th Birthday. Lecture Notes in Computer Science, vol. 11760, pp. 101–117. Springer (2019). https://doi.org/10.1007/978-3-030-31175-9_7
37. Vasconcelos, V.T.: Fundamentals of session types. Inf. Comput. **217**, 52–70 (2012). https://doi.org/10.1016/j.ic.2012.05.002

Correctness of Sequential Monte Carlo Inference for Probabilistic Programming Languages*

Daniel Lundén(✉)[1], Johannes Borgström[2], and David Broman[1]

[1] Digital Futures and EECS,
KTH Royal Institute of Technology, Stockholm, Sweden
{dlunde,dbro}@kth.se
[2] Uppsala University, Uppsala, Sweden
johannes.borgstrom@it.uu.se

Abstract. Probabilistic programming is an approach to reasoning under uncertainty by encoding inference problems as programs. In order to solve these inference problems, probabilistic programming languages (PPLs) employ different inference algorithms, such as sequential Monte Carlo (SMC), Markov chain Monte Carlo (MCMC), or variational methods. Existing research on such algorithms mainly concerns their implementation and efficiency, rather than the correctness of the algorithms themselves when applied in the context of expressive PPLs. To remedy this, we give a correctness proof for SMC methods in the context of an expressive PPL calculus, representative of popular PPLs such as WebPPL, Anglican, and Birch. Previous work have studied correctness of MCMC using an operational semantics, and correctness of SMC and MCMC in a denotational setting without term recursion. However, for SMC inference—one of the most commonly used algorithms in PPLs as of today—no formal correctness proof exists in an operational setting. In particular, an open question is if the resample locations in a probabilistic program affects the correctness of SMC. We solve this fundamental problem, and make four novel contributions: (i) we extend an untyped PPL lambda calculus and operational semantics to include explicit resample terms, expressing synchronization points in SMC inference; (ii) we prove, for the first time, that subject to mild restrictions, any placement of the explicit resample terms is valid for a generic form of SMC inference; (iii) as a result of (ii), our calculus benefits from classic results from the SMC literature: a law of large numbers and an unbiased estimate of the model evidence; and (iv) we formalize the bootstrap particle filter for the calculus and discuss how our results can be further extended to other SMC algorithms.

Keywords: Probabilistic Programming · Sequential Monte Carlo · Operational Semantics · Functional Programming · Measure Theory

* This project is financially supported by the Swedish Foundation for Strategic Research (ASSEMBLE RIT15-0012) and the Swedish Research Council (grant 2013-4853).

N. Yoshida (Ed.): ESOP 2021, LNCS 12648, pp. 404–431, 2021.
https://doi.org/10.1007/978-3-030-72019-3_15

1 Introduction

Probabilistic programming is a programming paradigm for probabilistic models, encompassing a wide range of programming languages, libraries, and platforms [5,13,14,25,32,37,38]. Such probabilistic models are typically created to express *inference problems*, which are ubiquitous and highly significant in, for instance, machine learning [1], artificial intelligence [31], phylogenetics [29,30], and topic modeling [2].

In order to solve such inference problems, an *inference algorithm* is required. Common general-purpose algorithm choices for inference problems include *sequential Monte Carlo (SMC)* methods [9], *Markov chain Monte Carlo (MCMC)* methods [12], and *variational* methods [42]. In traditional settings, correctness results for such algorithms often come in the form of laws of large numbers, central limit theorems, or optimality arguments. However, for general-purpose probabilistic programming languages (PPLs), the emphasis has predominantly been on algorithm implementations and their efficiency [14,25,37], rather than the correctness of the algorithms themselves. In particular, explicit connections between traditional theoretical SMC results and PPL semantics have been limited. In this paper, we bridge this gap by formally connecting fundamental SMC results to the context of an expressive PPL calculus.

Essentially, SMC works by simulating many executions of a probabilistic program concurrently, occasionally *resampling* the different executions. In this resampling step, SMC discards less likely executions, and replicates more likely executions, while remembering the average likelihood at each resampling step in order to estimate the overall likelihood. In expressive PPLs, there is freedom in choosing where in a program this resampling occurs. For example, most SMC implementations, such as WebPPL [14], Anglican [43], and Birch [25], always resample when all executions have reached a call to the *weighting* construct in the language. At possible resampling locations, Anglican takes a conservative approach by dynamically checking during runtime if all executions have either stopped at a weighting construct, or all have finished. If none of these two cases apply, report a runtime error. In contrast, WebPPL does not perform any checks and simply includes the executions that have finished in the resampling step. There are also heuristic approaches [21] that automatically *align* resampling locations in programs, ensuring that all executions finish after encountering the same number of them. The motivations for using the above approaches are all based on experimental validation. As such, an open research problem is whether there are any inherent restrictions when selecting resampling locations, or if the correctness of SMC is independent of this selection. This is not only important theoretically to guarantee the correctness of inference results, but also for inference performance, both since inference performance is affected by the locations of resampling locations [21] and since dynamic checks result in direct runtime overhead. We address this research problem in this paper.

In the following, we give an overview of the paper and our contributions. In Section 2, we begin by giving a motivating example from phylogenetics, illustrating the usefulness of our results. Next, in Section 3, we define the syntax and operational semantics of an expressive functional PPL calculus based on the operational formalization in Borgström et al. [3], representative of common PPLs. The operational semantics assign to each pair of term $\mathbf{t}$ and initial random *trace* (sequences of random samples) a non-negative weight. This weight is accumulated during evaluation through a `weight` construct, which, in current calculi and implementations of SMC, is (implicitly) always followed by a resampling. To decouple resampling from weighting, we present our first contribution.

(i) We extend the calculus from Borgström et al. [3] to include explicit `resample` terms, expressing explicit synchronization points for performing resampling in SMC. With this extension, we also define a semantics which limits the number of evaluated resample terms, laying the foundation for the remaining contributions.

In Section 4, we define the probabilistic semantics of the calculus. The weight from the operational semantics is used to define unnormalized distributions $\langle\langle \mathbf{t} \rangle\rangle$ over traces and $[\![\mathbf{t}]\!]$ over result terms. The measure $[\![\mathbf{t}]\!]$ is called the *target measure*, and finding a representation of this is the main objective of inference algorithms.

We give a formal definition of SMC inference based on Chopin [6] in Section 5. This includes both a generic SMC algorithm, and two standard correctness results from the SMC literature: a law of large numbers [6], and the unbiasedness of the likelihood estimate [26].

In Section 6, we proceed to present the main contributions.

(ii) From the SMC formulation by Chopin [6], we formalize a sequence of distributions $\langle\langle \mathbf{t} \rangle\rangle_n$, indexed by n, such that $\langle\langle \mathbf{t} \rangle\rangle_n$ allows for evaluating at most n `resamples`. This sequence is determined by the placement of `resamples` in $\mathbf{t}$. Our first result is Theorem 1, showing that $\langle\langle \mathbf{t} \rangle\rangle_n$ eventually equals $\langle\langle \mathbf{t} \rangle\rangle$ if the number of calls to `resample` is upper bounded. Because of the explicit `resample` construct, this also implies that, for *all* `resample` placements such that the number of calls to `resample` is upper bounded, $\langle\langle \mathbf{t} \rangle\rangle_n$ eventually equals $\langle\langle \mathbf{t} \rangle\rangle$. We further relax the finite upper bound restriction and investigate under which conditions $\lim_{n\to\infty}\langle\langle \mathbf{t} \rangle\rangle_n = \langle\langle \mathbf{t} \rangle\rangle$ pointwise. In particular, we relate this equality to the dominated convergence theorem in Theorem 2, which states that the limit converges as long as there exists a function dominating the weights encountered during evaluation. This gives an alternative set of conditions under which $\langle\langle \mathbf{t} \rangle\rangle_n$ converges to $\langle\langle \mathbf{t} \rangle\rangle$ (now asymptotically, in the number of resamplings n).

The contribution is fundamental, in that it provides us with a sequence of approximating distributions $\langle\langle \mathbf{t} \rangle\rangle_n$ of $\langle\langle \mathbf{t} \rangle\rangle$ that can be targeted by the SMC algorithm of Section 5. As a consequence, we can extend the standard correctness results of that section to our calculus. This is our next contribution.

(iii) Given a suitable sequence of transition kernels (ways of moving between the $\langle\langle \mathbf{t} \rangle\rangle_n$), we can *correctly* approximate $\langle\langle \mathbf{t} \rangle\rangle_n$ with the SMC algorithm from Section 5. The approximation is correct in the sense of Section 5: the law of large numbers and the unbiasedness of the likelihood estimate holds. As a consequence of (ii), SMC also correctly approximates $\langle\langle \mathbf{t} \rangle\rangle$, and in turn the target measure $[\![\mathbf{t}]\!]$. Crucially, this also means estimating the model evidence (likelihood), which allows for compositionality [15] and comparisons between different models [30]. This contribution is summarized in Theorem 3.

Related to the above contributions, Ścibior et al. [33] formalizes SMC and MCMC inference as transformations over monadic inference representations using a denotational approach (in contrast to our operational approach). They prove that their SMC transformations preserve the measure of the initial representation of the program (i.e., the target measure). Furthermore, their formalization is based on a simply-typed lambda calculus with primitive recursion, while our formalization is based on an untyped lambda calculus which naturally supports full term recursion. Our approach is also rather more elementary, only requiring basic measure theory compared to the relatively heavy mathematics (category theory and synthetic measure theory) used by them. Regarding generalizability, their approach is both general and compositional in the different inference transformations, while we abstract over parts of the SMC algorithm. This allows us, in particular, to relate directly to standard SMC correctness results.

Section 7 concerns the instantiation of the transition kernels from (iii), and also discusses other SMC algorithms. Our last contribution is the following.

(iv) We define a sequence of sub-probability kernels $k_{\mathbf{t},n}$ induced by a given program $\mathbf{t}$, corresponding to the fundamental SMC algorithm known as the *bootstrap particle filter (BPF)* for our calculus. This is the most common version of SMC, and we present a concrete SMC algorithm corresponding to these kernels. We also discuss other SMC algorithms and their relation to our formalization: the resample-move [11], alive [19], and auxiliary [28] particle filters.

Importantly, by combining the above contributions, we justify that the implementation strategies of the BPFs in WebPPL, Anglican, and Birch are indeed correct. In fact, our results show that the strategy in Anglican, in which every evaluation path must resample the same number of times, is too conservative.

An extended version of this paper is also available [20]. This extended version includes rigorous definitions and detailed proofs for many lemmas found in the paper, as well as further examples and comments. The lemmas proved in the extended version are explicitly marked with †.

2 A Motivating Example from Phylogenetics

In this section, we give a motivating example from phylogenetics. The example is written in a functional PPL[3] developed as part of this paper, in order to verify

[3] The implementation is an interpreter written in OCaml. It largely follows the same approach as Anglican and WebPPL, and uses continuation-passing style in order to

```
let tree = {
 left:{left:{age:0},right:{age:0},age:4},
 right:{left:{age:0},right:{age:0},age:6},
 age:10
} in

let lambda = 0.2 in let mu = 0.1 in

let crbdGoesExtinct startTime =
 let curTime = startTime
   - (sample (exponential (lambda + mu)))
 in
 if curTime < 0 then false
 else
  let speciation = sample
    (bernoulli (lambda / (lambda + mu))) in
  if !speciation then true
  else crbdGoesExtinct curTime
    && crbdGoesExtinct curTime in

let simBranch startTime stopTime =
 let curTime = startTime -
   sample (exponential lambda) in
 if curTime < stopTime then ()
 else if not (crbdGoesExtinct curTime)
 then weight (log 0) // #1
 else (weight (log 2); // #2
       simBranch curTime stopTime) in

let simTree tree parent =
 let w = -mu * (parent.age - tree.age) in
 weight w; // #3
 simBranch parent.age tree.age;
 match tree with
 | {left,right,age} ->
   simTree left tree; simTree right tree
 | {age} -> () in

simTree tree.left tree;
simTree tree.right tree
```

Fig. 1: A simplified version of a phylogenetic birth-death model from [30]. See the text for a description.

and experiment with the presented concepts and results. In particular, this PPL supports SMC inference (Algorithm 2) with decoupled `resample`s and `weight`s[4], as well as sampling from random distributions with a `sample` construct.

Consider the program in Fig. 1, encoding a simplified version of a phylogenetic birth-death model (see Ronquist et al. [30] for the full version). The problem is to find the model evidence for a particular birth rate (`lambda = 0.2`) and death rate (`mu = 0.1`), given an observed phylogenetic `tree`. The tree represents known lineages of evolution, where the leaves are extant (surviving to the present) species. Most importantly, for illustrating the usefulness of the results in this paper, the recursive function `simBranch`, with its two `weight` applications `#1` and `#2`, is called a random number of times for each branch in the observed `tree`. Thus, different SMC executions encounter differing numbers of calls to `weight`. When resampling is performed after every call to `weight` (`#1`, `#2`, and `#3`), it is, because of the differing numbers of resamples, not obvious that inference is correct (e.g., the equivalent program in Anglican gives a runtime error). Our results show that such a resampling strategy is indeed correct.

This strategy is far from optimal, however. For instance, only resampling at `#3`, which is encountered the same number of times in each execution, performs much better [21,30]. Our results show that this is correct as well, and that it gives the same asymptotic results as the naive strategy in the previous paragraph.

Another strategy is to resample only at `#1` and `#3`, again causing executions to encounter differing numbers of resamples. Because `#1` weights with (log) 0, this

pause and resume executions as part of inference. It is available at https://github.com/miking-lang/miking-dppl/tree/pplcore. The example in Fig. 1 can be found under `examples/crbd/crbd-esop.ppl`

[4] The implementation uses log weights as arguments to `weight` for numerical reasons.

approach gives the same accuracy as resampling only at #3, but avoids useless computation since a zero-weight execution can never obtain non-zero weight. Equivalently to resampling at #1, zero-weight executions can also be identified and stopped automatically at runtime. This gives a direct performance gain, and both are correct by our results. We compared the three strategies above for SMC inference with 50 000 particles[5]: resampling at #1,#2, and #3 resulted in a runtime of 15.0 seconds, at #3 in a runtime of 12.6 seconds, and at #1 and #3 in a runtime of 11.2 seconds. Furthermore, resampling at #1,#2, and #3 resulted in significantly worse accuracy compared to the other two strategies [21,30].

Summarizing the above, the results in this paper ensure correctness when exploring different resampling placement strategies. As just demonstrated, this is useful, because resampling strategies can have a large impact on SMC accuracy and performance.

3 A Calculus for Probabilistic Programming Languages

In this section, we define the calculus used throughout the paper. In Section 3.1, we begin by defining the syntax, and demonstrate how a simple probability distribution can be encoded using it. In Section 3.2, we define the semantics and demonstrate it on the previously encoded probability distribution. This semantics is used in Section 4 to define the *target measure* for any given program. In Section 3.3, we extend the semantics of Section 3.2 to limit the number of allowed resamples in an evaluation. This extended semantics forms the foundation for formalizing SMC in Sections 6 and 7.

3.1 Syntax

The main difference between the calculus presented in this section and the standard untyped lambda calculus is the addition of real numbers, functions operating on real numbers, a sampling construct for drawing random values from real-valued probability distributions, and a construct for weighting executions. The rationale for making these additions is that, in addition to discrete probability distributions, continuous distributions are ubiquitous in most real-world models, and the weighting construct is essential for encoding inference problems. In order to define the calculus, we let X be a countable set of variable names; $D \in \mathbb{D}$ range over a countable set $\mathbb{D}$ of identifiers for families of probability distributions over $\mathbb{R}$, where the family for each identifier D has a fixed number of real parameters $|D|$; and $g \in \mathbb{G}$ range over a countable set $\mathbb{G}$ of identifiers for real-valued functions with respective arities $|g|$. More precisely, for each g, there is a measurable function $\sigma_g : \mathbb{R}^{|g|} \to \mathbb{R}$. For simplicity, we often use g to denote both the identifier and its measurable function. We can now give an inductive definition of the abstract syntax, consisting of values $\mathbf{v}$ and terms $\mathbf{t}$.

[5] We repeated each experiment 20 times on a machine running Ubuntu 20.04 with an Intel i5-2500K CPU (4 cores) and 8GB memory. The standard deviation was under 0.1 seconds in all three cases.

$\texttt{sample}_{Beta}(2,2)$

(a)

```
let p = sample_Beta(2, 2) in
let observe o =
  weight(f_Bern(p, o)) in
iter observe [true, false, true] ; p
```

(b)

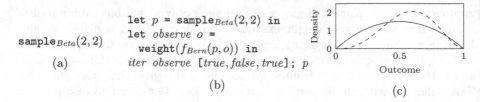

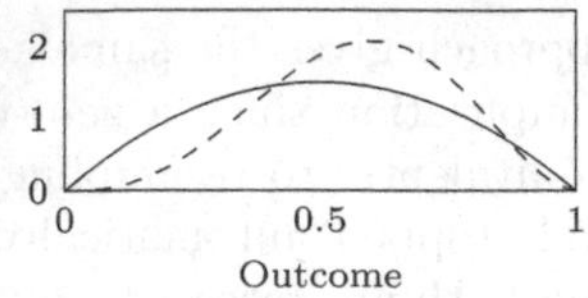

(c)

Fig. 2: The *Beta*(2, 2) distribution as a program in (a), and visualized with a solid line in (c). Also, the program $\mathbf{t}_{obs}$ in (b), visualized with a dashed line in (c). The *iter* function in (b) simply maps the given function over the given list and returns (). That is, it calls *observe true*, *observe false*, and *observe true* purely for the side-effect of weighting.

Definition 1.

$$\mathbf{v} ::= c \mid \lambda x.\mathbf{t} \qquad \begin{aligned} \mathbf{t} ::= {} & \mathbf{v} \mid x \mid \mathbf{t}\ \mathbf{t} \mid \texttt{if}\ \mathbf{t}\ \texttt{then}\ \mathbf{t}\ \texttt{else}\ \mathbf{t} \mid g(\mathbf{t}_1, \ldots, \mathbf{t}_{|g|}) \\ & \mid \texttt{sample}_D(\mathbf{t}_1, \ldots, \mathbf{t}_{|D|}) \mid \texttt{weight}(\mathbf{t}) \mid \texttt{resample} \end{aligned} \tag{1}$$

Here, $c \in \mathbb{R}$, $x \in X, D \in \mathbb{D}$, $g \in \mathbb{G}$. We denote the set of all terms by $\mathbb{T}$ and the set of all values by $\mathbb{V}$.

The formal semantics is given in Section 3.2. Here, we instead give an informal description of the various language constructs.

Some examples of distribution identifiers are $\mathcal{N} \in \mathbb{D}$, the identifier for the family of normal distributions, and $\mathcal{U} \in \mathbb{D}$, the identifier for the family of continuous uniform distributions. The semantics of the term $\texttt{sample}_{\mathcal{N}}(0,1)$ is, informally, "draw a random sample from the normal distribution with mean 0 and variance 1". The `weight` construct is illustrated later in this section, and we discuss the `resample` construct in detail in Sections 3.3 and 6.

We use common syntactic sugar throughout the paper. Most importantly, we use *false* and *true* as aliases for 0 and 1, respectively, and () (unit) as another alias for 0. Furthermore, we often write $g \in \mathbb{G}$ as infix operators. For instance, $1+2$ is a valid term, where $+ \in \mathbb{G}$. Now, let $\mathbb{R}_+$ denote the non-negative reals. We define $f_D : \mathbb{R}^{|D|+1} \to \mathbb{R}_+$ as the function $f_D \in \mathbb{G}$ such that $f_D(c_1, \ldots, c_{|D|}, \cdot)$ is the probability *density* (continuous distribution) or *mass* function (discrete distribution) for the probability distribution corresponding to $D \in \mathbb{D}$ and $(c_1, \ldots, c_{|D|})$. For example, $f_{\mathcal{N}}(0,1,x) = \frac{1}{\sqrt{2\pi}} \cdot e^{-\frac{1}{2}\cdot x^2}$ is the standard probability density of the normal distribution with mean 0 and variance 1. Lastly, we will also use `let` bindings, `let rec` bindings, sequencing using ;, and lists (all of which can be encoded in the calculus). Sequencing is required for the side-effects produced by `weight` (see Definition 5) and `resample` (see Sections 3.3 and 6).

We now consider an example. In Sections 3.2 and 4.3 this example will be further considered to illustrate the semantics, and target measure, respectively. Here, we first give the syntax, and informally visualize the probability distributions (i.e., the target measures, as we will see in Section 4.3) for the example.

Consider first the program in Fig. 2a, directly encoding the *Beta*(2, 2) distribution, illustrated in Fig. 2c. This distribution naturally represents the uncertainty in the bias of a coin—in this case, the coin is most likely unbiased (bias 0.5), and biases closer to 0 and 1 are less likely. In Fig. 2b, we extend Fig. 2a by observing the sequence [*true*, *false*, *true*] when flipping the coin. These observations are encoded using the `weight` construct, which simply accumulates a product (as a side-effect) of all real-valued arguments given to it throughout the execution. First, recall the standard mass function ($\sigma_{f_{Bern}}(p, \mathit{true}) = p$; $\sigma_{f_{Bern}}(p, \mathit{false}) = (1-p)$; $\sigma_{f_{Bern}}(p, x) = 0$ otherwise) for the Bernoulli distribution corresponding to $f_{Bern} \in \mathbb{G}$. The observations [*true*, *false*, *true*] are encoded using the *observe* function, which uses the `weight` construct internally to assign weights to the current value p according to the Bernoulli mass function. As an example, assume we have drawn $p = 0.4$. The weight for this execution is $\sigma_{f_{Bern}}(0.4, \mathit{true}) \cdot \sigma_{f_{Bern}}(0.4, \mathit{false}) \cdot \sigma_{f_{Bern}}(0.4, \mathit{true}) = 0.4^2 \cdot 0.6$. Now consider $p = 0.6$ instead. For this value of p the weight is instead $0.6^2 \cdot 0.4$. This explains the shift in Fig. 2c—a bias closer to 1 is more likely, since we have observed two *true* flips, but only one *false*.

3.2 Semantics

In this section, we define the semantics of our calculus. The definition is split into two parts: a *deterministic semantics* and a *stochastic semantics*. We use evaluation contexts to assist in defining our semantics. The evaluation contexts $\mathbf{E}$ induce a call-by-value semantics, and are defined as follows.

Definition 2.

$$\begin{aligned}\mathbf{E} ::= {} & [\cdot] \mid \mathbf{E}\ \mathbf{t} \mid (\lambda x.\mathbf{t})\ \mathbf{E} \mid \mathtt{if}\ \mathbf{E}\ \mathtt{then}\ \mathbf{t}\ \mathtt{else}\ \mathbf{t} \\ & \mid g(c_1, \ldots, c_m, \mathbf{E}, \mathbf{t}_{m+2}, \ldots, \mathbf{t}_{|g|}) \\ & \mid \mathtt{sample}_D(c_1, \ldots, c_m, \mathbf{E}, \mathbf{t}_{m+2}, \ldots, \mathbf{t}_{|D|}) \mid \mathtt{weight}(\mathbf{E})\end{aligned} \tag{2}$$

We denote the set of all evaluation contexts by $\mathbb{E}$.

With the evaluation contexts in place, we proceed to define the *deterministic semantics* through a small-step relation $\rightarrow_{\mathrm{DET}}$.

Definition 3.

$$\frac{}{\mathbf{E}[(\lambda x.\mathbf{t})\ \mathbf{v}] \rightarrow_{\mathrm{DET}} \mathbf{E}[[x \mapsto \mathbf{v}]\mathbf{t}]}(\textsc{App}) \qquad \frac{c = \sigma_g(c_1, \ldots, c_{|g|})}{\mathbf{E}[g(c_1, \ldots, c_{|g|})] \rightarrow_{\mathrm{DET}} \mathbf{E}[c]}(\textsc{Prim})$$

$$\frac{}{\mathbf{E}[\mathtt{if}\ \mathit{true}\ \mathtt{then}\ \mathbf{t}_1\ \mathtt{else}\ \mathbf{t}_2] \rightarrow_{\mathrm{DET}} \mathbf{E}[\mathbf{t}_1]}(\textsc{IfTrue}) \tag{3}$$

$$\frac{}{\mathbf{E}[\mathtt{if}\ \mathit{false}\ \mathtt{then}\ \mathbf{t}_1\ \mathtt{else}\ \mathbf{t}_2] \rightarrow_{\mathrm{DET}} \mathbf{E}[\mathbf{t}_2]}(\textsc{IfFalse})$$

The rules are straightforward, and will not be discussed in further detail here. We use the standard notation for transitive and reflexive closures (e.g. $\rightarrow^*_{\mathrm{DET}}$), and transitive closures (e.g. $\rightarrow^+_{\mathrm{DET}}$) of relations throughout the paper.

Following the tradition of Kozen [18] and Park et al. [27], sampling in our stochastic semantics works by consuming randomness from a tape of real numbers. We use inverse transform sampling, and therefore the tape consists of numbers from the interval $[0,1]$. In order to use inverse transform sampling, we require that for each $D \in \mathbb{D}$, there exists a measurable function $F_D^{-1} : \mathbb{R}^{|D|} \times [0,1] \to \mathbb{R}$, such that $F_D^{-1}(c_1, \ldots, c_{|D|}, \cdot)$ is the *inverse cumulative distribution function* for the probability distribution corresponding to D and $(c_1, \ldots, c_{|D|})$. We call the tape of real numbers a *trace*, and make the following definition.

Definition 4. *Let* $\mathbb{N}_0 = \mathbb{N} \cup \{0\}$. *The set of all traces is* $\mathbb{S} = \bigcup_{n \in \mathbb{N}_0} [0,1]^n$.

We use the notation $(c_1, c_2, \ldots, c_n)_{\mathbb{S}}$ to indicate the trace consisting of the n numbers $c_1, c_2, \ldots, c_n$. Given a trace s, we denote by $|s|$ the length of the trace. We also denote the concatenation of two traces s and s' with $s * s'$. Lastly, we let $c :: s$ denote the extension of the trace s with the real number c as head.

With the traces and F_D^{-1} defined, we can proceed to the stochastic[6] semantics $\to$ over $\mathbb{T} \times \mathbb{R}_+ \times \mathbb{S}$.

Definition 5.

$$\mathbf{t}_{stop} ::= \mathbf{v} \mid \mathbf{E}[\mathtt{sample}_D(c_1, \ldots, c_{|D|})] \mid \mathbf{E}[\mathtt{weight}(c)] \mid \mathbf{E}[\mathtt{resample}] \tag{4}$$

$$\frac{\mathbf{t} \to_{\text{DET}}^{+} \mathbf{t}_{stop}}{\mathbf{t}, w, s \to \mathbf{t}_{stop}, w, s}(\text{DET}) \qquad \frac{c \geq 0}{\mathbf{E}[\mathtt{weight}(c)], w, s \to \mathbf{E}[()], w \cdot c, s}(\text{WEIGHT})$$

$$\frac{c = F_D^{-1}(c_1, \ldots, c_{|D|}, p)}{\mathbf{E}[\mathtt{sample}_D(c_1, \ldots, c_{|D|})], w, p :: s \to \mathbf{E}[c], w, s}(\text{SAMPLE}) \tag{5}$$

$$\frac{}{\mathbf{E}[\mathtt{resample}], w, s \to \mathbf{E}[()], w, s}(\text{RESAMPLE})$$

The rule (DET) encapsulates the $\to_{\text{DET}}$ relation, and states that terms can move deterministically only to terms of the form $\mathbf{t}_{stop}$. Note that terms of the form $\mathbf{t}_{stop}$ are found at the left-hand side in the other rules. The (SAMPLE) rule describes how random values are drawn from the inverse cumulative distribution functions and the trace when terms of the form $\mathtt{sample}_D(c_1, \ldots, c_{|D|})$ are encountered. Similarly, the WEIGHT rule determines how the weight is updated when $\mathtt{weight}(c)$ terms are encountered. Finally, the `resample` construct always evaluates to unit, and is therefore meaningless from the perspective of this semantics. We elaborate on the role of the `resample` construct in Section 3.3.

With the semantics in place, we define two important functions over $\mathbb{S}$ for a given term. In the below definition, assume that a fixed term $\mathbf{t}$ is given.

Definition 6.

$$r_{\mathbf{t}}(s) = \begin{cases} \mathbf{v} & \textit{if } \mathbf{t}, 1, s \to^* \mathbf{v}, w, ()_{\mathbb{S}} \\ () & \textit{otherwise} \end{cases} \qquad f_{\mathbf{t}}(s) = \begin{cases} w & \textit{if } \mathbf{t}, 1, s \to^* \mathbf{v}, w, ()_{\mathbb{S}} \\ 0 & \textit{otherwise} \end{cases} \tag{6}$$

[6] Note that the semantics models stochastic behavior, but is itself a deterministic relation.

Intuitively, $r_{\mathbf{t}}$ is the function returning the *result value* after having repeatedly applied $\rightarrow$ on the initial trace s. Analogously, $f_{\mathbf{t}}$ gives the *density* or *weight* of a particular s. Note that, if $(\mathbf{t}, 1, s)$ gets stuck or diverges, the result value is $()$, and the weight is 0. In other words, we disregard such traces entirely, since we are in practice only interested in probability distributions over values. Furthermore, note that if the final $s \neq ()_{\mathbb{S}}$, the value and weight are again $()$ and 0, respectively. The motivation for this is discussed in Section 4.3.

To illustrate $r_{\mathbf{t}}$, $f_{\mathbf{t}}$, and the `weight` construct, consider the program $\mathbf{t}_{obs}$ in Fig. 2b, and the singleton trace $(0.8)_{\mathbb{S}}$. This program will, in total, evaluate one call to `sample`, and three calls to `weight`. Now, let $h(c) = F_{Beta}^{-1}(2, 2, c)$ and recall the function $\sigma_{f_{Bern}}$ from Section 3.1. Using the notation $\phi(c, x) = \sigma_{f_{Bern}}(h(c), x)$, we have, for some evaluation contexts $\mathbf{E}_1, \mathbf{E}_2, \mathbf{E}_3, \mathbf{E}_4$,

$$\begin{aligned}
&\mathbf{t}_{obs}, 1, (0.8)_{\mathbb{S}} = \mathbf{E}_1[\mathtt{sample}_{Beta}(2,2)], 1, (0.8)_{\mathbb{S}} \rightarrow \mathbf{E}_1[h(0.8)], 1, ()_{\mathbb{S}} \\
&\rightarrow \mathbf{E}_2[\mathtt{weight}(\phi(0.8, \mathit{true}))], 1, ()_{\mathbb{S}} \rightarrow \mathbf{E}_2[()], \phi(0.8, \mathit{true}), ()_{\mathbb{S}} \\
&= \mathbf{E}_2[()], h(0.8), ()_{\mathbb{S}} \rightarrow^{+} \mathbf{E}_3[()], \phi(0.8, \mathit{false}) \cdot h(0.8), ()_{\mathbb{S}} \qquad (7) \\
&\rightarrow^{+} \mathbf{E}_4[()], \phi(0.8, \mathit{true}) \cdot (1 - h(0.8)) \cdot h(0.8), ()_{\mathbb{S}} \\
&\rightarrow^{+} h(0.8), h(0.8) \cdot (1 - h(0.8)) \cdot h(0.8), ()_{\mathbb{S}}.
\end{aligned}$$

That is, $r_{\mathbf{t}_{obs}}((0.8)_{\mathbb{S}}) = h(0.8)$ and $f_{\mathbf{t}_{obs}}((0.8)_{\mathbb{S}}) = h(0.8)^2(1 - h(0.8))$. For arbitrary c, we see that $r_{\mathbf{t}_{obs}}((c)_{\mathbb{S}}) = h(c)$ and $f_{\mathbf{t}_{obs}}((c)_{\mathbb{S}}) = h(c)^2(1 - h(c))$. For any other trace s with $|s| \neq 1$, $r_{\mathbf{t}_{obs}}(s) = ()$ and $f_{\mathbf{t}_{obs}}(s) = 0$. We will apply this result when reconsidering this example in Section 4.3.

3.3 Resampling Semantics

In order to connect SMC in PPLs to the classical formalization of SMC presented in Section 5—and thus enabling the theoretical treatments in Sections 6 and 7—we need a relation in which terms "stop" after a certain number n of encountered `resample` terms. In this section, we define such a relation, denoted by $\hookrightarrow$. Its definition is given below.

Definition 7.

$$\frac{\mathbf{t} \neq \mathbf{E}[\mathtt{resample}] \quad \mathbf{t}, w, s \rightarrow \mathbf{t}', w', s'}{\mathbf{t}, w, s, n \hookrightarrow \mathbf{t}', w', s', n}(\textsc{Stoch-Fin})$$

$$\frac{n > 0 \quad \mathbf{E}[\mathtt{resample}], w, s \rightarrow \mathbf{E}[()], w, s}{\mathbf{E}[\mathtt{resample}], w, s, n \hookrightarrow \mathbf{E}[()], w, s, n-1}(\textsc{Resample-Fin}) \qquad (8)$$

This relation is $\rightarrow$ extended with a natural number n, indicating how many further `resample` terms can be evaluated. We implement this limitation by replacing the rule (Resample) of $\rightarrow$ with (Resample-Fin) of $\hookrightarrow$ above which decrements n each time it is applied, causing terms to get stuck at the $n+1$th resample encountered.

Now, assume that a fixed term $\mathbf{t}$ is given. We define $r_{\mathbf{t},n}$ and $f_{\mathbf{t},n}$ similar to $r_{\mathbf{t}}$ and $f_{\mathbf{t}}$.

Definition 8. $r_{\mathbf{t},n}(s) = \begin{cases} \mathbf{v} & \textit{if } \mathbf{t}, 1, s, n \hookrightarrow^* \mathbf{v}, w, ()_{\mathbb{S}}, n' \\ \mathbf{E}[\texttt{resample}] & \textit{if } \mathbf{t}, 1, s, n \hookrightarrow^* \mathbf{E}[\texttt{resample}], w, ()_{\mathbb{S}}, 0 \\ () & \textit{otherwise} \end{cases}$

Definition 9. $f_{\mathbf{t},n}(s) = \begin{cases} w & \textit{if } \mathbf{t}, 1, s, n \hookrightarrow^* \mathbf{v}, w, ()_{\mathbb{S}}, n' \\ w & \textit{if } \mathbf{t}, 1, s, n \hookrightarrow^* \mathbf{E}[\texttt{resample}], w, ()_{\mathbb{S}}, 0 \\ 0 & \textit{otherwise} \end{cases}$

As for $r_{\mathbf{t}}$ and $f_{\mathbf{t}}$, these functions return the result value and weight, respectively, after having repeatedly applied $\hookrightarrow$ on the initial trace s. There is one difference compared to $\rightarrow$: besides values, we now also allow stopping with non-zero weight at terms of the form $\mathbf{E}[\texttt{resample}]$.

To illustrate $\hookrightarrow$, $r_{\mathbf{t},n}(s)$, and $f_{\mathbf{t},n}(s)$, consider the term $\mathbf{t}_{seq}$ defined by

$$\begin{aligned}&\texttt{let } \textit{observe } x\ o = \texttt{weight}(f_{\mathcal{N}}(x,4,o))\texttt{; resample in}\\ &\texttt{let } \textit{sim } x_{n-1}\ o_n =\\ &\quad \texttt{let } x_n = \texttt{sample}_{\mathcal{N}}(x_{n-1}+2,1) \texttt{ in } \textit{observe } x_n\ o_n\texttt{; } x_n \texttt{ in}\\ &\texttt{let } x_0 = \texttt{sample}_{\mathcal{U}}(0,100) \texttt{ in}\\ &\texttt{let } f = \textit{foldl sim} \texttt{ in } f\ x_0\ \texttt{[}c_1, c_2, \ldots, c_{t-1}, c_t\texttt{]}.\end{aligned} \tag{9}$$

This term encodes a model in which an object moves along a real-valued axis in discrete time steps, but where the actual positions (x_1, x_2, ...) can only be observed through a noisy sensor (c_1, c_2, ...). The inference problem consists of finding the probability distribution for the very last position, x_t, given all collected observations (c_1, c_2, ..., c_t). Most importantly, note the position of `resample` in (9)—it is evaluated just after evaluating `weight` in every folding step. Because of this, for $n < t$ and all traces s such that $f_{\mathbf{t}_{seq},n}(s) > 0$, we have $r_{\mathbf{t}_{seq},n}(s) = \mathbf{E}^n_{seq}[\texttt{resample; } x_n]$, where $\mathbf{E}^n_{seq} = f\ [\cdot]\ \texttt{[}c_{n+1}, c_{n+2}, \ldots, c_{t-1}, c_t\texttt{]}$ and where x_n is the value sampled in *sim* at the nth folding step. That is, we can now "stop" evaluation at `resample`s. We will revisit this example in Section 6.

4 The Target Measure of a Program

In this section, we define the *target measure* induced by any given program in our calculus. We assume basic familiarity with measure theory, Lebesgue integration, and Borel spaces. McDonald and Weiss [23] provide a pedagogical introduction to the subject. In order to define the target measure of a program as a Lebesgue integral (Section 4.3), we require a *measure space* on traces (Section 4.1), and a *measurable space* on terms (Section 4.2). For illustration, we derive the target measure for the example program from Section 3 in Section 4.3. The concepts presented in this section are quite standard, and experienced readers might want to quickly skim it, or even skip it entirely.

4.1 A Measure Space over Traces

We use a standard measure space over traces of samples [22]. First, we define a measurable space over traces. We denote the Borel σ-algebra on $\mathbb{R}^n$ with $\mathcal{B}^n$, and the Borel σ-algebra on $[0,1]$ with $\mathcal{B}^n_{[0,1]}$.

Definition 10. *The σ-algebra $\mathcal{S}$ on $\mathbb{S}$ is the σ-algebra consisting of sets of the form $S = \bigcup_{n\in\mathbb{N}_0} B_n$ with $B_n \in \mathcal{B}^n_{[0,1]}$. Naturally, $[0,1]^0$ is the singleton set containing the empty trace. In other words, $([0,1]^0, \mathcal{B}^0_{[0,1]}) = (\{()_\mathbb{S}\}, \{\{()_\mathbb{S}\}, \emptyset\})$, where $()_\mathbb{S}$ denotes the empty trace.*

Lemma 1. $(\mathbb{S}, \mathcal{S})$ *is a measurable space.*†

The most common measure on $\mathcal{B}^n$ is the n-dimensional Lebesgue measure, denoted λ_n. For $n = 0$, we let $\lambda_0 = \delta_{()_\mathbb{S}}$, where δ denotes the standard Dirac measure. By combining the Lebesgue measures for each n, we construct a measure $\mu_\mathbb{S}$ over $(\mathbb{S}, \mathcal{S})$.

Definition 11. $\mu_\mathbb{S}(S) = \mu_\mathbb{S}\left(\bigcup_{n\in\mathbb{N}_0} B_n\right) = \sum_{n\in\mathbb{N}_0} \lambda_n(B_n)$

Lemma 2. $(\mathbb{S}, \mathcal{S}, \mu_\mathbb{S})$ *is a measure space. Furthermore, $\mu_\mathbb{S}$ is σ-finite.*†

A comment on notation: we denote universal sets by blackboard bold capital letters (e.g., $\mathbb{S}$), σ-algebras by calligraphic capital letters (e.g., $\mathcal{S}$), members of σ-algebras by capital letters (e.g., S), and individual elements by lower case letters (e.g., s).

4.2 A Measurable Space over Terms

In order to show that $r_\mathbf{t}$ is measurable, we need a measurable space over terms. We let $(\mathbb{T}, \mathcal{T})$ denote the measurable space that we seek to construct, and follow the approach in Staton et al. [35] and Vákár et al. [39]. Because our calculus includes the reals, we would like to at least have $\mathcal{B} \subset \mathcal{T}$. Furthermore, we would also like to extend the Borel measurable sets $\mathcal{B}^n$ to terms with n reals as subterms. For instance, we want sets of the form $\{(\lambda x.\ (\lambda y.\ x + y)\ c_2)\ c_1 \mid (c_1, c_2) \in B_2\}$ to be measurable, where $B_2 \in \mathcal{B}^2$. This leads us to consider terms in a language in which constants (i.e., reals) are replaced with placeholders $[\cdot]$.

Definition 12. *Let $\mathbf{v}_p ::= [\cdot] \mid \lambda x.\mathbf{t}$ replace the values $\mathbf{v}$ from Definition 1. The set of all terms in the resulting new calculus is denoted with $\mathbb{T}_p$.*

Most importantly, it is easy to verify that $\mathbb{T}_p$ is countable. Next, we make the following definitions.

Definition 13. *For $n \in \mathbb{N}_0$, we denote by $\mathbb{T}^n_p \subset \mathbb{T}_p$ the set of all terms with exactly n placeholders.*

Definition 14. *We let $\mathbf{t}^n_p$ range over the elements of $\mathbb{T}^n_p$. The $\mathbf{t}^n_p$ can be regarded as functions $\mathbf{t}^n_p : \mathbb{R}^n \to \mathbf{t}^n_p(\mathbb{R}_n)$ which replaces the n placeholders with the n reals given as arguments.*

Definition 15. $\mathcal{T}_{\mathbf{t}_p^n} = \{\mathbf{t}_p^n(B_n) \mid B_n \in \mathcal{B}^n\}$.

From the above definitions, we construct the required σ-algebra $\mathcal{T}$.

Definition 16. *The σ-algebra $\mathcal{T}$ on $\mathbb{T}$ is the σ-algebra consisting of sets of the form* $T = \bigcup_{n \in N_0} \bigcup_{\mathbf{t}_p^n \in \mathbb{T}_p^n} \mathbf{t}_p^n(B_n)$.

Lemma 3. $(\mathbb{T}, \mathcal{T})$ *is a measurable space.*†

4.3 The Target Measure

We are now in a position to define the target measure. We will first give the formal definitions, and then illustrate the definitions with an example. The definitions rely on the following result.

Lemma 4. $r_{\mathbf{t}} : (\mathbb{S}, \mathcal{S}) \to (\mathbb{T}, \mathcal{T})$ *and* $f_{\mathbf{t}} : (\mathbb{S}, \mathcal{S}) \to (\mathbb{R}_+, \mathcal{B}_+)$ *are measurable.*†

We can now proceed to define the measure $\langle\!\langle \mathbf{t} \rangle\!\rangle$ over $\mathbb{S}$ induced by a term $\mathbf{t}$ using Lebesgue integration.

Definition 17. $\langle\!\langle \mathbf{t} \rangle\!\rangle(S) = \int_S f_{\mathbf{t}}(s) \; d\mu_{\mathbb{S}}(s)$

Using Definition 17 and the measurability of $r_{\mathbf{t}}$, we can also define a corresponding pushforward measure $[\![\mathbf{t}]\!]$ over $\mathbb{T}$.

Definition 18. $[\![\mathbf{t}]\!](T) = \langle\!\langle \mathbf{t} \rangle\!\rangle(r_{\mathbf{t}}^{-1}(T)) = \int_{r_{\mathbf{t}}^{-1}(T)} f_{\mathbf{t}}(s) \; d\mu_{\mathbb{S}}(s)$.

The measure $[\![\mathbf{t}]\!]$ is our *target measure*, i.e., the measure encoded by our program that we are interested in.

Let us now consider the target measure for the program given by $\mathbf{t}_{obs}$. It is not too difficult to show that $[\![\mathbf{t}_{obs}]\!](T) = \int_{T \cap \mathbb{R}} c^3(1-c)^2 \; d\lambda(c)$. We recognize the integrand as the density for the *Beta*(4, 3) distribution, which, as expected, is exactly the graph shown in Fig. 2c.

We should in some way ensure the target measure is finite (i.e., can be normalized to a probability measure), since we are in the end most often only interested in probability measures. Unfortunately, as observed by Staton [34], there is no known useful syntactic restriction that enforces finite measures in PPLs while still admitting weights > 1. We will discuss this further in Section 6.2 in relation to SMC in our calculus.

Lastly, from Section 3.2, recall that we disallow non-empty final traces in $f_{\mathbf{t}}$ and $r_{\mathbf{t}}$. We see here why this is needed: if allowed, for every trace s with $f_{\mathbf{t}}(s) > 0$, *all* extensions $s * s'$ have the same density $f_{\mathbf{t}}(s * s') = f_{\mathbf{t}}(s) > 0$. From this, it is easy to check that if $[\![\mathbf{t}]\!] \neq 0$ (the zero measure), then $[\![\mathbf{t}]\!](\mathbb{T}) = \infty$ (i.e., the measure is not finite). In fact, for any $T \in \mathcal{T}$, $[\![\mathbf{t}]\!](T) > 0 \implies [\![\mathbf{t}]\!](T) = \infty$. Clearly, this is not a useful target measure.

5 Formal SMC

In this section, we give a generic formalization of SMC based on Chopin [6]. We assume a basic understanding of SMC. For a complete introduction to SMC, we recommend Naesseth et al. [26] and Doucet and Johansen [10].

First, in Section 5.1, we introduce transition kernels, which is a fundamental concept used in the remaining sections of the paper. Second, in Section 5.2, we describe Chopin's generic formalization of SMC as an algorithm for approximating a sequence of distributions based on a sequence of approximating transition kernels. Lastly, in Section 5.3, we give standard correctness results for the algorithm.

5.1 Preliminaries: Transition Kernels

Intuitively, transition kernels describe how elements move between measurable spaces. For a more comprehensive introduction, see Vákár and Ong [40].

Definition 19. *Let* $(\mathbb{A}, \mathcal{A})$ *and* $(\mathbb{A}', \mathcal{A}')$ *be measurable spaces, and let* $\mathcal{B}_+^* = \{B \mid B \setminus \{\infty\} \in \mathcal{B}_+\}$*. A function* $k : \mathbb{A} \times \mathcal{A}' \to \mathbb{R}_+^*$ *is a* (transition) kernel *if (1) for all* $a \in \mathbb{A}$, $k(a, \cdot) : \mathcal{A}' \to \mathbb{R}_+^*$ *is a measure on* $\mathcal{A}'$*, and (2) for all* $A' \in \mathcal{A}'$, $k(\cdot, A') : (\mathbb{A}, \mathcal{A}) \to (\mathbb{R}_+^*, \mathcal{B}_+^*)$ *is measurable.*

Additionally, we can classify transition kernels according to the below definition.

Definition 20. *Let* $(\mathbb{A}, \mathcal{A})$ *and* $(\mathbb{A}', \mathcal{A}')$ *be measurable spaces. A kernel* $k : \mathbb{A} \times \mathcal{A}' \to \mathbb{R}_+^*$ *is a* sub-probability kernel *if* $k(a, \cdot)$ *is a sub-probability measure for all* $a \in \mathbb{A}$*; a* probability kernel *if* $k(a, \cdot)$ *is a probability measure for all* $a \in \mathbb{A}$*; and a* finite kernel *if* $\sup_{a \in \mathbb{A}} k(a, \mathbb{A}') < \infty$.

5.2 Algorithm

The starting point in Chopin's formulation of SMC is a sequence of probability measures π_n (over respective measurable spaces $(\mathbb{A}_n, \mathcal{A}_n)$, with $n \in \mathbb{N}_0$) that are difficult or impossible to directly draw samples from.

The SMC approach is to generate samples from the π_n by first sampling from a sequence of *proposal measures* q_n, and then correcting for the discrepancy between these measures by weighting the proposal samples. The proposal distributions are generated from an initial measure q_0 and a sequence of transition kernels $k_n : \mathbb{A}_{n-1} \times \mathcal{A}_n \to [0, 1], n \in \mathbb{N}$ as

$$q_n(A_n) = \int_{\mathbb{A}_{n-1}} k_n(a_{n-1}, A_n)\, d\pi_{n-1}(a_{n-1}). \tag{10}$$

In order to approximate π_n by weighting samples from q_n, we need some way of obtaining the appropriate weights. Hence, we require each measurable space $(\mathbb{A}_n, \mathcal{A}_n)$ to have a default σ-finite measure $\mu_{\mathbb{A}_n}$, and the measures π_n and q_n to

Algorithm 1 A generic formulation of sequential Monte Carlo inference based on Chopin [6]. In each step, we let $1 \leq j \leq J$, where J is the number of samples.

1. **Initialization:** Set $n = 0$. Draw $a_0^j \sim q_0$ for $1 \leq j \leq J$.
   The empirical distribution given by $\{a_0^j\}_{j=1}^J$ approximates q_0.
2. **Correction:** Calculate $w_n^j = \frac{f_{\widetilde{\pi}_n}(a_n^j)}{f_{\widetilde{q}_n}(a_n^j)}$.
   The empirical distribution given by $\{(a_n^j, w_n^j)\}_{j=1}^J$ approximates π_n.
3. **Selection:** Resample the empirical distribution $\{(a_n^j, w_n^j)\}_{j=1}^J$.
   The new empirical distribution is unweighted and is given by $\{\hat{a}_n^j\}_{j=1}^J$. This distribution also approximates π_n.
4. **Mutation:** Increment n.
   Draw $a_n^j \sim k_n(\hat{a}_{n-1}^j, \cdot)$ for $1 \leq j \leq J$. The empirical distribution given by $\{a_n^j\}_{j=1}^J$ approximates q_n. Go to (2).

have densities f_{π_n} and f_{q_n} with respect to this default measure. Furthermore, we require that the functions f_{π_n} and f_{q_n} can be efficiently computed pointwise, up to an unknown constant factor per function and value of n. More precisely, we can efficiently compute the densities $f_{\widetilde{\pi}_n} = Z_{\widetilde{\pi}_n} \cdot f_{\pi_n}$ and $f_{\widetilde{q}_n} = Z_{\widetilde{q}_n} \cdot f_{q_n}$, corresponding to the unnormalized measures $\widetilde{\pi}_n = Z_{\widetilde{\pi}_n} \cdot \pi_n$ and $\widetilde{q}_n = Z_{\widetilde{q}_n} \cdot q_n$. Here, $Z_{\widetilde{\pi}_n} = \widetilde{\pi}_n(\mathbb{A}_n) \in \mathbb{R}_+$ and $Z_{\widetilde{q}_n} = \widetilde{q}_n(\mathbb{A}_n) \in \mathbb{R}_+$ denote the unknown *normalizing constants* for the distributions $\widetilde{\pi}_n$ and $\widetilde{q}_n$.

Algorithm 1 presents a generic version of SMC [6] for approximating π_n. We make the notion of approximation used in the algorithm precise in Section 5.3. Note that in the correction step, the unnormalized pointwise evaluation of f_{π_n} and f_{q_n} is used to calculate the weights. In the algorithm description, we also use some new terminology. First, an *empirical distribution* is the discrete probability measure formed by a finite set of possibly weighted samples $\{(a_n^j, w_n^j)\}_{j=1}^J$, where $a_n^j \in \mathbb{A}_n$ and $w_n^j \in \mathbb{R}_+$. Second, when *resampling* an empirical distribution, we sample J times from it (with replacement), with each sample having its normalized weight as probability of being sampled. More specifically, this is known as *multinomial resampling.* Other resampling schemes also exist [8], and are often used in practice to reduce variance. After resampling, the set of samples forms a new empirical distribution with J unweighted (all $w_n^j = 1$) samples.

An important feature of SMC compared to other inference algorithms is that SMC produces, as a by-product of inference, unbiased estimates $\hat{Z}_{\widetilde{\pi}_n}$ of the normalizing constants $Z_{\widetilde{\pi}_n}$. Stated differently, this means that Algorithm 1 not only approximates the π_n, but also the unnormalized versions $\widetilde{\pi}_n$. From the weights w_n^j in Algorithm 1, the estimates are given by

$$\hat{Z}_{\widetilde{\pi}_n} = \prod_{i=0}^{n} \frac{1}{J} \sum_{j=1}^{J} w_i^j \approx Z_{\widetilde{\pi}_n} \tag{11}$$

for each $\widetilde{\pi}_n$. We give the unbiasedness result of $\hat{Z}_{\widetilde{\pi}_n}$ in Lemma 5 (item 2) below. The normalizing constant is often used to compare the accuracy of different probabilistic models, and as such, it is also known as the *marginal likelihood*, or *model evidence*. For an example application, see Ronquist et al. [30].

To conclude this section, note that many sequences of probability kernels k_n can be used to approximate the same sequence of measures π_n. The only requirement on the k_n is that $f_{\pi_n}(a_n) > 0 \implies f_{q_n}(a_n) > 0$ must hold for all $n \in \mathbb{N}_0$ and $a_n \in \mathbb{A}_n$ (i.e., the proposals must "cover" the π_n) [9]. We call such a sequence of kernels k_n *valid*. Different choices of k_n induce different proposals q_n, and hence capture different SMC algorithms. The most common example is the BPF, which directly uses the kernels from the model as the sequence of kernels in the SMC algorithm (hence the "bootstrap"). In Section 7.1, we formalize the bootstrap kernels in the context of our calculus. However, we may want to choose other probability kernels that satisfy the covering condition, since the choice of kernels can have major implications for the rate of convergence [28].

5.3 Correctness

We begin by defining the notion of approximation used in Algorithm 1.

Definition 21 (Based on Chopin [6, p. 2387]). *Let* $(\mathbb{A}, \mathcal{A})$ *denote a measurable space,* $\{\{(a^{j,J}, w^{j,J})\}_{j=1}^{J}\}_{J\in\mathbb{N}}$ *a triangular array of random variables in* $\mathbb{A} \times \mathbb{R}$*, and* $\pi : \mathcal{A} \to \mathbb{R}_+^*$ *a probability measure. We say that* $\{\{(a^{j,J}, w^{j,J})\}_{j=1}^{J}\}_{J\in\mathbb{N}}$ *approximates* π *if the equality* $\lim_{J\to\infty} \frac{\sum_{j=1}^{J} w^{j,J}\varphi(a^{j,J})}{\sum_{j=1}^{J} w^{j,J}} = \mathbb{E}_\pi(\varphi)$ *holds almost surely for all measurable functions* $\varphi : (\mathbb{A}, \mathcal{A}) \to (\mathbb{R}, \mathcal{B})$ *such that* $\mathbb{E}_\pi(\varphi)$*—the expected value of the function* φ *over the distribution* π*—exists.*

First, note that the triangular array can also be viewed as a sequence of random empirical distributions (indexed by J). Precisely such sequences are formed by the random empirical distributions in Algorithm 1 when indexed by the increasing number of samples J. For simplicity, we often let context determine the sequence, and directly state that a random empirical distribution approximates some distribution (as in Algorithm 1).

Two classical results in SMC literature are given in the following lemma: a law of large numbers and the unbiasedness of the normalizing constant estimate. We take these results as the definition of SMC correctness used in this paper.

Lemma 5. *Let* π_n*,* $n \in \mathbb{N}_0$*, be a sequence of probability measures over measurable spaces* $(\mathbb{A}_n, \mathcal{A}_n)$ *with default* σ*-finite measures* $\mu_{\mathbb{A}_n}$*, such that the* π_n *have densities* f_{π_n} *with respect to these default measures. Furthermore, let* q_0 *be a probability measure with density* f_{q_0} *with respect to* $\mu_{\mathbb{A}_0}$*, and* k_n *a sequence of probability kernels inducing a sequence of proposal probability measures* q_n*, given by* (10)*, over* $(\mathbb{A}_n, \mathcal{A}_n)$ *with densities* f_{q_n} *with respect to* $\mu_{\mathbb{A}_n}$*. Also, assume the* k_n *are valid, i.e., that that* $f_{\pi_n}(a_n) > 0 \implies f_{q_n}(a_n) > 0$ *holds for all* $n \in \mathbb{N}_0$ *and* $a_n \in \mathbb{A}_n$*. Then*

1. *the empirical distributions* $\{(a_n^j, w_n^j)\}_{j=1}^{J}$ *and* $\{\hat{a}_n^j\}_{j=1}^{J}$ *produced by Algorithm 1 approximate* π_n *for each* $n \in \mathbb{N}_0$*; and*

2. $\mathbb{E}(\hat{Z}_{\widetilde{\pi}_n}) = Z_{\widetilde{\pi}_n}$ *for each* $n \in \mathbb{N}_0$*, where the expectation is taken with respect to the weights produced when running Algorithm 1, and* $\hat{Z}_{\widetilde{\pi}_n}$ *is given by* (11).

Proof. As referenced in Naesseth et al. [26], see Del Moral [7][Theorem 7.4.3] for 1. For 2, see Naesseth et al. [26][Appendix 4.A].

Chopin [6][Theorem 1] gives another SMC convergence result in the form of a central limit. This result, however, requires further restrictions on the weights w_n^j in Algorithm 1. It is not clear when these restrictions are fulfilled when applying SMC on a program in our calculus. This is an interesting topic for future work.

6 Formal SMC for Probabilistic Programming Languages

This section contains our main contribution: how to interpret the operational semantics of our calculus as the unnormalized sequence of measures $\widetilde{\pi}_n$ in Chopin's formalization (Section 6.1), as well as sufficient conditions for this sequence of approximating measures to converge to $\langle\!\langle \mathbf{t} \rangle\!\rangle$ and for the normalizing constant estimate to be correct (Section 6.2).

An important insight during this work was that it is more convenient to find an approximating sequence of measures $\langle\!\langle \mathbf{t} \rangle\!\rangle_n$ to the trace measure $\langle\!\langle \mathbf{t} \rangle\!\rangle$, compared to finding a sequence of measures $[\![\mathbf{t}]\!]_n$ directly approximating the target measure $[\![\mathbf{t}]\!]$. In Section 6.1, we define $\langle\!\langle \mathbf{t} \rangle\!\rangle_n$ similarly to $\langle\!\langle \mathbf{t} \rangle\!\rangle$, except that at most n evaluations of `resample` are allowed. This upper bound on the number of `resample`s is formalized through the relation $\hookrightarrow$ from Section 3.3.

In Section 6.2, we obtain two different conditions for the convergence of the sequence $\langle\!\langle \mathbf{t} \rangle\!\rangle_n$ to $\langle\!\langle \mathbf{t} \rangle\!\rangle$: Theorem 1 states that for programs with an upper bound N on the number of `resample`s they evaluate, $\langle\!\langle \mathbf{t} \rangle\!\rangle_N = \langle\!\langle \mathbf{t} \rangle\!\rangle$. This precondition holds in many practical settings, for instance where each resampling is connected to a datum collected before inference starts. Theorem 2 states another convergence result for programs without such an upper bound but with dominated weights. Because of these convergence results, we can often approximate $\langle\!\langle \mathbf{t} \rangle\!\rangle$ by approximating $\langle\!\langle \mathbf{t} \rangle\!\rangle_n$ with Algorithm 1. When this is the case, Lemma 5 implies that Algorithm 1, either after a sufficient number of time steps or asymptotically, correctly approximates $\langle\!\langle \mathbf{t} \rangle\!\rangle$ and the normalizing constant $Z_{\langle\!\langle \mathbf{t} \rangle\!\rangle}$. This is the content of Theorem 3. We conclude Section 6.2 by discussing `resample` placements and their relation to Theorem 3, as well as practical implications of Theorem 3.

6.1 The Sequence of Measures Generated by a Program

We now apply the formalization from Section 4.3 again, but with $f_{\mathbf{t},n}$ and $r_{\mathbf{t},n}$ (from Section 3.3) replacing $f_{\mathbf{t}}$ and $r_{\mathbf{t}}$. Intuitively, this yields a sequence of measures $[\![\mathbf{t}]\!]_n$ indexed by n, which are similar to $[\![\mathbf{t}]\!]$, but only allow for evaluating at most n resamples. To illustrate this idea, consider again the program $\mathbf{t}_{seq}$ in (9). Here, $[\![\mathbf{t}_{seq}]\!]_0$ is a distribution over terms of the form $\mathbf{E}^1_{seq}[$`resample;` $x_1]$, $[\![\mathbf{t}_{seq}]\!]_1$ a distribution over terms of the form $\mathbf{E}^2_{seq}[$`resample;` $x_2]$, and so forth.

For $n \geq t$, $[\![\mathbf{t}_{seq}]\!]_n = [\![\mathbf{t}_{seq}]\!]$, because it is clear that t is an upper bound on the number of resamples evaluated in $\mathbf{t}_{seq}$.

While the measures $[\![\mathbf{t}]\!]_n$ are useful for giving intuition, it is easier from a technical perspective to define and work with $\langle\!\langle \mathbf{t} \rangle\!\rangle_n$, the sequence of measures over *traces* where at most n `resamples` are allowed. First, we need the following result, analogous to Lemma 4.

Lemma 6. *$r_{\mathbf{t},n} : (\mathbb{S}, \mathcal{S}) \to (\mathbb{T}, \mathcal{T})$ and $f_{\mathbf{t},n} : (\mathbb{S}, \mathcal{S}) \to (\mathbb{R}_+, \mathcal{B}_+)$ are measurable.*†

This allows us to define $\langle\!\langle \mathbf{t} \rangle\!\rangle_n$ (cf. Definition 17).

Definition 22. $\langle\!\langle \mathbf{t} \rangle\!\rangle_n(S) = \int_S f_{\mathbf{t},n}(s)\ d\mu_{\mathbb{S}}(s)$

6.2 Correctness

We begin with a convergence result for when the number of calls to `resample` in a program is upper bounded.

Theorem 1. *If there is $N \in \mathbb{N}$ such that $f_{\mathbf{t},n} = f_{\mathbf{t}}$ whenever $n > N$, then $\langle\!\langle \mathbf{t} \rangle\!\rangle_n = \langle\!\langle \mathbf{t} \rangle\!\rangle$ for all $n > N$.*

This follows directly since $f_{\mathbf{t},n}$ not only converges to $f_{\mathbf{t}}$, but is also equal to $f_{\mathbf{t}}$ for all $n > N$. However, even if the number of calls to `resample` in $\mathbf{t}$ is upper bounded, there is still one concern with using $\langle\!\langle \mathbf{t} \rangle\!\rangle_n$ as $\widetilde{\pi}_n$ in Algorithm 1: there is no guarantee that the measures $\langle\!\langle \mathbf{t} \rangle\!\rangle_n$ can be normalized to probability measures and have unique densities (i.e., that they are finite). This is a requirement for the correctness results in Lemma 5. Unfortunately, recall from Section 4.3 that there is no known useful syntactic restriction that enforces finiteness of the target measure. This is clearly true for the measures $\langle\!\langle \mathbf{t} \rangle\!\rangle_n$ as well, and as such, we need to *make the assumption* that the $\langle\!\langle \mathbf{t} \rangle\!\rangle_n$ are finite—otherwise, it is not clear that Algorithm 1 produces the correct result, since the conditions in Lemma 5 are not fulfilled. Fortunately, this assumption is valid for most, if not all, models of practical interest. Nevertheless, investigating whether or not the restriction to probability measures in Lemma 5 can be lifted to some extent is an interesting topic for future work.

Although of limited practical interest, programs with an unbounded number of calls to `resample` are of interest from a semantic perspective. If we have $\lim_{n\to\infty} \langle\!\langle \mathbf{t} \rangle\!\rangle_n = \langle\!\langle \mathbf{t} \rangle\!\rangle$ pointwise, then any SMC algorithm approximating the sequence $\langle\!\langle \mathbf{t} \rangle\!\rangle_n$ also approximates $\langle\!\langle \mathbf{t} \rangle\!\rangle$, at least asymptotically in the number of steps n. First, consider the program $\mathbf{t}_{geo\text{-}res}$ given by

```
let rec geometric _ =
  resample; if sample_bern(0.6) then 1 + geometric () else 1        (12)
in geometric ().
```

Note that $\mathbf{t}_{geo\text{-}res}$ has no upper bound on the number of calls to `resample`, and therefore Theorem 1 is not applicable. It is easy, however, to check that $\lim_{n\to\infty} \langle\!\langle \mathbf{t}_{geo\text{-}res} \rangle\!\rangle_n = \langle\!\langle \mathbf{t}_{geo\text{-}res} \rangle\!\rangle$ pointwise. So does $\lim_{n\to\infty} \langle\!\langle \mathbf{t} \rangle\!\rangle_n = \langle\!\langle \mathbf{t} \rangle\!\rangle$ pointwise hold in general? The answer is no, as we demonstrate next.

For $\lim_{n\to\infty}\langle\!\langle \mathbf{t}\rangle\!\rangle_n = \langle\!\langle \mathbf{t}\rangle\!\rangle$ to hold pointwise, it must hold that $\lim_{n\to\infty} f_{\mathbf{t},n} = f_{\mathbf{t}}$ pointwise $\mu_{\mathbb{S}}$-ae. Unfortunately, this does not hold for all programs. Consider the program $\mathbf{t}_{loop}$ defined by `let rec loop _ = resample; loop () in loop ()`. Here, $f_{\mathbf{t}_{loop}} = 0$ since the program diverges deterministically, but $f_{\mathbf{t}_{loop},n}(()_{\mathbb{S}}) = 1$ for all n. Because $\mu_{\mathbb{S}}(\{()_{\mathbb{S}}\}) \neq 0$, we do not have $\lim_{n\to\infty} f_{\mathbf{t}_{loop},n} = f_{\mathbf{t}_{loop}}$ pointwise $\mu_{\mathbb{S}}$-ae.

Even if we have $\lim_{n\to\infty} f_{\mathbf{t},n} = f_{\mathbf{t}}$ pointwise $\mu_{\mathbb{S}}$-ae, we might not have $\lim_{n\to\infty}\langle\!\langle \mathbf{t}\rangle\!\rangle_n = \langle\!\langle \mathbf{t}\rangle\!\rangle$ pointwise. Consider, for instance, the program $\mathbf{t}_{unit}$ given by

```
let s = sampleU(0,1) in
let rec foo n =
  if s ≤ 1/n then resample; weight 2; foo (2·n) else weight 0 in      (13)
foo 1
```

We have $f_{\mathbf{t}_{unit}} = 0$ and $f_{\mathbf{t}_{unit},n} = 2^n \cdot \mathbf{1}_{[0,1/2^n]}$ for $n > 0$. Also, $\lim_{n\to\infty} f_{\mathbf{t}_{unit},n} = f_{\mathbf{t}_{unit}}$ pointwise. However, $\lim_{n\to\infty}\langle\!\langle \mathbf{t}_{unit}\rangle\!\rangle_n(\mathbb{S}) = 1 \neq 0 = \langle\!\langle \mathbf{t}_{unit}\rangle\!\rangle(\mathbb{S})$. This shows that the limit may fail to hold, even for programs that terminate almost surely, as is the case for the program $\mathbf{t}_{unit}$ in (13). In fact, this program is positively almost surely terminating [4] since the expected number of recursive calls to `foo` is 1.

Guided by the previous example, we now state the dominated convergence theorem—a fundamental result in measure theory—in the context of SMC inference in our calculus.

Theorem 2. *Assume that* $\lim_{n\to\infty} f_{\mathbf{t},n} = f_{\mathbf{t}}$ *holds pointwise* $\mu_{\mathbb{S}}$*-ae. Furthermore, assume that there exists a measurable function* $g : (\mathbb{S}, \mathcal{S}) \to (\mathbb{R}_+, \mathcal{B}_+)$ *such that* $f_{\mathbf{t},n} \leq g$ $\mu_{\mathbb{S}}$*-ae for all* n*, and* $\int_{\mathbb{S}} g(s) d\mu_{\mathbb{S}}(s) < \infty$*. Then* $\lim_{n\to\infty}\langle\!\langle \mathbf{t}\rangle\!\rangle_n = \langle\!\langle \mathbf{t}\rangle\!\rangle$ *pointwise.*

For a proof, see McDonald and Weiss [23, Theorem 4.9]. It is easy to check that for our example in (13), there is no dominating and integrable g as is required in Theorem 2. We have already seen that the conclusion of the theorem fails to hold here. As a corollary, if there exists a dominating and integrable g, the measures $\langle\!\langle \mathbf{t}\rangle\!\rangle_n$ are always finite.

Corollary 1. *If there exists a measurable function* $g : (\mathbb{S}, \mathcal{S}) \to (\mathbb{R}_+, \mathcal{B}_+)$ *such that* $f_{\mathbf{t},n} \leq g$ $\mu_{\mathbb{S}}$*-ae for all* n*, and* $\int_{\mathbb{S}} g(s) d\mu_{\mathbb{S}}(s) < \infty$*, then* $\langle\!\langle \mathbf{t}\rangle\!\rangle_n$ *is finite for each* $n \in \mathbb{N}_0$*.*

This holds because $\langle\!\langle \mathbf{t}\rangle\!\rangle_n(\mathbb{S}) = \int_{\mathbb{S}} f_{\mathbf{t},n}(s) d\mu_{\mathbb{S}}(s) \leq \int_{\mathbb{S}} g(s) d\mu_{\mathbb{S}}(s) < \infty$. Hence, we do not need to assume the finiteness of $\langle\!\langle \mathbf{t}\rangle\!\rangle_n$ in order for Algorithm 1 to be applicable, as was the case for the setting of Theorem 1.

In Theorem 3, we summarize and combine the above results with Lemma 5.

Theorem 3. *Let* $\mathbf{t}$ *be a term, and apply Algorithm 1 with* $\langle\!\langle \mathbf{t}\rangle\!\rangle_n$ *as* $\widetilde{\pi}_n$*, and with arbitrary valid kernels* k_n*. If the condition of Theorem 1 holds and* $\langle\!\langle \mathbf{t}\rangle\!\rangle_n$ *is finite for each* $n \in \mathbb{N}_0$*, then Algorithm 1 approximates* $\langle\!\langle \mathbf{t}\rangle\!\rangle$ *and its normalizing constant after a finite number of steps. Alternatively, if the condition of Theorem 2* *holds, then Algorithm 1 approximates* $\langle\!\langle \mathbf{t} \rangle\!\rangle$ *and its normalizing constant in the limit* $n \to \infty$.

This follows directly from Theorem 1, Theorem 2, and Lemma 5.

We conclude this section by discussing `resample` placements, and the practical implications of Theorem 3. First, we define a `resample` *placement* for a term $\mathbf{t}$ as the term resulting from replacing arbitrary subterms $\mathbf{t}'$ of $\mathbf{t}$ with `resample;` $\mathbf{t}'$. Note that such a placement directly corresponds to constructing the sequence $\langle\!\langle \mathbf{t} \rangle\!\rangle_n$. Second, note that the measure $\langle\!\langle \mathbf{t} \rangle\!\rangle$ and the target measure $[\![\mathbf{t}]\!]$ are clearly *unaffected* by such a placement—indeed, `resample` simply evaluates to (), and for $\langle\!\langle \mathbf{t} \rangle\!\rangle$ and $[\![\mathbf{t}]\!]$, there is no bound on how many `resamples` we can evaluate. As such, we conclude that *all* resample placements in $\mathbf{t}$ fulfilling one of the two conditions in Theorem 3 leads to a correct approximation of $\langle\!\langle \mathbf{t} \rangle\!\rangle$ when applying Algorithm 1. Furthermore, there is always, in practice, an upper bound on the number of calls to `resample`, since any concrete run of SMC has an (explicit or implicit) upper bound on its runtime. This is a powerful result, since it implies that when implementing SMC for PPLs, any method for selecting resampling locations in a program is correct under mild conditions (Theorem 1 or Theorem 2) that are most often, if not always, fulfilled in practice. Most importantly, this justifies the basic approach for placing `resamples` found in WebPPL, Anglican, and Birch, in which every call to `weight` is directly followed (implicitly) by a call to `resample`. It also justifies the approach to placing `resamples` described in Lundén et al. [21]. This latter approach is essential in, e.g., Ronquist et al. [30], in order to increase inference efficiency.

Our results also show that the restriction in Anglican requiring all executions to encounter the same number of `resamples`, is too conservative. Clearly, this is not a requirement in either Theorem 1 or Theorem 2. For instance, the number of calls to `resample` varies significantly in (12).

7 SMC Algorithms

In this section, we take a look at how the kernels k_n in Algorithm 1 can be instantiated to yield the concrete SMC algorithm known as the bootstrap particle filter (Section 7.1), and also discuss other SMC algorithms and how they relate to Algorithm 1 (Section 7.2).

7.1 The Bootstrap Particle Filter

We define for each term $\mathbf{t}$ a particular sequence of kernels $k_{\mathbf{t},n}$, that gives rise to the SMC algorithm known as the bootstrap particle filter (BPF). Informally, these kernels correspond to simply continuing to evaluate the program until either arriving at a value $\mathbf{v}$ or a term of the form $\mathbf{E}$[`resample`]. For the bootstrap kernel, calculating the weights w_n^j from Algorithm 1 is particularly simple.

Similarly to $\langle\!\langle \mathbf{t} \rangle\!\rangle_n$, it is more convenient to define and work with sequences of kernels over traces, rather than terms. We will define $k_{\mathbf{t},n}(s, \cdot)$ to be the sub-probability measure over extended traces $s * s'$ resulting from evaluating the term $r_{\mathbf{t},n-1}(s)$ until the next `resample` or value $\mathbf{v}$, ignoring any call to `weight`. First, we immediately have that the set of all traces that do not have s as prefix must have measure zero. To make this formal, we will use the inverse images of the functions $prepend_s(s') = s * s'$, $s \in \mathbb{S}$ in the definition of the kernel.

Lemma 7. *The functions* $prepend_s : (\mathbb{S}, \mathcal{S}) \to (\mathbb{S}, \mathcal{S})$ *are measurable.*†

The next ingredient for defining the kernels $k_{\mathbf{t},n}$ is a function $p_{\mathbf{t},n}$ that indicates what traces are possible when executing $\mathbf{t}$ until the $n+1$th `resample` or value.

Definition 23. $p_{\mathbf{t},n}(s) = \begin{cases} 1 & \textit{if}\, \mathbf{t}, \cdot, s, n \hookrightarrow^* \mathbf{v}, \cdot, ()_{\mathbb{S}}, \cdot \\ 1 & \textit{if}\, \mathbf{t}, \cdot, s, n \hookrightarrow^* \mathbf{E}[\texttt{resample}], \cdot, ()_{\mathbb{S}}, 0 \\ 0 & \textit{otherwise} \end{cases}$

Note the similarities to Definition 9. In particular, $f_{\mathbf{t},n}(s) > 0$ implies $p_{\mathbf{t},n}(s) = 1$. However, note that $f_{\mathbf{t},n}(s) = 0$ does not imply $p_{\mathbf{t},n}(s) = 0$, since $p_{\mathbf{t},n}$ ignores weights. As an example, $f_{(\texttt{weight}\ 0),n}(()_{\mathbb{S}}) = 0$, while $p_{(\texttt{weight}\ 0),n}(()_{\mathbb{S}}) = 1$.

Lemma 8. $p_{\mathbf{t},n} : (\mathbb{S}, \mathcal{S}) \to (\mathbb{R}_+, \mathcal{B}_+)$ *is measurable.*

The proof is analogous to that of Lemma 6. We can now formally define the kernels $k_{\mathbf{t},n}$.

Definition 24. $k_{\mathbf{t},n}(s, S) = \int_{prepend_s^{-1}(S)} p_{r_{\mathbf{t},n-1}(s),1}(s')\, d\mu_{\mathbb{S}}(s')$

By the definition of $p_{\mathbf{t},n}$, the $k_{\mathbf{t},n}$ are *sub-probability* kernels rather than probability kernels. Intuitively, the reason for this is that during evaluation, terms can get stuck, deterministically diverge, or even stochastically diverge. Such traces are assigned 0 weight by $p_{\mathbf{t},n}$.

Lemma 9. *The functions* $k_{\mathbf{t},n} : \mathbb{S} \times \mathcal{S} \to \mathbb{R}_+$ *are sub-probability kernels.*†[7]

We get a natural starting measure q_0 from the sub-probability distribution resulting from running the initial program $\mathbf{t}$ until reaching a value or a call to `resample`, ignoring weights.

Definition 25. $\langle \mathbf{t} \rangle_0(S) = \int_S p_{\mathbf{t},0}(s) d\mu_{\mathbb{S}}(s)$.

Now we have all the ingredients for the general SMC algorithm described in Section 5.2: a sequence of target measures $\langle\!\langle \mathbf{t} \rangle\!\rangle_n = \widetilde{\pi}_n$ (Definition 22), a starting measure $\langle \mathbf{t} \rangle_0 \propto q_0$ (Definition 25), and a sequence of kernels $k_{\mathbf{t},n} \propto k_n$ (Definition 24). These then induce a sequence of proposal measures $\langle \mathbf{t} \rangle_n = \widetilde{q}_n$ as in Equation (10), which we instantiate in the following definition.

Definition 26. $\langle \mathbf{t} \rangle_n(S) = \int_{\mathbb{S}} k_{\mathbf{t},n}(s, S) f_{\mathbf{t},n-1}(s) d\mu_{\mathbb{S}}(s), \quad n > 0$

Intuitively, the measures $\langle \mathbf{t} \rangle_n$ are obtained by evaluating the terms in the support of the measure $\langle\!\langle \mathbf{t} \rangle\!\rangle_{n-1}$ until reaching the next `resample` or value. For an efficient implementation, we need to factorize this definition into the history and the current step, which amounts to splitting the traces. Each feasible trace can be split in such a way.

[7] We only give a partial proof of this lemma.

Algorithm 2 A concrete instantiation of Algorithm 1 with $\widetilde{\pi}_n = \langle\!\langle \mathbf{t} \rangle\!\rangle_n$, $k_n \propto k_{\mathbf{t},n}$, $q_0 \propto \langle \mathbf{t} \rangle_0$, and as a consequence $\widetilde{q}_n = \langle \mathbf{t} \rangle_n$ (for $n > 0$). In each step, we let $1 \leq j \leq J$, where J is the number of samples.

1. **Initialization:** Set $n = 0$. Draw $s_0^j \sim \langle \mathbf{t} \rangle_0$ for $1 \leq j \leq J$.
   That is, run the program $\mathbf{t}$, and draw from $\mathcal{U}(0,1)$ whenever required by a $\texttt{sample}_D$. Record these draws as the trace s_0^j. Stop when reaching a term of the form $\mathbf{E}[\texttt{resample}]$ or a value $\mathbf{v}$. The empirical distribution $\{s_0^j\}_{j=1}^J$ approximates $\langle \mathbf{t} \rangle_0$.
2. **Correction:** Calculate $w_n^j = \frac{f_{\langle\!\langle \mathbf{t} \rangle\!\rangle_n}(s_n^j)}{f_{\langle \mathbf{t} \rangle_n}(s_n^j)}$ for $1 \leq j \leq J$.
   As a consequence of Lemma 13, this is trivial. Simply set w_n^j to the weight accumulated while running $\mathbf{t}$ in step (1), or $r_{\mathbf{t},n-1}(\hat{s}_{n-1}^j)$ in step (5). The empirical distribution given by $\{(s_n^j, w_n^j)\}_{j=1}^J$ approximates $\langle\!\langle \mathbf{t} \rangle\!\rangle_n / Z_{\langle\!\langle \mathbf{t} \rangle\!\rangle_n}$.
3. **Termination:** If all samples $r_{\mathbf{t}}(s_n^j)$ are values, terminate and output $\{(s_n^j, w_n^j)\}_{j=1}^J$. If not, go to the next step.
   We cannot evaluate values further, so running the algorithm further if all samples are values is pointless. When terminating, assuming the conditions in Theorem 1 or Theorem 2 holds, $\{(s_n^j, w_n^j)\}_{j=1}^J$ approximates $\langle\!\langle \mathbf{t} \rangle\!\rangle / Z_{\langle\!\langle \mathbf{t} \rangle\!\rangle_n}$. Also, by the definition of $[\![\mathbf{t}]\!]$, $\{(r_{\mathbf{t}}(s_n^j), w_n^j)\}_{j=1}^J$ approximates $[\![\mathbf{t}]\!] / Z_{[\![\mathbf{t}]\!]_n}$, the normalized version of $[\![\mathbf{t}]\!]$.
4. **Selection:** Resample the empirical distribution $\{(s_n^j, w_n^j)\}_{j=1}^J$. The new empirical distribution is unweighted and given by $\{\hat{s}_n^j\}_{j=1}^J$. This distribution also approximates $\langle\!\langle \mathbf{t} \rangle\!\rangle_n / Z_{\langle\!\langle \mathbf{t} \rangle\!\rangle_n}$.
5. **Mutation:** Increment n. Draw $s_n^j \sim k_{\mathbf{t},n}(\hat{s}_{n-1}^j, \cdot)$ for $1 \leq j \leq J$.
   That is, simply run the intermediate program $r_{\mathbf{t},n-1}(\hat{s}_{n-1}^j)$, and draw from $\mathcal{U}(0,1)$ whenever required by a $\texttt{sample}_D$. Record these draws and append them to $\hat{s}_{n-1}^j$, resulting in the trace s_n^j. Stop when reaching a term of the form $\mathbf{E}[\texttt{resample}]$ or a value $\mathbf{v}$. The empirical distribution $\{s_n^j\}_{j=1}^J$ approximates $\langle \mathbf{t} \rangle_n / Z_{\langle \mathbf{t} \rangle_n}$. Go to (2).

Lemma 10. *Let $n > 0$. If $f_{\mathbf{t},n}(s) > 0$, then $f_{\mathbf{t},n}(s) = f_{\mathbf{t},n-1}(\underline{s}) f_{r_{\mathbf{t},n-1}(\underline{s}),1}(\overline{s})$ for exactly one decomposition $\underline{s} * \overline{s} = s$. If $f_{\mathbf{t},n}(s) = 0$, then $f_{\mathbf{t},n-1}(\underline{s}) f_{r_{\mathbf{t},n-1}(\underline{s}),1}(\overline{s}) = 0$ for all decompositions $\underline{s} * \overline{s} = s$. As a consequence, if $f_{\mathbf{t},n}(s) > 0$, then $p_{r_{\mathbf{t},n-1}(\underline{s}),1}(\overline{s}) = 1$.*†

This gives a more efficiently computable definition of the density.

Lemma 11. *For $n \in \mathbb{N}$, $\langle \mathbf{t} \rangle_n(S) = \int_S f_{\mathbf{t},n-1}(\underline{s}) p_{r_{\mathbf{t},n-1}(\underline{s}),1}(\overline{s}) d\mu_{\mathbb{S}}(s)$, where $\underline{s} * \overline{s} = s$ is the unique decomposition from Lemma 10.*†[8]

Since the kernels $k_{\mathbf{t},n}$ are sub-probability kernels, the measures $\langle \mathbf{t} \rangle_n$ are finite given that the $\langle\!\langle \mathbf{t} \rangle\!\rangle_n$ are finite.

Lemma 12. *$\langle \mathbf{t} \rangle_0$ is a sub-probability measure. Also, if $\langle\!\langle \mathbf{t} \rangle\!\rangle_{n-1}$ is finite, then $\langle \mathbf{t} \rangle_n$ is finite.*†

As discussed in Section 6.2, the $\langle\!\langle \mathbf{t} \rangle\!\rangle_n$ are finite, either by assumption (Theorem 1) or as a consequence of the dominating function of Theorem 2. From this

[8] We only give a proof sketch for this lemma.

and Lemma 12, the $\langle \mathbf{t} \rangle_n$ are also finite. Furthermore, checking that $\langle \mathbf{t} \rangle_n$ are valid, i.e. that the density $f_{\langle \mathbf{t} \rangle_n}$ of each $\langle \mathbf{t} \rangle_n$ covers the density $f_{\langle\langle \mathbf{t} \rangle\rangle_n}$ of $\langle\langle \mathbf{t} \rangle\rangle_n$ is trivial. As such, by Lemma 5, we can now correctly approximate $\langle\langle \mathbf{t} \rangle\rangle_n$ using Algorithm 1. The details are given in Algorithm 2, which closely resembles the standard SMC algorithm in WebPPL. For ease of notation, we assume it possible to draw samples from $\langle \mathbf{t} \rangle_0$ and $k_{\mathbf{t},n}(s, \cdot)$, even though these are sub-probability measures. This essentially corresponds to assuming evaluation never gets stuck or diverges. Making sure this is the case is not within the scope of this paper. The weights in Algorithm 2 at time step n can easily be calculated according to the following lemma.

Lemma 13. $w_n(s) = \dfrac{f_{\langle\langle \mathbf{t} \rangle\rangle_n}(s)}{f_{\langle \mathbf{t} \rangle_n}(s)} = \begin{cases} f_{r_{\mathbf{t},n-1}(\underline{s}),1}(\overline{s}) & \text{if } n > 0 \\ f_{\mathbf{t},0}(s) & \text{if } n = 0 \end{cases}$ *when* $f_{\langle \mathbf{t} \rangle_n}(s) > 0$. *Here,* $\underline{s} * \overline{s} = s$ *is the unique decomposition from Lemma 10.*†

7.2 Other SMC Algorithms

In this section, we discuss SMC algorithms other than the BPF.

First, we have the *resample-move* algorithm by Gilks and Berzuini [11], which is also implemented in WebPPL [13], and treated by Chopin [6] and Ścibior et al. [33]. In this algorithm, the SMC kernel is composed with a suitable MCMC kernel, such that one or more MCMC steps are taken for each sample after each resampling. This helps with the so-called degeneracy problem in SMC, which refers to the tendency of SMC samples to share a common ancestry as a result of resampling. We can directly achieve this algorithm in our context by simply choosing appropriate transition kernels in Algorithm 1. Let $k_{\mathrm{MCMC},n}$ be MCMC transition kernels with $\widetilde{\pi}_{n-1} = \langle\langle \mathbf{t} \rangle\rangle_{n-1}$ as *invariant distributions*. Using the bootstrap kernels as the main kernels, we let $k_n = k_{\mathbf{t},n} \circ k_{\mathrm{MCMC},n}$ where $\circ$ denotes kernel composition. The sequence k_n is valid because of the validity of the main SMC kernels and the invariance of the MCMC kernels.

While Algorithm 1 captures different SMC algorithms by allowing the use of different kernels, some algorithms require changes to Algorithm 1 itself. The first such variation of Algorithm 1 is the *alive* particle filter, recently discussed by Kudlicka et al. [19], which reduces the tendency to degeneracy by not including sample traces with zero weight in resampling. This is done by repeating the selection and mutation steps (for each sample individually) until a trace with non-zero weight is proposed; the corresponding modifications to Algorithm 1 are straightforward. The unbiasedness result of Kudlicka et al. [19] can easily be extended to our PPL context, with another minor modification to Algorithm 1.

Another variation of Algorithm 1 is the auxiliary particle filter [28]. Informally, this algorithm allows the selection and mutation steps of Algorithm 1 to be guided by future information regarding the weights w_n. For many models, this is possible since the weighting functions w_n from Algorithm 1 are often parametric in an explicitly available sequence of *observation data points*, which can also be used to derive better kernels k_n. Clearly, such optimizations are model-specific, and can not directly be applied in expressive PPL calculi such as ours. However, the general idea of using look-ahead in general-purpose PPLs to guide selection and mutation is interesting, and should be explored.

8 Related Work

The only major previous work related to formal SMC correctness in PPLs is Ścibior et al. [33] (see Section 1). They validate both the BPF and the resample-move SMC algorithms in a denotational setting. In a companion paper, Ścibior et al. [32] also give a Haskell implementation of these inference techniques.

Although formal correctness proofs of SMC in PPLs are sparse, there are many languages that implement SMC algorithms. Goodman and Stuhlmüller [14] describe SMC for the probabilistic programming language WebPPL. They implement a basic BPF very similar to Algorithm 2, but do not show correctness with respect to any language semantics. Also, related to WebPPL, Stuhlmüller et al. [36] discuss a coarse-to-fine SMC inference technique for probabilistic programs with independent sample statements.

Wood et al. [43] describe PMCMC, an MCMC inference technique that uses SMC internally, for the probabilistic programming language Anglican [37]. Similarly to WebPPL, Anglican also includes a basic BPF similar to Algorithm 2, with the exception that every execution needs to encounter the same number of calls to `resample`. They use various types of empirical tests to validate correctness, in contrast to the formal proof found in this paper. Related to Anglican, a brief discussion on resample placement requirements can be found in van de Meent et al. [41].

Birch [25] is an imperative object-oriented PPL, with a particular focus on SMC. It supports a number of SMC algorithms, including the BPF [16] and the auxiliary particle filter [28]. Furthermore, they support dynamic analytical optimizations, for instance using locally-optimal proposals and Rao–Blackwellization [24]. As with WebPPL and Anglican, the focus is on performance and efficiency, and not on formal correctness.

There are quite a few papers studying the correctness of MCMC algorithms for PPLs. Using the same underlying framework as for their SMC correctness proof, Ścibior et al. [33] also validates a trace MCMC algorithm. Another proof of correctness for trace MCMC is given in Borgström et al. [3], which instead uses an untyped lambda calculus and an operational semantics. Much of the formalization in this paper is based on constructions used as part of their paper. For instance, the functions $f_{\mathbf{t}}$ and $r_{\mathbf{t}}$ are defined similarly, as well as the measure space $(\mathbb{S}, \mathcal{S}, \mu_{\mathbb{S}})$ and the measurable space $(\mathbb{T}, \mathcal{T})$. Our measurability proofs of $f_{\mathbf{t}}$, $r_{\mathbf{t}}$, $f_{\mathbf{t},n}$, and $r_{\mathbf{t},n}$ largely follow the same strategies as found in their paper. Similarly to us, they also relate their proof of correctness to classical results from the MCMC literature. A difference is that we use inverse transform sampling, whereas they use probability density functions. As a result of this, our traces consist of numbers on $[0,1]$, while their traces consist of numbers on $\mathbb{R}$. Also, inverse transform sampling naturally allows for built-in discrete distributions. In contrast, discrete distributions must be encoded in the language itself when using probability densities. Another difference is that they restrict the arguments to `weight` to [0, 1], in order to ensure the finiteness of the target measure.

Other work related to ours include Jacobs [17], Vákár et al. [39], and Staton et al. [35]. Jacobs [17] discusses problems with models in which `observe` (related to `weight`) statements occur conditionally. While our results show that SMC inference for such models is correct, the models themselves may not be useful. Vákár et al. [39] develops a powerful domain theory for term recursion in PPLs, but does not cover SMC inference in particular. Staton et al. [35] develops both operational and denotational semantics for a PPL calculus with higher-order functions, but without recursion. They also briefly mention SMC as a program transformation.

Classical work on SMC includes Chopin [6], which we use as a basis for our formalization. In particular, Chopin [6] provides a general formulation of SMC, placing few requirements on the underlying model. The book by Del Moral [7] contains a vast number of classical SMC results, including the law of large numbers and unbiasedness result from Lemma 5. A more accessible summary of the important SMC convergence results from Del Moral [7] can be found in Naesseth et al. [26].

9 Conclusions

In conclusion, we have formalized SMC inference for an expressive functional PPL calculus, based on the formalization by Chopin [6]. We showed that in this context, SMC is correct in that it approximates the target measures encoded by programs in the calculus under mild conditions. Furthermore, we illustrated a particular instance of SMC for our calculus, the bootstrap particle filter, and discussed other variations of SMC and their relation to our calculus.

As indicated in Section 2, the approach used for selecting resampling locations can have a large impact on SMC accuracy and performance. This leads us to the following general question: can we select optimal resampling locations in a given program, according to some formally defined measure of optimality? We leave this important research direction for future work.

Acknowledgments

We thank our colleagues Lawrence Murray and Fredrik Ronquist for fruitful discussions and ideas. We also thank Sam Staton and the anonymous reviewers at ESOP for their detailed and helpful comments.

References

1. Bishop, C.M.: Pattern Recognition and Machine Learning (Information Science and Statistics). Springer-Verlag (2006)
2. Blei, D.M., Ng, A.Y., Jordan, M.I.: Latent Dirichlet allocation. Journal of Machine Learning Research **3**, 993–1022 (2003)
3. Borgström, J., Dal Lago, U., Gordon, A.D., Szymczak, M.: A lambda-calculus foundation for universal probabilistic programming. In: Proceedings of the 21st ACM SIGPLAN International Conference on Functional Programming. pp. 33–46. Association for Computing Machinery (2016)
4. Bournez, O., Garnier, F.: Proving positive almost-sure termination. In: Term Rewriting and Applications. pp. 323–337. Springer Berlin Heidelberg (2005)
5. Carpenter, B., Gelman, A., Hoffman, M., Lee, D., Goodrich, B., Betancourt, M., Brubaker, M., Guo, J., Li, P., Riddell, A.: Stan: A probabilistic programming language. Journal of Statistical Software, Articles **76**(1), 1–32 (2017)
6. Chopin, N.: Central limit theorem for sequential Monte Carlo methods and its application to Bayesian inference. Annals of Statistics **32**(6), 2385–2411 (2004)
7. Del Moral, P.: Feynman-Kac Formulae: Genealogical and Interacting Particle Systems With Applications, Probability and Its Applications, vol. 100. Springer-Verlag New York (2004)
8. Douc, R., Cappe, O.: Comparison of resampling schemes for particle filtering. In: Proceedings of the 4th International Symposium on Image and Signal Processing and Analysis. pp. 64–69 (2005)
9. Doucet, A., de Freitas, N., Gordon, N.: Sequential Monte Carlo Methods in Practice. Information Science and Statistics, Springer New York (2001)
10. Doucet, A., Johansen, A.: The Oxford Handbook of Nonlinear Filtering, chap. A Tutorial on Particle Filtering and Smoothing: Fifteen Years Later. Oxford University Press (2009)
11. Gilks, W.R., Berzuini, C.: Following a moving target-Monte Carlo inference for dynamic Bayesian models. Journal of the Royal Statistical Society. Series B (Statistical Methodology) **63**(1), 127–146 (2001)
12. Gilks, W., Richardson, S., Spiegelhalter, D.: Markov Chain Monte Carlo in Practice. Chapman & Hall/CRC Interdisciplinary Statistics, Taylor & Francis (1995)
13. Goodman, N.D., Mansinghka, V.K., Roy, D., Bonawitz, K., Tenenbaum, J.B.: Church: A language for generative models. In: Proceedings of the Twenty-Fourth Conference on Uncertainty in Artificial Intelligence. pp. 220–229. AUAI Press (2008)
14. Goodman, N.D., Stuhlmüller, A.: The design and implementation of probabilistic programming languages. http://dippl.org (2014), accessed: 2020-07-09
15. Gordon, A.D., Aizatulin, M., Borgstrom, J., Claret, G., Graepel, T., Nori, A.V., Rajamani, S.K., Russo, C.: A model-learner pattern for Bayesian reasoning. In: Proceedings of the 40th Annual ACM SIGPLAN-SIGACT Symposium on Principles of Programming Languages. pp. 403–416. Association for Computing Machinery (2013)
16. Gordon, N.J., Salmond, D.J., Smith, A.F.M.: Novel approach to nonlinear/non-Gaussian Bayesian state estimation. IEE Proceedings F - Radar and Signal Processing **140**(2), 107–113 (1993)
17. Jacobs, J.: Paradoxes of probabilistic programming: And how to condition on events of measure zero with infinitesimal probabilities. Proceedings of the ACM on Programming Languages **5**(POPL) (2021)

18. Kozen, D.: Semantics of probabilistic programs. Journal of Computer and System Sciences **22**(3), 328–350 (1981)
19. Kudlicka, J., Murray, L.M., Ronquist, F., Schön, T.B.: Probabilistic programming for birth-death models of evolution using an alive particle filter with delayed sampling. In: Conference on Uncertainty in Artificial Intelligence (2019)
20. Lundén, D., Borgström, J., Broman, D.: Correctness of sequential monte carlo inference for probabilistic programming languages. arXiv e-prints p. arXiv:2003.05191 (2020)
21. Lundén, D., Broman, D., Ronquist, F., Murray, L.M.: Automatic alignment of sequential monte carlo inference in higher-order probabilistic programs. arXiv e-prints p. arXiv:1812.07439 (2018)
22. Mak, C., Ong, C.H.L., Paquet, H., Wagner, D.: Densities of almost-surely terminating probabilistic programs are differentiable almost everywhere. arXiv e-prints p. arXiv:2004.03924 (2020)
23. McDonald, J.N., Weiss, N.A.: A Course in Real Analysis. Elsevier Science (2012)
24. Murray, L., Lundén, D., Kudlicka, J., Broman, D., Schön, T.: Delayed sampling and automatic rao-blackwellization of probabilistic programs. In: Proceedings of the Twenty-First International Conference on Artificial Intelligence and Statistics. vol. 84, pp. 1037–1046. PMLR (2018)
25. Murray, L.M., Schön, T.B.: Automated learning with a probabilistic programming language: Birch. arXiv e-prints p. arXiv:1810.01539 (2018)
26. Naesseth, C.A., Lindsten, F., Schön, T.B.: Elements of sequential monte carlo. arXiv e-prints p. arXiv:1903.04797 (2019)
27. Park, S., Pfenning, F., Thrun, S.: A probabilistic language based on sampling functions. ACM Transactions on Programming Languages and Systems **31**(1) (2008)
28. Pitt, M.K., Shephard, N.: Filtering via simulation: Auxiliary particle filters. Journal of the American Statistical Association **94**(446), 590–599 (1999)
29. Ronquist, F., Huelsenbeck, J.P.: MrBayes 3: Bayesian phylogenetic inference under mixed models. Bioinformatics **19**(12), 1572–1574 (2003)
30. Ronquist, F., Kudlicka, J., Senderov, V., Borgström, J., Lartillot, N., Lundén, D., Murray, L., Schön, T.B., Broman, D.: Universal probabilistic programming offers a powerful approach to statistical phylogenetics. bioRxiv (2020)
31. Russell, S., Norvig, P.: Artificial Intelligence: A Modern Approach. Prentice Hall Press, 3rd edn. (2009)
32. Ścibior, A., Kammar, O., Ghahramani, Z.: Functional programming for modular Bayesian inference. Proceedings of the ACM on Programming Languages **2**(ICFP) (2018)
33. Ścibior, A., Kammar, O., Vákár, M., Staton, S., Yang, H., Cai, Y., Ostermann, K., Moss, S.K., Heunen, C., Ghahramani, Z.: Denotational validation of higher-order Bayesian inference. Proceedings of the ACM on Programming Languages **2**(POPL) (2017)
34. Staton, S.: Commutative semantics for probabilistic programming. In: Programming Languages and Systems. pp. 855–879. Springer Berlin Heidelberg (2017)
35. Staton, S., Yang, H., Wood, F., Heunen, C., Kammar, O.: Semantics for probabilistic programming: Higher-order functions, continuous distributions, and soft constraints. In: Proceedings of the 31st Annual ACM/IEEE Symposium on Logic in Computer Science. pp. 525–534. Association for Computing Machinery (2016)
36. Stuhlmüller, A., Hawkins, R.X.D., Siddharth, N., Goodman, N.D.: Coarse-to-fine sequential monte carlo for probabilistic programs. arXiv e-prints p. arXiv:1509.02962 (2015)

37. Tolpin, D., van de Meent, J.W., Yang, H., Wood, F.: Design and implementation of probabilistic programming language Anglican. In: Proceedings of the 28th Symposium on the Implementation and Application of Functional Programming Languages. Association for Computing Machinery (2016)
38. Tran, D., Kucukelbir, A., Dieng, A.B., Rudolph, M., Liang, D., Blei, D.M.: Edward: A library for probabilistic modeling, inference, and criticism. arXiv e-prints p. arXiv:1610.09787 (2016)
39. Vákár, M., Kammar, O., Staton, S.: A domain theory for statistical probabilistic programming. Proceedings of the ACM on Programming Languages **3**(POPL) (2019)
40. Vákár, M., Ong, L.: On s-finite measures and kernels. arXiv e-prints p. arXiv:1810.01837 (2018)
41. van de Meent, J.W., Paige, B., Yang, H., Wood, F.: An introduction to probabilistic programming. arXiv e-prints p. arXiv:1809.10756 (2018)
42. Wainwright, M.J., Jordan, M.I.: Graphical models, exponential families, and variational inference. Foundations and Trends in Machine Learning **1**(1–2), 1–305 (2008)
43. Wood, F., Meent, J.W., Mansinghka, V.: A new approach to probabilistic programming inference. In: Proceedings of the Seventeenth International Conference on Artificial Intelligence and Statistics. vol. 33, pp. 1024–1032. PMLR (2014)

Densities of Almost Surely Terminating Probabilistic Programs are Differentiable Almost Everywhere

Carol Mak, C.-H. Luke Ong, Hugo Paquet, and Dominik Wagner(✉)

Department of Computer Science, University of Oxford, Oxford, UK
{pui.mak,luke.ong,hugo.paquet,dominik.wagner}@cs.ox.ac.uk

Abstract. We study the differential properties of higher-order statistical probabilistic programs with recursion and conditioning. Our starting point is an open problem posed by Hongseok Yang: what class of statistical probabilistic programs have densities that are differentiable almost everywhere? To formalise the problem, we consider Statistical PCF (SPCF), an extension of call-by-value PCF with real numbers, and constructs for sampling and conditioning. We give SPCF a sampling-style operational semantics à la Borgström et al., and study the associated weight (commonly referred to as the density) function and value function on the set of possible execution traces.

Our main result is that almost surely terminating SPCF programs, generated from a set of primitive functions (e.g. the set of analytic functions) satisfying mild closure properties, have weight and value functions that are almost everywhere differentiable. We use a stochastic form of symbolic execution to reason about almost everywhere differentiability. A by-product of this work is that almost surely terminating *deterministic* (S)PCF programs with real parameters denote functions that are almost everywhere differentiable.

Our result is of practical interest, as almost everywhere differentiability of the density function is required to hold for the correctness of major gradient-based inference algorithms.

1 Introduction

Probabilistic programming refers to a set of tools and techniques for the systematic use of programming languages in Bayesian statistical modelling. Users of probabilistic programming — those wishing to make inferences or predictions — **(i)** encode their domain knowledge in program form; **(ii)** *condition* certain program variables based on observed data; and **(iii)** make a query. The resulting code is then passed to an *inference engine* which performs the necessary computation to answer the query, usually following a generic approximate Bayesian inference algorithm. (In some recent systems [5,14], users may also write their own inference code.) The Programming Language community has contributed to the field by developing formal methods for probabilistic programming languages (PPLs), seen as usual languages enriched with primitives for **(i)** sampling and

N. Yoshida (Ed.): ESOP 2021, LNCS 12648, pp. 432–461, 2021.
https://doi.org/10.1007/978-3-030-72019-3_16

(ii) conditioning. (The query **(iii)** can usually be encoded as the return value of the program.)

It is crucial to have access to reasoning principles in this context. The combination of these new primitives with the traditional constructs of programming languages leads to a variety of new computational phenomena, and a major concern is the *correctness of inference*: given a query, will the algorithm converge, in some appropriate sense, to a correct answer? In a *universal* PPL (i.e. one whose underlying language is Turing-complete), this is not obvious: the inference engine must account for a wide class of programs, going beyond the more well-behaved models found in many of the current statistical applications. Thus the design of inference algorithms, and the associated correctness proofs, are quite delicate. It is well-known, for instance, that in its original version the popular lightweight Metropolis-Hastings algorithm [53] contained a bug affecting the result of inference [20,25].

Fortunately, research in this area benefits from decades of work on the semantics of programs with random features, starting with pioneering work by Kozen [26] and Saheb-Djahromi [44]. Both operational and denotational models have recently been applied to the validation of inference algorithms: see e.g. [20,8] for the former and [45,10] for the latter. There are other approaches, e.g. using refined type systems [33].

Inference algorithms in probabilistic programming are often based on the concept of *program trace*, because the operational behaviour of a program is parametrised by the sequence of random numbers it draws along the way. Accordingly a probabilistic program has an associated *value function* which maps traces to output values. But the inference procedure relies on another function on traces, commonly called the *density*[1] of the program, which records a cumulative likelihood for the samples in a given trace. Approximating a normalised version of the density is the main challenge that inference algorithms aim to tackle. We will formalise these notions: in Sec. 3 we demonstrate how the value function and density of a program are defined in terms of its operational semantics.

Contributions. The main result of this paper is that both the density and value function are *differentiable almost everywhere* (that is, everywhere but on a set of measure zero), provided the program is *almost surely terminating* in a suitable sense. Our result holds for a universal language with recursion and higher-order functions. We emphasise that it follows immediately that *purely deterministic programs with real parameters* denote functions that are almost everywhere differentiable. This class of programs is important, because they can express machine learning models which rely on gradient descent [30].

This result is of practical interest, because many modern inference algorithms are "gradient-based": they exploit the derivative of the density function in order to optimise the approximation process. This includes the well-known methods of Hamiltonian Monte-Carlo [15,37] and stochastic variational inference [18,40,6,27]. But these techniques can only be applied when the derivative

[1] For some readers this terminology may be ambiguous; see Remark 1 for clarification.

exists "often enough", and thus, in the context of probabilistic programming, almost everywhere differentiability is often cited as a requirement for correctness [55,31]. The question of which probabilistic programs satisfy this property was selected by Hongseok Yang in his FSCD 2019 invited lecture [54] as one of three open problems in the field of semantics for probabilistic programs.

Points of non-differentiability exist largely because of *branching*, which typically arises in a program when the control flow reaches a conditional statement. Hence our work is a study of the connections between the traces of a probabilistic program and its branching structure. To achieve this we introduce *stochastic symbolic execution*, a form of operational semantics for probabilistic programs, designed to identify sets of traces corresponding to the same control-flow branch. Roughly, a reduction sequence in this semantics corresponds to a control flow branch, and the rules additionally provide for every branch a symbolic expression of the trace density, parametrised by the outcome of the random draws that the branch contains. We obtain our main result in conjunction with a careful analysis of the branching structure of almost surely terminating programs.

Outline. We devote Sec. 2 to a more detailed introduction to the problem of trace-based inference in probabilistic programming, and the issue of differentiability in this context. In Sec. 3, we present a trace-based operational semantics to Statistical PCF, a prototypical higher-order functional language previously studied in the literature. This is followed by a discussion of differentiability and almost sure termination of programs (Sec. 4). In Sec. 5 we define the "symbolic" operational semantics required for the proof of our main result, which we present in Sec. 6. We discuss related work and further directions in Sec. 7.

For the extended version of the paper refer to [34].

2 Probabilistic Programming and Trace-Based Inference

In this section we give a short introduction to probabilistic programs and the densities they denote, and we motivate the need for gradient-based inference methods. Our account relies on classical notions from measure theory, so we start with a short recap.

2.1 Measures and Densities

A ***measurable space*** is a pair (X, Σ_X) consisting of a set together with a ***σ-algebra*** of subsets, i.e. $\Sigma_X \subseteq \mathcal{P}(X)$ contains $\emptyset$ and is closed under complements and countable unions and intersections. Elements of Σ_X are called ***measurable sets***. A ***measure*** on (X, Σ_X) is a function $\mu : \Sigma_X \to [0, \infty]$ satisfying $\mu(\emptyset) = 0$, and $\mu(\bigcup_{i\in I} U_i) = \sum_{i\in I} \mu(U_i)$ for every countable family $\{U_i\}_{i\in I}$ of pairwise disjoint measurable subsets. A (possibly partial) function $X \rightharpoonup Y$ is ***measurable*** if for every $U \in \Sigma_Y$ we have $f^{-1}(U) \in \Sigma_X$.

The space $\mathbb{R}$ of real numbers is an important example. The (Borel) σ-algebra $\Sigma_{\mathbb{R}}$ is the smallest one containing all intervals $[a, b)$, and the ***Lebesgue measure***

Leb is the unique measure on $(\mathbb{R}, \Sigma_{\mathbb{R}})$ satisfying $\text{Leb}([a, b)) = b - a$. For measurable spaces (X, Σ_X) and (Y, Σ_Y), the ***product σ-algebra*** $\Sigma_{X \times Y}$ is the smallest one containing all $U \times V$, where $U \in \Sigma_X$ and $V \in \Sigma_Y$. So in particular we get for each $n \in \mathbb{N}$ a space $(\mathbb{R}^n, \Sigma_{\mathbb{R}^n})$, and additionally there is a unique measure Leb_n on $\mathbb{R}^n$ satisfying $\text{Leb}_n(\prod_i U_i) = \prod_i \text{Leb}(U_i)$.

When a function $f : X \to \mathbb{R}$ is measurable and non-negative and μ is a measure on X, for each $U \in \Sigma_X$ we can define the ***integral*** $\int_U (\mathrm{d}\mu) f \in [0, \infty]$. Common families of probability distributions on the reals (Uniform, Normal, etc.) are examples of measures on $(\mathbb{R}, \Sigma_{\mathbb{R}})$. Most often these are defined in terms of *probability density functions* with respect to the Lebesgue measure, meaning that for each μ_D there is a measurable function $\text{pdf}_D : \mathbb{R} \to \mathbb{R}_{\geq 0}$ which determines it: $\mu_D(U) = \int_U (\mathrm{d}\,\text{Leb})\ \text{pdf}_D$. As we will see, density functions such as pdf_D have a central place in Bayesian inference.

Formally, if μ is a measure on a measurable space X, a ***density*** for μ with respect to another measure ν on X (most often ν is the Lebesgue measure) is a measurable function $f : X \to \mathbb{R}$ such that $\mu(U) = \int_U (\mathrm{d}\nu) f$ for every $U \in \Sigma_X$. In the context of the present work, an *inference algorithm* can be understood as a method for approximating a distribution of which we only know the density up to a normalising constant. In other words, if the algorithm is fed a (measurable) function $g : X \to \mathbb{R}$, it should produce samples approximating the probability measure $U \mapsto \frac{\int_U (\mathrm{d}\nu) g}{\int_X (\mathrm{d}\nu) g}$ on X.

We will make use of some basic notions from topology: given a topological space X and an set $A \subseteq X$, the ***interior*** of A is the largest open set $\mathring{A}$ contained in A. Dually the ***closure*** of A is the smallest closed set $\overline{A}$ containing A, and the ***boundary*** of A is defined as $\partial A := \overline{A} \setminus \mathring{A}$. Note that for all $U \subseteq \mathbb{R}^n$, all of $\mathring{U}$, $\overline{U}$ and ∂U are measurable (in $\Sigma_{\mathbb{R}^n}$).

2.2 Probabilistic Programming: a (Running) Example

Our running example is based on a random walk in $\mathbb{R}_{\geq 0}$.

The story is as follows: a pedestrian has gone on a walk on a certain semi-infinite street (i.e. extending infinitely on one side), where she may periodically change directions. Upon reaching the end of the street she has forgotten her starting point, only remembering that she started no more than 3km away. Thanks to an odometer, she knows the total distance she has walked is 1.1km, although there is a small margin of error. Her starting point can be inferred using probabilistic programming, via the program in Fig. 1a.

The function walk in Fig. 1a is a recursive simulation of the random walk: note that in this model a new direction is sampled after at most 1km. Once the pedestrian has travelled past 0 the function returns the total distance travelled. The rest of the program first specifies a *prior distribution* for the starting point, representing the pedestrian's belief — uniform distribution on $[0, 3]$ — before observing the distance measured by the odometer. After drawing a value for start the program simulates a random walk, and the execution is weighted (via score) according to how close distance is to the observed value of 1.1. The return

```
(* returns total distance travelled *)
let rec walk start =
  if (start <= 0) then
    0
  else
    (* each leg < 1km *)
    let step = Uniform(0, 1) in
    if (flip ()) then
      (* go towards +infty *)
      step + walk (start+step)
    else
      (* go towards 0 *)
      step + walk (start-step)
in
(* prior *)
let start = Uniform(0, 3) in
let distance = walk start in
(* likelihood *)
score ((pdfN distance 0.1) 1.1);
(* query *)
start
```

(a) Running example in pseudo-code.

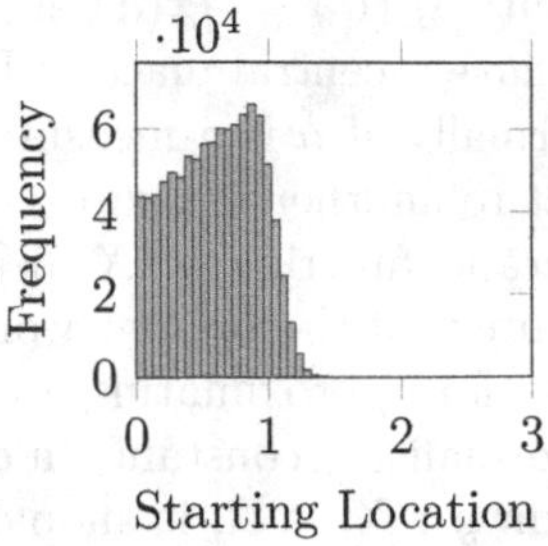

(b) Resulting histogram.

Fig. 1: Inferring the starting point of a random walk on $\mathbb{R}_{\geq 0}$, in a PPL.

value is our query: it indicates that we are interested in the *posterior* distribution on the starting point.

The histogram in Fig. 1b is obtained by sampling repeatedly from the posterior of a Python model of our running example. It shows the mode of the pedestrian's starting point to be around the 0.8km mark.

To approximate the posterior, inference engines for probabilistic programs often proceed indirectly and operate on the space of *program traces*, rather than on the space of possible return values. By *trace*, we mean the sequence of samples drawn in the course of a particular run, one for each random primitive encountered. Because each random primitive (qua probability distribution) in the language comes with a density, given a particular trace we can compute a coefficient as the appropriate product. We can then multiply this coefficient by all scores encountered in the execution, and this yields a (*weight*) function, mapping traces to the non-negative reals, over which the chosen inference algorithm may operate. This indirect approach is more practical, and enough to answer the query, since every trace unambiguously induces a return value.

Remark 1. In much of the probabilistic programming literature (e.g. [31,55,54], including this paper), the above-mentioned weight function on traces is called the *density* of the probabilistic program. This may be confusing: as we have seen, a probabilistic program induces a posterior probability distribution on return values, and it is natural to ask whether this distribution admits a probability density function (Radon-Nikodym derivative) w.r.t. some base measure. This problem is of current interest [2,3,21] but unrelated to the present work.

2.3 Gradient-Based Approximate Inference

Some of the most influential and practically important inference algorithms make use of the gradient of the density functions they operate on, when these are differentiable. Generally the use of gradient-based techniques allow for much greater efficiency in inference.

A popular example is the Markov Chain Monte Carlo algorithm known as Hamiltonian Monte Carlo (HMC) [15,37]. Given a density function $g : X \to \mathbb{R}$, HMC samples are obtained as the states of a Markov chain by (approximately) simulating Hamilton's equations via an integrator that uses the gradient $\nabla_x g(x)$. Another important example is (stochastic) variational inference [18,40,6,27], which transforms the posterior inference problem to an optimisation problem. This method takes two inputs: the posterior density function of interest $g : X \to \mathbb{R}$, and a function $h : \Theta \times X \to \mathbb{R}$; typically, the latter function is a member of an expressive and mathematically well-behaved family of densities that are parameterised in Θ. The idea is to use stochastic gradient descent to find the parameter $\theta \in \Theta$ that minimises the "distance" (typically the Kullback–Leibler divergence) between $h(\theta, -)$ and g, relying on a suitable estimate of the gradient of the objective function. When g is the density of a probabilistic program (the *model*), h can be specified as the density of a second program (the *guide*) whose traces have additional θ-parameters. The gradient of the objective function is then estimated in one approach (score function [41]) by computing the gradient $\nabla_\theta h(\theta, x)$, and in another (reparameterised gradient [24,42,49]) by computing the gradient $\nabla_x g(x)$.

In probabilistic programming, the above inference methods must be adapted to deal with the fact that in a universal PPL, the set of random primitives encountered can vary between executions, and traces can have arbitrary and unbounded dimension; moreover, the density function of a probabilistic program is generally not (everywhere) differentiable. Crucially these adapted algorithms are only valid when the input densities are *almost everywhere* differentiable [55,38,32]; this is the subject of this paper.

Our main result (Thm. 3) states that the weight function and value function of almost surely terminating SPCF programs are almost everywhere differentiable. This applies to our running example: the program in Fig. 1a (expressible in SPCF using primitive functions that satisfy Assumption 1 – see Ex. 1) is almost surely terminating.

3 Sampling Semantics for Statistical PCF

In this section, we present a simply-typed statistical probabilistic programming language with recursion and its operational semantics.

$$\sigma, \tau ::= \mathsf{R} \mid \sigma \Rightarrow \tau$$
$$M, N, L ::= y \mid \underline{r} \mid \underline{f}(M_1, \ldots, M_\ell) \mid \lambda y.\, M \mid M\, N \mid \mathsf{Y} M \mid \mathsf{if}(L \leq 0, M, N)$$
$$\mid \boxed{\mathsf{sample}} \mid \boxed{\mathsf{score}(M)}$$

$$\frac{}{\Gamma \vdash \mathsf{sample} : \mathsf{R}} \qquad \frac{\Gamma \vdash M : \mathsf{R}}{\Gamma \vdash \mathsf{score}(M) : \mathsf{R}} \qquad \frac{\Gamma \vdash M : (\sigma \Rightarrow \tau) \Rightarrow (\sigma \Rightarrow \tau)}{\Gamma \vdash \mathsf{Y} M : \sigma \Rightarrow \tau}$$

Fig. 2: Syntax of SPCF, where $r \in \mathbb{R}$, x, y are variables, and $f : \mathbb{R}^n \rightharpoonup \mathbb{R}$ ranges over a set $\mathcal{F}$ of partial, measurable ***primitive functions*** (see Sec. 4.2).

3.1 Statistical PCF

Statistical PCF (SPCF) is higher-order probabilistic programming with recursion in purified form. The terms and part of the (standard) typing system of SPCF are presented in Fig. 2 [2]. In the rest of the paper we write $\boldsymbol{x}$ to represent a sequence of variables $x_1, \ldots, x_n$, Λ for the set of SPCF terms, and Λ^0 for the set of closed SPCF terms. In the interest of readability, we sometimes use pseudo code (e.g. Fig. 1a) in the style of Core ML to express SPCF terms.

SPCF is a statistical probabilistic version of call-by-value PCF [46,47] with reals as the ground type. The probabilistic constructs of SPCF are relatively standard (see for example [48]): the sampling construct sample draws from $\mathcal{U}(0,1)$, the standard uniform distribution with end points 0 and 1; the scoring construct $\mathsf{score}(M)$ enables conditioning on observed data by multiplying the weight of the current execution with the (non-negative) real number denoted by M. Sampling from other real-valued distributions can be obtained from $\mathcal{U}(0,1)$ by applying the inverse of the distribution's cumulative distribution function.

Our SPCF is an (inconsequential) variant of CBV SPCF [51] and a (CBV) extension of PPCF [16] with scoring; it may be viewed as a simply-typed version of the untyped probabilistic languages of [8,13,52].

Example 1 (Running Example Ped*).* We express in SPCF the example in Fig. 1a.

$$\mathsf{Ped} \equiv \begin{pmatrix} \mathsf{let}\ x = \mathsf{sample} \cdot \underline{3}\ \mathsf{in} \\ \mathsf{let}\ d = \mathsf{walk}\, x\ \mathsf{in} \\ \mathsf{let}\ w = \mathsf{score}(\underline{\mathrm{pdf}_{\mathcal{N}(1.1,0.1)}}(d))\ \mathsf{in}\ x \end{pmatrix} \quad \text{where}$$

$$\mathsf{walk} \equiv \mathsf{Y}\left(\begin{array}{l} \lambda f x.\ \mathsf{if}\ x \leq \underline{0}\ \mathsf{then}\ \underline{0} \\ \qquad \mathsf{else} \begin{pmatrix} \mathsf{let}\ s = \mathsf{sample}\ \mathsf{in} \\ \mathsf{if}\big((\mathsf{sample} \leq \underline{0.5}), (s + f(x+s)), (s + f(x-s))\big) \end{pmatrix} \end{array} \right)$$

The let construct, $\mathsf{let}\ x = N\ \mathsf{in}\ M$, is syntactic sugar for the term $(\lambda x.M)\, N$; and $\mathrm{pdf}_{\mathcal{N}(1.1,0.1)}$, the density function of the normal distribution with mean 1.1 and variance 0.1, is a primitive function. To enhance readability we use infix notation and omit the underline for standard functions such as addition.

[2] In Fig. 2 and in other figures, we highlight the elements that are new or otherwise noteworthy.

3.2 Operational Semantics

The execution of a probabilistic program generates a *trace*: a sequence containing the values sampled during a run. Our operational semantics captures this dynamic perspective. This is closely related to the treatment in [8] which, following [26], views a probabilistic program as a deterministic program parametrized by the sequence of random draws made during the evaluation.

Traces. Recall that in our language, sample produces a random value in the open unit interval; accordingly a ***trace*** is a finite sequence of elements of $(0,1)$. We define a ***measure space*** $\mathbb{S}$ ***of traces*** to be the set $\bigcup_{n\in\mathbb{N}}(0,1)^n$, equipped with the standard disjoint union σ-algebra, and the sum of the respective (higher-dimensional) Lebesgue measures. Formally, writing $\mathbb{S}_n := (0,1)^n$, we define:

$$\mathbb{S} := \left(\bigcup_{n\in\mathbb{N}} \mathbb{S}_n, \left\{\bigcup_{n\in\mathbb{N}} U_n \mid U_n \in \Sigma_{\mathbb{S}_n}\right\}, \mu_{\mathbb{S}}\right) \text{ and } \mu_{\mathbb{S}}\left(\bigcup_{n\in\mathbb{N}} U_n\right) := \sum_{n\in\mathbb{N}} \mathrm{Leb}_n(U_n).$$

Henceforth we write traces as lists, such as $[0.5, 0.999, 0.12]$; the empty trace as $[]$; and the concatenation of traces $\boldsymbol{s}, \boldsymbol{s}' \in \mathbb{S}$ as $\boldsymbol{s} +\!\!+ \boldsymbol{s}'$.

More generally, to account for open terms, we define, for each $m \in \mathbb{N}$, the measure space

$$\mathbb{R}^m \times \mathbb{S} := \left(\bigcup_{n\in\mathbb{N}} \mathbb{R}^m \times \mathbb{S}_n, \left\{\bigcup_{n\in\mathbb{N}} V_n \mid V_n \in \Sigma_{\mathbb{R}^m\times\mathbb{S}_n}\right\}, \mu_{\mathbb{R}^m\times\mathbb{S}}\right)$$

where $\mu_{\mathbb{R}^m\times\mathbb{S}}\left(\bigcup_{n\in\mathbb{N}} V_n\right) := \sum_{n\in\mathbb{N}} \mathrm{Leb}_{m+n}(V_n)$. To avoid clutter, we will elide the subscript from $\mu_{\mathbb{R}^m\times\mathbb{S}}$ whenever it is clear from the context.

Small-Step Reduction. Next, we define the ***values*** (typically denoted V), ***redexes*** (typically R) and ***evaluation contexts*** (typically E):

$$\begin{aligned} V &::= \underline{r} \mid \lambda y.M \\ R &::= (\lambda y.\, M)\, V \mid \underline{f}(\underline{r_1}, \ldots, \underline{r_\ell}) \mid \mathsf{Y}(\lambda y.\, M) \mid \mathsf{if}\left(\underline{r} \leq 0, M, N\right) \mid \mathsf{sample} \mid \mathsf{score}(\underline{r}) \\ E &::= [] \mid E\, M \mid (\lambda y.M)\, E \mid \underline{f}(\underline{r_1}, \ldots, \underline{r_{i-1}}, E, M_{i+1}, \ldots, M_\ell) \mid \mathsf{Y}E \\ &\quad\ \mid \mathsf{if}\left(E \leq 0, M, N\right) \mid \mathsf{score}(E) \end{aligned}$$

We write Λ_v for the set of SPCF values, and Λ_v^0 for the set of closed SPCF values.

It is easy to see that every closed SPCF term M is either a value, or there exists a unique pair of context E and redex R such that $M \equiv E[R]$.

We now present the operational semantics of SPCF as a rewrite system of ***configurations***, which are triples of the form $\langle M, w, \boldsymbol{s}\rangle$ where M is a closed SPCF term, $w \in \mathbb{R}_{\geq 0}$ is a ***weight***, and $\boldsymbol{s} \in \mathbb{S}$ a trace. (We will sometimes refer to

Redex Contractions:

$$\langle (\lambda y.\, M)\, V, w, \boldsymbol{s}\rangle \to \langle M[V/y], w, \boldsymbol{s}\rangle$$

$$\langle \underline{f}(\underline{r_1}, \ldots, \underline{r_\ell}), w, \boldsymbol{s}\rangle \to \left\langle \underline{f(r_1, \ldots, r_\ell)}, w, \boldsymbol{s}\right\rangle \qquad (\text{if } (r_1, \ldots, r_\ell) \in \mathsf{dom}(f))$$

$$\langle \underline{f}(\underline{r_1}, \ldots, \underline{r_\ell}), w, \boldsymbol{s}\rangle \to \mathsf{fail} \qquad (\text{if } (r_1, \ldots, r_\ell) \notin \mathsf{dom}(f))$$

$$\langle \mathsf{Y}(\lambda y.M), w, \boldsymbol{s}\rangle \to \langle \lambda z.M[\mathsf{Y}(\lambda y.M)/y]\, z, w, \boldsymbol{s}\rangle \qquad (\text{for fresh variable } z)$$

$$\langle \mathsf{if}(\underline{r} \leq 0, M, N), w, \boldsymbol{s}\rangle \to \langle M, w, \boldsymbol{s}\rangle \qquad (\text{if } r \leq 0)$$

$$\langle \mathsf{if}(\underline{r} \leq 0, M, N), w, \boldsymbol{s}\rangle \to \langle N, w, \boldsymbol{s}\rangle \qquad (\text{if } r > 0)$$

$$\langle \mathsf{sample}, w, \boldsymbol{s}\rangle \to \langle \underline{r}, w, \boldsymbol{s} +\!\!+ [r]\rangle \qquad (\text{for some } r \in (0,1))$$

$$\langle \mathsf{score}(\underline{r}), w, \boldsymbol{s}\rangle \to \langle \underline{r}, r \cdot w, \boldsymbol{s}\rangle \qquad (\text{if } r \geq 0)$$

$$\langle \mathsf{score}(\underline{r}), w, \boldsymbol{s}\rangle \to \mathsf{fail} \qquad (\text{if } r < 0)$$

Evaluation Contexts:

$$\frac{\langle R, w, \boldsymbol{s}\rangle \to \langle R', w', \boldsymbol{s}'\rangle}{\langle E[R], w, \boldsymbol{s}\rangle \to \langle E[R'], w', \boldsymbol{s}'\rangle} \qquad \frac{\langle R, w, \boldsymbol{s}\rangle \to \mathsf{fail}}{\langle E[R], w, \boldsymbol{s}\rangle \to \mathsf{fail}}$$

Fig. 3: Operational small-step semantics of SPCF

these as the *concrete* configurations, in contrast with the *abstract* configurations of our symbolic operational semantics, see Sec. 5.2.)

The small-step reduction relation $\to$ is defined in Fig. 3. In the rule for sample, a random value $r \in (0,1)$ is generated and recorded in the trace, while the weight remains unchanged: in a uniform distribution on $(0,1)$ each value is drawn with likelihood 1. In the rule for score($\underline{r}$), the current weight is multiplied by non-negative $r \in \mathbb{R}$: typically this reflects the likelihood of the current execution given some observed data. Similarly to [8] we reduce terms which cannot be reduced in a reasonable way (i.e. scoring with negative constants or evaluating functions outside their domain) to fail.

Example 2. We present a possible reduction sequence for the program in Ex. 1:

$$\langle \mathsf{Ped}, 1, []\rangle \to^* \left\langle \begin{pmatrix} \mathsf{let}\ x = \underline{0.2} \cdot \underline{3}\ \mathsf{in} \\ \mathsf{let}\ d = \mathsf{walk}\, x\ \mathsf{in} \\ \mathsf{let}\ w = \mathsf{score}(\underline{\mathrm{pdf}_{\mathcal{N}(1.1,0.1)}}(d))\ \mathsf{in}\ x \end{pmatrix}, 1, [0.2] \right\rangle$$

$$\to^* \left\langle \begin{pmatrix} \mathsf{let}\ d = \mathsf{walk}\, \underline{0.6}\ \mathsf{in} \\ \mathsf{let}\ w = \mathsf{score}(\underline{\mathrm{pdf}_{\mathcal{N}(1.1,0.1)}}(d))\ \mathsf{in}\ \underline{0.6} \end{pmatrix}, 1, [0.2] \right\rangle$$

$$\to^* \left\langle \mathsf{let}\ w = \mathsf{score}(\underline{\mathrm{pdf}_{\mathcal{N}(1.1,0.1)}}(\underline{0.9}))\ \mathsf{in}\ \underline{0.6}, 1, [0.2, 0.9, 0.7] \right\rangle \qquad (\star)$$

$$\to^* \langle \mathsf{let}\ w = \mathsf{score}(\underline{0.54})\ \mathsf{in}\ \underline{0.6}, 1, [0.2, 0.9, 0.7]\rangle$$

$$\to^* \langle \underline{0.6}, 0.54, [0.2, 0.9, 0.7]\rangle$$

In this execution, the initial sample yields $\underline{0.2}$, which is appended to the trace. At step $(\star)$, we assume given a reduction sequence $\langle \mathsf{walk}\, \underline{0.6}, 1, [0.2]\rangle \to^*$

$\langle \underline{0.9}, 1, [0.2, 0.9, 0.7] \rangle$; this means that in the call to walk, 0.9 was sampled as the the step size and 0.7 as the direction factor; this makes the new location -0.3, which is negative, so the return value is 0.9. In the final step, we perform *conditioning* using the likelihood of observing 0.9 given the data 1.1: the score() expression updates the current weight using the the density of 0.9 in the normal distribution with parameters (1.1, 0.1).

Value and Weight Functions. Using the relation $\to$, we now aim to reason more globally about probabilistic programs in terms of the traces they produce. Let M be an SPCF term with free variables amongst $x_1, \ldots, x_m$ of type R. Its ***value function*** $\mathsf{value}_M : \mathbb{R}^m \times \mathbb{S} \to \Lambda_v^0 \cup \{\bot\}$ returns, given values for each free variable and a trace, the output value of the program, if the program terminates in a value. The ***weight function*** $\mathsf{weight}_M : \mathbb{R}^m \times \mathbb{S} \to \mathbb{R}_{\geq 0}$ returns the final weight of the corresponding execution. Formally:

$$\mathsf{value}_M(\boldsymbol{r}, \boldsymbol{s}) := \begin{cases} V & \text{if } \langle M[\underline{\boldsymbol{r}}/\boldsymbol{x}], 1, [] \rangle \to^* \langle V, w, \boldsymbol{s} \rangle \\ \bot & \text{otherwise} \end{cases}$$

$$\mathsf{weight}_M(\boldsymbol{r}, \boldsymbol{s}) := \begin{cases} w & \text{if } \langle M[\underline{\boldsymbol{r}}/\boldsymbol{x}], 1, [] \rangle \to^* \langle V, w, \boldsymbol{s} \rangle \\ 0 & \text{otherwise} \end{cases}$$

For closed SPCF terms M we just write $\mathsf{weight}_M(\boldsymbol{s})$ for $\mathsf{weight}_M([], \boldsymbol{s})$ (similarly for value_M), and it follows already from [8, Lemma 9] that the functions value_M and weight_M are measurable (see also Sec. 4.1).

Finally, every closed SPCF term M has an associated ***value measure***

$$[\![M]\!] : \Sigma_{\Lambda_v^0} \to \mathbb{R}_{\geq 0}$$

defined by $[\![M]\!](U) := \int_{\mathsf{value}_M{}^{-1}(U)} \mathrm{d}\mu_{\mathbb{S}} \, \mathsf{weight}_M$. This corresponds to the denotational semantics of SPCF in the ω-quasi-Borel space model via computational adequacy [51].

Returning to Remark 1, what are the connections, if any, between the two types of density of a program? To distinguish them, let's refer to the weight function of the program, weight_M, as its *trace density*, and the Radon-Nikodyn derivative of the program's value-measure, $\frac{d[\![M]\!]}{d\nu}$ where ν is the reference measure of the measurable space $\Sigma_{\Lambda_v^0}$, as the *output density*. Observe that, for any measurable function $f : \Lambda_v^0 \to [0, \infty]$, $\int_{\Lambda_v^0} d\,[\![M]\!]\, f = \int_{\mathsf{value}_M^{-1}(\Lambda_v^0)} d\mu_{\mathbb{S}} \, \mathsf{weight}_M \cdot (f \circ \mathsf{value}_M) = \int_{\mathbb{S}} d\mu_{\mathbb{S}} \, \mathsf{weight}_M \cdot (f \circ \mathsf{value}_M)$ (because if $\boldsymbol{s} \notin \mathsf{value}_M^{-1}(\Sigma_{\Lambda_v^0})$ then $\mathsf{weight}_M(\boldsymbol{s}) = 0$). It follows that we can express any expectation w.r.t. the output density $\frac{d[\![M]\!]}{d\nu}$ as an expectation w.r.t. the trace density weight_M. If our aim is, instead, to generate samples from $\frac{d[\![M]\!]}{d\nu}$ then we can simply generate samples from weight_M, and deterministically convert each sample to the space $(\Lambda_v^0, \Sigma_{\Lambda_v^0})$ via the value function value_M. In other words, if our intended output is just a sequence of samples, then our inference engine does not need to concern itself with the consequences of change of variables.

4 Differentiability of the Weight and Value Functions

To reason about the differential properties of these functions we place ourselves in a setting in which differentiation makes sense. We start with some preliminaries.

4.1 Background on Differentiable Functions

Basic real analysis gives a standard notion of differentiability at a point $\boldsymbol{x} \in \mathbb{R}^n$ for functions between Euclidean spaces $\mathbb{R}^n \to \mathbb{R}^m$. In this context a function $f : \mathbb{R}^n \to \mathbb{R}^m$ is ***smooth*** on an open $U \subseteq \mathbb{R}^n$ if it has derivatives of all orders at every point of U. The theory of *differential geometry* (see e.g. the textbooks [50,29,28]) abstracts away from Euclidean spaces to *smooth manifolds*. We recall the formal definitions.

A topological space $\mathcal{M}$ is ***locally Euclidean at a point*** $x \in \mathcal{M}$ if x has a neighbourhood U such that there is a homeomorphism ϕ from U onto an open subset of $\mathbb{R}^n$, for some n. The pair $(U, \phi : U \to \mathbb{R}^n)$ is called a ***chart*** (of dimension n). We say $\mathcal{M}$ is ***locally Euclidean*** if it is locally Euclidean at every point. A ***manifold*** $\mathcal{M}$ is a Hausdorff, second countable, locally Euclidean space.

Two charts, $(U, \phi : U \to \mathbb{R}^n)$ and $(V, \psi : V \to \mathbb{R}^m)$, are ***compatible*** if the function $\psi \circ \phi^{-1} : \phi(U \cap V) \to \psi(U \cap V)$ is smooth, with a smooth inverse. An ***atlas*** on $\mathcal{M}$ is a family $\{(U_\alpha, \phi_\alpha)\}$ of pairwise compatible charts that cover $\mathcal{M}$. A ***smooth manifold*** is a manifold equipped with an atlas.

It follows from the topological invariance of dimension that charts that cover a part of the same connected component have the same dimension. We emphasise that, although this might be considered slightly unusual, distinct connected components need not have the same dimension. This is important for our purposes: $\mathbb{S}$ is easily seen to be a smooth manifold since each connected component $\mathbb{S}_i$ is diffeomorphic to $\mathbb{R}^i$. It is also straightforward to endow the set Λ of SPCF terms with a (smooth) manifold structure. Following [8] we view Λ as $\bigcup_{m \in \mathbb{N}} (\mathsf{SK}_m \times \mathbb{R}^m)$, where SK_m is the set of SPCF terms with exactly m place-holders (a.k.a. *skeleton terms*) for numerals. Thus identified, we give Λ the countable disjoint union topology of the product topology of the discrete topology on SK_m and the standard topology on $\mathbb{R}^m$. Note that the connected components of Λ have the form $\{M\} \times \mathbb{R}^m$, with M ranging over SK_m, and m over $\mathbb{N}$. So in particular, the subspace $\Lambda_v \subseteq \Lambda$ of values inherits the manifold structure. We fix the Borel algebra of this topology to be the σ-algebra on Λ.

Given manifolds $(\mathcal{M}, \{U_\alpha, \phi_\alpha\})$ and $(\mathcal{M}', \{V_\beta, \psi_\beta\})$, a function $f : \mathcal{M} \to \mathcal{M}'$ is ***differentiable*** at a point $x \in \mathcal{M}$ if there are charts (U_α, ϕ_α) about x and (V_β, ψ_β) about $f(x)$ such that the composite $\psi_\beta \circ f \circ \phi_\alpha^{-1}$ restricted to the open subset $\phi_\alpha(f^{-1}(V_\beta) \cap U_\alpha)$ is differentiable at $\phi_\alpha(x)$.

The definitions above are useful because they allow for a uniform presentation. But it is helpful to unpack the definition of differentiability in a few instances, and we see that they boil down to the standard sense in real analysis. Take an SPCF term M with free variables amongst $x_1, \ldots, x_m$ (all of type R), and $(\boldsymbol{r}, \boldsymbol{s}) \in \mathbb{R}^m \times \mathbb{S}_n$.

- The function $\mathsf{weight}_M : \mathbb{R}^m \times \mathbb{S} \to \mathbb{R}_{\geq 0}$ is differentiable at $(\boldsymbol{r}, \boldsymbol{s}) \in \mathbb{R}^m \times \mathbb{S}_n$ just if its restriction $\mathsf{weight}_M|_{\mathbb{R}^m \times \mathbb{S}_n} : \mathbb{R}^m \times \mathbb{S}_n \to \mathbb{R}_{\geq 0}$ is differentiable at $(\boldsymbol{r}, \boldsymbol{s})$.
- In case M is of type R, $\mathsf{value}_M : \mathbb{R}^m \times \mathbb{S} \to \Lambda_v^0 \cup \{\bot\}$ is in essence a partial function $\mathbb{R}^m \times \mathbb{S} \rightharpoonup \mathbb{R}$. Precisely value_M is differentiable at $(\boldsymbol{r}, \boldsymbol{s})$ just if for some open neighbourhood $U \subseteq \mathbb{R}^m \times \mathbb{S}_n$ of $(\boldsymbol{r}, \boldsymbol{s})$:
  1. $\mathsf{value}_M(\boldsymbol{r}', \boldsymbol{s}') = \bot$ for all $(\boldsymbol{r}', \boldsymbol{s}') \in U$; or
  2. $\mathsf{value}_M(\boldsymbol{r}', \boldsymbol{s}') \neq \bot$ for all $(\boldsymbol{r}', \boldsymbol{s}') \in U$, and $\mathsf{value}'_M : U \to \mathbb{R}$ is differentiable at $(\boldsymbol{r}, \boldsymbol{s})$, where we define $\mathsf{value}'_M(\boldsymbol{r}', \boldsymbol{s}') := r''$ whenever $\mathsf{value}_M(\boldsymbol{r}', \boldsymbol{s}') = \underline{r''}$.

4.2 Why Almost Everywhere Differentiability Can Fail

Conditional statements break differentiability. This is easy to see with an example: the weight function of the term

$$\mathsf{if}\big(\mathsf{sample} \leq \mathsf{sample}, \mathsf{score}(\underline{1}), \mathsf{score}(\underline{0})\big)$$

is exactly the characteristic function of $\{[s_1, s_2] \in \mathbb{S} \mid s_1 \leq s_2\}$, which is not differentiable on the diagonal $\{[s, s] \in \mathbb{S}_2 \mid s \in (0, 1)\}$.

This function is however differentiable *almost everywhere*: the diagonal is an uncountable set but has Leb_2 measure zero in the space $\mathbb{S}_2$. Unfortunately, this is not true in general. Without sufficient restrictions, conditional statements also break almost everywhere differentiability. This can happen for two reasons.

Problem 1: Pathological Primitive Functions. Recall that our definition of SPCF is parametrised by a set $\mathcal{F}$ of primitive functions. It is tempting in this context to take $\mathcal{F}$ to be the set of all differentiable functions, but this is too general, as we show now. Consider that for every $f : \mathbb{R} \to \mathbb{R}$ the term

$$\mathsf{if}\big(\underline{f}(\mathsf{sample}) \leq 0, \mathsf{score}(\underline{1}), \mathsf{score}(\underline{0})\big)$$

has weight function the characteristic function of $\{[s_1] \in \mathbb{S} \mid f(s_1) \leq 0\}$. This function is non-differentiable at every $s_1 \in \mathbb{S}_1 \cap \partial f^{-1}(-\infty, 0]$: in every neighbourhood of s_1 there are s_1' and s_1'' such that $f(s_1') \leq 0$ and $f(s_1'') > 0$. One can construct a differentiable f for which this is *not* a measure zero set. (For example, there exists a non-negative function f which is zero exactly on a *fat* Cantor set, i.e., a Cantor-like set with strictly positive measure. See [43, Ex. 5.21].)

Problem 2: Non-Terminating Runs. Our language has recursion, so we can construct a term which samples a random number, halts if this number is in $\mathbb{Q} \cap [0, 1]$, and diverges otherwise. In pseudo-code:

```
let rec enumQ p q r =
  if (r = p/q) then (score 1) else
    if (r < p/q) then
```

```
        enumQ p (q+1) r
    else
        enumQ (p+1) q r
in enumQ 0 1 sample
```

The induced weight function is the characteristic function of $\{[s_1] \in \mathbb{S} \mid s_1 \in \mathbb{Q}\}$; the set of points at which this function is non-differentiable is $\mathbb{S}_1$, which has measure 1.

We proceed to overcome Problem 1 by making appropriate assumptions on the set of primitives. We will then address Problem 2 by focusing on *almost surely terminating* programs.

4.3 Admissible Primitive Functions

One contribution of this work is to identify sufficient conditions for $\mathcal{F}$. We will show in Sec. 6 that our main result holds provided:

Assumption 1 (Admissible Primitive Functions). *$\mathcal{F}$ is a set of partial, measurable functions $\mathbb{R}^\ell \rightharpoonup \mathbb{R}$ including all constant and projection functions which satisfies*

1. *if $f : \mathbb{R}^\ell \rightharpoonup \mathbb{R}$ and $g_i : \mathbb{R}^m \rightharpoonup \mathbb{R}$ are elements of $\mathcal{F}$ for $i = 1, \ldots, \ell$, then $f \circ \langle g_i \rangle_{i=1}^{\ell} : \mathbb{R}^m \rightharpoonup \mathbb{R}$ is in $\mathcal{F}$*
2. *if $(f : \mathbb{R}^\ell \rightharpoonup \mathbb{R}) \in \mathcal{F}$, then f is differentiable in the interior of* $\mathsf{dom}(f)$
3. *if $(f : \mathbb{R}^\ell \rightharpoonup \mathbb{R}) \in \mathcal{F}$, then $\mathrm{Leb}_\ell(\partial f^{-1}[0, \infty)) = 0$.*

Example 3. The following sets of primitive operations satisfy the above sufficient conditions. (See [34] for a proof.)

1. The set $\mathcal{F}_1$ of analytic functions with co-domain $\mathbb{R}$. Recall that a function $f : \mathbb{R}^\ell \to \mathbb{R}^n$ is *analytic* if it is infinitely differentiable and its multivariate Taylor expansion at every point $x_0 \in \mathbb{R}^\ell$ converges pointwise to f in a neighbourhood of x_0.
2. The set $\mathcal{F}_2$ of (partial) functions $f : \mathbb{R}^\ell \rightharpoonup \mathbb{R}$ such that $\mathsf{dom}(f)$ is open[3], and f is differentiable everywhere in $\mathsf{dom}(f)$, and $f^{-1}(I)$ is a finite union of (possibly unbounded) rectangles[4] for (possibly unbounded) intervals I.

Note that all primitive functions mentioned in our examples (and in particular the density of the normal distribution) are included in both $\mathcal{F}_1$ and $\mathcal{F}_2$.

It is worth noting that both $\mathcal{F}_1$ and $\mathcal{F}_2$ satisfy the following stronger (than Assumption 1.3) property: $\mathrm{Leb}_n(\partial f^{-1} I) = 0$ for every interval I, for every primitive function f.

[3] This requirement is crucial, and cannot be relaxed.

[4] i.e. a finite union of $I_1 \times \cdots \times I_\ell$ for (possibly unbounded) intervals I_i

4.4 Almost Sure Termination

To rule out the contrived counterexamples which diverge we restrict attention to *almost surely terminating* SPCF terms. Intuitively, a program M (closed term of ground type) is almost surely terminating if the probability that a run of M terminates is 1.

Take an SPCF term M with variables amongst $x_1, \ldots, x_m$ (all of type $\mathbb{R}$), and set

$$\mathbb{T}_{M,\mathsf{term}} := \left\{(\boldsymbol{r}, \boldsymbol{s}) \in \mathbb{R}^m \times \mathbb{S} \mid \exists V, w \,.\, \langle M[\boldsymbol{r}/\boldsymbol{x}], 1, []\rangle \to^* \langle V, w, \boldsymbol{s}\rangle \right\}. \quad (1)$$

Let us first consider the case of closed $M \in \Lambda^0$ i.e. $m = 0$ (notice that the measure $\mu_{\mathbb{R}^m \times \mathbb{S}}$ is not finite, for $m \geq 1$). As $\mathbb{T}_{M,\mathsf{term}}$ now coincides with $\mathsf{value}_M^{-1}(\Lambda_v^0)$, $\mathbb{T}_{M,\mathsf{term}}$ is a measurable subset of $\mathbb{S}$. Plainly if M is deterministic (i.e. sample-free), then $\mu_{\mathbb{S}}(\mathbb{T}_{M,\mathsf{term}}) = 1$ if M converges to a value, and 0 otherwise. Generally for an arbitrary (stochastic) term M we can regard $\mu_{\mathbb{S}}(\mathbb{T}_{M,\mathsf{term}})$ as the probability that a run of M converges to a value, because of Lem. 1.

Lemma 1. *If $M \in \Lambda^0$ then $\mu_{\mathbb{S}}(\mathbb{T}_{M,\mathsf{term}}) \leq 1$.*

More generally, if M has free variables amongst $x_1, \ldots, x_m$ (all of type R), then we say that M is almost surely terminating if for almost every (instantiation of the free variables by) $\boldsymbol{r} \in \mathbb{R}^m$, $M[\boldsymbol{r}/\boldsymbol{x}]$ terminates with probability 1.

We formalise the notion of almost sure termination as follows.

Definition 1. Let M be an SPCF term. We say that M ***terminates almost surely*** if

1. M is closed and $\mu(\mathbb{T}_{M,\mathsf{term}}) = \mu(\mathsf{value}_M^{-1}(\Lambda_v^0)) = 1$; or
2. M has free variables amongst $x_1, \ldots, x_m$ (all of which are of type R), and there exists $T \in \Sigma_{\mathbb{R}^m}$ such that $\mathrm{Leb}_m(\mathbb{R}^m \setminus T) = 0$ and for each $\boldsymbol{r} \in T$, $M[\underline{\boldsymbol{r}}/\boldsymbol{x}]$ terminates almost surely.

Suppose that M is a closed term and $M^\flat$ is obtained from M by recursively replacing subterms $\mathsf{score}(L)$ with the term $\mathsf{if}(L < 0, N_{\mathsf{fail}}, L)$, where N_{fail} is a term that reduces to fail such as $\underline{1}/\underline{0}$. It is easy to see that for all $\boldsymbol{s} \in \mathbb{S}$, $\langle M^\flat, 1, []\rangle \to^* \langle V, 1, \boldsymbol{s}\rangle$ iff for some (unique) $w \in \mathbb{R}_{\geq 0}$, $\langle M, 1, []\rangle \to^* \langle V, w, \boldsymbol{s}\rangle$. Therefore,

$$\begin{aligned}\llbracket M^\flat \rrbracket(\Lambda_v) &= \int_{\mathsf{value}_{M^\flat}^{-1}(\Lambda_v)} d\mu_{\mathbb{S}}\ \mathsf{weight}_{M^\flat} \\ &= \mu_{\mathbb{S}}(\{\boldsymbol{s} \in \mathbb{S} \mid \exists V \,.\, \left\langle M^\flat, 1, []\right\rangle \to^* \langle V, 1, \boldsymbol{s}\rangle\}) = \mu_{\mathbb{S}}(\mathbb{T}_{M,\mathsf{term}})\end{aligned}$$

Consequently, the closed term M terminates almost surely iff $\llbracket M^\flat \rrbracket$ is a probability measure.

Remark 2. – Like many treatments of semantics of probabilistic programs in the literature, we make no distinction between non-terminating runs and aborted runs of a (closed) term M: both could result in the value semantics $\llbracket M^\flat \rrbracket$ being a sub-probabilty measure (cf. [4]).

– Even so, current probabilistic programming systems do not place any restrictions on the code that users can write: it is perfectly possible to construct invalid models because catching programs that do not define valid probability distributions can be hard, or even impossible. This is not surprising, because almost sure termination is hard to decide: it is Π_2^0-complete in the arithmetic hierarchy [22]. Nevertheless, because a.s. termination is an important correctness property of probabilistic programs (not least because of the main result of this paper, Thm. 3), the development of methods to prove a.s. termination is a hot research topic.

Accordingly the main theorem of this paper is stated as follows:

Theorem 3. *Let M be an SPCF term (possibly with free variables of type* R*) which terminates almost surely. Then its weight function* weight_M *and value function* value_M *are differentiable almost everywhere.*

5 Stochastic Symbolic Execution

We have seen that a source of discontinuity is the use of if-statements. Our main result therefore relies on an in-depth understanding of the branching behaviour of programs. The operational semantics given in Sec. 3 is unsatisfactory in this respect: any two execution paths are treated independently, whether they go through different branches of an if-statement or one is obtained from the other by using slightly perturbed random samples not affecting the control flow.

More concretely, note that although we have derived $\mathsf{weight}_{\mathsf{Ped}}[0.2, 0.9, 0.7] = 0.54$ and $\mathsf{value}_{\mathsf{Ped}}[0.2, 0.9, 0.7] = \underline{0.6}$ in Ex. 2, we cannot infer anything about $\mathsf{weight}_{\mathsf{Ped}}[0.21, 0.91, 0.71]$ and $\mathsf{value}_{\mathsf{Ped}}[0.21, 0.91, 0.71]$ unless we perform the corresponding reduction.

So we propose an alternative *symbolic* operational semantics (similar to the "compilation scheme" in [55]), in which no sampling is performed: whenever a sample command is encountered, we simply substitute a fresh variable α_i for it, and continue on with the execution. We can view this style of semantics as a stochastic form of symbolic execution [12,23], i.e., a means of analysing a program so as to determine what *inputs*, and *random draws* (from sample) cause each part of a program to execute.

Consider the term $M \equiv \mathsf{let}\ x = \mathsf{sample} \cdot \underline{3}\ \mathsf{in}\ (\mathsf{walk}\, x)$, defined using the function walk of Ex. 1. We have a reduction path

$$M \Rightarrow \mathsf{let}\ (x = \alpha_1 \cdot \underline{3})\ \mathsf{in}\ (\mathsf{walk}\, x) \Rightarrow \mathsf{walk}\,(\alpha_1 \cdot \underline{3})$$

but at this point we are stuck: the CBV strategy requires a value for α_1. We will "delay" the evaluation of the multiplication $\alpha_1 \cdot \underline{3}$; we signal this by drawing a box around the delayed operation: $\alpha_1 \boxdot \underline{3}$. We continue the execution, inspecting the definition of walk, and get:

$$M \Rightarrow^* \mathsf{walk}\,(\alpha_1 \boxdot \underline{3}) \Rightarrow^* N \equiv \mathsf{if}\big(\alpha_1 \boxdot \underline{3} \leq 0, \underline{0}, P\big)$$

where

$$P \equiv \begin{pmatrix} \text{let } s = \text{sample in} \\ \text{if}((\text{sample} \leq \underline{0.5}), (s + \text{walk}(\alpha_1 \boxdot \underline{3} + s)), (s + \text{walk}(\alpha_1 \boxdot \underline{3} - s))) \end{pmatrix}.$$

We are stuck again: the value of α_1 is needed in order to know which branch to follow. Our approach consists in considering the space $\mathbb{S}_1 = (0,1)$ of possible values for α_1, and splitting it into $\{s_1 \in (0,1) \mid s_1 \cdot 3 \leq 0\} = \emptyset$ and $\{s_1 \in (0,1) \mid s_1 \cdot 3 > 0\} = (0,1)$. Each of the two branches will then yield a weight function restricted to the appropriate subspace.

Formally, our symbolic operational semantics is a rewrite system of configurations of the form $\langle\!\langle \mathcal{M}, w, U \rangle\!\rangle$, where $\mathcal{M}$ is a term with delayed (boxed) operations, and free "sampling" variables[5] $\alpha_1, \ldots, \alpha_n$; $U \subseteq \mathbb{S}_n$ is the subspace of sampling values compatible with the current branch; and $w : U \to \mathbb{R}_{\geq 0}$ is a function assigning to each $s \in U$ a weight $w(s)$. In particular, for our running example[6]

$$\langle\!\langle M, \lambda[].\, 1, \mathbb{S}_0 \rangle\!\rangle \Rightarrow^* \langle\!\langle N, \lambda[s_1].\, 1, (0,1) \rangle\!\rangle.$$

As explained above, this leads to two branches:

$$\langle\!\langle N, \lambda[s_1].\, 1, (0,1) \rangle\!\rangle \begin{array}{l} \nearrow^* \langle\!\langle \underline{0}, \lambda[s_1].\, 1, \emptyset \rangle\!\rangle \\ \searrow^* \langle\!\langle P, \lambda[s_1].\, 1, (0,1) \rangle\!\rangle \end{array}$$

The first branch has reached a value, and the reader can check that the second branch continues as

$$\langle\!\langle P, \lambda[s_1].\, 1, (0,1) \rangle\!\rangle \Rightarrow^*$$
$$\langle\!\langle \text{if}(\alpha_3 \leq \underline{0.5}, \alpha_2 + \text{walk}(\alpha_1 \boxdot \underline{3} + \alpha_2), \alpha_2 + \text{walk}(\alpha_1 \boxdot \underline{3} - \alpha_2)), \lambda[s_1, s_2, s_3].\, 1, (0,1)^3 \rangle\!\rangle$$

where α_2 and α_3 stand for the two sample statements in P. From here we proceed by splitting $(0,1)^3$ into $(0,1) \times (0,1) \times (0,0.5]$ and $(0,1) \times (0,1) \times (0.5,1)$ and after having branched again (on whether we have passed 0) the evaluation of walk can terminate in the configuration

$$\langle\!\langle \alpha_2 \boxplus 0, \lambda[s_1, s_2, s_3].\, 1, U \rangle\!\rangle$$

where $U := \{[s_1, s_2, s_3] \in \mathbb{S}_3 \mid s_3 > 0.5 \wedge s_1 \cdot 3 - s_2 \leq 0\}$.

Recall that M appears in the context of our running example Ped. Using our calculations above we derive one of its branches:

$$\langle\!\langle \text{Ped}, \lambda[].\, 1, \{[]\} \rangle\!\rangle \Rightarrow^* \langle\!\langle \text{let w} = \text{score}(\underline{\text{pdf}_{\mathcal{N}(1.1,0.1)}(\alpha_2)}) \text{ in } \alpha_1 \boxdot \underline{3}, \lambda[s_1, s_2, s_3].\, 1, U \rangle\!\rangle$$
$$\Rightarrow \langle\!\langle \text{let } w = \text{score}(\boxed{\text{pdf}_{\mathcal{N}(1.1,0.1)}}(\alpha_2)) \text{ in } \alpha_1 \boxdot \underline{3}, \lambda[s_1, s_2, s_3].\, 1, U \rangle\!\rangle$$
$$\Rightarrow^* \langle\!\langle \text{let } w = \boxed{\text{pdf}_{\mathcal{N}(1.1,0.1)}}(\alpha_2) \text{ in } \alpha_1 \boxdot \underline{3}, \lambda[s_1, s_2, s_3].\, \text{pdf}_{\mathcal{N}(1.1,0.1)}(s_2), U \rangle\!\rangle$$
$$\Rightarrow^* \langle\!\langle \alpha_1 \boxdot \underline{3}, \lambda[s_1, s_2, s_3].\, \text{pdf}_{\mathcal{N}(1.1,0.1)}(s_2), U \rangle\!\rangle$$

[5] Note that $\mathcal{M}$ may be open and contain other free "non-sampling" variables, usually denoted $x_1, \ldots, x_m$.

[6] We use the meta-lambda-abstraction $\lambda x.\, f(x)$ to denote the set-theoretic function $x \mapsto f(x)$.

In particular the trace $[0.2, 0.9, 0.7]$ of Ex. 2 lies in the subspace U. We can immediately read off the corresponding value and weight functions for *all* $[s_1, s_2, s_3] \in U$ simply by evaluating the computation $\alpha_1 \cdot \underline{3}$, which we have delayed until now:

$$\mathsf{value}_{\mathsf{Ped}}[s_1, s_2, s_3] = \underline{s_1 \cdot 3} \qquad \mathsf{weight}_{\mathsf{Ped}}[s_1, s_2, s_3] = \mathrm{pdf}_{\mathcal{N}(1.1,0.1)}(s_2)$$

5.1 Symbolic Terms and Values

We have just described informally our symbolic execution approach, which involves delaying the evaluation of primitive operations. We make this formal by introducing an extended notion of terms, which we call ***symbolic terms*** and define in Fig. 4a along with a notion of ***symbolic values***. For this we assume fixed denumerable sequences of ***distinguished*** variables: $\alpha_1, \alpha_2, \ldots$, used to represent sampling, and $x_1, x_2, \ldots$ used for free variables of type R. Symbolic terms are typically denoted $\mathcal{M}$, $\mathcal{N}$, or $\mathcal{L}$. They contain terms of the form $\boxed{f}(\mathcal{V}_1, \ldots, \mathcal{V}_\ell)$ for $f : \mathbb{R}^\ell \rightharpoonup \mathbb{R} \in \mathcal{F}$ a primitive function, representing delayed evaluations, and they also contain the sampling variables α_j. The type system is adapted in a straightforward way, see Fig. 4b.

We use $\Lambda_{(m,n)}$ to refer to the set of well-typed symbolic terms with free variables amongst $x_1, \ldots, x_m$ and $\alpha_1, \ldots, \alpha_n$ (and all are of type R). Note that every term in the sense of Fig. 2 is also a symbolic term.

Each symbolic term $\mathcal{M} \in \Lambda_{(m,n)}$ has a corresponding set of regular terms, accounting for all possible values for its sampling variables $\alpha_1, \ldots, \alpha_n$ and its (other) free variables $x_1, \ldots, x_m$. For $\boldsymbol{r} \in \mathbb{R}^m$ and $\boldsymbol{s} \in \mathbb{S}_n$, we call ***partially evaluated instantiation*** of $\mathcal{M}$ the term $\lfloor \mathcal{M} \rfloor (\boldsymbol{r}, \boldsymbol{s})$ obtained from $\mathcal{M}[\underline{\boldsymbol{r}}/\boldsymbol{x}, \underline{\boldsymbol{s}}/\boldsymbol{\alpha}]$ by recursively "evaluating" subterms of the form $\boxed{f}(\underline{r_1}, \ldots, \underline{r_\ell})$ to $\underline{f(r_1, \ldots, r_\ell)}$, provided $(r_1, \ldots, r_\ell) \in \mathsf{dom}(f)$. In this operation, subterms of the form $\underline{f}(\underline{r_1}, \ldots, \underline{r_\ell})$ are left unchanged, and so are any other redexes. $\lfloor \mathcal{M} \rfloor$ can be viewed as a partial function $\lfloor \mathcal{M} \rfloor : \mathbb{R}^m \times \mathbb{S}_n \rightharpoonup \Lambda$ and a formal definition is presented in Fig. 5b. (To be completely rigorous, we define for *fixed* m and n, partial functions $\lfloor \mathcal{M} \rfloor_{m,n} : \mathbb{R}^m \times \mathbb{S}_n \rightharpoonup \Lambda$ for symbolic terms $\mathcal{M}$ whose distinguished variables are amongst $x_1, \ldots, x_m$ and $\alpha_1, \ldots, \alpha_n$. $\mathcal{M}$ may contain other variables $y, z, \ldots$ of any type. Since m and n are usually clear from the context, we omit them.) Observe that for $\mathcal{M} \in \Lambda_{(m,n)}$ and $(\boldsymbol{r}, \boldsymbol{s}) \in \mathsf{dom} \lfloor \mathcal{M} \rfloor$, $\lfloor \mathcal{M} \rfloor (\boldsymbol{r}, \boldsymbol{s})$ is a closed term.

Example 4. Consider $\mathcal{M} \equiv (\lambda z. \alpha_1 \boxdot \underline{3})\,(\mathsf{score}(\underline{\mathrm{pdf}_{\mathcal{N}(1.1,0.1)}}(\alpha_2)))$. Then, for $\boldsymbol{r} = []$ and $\boldsymbol{s} = [0.2, 0.9, 0.7]$, we have $\lfloor \mathcal{M} \rfloor (\boldsymbol{r}, \boldsymbol{s}) = (\lambda z. \underline{0.6})\,(\mathsf{score}(\underline{\mathrm{pdf}_{\mathcal{N}(1.1,0.1)}}(\underline{0.9})))$.

More generally, observe that if $\Gamma \vdash \mathcal{M} : \sigma$ and $(\boldsymbol{r}, \boldsymbol{s}) \in \mathsf{dom} \lfloor \mathcal{M} \rfloor$ then $\Gamma \vdash \lfloor \mathcal{M} \rfloor (\boldsymbol{r}, \boldsymbol{s}) : \sigma$. In order to evaluate conditionals $\mathsf{if}(\mathcal{L} \leq 0, \mathcal{M}, \mathcal{N})$ we need to reduce $\mathcal{L}$ to a real constant, i.e., we need to have $\lfloor \mathcal{L} \rfloor (\boldsymbol{r}, \boldsymbol{s}) = \underline{r}$ for some $r \in \mathbb{R}$. This is the case whenever $\mathcal{L}$ is a symbolic value of type R, since these are built only out of delayed operations, real constants and distinguished variables x_i or α_j. Indeed we can show the following:

Lemma 2. *Let* $(\boldsymbol{r}, \boldsymbol{s}) \in \mathsf{dom} \lfloor \mathcal{M} \rfloor$. *Then* $\mathcal{M}$ *is a symbolic value iff* $\lfloor \mathcal{M} \rfloor (\boldsymbol{r}, \boldsymbol{s})$ *is a value.*

$$\mathcal{V} ::= \underline{r} \mid x_i \mid \alpha_j \mid \boxed{f}(\mathcal{V}_1,\dots,\mathcal{V}_\ell) \mid \lambda y.\,\mathcal{M}$$

$$\mathcal{M},\mathcal{N},\mathcal{L} ::= \mathcal{V} \mid y \mid \underline{f}(\mathcal{M}_1,\dots,\mathcal{M}_\ell) \mid \mathcal{M}\,\mathcal{N} \mid \mathsf{Y}\mathcal{M} \mid \mathsf{if}(\mathcal{L}\le 0,\mathcal{M},\mathcal{N}) \mid \mathsf{sample} \mid \mathsf{score}(\mathcal{M})$$

(a) Symbolic values (typically $\mathcal{V}$) and symbolic terms (typically $\mathcal{M}$, $\mathcal{N}$ or $\mathcal{L}$)

$$\frac{\Gamma\vdash\mathcal{V}_1:\mathsf{R}\cdots\Gamma\vdash\mathcal{V}_\ell:\mathsf{R}}{\Gamma\vdash\boxed{f}(\mathcal{V}_1,\dots,\mathcal{V}_\ell):\mathsf{R}} \qquad \frac{}{\Gamma\vdash x_i:\mathsf{R}} \qquad \frac{}{\Gamma\vdash\alpha_j:\mathsf{R}}$$

$$\frac{}{\Gamma,y:\sigma\vdash y:\sigma} \qquad \frac{}{\Gamma\vdash\underline{r}:\mathsf{R}}\;r\in\mathbb{R} \qquad \frac{\Gamma\vdash\mathcal{M}_1:\mathsf{R}\cdots\Gamma\vdash\mathcal{M}_\ell:\mathsf{R}}{\Gamma\vdash\underline{f}(\mathcal{M}_1,\dots,\mathcal{M}_\ell):\mathsf{R}}$$

$$\frac{\Gamma,y:\sigma\vdash\mathcal{M}:\tau}{\Gamma\vdash\lambda y.\,\mathcal{M}:\sigma\to\tau} \qquad \frac{\Gamma\vdash\mathcal{M}:\sigma\to\tau\quad\Gamma\vdash\mathcal{N}:\sigma}{\Gamma\vdash\mathcal{M}\,\mathcal{N}:\tau} \qquad \frac{\Gamma\vdash\mathcal{M}:(\sigma\Rightarrow\tau)\Rightarrow\sigma\Rightarrow\tau}{\Gamma\vdash\mathsf{Y}\mathcal{M}:\sigma\Rightarrow\tau}$$

$$\frac{\Gamma\vdash\mathcal{L}:\mathsf{R}\quad\Gamma\vdash\mathcal{M}:\sigma\quad\Gamma\vdash\mathcal{N}:\sigma}{\Gamma\vdash\mathsf{if}(\mathcal{L}\le 0,\mathcal{M},\mathcal{N}):\sigma} \qquad \frac{}{\Gamma\vdash\mathsf{sample}:\mathsf{R}} \qquad \frac{\Gamma\vdash\mathcal{M}:\mathsf{R}}{\Gamma\vdash\mathsf{score}(\mathcal{M}):\mathsf{R}}$$

(b) Type system for symbolic terms

$$\mathcal{R} ::= (\lambda y.\,\mathcal{M})\,\mathcal{V} \mid \underline{f}(\mathcal{V}_1,\dots,\mathcal{V}_\ell) \mid \mathsf{Y}(\lambda y.\,\mathcal{M}) \mid \mathsf{if}(\mathcal{V}\le 0,\mathcal{M},\mathcal{N}) \mid \mathsf{sample} \mid \mathsf{score}(\mathcal{V})$$

$$\mathcal{E} ::= [\,] \mid \mathcal{E}\,\mathcal{M} \mid (\lambda y.\,\mathcal{M})\,\mathcal{E} \mid \underline{f}(\mathcal{V}_1,\dots,\mathcal{V}_{i-1},\mathcal{E},\mathcal{M}_{i+1},\dots,\mathcal{M}_\ell) \mid \mathsf{Y}\mathcal{E} \mid$$
$$\mathsf{if}(\mathcal{E}\le 0,\mathcal{M},\mathcal{N}) \mid \mathsf{score}(\mathcal{E})$$

(c) Symbolic values (typically $\mathcal{V}$), redexes ($\mathcal{R}$) and reduction contexts ($\mathcal{E}$).

Fig. 4: Symbolic terms and values, type system, reduction contexts, and redexes. As usual $f\in\mathcal{F}$ and $r\in\mathbb{R}$.

For symbolic values $\mathcal{V}:\mathsf{R}$ and $(\boldsymbol{r},\boldsymbol{s})\in\mathsf{dom}\lfloor\mathcal{V}\rfloor$ we employ the notation $\|\mathcal{V}\|(\boldsymbol{r},\boldsymbol{s}):=r'$ provided that $\lfloor\mathcal{V}\rfloor(\boldsymbol{r},\boldsymbol{s})=\underline{r'}$.

A simple induction on symbolic terms and values yields the following property, which is crucial for the proof of our main result (Thm. 3):

Lemma 3. *Suppose the set $\mathcal{F}$ of primitives satisfies Item 1 of Assumption 1.*

1. *For each symbolic value $\mathcal{V}$ of type* R*, by identifying* $\mathsf{dom}\,\|\mathcal{V}\|$ *with a subset of $\mathbb{R}^{m+n}$, we have $\|\mathcal{V}\|\in\mathcal{F}$.*
2. *If $\mathcal{F}$ also satisfies item 2 of Assumption 1 then for each symbolic term $\mathcal{M}$, $\lfloor\mathcal{M}\rfloor:\mathbb{R}^m\times\mathbb{S}_n\rightharpoonup\Lambda$ is differentiable in the interior of its domain.*

5.2 Symbolic Operational Semantics

We aim to develop a symbolic operational semantics that provides a sound and complete abstraction of the (concrete) operational trace semantics. The symbolic

$$\begin{aligned}
\mathsf{dom}\left\lfloor \boxed{f}(\mathcal{V}_1,\ldots,\mathcal{V}_\ell)\right\rfloor &:= \{(\boldsymbol{r},\boldsymbol{s}) \in \mathsf{dom}\lfloor \mathcal{V}_1\rfloor \cap\cdots\cap \mathsf{dom}\lfloor \mathcal{V}_\ell\rfloor \mid (r'_1,\ldots,r'_\ell) \in \mathsf{dom}(f),\\
&\qquad \text{where } \underline{r'_1} = \lfloor \mathcal{V}_1\rfloor(\boldsymbol{r},\boldsymbol{s}),\cdots,\underline{r'_\ell} = \lfloor \mathcal{V}_\ell\rfloor(\boldsymbol{r},\boldsymbol{s})\}\\
\mathsf{dom}\lfloor \mathsf{sample}\rfloor &:= \mathsf{dom}\lfloor x_i\rfloor := \mathsf{dom}\lfloor \alpha_j\rfloor := \mathsf{dom}\lfloor y\rfloor := \mathsf{dom}\lfloor \underline{r'}\rfloor := \mathbb{R}^m \times \mathbb{S}_n\\
\mathsf{dom}\underline{f}(\mathcal{M}_1,\ldots,\mathcal{M}_\ell) &:= \mathsf{dom}\lfloor \mathcal{M}_1\rfloor \cap\cdots\cap \mathsf{dom}\lfloor \mathcal{M}_\ell\rfloor\\
\mathsf{dom}\lfloor \lambda y.\, \mathcal{M}\rfloor &:= \mathsf{dom}\lfloor \mathsf{Y}\mathcal{M}\rfloor := \mathsf{dom}\lfloor \mathsf{score}(\mathcal{M})\rfloor := \mathsf{dom}\lfloor \mathcal{M}\rfloor\\
\mathsf{dom}\lfloor \mathcal{M}\,\mathcal{N}\rfloor &:= \mathsf{dom}\lfloor \mathcal{M}\rfloor \cap \mathsf{dom}\lfloor \mathcal{N}\rfloor\\
\mathsf{dom}\left\lfloor \mathsf{if}(\mathcal{L} \le 0,\mathcal{M},\mathcal{N})\right\rfloor &:= \mathsf{dom}\lfloor \mathcal{L}\rfloor \cap \mathsf{dom}\lfloor \mathcal{M}\rfloor \cap \mathsf{dom}\lfloor \mathcal{N}\rfloor
\end{aligned}$$

(a) Domain of $\lfloor\cdot\rfloor$

$$\begin{aligned}
\left\lfloor \boxed{f}(\mathcal{V}_1,\ldots,\mathcal{V}_\ell)\right\rfloor(\boldsymbol{r},\boldsymbol{s}) &:= \underline{f(r'_1,\ldots,r'_\ell)}\text{, where for } 1 \le i \le \ell,\ \lfloor \mathcal{V}_i\rfloor(\boldsymbol{r},\boldsymbol{s}) = \underline{r'_i}\\
\lfloor x_i\rfloor(\boldsymbol{r},\boldsymbol{s}) &:= \underline{r_i}\\
\lfloor \alpha_j\rfloor(\boldsymbol{r},\boldsymbol{s}) &:= \underline{s_j}\\
\lfloor y\rfloor(\boldsymbol{r},\boldsymbol{s}) &:= y\\
\lfloor \underline{r'}\rfloor(\boldsymbol{r},\boldsymbol{s}) &:= \underline{r'}\\
\left\lfloor \underline{f}(\mathcal{M}_1,\ldots,\mathcal{M}_\ell)\right\rfloor(\boldsymbol{r},\boldsymbol{s}) &:= \underline{f}(\lfloor \mathcal{M}_1\rfloor(\boldsymbol{r},\boldsymbol{s}),\ldots,\lfloor \mathcal{M}_\ell\rfloor(\boldsymbol{r},\boldsymbol{s}))\\
\lfloor \lambda y.\, \mathcal{M}\rfloor(\boldsymbol{r},\boldsymbol{s}) &:= \lambda y.\, \lfloor \mathcal{M}\rfloor(\boldsymbol{r},\boldsymbol{s})\\
\lfloor \mathcal{M}\,\mathcal{N}\rfloor(\boldsymbol{r},\boldsymbol{s}) &:= (\lfloor \mathcal{M}\rfloor(\boldsymbol{r},\boldsymbol{s}))\,(\lfloor \mathcal{N}\rfloor(\boldsymbol{r},\boldsymbol{s}))\\
\lfloor \mathsf{Y}\mathcal{M}\rfloor(\boldsymbol{r},\boldsymbol{s}) &:= \mathsf{Y}(\lfloor \mathcal{M}\rfloor(\boldsymbol{r},\boldsymbol{s}))\\
\left\lfloor \mathsf{if}(\mathcal{L} \le 0,\mathcal{M},\mathcal{N})\right\rfloor(\boldsymbol{r},\boldsymbol{s}) &:= \mathsf{if}(\lfloor \mathcal{L}\rfloor(\boldsymbol{r},\boldsymbol{s}) \le 0, \lfloor \mathcal{M}\rfloor(\boldsymbol{r},\boldsymbol{s}), \lfloor \mathcal{N}\rfloor(\boldsymbol{r},\boldsymbol{s}))\\
\lfloor \mathsf{sample}\rfloor(\boldsymbol{r},\boldsymbol{s}) &:= \mathsf{sample}\\
\lfloor \mathsf{score}(\mathcal{M})\rfloor(\boldsymbol{r},\boldsymbol{s}) &:= \mathsf{score}(\lfloor \mathcal{M}\rfloor(\boldsymbol{r},\boldsymbol{s}))
\end{aligned}$$

(b) Definition of $\lfloor\cdot\rfloor$ on $\mathsf{dom}\lfloor\cdot\rfloor$

Fig. 5: Formal definition of the instantiation and partial evaluation function $\lfloor\cdot\rfloor$

semantics is presented as a rewrite system of ***symbolic configurations***, which are defined to be triples of the form $\langle\!\langle \mathcal{M}, w, U\rangle\!\rangle$, where for some m and n, $\mathcal{M} \in \Lambda_{(m,n)}$, $U \subseteq \mathsf{dom}\lfloor \mathcal{M}\rfloor \subseteq \mathbb{R}^m \times \mathbb{S}_n$ is measurable, and $w : \mathbb{R}^m \times \mathbb{S} \rightharpoonup \mathbb{R}_{\ge 0}$ with $\mathsf{dom}(w) = U$. Thus we aim to prove the following result (writing *1* for the constant function $\lambda\!\!\lambda(\boldsymbol{r},\boldsymbol{s}).\,1$):

Theorem 1. *Let M be a term with free variables amongst $x_1,\ldots,x_m$.*

1. *(Soundness). If $\langle\!\langle M, 1, \mathbb{R}^m\rangle\!\rangle \Rightarrow^* \langle\!\langle \mathcal{V}, w, U\rangle\!\rangle$ then for all $(\boldsymbol{r},\boldsymbol{s}) \in U$ it holds $\mathsf{weight}_M(\boldsymbol{r},\boldsymbol{s}) = w(\boldsymbol{r},\boldsymbol{s})$ and $\mathsf{value}_M(\boldsymbol{r},\boldsymbol{s}) = \lfloor \mathcal{V}\rfloor(\boldsymbol{r},\boldsymbol{s})$.*
2. *(Completeness). If $\boldsymbol{r} \in \mathbb{R}^m$ and $\langle M[\underline{\boldsymbol{r}}/\boldsymbol{x}], 1, []\rangle \to^* \langle V, w, \boldsymbol{s}\rangle$ then there exists $\langle\!\langle M, 1, \mathbb{R}^m\rangle\!\rangle \Rightarrow^* \langle\!\langle \mathcal{V}, w, U\rangle\!\rangle$ such that $(\boldsymbol{r},\boldsymbol{s}) \in U$.*

As formalised by Thm. 1, the key intuition behind symbolic configurations $\langle\!\langle \mathcal{M}, w, U\rangle\!\rangle$ (that are reachable from a given $\langle\!\langle M, 1, \mathbb{R}^m\rangle\!\rangle$) is that, whenever $\mathcal{M}$ is a symbolic value:

- $\mathcal{M}$ gives a correct *local* view of value_M (restricted to U), and
- w gives a correct *local* view of weight_M (restricted to U);

moreover, the respective third components U (of the symbolic configurations $\langle\!\langle \mathcal{M}, w, U\rangle\!\rangle$) cover $\mathbb{T}_{M,\mathsf{term}}$.

To establish Thm. 1, we introduce ***symbolic reduction contexts*** and ***symbolic redexes***. These are presented in Fig. 4c and extend the usual notions (replacing real constants with arbitrary symbolic values of type R).

Using Lem. 2 we obtain:

Lemma 4. *If $\mathcal{R}$ is a symbolic redex and $(\boldsymbol{r}, \boldsymbol{s}) \in \mathsf{dom}\lfloor \mathcal{R}\rfloor$ then $\lfloor \mathcal{R}\rfloor(\boldsymbol{r}, \boldsymbol{s})$ is a redex.*

The following can be proven by a straightforward induction:

Lemma 5 (Subject Construction). *Let $\mathcal{M}$ be a symbolic term.*

1. *If $\mathcal{M}$ is a symbolic value then for all symbolic contexts $\mathcal{E}$ and symbolic redexes $\mathcal{R}$, $\mathcal{M} \not\equiv \mathcal{E}[\mathcal{R}]$.*
2. *If $\mathcal{M} \equiv \mathcal{E}_1[\mathcal{R}_1] \equiv \mathcal{E}_2[\mathcal{R}_2]$ then $\mathcal{E}_1 \equiv \mathcal{E}_2$ and $\mathcal{R}_1 \equiv \mathcal{R}_2$.*
3. *If $\mathcal{M}$ is not a symbolic value and $\mathsf{dom}\lfloor \mathcal{M}\rfloor \neq \emptyset$ then there exist $\mathcal{E}$ and $\mathcal{R}$ such that $\mathcal{M} \equiv \mathcal{E}[\mathcal{R}]$.*

The partial instantiation function also extends to symbolic contexts $\mathcal{E}$ in the evident way – we give the full definition in [34].

Now, we introduce the following rules for ***symbolic redex contractions***:

$$\begin{aligned}
\langle\!\langle (\lambda y.\, \mathcal{M})\, \mathcal{V}, w, U\rangle\!\rangle &\Rightarrow \langle\!\langle \mathcal{M}[\mathcal{V}/y], w, U\rangle\!\rangle \\
\langle\!\langle \underline{f}(\mathcal{V}_1, \dots, \mathcal{V}_\ell), w, U\rangle\!\rangle &\Rightarrow \langle\!\langle \boxed{f}(\mathcal{V}_1, \dots, \mathcal{V}_\ell), w, \mathsf{dom}\, \|\boxed{f}(\mathcal{V}_1, \dots, \mathcal{V}_\ell)\| \cap U\rangle\!\rangle \\
\langle\!\langle \mathsf{Y}(\lambda y.\, \mathcal{M}), w, U\rangle\!\rangle &\Rightarrow \langle\!\langle \lambda z.\, \mathcal{M}[\mathsf{Y}(\lambda y.\, \mathcal{M})/y]\, z, w, U\rangle\!\rangle \\
\langle\!\langle \mathsf{if}(\mathcal{V} \le 0, \mathcal{M}, \mathcal{N}), w, U\rangle\!\rangle &\Rightarrow \langle\!\langle \mathcal{M}, w, \|\mathcal{V}\|^{-1}(-\infty, 0] \cap U\rangle\!\rangle \\
\langle\!\langle \mathsf{if}(\mathcal{V} \le 0, \mathcal{M}, \mathcal{N}), w, U\rangle\!\rangle &\Rightarrow \langle\!\langle \mathcal{N}, w, \|\mathcal{V}\|^{-1}(0, \infty) \cap U\rangle\!\rangle \\
\langle\!\langle \mathsf{sample}, w, U\rangle\!\rangle &\Rightarrow \langle\!\langle \alpha_{n+1}, w', U'\rangle\!\rangle \qquad (U \subseteq \mathbb{R}^m \times \mathbb{S}_n) \\
\langle\!\langle \mathsf{score}(\mathcal{V}), w, U\rangle\!\rangle &\Rightarrow \langle\!\langle \mathcal{V}, \|\mathcal{V}\| \cdot w, \|\mathcal{V}\|^{-1}[0, \infty) \cap U\rangle\!\rangle
\end{aligned}$$

In the rule for sample, $U' := \{(\boldsymbol{r}, \boldsymbol{s} +\!\!+ [s']) \mid (\boldsymbol{r}, \boldsymbol{s}) \in U \land s' \in (0,1)\}$ and $w'(\boldsymbol{r}, \boldsymbol{s} +\!\!+ [s']) := w(\boldsymbol{r}, \boldsymbol{s})$; in the rule for $\mathsf{score}(\mathcal{V})$, $(\|\mathcal{V}\| \cdot w)(\boldsymbol{r}, \boldsymbol{s}) := \|\mathcal{V}\|(\boldsymbol{r}, \boldsymbol{s}) \cdot w(\boldsymbol{r}, \boldsymbol{s})$.

The rules are designed to closely mirror their concrete counterparts. Crucially, the rule for sample introduces a "fresh" sampling variable, and the two rules for conditionals split the last component $U \subseteq \mathbb{R}^m \times \mathbb{S}_n$ according to whether $\|\mathcal{V}\|(\boldsymbol{r}, \boldsymbol{s}) \le 0$ or $\|\mathcal{V}\|(\boldsymbol{r}, \boldsymbol{s}) > 0$. The "delay" contraction (second rule) is introduced for a technical reason: ultimately, to enable item 1 (Soundness). Otherwise it is, for example, unclear whether $\lambda y.\, \alpha_1 + \underline{1}$ should correspond to $\lambda y.\, \underline{0.5} + \underline{1}$ or $\lambda y.\, \underline{1.5}$ for $s_1 = 0.5$.

Finally we lift this to arbitrary symbolic terms using the obvious rule for symbolic evaluation contexts:

$$\frac{\langle\!\langle \mathcal{R}, w, U \rangle\!\rangle \Rightarrow \langle\!\langle \mathcal{R}', w', U' \rangle\!\rangle}{\langle\!\langle \mathcal{E}[\mathcal{R}], w, U \rangle\!\rangle \Rightarrow \langle\!\langle \mathcal{E}[\mathcal{R}'], w', U' \rangle\!\rangle}$$

Note that we do not need rules corresponding to reductions to fail because the third component of the symbolic configurations "filters out" the pairs $(\boldsymbol{r}, \boldsymbol{s})$ corresponding to undefined behaviour. In particular, the following holds:

Lemma 6. *Suppose $\langle\!\langle \mathcal{M}, w, U \rangle\!\rangle$ is a symbolic configuration and $\langle\!\langle \mathcal{M}, w, U \rangle\!\rangle \Rightarrow \langle\!\langle \mathcal{N}, w', U' \rangle\!\rangle$. Then $\langle\!\langle \mathcal{N}, w', U' \rangle\!\rangle$ is a symbolic configuration.*

A key advantage of the symbolic execution is that the induced computation tree is finitely branching, since branching only arises from conditionals, splitting the trace space into disjoint subsets. This contrasts with the concrete situation (from Sec. 3), in which sampling creates uncountably many branches.

Lemma 7 (Basic Properties). *Let $\langle\!\langle \mathcal{M}, w, U \rangle\!\rangle$ be a symbolic configuration. Then*

1. *There are at most countably distinct such U' that $\langle\!\langle \mathcal{M}, w, U \rangle\!\rangle \Rightarrow^* \langle\!\langle \mathcal{N}, w', U' \rangle\!\rangle$.*
2. *If $\langle\!\langle \mathcal{M}, w, U \rangle\!\rangle \Rightarrow^* \langle\!\langle \mathcal{V}_i, w_i, U_i \rangle\!\rangle$ for $i \in \{1, 2\}$ then $U_1 = U_2$ or $U_1 \cap U_2 = \emptyset$.*
3. *If $\langle\!\langle \mathcal{M}, w, U \rangle\!\rangle \Rightarrow^* \langle\!\langle \mathcal{E}_i[\mathsf{sample}], w_i, U_i \rangle\!\rangle$ for $i \in \{1, 2\}$ then $U_1 = U_2$ or $U_1 \cap U_2 = \emptyset$.*

Crucially, there is a correspondence between the concrete and symbolic semantics in that they can "simulate" each other:

Proposition 1 (Correspondence). *Suppose $\langle\!\langle \mathcal{M}, w, U \rangle\!\rangle$ is a symbolic configuration, and $(\boldsymbol{r}, \boldsymbol{s}) \in U$. Let $M \equiv \lfloor \mathcal{M} \rfloor (\boldsymbol{r}, \boldsymbol{s})$ and $w := w(\boldsymbol{r}, \boldsymbol{s})$. Then*

1. *If $\langle\!\langle \mathcal{M}, w, U \rangle\!\rangle \Rightarrow \langle\!\langle \mathcal{N}, w', U' \rangle\!\rangle$ and $(\boldsymbol{r}, \boldsymbol{s} +\!\!+\, \boldsymbol{s}') \in U'$ then*
$$\langle M, w, \boldsymbol{s} \rangle \to \langle \lfloor \mathcal{N} \rfloor (\boldsymbol{r}, \boldsymbol{s} +\!\!+\, \boldsymbol{s}'), w(\boldsymbol{r}, \boldsymbol{s}'), \boldsymbol{s} +\!\!+\, \boldsymbol{s}' \rangle\,.$$
2. *If $\langle M, w, \boldsymbol{s} \rangle \to \langle N, w', \boldsymbol{s}' \rangle$ then there exists $\langle\!\langle \mathcal{M}, w, U \rangle\!\rangle \Rightarrow \langle\!\langle \mathcal{N}, w', U' \rangle\!\rangle$ such that $\lfloor \mathcal{N} \rfloor (\boldsymbol{r}, \boldsymbol{s}') \equiv N$, $w'(\boldsymbol{r}, \boldsymbol{s}') = w'$ and $(\boldsymbol{r}, \boldsymbol{s}') \in U'$.*

As a consequence of Lem. 2, we obtain a proof of Thm. 1.

6 Densities of Almost Surely Terminating Programs are Differentiable Almost Everywhere

So far we have seen that the symbolic execution semantics provides a sound and complete way to reason about the weight and value functions. In this section we impose further restrictions on the primitive operations and the terms to obtain results about the differentiability of these functions.

Henceforth we assume Assumption 1 and we fix a term M with free variables amongst $x_1, \ldots, x_m$.

From Lem. 3 we immediately obtain the following:

Lemma 8. *Let $\langle\!\langle \mathcal{M}, w, U \rangle\!\rangle$ be a symbolic configuration such that w is differentiable on $\mathring{U}$ and $\mu(\partial U) = 0$. If $\langle\!\langle \mathcal{M}, w, U \rangle\!\rangle \Rightarrow \langle\!\langle \mathcal{M}', w', U' \rangle\!\rangle$ then w' is differentiable on $\mathring{U}'$ and $\mu(\partial U') = 0$.*

6.1 Differentiability on Terminating Traces

As an immediate consequence of the preceding, Lem. 3 and the Soundness (item 1 of Thm. 1), whenever $\langle\!\langle M, 1, \mathbb{R}^m \rangle\!\rangle \Rightarrow^* \langle\!\langle \mathcal{V}, w, U \rangle\!\rangle$ then weight_M and value_M are differentiable everywhere in $\mathring{U}$.

Recall the set $\mathbb{T}_{M,\mathsf{term}}$ of $(\boldsymbol{r}, \boldsymbol{s}) \in \mathbb{R}^m \times \mathbb{S}$ from Eq. (1) for which M terminates. We abbreviate $\mathbb{T}_{M,\mathsf{term}}$ to $\mathbb{T}_{\mathsf{term}}$ and define

$$\mathbb{T}_{\mathsf{term}} := \mathbb{T}_{M,\mathsf{term}} = \{(\boldsymbol{r}, \boldsymbol{s}) \in \mathbb{R}^m \times \mathbb{S} \mid \exists V, w \,.\, \langle M[\boldsymbol{r}/\boldsymbol{x}], 1, [] \rangle \to^* \langle V, w, \boldsymbol{s} \rangle\}$$
$$\mathbb{T}^{\mathsf{int}}_{\mathsf{term}} := \bigcup \{\mathring{U} \mid \exists \mathcal{V}, w \,.\, \langle\!\langle M, 1, \mathbb{R}^m \rangle\!\rangle \Rightarrow^* \langle\!\langle \mathcal{V}, w, U \rangle\!\rangle\}$$

By Completeness (item 2 of Thm. 1), $\mathbb{T}_{\mathsf{term}} = \bigcup \{U \mid \exists \mathcal{V}, w \,.\, \langle\!\langle M, 1, \mathbb{R}^m \rangle\!\rangle \Rightarrow^* \langle\!\langle \mathcal{V}, w, U \rangle\!\rangle\}$. Therefore, being countable unions of measurable sets (Lemmas 6 and 7), $\mathbb{T}_{\mathsf{term}}$ and $\mathbb{T}^{\mathsf{int}}_{\mathsf{term}}$ are measurable.

By what we have said above, weight_M and value_M are differentiable everywhere on $\mathbb{T}^{\mathsf{int}}_{\mathsf{term}}$. Observe that in general, $\mathbb{T}^{\mathsf{int}}_{\mathsf{term}} \subsetneq \mathring{\mathbb{T}}_{\mathsf{term}}$. However,

$$\mu\left(\mathbb{T}_{\mathsf{term}} \setminus \mathbb{T}^{\mathsf{int}}_{\mathsf{term}}\right) = \mu\Bigg(\bigcup_{\substack{U : \langle\!\langle M, 1, \mathbb{R}^m \rangle\!\rangle \Rightarrow^* \\ \langle\!\langle \mathcal{V}, w, U \rangle\!\rangle}} (U \setminus \mathring{U})\Bigg) \leq \sum_{\substack{U : \langle\!\langle M, 1, \mathbb{R}^m \rangle\!\rangle \Rightarrow^* \\ \langle\!\langle \mathcal{V}, w, U \rangle\!\rangle}} \mu(\partial U) = 0 \quad (2)$$

The first equation holds because the U-indexed union is of pairwise disjoint sets. The inequality is due to $(U \setminus \mathring{U}) \subseteq \partial U$. The last equation above holds because each $\mu(\partial U) = 0$ (Assumption 1 and Lem. 8).

Thus we conclude:

Theorem 2. *Let M be an SPCF term. Then its weight function* weight_M *and value function* value_M *are differentiable for almost all terminating traces.*

6.2 Differentiability for Almost Surely Terminating Terms

Next, we would like to extend this insight for almost surely terminating terms to suitable subsets of $\mathbb{R}^m \times \mathbb{S}$, the union of which constitutes almost the entirety of $\mathbb{R}^m \times \mathbb{S}$. Therefore, it is worth examining consequences of almost sure termination (see Def. 1).

We say that $(\boldsymbol{r}, \boldsymbol{s}) \in \mathbb{R}^m \times \mathbb{S}$ is ***maximal*** (for M) if $\langle M[\underline{\boldsymbol{r}}/\boldsymbol{x}], 1, [] \rangle \to^* \langle N, w, \boldsymbol{s} \rangle$ and for all $\boldsymbol{s}' \in \mathbb{S} \setminus \{[]\}$ and N', $\langle N, w, \boldsymbol{s} \rangle \not\to^* \langle N', w', \boldsymbol{s} \mathbin{+\!\!+} \boldsymbol{s}' \rangle$. Intuitively, $\boldsymbol{s}$ contains a maximal number of samples to reduce $M[\boldsymbol{r}/\boldsymbol{x}]$. Let $\mathbb{T}_{\mathsf{max}}$ be the set of maximal $(\boldsymbol{r}, \boldsymbol{s})$.

Note that $\mathbb{T}_{\mathsf{term}} \subseteq \mathbb{T}_{\mathsf{max}}$ and there are terms for which the inclusion is strict (e.g. for the diverging term $M \equiv \mathsf{Y}(\lambda f.\, f)$, $[] \in \mathbb{T}_{\mathsf{max}}$ but $[] \notin \mathbb{T}_{\mathsf{term}}$). Besides,

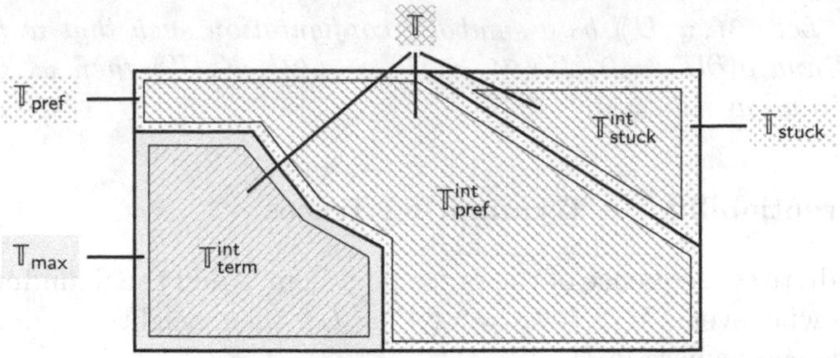

Fig. 6: Illustration of how $\mathbb{R}^m \times \mathbb{S}$ – visualised as the entire rectangle – is partitioned to prove Thm. 3. The value function returns $\perp$ in the red dotted area and a closed value elsewhere (i.e. in the blue shaded area).

$\mathbb{T}_{\mathsf{max}}$ is measurable because, thanks to Prop. 1, for every $n \in \mathbb{N}$,

$$\{(\boldsymbol{r}, \boldsymbol{s}) \in \mathbb{R}^m \times \mathbb{S}_n \mid \langle M[\underline{\boldsymbol{r}}/\boldsymbol{x}], 1, []\rangle \to^* \langle N, w, \boldsymbol{s}\rangle\} = \bigcup_{\substack{U : \langle\!\langle M, 1, \mathbb{R}^m \rangle\!\rangle \Rightarrow^* \\ \langle\!\langle \mathcal{N}, w, U \rangle\!\rangle}} U \cap (\mathbb{R}^m \times \mathbb{S}_n)$$

and the RHS is a countable union of measurable sets (Lemmas 6 and 7).

The following is a consequnce of the definition of almost sure termination and a corollary of Fubini's theorem (see [34] for details):

Lemma 9. *If M terminates almost surely then* $\mu(\mathbb{T}_{\mathsf{max}} \setminus \mathbb{T}_{\mathsf{term}}) = 0$.

Now, observe that for all $(\boldsymbol{r}, \boldsymbol{s}) \in \mathbb{R}^m \times \mathbb{S}$, exactly one of the following holds:
1. $(\boldsymbol{r}, \boldsymbol{s})$ is maximal
2. for a proper prefix $\boldsymbol{s}'$ of $\boldsymbol{s}$, $(\boldsymbol{r}, \boldsymbol{s}')$ is maximal
3. $(\boldsymbol{r}, \boldsymbol{s})$ is *stuck*, because $\boldsymbol{s}$ does not contain enough randomness.

Formally, we say $(\boldsymbol{r}, \boldsymbol{s})$ is ***stuck*** if $\langle M[\underline{\boldsymbol{r}}/\boldsymbol{x}], 1, []\rangle \to^* \langle E[\mathsf{sample}], w, \boldsymbol{s}\rangle$, and we let $\mathbb{T}_{\mathsf{stuck}}$ be the set of all $(\boldsymbol{r}, \boldsymbol{s})$ which get stuck. Thus,

$$\mathbb{R}^m \times \mathbb{S} = \mathbb{T}_{\mathsf{max}} \cup \mathbb{T}_{\mathsf{pref}} \cup \mathbb{T}_{\mathsf{stuck}}$$

where $\mathbb{T}_{\mathsf{pref}} := \{(\boldsymbol{r}, \boldsymbol{s} +\!\!+ \boldsymbol{s}') \mid (\boldsymbol{r}, \boldsymbol{s}) \in \mathbb{T}_{\mathsf{max}} \wedge \boldsymbol{s}' \neq []\}$, and the union is disjoint.

Defining $\mathbb{T}_{\mathsf{stuck}}^{\mathsf{int}} := \bigcup\{\mathring{U} \mid \langle\!\langle M, 1, \mathbb{R}^m \rangle\!\rangle \Rightarrow^* \langle\!\langle \mathcal{E}[\mathsf{sample}], w, U \rangle\!\rangle\}$ we can argue analogously to Eq. (2) that $\mu(\mathbb{T}_{\mathsf{stuck}} \setminus \mathbb{T}_{\mathsf{stuck}}^{\mathsf{int}}) = 0$.

Moreover, for $\mathbb{T}_{\mathsf{pref}}^{\mathsf{int}} := \{(\boldsymbol{r}, \boldsymbol{s} +\!\!+ \boldsymbol{s}') \mid (\boldsymbol{r}, \boldsymbol{s}) \in \mathbb{T}_{\mathsf{term}}^{\mathsf{int}}$ and $[] \neq \boldsymbol{s}' \in \mathbb{S}\}$ it holds

$$\mathbb{T}_{\mathsf{pref}} \setminus \mathbb{T}_{\mathsf{pref}}^{\mathsf{int}} = \bigcup_{n \in \mathbb{N}} \{(\boldsymbol{r}, \boldsymbol{s} +\!\!+ \boldsymbol{s}') \mid (\boldsymbol{r}, \boldsymbol{s}) \in \mathbb{T}_{\mathsf{max}} \setminus \mathbb{T}_{\mathsf{term}}^{\mathsf{int}} \wedge \boldsymbol{s}' \in \mathbb{S}_n\}$$

and hence, $\mu(\mathbb{T}_{\mathsf{pref}} \setminus \mathbb{T}_{\mathsf{pref}}^{\mathsf{int}}) \leq \sum_{n \in \mathbb{N}} \mu(\mathbb{T}_{\mathsf{max}} \setminus \mathbb{T}_{\mathsf{term}}^{\mathsf{int}}) \leq 0$.

Finally, we define

$$\mathbb{T} := \mathbb{T}_{\mathsf{term}}^{\mathsf{int}} \cup \mathbb{T}_{\mathsf{pref}}^{\mathsf{int}} \cup \mathbb{T}_{\mathsf{stuck}}^{\mathsf{int}}$$

Clearly, this is an open set and the situation is illustrated in Fig. 6. By what we have seen,

$$\mu\left((\mathbb{R}^m \times \mathbb{S}) \setminus \mathbb{T}\right) = \mu(\mathbb{T}_{\mathsf{term}} \setminus \mathbb{T}_{\mathsf{term}}^{\mathsf{int}}) + \mu(\mathbb{T}_{\mathsf{pref}}^{\mathsf{int}} \setminus \mathbb{T}_{\mathsf{pref}}) + \mu(\mathbb{T}_{\mathsf{stuck}} \setminus \mathbb{T}_{\mathsf{stuck}}^{\mathsf{int}}) = 0$$

Moreover, to conclude the proof of our main result Thm. 3 it suffices to note:

1. weight_M and value_M are differentiable everywhere on $\mathbb{T}_{\mathsf{term}}^{\mathsf{int}}$ (as for Thm. 2), and
2. $\mathsf{weight}_M(\boldsymbol{r}, \boldsymbol{s}) = 0$ and $\mathsf{value}_M(\boldsymbol{r}, \boldsymbol{s}) = \bot$ for $(\boldsymbol{r}, \boldsymbol{s}) \in \mathbb{T}_{\mathsf{pref}}^{\mathsf{int}} \cup \mathbb{T}_{\mathsf{stuck}}^{\mathsf{int}}$.

Theorem 3. *Let M be an SPCF term (possibly with free variables of type* R*) which terminates almost surely. Then its weight function* weight_M *and value function* value_M *are differentiable almost everywhere.*

We remark that almost sure termination was not used in our development until the proof of Lem. 9. For Thm. 3 we could have instead directly assumed the conclusion of Lem. 9; that is, almost all maximal traces are terminating. This is a strictly weaker condition than almost sure termination. The exposition we give is more appropriate: almost sure termination is a standard notion, and the development of methods to prove almost sure termination is a subject of active research.

We also note that the technique used in this paper to establish almost everywhere differentiability could be used to target another "almost everywhere" property instead: one can simply remove the requirement that elements of $\mathcal{F}$ are differentiable, and replace it with the desired property. A basic example of this is *smoothness*.

7 Conclusion

We have solved an open problem in the theory of probabilistic programming. This is mathematically interesting, and motivated the development of stochastic symbolic execution, a more informative form of operational semantics in this context. The result is also of major practical interest, since almost everywhere differentiability is necessary for correct gradient-based inference.

Related Work. This problem was partially addressed in the work of Zhou et al. [55] who prove a restricted form of our theorem for recursion-free first-order programs with analytic primitives. Our stochastic symbolic execution is related to their *compilation scheme*, which we extend to a more general language.

The idea of considering the possible control paths through a probabilistic programs is fairly natural and not new to this paper; it has been used towards the design of specialised inference algorithms for probabilistic programming, see [11,56]. To our knowledge, this is the first semantic formalisation of the concept, and the first time it is used to reason about whole-program density.

The notions of *weight function* and *value function* in this paper are inspired by the more standard trace-based operational semantics of Borgström et al. [8] (see also [52,31]).

Mazza and Pagani [35] study the correctness of automatic differentiation (AD) of purely *deterministic* programs. This problem is orthogonal to the work reported here, but it is interesting to combine their result with ours. Specifically, we show a.e. differentiability whilst [35] proves a.s. correctness of AD on the *differentiable* domain. Combining both results one concludes that for a deterministic program, AD returns a correct gradient a.s. on the *entire* domain. Going deeper into the comparison, Mazza and Pagani propose a notion of admissible primitive function strikingly similar to ours: given continuity, their condition 2 and our condition 3 are equivalent. On the other hand we require admissible functions to be differentiable, when they are merely continuous in [35]. Finally, we conjecture that "stable points", a central notion in [35], have a clear counterpart within our framework: for a symbolic evaluation path arriving at $\langle\!\langle \mathcal{V}, w, U \rangle\!\rangle$, for $\mathcal{V}$ a symbolic value, the points of $\mathring{U}$ are precisely the stable points.

Our work is also connected to recent developments in differentiable programming. Lee et al. [30] study the family of *piecewise functions under analytic partition*, or just "PAP" functions. PAP functions are a well-behaved family of almost everywhere differentiable functions, which can be used to reason about automatic differentiation in recursion-free first-order programs. An interesting question is whether this can be extended to a more general language, and whether densities of almost surely terminating SPCF programs are PAP functions. (See also [19,9] for work on differentiable programs *without* conditionals.)

A similar class of functions is also introduced by Bolte and Pauwels [7] in very recent work; this is used to prove a convergence result for stochastic gradient descent in deep learning. Whether this class of functions can be used to reason about probabilistic program densities remains to be explored.

Finally we note that *open logical relations* [1] are a convenient proof technique for establishing properties of programs which hold at first order, such as almost everywhere differentiability. This approach remains to be investigated in this context, as the connection with probabilistic densities is not immediate.

Further Directions. This investigation would benefit from a denotational treatment; this is not currently possible as existing models of probabilistic programming do not account for differentiability.

In another direction, it is likely that we can generalise the main result by extending SPCF with recursive types, as in [51], and, more speculatively, first-class differential operators as in [17]. It would also be useful to add to SPCF a family of *discrete* distributions, and more generally continuous-discrete mixtures, which have practical applications [36].

Our work will have interesting implications in the correctness of various gradient-based inference algorithms, such as the recent discontinuous HMC [39] and reparameterisation gradient for non-differentiable models [32]. But given the lack of guarantees of correctness properties available until now, these algorithms have not yet been developed in full generality, leaving many perspectives open.

Acknowledgements. We thank Wonyeol Lee for spotting an error in an example.
We gratefully acknowledge support from EPSRC and the Royal Society.

References

1. Gilles Barthe, Raphaëlle Crubillé, Ugo Dal Lago, and Francesco Gavazzo. On the versatility of open logical relations. In *European Symposium on Programming*, pages 56–83. Springer, 2020.
2. Sooraj Bhat, Ashish Agarwal, Richard W. Vuduc, and Alexander G. Gray. A type theory for probability density functions. In John Field and Michael Hicks, editors, *Proceedings of the 39th ACM SIGPLAN-SIGACT Symposium on Principles of Programming Languages, POPL 2012, Philadelphia, Pennsylvania, USA, January 22-28, 2012*, pages 545–556. ACM, 2012.
3. Sooraj Bhat, Johannes Borgström, Andrew D. Gordon, and Claudio V. Russo. Deriving probability density functions from probabilistic functional programs. *Logical Methods in Computer Science*, 13(2), 2017.
4. Benjamin Bichsel, Timon Gehr, and Martin T. Vechev. Fine-grained semantics for probabilistic programs. In Amal Ahmed, editor, *Programming Languages and Systems - 27th European Symposium on Programming, ESOP 2018, Held as Part of the European Joint Conferences on Theory and Practice of Software, ETAPS 2018, Thessaloniki, Greece, April 14-20, 2018, Proceedings*, volume 10801 of *Lecture Notes in Computer Science*, pages 145–185. Springer, 2018.
5. Eli Bingham, Jonathan P. Chen, Martin Jankowiak, Fritz Obermeyer, Neeraj Pradhan, Theofanis Karaletsos, Rohit Singh, Paul A. Szerlip, Paul Horsfall, and Noah D. Goodman. Pyro: Deep universal probabilistic programming. *J. Mach. Learn. Res.*, 20:28:1–28:6, 2019.
6. David M Blei, Alp Kucukelbir, and Jon D McAuliffe. Variational inference: A review for statisticians. *Journal of the American statistical Association*, 112(518):859–877, 2017.
7. Jérôme Bolte and Edouard Pauwels. A mathematical model for automatic differentiation in machine learning. *CoRR*, abs/2006.02080, 2020.
8. Johannes Borgström, Ugo Dal Lago, Andrew D. Gordon, and Marcin Szymczak. A lambda-calculus foundation for universal probabilistic programming. In *Proceedings of the 21st ACM SIGPLAN International Conference on Functional Programming, ICFP 2016, Nara, Japan, September 18-22, 2016*, pages 33–46, 2016.
9. Aloïs Brunel, Damiano Mazza, and Michele Pagani. Backpropagation in the simply typed lambda-calculus with linear negation. *Proc. ACM Program. Lang.*, 4(POPL):64:1–64:27, 2020.
10. Simon Castellan and Hugo Paquet. Probabilistic programming inference via intensional semantics. In *European Symposium on Programming*, pages 322–349. Springer, 2019.
11. Arun Chaganty, Aditya Nori, and Sriram Rajamani. Efficiently sampling probabilistic programs via program analysis. In *Artificial Intelligence and Statistics*, pages 153–160, 2013.
12. Lori A. Clarke. A system to generate test data and symbolically execute programs. *IEEE Trans. Software Eng.*, 2(3):215–222, 1976.
13. Ryan Culpepper and Andrew Cobb. Contextual equivalence for probabilistic programs with continuous random variables and scoring. In Hongseok Yang, editor, *Programming Languages and Systems - 26th European Symposium on Programming, ESOP 2017, Held as Part of the European Joint Conferences on Theory and Practice of Software, ETAPS 2017, Uppsala, Sweden, April 22-29, 2017, Proceedings*, volume 10201 of *Lecture Notes in Computer Science*, pages 368–392. Springer, 2017.

14. Marco F. Cusumano-Towner, Feras A. Saad, Alexander K. Lew, and Vikash K. Mansinghka. Gen: a general-purpose probabilistic programming system with programmable inference. In Kathryn S. McKinley and Kathleen Fisher, editors, *Proceedings of the 40th ACM SIGPLAN Conference on Programming Language Design and Implementation, PLDI 2019, Phoenix, AZ, USA, June 22-26, 2019*, pages 221–236. ACM, 2019.
15. S. Duane, A. D. Kennedy, B. J. Pendleton, and D. Roweth. Hybrid monte carlo. *Physics letters B*, 1987.
16. Thomas Ehrhard, Michele Pagani, and Christine Tasson. Measurable cones and stable, measurable functions: a model for probabilistic higher-order programming. *PACMPL*, 2(POPL):59:1–59:28, 2018.
17. Thomas Ehrhard and Laurent Regnier. The differential lambda-calculus. *Theor. Comput. Sci.*, 309(1-3):1–41, 2003.
18. Matthew D. Hoffman, David M. Blei, Chong Wang, and John W. Paisley. Stochastic variational inference. *J. Mach. Learn. Res.*, 14(1):1303–1347, 2013.
19. Mathieu Huot, Sam Staton, and Matthijs Vákár. Correctness of automatic differentiation via diffeologies and categorical gluing. In Jean Goubault-Larrecq and Barbara König, editors, *Foundations of Software Science and Computation Structures - 23rd International Conference, FOSSACS 2020, Held as Part of the European Joint Conferences on Theory and Practice of Software, ETAPS 2020, Dublin, Ireland, April 25-30, 2020, Proceedings*, volume 12077 of *Lecture Notes in Computer Science*, pages 319–338. Springer, 2020.
20. Chung-Kil Hur, Aditya V Nori, Sriram K Rajamani, and Selva Samuel. A provably correct sampler for probabilistic programs. In *35th IARCS Annual Conference on Foundations of Software Technology and Theoretical Computer Science (FSTTCS 2015)*. Schloss Dagstuhl-Leibniz-Zentrum fuer Informatik, 2015.
21. Wazim Mohammed Ismail and Chung-chieh Shan. Deriving a probability density calculator (functional pearl). In Jacques Garrigue, Gabriele Keller, and Eijiro Sumii, editors, *Proceedings of the 21st ACM SIGPLAN International Conference on Functional Programming, ICFP 2016, Nara, Japan, September 18-22, 2016*, pages 47–59. ACM, 2016.
22. Benjamin Lucien Kaminski, Joost-Pieter Katoen, and Christoph Matheja. On the hardness of analyzing probabilistic programs. *Acta Inf.*, 56(3):255–285, 2019.
23. James C. King. Symbolic execution and program testing. *Commun. ACM*, 19(7):385–394, 1976.
24. Diederik P. Kingma and Max Welling. Auto-encoding variational bayes. In Yoshua Bengio and Yann LeCun, editors, *2nd International Conference on Learning Representations, ICLR 2014, Banff, AB, Canada, April 14-16, 2014, Conference Track Proceedings*, 2014.
25. Oleg Kiselyov. Problems of the Lightweight Implementation of Probabilistic Programming. In *PPS Workshop*, 2016.
26. Dexter Kozen. Semantics of probabilistic programs. In *20th Annual Symposium on Foundations of Computer Science, San Juan, Puerto Rico, 29-31 October 1979*, pages 101–114, 1979.
27. Alp Kucukelbir, Rajesh Ranganath, Andrew Gelman, and David M. Blei. Automatic variational inference in stan. In *Advances in Neural Information Processing Systems 28: Annual Conference on Neural Information Processing Systems 2015, December 7-12, 2015, Montreal, Quebec, Canada*, pages 568–576, 2015.
28. Jeffrey M. Lee. *Manifolds and Differential Geometry*, volume 107 of *Graduate Studies in Mathematics*. AMS, 2009.

29. John M. Lee. *An introduction to smooth manifolds*, volume 218 of *Graduate Texts in Mathematics*. Springer, second edition, 2013.
30. Wonyeol Lee, Hangyeol Yu, Xavier Rival, and Hongseok Yang. On correctness of automatic differentiation for non-differentiable functions. *CoRR*, abs/2006.06903, 2020.
31. Wonyeol Lee, Hangyeol Yu, Xavier Rival, and Hongseok Yang. Towards verified stochastic variational inference for probabilistic programs. *PACMPL*, 4(POPL):16:1–16:33, 2020.
32. Wonyeol Lee, Hangyeol Yu, and Hongseok Yang. Reparameterization gradient for non-differentiable models. In Samy Bengio, Hanna M. Wallach, Hugo Larochelle, Kristen Grauman, Nicolò Cesa-Bianchi, and Roman Garnett, editors, *Advances in Neural Information Processing Systems 31: Annual Conference on Neural Information Processing Systems 2018, NeurIPS 2018, 3-8 December 2018, Montréal, Canada*, pages 5558–5568, 2018.
33. Alexander K Lew, Marco F Cusumano-Towner, Benjamin Sherman, Michael Carbin, and Vikash K Mansinghka. Trace types and denotational semantics for sound programmable inference in probabilistic languages. *Proceedings of the ACM on Programming Languages*, 4(POPL):1–32, 2019.
34. Carol Mak, C.-H. Luke Ong, Hugo Paquet, and Dominik Wagner. Densities of almost-surely terminating probabilistic programs are differentiable almost everywhere. *CoRR*, abs/2004.03924, 2020.
35. Damiano Mazza and Michele Pagani. Automatic differentiation in pcf. *Proc. ACM Program. Lang.*, 5(POPL), January 2021.
36. Praveen Narayanan and Chung-chieh Shan. Symbolic disintegration with a variety of base measures. *ACM Transactions on Programming Languages and Systems (TOPLAS)*, 42(2):1–60, 2020.
37. Radford M Neal. Mcmc using hamiltonian dynamics. *Handbook of Markov Chain Monte Carlo*, page 113, 2011.
38. Akihiko Nishimura, David B Dunson, and Jianfeng Lu. Discontinuous hamiltonian monte carlo for discrete parameters and discontinuous likelihoods. *Biometrika*, 107(2):365–380, Mar 2020.
39. Akihiko Nishimura, David B Dunson, and Jianfeng Lu. Discontinuous Hamiltonian Monte Carlo for discrete parameters and discontinuous likelihoods. *Biometrika*, 03 2020. asz083.
40. Rajesh Ranganath, Sean Gerrish, and David M. Blei. Black box variational inference. In *Proceedings of the Seventeenth International Conference on Artificial Intelligence and Statistics, AISTATS 2014, Reykjavik, Iceland, April 22-25, 2014*, pages 814–822, 2014.
41. Rajesh Ranganath, Sean Gerrish, and David M. Blei. Black box variational inference. In *Proceedings of the Seventeenth International Conference on Artificial Intelligence and Statistics, AISTATS 2014, Reykjavik, Iceland, April 22-25, 2014*, volume 33 of *JMLR Workshop and Conference Proceedings*, pages 814–822. JMLR.org, 2014.
42. Danilo Jimenez Rezende, Shakir Mohamed, and Daan Wierstra. Stochastic backpropagation and approximate inference in deep generative models. In *Proceedings of the 31th International Conference on Machine Learning, ICML 2014, Beijing, China, 21-26 June 2014*, volume 32 of *JMLR Workshop and Conference Proceedings*, pages 1278–1286. JMLR.org, 2014.
43. Walter Rudin. *Principles of Mathematical Analysis*. International Series in Pure and Applied Mathematics. McGraw-Hill Education, 3rd edition edition, 1976.

44. Nasser Saheb-Djahromi. Probabilistic lcf. In *International Symposium on Mathematical Foundations of Computer Science*, pages 442–451. Springer, 1978.
45. Adam Ścibior, Ohad Kammar, Matthijs Vákár, Sam Staton, Hongseok Yang, Yufei Cai, Klaus Ostermann, Sean K Moss, Chris Heunen, and Zoubin Ghahramani. Denotational validation of higher-order bayesian inference. *Proceedings of the ACM on Programming Languages*, 2(POPL):60, 2017.
46. Dana S. Scott. A type-theoretical alternative to ISWIM, CUCH, OWHY. *Theor. Comput. Sci.*, 121(1&2):411–440, 1993.
47. Kurt Sieber. Relating full abstraction results for different programming languages. In *Foundations of Software Technology and Theoretical Computer Science, Tenth Conference, Bangalore, India, December 17-19, 1990, Proceedings*, pages 373–387, 1990.
48. Sam Staton. Commutative semantics for probabilistic programming. In Hongseok Yang, editor, *Programming Languages and Systems - 26th European Symposium on Programming, ESOP 2017, Held as Part of the European Joint Conferences on Theory and Practice of Software, ETAPS 2017, Uppsala, Sweden, April 22-29, 2017, Proceedings*, volume 10201 of *Lecture Notes in Computer Science*, pages 855–879. Springer, 2017.
49. Michalis K. Titsias and Miguel Lázaro-Gredilla. Doubly stochastic variational bayes for non-conjugate inference. In *Proceedings of the 31th International Conference on Machine Learning, ICML 2014, Beijing, China, 21-26 June 2014*, volume 32 of *JMLR Workshop and Conference Proceedings*, pages 1971–1979. JMLR.org, 2014.
50. Loring W. Tu. *An introduction to manifolds.* Universitext. Springer-Verlag, 2011.
51. Matthijs Vákár, Ohad Kammar, and Sam Staton. A domain theory for statistical probabilistic programming. *PACMPL*, 3(POPL):36:1–36:29, 2019.
52. Mitchell Wand, Ryan Culpepper, Theophilos Giannakopoulos, and Andrew Cobb. Contextual equivalence for a probabilistic language with continuous random variables and recursion. *PACMPL*, 2(ICFP):87:1–87:30, 2018.
53. David Wingate, Andreas Stuhlmüller, and Noah D. Goodman. Lightweight implementations of probabilistic programming languages via transformational compilation. In Geoffrey J. Gordon, David B. Dunson, and Miroslav Dudík, editors, *Proceedings of the Fourteenth International Conference on Artificial Intelligence and Statistics, AISTATS 2011, Fort Lauderdale, USA, April 11-13, 2011*, volume 15 of *JMLR Proceedings*, pages 770–778. JMLR.org, 2011.
54. Hongseok Yang. Some semantic issues in probabilistic programming languages (invited talk). In Herman Geuvers, editor, *4th International Conference on Formal Structures for Computation and Deduction, FSCD 2019, June 24-30, 2019, Dortmund, Germany*, volume 131 of *LIPIcs*, pages 4:1–4:6. Schloss Dagstuhl - Leibniz-Zentrum für Informatik, 2019.
55. Yuan Zhou, Bradley J. Gram-Hansen, Tobias Kohn, Tom Rainforth, Hongseok Yang, and Frank Wood. LF-PPL: A low-level first order probabilistic programming language for non-differentiable models. In Kamalika Chaudhuri and Masashi Sugiyama, editors, *The 22nd International Conference on Artificial Intelligence and Statistics, AISTATS 2019, 16-18 April 2019, Naha, Okinawa, Japan*, volume 89 of *Proceedings of Machine Learning Research*, pages 148–157. PMLR, 2019.
56. Yuan Zhou, Hongseok Yang, Yee Whye Teh, and Tom Rainforth. Divide, conquer, and combine: a new inference strategy for probabilistic programs with stochastic support. *CoRR*, abs/1910.13324, 2019.

Graded Modal Dependent Type Theory

Benjamin Moon[1(✉)], Harley Eades III[2], and Dominic Orchard[1]

[1] University of Kent, Canterbury, UK
{bgm4,d.a.orchard}@kent.ac.uk
[2] Augusta University, Augusta, USA
harley.eades@gmail.com

Abstract. Graded type theories are an emerging paradigm for augmenting the reasoning power of types with parameterizable, fine-grained analyses of program properties. There have been many such theories in recent years which equip a type theory with quantitative dataflow tracking, usually via a semiring-like structure which provides analysis on variables (often called 'quantitative' or 'coeffect' theories). We present Graded Modal Dependent Type Theory (GRTT for short), which equips a dependent type theory with a general, parameterizable analysis of the flow of data, both in and between computational terms and types. In this theory, it is possible to study, restrict, and reason about data use in programs and types, enabling, for example, parametric quantifiers and linearity to be captured in a dependent setting. We propose GRTT, study its metatheory, and explore various case studies of its use in reasoning about programs and studying other type theories. We have implemented the theory and highlight the interesting details, including showing an application of grading to optimising the type checking procedure itself.

1 Introduction

The difference between simply-typed, polymorphically-typed, and dependently-typed languages can be characterised by the *dataflow* permitted by each type theory. In each, dataflow can be enacted by *substituting* a term for occurrences of a variable in another term, the scope of which is delineated by a binder. In the simply-typed λ-calculus, data can only flow in 'computational' terms; computations and types are separate syntactic categories, with variables, bindings (λ), and substitution—and thus dataflow—only at the computational level. In contrast, polymorphic calculi like System F [26,52] permit dataflow within types, via type quantification ($\forall$), and a limited form of dataflow from computations to types, via type abstraction (Λ) and type application. Dependently-typed calculi (e.g., [14,40,41,42]) break down the barrier between computations and types further: variables are bound simultaneously in types and computations, such that data can flow both to computations and types via dependent functions (Π) and application. This pervasive dataflow enables the Curry-Howard correspondence to be leveraged for program reasoning and theorem proving [59]. However, unrestricted dataflow between computations and types can impede reasoning and can interact poorly with other type theoretic ideas.

N. Yoshida (Ed.): ESOP 2021, LNCS 12648, pp. 462–490, 2021.
https://doi.org/10.1007/978-3-030-72019-3_17

Firstly, System F allows *parametric reasoning* and notions of representation independence [53,57], but this is lost in general in dependently-typed languages when quantifying over higher-kinded types [45] (rather than just 'small' types [7,36]). Furthermore, unrestricted dataflow impedes efficient compilation as compilers do not know, from the types alone, where a term is actually needed. Additional static analyses are needed to recover dataflow information for optimisation and reasoning. For example, a term shown to be used only for type checking (not flowing to the computational 'run time' level) can be erased [9]. Thus, dependent theories do not expose the distinction between proof relevant and irrelevant terms, requiring extensions to capture irrelevance [4,50,51]. Whilst unrestricted dataflow between computations and terms has its benefits, the permissive nature of dependent types can hide useful information. This permissiveness also interacts poorly with other type theories which seek to deliberately restrict dataflow, notably *linear types.*

Linear types allow data to be treated as a 'resource' which must be consumed exactly once: linearly-typed values are restricted to linear dataflow [27,58,60]. Reasoning about resourceful data has been exploited by several languages, e.g., ATS [54], Alms [56], Clean [18], Granule [46], and Linear Haskell [8]. However, linear dataflow is rare in a dependently-typed setting. Consider typing the body of the polymorphic identity function in Martin-Löf type theory:

$$a : \mathsf{Type}, x : a \vdash x : a$$

This judgment uses a twice (typing x in the context and the subject of the judgment) and x once in the term but not at all in the type. There have been various attempts to meaningfully reconcile linear and dependent types [12,15,37,39] usually by keeping them separate, allowing types to depend only on non-linear variables. All such theories cannot distinguish variables used for computation from those used purely for type formation, which could be erased at runtime.

Recent work by McBride [43], refined by Atkey [6], generalises ideas from 'coeffect analyses' (variable usage analyses, like that of Petricek et al. [49]) to a dependently-typed setting to reconcile the ubiquitous flow of data in dependent types with the restricted dataflow of linearity. This approach, called Quantitative Type Theory (QTT), types the above example as:

$$a \overset{0}{:} \mathsf{Type}, x \overset{1}{:} a \vdash x \overset{1}{:} a$$

The annotation 0 on a explains that we can use a to form a type, but we cannot, or do not, use it at the term level, thus it can be erased at runtime. The cornerstone of QTT's approach is that dataflow of a term to the type level counts as 0 use, so arbitrary type-level use is allowed whilst still permitting quantitative analysis of computation-level dataflow. Whilst this gives a useful way to relate linear and dependent types, it cannot however reason about dataflow at the type-level (all type-level usage counts as 0). Thus, for example, QTT cannot express that a variable is used just computationally but not at all in types.

In an extended abstract, Abel proposes a generalisation of QTT to track variable use in both types and computations [2], suggesting that tracking in types enables type checking optimisations and increased expressivity. We develop a core dependent type theory along the same lines, using the paradigm of *grading*: graded systems augment types with additional information, capturing the structure of programs [23,46]. We therefore name our approach *Graded Modal Dependent Type Theory* (GrTT for short). Our type theory is parameterised by a semiring which, like other coeffect and quantitative approaches [3,6,10,25,43,49,61], describes dataflow through a program, but in *both types and computations equally*, remedying QTT's inability to track type-level use. We extend Abel's initial idea by presenting a rich language, including dependent tensors, a complete metatheory, and a *graded modality* which aids the practical use of this approach (e.g., enabling functions to use components of data non-uniformly). The result is a calculus which extends the power of existing non-dependent graded languages, like Granule [46], to a dependent setting.

We begin with the definition of GrTT in Section 2, before demonstrating the power of GrTT through case studies in Section 3, where we show how to use grading to restrict GrTT terms to simply-typed reasoning, parametric reasoning (regaining universal quantification smoothly within a dependent theory), existential types, and linear types. The calculus can be instantiated to different kinds of dataflow reasoning: we show an example application to information-flow security. We then show the metatheory of GrTT in Section 4: admissibility of graded structural rules, substitution, type preservation, and strong normalisation.

We implemented a prototype language based on GrTT called **Gerty**.[3] We briefly mention its syntax in Section 2.5 for use in examples. Later, Section 5 describes how the formal definition of GrTT is implemented as a bidirectional type checking algorithm, interfacing with an SMT solver to solve constraints over grades. Furthermore, Abel conjectured that a quantitative dependent theory could enable usage-based optimisation of type-checking itself [2], which would assist dependently-typed programming at scale. We validate this claim in Section 5 showing a grade-directed optimisation to **Gerty**'s type checker.

Section 6 discusses next steps for increasing the expressive power of GrTT. Full proofs and details are provided in the extended version of this paper [44].

Gerty has some similarity to Granule [46]: both are functional languages with graded types. However, Granule has a linearly typed core and no dependent types (only indexed types), thus has no need for resource tracking at the type level (type indices are not subject to tracking and their syntax is restricted).

2 GrTT: Graded Modal Dependent Type Theory

GrTT augments a standard presentation of dependent type theory with 'grades' (elements of a semiring) which account for how variables are used, i.e., their *dataflow*. Whilst existing work uses grades to describe usage only in computational terms (e.g. [10]), GrTT incorporates additional grades to account for how variables are used in types. We introduce here the syntax and typing, and briefly show the syntax of the implementation. Section 4 describes its metatheory.

[3] https://github.com/granule-project/gerty/releases/tag/esop2021

2.1 Syntax

The syntax of GRTT is that of a standard Martin-Löf type theory, with the addition of a *graded modality* and grade annotations on function and tensor binders. Throughout, s and r range over grades, which are elements of a semiring $(\mathcal{R}, *, 1, +, 0)$. It is instructive to instantiate this semiring to the natural number semiring $(\mathbb{N}, \times, 1, +, 0)$, which captures the exact number of times variables are used. We appeal to this example in descriptions here.

GRTT has a single syntactic sort for computations and types:

$$\begin{array}{llll}
(\textit{terms}) & t, A, B, C ::= x & \mid \mathsf{Type}_l & \\
& \mid (x :_{(s,r)} A) \to B & \mid \lambda x.t & \mid t_1\, t_2 \\
& \mid (x :_r A) \otimes B & \mid (t_1, t_2) & \mid \mathsf{let}\,(x, y) = t_1 \,\mathsf{in}\, t_2 \\
& \mid \Box_s A & \mid \Box t & \mid \mathsf{let}\,\Box x = t_1 \,\mathsf{in}\, t_2 \\
(\textit{levels}) & l ::= 0 \mid \mathsf{suc}\, l \mid l_1 \sqcup l_2 & &
\end{array}$$

Terms include variables and a constructor for an inductive hierarchy of universes, annotated by a level l. Dependent function types are annotated with a pair of grades s and r, with s capturing how x is used in the body of the inhabiting function and r capturing how x is used in the codomain B. Dependent tensors have a single grade r, which describes how the first element is used in the typing of the second. The graded modal type operator $\Box_s A$ 'packages' a term and its dependencies so that values of type A can be used with grade s in the future. Graded modal types are introduced via *promotion* $\Box t$ and eliminated via $\mathsf{let}\,\Box x = t_1 \,\mathsf{in}\, t_2$. The following sections explain the semantics of each piece of syntax with respect to its typing. We typically use A and B to connote terms used as types.

2.2 Typing Judgments, Contexts, and Grading

Typing judgments are written in either of the following two equivalent forms:

$$(\Delta \mid \sigma_1 \mid \sigma_2) \odot \Gamma \vdash t : A \qquad\qquad \begin{pmatrix}\Delta\\ \sigma_1\\ \sigma_2\end{pmatrix} \odot \Gamma \vdash t : A$$

The 'horizontal' syntax (left) is used most often, with the equivalent 'vertical' form (right) used for clarity in some places. Ignoring the part to the left of $\odot$, typing judgments and their rules are essentially those of Martin-Löf type theory (with the addition of the modality) where Γ ranges over usual dependently-typed typing *contexts*. The left of $\odot$ provides the grading information, where σ and Δ range over *grade vectors* and *context grade vectors* respectively, of the form:

$$\begin{array}{ccc}
(\textit{contexts}) & (\textit{grade vectors}) & (\textit{context grade vectors}) \\
\Gamma ::= \emptyset \mid \Gamma, x : A & \sigma ::= \emptyset \mid \sigma, s & \Delta ::= \emptyset \mid \Delta, \sigma
\end{array}$$

A grade vector σ is a vector of semiring elements, and a context vector Δ is a vector of grade vectors. We write $(s_1, \ldots, s_n)$ to denote an n-vector and likewise for context grade vectors. We omit parentheses when this would not cause ambiguity. Throughout, a comma is used to concatenate vectors and disjoint contexts, and to extend vectors with a single grade, grade vector, or typing assumption.

For a judgment $(\Delta \mid \sigma_s \mid \sigma_r) \odot \Gamma \vdash t : A$ the vectors Γ, Δ, σ_s, and σ_r are all of equal size. Given a typing assumption $y : B$ at index i in Γ, the grade $\sigma_s[i] \in \mathcal{R}$ denotes the use of y in t (the *subject* of the judgment), the grade $\sigma_r[i] \in \mathcal{R}$ denotes the use of y in A (the *subject's type*), and $\Delta[i] \in \mathcal{R}^i$ (of size i) describes how assumptions prior to y are used to form y's type, B.

Consider the following example, which types the body of a function that takes two arguments of type a, and returns only the first:

$$\begin{pmatrix} (),(1),(1,0) \\ 0,1,0 \\ 1,0,0 \end{pmatrix} \odot a : \mathsf{Type}_l, x : a, y : a \vdash x : a$$

Let the context grade vector be called Δ. Then, $\Delta[0] = ()$ (empty vector) explains that there are no assumptions that are used to type a in the context, as Type_l is a closed term and the first assumption. $\Delta[1] = (1)$ explains that the first assumption a is used (grade 1) in the typing of x in the context, and $\Delta[2] = (1, 0)$, explains that a is used once in the typing of y in the context, and x is unused in the typing of y. The subject grade vector $\sigma_s = (0, 1, 0)$ explains that a is unused in the subject, x is used once, and y is unused. Finally, the subject type vector $\sigma_r = (1, 0, 0)$ explains that a appears once in the subject's type (which is just a), and x and y are unused in the formation of the subject's type.

To aid reading, recall that standard typing rules typically have the form *context* $\vdash$ *subject* : *subject-type*, the order of which is reflected by $(\Delta \mid \sigma_s \mid \sigma_r)\odot\ldots$ giving the context, subject, and subject-type grading respectively.

Well-formed Contexts The relation $\Delta \odot \Gamma \vdash$ identifies a context Γ as well-formed with respect to context grade vector Δ, defined by the following rules:

$$\frac{}{\emptyset \odot \emptyset \vdash}\textsc{wf}\emptyset \qquad \frac{(\Delta \mid \sigma \mid \mathbf{0}) \odot \Gamma \vdash A : \mathsf{Type}_l}{\Delta, \sigma \odot \Gamma, x : A \vdash}\textsc{wfExt}$$

Unlike typing, well-formedness does not need to include subject and subject-type grade vectors, as it considers only the well-formedness of the assumptions in a context with respect to prior assumptions in the context. The WF∅ rule states that the empty context is well-formed with an empty context grade vector as there are no assumptions to account for. The WFEXT rule states that given A is a type under the assumptions in Γ, with σ accounting for the usage of Γ variables in A, and Δ accounting for usage within Γ, then we can form the well-formed context $\Gamma, x : A$ by extending Δ with σ to account for the usage of A in forming the context. The notation $\mathbf{0}$ denotes a vector for which each element is the semiring 0. Note that the well-formedness $\Delta \odot \Gamma \vdash$ is inherent from the premise of WFEXT due to the following lemma:

Lemma 1 (Typing contexts are well-formed). *If* $(\Delta \mid \sigma_1 \mid \sigma_2) \odot \Gamma \vdash t : A$ *then* $\Delta \odot \Gamma \vdash$.

2.3 Typing Rules

We examine the typing rules of GRTT one at a time.

Variables are introduced as follows:

$$\frac{(\Delta_1, \sigma, \Delta_2) \odot \Gamma_1, x : A, \Gamma_2 \vdash \quad |\Delta_1| = |\Gamma_1|}{(\Delta_1, \sigma, \Delta_2 \mid \mathbf{0}^{|\Delta_1|}, 1, \mathbf{0} \mid \sigma, 0, \mathbf{0}) \odot \Gamma_1, x : A, \Gamma_2 \vdash x : A} \text{VAR}$$

The premise identifies $\Gamma_1, x : A, \Gamma_2$ as well-formed under the context grade vector $\Delta_1, \sigma, \Delta_2$. By the size condition $|\Delta_1| = |\Gamma_1|$, we are able to identify σ as capturing the usage of the variables Γ_1 in forming A. This information is used in the conclusion, capturing type-level variable usage as $\sigma, 0, \mathbf{0}$, which describes that Γ_1 is used according to σ in the subject's type (A), and that the x and the variables of Γ_2 are used with grade 0. For subject usage, we annotate the first zero vector with a size $|\Delta_1|$, allowing us to single out x as being the only assumption used with grade 1 in the subject; all other assumptions are used with grade 0.

For example, typing the body of the polymorphic identity ends with VAR:

$$\frac{\dfrac{\dots}{((), (1)) \odot a : \mathsf{Type}, x : a \vdash} \text{WFEXT} \qquad |(())| = |a : \mathsf{Type}|}{(((), (1)) \mid 0, 1 \mid 1, 0) \odot a : \mathsf{Type}, x : a \vdash x : a} \text{VAR}$$

The premise implies that $((), 1, 0) \odot a : \mathsf{Type} \vdash a : \mathsf{Type}$ by the following lemma:

Lemma 2 (Typing an assumption in a well-formed context). *If* $\Delta_1, \sigma, \Delta_2 \odot \Gamma_1, x : A, \Gamma_2 \vdash$ *with* $|\Delta_1| = |\Gamma_1|$, *then* $(\Delta_1 \mid \sigma \mid 0) \odot \Gamma_1 \vdash A : \mathsf{Type}_l$ *for some* l.

In the conclusion of VAR, the typing $((), 1, 0) \odot a : \mathsf{Type} \vdash a : \mathsf{Type}$ is 'distributed' to the typing of x in the context and to the formation the subject's type. Thus subject grade $(0, 1)$ corresponds to the absence of a from the subject and the presence of x, and subject-type grade $(1, 0)$ corresponds to the presence of a in the subject's type (a), and the absence of x.

Typing universes are formed as follows:

$$\frac{\Delta \odot \Gamma \vdash}{(\Delta \mid \mathbf{0} \mid \mathbf{0}) \odot \Gamma \vdash \mathsf{Type}_l : \mathsf{Type}_{\mathsf{suc}\ l}} \mathsf{Type}$$

We use an inductive hierarchy of universes [47] with ordering $<$ such that $l < \mathsf{suc}\ l$. Universes can be formed under any well-formed context, with every assumption graded with 0 subject and subject-type use, capturing the absence of any assumptions from the universes, which are closed forms.

Functions Function types $(x :_{(s,r)} A) \to B$ are annotated with two grades: explaining that x is used with grade s in the body of the inhabiting function and with grade r in B. Function types have the following formation rule:

$$\frac{(\Delta \mid \sigma_1 \mid \mathbf{0}) \odot \Gamma \vdash A : \mathsf{Type}_{l_1} \quad (\Delta, \sigma_1 \mid \sigma_2, r \mid \mathbf{0}) \odot \Gamma, x : A \vdash B : \mathsf{Type}_{l_2}}{(\Delta \mid \sigma_1 + \sigma_2 \mid \mathbf{0}) \odot \Gamma \vdash (x :_{(s,r)} A) \to B : \mathsf{Type}_{l_1 \sqcup l_2}} \to$$

The usage of the dependencies of A and B (excepting x) are given by σ_1 and σ_2 in the premises (in the 'subject' position) which are combined as $\sigma_1 + \sigma_2$ (via pointwise vector addition using the + of the semiring), which serves to *contract* the dependencies of the two types. The usage of x in B is captured by r, and then internalised to the binder in the conclusion of the rule. An arbitrary grade for s is allowed here as there is no information on how x is used in an inhabiting function body. Function terms are then typed by the following rule:

$$\frac{(\Delta, \sigma_1 \mid \sigma_3, r \mid \mathbf{0}) \odot \Gamma, x : A \vdash B : \mathsf{Type}_l \quad (\Delta, \sigma_1 \mid \sigma_2, s \mid \sigma_3, r) \odot \Gamma, x : A \vdash t : B}{(\Delta \mid \sigma_2 \mid \sigma_1 + \sigma_3) \odot \Gamma \vdash \lambda x.t : (x :_{(s,r)} A) \to B} \lambda_i$$

The second premise types the body of the λ-term, showing that s captures the usage of x in t and r captures the usage of x in B; the subject and subject-type grades of x are then internalised as annotations on the function type's binder.

Dependent functions are eliminated through application:

$$\frac{\begin{array}{l}(\Delta, \sigma_1 \mid \sigma_3, r \mid \mathbf{0}) \odot \Gamma, x : A \vdash B : \mathsf{Type}_l \\ (\Delta \mid \sigma_2 \mid \sigma_1 + \sigma_3) \odot \Gamma \vdash t_1 : (x :_{(s,r)} A) \to B \quad (\Delta \mid \sigma_4 \mid \sigma_1) \odot \Gamma \vdash t_2 : A\end{array}}{(\Delta \mid \sigma_2 + s * \sigma_4 \mid \sigma_3 + r * \sigma_4) \odot \Gamma \vdash t_1\, t_2 : [t_2/x]B} \lambda_e$$

where $*$ is the scalar multiplication of a vector, using the semiring multiplication. Given a function t_1 which uses its parameter with grade s to compute and with grade r in the typing of the result, we can apply it to a term t_2, provided that we have the resources required to form t_2 scaled by s at the subject level and by r at the subject-type level, since t_2 is substituted into the return type B. This scaling behaviour is akin to that used in coeffect calculi [25,49], QTT [6,43] and Linear Haskell [8], but scalar multiplication happens here at both the subject and subject-type level. The use of variables in A is accounted for by σ_1 as explained in the third premise, but these usages are not present in the resulting application since A no longer appears in the types or the terms.

Consider the constant function $\lambda x.\lambda y.x : (x :_{(1,0)} A) \to (y :_{(0,0)} B) \to A$ (for some A and B). Here the resources required for the second parameter will always be scaled by 0, which is absorbing, meaning that anything passed as the second argument has 0 subject and subject-type use. This example begins to show some of the power of grading—the grades capture the program structure at all levels.

Tensors The rule for forming dependent tensor types is as follows:

$$\frac{(\Delta \mid \sigma_1 \mid \mathbf{0}) \odot \Gamma \vdash A : \mathsf{Type}_l \quad (\Delta, \sigma_1 \mid \sigma_2, r \mid \mathbf{0}) \odot \Gamma, x : A \vdash B : \mathsf{Type}_l}{(\Delta \mid \sigma_1 + \sigma_2 \mid \mathbf{0}) \odot \Gamma \vdash (x :_r A) \otimes B : \mathsf{Type}_l} \otimes$$

This rule is almost identical to function type formation $\to$ but with only a single grade r on the binder, since x is only bound in B (the type of the second component), and not computationally. For 'quantitative' semirings, where 0 really means unused (see Section 3), $(x :_0 A) \otimes B$ is then a product $A \times B$.

Dependent tensors are introduced as follows:

$$\frac{\begin{array}{l}(\Delta, \sigma_1 \mid \sigma_3, r \mid \mathbf{0}) \odot \Gamma, x : A \vdash B : \mathsf{Type}_l \\ (\Delta \mid \sigma_2 \mid \sigma_1) \odot \Gamma \vdash t_1 : A \qquad (\Delta \mid \sigma_4 \mid \sigma_3 + r * \sigma_2) \odot \Gamma \vdash t_2 : [t_1/x]B\end{array}}{(\Delta \mid \sigma_2 + \sigma_4 \mid \sigma_1 + \sigma_3) \odot \Gamma \vdash (t_1, t_2) : (x :_r A) \otimes B} \otimes_i$$

In the typing premise for t_2, occurrences of x are replaced with t_1 in the type, ensuring that the type of the second component (t_2) is calculated using the first component (t_1). The resources for t_1 in this substitution are scaled by r, accounting for the existing usage of x in B. In the conclusion, we see the resources for the two components (and their types) combined via the semiring addition.

Finally, tensors are eliminated with the following rule:

$$\frac{\begin{array}{l}(\Delta \mid \sigma_3 \mid \sigma_1 + \sigma_2) \odot \Gamma \vdash t_1 : (x :_r A) \otimes B \\ (\Delta, (\sigma_1 + \sigma_2) \mid \sigma_5, r' \mid \mathbf{0}) \odot \Gamma, z : (x :_r A) \otimes B \vdash C : \mathsf{Type}_l \\ (\Delta, \sigma_1, (\sigma_2, r) \mid \sigma_4, s, s \mid \sigma_5, r', r') \odot \Gamma, x : A, y : B \vdash t_2 : [(x, y)/z]C\end{array}}{(\Delta \mid \sigma_4 + s * \sigma_3 \mid \sigma_5 + r' * \sigma_3) \odot \Gamma \vdash \mathsf{let}\,(x, y) = t_1 \,\mathsf{in}\, t_2 : [t_1/z]C} \otimes_e$$

As this is a dependent eliminator, we allow the result type C to depend upon the value of the tensor as a whole, bound as z in the second premise with grade r', into which is substituted our actual tensor term t_1 in the conclusion.

Eliminating a tensor (t_1) requires that we consider each component (x and y) is used with the same grade s in the resulting expression t_2, and that we scale the resources of t_1 by s. This is because we cannot inspect t_1 itself, and semiring addition is not injective (preventing us from splitting the grades required to form t_1). This prevents forming certain functions (e.g., projections) under some semirings, but this can be overcome by the introduction of *graded modalities.*

Graded Modality Graded binders alone do not allow different parts of a value to be used differently, e.g., computing the length of a list ignores the elements, projecting from a pair discards one component. We therefore introduce a *graded modality* (à la [10,46]) allowing us to capture the notion of local inspection on data and internalising usage information into types. A type $\Box_s A$ denotes terms of type A that are used with grade s. Type formation and introduction rules are:

$$\frac{(\Delta \mid \sigma \mid \mathbf{0}) \odot \Gamma \vdash A : \mathsf{Type}_l}{(\Delta \mid \sigma \mid \mathbf{0}) \odot \Gamma \vdash \Box_s A : \mathsf{Type}_l} \Box \qquad \frac{(\Delta \mid \sigma_1 \mid \sigma_2) \odot \Gamma \vdash t : A}{(\Delta \mid s * \sigma_1 \mid \sigma_2) \odot \Gamma \vdash \Box t : \Box_s A} \Box_i$$

To form a term of type $\Box_s A$, we 'promote' a term t of type A by requiring that we can use the resources used to form t (σ_1) according to grade s. This 'promotion' resembles that of other graded modal systems (e.g., [3,10,23,46]), but the elimination needs to also account for type usage due to dependent elimination.

We can see promotion $\Box_i$ as capturing t for later use according to grade s. Thus, when eliminating a term of type $\Box_s A$, we must consider how the 'unboxed' term is used with grade s, as per the following dependent eliminator:

$$\frac{\begin{array}{l}(\Delta, \sigma_2 \mid \sigma_4, r \mid \mathbf{0}) \odot \Gamma, z : \Box_s A \vdash B : \mathsf{Type}_l \\ (\Delta \mid \sigma_1 \mid \sigma_2) \odot \Gamma \vdash t_1 : \Box_s A \quad (\Delta, \sigma_2 \mid \sigma_3, s \mid \sigma_4, (s * r)) \odot \Gamma, x : A \vdash t_2 : [\Box x/z]B\end{array}}{(\Delta \mid \sigma_1 + \sigma_3 \mid \sigma_4 + r * \sigma_1) \odot \Gamma \vdash \mathsf{let}\,\Box x = t_1 \,\mathsf{in}\, t_2 : [t_1/z]B} \Box_e$$

This rule can be understood as a kind of 'cut', connecting a 'capability' to use a term of type A according to grade s with the requirement that $x : A$ is used according to grade s as a dependency of t_2. Since we are in a dependently-typed setting, we also substitute t_1 into the type level such that B can depend on t_1 according to grade r which then causes the dependencies of t_1 (σ_1) to be scaled-up by r and added to the subject-type grading.

Equality, Conversion, and Subtyping A key part of dependent type theories is a notion of term equality and type conversion [33]. GRTT term equality is via judgments $(\Delta \mid \sigma_1 \mid \sigma_2) \odot \Gamma \vdash t_1 = t_2 : A$ equating terms t_1 and t_2 of type A. Equality includes full congruences as well as $\beta\eta$-equality for functions, tensors, and graded modalities, of which the latter are:

$$\frac{\begin{array}{l}(\Delta, \sigma_2 \mid \sigma_4, r \mid \mathbf{0}) \odot \Gamma, z : \Box_s A \vdash B : \mathsf{Type}_l \\ (\Delta \mid \sigma_1 \mid \sigma_2) \odot \Gamma \vdash t_1 : A \quad (\Delta, \sigma_2 \mid \sigma_3, s \mid \sigma_4, (s * r)) \odot \Gamma, x : A \vdash t_2 : [\Box x/z]B\end{array}}{(\Delta \mid \sigma_3 + s * \sigma_1 \mid \sigma_4 + s * r * \sigma_1) \odot \Gamma \vdash (\mathsf{let}\,\Box x = \Box t_1\,\mathsf{in}\,t_2) = [t_1/x]t_2 : [\Box t_1/z]B} \text{EQ}_{\Box_c}$$

$$\frac{(\Delta \mid \sigma_1 \mid \sigma_2) \odot \Gamma \vdash t : \Box_s A}{(\Delta \mid \sigma_1 \mid \sigma_2) \odot \Gamma \vdash t = (\mathsf{let}\,\Box x = t\,\mathsf{in}\,\Box x) : \Box_s A} \text{EQ}_{\Box_u}$$

A subtyping relation ($(\Delta \mid \sigma) \odot \Gamma \vdash A \leq B$) subsumes equality, adding ordering of universe levels. *Type conversion* allows re-typing terms based on the judgment:

$$\frac{(\Delta \mid \sigma_1 \mid \sigma_2) \odot \Gamma \vdash t : A \quad (\Delta \mid \sigma_2) \odot \Gamma \vdash A \leq B}{(\Delta \mid \sigma_1 \mid \sigma_2) \odot \Gamma \vdash t : B} \text{CONV}$$

The full rules for equality and subtyping are in this paper's extended version [44].

2.4 Operational Semantics

As with other graded modal calculi (e.g., [3,10,23]), the core calculus of GRTT has a Call-by-Name small-step operational semantics with reductions $t \rightsquigarrow t'$. The rules are standard, with the addition of the β-rule for the graded modality:

$$\mathsf{let}\,\Box x = \Box t_1\,\mathsf{in}\,t_2 \rightsquigarrow [t_1/x]t_2 \qquad (\beta\Box)$$

Type preservation and normalisation are considered in Section 4.

2.5 Implementation and Examples

To explore our theory, we provide an implementation, **Gerty**. Section 5 describes how the declarative definition of the type theory is implemented as a bidirectional type checking algorithm. We briefly mention the syntax here for use in later examples. The following is the polymorphic identity function in **Gerty**:

```
id : (a : (.0, .2) Type 0) -> (x : (.1, .0) a) -> a
id = \a -> \x -> x
```

The syntax resembles the theory, where grading terms `.n` are syntactic sugar for a unary encoding of grades in terms of 0 and repeated addition of 1, e.g., `.2` = `(.0 + .1) + .1`. This syntax can be used for grade terms of any semiring, which can be resolved to particular built-in semirings at other points of type checking.

The following shows first projection on (non-dependent) pairs, using the graded modality (at grade 0 here) to give fine-grained usage on compound data:

```
fst : (a : (.0, .2) Type 0) (b : (.0, .1) Type 0) -> <a * [.0] b> -> a
fst = \a b p -> case p of <x, y> -> let [z] = y in x
```

The implementation adds various built-in semirings, some syntactic sugar, and extras such as: a singleton *unit* type, extensions of the theory to semirings with a pre-ordering (discussed further in Section 6), and some implicit resolution. Anywhere a grade is expected, an underscore can be supplied to indicate that **Gerty** should try to resolve the grade implicitly. Grades may also be omitted from binders (see above in `fst`), in which case they are treated as implicits. Currently, implicits are handled by generating existentially quantified grade variables, and using SMT to solve the necessary constraints (see Section 5).

So far we have considered the natural numbers semiring providing an analysis of usage. We come back to this and similar examples in Section 3. To show another kind of example, we consider a lattice semiring of privacy levels (appearing elsewhere [3,23,46]) which enforces information-flow control, akin to DCC [1]. Differently to DCC, dataflow is tracked through variable dependencies, rather than through the results of computations in the monadic style of DCC.

Definition 1. [Security levels] Let $\mathcal{R} = \texttt{Lo} \leq \texttt{Hi}$ be a set of labels with $0 = \texttt{Hi}$ and $1 = \texttt{Lo}$, semiring addition as the meet and multiplication as join. Here, $1 = \texttt{Lo}$ treats the base notion of dataflow as being in the low security (public) domain. Variables graded with `Hi` must then be unused, or guarded by a graded modality. This semiring is primitive in **Gerty**; we can express the following example:

```
idLo : (a : (.0, .2) Type 0) -> (x : (Lo, Hi) a) -> a
idLo = \a -> \x -> x
-- The following is rejected as ill-typed
leak : (a : (.0, .2) Type 0) -> (x : (Hi, Hi) a) -> a
leak = \a -> \x -> idLo a x
```

The first definition is well-typed, but the second yields a typing error originating from the application in its body:

```
At subject stage got the following mismatched grades:
 For 'x' expected Hi but got .1
```

where grade `1` is `Lo` here. Thus we can use this abstract label semiring as a way of restricting flow of data between regions (*cf.* region typing systems [31,55]). Note that the ordering is not leveraged here other than in the lattice operations.

3 Case Studies

We now demonstrate GRTT via several cases studies that focus the reasoning power of dependent types via grading. Since grading in GRTT serves to explain dataflow, we can characterise subsets of GRTT that correspond to various type theories. We demonstrate the approach with simple types, parametric polymorphism, and linearity. In each case study, we restrict GRTT to a subset by *a characterisation of the grades*, rather than by, say, placing detailed syntactic restrictions or employing meta-level operations or predicates that restrict syntax (as one might do for example to map a subset of Martin-Löf type theory into the simply-typed λ-calculus by restriction to closed types, requiring deep inspection of type terms). Since this restriction is only on grades, we can harness the specific reasoning power of particular calculi from within the language itself, simply by specifications on grades. In the context of an implementation like **Gerty**, this amounts to using type signatures to restrict dataflow.

This section shows the power of tracking dataflow in types via grades, going beyond QTT [6] and GRAD [13]. For 'quantitative' semirings, a 0 type-grade means that we can recover simply-typed reasoning (Section 3.3) and distinguish computational functions from type-parameter functions for parametric reasoning (Section 3.4), embedding a grade-restricted subset of GRTT into System F.

Section 5 returns to a case study that builds on the implementation.

3.1 Recovering Martin-Löf Type Theory

When the semiring parameterising GRTT is the singleton semiring (i.e., any semiring where $1 = 0$), we have an isomorphism $\Box_r A \cong A$, and grade annotations become redundant, as all grades are equal. All vectors and grades on binders may then be omitted, and we can write typing judgments as $\Gamma \vdash t : A$, giving rise to a standard Martin-Löf type theory as a special case of GRTT.

3.2 Determining Usage via Quantitative Semirings

Unlike existing systems, we can use the fine-grained grading to *guarantee* the relevance or irrelevance of assumptions in types. To do this we must consider a subset of semirings $(\mathcal{R}, *, 1, +, 0)$ called *quantitative* semirings, satisfying:

$$\begin{aligned} &\text{(zero-unique)} \quad 1 \neq 0; \\ &\text{(positivity)} \quad \forall r, s.\ r + s = 0 \implies r = 0 \wedge s = 0; \\ &\text{(zero-product)} \quad \forall r, s.\ r * s = 0 \implies r = 0 \vee s = 0. \end{aligned}$$

These axioms[4] ensure that a 0-grade in a quantitative semiring represents irrelevant variable use. This notion has recently been proved for computational use by Choudhury et al. [13] via a heap-based semantics for grading (on computations) and the same result applies here. Conversely, in a quantitative semiring any grade other than 0 denotes relevance. From this, we can *directly* encode non-dependent tensors and arrows: in $(x :_0 A) \otimes B$ the grade 0 captures that x cannot have any computational content in B, and likewise for $(x :_{(s,0)} A) \to B$ the grade 0 explains that x cannot have any computational content in B, but may have computational use according to s in the inhabiting function. Thus,

[4] Atkey requires *positivity* and *zero-product* for all semirings parameterising QTT [6] (as does Abel [2]). Atkey imposes this for admissibility of substitution. We need not place this restriction on GRTT to have substitution in general (Sec. 4.1).

the grade 0 here describes that elimination forms *cannot* ever inspect the variable during normalisation. Additionally, quantitative semirings can be used for encoding simply-typed and polymorphic reasoning.

Example 1. Some quantitative semirings are:
- (*Exact usage*) $(\mathbb{N}, \times, 1, +, 0)$;
- (*0-1*) The semiring over $\mathcal{R} = \{0, 1\}$ with $1 + 1 = 1$ which describes relevant *vs.* irrelevant dependencies, but no further information.
- (*None-One-Tons* [43]) The semiring on $\mathcal{R} = \{0, 1, \infty\}$ is more fine-grained than 0-1, where ∞ represents more than 1 usage, with $1 + 1 = \infty = 1 + \infty$.

3.3 Simply-typed Reasoning

As discussed in Section 1, the simply-typed λ-calculus (STLC) can be distinguished from dependently-typed calculi via the restriction of dataflow: in simple types, data can only flow at the computational level, with no dataflow within, into, or from types. We can thus view a GRTT function as simply typed when its variable is irrelevant in the type, e.g., $(x :_{(s,0)} A) \to B$ for quantitative semirings. We define a subset of GRTT restricted to simply-typed reasoning:

Definition 2. [Simply-typed GRTT] For a quantitative semiring, the following predicate STLC(−) determines a subset of simply-typed GRTT programs:

$\textsc{Stlc}((\emptyset \mid \emptyset \mid \emptyset) \odot \emptyset \vdash t : A)$

$\textsc{Stlc}((\Delta \mid \sigma_1 \mid \sigma_2) \odot \Gamma \vdash t : A) \implies \textsc{Stlc}((\Delta, \mathbf{0} \mid \sigma_1, s \mid \sigma_2, 0) \odot \Gamma, x : B \vdash t : A)$

That is, all subject-type grades are 0 (thus function types are of the form $(x :_{(s,0)} A) \to B$). A similar predicate is defined on well-formed contexts (elided), restricting context grades of well-formed contexts to only zero grading vectors.

Under the restriction of Definition 2, a subset of GRTT terms embeds into the simply-typed λ-calculus in a sound and complete way. Since STLC does not have a notion of tensor or modality, this is omitted from the encoding:

$$[\![x]\!] = x \quad [\![\lambda x.t]\!] = \lambda x.[\![t]\!] \quad [\![t_1\, t_2]\!] = [\![t_1]\!][\![t_2]\!] \quad [\![(x :_{(s,0)} A) \to B]\!]_\tau = [\![A]\!]_\tau \to [\![B]\!]_\tau$$

Variable contexts of GRTT are interpreted by point-wise applying $[\![-]\!]_\tau$ to typing assumptions. We then get the following preservation of typing into the simply-typed λ-calculus, and soundness and completeness of this encoding:

Lemma 3 (Soundness of typing). *Given a derivation of* $(\Delta \mid \sigma_1 \mid \sigma_2) \odot \Gamma \vdash t : A$ *such that* $\textsc{Stlc}((\Delta \mid \sigma_1 \mid \sigma_2) \odot \Gamma \vdash t : A)$ *then* $[\![\Gamma]\!]_\tau \vdash [\![t]\!] : [\![A]\!]_\tau$ *in STLC.*

Theorem 1 (Soundness and completeness of the embedding). *Given* $\textsc{Stlc}((\Delta \mid \sigma_1 \mid \sigma_2) \odot \Gamma \vdash t : A)$ *and* $[\![(\Delta \mid \sigma_1 \mid \sigma_2) \odot \Gamma \vdash t : A]\!]$ *then for CBN reduction* $\rightsquigarrow^{\text{STLC}}$ *in simply-typed λ-calculus:*

$$\begin{array}{ll} \textit{(soundness)}\ \forall t'.\ \textit{if}\ t \rightsquigarrow t' & \textit{then}\ [\![t]\!] \rightsquigarrow^{\text{STLC}} [\![t']\!] \\ \textit{(completeness)}\ \forall t_a.\ \textit{if}\ [\![t]\!] \rightsquigarrow^{\text{STLC}} t_a & \textit{then}\ \exists t'.\ t \rightsquigarrow t' \wedge [\![t']\!] \equiv_{\beta\eta} t_a \end{array}$$

Thus, we capture simply-typed reasoning just by restricting type grades to 0 for quantitative semirings. We consider quantitative semirings again for parametric reasoning, but first recall issues with parametricity and dependent types.

3.4 Recovering Parametricity via Grading

One powerful feature of grading in a dependent type setting is the ability to recover parametricity from dependent function types. Consider the following type of functions in System F (we borrow this example from Nuyts et al. [45]):

$$\mathsf{RI}\ A\ B \triangleq \forall\gamma.(\gamma \to A) \to (\gamma \to B)$$

Due to parametricity, we get the following notion of *representation independence* in System F: for a function $f : \mathsf{RI}\ A\ B$, some type γ', and terms $h : \gamma' \to A$ and $c : \gamma'$, then we know that f can only use c by applying $h\ c$. Subsequently, $\mathsf{RI}\ A\ B \cong A \to B$ by parametricity [52], defined uniquely as:

$$\begin{array}{ll} \mathit{iso} : \mathsf{RI}\ A\ B \to (A \to B) & \mathit{iso}^{-1} : (A \to B) \to \mathsf{RI}\ A\ B \\ \mathit{iso}\ f = f\ A\ (\mathit{id}\ A) & \mathit{iso}^{-1}\ g = \Lambda\gamma.\ \lambda h.\ \lambda(c : \gamma).\ g(h\,c) \end{array}$$

In a dependently-typed language, one might seek to replace System F's universal quantifier with Π-types, i.e.

$$\mathsf{RI}'\ A\ B \triangleq (\gamma : \mathsf{Type}) \to (\gamma \to A) \to (\gamma \to B)$$

However, we can no longer reason parametrically about the inhabitants of such types (we cannot prove that $\mathsf{RI}'\ A\ B \cong A \to B$) as the free interaction of types and computational terms allows us to give the following non-parametric element of $\mathsf{RI}'\ A\ B$ over 'large' type instances:

$$\mathit{leak} = \lambda\gamma.\ \lambda h.\ \lambda c.\ \gamma : \mathsf{RI}'\ A\ \mathsf{Type}$$

Instead of applying $h\ c$, the above "leaks" the type parameter γ. GRTT can recover universal quantification, and hence parametric reasoning, by using grading to restrict the data-flow capabilities of a Π-type. We can refine representation independence to the following:

$$\mathsf{RI}''\ A\ B \triangleq (\gamma :_{(0,2)} \mathsf{Type}) \to (h :_{(s_1,0)} (x :_{(s_2,0)} \gamma) \to A) \to (c :_{(s_3,0)} \gamma) \to B$$

for some grades s_1, s_2, and s_3, and with shorthand $2 = 1 + 1$.

If we look at the definition of *leak* above, we see that γ is used in the body of the function and thus requires usage 1, so *leak* cannot inhabit $\mathsf{RI}''\ A\ \mathsf{Type}$. Instead, *leak* would be typed differently as:

$$\mathit{leak} : (\gamma :_{(1,2)} \mathsf{Type}) \to (h :_{(0,0)} (x :_{(s,0)} \gamma) \to A) \to (c :_{(0,0)} \gamma) \to \mathsf{Type}$$

The problematic behaviour (that the type parameter γ is returned by the inner function) is exposed by the subject grade 1 on the binder of γ. We can thus define a graded universal quantification from a graded Π-typed:

$$\forall_r(\gamma : A).B \triangleq (\gamma :_{(0,r)} A) \to B \qquad (1)$$

This denotes that the type parameter γ can appear freely in B described by grade r, but is irrelevant in the body of any corresponding λ-abstraction. This is akin to the work of Nuyts et al. who develop a system with several modalities for regaining parametricity within a dependent type theory [45]. Note however that parametricity is recovered for us here as one of many possible options coming from systematically specialising the grading.

Capturing Existential Types With the ability to capture universal quantifier, we can similarly define existentials (allowing, e.g., abstraction [11]). We define the existential type via a Church-encoding as follows:

$$\exists_r(x : A).B \triangleq \forall_2(C : \mathsf{Type}_l).(f :_{(1,0)} \forall_r(x : A).(b :_{(s,0)} B) \to C) \to C$$

Embedding into Stratified System F We show that parametricity is regained here (and thus eqn. (1) really behaves as a universal quantifier and not a general Π-type) by showing that we can embed a subset of GRTT into System F, based solely on a classification of the grades. We follow a similar approach to Section 3.3 for simply-typed reasoning but rather than defining a purely syntactic encoding (and then proving it type sound) our encoding is type directed since we embed GRTT functions of type $(x :_{(0,r)} \mathsf{Type}_l) \to B$ as universal types in System F with corresponding type abstractions (Λ) as their inhabitants. Since GRTT employs a predicative hierarchy of universes, we target Stratified System F (hereafter SSF) since it includes the analogous inductive hierarchy of kinds [38]. We use the formulation of Eades and Stump [21] with terms t_s and types T:

$$t_s ::= x \mid \lambda(x : T).t_s \mid t_s\, t'_s \mid \Lambda(X : K).t_s \mid t_s\, [T] \qquad T ::= X \mid T \to T' \mid \forall(X : K).T$$

with kinds $K ::= \star_l$ where $l \in \mathbb{N}$ providing the stratified kind hierarchy. Capitalised variables X are System F type variables and $t_s\,[T]$ is type application. Contexts may contain both type and computational variables, and so free-variable type assumptions may have dependencies, akin to dependent type systems. Kinding is via judgments $\Gamma \vdash T : \star_l$ and typing via $\Gamma \vdash t : T$.

We define a type directed encoding on a subset of GRTT typing derivations characterised by the following predicate:

$$\begin{aligned}
&\textsc{Ssf}((\emptyset \mid \emptyset \mid \emptyset) \odot \emptyset \vdash t : A)\\
&\textsc{Ssf}((\Delta \mid \sigma_1 \mid \sigma_2) \odot \Gamma \vdash t : A) \implies \textsc{Ssf}((\Delta, \mathbf{0} \mid \sigma_1, 0 \mid \sigma_2, r) \odot \Gamma, x : \mathsf{Type}_l \vdash t : A)\\
&\textsc{Ssf}((\Delta \mid \sigma_1 \mid \sigma_2) \odot \Gamma \vdash t : A) \wedge \mathsf{Type}_l \not\in^{+ve} B\\
&\qquad\qquad\qquad\qquad \implies \textsc{Ssf}((\Delta, \sigma_3 \mid \sigma_1, s \mid \sigma_2, 0) \odot \Gamma, x : B \vdash t : A)
\end{aligned}$$

By $\mathsf{Type}_l \not\in^{+ve} B$ we mean Type_l is not a positive subterm of B, avoiding higher-order typing terms (e.g., type constructors) which do not exist in SSF.

Under this restriction, we give a type-directed encoding mapping derivations of GRTT to SSF: given a GRTT derivation of judgment $(\Delta \mid \sigma_1 \mid \sigma_2) \odot \Gamma \vdash t : A$ we have that $\exists t_s$ (an SSF term) such that there is a derivation of judgment $[\![\Gamma]\!] \vdash t_s : [\![A]\!]_\tau$ in SSF where we interpret a subset of GRTT terms A as types:

$$\begin{aligned}
[\![x]\!]_\tau &= x\\
[\![\mathsf{Type}_l]\!]_\tau &= \star_l\\
[\![(x :_{(0,r)} \mathsf{Type}_l) \to B]\!]_\tau &= \forall x : \star_l.[\![B]\!]_\tau && \textit{where } \mathsf{Type}_l \not\in^{+ve} B\\
[\![(x :_{(s,0)} A) \to B]\!]_\tau &= [\![A]\!]_\tau \to [\![B]\!]_\tau && \textit{where } \mathsf{Type}_l \not\in^{+ve} A, B
\end{aligned}$$

Thus, dependent functions with Type parameters that are computationally irrelevant (subject grade 0) map to $\forall$ types, and dependent functions with parameters irrelevant in types (subject-type grade 0) map to regular function types.

We elide the full details but sketch key parts where functions and applications are translated inductively (where Ty_l is shorthand for Type_l):

$$[\![\frac{(\Delta, \sigma_1 \mid \sigma_2, 0 \mid \sigma_3, r) \odot \Gamma, x : \mathsf{Ty}_l \vdash t : B}{(\Delta \mid \sigma_2 \mid \sigma_1 + \sigma_3) \odot \Gamma \vdash \lambda x.t : (x :_{(0,r)} \mathsf{Ty}_l) \to B}]\!] = \frac{[\![\Gamma]\!], x : \star_l \vdash t_s : [\![B]\!]_\tau}{[\![\Gamma]\!] \vdash \Lambda(x : \star_l).t_s : \forall x : \star_l.[\![B]\!]_\tau}$$

$$[\![\frac{(\Delta, \sigma_1 \mid \sigma_2, s \mid \sigma_3, 0) \odot \Gamma, x : A \vdash t : B}{(\Delta \mid \sigma_2 \mid \sigma_1 + \sigma_3) \odot \Gamma \vdash \lambda x.t : (x :_{(s,0)} A) \to B}]\!] = \frac{[\![\Gamma]\!], x : [\![A]\!]_\tau \vdash t_s : [\![B]\!]_\tau}{[\![\Gamma]\!] \vdash \lambda(x : [\![A]\!]_\tau).t_s : [\![A]\!]_\tau \to [\![B]\!]_\tau}$$

$$[\![\frac{\begin{array}{l}(\Delta \mid \sigma_2 \mid \sigma_1 + \sigma_3) \odot \Gamma \vdash t_1 : (x :_{(0,r)} \mathsf{Ty}_l) \to B \\ (\Delta \mid \sigma_4 \mid \sigma_1) \odot \Gamma \vdash t_2 : \mathsf{Ty}_l\end{array}}{(\Delta \mid \sigma_2 \mid \sigma_3 + r * \sigma_4) \odot \Gamma \vdash t_1\, t_2 : [t_2/x]B}]\!] = \frac{\begin{array}{l}[\![\Gamma]\!] \vdash t_s : \forall (x : \star_l).[\![B]\!]_\tau \\ [\![\Gamma]\!] \vdash T : \star_l\end{array}}{[\![\Gamma]\!] \vdash t_s[T] : [T/x][\![B]\!]_\tau}$$

$$[\![\frac{\begin{array}{l}(\Delta \mid \sigma_2 \mid \sigma_1 + \sigma_3) \odot \Gamma \vdash t_1 : (x :_{(s,0)} A) \to B \\ (\Delta \mid \sigma_4 \mid \sigma_1) \odot \Gamma \vdash t_2 : A\end{array}}{(\Delta \mid \sigma_2 + s * \sigma_4 \mid \sigma_3) \odot \Gamma \vdash t_1\, t_2 : [t_2/x]B}]\!] = \frac{\begin{array}{l}[\![\Gamma]\!] \vdash t_s : [\![A]\!]_\tau \to [\![B]\!]_\tau \\ [\![\Gamma]\!] \vdash t'_s : [\![A]\!]_\tau\end{array}}{[\![\Gamma]\!] \vdash t_s\, t'_s : [t'_s/x][\![B]\!]_\tau}$$

In the last case, note the presence of $[t'_s/x][\![B]\!]_\tau$. Reasoning under the context of the encoding, this is proven equivalent to $[\![B]\!]_\tau$ since the subject type grade is 0 and therefore use of x in B is irrelevant.

Theorem 2 (Soundness and completeness of SSF embedding). *Given* $\textsc{Ssf}((\Delta \mid \sigma_1 \mid \sigma_2) \odot \Gamma \vdash t : A)$ *and* t_a *in SSF where* $[\![(\Delta \mid \sigma_1 \mid \sigma_2) \odot \Gamma \vdash t : A]\!] = [\![\Gamma]\!] \vdash t_s : [\![A]\!]_\tau$ *then for CBN reduction* $\rightsquigarrow^{\text{SSF}}$ *in Stratified System F:*

$$\begin{array}{rl}\textit{(soundness)}\ \forall t'.\, t \rightsquigarrow t' \implies & \exists t'_s.t_s \rightsquigarrow^{\text{SSF}} t'_s \\ & \wedge\ [\![(\Delta \mid \sigma_1 \mid \sigma_2) \odot \Gamma \vdash t' : A]\!] = [\![\Gamma]\!] \vdash t'_s : [\![A]\!]_\tau \\ \textit{(completeness)}\ \forall t'_s.\, t_s \rightsquigarrow^{\text{SSF}} t'_s \implies & \exists t'.t \rightsquigarrow t' \\ & \wedge\ [\![(\Delta \mid \sigma_1 \mid \sigma_2) \odot \Gamma \vdash t' : A]\!] = [\![\Gamma]\!] \vdash t'_s : [\![A]\!]_\tau\end{array}$$

Thus, we can capture parametricity in GRTT via the judicious use of 0 grading (at either the type or computational level) for quantitative semirings. This embedding is not possible from QTT since QTT variables graded with 0 may be used arbitrarily in the types; the embedding here relies on GRTT's 0 type-grade capturing abscence in types for quantitative semirings.

3.5 Graded Modal Types and Non-dependent Linear Types

GRTT can embed the reasoning present in other graded modal type theories (which often have a linear base), for example the explicit semiring-graded necessity modality found in coeffect calculi [10,23] and Granule [46]. We can recover the axioms of a graded necessity modality (usually modelled by an exponential graded comonad [23]). For example, in **Gerty** the following are well typed:

```
counit : (a : (.0, .2) Type) -> (z : (.1 , .0) [.1] a) -> a
counit = \a z -> case z of [y] -> y
comult : (a : (.0, .2) Type) -> (z : (.1 , .0) [.6] a) -> [.2] ([.3] a)
comult = \a z -> case z of [y] -> [[y]]
```

corresponding to $\varepsilon : \Box_1 A \to A$ and $\delta_{r,s} : \Box_{r*s} A \to \Box_r(\Box_s A)$: operations of graded necessity / graded comonads. Since we cannot use arbitrary terms for grades in the implementation, we have picked some particular grades here for `comult`. First-class grading is future work, discussed in Section 6.

Linear functions can be captured as $A \multimap B \triangleq (x :_{(1,r)} A) \to B$ for an exact usage semiring. It is straightforward to characterise a subset of GRTT programs that maps to the linear λ-calculus akin to the encodings above. Thus, GRTT provides a suitable basis for studying both linear and non-linear theories alike.

4 Metatheory

We now study GRTT's metatheory. We first explain how substitution presents itself in the theory, and how type preservation follows from a relationship between equality and reduction. We then show admissibility of graded structural rules for contraction, exchange, and weakening, and strong normalization.

4.1 Substitution

We introducing substitution for well-formed contexts and then typing.

Lemma 4 (Substitution for well-formed contexts). *If the following hold:*

1. $(\Delta \mid \sigma_2 \mid \sigma_1) \odot \Gamma_1 \vdash t : A$ *and* *2.* $(\Delta, \sigma_1, \Delta') \odot \Gamma_1, x : A, \Gamma_2 \vdash$

Then: $\Delta, (\Delta' \backslash |\Delta| + (\Delta' / |\Delta|) * \sigma_2) \odot \Gamma_1, [t/x]\Gamma_2 \vdash$

That is, given $\Gamma_1, x : A, \Gamma_2$ is well-formed, we can cut out x by substituting t for x in Γ_2, accounting for the new usage in the context grade vectors. The usage of Γ_1 in t is given by σ_2, and the usage in A by σ_1. When substituting, Δ remains the same, as Γ_1 is unchanged. However, to account for the usage in $[t/x]\Gamma_2$, we have to form a new context grade vector $\Delta' \backslash |\Delta| + (\Delta' / |\Delta|) * \sigma_2$.

The operation $\Delta' \backslash |\Delta|$ (pronounced 'discard') removes grades corresponding to x, by removing the grade at index $|\Delta|$ from each grade vector in Δ'. Everything previously used in the typing of x in the context must now be distributed across $[t/x]\Gamma_2$, which is done by adding on $(\Delta' / |\Delta|) * \sigma_2$, which uses $\Delta' / |\Delta|$ (pronounced 'choose') to produce a vector of grades, which correspond to the grades cut out in $\Delta' \backslash |\Delta|$. The multiplication of $(\Delta' / |\Delta|) * \sigma_2$ produces a context grade vector by scaling σ_2 by each element of $(\Delta' / |\Delta|)$. When adding vectors, if the sizes of the vectors are different, then the shorter vector is right-padded with zeroes. Thus $\Delta' \backslash |\Delta| + (\Delta' / |\Delta|) * \sigma_2$ can be read as *'Δ' without the grades corresponding to x, plus the usage of t scaled by the prior usage of x'*.

For example, given typing $((), (1) \mid 0, 1 \mid 1, 0) \odot a : \mathsf{Type}, y : a \vdash y : a$ and well-formed context $((), (1), (1, 0), (0, 0, 2)) \odot a : \mathsf{Type}, y : a, x : a, z : t' \vdash$, where t' uses x twice, we can substitute y for x. Therefore, let $\Gamma_1 = a : \mathsf{Type}, y : a$ thus $|\Gamma_1| = 2$ and $\Gamma_2 = z : x$ and $\Delta' = ((0, 0, 2))$ and $\sigma_1 = 1, 0$ and $\sigma_2 = 0, 1$. Then the context grade of the substitution $[y/x]\Gamma_2$ is calculated as:

$$((0, 0, 2)) \backslash |\Gamma_1| = ((0, 0)) \qquad (((0, 1, 2)) / |\Gamma_1|) * \sigma_2 = (2) * (0, 1) = ((0, 2))$$

Thus the resulting judgment is $((),(1),(0,2)) \odot a : \mathsf{Type}, y : a, z : [y/x]t' \vdash$.

Lemma 5 (Substitution for typing). *If the following premises hold:*

1. $(\Delta \mid \sigma_2 \mid \sigma_1) \odot \Gamma_1 \vdash t : A$
2. $(\Delta, \sigma_1, \Delta' \mid \sigma_3, s, \sigma_4 \mid \sigma_5, r, \sigma_6) \odot \Gamma_1, x : A, \Gamma_2 \vdash t' : B$
3. $|\sigma_3| = |\sigma_5| = |\Gamma_1|$

Then $\begin{pmatrix} \Delta,(\Delta'\backslash|\Delta|+(\Delta'/|\Delta|)*\sigma_2) \\ (\sigma_3+s*\sigma_2),\sigma_4 \\ (\sigma_5+r*\sigma_2),\sigma_6 \end{pmatrix} \odot \Gamma_1, [t/x]\Gamma_2 \vdash [t/x]t' : [t/x]B.$

As with substitution for well-formed contexts, we account for the replacement of x with t in Γ_2 by 'cutting out' x from the context grade vectors, and adding on the grades required to form t, scaled by the grades that described x's usage. We additionally must account for the altered subject and subject-type usage. We do this in a similar manner, by taking, for example, the usage of Γ_1 in the subject (σ_3), and adding on the grades required to form t, scaled by the grade with which x was previously used (s). Subject-type grades are calculated similarly.

4.2 Type Preservation

Lemma 6. *Reduction implies equality If* $(\Delta \mid \sigma_1 \mid \sigma_2) \odot \Gamma \vdash t_1 : A$ *and* $t_1 \rightsquigarrow t_2$, *then* $(\Delta \mid \sigma_1 \mid \sigma_2) \odot \Gamma \vdash t_1 = t_2 : A$.

Lemma 7. *Equality inversion If* $(\Delta \mid \sigma_1 \mid \sigma_2) \odot \Gamma \vdash t_1 = t_2 : A$, *then* $(\Delta \mid \sigma_1 \mid \sigma_2) \odot \Gamma \vdash t_1 : A$ *and* $(\Delta \mid \sigma_1 \mid \sigma_2) \odot \Gamma \vdash t_2 : A$.

Lemma 8. *Type preservation If* $(\Delta \mid \sigma_1 \mid \sigma_2) \odot \Gamma \vdash t : A$ *and* $t \rightsquigarrow t'$, *then* $(\Delta \mid \sigma_1 \mid \sigma_2) \odot \Gamma \vdash t' : A$.

Proof. By Lemma 6 we have $(\Delta \mid \sigma_1 \mid \sigma_2) \odot \Gamma \vdash t = t' : A$, and therefore by Lemma 7 we have $(\Delta \mid \sigma_1 \mid \sigma_2) \odot \Gamma \vdash t' : A$, as required.

4.3 Structural Rules

We now consider the structural rules of *contraction*, *exchange*, and *weakening*.

Lemma 9 (Contraction). *The following rule is admissible:*

$$\frac{\begin{pmatrix} \Delta_1,\sigma_1,(\sigma_1,0),\Delta_2 \\ \sigma_2,s_1,s_2,\sigma_3 \\ \sigma_4,r_1,r_2,\sigma_5 \end{pmatrix} \odot \Gamma_1, x : A, y : A, \Gamma_2 \vdash t : B \quad |\Delta_1| = |\sigma_2| = |\sigma_4| = |\Gamma_1|}{\begin{pmatrix} \Delta_1,\sigma_1,\mathsf{contr}(|\Delta_1|;\Delta_2) \\ \sigma_2,(s_1+s_2),\sigma_3 \\ \sigma_4,(r_1+r_2),\sigma_5 \end{pmatrix} \odot \Gamma_1, z : A, [z,z/x,y]\Gamma_2 \vdash [z,z/x,y]t : [z,z/x,y]B} \textsc{Contr}$$

The operation $\mathsf{contr}(\pi;\Delta)$ contracts the elements at index π and $\pi+1$ for each vector in Δ by combining them with the semiring addition, defined $\mathsf{contr}(\pi;\Delta) = \Delta\backslash(\pi+1) + \Delta/(\pi+1) * (\mathbf{0}^{\pi}, 1)$. Admissibility follows from the semiring addition, which serves to contract dependencies, being threaded throughout the rules.

Lemma 10 (Exchange). *The following rule is admissible:*

$$\frac{x \notin \mathsf{FV}(B) \qquad |\Delta_1| = |\sigma_3| = |\sigma_5| = |\Gamma_1| \qquad \begin{pmatrix} \Delta_1,\sigma_1,(\sigma_2,0),\Delta_2 \\ \sigma_3,s_1,s_2,\sigma_4 \\ \sigma_5,r_1,r_2,\sigma_6 \end{pmatrix} \odot \Gamma_1, x : A, y : B, \Gamma_2 \vdash t : C}{\begin{pmatrix} \Delta_1,\sigma_2,(\sigma_1,0),\mathsf{exch}(|\Delta_1|;\Delta_2) \\ \sigma_3,s_2,s_1,\sigma_4 \\ \sigma_5,r_2,r_1,\sigma_6 \end{pmatrix} \odot \Gamma_1, y : B, x : A, \Gamma_2 \vdash t : C} \text{ EXC}$$

Notice that if you strip away the vector fragment and sizing premise, this is exactly the form of exchange we would expect in a dependent type theory: if x and y are assumptions in a context typing $t : C$, and the type of y does not depend upon x, then we can type $t : C$ when we swap the order of x and y.

The action on grade vectors is simple: we swap the grades associated with each of the variables. For the context grade vector however, we must do two things: first, we capture the formation of A with σ_1, and the formation of B with $\sigma_1, 0$ (indicating x being used with grade 0 in B), then swap these around, cutting the final grade from $\sigma_2, 0$, and adding 0 to the end of σ_1 to ensure correct sizing. Next, the operation $\mathsf{exch}(|\Delta_1|\,;\Delta_2)$ swaps the element at index $|\Delta_1|$ (i.e., that corresponding to usage of x) with the element at index $|\Delta_1| + 1$ (corresponding to y) for every vector in Δ_2; this exchange operation ensures that usage in the trailing context is reordered appropriately.

Lemma 11 (Weakening). *The following rule is admissible:*

$$\frac{\begin{array}{l}(\Delta_1, \Delta_2 \mid \sigma_1, \sigma_1' \mid \sigma_2, \sigma_2') \odot \Gamma_1, \Gamma_2 \vdash t : B \\ (\Delta_1 \mid \sigma_3 \mid \mathit{0}) \odot \Gamma_1 \vdash A : \mathsf{Type}_l \qquad |\sigma_1| = |\sigma_2| = |\Gamma_1|\end{array}}{(\Delta_1, \sigma_3, \mathsf{ins}(|\Delta_1|\,; 0; \Delta_2) \mid \sigma_1, 0, \sigma_1' \mid \sigma_2, 0, \sigma_2') \odot \Gamma_1, x : A, \Gamma_2 \vdash t : B} \text{ WEAK}$$

Weakening introduces irrelevant assumptions to a context. We do this by capturing the usage in the formation of the assumption's type with σ_3 to preserve the well-formedness of the context. We then indicate irrelevance of the assumption by grading with 0 in appropriate places. The operation $\mathsf{ins}(\pi; s; \Delta)$ inserts the element s at index π for each σ in Δ, such that all elements preceding index π (in σ) keep their positions, and every element at index π or greater (in σ) will be shifted one index later in the new vector. The 0 grades in the subject and subject-type grade vector positions correspond to the absence of the irrelevant assumption from the subject and subject's type.

4.4 Strong Normalization

We adapt Geuvers' strong normalization proof for the Calculus of Constructions (CC) [24] to a fragment of GRTT (called $\text{GRTT}^{\{0,1\}}$) restricted to two universe levels and without variables of type Type_1. This results in a less expressive system than full GRTT when it comes to higher kinds, but this is orthogonal to the main idea here of grading. We briefly overview the strong normalization proof; details can be found in the extended version [44]. Note this strong normalization result is with respect to β-reduction only (our semantics does not include η-reduction).

We use the proof technique of saturated sets, based on the reducibility candidates of Girard [29]. While $\text{GRTT}^{\{0,1\}}$ has a collapsed syntax we use judgments to break typing up into stages. We use these sets to match on whether a term is a kind, type, constructor, or a function (we will refer to these as terms).

Definition 3. Typing can be broken up into the following stages:

$$\begin{aligned}
\mathsf{Kind} &:= \{A \mid \exists \Delta, \sigma_1, \Gamma.(\Delta \mid \sigma_1 \mid \mathbf{0}) \odot \Gamma \vdash A : \mathsf{Type}_1\} \\
\mathsf{Type} &:= \{A \mid \exists \Delta, \sigma_1, \Gamma.(\Delta \mid \sigma_1 \mid \mathbf{0}) \odot \Gamma \vdash A : \mathsf{Type}_0\} \\
\mathsf{Con} &:= \{t \mid \exists \Delta, \sigma_1, \sigma_2, \Gamma, A.(\Delta \mid \sigma_1 \mid \sigma_2) \odot \Gamma \vdash t : A \wedge (\Delta \mid \sigma_2 \mid \mathbf{0}) \odot \Gamma \vdash A : \mathsf{Type}_1\} \\
\mathsf{Term} &:= \{t \mid \exists \Delta, \sigma_1, \sigma_2, \Gamma, A.(\Delta \mid \sigma_1 \mid \sigma_2) \odot \Gamma \vdash t : A \wedge (\Delta \mid \sigma_2 \mid \mathbf{0}) \odot \Gamma \vdash A : \mathsf{Type}_0\}
\end{aligned}$$

Lemma 12 (Classification). *We have* $\mathsf{Kind} \cap \mathsf{Type} = \emptyset$ *and* $\mathsf{Con} \cap \mathsf{Term} = \emptyset$.

The classification lemma states that we can safely case split over kinds and types, or constructors and terms without fear of an overlap occurring.

Saturated sets are essentially collections of strongly normalizing terms that are closed under β-reduction. The intuition behind this proof is that every typable program ends up in some saturated set, and hence, is strongly normalizing.

Definition 4. [Base terms and saturated terms] Informally, the set of base terms $\mathcal{B}$ is inductively defined from variables and Type_0 and Type_1, and compound terms over base $\mathcal{B}$ and strongly normalising terms SN.

A set of terms X is *saturated* if $X \subset \mathsf{SN}$, $\mathcal{B} \subset X$, and if $\mathsf{red}_\mathsf{k}\, t \in X$ and $t \in \mathsf{SN}$, then $t \in X$. Thus saturated sets are closed under strongly normalizing terms with a *key redex*, denoted $\mathsf{red}_\mathsf{k}\, t$, which are redexes or a redex at the head of an elimination form. SAT denotes the collection of saturated sets.

Lemma 13 (SN saturated). *All saturated sets are non-empty;* SN *is saturated.*

Since $\text{GRTT}^{\{0,1\}}$ allows computation in types as well as in types, we separate the interpretations for kinds and types, where the former is a set of the latter.

Definition 5. For $A \in \mathsf{Kind}$, the kind interpretation, $\mathcal{K}[\![A]\!]$, is defined:

$$\begin{aligned}
&\mathcal{K}[\![\mathsf{Type}_0]\!] = \mathsf{SAT} && \mathcal{K}[\![(x :_{(s,r)} A) \to B]\!] = \{f \mid f : \mathcal{K}[\![A]\!] \to \mathcal{K}[\![B]\!]\}, \text{ if } A, B \in \mathsf{Kind} \\
&\mathcal{K}[\![\Box_s A]\!] \;\; = \mathcal{K}[\![A]\!] && \mathcal{K}[\![(x :_{(s,r)} A) \to B]\!] = \mathcal{K}[\![A]\!], \text{ if } A \in \mathsf{Kind}, B \in \mathsf{Type} \\
& && \mathcal{K}[\![(x :_{(s,r)} A) \to B]\!] = \mathcal{K}[\![B]\!], \text{ if } A \in \mathsf{Type}, B \in \mathsf{Kind} \\
& && \mathcal{K}[\![(x :_r A) \otimes B]\!] \quad = \mathcal{K}[\![A]\!] \times \mathcal{K}[\![B]\!], \text{ if } A, B \in \mathsf{Kind} \\
& && \mathcal{K}[\![(x :_r A) \otimes B]\!] \quad = \mathcal{K}[\![A]\!], \text{ if } A \in \mathsf{Kind}, B \in \mathsf{Type} \\
& && \mathcal{K}[\![(x :_r A) \otimes B]\!] \quad = \mathcal{K}[\![B]\!], \text{ if } A \in \mathsf{Type}, B \in \mathsf{Kind}
\end{aligned}$$

Next we define the interpretation of types, which requires the interpretation to be parametric on an interpretation of type variables called a type evaluation. This is necessary to make the interpretation well-founded (first realized by Girard [29]).

Definition 6. *Type valuations,* $\Delta \odot \Gamma \models \varepsilon$, are defined as follows:

$$\frac{}{\emptyset \odot \emptyset \models \emptyset}\,\text{E} \qquad \frac{X \in \mathcal{K}[\![A]\!] \quad \Delta \odot \Gamma \models \varepsilon \quad (\Delta \mid \sigma \mid \mathbf{0}) \odot \Gamma \vdash A : \mathsf{Type}_1}{(\Delta, \sigma) \odot (\Gamma, x : A) \models \varepsilon[x \mapsto X]}\,\text{TY} \qquad \frac{\Delta \odot \Gamma \models \varepsilon \quad (\Delta \mid \sigma \mid \mathbf{0}) \odot \Gamma \vdash A : \mathsf{Type}_0}{(\Delta, \sigma) \odot (\Gamma, x : A) \models \varepsilon}\,\text{TM}$$

Type valuations ignore term variables (rule TM), in fact, the interpretations of both types and kinds ignores them because we are defining sets of terms over types, and thus terms in types do not contribute to the definition of these sets. However as these interpretations define sets of open terms we must carry a graded context around where necessary. Thus, type valuations are with respect to a well-formed graded context $\Delta \odot \Gamma$. We now outline the type interpretation.

Definition 7. For type valuation $\Delta \odot \Gamma \models \varepsilon$ and a type $A \in (\mathsf{Kind} \cup \mathsf{Type} \cup \mathsf{Con})$ with A typable in $\Delta \odot \Gamma$, the interpretation of types $[\![A]\!]_\varepsilon$ is defined inductively. For brevity, we list just a few illustrative cases, including modalities and some function cases; the complete definition is given in the extended version [44].

$$\begin{aligned}
[\![\mathsf{Type}_1]\!]_\varepsilon &= \mathsf{SN} \\
[\![\mathsf{Type}_0]\!]_\varepsilon &= \lambda X \in \mathsf{SAT}.\mathsf{SN} \\
[\![x]\!]_\varepsilon &= \varepsilon\, x && \text{if } x \in \mathsf{Con} \\
[\![\Box_s A]\!]_\varepsilon &= [\![A]\!]_\varepsilon \\
[\![\lambda x : A.B]\!]_\varepsilon &= \lambda X \in \mathcal{K}[\![A]\!].[\![B]\!]_{\varepsilon[x \mapsto X]} && \text{if } A \in \mathsf{Kind}, B \in \mathsf{Con} \\
[\![A\, B]\!]_\varepsilon &= [\![A]\!]_\varepsilon([\![B]\!]_\varepsilon) && \text{if } B \in \mathsf{Con} \\
[\![(x :_{(s,r)} A) \to B]\!]_\varepsilon &= \lambda X \in \mathcal{K}[\![A]\!] \to \mathcal{K}[\![B]\!].\textstyle\bigcap_{Y \in \mathcal{K}[\![A]\!]}([\![A]\!]_\varepsilon\, Y \to [\![B]\!]_{\varepsilon[x \mapsto Y]}\,(X\,(Y))) \\
& && \text{if } A, B \in \mathsf{Kind}
\end{aligned}$$

Grades play no role in the reduction relation for GRTT, and hence, our interpretation erases graded modalities and their introductory and elimination forms (translated into substitutions). In fact, the above interpretation can be seen as a translation of $\text{GRTT}^{\{0,1\}}$ into non-substructural set theory; there is no data-usage tracking in the image of the interpretation. Tensors are translated into Cartesian products whose eliminators are translated into substitutions similarly to graded modalities. All terms however remain well-typed through the interpretation.

The interpretation of terms corresponds to term valuations that are used to close the term before interpreting it into the interpretation of its type.

Definition 8. *Valid term valuations*, $\Delta \odot \Gamma \models_\varepsilon \rho$, are defined as follows:

$$\frac{}{\emptyset \odot \emptyset \models_\emptyset \emptyset}\,\textsc{E} \qquad \frac{t \in ([\![A]\!]_\varepsilon)\,(\varepsilon\, x) \quad \Delta \odot \Gamma \models_\varepsilon \rho \quad (\Delta \mid \sigma \mid \mathbf{0}) \odot \Gamma \vdash A : \mathsf{Type}_1}{(\Delta, \sigma) \odot \Gamma, x : A \models_\varepsilon \rho[x \mapsto t]}\,\textsc{Ty} \qquad \frac{t \in [\![A]\!]_\varepsilon \quad \Delta \odot \Gamma \models_\varepsilon \rho \quad (\Delta \mid \sigma \mid \mathbf{0}) \odot \Gamma \vdash A : \mathsf{Type}_0}{(\Delta, \sigma) \odot \Gamma, x : A \models_\varepsilon \rho[x \mapsto t]}\,\textsc{Tm}$$

We interpret terms as substitutions, but graded modalities must be erased and their elimination forms converted into substitutions (and similarly for the eliminator for tensor products).

Definition 9. Suppose $\Delta \odot \Gamma \models_\varepsilon \rho$. Then the *interpretation of a term* t typable in $\Delta \odot \Gamma$ is $(\!|t|\!)_\rho = \rho t$, but where all let-expressions are translated into substitutions, and all graded modalities are erased.

Finally, we prove our main result using semantic typing which will imply strong normalization. Suppose $(\Delta \mid \sigma_1 \mid \sigma_2) \odot \Gamma \vdash t : A$, then:

Definition 10. *Semantic typing,* $(\Delta \mid \sigma_1 \mid \sigma_2) \odot \Gamma \models t : A$, is defined as follows:

1. If $(\Delta \mid \sigma \mid \mathbf{0}) \odot \Gamma \vdash A : \mathsf{Type}_1$, then for every $\Delta \odot \Gamma \models_\varepsilon \rho$, $(\!|t|\!)_\rho \in [\![A]\!]_\varepsilon\, ([\![t]\!]_\varepsilon)$.
2. If $(\Delta \mid \sigma \mid \mathbf{0}) \odot \Gamma \vdash A : \mathsf{Type}_0$, then for every $\Delta \odot \Gamma \models_\varepsilon \rho$, $(\!|t|\!)_\rho \in [\![A]\!]_\varepsilon$.

Theorem 3 (Soundness for Semantic Typing). $(\Delta \mid \sigma_1 \mid \sigma_2) \odot \Gamma \models t : A$.

Corollary 1 (Strong Normalization). *We have* $t \in \mathsf{SN}$.

5 Implementation

Our implementation **Gerty** is based on a bidirectionalised version of the typing rules here, somewhat following traditional schemes of bidirectional typing [19,20] but with grading (similar to Granule [46] but adapted considerably for the dependent setting). We briefly outline the implementation scheme and highlight a few key points, rules, and examples. We use this implementation to explore further applications of GRTT, namely optimising type checking algorithms.

Bidirectional typing splits declarative typing rules into *check* and *infer* modes. Furthermore, bidirectional GRTT rules split the grading context (left of $\odot$) into *input* and *output* contexts where $(\Delta \mid \sigma_1 \mid \sigma_2) \odot \Gamma \vdash t : A$ is implemented via:

$$(\textit{check})\ \ \Delta; \Gamma \vdash t \Leftarrow A; \sigma_1; \sigma_2 \quad \textit{or} \quad (\textit{infer})\ \ \Delta; \Gamma \vdash t \Rightarrow A; \sigma_1; \sigma_2$$

where $\Leftarrow$ rules *check* that t has type A and $\Rightarrow$ rules *infer* (calculate) that t has type A. In both judgments, the context grading Δ and context Γ left of $\vdash$ are inputs whereas the grade vectors σ_1 and σ_2 to the right of A are outputs. This input-output context approach resembles that employed in linear type checking [5,32,62]. Rather than following a "left over" scheme as in these works (where the output context explains what resources are left), the output grades here explain what has been used according to the analysis of grading ('adding up' rather than 'taking away').

For example, the following is the *infer* rule for function elimination:

$$\frac{\begin{array}{l}\Delta; \Gamma \vdash t_1 \Rightarrow (x :_{(s,r)} A) \to B; \sigma_2; \sigma_{13} \\ \Delta; \Gamma \vdash t_2 \Leftarrow A; \sigma_4; \sigma_1 \\ \Delta, \sigma_1; \Gamma, x : A \vdash B \Rightarrow \mathsf{Type}_l; \sigma_3, r; \mathbf{0} \qquad \sigma_{13} = \sigma_1 + \sigma_3\end{array}}{\Delta; \Gamma \vdash t_1\, t_2 \Rightarrow [t_2/x]B; \sigma_2 + s * \sigma_4; \sigma_3 + r * \sigma_4} \Rightarrow \lambda_e$$

The rule can be read by starting at the input of the conclusion (left of $\vdash$), then reading top down through each premise, to calculate the output grades in the rule's conclusion. Any concrete value or already-bound variable appearing in the output grades of a premise can be read as causing an equality check in the type checker. The last premise checks that the output subject-type grade σ_{13} from the first premise matches $\sigma_1 + \sigma_3$ (which were calculated by later premises).

In contrast, function introduction is a *check* rule:

$$\frac{\Delta; \Gamma \vdash A \Rightarrow \mathsf{Type}_l; \sigma_1; \mathbf{0} \qquad \Delta, \sigma_1; \Gamma, x : A \vdash t \Leftarrow B; \sigma_2, s; \sigma_3, r}{\Delta; \Gamma \vdash \lambda x.t \Leftarrow (x :_{(s,r)} A) \to B; \sigma_2; \sigma_1 + \sigma_3} \Leftarrow \lambda_i$$

Thus, dependent functions can be checked against type $(x :_{(s,r)} A) \to B$ given input $\Delta; \Gamma$ by first inferring the type of A and checking that its output subject-type grade comprises all zeros $\mathbf{0}$. Then the body of the function t is checked against B under the context $\Delta, \sigma_1; \Gamma, x : A$ producing grade vectors σ_2, s' and σ_1, r' where it is checked that $s = s'$ and $r = r'$ (described implicitly in the rule), i.e., the calculated grades match those of the binder.

The implementation anticipates some further work for GRTT: the potential for grades which are first-class terms, for which we anticipate complex equations on grades. For grade equality, **Gerty** has two modes: one which normalises terms and then compares for syntactic equality, and the other which discharges constraints via an off-the-shelf SMT solver (we use Z3 [17]). We discuss briefly some performance implications in the next section.

Using Grades to Optimise Type Checking Abel posited that a dependent theory with quantitative resource tracking at the type level could leverage linearity-like optimisations in type checking [2]. Our implementation provides a research vehicle for exploring this idea; we consider one possible optimisation here.

Key to dependent type checking is the substitution of terms into types in elimination forms (i.e., application, tensor elimination). However, in a quantitative semiring setting, if a variable has 0 subject-type grade, then we know it is irrelevant to type formation (it is not semantically depended upon, i.e., during normalisation). Subsequently, substitutions into a 0-graded variable can be elided (or allocations to a closure environment can be avoided). We implemented this optimisation in **Gerty** when inferring the type of an application for $t_1\, t_2$ (rule $\Rightarrow \lambda_e$ above), where the type of t_1 is inferred as $(x :_{(s,0)} A) \to B$. For a quantitative semiring we know that x irrelevant in B, thus we need not perform the substitution $[t_2/x]B$ when type checking the application.

We evaluate this on simple **Gerty** programs of an n-ary "fanout" combinator implemented via an n-ary application combinator, e.g., for arity 3:

```
app3 : (a : (0, 6) Type 0) -> (b : (0, 2) Type 0)
-> (x0 : (1, 0) a) -> (x1 : (1, 0) a) -> (x2 : (1, 0) a)
-> (f:(1, 0) ((y0:(1,0) a) -> (y1:(1,0) a) -> (y2:(1,0) a) -> b)) -> b
app3 = \a -> \b -> \x0 -> \x1 -> \x2 -> \f -> f x0 x1 x2

fan3 : (a : (0, 4) Type 0) -> (b : (0, 2) Type 0)
-> (f : (1,0) ((z0 : (1,0) a) -> (z1 : (1,0) a) -> (z2 : (1,0) a) -> b))
-> (x : (3, 0) a) -> b
fan3 = \a -> \b -> \f -> \x -> app3 a b x x x f
```

Note that `fan3` uses its parameter `x` three times (hence the grade 3) which then incurs substitutions into the type of `app3` during type checking, but each such substitution is redundant since the type does not depend on these parameters, as reflected by the 0 subject-type grades.

To evaluate the optimisation and SMT solving vs. normalisation-based equality, we ran **Gerty** on the fan out program for arities from 3 to 8, with and without the optimisation and under the two equality approaches.

	Normalisation			SMT		
n	Base ms	Optimised ms	Speedup	Base ms	Optimised ms	Speedup
3	45.71 (1.72)	44.08 (1.28)	1.04	77.12 (2.65)	76.91 (2.36)	1.00
4	108.75 (4.09)	89.73 (4.73)	1.21	136.18 (5.23)	162.95 (3.62)	0.84
5	190.57 (8.31)	191.25 (8.13)	1.00	279.49 (15.73)	289.73 (23.30)	0.96
6	552.11 (29.00)	445.26 (23.50)	1.24	680.11 (16.28)	557.08 (13.87)	1.22
7	1821.49 (49.44)	1348.85 (26.37)	1.35	1797.09 (43.53)	1368.45 (20.16)	1.31
8	6059.30 (132.01)	4403.10 (86.57)	1.38	5913.06 (118.83)	4396.90 (59.82)	1.34

Table 1. Performance analysis of grade-based optimisations to type checking. Times in milliseconds to 2 d.p. with the standard error given in brackets. Measurements are the mean of 10 trials (run on a 2.7 Ghz Intel Core, 8Gb of RAM, Z3 4.8.8).

Table 1 gives the results. For grade equality by normalisation, the optimisation has a positive effect on speedup, getting increasingly significant (up to 38%) as the overall cost increases. For SMT-based grade equality, the optimisation causes some slow down for arity 4 and 5 (and just breaking even for arity 3). This is because working out whether the optimisation can be applied requires checking whether grades are equal to 0, which incurs extra SMT solver calls. Eventually, this cost is outweighed by the time saved by reducing substitutions. Since the grades here are all relatively simple, it is usually more efficient for the type checker to normalise and compare terms rather than compiling to SMT and starting up the external solver, as seen by longer times for the SMT approach.

The baseline performance here is poor (the implementation is not highly optimised) partly due to the overhead of computing type formation judgments often to accurately account for grading. However, such checks are often recomputed and could be optimised away by memoisation. Nevertheless this experiment gives the evidence that grades can indeed be used to optimise type checking. A thorough investigation of grade-directed optimisations is future work.

6 Discussion

Grading, Coeffects, and Quantitative Types The notion of *coeffects*, describing how a program depends on its context, arose in the literature from two directions: as a dualisation of effect types [48,49] and a generalisation of Bounded Linear Logic to general resource semirings [25,10]. Coeffect systems can capture reuse bounds, information flow security [23], hardware scheduling constraints [25], and sensitivity for differential privacy [16,22]. A coeffect-style approach also enables linear types to be retrofitted to Haskell [8]. A common thread is the annotation of variables in the context with usage information, drawn from a semiring. Our approach generalises this idea to capture type, context, and computational usage.

McBride [43] reconciles linear and dependent types, allowing types to depend on linear values, refined by Atkey [6] as Quantitative Type Theory. QTT employs coeffect-style annotation of each assumption in a context with an element of a resource accounting algebra, with judgments of the form:

$$x_1 \overset{\rho_1}{:} A_1, \ldots, x_n \overset{\rho_n}{:} A_n \vdash M \overset{\rho}{:} B$$

where ρ_i, ρ are elements of a semiring, and $\rho = 0$ or $\rho = 1$, respectively denoting a term which can be used in type formation (erased at runtime) or at runtime. Dependent function arrows are of the form $(x \overset{\rho}{:} A) \to B$, where ρ is a semiring element that denotes the computational usage of the parameter.

Variables used for type formation but not computation are annotated by 0. Subsequently, type formation rules are all of the form $0\Gamma \vdash T$, meaning every variable assumption has a 0 annotation. GRTT is similar to QTT, but differs in its more extensive grading to track usage in types, rather than blanketing all type usage with 0. In Atkey's formulation, a term can be promoted to a type if its result and dependency quantities are all 0. A set of rules provide formation of computational type terms, but these are also graded at 0. Subsequently, it is not possible to construct an inhabitant of Type that can be used at runtime. We avoid this shortcoming allowing matching on types. For example, a computation t that inspects a type variable a would be typed as: $(\Delta, \mathbf{0}, \Delta' \mid \sigma_1, 1, \sigma_1' \mid \sigma_2, r, \sigma_2') \odot \Gamma, a : \mathsf{Type}, \Gamma' \vdash t : B$ denoting 1 computational use and r type uses in B.

At first glance, it seems QTT could be encoded into GRTT taking the semiring $\mathcal{R}$ of QTT and parameterising GRTT by the semiring $\mathcal{R} \cup \{\hat{0}\}$ where $\hat{0}$ denotes arbitrary usage in type formation. However, there is impedance between the two systems as QTT always annotates type use with 0. It is not clear how to make this happen in GRTT whilst still having non-0 tracking at the computational level, since we use one semiring for both. Exploring an encoding is future work.

Choudhury et al. [13] give a system closely related (but arguably simpler) to QTT called GRAD. One key difference is that rather than annotating type usage with 0, grades are simply ignored in types. This makes for a surprisingly flexible system. In addition, they show that irrelevance is captured by the 0 grade using a heap-based semantics (a result leveraged in Section 3). GRAD however does not have the power of type-grades presented here.

Dependent Types and Modalities Dal Lago and Gaboardi extend PCF with linear and lightweight dependent types [15] (then adapted for differential privacy analysis [22]). They add a natural number type indexed by upper and lower bound terms which index a modality. Combined with linear arrows of the form $[a < I].\sigma \multimap \tau$ these describe functions using the parameter at most I times (where the modality acts as a binder for index variable a which denotes instantiations). Their system is leveraged to give fine-grained cost analyses in the context of Implicit Computational Complexity. Whilst a powerful system, their approach is restricted in terms of dependency, where only a specialised type can depend on specialised natural-number indexed terms (which are non-linear).

Gratzer et al. define a dependently-typed language with a Fitch-style modality [30]. It seems that such an approach could also be generalised to a graded modality, although we have used the natural-deduction style for our graded modality rather than the Fitch-style.

As discussed in Section 1, our approach closely resembles Abel's *resourceful dependent types* [2]. Our work expands on the idea, including tensors and the graded modalities. We considerably developed the associated metatheory, provide an implementation, and study applications.

Further Work One expressive extension is to capture analyses which have an ordering, e.g., grading by a *pre-ordered* semiring, allowing a notion of *approximation*. This would enable analyses such as bounded reuse from Bounded Linear Logic [28], intervals with least- and upper-bounds on use [46], and top-completed semirings, with an ∞-element denoting arbitrary usage as a fall-back. We have made progress into exploring the interaction between approximation and dependent types, and the remainder of this is left as future work.

A powerful extension of GRTT for future work is to allow grades to be first-class terms. Typing rules in GRTT involving grades could be adapted to internalise the elements as first-class terms. We could then, e.g., define the map function over sized vectors, which requires that the parameter function is used exactly the same number of times as the length of the vector:

$$\begin{aligned} &map : (n :_{(0,5)} \mathsf{nat}) \rightarrow (a :_{(0,n+1)} \mathsf{Type}) \rightarrow (b :_{(0,n+1)} \mathsf{Type}) \rightarrow \\ &\qquad (f :_{(n,0)} (x :_{(1,0)} a) \rightarrow b) \rightarrow (xs :_{(1,0)} \mathsf{Vec}\, n\, a) \rightarrow \mathsf{Vec}\, n\, b \end{aligned}$$

This type provides strong guarantees: the only well-typed implementations do the correct thing, up to permutations of the result vector. Without the grading, an implementation could apply f fewer than n times, replicating some of the transformed elements; here we know that f must be applied exactly n-times.

A further appealing possibility for GRTT is to allow the semiring to be defined internally, rather than as a meta-level parameter, leveraging dependent types for proofs of key properties. An implementation could specify what is required for a semiring instance, e.g., a record type capturing the operations and properties of a semiring. The rules of GRTT could then be extended, similarly to the extension to first-class grades, with the provision of the semiring(s) coming from GRTT terms. Thus, anywhere with a grading premise $(\Delta \mid \sigma_1 \mid \sigma_2) \odot \Gamma \vdash r : \mathcal{R}$ would also require a premise $(\Delta \mid \sigma_2 \mid \mathbf{0}) \odot \Gamma \vdash \mathcal{R} : \mathsf{Semiring}$. This opens up the ability for programmers and library developers to provide custom modes of resource tracking with their libraries, allowing domain-specific program verification.

Conclusions The paradigm of 'grading' exposes the inherent structure of a type theory, proof theory, or semantics by matching the underlying structure with some algebraic structure augmenting the types. This idea has been employed for reasoning about side effects via graded monads [35], and reasoning about data flow as discussed here by semiring grading. Richer algebras could be employed to capture other aspects, such as *ordered logics* in which the exchange rule can be controlled via grading (existing work has done this via modalities [34]).

We developed the core of grading in the context of dependent-types, treating types and terms equally (as one comes to expect in dependent-type theories). The tracking of data flow in types appears complex since we must account for how variables are used to form types in both the context and in the subject type, making sure not to repeat context formation use. The result however is a powerful system for studying dependencies in type theories, as shown by our ability to study different theories just be specialising grades. Whilst not yet a fully fledged implementation, **Gerty** is a useful test bed for further exploration.

Acknowledgments Orchard is supported by EPSRC grant EP/T013516/1.

References

1. Abadi, M., Banerjee, A., Heintze, N., Riecke, J.: A Core Calculus of Dependency. In: POPL. ACM (1999). https://doi.org/10.1145/292540.292555
2. Abel, A.: Resourceful Dependent Types. In: 24th International Conference on Types for Proofs and Programs, Abstracts (2018)
3. Abel, A., Bernardy, J.: A unified view of modalities in type systems. Proc. ACM Program. Lang. **4**(ICFP), 90:1–90:28 (2020). https://doi.org/10.1145/3408972
4. Abel, A., Scherer, G.: On irrelevance and algorithmic equality in predicative type theory. Log. Methods Comput. Sci. **8**(1) (2012). https://doi.org/10.2168/LMCS-8(1:29)2012
5. Allais, G.: Typing with Leftovers - A mechanization of Intuitionistic Multiplicative-Additive Linear Logic. In: Abel, A., Forsberg, F.N., Kaposi, A. (eds.) 23rd International Conference on Types for Proofs and Programs (TYPES 2017). Leibniz International Proceedings in Informatics (LIPIcs), vol. 104, pp. 1:1–1:22. Schloss Dagstuhl–Leibniz-Zentrum fuer Informatik, Dagstuhl, Germany (2018). https://doi.org/10.4230/LIPIcs.TYPES.2017.1
6. Atkey, R.: Syntax and Semantics of Quantitative Type Theory. In: Proceedings of the 33rd Annual ACM/IEEE Symposium on Logic in Computer Science, LICS 2018, Oxford, UK, July 09-12, 2018. pp. 56–65 (2018). https://doi.org/10.1145/3209108.3209189
7. Atkey, R., Ghani, N., Johann, P.: A relationally parametric model of dependent type theory. In: Proceedings of the 41st ACM SIGPLAN-SIGACT Symposium on Principles of Programming Languages. pp. 503–515 (2014). https://doi.org/10.1145/2535838.2535852
8. Bernardy, J.P., Boespflug, M., Newton, R.R., Peyton Jones, S., Spiwack, A.: Linear Haskell: practical linearity in a higher-order polymorphic language. Proceedings of the ACM on Programming Languages **2**(POPL), 5 (2017). https://doi.org/10.1145/3158093
9. Brady, E., McBride, C., McKinna, J.: Inductive families need not store their indices. In: International Workshop on Types for Proofs and Programs. pp. 115–129. Springer (2003). https://doi.org/10.1007/978-3-540-24849-1_8
10. Brunel, A., Gaboardi, M., Mazza, D., Zdancewic, S.: A Core Quantitative Coeffect Calculus. In: Shao, Z. (ed.) Programming Languages and Systems - 23rd European Symposium on Programming, ESOP 2014, Held as Part of the European Joint Conferences on Theory and Practice of Software, ETAPS 2014, Grenoble, France, April 5-13, 2014, Proceedings. Lecture Notes in Computer Science, vol. 8410, pp. 351–370. Springer (2014). https://doi.org/10.1007/978-3-642-54833-8_19
11. Cardelli, L., Wegner, P.: On understanding types, data abstraction, and polymorphism. ACM Computing Surveys **17**(4), 471–523 (Dec 1985). https://doi.org/10.1145/6041.6042
12. Cervesato, I., Pfenning, F.: A linear logical framework. Information and Computation **179**(1), 19–75 (2002). https://doi.org/10.1109/LICS.1996.561339
13. Choudhury, P., Eades III, H., Eisenberg, R.A., Weirich, S.: A Graded Dependent Type System with a Usage-Aware Semantics. Proc. ACM Program. Lang. **5**(POPL) (Jan 2021). https://doi.org/10.1145/3434331
14. Coquand, T., Huet, G.: The Calculus of Constructions. Ph.D. thesis, INRIA (1986)
15. Dal Lago, U., Gaboardi, M.: Linear dependent types and relative completeness. In: Logic in Computer Science (LICS), 2011 26th Annual IEEE Symposium on. pp. 133–142. IEEE (2011). https://doi.org/10.1109/LICS.2011.22

16. De Amorim, A.A., Gaboardi, M., Gallego Arias, E.J., Hsu, J.: Really Natural Linear Indexed Type Checking. In: Proceedings of the 26nd 2014 International Symposium on Implementation and Application of Functional Languages. p. 5. ACM (2014). https://doi.org/10.1145/2746325.2746335
17. De Moura, L., Bjørner, N.: Z3: An efficient SMT solver. In: International conference on Tools and Algorithms for the Construction and Analysis of Systems. pp. 337–340. Springer (2008). https://doi.org/10.1007/978-3-540-78800-3_24
18. De Vries, E., Plasmeijer, R., Abrahamson, D.M.: Uniqueness typing simplified. In: Symposium on Implementation and Application of Functional Languages. pp. 201–218. Springer (2007). https://doi.org/10.1007/978-3-540-85373-2_12
19. Dunfield, J., Krishnaswami, N.R.: Sound and complete bidirectional typechecking for higher-rank polymorphism with existentials and indexed types. PACMPL **3**(POPL), 9:1–9:28 (2019). https://doi.org/10.1145/3290322
20. Dunfield, J., Pfenning, F.: Tridirectional typechecking. In: Proceedings of the 31st ACM SIGPLAN-SIGACT Symposium on Principles of Programming Languages. pp. 281–292. POPL '04, ACM, New York, NY, USA (2004). https://doi.org/10.1145/964001.964025
21. Eades, H., Stump, A.: Hereditary substitution for Stratified System F. In: International Workshop on Proof-Search in Type Theories, PSTT. vol. 10 (2010)
22. Gaboardi, M., Haeberlen, A., Hsu, J., Narayan, A., Pierce, B.C.: Linear dependent types for differential privacy. In: POPL. pp. 357–370 (2013). https://doi.org/10.1145/2429069.2429113
23. Gaboardi, M., Katsumata, S.y., Orchard, D., Breuvart, F., Uustalu, T.: Combining Effects and Coeffects via Grading. In: Proceedings of the 21st ACM SIGPLAN International Conference on Functional Programming. p. 476–489. ICFP 2016, Association for Computing Machinery, New York, NY, USA (2016). https://doi.org/10.1145/2951913.2951939
24. Geuvers, H.: A short and flexible proof of strong normalization for the calculus of constructions. In: Dybjer, P., Nordström, B., Smith, J. (eds.) Types for Proofs and Programs. pp. 14–38. Springer Berlin Heidelberg, Berlin, Heidelberg (1995). https://doi.org/10.1007/3-540-60579-7_2
25. Ghica, D.R., Smith, A.I.: Bounded linear types in a resource semiring. In: ESOP. pp. 331–350 (2014). https://doi.org/10.1007/978-3-642-54833-8_18
26. Girard, J.Y.: Une extension de l'interpretation de gödel a l'analyse, et son application a l'elimination des coupures dans l'analyse et la theorie des types. In: Studies in Logic and the Foundations of Mathematics, vol. 63, pp. 63–92. Elsevier (1971)
27. Girard, J.Y.: Linear logic. Theoretical Computer Science **50**, 1–102 (1987)
28. Girard, J.Y., Scedrov, A., Scott, P.J.: Bounded linear logic: a modular approach to polynomial-time computability. Theoretical computer science **97**(1), 1–66 (1992). https://doi.org/10.1016/0304-3975(92)90386-T
29. Girard, J., Taylor, P., Lafont, Y.: Proofs and types, vol. 7. Cambridge University Press Cambridge (1989)
30. Gratzer, D., Sterling, J., Birkedal, L.: Implementing a modal dependent type theory. Proc. ACM Program. Lang. **3**(ICFP), 107:1–107:29 (2019). https://doi.org/10.1145/3341711
31. Henglein, F., Makholm, H., Niss, H.: Effect types and region-based memory management. Advanced Topics in Types and Programming Languages pp. 87–135 (2005)
32. Hodas, J.S.: Logic programming in intutionistic linear logic: Theory, design and implementation. PhD Thesis, University of Pennsylvania, Department of Computer and Information Science (1994)

33. Hofmann, M.: Syntax and semantics of dependent types. Semantics and logics of computation **14**, 79 (1997)
34. Jiang, J., Eades III, H., de Paiva, V.: On the lambek calculus with an exchange modality. In: Ehrhard, T., Fernández, M., de Paiva, V., de Falco, L.T. (eds.) Proceedings Joint International Workshop on Linearity & Trends in Linear Logic and Applications, Linearity-TLLA@FLoC 2018, Oxford, UK, 7-8 July 2018. EPTCS, vol. 292, pp. 43–89 (2018). https://doi.org/10.4204/EPTCS.292.4
35. Katsumata, S.: Parametric effect monads and semantics of effect systems. In: Proceedings of POPL. pp. 633–646. ACM (2014). https://doi.org/10.1145/2535838.2535846
36. Krishnaswami, N.R., Dreyer, D.: Internalizing relational parametricity in the extensional calculus of constructions. In: Computer Science Logic 2013 (CSL 2013). Schloss Dagstuhl-Leibniz-Zentrum fuer Informatik (2013). https://doi.org/10.4230/LIPIcs.CSL.2013.432
37. Krishnaswami, N.R., Pradic, P., Benton, N.: Integrating linear and dependent types. In: ACM SIGPLAN Notices. vol. 50, pp. 17–30. ACM (2015)
38. Leivant, D.: Finitely stratified polymorphism. Information and Computation **93**(1), 93–113 (1991). https://doi.org/10.1016/0890-5401(91)90053-5
39. Luo, Z., Zhang, Y.: A linear dependent type theory. Types for Proofs and Programs (TYPES 2016), Novi Sad (2016)
40. Martin-Löf, P.: An Intuitionistic Theory of Types: Predicative Part. In: Rose, H.E., Shepherdson, J.C. (eds.) Studies in Logic and the Foundations of Mathematics, Logic Colloquium '73, vol. 80, pp. 73–118. Elsevier (Jan 1975). https://doi.org/10.1016/S0049-237X(08)71945-1
41. Martin-Löf, P.: Intuitionistic Type Theory (Jun 1980)
42. Martin-Löf, P.: Constructive Mathematics and Computer Programming. In: Cohen, L.J., Łoś, J., Pfeiffer, H., Podewski, K.P. (eds.) Studies in Logic and the Foundations of Mathematics, Logic, Methodology and Philosophy of Science VI, vol. 104, pp. 153–175. Elsevier (Jan 1982). https://doi.org/10.1016/S0049-237X(09)70189-2
43. McBride, C.: I Got Plenty o' Nuttin', pp. 207–233. Springer International Publishing, Cham (2016). https://doi.org/10.1007/978-3-319-30936-1_12
44. Moon, B., Eades III, H., Orchard, D.: Graded modal dependent type theory. CoRR **abs/2010.13163** (2020), https://arxiv.org/abs/2010.13163
45. Nuyts, A., Vezzosi, A., Devriese, D.: Parametric quantifiers for dependent type theory. Proceedings of the ACM on Programming Languages **1**(ICFP), 32:1–32:29 (Aug 2017). https://doi.org/10.1145/3110276
46. Orchard, D., Liepelt, V.B., Eades III, H.: Quantitative Program Reasoning with Graded Modal Types. Proc. ACM Program. Lang. **3**(ICFP), 110:1–110:30 (Jul 2019). https://doi.org/10.1145/3341714
47. Palmgren, E.: On universes in type theory. Twenty-five years of constructive type theory **36**, 191–204 (1998)
48. Petricek, T., Orchard, D., Mycroft, A.: Coeffects: Unified Static Analysis of Context-Dependence. In: ICALP (2). pp. 385–397 (2013). https://doi.org/10.1007/978-3-642-39212-2_35
49. Petricek, T., Orchard, D., Mycroft, A.: Coeffects: A calculus of context-dependent computation. In: Proceedings of the 19th ACM SIGPLAN International Conference on Functional Programming. pp. 123–135. ICFP '14, ACM (2014). https://doi.org/10.1145/2628136.2628160

50. Pfenning, F.: Intensionality, extensionality, and proof irrelevance in modal type theory. In: Proceedings 16th Annual IEEE Symposium on Logic in Computer Science. pp. 221–230. IEEE (2001). https://doi.org/10.1109/LICS.2001.932499
51. Reed, J.: Extending higher-order unification to support proof irrelevance. In: International Conference on Theorem Proving in Higher Order Logics. pp. 238–252. Springer (2003). https://doi.org/10.1007/10930755_16
52. Reynolds, J.C.: Towards a theory of type structure. In: Programming Symposium. pp. 408–425. Springer (1974). https://doi.org/10.1007/3-540-06859-7_148
53. Reynolds, J.C.: Types, abstraction and parametric polymorphism. In: Information Processing 83, Proceedings of the IFIP 9th World Computer Congres. pp. 513–523 (1983)
54. Shi, R., Xi, H.: A linear type system for multicore programming in ATS. Science of Computer Programming **78**(8), 1176–1192 (2013). https://doi.org/10.1016/j.scico.2012.09.005
55. Tofte, M., Talpin, J.P.: Region-based memory management. Information and computation **132**(2), 109–176 (1997). https://doi.org/10.1006/inco.1996.2613
56. Tov, J.A., Pucella, R.: Practical affine types. In: Proceedings of the 38th ACM SIGPLAN-SIGACT Symposium on Principles of Programming Languages, POPL 2011, Austin, TX, USA, January 26-28, 2011. pp. 447–458 (2011). https://doi.org/10.1145/1926385.1926436
57. Wadler, P.: Theorems for free! In: Proceedings of the fourth international conference on Functional programming languages and computer architecture. pp. 347–359 (1989). https://doi.org/10.1145/99370.99404
58. Wadler, P.: Linear Types Can Change the World! In: Programming Concepts and Methods. North (1990)
59. Wadler, P.: Propositions as types. Communications of the ACM **58**(12), 75–84 (2015). https://doi.org/10.1145/2699407
60. Walker, D.: Substructural type systems. Advanced Topics in Types and Programming Languages pp. 3–44 (2005)
61. Wood, J., Atkey, R.: A Linear Algebra Approach to Linear Metatheory. CoRR **abs/2005.02247** (2020), https://arxiv.org/abs/2005.02247
62. Zalakain, U., Dardha, O.: Pi with leftovers: a mechanisation in Agda. arXiv preprint arXiv:2005.05902 (2020)

Automated Termination Analysis of Polynomial Probabilistic Programs *

Marcel Moosbrugger[1(✉)], Ezio Bartocci[1], Joost-Pieter Katoen[2], and Laura Kovács[1]

[1] TU Wien, Vienna, Austria
marcel.moosbrugger@tuwien.ac.at
[2] RWTH Aachen University, Aachen, Germany

Abstract. The termination behavior of probabilistic programs depends on the outcomes of random assignments. Almost sure termination (AST) is concerned with the question whether a program terminates with probability one on all possible inputs. Positive almost sure termination (PAST) focuses on termination in a finite expected number of steps. This paper presents a fully automated approach to the termination analysis of probabilistic while-programs whose guards and expressions are polynomial expressions. As proving (positive) AST is undecidable in general, existing proof rules typically provide sufficient conditions. These conditions mostly involve constraints on supermartingales. We consider four proof rules from the literature and extend these with generalizations of existing proof rules for (P)AST. We automate the resulting set of proof rules by effectively computing asymptotic bounds on polynomials over the program variables. These bounds are used to decide the sufficient conditions – including the constraints on supermartingales – of a proof rule. Our software tool AMBER can thus check AST, PAST, as well as their negations for a large class of polynomial probabilistic programs, while carrying out the termination reasoning fully with polynomial witnesses. Experimental results show the merits of our generalized proof rules and demonstrate that AMBER can handle probabilistic programs that are out of reach for other state-of-the-art tools.

Keywords: Probabilistic Programming · Almost sure Termination · Martingales · Asymptotic Bounds · Linear Recurrences

1 Introduction

Classical program termination. Termination is a key property in program analysis [16]. The question whether a program terminates on all possible inputs – the universal halting problem – is undecidable. Proof rules based on ranking functions have been developed that impose sufficient conditions implying (non-)termination. Automated termination checking has given rise to powerful software tools such as AProVE [21] and NaTT [44] (using term rewriting), and UltimateAutomizer [26] (using automata theory). These tools have shown to be able to determine the termination of several intricate programs. The industrial

* This research was supported by the WWTF ICT19-018 grant ProbInG, the ERC Starting Grant SYMCAR 639270, the ERC AdG Grant FRAPPANT 787914, and the Austrian FWF project W1255-N23.

N. Yoshida (Ed.): ESOP 2021, LNCS 12648, pp. 491–518, 2021.
https://doi.org/10.1007/978-3-030-72019-3_18

```
x := 10
while x > 0 do
 | x := x+1 [1/2] x−1
end
```
(a)

```
x := 10
while x > 0 do
 | x := x−1 [1/2] x+2
end
```
(b)

```
x := 0, y := 0
while x^2 + y^2 < 100 do
 | x := x+1 [1/2] x−1
 | y := y+x [1/2] y−x
end
```
(c)

```
x := 10, y := 0
while x > 0 do
 | y := y+1
 | x := x+4y [1/2] x−y^2
end
```
(d)

Fig. 1: Examples of probabilistic programs in our probabilistic language. Program 1a is a symmetric 1D random walk. The program is almost surely terminating (AST) but not positively almost surely terminating (PAST). Program 1b is not AST. Programs 1c and 1d contain dependent variable updates with polynomial guards and both programs are PAST.

tool Terminator [15] has taken termination proving into practice and is able to prove termination – or even more general liveness properties – of e.g., device driver software. Rather than seeking a single ranking function, it takes a disjunctive termination argument using sets of ranking functions. Other results include termination proving methods for specific program classes such as linear and polynomial programs, see, e.g., [9,24].

Termination of probabilistic program. Probabilistic programs extend sequential programs with the ability to draw samples from probability distributions. They are used e.g. for, encoding randomized algorithms, planning in AI, security mechanisms, and in cognitive science. In this paper, we consider probabilistic while-programs with discrete probabilistic choices, in the vein of the seminal works [34] and [37]. Termination of probabilistic programs differs from the classical halting problem in several respects, e.g., probabilistic programs may exhibit diverging runs that have probability mass zero in total. Such programs do not always terminate, but terminate with probability one – they *almost surely* terminate. An example of such a program is given in Figure 1a where variable x is incremented by 1 with probability $1/2$, and otherwise decremented with this amount. This program encodes a one-dimensional (1D) left-bounded random walk starting at position 10. Another important difference to classical termination is that the expected number of program steps until termination may be infinite, even if the program almost surely terminates. Thus, almost sure termination (AST) does not imply that the expected number of steps until termination is finite. Programs that have a finite expected runtime are referred to as *positively almost surely* terminating (PAST). Figure 1c is a sample program that is PAST. While PAST implies AST, the converse does not hold, as evidenced by Figure 1a: the program of Figure 1a terminates with probability one but needs infinitely many steps on average to reach $x{=}0$, hence is not PAST. (The terminology AST and PAST was coined in [8] and has its roots in the theory of Markov processes.)

Proof rules for AST and PAST. Proving termination of probabilistic programs is hard: AST for a single input is as hard as the universal halting problem, whereas PAST is even harder [30]. Termination analysis of probabilistic programs is currently attracting quite some attention. It is not just of theoretical interest. For instance, a popular way to analyze probabilistic programs in machine learning is by using some advanced form of simulation. If, however, a program is not PAST, the simulation may take forever. In addition, the use of probabilistic programs in safety-critical environments [2,7,20] necessitates providing formal guarantees on termination. Different techniques are considered for probabilistic program termination ranging from probabilistic term rewriting [3], sized types [17], and

Büchi automata theory [14], to weakest pre-condition calculi for checking PAST [31]. A large body of works considers *proof rules* that provide sufficient conditions for proving AST, PAST, or their negations. These rules are based on martingale theory, in particular supermartingales. They are stochastic processes that can be (phrased in a simplified manner) viewed as the probabilistic analog of ranking functions: the value of a random variable represents the "value" of the function at the beginning of a loop iteration. Successive random variables model the evolution of the program loop. Being a supermartingale means that the expected value of the random variables at the end of a loop does not exceed its value at the start of the loop. Constraints on supermartingales form the essential part of proof rules. For example, the AST proof rule in [38] requires the existence of a supermartingale whose value decreases at least with a certain amount by at least a certain probability on each loop iteration. Intuitively speaking, the closer the supermartingales comes to zero – indicating termination – the more probable it is that it increases more. The AST proof rule in [38] is applicable to prove AST for the program in Figure 1a; yet, it cannot be used to prove PAST of Figures 1c-1d. On the other hand, the PAST proof rule in [10,19] requires that the expected decrease of the supermartingale on each loop iteration is at least some positive constant ϵ and on loop termination needs to be at most zero – very similar to the usual constraint on ranking functions. While [10,19] can be used to prove the program in Figure 1c to be PAST, these works cannot be used for Figure 1a. They cannot be used for proving Figure 1d to be PAST either. The rule for showing non-AST [13] requires the supermartingale to be repulsing. This intuitively means that the supermartingale decreases on average with at least ε and is positive on termination. Figuratively speaking, it repulses terminating states. It can be used to prove the program in Figure 1b to be not AST. In summary, while existing works for proving AST, PAST, and their negations are generic in nature, they are also restricted for classes of probabilistic programs. *In this paper, we propose relaxed versions of existing proof rules for probabilistic termination that turn out to treat quite a number of programs that could not be proven otherwise (Section 4).* In particular, (non-)termination of all four programs of Figure 1 can be proven using our proof rules.

Automated termination checking of AST and PAST. Whereas there is a large body of techniques and proof rules, software tool support to automate checking termination of probabilistic programs is still in its infancy. *This paper presents novel algorithms to automate various proof rules for probabilistic programs:* the three aforementioned proof rules [10,19,38,13] and a variant of the non-AST proof rule to prove non-PAST [13][3]. We also present relaxed versions of each of the proof rules, going beyond the state-of-the-art in the termination analysis of probabilistic programs. We focus on so-called Prob-solvable loops, extending [4]. Namely, we define Prob-solvable loops as probabilistic while-programs whose guards compare two polynomials (over program variables) and whose body is a sequence of random assignments with polynomials as right-hand side such that a variable x, say, only depends on variables preceding x in the loop body. While restrictive, Prob-solvable loops cover a vast set of interesting probabilistic programs (see Remark 1). An essential property of our programs is that the statistical moments of program variables can be obtained as closed-form formulas [4]. *The key of our algorithmic*

---

[3] For automation, the proof rule of [38] is considered for constant decrease and probability functions.

approach is a procedure for computing asymptotic lower, upper and absolute bounds on polynomial expressions over program variables in our programs (Section 5). This enables a novel method for automating probabilistic termination and non-termination proof rules based on (super)martingales, going beyond the state-of-the-art in probabilistic termination. Our relaxed proof rules allow us to fully automate (P)AST analysis by using only polynomial witnesses. Our experiments provide practical evidence that polynomial witnesses within Prob-solvable loops are sufficient to certify most examples from the literature and even beyond (Section 6).

Our termination tool AMBER. We have implemented our algorithmic approach in the publicly available tool AMBER. It exploits asymptotic bounds over polynomial martingales and uses the tool MORA [4] for computing the first-order moments of program variables and the computer algebra system package `diofant`. It employs over- and under-approximations realized by a simple static analysis. AMBER *establishes probabilistic termination in a fully automated manner* and has the following unique characteristics:

- it includes the first implementation of the AST proof rule of [38], and
- it is the first tool capable of certifying AST for programs that are not PAST and cannot be split into PAST subprograms, and
- it is the first tool that brings the various proof rules under a single umbrella: AST, PAST, non-AST and non-PAST.

An experimental evaluation on various benchmarks shows that: (1) AMBER is superior to existing tools for automating PAST [42] and AST [10], (2) the relaxed proof rules enable proving substantially more programs, and (3) AMBER is able to automate the termination checking of intricate probabilistic programs (within the class of programs considered) that could not be automatically handled so far (Section 6). For example, AMBER *solves 23 termination benchmarks that no other automated approach could so far handle.*

Main contributions. To summarize, the main contributions of this paper are:

1. Relaxed proof rules for (non-)termination, enabling treating a wider class of programs (Section 4).
2. Efficient algorithms to compute asymptotic bounds on polynomial expressions of program variables (Section 5).
3. Automation: a realisation of our algorithms in the tool AMBER (Section 6).
4. Experiments showing the superiority of AMBER over existing tools for proving (P)AST (Section 6).

2 Preliminaries

We denote by $\mathbb{N}$ and $\mathbb{R}$ the set of natural and real numbers, respectively. Further, let $\overline{\mathbb{R}}$ denote $\mathbb{R} \cup \{+\infty, -\infty\}$, $\mathbb{R}_0^+$ the non-negative reals and $\mathbb{R}[x_1,...,x_m]$ the polynomial ring in $x_1,...,x_m$ over $\mathbb{R}$. We write $x := E_{(1)}\ [p_1]\ E_{(2)}\ [p_2] ... [p_{m-1}]\ E_{(m)}$ for the probabilistic update of program variable x, denoting the execution of $x := E_{(j)}$ with probability p_j, for $j = 1,...,m-1$, and the execution of $x := E_{(m)}$ with probability $1 - \sum_{j=1}^{m-1} p_j$, where $m \in \mathbb{N}$. We write indices of expressions over program variables in round brackets and use E_i for the stochastic process induced by expression E. This section introduces our programming language extending *Prob-solvable loops* [4] and defines the probability space introduced by such programs. Let $\mathbb{E}$ denote the expectation operator with respect to a probability space. We assume the reader to be familiar with probability theory [33].

2.1 Programming Model: Prob-Solvable Loops

Prob-solvable loops [4] are syntactically restricted probabilistic programs with polynomial expressions over program variables. The statistical higher-order moments of program variables, like expectation and variance of such loops, can always be computed as functions of the loop counter. In this paper, we extend Prob-solvable loops with polynomial loop guards in order to study their termination behavior, as follows.

Definition 1 (Prob-solvable loop $\mathcal{L}$). *A Prob-solvable loop $\mathcal{L}$ with real-valued variables $x_{(1)},\dots,x_{(m)}$, where $m \in \mathbb{N}$, is a program of the form: $\mathcal{I}_\mathcal{L}$ while $\mathcal{G}_\mathcal{L}$ do $\mathcal{U}_\mathcal{L}$ end, with*

- *(Init) $\mathcal{I}_\mathcal{L}$ is a sequence $x_{(1)} := r_{(1)},\dots,x_{(m)} := r_{(m)}$ of m assignments, with $r_{(j)} \in \mathbb{R}$*
- *(Guard) $\mathcal{G}_\mathcal{L}$ is a strict inequality $P > Q$, where $P, Q \in \mathbb{R}[x_{(1)},\dots,x_{(m)}]$*
- *(Update) $\mathcal{U}_\mathcal{L}$ is a sequence of m probabilistic updates of the form*

$$x_{(j)} := a_{(j1)}x_{(j)} + P_{(j1)}\ [p_{j1}]\ a_{(j2)}x_{(j)} + P_{(j2)}\ [p_{j2}] \dots [p_{j(l_j-1)}]\ a_{(jl_j)}x_{(j)} + P_{(jl_j)},$$

where $a_{(jk)} \in \mathbb{R}_0^+$ are constants, $P_{(jk)} \in \mathbb{R}[x_{(1)},\dots,x_{(j-1)}]$ are polynomials, $p_{(jk)} \in [0,1]$ and $\sum_k p_{jk} < 1$.

If $\mathcal{L}$ is clear from the context, the subscript $\mathcal{L}$ is omitted from $\mathcal{I}_\mathcal{L}$, $\mathcal{G}_\mathcal{L}$, and $\mathcal{U}_\mathcal{L}$. Figure 1 gives four example Prob-solvable loops.

Remark 1 (Prob-solvable expressiveness). The enforced order of assignments in the loop body of Prob-solvable loops seems restrictive. However, many non-trivial probabilistic programs can be naturally modeled as succinct Prob-solvable loops. These include complex stochastic processes such as 2D random walks and dynamic Bayesian networks [5]. Almost all existing benchmarks on automated probabilistic termination analysis fall within the scope of Prob-solvable loops (cf. Section 6).

In the sequel, we consider an arbitrary Prob-solvable loop $\mathcal{L}$ and provide all definitions relative to $\mathcal{L}$. The semantics of $\mathcal{L}$ is defined next, by associating $\mathcal{L}$ with a probability space.

2.2 Canonical Probability Space

A probabilistic program, and thus a Prob-solvable loop, can be semantically described as a probabilistic transition system [10] or as a probabilistic control flow graph [13], which in turn induce an infinite Markov chain (MC) [4]. An MC is associated with a *sequence space* [33], a special probability space. In the sequel, we associate $\mathcal{L}$ with the sequence space of its corresponding MC, similarly as in [25].

[4] In fact, [13] consider Markov decision processes, but in absence of non-determinism in Prob-solvable loops, Markov chains suffice for our purpose.

Definition 2 (State, Run of $\mathcal{L}$). *The* state *of Prob-solvable loop $\mathcal{L}$ over m variables, is a vector $s \in \mathbb{R}^m$. Let $s[j]$ or $s[x_{(j)}]$ denote the j-th component of s representing the value of the variable $x_{(j)}$ in state s. A* run *ϑ of $\mathcal{L}$ is an infinite sequence of states.*

Note that any infinite sequence of states is a run. Infeasible runs will however be assigned measure 0. We write $s \models B$ to denote that the logical formula B holds in state s.

Definition 3 (Loop Space of $\mathcal{L}$). *The Prob-solvable loop $\mathcal{L}$ induces a canonical filtered probability space $(\Omega^{\mathcal{L}}, \Sigma^{\mathcal{L}}, (\mathcal{F}_i^{\mathcal{L}})_{i\in\mathbb{N}}, \mathbb{P}^{\mathcal{L}})$, called* loop space, *where*
- *the* sample space *$\Omega^{\mathcal{L}} := (\mathbb{R}^m)^\omega$ is the set of all program runs,*
- *the* σ-algebra *$\Sigma^{\mathcal{L}}$ is the smallest σ-algebra containing all cylinder sets $Cyl(\pi) := \{\pi\vartheta \mid \vartheta \in (\mathbb{R}^m)^\omega\}$ for all finite prefixes $\pi \in (\mathbb{R}^m)^+$, that is $\Sigma^{\mathcal{L}} := \langle \{Cyl(\pi) \mid \pi \in (\mathbb{R}^m)^+\} \rangle_\sigma$,*
- *the* filtration *$(\mathcal{F}_i^{\mathcal{L}})_{i\in\mathbb{N}}$ contains the smallest σ-algebras containing all cylinder sets for all prefixes of length $i+1$, i.e. $\mathcal{F}_i^{\mathcal{L}} := \langle \{Cyl(\pi) \mid \pi \in (\mathbb{R}^m)^+, |\pi| = i+1\} \rangle_\sigma$.*
- *the* probability measure *$\mathbb{P}^{\mathcal{L}}$ is defined as $\mathbb{P}^{\mathcal{L}}(Cyl(\pi)) := p(\pi)$, where p is given by*

$$p(s) := \mu_{\mathcal{I}}(s), \quad p(\pi s s') := \begin{cases} p(\pi s) \cdot [s' = s], \text{if } s \models \neg \mathcal{G}_{\mathcal{L}} \\ p(\pi s) \cdot \mu_{\mathcal{U}}(s, s'), \text{if } s \models \mathcal{G}_{\mathcal{L}}. \end{cases}$$

$\mu_{\mathcal{I}}(s)$ denotes the probability that, after initialization $\mathcal{I}_{\mathcal{L}}$, the loop $\mathcal{L}$ is in state s. $\mu_{\mathcal{U}}(s, s')$ denotes the probability that, after one loop iteration starting in state s, the resulting program state is s'. [...] represent the Iverson brackets, i.e. $[s' = s]$ is 1 iff $s' = s$.

Intuitively, $\mathbb{P}(Cyl(\pi))$ is the probability that prefix π is the sequence of the first $|\pi|$ program states when executing $\mathcal{L}$. Moreover, the σ-algebra $\mathcal{F}_i$ intuitively captures the information about the program run after the loop body $\mathcal{U}$ has been executed i times. We note that the effect of the loop body $\mathcal{U}$ is considered as atomic.

In order to formalize termination properties of a Prob-solvable loop $\mathcal{L}$, we define the *looping time* of $\mathcal{L}$ to be a random variable in $\mathcal{L}$'s loop space.

Definition 4 (Looping Time of $\mathcal{L}$). *The* looping time *of $\mathcal{L}$ is the random variable $T^{\neg\mathcal{G}} : \Omega \to \mathbb{N} \cup \{\infty\}$, where $T^{\neg\mathcal{G}}(\vartheta) := \inf\{i \in \mathbb{N} \mid \vartheta_i \models \neg\mathcal{G}\}$.*

Intuitively, the looping time $T^{\neg\mathcal{G}}$ maps a program run of $\mathcal{L}$ to the index of the first state falsifying the loop guard $\mathcal{G}$ of $\mathcal{L}$ or to ∞ if no such state exists. We now formalize termination properties of $\mathcal{L}$ using the looping time $T^{\neg\mathcal{G}}$.

Definition 5 (Termination of $\mathcal{L}$). *The Prob-solvable loop $\mathcal{L}$ is* AST *if $\mathbb{P}(T^{\neg\mathcal{G}} < \infty) = 1$. $\mathcal{L}$ is PAST if $\mathbb{E}(T^{\neg\mathcal{G}}) < \infty$.*

2.3 Martingales

While for arbitrary probabilistic programs, answering $\mathbb{P}(T^{\neg\mathcal{G}} < \infty)$ and $\mathbb{E}(T^{\neg\mathcal{G}} < \infty)$ is undecidable, sufficient conditions for AST, PAST and their negations have been developed [10,19,38,13]. These works use (super)martingales which are special stochastic processes. In this section, we adopt the general setting of martingale theory to a Prob-solvable loop $\mathcal{L}$ and then formalize sufficient termination conditions for $\mathcal{L}$ in Section 3.

Definition 6 (Stochastic Process of $\mathcal{L}$). *Every arithmetic expression E over the program variables of $\mathcal{L}$ induces the stochastic process $(E_i)_{i\in\mathbb{N}}$, $E_i:\Omega\to\mathbb{R}$ with $E_i(\vartheta):=E(\vartheta_i)$. For a run ϑ of $\mathcal{L}$, $E_i(\vartheta)$ is the evaluation of E in the i-th state of ϑ.*

In the sequel, for a boolean condition B over program variables x of $\mathcal{L}$, we write B_i to refer to the result of substituting x by x_i in B.

Definition 7 (Martingales). *Let $(\Omega,\Sigma,(\mathcal{F}_i)_{i\in\mathbb{N}},\mathbb{P})$ be a filtered probability space and $(M_i)_{i\in\mathbb{N}}$ be an integrable stochastic process adapted to $(\mathcal{F}_i)_{i\in\mathbb{N}}$. Then $(M_i)_{i\in\mathbb{N}}$ is a* martingale *if $\mathbb{E}(M_{i+1}\mid\mathcal{F}_i)=M_i$ (or equivalently $\mathbb{E}(M_{i+1}-M_i\mid\mathcal{F}_i)=0$). Moreover, $(M_i)_{i\in\mathbb{N}}$ is called a* supermartingale (SM) *if $\mathbb{E}(M_{i+1}\mid\mathcal{F}_i)\le M_i$ (or equivalently $\mathbb{E}(M_{i+1}-M_i\mid\mathcal{F}_i)\le 0$). For an arithmetic expression E over the program variables of $\mathcal{L}$, the conditional expected value $\mathbb{E}(E_{i+1}-E_i\mid\mathcal{F}_i)$ is called* the martingale expression of E.

3 Proof Rules for Probabilistic Termination

While AST and PAST are undecidable in general [30], sufficient conditions, called *proof rules*, for AST and PAST have been introduced, see e.g. [10,19,38,13]. In this section, we survey four proof rules, adapted to Prob-solvable loops. In the sequel, a *pure invariant* is a loop invariant in the classical deterministic sense [27]. Based on the probability space corresponding to $\mathcal{L}$, a pure invariant holds before and after every iteration of $\mathcal{L}$.

3.1 Positive Almost Sure Termination (PAST)

The proof rule for PAST introduced in [10] relies on the notion of ranking supermartingales (RSMs), which is a SM that decreases by a fixed positive ϵ on average at every loop iteration. Intuitively, RSMs resemble ranking functions for deterministic programs, yet for probabilistic programs.

Theorem 1 (Ranking-Supermartingale-Rule (RSM-Rule) [10], [19]). *Let $M:\mathbb{R}^m\to\mathbb{R}$ be an expression over the program variables of $\mathcal{L}$ and I a pure invariant of $\mathcal{L}$. Assume the following conditions hold for all $i\in\mathbb{N}$:*

1. *(Termination) $\mathcal{G}\wedge I\implies M>0$*
2. *(RSM Condition) $\mathcal{G}_i\wedge I_i\implies\mathbb{E}(M_{i+1}-M_i\mid\mathcal{F}_i)\le-\epsilon$, for some $\epsilon>0$.*

Then, $\mathcal{L}$ is PAST. Further, M is called an ϵ-ranking supermartingale.

Example 1. Consider Figure 1c, set $M:=100-x^2-y^2$ and $\epsilon:=2$ and let I be $true$. Condition (1) of Theorem 1 trivially holds. Further, M is also an ϵ-ranking supermartingale, as $\mathbb{E}(M_{i+1}-M_i\mid\mathcal{F}_i)=100-\mathbb{E}(x_{i+1}^2\mid\mathcal{F}_i)-\mathbb{E}(y_{i+1}^2\mid\mathcal{F}_i)-100+x_i^2+y_i^2=-2-x_i^2\le-2$. That is because $\mathbb{E}(x_{i+1}^2\mid\mathcal{F}_i)=x_i^2+1$ and $\mathbb{E}(y_{i+1}^2\mid\mathcal{F}_i)=y_i^2+x_i^2+1$. Figure 1c is thus proved PAST using the RSM-Rule.

3.2 Almost Sure Termination (AST)

Recall that Figure 1a is AST but not PAST, and hence the RSM-rule cannot be used for Figure 1a. By relaxing the ranking conditions, the proof rule in [38] uses general supermartingales to prove AST of programs that are not necessarily PAST.

Theorem 2 (Supermartingale-Rule (SM-Rule) [38]). *Let $M:\mathbb{R}^m \to \mathbb{R}_{\geq 0}$ be an expression over the program variables of $\mathcal{L}$ and I a pure invariant of $\mathcal{L}$. Let $p:\mathbb{R}_{\geq 0} \to (0,1]$ (for* probability*) and $d:\mathbb{R}_{\geq 0} \to \mathbb{R}_{>0}$ (for* decrease*) be antitone (i.e. monotonically decreasing) functions. Assume the following conditions hold for all $i \in \mathbb{N}$:*
1. (Termination) $\mathcal{G} \wedge I \Longrightarrow M > 0$
2. (Decrease) $\mathcal{G}_i \wedge I_i \Longrightarrow \mathbb{P}(M_{i+1} - M_i \leq -d(M_i) \mid \mathcal{F}_i) \geq p(M_i)$
3. (SM Condition) $\mathcal{G}_i \wedge I_i \Longrightarrow \mathbb{E}(M_{i+1} - M_i \mid \mathcal{F}_i) \leq 0$.
Then, $\mathcal{L}$ is AST.

Intuitively, the requirement of d and p being antitone forbids that the "execution progress" of $\mathcal{L}$ towards termination becomes infinitely small while still being positive.

Example 2. The SM-Rule can be used to prove AST for Figure 1a. Consider $M := x$, $p := 1/2$, $d := 1$ and $I := true$. Clearly, p and d are antitone. The remaining conditions of Theorem 2 also hold as (1) $x > 0 \Longrightarrow x > 0$; (2) x decreases by d with probability p in every iteration; and (3) $\mathbb{E}(M_{i+1} - M_i \mid \mathcal{F}_i) = x_i - x_i \leq 0$.

3.3 Non-Termination

While Theorems 1 and 2 can be used for proving AST and PAST, respectively, they are not applicable to the analysis of non-terminating Prob-solvable loops. Two sufficient conditions for certifying the negations of AST and PAST have been introduced in [13] using so-called *repulsing-supermartingales*. Intuitively, a *repulsing-supermartingale* M on average decreases in every iteration of $\mathcal{L}$ and on termination is non-negative. Figuratively, M repulses terminating states.

Theorem 3 (Repulsing-AST-Rule (R-AST-Rule) [13]). *Let $M:\mathbb{R}^m \to \mathbb{R}$ be an expression over the program variables of $\mathcal{L}$ and I a pure invariant of $\mathcal{L}$. Assume the following conditions hold for all $i \in \mathbb{N}$:*
1. (Negative) $M_0 < 0$
2. (Non-Termination) $\neg\mathcal{G} \wedge I \Longrightarrow M \geq 0$
3. (RSM Condition) $\mathcal{G}_i \wedge I_i \Longrightarrow \mathbb{E}(M_{i+1} - M_i \mid \mathcal{F}_i) \leq -\epsilon$, for some $\epsilon > 0$
4. (c-Bounded Differences) $|M_{i+1} - M_i| < c$, for some $c > 0$.
Then, $\mathcal{L}$ is not *AST. M is called an ϵ-*repulsing supermartingale *with c-*bounded differences.

Example 3. Consider Figure 1b and let $M := -x$, $c := 3$, $\epsilon := 1/2$ and $I := true$. All four above conditions hold: (1) $-x_0 = -10 < 0$; (2) $x \leq 0 \Longrightarrow -x \geq 0$; (3) $\mathbb{E}(M_{i+1} - M_i \mid \mathcal{F}_i) = -x_i - 1/2 + x_i = -1/2 \leq -\epsilon$; and (4) $|x_i - x_{i+1}| < 3$. Thus, Figure 1b is not AST.

While Theorem 3 can prove programs not to be AST, and thus also not PAST, it cannot be used to prove programs not to be PAST when they are AST. For example, Theorem 3 cannot be used to prove that Figure 1a is not PAST. To address such cases, a variation of the R-AST-Rule [13] for certifying programs not to be PAST arises by relaxing the condition $\epsilon > 0$ of the R-AST-Rule to $\epsilon \geq 0$. We refer to this variation by *Repulsing-PAST-Rule (R-PAST-Rule)*.

4 Relaxed Proof Rules for Probabilistic Termination

While Theorems 1-3 provide sufficient conditions proving PAST, AST and their negations, the applicability to Prob-solvable loops is somewhat restricted. For example, the RSM-Rule cannot be used to prove Figure 1d to be PAST using the simple expression $M := x$, as explained in detail with Example 4, but may require more complex witnesses for certifying PAST, complicating automation. In this section, we relax the conditions of Theorems 1-3 by requiring these conditions to only hold "eventually". A property $P(i)$ parameterized by a natural number $i \in \mathbb{N}$ *holds eventually* if there is an $i_0 \in \mathbb{N}$ such that $P(i)$ holds for all $i \geq i_0$. Our relaxations of probabilistic termination proof rules can intuitively be described as follows: If $\mathcal{L}$, after a fixed number of steps, almost surely reaches a state from which the program is PAST or AST, then the program is PAST or AST, respectively. Let us first illustrate the benefits of reasoning with "eventually" holding properties for probabilistic termination in the following example.

```
x := x0, y := 0
while x > 0 do
 |  y := y+1
 |  x := x+(y−5) [1/2] x−(y−5)
end
```

(a)

```
x := 1, y := 2
while x > 0 do
 |  y := 1/2·y
 |  x := x+1−y [2/3] x−1+y
end
```

(b)

Fig. 2: Prob-solvable loops which require our relaxed proof rules for termination analysis.

Example 4 (Limits of the RSM-Rule and SM-Rule). Consider Figure 1d. Setting $M := x$, we have the martingale expression $\mathbb{E}(M_{i+1} - M_i \mid \mathcal{F}_i) = -y_i^2/2 + y_i + 3/2 = -i^2/2 + i + 3/2$. Since $\mathbb{E}(x_{i+1} - x_i \mid \mathcal{F}_i)$ is non-negative for $i \in \{0,1,2,3\}$, we conclude that M is not an RSM. However, Figure 1d either terminates within the first three iterations or, after three loop iterations, is in a state such that the RSM-Rule is applicable. Therefore, Figure 1d is PAST but the RSM-Rule cannot directly prove using $M := x$. A similar restriction of the SM-Rule can be observed for Figure 2a. By considering $M := x$, we derive the martingale expression $\mathbb{E}(x_{i+1} - x_i \mid \mathcal{F}_i) = 0$, implying that M is a martingale for Figure 2a. However, the decrease function d for the SM-Rule cannot be defined because, for example, in the fifth loop iteration of Figure 2a, there is no progress as x is almost surely updated with its previous value. However, after the fifth iteration of Figure 2a, x always decreases by at least 1 with probability $1/2$ and all conditions of the SM-Rule are satisfied. Thus, Figure 2a either terminates within the first five iterations or reaches a state from which it terminates almost surely. Consequently, Figure 2a is AST but the SM-Rule cannot directly prove it using $M := x$.

We therefore relax the RSM-Rule and SM-Rule of Theorems 1 and 2 as follows.

Theorem 4 (Relaxed Termination Proof Rules). *For the RSM-Rule to certify PAST of $\mathcal{L}$, it is sufficient that conditions* (1)-(2) *of Theorem 1 hold eventually (instead of for all $i \in \mathbb{N}$). Similarly, for the SM-Rule to certify AST of $\mathcal{L}$, it is sufficient that conditions* (1)-(3) *of Theorem 2 hold eventually.*

Proof. We prove the relaxation of the RSM-Rule. The proof of the relaxed SM-Rule is analogous. Let $\mathcal{L} := \mathcal{I}\ \mathit{while}\ \mathcal{G}\ \mathit{do}\ \mathcal{U}\ \mathit{end}$ be as in Definition 1. Assume $\mathcal{L}$ satisfies the conditions (1)-(2) of Theorem 1 after some $i_0 \in \mathbb{N}$. We construct the following probabilistic program $\mathcal{P}$, where i is a new variable not appearing in $\mathcal{L}$:

$$\begin{array}{l}\mathcal{I}; i := 0 \\ \mathit{while}\ i < i_0\ \mathit{do}\ \mathcal{U}; i := i+1\ \mathit{end} \\ \mathit{while}\ \mathcal{G}\ \mathit{do}\ \mathcal{U}\ \mathit{end}\end{array} \tag{1}$$

We first argue that if $\mathcal{P}$ is PAST, then so is $\mathcal{L}$. Assume $\mathcal{P}$ to be PAST. Then, the looping time of $\mathcal{L}$ is either bounded by i_0 or it is PAST, by the definition of $\mathcal{P}$. In both cases, $\mathcal{L}$ is PAST. Finally, observe that $\mathcal{P}$ is PAST if and only if its second while-loop is PAST. However, the second while-loop of $\mathcal{P}$ can be certified to be PAST using the RSM-Rule and additionally using $i \geq i_0$ as an invariant. □

Remark 2. The central point of our proof rule relaxations is that they allow for simpler witnesses. While for Example 4 it can be checked that $M := x + 2^{y+5}$ is an RSM, the example illustrates that the relaxed proof rule allows for a much simpler PAST witness (linear instead of exponential). This simplicity is key for automation.

Similar to Theorem 4, we relax the R-AST-Rule and the R-PAST-Rule. However, compared to Theorem 4, it is not enough for a non-termination proof rule to certify non-AST from some state onward, because $\mathcal{L}$ may never reach this state as it might terminate earlier. Therefore, a necessary assumption when relaxing non-termination proof rules comes with ensuring that $\mathcal{L}$ has a positive probability of reaching the state after which a proof rule witnesses non-termination. This is illustrated in the following example .

Example 5 (Limits of the R-AST-Rule). Consider Figure 2b and set $M := -x$. As a result, we get $\mathbb{E}(M_{i+1} - M_i \mid \mathcal{F}_i) = {}^{y_i}/_6 - {}^1/_3 = {}^{2^{-i}}/_3 - {}^1/_3$. Thus, $\mathbb{E}(M_{i+1} - M_i \mid \mathcal{F}_i) = 0$ for $i = 0$, implying that M cannot be an ϵ-repulsing supermartingale with $\epsilon > 0$ for all $i \in \mathbb{N}$. However, after the first iteration of $\mathcal{L}$, M satisfies all requirements of the R-AST-Rule. Moreover, $\mathcal{L}$ always reaches the second iteration because in the first iteration x almost surely does not change. From this follows that Figure 2b is not AST.

The following theorem formalizes the observation of Example 5 relaxing the R-AST-Rule and R-PAST-Rule of Theorem 3.

Theorem 5 (Relaxed Non-Termination Proof Rules for). *For the R-AST-Rule to certify non-AST for $\mathcal{L}$ (Theorem 3), as well as for the R-PAST-Rule to certify non-PAST for $\mathcal{L}$ (Theorem 3), if $\mathbb{P}(M_{i_0} < 0) > 0$ for some $i_0 \geq 0$, it suffices that conditions* (2)-(4) *hold for all $i \geq i_0$ (instead of for all $i \in \mathbb{N}$).*

The proof of Theorem 5 is similar to the one of Theorem 4 and available in [40]. In what follows, whenever we write RSM-Rule, SM-Rule, R-AST-Rule or R-PAST-Rule we refer to our relaxed versions of the proof rules.

5 Algorithmic Termination Analysis through Asymptotic Bounds

The *two major challenges when automating reasoning* with the proof rules of Sections 3 and 4 are (i) constructing expressions M over the program variables and (ii) proving inequalities involving $\mathbb{E}(M_{i+1} - M_i \mid \mathcal{F}_i)$. In this section, we address these two challenges for Prob-solvable loops. For the loop guard $\mathcal{G}_\mathcal{L} = P > Q$, let $G_\mathcal{L}$ denote the polynomial $P - Q$. As before, if $\mathcal{L}$ is clear from the context, we omit the subscript $\mathcal{L}$. It holds that $G > 0$ is equivalent to $\mathcal{G}$.

(i) Constructing (super)martingales M: For a Prob-solvable loop $\mathcal{L}$, the polynomial G is a natural candidate for the expression M in termination proof rules (RSM-Rule, SM-Rule) and $-G$ in the non-termination proof rules (R-AST-Rule, R-PAST-Rule). Hence, we construct potential (super)martingales M by setting $M := G$ for the RSM-Rule and the SM-Rule, and $M := -G$ for the R-AST-Rule and the R-PAST-Rule. The property $\mathcal{G} \implies G > 0$, a condition of the RSM-Rule and the SM-Rule, trivially holds. Moreover, for the R-AST-Rule and R-PAST-Rule the condition $\neg\mathcal{G} \implies -G \geq 0$ is satisfied. The remaining conditions of the proof rules are:

- RSM-Rule: (a) $\mathcal{G}_i \implies \mathbb{E}(G_{i+1} - G_i \mid \mathcal{F}_i) \leq -\epsilon$ for some $\epsilon > 0$
- SM-Rule: (a) $\mathcal{G}_i \implies \mathbb{E}(G_{i+1} - G_i \mid \mathcal{F}_i) \leq 0$ and (b) $\mathcal{G}_i \implies \mathbb{P}(G_{i+1} - G_i \leq -d \mid \mathcal{F}_i) \geq p$ for some $p \in (0,1]$ and $d \in \mathbb{R}^+$ (for the purpose of efficient automation, we restrict the functions $d(r)$ and $p(r)$ to be constant)
- R-AST-Rule: (a) $\mathcal{G}_i \implies \mathbb{E}(-G_{i+1} + G_i \mid \mathcal{F}_i) \leq -\epsilon$ for some $\epsilon > 0$ and (b) $|G_{i+1} - G_i| \leq c$, for some $c > 0$.

All these conditions express bounds over G_i. Choosing G as the potential witness may seem simplistic. However, Example 4 already illustrated how our relaxed proof rules can mitigate the need for more complex witnesses (even exponential ones). *The computational effort in our approach does not lie in synthesizing a complex witness but in constructing asymptotic bounds for the loop guard.* Our approach can therefore be seen as complementary to approaches synthesizing more complex witnesses [10,11,13]. The martingale expression $\mathbb{E}(G_{i+1} - G_i \mid \mathcal{F}_i)$ is an expression over program variables, whereas $G_{i+1} - G_i$ cannot be interpreted as a single expression but through a distribution of expressions.

Definition 8 (One-step Distribution). *For expression H over the program variables of Prob-solvable loop $\mathcal{L}$, let the* one-step distribution $\mathcal{U}_\mathcal{L}^H$ *be defined by $E \mapsto \mathbb{P}(H_{i+1} = E \mid \mathcal{F}_i)$ with support set $supp(\mathcal{U}_\mathcal{L}^H) := \{B \mid \mathcal{U}_\mathcal{L}^H(B) > 0\}$. We refer to expressions $B \in supp(\mathcal{U}_\mathcal{L}^H)$ by* branches of *H.*

The notation $\mathcal{U}_\mathcal{L}^H$ is chosen to suggest that the loop body $\mathcal{U}_\mathcal{L}$ is "applied" to the expression H, leading to a distribution over expressions. Intuitively, the support $supp(\mathcal{U}_\mathcal{L}^H)$ of an expression H contains all possible updates of H after executing a single iteration of $\mathcal{U}_\mathcal{L}$.

(ii) Proving inequalities involving $\mathbb{E}(M_{i+1} - M_i \mid \mathcal{F}_i)$: To automate the termination analysis of $\mathcal{L}$ with the proof rules from Section 3, we need to compute bounds for the expression $\mathbb{E}(G_{i+1} - G_i \mid \mathcal{F}_i)$ as well as for the branches of G. In addition, our relaxed proof rules from Section 4 only need asymptotic bounds, i.e. bounds which hold eventually. In Section 5.2, we propose Algorithm 1 for computing *asymptotic lower and upper bounds* for any polynomial expression over program variables of $\mathcal{L}$. Our procedure allows us to derive bounds

for $\mathbb{E}(G_{i+1} - G_i \mid \mathcal{F}_i)$ and the branches of G. Before formalizing our method, let us first illustrate how reasoning with asymptotic bounds helps to apply termination proof rules to $\mathcal{L}$.

Example 6 (Asymptotic Bounds for the RSM-Rule). Consider the following program:

```
x := 1, y := 0
while x < 100 do
 | y := y+1
 | x := 2x+y^2 [1/2] 1/2·x
end
```

Observe $y_i = i$. The martingale expression for $G = 100 - x$ is $\mathbb{E}(G_{i+1} - G_i \mid \mathcal{F}_i) = {}^1\!/\!_2(100 - 2x_i - (i+1)^2) + {}^1\!/\!_2(100 - {}^{x_i}\!/\!_2) - (100 - x_i) = -{}^{x_i}\!/\!_4 - {}^{i^2}\!/\!_2 - i - {}^1\!/\!_2$. Note that if the term $-{}^{x_i}\!/\!_4$ would not be present in $\mathbb{E}(G_{i+1} - G_i \mid \mathcal{F}_i)$, we could certify the program to be PAST using the RSM-Rule because $-{}^{i^2}\!/\!_2 - i - {}^1\!/\!_2 \leq -{}^1\!/\!_2$ for all $i \geq 0$. However, by taking a closer look at the variable x, we observe that it is *eventually* and almost surely lower bounded by the function $\alpha \cdot 2^{-i}$ for some $\alpha \in \mathbb{R}^+$. Therefore, *eventually* $-{}^{x_i}\!/\!_4 \leq -\beta \cdot 2^{-i}$ for some $\beta \in \mathbb{R}^+$. Thus, *eventually* $\mathbb{E}(G_{i+1} - G_i \mid \mathcal{F}_i) \leq -\gamma \cdot i^2$ for some $\gamma \in \mathbb{R}^+$. By our RSM-Rule, the program is PAST.

Now, the question arises how the asymptotic lower bound $\alpha \cdot 2^{-i}$ for x can be computed automatically. In every iteration, x is either updated with $2x + y^2$ or ${}^1\!/\!_2 \cdot x$. Considering the updates as recurrences, we have the inhomogeneous parts y^2 and 0. Asymptotic lower bounds for these parts are i^2 and 0, respectively, where 0 is the "asymptotically smallest one". Taking 0 as the inhomogeneous part, we construct two recurrences: (1) $l_0 = \alpha$, $l_{i+1} = 2l_i + 0$ and (2) $l_0 = \alpha$, $l_{i+1} = {}^1\!/\!_2 \cdot l_i + 0$, for some $\alpha \in \mathbb{R}^+$. Solutions to these recurrences are $\alpha \cdot 2^i$ and $\alpha \cdot 2^{-i}$, where the last one is the desired lower bound because it is "asymptotically smaller". We will formalize this idea of computing asymptotic bounds in Algorithm 1.

We next present our method for computing asymptotic bounds over martingale expressions in Sections 5.1-5.2. Based on these asymptotic bounds, in Section 5.3 we introduce algorithmic approaches for our proof rules from Section 4, solving our aforementioned challenges (i)-(ii) in a fully automated manner (Section 5.4).

5.1 Prob-solvable Loops and Monomials

Algorithm 1 computes asymptotic bounds on monomials over program variables in a recursive manner. To ensure termination of Algorithm 1, it is important that there are no circular dependencies among monomials. By the definition of Prob-solvable loops, this indeed holds for program variables (monomials of order 1). Every Prob-solvable loop $\mathcal{L}$ comes with an ordering on its variables and every variable is restricted to only depend linearly on itself and polynomially on previous variables. Acyclic dependencies naturally extend from single variables to monomials.

Definition 9 (Monomial Ordering). *Let $\mathcal{L}$ be a Prob-solvable loop with variables $x_{(1)},\ldots,x_{(m)}$. Let $y_1 = \prod_{j=1}^{m} x_{(j)}^{p_j}$ and $y_2 = \prod_{j=1}^{m} x_{(j)}^{q_j}$, where $p_j, q_j \in \mathbb{N}$, be two monomials over the program variables. The* order $\preceq$ on monomials *over the program variables of $\mathcal{L}$ is defined by $y_1 \preceq y_2 \iff (p_m,\ldots,p_1) \leq_{lex} (q_m,\ldots,q_1)$, where $\leq_{lex}$ is the lexicographic order on $\mathbb{N}^m$. The order $\preceq$ is total because $\leq_{lex}$ is total. With $y_1 \prec y_2$ we denote $y_1 \preceq y_2 \wedge y_1 \neq y_2$.*

To prove acyclic dependencies for monomials we exploit the following fact.

Lemma 1. *Let y_1, y_2, z_1, z_2 be monomials. If $y_1 \preceq z_1$ and $y_2 \preceq z_2$ then $y_1 \cdot y_2 \preceq z_1 \cdot z_2$.*

By structural induction over monomials and Lemma 1, we establish:

Lemma 2 (Monomial Acyclic Dependency). *Let x be a monomial over the program variables of $\mathcal{L}$. For every branch $B \in supp(\mathcal{U}_{\mathcal{L}}^{x})$ and monomial y in B, $y \preceq x$ holds.*

Lemma 2 states that the value of a monomial x over the program variables of $\mathcal{L}$ only depends on the value of monomials y which precede x in the monomial ordering $\preceq$. This ensures the dependencies among monomials over the program variables of $\mathcal{L}$ to be acyclic.

5.2 Computing Asymptotic Bounds for Prob-solvable Loops

The structural result on monomial dependencies from Lemma 2 allows for recursive procedures over monomials. This is exploited in Algorithm 1 for computing asymptotic bounds for monomials. The standard Big-O notation does not differentiate between positive and negative functions, as it considers the absolute value of functions. We, however, need to differentiate between functions like 2^i and -2^i. Therefore, we introduce the notions of *Domination* and *Bounding Functions.*

Definition 10 (Domination). *Let F be a finite set of functions from $\mathbb{N}$ to $\mathbb{R}$. A function $g : \mathbb{N} \to \mathbb{R}$ is* dominating *F if eventually $\alpha \cdot g(i) \geq f(i)$ for all $f \in F$ and some $\alpha \in \mathbb{R}^+$. A function $g : \mathbb{N} \to \mathbb{R}$ is* dominated by *F if all $f \in F$ dominate $\{g\}$.*

Intuitively, a function f dominates a function g if f eventually surpasses g modulo a positive constant factor. *Exponential polynomials* are sums of products of polynomials with exponential functions, i.e. $\sum_j p_j(x) \cdot c_j^x$, where $c_j \in \mathbb{R}_0^+$. All functions arising in Algorithms 1-4 are exponential polynomials. For a finite set F of exponential polynomials, a function dominating F and a function dominated by F are easily computable with standard techniques, by analyzing the terms of the functions in the finite set F. With $dominating(F)$ we denote an algorithm computing an exponential polynomial dominating F. With $dominated(F)$ we denote an algorithm computing an exponential polynomial dominated by F. We assume the functions returned by the algorithms $dominating(F)$ and $dominated(F)$ to be monotone and either non-negative or non-positive.

Example 7 (Domination). The following statements are true: 0 dominates $\{-i^3+i^2+5\}$, i^2 dominates $\{2i^2\}$, $i^2 \cdot 2^i$ dominates $\{i^2 \cdot 2^i + i^9, i^5 + i^3, 2^{-i}\}$, i is dominated by $\{i^2 - 2i + 1, \frac{1}{2}i - 5\}$ and -2^i is dominated by $\{2^i - i^2, -10 \cdot 2^{-i}\}$.

Definition 11 (Bounding Function for $\mathcal{L}$). *Let E be an arithmetic expression over the program variables of $\mathcal{L}$. Let $l, u : \mathbb{N} \to \mathbb{R}$ be monotone and non-negative or non-positive.*

1. *l is a* lower bounding function *for E if eventually $\mathbb{P}(\alpha \cdot l(i) \leq E_i \mid T^{\neg \mathcal{G}} > i) = 1$ for some $\alpha \in \mathbb{R}^+$.*
2. *u is an* upper bounding function *for E if eventually $\mathbb{P}(E_i \leq \alpha \cdot u(i) \mid T^{\neg \mathcal{G}} > i) = 1$ for some $\alpha \in \mathbb{R}^+$.*
3. *An* absolute bounding function *for E is an upper bounding function for $|E|$.*

A bounding function imposes a bound on an expression E over the program variables holding eventually, almost surely, and modulo a positive constant factor. Moreover, bounds on E only need to hold as long as the program has not yet terminated.

Given a Prob-solvable loop $\mathcal{L}$ and a monomial x over the program variables of $\mathcal{L}$, Algorithm 1 computes a lower and upper bounding function for x. Because every polynomial expression is a linear combination of monomials, the procedure can be used to compute lower and upper bounding functions for any polynomial expression over $\mathcal{L}$'s program variables by substituting every monomial with its lower or upper bounding function depending on the sign of the monomial's coefficient. Once a lower bounding function l and an upper bounding function u are computed, an absolute bounding function can be computed by $dominating(\{u,-l\})$.

In Algorithm 1, candidates for bounding functions are modeled using recurrence relations. Solutions $s(i)$ of these recurrences are closed-form candidates for bounding functions parameterized by loop iteration i. Algorithm 1 relies on the existence of closed-form solutions of recurrences. While closed-forms of general recurrences do not always exist, a property of *C-finite recurrences*, linear recurrences with constant coefficients, is that their closed-forms always exist and are computable [32]. In all occurring recurrences, we consider a monomial over program variables as a single function. Therefore, throughout this section, all recurrences arising from a Prob-solvable loop $\mathcal{L}$ in Algorithm 1 are C-finite or can be turned into C-finite recurrences. Moreover, closed-forms $s(i)$ of C-finite recurrences are given by exponential polynomials. Therefore, for any solution $s(i)$ to a C-finite recurrence and any constant $r \in \mathbb{R}$, the following holds:

$$\exists \alpha,\beta \in \mathbb{R}^+, \exists i_0 \in \mathbb{N} : \forall i \geq i_0 : \alpha \cdot s(i) \leq s(i+r) \leq \beta \cdot s(i). \tag{2}$$

Intuitively, the property states that constant shifts do not change the asymptotic behavior of s. We use this property at various proof steps in this section. Moreover, we recall that limits of exponential polynomials are computable [23].

For every monomial x, every branch $B \in supp(\mathcal{U}^{x}_{\mathcal{L}})$ is a polynomial over the program variables. Let $Rec(x) := \{\text{coefficient of } x \text{ in } B \mid B \in supp(\mathcal{U}^{x}_{\mathcal{L}})\}$ denote the set of coefficients of the monomial x in all branches of $\mathcal{L}$. Let $Inhom(x) := \{B - c \cdot x \mid B \in supp(\mathcal{U}^{x}_{\mathcal{L}}) \text{ and } c = \text{coefficient of } x \text{ in } B\}$ denote all the branches of the monomial x without x and its coefficient. The symbolic constants c_1 and c_2 in Algorithm 1 represent arbitrary initial values of the monomial x for which bounding functions are computed. The fact that they are symbolic ensures that all potential initial values are accounted for. c_1 represents positive initial values and $-c_2$ negative initial values. The symbolic constant d is used in the recurrences to account for the fact that the bounding functions only hold modulo a constant. Intuitively, if we use the bounding function in a recurrence we need to restore the lost constant. $Sign(x)$ is an over-approximation of the sign of the monomial x, i.e., if $\exists i : \mathbb{P}(x_i > 0) > 0$, then $+ \in Sign(x)$ and if $\exists i : \mathbb{P}(x_i < 0) > 0$, then $- \in Sign(x)$.

Lemma 2, the computability of closed-forms of C-finite recurrences and the fact that within a Prob-solvable loop only finitely many monomials can occur, implies the termination of Algorithm 1. Its correctness is stated in the next theorem.

Theorem 6 (Correctness of Algorithm 1). *The functions $l(i), u(i)$ returned by Algorithm 1 on input $\mathcal{L}$ and x are a lower- and an upper bounding function for x, respectively.*

Algorithm 1: Computing bounding functions for monomials

Input: A Prob-solvable loop $\mathcal{L}$ and a monomial x over $\mathcal{L}$'s variables
Output: Lower and upper bounding functions $l(i)$, $u(i)$ for x

1 $\mathit{inhomBoundsUpper} := \{\text{upper bounding function of } P \mid P \in \mathit{Inhom}(x)\}$ (recursive call)
2 $\mathit{inhomBoundsLower} := \{\text{lower bounding function of } P \mid P \in \mathit{Inhom}(x)\}$ (recursive call)
3 $U(i) := \mathit{dominating}(\mathit{inhomBoundsUpper})$
4 $L(i) := \mathit{dominated}(\mathit{inhomBoundsLower})$
5 $\mathit{maxRec} := \max \mathit{Rec}(x)$
6 $\mathit{minRec} := \min \mathit{Rec}(x)$
7 $I := \emptyset$
8 **if** $+ \in \mathit{Sign}(x)$ **then** $I := I \cup \{c_1\}$;
9 **if** $- \in \mathit{Sign}(x)$ **then** $I := I \cup \{-c_2\}$;
10 $\mathit{uCand} :=$ closed-forms of $\{y_{i+1} = r \cdot y_i + d \cdot U(i) \mid r \in \{\mathit{minRec}, \mathit{maxRec}\}, y_0 \in I\}$
11 $\mathit{lCand} :=$ closed-forms of $\{y_{i+1} = r \cdot y_i + d \cdot L(i) \mid r \in \{\mathit{minRec}, \mathit{maxRec}\}, y_0 \in I\}$
12 $u(i) := \mathit{dominating}(\mathit{uCand})$
13 $l(i) := \mathit{dominated}(\mathit{lCand})$
14 **return** $l(i), u(i)$

Proof. Intuitively, it has to be shown that regardless of the paths through the loop body taken by any program run, the value of x is always eventually upper bounded by some function in uCand and eventually lower bounded by some function in lCand (almost surely and modulo positive constant factors). We show that x is always eventually upper bounded by some function in uCand. The proof for the lower bounding function is analogous.

Let $\vartheta \in \Sigma$ be a *possible* program run, i.e. $\mathbb{P}(\mathit{Cyl}(\pi)) > 0$ for all finite prefixes π of ϑ. Then, for every $i \in \mathbb{N}$, if $T^{\neg\mathcal{G}}(\vartheta) > i$, the following holds:

$$x_{i+1}(\vartheta) = a_{(1)} \cdot x_i(\vartheta) + P_{(1)i}(\vartheta) \text{ or } x_{i+1}(\vartheta) = a_{(2)} \cdot x_i(\vartheta) + P_{(2)i}(\vartheta)$$
$$\text{or ... or } x_{i+1}(\vartheta) = a_{(k)} \cdot x_i(\vartheta) + P_{(k)i}(\vartheta),$$

where $a_{(j)} \in \mathit{Rec}(x)$ and $P_{(j)} \in \mathit{Inhom}(x)$ are polynomials over program variables. Let $u_1(i), ..., u_k(i)$ be upper bounding functions of $P_{(1)}, ..., P_{(k)}$, which are computed recursively at line 10. Moreover, let $U(i) := \mathit{dominating}(\{u_1(i), ..., u_k(i)\})$, $\mathit{minRec} = \min \mathit{Rec}(x)$ and $\mathit{maxRec} = \max \mathit{Rec}(x)$. Let $l_0 \in \mathbb{N}$ be the smallest number such that for all $j \in \{1, ..., k\}$ and $i \geq l_0$:

$$\mathbb{P}(P_{(j)i} \leq \alpha_j \cdot u_j(i) \mid T^{\neg\mathcal{G}} > i) = 1 \text{ for some } \alpha_j \in \mathbb{R}^+\text{, and} \tag{3}$$
$$u_j(i) \leq \beta \cdot U(i) \text{ for some } \beta \in \mathbb{R}^+ \tag{4}$$

Thus, all inequalities from the bounding functions u_j and the dominating function U hold from l_0 onward. Because U is a dominating function, it is by definition either non-negative or non-positive. Assume $U(i)$ to be non-negative, the case for which $U(i)$ is non-positive is symmetric. Using the facts (3) and (4), we establish: For the constant $\gamma := \beta \cdot \max_{j=1..k} \alpha_j$, it holds that $\mathbb{P}(P_{(j)i} \leq \gamma \cdot U(i) \mid T^{\neg\mathcal{G}} > i) = 1$ for all $j \in \{1, ..., k\}$ and all $i \geq l_0$. Let l_1 be the smallest number such that $l_1 \geq l_0$ and $U(i + l_0) \leq \delta \cdot U(i)$ for all $i \geq l_1$ and some $\delta \in \mathbb{R}^+$.

Case 1, x_i is almost surely negative for all $i \geq l_1$: Consider the recurrence relation $y_0 = m$, $y_{i+1} = \mathit{minRec} \cdot y_i + \eta \cdot U(i)$, where $\eta := \max(\gamma, \delta)$ and m is the maximum value of $x_{l_1}(\vartheta)$ among all possible program runs ϑ. Note that m exists because there are only finitely many values $x_{l_1}(\vartheta)$ for possible program runs ϑ. Moreover, m is negative by our case assumption. By induction, we get $\mathbb{P}(x_i \leq y_{i-l_1} \mid T^{\neg\mathcal{G}} > i) = 1$ for all $i \geq l_1$. Therefore, for a closed-form solution $s(i)$ of the recurrence relation y_i, we get $\mathbb{P}(x_i \leq s(i-l_1) \mid T^{\neg\mathcal{G}} > i) = 1$ for all $i \geq l_1$. We emphasize that s exists and can effectively be computed because y_i is C-finite. Moreover, $s(i-l_1) \leq \theta \cdot s(i)$ for all $i \geq l_2$ for some $l_2 \geq l_1$ and some $\theta \in \mathbb{R}^+$. Therefore, s satisfies the bound condition of an upper bounding function. Also, s is present in $uCand$ by choosing the symbolic constants c_2 and d to represent $-m$ and η respectively. The function $u(i) := dominating(uCand)$, at line 12, is dominating $uCand$ (hence also s), is monotone and either non-positive or non-negative. Therefore, $u(i)$ is an upper bounding function for x.

Case 2, x_i is not almost surely negative for all $i \geq l_1$: Thus, there is a possible program run ϑ' such that $x_i(\vartheta') \geq 0$ for some $i \geq l_1$. Let $l_2 \geq l_1$ be the smallest number such that $x_{l_2}(\hat{\vartheta}) \geq 0$ for some possible program run $\hat{\vartheta}$. This number certainly exists, as $x_i(\vartheta')$ is non-negative for some $i \geq l_1$. Consider the recurrence relation $y_0 = m$, $y_{i+1} = maxRec \cdot y_i + \eta \cdot U(i)$, where $\eta := \max(\gamma, \delta)$ and m is the maximum value of $x_{l_2}(\vartheta)$ among all possible program runs ϑ. Note that m exists because there are only finitely many values $x_{l_2}(\vartheta)$ for possible program runs ϑ. Moreover, m is non-negative because $m \geq x_{l_2}(\hat{\vartheta}) \geq 0$. By induction, we get $\mathbb{P}(x_i \leq y_{i-l_2} \mid T^{\neg\mathcal{G}} > i) = 1$ for all $i \geq l_2$. Therefore, for a solution $s(i)$ of the recurrence relation y_i, we get $\mathbb{P}(x_i \leq s(i-l_2) \mid T^{\neg\mathcal{G}} > i) = 1$ for all $i \geq l_2$. As above, s exists and can effectively be computed because y_i is C-finite. Moreover, $s(i-l_2) \leq \theta \cdot s(i)$ for all $i \geq l_3$ for some $l_3 \geq l_2$ and some $\theta \in \mathbb{R}^+$. Therefore, s satisfies the bound condition of an upper bounding function Also, s is present in $uCand$ by choosing the symbolic constants c_1 and d to represent m and η respectively. The function $u(i) := dominating(uCand)$, at line 12, is dominating $uCand$ (hence also s), is monotone and either non-positive or non-negative. Therefore, $u(i)$ is an upper bounding function for x. □

Example 8 (Bounding functions). We illustrate Algorithm 1 by computing bounding functions for x and the Prob-solvable loop from Example 6: We have $Rec(x) := \{2, \frac{1}{2}\}$ and $Inhom(x) = \{y^2, 0\}$. Computing bounding functions recursively for $P \in Inhom(x) = \{y^2, 0\}$ is simple, as we can give exact bounds leading to $inhomBoundsUpper = \{i^2, 0\}$ and $inhomBoundsLower = \{i^2, 0\}$. Consequently, we get $U(i) = i^2$, $L(i) = 0$, $maxRec = 2$ and $minRec = \frac{1}{2}$. With a rudimentary static analysis of the loop, we determine the (exact) over-approximation $Sign(x) := \{+\}$ by observing that $x_0 > 0$ and all $P \in Inhom(x)$ are strictly positive. Therefore, $uCand$ is the set of closed-form solutions of the recurrences $y_0 := c_1$, $y_{i+1} := 2y_i + d \cdot i^2$ and $y_0 := c_1$, $y_{i+1} := \frac{1}{2}y_i + d \cdot i^2$. Similarly, $lCand$ is the set of closed-form solutions of the recurrences $y_0 := c_1$, $y_{i+1} := 2y_i$ and $y_0 := c_1$, $y_{i+1} := \frac{1}{2}y_i$. Using any algorithm for computing closed-forms of C-finite recurrences, we obtain $uCand = \{c_1 2^i - di^2 - 2di + 3d2^i - 3d,\ c_1 2^{-i} + 2di^2 - 8di - 12d2^{-i} + 12d\}$ and $lCand = \{c_1 2^i, c_1 2^{-i}\}$. This leads to the upper bounding function $u(i) = 2^i$ and the lower bounding function $l(i) = 2^{-i}$. The bounding functions $l(i)$ and $u(i)$ can be used to compute bounding functions for expressions containing x linearly by replacing x by $l(i)$ or $u(i)$ depending on the sign of the coefficient of x. For instance, eventually and almost surely the following inequality holds: $-\frac{x_i}{4} - \frac{i^2}{2} - i - \frac{1}{2} \leq -\frac{1}{4} \cdot \alpha \cdot 2^{-i} - \frac{i^2}{2} - i - \frac{1}{2}$ for some $\alpha \in \mathbb{R}^+$. The inequality results from replacing x_i by $l(i)$. Therefore, eventually and almost surely $-\frac{x_i}{4}-\frac{i^2}{2}-i-\frac{1}{2}\leq-\beta\cdot i^2$ for some $\beta\in\mathbb{R}^+$. Thus, $-i^2$ is an upper bounding function for the expression $-\frac{x_i}{4}-\frac{i^2}{2}-i-\frac{1}{2}$.

Remark 3. Algorithm 1 describes a general procedure computing bounding functions for special sequences. Figuratively, that is for sequences s such that $s_{i+1}=f(s_i,i)$ but in every step the function f is chosen non-deterministically among a fixed set of special functions (corresponding to branches in our case). We reserve the investigation of applications of bounding functions for such sequences beyond the probabilistic setting for future work.

5.3 Algorithms for Termination Analysis of Prob-solvable Loops

Using Algorithm 1 to compute bounding functions for polynomial expressions over program variables at hand, we are now able to formalize our algorithmic approaches automating the termination analysis of Prob-solvable loops using the proof rules from Section 4. Given a Prob-solvable loop $\mathcal{L}$ and a polynomial expression E over $\mathcal{L}$'s variables, we denote with $lbf(E)$, $ubf(E)$ and $abf(E)$ functions computing a lower, upper and absolute bounding function for E respectively. Our algorithmic approach for proving PAST using the RSM-Rule is given in Algorithm 2.

Algorithm 2: Ranking-Supermartingale-Rule for proving PAST

Input: Prob-solvable loop $\mathcal{L}$

Output: If *true* then $\mathcal{L}$ with G satisfies the RSM-Rule; hence $\mathcal{L}$ is PAST

```
1 E := 𝔼(G_{i+1} − G_i | F_i)
2 u(i) := ubf(E)
3 limit := lim_{i→∞} u(i)
4 return limit < 0
```

Example 9 (Algorithm 2). Let us illustrate Algorithm 2 with the Prob-solvable loop from Examples 6 and 8. Applying Algorithm 2 on $\mathcal{L}$ leads to $E=-\frac{x_i}{4}-\frac{i^2}{2}-i-\frac{1}{2}$. We obtain the upper bounding function $u(i):=-i^2$ for E. Because $\lim_{i\to\infty}u(i)<0$, Algorithm 2 returns true. This is valid because $u(i)$ having a negative limit witnesses that E is eventually bounded by a negative constant and therefore is eventually an RSM.

We recall that all functions arising from $\mathcal{L}$ are exponential polynomials (see Section 5.2) and that limits of exponential polynomials are computable [23]. Therefore, the termination of Algorithm 2 is guaranteed and its correctness is stated next.

Theorem 7 (Correctness of Algorithm 2). *If Algorithm 2 returns* true *on input $\mathcal{L}$, then $\mathcal{L}$ with $G_{\mathcal{L}}$ satisfies the RSM-Rule.*

Proof. When returning *true* at line 4 we have $\mathbb{P}(E_i \leq \alpha\cdot u(i) \mid T^{\neg\mathcal{G}} > i) = 1$ for all $i \geq i_0$ and some $i_0 \in \mathbb{N}$, $\alpha \in \mathbb{R}^+$. Moreover, $u(i) < -\epsilon$ for all $i \geq i_1$ for some $i_1 \in \mathbb{N}$, by the definition of lim. From this follows that $\forall i \geq \max(i_0,i_1)$ almost surely $\mathcal{G}_i \Longrightarrow \mathbb{E}(G_{i+1}-G_i \mid \mathcal{F}_i)\leq-\alpha\cdot\epsilon$, which means G is eventually an RSM. □

Our approach proving AST using the SM-Rule is captured with Algorithm 3.

Algorithm 3: Supermartingale-Rule for proving AST

Input: Prob-solvable loop $\mathcal{L}$
Output: If *true*, $\mathcal{L}$ with G satisfies the SM-Rule with constant d and p; hence $\mathcal{L}$ is AST

1 $E := \mathbb{E}(G_{i+1} - G_i \mid \mathcal{F}_i)$
2 $u(i) := \mathit{ubf}(E)$
3 **if** *not eventually* $u(i) \leq 0$ **then return** false ;
4 **for** $B \in \mathit{supp}(\mathcal{U}_{\mathcal{L}}^{G})$ **do**
5     $d(i) := \mathit{ubf}(B - G)$
6     $\mathit{limit} := \lim_{i\to\infty} d(i)$
7   **if** $\mathit{limit} < 0$ **then return** true ;
8 **end**
9 **return** false

Example 10 (Algorithm 3). Let us illustrate Algorithm 3 for the Prob-solvable loop $\mathcal{L}$ from Figure 2a: Applying Algorithm 3 on $\mathcal{L}$ yields $E \equiv 0$ and $u(i) = 0$. The expression G $(= x)$ has two branches. One of them is $x_i - y_i + 4$, which occurs with probability $1/2$. When the for-loop of Algorithm 3 reaches this branch $B = x_i - y_i + 4$ on line 4, it computes the difference $B - G = -y_i + 4$. An upper bounding function for $B - G$ is given by $d(i) = -i$. Because $\lim_{i\to\infty} d(i) < 0$, Algorithm 3 returns true. This is valid because of the branch B witnessing that G eventually decreases by at least a constant with probability $1/2$. Therefore, all conditions of the SM-Rule are satisfied and $\mathcal{L}$ is AST.

Theorem 8 (Correctness of Algorithm 3). *If Algorithm 3 returns* true *on input $\mathcal{L}$, then $\mathcal{L}$ with $G_{\mathcal{L}}$ satisfies the SM-Rule with constant d and p.*

The proof of Theorem 8, as well as of Theorem 9, are similar to the one of Theorem 7 and can be found in [40].

As established in Section 4, the relaxation of the R-AST-Rule requires that there is a positive probability of reaching the iteration i_0 after which the conditions of the proof rule hold. Regarding automation, we strengthen this condition by ensuring that there is a positive probability of reaching any iteration, i.e. $\forall i \in \mathbb{N} : \mathbb{P}(\mathcal{G}_i) > 0$. Obviously, this implies $\mathbb{P}(\mathcal{G}_{i_0}) > 0$. Furthermore, with $\mathit{CanReachAnyIteration}(\mathcal{L})$ we denote a computable under-approximation of $\forall i \in \mathbb{N} : \mathbb{P}(\mathcal{G}_i) > 0$. That means, $\mathit{CanReachAnyIteration}(\mathcal{L})$ implies $\forall i \in \mathbb{N} : \mathbb{P}(\mathcal{G}_i) > 0$. Our approach proving non-AST is summarized in Algorithm 4.

Example 11 (Algorithm 4). Let us illustrate Algorithm 4 for the Prob-solvable loop $\mathcal{L}$ from Figure 2a: Applying Algorithm 4 on $\mathcal{L}$ leads to $E = \frac{y_i}{6} - \frac{1}{3} = \frac{2^{-i}}{3} - \frac{1}{3}$ and to the upper bounding function $u(i) = -1$ for E on line 2. Therefore, the if-statement on line 3 is not executed, which means $-G$ is eventually a ϵ-repulsing supermartingale. Moreover, with a simple static analysis of the loop, we establish $\mathit{CanReachAnyIteration}(\mathcal{L})$ to be true, as there is a positive probability that the loop guard does not decrease. Thus, the if-statement on line 4 is not executed. Also, the if-statement on line 6 is not executed, because $\epsilon(i) = -u(i) = 1$ is constant and therefore in $\Omega(1)$. E eventually decreases by $\epsilon = 1$ (modulo a positive constant factor), because $u(i) = -1$ is an upper bounding function for E. We have $\mathit{differences} = \{1 - \frac{y_i}{2}, 1 + \frac{y_i}{2}\}$. Both expressions in *differences* have an absolute bounding function of 1. Therefore, $\mathit{diffBounds} = \{1\}$. As a result on line 9 we have $c(i) = 1$, which eventually and almost surely is an upper bound on $|-G_{i+1} + G_i|$

Algorithm 4: Repulsing-AST-Rule for proving non-AST

Input: Prob-solvable loop $\mathcal{L}$

Output: if *true*, $\mathcal{L}$ with $-G$ satisfies the R-AST-Rule; hence $\mathcal{L}$ is not AST

$E := \mathbb{E}(-G_{i+1} + G_i \mid \mathcal{F}_i)$

$u(i) := \mathit{ubf}(E)$

if *not eventually* $u(i) \leq 0$ **then return** false ;

if $\neg \mathit{CanReachAnyIteration}(\mathcal{L})$ **then return** false ;

$\epsilon(i) := -u(i)$

if $\epsilon(i) \notin \Omega(1)$ **then return** false ;

$\mathit{differences} := \{B + G \mid B \in \mathit{supp}(\mathcal{U}_{\mathcal{L}}^{-G})\}$

$\mathit{diffBounds} := \{\mathit{abf}(d) \mid d \in \mathit{differences}\}$

$c(i) := \mathit{dominating}(\mathit{diffBounds})$

return $c(i) \in O(1)$

(modulo a positive constant factor). Therefore, the algorithm returns true. This is correct, as all the preconditions of the R-AST-Rule are satisfied (and therefore $\mathcal{L}$ is not AST).

Theorem 9 (Correctness of Algorithm 4). *If Algorithm 4 returns* true *on input* $\mathcal{L}$*, then* $\mathcal{L}$ *with* $-G_{\mathcal{L}}$ *satisfies the R-AST-Rule.*

Because the R-PAST-Rule is a slight variation of the R-AST-Rule, Algorithm 4 can be slightly modified to yield a procedure for the R-PAST-Rule. An algorithm for the R-PAST-Rule is provided in [40].

5.4 Ruling out Proof Rules for Prob-Solvable Loops

A question arising when combining our algorithmic approaches from Section 5.3 into a unifying framework is that, given a Prob-solvable loop $\mathcal{L}$, what algorithm to apply first for determining $\mathcal{L}$'s termination behavior? In [4] the authors provide an algorithm for computing an algebraically closed-form of $\mathbb{E}(M_i)$, where M is a polynomial over $\mathcal{L}$'s variables. The following lemma explains how the expression $\mathbb{E}(M_{i+1} - M_i)$ relates to the expression $\mathbb{E}(M_{i+1} - M_i \mid \mathcal{F}_i)$. The lemma follows from the monotonicity of $\mathbb{E}$.

Lemma 3 (Rule out Rules for $\mathcal{L}$). *Let* $(M_i)_{i \in \mathbb{N}}$ *be a stochastic process. If* $\mathbb{E}(M_{i+1} - M_i \mid \mathcal{F}_i) \leq -\epsilon$ *then* $\mathbb{E}(M_{i+1} - M_i) \leq -\epsilon$*, for any* $\epsilon \in \mathbb{R}^+$.

The contrapositive of Lemma 3 provides a criterion to rule out the viability of a given proof rule. For a Prob-solvable loop $\mathcal{L}$, if $\mathbb{E}(G_{i+1} - G_i) \not\leq 0$ then $\mathbb{E}(G_{i+1} - G_i \mid \mathcal{F}_i) \not\leq 0$, meaning G is not a supermartingale. The expression $\mathbb{E}(G_{i+1} - G_i)$ depends only on i and can be computed by $\mathbb{E}(G_{i+1} - G_i) = \mathbb{E}(G_{i+1}) - \mathbb{E}(G_i)$, where the expected value $\mathbb{E}(G_i)$ is computed as in [4]. Therefore, in some cases, proof rules can automatically be deemed nonviable, without the need to compute bounding functions.

6 Implementation and Evaluation

6.1 Implementation

We implemented and combined our algorithmic approaches from Section 5 in the new software tool AMBER to stand for *Asymptotic Martingale Bounds*. AMBER and all benchmarks are available at https://github.com/probing-lab/amber. AMBER uses MORA [4][6] for computing the first-order moments of program variables and the DIOFANT package[5] as its computer algebra system.

Computing dominating and dominated The *dominating* and *dominated* procedures used in Algorithms 1 and 4 are implemented by combining standard algorithms for Big-O analysis and bookkeeping of the asymptotic polarity of the input functions. Let us illustrate this. Consider the following two input-output-pairs which our implementation would produce: (a) $dominating(\{i^2+10, 10\cdot i^5-i^3\}) = i^5$ and (b) $dominating(\{-i+50, -i^8+i^2-3\cdot i^3\}) = -i$. For (a) i^5 is eventually greater than all functions in the input set modulo a constant factor because all functions in the input set are $O(i^5)$. Therefore, i^5 dominates the input set. For (b), the first function is $O(i)$ and the second is $O(i^8)$. In this case, however, both functions are eventually negative. Therefore, $-i$ is a function dominating the input set. Important is the fact that an exponential polynomial $\sum_j p_j(i) \cdot c_j^i$, where $c_j \in \mathbb{R}_0^+$ will always be eventually either only positive or only negative (or 0 if identical to 0).

Sign Over-Approximation The over-approximation $Sign(x)$ of the signs of a monomial x used in Algorithm 1 is implemented by a simple static analysis: For a monomial x consisting solely of even powers, $Sign(x) = \{+\}$. For a general monomial x, if $x_0 \geq 0$ and all monomials on which x depends, together with their associated coefficients are always positive, then $- \notin Sign(x)$. For example, if $supp(\mathcal{U}_{\mathcal{L}}^x) = \{x_i + 2y_i - 3z_i, x_i + u_i\}$, then $- \notin Sign(x)$ if $x_0 \geq 0$ as well as $- \notin Sign(y)$, $+ \notin Sign(z)$ and $- \notin Sign(u)$. Otherwise, $- \in Sign(x)$. The over-approximation for $+ \notin Sign(x)$ is analogous.

Reachability Under-Approximation $CanReachAnyIteration(\mathcal{L})$, used in Algorithm 4, needs to satisfy the property that if it returns true, then loop $\mathcal{L}$ reaches any iteration with positive probability. In AMBER, we implement this under-approximation as follows: $CanReachAnyIteration(\mathcal{L})$ is true if there is a branch B of the loop guard polynomial $G_{\mathcal{L}}$ such that $B - G_{\mathcal{L}i}$ is non-negative for all $i \in \mathbb{N}$. Otherwise, $CanReachAnyIteration(\mathcal{L})$ is false. In other words, if $CanReachAnyIteration(\mathcal{L})$ is true, then in any iteration there is a positive probability of $G_{\mathcal{L}}$ not decreasing.

Bound Computation Improvements In addition to Algorithm 1 computing bounding functions for monomials of program variables, AMBER implements the following refinements:

1. A monomial x is deterministic, which means it is independent of probabilistic choices, if x has a single branch and only depends on monomials having single branches. In this case, the exact value of x in any iteration is given by its first-order moments and bounding functions can be obtained by using these exact representations.
2. Bounding functions for an odd power p of a monomial x can be computed by $u(i)^p$ and $l(i)^p$, where $u(i)$ is an upper- and $l(i)$ a lower bounding function for x.

Whenever the above enhancements are applicable, AMBER prefers them over Algorithm 1.

[5] https://github.com/diofant/diofant

6.2 Experimental Setting and Results

Experimental Setting and Comparisons Regarding programs which are PAST, we compare AMBER against the tool ABSYNTH [42] and the tool in [10] which we refer to as MGEN. ABSYNTH uses a system of inference rules over the syntax of probabilistic programs to derive bounds on the expected resource consumption of a program and can, therefore, be used to certify PAST. In comparison to AMBER, ABSYNTH requires the degree of the bound to be provided upfront. Moreover, ABSYNTH cannot refute the existence of a bound and therefore cannot handle programs that are not PAST. MGEN uses linear programming to synthesize linear martingales and supermartingales for probabilistic transition systems with linear variable updates. To certify PAST, we extended MGEN [10] with the SMT solver Z3 [41] in order to find or refute the existence of conical combinations of the (super)martingales derived by MGEN which yield RSMs.

With AMBER-LIGHT we refer to a variant of AMBER without the relaxations of the proof rules introduced in Section 4. That is, with AMBER-LIGHT the conditions of the proof rules need to hold for all $i \in \mathbb{N}$, whereas with AMBER the conditions are allowed to only hold eventually. For all benchmarks, we compare AMBER against AMBER-LIGHT to show the effectiveness of the respective relaxations. For each experimental table (Tables 1-3), ✓ symbolizes that the respective tool successfully certified PAST/AST/non-AST for the given program; ✗ means it failed to certify PAST/AST/non-AST. Further, **NA** indicates the respective tool failed to certify PAST/AST/non-AST because the given program is out-of-scope of the tool's capabilities. Every benchmark has been run on a machine with a 2.2 GHz Intel i7 (Gen 6) processor and 16 GB of RAM and finished within a timeout of 50 seconds, where most benchmarks terminated within a few seconds.

Benchmarks We evaluated AMBER against 38 probabilistic programs. We present our experimental results by separating our benchmarks within three categories: (i) 21 programs which are PAST (Table 1), (ii) 11 programs which are AST (Table 2) but not necessarily PAST, and (iii) 6 programs which are not AST (Table 3). The benchmarks have either been introduced in the literature on probabilistic programming [42,10,4,22,38], are adaptations of well-known stochastic processes or have been designed specifically to test unique features of AMBER, like the ability to handle polynomial real arithmetic.

The 21 PAST benchmarks consist of 10 programs representing the original benchmarks of MGEN [10] and ABSYNTH [42] augmented with 11 additional probabilistic programs. Not all benchmarks of MGEN and ABSYNTH could be used for our comparison as MGEN and ABSYNTH target related but different computation tasks than certifying PAST. Namely, MGEN aims to synthesize (super)martingales, but not ranking ones, whereas ABSYNTH focuses on computing bounds on the expected runtime. Therefore, we adopted *all* (50) benchmarks from [10] (11) and [42] (39) for which the termination behavior is non-trivial. A benchmark is trivial regarding PAST if either (i) there is no loop, (ii) the loop is bounded by a constant, or (iii) the program is meant to run forever. Moreover, we cleansed the benchmarks of programs for which the witness for PAST is just a trivial combination of witnesses for already included programs. For instance, the benchmarks of [42] contain multiple programs that are concatenated constant biased-random-walks. These are relevant benchmarks when evaluating ABSYNTH for discovering bounds, but would blur the picture when comparing against AMBER for PAST certification. With

Program	AMBER	AMBER-LIGHT	ABSYNTH	MGEN+Z3
2d_bounded_random_walk	✓	✓	✗	NA
biased_random_walk_constant	✓	✓	✓	✓
biased_random_walk_exp	✓	✓	✗	✓
biased_random_walk_poly	✓	✗	✗	✗
binomial_past	✓	✓	✓	✓
complex_past	✓	✗	✗	NA
consecutive_bernoulli_trails	✓	✓	✓	✓
coupon_collector_4	✓	✗	✗	✓
coupon_collector_5	✓	✗	✗	✓
dueling_cowboys	✓	✓	✓	✓
exponential_past_1	✓	✓	NA	NA
exponential_past_2	✓	✓	NA	NA
geometric	✓	✓	✓	✓
geometric_exponential	✗	✗	✗	✗
linear_past_1	✓	✓	✗	✗
linear_past_2	✓	✓	✗	NA
nested_loops	NA	NA	✓	✗
polynomial_past_1	✓	✗	✗	NA
polynomial_past_2	✓	✗	✗	NA
sequential_loops	NA	NA	✓	✗
tortoise_hare_race	✓	✓	✓	✓
Total ✓	18	12	8	9

Table 1: 21 programs which are PAST.

these criteria, 10 out of the 50 original benchmarks of [10] and [42] remain. We add 11 additional benchmarks which have either been introduced in the literature on probabilistic programming [4,22,38], are adaptations of well-known stochastic processes or have been designed specifically to test unique features of AMBER. Notably, out of the 50 original benchmarks from [42] and [10], only 2 remain which are included in our benchmarks and which AMBER cannot prove PAST (because they are not Prob-solvable). All our benchmarks are available at https://github.com/probing-lab/amber.

Experiments with PAST – Table 1: Out of the 21 PAST benchmarks, AMBER certifies 18 programs. AMBER cannot handle the benchmarks *nested_loops* and *sequential_loops*, as these examples use nested or sequential loops and thus are not expressible as Prob-solvable loops. The benchmarks *exponential_past_1* and *exponential_past_2* are out of scope of ABSYNTH because they require real numbers, while ABSYNTH can only handle integers. MGEN+Z3 cannot handle benchmarks containing non-linear variable updates or non-linear guards. Table 1 shows that AMBER outperforms both ABSYNTH and MGEN+Z3 for Prob-solvable loops, even when our relaxed proof rules from Section 4 are not used. Yet, our experiments show that our relaxed proof rules enable AMBER to certify 6 examples to be PAST, which could not be proved without these relaxations by AMBER-LIGHT.

Experiments with AST – Table 2: We compare AMBER against AMBER-LIGHT on 11 benchmarks which are AST but not necessarily PAST and also cannot be split into PAST subprograms. Therefore, the SM-Rule is needed to certify AST. To the best of our knowledge, AMBER is the first tool able to certify AST for such programs. Existing approaches like [1] and [14] can only witness AST for non-PAST programs, if - intuitively speaking - the programs contain subprograms which are PAST. Therefore, we compared

AMBER only against AMBER-LIGHT on this set of examples. The benchmark *symmetric_2d_random_walk*, which AMBER fails to certify as AST, models the symmetric random walk in $\mathbb{R}^2$ and is still out of reach of current automation techniques. In [38] the authors mention that a closed-form expression M and functions p and d satisfying the conditions of the SM-Rule have not been discovered yet. The benchmark *fair_in_limit_random_walk* involves non-constant probabilities and can therefore not be modeled as a Prob-solvable loop.

Experiments with non-AST – Table 3: We compare AMBER against AMBER-LIGHT on 6 benchmarks which are not AST. To the best of our knowledge, AMBER is the first tool able to certify non-AST for such programs, and thus we compared AMBER only against AMBER-LIGHT. In [13], where the notion of repulsing supermartingales and the R-AST-Rule are introduced, the authors also propose automation techniques. However, the authors of [13] claim that their "experimental results are basic" and their computational methods are evaluated on only 3 examples, without having any available tool support. For the benchmarks in Table 3, the outcomes of AMBER and AMBER-LIGHT coincide. The reason for this is R-AST-Rule's condition that the martingale expression has to have c-bounded differences. This condition forces a suitable martingale expression to be bounded by a linear function, which is also the reason why AMBER cannot certify the benchmark *polynomial_nast*.

Experimental Summary Our results from Tables 1-3 demonstrate that:

- AMBER outperforms the state-of-the-art in automating PAST certification for Prob-solvable loops (Table 1).
- Complex probabilistic programs which are AST and not PAST as well as programs which are not AST can automatically be certified as such by AMBER (Tables 2, 3).
- The relaxations of the proof rules introduced in Section 4 are helpful in automating the termination analysis of probabilistic programs, as evidenced by the performance of AMBER against AMBER-LIGHT (Tables 1-3).

7 Related Work

Proof Rules for Probabilistic Termination Several proof rules have been proposed in the literature to provide sufficient conditions for the termination behavior of probabilistic programs. The work of [10] uses martingale theory to characterize *positive almost sure termination (PAST)*. In particular, the notion of a ranking supermartingale (RSM) is introduced together with a proof rule (RSM-Rule) to certify PAST, as discussed in Section 3.1. The approach of [19] extended this method to include (demonic) non-determinism and continuous probability distributions, showing the completeness of the RSM-Rule for this program class. The compositional approach proposed in [19] was further strengthened in [29] to a sound approach using the notion of *descent supermartingale map*. In [1], the authors introduced *lexicographic* RSMs.

The SM-Rule discussed in Section 3.2 was introduced in [38]. It is worth mentioning that this proof rule is also applicable to non-deterministic probabilistic programs. The work of [28] presented an independent proof rule based on supermartingales with lower bounds on conditional absolute differences. Both proof rules are based on supermartingales and

Program	Amber	Amber-Light
fair_in_limit_random_walk	**NA**	**NA**
gambling	✓	✓
symmetric_2d_random_walk	✗	✗
symmetric_random_walk_constant_1	✓	✓
symmetric_random_walk_constant_2	✓	✓
symmetric_random_walk_exp_1	✓	✗
symmetric_random_walk_exp_2	✓	✗
symmetric_random_walk_linear_1	✓	✗
symmetric_random_walk_linear_2	✓	✓
symmetric_random_walk_poly_1	✓	✗
symmetric_random_walk_poly_2	✓	✗
Total ✓	9	4

Table 2: 11 programs which are AST and not necessarily PAST.

Program	Amber	Amber-Light
biased_random_walk_nast_1	✓	✓
biased_random_walk_nast_2	✓	✓
biased_random_walk_nast_3	✓	✓
biased_random_walk_nast_4	✓	✓
binomial_nast	✓	✓
polynomial_nast	✗	✗
Total ✓	5	5

Table 3: 6 programs which are not AST.

can certify AST for programs that are not necessarily PAST. The approach of [43] examined martingale-based techniques for obtaining bounds on reachability probabilities — and thus termination probabilities— from an order-theoretic viewpoint. The notions of *nonnegative repulsing supermartingales* and γ*-scaled submartingales*, accompanied by sound and complete proof rules, have also been introduced. The R-AST-Rule from Section 3.3 was proposed in [13] mainly for obtaining bounds on the probability of stochastic invariants.

An alternative approach is to exploit weakest precondition techniques for probabilistic programs, as presented in the seminal works [34,35] that can be used to certify AST. The work of [37] extended this approach to programs with non-determinism and provided several proof rules for termination. These techniques are purely syntax-based. In [31] a weakest precondition calculus for obtaining bounds on expected termination times was proposed. This calculus comes with proof rules to reason about loops.

Automation of Martingale Techniques The work of [10] proposed an automated procedure — by using Farkas' lemma — to synthesize *linear* (super)martingales for probabilistic programs with linear variable updates. This technique was considered in our experimental evaluation, cf. Section 6. The algorithmic construction of supermartingales was extended to treat (demonic) non-determinism in [12] and to polynomial supermartingales in [11] using semi-definite programming. The recent work of [14] uses ω-regular decomposition to certify AST. They exploit so-called *localized* ranking supermartingales, which can be synthesized efficiently but must be linear.

Other Approaches Abstract interpretation is used in [39] to prove the probabilistic termination of programs for which the probability of taking a loop k times decreases at least exponentially with k. In [18], a sound and complete procedure deciding AST is given for probabilistic programs with a finite number of reachable states from any initial state.

The work of [42] gave an algorithmic approach based on potential functions for computing bounds on the expected resource consumption of probabilistic programs. In [36], model checking is exploited to automatically verify whether a parameterized family of probabilistic concurrent systems is AST.

Finally, the class of Prob-solvable loops considered in this paper extends [4] to a wider class of loops. While [4] focused on computing statistical higher-order moments, our work addresses the termination behavior of probabilistic programs. The related approach of [22] computes exact expected runtimes of constant probability programs and provides a decision procedure for AST and PAST for such programs. Our programming model strictly generalizes the constant probability programs of [22], by supporting polynomial loop guards, updates and martingale expressions.

8 Conclusion

This paper reported on the automation of termination analysis of probabilistic while-programs whose guards and expressions are polynomial expressions. To this end, we introduced mild relaxations of existing proof rules for AST, PAST, and their negations, by requiring their sufficient conditions to hold only eventually. The key to our approach is that the structural constraints of Prob-solvable loops allow for automatically computing almost sure asymptotic bounds on polynomials over program variables. Prob-solvable loops cover a vast set of complex and relevant probabilistic processes including random walks and dynamic Bayesian networks [5]. Only two out of 50 benchmarks in [10,42] are outside the scope of Prob-solvable loops regarding PAST certification. The almost sure asymptotic bounds were used to formalize algorithmic approaches for proving AST, PAST, and their negations. Moreover, for Prob-solvable loops four different proof rules from the literature uniformly come together in our work.

Our approach is implemented in the software tool AMBER (github.com/probing-lab/amber), offering a fully automated approach to probabilistic termination. Our experimental results show that our relaxed proof rules enable proving probabilistic (non-) termination of more programs than could be treated before. A comparison to the state-of-art in automated analysis of probabilistic termination reveals that AMBER significantly outperforms related approaches. To the best of our knowledge, AMBER is the first tool to automate AST, PAST, non-AST and non-PAST in a single tool-chain.

There are several directions for future work. These include extensions to Prob-solvable loops such as symbolic distributions, more complex control flow, and non-determinism. We will also consider program transformations that translate programs into our format. Extensions of the SM-Rule algorithm with non-constant probability and decrease functions are also in our interest.

References

1. Agrawal, S., Chatterjee, K., Novotný, P.: Lexicographic ranking supermartingales: an efficient approach to termination of probabilistic programs. Proc. of POPL (2017). https://doi.org/10.1145/3158122
2. Arora, N.S., Russell, S.J., Sudderth, E.B.: NET-VISA: Network Processing Vertically Integrated Seismic Analysis. Seismol. Soc. Am., Bull. (2013). https://doi.org/10.1785/0120120107
3. Avanzini, M., Lago, U.D., Yamada, A.: On probabilistic term rewriting. Sci. Comput. Program. (2020). https://doi.org/10.1016/j.scico.2019.102338
4. Bartocci, E., Kovács, L., Stankovic, M.: Automatic generation of moment-based invariants for prob-solvable loops. In: Proc. of ATVA (2019). https://doi.org/10.1007/978-3-030-31784-3_15
5. Bartocci, E., Kovács, L., Stankovic, M.: Analysis of bayesian networks via prob-solvable loops. In: Proc. of ICTAC (2020). https://doi.org/10.1007/978-3-030-64276-1_12
6. Bartocci, E., Kovács, L., Stankovic, M.: Mora - automatic generation of moment-based invariants. In: Proc. of TACAS (2020). https://doi.org/10.1007/978-3-030-45190-5
7. Bistline, J.E., Blum, D.M., Rinaldi, C., Shields-Estrada, G., Hecker, S.S., Paté-Cornell, M.E.: A Bayesian Model to Assess the Size of North Korea's Uranium Enrichment Program. Sci. Global Secur. (2015). https://doi.org/10.1080/08929882.2015.1039431
8. Bournez, O., Garnier, F.: Proving positive almost-sure termination. In: Proc. of RTA (2005). https://doi.org/10.1007/978-3-540-32033-3_24
9. Bradley, A.R., Manna, Z., Sipma, H.B.: Termination of Polynomial Programs. In: Proc. of VMCAI (2005). https://doi.org/10.1007/b105073
10. Chakarov, A., Sankaranarayanan, S.: Probabilistic Program Analysis with Martingales. In: Proc. of CAV (2013). https://doi.org/10.1007/978-3-642-39799-8_34
11. Chatterjee, K., Fu, H., Goharshady, A.K.: Termination Analysis of Probabilistic Programs Through Positivstellensatz's. In: Proc. of CAV (2016). https://doi.org/10.1007/978-3-319-41528-4_1
12. Chatterjee, K., Fu, H., Novotný, P., Hasheminezhad, R.: Algorithmic Analysis of Qualitative and Quantitative Termination Problems for Affine Probabilistic Programs. ACM Trans. Program. Lang. Syst. (2018). https://doi.org/10.1145/3174800
13. Chatterjee, K., Novotný, P., Zikelic, D.: Stochastic Invariants for Probabilistic Termination. In: Proc. of POPL (2017). https://doi.org/10.1145/3009837.3009873
14. Chen, J., He, F.: Proving almost-sure termination by omega-regular decomposition. In: Proc. of PLDI (2020). https://doi.org/10.1145/3385412.3386002
15. Cook, B., Podelski, A., Rybalchenko, A.: Terminator: Beyond Safety. In: Proc. of CAV (2006). https://doi.org/10.1007/11817963_37
16. Cook, B., Podelski, A., Rybalchenko, A.: Proving program termination. Commun. ACM (2011). https://doi.org/10.1145/1941487.1941509
17. Dal Lago, U., Grellois, C.: Probabilistic termination by monadic affine sized typing. ACM Trans. Program. Lang. Syst. (2019). https://doi.org/10.1145/3293605
18. Esparza, J., Gaiser, A., Kiefer, S.: Proving Termination of Probabilistic Programs Using Patterns. In: Proc. of CAV (2012). https://doi.org/10.1007/978-3-642-31424-7_14
19. Ferrer Fioriti, L.L.M., Hermanns, H.: Probabilistic Termination: Soundness, Completeness, and Compositionality. In: Proc. of POPL (2015). https://doi.org/10.1145/2676726.2677001
20. Fremont, D.J., Dreossi, T., Ghosh, S., Yue, X., Sangiovanni-Vincentelli, A.L., Seshia, S.A.: Scenic: a language for scenario specification and scene generation. In: Proc. of PLDI (2019). https://doi.org/10.1145/3314221.3314633
21. Giesl, J., Aschermann, C., Brockschmidt, M., Emmes, F., Frohn, F., Fuhs, C., Hensel, J., Otto, C., Plücker, M., Schneider-Kamp, P., Ströder, T., Swiderski, S., Thiemann, R.: Analyzing program termination and complexity automatically with aprove. J. Autom. Reasoning (2017). https://doi.org/10.1007/s10817-016-9388-y

22. Giesl, J., Giesl, P., Hark, M.: Computing expected runtimes for constant probability programs. In: Proc. of CADE (2019). https://doi.org/10.1007/978-3-030-29436-6_16
23. Gruntz, D.: On computing limits in a symbolic manipulation system. Ph.D. thesis, ETH Zürich (1996). https://doi.org/10.3929/ETHZ-A-001631582
24. Hark, M., Frohn, F., Giesl, J.: Polynomial loops: Beyond termination. In: Proc. of LPAR (2020). https://doi.org/10.29007/nxv1
25. Hark, M., Kaminski, B.L., Giesl, J., Katoen, J.: Aiming low is harder: induction for lower bounds in probabilistic program verification. In: Proc. of POPL (2020). https://doi.org/10.1145/3371105
26. Heizmann, M., Chen, Y., Dietsch, D., Greitschus, M., Hoenicke, J., Li, Y., Nutz, A., Musa, B., Schilling, C., Schindler, T., Podelski, A.: Ultimate automizer and the search for perfect interpolants - (competition contribution). In: Proc. of TACAS (2018). https://doi.org/10.1007/978-3-319-89963-3_30
27. Hoare, C.A.R.: An Axiomatic Basis for Computer Programming. Commun. ACM (1969). https://doi.org/10.1145/363235.363259
28. Huang, M., Fu, H., Chatterjee, K.: New Approaches for Almost-Sure Termination of Probabilistic Programs. In: Proc. of APLAS (2018). https://doi.org/10.1007/978-3-030-02768-1_11
29. Huang, M., Fu, H., Chatterjee, K., Goharshady, A.K.: Modular verification for almost-sure termination of probabilistic programs. Proc. ACM Program. Lang. (2019). https://doi.org/10.1145/3360555
30. Kaminski, B.L., Katoen, J.P.: On the hardness of almost-sure termination. In: Proc. of MFCS (2015). https://doi.org/10.1007/978-3-662-48057-1_24
31. Kaminski, B.L., Katoen, J., Matheja, C., Olmedo, F.: Weakest precondition reasoning for expected runtimes of randomized algorithms. J. ACM (2018). https://doi.org/10.1145/3208102
32. Kauers, M., Paule, P.: The Concrete Tetrahedron: Symbolic Sums, Recurrence Equations, Generating Functions, Asymptotic Estimates. Springer (2011)
33. Kemeny, J.G., Snell, J.L., Knapp, A.W.: Denumerable Markov Chains: with a chapter of Markov Random Fields by David Griffeath. Springer, 2 edn. (1976)
34. Kozen, D.: Semantics of probabilistic programs. J. Comput. Syst. Sci. (1981). https://doi.org/10.1016/0022-0000(81)90036-2
35. Kozen, D.: A probabilistic PDL. J. Comput. Syst. Sci. (1985). https://doi.org/10.1016/0022-0000(85)90012-1
36. Lengál, O., Lin, A.W., Majumdar, R., Rümmer, P.: Fair termination for parameterized probabilistic concurrent systems. In: Proc. of TACAS (2017). https://doi.org/10.1007/978-3-662-54577-5_29
37. McIver, A., Morgan, C.: Abstraction, Refinement and Proof for Probabilistic Systems. Springer (2005)
38. McIver, A., Morgan, C., Kaminski, B.L., Katoen, J.P.: A New Proof Rule for Almost-sure Termination. Proc. ACM Program. Lang. (2018). https://doi.org/10.1145/3158121
39. Monniaux, D.: An abstract analysis of the probabilistic termination of programs. In: Proc. of SAS (2001). https://doi.org/10.1007/3-540-47764-0
40. Moosbrugger, M., Bartocci, E., Katoen, J.P., Kovács, L.: Automated termination analysis of polynomial probabilistic programs (2020)
41. de Moura, L.M., Bjørner, N.: Z3: an efficient SMT solver. In: Proc. of TACAS (2008). https://doi.org/10.1007/978-3-540-78800-3
42. Ngo, V.C., Carbonneaux, Q., Hoffmann, J.: Bounded expectations: resource analysis for probabilistic programs. In: Proc. of PLDI (2018). https://doi.org/10.1145/3192366.3192394
43. Takisaka, T., Oyabu, Y., Urabe, N., Hasuo, I.: Ranking and repulsing supermartingales for reachability in probabilistic programs. In: Proc. of ATVA (2018). https://doi.org/10.1007/978-3-030-01090-4_28

44. Yamada, A., Kusakari, K., Sakabe, T.: Nagoya termination tool. In: Proc. of RTA-TLCA (2014). https://doi.org/10.1007/978-3-319-08918-8_32

Bayesian strategies: probabilistic programs as generalised graphical models

Hugo Paquet

Department of Computer Science, University of Oxford, Oxford, UK
hugo.paquet@cs.ox.ac.uk

Abstract. We introduce *Bayesian strategies*, a new interpretation of probabilistic programs in game semantics. This interpretation can be seen as a refinement of Bayesian networks.
Bayesian strategies are based on a new form of *event structure*, with two causal dependency relations respectively modelling control flow and data flow. This gives a graphical representation for probabilistic programs which resembles the concrete representations used in modern implementations of probabilistic programming.
From a theoretical viewpoint, Bayesian strategies provide a rich setting for denotational semantics. To demonstrate this we give a model for a general higher-order programming language with recursion, conditional statements, and primitives for sampling from continuous distributions and trace re-weighting. This is significant because Bayesian networks do not easily support higher-order functions or conditionals.

1 Introduction

One promise of probabilistic programming languages (PPLs) is to make Bayesian statistics accessible to anyone with a programming background. In a PPL, the programmer can express complex statistical models clearly and precisely, and they additionally gain access to the set of inference tools provided by the probabilistic programming system, which they can use for simulation, data analysis, *etc.* Such tools are usually designed so that the user does not require any in-depth knowledge of Bayesian inference algorithms.

A challenge for language designers is to provide efficient inference algorithms. This can be intricate, because programs can be arbitrarily complex, and inference requires a close interaction between the inference engine and the language interpreter [42, Ch.6]. In practice, many modern inference engines do not manipulate the program syntax direcly but instead exploit some *representation* of it, more suited to the type of inference method at hand (Metropolis-Hastings (MH), Sequential Monte Carlo (SMC), Hamiltonian Monte Carlo, variational inference, *etc.*).

While many authors have recently given proofs of correctness for inference algorithms (see for example [11,24,32]), most have focused on idealised descriptions of the algorithms, based on syntax or operational semantics, rather than on the concrete program representations used in practice. In this paper we instead

N. Yoshida (Ed.): ESOP 2021, LNCS 12648, pp. 519–547, 2021.
https://doi.org/10.1007/978-3-030-72019-3_19

put forward a mathematical semantics for probabilistic programs designed to provide reasoning tools for existing implementations of inference.

Our work targets a specific class of representations which we call *data flow* representations. We understand **data flow** as describing the dependence relationships between random variables of a program. This is in contrast with **control flow**, which describes *in what order* samples are performed. Such data flow representations are widely used in practice. We give a few examples. For Metropolis-Hastings inference, Church [30] and Venture [41] manipulate dependency graphs for random variables ("computation traces" or "probabilistic execution traces"); Infer.NET [22] compiles programs to *factor graphs* in order to apply message passing algorithms; for a subset of well-behaved programs, Gen [23] statically constructs a representation based on certain *combinators* which is then exploited by a number of inference algorithms; and finally, for variational inference, Pyro [9] and Edward [55] rely on data flow graphs for efficient computation of gradients by automatic differentiation. (Also [52,28].)

In this paper, we make a step towards correctness of these implementations and introduce **Bayesian strategies**, a new representation based on Winskel's event structures [46] which tracks *both* data flow and control flow. The Bayesian strategy corresponding to a program is obtained compositionally as is standard in concurrent game semantics [63], and provides an intensional foundation for probabilistic programs, complementary to existing approaches [24,57].

This paper was inspired by the pioneering work of Ścibior et al. [53], which provides the first denotational analysis for concrete inference representations. In particular, their work provides a general framework for proving correct inference algorithms based on static representations. But the authors do not show how their framework can be used to accommodate data flow representations or verify any of the concrete implementations mentioned above. The work of this paper does *not* fill this gap, as we make no attempt to connect our semantic constructions with those of [53], or indeed to prove correct any inference algorithms. This could be difficult, because our presentation arises out of previous work on game semantics and thus does not immediately fit in with the monadic techniques employed in [53]. Nonetheless, efforts to construct game semantics monadically are underway [14], and it is hoped that the results presented here will set the ground for the development of event structure-based validation of inference.

1.1 From Bayesian networks to Bayesian strategies

Consider the following basic model, found in the Pyro tutorials (and also used in [39]), used to infer the weight of an object based on two noisy measurements. The measurements are represented by random variables $meas_1$ and $meas_2$, whose values are drawn from a normal distribution around the true weight (*weight*), whose *prior* distribution is also normal, and centered at 2. (In this situation, $meas_1$ and $meas_2$ are destined to be *conditioned* on actual observed values, and the problem is then to infer the *posterior* distribution of *weight* based on these observations. We leave out conditioning in this example and focus on the model specification.)

To describe this model it is convenient to use a *Bayesian network*, *i.e.* a DAG of random variables in which the distribution of each variable depends only on the value of its parents:

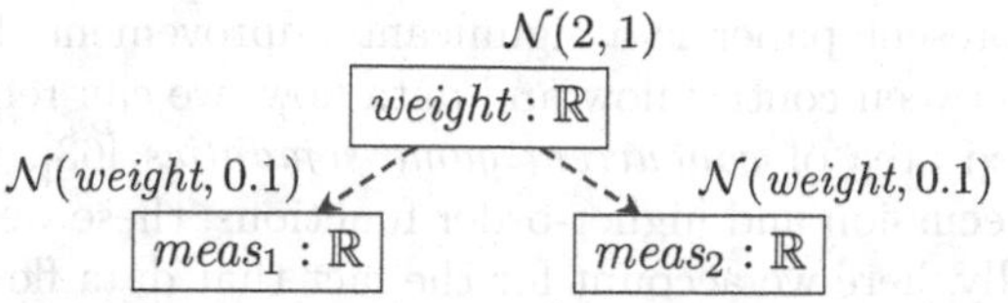

The same probabilistic model can be encoded in an ML-style language:

$$
\begin{array}{l}
\textbf{let } \text{weight} = \textbf{sample}_{weight}\ \textbf{normal}(2,1)\ \textbf{in} \\
\textbf{sample}_{meas_1}\ \textbf{normal}(\text{weight}, 0.1); \\
\textbf{sample}_{meas_2}\ \textbf{normal}(\text{weight}, 0.1); \\
()
\end{array}
$$

Our choice of sampling $meas_1$ before $meas_2$ is arbitrary: the same program with the second and third lines swapped corresponds to the same probabilistic model. This redundancy is unavoidable because programs are inherently sequential. It is the purpose of "commutative" semantics for probabilistic programs, as introduced by Staton et al. [54,57], to clarify this situation. They show that reordering program lines does not change the semantics, even in the presence of conditioning. This result says that when specifying a probabilistic model, only data flow matters, and not control flow. This motivates the use of program representations based on data flow such as the examples listed above.

In our game semantics, a probabilistic program is interpreted as a control flow graph *annotated* by a data dependency relation. The Bayesian strategy associated with the program above is as follows:

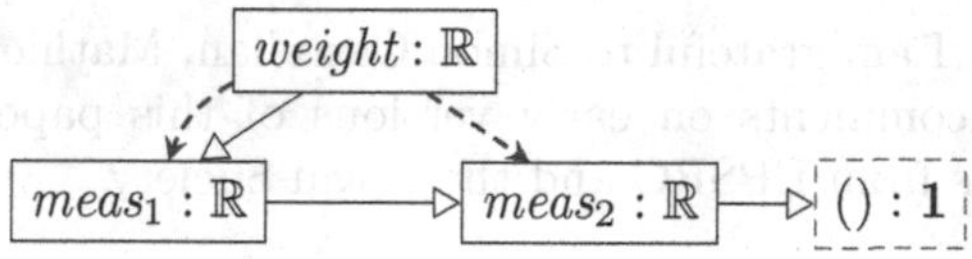

where (in brief), ⇢ is data flow, → is control flow, and the dashed node is the program output. (Probability distributions are as in the Bayesian network.)

The semantics is not commutative, simply because reordering lines affects control flow; we emphasise that the point of this work is not to prove any new program equations, but instead to provide a formal framework for the representations involved in practical inference settings.

1.2 Our approach

To formalise this idea we use event structures, which naturally model control flow, enriched with additional structure for probability and an explicit data flow relation. Event structures were used in previous work by the author and Castellan on probabilistic programming [18], and were shown to be a good fit for reasoning about MH inference. But the representation in [18] combines data flow and control flow in a single transitive relation, and thus suffers from important limitations. The present paper is a significant improvement: by maintaining a clear separation between control flow and data flow, we can reframe the ideas in the well-established area of *concurrent game semantics* [63], which enables an interpretation of recursion and higher-order functions; these were not considered in [18]. Additionally, here we account for the fact that data flow in probabilistic programming is *not* in general a transitive relation.

While there is some work in setting up the right notion of event structure, the standard methods of concurrent game semantics adapt well to this setting. This is not surprising, as event structures and games are known to be resistant to the addition of extra structure, see e.g. [21,5,15]. One difficulty is to correctly define composition, keeping track of potential hidden data dependencies. In summary:

- We introduce a general notion of Bayesian event structure, modelling control flow, data flow, and probability.
- We set up a compositional framework for these event structures based on concurrent games. Specifically, we define a category **BG** of *arenas* and *Bayesian strategies*, and give a description of its abstract properties.
- We give a denotational semantics for a higher-order statistical language. Our semantics gives an operationally intuitive representation for programs and their data flow structure, while only relying on standard mathematical tools.

Paper outline. We start by recalling the basics of probability and Bayesian networks, and we then describe the syntax of our language (Sec. 2). In Sec. 3, we introduce event structures and Bayesian event structures, and informally describe our semantics using examples. In Sec. 4 we define our category of arenas and strategies, which we apply to the denotational semantics of the language in Sec. 5. We give some context and perspectives in Sec. 6.

Acknowledgements. I am grateful to Simon Castellan, Mathieu Huot and Philip Saville for helpful comments on early versions of this paper. This work was supported by grants from EPSRC and the Royal Society.

2 Probability distributions, Bayesian networks, and probabilistic programming

2.1 Probability and measure

We recall the basic notions, see *e.g.* [8] for a reference.

Measures. A **measurable space** is a set X equipped with a **σ-algebra**, that is, a set Σ_X of subsets of X containing X itself, and closed under completements and countable unions. The elements of Σ_X are called **measurable subsets** of X. An important example of measurable space is the set $\mathbb{R}$ equipped with its

σ-algebra $\Sigma_{\mathbb{R}}$ of Borel sets, the smallest one containing all intervals. Another basic example is the discrete space $\mathbb{N}$, in which all subsets are measurable.

A **measure** on (X, Σ_X) is a function $\mu : \Sigma_X \to [0, \infty]$ which is countably additive, *i.e.* $\mu(\biguplus_{i \in I} U_i) = \sum_{i \in I} U_i$ for I countable, and satisfies $\mu(\emptyset) = 0$. A fundamental example is the **Lebesgue measure** λ on $\mathbb{R}$, defined on intervals as $\lambda([a, b]) = b - a$ and extended to all Borel sets. Another example (for arbitrary X) is the **Dirac measure** at a point $x \in X$: for any $U \in \Sigma_X$, $\delta_x(U) = 1$ if $x \in U$, 0 otherwise. A **sub-probability measure** on (X, Σ_X) is a measure μ satisfying $\mu(X) \leq 1$.

A function $f : X \to Y$ is measurable if $U \in \Sigma_Y \implies f^{-1}U \in \Sigma_X$. Given a measure on a space X and a measurable function $f : X \to \mathbb{R}$, for every measurable subset U of X we can define the **integral** $\int_U \mathrm{d}\mu f$, an element of $\mathbb{R} \cup \{\infty\}$. This construction yields a measure on X. (Many well-known probability distributions on the reals arise in this way from their *density*.)

Kernels. We will make extensive use of *kernels*, which can be seen as parametrised families of measures. Formally a **kernel** from X to Y is a map $k : X \times \Sigma_Y \to [0, \infty]$ such that for every $x \in X$, $k(x, -)$ is a measure on Y, and for every $V \in \Sigma_Y$, $k(-, V)$ is a measurable function. It is a **sub-probability kernel** if each $k(x, -)$ is a sub-probability measure, and it is an **s-finite kernel** if it is a countable (pointwise) sum of sub-probability kernels. Every measurable function $f : X \to Y$ induces a Dirac kernel $\delta_f : X \rightsquigarrow Y : x \mapsto \delta_{f(x)}$. Kernels compose: if $k : X \rightsquigarrow Y$ and $h : Y \rightsquigarrow Z$ then the map $h \circ k : X \times \Sigma_Z \to [0, 1]$ defined as $(x, W) \mapsto \int_Y \mathrm{d}k(x, -)h(-, W)$ is also a kernel, and the Dirac kernel δ_{id} (often just δ) is an identity for this composition. We note that if both h and k are sub-probability kernels, then $h \circ k$ is a sub-probability kernel. Finally, observe that a kernel $\mathbf{1} \rightsquigarrow X$, for $\mathbf{1}$ a singleton space, is the same thing as a measure on X.

In this paper we will refer to the bernoulli, normal, and uniform families of distributions; all of these are sub-probability kernels from their parameters spaces to $\mathbb{N}$ or $\mathbb{R}$. For example, there is a kernel $\mathbb{R}^2 \rightsquigarrow \mathbb{R} : ((x, y), U) \mapsto \mu_{\mathcal{N}(x,y)}(U)$, where $\mu_{\mathcal{N}(x,y)}$ is the measure associated with a normal distribution with parameters (x, y), if $y > 0$, and the 0 measure otherwise. We understand the bernoulli distribution as returning either 0 or $1 \in \mathbb{N}$.

Product spaces and independence. When several random quantities are under study one uses the notion of **product space**: given (X, Σ_X) and (Y, Σ_Y) we can equip the set $X \times Y$ with the product σ-algebra, written $\Sigma_{X \times Y}$, defined as the smallest one containing $U \times V$, for $U \in \Sigma_X$ and $V \in \Sigma_Y$.

A measure μ on $X \times Y$ gives rise to **marginals** μ_X and μ_Y, measures on X and Y respectively, defined by $\mu_X(U) = \mu(U \times Y)$ and $\mu_Y(V) = \mu(X \times V)$ for $U \in \Sigma_X$ and $V \in \Sigma_Y$.

Given kernels $k : X \rightsquigarrow Y$ and $h : Z \rightsquigarrow W$ we define the **product kernel** $k \times h : X \times Z \rightsquigarrow Y \times W$ via iterated integration:

$$((x, z), U) \mapsto \int_{y \in Y} \mathrm{d}k(x, -) \int_{w \in W} \mathrm{d}h(z, -)\chi_U(y, w),$$

where χ_U is the characteristic function of $U \in \Sigma_{Y \times V}$. When $X = Z = \mathbf{1}$ this gives the notion of **product measure**.

The definitions above extend with no difficulty to product spaces $\prod_{i \in I} X_i$. A measure P on $\prod_{i \in I} X_i$ has marginals P_J for any $J \subseteq I$, and we say that X_i and X_j are **independent w.r.t. P** if the marginal $P_{i,j}$ is equal to the product measure $P_i \times P_j$.

2.2 Bayesian networks

An efficient way to define measures on product spaces is using probabilistic graphical models [37], for example Bayesian networks, whose definition we briefly recall now. The idea is to use a graph structure to encode a set of independence constraints between the components of a product space. We recall the definition of conditional independence. With respect to a joint distribution P on $\prod_{i \in I} X_i$, we say X_i and X_j are **conditionally independent given** X_k if there exists a kernel $k : X_k \rightsquigarrow X_i \times X_j$ such that $P_{i,j,k}(U_i \times U_j \times U_k) = \int_{U_k} k(-, U_i \times U_j) \mathrm{d}P_k$ for all measurable U_i, U_j, U_k, and X_i and X_j are independent w.r.t. $k(x_k, -)$ for all $x_k \in X_k$. In this definition, k is a *conditional distribution* of $X_i \times X_j$ given X_k (w.r.t. P); under some reasonable conditions [8] this always exists, and the independence condition is the main requirement.

Adapting the presentation used in [27], we define a **Bayesian network** as a directed acyclic graph $G = (V, \dashrightarrow)$ where each node $v \in V$ is assigned a measurable space $\mathcal{M}(v)$. We define the **parents** $\mathrm{pa}(v)$ of v to be the set of nodes u with $u \dashrightarrow v$, and its **non-descendants** $\mathrm{nd}(v)$ to contain the nodes u such that there is no path $v \dashrightarrow \cdots \dashrightarrow u$. Writing $\mathcal{M}(S) = \prod_{v \in S} \mathcal{M}(v)$ for any subset $S \subseteq V$, a measure P on $\mathcal{M}(V)$ is said to be **compatible with** G if for every $v \in V$, $\mathcal{M}(v)$ and $\mathcal{M}(\mathrm{nd}(v))$ are independent given $\mathcal{M}(\mathrm{pa}(v))$. It is straightforward to verify that given a Bayesian network G, we can construct a compatible measure by supplying for every $v \in V$, an s-finite kernel $k_v : \mathcal{M}(\mathrm{pa}(v)) \rightsquigarrow \mathcal{M}(v)$.

(In practice, Bayesian networks are used to represent probabilistic models, and so typically every kernel k_v is strictly probabilistic. Here the k_v are only required to be s-finite, so they are in general unnormalised. As we will see, this is because we consider possibly *conditioned* models.)

Bayesian networks are an elegant way of constructing models, but they are limited. We now present a programming language whose expressivity goes beyond them.

2.3 A language for probabilistic modelling

Our language of study is a call-by-value statistical language with sums, products, and higher-order types, as well as recursive functions. Languages with comparable features are considered in [11,57,40].

The syntax of this language is described in Fig. 1. Note the distinction between general terms M, N and values V. The language includes the usual term constructors and pattern matching. Base types are the unit type, the real numbers and the natural numbers, and for each of them there are associated constants. The language is parametrised by a set $\mathcal{L}$ of *labels*, a set $\mathcal{F}$ of partial measurable functions $\mathbb{R}^n \to \mathbb{R}$ or $\mathbb{R}^n \to \mathbb{N}$, and a set $\mathcal{D}$ of standard distribution families, which are sub-probability kernels[1] $\mathbb{R}^n \rightsquigarrow \mathbb{R}$ or $\mathbb{R}^n \rightsquigarrow \mathbb{N}$. There is also a primitive **score** which multiplies the weight of the current trace by the value of its argument. This is an idealised form of conditioning via *soft constraints*, which justifies the move from sub-probability to s-finite kernels (see [54]).

$$\begin{aligned}
A, B &::= \mathbf{1} \mid \mathbb{N} \mid \mathbb{R} \mid A \times B \mid A + B \mid A \to B \\
V, W &::= () \mid \underline{n} \mid \underline{r} \mid \underline{f} \mid (V, W) \mid \mathbf{inl}\, V \mid \mathbf{inr}\, V \mid \lambda x.M \\
M, N &::= V \mid x \mid M\, N \mid M =^? 0 \mid \mu x : A \to B.M \mid \mathbf{sample}_\ell\ \mathbf{dist}(M_1, \ldots, M_n) \\
&\qquad (M, N) \mid \mathbf{match}\ M\ \mathbf{with}\ (x, y) \to P \mid \mathbf{score}\ M \\
&\qquad \mathbf{inl}\, M \mid \mathbf{inr}\, M \mid \mathbf{match}\ M\ \mathbf{with}\ [\mathbf{inl}\, x \to N_1 \mid \mathbf{inr}\, x \to N_2]
\end{aligned}$$

Fig. 1: Syntax.

$$\frac{r \in \mathbb{R}}{\Gamma \vdash \underline{r} : \mathbb{R}} \qquad \frac{\Gamma \vdash M : \mathbb{N}}{\Gamma \vdash M =^? 0 : \mathbb{B}} \qquad \frac{\Gamma \vdash M : \mathbb{R}}{\Gamma \vdash \mathbf{score}\ M : \mathbf{1}} \qquad \frac{\Gamma, x : A \to B \vdash M : A \to B}{\Gamma \vdash \mu x : A \to B.M : A \to B}$$

$$\frac{(f : \mathbb{R}^n \rightharpoonup \mathbb{X}) \in \mathcal{F}}{\Gamma \vdash \underline{f} : \mathbb{R}^n \to \mathbb{X}} \qquad \frac{(\mathbf{dist} : \mathbb{R}^n \to \mathbb{X}) \in \mathcal{D} \quad \text{For } i = 1, \ldots, n,\ \Gamma \vdash M_i : \mathbb{R} \quad \ell \in \mathcal{L}}{\Gamma \vdash \mathbf{sample}_\ell\ \mathbf{dist}(M_1, \ldots, M_n) : \mathbb{X}}$$

Fig. 2: Subset of typing rules.

Terms of the language are typed in the standard way; in Fig. 2 we present a subset of the rules which could be considered non-standard. We use $\mathbb{X}$ to stand for either $\mathbb{N}$ or $\mathbb{R}$, and we do not distinguish between the type and the corresponding measurable space. We also write $\mathbb{B}$ for $\mathbf{1} + \mathbf{1}$, and use syntactic sugar for let-bindings, sequencing, and conditionals:

$$\begin{aligned}
\mathbf{let}\ x : A = M\ \mathbf{in}\ N &:= (\lambda x : A.N)\, M \\
M; N &:= \mathbf{let}\ x : A = M\ \mathbf{in}\ N \quad (\text{for } x \text{ not free in } N) \\
\mathbf{if}\, M\ \mathbf{then}\ N_1\ \mathbf{else}\ N_2 &:= \mathbf{match}\ M\ \mathbf{with}\ [\mathbf{inl}\, x \to N_1 \mid \mathbf{inr}\, x \to N_2]
\end{aligned}$$

3 Programs as event structures

In this section, we introduce our causal approach. We give a series of examples illustrating how programs can be understood as graph-like structures known as *event structures*, of which we assume no prior knowledge. Event structures were introduced by Winskel et al. [46], though for the purposes of this work the traditional notion must be significantly enriched.

[1] In any practical instance of the language it would be expected that every kernel in $\mathcal{D}$ has a density in $\mathcal{F}$, but this is not strictly necessary here.

let weight = **sample**$_{weight}$ **normal**(2, 1) **in**
sample$_{meas_1}$ **normal**(weight, 0.1);
sample$_{meas_2}$ **normal**(weight, 0.1); ()

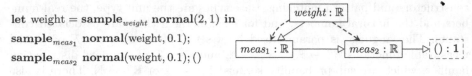

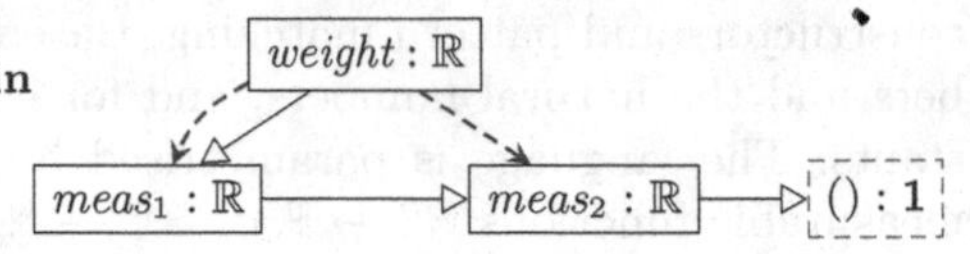

Fig. 3

The examples which follow are designed to showcase the following features of the semantics: combination of data flow and control flow with probability (Sec. 3.1), conditional branching (Sec. 3.2), open programs with multiple arguments (Sec. 3.3) and finally higher-order programs (Sec. 3.4). We will then give further definitions in Sec. 3.5 and Sec. 3.6.

Our presentation in Sec. 3.1 and Sec. 3.2 is intended to be informal; we give all the necessary definitions starting from Sec. 3.3.

3.1 Control flow, data flow, and probability

We briefly recall the example of the introduction; the program and its semantics are given in Fig. 3. As before, $\rightarrowtriangle$ represents control flow, and $\dashrightarrow$ represents data flow. There is a node for each random choice in the program, and the dependency relationships are pictured using the appropriate arrows. Naturally, a data dependency imposes constraints on the control flow: every arrow $\dashrightarrow$ must be realised by a control flow path $\rightarrowtriangle^*$. There is an additional node for the output value, drawn in a dashed box, which indicates that it is a possible point of interaction with other programs. This will be discussed in Sec. 3.3.

Although this is not pictured in the above diagram, the semantics also comprises a family of kernels, modelling the probabilistic execution according to the distributions specified by the program. Intuitively, each node has a distribution whose parameters are its parents for the relation $\dashrightarrow$. For example, the node labelled $meas_2$ will be assigned a kernel $k_{meas_2} : \mathbb{R} \rightsquigarrow \mathbb{R}$ defined so that $k_{meas_2}(weight, -)$ is a normal distribution with parameters $(weight, 0.1)$.

3.2 Branching

Consider a modified scenario in which only one measurement is performed, but with probability 0.01 an error occurs and the scales display a random number between 0 and 10. The corresponding program and its semantics are given in Fig. 4.

In order to represent the conditional statement we have introduced a new element to the graph: a binary relation known as *conflict*, pictured $\rightsquigarrow$, and indicating that two nodes are incompatible and any execution of the program will only encounter one of them. Conflict is *hereditary*, in the sense that the respective futures of two nodes in conflict are also incompatible. Hence we need two copies of (); one for each branch of the conditional statement. Unsurprisingly,

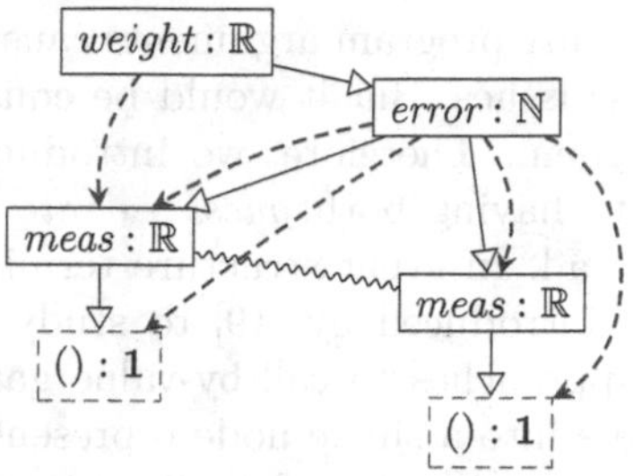

let weight = $\textbf{sample}_{weight}$ **normal**(2, 1) **in**
let error = $\textbf{sample}_{error}$ **bernoulli**(0.01) **in**
if error $=^?$ 0
then $\textbf{sample}_{meas}$ **uniform**(0, 10)
else $\textbf{sample}_{meas}$ **normal**(weight, 0.1); ()

Fig. 4

beyond the branching point all events depend on *error*, since their very existence depends on its value.

We continue our informal presentation with a description of the semantics of open terms. This will provide enough context to formally define the notion of event structure we use in this paper, which differs from others found in the literature.

3.3 Programs with free variables

We turn the example in Sec. 3.2 into one involving two free variables, *guess* and *rate*, used as parameters for the distributions of *weight* and *error*, respectively. These allow the same program to serve as a model for different situations. Formally we have a term M such that $guess : \mathbb{R}, rate : \mathbb{R} \vdash M : \mathbf{1}$, given in Fig. 5 with its semantics. We see that the two parameters are themselves represented

let weight = $\textbf{sample}_{weight}$ **normal**(*guess*, 1) **in**
let error = $\textbf{sample}_{error}$ **bernoulli**(*rate*) **in**
if error $=^?$ 0
then $\textbf{sample}_{meas}$ **uniform**(0, 10)
else $\textbf{sample}_{meas}$ **normal**(weight, 0.1); ()

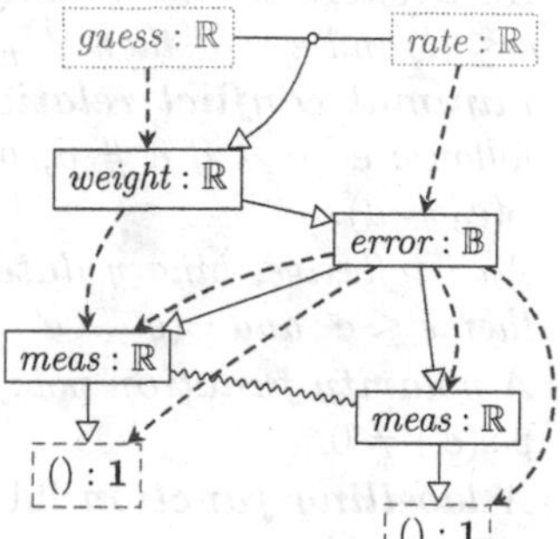

Fig. 5

by nodes, drawn in dotted boxes, showing that (like the output nodes) they are a point of interaction with the program's external environment; this time, a value is received rather than sent. Below, we will distinguish between the different types of nodes by means of a *polarity* function.

We attach to the parameter nodes the appropriate data dependency arrows. The subtlety here is with control flow: while is it clear that parameter values must be obtained before the start of the execution, and that necessarily *guess* $\rightarrow$ *weight* and *rate* $\rightarrow$ *weight*, it is less clear what relationship *guess* and *rate* should have with each other.

In a call-by-value language, we find that leaving program arguments causally independent (of each other) leads to soundness issues. But it would be equally unsound to impose a causal order between them. Therefore, we introduce a form of synchronisation relation, amounting to having both *guess* $\rightarrow$ *rate* and *rate* $\rightarrow$ *guess*, but we write *guess* $\multimapboth$ *rate* instead. In event structure terminology this is known as a *coincidence*, and was introduced by [19] to study the synchronous π-calculus. Note that in many approaches to call-by-value games (*e.g.* [31,26]) one would bundle both parameters into a single node representing the pair (*guess*, *rate*), but this is not suitable here since our data flow analysis requires separate nodes.

We proceed to define event structures, combining the ingredients we have described so far: control dependency, data dependency, conflict, and coincidence, together with a *polarity* function, used implicitly above to distinguish between input nodes (−), output nodes (+), and internal random choices (0).

Definition 1. *An* ***event structure*** *E is a set E of* events *(or* nodes*) together with the following structure:*

- *A* ***control flow preorder*** *$\leq$ on E, and such that each event has a finite history: $\forall e \in E$, the set $[e] := \{e' \in E \mid e' \leq e\}$ is finite. This preorder is designed to be generated from the* ***immediate dependency relation*** *$\rightarrow$ and the* ***coincidence relation*** *$\multimapboth$, which can both be recovered from $\leq$, as follows: we write $e \multimapboth e'$ when e and e' are equivalent in the preorder,* i.e. *$e \leq e'$ and $e' \leq e$; and $e \rightarrow e'$ whenever the following holds: $e < e'$, $\neg(e' > e)$, and if $e \leq d \leq e'$ then either $d \multimapboth e$ or $d \multimapboth e'$; .*
- *An irreflexive, binary* ***conflict relation*** *$\#$ on E, which is* hereditary*: if $e \leq e'$ and $e \# d$ then $e' \# d$. Observe that this applies when $e \multimapboth e'$. The* ***minimal conflict relation*** *$\sim\!\sim$ (typically used in diagrams) is defined as follows: $e \sim\!\sim d$ if $e \# d$, but for every $d_0 < d$ and $e_0 < e$, $\neg(e \# d_0)$ and $\neg(e_0 \# d)$.*
- *An irreflexive, binary* ***data flow relation*** *$\dashrightarrow$ on E, such that if $e \dashrightarrow e'$ then $e \leq e'$ and $\neg(e \multimapboth e')$. Note that this is not required to be transitive.*
- *A* ***polarity function*** *$pol : E \to \{+, 0, -\}$, such that if $e \multimapboth e'$ then $pol(e) = pol(e') \neq 0$.*
- *A* ***labelling function*** *$\mathrm{lbl} : E_0 \to \mathcal{L}$, defined on the set $E_0 := \{e \in E \mid pol(e) = 0\}$.*

Often we write E instead of the whole tuple $(E, \leq, \#, \dashrightarrow, \mathrm{pol})$. It is sometimes useful to quotient out coincidences: we write $E_{\multimapboth}$ for the **set of $\multimapboth$-equivalence classes**, which we denote as boldface letters $(\mathbf{e}, \mathbf{a}, \mathbf{s}, \dots)$. It is easy to check that this is also an event structure with $\mathbf{e} \leq \mathbf{e}'$ (resp. $\#, \dashrightarrow$) if there is $e \in \mathbf{e}$ and $e' \in \mathbf{e}'$ with $e \leq e'$ (resp. $\#, \dashrightarrow$), and evident polarity function.

We will see in Sec. 3.5 how this structure can be equipped with quantitative information (in the form of measurable spaces and kernels). Before discussing higher-order programs, we introduce the fundamental concept of *configuration*, which will play an essential role in the technical development of this paper.

Definition 2. *A **configuration** of E is a finite subset $x \subseteq E$ which is down-closed (if $e \leq e'$ and $e' \in x$ then $e \in x$) and conflict-free (if $e, e' \in x$ then $\neg(e \# e')$). The **set of all configurations** of E is denoted $\mathscr{C}(E)$ and it is a partial order under $\subseteq$.*

We introduce some important terminology. For an event $e \in E$, we have defined its **history** $[e]$ above. This is always a configuration of E, and the smallest one containing e. More generally we can define $[\mathbf{e}] = \{e' \mid \forall e \in \mathbf{e}.\, e' \leq e\}$, and $[\mathbf{e}) = [\mathbf{e}] \setminus \mathbf{e}$.

The **covering relation** $-\!\!\subset$ defines the smallest non-trivial extensions to a configuration; it is defined as follows: $x -\!\!\subset y$ if there is $\mathbf{e} \in E_{\infty}$ such that $x \cap \mathbf{e} = \emptyset$ and $y = x \cup \mathbf{e}$. We will sometimes write $x -\!\!\subset^{\mathbf{e}} y$. We sometimes annotate $-\!\!\subset$ and $\subseteq$ with the polarities of the added events: so for instance $x \subseteq_{+,0} y$ if each $e_i \in y \setminus x$ has polarity $+$ or 0.

3.4 Higher-order programs

We return to a fairly informal presentation; our goal now is to convey intuition about the representation of higher-order programs in the framework of event structures. We will see in Sec. 4 how this representation is obtained from the usual categorical approach to denotational semantics.

Consider yet another faulty-scales scenario, in which the probability of error now depends on the object's weight. Suppose that this dependency is not known by the program, and thus left as a parameter $rate : \mathbb{R} \to \mathbb{R}$. The resulting program has type $rate : \mathbb{R} \to \mathbb{R}, guess : \mathbb{R} \vdash \mathbb{R}$, as follows:

$$\textbf{let } \text{weight} = \textbf{sample}_{weight}\ \textbf{normal}(guess, 1)\ \textbf{in}$$
$$\textbf{let } \text{error} = \textbf{sample}_{error}\ \textbf{bernoulli}\ (rate\ \text{weight})\ \textbf{in}\ \text{error}$$

We give its semantics in Fig. 6. (To keep things simple this scenario involves no measurements.)

It is an important feature of the semantics presented here that higher-order programs are interpreted as causal structures involving only values of ground type. In the example, the argument *rate* is initially received not as a mathematical function, but as a single message of unit type (labelled λ^{rate}), which gives the program the possibility to call the function *rate* by feeding it an input value. Because the behaviour of *rate* is unknown, its output is treated as a new argument to the program, represented by the negative *out* node. The shaded region

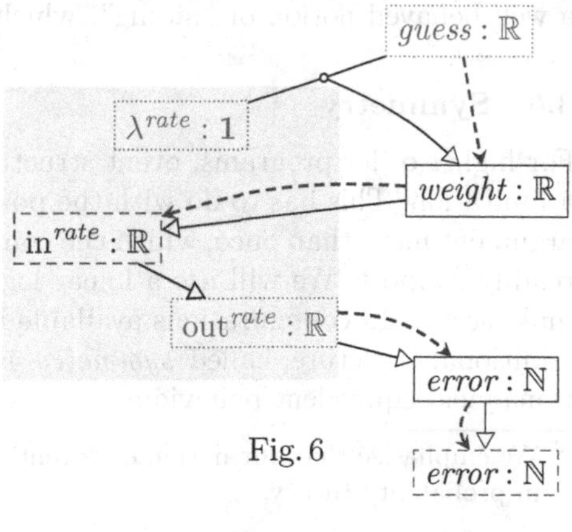

Fig. 6

highlights the part of computation during which the program interacts with its argument *rate*. The semantics accommodates the possibiliy that *rate* itself has internal random choices; this will be accounted for in the compositional framework of Sec. 4.

3.5 Bayesian event structures

We show now that event structures admit a probabilistic enrichment.[2]

Definition 3. *A* ***measurable event structure*** *is an event structure together with the assignment of a measurable space $\mathcal{M}(e)$ for every event $e \in E$. For any $X \subseteq E$ we set $\mathcal{M}(X) = \prod_{e \in X} \mathcal{M}(e)$.*

As is common in statistics, we often call $\underline{e}$ (or $\underline{X}$) an element of $\mathcal{M}(e)$ (or $\mathcal{M}(X)$). We now proceed to equip this with a kernel for each event.

Definition 4. *For E an event structure and $e \in E$, we define the* **parents** $\mathrm{pa}(e)$ *of e as $\{d \in E \mid d \dashrightarrow e\}$.*

Definition 5. *A* ***quantitative event structure*** *is a measurable event structure E with, for every non-negative $e \in E$, a kernel $k_e : \mathcal{M}(\mathrm{pa}(e)) \rightsquigarrow \mathcal{M}(e)$.*

Our *Bayesian* event structures are quantitative event structures satisfying an additional axiom, which we introduce next. This axiom is necessary for a smooth combination of data flow and control flow; without it, the compositional framework of the next section is not possible.

Definition 6. *Let E be a quantitative event structure. We say that $e \in E$ is* ***non-uniform*** *if there are distinct $\underline{\mathrm{pa}}(e), \underline{\mathrm{pa}}'(e) \in \mathcal{M}(\mathrm{pa}(e))$ such that*

$$k_e(\underline{\mathrm{pa}}(e), \mathcal{M}(e)) \neq k_e(\underline{\mathrm{pa}}'(e), \mathcal{M}(e)).$$

We finally define:

Definition 7. *A* ***Bayesian event structure*** *is a quantitative event structure such that if $e \in E$ is non-uniform, and $e \leq e'$ with e and e' not coincident, then $\mathrm{pa}(e) \subseteq \mathrm{pa}(e')$.*

The purpose of this condition is to ensure that Bayesian event structures support a well-behaved notion of "hiding", which we will define in the next section.

3.6 Symmetry

For higher-order programs, event structures in the sense of Definition 1 present a limitation. This has to do with the possibility for a program to call a function argument more than once, which the compositional framework of Sec. 4 does not readily support. We will use a linear logic-inspired "!" to duplicate nodes, thus making certain configurations available in infinitely many copies. The following additional structure, called *symmetry*, is there to enforce that these configurations yield equivalent behaviour.

---

[2] We emphasise that our notion of "event" is *not* related to the usual notion of event in probability theory.

Definition 8 (Winskel [61]). *A **symmetry** on an event structure E is a family $\cong_E$ of bijections $\theta : x \cong y$, with $x, y \in \mathscr{C}(E)$, containing all identity bijections and closed under composition and inverses, satisfying the following axioms.*

- *For each $\theta : x \cong y$ in $\cong_E$, if $x \subseteq x'$ then there is a bijection $\theta' : x' \cong y'$ in $\cong_E$, such that $\theta \subseteq \theta'$. The analogous property is required for every restriction $x' \subseteq x$.*
- *Each $\theta \in \cong_E$ preserves polarity ($pol(e) = pol(\theta(e))$), data flow ($e \dashrightarrow e' \implies \theta(e) \dashrightarrow \theta(e')$), and measurable structure ($\mathcal{M}(e) = \mathcal{M}(\theta(e))$).*

We write $\theta : x \cong_E y$ if $(\theta : x \cong y) \in \cong_E$. When E is Bayesian, we additionally require $k_e = k_{\theta(e)}$ for every non-negative $e \in x$. (This is well-defined because θ preserves data flow and thus $\mathrm{pa}(\theta(\mathbf{e})) = \theta\, \mathrm{pa}(\mathbf{e})$.)

Although symmetry can be mathematically subtle, combining it with additional data on event structures does not usually pose any difficulty [15,48].

In this section we have described Bayesian event structures with symmetry, which are the basic mathematical objects we use to represent programs. A central contribution of this paper is to define a *compositional* semantics, in which the interpretation of a program is obtained from that of its sub-programs. This is the topic of the next section.

4 Games and Bayesian strategies

The presentation is based on *game semantics*, a line of research in the semantics of programming languages initiated in [3,33], though the subject has earlier roots in the semantics of linear logic proofs (e.g. [10]).

It is typical of game semantics that programs are interpreted as concrete computational trees, and that higher-order terms are described in terms of the possible interactions with their arguments. As we have seen in the examples of the previous section, this interaction takes the form of an exchange of first-order values. The central technical achievement of game semantics is to provide a method for *composing* such representations.

To the reader not familiar with game semantics, the terminology may be misleading: the work of this paper hardly retains any connection to game theory. In particular there is no notion of *winning*. The analogy may be understood as follows for a given program of type $\Gamma \vdash M : A$. There are two players: the program itself, and its environment. The "game", which we study from the point of view of the program, takes place in the *arena* $[\![\Gamma \vdash A]\!]$, which specifies which moves are allowed (calls to arguments in Γ, internal samples, return values in A, *etc.*). The semantics of M is a *strategy* (written $[\![M]\!]$), which specifies a plan of action for the program to follow in reaction to the moves played by the environment; this plan has to obey the constraints specified by the arena.

4.1 An introduction to game semantics based on event structures

There are many formulations of game semantics in the literature, with varying advantages. This paper proposes to use *concurrent games*, based on event structures, for reasoning about data flow in probabilistic programs. Originally introduced in [51] (though some important ideas appeared earlier: [25,44]), concurrent games based on event structures have been extensively developed and have found a range of applications.

In Sec. 2, we motivated our approach by assigning event structures to programs; these event structures are examples of *strategies*, which we will shortly define. First we define *arenas*, which are the objects of the category we will eventually build. (The morphisms will be strategies.)

Perhaps surprisingly, an arena is also defined as an event structure, though a much simpler one, with no probabilistic information, empty data dependency relation $\dashrightarrow$, and no neutral polarity events. We call this a **simple event structure**. This event structure does not itself represent any computation, but is simply there to constrain the shape of strategies, just as types constrain programs. Before giving the definition, we present in Fig. 7 the arenas associated with the strategies in Sec. 3.3 and Sec. 3.4, stating which types they represent. Note the **copy indices** (0, 1, ...) in Fig. 7b; these point to duplicated (*i.e. symmetric*) branches.

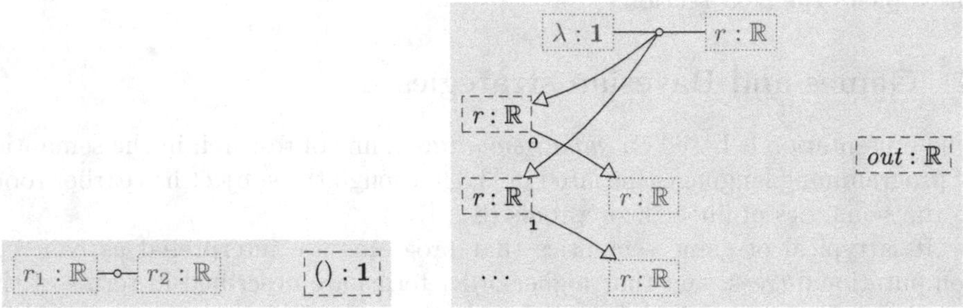

(a) The arena $[\![\mathbb{R}, \mathbb{R} \vdash \mathbf{1}]\!]$. (b) The arena $[\![\mathbb{R} \to \mathbb{R}, \mathbb{R} \vdash \mathbb{R}]\!]$.

Fig. 7: Examples of arenas.

Definition 9. *An* ***arena*** *is a simple, measurable event structure with symmetry $\mathcal{A} = (A, \cong_A)$, together with two sub-symmetries $\cong_A^+$ and $\cong_A^-$, subject to the following conditions:*

- *A is a simple event structure which is* ***alternating****: if $a \rightarrowtriangle b$ then $pol(a) \neq pol(b)$;* ***forest-shaped****: if $a \leq b$ and $c \leq b$ then $a \leq c$ or $c \leq a$ (or both); and* ***race-free****: if $a \rightsquigarrow b$ then $pol(a) = pol(b)$.*
- *$\cong_A$, $\cong_A^-$ and $\cong_A^+$ satisfy the axioms of* thin concurrent games *[17, 3.17].*
- *If a, a' are symmetric moves (*i.e. *there is $\theta \in \cong_A$ such that $\theta(a) = a'$) then $\mathcal{M}(a) = \mathcal{M}(a')$.*

Write $init(A)$ for the set of ***initial events****,* i.e. *those minimal for $\leq$. We say that $\mathcal{A}$ is* ***positive*** *if every $a \in init(A)$ is positive. (****Negative*** *arenas are defined* *similarly.) We say that $\mathcal{A}$ is* **regular** *if whenever $a, b \in init(A)$, either $a \multimap b$ or $a \rightsquigarrow b$.*

So, arenas provide a set of moves together with certain constraints for playing those moves. Our definition of strategy is slightly technical, but the various conditions ensure that strategies can be composed soundly; we will explore this second point in Sec. 4.2.

For a strategy S to be well-defined relative to an arena A, each positive or negative move of S must correspond to a move of A; however neutral moves of S correspond to internal samples of the program; these should not be constrained by the type. Accordingly, a strategy comprises a partial map $S \rightharpoonup A$ defined precisely on the non-neutral events. The reader should be able to reconstruct this map for the examples of Sec. 3.3 and Sec. 3.4.

Definition 10. *A* ***strategy*** *on an arena $\mathcal{A}$ is a Bayesian event structure with symmetry $\mathcal{S} = (S, \cong_S)$, together with a partial function $\sigma : S \rightharpoonup A$, whose domain of definition is exactly the subset $\{s \in S \mid pol(s) \neq 0\}$, and such that whenever $\sigma(s)$ is defined, $\mathcal{M}(\sigma(s)) = \mathcal{M}(s)$ and $pol(\sigma(s)) = pol(s)$. This data is subject to the following additional conditions:*

(1) σ ***preserves configurations****: if $x \in \mathscr{C}(S)$ then $\sigma x \in \mathscr{C}(A)$; and is* ***locally injective****: for $s, s' \in x \in \mathscr{C}(S)$, if $\sigma(s) = \sigma(s')$ then $s = s'$.*
(2) σ is ***courteous****: if $s \twoheadrightarrow s'$ in S and either $pol(s) = +$ or $pol(s') = -$, then $\sigma(s) \twoheadrightarrow \sigma(s')$.*
(3) σ ***preserves symmetry*** *($\theta : x \cong_S y \implies \sigma\theta : \sigma x \cong_A \sigma y$), and it is $\cong$-***receptive***: if $\theta : x \cong_S y$ and $\sigma\theta \multimap\!\!\subset_- \psi \in \cong_A$ then there exists a unique $\theta' \in \cong_S$ such that $\theta \multimap\!\!\subset_- \theta'$ and $\sigma\theta' = \psi$; and* ***thin****: if $x \in \mathscr{C}(S)$ and $\mathrm{id}_x \multimap\!\!\subset_{+,0} \theta$ for some $\theta \in \cong_S$, then $\theta = \mathrm{id}_{x'}$ for some $x' \in \mathscr{C}(S)$.*
(4) If $s \dashrightarrow s'$ in S, then $pol(s') \neq -$ and $pol(s) \neq +$.

Condition (1) amounts to σ being a map of event structures [60]. Combined with (2) and (3), we get the usual notion of a concurrent strategy on an arena with symmetry [17]; and finally (4) is a form of $\dashrightarrow$-courtesy.

To these four conditions we add the following:

Definition 11. *A strategy $\mathcal{S}$ is* ***innocent*** *if conflict is local: $s \rightsquigarrow s' \implies [s) = [s')$, and for every $s \in S$, the following conditions hold:*

– (backwards sequentiality) *the history $[s]$ is a total preorder; and*
– (forward sequentiality) *if $[s] \multimap\!\!\subset^{\mathbf{s}_1}_{0,+}$ and $[s] \multimap\!\!\subset^{\mathbf{s}_2}_{0,+}$ and $\mathbf{s}_1 \neq \mathbf{s}_2$, then $\mathbf{s}_1 \rightsquigarrow \mathbf{s}_2$.*

Innocence [33,56,16] prevents any non-local or concurrent behaviour. It is typically used to characterise "purely functional" sequential programs, *i.e.* those using no state or control features. Here, we use innocence as a way to confine ourselves to a simpler semantic universe. In particular we avoid the need to deal with the difficulties of combining concurrency and probability [62].

In the rest of the paper, a **Bayesian strategy** is an innocent strategy in the sense of Definition 10 and Definition 11.

4.2 Composition of strategies

At this point, we have seen how to define *arenas*, and we have said that the event structures of Sec. 2 arise as *strategies* $\sigma : \mathcal{S} \rightharpoonup \mathcal{A}$ for an arena $\mathcal{A}$. As usual in denotational semantics, these will be obtained compositionally, by induction on the syntax. For this we must move to a categorical setting, in which arenas are objects and strategies are morphisms.

Strategies as morphisms. Before we introduce the notion of strategy *from* $\mathcal{A}$ *to* $\mathcal{B}$ we must introduce some important construction on event structures.

Definition 12. *If* A *is an event structure, its* **dual** $A^\perp$ *is the event structure whose structure is the same as* A *but for polarity, which is defined at* $pol_{A^\perp}(a) = -pol_A(a)$. *(Negative moves become positive, and vice-versa, with neutral moves not affected.) For arenas, we define* $(A, \cong_A, \cong_A^-, \cong_A^+)^\perp = (A^\perp, \cong_A, \cong_A^+, \cong_A^-)$.

Given a family $(\mathcal{A}_i)_{i\in I}$ *of event structures with symmetry, we define their* ***parallel composition*** *to have events* $\|_{i\in I} A_i = \bigcup_{i\in I} A_i \times \{i\}$ *with polarity, conflict and both kinds of dependency obtained componentwise. Noticing that a configuration* $x \in \mathscr{C}(\|_{i\in I} A_i)$ *corresponds to* $\|_{i\in I} x_i$ *where each* $x_i \in \mathscr{C}(A_i)$, *and* $x_i = \emptyset$ *for all but finitely many* i, *we define the symmetry* $\cong_{\|_{i\in I} A_i}$ *to contain bijections* $\|_i \theta_i : \|_i x_i \cong \|_i y_i$ *where each* $\theta_i \in \cong_{A_i}$. *If the* $\mathcal{A}_i$ *are arenas we define the two other symmetries in the same way.*

We can now define our morphisms: a **strategy from** $\mathcal{A}$ **to** $\mathcal{B}$ is a strategy on the arena $\mathcal{A}^\perp \parallel \mathcal{B}$, *i.e.* a map $\sigma : \mathcal{S} \rightharpoonup \mathcal{A}^\perp \parallel \mathcal{B}$. The event structure S consists of A-*moves* (those mapped to the $A^\perp$ component), B-*moves*, and internal (*i.e.* neutral) events. We sometimes write $\mathcal{S} : A \nrightarrow B$.

The purpose of the composition operation $\odot$ which we proceed to define is therefore to produce, from a pair of strategies $\sigma : \mathcal{S} \rightharpoonup \mathcal{A}^\perp \parallel \mathcal{B}$ and $\tau : \mathcal{T} \rightharpoonup \mathcal{B}^\perp \parallel \mathcal{C}$, a strategy $\tau \odot \sigma : \mathcal{T} \odot \mathcal{S} \rightharpoonup \mathcal{A}^\perp \parallel \mathcal{C}$. A constant feature of denotational games models is that composition is defined in two steps: *interaction*, in which $\mathcal{S}$ and $\mathcal{T}$ synchronise by playing matching B-moves, and *hiding*, where the matching pairs of events are deleted. The setting of this paper allows both σ and τ to be partial maps, so that in general there can be neutral events in both $\mathcal{S}$ and $\mathcal{T}$; these *never* synchronise, and indeed they should not be hidden, since we aim to give an account of internal sampling.

Before moving on to composition, a word of warning: the resulting structure will *not* be a category. Instead, arenas and strategies assemble into a weaker structure called a *bicategory* [6]. Bicategories have objects, morphisms, and *2-cells* (morphisms between morphisms), and the associativity and identity laws are relaxed, and only need to hold up to isomorphisms. (This situation is relatively common for intensional models of non-determinism.)

Definition 13. *Two strategies* $\sigma : \mathcal{S} \rightharpoonup \mathcal{A}^\perp \parallel \mathcal{B}$ *and* $\sigma' : \mathcal{S}' \rightharpoonup \mathcal{A}^\perp \parallel \mathcal{B}$ *are* ***isomorphic*** *if there is a bijection* $f : S \cong S'$ *preserving all structure, and such that for every* $x \in \mathscr{C}(S)$, *the bijection with graph* $\{(\sigma(s), \sigma'(f(s))) \mid s \in x\}$ *is in* $\cong_A^+$.

Intuitively, $\mathcal{S}$ and $\mathcal{S}'$ have the same moves up to the choice of copy indices. We know from [17] that isomorphism is preserved by composition (and all other constructions), so from now on we always consider strategies up to isomorphism; then we will get a category.

Interaction. In what follows we assume fixed Bayesian innocent strategies $\mathcal{S} : \mathcal{A} \nrightarrow \mathcal{B}$ and $\mathcal{T} : \mathcal{B} \nrightarrow \mathcal{C}$ as above, and study their interaction. We have hinted at the concept of "matching events" but the more convenient notion is that of *matching configurations*, which we define next.

Definition 14. *Configurations $x_S \in \mathscr{C}(S)$ and $x_T \in \mathscr{C}(T)$ are* **matching** *if there are $x_A \in \mathscr{C}(A)$ and $x_C \in \mathscr{C}(C)$ such that $\sigma x_S \parallel x_C = x_A \parallel \tau x_T$.*

There is an event structure with symmetry $\mathcal{T} \circledast \mathcal{S}$ whose configurations correspond precisely to matching pairs; it is a well-known fact in game semantics that innocent strategies compose "like relations" [43,15]. Because "matching" B-moves have a different polarity in $\mathcal{S}$ and $\mathcal{T}$, there is an ambiguity in the polarity of some events in $T \circledast S$; we address this after the lemma.

Lemma 1. *Ignoring polarity, there is, up to isomorphism, a unique event structure with symmetry $\mathcal{T} \circledast \mathcal{S}$, such that:*

- *There is an order-isomorphism $\mathscr{C}(T \circledast S) \cong \{(x_S, x_T) \in \mathscr{C}(S) \times \mathscr{C}(T) \mid x_S \text{ and } x_T \text{ matching}\}$. Write $x_T \circledast x_S$ for the configuration corresponding to (x_S, x_T).*
- *There are partial functions $\Pi_S : T \circledast S \rightharpoonup S$ and $\Pi_T : T \circledast S \rightharpoonup T$, such that for every $x_T \circledast x_S \in \mathscr{C}(T \circledast S)$, $\Pi_S(x_T \circledast x_S) = x_S$ and $\Pi_S(x_T \circledast x_S) = x_T$.*
- *For every $e, e' \in T \circledast S$, $e \rightarrow e'$ iff either $\Pi_S(e) \rightarrow \Pi_S(e')$ or $\Pi_T(e) \rightarrow \Pi_T(e')$, and the same property holds for the conflict and data dependency relations.*
- *Π_S and Π_T preserve and reflect labels.*
- *A bijection $\theta : x_T \circledast x_S \cong y_T \circledast y_S$ is in $\cong_{T \circledast S}$ if both $\Pi_T \theta : x_T \cong_T y_T$ and $\Pi_S \theta : x_S \cong_S y_S$.*

Furthermore, for every $e \in T \circledast S$, at least one of $\Pi_S(e)$ and $\Pi_T(e)$ is defined.

When reasoning about the polarity of events in $T \circledast S$, a subtlety arises because B-moves are not assigned the same polarity in $\mathcal{S}$ and $\mathcal{T}$. This is not surprising: polarity is there precisely to allow strategies to communicate by sending $(+)$ and receiving $(-)$ values; in this interaction, $\mathcal{S}$ and $\mathcal{T}$ play complementary roles. To reason about the flow of information in the event structure $\mathcal{T} \circledast \mathcal{S}$ it will be important, for each B-move e of $T \circledast S$, to know whether it is positive in $\mathcal{S}$ or in $\mathcal{T}$; in other words, whether information is flowing *from $\mathcal{S}$ to $\mathcal{T}$*, or vice-versa.

Accordingly, we define $\mathrm{pol}^{\circledast} : T \circledast S \to \{+^{\mathcal{S}}, +^{\mathcal{T}}, 0^{\mathcal{S}}, 0^{\mathcal{T}}, -\}$, as follows:

$$\mathrm{pol}^{\circledast}(e) = \begin{cases} +^{\mathcal{S}} \text{ (resp. } 0^{\mathcal{S}}) & \text{if } \Pi_S(e) \text{ is defined and } \mathrm{pol}(\Pi_S(e)) = + \text{ (resp. 0)} \\ +^{\mathcal{T}} \text{ (resp. } 0^{\mathcal{T}}) & \text{if } \Pi_T(e) \text{ is defined and } \mathrm{pol}(\Pi_T(e)) = + \text{ (resp. 0)}, \\ - & \text{otherwise.} \end{cases}$$

Probability in the interaction. Unlike with polarity, $\mathcal{S}$ and $\mathcal{T}$ agree on what measurable space to assign to each B-move, since by the conditions on strategies, this is determined by the arena. So for each $e \in T \circledast S$ we can set $\mathcal{M}(e) = \mathcal{M}(\Pi_S(e))$ or $\mathcal{M}(\Pi_T(e))$, unambiguously, and an easy argument shows that this makes $\mathcal{T} \circledast \mathcal{S}$ a well-defined *measurable* event structure with symmetry.

We can turn $\mathcal{T} \circledast \mathcal{S}$ into a quantitative event structure by defining a kernel $k_e^{\circledast} : \mathcal{M}(\mathrm{pa}^{\circledast}(e)) \rightsquigarrow \mathcal{M}(e)$ for every $e \in T \circledast S$ such that $\mathrm{pol}^{\circledast}(e) \neq -$. The key observation is that when $\mathrm{pol}^{\circledast}(e) \in \{+^S, 0^S\}$, the parents of e correspond precisely to the parents of $\Pi_S(e)$ in $\mathcal{S}$. Since Π_S preserves the measurable space associated to an event, we may then take $k_e^{\circledast} = k_{\Pi_S(e)}$.

Hiding. Hiding is the process of deleting the B-moves from $T \circledast S$, yielding a strategy from $\mathcal{A}$ to $\mathcal{C}$. The B-moves are exactly those on which both projections are defined, so the new set of events is obtained as follows:

$$T \odot S = \{e \in T \circledast S \mid \Pi_S(e) \text{ and } \Pi_T(e) \text{ are not both defined}\}.$$

This set inherits a preorder $\leq$, conflict relation $\#$, and measurable structure directly from $T \circledast S$. Polarity is lifted from either S or T via the projections. (Note that by removing the B-moves we resolved the mismatch.) To define the data flow dependency, we must take care to ensure that the resulting $T \odot S$ is Bayesian. For $e, e' \in T \odot S$, we say $e \dashrightarrow e'$ if one of the following holds:

(1) There exist $n \geq 0$ and $e_1, \ldots, e_n \in T \circledast S$, all B-moves, such that $e \dashrightarrow e_1 \dashrightarrow \cdots \dashrightarrow e_n \dashrightarrow e'$ (in $T \circledast S$).
(2) There exist a non-uniform $\mathbf{d} \in T \circledast S$, $n \geq 0$ and $e_1, \ldots, e_n \in T \circledast S$, all B-moves, such that such that $e \dashrightarrow e_1 \dashrightarrow \cdots \dashrightarrow e_n \dashrightarrow \mathbf{d}$ and $\mathbf{d} \leq e'$.

From a configuration $x \in \mathscr{C}(T \odot S)$ we can recover the hidden moves to get an **interaction witness** $\overline{x} = \{e \in T \circledast S \mid e \leq e' \in x\}$, a configuration of $\mathscr{C}(T \circledast S)$. For $x, y \in \mathscr{C}(T \odot S)$, a bijection $\theta : x \cong y$ is in $\cong_{T \odot S}$ if there is $\overline{\theta} : \overline{x} \cong_{T \circledast S} \overline{y}$ which restricts to θ. This gives a measurable event structure with symmetry $\mathcal{T} \odot \mathcal{S}$.

To make $\mathcal{T} \odot \mathcal{S}$ a Bayesian event structure, we must define for every $e \in T \odot S$ a kernel k_e, which we denote $k_e^{\odot}$ to emphasise the difference with the kernel $k_e^{\circledast}$ defined above. Indeed the parents $\mathrm{pa}^{\circledast}(e)$ of e in $T \circledast S$ may no longer exist in $T \odot S$, where e has a different set of parents $\mathrm{pa}^{\odot}(e)$.

We therefore consider the subset of hidden ancestors of $\mathbf{e}$ which ought to affect the kernel $k_e^{\odot}$:

Definition 15. *For strategies $\mathcal{S} : \mathcal{A} \nrightarrow \mathcal{B}$ and $\mathcal{T} : \mathcal{B} \nrightarrow \mathcal{C}$, and $e \in T \odot S$, an* ***essential hidden ancestor*** *of e is a B-move $d \in T \circledast S$, such that $d \leq e$ and one of the following holds:*

(1) There are $e_1 \in \mathrm{pa}^{\odot}(e), e_2 \in \mathrm{pa}^{\circledast}(e)$ such that $e_1 \dashrightarrow \cdots \dashrightarrow d \dashrightarrow \cdots \dashrightarrow e_2$.
(2) There are $e_0 \in \mathrm{pa}^{\odot}(e)$, B-moves d' and $e_1, \ldots, e_n$, with d' non-uniform, such that $e_0 \dashrightarrow e_1 \dashrightarrow \cdots \dashrightarrow e_j \dashrightarrow d \dashrightarrow e_{j+1} \dashrightarrow \cdots \dashrightarrow e_n \dashrightarrow d'$.

Since $\mathcal{T} \odot \mathcal{S}$ is innocent, e has a sequential history, and thus the set of essential hidden ancestors of e forms a finite, total preorder, for which there exists a linear enumeration $d_1 \leq \cdots \leq d_n$. We then define $k_e^{\odot} : \mathcal{M}(\mathrm{pa}(e)) \rightsquigarrow \mathcal{M}(e)$ as follows:

$$k_e^{\odot}(\underline{\mathrm{pa}}^{\odot}(e), U) = \int_{\underline{d}_1} k(\underline{\mathrm{pa}}^{\circledast}(d_1), \mathrm{d}\underline{d}_1) \cdots \int_{\underline{d}_n} k(\underline{\mathrm{pa}}^{\circledast}(d_n), \mathrm{d}\underline{d}_n)\ [k_e^{\circledast}(\underline{\mathrm{pa}}^{\circledast}(e), U)]$$

where we abuse notation: using that for every $i \leq n$, $\mathrm{pa}^{\circledast}(d_i) \subseteq \mathrm{pa}^{\odot}(e) \cup \{d_j \mid j < i\}$, we may write $\underline{\mathrm{pa}}^{\circledast}(d_i)$ for the only element of $\mathcal{M}(\mathrm{pa}^{\circledast}(d_i))$ compatible with $\underline{\mathrm{pa}}^{\odot}(e)$ and $\underline{d}_1, \ldots, \underline{d}_{i-1}$. The particular choice of linear enumeration does not matter by Fubini's theorem for s-finite kernels.

Lemma 2. *There is a map $\tau \odot \sigma : \mathcal{T} \odot \mathcal{S} \rightharpoonup \mathcal{A}^{\perp} \parallel \mathcal{C}$ making $\mathcal{T} \odot \mathcal{S}$ a Bayesian strategy. We call this the* ***composition*** *of $\mathcal{S}$ and $\mathcal{T}$.*

Copycat. We have defined morphisms between arenas, and how they compose. We now define identities, called *copycat strategies.* In the semantics of our language, these are used to interpret typing judgements of the form $x : A \vdash x : A$, and the copycat acts by forwarding values received on one side across to the other. To guide the intuition, the copycat strategy for the game $[\![\mathbb{R}]\!] \multimap [\![\mathbb{R}]\!]$ is pictured in Fig. 8. (We will define the $\multimap$ construction later.)

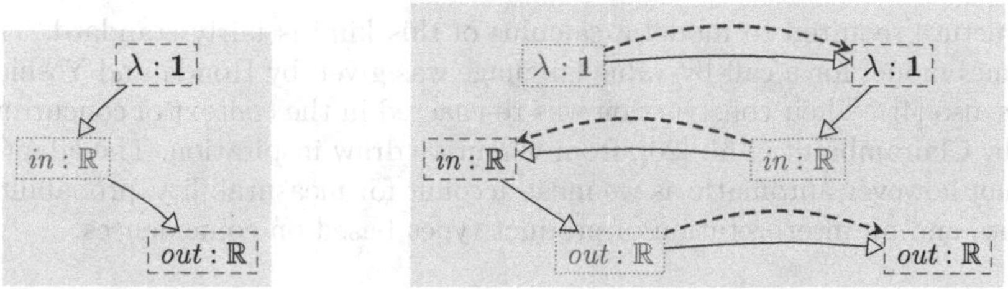

(a) (b)

Fig. 8: The arena $[\![\mathbb{R}]\!] \multimap [\![\mathbb{R}]\!]$ (a), and the copycat strategy on it (b).

Formally, the copycat strategy on an arena $\mathcal{A}$ is a Bayesian event structure (with symmetry) $\mathbb{C}_{\mathcal{A}}$, together with a (total) map $\mathbb{c}_{\mathcal{A}} : \mathbb{C}_{\mathcal{A}} \to \mathcal{A}^{\perp} \parallel \mathcal{A}$. As should be clear in the example of Fig. 8, the events, polarity, conflict, and measurable structure of $\mathbb{C}_A$ are those of $A^{\perp} \parallel A$. The order $\leq$ is the transitive closure of that in $A^{\perp} \parallel A$ enriched with the pairs $\{((a,1),(a,2)) \mid a \in A \text{ and } \mathrm{pol}_A(a) = +\} \cup \{((a,2),(a,1)) \mid \mathrm{pol}_A(a) = -\}$. The same sets of pairs also make up the data dependency relation in $\mathbb{C}_A$; recall that there is no data dependency in the event structure A. Note that because $\mathbb{C}_A$ is just $A^{\perp} \parallel A$ with added constraints, configurations of $\mathbb{C}_A$ can be seen as a subset of those of $A^{\perp} \parallel A$, and thus the symmetry $\cong_{\mathbb{C}_A}$ is inherited from $\cong_{A^{\perp} \parallel A}$.

To make copycat a Bayesian strategy, we observe that for every positive $e \in \mathbb{C}_A$, $\mathrm{pa}(e)$ contains a single element, the correponding negative move in $A^\perp \parallel A$, which carries the same measurable space. Naturally, we take $k_e : \mathcal{M}(e) \rightsquigarrow \mathcal{M}(e)$ to be the identity kernel.

We have defined objects, morphisms, composition, and identities. They assemble into a category.

Theorem 1. *Arenas and Bayesian strategies, with the latter considered up to isomorphism, form a category* **BG**. **BG** *has a subcategory* $\mathbf{BG}^+$ *whose objects are positive, regular arenas and whose morphisms are* ***negative strategies*** *(*i.e. *strategies whose inital moves are negative), up to isomorphism.*

The restriction implies (using receptivity) that for every strategy $\mathcal{A} \nrightarrow \mathcal{B}$ in $\mathbf{BG}^+$, initial moves of $\mathcal{S}$ correspond to $\mathrm{init}(A)$. This reflects the dynamics of a call-by-value language, where arguments are received before anything else. We now set out to define the semantics of our language in $\mathbf{BG}^+$.

5 A denotational model

In Sec. 5.1, we describe some abstract constructions in the category, which provide the necessary ingredients for interpreting types and terms in Sec. 5.2.

5.1 Categorical structure

The structure required to model a calculus of this kind is fairly standard. The first games model for a call-by-value language was given by Honda and Yoshida [31] (see also [4]). Their construction was re-enacted in the context of concurrent games by Clairambault et al. [20], from whom we draw inspiration. The adaptation is not however automatic as we must account for measurability, probability, data flow, and an interpretation of product types based on coincidences.

Coproducts. Given arenas $\mathcal{A}$ and $\mathcal{B}$, their **sum** $\mathcal{A}+\mathcal{B}$ has events those of $A \parallel B$, and inherited polarity, preorder, and measurable structure, but the conflict relation is extended so that $a \# b$ for every $a \in A$ and $b \in B$. The symmetries $\cong_{A+B}, \cong^-_{A+B}$ and $\cong^+_{A+B}$ are restricted from $\cong_{A\parallel B}, \cong^-_{A\parallel B}$ and $\cong^+_{A\parallel B}$.

The arena $\mathcal{A}+\mathcal{B}$ is a coproduct of $\mathcal{A}$ and $\mathcal{B}$ in $\mathbf{BG}^+$. This means that there are injections $\iota_\mathcal{A} : \mathcal{A} \nrightarrow \mathcal{A}+\mathcal{B}$ and $\iota_\mathcal{B} : \mathcal{B} \nrightarrow \mathcal{A}+\mathcal{B}$ behaving as copycat on the appropriate component, and that any two strategies $\sigma : \mathcal{A} \nrightarrow \mathcal{C}$ and $\tau : \mathcal{B} \nrightarrow \mathcal{C}$ induce a unique co-pairing strategy denoted $[\sigma, \tau] : \mathcal{A}+\mathcal{B} \nrightarrow \mathcal{C}$. This construction can be performed for any arity, giving coproducts $\sum_{i \in I} \mathcal{A}_i$.

Tensor. Tensor products are more subtle, partly because in this paper we use *coincidence* to deal with pairs, as motivated in Sec. 3.3. For example, given two arenas each having a single initial move, we construct their tensor product by taking their parallel composition and making the two initial moves coincident.

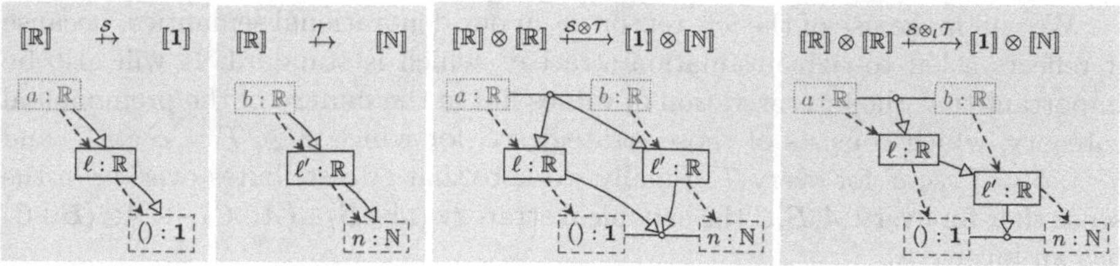

Fig. 9: Example of tensor construction.

More generally, suppose $\mathcal{A}$ and $\mathcal{B}$ are arenas in which all inital events are coincident; we call these **elementary arenas.** Then $A \otimes B$ has all structure inherited from $A \parallel B$, and additionally we set $a \multimapdot b$ for every $a \in \text{init}(A)$ and $b \in \text{init}(B)$. Since $\mathscr{C}(A \otimes B) \subseteq \mathscr{C}(A \parallel B)$, we can define symmetries on $A \otimes B$ by restricting those in $A \parallel B$.

Now, because arenas in $\mathbf{BG}^+$ are *regular* (Definition 9), it is easy to see that each $\mathcal{A}$ is isomorphic to a sum $\sum_{i \in I} \mathcal{A}_i$ with each $\mathcal{A}_i$ elementary. If $\mathcal{B} \in \mathbf{BG}^+$ is isomorphic to $\sum_{j \in J} \mathcal{B}_j$ with the $\mathcal{B}_j$ elementary, we define $\mathcal{A} \otimes \mathcal{B} = \sum_{i,j} \mathcal{A}_i \otimes \mathcal{B}_j$.

In order to give semantics to pairs of terms, we must define the action of $\otimes$ of strategies. Consider two strategies $\sigma : \mathcal{S} \rightharpoonup \mathcal{A}^\perp \parallel \mathcal{A}'$ and $\tau : \mathcal{T} \rightharpoonup \mathcal{B}^\perp \parallel \mathcal{B}'$. Let $\sigma \parallel \tau : \mathcal{S} \parallel \mathcal{T} \rightharpoonup (\mathcal{A} \parallel \mathcal{B})^\perp \parallel (\mathcal{A}' \parallel \mathcal{B}')$ be defined in the obvious way from σ and τ (note the codomain was rearranged). We observe that $\mathscr{C}((\mathcal{A} \otimes \mathcal{B})^\perp \parallel (\mathcal{A}' \otimes \mathcal{B}')) \subseteq \mathscr{C}((\mathcal{A} \parallel \mathcal{B})^\perp \parallel (\mathcal{A}' \parallel \mathcal{B}'))$ and show:

Lemma 3. *Up to symmetry, there is a unique event structure $S \otimes T$ such that $\mathscr{C}(S \otimes T) = \{x \in \mathscr{C}(S \parallel T) \mid (\sigma \parallel \tau)\, x \in \mathscr{C}((\mathcal{A} \otimes \mathcal{B})^\perp \parallel (\mathcal{A}' \otimes \mathcal{B}'))\}$ and such that polarity, labelling, and data flow are lifted from $S \parallel T$ via a projection function $S \otimes T \to S \parallel T$.*

Informally, the strategies synchronise at the start, *i.e.* all initial moves are received at the same time, and they synchronise again when they are both ready to move to the $\mathcal{A}' \otimes \mathcal{B}'$ side for the first time.

The operations $- \otimes \mathcal{B}$ and $\mathcal{A} \otimes -$ on $\mathbf{BG}^+$ define functors. However, as is typically the case for models of call-by-value, the tensor fails to be *bifunctorial*, and thus $\mathbf{BG}^+$ is not monoidal but only *premonoidal* [50]. The unit for $\otimes$ is the arena $\mathbf{1}$ with one (positive) event $() : \mathbf{1}$. There are "copycat-like" associativity, unit and braiding strategies, which we omit.

The failure of bifunctoriality in this setting means that for $\sigma : \mathcal{A} \nrightarrow \mathcal{A}'$ and $\tau : \mathcal{B} \nrightarrow \mathcal{B}'$, the strategy $\mathcal{S} \otimes \mathcal{T}$ is in general distinct from the following two strategies:

$$\mathcal{S} \otimes_l \mathcal{T} = (\mathbb{C}_{\mathcal{A}'} \otimes \mathcal{T}) \odot (\mathcal{S} \otimes \mathbb{C}_{\mathcal{B}}) \qquad \mathcal{S} \otimes_r \mathcal{T} = (\mathcal{S} \otimes \mathbb{C}_{\mathcal{B}'}) \odot (\mathbb{C}_{\mathcal{A}} \otimes \mathcal{T})$$

See Fig. 9 for an example of the $\otimes$ and $\otimes_l$ constructions on simple strategies. Observe that the data flow relation is *not* affected by the choice of tensor: this is related to our discussion of commutativity in Sec. 1.1: a commutative semantics is one that satisfies $\otimes_l = \otimes_r = \otimes$.

We will make use of the left tensor $\otimes_l$ in our denotational semantics, because it reflects a left-to-right evaluation strategy, which is standard. It will also be important that the interpretation of values lies in the **centre** of the premonoidal category, which consists of those strategies $\mathcal{S}$ for which $\mathcal{S} \otimes_l \mathcal{T} = \mathcal{S} \otimes_r \mathcal{T}$ and $\mathcal{T} \otimes_l \mathcal{S} = \mathcal{T} \otimes_r \mathcal{S}$ for every $\mathcal{T}$. Finally we note that $\otimes$ distributes over $+$, in the sense that for every $\mathcal{A}, \mathcal{B}, \mathcal{C}$ the canonical strategy $(\mathcal{A}\otimes\mathcal{B})+(\mathcal{A}\otimes\mathcal{C}) \nrightarrow \mathcal{A}\otimes(\mathcal{B}+\mathcal{C})$ has an inverse λ.

Function spaces. We now investigate the construction of arenas of the form $\mathcal{A} \multimap \mathcal{B}$. This is a *linear* function space construction, allowing at most one call to the argument $\mathcal{A}$; in Sec. 5.1 we will construct an extended arena $!(\mathcal{A} \multimap \mathcal{B})$ permitting arbitrary usage. Given $\mathcal{A}$ and $\mathcal{B}$ we construct $\mathcal{A} \multimap \mathcal{B}$ as follows. (This construction is the same as in other call-by-value game semantics, *e.g.* [31,20].) Recall that we can write $\mathcal{A} = \sum_{i \in I} \mathcal{A}_i$ with each $\mathcal{A}_i$ an elementary arena. Then, $A \multimap B$ has the same set of events as $\mathbf{1} \parallel \sum_{i \in I}(A_i^{\perp} \parallel \mathcal{B})$, with inherited polarity and measurable structure, but with a preorder enriched with the pairs $\{(\lambda, a) \mid a \in \mathrm{init}(A)\} \cup \{(a_i, (i, b)) \mid a \in \mathrm{init}(A_i), b \in \mathrm{init}(B)\}$, where in this case we call λ the unique move of $\mathbf{1}$.

For every strategy $\sigma : \mathcal{A} \otimes \mathcal{B} \nrightarrow \mathcal{C}$ we call $\Lambda(\sigma) : \mathcal{A} \nrightarrow \mathcal{B} \multimap \mathcal{C}$ the strategy which, upon receiving an opening $\mathcal{A}$-move (or coincidence) $\mathbf{a}$, deterministically (and with no data-flow link) plays the move λ in $\mathcal{B} \multimap \mathcal{C}$, waits for Opponent to play a B-move (or coincidence) $\mathbf{b}$ and continues as σ would on input $\mathbf{a} \multimap \mathbf{b}$. Additionally there is for every $\mathcal{B}$ and $\mathcal{C}$ an evaluation morphism $\mathrm{ev}_{\mathcal{B},\mathcal{C}} : (\mathcal{B} \multimap \mathcal{C}) \otimes \mathcal{B} \nrightarrow \mathcal{C}$ defined as in [20].

Lemma 4. *For a strategy $\sigma : \mathcal{A} \otimes \mathcal{B} \nrightarrow \mathcal{C}$, the strategy $\Lambda(\sigma)$ is central and satisfies* $\mathrm{ev} \odot (\Lambda(\sigma) \otimes \mathrm{cc}) = \sigma$.

Duplication. We define, for every arena $\mathcal{A}$, a "reusable" arena $!\mathcal{A}$. Its precise purpose will become clear when we define the semantics of our language. It is helpful to start with the observation that ground type values are readily duplicable, in the sense that there is a strategy $[\![\mathbb{R}]\!] \nrightarrow [\![\mathbb{R}]\!] \otimes [\![\mathbb{R}]\!]$ in **BG**. Therefore ! will have no effect on $[\![\mathbb{R}]\!]$, but only on more sophisticated arenas (*e.g.* $[\![\mathbb{R}]\!] \multimap [\![\mathbb{R}]\!]$) for which no such (well-behaved) map exists. We start by studying *negative* arenas.

Definition 16. *Let $\mathcal{A}$ be a* negative *arena. We define $!\mathcal{A}$ to be the measurable event structure $!A = \parallel_{i \in \omega} A$, equipped with the following symmetries:*

- *$\cong_{!A}$ contains those $\theta : \parallel_{i \in \omega} x_i \cong \parallel_{i \in \omega} y_i$ for which there is $\pi : \omega \cong \omega$ and $\theta_i : x_i \cong_{A_i} x_{\pi(i)}$ such that $\theta(a, i) = (\theta_i(a), \pi(i))$ for each $(a, i) \in !A$.*
- *$\cong_{!A}^-$ contains bijections $\theta : x \cong_{!A} y$ such that for each $i \in \omega$, $\theta_i : x_i \cong_A^- y_{\pi(i)}$.*
- *$\cong_{!A}^+$ contains bijections $\theta : x \cong_{!A} y$ s.t. $\pi = \mathrm{id}$ and for each i, $\theta_i : x_i \cong_A^+ y_i$.*

It can be shown that $!\mathcal{A}$ is a well-defined negative arena, *i.e.* meets the conditions of Definition 9. Observe that an elementary *positive* arena $\mathcal{B}$ corresponds precisely to a set $\mathbf{e}$ of coincident positive events, all initial for $\rightarrow$, immediately followed by a negative arena which we call $\mathcal{B}_-$. *Followed* here means that $e \leq b$

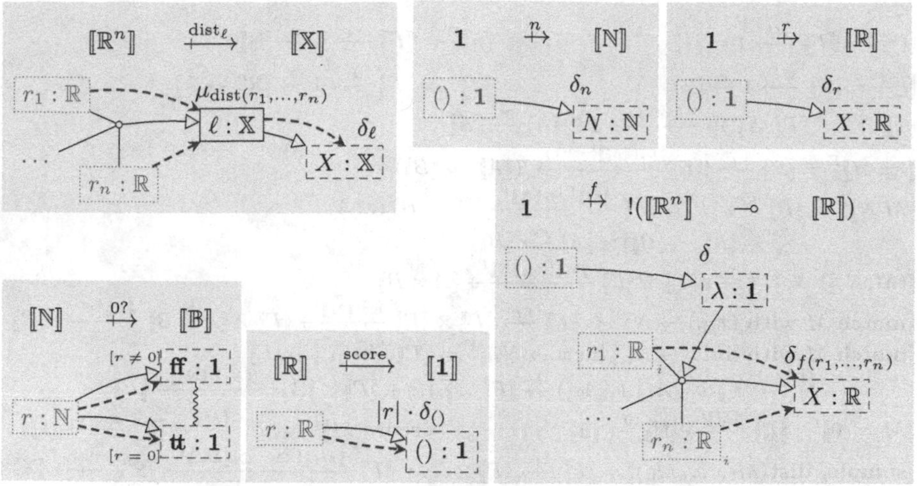

Fig. 10: Constant strategies. (The copy indices i in f indicate that we have ω symmetric branches.)

for all $e \in \mathbf{e}$ and $b \in B_-$, and we write $\mathcal{B} = \mathbf{e} \cdot \mathcal{B}_-$. We define $!\mathcal{B} = \mathbf{e} \cdot !\mathcal{B}_-$. Finally, recall that an arbitrary positive arena $\mathcal{B}$ can be written as a sum of elementary ones: $\mathcal{B} = \sum_{i \in I} \mathcal{B}_i$. We then define $!\mathcal{B} = \sum_{i \in I} !\mathcal{B}_i$.

For positive $\mathcal{A}$ and $\mathcal{B}$, a *central* strategy $\sigma : \mathcal{A} \nrightarrow \mathcal{B}$ induces a strategy $!\sigma : !\mathcal{A} \nrightarrow !\mathcal{B}$, and this is functorial. The functor ! extends to a linear exponential comonad on the category with elementary arenas as objects and central strategies as morphisms (see [20] for the details of a similar construction).

Recursion. To interpret fixed points, we consider an ordering relation on strategies. We momentarily break our habit of considering strategies up to isomorphism, as in this instance it becomes technically inconvenient [17].

Definition 17. *If $\sigma : \mathcal{S} \rightharpoonup \mathcal{A}$ and $\tau : \mathcal{T} \rightharpoonup \mathcal{A}$ are strategies, we write $\mathcal{S} \sqsubseteq \mathcal{T}$ if $\mathcal{S} \subseteq \mathcal{T}$, the inclusion map is a map of event structures, preserves all structure, including kernels, and for every $s \in \mathcal{S}$, $\sigma(s) = \tau(s)$.*

Lemma 5. *Every ω-chain $\mathcal{S}_0 \sqsubseteq \mathcal{S}_1 \sqsubseteq \ldots$ has a least upper bound $\bigvee_{i \in \omega} \mathcal{S}_i$, given by the union $\bigcup_{i \in \omega} \mathcal{S}_i$, with all structure obtained by componentwise union.*

There is also a least strategy $\perp$ on every arena, unique up to isomorphism. We are now ready to give the semantics of our language.

5.2 Denotational semantics

The interpretation of types is as follows:

$$[\![\mathbf{1}]\!] = \boxed{() : \mathbf{1}} \qquad [\![\mathbb{R}]\!] = \boxed{a : \mathbb{R}} \qquad [\![\mathbb{N}]\!] = \boxed{a : \mathbb{N}}$$

$$
\begin{array}{ll}
[\![()]\!]^{\Gamma} = [\![\Gamma]\!] \xrightarrow{\mathrm{w}_\Gamma} \mathbf{1} = [\![\mathbf{1}]\!] & [\![\underline{n}]\!]^{\Gamma} = [\![\Gamma]\!] \xrightarrow{\mathrm{w}_\Gamma} \mathbf{1} \xrightarrow{n} [\![\mathbb{N}]\!] \\
[\![\underline{r}]\!]^{\Gamma} = [\![\Gamma]\!] \xrightarrow{\mathrm{w}_\Gamma} \mathbf{1} \xrightarrow{r} [\![\mathbb{R}]\!] & [\![\underline{f}]\!]^{\Gamma} = [\![\Gamma]\!] \xrightarrow{\mathrm{w}_\Gamma} \mathbf{1} \xrightarrow{f} [\![\mathbb{R}^n \to \mathbb{R}]\!]
\end{array}
$$

$$
\begin{aligned}
&[\![x]\!]^{\Gamma, x:A} = [\![\Gamma]\!] \otimes [\![A]\!] \xrightarrow{\mathrm{w}_\Gamma \otimes \mathrm{æ}_{[\![A]\!]}} \mathbf{1} \otimes [\![A]\!] \xrightarrow{\cong} [\![A]\!] \\
&[\![\lambda x.M]\!]^{\Gamma} = [\![\Gamma]\!] \xrightarrow{h_\Gamma} ![\![\Gamma]\!] \xrightarrow{!\Lambda([\![M]\!]^{\Gamma, x:A})} !([\![A]\!] \multimap [\![B]\!]) \\
&[\![M\, N]\!]^{\Gamma} = [\![\Gamma]\!] \xrightarrow{\mathrm{c}_\Gamma} [\![\Gamma]\!] \otimes [\![\Gamma]\!] \xrightarrow{[\![M]\!]^{\Gamma} \otimes_l [\![N]\!]^{\Gamma}} [\![A \to B]\!] \otimes [\![A]\!] \\
&\qquad\qquad \xrightarrow{\varepsilon \otimes \mathrm{æ}} ([\![A]\!] \multimap [\![B]\!]) \otimes [\![A]\!] \xrightarrow{\mathrm{ev}} [\![B]\!] \\
&[\![(M, N)]\!]^{\Gamma} = [\![\Gamma]\!] \xrightarrow{\mathrm{c}_\Gamma} [\![\Gamma]\!] \otimes [\![\Gamma]\!] \xrightarrow{[\![M]\!]^{\Gamma} \otimes_l [\![N]\!]^{\Gamma}} [\![A \times B]\!] \\
&[\![\mathbf{match}\ M\ \mathbf{with}\ (x, y) \to N]\!]^{\Gamma} = [\![\Gamma]\!] \xrightarrow{\mathrm{c}_\Gamma} [\![\Gamma]\!] \otimes [\![\Gamma]\!] \xrightarrow{\mathrm{æ} \otimes [\![M]\!]^{\Gamma}} [\![\Gamma]\!] \otimes [\![A \times B]\!] \xrightarrow{[\![N]\!]^{\Gamma, x, y}} [\![C]\!] \\
&[\![\mathbf{match}\ M\ \mathbf{with}\ [\mathbf{inl}\, x \to N_1 \mid \mathbf{inr}\, x \to N_2]]\!]^{\Gamma} = [\![\Gamma]\!] \xrightarrow{\mathrm{c}_\Gamma} [\![\Gamma]\!] \otimes [\![\Gamma]\!] \\
&\qquad \xrightarrow{\mathrm{æ} \otimes [\![M]\!]^{\Gamma}} [\![\Gamma]\!] \otimes ([\![A_1]\!] + [\![A_2]\!]) \xrightarrow{\lambda} [\![\Gamma]\!] \otimes [\![A_1]\!] + [\![\Gamma]\!] \otimes [\![A_2]\!] \xrightarrow{[[\![N_1]\!], [\![N_2]\!]]} [\![B]\!]
\end{aligned}
$$

$$
\begin{array}{ll}
[\![M =^? 0]\!]^{\Gamma} : [\![\Gamma]\!] \xrightarrow{[\![M]\!]^{\Gamma}} [\![\mathbb{N}]\!] \xrightarrow{0?} [\![\mathbb{B}]\!] & [\![\mathbf{score}\ M]\!]^{\Gamma} = [\![\Gamma]\!] \xrightarrow{[\![M]\!]^{\Gamma}} [\![\mathbb{R}]\!] \xrightarrow{\mathbf{score}} [\![\mathbf{1}]\!]
\end{array}
$$

$$
\begin{aligned}
&[\![\mathbf{sample}_\ell\ \mathbf{dist}(M_1, \ldots, M_n)]\!] = [\![\Gamma]\!] \xrightarrow{\mathrm{c}_\Gamma} [\![\Gamma]\!] \otimes \ldots \otimes [\![\Gamma]\!] \xrightarrow{[\![M_1]\!]^{\Gamma} \otimes_l \ldots \otimes_l [\![M_n]\!]^{\Gamma}} [\![\mathbb{R}^n]\!] \xrightarrow{\mathrm{dist}_\ell} [\![\mathbb{X}]\!] \\
&[\![\mu x.M]\!]^{\Gamma} = \textstyle\bigvee_{i \in \omega} [\![M]\!]_i^{\Gamma, x}(\bot), \\
&\quad \text{where } [\![M]\!]_0^{\Gamma, x}(\bot) = \bot \text{ and } [\![M]\!]_{n+1}^{\Gamma, x}(\bot) = [\![M]\!]^{\Gamma, x} \odot (\mathrm{æ}_\Gamma \otimes [\![M]\!]_n^{\Gamma, x}(\bot)) \odot \mathrm{c}_\Gamma
\end{aligned}
$$

Fig. 11: Interpretation of terms as strategies.

$$
[\![A + B]\!] = [\![A]\!] + [\![B]\!] \quad [\![A \times B]\!] = [\![A]\!] \otimes [\![B]\!] \quad [\![A \to B]\!] = !([\![A]\!] \multimap [\![B]\!])
$$

This interpretation extends to contexts via $[\![\cdot]\!] = \mathbf{1}$ and $[\![x_1 : A_1, \ldots, x_n : A_n]\!] = [\![A_1]\!] \otimes \ldots \otimes [\![A_n]\!]$. (In Fig. 7 we used $[\![\Gamma \vdash A]\!]$ to refer to the arena $[\![\Gamma]\!]^{\perp} \parallel [\![A]\!]$.)

A term $\Gamma \vdash M : A$ is interpreted as a strategy $[\![M]\!]^{\Gamma} : [\![\Gamma]\!] \nrightarrow [\![A]\!]$, defined inductively. For every type A, the arena $[\![A]\!]$ is both a !-coalgebra and a commutative comonoid, so there are strategies $\mathrm{w}_A : [\![A]\!] \nrightarrow \mathbf{1}$, $\mathrm{c}_A : [\![A]\!] \nrightarrow [\![A]\!] \otimes [\![A]\!]$, and $h_A : [\![A]\!] \nrightarrow ![\![A]\!]$. Using that the comonad ! is monoidal, this structure extends to contexts; we write $\mathrm{c}_\Gamma, \mathrm{w}_\Gamma$ and h_Γ for the induced maps. The interpretation of constants is shown in Fig. 10, and the rest of the semantics is given in Fig. 11.

Lemma 6. *For a value $\Gamma \vdash V : A$, the strategy $[\![V]\!]^{\Gamma}$ is central.*

The semantics is sound for the usual call-by-value equations.

Proposition 1. *For arbitrary terms M, P, N_1, N_2 and values V, W,*

$$
\begin{aligned}
&[\![(\lambda x.M)\, V]\!]^{\Gamma} = [\![M[V/x]]\!]^{\Gamma} \\
&[\![\mathbf{match}\ (V, W)\ \mathbf{with}\ (x, y) \to P]\!]^{\Gamma} = [\![P[V/x][W/y]]\!]^{\Gamma} \\
&[\![\mathbf{match}\ \mathbf{inl}\, V\ \mathbf{with}\ [\mathbf{inl}\, x \to N_1 \mid \mathbf{inr}\, x \to N_2]]\!]^{\Gamma} = [\![N_1[V/x]]\!]^{\Gamma}.
\end{aligned}
$$

The equations are directly verified. Standard reasoning principles apply given the categorical structure we have outlined above. (It is well known that premonoidal categories provide models for call-by-value [50], and our interpretation is a version of Girard's translation of call-by-value into linear logic [29].)

6 Conclusion and perspectives

We have defined, for every term $\Gamma \vdash M : A$, a strategy $[\![M]\!]^\Gamma$. This gives a model for probabilistic programming which provides an explicit representation of data flow. In particular, if $\vdash M : \mathbf{1}$, and M has no subterm of type $B + C$, then the Bayesian strategy $[\![M]\!]$ is a Bayesian network equipped with a total ordering of its nodes: the control flow relation $\leq$. Our proposed compositional semantics additionally supports sum types, higher types, and open terms.

This paper does not contain an adequacy result, largely for lack of space: the 'Monte Carlo' operational semantics of probabilistic programs is difficult to define in full rigour. In further work I hope to address this and carry out the integration of causal models into the framework of [53]. The objective remains to obtain proofs of correctness for existing and new inference algorithms.

Related work on denotational semantics. Our representation of data flow based on coincidences and a relation $\dashrightarrow$ is novel, but the underlying machinery relies on existing work in concurrent game semantics, in particular the framework of games with symmetry developed by Castellan et al. [17]. This was applied to a language with *discrete* probability in [15], and to a *call-by-name* and *affine* language with continuous probability in [49]. This paper is the first instance of a concurrent games model for a higher-order language with recursion and continuous probability, and the first to track internal sampling and data flow.

There are other interactive models for statistical languages, e.g. by Ong and Vákár [47] and Dal Lago et al. [38]. Their objectives are different: they do not address data flow (*i.e.* their semantics only represents the control flow), and do not record internal samples.

Prior to the development of probabilistic concurrent games, probabilistic notions of event structures were considered by several authors (see [58,1,59]). The literature on probabilistic Petri nets important related work, as Petri nets can sometimes provide finite representations for infinite event structures. *Markov nets* [7,2] satisfy conditional independence conditions based on the causal structure of Petri nets. More recently Bruni et al. [12,13] relate a form of Petri nets to Bayesian networks and inference, though their probability spaces are discrete.

Related work on graphical representations. Our event structures are reminiscent of Jeffrey's graphical language for premonoidal categories [35], which combines string diagrams [36] with a control flow relation. Note that in event structures the conflict relation provides a model for sum types, which is difficult to obtain in Jeffrey's setting. The problem of representing sum types arises also in probabilistic modelling, because Bayesian networks do not support them: [45] propose an extended graphical language, which could serve to interpret first-order probabilistic programs with conditionals. Another approach is by [42], whose Bayesian networks have edges labelled by predicates describing the branching condition. Finally, the theory of Bayesian networks has also been investigated extensively by Jacobs [34] with a categorical viewpoint. It will be important to understand the formal connections between our work and the above.

References

1. Abbes, S., Benveniste, A.: True-concurrency probabilistic models: Branching cells and distributed probabilities for event structures. Information and Computation **204**(2), 231–274 (2006)
2. Abbes, S., Benveniste, A.: True-concurrency probabilistic models: Markov nets and a law of large numbers. Theoretical computer science **390**(2-3), 129–170 (2008)
3. Abramsky, S., Jagadeesan, R., Malacaria, P.: Full abstraction for PCF. Information and Computation **163**(2), 409–470 (2000)
4. Abramsky, S., McCusker, G.: Call-by-value games. In: International Workshop on Computer Science Logic. pp. 1–17. Springer (1997)
5. Alcolei, A.: Jeux concurrents enrichis: témoins pour les preuves et les ressources. Ph.D. thesis, ENS Lyon (2019)
6. Bénabou, J.: Introduction to bicategories. In: Reports of the midwest category seminar. pp. 1–77. Springer (1967)
7. Benveniste, A., Fabre, E., Haar, S.: Markov nets: probabilistic models for distributed and concurrent systems. IEEE Transactions on Automatic Control **48**(11), 1936–1950 (2003)
8. Billingsley, P.: Probability and measure. John Wiley & Sons (2008)
9. Bingham, E., Chen, J.P., Jankowiak, M., Obermeyer, F., Pradhan, N., Karaletsos, T., Singh, R., Szerlip, P., Horsfall, P., Goodman, N.D.: Pyro: Deep universal probabilistic programming. The Journal of Machine Learning Research **20**(1), 973–978 (2019)
10. Blass, A.: A game semantics for linear logic. Annals of Pure and Applied logic **56**(1-3), 183–220 (1992)
11. Borgström, J., Dal Lago, U., Gordon, A.D., Szymczak, M.: A lambda-calculus foundation for universal probabilistic programming. In: ACM SIGPLAN Notices. vol. 51, pp. 33–46. ACM (2016)
12. Bruni, R., Melgratti, H., Montanari, U.: Concurrency and probability: Removing confusion, compositionally. In: Proceedings of the 33rd Annual ACM/IEEE Symposium on Logic in Computer Science. pp. 195–204 (2018)
13. Bruni, R., Melgratti, H., Montanari, U.: Bayesian network semantics for petri nets. Theoretical Computer Science **807**, 95–113 (2020)
14. Castellan, S.: The causality project, http://iso.mor.phis.me/software/causality/
15. Castellan, S., Clairambault, P., Paquet, H., Winskel, G.: The concurrent game semantics of probabilistic PCF. In: Logic in Computer Science (LICS), 2018 33rd Annual ACM/IEEE Symposium on, ACM/IEEE (2018)
16. Castellan, S., Clairambault, P., Winskel, G.: The parallel intensionally fully abstract games model of PCF. In: 2015 30th Annual ACM/IEEE Symposium on Logic in Computer Science. pp. 232–243. IEEE (2015)
17. Castellan, S., Clairambault, P., Winskel, G.: Thin games with symmetry and concurrent Hyland-Ong games. Logical Methods in Computer Science (2019)
18. Castellan, S., Paquet, H.: Probabilistic programming inference via intensional semantics. In: European Symposium on Programming. pp. 322–349. Springer (2019)
19. Castellan, S., Yoshida, N.: Two sides of the same coin: session types and game semantics: a synchronous side and an asynchronous side. Proceedings of the ACM on Programming Languages **3**(POPL), 1–29 (2019)
20. Clairambault, P., De Visme, M., Winskel, G.: Game semantics for quantum programming. Proceedings of the ACM on Programming Languages **3**(POPL), 1–29 (2019)

21. Clairambault, P., de Visme, M.: Full abstraction for the quantum lambda-calculus. Proceedings of the ACM on Programming Languages **4**(POPL), 1–28 (2019)
22. Claret, G., Rajamani, S.K., Nori, A.V., Gordon, A.D., Borgström, J.: Bayesian inference using data flow analysis. In: Proceedings of the 2013 9th Joint Meeting on Foundations of Software Engineering. pp. 92–102 (2013)
23. Cusumano-Towner, M.F., Saad, F.A., Lew, A.K., Mansinghka, V.K.: Gen: a general-purpose probabilistic programming system with programmable inference. In: Proceedings of the 40th ACM SIGPLAN Conference on Programming Language Design and Implementation. pp. 221–236 (2019)
24. Dahlqvist, F., Kozen, D.: Semantics of higher-order probabilistic programs with conditioning. Proceedings of the ACM on Programming Languages **4**(POPL), 1–29 (2019)
25. Faggian, C., Piccolo, M.: Partial orders, event structures and linear strategies. In: International Conference on Typed Lambda Calculi and Applications. pp. 95–111. Springer (2009)
26. Fiore, M., Honda, K.: Recursive types in games: Axiomatics and process representation. In: Proceedings. Thirteenth Annual IEEE Symposium on Logic in Computer Science (Cat. No. 98CB36226). pp. 345–356. IEEE (1998)
27. Fong, B.: Causal theories: A categorical perspective on Bayesian networks. arXiv preprint arXiv:1301.6201 (2013)
28. Gabler, P., Trapp, M., Ge, H., Pernkopf, F.: Graph tracking in dynamic probabilistic programs via source transformations. In: Symposium on Advances in Approximate Bayesian Inference (AABI) (2019)
29. Girard, J.Y.: Linear logic. Theoretical computer science **50**(1), 1–101 (1987)
30. Goodman, N.D., Mansinghka, V.K., Roy, D., Bonawitz, K., Tenenbaum, J.B.: Church: a language for generative models. In: Proceedings of the Twenty-Fourth Conference on Uncertainty in Artificial Intelligence. pp. 220–229 (2008)
31. Honda, K., Yoshida, N.: Game theoretic analysis of call-by-value computation. In: International Colloquium on Automata, Languages, and Programming. pp. 225–236. Springer (1997)
32. Hur, C.K., Nori, A.V., Rajamani, S.K., Samuel, S.: A provably correct sampler for probabilistic programs. In: LIPIcs-Leibniz International Proceedings in Informatics. vol. 45. Schloss Dagstuhl-Leibniz-Zentrum fuer Informatik (2015)
33. Hyland, J.M.E., Ong, C.H.: On full abstraction for PCF: I, II, and III. Information and computation **163**(2) (2000)
34. Jacobs, B.: A channel-based exact inference algorithm for bayesian networks. arXiv preprint arXiv:1804.08032 (2018)
35. Jeffrey, A.: Premonoidal categories and a graphical view of programs. Preprint, Dec (1997)
36. Joyal, A., Street, R.: The geometry of tensor calculus, I. Advances in mathematics **88**(1), 55–112 (1991)
37. Koller, D., Friedman, N.: Probabilistic graphical models: principles and techniques. MIT press (2009)
38. Lago, U., Hoshino, N.: The geometry of Bayesian programming. In: 2019 34th Annual ACM/IEEE Symposium on Logic in Computer Science (LICS). pp. 1–13 (2019)
39. Lew, A.K., Cusumano-Towner, M.F., Sherman, B., Carbin, M., Mansinghka, V.K.: Trace types and denotational semantics for sound programmable inference in probabilistic languages. Proceedings of the ACM on Programming Languages **4**(POPL), 1–32 (2019)

40. Mak, C., Ong, C.H.L., Paquet, H., Wagner, D.: Densities of almost-surely terminating probabilistic programs are differentiable almost everywhere. In: European Symposium on Programming. Springer (2021)
41. Mansinghka, V., Selsam, D., Perov, Y.: Venture: a higher-order probabilistic programming platform with programmable inference. arXiv preprint arXiv:1404.0099 (2014)
42. van de Meent, J.W., Paige, B., Yang, H., Wood, F.: An introduction to probabilistic programming. arXiv preprint arXiv:1809.10756 (2018)
43. Mellies, P.A.: Asynchronous games 4: A fully complete model of propositional linear logic. In: 20th Annual IEEE Symposium on Logic in Computer Science (LICS'05). pp. 386–395. IEEE (2005)
44. Melliès, P.A., Mimram, S.: Asynchronous games: Innocence without alternation. In: International Conference on Concurrency Theory. pp. 395–411. Springer (2007)
45. Minka, T., Winn, J.: Gates. In: Advances in Neural Information Processing Systems. pp. 1073–1080 (2009)
46. Nielsen, M., Plotkin, G., Winskel, G.: Petri nets, event structures and domains, part i. Theoretical Computer Science **13**(1), 85–108 (1981)
47. Ong, L., Vákár, M.: S-finite kernels and game semantics for probabilistic programming. In: POPL'18 Workshop on Probabilistic Programming Semantics (PPS) (2018)
48. Paquet, H.: Probabilistic concurrent game semantics. Ph.D. thesis, University of Cambridge (2020)
49. Paquet, H., Winskel, G.: Continuous probability distributions in concurrent games. Electronic Notes in Theoretical Computer Science **341**, 321–344 (2018)
50. Power, J., Robinson, E.: Premonoidal categories and notions of computation. Mathematical structures in computer science **7**(5), 453–468 (1997)
51. Rideau, S., Winskel, G.: Concurrent strategies. In: 2011 IEEE 26th Annual Symposium on Logic in Computer Science. pp. 409–418. IEEE (2011)
52. Schulman, J., Heess, N., Weber, T., Abbeel, P.: Gradient estimation using stochastic computation graphs. In: Advances in Neural Information Processing Systems. pp. 3528–3536 (2015)
53. Ścibior, A., Kammar, O., Vákár, M., Staton, S., Yang, H., Cai, Y., Ostermann, K., Moss, S.K., Heunen, C., Ghahramani, Z.: Denotational validation of higher-order bayesian inference. Proceedings of the ACM on Programming Languages **2**(POPL), 60 (2017)
54. Staton, S.: Commutative semantics for probabilistic programming. In: European Symposium on Programming. pp. 855–879. Springer (2017)
55. Tran, D., Kucukelbir, A., Dieng, A.B., Rudolph, M., Liang, D., Blei, D.M.: Edward: A library for probabilistic modeling, inference, and criticism. arXiv preprint arXiv:1610.09787 (2016)
56. Tsukada, T., Ong, C.L.: Nondeterminism in game semantics via sheaves. In: 2015 30th Annual ACM/IEEE Symposium on Logic in Computer Science. pp. 220–231. IEEE (2015)
57. Vákár, M., Kammar, O., Staton, S.: A domain theory for statistical probabilistic programming. Proceedings of the ACM on Programming Languages **3**(POPL), 1–29 (2019)
58. Varacca, D., Völzer, H., Winskel, G.: Probabilistic event structures and domains. In: International Conference on Concurrency Theory. pp. 481–496. Springer (2004)
59. Varacca, D., Yoshida, N.: Probabilistic π-calculus and event structures. Electronic Notes in Theoretical Computer Science **190**(3), 147–166 (2007)

60. Winskel, G.: Event structures. In: Advances in Petri Nets. pp. 325–392 (1986)
61. Winskel, G.: Event structures with symmetry. Electronic Notes in Theoretical Computer Science **172**, 611–652 (2007)
62. Winskel, G.: Distributed probabilistic and quantum strategies. Electr. Notes Theor. Comput. Sci. **298**, 403–425 (2013)
63. Winskel, G., Rideau, S., Clairambault, P., Castellan, S.: Games and strategies as event structures. Logical Methods in Computer Science **13** (2017)

Temporal Refinements for Guarded Recursive Types*

Guilhem Jaber[1] and Colin Riba[2] (✉)

Université de Nantes, LS2N CNRS, Inria, Nantes, France
guilhem.jaber@univ-nantes.fr
Univ Lyon, EnsL, UCBL, CNRS, LIP, F-69342, Lyon Cedex 07, France
colin.riba@ens-lyon.fr

Abstract. We propose a logic for temporal properties of higher-order programs that handle infinite objects like streams or infinite trees, represented via coinductive types. Specifications of programs use safety and liveness properties. Programs can then be proven to satisfy their specification in a compositional way, our logic being based on a type system. The logic is presented as a refinement type system over the guarded λ-calculus, a λ-calculus with guarded recursive types. The refinements are formulae of a modal μ-calculus which embeds usual temporal modal logics such as LTL and CTL. The semantics of our system is given within a rich structure, the topos of trees, in which we build a realizability model of the temporal refinement type system.

Keywords: coinductive types, guarded recursive types, μ-calculus, refinement types, topos of trees.

1 Introduction

Functional programming is by now well established to handle infinite data, thanks to declarative definitions and equational reasoning on high-level abstractions, in particular when infinite objects are represented with coinductive types. In such settings, programs in general do not terminate, but are expected to compute a part of their output in finite time. For example, a program expected to generate a stream should produce the next element in finite time: it is *productive*.

Our goal is to prove input-output temporal properties of higher-order programs that handle coinductive types. Logics like LTL, CTL or the modal μ-calculus are widely used to formulate, on infinite objects, safety and liveness properties. Safety properties state that some "bad" event will not occur, while liveness properties specify that "something good" will happen (see e.g. [9]). Typically, modalities like $\Box$ (*always*) or $\Diamond$ (*eventually*) are used to write properties of streams or infinite trees and specifications of programs over such data.

We consider temporal refinement types $\{A \mid \varphi\}$, where A is a standard type of our programming language, and φ is a formula of the modal μ-calculus. Using

* This work was partially supported by the ANR-14-CE25-0007 - RAPIDO and by the LABEX MILYON (ANR-10-LABX-0070) of Université de Lyon.

N. Yoshida (Ed.): ESOP 2021, LNCS 12648, pp. 548–578, 2021.
https://doi.org/10.1007/978-3-030-72019-3_20

refinement types [22], temporal connectives are not reflected in the programming language, and programs are formally independent from the shape of their temporal specifications. One can thus give different refinement types to the same program. For example, the following two types can be given to the same map function on streams:

$$\begin{array}{l}\mathsf{map} : (\{B \mid \psi\} \to \{A \mid \varphi\}) \longrightarrow \{\mathsf{Str}\, B \mid \Box\Diamond[\mathsf{hd}]\psi\} \longrightarrow \{\mathsf{Str}\, A \mid \Box\Diamond[\mathsf{hd}]\varphi\} \\ \mathsf{map} : (\{B \mid \psi\} \to \{A \mid \varphi\}) \longrightarrow \{\mathsf{Str}\, B \mid \Diamond\Box[\mathsf{hd}]\psi\} \longrightarrow \{\mathsf{Str}\, A \mid \Diamond\Box[\mathsf{hd}]\varphi\}\end{array} \quad (\star)$$

These types mean that given $f : B \to A$ s.t. $f(b)$ satisfies φ if b satisfies ψ, the function $(\mathsf{map}\ f)$ takes a stream with infinitely many (resp. ultimately all) elements satisfying ψ to one with infinitely many (resp. ultimately all) elements satisfying φ. For φ a formula over A, $[\mathsf{hd}]\varphi$ is a formula over streams of A's which holds on a given stream if φ holds on its head element.

It is undecidable whether a given higher-order program satisfies a given input-output temporal property written with formulae of the modal μ-calculus [41]. Having a type system is a partial workaround to this obstacle, which moreover enables to reason compositionally on programs, by decomposing a specification to the various components of a program in order to prove its global specification.

Our system is built on top of the guarded λ-calculus [18], a higher-order programming language with guarded recursion [52]. Guarded recursion is a simple device to control and reason about unfoldings of fixpoints. It can represent coinductive types [50] and provides a syntactic compositional productivity check [5].

Safety properties (e.g. $\Box[\mathsf{hd}]\varphi$) can be correctly represented with guarded fixpoints, but not liveness properties (e.g. $\Diamond[\mathsf{hd}]\varphi$, $\Diamond\Box[\mathsf{hd}]\varphi$, $\Box\Diamond[\mathsf{hd}]\varphi$). Combining liveness with guarded recursion is a challenging problem since guarded fixpoints tend to have unique solutions. Existing approaches to handle temporal types in presence of guarded recursion face similar difficulties. Functional reactive programming (FRP) [21] provides a Curry-Howard correspondence for temporal logics [32,33,17] in which logical connectives are reflected as programming constructs. When combining FRP with guarded recursion [44,7], and in particular to handle liveness properties [8], uniqueness of guarded fixpoints is tempered by specific recursors for temporal types.

Our approach is different from [8], as we wish as much as possible the logical level not to impact the program level. We propose a two level system, with the lower or *internal* level, which interacts with guarded recursion and at which only safety properties are correctly represented, and the higher or *external* one, at which liveness properties are correctly handled, but without direct access to guarded recursion. By restricting to the alternation-free modal μ-calculus, in which fixpoints can always be computed in ω-steps, one can syntactically reason on finite unfoldings of liveness properties, thus allowing for crossing down the safety barrier. Soundness is proved by a realizability interpretation based on the semantics of guarded recursion in the topos of trees [13], which correctly represents the usual set-theoretic final coalgebras of polynomial coinductive types [50].

We provide example programs involving linear structures (colists, streams, fair streams [17,8]) and branching structures (resumptions *à la* [44]), for which

$$
\begin{array}{rll}
\mathsf{Cons}^{\mathsf{g}} &:= \lambda x.\lambda s.\,\mathsf{fold}(\langle x, s\rangle) &: A \to \blacktriangleright \mathsf{Str}^{\mathsf{g}} A \to \mathsf{Str}^{\mathsf{g}} A \\
\mathsf{hd}^{\mathsf{g}} &:= \lambda s.\pi_0(\mathsf{unfold}\ s) &: \mathsf{Str}^{\mathsf{g}} A \to A \\
\mathsf{tl}^{\mathsf{g}} &:= \lambda s.\pi_1(\mathsf{unfold}\ s) &: \mathsf{Str}^{\mathsf{g}} A \to \blacktriangleright \mathsf{Str}^{\mathsf{g}} A \\
\mathsf{map}^{\mathsf{g}} &:= \lambda f.\mathsf{fix}(g).\lambda s.\,\mathsf{Cons}^{\mathsf{g}}\ (f(\mathsf{hd}^{\mathsf{g}}\ s))\ (g \circledast (\mathsf{tl}^{\mathsf{g}}\ s)) &: (B \to A) \to \mathsf{Str}^{\mathsf{g}} B \to \mathsf{Str}^{\mathsf{g}} A
\end{array}
$$

Fig. 1. Constructor, Destructors and Map on Guarded Streams.

we prove liveness properties similar to ($\star$) above. Our system also handles safety properties on breadth-first (infinite) tree traversals *à la* [35] and [10].

Organization of the paper. We give an overview of our approach in §2. Then §3 presents the syntax of the guarded λ-calculus. Our base temporal logic (without liveness) is introduced in §4, and is used to define our refinement type system in §5. Liveness properties are handled in §6. The semantics is given in §7, and §8 presents examples. Finally, we discuss related work in §9 and future work in §10. Table 4 (§8) gathers the main refinement types we can give to example functions, most of them defined in Table 3. Omitted material is available in [28].

2 Outline

Overview of the Guarded λ-Calculus. Guarded recursion enforces productivity of programs using a type system equipped with a type modality $\blacktriangleright$, in order to indicate that one has access to a value not right now but only "later". One can define guarded streams $\mathsf{Str}^{\mathsf{g}} A$ over a type A via the guarded recursive definition $\mathsf{Str}^{\mathsf{g}} A = A \times \blacktriangleright \mathsf{Str}^{\mathsf{g}} A$. Streams that inhabit this type have their head available now, but their tail only one step in the future. The type modality $\blacktriangleright$ is reflected in programs with the next operation. One also has a fixpoint constructor on terms $\mathsf{fix}(x).M$ for guarded recursive definitions. They are typed with

$$
\frac{\mathcal{E} \vdash M : A}{\mathcal{E} \vdash \mathsf{next}(M) : \blacktriangleright A}
\qquad\qquad
\frac{\mathcal{E}, x : \blacktriangleright A \vdash M : A}{\mathcal{E} \vdash \mathsf{fix}(x).M : A}
$$

This allows for the constructor and basic destructors on guarded streams to be defined as in Fig. 1, where $\mathsf{fold}(-)$ and $\mathsf{unfold}(-)$ are explicit operations for folding and unfolding guarded recursive types. In the following, we use the infix notation $a ::^{\mathsf{g}} s$ for $\mathsf{Cons}^{\mathsf{g}}\ a\ s$. Using the fact that the type modality $\blacktriangleright$ is an applicative functor [49], we can distribute $\blacktriangleright$ over the arrow type. This is represented in the programming language by the infix applicative operator $\circledast$. With it, one can define the usual map function on guarded streams as in Fig. 1.

Compositional Safety Reasoning on Streams. Given a property φ on a type A, we would like to consider a subtype of $\mathsf{Str}^{\mathsf{g}} A$ that selects those streams whose elements all satisfy φ. To do so, we use a temporal modal formula $\Box[\mathsf{hd}]\varphi$,

Typed Formulae	Provability	Refinement Types	Subtyping	Typing
$\Sigma \vdash \varphi : A$ (§4)	$\vdash^A \varphi$ (where $\vdash \varphi : A$, §4)	$\{A \mid \varphi\}$ (where $\vdash \varphi : A$, §5)	$T \leq U$ (T, U refinement types, §5)	$\mathcal{E} \vdash M : T$

Table 1. Syntactic Classes and Judgments.

and consider the *refinement type* $\{\mathsf{Str}^{\mathsf{g}}\, A \mid \Box[\mathsf{hd}]\varphi\}$. Suppose for now that we can give the following refinement types to the basic stream operations:

$$\begin{aligned}
\mathsf{hd}^{\mathsf{g}} &: \{\mathsf{Str}^{\mathsf{g}}\, A \mid \Box[\mathsf{hd}]\varphi\} \longrightarrow \{A \mid \varphi\} \\
\mathsf{tl}^{\mathsf{g}} &: \{\mathsf{Str}^{\mathsf{g}}\, A \mid \Box[\mathsf{hd}]\varphi\} \longrightarrow \blacktriangleright \{\mathsf{Str}^{\mathsf{g}}\, A \mid \Box[\mathsf{hd}]\varphi\} \\
\mathsf{Cons}^{\mathsf{g}} &: \{A \mid \varphi\} \longrightarrow \blacktriangleright \{\mathsf{Str}^{\mathsf{g}}\, A \mid \Box[\mathsf{hd}]\varphi\} \longrightarrow \{\mathsf{Str}^{\mathsf{g}}\, A \mid \Box[\mathsf{hd}]\varphi\}
\end{aligned}$$

By using the standard typing rules for λ-abstraction and application, together with the rules to type $\mathsf{fix}(x).M$ and $\circledast$, we can type the function $\mathsf{map}^{\mathsf{g}}$ as

$$\mathsf{map}^{\mathsf{g}} : (\{B \mid \psi\} \to \{A \mid \varphi\}) \longrightarrow \{\mathsf{Str}^{\mathsf{g}}\, B \mid \Box[\mathsf{hd}]\psi\} \longrightarrow \{\mathsf{Str}^{\mathsf{g}}\, A \mid \Box[\mathsf{hd}]\varphi\}$$

A Manysorted Temporal Logic. Our logical language, taken with minor adaptations from [30], is *manysorted*: for each type A we have formulae *of type* A (notation $\vdash \varphi : A$), where φ selects inhabitants of A.

We use atomic modalities ($[\pi_i]$, $[\mathsf{fold}]$, $[\mathsf{next}]$, ...) in refinements to navigate between types (see Fig. 5, §4). For instance, a formula φ of type A_0, specifying a property over the inhabitants of A_0, can be lifted to the formula $[\pi_0]\varphi$ of type $A_0 \times A_1$, which intuitively describes those inhabitants of $A_0 \times A_1$ whose first component satisfy φ. Given a formula φ of type A, one can define its "head lift" $[\mathsf{hd}]\varphi$ of type $\mathsf{Str}^{\mathsf{g}}\, A$, that enforces φ to be satisfied on the head of the provided stream. Also, one can define a modality $\bigcirc$ such that given a formula $\psi : \mathsf{Str}^{\mathsf{g}}\, A$, the formula $\bigcirc\psi : \mathsf{Str}^{\mathsf{g}}\, A$ enforces ψ to be satisfied on the tail of the provided stream. These modalities are obtained resp. as $[\mathsf{hd}]\varphi := [\mathsf{fold}][\pi_0]\varphi$ and $\bigcirc\varphi := [\mathsf{fold}][\pi_1][\mathsf{next}]\varphi$. We similarly have atomic modalities $[\mathsf{in}_0], [\mathsf{in}_1]$ on sum types. For instance, on the type of guarded colists defined as $\mathsf{CoList}^{\mathsf{g}}\, A := \mathsf{Fix}(X).\ \mathbf{1} + A \times \blacktriangleright X$, we can express the fact that a colist is empty (resp. non-empty) with the formula $[\mathsf{nil}] := [\mathsf{fold}][\mathsf{in}_0]\top$ (resp. $[\neg\mathsf{nil}] := [\mathsf{fold}][\mathsf{in}_1]\top$).

We also provide a deduction system $\vdash^A \varphi$ on temporal modal formulae. This deduction system is used to define a subtyping relation $T \leq U$ between refinement types, with $\{A \mid \varphi\} \leq \{A \mid \psi\}$ when $\vdash^A \varphi \Rightarrow \psi$. The subtyping relation thus incorporates logical reasoning in the type system.

In addition, we have greatest fixpoints formulae $\nu\alpha\varphi$ (so that formulae can have free typed propositional variables), equipped with Kozen's reasoning principles [43]. In particular, we can form an *always* modality as $\Box\varphi := \nu\alpha.\ \varphi \wedge \bigcirc\alpha$, with $\Box\varphi : \mathsf{Str}^{\mathsf{g}}\, A$ if $\varphi : \mathsf{Str}^{\mathsf{g}}\, A$. The formula $\Box\varphi$ holds on a stream $s = (s_i \mid i \geq 0)$, iff φ holds on every substream $(s_i \mid i \geq n)$ for $n \geq 0$. If we rather start with $\psi : A$, one first need to lift it to $[\mathsf{hd}]\psi : \mathsf{Str}^{\mathsf{g}} A$. Then $\Box[\mathsf{hd}]\psi$ means that all the elements of the stream satisfies ψ, since all its suffixes satisfy $[\mathsf{hd}]\psi$.

Table 1 summarizes the different judgments used in this paper.

Beyond Safety. In order to handle liveness properties, we also need to have least fixpoints formulae $\mu\alpha\varphi$. For example, this would give the *eventually* modality $\Diamond\varphi := \mu\alpha.\ \varphi \vee \bigcirc\alpha$. With Kozen-style rules, one could then give the following two types to the guarded stream constructor:

$$\begin{aligned}\mathsf{Cons}^{\mathsf{g}} &: \{A \mid \varphi\} \longrightarrow \blacktriangleright \mathsf{Str}^{\mathsf{g}} A \longrightarrow \{\mathsf{Str}^{\mathsf{g}} A \mid \Diamond[\mathsf{hd}]\varphi\}\\ \mathsf{Cons}^{\mathsf{g}} &: A \longrightarrow \blacktriangleright \{\mathsf{Str}^{\mathsf{g}} A \mid \Diamond[\mathsf{hd}]\varphi\} \longrightarrow \{\mathsf{Str}^{\mathsf{g}} A \mid \Diamond[\mathsf{hd}]\varphi\}\end{aligned}$$

But consider a finite base type $\mathtt{B}$ with two distinguished elements $\mathtt{a}, \mathtt{b}$, and suppose that we have access to a modality $[\mathtt{b}]$ on $\mathtt{B}$ so that terms inhabiting $\{\mathtt{B} \mid [\mathtt{b}]\}$ must be equal to $\mathtt{b}$. Using the above types for $\mathsf{Cons}^{\mathsf{g}}$, we could type the stream with constant value $\mathtt{a}$, defined as $\mathsf{fix}(s).\mathtt{a} ::^{\mathsf{g}} s$, with the type $\{\mathsf{Str}^{\mathsf{g}}\,\mathtt{B} \mid \Diamond[\mathsf{hd}][\mathtt{b}]\}$ that is supposed to enforce the existence of an occurrence of $\mathtt{b}$ in the stream. Similarly, on colists we would have $\mathsf{fix}(s).\mathtt{a} ::^{\mathsf{g}} s$ of type $\{\mathsf{CoList}^{\mathsf{g}}\,\mathtt{B} \mid \Diamond[\mathsf{nil}]\}$, while $\Diamond[\mathsf{nil}]$ expresses that a colist will eventually contain a nil, and is thus finite. Hence, liveness properties may interact quite badly with guarded recursion. Let us look at this in a semantic model of guarded recursion.

***Internal* Semantics in the Topos of Trees.** The types of the guarded λ-calculus can be interpreted as sequences of sets $(X(n))_{n>0}$ where $X(n)$ represents the values available "at time n". In order to interpret guarded recursion, one also needs to have access to functions $r_n^X : X(n+1) \to X(n)$, which tell how values "at $n+1$" can be restricted (actually most often truncated) to values "at n". This means that the objects used to represent types are in fact *presheaves* over the poset $(\mathbb{N} \setminus \{0\}, \leq)$. The category $\mathcal{S}$ of such presheaves is the *topos of trees* [13]. For instance, the type $\mathsf{Str}^{\mathsf{g}}\,\mathtt{B}$ of guarded streams over a finite base type $\mathtt{B}$ is interpreted in $\mathcal{S}$ as $(\mathtt{B}^n)_{n>0}$, with restriction maps taking $(\mathtt{b}_0, \ldots, \mathtt{b}_{n-1}, \mathtt{b}_n)$ to $(\mathtt{b}_0, \ldots, \mathtt{b}_{n-1})$. We write $[\![A]\!]$ for the interpretation of a type A in $\mathcal{S}$.

The Necessity of an *External* Semantics. The topos of trees cannot correctly handle liveness properties. For instance, the formula $\Diamond[\mathsf{hd}][\mathtt{b}]$ cannot describe in $\mathcal{S}$ the set of streams that contain at least one occurrence of $\mathtt{b}$. Indeed, the interpretation of $\Diamond[\mathsf{hd}][\mathtt{b}]$ in $\mathcal{S}$ is a sequence $(C(n))_{n>0}$ with $C(n) \subseteq \mathtt{B}^n$. But any element of $\mathtt{B}^n$ can be extended to a stream which contains an occurrence of $\mathtt{b}$. Hence $C(n)$ should be equal to $\mathtt{B}^n$, and the interpretation of $\Diamond[\mathsf{hd}][\mathtt{b}]$ is the whole $[\![\mathsf{Str}^{\mathsf{g}}\,\mathtt{B}]\!]$. More generally, guarded fixpoints have unique solutions in the topos of trees [13], and $\Diamond\varphi = \mu\alpha.\ \varphi \vee \bigcirc\varphi$ gets the same interpretation as $\nu\alpha.\ \varphi \vee \bigcirc\alpha$.

We thus have a formal system with least and greatest fixpoints, that has a semantics inside the topos of trees, but which does not correctly handle least fixpoints. On the other hand, it was shown by [50] that the interpretation of guarded polynomial (*i.e.* first-order) recursive types in $\mathcal{S}$ induces final coalgebras for the corresponding polynomial functors on the category **Set** of usual sets and functions. This applies e.g. to streams and colists. Hence, it makes sense to think of interpreting least fixpoint formulae over such types *externally*, in **Set**.

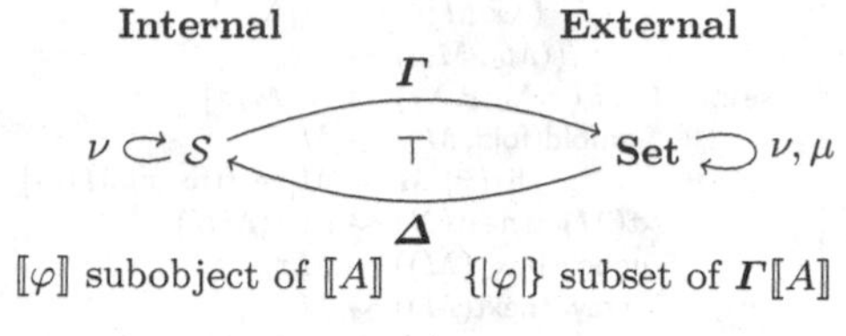

$$[\![\blacksquare A]\!] := \boldsymbol{\Delta}\boldsymbol{\Gamma}[\![A]\!]$$
$$[\![[\mathsf{box}]\varphi]\!] := \boldsymbol{\Delta}\,\{\!|\varphi|\!\} \quad (\varphi : A,\ [\mathsf{box}]\varphi : \blacksquare A)$$
$$\{\!|\varphi|\!\} = \boldsymbol{\Gamma}[\![\varphi]\!] \quad (\text{if } \varphi \text{ is safe})$$

Fig. 2. Internal and External Semantics

The Constant Type Modality. Figure 2 represents adjoint functors $\boldsymbol{\Gamma} : \mathcal{S} \to \mathbf{Set}$ and $\boldsymbol{\Delta} : \mathbf{Set} \to \mathcal{S}$. To correctly handle least fixpoints $\mu\alpha\varphi : A$, we would like to see them as subsets of $\boldsymbol{\Gamma}[\![A]\!]$ in **Set** rather than subobjects of $[\![A]\!]$ in $\mathcal{S}$. On the other hand, the internal semantics in $\mathcal{S}$ is still necessary to handle definitions by guarded recursion. We navigate between the internal semantics in $\mathcal{S}$ and the external semantics in **Set** via the adjunction $\boldsymbol{\Delta} \dashv \boldsymbol{\Gamma}$. This adjunction induces a comonad $\boldsymbol{\Delta}\boldsymbol{\Gamma}$ on $\mathcal{S}$, which is represented in the guarded λ-calculus of [18] by the *constant* type modality $\blacksquare$. This gives *coinductive* versions of guarded recursive types, e.g. $\mathsf{Str}\,A := \blacksquare\,\mathsf{Str}^{\mathsf{g}}\,A$ for streams and $\mathsf{CoList}\,A := \blacksquare\,\mathsf{CoList}^{\mathsf{g}}\,A$ for colists, which allow for productive but not causal programs [18, Ex. 1.10.(3)].

Each formula gets two interpretations: $[\![\varphi]\!]$ in $\mathcal{S}$ and $\{\!|\varphi|\!\}$ in **Set**. The external semantics $\{\!|\varphi|\!\}$ handles least fixpoints in the standard set-theoretic way, thus the two interpretations differ in general. But we do have $\{\!|\varphi|\!\} = \boldsymbol{\Gamma}[\![\varphi]\!]$ when φ is *safe* (Def. 6.5), that is, when φ describes a safety property. We have a modality $[\mathsf{box}]\varphi$ which lifts $\varphi : A$ to $\blacksquare A$. By defining $[\![[\mathsf{box}]\varphi]\!] := \boldsymbol{\Delta}\,\{\!|\varphi|\!\}$, we correctly handle the least fixpoints which are guarded by a $[\mathsf{box}]$ modality. When φ is safe, we can navigate between $\{\blacksquare A \mid [\mathsf{box}]\varphi\}$ and $\blacksquare\,\{A \mid \varphi\}$, thus making available the comonad structure of $\blacksquare$ on $[\mathsf{box}]\varphi$. Note that $[\mathsf{box}]$ is unrelated to $\Box$.

Approximating Least Fixpoints. For proving liveness properties on functions defined by guarded recursion, one needs to navigate between e.g. $[\mathsf{box}]\Diamond\varphi$ and $\Diamond\varphi$, while $\Diamond\varphi$ is in general unsafe. The fixpoint $\Diamond\varphi = \mu\alpha.\varphi \vee \bigcirc\alpha$ is *alternation-free* (see e.g. [16, §4.1]). This implies that $\Diamond\varphi$ can be seen as the supremum of the $\bigcirc^m\varphi$ for $m \in \mathbb{N}$, where each $\bigcirc^m\varphi$ is safe when φ is safe. More generally, we can approximate alternation-free $\mu\alpha\varphi$ by their finite unfoldings $\varphi^m(\bot)$, *à la* Kleene. We extend the logic with finite iterations $\mu^k\alpha\varphi$, where k is an *iteration variable*, and where $\mu^k\alpha\varphi$ is seen as $\varphi^k(\bot)$. Let $\Diamond^k\varphi := \mu^k\alpha.\ \varphi\vee\bigcirc\alpha$. If φ is safe then so is $\Diamond^k\varphi$. For safe φ, ψ, we have the following refinement typings for the guarded recursive $\mathsf{map}^{\mathsf{g}}$ and its coinductive lift map:

$$\begin{aligned}
\mathsf{map}^{\mathsf{g}} &: (\{B \mid \psi\} \to \{A \mid \varphi\}) \to \left\{\mathsf{Str}^{\mathsf{g}}\,B \,\middle|\, \Diamond^k[\mathsf{hd}]\psi\right\} \to \left\{\mathsf{Str}^{\mathsf{g}}\,A \,\middle|\, \Diamond^k[\mathsf{hd}]\varphi\right\}\\
\mathsf{map} &: (\{B \mid \psi\} \to \{A \mid \varphi\}) \to \{\mathsf{Str}\,B \mid [\mathsf{box}]\Diamond[\mathsf{hd}]\psi\} \to \{\mathsf{Str}\,A \mid [\mathsf{box}]\Diamond[\mathsf{hd}]\varphi\}
\end{aligned}$$

3 The Pure Calculus

Our system lies on top of the guarded λ-calculus of [18]. We briefly review it here. We consider values and terms from the grammar given in Fig. 3 (left). In

$$
\begin{array}{lll}
v ::= \lambda x.M \mid \langle M_0, M_1\rangle \mid \langle\rangle \mid \mathsf{in}_0(M) \mid \mathsf{in}_1(M) \mid \mathsf{fold}(M) \mid \mathsf{box}_\sigma(M) \mid \mathsf{next}(M)
\end{array}
$$

$$
M, N ::= v \mid x \mid MN \mid \pi_0(M) \mid \pi_1(M) \mid \mathsf{case}\ M\ \mathsf{of}\ (x.M_0|x.M_1) \mid \mathsf{unfold}(M) \mid \mathsf{unbox}(M) \mid \mathsf{prev}_\sigma(M) \mid M \circledast N \mid \mathsf{fix}(x).M
$$

$$
E ::= \bullet \mid EM \mid \pi_0(E) \mid \pi_1(E) \mid \mathsf{case}\ E\ \mathsf{of}\ (x.M_0|x.M_1) \mid \mathsf{unfold}(E) \mid \mathsf{unbox}(E) \mid \mathsf{prev}_{[]}(E) \mid E \circledast M \mid v \circledast E
$$

$$
\begin{array}{rcl}
(\lambda x.M)N & \rightsquigarrow & M[N/x] \\
\pi_i(\langle M_0, M_1\rangle) & \rightsquigarrow & M_i \\
\mathsf{case}\ \mathsf{in}_i(M)\ \mathsf{of}\ (x.N_0|x.N_1) & \rightsquigarrow & N_i[M/x] \\
\mathsf{unfold}(\mathsf{fold}(M)) & \rightsquigarrow & M \\
\mathsf{fix}(x).M & \rightsquigarrow & M[\mathsf{next}(\mathsf{fix}(x).M)/x] \\
\mathsf{next}(M) \circledast \mathsf{next}(N) & \rightsquigarrow & \mathsf{next}(MN) \\
\mathsf{unbox}(\mathsf{box}_\sigma(M)) & \rightsquigarrow & M\sigma \\
\mathsf{prev}_{[]}(\mathsf{next}(M)) & \rightsquigarrow & M \\
\mathsf{prev}_\sigma(M) & \rightsquigarrow & \mathsf{prev}_{[]}(M\sigma) \quad (\sigma \neq [])
\end{array}
\qquad
\frac{M \rightsquigarrow N}{E[M] \rightsquigarrow E[N]}
$$

Fig. 3. Syntax and Operational Semantics of the Pure Calculus.

both $\mathsf{box}_\sigma(M)$ and $\mathsf{prev}_\sigma(M)$, σ is a *delayed substitution* of the form $\sigma = [x_1 \mapsto M_1, \ldots, x_k \mapsto M_k]$ and such that $\mathsf{box}_\sigma(M)$ and $\mathsf{prev}_\sigma(M)$ bind $x_1, \ldots, x_k$ in M. We use the following conventions of [18]: $\mathsf{box}(M)$ and $\mathsf{prev}(M)$ (without indicated substitution) stand resp. for $\mathsf{box}_{[]}(M)$ and $\mathsf{prev}_{[]}(M)$ *i.e.* bind no variable of M. Moreover, $\mathsf{box}_\iota(M)$ stands for $\mathsf{box}_{[x_1 \mapsto x_1, \ldots, x_k \mapsto x_k]}(M)$ where $x_1, \ldots, x_k$ is a list of all free variables of M, and similarly for $\mathsf{prev}_\iota(M)$. We consider the weak call-by-name reduction of [18], recalled in Fig. 3 (right).

Pure types (notation A, B, etc.) are the closed types over the grammar

$$A ::= \mathbf{1} \mid A + A \mid A \times A \mid A \to A \mid \blacktriangleright A \mid X \mid \mathsf{Fix}(X).A \mid \blacksquare A$$

where, (1) in the case $\mathsf{Fix}(X).A$, each occurrence of X in A must be guarded by a $\blacktriangleright$, and (2) in the case of $\blacksquare A$, the type A is closed (*i.e.* has no free type variable). Guarded recursive types are built with the fixpoint constructor $\mathsf{Fix}(X).A$, which allows for X to appear in A both at positive and negative positions, but only under a $\blacktriangleright$. In this paper we shall only consider positive types.

Example 3.1. We can code a finite base type $\mathtt{B} = \{\mathtt{b}_1, \ldots, \mathtt{b}_n\}$ as a sum of unit types $\sum_{i=1}^{n} \mathbf{1} = \mathbf{1} + (\cdots + \mathbf{1})$, where the ith component of the sum is intended to represent the element $\mathtt{b}_i$ of $\mathtt{B}$. At the term level, the elements of $\mathtt{B}$ are represented as compositions of injections $\mathsf{in}_{j_1}(\mathsf{in}_{j_2}(\ldots \mathsf{in}_{j_i}\langle\rangle))$. For instance, Booleans are represented by $\mathsf{Bool} := \mathbf{1} + \mathbf{1}$, with $\mathsf{tt} := \mathsf{in}_0(\langle\rangle)$ and $\mathsf{ff} := \mathsf{in}_1(\langle\rangle)$.

Example 3.2. Besides streams ($\mathsf{Str}^{\mathsf{g}} A$), colists ($\mathsf{CoList}^{\mathsf{g}} A$), conatural numbers ($\mathsf{CoNat}^{\mathsf{g}}$) and infinite binary trees ($\mathsf{Tree}^{\mathsf{g}} A$), we consider a type $\mathsf{Res}^{\mathsf{g}} A$ of *resumptions* (parametrized by $\mathtt{I}$, $\mathtt{O}$) adapted from [44], and a higher-order recursive type $\mathsf{Rou}^{\mathsf{g}} A$, used in Martin Hofmann's breadth-first tree traversal (see e.g. [10]):

$$
\begin{array}{ll}
\mathsf{Tree}^{\mathsf{g}} A := \mathsf{Fix}(X).\ A \times (\blacktriangleright X \times \blacktriangleright X) & \mathsf{CoNat}^{\mathsf{g}} := \mathsf{Fix}(X).\ \mathbf{1} + \blacktriangleright X \\
\mathsf{Res}^{\mathsf{g}} A := \mathsf{Fix}(X).\ A + (\mathtt{I} \to (\mathtt{O} \times \blacktriangleright X)) & \mathsf{Rou}^{\mathsf{g}} A := \mathsf{Fix}(X).\ \mathbf{1} + ((\blacktriangleright X \to \blacktriangleright A) \to A)
\end{array}
$$

Some typing rules of the pure calculus are given in Fig. 4, where a pure type A is *constant* if each occurrence of $\blacktriangleright$ in A is guarded by a $\blacksquare$. The omitted rules are the standard ones for simple types with finite sums and products [28, §A].

$$\frac{\mathcal{E} \vdash M : A[\mathsf{Fix}(X).A/X]}{\mathcal{E} \vdash \mathsf{fold}(M) : \mathsf{Fix}(X).A} \qquad \frac{\mathcal{E} \vdash M : \mathsf{Fix}(X).A}{\mathcal{E} \vdash \mathsf{unfold}(M) : A[\mathsf{Fix}(X).A/X]} \qquad \frac{\mathcal{E} \vdash M : \blacktriangleright(B \to A) \qquad \mathcal{E} \vdash N : \blacktriangleright B}{\mathcal{E} \vdash M \circledast N : \blacktriangleright A}$$

$$\frac{\mathcal{E} \vdash M : A}{\mathcal{E} \vdash \mathsf{next}(M) : \blacktriangleright A} \qquad \frac{x_1 : A_1, \dots, x_k : A_k \vdash M : \blacktriangleright A \qquad \mathcal{E} \vdash M_i : A_i \text{ with } A_i \text{ constant for } 1 \le i \le k}{\mathcal{E} \vdash \mathsf{prev}_{[x_1 \mapsto M_1, \dots, x_k \mapsto M_k]}(M) : A}$$

$$\frac{x_1 : A_1, \dots, x_k : A_k \vdash M : A \qquad \mathcal{E} \vdash M_i : A_i \text{ with } A_i \text{ constant for } 1 \le i \le k}{\mathcal{E} \vdash \mathsf{box}_{[x_1 \mapsto M_1, \dots, x_k \mapsto M_k]}(M) : \blacksquare A} \qquad \frac{\mathcal{E} \vdash M : \blacksquare A}{\mathcal{E} \vdash \mathsf{unbox}(M) : A}$$

Fig. 4. Typing Rules of the Pure Calculus (excerpt).

Example 3.3. Figure 1 defines some operations on guarded streams. On other types of Ex. 3.2, we have e.g. the constructors of colists $\mathsf{Nil}^{\mathsf{g}} := \mathsf{fold}(\mathsf{in}_0\langle\rangle) : \mathsf{CoList}^{\mathsf{g}}\, A$ and $\mathsf{Cons}^{\mathsf{g}} := \lambda x.\lambda xs.\mathsf{fold}(\mathsf{in}_1\langle x, xs\rangle) : A \to \blacktriangleright \mathsf{CoList}^{\mathsf{g}}\, A \to \mathsf{CoList}^{\mathsf{g}}\, A$. Infinite binary trees $\mathsf{Tree}^{\mathsf{g}}\, A$ have operations $\mathsf{son}^{\mathsf{g}}_d : \mathsf{Tree}^{\mathsf{g}}\, A \to \blacktriangleright \mathsf{Tree}^{\mathsf{g}}\, A$ for $d \in \{\ell, r\}$, $\mathsf{Node}^{\mathsf{g}} : A \to \blacktriangleright \mathsf{Tree}^{\mathsf{g}}\, A \to \blacktriangleright \mathsf{Tree}^{\mathsf{g}}\, A \to \mathsf{Tree}^{\mathsf{g}}\, A$ and $\mathsf{label}^{\mathsf{g}} : \mathsf{Tree}^{\mathsf{g}}\, A \to A$.

Example 3.4. Coinductive types are guarded recursive types under a $\blacksquare$. For instance $\mathsf{Str}\, A := \blacksquare \mathsf{Str}^{\mathsf{g}}\, A$, $\mathsf{CoList}\, A := \blacksquare \mathsf{CoList}^{\mathsf{g}}\, A$, $\mathsf{CoNat} := \blacksquare \mathsf{CoNat}^{\mathsf{g}}$ and $\mathsf{Res}\, A := \blacksquare \mathsf{Res}^{\mathsf{g}}\, A$, with A, $\mathtt{I}$, $\mathtt{O}$ *constant.* Basic operations on guarded types lift to coinductive ones. For instance

$$\begin{aligned}
\mathsf{Cons} &:= \lambda x.\lambda s.\mathsf{box}_\iota(\mathsf{Cons}^{\mathsf{g}}\ x\ \mathsf{next}(\mathsf{unbox}\ s)) &&: A \to \mathsf{Str}\, A \to \mathsf{Str}\, A \\
\mathsf{hd} &:= \lambda s.\mathsf{hd}^{\mathsf{g}}\ (\mathsf{unbox}\ s) &&: \mathsf{Str}\, A \to A \\
\mathsf{tl} &:= \lambda s.\mathsf{box}_\iota(\mathsf{prev}_\iota(\mathsf{tl}^{\mathsf{g}}\ (\mathsf{unbox}\ s))) &&: \mathsf{Str}\, A \to \mathsf{Str}\, A
\end{aligned}$$

These definitions follow a general pattern to lift a function over a guarded recursive type into one over its coinductive version, by performing an η-expansion with some box and unbox inserted in the right places. For example, one can define the map function on coinductive streams as:

$$\mathsf{map} := \lambda f.\lambda s.\mathsf{box}_\iota(\mathsf{map}^{\mathsf{g}}\ f\ (\mathsf{unbox}\ s)) : (B \to A) \longrightarrow \mathsf{Str}\, B \longrightarrow \mathsf{Str}\, A$$

4 A Temporal Modal Logic

We present here a logic of (modal) temporal specifications. We focus on syntactic aspects. The semantics is discussed in §7. For the moment the logic has only one form of fixpoints ($\nu\alpha\varphi$). It is extended with least fixpoints ($\mu\alpha\varphi$) in §6.

Manysorted Modal Temporal Formulae. The main ingredient of this paper is the logical language we use to annotate pure types when forming refinement types. This language, that we took with minor adaptations from [30], is *manysorted*: for each pure type A we have formulae φ *of type* A (notation $\vdash \varphi : A$). The formulation rules of formulae are given in Fig. 5.

Example 4.1. Given a finite base type $\mathtt{B} = \{\mathtt{b}_1, \dots, \mathtt{b}_n\}$ as in Ex. 3.1, with element $\mathtt{b}_i$ represented by $\mathsf{in}_{j_1}(\mathsf{in}_{j_2}(\dots \mathsf{in}_{j_i}\langle\rangle))$, the formula $[\mathsf{in}_{j_1}][\mathsf{in}_{j_2}]\dots[\mathsf{in}_{j_i}]\top$ represents the singleton subset $\{\mathtt{b}_k\}$ of $\mathtt{B}$. On Bool, we have the formulae $[\mathsf{tt}] := [\mathsf{in}_0]\top$ and $[\mathsf{ff}] := [\mathsf{in}_1]\top$ representing resp. tt and ff.

$$\frac{(\alpha : A) \in \Sigma}{\Sigma \vdash \alpha : A} \qquad \frac{}{\Sigma \vdash \bot : A} \qquad \frac{}{\Sigma \vdash \top : A} \qquad \frac{\Sigma \vdash \varphi : A}{\Sigma, \alpha : B \vdash \varphi : A}$$

$$\frac{\Sigma \vdash \varphi : A \qquad \Sigma \vdash \psi : A}{\Sigma \vdash \varphi \Rightarrow \psi : A} \qquad \frac{\Sigma \vdash \varphi : A \qquad \Sigma \vdash \psi : A}{\Sigma \vdash \varphi \wedge \psi : A} \qquad \frac{\Sigma \vdash \varphi : A \qquad \Sigma \vdash \psi : A}{\Sigma \vdash \varphi \vee \psi : A}$$

$$\frac{\Sigma \vdash \varphi : A_i}{\Sigma \vdash [\pi_i]\varphi : A_0 \times A_1} \qquad \frac{\Sigma \vdash \varphi : A_i}{\Sigma \vdash [\mathsf{in}_i]\varphi : A_0 + A_1} \qquad \frac{\Sigma \vdash \psi : B \quad \Sigma \vdash \varphi : A}{\Sigma \vdash [\mathsf{ev}(\psi)]\varphi : B \to A}$$

$$\frac{\Sigma \vdash \varphi : A[\mathsf{Fix}(X).A/X]}{\Sigma \vdash [\mathsf{fold}]\varphi : \mathsf{Fix}(X).A} \qquad \frac{\Sigma \vdash \varphi : A}{\Sigma \vdash [\mathsf{next}]\varphi : \blacktriangleright A} \qquad \frac{\vdash \varphi : A}{\vdash [\mathsf{box}]\varphi : \blacksquare A}$$

$$(\nu\text{-F}) \ \frac{\Sigma, \alpha : A \vdash \varphi : A \qquad \alpha \text{ Pos } \varphi}{\Sigma \vdash \nu\alpha\varphi : A} \ (\alpha \text{ guarded in } \varphi)$$

Fig. 5. Formation Rules of Formulae (where A, B are pure types).

Example 4.2. (a) The formula $[\mathsf{hd}][\mathsf{a}] \Rightarrow \bigcirc[\mathsf{hd}][\mathsf{b}]$ means that if the head of a stream is a, then its second element (the head of its tail) should be b.
(b) On colists, we let $[\mathsf{hd}]\varphi := [\mathsf{fold}][\mathsf{in}_1][\pi_0]\varphi$ and $\bigcirc\psi := [\mathsf{fold}][\mathsf{in}_1][\pi_1][\mathsf{next}]\psi$.
(c) On (guarded) infinite binary trees over A, we also have a modality $[\mathsf{lbl}]\varphi := [\mathsf{fold}][\pi_0]\varphi : \mathsf{Tree}^{\mathsf{g}} A$ (provided $\varphi : A$). Moreover, we have modalities $\bigcirc_\ell$ and $\bigcirc_r$ defined on formulae $\varphi : \mathsf{Tree}^{\mathsf{g}} A$ as $\bigcirc_\ell\varphi := [\mathsf{fold}][\pi_1][\pi_0][\mathsf{next}]\varphi$ and $\bigcirc_r\varphi := [\mathsf{fold}][\pi_1][\pi_1][\mathsf{next}]\varphi$. Intuitively, $[\mathsf{lbl}]\varphi$ should hold on a tree t over A iff the root label of t satisfies φ, and $\bigcirc_\ell\varphi$ (resp. $\bigcirc_r\varphi$) should hold on t iff φ holds on the left (resp. right) immediate subtree of t.

Formulae have fixpoints $\nu\alpha\varphi$. The rules of Fig. 5 thus allow for the formation of formulae with free typed propositional variables (ranged over by $\alpha, \beta, \dots$), and involve contexts Σ of the form $\alpha_1 : A_1, \dots, \alpha_n : A_n$. In the formation of a fixpoint, the side condition "α guarded in φ" asks that each occurrence of α is beneath a [next] modality. Because we are ultimately interested in the *external* set-theoretic semantics of formulae, we assume a usual positivity condition of α in φ. It is defined with relations α Pos φ and α Neg φ (see [28, §B]). We just mention here that $[\mathsf{ev}(-)](-)$ is contravariant in its first argument. Note that $[\mathsf{box}]\varphi$ can only be formed for *closed* φ.

Example 4.3. (a) The modality $\Box$ makes it possible to express a range of safety properties. For instance, assuming $\varphi, \psi : \mathsf{Str}^{\mathsf{g}} A$, the formula $\Box(\psi \Rightarrow \bigcirc\varphi)$ is intended to hold on a stream $s = (s_i \mid i \geq 0)$ iff, for all $n \in \mathbb{N}$, if $(s_i \mid i \geq n)$ satisfies ψ, then $(s_i \mid i \geq n+1)$ satisfies φ.
(b) The modality $\Box$ has its two CTL-like variants on $\mathsf{Tree}^{\mathsf{g}} A$, namely $\forall\Box\varphi := \nu\alpha.\ \varphi \wedge (\bigcirc_\ell\alpha \wedge \bigcirc_r\alpha)$ and $\exists\Box\varphi := \nu\alpha.\ \varphi \wedge (\bigcirc_\ell\alpha \vee \bigcirc_r\alpha)$. Assuming $\psi : A$, $\forall\Box[\mathsf{lbl}]\psi$ is intended to hold on a tree $t : \mathsf{Tree}^{\mathsf{g}} A$ iff all node-labels of t satisfy ψ, while $\exists\Box[\mathsf{lbl}]\psi$ holds on t iff ψ holds on all nodes of *some* infinite path from the root of t.

Name	Formulation	$[\pi_i]$	[fold]	[next]	$[\mathsf{in}_i]$	$[\mathsf{ev}(\psi)]$	[box]	[hd]	$\bigcirc$
(RM)	$\dfrac{\vdash \psi \Rightarrow \varphi}{\vdash [\Delta]\psi \Rightarrow [\Delta]\varphi}$	✓	✓	✓	✓	✓	✓	✓	✓
(C)	$[\Delta]\varphi \wedge [\Delta]\psi \implies [\Delta](\varphi \wedge \psi)$	✓	✓	✓	✓	✓	✓	✓	✓
(N)	$[\Delta]\top$	✓	✓	✓		✓	✓	✓	✓
(P)	$[\Delta]\bot \implies \bot$	✓	✓	**(C)**	✓		✓	✓	**(C)**
$(\mathsf{C}_\vee)$	$[\Delta](\varphi \vee \psi) \implies [\Delta]\varphi \vee [\Delta]\psi$	✓	✓	✓	✓		✓	✓	✓
$(\mathsf{C}_\Rightarrow)$	$([\Delta]\psi \Rightarrow [\Delta]\varphi) \Rightarrow [\Delta](\psi \Rightarrow \varphi)$	✓	✓	**(C)**			✓	✓	**(C)**

Table 2. Modal Axioms and Rules. Types are omitted in $\vdash$ and **(C)** marks axioms assumed for $\vdash_{\mathsf{c}}$ but not for $\vdash$. Properties of the non-atomic [hd] and $\bigcirc$ are derived.

Modal Theories. Formulae are equipped with a modal deduction system which enters the type system via a subtyping relation (§5). For each pure type A, we have an intuitionistic theory $\vdash^A$ (the general case) and a classical theory $\vdash^A_{\mathsf{c}}$ (which is only assumed under $\blacksquare$/[box]), summarized in Fig. 6 and Table 2 (where we also give properties of the derived modalities [hd], $\bigcirc$). In any case, $\vdash^A_{(\mathsf{c})} \varphi$ is only defined when $\vdash \varphi : A$ (and so when φ has no free propositional variable).

Fixpoints $\nu\alpha\varphi$ are equipped with their usual Kozen axioms [43]. The atomic modalities $[\pi_i]$, [fold], [next], $[\mathsf{in}_i]$ and [box] have deterministic branching (see Fig. 12, §7). We can get the axioms of the intuitionistic (normal) modal logic **IK** [56] (see also e.g. [60,48]) for $[\pi_i]$, [fold] and [box] but not for $[\mathsf{in}_i]$ nor for the intuitionistic [next]. For [next], in the intuitionistic case this is due to semantic issues with step indexing (discussed in §7) which are absent from the classical case. As for $[\mathsf{in}_i]$, we have a logical theory allowing for a coding of finite base types as finite sum types, which allows to derive, for a finite base type B:

$$\vdash^{\mathsf{B}} \bigvee_{\mathsf{a} \in \mathsf{B}} \Big([\mathsf{a}] \;\wedge\; \bigwedge_{\substack{\mathsf{b} \in \mathsf{B} \\ \mathsf{b} \neq \mathsf{a}}} \neg[\mathsf{b}] \Big)$$

Definition 4.4 (Modal Theories). *For each pure type A, the* intuitionistic *and* classical *modal theories $\vdash^A \varphi$ and $\vdash^A_{\mathsf{c}} \varphi$ (where $\vdash \varphi : A$) are defined by mutual induction:*

- *The theory $\vdash^A$ is deduction for intuitionistic propositional logic augmented with the check-marked (✓) axioms and rules of Table 2 and the axioms and rules of Fig. 6 (for $\vdash^A$).*
- *The theory $\vdash^A_{\mathsf{c}}$ is $\vdash^A$ augmented with the axioms* (P) *and* $(\mathsf{C}_\Rightarrow)$ *for* [next] *and with the axiom* (CL) *(Fig. 6).*

For example, we have $\vdash^{\mathsf{Str}^{\mathsf{g}} A} \Box\psi \Rightarrow (\psi \wedge \bigcirc\Box\psi)$ and $\vdash^{\mathsf{Str}^{\mathsf{g}} A} (\psi \wedge \bigcirc\Box\psi) \Rightarrow \Box\psi$.

$$\frac{\vdash^B \psi \Rightarrow \phi \qquad \vdash \varphi : A}{\vdash^{B \to A} [\mathsf{ev}(\phi)]\varphi \Rightarrow [\mathsf{ev}(\psi)]\varphi} \qquad \frac{}{\vdash^{B \to A} ([\mathsf{ev}(\psi_0)]\varphi \wedge [\mathsf{ev}(\psi_1)]\varphi) \Rightarrow [\mathsf{ev}(\psi_0 \vee \psi_1)]\varphi}$$

$$\frac{}{\vdash^A_{\mathsf{c}} ((\varphi \Rightarrow \psi) \Rightarrow \varphi) \Rightarrow \varphi}\ (\mathsf{CL}) \qquad \frac{\vdash^A_{\mathsf{c}} \varphi}{\vdash^{\blacksquare A} [\mathsf{box}]\varphi} \qquad \frac{}{\vdash^{A_0+A_1} ([\mathsf{in}_0]\top \vee [\mathsf{in}_1]\top) \wedge \neg([\mathsf{in}_0]\top \wedge [\mathsf{in}_1]\top)}$$

$$\frac{}{\vdash^{A_0+A_1} ([\mathsf{in}_i]\top) \Rightarrow (\neg[\mathsf{in}_i]\varphi \Leftrightarrow [\mathsf{in}_i]\neg\varphi)} \qquad \frac{}{\vdash^A \nu\alpha\varphi \Rightarrow \varphi[\nu\alpha\varphi/\alpha]} \qquad \frac{\vdash^A \psi \Rightarrow \varphi[\psi/\alpha]}{\vdash^A \psi \Rightarrow \nu\alpha\varphi}$$

Fig. 6. Modal Axioms and Rules.

$$\frac{}{T \leq |T|} \qquad \frac{}{A \leq \{A \mid \top\}} \qquad \frac{\vdash^A \varphi \Rightarrow \psi}{\{A \mid \varphi\} \leq \{A \mid \psi\}} \qquad \frac{\vdash^A_{\mathsf{c}} \varphi \Rightarrow \psi}{\{\blacksquare A \mid [\mathsf{box}]\varphi\} \leq \{\blacksquare A \mid [\mathsf{box}]\psi\}}$$

$$\frac{}{\{\blacktriangleright A \mid [\mathsf{next}]\varphi\} \equiv \blacktriangleright \{A \mid \varphi\}} \qquad \frac{}{\{B \to A \mid [\mathsf{ev}(\psi)]\varphi\} \equiv \{B \mid \psi\} \to \{A \mid \varphi\}}$$

Fig. 7. Subtyping Rules (excerpt).

5 A Temporally Refined Type System

Temporal refinement types (or *types*), notation T, U, V, etc., are defined by:

$$T, U ::= A \mid \{A \mid \varphi\} \mid T + T \mid T \times T \mid T \to T \mid \blacktriangleright T \mid \blacksquare T$$

where $\vdash \varphi : A$ and, in the case of $\blacksquare T$, the type T has no free type variable. So types are built from (closed) pure types A and temporal refinements $\{A \mid \varphi\}$. They allow for all the type constructors of pure types.

As a refinement type $\{A \mid \varphi\}$ intuitively represents a subset of the inhabitants of A, it is natural to equip our system with a notion of *subtyping*. In addition to the usual rules for product, arrow and sum types, our subtyping relation is made of two more ingredients. The first follows the principle that our refinement type system is meant to prove properties of programs, and not to type more programs, so that (say) a type of the form $\{A \mid \varphi\} \to \{B \mid \psi\}$ is a subtype of $A \to B$. We formalize this with the notion of *underlying pure type* $|T|$ of a type T. The second ingredient is the modal theory $\vdash^A \varphi$ of §4. The subtyping rules concerning refinements are given in Fig. 7, where $T \equiv U$ enforces both $T \leq U$ and $U \leq T$. The full set of rules is given in [28, §C]. Notice that subtyping does not incorporate (un)folding of guarded recursive types.

Typing for refinement types is given by the rules of Fig. 8, together with the rules of §3 *extended to refinement types*, where T is *constant* if $|T|$ is constant. Modalities $[\pi_i]$, $[\mathsf{in}_i]$, $[\mathsf{fold}]$ and $[\mathsf{ev}(-)]$ (but not $[\mathsf{next}]$) have introduction rules extending those of the corresponding term formers.

$$(\text{Pi}_i\text{-I})\ \frac{\mathcal{E} \vdash M_i : \{A_i \mid \varphi\} \qquad \mathcal{E} \vdash M_{1-i} : A_{1-i}}{\mathcal{E} \vdash \langle M_0, M_1\rangle : \{A_0 \times A_1 \mid [\pi_i]\varphi\}} \qquad (\text{Pi}_i\text{-E})\ \frac{\mathcal{E} \vdash M : \{A_0 \times A_1 \mid [\pi_i]\varphi\}}{\mathcal{E} \vdash \pi_i(M) : \{A_i \mid \varphi\}}$$

$$(\text{Ev-I})\ \frac{\mathcal{E}, x : \{B \mid \psi\} \vdash M : \{A \mid \varphi\}}{\mathcal{E} \vdash \lambda x.M : \{B \to A \mid [\mathsf{ev}(\psi)]\varphi\}} \qquad (\text{Ev-E})\ \frac{\mathcal{E} \vdash M : \{B \to A \mid [\mathsf{ev}(\psi)]\varphi\} \qquad \mathcal{E} \vdash N : \{B \mid \psi\}}{\mathcal{E} \vdash MN : \{A \mid \varphi\}}$$

$$(\text{Fd-I})\ \frac{\mathcal{E} \vdash M : \{A[\mathsf{Fix}(X).A/X] \mid \varphi\}}{\mathcal{E} \vdash \mathsf{fold}(M) : \{\mathsf{Fix}(X).A \mid [\mathsf{fold}]\varphi\}} \qquad (\text{Fd-E})\ \frac{\mathcal{E} \vdash M : \{\mathsf{Fix}(X).A \mid [\mathsf{fold}]\varphi\}}{\mathcal{E} \vdash \mathsf{unfold}(M) : \{A[\mathsf{Fix}(X).A/X] \mid \varphi\}}$$

$$(\text{Inj}_i\text{-E})\ \frac{\mathcal{E} \vdash M : \{A_0 + A_1 \mid [\mathsf{in}_i]\varphi\} \qquad \mathcal{E}, x : \{A_i \mid \varphi\} \vdash N_i : U \qquad \mathcal{E}, x : A_{1-i} \vdash N_{1-i} : U}{\mathcal{E} \vdash \mathsf{case}\ M\ \mathsf{of}\ (x.N_0 | x.N_1) : U}$$

$$\text{for } i \in \{0,1\},\quad (\vee\text{-E})\ \frac{\mathcal{E} \vdash M : \{A \mid \varphi_0 \vee \varphi_1\} \qquad \mathcal{E}, x : \{A \mid \varphi_i\} \vdash N : U}{\mathcal{E} \vdash N[M/x] : U} \qquad (\text{Inj}_i\text{-I})\ \frac{\mathcal{E} \vdash M : \{A_i \mid \varphi\}}{\mathcal{E} \vdash \mathsf{in}_i(M) : \{A_0 + A_1 \mid [\mathsf{in}_i]\varphi\}}$$

$$(\text{MP})\ \frac{\mathcal{E} \vdash M : \{A \mid \psi \Rightarrow \varphi\} \quad \mathcal{E} \vdash M : \{A \mid \psi\}}{\mathcal{E} \vdash M : \{A \mid \varphi\}} \qquad (\text{ExF})\ \frac{\mathcal{E} \vdash M : \{A \mid \bot\} \quad \mathcal{E} \vdash N : |U|}{\mathcal{E} \vdash N : U}$$

$$(\text{Sub})\ \frac{\mathcal{E} \vdash M : T \quad T \leq U}{\mathcal{E} \vdash M : U}$$

Fig. 8. Typing Rules for Refined Modal Types.

Example 5.1. Since $\varphi \Rightarrow \psi \Rightarrow (\varphi \wedge \psi)$ and using two times the rule (MP), we get the first derived rule below, from which we can deduce the second one:

$$\frac{\mathcal{E} \vdash M : \{A \mid \varphi\} \quad \mathcal{E} \vdash M : \{A \mid \psi\}}{\mathcal{E} \vdash M : \{A \mid \varphi \wedge \psi\}} \qquad \frac{\mathcal{E} \vdash M : \{A \mid \varphi\} \quad \mathcal{E} \vdash N : \{B \mid \psi\}}{\mathcal{E} \vdash \langle M, N\rangle : \{A \times B \mid [\pi_0]\varphi \wedge [\pi_1]\psi\}}$$

Example 5.2. We have the following derived rules:

$$\frac{\mathcal{E} \vdash M : \{\mathsf{Str}^{\mathsf{g}}\, A \mid \Box\varphi\}}{\mathcal{E} \vdash M : \{\mathsf{Str}^{\mathsf{g}}\, A \mid \varphi \wedge \bigcirc\Box\varphi\}} \quad \text{and} \quad \frac{\mathcal{E} \vdash M : \{\mathsf{Str}^{\mathsf{g}}\, A \mid \varphi \wedge \bigcirc\Box\varphi\}}{\mathcal{E} \vdash M : \{\mathsf{Str}^{\mathsf{g}}\, A \mid \Box\varphi\}}$$

Example 5.3. We have $\mathsf{Cons}^{\mathsf{g}} : A \to \blacktriangleright\{\mathsf{Str}^{\mathsf{g}}\, A \mid \varphi\} \to \{\mathsf{Str}^{\mathsf{g}}\, A \mid \bigcirc\varphi\}$ as well as $\mathsf{tl}^{\mathsf{g}} : \{\mathsf{Str}^{\mathsf{g}}\, A \mid \bigcirc\varphi\} \to \blacktriangleright\{\mathsf{Str}^{\mathsf{g}}\, A \mid \varphi\}$.

Example 5.4 ("Always" ($\Box$) on Guarded Streams). The refined types of $\mathsf{Cons}^{\mathsf{g}}$, hd^{g}, tl^{g} and $\mathsf{map}^{\mathsf{g}}$ mentioned in §2 are easy to derive. We also have the type

$$\{\mathsf{Str}^{\mathsf{g}}\, A \mid \Box[\mathsf{hd}]\varphi_0\} \longrightarrow \{\mathsf{Str}^{\mathsf{g}}\, A \mid \Box[\mathsf{hd}]\varphi_1\} \longrightarrow \{\mathsf{Str}^{\mathsf{g}}\, A \mid \Box([\mathsf{hd}]\varphi_0 \vee [\mathsf{hd}]\varphi_1)\}$$

for the $\mathsf{merge}^{\mathsf{g}}$ function which takes two guarded streams and interleaves them:

$$\begin{aligned} \mathsf{merge}^{\mathsf{g}} :\ & \mathsf{Str}^{\mathsf{g}}\, A \longrightarrow \mathsf{Str}^{\mathsf{g}}\, A \longrightarrow \mathsf{Str}^{\mathsf{g}}\, A \\ :=\ & \mathsf{fix}(g).\lambda s_0.\lambda s_1.\ (\mathsf{hd}^{\mathsf{g}}\, s_0) ::^{\mathsf{g}} \mathsf{next}\big((\mathsf{hd}^{\mathsf{g}}\, s_1) ::^{\mathsf{g}} (g \circledast (\mathsf{tl}^{\mathsf{g}}\, s_0) \circledast (\mathsf{tl}^{\mathsf{g}}\, s_1))\big) \end{aligned}$$

6 The Full System

The system presented so far has only one form of fixpoints in formulae ($\nu\alpha\varphi$). We now present our full system, which also handles least fixpoints ($\mu\alpha\varphi$) and thus liveness properties. A key role is played by *polynomial* guarded recursive types, that we discuss first.

$$(\mu\text{-F})\ \frac{\Sigma, \alpha : A \vdash \varphi : A}{\Sigma \vdash \mu\alpha\varphi : A} \qquad \frac{\Sigma, \alpha : A \vdash \varphi : A}{\Sigma \vdash \mu^{\mathtt{t}}\alpha\varphi : A} \qquad \frac{\Sigma, \alpha : A \vdash \varphi : A}{\Sigma \vdash \nu^{\mathtt{t}}\alpha\varphi : A}$$

Fig. 9. Extended Formation Rules of Formulae (with α Pos φ and α guarded in φ).

$$\frac{}{\vdash^A \varphi[\mu\alpha\varphi/\alpha] \Rightarrow \mu\alpha\varphi} \qquad \frac{\vdash^A \varphi[\psi/\alpha] \Rightarrow \psi}{\vdash^A \mu\alpha\varphi \Rightarrow \psi}$$

$$\frac{}{\vdash^A \theta^{\mathtt{t}+1}\alpha\varphi \Leftrightarrow \varphi[\theta^{\mathtt{t}}\alpha\varphi/\alpha]} \qquad \frac{}{\vdash^A \mu^0\alpha\varphi \Leftrightarrow \bot} \qquad \frac{}{\vdash^A \nu^0\alpha\varphi \Leftrightarrow \top}$$

$$\frac{[\![\mathtt{t}]\!] \leq [\![\mathtt{u}]\!]}{\vdash^A \mu^{\mathtt{t}}\alpha\varphi \Rightarrow \mu^{\mathtt{u}}\alpha\varphi} \qquad \frac{}{\vdash^A \mu^{\mathtt{t}}\alpha\varphi \Rightarrow \mu\alpha\varphi} \qquad \frac{[\![\mathtt{t}]\!] \geq [\![\mathtt{u}]\!]}{\vdash^A \nu^{\mathtt{t}}\alpha\varphi \Rightarrow \nu^{\mathtt{u}}\alpha\varphi} \qquad \frac{}{\vdash^A \nu\alpha\varphi \Rightarrow \nu^{\mathtt{t}}\alpha\varphi}$$

Fig. 10. Extended Modal Axioms and Rules (with A a pure type and θ either μ or ν).

Strictly Positive and Polynomial Types. *Strictly positive types* (notation P^+, Q^+, etc.) are given by

$$P^+ ::= A \mid X \mid \blacktriangleright P^+ \mid P^+ + P^+ \mid P^+ \times P^+ \mid \mathsf{Fix}(X).P^+ \mid B \to P^+$$

where A, B are (closed) *constant* pure types. Strictly positive types are a convenient generalization of polynomial types. A guarded recursive type $\mathsf{Fix}(X).P(X)$ is *polynomial* if $P(X)$ is induced by

$$P(X) ::= A \mid \blacktriangleright X \mid P(X) + P(X) \mid P(X) \times P(X) \mid B \to P(X)$$

where A, B are (closed) *constant* pure types. Note that if $\mathsf{Fix}(X).P(X)$ is polynomial, X cannot occur on the left of an arrow ($\to$) in $P(X)$. We say that $\mathsf{Fix}(X).P(X)$ (resp. P^+) is *finitary* polynomial (resp. *finitary* strictly positive) if B is a finite base type (see Ex. 3.1) in the above grammars. The set-theoretic counterpart of our polynomial recursive types are the *exponent* polynomial functors of [31], which all have final **Set**-coalgebras (see e.g. [31, Cor. 4.6.3]).

Example 6.1. For A a constant pure type, e.g. $\mathsf{Str}^{\mathsf{g}} A$, $\mathsf{CoList}^{\mathsf{g}} A$ and $\mathsf{Tree}^{\mathsf{g}} A$ as well as $\mathsf{Str}^{\mathsf{g}}(\mathsf{Str}\, A)$, $\mathsf{CoList}^{\mathsf{g}}(\mathsf{Str}\, A)$ and $\mathsf{Res}^{\mathsf{g}} A$ (with $\mathtt{I}$, $\mathtt{O}$ constant) are polynomial. More generally, polynomial types include all recursive types $\mathsf{Fix}(X).P(X)$ where $P(X)$ is of the form $\sum_{i=0}^{n} A_i \times (\blacktriangleright X)^{B_i}$ with A_i, B_i constant. The non-strictly positive recursive type $\mathsf{Rou}^{\mathsf{g}} A$ of Ex. 3.2, used in Hofmann's breadth-first traversal (see e.g. [10]), is *not* polynomial.

The Full Temporal Modal Logic. We assume given a first-order signature of *iteration terms* (notation $\mathtt{t}, \mathtt{u}$, etc.), with *iteration variables* k, ℓ, etc., and for each iteration term $\mathtt{t}(k_1, \ldots, k_m)$ with variables as shown, a given primitive recursive function $[\![\mathtt{t}]\!] : \mathbb{N}^m \to \mathbb{N}$. We assume a term $\mathsf{0}$ for $0 \in \mathbb{N}$ and a term $k{+}1$ for the successor function $n \in \mathbb{N} \mapsto n + 1 \in \mathbb{N}$.

The formulae of the *full temporal modal logic* extend those of Fig. 5 with least fixpoints $\mu\alpha\varphi$ and with *approximated fixpoints* $\mu^{\mathsf{t}}\alpha\varphi$ and $\nu^{\mathsf{t}}\alpha\varphi$ where t is an iteration term. The additional formation rule for formulae are given in Fig. 9. We use θ as a generic notation for μ and ν. Least fixpoints $\mu\alpha\varphi$ are equipped with their usual Kozen axioms. In addition, iteration formulae $\nu^{\mathsf{t}}\alpha\varphi(\alpha)$ and $\mu^{\mathsf{t}}\alpha\varphi(\alpha)$ have axioms expressing that they are indeed iterations of $\varphi(\alpha)$ from resp. $\top$ and $\bot$. A fixpoint logic with iteration variables was already considered in [63].

Definition 6.2 (Full Modal Theories). *The* full *intuitionistic and classical modal theories (still denoted* $\vdash^A$ *and* $\vdash^A_{\mathrm{c}}$*) are defined by extending Def. 4.4 with the axioms and rules of Fig. 10.*

Example 6.3. Least fixpoints allow us to define liveness properties. On streams and colists, we have $\Diamond\varphi := \mu\alpha.\ \varphi \vee \bigcirc\alpha$ and $\varphi \mathbin{\mathsf{U}} \psi := \mu\alpha.\ \psi \vee (\varphi \wedge \bigcirc\alpha)$. On trees, we have the CTL-like $\exists\Diamond\varphi := \mu\alpha.\ \varphi \vee (\bigcirc_\ell\alpha \vee \bigcirc_r\alpha)$ and $\forall\Diamond\varphi := \mu\alpha.\ \varphi \vee (\bigcirc_\ell\alpha \wedge \bigcirc_r\alpha)$. The formula $\exists\Diamond\varphi$ is intended to hold on a tree if there is a finite path which leads to a subtree satisfying φ, while $\forall\Diamond\varphi$ is intended to hold if every infinite path crosses a subtree satisfying φ.

Remark 6.4. On *finitary trees* (as in Ex. 6.1 but with A_i, B_i finite base types), we have all formulae of the modal μ-calculus. For this fragment, satisfiability is decidable (see e.g. [16]), as well as the *classical* theory $\vdash_{\mathrm{c}}$ by completeness of Kozen's axiomatization [68] (see [58] for completeness results on fragments of the μ-calculus).

The Safe and Smooth Fragments. We now discuss two related but distinct fragments of the temporal modal logic. Both fragments directly impact the refinement type system by allowing for more typing rules.

The *safe* fragment plays a crucial role, because it reconciles the internal and external semantics of our system (see §7). It gives subtyping rules for $\blacksquare$ (Fig. 11), which makes available the comonad structure of $\blacksquare$ on $[\mathsf{box}]\varphi$ when φ is safe.

Definition 6.5 (Safe Formula). *Say* $\alpha_1 : A_1, \ldots, \alpha_n : A_n \vdash \varphi : A$ *is* safe *if*

(i) the types $A_1, \ldots, A_n, A$ *are strictly positive, and*
(ii) for each occurrence in φ *of a modality* $[\mathsf{ev}(\psi)]$*, the formula* ψ *is closed, and*
(iii) each occurrence in φ *of a least fixpoint* $(\mu\alpha(-))$ *and of an implication* $(\Rightarrow)$ *is guarded by a* $[\mathsf{box}]$.

Note that the safe restriction imposes no condition on approximated fixpoints $\theta^{\mathsf{t}}\alpha$. Recalling that the theory under a $[\mathsf{box}]$ is $\vdash^A_{\mathrm{c}}$, the only propositional connectives accessible to $\vdash^A$ in safe formulae are those on which $\vdash^A$ and $\vdash^A_{\mathrm{c}}$ coincide. The formula $[\neg\mathsf{nil}] = [\mathsf{fold}][\mathsf{in}_1]\top$ is safe. Moreover:

Example 6.6. Any formula without fixpoint nor $[\mathsf{ev}(-)]$ is equivalent in $\vdash_{\mathrm{c}}$ to a safe one. It φ is safe, then so are $[\mathsf{hd}]\varphi$, $[\mathsf{lbl}]\varphi$, as well as $\triangle\varphi$ (for $\triangle \in \{\Box, \forall\Box, \exists\Box\}$) and $[\mathsf{box}]\triangle\varphi$ (for $\triangle \in \{\Diamond, \exists\Diamond, \forall\Diamond\}$).

Definition 6.7 (Smooth Formula). *A formula* $\alpha_1 : A_1, \ldots, \alpha_n : A_n \vdash \varphi : A$ *is* smooth *if*

(i) the types $A_1, \ldots, A_n, A$ *are* finitary *strictly positive, and*
(ii) for each occurrence in φ *of a modality* $[\mathsf{ev}(\psi)]$, *the formula* ψ *is closed, and*
(iii) φ *is* alternation-free: *for* $\theta, \theta' \in \{\mu, \nu\}$, *(1) if* $\theta\beta_0\psi_0$ *is a subformula of* φ, *and* $\theta'\beta_1\psi_1$ *is a subformula of* ψ_0 *s.t.* β_0 *occurs free in* ψ_1, *then* $\theta = \theta'$, *(2) if some* α_i *occurs in two subformulae* $\theta\beta_0\psi_0$ *and* $\theta'\beta_1\psi_1$ *of* φ, *then* $\theta = \theta'$, *and (3) if some* α_i *occurs in a subformula* $\theta'\beta\psi$ *of* φ, *then* α_i Pos ψ.

Our notion of alternation freedom is adapted from [16], in which propositional (fixpoint) variables are always positive. Note that the smooth restriction imposes no further conditions on approximated fixpoints $\theta^{\mathtt{t}}\alpha$. In the smooth fragment, greatest and least fixpoints can be thought about resp. as

$$\bigwedge_{m \in \mathbb{N}} \varphi^m(\top) \qquad \text{and} \qquad \bigvee_{m \in \mathbb{N}} \varphi^m(\bot)$$

Iteration terms allow for formal reasoning about such unfoldings. Assuming $[\![\mathtt{t}]\!] = m \in \mathbb{N}$, the formula $\nu^{\mathtt{t}}\alpha\varphi(\alpha)$ (resp. $\mu^{\mathtt{t}}\alpha\varphi(\alpha)$) can be read as $\varphi^m(\top)$ (resp. $\varphi^m(\bot)$). This gives the rules (ν-I) and (μ-E) (Fig. 11), which allow for reductions to the safe case (see examples in §8).

Remark 6.8. It is well-known (see e.g. [16, §4.1]) that on *finitary trees* (see Rem. 6.4) the alternation-free fragment is equivalent to *Weak* MSO (MSO with second-order variables restricted to *finite* sets). In the case of streams Str B (for a finite base type B), Weak MSO is in turn equivalent to the full modal μ-calculus. In particular, the alternation-free fragment contains all the *flat* fixpoints of [58] and thus LTL on Str B and CTL on Tree B and on Res B with I, O, B finite base types. A typical property on Tree B which *cannot* be expressed with alternation-free formulae is "there is an infinite path with infinitely many occurrences of b" for a fixed b : B (see e.g. [16, §2.2]).

Example 6.9. Any formula without fixpoint nor $[\mathsf{ev}(-)]$ is smooth. It φ is smooth, then so are $[\mathsf{hd}]\varphi$, $[\mathsf{lbl}]\varphi$ and $\triangle\varphi$ for $\triangle \in \{\Box, \forall\Box, \exists\Box, \Diamond, \exists\Diamond, \forall\Diamond\}$.

The Full System. We extend the types of §5 with universal quantification over iteration variables ($\forall k \cdot T$). The type system of §5 is extended with the rules of Fig. 11.

Example 6.10. The logical rules of Fig. 10 give the following derived typing rules (where β Pos γ):

$$(\mu\text{-I})\ \frac{\mathcal{E} \vdash M : \{\blacksquare A \mid [\mathsf{box}]\gamma[\mu^{\mathtt{t}}\alpha\varphi/\beta]\}}{\mathcal{E} \vdash M : \{\blacksquare A \mid [\mathsf{box}]\gamma[\mu\alpha\varphi/\beta]\}} \qquad (\nu\text{-E})\ \frac{\mathcal{E} \vdash M : \{\blacksquare A \mid [\mathsf{box}]\gamma[\nu\alpha\varphi/\beta]\}}{\mathcal{E} \vdash M : \{\blacksquare A \mid [\mathsf{box}]\gamma[\nu^{\mathtt{t}}\alpha\varphi/\beta]\}}$$

$$\frac{\varphi \text{ safe}}{\{\blacksquare A \mid [\mathsf{box}]\varphi\} \equiv \blacksquare\{A \mid \varphi\}} \qquad \frac{}{\forall k \cdot \blacktriangleright T \equiv \blacktriangleright \forall k \cdot T}$$

$$(\forall\text{-I})\ \frac{\mathcal{E} \vdash M : T}{\mathcal{E} \vdash M : \forall k \cdot T} \qquad (\forall\text{-CI})\ \frac{\mathcal{E} \vdash M : T[0/k] \qquad \mathcal{E} \vdash M : T[k{+}1/k]}{\mathcal{E} \vdash M : \forall k \cdot T}$$

$$(\nu\text{-I})\ \frac{\mathcal{E} \vdash M : \{\blacksquare A \mid [\mathsf{box}]\gamma[\nu^\ell \alpha\psi/\beta]\}}{\mathcal{E} \vdash M : \{\blacksquare A \mid [\mathsf{box}]\gamma[\nu\alpha\psi/\beta]\}} \qquad (\forall\text{-E})\ \frac{\mathcal{E} \vdash M : \forall k \cdot T}{\mathcal{E} \vdash M : T[\mathtt{t}/k]}$$

$$(\mu\text{-E})\ \frac{\mathcal{E} \vdash M : \{\blacksquare A \mid [\mathsf{box}]\gamma[\mu\alpha\psi/\beta]\} \qquad \mathcal{E}, x : \{\blacksquare A \mid [\mathsf{box}]\gamma[\mu^\ell\alpha\psi/\beta]\} \vdash N : U}{\mathcal{E} \vdash N[M/x] : U}$$

Fig. 11. Extended (Sub)Typing Rules for Refinement Types (where k is not free in $\mathcal{E}$ in ($\forall$-I) & ($\forall$-CI), ℓ is fresh in (ν-I) & (μ-E), $\theta\alpha\psi$ and γ are smooth, and β Pos γ).

7 Semantics

We present the main ingredients of the semantics of our type system. We take as base the denotational semantics of guarded recursion in the topos of trees.

Denotational Semantics in the Topos of Trees. The *topos of trees* $\mathcal{S}$ provides a natural model of guarded recursion [13]. Formally, $\mathcal{S}$ is the category of presheaves over $(\mathbb{N} \setminus \{0\}, \leq)$. In words, the objects of $\mathcal{S}$ are indexed sets $X = (X(n))_{n>0}$ equipped with *restriction maps* $r^X_n : X(n+1) \to X(n)$. Excluding 0 from the indexes is a customary notational convenience ([13]). The morphisms from X to Y are families of functions $f = (f_n : X(n) \to Y(n))_{n>0}$ which commute with restriction, that is $f_n \circ r^X_n = r^Y_n \circ f_{n+1}$. As any presheaf category, $\mathcal{S}$ has (pointwise) limits and colimits, and is Cartesian closed (see e.g. [47, §I.6]). We write $\boldsymbol{\Gamma} : \mathcal{S} \to \mathbf{Set}$ for the *global section functor*, which takes X to $\mathcal{S}[\mathbf{1}, X]$, the set of morphisms $\mathbf{1} \to X$ in $\mathcal{S}$, where $\mathbf{1} = (\{\bullet\})_{n>0}$ is terminal in $\mathcal{S}$.

A typed term $\mathcal{E} \vdash M : T$ is to be interpreted in $\mathcal{S}$ as a morphism

$$[\![M]\!] : [\![|\mathcal{E}|]\!] \longrightarrow [\![|T|]\!]$$

where $[\![|\mathcal{E}|]\!] = [\![|T_1|]\!] \times \cdots \times [\![|T_n|]\!]$ for $\mathcal{E} = x_1 : T_1, \ldots, x_n : T_n$. In particular, a closed term $M : T$ is to be interpreted as a global section $[\![M]\!] \in \boldsymbol{\Gamma}[\![|T|]\!]$. The $\times/+/\to$ fragment of the calculus is interpreted by the corresponding structure in $\mathcal{S}$. The $\blacktriangleright$ modality is interpreted by the functor $\blacktriangleright : \mathcal{S} \to \mathcal{S}$ of [13]. This functor shifts indexes by 1 and inserts a singleton set $\mathbf{1}$ at index 1. The term constructor next is interpreted by the natural map with component $\mathsf{next}^X : X \to \blacktriangleright X$ as in

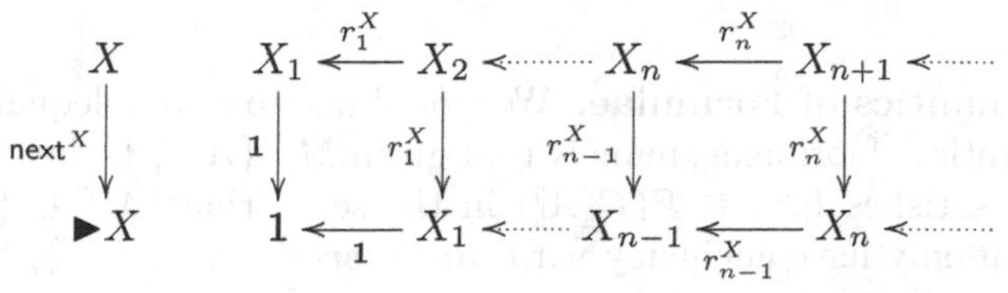

$$
\begin{array}{rlrl}
\{\![[\pi_i]\varphi]\!\} &:= \{x \in \boldsymbol{\Gamma}[\![A_0 \times A_1]\!] \mid \pi_i \circ x \in \{\![\varphi]\!\}\} & \{\![[\mathsf{next}]\varphi]\!\} &:= \{\mathsf{next} \circ x \in \boldsymbol{\Gamma}[\![\blacktriangleright A]\!] \mid x \in \{\![\varphi]\!\}\} \\
\{\![[\mathsf{fold}]\varphi]\!\} &:= \{x \in \boldsymbol{\Gamma}[\![\mathsf{Fix}(X).A]\!] \mid \mathsf{unfold} \circ x \in \{\![\varphi]\!\}\} & \{\![[\mathsf{box}]\varphi]\!\} &:= \{x \in \boldsymbol{\Gamma}[\![\blacksquare A]\!] \mid x_1(\bullet) \in \{\![\varphi]\!\}\} \\
\{\![[\mathsf{in}_i]\varphi]\!\} &:= \{x \in \boldsymbol{\Gamma}[\![A_0 + A_1]\!] \mid \exists y \in \boldsymbol{\Gamma}[\![A_i]\!]\big(x = \mathsf{in}_i \circ y \text{ and } y \in \{\![\varphi]\!\}\big)\} && \\
\{\![[\mathsf{ev}(\psi)]\varphi]\!\} &:= \{x \in \boldsymbol{\Gamma}[\![B \to A]\!] \mid \forall y \in \boldsymbol{\Gamma}[\![B]\!]\big(y \in \{\![\psi]\!\} \implies \mathsf{ev} \circ \langle x, y\rangle \in \{\![\varphi]\!\}\big)\} &&
\end{array}
$$

Fig. 12. External Semantics (for closed formulae).

The guarded fixpoint combinator fix is interpreted by the morphism $\mathsf{fix}^X : X^{\blacktriangleright X} \to X$ of [13, Thm. 2.4].

The constant type modality $\blacksquare$ is interpreted as the comonad $\boldsymbol{\Delta\Gamma} : \mathcal{S} \to \mathcal{S}$, where the left adjoint $\boldsymbol{\Delta} : \mathbf{Set} \to \mathcal{S}$ is the *constant object functor*, which takes a set S to the constant family $(S)_{n>0}$. In words, all components $[\![\blacksquare A]\!](n)$ are equal to $\boldsymbol{\Gamma}[\![A]\!]$, and the restriction maps of $[\![\blacksquare A]\!]$ are identities. In particular, a global section $x \in \boldsymbol{\Gamma}[\![\blacksquare A]\!]$ is a constant family $(x_n)_n$ describing a unique global section $x_{n+1}(\bullet) = x_n(\bullet) \in \boldsymbol{\Gamma}[\![A]\!]$. We refer to [18] and [28, §D] for the interpretation of prev, box and unbox. Just note that the unit $\eta : \mathrm{Id}_{\mathbf{Set}} \to \boldsymbol{\Gamma\Delta}$ is an iso.

Together with an interpretation of guarded recursive types, this gives a denotational semantics of the pure calculus of §3. See [13,18] for details. We write fold : $[\![A[\mathsf{Fix}(X).A/X]]\!] \to [\![\mathsf{Fix}(X).A]\!]$ and unfold : $[\![\mathsf{Fix}(X).A]\!] \to [\![A[\mathsf{Fix}(X).A/X]]\!]$ for the two components of the iso $[\![\mathsf{Fix}(X).A]\!] \simeq [\![A[\mathsf{Fix}(X).A/X]]\!]$.

External Semantics. Møgelberg [50] has shown that for polynomial types such as $\mathsf{Str}^{\mathsf{g}}\, B$ with B a constant type, the set of global sections $\boldsymbol{\Gamma}[\![\mathsf{Str}^{\mathsf{g}}\, B]\!]$ is equipped with the usual final coalgebra structure of streams over B in **Set**. To each polynomial recursive type $\mathsf{Fix}(X).P(X)$, we associate a polynomial functor $P_{\mathbf{Set}} : \mathbf{Set} \to \mathbf{Set}$ in the obvious way.

Theorem 7.1 ([50] (see also [18])). *If* $\mathsf{Fix}(X).P(X)$ *is polynomial, then the set* $\boldsymbol{\Gamma}[\![\mathsf{Fix}(X).P(X)]\!]$ *carries a final* **Set***-coalgebra structure for* $P_{\mathbf{Set}}$.

We devise a **Set** interpretation $\{\![\varphi]\!\} \in \mathcal{P}(\boldsymbol{\Gamma}[\![A]\!])$ of formulae $\varphi : A$. We rely on the (complete) Boolean algebra structure of powersets for propositional connectives and on Knaster-Tarski Fixpoint Theorem for fixpoints μ and ν. The interpretations of $\nu^{\mathtt{t}}\alpha\varphi(\alpha)$ and $\mu^{\mathtt{t}}\alpha\varphi(\alpha)$ (for $\mathtt{t}$ closed) are defined to be the interpretations resp. of $\varphi^{[\![\mathtt{t}]\!]}(\top)$ and $\varphi^{[\![\mathtt{t}]\!]}(\bot)$, where e.g. $\varphi^0(\top) := \top$ and $\varphi^{n+1}(\top) := \varphi(\varphi^n(\top))$. We give the cases of the atomic modalities in Fig. 12 (where for simplicity we assume formulae to be closed). It can be checked that, when restricting to polynomial types, one gets the coalgebraic semantics of [30] (with sums as in [31]) extended to fixpoints.

Internal Semantics of Formulae. We would like to have adequacy w.r.t. the external semantics of formulae, namely that given $M : \{A \mid \varphi\}$, the global section $[\![M]\!] \in \boldsymbol{\Gamma}[\![A]\!]$ satisfies $\{\![\varphi]\!\} \in \mathcal{P}(\boldsymbol{\Gamma}[\![A]\!])$ in the sense that $[\![M]\!] \in \{\![\varphi]\!\}$. But in general we can only have adequacy w.r.t. an *internal* semantics $[\![\varphi]\!] \in \mathrm{Sub}([\![A]\!])$

of formulae $\varphi : A$. We sketch it here. First, $\mathrm{Sub}(X)$ is the (complete) Heyting algebra of *subobjects* of an object X of $\mathcal{S}$. Explicitly, we have $S = (S(n))_n \in \mathrm{Sub}(X)$ iff for all $n > 0$, $S(n) \subseteq X(n)$ and $r^X_n(t) \in S(n)$ whenever $t \in S(n+1)$. For propositional connectives and fixpoints, the internal $[\![-]\!]$ is defined similarly as the external $\{\!|-|\!\}$, but using (complete) Heyting algebras of subobjects rather than (complete) Boolean algebras of subsets.

As for modalities, let $[\triangle]$ be of the form $[\pi_i]$, $[\mathsf{in}_i]$, $[\mathsf{next}]$ or $[\mathsf{fold}]$, and assume $[\triangle]\varphi : B$ whenever $\varphi : A$. Standard topos theoretic constructions give posets morphisms $[\![[\triangle]]\!] : \mathrm{Sub}([\![A]\!]) \to \mathrm{Sub}([\![B]\!])$ such that $[\![[\pi_i]]\!]$, $[\![[\mathsf{fold}]]\!]$ are maps of Heyting algebras, $[\![[\mathsf{in}_i]]\!]$ preserves $\vee, \bot$ and $\wedge$, while $[\![[\mathsf{next}]]\!]$ preserves $\wedge, \top$ and $\vee$. With $[\![[\triangle]\varphi]\!] := [\![[\triangle]]\!]([\![\varphi]\!])$, all the axioms and rules of Table 2 are validated for these modalities. To handle guarded recursion, it is crucial to have $[\![[\mathsf{next}]\varphi]\!] := \blacktriangleright([\![\varphi]\!])$, with $[\![[\mathsf{next}]\varphi]\!]$ true at time 1, independently from φ. As a consequence, $[\mathsf{next}]$ and $\bigcirc$ do not validate axiom (P) (Table 2), and $\Diamond[\mathsf{hd}]\varphi$ can "lie" about the next time step. We let $[\![[\mathsf{box}]\varphi]\!] := \boldsymbol{\Delta}(\{\!|\varphi|\!\})$.

The modality $[\mathsf{ev}(\psi)]$ is a bit more complex. For $\psi : B$ and $\varphi : A$, the formula $[\mathsf{ev}(\psi)]\varphi$ is interpreted as a *logical predicate* in the sense of [29, §9.2 & Prop. 9.2.4]. The idea is that for a term $M : \{B \to A \mid [\mathsf{ev}(\psi)]\varphi\}$, the global section $\mathsf{ev} \circ \langle [\![M]\!], x\rangle \in \boldsymbol{\Gamma}[\![A]\!]$ should satisfy φ whenever $x \in \boldsymbol{\Gamma}[\![B]\!]$ satisfies ψ. We refer to [28, §D] for details.

Our semantics are both correct w.r.t. the full modal theories of Def. 6.2.

Lemma 7.2. *If* $\vdash^A_{\mathsf{c}} \varphi$ *then* $\{\!|\varphi|\!\} = \{\!|\top|\!\}$. *If* $\vdash^A \varphi$ *then* $[\![\varphi]\!] = [\![\top]\!]$.

The Safe Fragment. For α (positive and) guarded in φ, the internal semantics of $\theta\alpha\varphi$ is somewhat meaningless because $\mathcal{S}$ has *unique* guarded fixpoints [13, §2.5]. In particular, the typing $\mathsf{fix}(s).\mathsf{Cons}^{\mathsf{g}}\ a\ s : \{\mathsf{Str}^{\mathsf{g}} A \mid \Diamond[\varphi]\}$ for arbitrary $a : A$ and $\varphi : \mathsf{Str}^{\mathsf{g}} A$ (extending §2) is indeed verified by the $\mathcal{S}$ semantics $[\![-]\!]$. This prevents us from adequacy w.r.t. the external semantics in general. But this is possible for *safe* formulae since in this case we have:

Proposition 7.3. *If* $\varphi : A$ *is safe then* $\{\!|\varphi|\!\} = \boldsymbol{\Gamma}[\![\varphi]\!]$.

Proposition 7.3 gives the subtyping rule $\{\blacksquare A \mid [\mathsf{box}]\varphi\} \equiv \blacksquare\{A \mid \varphi\}$ (Fig. 11), which makes available the comonad structure of $\blacksquare$ on $[\mathsf{box}]\varphi$ when φ is safe. Recall that in safe formulae, implications can only occur under a $[\mathsf{box}]$ modality and thus in *closed* subformulae. It is crucial for Prop. 7.3 that infs and sups are pointwise in the subobject lattices of $\mathcal{S}$, so that conjunctions and disjunctions are interpreted as with the usual classical Kripke semantics (see e.g. [47, §VI.7]). This does not hold for implications!

The second key to Prop. 7.3 is the following. For L a complete lattice, a Scott *cocontinuous* function $L \to L$ is a Scott continuous function $L^{\mathrm{op}} \to L^{\mathrm{op}}$, *i.e.* which preserves codirected infs. For a safe $\alpha : A \vdash \varphi : A$, the poset maps $[\![\varphi]\!] : \mathrm{Sub}([\![A]\!]) \to \mathrm{Sub}([\![A]\!])$ and $\{\!|\varphi|\!\} : \mathcal{P}(\boldsymbol{\Gamma}[\![A]\!]) \to \mathcal{P}(\boldsymbol{\Gamma}[\![A]\!])$ are Scott cocontinuous. The greatest fixpoint $\nu\alpha\varphi(\alpha)$ can thus be interpreted, *both in* **Set** *and* $\mathcal{S}$, using Kleene's Fixpoint Theorem, as the infs of the interpretations of $\varphi^m(\top)$ for $m \in \mathbb{N}$. This leads to the expected coincidence of the two semantics for safe formulae.

$$
\begin{array}{lll}
x \Vdash_n \{A \mid \varphi\} & \text{iff } x_n(\bullet) \in [\![\varphi]\!]^A(n) & x \Vdash_n \mathsf{Fix}(X).A \text{ iff } \mathsf{unfold} \circ x \Vdash_n A[\mathsf{Fix}(X).A/X] \\
x \Vdash_n T_0 + T_1 & \text{iff } \exists i \in \{0,1\},\ \exists y \in \boldsymbol{\Gamma}[\![|T_i|]\!],\ x = \mathsf{in}_i \circ y \text{ and } y \Vdash_n T_i & \\
x \Vdash_n T_0 \times T_1 & \text{iff } \pi_0 \circ x \Vdash_n T_0 \text{ and } \pi_1 \circ x \Vdash_n T_1 & x \Vdash_n \mathbf{1} \\
x \Vdash_n U \to T & \text{iff } \forall k \leq n,\ \forall y \in \boldsymbol{\Gamma}[\![|U|]\!],\ y \Vdash_k U \implies \mathsf{ev} \circ \langle x, y\rangle \Vdash_k T & \\
x \Vdash_{n+1} \blacktriangleright T & \text{iff } \exists y \in \boldsymbol{\Gamma}[\![|T|]\!],\ x = \mathsf{next} \circ y \text{ and } y \Vdash_n T & x \Vdash_1 \blacktriangleright T \\
x \Vdash_n \blacksquare T & \text{iff } \forall m > 0,\ x_n(\bullet) \Vdash_m T & (\text{where } x \in \boldsymbol{\Gamma}[\![|\blacksquare T|]\!]) \\
x \Vdash_n \forall k \cdot T & \text{iff } x \Vdash_n T[\mathtt{t}/k] \text{ for all closed iteration terms } \mathtt{t} &
\end{array}
$$

Fig. 13. The Realizability Semantics.

The Smooth Fragment. The *smooth* restriction allows for continuity properties needed to compute fixpoints iteratively, following Kleene's Fixpoint Theorem. This implies the correctness of the typing rules (ν-I) and (μ-E) of Fig. 11.

Lemma 7.4. *Given a closed smooth $\nu\alpha\varphi(\alpha) : A$ (resp. $\mu\alpha\varphi(\alpha) : A$), the function $\{|\varphi|\} : \mathcal{P}(\boldsymbol{\Gamma}[\![A]\!]) \to \mathcal{P}(\boldsymbol{\Gamma}[\![A]\!])$ is Scott-cocontinuous (resp. Scott-continuous). We have $\{|\nu\alpha\varphi(\alpha)|\} = \bigcap_{m\in\mathbb{N}} \{|\varphi^m(\top)|\}$ (resp. $\{|\mu\alpha\varphi(\alpha)|\} = \bigcup_{m\in\mathbb{N}} \{|\varphi^m(\bot)|\}$).*

The Realizability Semantics. The correctness of the type system w.r.t. its semantics in $\mathcal{S}$ is proved with a realizability relation.

Definition 7.5 (Realizability). *Given a type T without free iteration variable, a global section $x \in \boldsymbol{\Gamma}[\![|T|]\!]$ and $n > 0$, we define the realizability relation $x \Vdash_n T$ by induction on lexicographicaly ordered pairs (n, T) in Fig. 13.*

Lemma 7.6. *Given types T, U without free iteration variable, if $x \Vdash_n U$ and $U \leq T$ then $x \Vdash_n T$.*

Theorem 7.7 (Adequacy). *If $\vdash M : T$, where T has no free iteration variable, then $[\![M]\!] \Vdash_n T$ for all $n > 0$.*

By Thm. 7.7, a program $M : B \to A$ induces a set-theoretic function $\boldsymbol{\Gamma}[\![M]\!] : \boldsymbol{\Gamma}[\![B]\!] \to \boldsymbol{\Gamma}[\![A]\!]$, $x \mapsto [\![M]\!] \circ x$. When B and A are polynomial (e.g. streams $\mathsf{Str}^{\mathsf{g}}\ \mathtt{B}$, $\mathsf{Str}^{\mathsf{g}}\ \mathtt{A}$ with $\mathtt{B}$, $\mathtt{A}$ constant), Møgelberg's Thm. 7.1 says that $\boldsymbol{\Gamma}[\![M]\!]$ is a function on the usual final coalgebra for B, A in **Set** (e.g. the set of usual streams over $\mathtt{B}$ and $\mathtt{A}$). Moreover, if e.g. $M : \{\mathsf{Str}\,\mathtt{B} \mid [\mathsf{box}]\psi\} \to \{\mathsf{Str}\,\mathtt{A} \mid [\mathsf{box}]\varphi\}$, then (modulo $\boldsymbol{\Gamma\Delta} \simeq \mathrm{Id}_{\mathbf{Set}}$) given a stream x that satisfies ψ (*i.e.* $x \in \{|\psi|\}$) the stream $\boldsymbol{\Gamma}[\![M]\!](x)$ satisfies φ (*i.e.* $\boldsymbol{\Gamma}[\![M]\!](x) \in \{|\varphi|\}$). See §8 for examples.

8 Examples

We exemplified basic manipulations of our system over §3-6. We give further examples here. The functions used in our main examples are gathered in Table 3, with the following conventions. We use the infix notation $a ::^{\mathsf{g}} s$ for $\mathsf{Cons}^{\mathsf{g}}\ a\ s$ and write $[]^{\mathsf{g}}$ for the empty colist $\mathsf{Nil}^{\mathsf{g}}$. Moreover, we use some syntactic sugar for pattern matching, e.g. assuming $s : \mathsf{CoList}^{\mathsf{g}}\ A$ we write $\mathsf{case}\ s\ \mathsf{of}\ ([]^{\mathsf{g}} \mapsto N | x ::^{\mathsf{g}} xs \mapsto M)$ for $\mathsf{case}(\mathsf{unfold}\ s)\ \mathsf{of}\ (y.N[\langle\rangle/y] | y.M[\pi_0(y)/x\,,\ \pi_1(y)/xs])$. Most of the

$$\begin{array}{lll}
\textbf{append} & : & \mathsf{CoList}\,A \longrightarrow \mathsf{CoList}\,A \longrightarrow \mathsf{CoList}\,A \\
 & := & \lambda s.\lambda t. \\
 & & \quad \mathsf{box}_\iota(\mathsf{append}^{\mathsf{g}}\ (\mathsf{unbox}\ s)\ (\mathsf{unbox}\ t))
\end{array}$$

$$\begin{array}{lll}
\textbf{sched} & : & \mathsf{Res}\,A \longrightarrow \mathsf{Res}\,A \longrightarrow \mathsf{Res}\,A \\
 & := & \lambda p.\lambda q. \\
 & & \quad \mathsf{box}_\iota(\mathsf{sched}^{\mathsf{g}}\ (\mathsf{unbox}\ p)\ (\mathsf{unbox}\ q))
\end{array}$$

$$\begin{array}{lll}
\textbf{append}^{\mathsf{g}} & : & \mathsf{CoList}^{\mathsf{g}}\,A \to \mathsf{CoList}^{\mathsf{g}}\,A \to \mathsf{CoList}^{\mathsf{g}}\,A \\
 & := & \mathsf{fix}(g).\lambda s.\lambda t.\mathsf{case}\ s\ \mathsf{of} \\
 & & \mid []^{\mathsf{g}} \ \mapsto\ t \\
 & & \mid x ::^{\mathsf{g}} xs \ \mapsto\ x ::^{\mathsf{g}} (g \circledast xs \circledast (\mathsf{next}\ t))
\end{array}$$

$$\begin{array}{lll}
\textbf{sched}^{\mathsf{g}} & : & \mathsf{Res}^{\mathsf{g}}\,A \longrightarrow \mathsf{Res}^{\mathsf{g}}\,A \longrightarrow \mathsf{Res}^{\mathsf{g}}\,A \\
 & := & \mathsf{fix}(g).\lambda p.\lambda q.\ \mathsf{case}\ p\ \mathsf{of} \\
 & & \mid \mathsf{Ret}^{\mathsf{g}}\ a \ \mapsto\ \mathsf{Ret}^{\mathsf{g}}\ a \\
 & & \mid \mathsf{Cont}^{\mathsf{g}}\ k \ \mapsto \\
 & & \mathsf{let}\ h = \lambda i.\ \mathsf{let}\ \langle o, t\rangle = ki \\
 & & \qquad\qquad\qquad \mathsf{in}\ \langle o, g \circledast (\mathsf{next}\ q) \circledast t\rangle \\
 & & \mathsf{in}\ \mathsf{Cont}^{\mathsf{g}}\ h
\end{array}$$

$$\begin{array}{rll}
\textbf{diag} & := \lambda s.\mathsf{box}_\iota\big(\mathsf{diag}^{\mathsf{g}}\ (\mathsf{unbox}\ s)\big) & : \mathsf{Str}(\mathsf{Str}\,A) \longrightarrow \mathsf{Str}\,A \\
\textbf{diag}^{\mathsf{g}} & := \mathsf{diagaux}^{\mathsf{g}}\ (\lambda x.x) & : \mathsf{Str}^{\mathsf{g}}(\mathsf{Str}\,A) \longrightarrow \mathsf{Str}^{\mathsf{g}}\,A \\
\textbf{diagaux}^{\mathsf{g}} & : \ (\mathsf{Str}\,A \to \mathsf{Str}\,A) \longrightarrow \mathsf{Str}^{\mathsf{g}}(\mathsf{Str}\,A) \longrightarrow \mathsf{Str}^{\mathsf{g}}\,A & \\
 & := \mathsf{fix}(g).\lambda t.\lambda s.\ \mathsf{Cons}^{\mathsf{g}}\ \big((\mathsf{hd} \circ t)(\mathsf{hd}^{\mathsf{g}}\ s)\big)\ \big(g \circledast \mathsf{next}(t \circ \mathsf{tl}) \circledast (\mathsf{tl}^{\mathsf{g}}\ s)\big) &
\end{array}$$

$$\begin{array}{lll}
\textbf{fb} & : & \mathsf{CoNat} \longrightarrow \mathsf{CoNat} \longrightarrow \mathsf{Str}\,\mathsf{Bool} \\
 & := & \lambda c.\lambda m.\ \mathsf{box}_\iota(\mathsf{fb}^{\mathsf{g}}\ (\mathsf{unbox}\ c)\ (\mathsf{unbox}\ m))
\end{array}$$

$$\begin{array}{lll}
\textbf{fb}^{\mathsf{g}} & : & \mathsf{CoNat}^{\mathsf{g}} \longrightarrow \mathsf{CoNat}^{\mathsf{g}} \longrightarrow \mathsf{Str}^{\mathsf{g}}\,\mathsf{Bool} \\
 & := & \mathsf{fix}(g).\lambda c.\lambda m.\ \mathsf{case}\ c\ \mathsf{of} \\
 & & \mid \mathsf{Z}^{\mathsf{g}} \ \mapsto\ \mathsf{ff} ::^{\mathsf{g}} g \circledast (\mathsf{next}\ m) \circledast \mathsf{next}(\mathsf{S}^{\mathsf{g}}\ (\mathsf{next}\ m)) \\
 & & \mid \mathsf{S}^{\mathsf{g}} n \ \mapsto\ \mathsf{tt} ::^{\mathsf{g}} g \circledast n \circledast (\mathsf{next}\ m)
\end{array}$$

$$\begin{array}{lll}
\textbf{extract} & : & \mathsf{Rou}^{\mathsf{g}}(\mathsf{CoList}^{\mathsf{g}}\,A) \longrightarrow \mathsf{CoList}^{\mathsf{g}}\,A \\
 & := & \mathsf{fix}(g).\lambda c.\ \mathsf{case}\ c\ \mathsf{of} \\
 & & \mid \mathsf{Over}^{\mathsf{g}} \ \mapsto\ \mathsf{Nil}^{\mathsf{g}} \\
 & & \mid \mathsf{Cont}^{\mathsf{g}} f \ \mapsto\ f g^{\circledast}
\end{array}$$

$$\begin{array}{lll}
\textbf{unfold} & : & \mathsf{Rou}^{\mathsf{g}}\,A \longrightarrow (\blacktriangleright \mathsf{Rou}^{\mathsf{g}}\,A \to \blacktriangleright A) \longrightarrow \blacktriangleright A \\
 & := & \lambda c.\ \mathsf{case}\ c\ \mathsf{of} \\
 & & \mid \mathsf{Over}^{\mathsf{g}} \ \mapsto\ \lambda k.\ k\ (\mathsf{next}\ \mathsf{Over}^{\mathsf{g}}) \\
 & & \mid \mathsf{Cont}^{\mathsf{g}} f \ \mapsto\ \lambda k.\ \mathsf{next}(fk)
\end{array}$$

$$\begin{array}{ll}
\textbf{bft}^{\mathsf{g}} := & \lambda t.\ \mathsf{extract}\ (\mathsf{bftaux}\ t\ \mathsf{Over}^{\mathsf{g}}) : \mathsf{Tree}^{\mathsf{g}}\,A \longrightarrow \mathsf{CoList}^{\mathsf{g}}\,A \\
\textbf{bftaux} : & \mathsf{Tree}^{\mathsf{g}}\,A \longrightarrow \mathsf{Rou}^{\mathsf{g}}(\mathsf{CoList}^{\mathsf{g}}\,A) \longrightarrow \mathsf{Rou}^{\mathsf{g}}(\mathsf{CoList}^{\mathsf{g}}\,A) \\
:= & \mathsf{fix}(g).\lambda t.\lambda c.\ \mathsf{Cont}\ \big(\lambda k.\ (\mathsf{label}^{\mathsf{g}}\ t) ::^{\mathsf{g}} \mathsf{unfold}\ c\ \big(k \circ (g \circledast (\mathsf{son}^{\mathsf{g}}_{\ell} t))^{\circledast} \circ (g \circledast (\mathsf{son}^{\mathsf{g}}_{r} t))^{\circledast}\big)\big)
\end{array}$$

Table 3. Code of the Examples.

functions of Table 3 are obtained from usual recursive definitions by inserting $\circledast$ and next at the right places. We often write $\psi \Vdash\!\!\to \varphi$ for $[\mathsf{ev}(\psi)]\varphi$. Table 4 recaps our main examples of refinement typings, all of which (for A, B, $\mathtt{O}$, $\mathtt{I}$ constant, $\mathtt{I}$ finite and φ, ψ safe and smooth) can be derived syntactically for the functions of Table 3. We use intermediate typings requiring iteration terms whenever a $\Diamond$ is involved. Below, "$\boldsymbol{\Gamma}[\![M]\!]$ satisfies φ" means $\boldsymbol{\Gamma}[\![M]\!] \in \{\!|\varphi|\!\}$ (modulo $\boldsymbol{\Gamma}\boldsymbol{\Delta} \simeq \mathrm{Id}_{\mathbf{Set}}$, see §7). We refer to [28, §E] for details.

Example 8.1 (The Append Function on CoLists). Our system can derive that $\boldsymbol{\Gamma}[\![\mathsf{append}]\!]$ returns a non-empty colist if one of its argument is non-empty. Using $\Diamond[\mathsf{nil}]$ (which says that a colist is finite), we can derive that $\boldsymbol{\Gamma}[\![\mathsf{append}]\!]$ returns a finite colist if its arguments are both finite. This involves the intermediate typing

$$\forall k\cdot\forall \ell\cdot\big(\{\mathsf{CoList}^{\mathsf{g}}\,A \mid \Diamond^{k}[\mathsf{nil}]\} \to \{\mathsf{CoList}^{\mathsf{g}}\,A \mid \Diamond^{\ell}[\mathsf{nil}]\} \to \{\mathsf{CoList}^{\mathsf{g}}\,A \mid \Diamond^{k+\ell}[\mathsf{nil}]\}\big)$$

In addition, if the first argument of $\boldsymbol{\Gamma}[\![\mathsf{append}]\!]$ has an element which satisfies φ, then the result has an element which satisfies φ. The same holds if the first argument is finite while the second one has an element which satisfies φ [28, §E.6]. □

Map over coinductive streams (with $\triangle$ either $\Box$, $\Diamond$, $\Diamond\Box$ or $\Box\Diamond$)

$$\mathsf{map} : (\{B \mid \psi\} \to \{A \mid \varphi\}) \longrightarrow \{\mathsf{Str}\, B \mid [\mathsf{box}]\triangle[\mathsf{hd}]\psi\} \longrightarrow \{\mathsf{Str}\, A \mid [\mathsf{box}]\triangle[\mathsf{hd}]\varphi\}$$

Diagonal of coinductive streams of streams (with $\triangle$ either $\Box$ or $\Diamond\Box$)

$$\mathsf{diag} : \{\mathsf{Str}(\mathsf{Str}\, A) \mid [\mathsf{box}]\triangle[\mathsf{hd}][\mathsf{box}]\Box[\mathsf{hd}]\varphi\} \longrightarrow \{\mathsf{Str}\, A \mid [\mathsf{box}]\triangle[\mathsf{hd}]\varphi\}$$

A fair stream of Booleans (adapted from [17,8])

$$\mathsf{fb} \quad : \mathsf{CoNat} \longrightarrow \mathsf{CoNat} \longrightarrow \mathsf{Str\,Bool}$$

$$\mathsf{fb}\ 0\ 1 : \{\mathsf{Str\,Bool} \mid [\mathsf{box}]\Box\Diamond[\mathsf{hd}][\mathsf{tt}] \quad \wedge \quad [\mathsf{box}]\Box\Diamond[\mathsf{hd}][\mathsf{ff}]\}$$

Append on guarded recursive colists

$$\mathsf{append}^{\mathsf{g}} : \{\mathsf{CoList}^{\mathsf{g}}\, A \mid [\neg\mathsf{nil}]\} \longrightarrow \mathsf{CoList}^{\mathsf{g}}\, A \longrightarrow \{\mathsf{CoList}^{\mathsf{g}}\, A \mid [\neg\mathsf{nil}]\}$$

$$\mathsf{append}^{\mathsf{g}} : \mathsf{CoList}^{\mathsf{g}}\, A \longrightarrow \{\mathsf{CoList}^{\mathsf{g}}\, A \mid [\neg\mathsf{nil}]\} \longrightarrow \{\mathsf{CoList}^{\mathsf{g}}\, A \mid [\neg\mathsf{nil}]\}$$

Append on coinductive colists

$$\mathsf{append} : \{\mathsf{CoList}\, A \mid [\mathsf{box}]\Diamond[\mathsf{hd}]\varphi\} \longrightarrow \mathsf{CoList}\, A \longrightarrow \{\mathsf{CoList}\, A \mid [\mathsf{box}]\Diamond[\mathsf{hd}]\varphi\}$$

$$\mathsf{append} : \{\mathsf{CoList}\, A \mid [\mathsf{box}]\Diamond[\mathsf{nil}]\} \longrightarrow \{\mathsf{CoList}\, A \mid [\mathsf{box}]\Diamond[\mathsf{hd}]\varphi\} \longrightarrow \{\mathsf{CoList}\, A \mid [\mathsf{box}]\Diamond[\mathsf{hd}]\varphi\}$$

$$\mathsf{append} : \{\mathsf{CoList}\, A \mid [\mathsf{box}]\Diamond[\mathsf{nil}]\} \longrightarrow \{\mathsf{CoList}\, A \mid [\mathsf{box}]\Diamond[\mathsf{nil}]\} \longrightarrow \{\mathsf{CoList}\, A \mid [\mathsf{box}]\Diamond[\mathsf{nil}]\}$$

Breadth-first tree traversal

$$\mathsf{bft}^{\mathsf{g}} : \{\mathsf{Tree}^{\mathsf{g}}\, C \mid \forall\Box[\mathsf{lbl}]\vartheta\} \longrightarrow \{\mathsf{CoList}^{\mathsf{g}}\, C \mid \Box[\mathsf{hd}]\vartheta\}$$

(à la [35] or with Hofmann's algorithm (see e.g. [10]))

A scheduler of resumptions (adapted from [44])

$$\mathsf{sched} : \{\mathsf{Res}\, A \mid [\mathsf{box}]\Diamond[\mathsf{Ret}]\} \longrightarrow \{\mathsf{Res}\, A \mid [\mathsf{box}]\Diamond[\mathsf{Ret}]\} \longrightarrow \{\mathsf{Res}\, A \mid [\mathsf{box}]\Diamond[\mathsf{Ret}]\}$$

$$\mathsf{sched} : \{\mathsf{Res}\, A \mid [\mathsf{box}]\Diamond[\mathsf{now}]\psi\} \longrightarrow \{\mathsf{Res}\, A \mid [\mathsf{box}]\Diamond[\mathsf{now}]\psi\} \longrightarrow \{\mathsf{Res}\, A \mid [\mathsf{box}]\Diamond[\mathsf{now}]\psi\}$$

$$\mathsf{sched} : \{\mathsf{Res}\, A \mid [\mathsf{box}]\Box\Diamond[\mathsf{Ret}]\} \longrightarrow \{\mathsf{Res}\, A \mid [\mathsf{box}]\Box\Diamond[\mathsf{Ret}]\} \longrightarrow \{\mathsf{Res}\, A \mid [\mathsf{box}]\Box\Diamond[\mathsf{Ret}]\}$$

$$\mathsf{sched} : \{\mathsf{Res}\, A \mid [\mathsf{box}]\Box\Diamond[\mathsf{out}]\vartheta\} \longrightarrow \{\mathsf{Res}\, A \mid [\mathsf{box}]\Box\Diamond[\mathsf{out}]\vartheta\} \longrightarrow \{\mathsf{Res}\, A \mid [\mathsf{box}]\Box\Diamond[\mathsf{out}]\vartheta\}$$

(where $\Diamond$ is either $\forall\Diamond$ or $\exists\Diamond$, $\Box$ is either $\forall\Box$ or $\exists\Box$, and $[\mathsf{out}]$ is either $[\wedge\mathsf{out}]$ or $[\vee\mathsf{out}]$)

Table 4. Some Refinement Typings (functions defined in Table 3).

Example 8.2 (The Map Function on Streams). The composite modalities $\Box\Diamond$ and $\Diamond\Box$ over streams are read resp. as "infinitely often" and "eventually always". Provided with a function $f : \boldsymbol{\Gamma}[\![B]\!] \to \boldsymbol{\Gamma}[\![A]\!]$ taking $b \in \boldsymbol{\Gamma}[\![B]\!]$ satisfying ψ to $f(b) \in \boldsymbol{\Gamma}[\![B]\!]$ satisfying φ, the function $\boldsymbol{\Gamma}[\![\mathsf{map}]\!]$ on set-theoretic streams returns a stream which infinitely often (resp. eventually always) satisfies φ if its stream argument infinitely often (resp. eventually always) satisfies ψ [28, §E.3]. $\Box$

Example 8.3 (The Diagonal Function). Consider a stream of streams s. We have $s = (s_i \mid i \geq 0)$ where each s_i is itself a stream $s_i = (s_{i,j} \mid j \geq 0)$. The *diagonal* of s is then the stream $(s_{i,i} \mid i \geq 0)$. Note that $s_{i,i} = \mathsf{hd}(\mathsf{tl}^i(\mathsf{hd}(\mathsf{tl}^i(s))))$. Indeed, $\mathsf{tl}^i(s)$ is the stream of streams $(s_k \mid k \geq i)$, so that $\mathsf{hd}(\mathsf{tl}^i(s))$ is the stream s_i and $\mathsf{tl}^i(\mathsf{hd}(\mathsf{tl}^i(s)))$ is the stream $(s_{i,k} \mid k \geq i)$. Taking its head thus gives $s_{i,i}$. In the diag function of Table 3, the auxiliary higher-order function $\mathsf{diagaux}^{\mathsf{g}}$ iterates the coinductive tl over the head of the stream of streams s. We write $\circ$ for function composition, so that assuming $s : \mathsf{Str}^{\mathsf{g}}(\mathsf{Str}\, A)$ and $t : \mathsf{Str}\, A \to \mathsf{Str}\, A$, we have (on the *coinductive* type $\mathsf{Str}\, A$), $(\mathsf{hd}^{\mathsf{g}}\ s) : \mathsf{Str}\, A$ and

$$(\mathsf{hd} \circ t) : \mathsf{Str}\, A \to A \qquad (\mathsf{hd} \circ t)(\mathsf{hd}^{\mathsf{g}}\ s) : A \qquad (t \circ \mathsf{tl}) : \mathsf{Str}\, A \to \mathsf{Str}\, A$$

The expected refinement types for diag (Table 4) say that if its argument is a stream whose component streams all satisfy $\Box\varphi$, then $\boldsymbol{\Gamma}[\![\mathsf{diag}]\!]$ returns a stream whose elements all satisfy φ. Also, if the argument of $\Gamma[\![\mathsf{diag}]\!]$ is a stream such that eventually all its component streams satisfy $\Box\varphi$, then it returns a stream which eventually always satisfies φ. See [28, §E.4] for details. □

Example 8.4 (A Fair Stream of Booleans). The non-regular stream $(\mathsf{fb}\ 0\ 1)$, adapted from [17,8], is of the form $\mathsf{ff}\cdot\mathsf{tt}\cdot\mathsf{ff}\cdot\mathsf{tt}^2\cdot\mathsf{ff}\cdots\mathsf{ff}\cdot\mathsf{tt}^m\cdot\mathsf{ff}\cdot\mathsf{tt}^{m+1}\cdot\mathsf{ff}\cdots$. It thus contains infinitely many tt's and infinitely many ff's. We indeed have (see [28, §E.5] for details) $(\mathsf{fb}\ 0\ 1) : \{\mathsf{Str\,Bool} \mid [\mathsf{box}]\Box\Diamond[\mathsf{hd}][\mathsf{tt}] \ \wedge\ [\mathsf{box}]\Box\Diamond[\mathsf{hd}][\mathsf{ff}]\}$. □

Example 8.5 (Resumptions). The type of resumptions $\mathsf{Res}^{\mathsf{g}}\,A$ (see Ex. 3.2) is adapted from [44]. Its guarded constructors are

$$\begin{aligned}\mathsf{Ret}^{\mathsf{g}} &:= \lambda a.\ \mathsf{fold}(\mathsf{in}_0\ a) : A \longrightarrow \mathsf{Res}^{\mathsf{g}}\,A\\ \mathsf{Cont}^{\mathsf{g}} &:= \lambda k.\ \mathsf{fold}(\mathsf{in}_1\ k) : (\mathtt{I} \to (\mathtt{0} \times \blacktriangleright \mathsf{Res}^{\mathsf{g}}\,A)) \longrightarrow \mathsf{Res}^{\mathsf{g}}\,A\end{aligned}$$

$\mathsf{Ret}^{\mathsf{g}}(a)$ represents a computation which returns the value $a : A$, while $\mathsf{Cont}^{\mathsf{g}}\langle f, k\rangle$ (with $\langle f, k\rangle : \mathtt{I} \to (\mathtt{0} \times \blacktriangleright \mathsf{Res}^{\mathsf{g}}\,A))$ represents a computation which on input $\mathtt{i} : \mathtt{I}$ outputs $f\mathtt{i} : \mathtt{0}$ and continues with $k\mathtt{i} : \blacktriangleright \mathsf{Res}^{\mathsf{g}}\,A$. Given $p, q : \mathsf{Res}^{\mathsf{g}}\,A$, the scheduler $(\mathsf{sched}^{\mathsf{g}}\ p\ q)$, adapted from [44], first evaluates p. If p returns, then the whole computation returns, with the same value. Otherwise, p evaluates to say $\mathsf{Cont}^{\mathsf{g}}\langle f, k\rangle$. Then $(\mathsf{sched}^{\mathsf{g}}\ p\ q)$ produces a computation which on input $\mathtt{i} : \mathtt{I}$ outputs $f\mathtt{i}$ and continues with $(\mathsf{sched}^{\mathsf{g}}\ q\ (k\mathtt{i}))$, thus switching arguments.

Let $\mathtt{I}$ be a finite base type (so that $\mathsf{Res}^{\mathsf{g}}\,A$ is *finitary* polynomial). Let $\psi : A$, $\vartheta : \mathtt{0}$ and $\varphi : \mathsf{Res}^{\mathsf{g}}\,A$. We have the following formulae (where $\mathtt{i} : \mathtt{I}$):

$$\begin{aligned}[\mathsf{Ret}] &:= [\mathsf{fold}][\mathsf{in}_0]\top & [\mathsf{out}_{\mathtt{i}}]\vartheta &:= [\mathsf{fold}][\mathsf{in}_1]\,([\mathtt{i}] \Vdash\!\!\to [\pi_0]\vartheta)\\ [\mathsf{now}]\psi &:= [\mathsf{fold}][\mathsf{in}_0]\psi & \bigcirc_{\mathtt{i}}\varphi &:= [\mathsf{fold}][\mathsf{in}_1]\,([\mathtt{i}] \Vdash\!\!\to [\pi_1][\mathsf{next}]\varphi)\end{aligned}$$

The formula $[\mathsf{Ret}]$ (resp. $[\mathsf{now}]\psi$) holds on a resumption which immediately returns (resp. with a value satisfying ψ) and we have $\mathsf{Ret}^{\mathsf{g}} : A \to \{\mathsf{Res}^{\mathsf{g}}\,A \mid [\mathsf{Ret}]\}$, $\mathsf{Ret}^{\mathsf{g}} : \{A \mid \psi\} \to \{\mathsf{Res}^{\mathsf{g}}\,A \mid [\mathsf{now}]\psi\}$. Moreover, the typings

$$\begin{aligned}&\mathsf{Cont}^{\mathsf{g}} : \{\mathtt{I} \to (\mathtt{0} \times \blacktriangleright \mathsf{Res}^{\mathsf{g}}\,A) \mid [\mathtt{i}] \Vdash\!\!\to [\pi_0]\vartheta\} \longrightarrow \{\mathsf{Res}^{\mathsf{g}}\,A \mid [\mathsf{out}_{\mathtt{i}}]\vartheta\}\\ &\mathsf{Cont}^{\mathsf{g}} : \{\mathtt{I} \to (\mathtt{0} \times \blacktriangleright \mathsf{Res}^{\mathsf{g}}A) \mid [\mathtt{i}] \Vdash\!\!\to [\pi_1][\mathsf{next}]\varphi\} \longrightarrow \{\mathsf{Res}^{\mathsf{g}}\,A \mid \bigcirc_{\mathtt{i}}\varphi\}\end{aligned}$$

express that $[\mathsf{out}_{\mathtt{i}}]\vartheta : \mathsf{Res}^{\mathsf{g}}\,A$ is satisfied by $\mathsf{Cont}^{\mathsf{g}}\langle f, k\rangle$ if $f\mathtt{i}$ satisfies ϑ, and that $\bigcirc_{\mathtt{i}}\varphi : \mathsf{Res}^{\mathsf{g}}\,A$ is satisfied by $\mathsf{Cont}^{\mathsf{g}}\langle f, k\rangle$ if $k\mathtt{i}$ satisfies $[\mathsf{next}]\varphi$. Since $\mathtt{I}$ is a finite base type, it is possible to quantify over its inhabitants. We thus obtain CTL-like variants of $\Box$ and $\Diamond$ (Ex. 4.3.(b) and Ex. 6.3). Namely:

$$\begin{aligned}[\wedge\mathsf{out}]\vartheta &:= \textstyle\bigwedge_{\mathtt{i}\in\mathtt{I}}[\mathsf{out}_{\mathtt{i}}]\vartheta : \mathsf{Res}^{\mathsf{g}}\,A & \circledA\,\varphi &:= \textstyle\bigwedge_{\mathtt{i}\in\mathtt{I}} \bigcirc_{\mathtt{i}}\,\varphi \ : \mathsf{Res}^{\mathsf{g}}\,A\\ [\vee\mathsf{out}]\vartheta &:= \textstyle\bigvee_{\mathtt{i}\in\mathtt{I}}[\mathsf{out}_{\mathtt{i}}]\vartheta : \mathsf{Res}^{\mathsf{g}}\,A & \circledE\,\varphi &:= \textstyle\bigvee_{\mathtt{i}\in\mathtt{I}} \bigcirc_{\mathtt{i}}\,\varphi \ : \mathsf{Res}^{\mathsf{g}}\,\varphi\\ \forall\Box\varphi &:= \nu\alpha.\ \varphi \wedge \circledA\,\alpha : \mathsf{Res}^{\mathsf{g}}\,A & \forall\Diamond\varphi &:= \mu\alpha.\ \varphi \vee \circledA\,\alpha : \mathsf{Res}^{\mathsf{g}}\,A\\ \exists\Box\varphi &:= \nu\alpha.\ \varphi \wedge \circledE\,\alpha : \mathsf{Res}^{\mathsf{g}}\,A & \exists\Diamond\varphi &:= \mu\alpha.\ \varphi \vee \circledE\,\alpha : \mathsf{Res}^{\mathsf{g}}\,A\end{aligned}$$

Our system can prove that $\Gamma[\![\mathsf{sched}]\!]$ returns in finite time when so do its arguments, either along *some* or along *any* sequence of inputs. We moreover have expected $\Box\Diamond$ properties for all possible (consistent) combinations of $\exists/\forall$ and $[\mathsf{Ret}]/[\vee\mathsf{out}]/[\wedge\mathsf{out}]$ (Table 4, with $\psi : A$, $\vartheta : \mathtt{0}$ safe and smooth) [28, §E.7]. □

Example 8.6 (Breadth-First Traversal). The function $\mathsf{bft}^{\mathsf{g}}$ of Table 3 (where $g^{\circledast}$ stands for $\lambda x.g \circledast x$) implements Martin Hofmann's algorithm for breadth-first tree traversal. This algorithm involves the higher-order type $\mathsf{Rou}^{\mathsf{g}}\, A$ (see Ex. 3.2) with constructors $\mathsf{Over}^{\mathsf{g}} := \mathsf{fold}(\mathsf{in}_0\langle\rangle) : \mathsf{Rou}^{\mathsf{g}}\, A$ and

$$\mathsf{Cont}^{\mathsf{g}} := \lambda f.\mathsf{fold}(\mathsf{in}_1 f) : ((\blacktriangleright \mathsf{Rou}^{\mathsf{g}}\, A \to \blacktriangleright A) \to A) \to \mathsf{Rou}^{\mathsf{g}}\, A$$

We refer to [10] for explanations. Consider a formula $\varphi : A$. We can lift φ to

$$[\mathsf{Rou}]\varphi := \nu\alpha.\ [\mathsf{fold}][\mathsf{in}_1]((([\mathsf{next}]\alpha \Vdash\!\!\to [\mathsf{next}]\varphi) \Vdash\!\!\to \varphi) : \mathsf{Rou}^{\mathsf{g}}\, A$$

We then easily derive the expected refinement type of $\mathsf{bft}^{\mathsf{g}}$ (Table 4, where $\vartheta : C$). Assume that ϑ is safe. On the one hand it is not clear what the meaning of $[\mathsf{Rou}]\vartheta$ is, because it is an unsafe formula over a non-polynomial type. On the other hand, the type of $\mathsf{bft}^{\mathsf{g}}$ in Tab. 4 has its standard expected meaning (namely: if all nodes of a tree satisfy ϑ then so do all elements of its traversal) because the types $\mathsf{Tree}^{\mathsf{g}}\, C$, $\mathsf{CoList}^{\mathsf{g}}\, C$ are polynomial and the formulae $\forall\Box[\mathsf{lbl}]\vartheta$, $\Box[\mathsf{hd}]\vartheta$ are safe. Hence, our system can prove standard statements via detours through non-standard ones, which illustrates its compositionality. We have the same typing for a usual breadth-first tree traversal with forests (*à la* [35]). See [28, §E.8]. □

9 Related Work

Type systems based on guarded recursion have been designed to enforce properties of programs handling coinductive types, like causality [45], productivity [5,50,18,6,25,24], or termination [62]. These properties are captured by the type systems, meaning that all well-typed programs satisfy these properties.

In an initially different line of work, temporal logics have been used as type systems for functional reactive programming (FRP), starting from LTL [32,33] to the intuitionistic modal μ-calculus [17]. These works follow the Curry-Howard "proof-as-programs" paradigm, and reflect in the programming languages the constructions of the temporal logic.

The FRP approach has been adapted to guarded recursion, e.g. for the absence of space leaks [44], or the absence of time leaks, with the Fitch-style system of [7]. This more recently lead [8] to consider liveness properties with an FRP approach based on guarded recursion. In this system, the guarded λ-calculus (presented in a Fitch-style type system) is extended with a delay modality (written $\bigcirc$) together with a "until type" A Until B. Following the Curry-Howard correspondence, A Until B is eliminated with a specific recursor, based on the usual unfolding of Until in LTL, and distinct from the guarded fixpoint operator.

In these Curry-Howard approaches, temporal operators are wired into the structure of types. This means that there is no separation between the program and the proof that it satisfies a given temporal property. Different type formers having different program constructs, different temporal specifications for the same program may lead to different actual code.

We have chosen a different approach, based on refinement types, with which the structure of formulae is not reflected in the structure of types. This allows for our examples to be mostly written in a usual guarded recursive fashion (see Table 3). Of course, we indeed use the modality ■ at the type level as a separation between safety and liveness properties. But different liveness properties (e.g. $\Diamond$, $\Diamond\Box$, $\Box\Diamond$) are uniformly handled with the same ■-type, which is moreover the expected one in the guarded λ-calculus [18].

Higher-order model checking (HOMC) [54,39] has been introduced to check *automatically* that higher-order recursion schemes, a simple form of higher-order programs with *finite* data-types, satisfy a μ-calculus formula. Automatic verification of higher-order programs with infinite data-types (integers) has been explored for safety [40], termination [46], and more generally ω-regular [51] properties. In presence of infinite datatypes, semi-automatic extensions of HOMC have recently been proposed [69]. In contrast with this paper, most HOMC approaches do not consider input-output behaviors on coalgebraic data. A notable exception is [41,23], but it does not handle higher-order functions (such as map), nor polynomial types such as $\mathsf{Str}(\mathsf{Str}\,A)$ (Ex. 8.3) or non-positive types such as $\mathsf{Rou}\,A$ (Ex. 8.6) and imposes a strong linearity constraint on pattern matching.

Event-driven approaches consider effects generating streams of events [61], which can be checked for temporal properties with algorithms based on (HO)MC [26,27], or, in presence of infinite datatypes, with refinement type systems [42,53]. Our iteration terms can be seen as oracles, as required by [42] to handle liveness properties, but we do not know if they allow for the non-regular specifications of [53]. While such approaches can handle infinite data types with good levels of automation, they do not have coinductive types nor branching time properties, such as the temporal specification of sched on resumptions (Ex. 8.5)

Along similar lines, branching was approached via non-determinism in [64], which also handles universal and existential properties on traces. This framework can handle CTL-like properties of the form $\exists/\forall$-$\Box/\Diamond$ (with our notation of Ex. 8.5), but not nested combinations of these (as e.g. $\exists\Box\forall\Diamond$ for sched in Ex. 8.5). It moreover does not handle coinductive types.

10 Conclusion and Future Work

We have presented a refinement type system for the guarded λ-calculus, with refinements expressing temporal properties stated as (alternation-free) μ-calculus formulae. As we have seen, the system is general enough to prove precise behavioral input/output properties of coinductively-typed programs. Our main contribution is to handle liveness properties in presence of guarded recursive types. As seen in §2, this comes with inherent difficulties. In general, once guarded recursive functions are packed into coinductive ones using ■, the logical reasoning is made in our system directly on top of programs, following their shape, but requiring no further modification. We thus believe to have achieved some separation between programs and proofs.

We provided several examples. While they demonstrate the flexibility of our system, they also show that more abstraction would be welcomed when proving liveness properties. In addition, our system lacks expressiveness to prove e.g. liveness properties on breadth-first tree traversals.

We believe that our approach could be generalized to other programming languages with inductive or coinductive types. The key requirement are: (1) modalities in the temporal logic to navigate through the types of the languages, (2) a semantics to indicate when a program satisfies a formula of the temporal logic, which is sufficiently closed to the set-theoretic one for liveness properties to get their expected meaning, and (3) inference rules to reason over this realizability semantics.

Extensions of the guarded λ-calculus with dependent types have been explored [14,11,6,24]. It may be possible to extend our work to these systems. This would require to work in a Fitch-style presentation of the $\blacksquare$ modality, as in [7,12], since it is not known how to extend delayed substitutions to dependent types while retaining decidability of type-checking [15]. Also, it is appealing to investigate the generalization of our approach to sized types [1], in which guarded recursive types are representable [67].

We plan to investigate type checking. For instance, in a decidable fragment like the μ-calculus on streams, one can check that a function of type $\{\mathsf{Str}^{\mathsf{g}}\, C \mid \Diamond\Box[\mathsf{hd}]\vartheta\} \to \{\mathsf{Str}^{\mathsf{g}}\, B \mid \Diamond\Box[\mathsf{hd}]\psi\}$ can be postcomposed with one of type $\{\mathsf{Str}^{\mathsf{g}}\, B \mid \Box\Diamond[\mathsf{hd}]\psi\} \to \{\mathsf{Str}^{\mathsf{g}}\, A \mid \Box\Diamond[\mathsf{hd}]\varphi\}$ (since $\Diamond\Box[\mathsf{hd}]\psi \Rightarrow \Box\Diamond[\mathsf{hd}]\psi$). Hence, we expect that some automation is possible for fragments of our logic. In presence of iteration terms, arithmetic extensions of the μ-calculus [37,38] may provide interesting backends. An other direction is the interaction with HOMC. If (say) a stream over A is representable in a suitable format, one may use HOMC to check whether it can be argument of a function expecting e.g. a stream of type $\{\mathsf{Str}^{\mathsf{g}}\, A \mid \Box\Diamond[\mathsf{hd}]\varphi\}$. This might provide automation for fragments of the guarded λ-calculus. Besides, the combination of refinement types with automatic techniques like predicate abstraction [57], abstract interpretation [34], or SMT solvers [66,65] has been particularly successful. More recently, the combination of refinement types inference with HOMC has been investigated [59].

We would like to explore temporal specification of general, effectful programs. To do so, we wish to develop the treatment of the coinductive resumptions monad [55], that provides a general framework to reason on effectful computations, as shown by interaction trees [70]. It would be interesting to study temporal specifications we could give to effectful programs encoded in this setting. To formalize reasoning on such examples, we would like to design an embedding of our system in a proof assistant like Coq.

Following [3], guarded recursion has been used to abstract the reasoning on step-indexing [4] that has been used to design Kripke Logical Relations [2] for typed higher-order effectful programming languages. Program logics for reasoning on such logical relations [19,20] uses this representation of step-indexing via guarded recursion. It is also found in Iris [36], a framework for higher-order concurrent separation logic. It would be interesting to explore the incorporation of temporal reasoning, especially liveness properties, in such logics.

References

1. Abel, A., Pientka, B.: Well-founded recursion with copatterns and sized types. J. Funct. Program. **26**, e2 (2016). https://doi.org/10.1017/S0956796816000022, https://doi.org/10.1017/S0956796816000022
2. Ahmed, A.: Step-Indexed Syntactic Logical Relations for Recursive and Quantified Types. In: Proceedings of the 15th European Conference on Programming Languages and Systems. pp. 69–83. ESOP'06, Springer-Verlag, Berlin, Heidelberg (2006). https://doi.org/10.1007/11693024_6, https://doi.org/10.1007/11693024_6
3. Appel, A., Melliès, P.A., Richards, C., Vouillon, J.: A Very Modal Model of a Modern, Major, General Type System. SIGPLAN Not. **42**(1), 109–122 (2007). https://doi.org/10.1145/1190215.1190235, https://doi.org/10.1145/1190215.1190235
4. Appel, A.W., McAllester, D.: An Indexed Model of Recursive Types for Foundational Proof-Carrying Code. ACM Trans. Program. Lang. Syst. **23**(5), 657–683 (2001). https://doi.org/10.1145/504709.504712, https://doi.org/10.1145/504709.504712
5. Atkey, R., McBride, C.: Productive coprogramming with guarded recursion. In: Proceedings of the 18th ACM SIGPLAN International Conference on Functional Programming. pp. 197–208. ICFP '13, ACM, New York, NY, USA (2013). https://doi.org/10.1145/2500365.2500597
6. Bahr, P., Grathwohl, H.B., Møgelberg, R.E.: The Clocks Are Ticking: No More Delays! In: 2017 32nd Annual ACM/IEEE Symposium on Logic in Computer Science (LICS). pp. 1–12 (2017). https://doi.org/10.1109/LICS.2017.8005097
7. Bahr, P., Graulund, C., Møgelberg, R.: Simply RaTT: A Fitch-Style Modal Calculus for Reactive Programming without Space Leaks. Proc. ACM Program. Lang. **3**(ICFP), 109:1–109:27 (2019). https://doi.org/10.1145/3341713
8. Bahr, P., Graulund, C., Møgelberg, R.: Diamonds are not Forever: Liveness in Reactive Programming with Guarded Recursion (2020), https://arxiv.org/abs/2003.03170, To Appear in POPL'21
9. Baier, C., Katoen, J.P.: Principles of Model Checking. The MIT Press (2008)
10. Berger, U., Matthes, R., Setzer, A.: Martin Hofmann's Case for Non-Strictly Positive Data Types. In: Dybjer, P., Espírito Santo, J., Pinto, L. (eds.) 24th International Conference on Types for Proofs and Programs (TYPES 2018), Leibniz International Proceedings in Informatics (LIPIcs), vol. 130, pp. 1:1–1:22. Schloss Dagstuhl - Leibniz-Zentrum fuer Informatik (2019). https://doi.org/10.4230/LIPIcs.TYPES.2018.1, https://hal.archives-ouvertes.fr/hal-02365814
11. Birkedal, L., Bizjak, A., Clouston, R., Grathwohl, H.B., Spitters, B., Vezzosi, A.: Guarded cubical type theory. Journal of Automated Reasoning **63**(2), 211–253 (2019). https://doi.org/10.1007/s10817-018-9471-7
12. Birkedal, L., Clouston, R., Mannaa, B., Møgelberg, R., Pitts, A.M., Spitters, B.: Modal dependent type theory and dependent right adjoints. Mathematical Structures in Computer Science **30**(2), 118–138 (2020). https://doi.org/10.1017/S0960129519000197
13. Birkedal, L., Møgelberg, R.E., Schwinghammer, J., Støvring, K.: First steps in synthetic guarded domain theory: step-indexing in the topos of trees. Logical Methods in Computer Science **8**(4) (2012)
14. Bizjak, A., Grathwohl, H.B., Clouston, R., Møgelberg, R.E., Birkedal, L.: Guarded Dependent Type Theory with Coinductive Types. In: Jacobs, B., Löding, C. (eds.)

Foundations of Software Science and Computation Structures. pp. 20–35. Springer Berlin Heidelberg, Berlin, Heidelberg (2016)
15. Bizjak, A., Møgelberg, R.E.: Denotational semantics for guarded dependent type theory. Mathematical Structures in Computer Science **30**(4), 342–378 (2020). https://doi.org/10.1017/S0960129520000080
16. Bradfield, J.C., Walukiewicz, I.: The mu-calculus and Model Checking. In: Clarke, E.M., Henzinger, T.A., Veith, H., Bloem, R. (eds.) Handbook of Model Checking, pp. 871–919. Springer (2018)
17. Cave, A., Ferreira, F., Panangaden, P., Pientka, B.: Fair Reactive Programming. In: Proceedings of the 41st ACM SIGPLAN-SIGACT Symposium on Principles of Programming Languages. pp. 361–372. POPL '14, ACM, New York, NY, USA (2014)
18. Clouston, R., Bizjak, A., Bugge Grathwohl, H., Birkedal, L.: The Guarded Lambda-Calculus: Programming and Reasoning with Guarded Recursion for Coinductive Types. Logical Methods in Computer Science **12**(3) (2016)
19. Dreyer, D., Ahmed, A., Birkedal, L.: Logical Step-Indexed Logical Relations. Logical Methods in Computer Science **Volume 7, Issue 2** (2011). https://doi.org/10.2168/LMCS-7(2:16)2011, https://lmcs.episciences.org/698
20. Dreyer, D., Neis, G., Rossberg, A., Birkedal, L.: A Relational Modal Logic for Higher-order Stateful ADTs. In: Proceedings POPL'10. pp. 185–198. ACM (2010)
21. Elliott, C., Hudak, P.: Functional Reactive Animation. In: Proceedings of the Second ACM SIGPLAN International Conference on Functional Programming. pp. 263–273. ICFP'97, ACM, New York, NY, USA (1997). https://doi.org/10.1145/258948.258973, http://doi.acm.org/10.1145/258948.258973
22. Freeman, T., Pfenning, F.: Refinement Types for ML. In: Proceedings of the ACM SIGPLAN 1991 Conference on Programming Language Design and Implementation. pp. 268–277. PLDI'91, Association for Computing Machinery, New York, NY, USA (1991). https://doi.org/10.1145/113445.113468, https://doi.org/10.1145/113445.113468
23. Fujima, K., Ito, S., Kobayashi, N.: Practical Alternating Parity Tree Automata Model Checking of Higher-Order Recursion Schemes. In: APLAS '13: Proceedings of the 11th Asian Symposium on Programming Languages and Systems - Volume 8301. pp. 17–32. Springer-Verlag, Berlin, Heidelberg (2013). https://doi.org/10.1007/978-3-319-03542-0_2, https://doi.org/10.1007/978-3-319-03542-0_2
24. Gratzer, D., Kavvos, G.A., Nuyts, A., Birkedal, L.: Multimodal dependent type theory. In: Proceedings of the 35th Annual ACM/IEEE Symposium on Logic in Computer Science. pp. 492–506. LICS '20, Association for Computing Machinery, New York, NY, USA (2020). https://doi.org/10.1145/3373718.3394736, https://doi.org/10.1145/3373718.3394736
25. Guatto, A.: A Generalized Modality for Recursion. In: Proceedings of the 33rd Annual ACM/IEEE Symposium on Logic in Computer Science. pp. 482–491. LICS '18, ACM, New York, NY, USA (2018). https://doi.org/10.1145/3209108.3209148
26. Hofmann, M., Chen, W.: Abstract interpretation from büchi automata. In: Henzinger, T.A., Miller, D. (eds.) Joint Meeting of the Twenty-Third EACSL Annual Conference on Computer Science Logic (CSL) and the Twenty-Ninth Annual ACM/IEEE Symposium on Logic in Computer Science (LICS), CSL-LICS '14, Vienna, Austria, July 14 - 18, 2014. pp. 51:1–51:10. ACM (2014). https://doi.org/10.1145/2603088.2603127, https://doi.org/10.1145/2603088.2603127

27. Hofmann, M., Ledent, J.: A cartesian-closed category for higher-order model checking. In: 32nd Annual ACM/IEEE Symposium on Logic in Computer Science, LICS 2017, Reykjavik, Iceland, June 20-23, 2017. pp. 1–12. IEEE Computer Society (2017). https://doi.org/10.1109/LICS.2017.8005120, https://doi.org/10.1109/LICS.2017.8005120
28. Jaber, G., Riba, C.: Temporal Refinements for Guarded Recursive Types (Jan 2021), https://hal.archives-ouvertes.fr/hal-02512655, full version. Available on HAL (hal-02512655)
29. Jacobs, B.: Categorical Logic and Type Theory. Studies in logic and the foundations of mathematics, Elsevier (2001)
30. Jacobs, B.: Many-Sorted Coalgebraic Modal Logic: a Model-theoretic Study. ITA **35**(1), 31–59 (2001)
31. Jacobs, B.: Introduction to Coalgebra: Towards Mathematics of States and Observation. Cambridge Tracts in Theoretical Computer Science, Cambridge University Press (2016)
32. Jeffrey, A.: LTL Types FRP: Linear-time Temporal Logic Propositions As Types, Proofs As Functional Reactive Programs. In: Proceedings of the Sixth Workshop on Programming Languages Meets Program Verification. pp. 49–60. PLPV'12, ACM, New York, NY, USA (2012). https://doi.org/10.1145/2103776.2103783, http://doi.acm.org/10.1145/2103776.2103783
33. Jeltsch, W.: An Abstract Categorical Semantics for Functional Reactive Programming with Processes. In: Proceedings of the ACM SIGPLAN 2014 Workshop on Programming Languages Meets Program Verification. pp. 47–58. PLPV'14, ACM, New York, NY, USA (2014). https://doi.org/10.1145/2541568.2541573, http://doi.acm.org/10.1145/2541568.2541573
34. Jhala, R., Majumdar, R., Rybalchenko, A.: HMC: Verifying functional programs using abstract interpreters. In: International Conference on Computer Aided Verification. pp. 470–485. Springer (2011)
35. Jones, G., Gibbons, J.: Linear-time Breadth-first Tree Algorithms: An Exercise in the Arithmetic of Folds and Zips. Technical report, University of Auckland (1993)
36. Jung, R., Krebbers, R., Jourdan, J.H., Bizjak, A., Birkedal, L., Dreyer, D.: Iris from the ground up: A modular foundation for higher-order concurrent separation logic. Journal of Functional Programming **28** (2018)
37. Kobayashi, K., Nishikawa, T., Igarashi, A., Unno, H.: Temporal Verification of Programs via First-Order Fixpoint Logic. In: Chang, B.E. (ed.) Static Analysis - 26th International Symposium, SAS 2019, Porto, Portugal, October 8-11, 2019, Proceedings. Lecture Notes in Computer Science, vol. 11822, pp. 413–436. Springer (2019). https://doi.org/10.1007/978-3-030-32304-2_20, https://doi.org/10.1007/978-3-030-32304-2_20
38. Kobayashi, N., Fedyukovich, G., Gupta, A.: Fold/Unfold Transformations for Fixpoint Logic. In: Biere, A., Parker, D. (eds.) Tools and Algorithms for the Construction and Analysis of Systems - 26th International Conference, TACAS 2020, Held as Part of the European Joint Conferences on Theory and Practice of Software, ETAPS 2020, Dublin, Ireland, April 25-30, 2020, Proceedings, Part II. Lecture Notes in Computer Science, vol. 12079, pp. 195–214. Springer (2020). https://doi.org/10.1007/978-3-030-45237-7_12, https://doi.org/10.1007/978-3-030-45237-7_12
39. Kobayashi, N., Ong, C.H.L.: A type system equivalent to the modal mu-calculus model checking of higher-order recursion schemes. In: 2009 24th Annual IEEE Symposium on Logic In Computer Science. pp. 179–188. IEEE (2009)

40. Kobayashi, N., Sato, R., Unno, H.: Predicate abstraction and CEGAR for higher-order model checking. SIGPLAN Not. **46**(6), 222–233 (2011). https://doi.org/10.1145/1993316.1993525, https://doi.org/10.1145/1993316.1993525
41. Kobayashi, N., Tabuchi, N., Unno, H.: Higher-Order Multi-Parameter Tree Transducers and Recursion Schemes for Program Verification. In: POPL '10: Proceedings of the 37th annual ACM SIGPLAN-SIGACT symposium on Principles of programming languages. pp. 495–508. Association for Computing Machinery, New York, NY, USA (2010). https://doi.org/10.1145/1707801.1706355, https://doi.org/10.1145/1707801.1706355
42. Koskinen, E., Terauchi, T.: Local Temporal Reasoning. In: Proceedings of the Joint Meeting of the Twenty-Third EACSL Annual Conference on Computer Science Logic (CSL) and the Twenty-Ninth Annual ACM/IEEE Symposium on Logic in Computer Science (LICS). CSL-LICS'14, Association for Computing Machinery, New York, NY, USA (2014). https://doi.org/10.1145/2603088.2603138, https://doi.org/10.1145/2603088.2603138
43. Kozen, D.: Results on the propositional μ-calculus. Theoretical Computer Science **27**(3), 333 – 354 (1983), special Issue Ninth International Colloquium on Automata, Languages and Programming (ICALP) Aarhus, Summer 1982
44. Krishnaswami, N.R.: Higher-order functional reactive programming without spacetime leaks. In: Proceedings of ICFP'13. pp. 221–232. ACM, New York, NY, USA (2013)
45. Krishnaswami, N.R., Benton, N.: Ultrametric Semantics of Reactive Programs. In: 2011 IEEE 26th Annual Symposium on Logic in Computer Science. pp. 257–266 (2011). https://doi.org/10.1109/LICS.2011.38
46. Kuwahara, T., Terauchi, T., Unno, H., Kobayashi, N.: Automatic Termination Verification for Higher-Order Functional Programs. In: Shao, Z. (ed.) Programming Languages and Systems. pp. 392–411. ESOP'14, Springer Berlin Heidelberg, Berlin, Heidelberg (2014)
47. Mac Lane, S., Moerdijk, I.: Sheaves in geometry and logic: A first introduction to topos theory. Springer (1992)
48. Marin, S.: Modal proof theory through a focused telescope. Phd thesis, Université Paris Saclay (Jan 2018), https://hal.archives-ouvertes.fr/tel-01951291
49. McBride, C., Paterson, R.: Applicative programming with effects. Journal of Functional Programming **18**(1) (2008). https://doi.org/10.1017/S0956796807006326
50. Møgelberg, R.E.: A type theory for productive coprogramming via guarded recursion. In: Proceedings of CSL-LICS 2014. CSL-LICS '14, ACM (2014)
51. Murase, A., Terauchi, T., Kobayashi, N., Sato, R., Unno, H.: Temporal Verification of Higher-Order Functional Programs. In: Proceedings of the 43rd Annual ACM SIGPLAN-SIGACT Symposium on Principles of Programming Languages. pp. 57–68. POPL'16, Association for Computing Machinery, New York, NY, USA (2016). https://doi.org/10.1145/2837614.2837667, https://doi.org/10.1145/2837614.2837667
52. Nakano, H.: A Modality for Recursion. In: Proceedings of LICS'00. pp. 255–266. IEEE Computer Society (2000)
53. Nanjo, Y., Unno, H., Koskinen, E., Terauchi, T.: A Fixpoint Logic and Dependent Effects for Temporal Property Verification. In: Proceedings of the 33rd Annual ACM/IEEE Symposium on Logic in Computer Science. pp. 759–768. LICS'18, Association for Computing Machinery, New York, NY, USA (2018). https://doi.org/10.1145/3209108.3209204, https://doi.org/10.1145/3209108.3209204

54. Ong, C.H.L.: On Model-Checking Trees Generated by Higher-Order Recursion Schemes. In: Proceedings of LICS 2006. pp. 81–90. IEEE Computer Society (2006)
55. Piróg, M., Gibbons, J.: The coinductive resumption monad. Electronic Notes in Theoretical Computer Science **308**, 273–288 (2014)
56. Plotkin, G., Stirling, C.: A Framework for Intuitionistic Modal Logics: Extended Abstract. In: Proceedings of the 1986 Conference on Theoretical Aspects of Reasoning About Knowledge. pp. 399–406. TARK '86, Morgan Kaufmann Publishers Inc., San Francisco, CA, USA (1986)
57. Rondon, P.M., Kawaguci, M., Jhala, R.: Liquid Types. In: Proceedings of the 29th ACM SIGPLAN Conference on Programming Language Design and Implementation. pp. 159–169. PLDI'08, Association for Computing Machinery, New York, NY, USA (2008). https://doi.org/10.1145/1375581.1375602, https://doi.org/10.1145/1375581.1375602
58. Santocanale, L., Venema, Y.: Completeness for flat modal fixpoint logics. Ann. Pure Appl. Logic **162**(1), 55–82 (2010)
59. Sato, R., Iwayama, N., Kobayashi, N.: Combining higher-order model checking with refinement type inference. In: Hermenegildo, M.V., Igarashi, A. (eds.) Proceedings of the 2019 ACM SIGPLAN Workshop on Partial Evaluation and Program Manipulation, PEPM@POPL 2019, Cascais, Portugal, January 14-15, 2019. pp. 47–53. ACM (2019). https://doi.org/10.1145/3294032.3294081, https://doi.org/10.1145/3294032.3294081
60. Simpson, A.K.: The Proof Theory and Semantics of Intuitionistic Modal Logic. Phd thesis, University of Edinburgh (Jul 1994), https://www.era.lib.ed.ac.uk/handle/1842/407
61. Skalka, C., Smith, S., Van horn, D.: Types and Trace Effects of Higher Order Programs. J. Funct. Program. **18**(2), 179–249 (Mar 2008). https://doi.org/10.1017/S0956796807006466, https://doi.org/10.1017/S0956796807006466
62. Spies, S., Krishnaswami, N., Dreyer, D.: Transfinite Step-Indexing for Termination. Proc. ACM Program. Lang. **5**(POPL) (Jan 2021). https://doi.org/10.1145/3434294, https://doi.org/10.1145/3434294
63. Sprenger, C., Dam, M.: On the Structure of Inductive Reasoning: Circular and Tree-Shaped Proofs in the μ-Calculus. In: Gordon, A.D. (ed.) Foundations of Software Science and Computational Structures, 6th International Conference, FOSSACS 2003 Held as Part of the Joint European Conference on Theory and Practice of Software, ETAPS 2003, Warsaw, Poland, April 7-11, 2003, Proceedings. Lecture Notes in Computer Science, vol. 2620, pp. 425–440. Springer (2003). https://doi.org/10.1007/3-540-36576-1_27, https://doi.org/10.1007/3-540-36576-1_27
64. Unno, H., Satake, Y., Terauchi, T.: Relatively complete refinement type system for verification of higher-order non-deterministic programs. Proc. ACM Program. Lang. **2**(POPL), 12:1–12:29 (2018). https://doi.org/10.1145/3158100, https://doi.org/10.1145/3158100
65. Vazou, N.: Liquid Haskell: Haskell as a theorem prover. Ph.D. thesis, UC San Diego (2016)
66. Vazou, N., Seidel, E.L., Jhala, R., Vytiniotis, D., Peyton-Jones, S.: Refinement Types for Haskell. In: Proceedings of the 19th ACM SIGPLAN International Conference on Functional Programming. pp. 269–282. ICFP'14, Association for Computing Machinery, New York, NY, USA (2014). https://doi.org/10.1145/2628136.2628161, https://doi.org/10.1145/2628136.2628161

67. Veltri, N., van der Weide, N.: Guarded Recursion in Agda via Sized Types. In: Geuvers, H. (ed.) 4th International Conference on Formal Structures for Computation and Deduction (FSCD 2019). Leibniz International Proceedings in Informatics (LIPIcs), vol. 131, pp. 32:1–32:19. Schloss Dagstuhl–Leibniz-Zentrum fuer Informatik, Dagstuhl, Germany (2019). https://doi.org/10.4230/LIPIcs.FSCD.2019.32, http://drops.dagstuhl.de/opus/volltexte/2019/10539
68. Walukiewicz, I.: Completeness of Kozen's Axiomatisation of the Propositional μ-Calculus. Information and Computation **157**(1-2), 142–182 (2000)
69. Watanabe, K., Tsukada, T., Oshikawa, H., Kobayashi, N.: Reduction from Branching-Time Property Verification of Higher-Order Programs to HFL Validity Checking. In: Proceedings of the 2019 ACM SIGPLAN Workshop on Partial Evaluation and Program Manipulation. pp. 22–34. PEPM 2019, Association for Computing Machinery, New York, NY, USA (2019). https://doi.org/10.1145/3294032.3294077, https://doi.org/10.1145/3294032.3294077
70. Xia, L.Y., Zakowski, Y., He, P., Hur, C.K., Malecha, G., Pierce, B.C., Zdancewic, S.: Interaction Trees: Representing Recursive and Impure Programs in Coq. Proc. ACM Program. Lang. **4**(POPL) (2019). https://doi.org/10.1145/3371119, https://doi.org/10.1145/3371119

Query Lifting

Language-integrated query for heterogeneous nested collections

Wilmer Ricciotti[1] (✉) and James Cheney[1,2]

[1] Laboratory for Foundations of Computer Science
University of Edinburgh, Edinburgh, United Kingdom
research@wilmer-ricciotti.net
jcheney@inf.ed.ac.uk
[2] The Alan Turing Institute, London, United Kingdom

Abstract. Language-integrated query based on comprehension syntax is a powerful technique for safe database programming, and provides a basis for advanced techniques such as *query shredding* or *query flattening* that allow efficient programming with complex nested collections. However, the foundations of these techniques are lacking: although SQL, the most widely-used database query language, supports *heterogeneous* queries that mix set and multiset semantics, these important capabilities are not supported by known correctness results or implementations that assume *homogeneous* collections. In this paper we study language-integrated query for a heterogeneous query language $\mathcal{NRC}_\lambda(Set, Bag)$ that combines set and multiset constructs. We show how to normalize and translate queries to SQL, and develop a novel approach to querying heterogeneous nested collections, based on the insight that "local" query subexpressions that calculate nested subcollections can be "lifted" to the top level analogously to lambda-lifting for local function definitions.

Keywords: language-integrated query · nested relations · multisets

1 Introduction

Since the rise of relational databases as important software components in the 1980s, it has been widely appreciated that database programming is hard [13]. Databases offer efficient access to flat tabular data using declarative SQL queries, a computational model very different from that of most general-purpose languages. To get the best performance from the database, programmers typically need to formulate important parts of their program's logic as queries, thus effectively programming in two languages: their usual general-purpose language (e.g. Java, Python, Scala) and SQL, with the latter query code typically constructed as unchecked, dynamic strings. Programming in two languages is more than twice as difficult as programming in one language [35]. The result is a hybrid programming model where important parts of the program's functionality are not statically checked and may lead to run-time failures, or worse, vulnerabilities

N. Yoshida (Ed.): ESOP 2021, LNCS 12648, pp. 579–606, 2021.
https://doi.org/10.1007/978-3-030-72019-3_21

such as SQL injection attacks. This undesirable state of affairs was recognized by Copeland and Maier [13] who coined the term *impedance mismatch* for it.

Though higher-level wrapper libraries and tools such as *object-relational mappings* (ORM) can help ameliorate the impedance mismatch, they often come at a price of performance and lack of transparency, as high-level operations on in-memory objects representing database data are not always mapped efficiently to queries [45]. An alternative approach, which has almost as long a history as the impedance mismatch problem itself, is to elevate queries in the host language from unchecked strings to a typed, domain-specific sublanguage, whose interactions with the rest of the program can be checked and which can be mapped to database queries safely while providing strong guarantees. This approach is nowadays typically called *language-integrated query* following Microsoft's successful LINQ extensions to .NET languages such as C# and F# [36,49]. It is ultimately based on Trinder and Wadler's insight that database queries can be modeled by a form of monadic comprehension syntax [50].

Comprehension-based query languages were placed on strong foundations in the database community in the 1990s [3,4,40,55,33]. A key insight due to Paredaens and van Gucht [40] is that although comprehension-based queries can manipulate nested collections, any expression whose input and output are *flat* collections (i.e. tables of records without other collections nested inside field values) can always be translated to an equivalent query only using flat relations (i.e. can be expressed in an SQL-like language). Wong [55] subsequently generalized this result and gave a constructive proof, in which the translation from nested to flat queries is accomplished through a strongly normalizing rewriting system.

Wong's work has informed a number of successful implementations, such as the influential Kleisli system [56] for biomedical data integration, and the Links programming language [12]. Although the implementation of LINQ in C# and F# was not directly based on normalization, Cheney et al. [7] showed that normalization can be performed as a pre-processing step to improve both reliability and performance of queries, and guarantee that a well-formed query expression evaluates to (at most) one equivalent SQL expression at run time.

Comprehension-based language-integrated query also forms the basis for libraries such as Quill for Scala [41] and Database-Supported Haskell [21]. Most recently, language-integrated query has been extended further to support efficient execution of queries that construct *nested* results [25,8,21,53], by translating such queries to a bounded number of flat queries. This technique, currently implemented in Links and DSH, has several benefits: for example to implement *provenance-tracking* efficiently in queries [17,47]. Fowler et al. [19] showed that in some cases, Links's support for nested query results decreased both the number of queries issued and the total query evaluation time by an order of magnitude or more compared to a Java database application. Unfortunately, there is still a gap between the theory and practice of language-integrated query. Widely-used and practically important SQL features that mix set and multiset collections, such as duplicate elimination, are supported by some implementations, but without guarantees regarding correctness or reliability. So far, such results have only been proved for special cases [7,8], typically for *homogeneous* queries operating on one uniform collection type. For example, in Links, queries have multiset semantics and cannot use duplicate elimination or set-valued operations. To the best of our knowledge the questions of how to correctly translate flat or nested *heterogeneous* queries to SQL are open problems.

In this paper, we solve both open problems. We study a heterogeneous query language $\mathcal{NRC}_\lambda(Set, Bag)$, which was introduced and studied in our recent work [42]. We have previously extended the key results on query normalization to $\mathcal{NRC}_\lambda(Set, Bag)$ [43], but unlike the homogeneous case, the resulting normal forms do not directly correspond to SQL. In this paper, we first show how flat $\mathcal{NRC}_\lambda(Set, Bag)$ queries can be translated to SQL, and we then develop a new approach for evaluating queries over nested heterogeneous collections. The key (and, to us at least, surprising) insight is to recognize that these two subproblems are really just different facets of one problem. That is, when translating flat $\mathcal{NRC}_\lambda(Set, Bag)$ queries to SQL, the main obstacle is how to deal with query expressions that depend on local variables; when translating nested $\mathcal{NRC}_\lambda(Set, Bag)$ queries to equivalent flat ones, the main obstacle is also how to deal with query expressions that depend on local variables. We solve this problem by observing that such query subexpressions can be *lifted*, analogously to *lambda-lifting* of local function definitions in functional programming [30], by abstracting over their free variables. Differently to lambda-lifting, however, we lift such expressions by converting them to *tabular functions*, or *graphs*, which can be calculated using database query constructs.

The remainder of this paper presents our contributions as follows:

- In section 2 we review the most relevant prior work and present our approach at a high, and we hope accessible, level.
- In sections 3 and 4 we present the core languages $\mathcal{NRC}_\lambda(Set, Bag)$ and $\mathcal{NRC}_\mathcal{G}$ which will be used in the rest of the paper.
- Section 5 presents our results on translation of flat $\mathcal{NRC}_\lambda(Set, Bag)$ queries to SQL, via $\mathcal{NRC}_\mathcal{G}$.
- Section 6 presents our results on translation of $\mathcal{NRC}_\lambda(Set, Bag)$ queries that construct nested results to a bounded number of flat $\mathcal{NRC}_\mathcal{G}$ queries.
- Sections 7 and 8 discuss related work and conclude.

2 Overview

In this section we sketch our approach. We use Links syntax [12], which differs in superficial respects from the core calculus in the rest of the paper but is more readable. We rely without further comment on existing capabilities of language-integrated query in Links, which are described elsewhere [11,34,8]. Suppose, hypothetically, we are interested in certain presidential candidates and prescription drugs they may be taking[3]. In Links, an expression querying a small database of presidential candidates and their drug prescriptions can be written as follows:

[3] For example, to see whether drug interactions might explain erratic behavior such as rage tweeting, creeping authoritarianism, or creepiness more generally.

Cand

name	cid
DJT	45
JRB	46

Pres

cid	did	day
45	101	Mon
45	223	Tue
45	223	Thu
46	765	Fri

Drug

did	drug
101	hydrochloroquine
223	adderall
765	caffeine

Q_F

in	out
(DJT,45)	hydrochloroquine
(DJT,45)	adderall
(JRB,46)	caffeine

Q_I

name	drug
DJT	hydrochloroquine
DJT	adderall
JRB	caffeine

Fig. 1. Input tables *Cand*, *Pres*, *Drug*, intermediate result of Q_F and result of Q_1.

```
Q0 = for (c <- Cand, p <- Pres, d <- Drug)
     where (c.cid == p.cid && p.did == d.did)
      [(name=c.name,drug=d.drug)]
```

Some (totally fictitious and not legally actionable) example data is shown in Figure 1; note that the prescriptions table *Pres* is a multiset containing duplicate entries. Executing this query in Links results in the following SQL query:

```
SELECT c.name, d.drug
FROM Cand c, Pres p, Drug d
WHERE c.cid = p.cid AND p.did = d.did
```

In Links, query results from the database are mapped back to list values non-deterministically, and the result of the above query Q_0 will be a list containing two copies of the tuple (`DJT`, `adderall`) and one copy of each of the tuples (`DJT`, `hydrochloroquine`) and (`JRB`, `caffeine`). If we are just interested in which candidates take which drugs and not how many times each drug was taken, we want to remove these duplicates. This can be accomplished in a basic SQL query using the `DISTINCT` keyword after `SELECT`. Currently, in Links there is no way to generate queries involving `DISTINCT`, and this duplicate elimination can only be performed in-memory. While this is not hard to do when the duplicate elimination happens at the end of the query, it is not as clear how to handle deduplication operations correctly in arbitrary places inside queries. Furthermore, SQL has several other operations that can have either set or multiset semantics such as `UNION` and `EXCEPT`: how should they be handled?

To study this problem we introduced a core calculus $\mathcal{NRC}_\lambda(Set, Bag)$ [42] (reviewed in the next section) in which there are two collection types, sets and multisets (or *bags*); duplicate elimination maps a multiset to a set with the same elements, and *promotion* maps a set to the least multiset with the same elements.

We considered, but were not previously able to solve, two problems in the context of $\mathcal{NRC}_\lambda(Set, Bag)$ which are addressed in this paper. First, the fundamental results regarding normalization and translation to SQL have been studied only for *homogeneous* query languages with collections consisting of either sets, bags, or lists. We recently extended the normalization results to $\mathcal{NRC}_\lambda(Set, Bag)$ [43], but the resulting normal forms do not correspond directly to SQL queries if operations such as deduplication, promotion, or bag difference are present. Second, query expressions that construct nested collections cannot be translated directly to SQL and can be very expensive to execute in-memory using nested loops, leading to the $N+1$ *query problem* (or *query avalanche problem* [26]) in which one query is performed for the outer loop and then another N queries are performed, one per iteration of the inner loop. Some techniques have been developed for translating nested queries to a fixed number of flat queries, but to date they either handle only homogeneous set or bag collections [54,8], or lack detailed correctness proofs [26,52].

Regarding the first problem, the closest work in this respect is by Libkin and Wong [33], who studied and related the expressiveness of comprehension-based homogeneous set and bag query languages but did not consider their heterogeneous combination or translation to SQL. The following query illustrates the fundamental obstacle:

```
Q1 = for (c <- Cand)
     for (d <- dedup(for (p <- Pres, d <- Drug)
                     where (c.cid == p.cid && p.did == d.did)
                     [d.drug]))
     [(name=c.name, drug=d)]
```

This query is similar to Q_0, but eliminates duplicates among the drugs for each candidate. The query contains a duplicate elimination operation (dedup) applied to another query subexpression that refers to c, which is introduced in an earlier generator. This is not directly supported in classic SQL: by default the subqueries in FROM clauses cannot refer to tuple variables introduced by earlier parts of the FROM clause. In fact, this query is expressible in SQL:1999 using the LATERAL keyword, which does allow such sideways information-passing:

```
SELECT c.name,d.drug
FROM Cand c, LATERAL (SELECT DISTINCT d.drug
                      FROM Pres p, Drug d
                      WHERE p.cid = c.cid AND p.did = d.did) d
```

(Without the LATERAL keyword, this query is not well-formed SQL.) However, such queries have only recently become widely supported, so are not available on legacy databases, and even when supported, are not typically optimized effectively; for example PostgreSQL will evaluate it as a nested loop, with quadratic complexity or worse.

Regarding the second problem, Van den Bussche [54] showed that any query returning nested set collections can be simulated by n flat queries, where n is the number of occurrences of the set collection type in the result. However, this translation has not been used as the basis for a practical system to our knowledge, and does not respect multiset semantics. Cheney et al. [8] provided an analogous *shredding* translation for nested multiset queries, but translated to a richer target language (including SQL:1999 features such as ROW_NUMBER) and did not handle operations such as multiset difference or duplicate elimination. Thus, neither approach handles the full expressiveness of a heterogeneous query language over bags and sets. The following query illustrates the fundamental obstacle:

```
Q2 = for (x <- Cand)
    [(name=x.name, drugs=dedup(for (p <- Pres, d <- Drug)
                               where (x.cid == p.cid and p.did == d.did)
                               [d.drug]))]
```

Much like Q_1, Q_2 builds a multiset of pairs (*name*, *drugs*) but here *drugs* is a *set* of all of the drugs taken by candidate *name*. Such a query is, of course, not even syntactically expressible in SQL because it returns a nested collection; it is not expressible in previous work on nested query evaluation either, because the result is a multiset of records, one component of which is a set.

We will now illustrate how to translate Q_1 to a plain SQL query (not using LATERAL), and how to translate Q_2 to two flat queries such that the nested result can be constructed easily from their flat results. First, note that we can rewrite both queries as follows, introducing an abbreviation $F(x)$ for a query subexpression parameterized by x:

```
F(x) = for (p <- Pres, d <- Drug)
       where (x.cid == p.cid and p.did == d.did)
       [d.drug]
Q1   = for (c <- Cand) for (d <- dedup(F(c))) [(name=c.name, drug=d)]
Q2   = for (c <- Cand) [(name=c.name, drugs=dedup(F(c)))]
```

Next, observe that the set of all possible values for x appearing in some call to $F(x)$ is finite, and can even be computed by a query. Therefore, we can write a *closed* query Q_F that builds a lookup table that calculates the *graph* of F (or at least, as much of it as is needed to evaluate the queries) as follows:

```
Q_F = dedup(for (x <- Cand, y <- F(x)) [(in=x,out=y)])
```

Notice that the use of deduplication here is really essential to define Q_F correctly: if we did not deduplicate then there would be repeated tuples in Q_F, leading to incorrect results later. If we inline and simplify $F(x)$ in the above query, we get the following:

```
Q_F' = dedup(for (x <- Cand, y <- Pres, z <- Drug)
             where (x.cid == y.cid && y.did = z.did)
             [(in=x,out=z.drug)])
```

Finally we may replace the call to $F(x)$ in Q_1 with a lookup to Q'_F, as follows:

```
Q1' = for (c <- Cand, f <- Q_F') where (c == f.in)
      [(name=c.name, drug=f.out)]
```

This expression may now be translated directly to SQL, because the argument to dedup is now closed:

```
SELECT c.name,f.drug
FROM Cand c, (SELECT DISTINCT x.name,x.cid,z.drug
              FROM Cand x, Pres y, Drug z
              WHERE x.cid = y.cid AND y.did = z.did) f
WHERE c.cid = f.cid AND c.name = f.name
```

Q_{21}

name	drugs
DJT	(DJT,45)
JRB	(JRB,46)

Q_{22}

in	out
(DJT,45)	hydrochloroquine
(DJT,45)	adderall
(JRB,46)	caffeine

Q_2

name	drugs
DJT	{hydrochloroquine, adderall}
JRB	{caffeine}

Fig. 2. Intermediate results of Q_{21}, Q_{22} and result of Q_2.

Although this query looks a bit more complex than the one given earlier using LATERAL, it can be optimized more effectively, for example PostgreSQL generates a query plan that uses a hash join, giving quasi-linear complexity.

On the other hand, to deal with Q_2, we refactor it into two closed, flat queries Q_{21}, Q_{22} and an expression Q_2' that builds the nested result from their flat results (illustrated in Figure 2):

```
Q_21 = for (x <- Cand) [(name=x.name, drugs=x)]
Q_22 = Q_F
Q2'  = for (x <- Q21)
         [(name=x.name,
           drugs=for (y <- Q_22) where(x.drugs == y.in) [y.out])]
```

Notice that in Q_{21} we replaced the call to F with the argument x, while Q_{22} is just Q_F again. The final expression Q_2' builds the nested result (in the host language's memory) by traversing Q_{21} and computing the set value of each cs field by looking up the appropriate values from Q_{22}. Thus, the original query result can be computed by first evaluating Q_{21} and Q_{22} on the database, and then evaluating the final *stitching* query expression in-memory. (In practice, as discussed in Cheney et al. [8], it is important for performance to use a more sophisticated stitching algorithm than the above naive nested loop, but in this paper we are primarily concerned with the correctness of the transformation.)

The above examples are a bit simplistic, but illustrate the key idea of *query lifting*. In the rest of this paper we place this approach on a solid foundation, and (partially inspired by Gibbons et al. [20]), to help clarify the reasoning we extend the calculus with a type of *tabulated functions* or *graphs* $\overrightarrow{\sigma} \dashrightarrow \{\tau\}$, with *graph abstraction* introduction form $\mathcal{G}(-;-)$ and *graph application* $M \circledast \langle \overrightarrow{x} \rangle$. In our running example we could define $Q_F = \mathcal{G}(x \leftarrow R; F(x))$, and we would use the application operation $M \circledast \langle \overrightarrow{x} \rangle$ to extract the set of elements corresponding to x in Q_F. We will also consider tabular functions that return multisets rather than sets, in order to deal with queries that return nested multisets.

3 Background

We recap the main points from [42], which introduced a calculus $\mathcal{NRC}_\lambda(Set, Bag)$ with the following syntax:

$$
\begin{array}{lrl}
\textbf{Types} & \sigma,\tau ::= & b \mid \langle\overrightarrow{\ell:\sigma}\rangle \mid \{\sigma\} \mid \Lbag\sigma\Rbag \mid \sigma\to\tau \\
\textbf{Terms} & M,N ::= & x \mid t \mid c(\overrightarrow{M}) \mid \langle\overrightarrow{\ell=M}\rangle \mid M.\ell \mid \lambda x.M \mid M\ N \\
& \mid & \emptyset \mid \{M\} \mid M\cup N \mid \bigcup\{M|\Theta\} \\
& \mid & \mho \mid \Lbag M\Rbag \mid M\uplus N \mid M-N \mid \biguplus\Lbag M|\Theta\Rbag \\
& \mid & \delta M \mid \iota M \mid M\ \mathbf{where}_{\mathsf{set}}\ N \mid M\ \mathbf{where}_{\mathsf{bag}}\ N \\
& \mid & \mathbf{empty}_{\mathsf{set}}(M) \mid \mathbf{empty}_{\mathsf{bag}}(M) \\
\textbf{Generators} & \Theta ::= & \overrightarrow{x\leftarrow M}
\end{array}
$$

We distinguish between (local) variables x and (global) table names t, and assume standard primitive types b and primitive operations $c(\overrightarrow{M})$ including respectively Booleans $\mathbf{B}$ and equality at every base type. The syntax for records and record projection $\langle\overrightarrow{\ell=M}\rangle, M.\ell$, and for lambda-abstraction and application $\lambda x.M, M\ N$ is standard; as usual, let-binding is definable. Set operations include empty set $\emptyset$, singleton construction $\{M\}$, union $M\cup N$, one-armed conditional M $\mathbf{where}_{\mathsf{set}}$ N, emptiness test $\mathbf{empty}_{\mathsf{set}}(M)$, and comprehension $\bigcup\{M \mid \Theta\}$, where Θ is a sequence of generators $x\leftarrow M$. Similarly, multiset operations include empty bag $\mho$, singleton $\Lbag M\Rbag$, bag union $M\uplus N$, bag difference $M-N$, conditional M $\mathbf{where}_{\mathsf{bag}}$ N, emptiness test $\mathbf{empty}_{\mathsf{bag}}(M)$. The syntax is completed by duplicate elimination δM (converting a bag M into a set with the same object type) and promotion ιM (which produces the bag containing all the elements of the set M, with multiplicity 1).

The one-way conditional operations M $\mathbf{where}_{\mathsf{set}}$ N and M $\mathbf{where}_{\mathsf{bag}}$ N evaluate Boolean test N, and return collection M if N is true, otherwise the empty set/bag; two-way conditionals can supported without problems. Other set operations, such as intersection, membership, subset, and equality are also definable, as are bag operations such as intersection [4,33]. Also, we may define $\mathbf{empty}_{\mathsf{bag}}(M)$ as $\mathbf{empty}_{\mathsf{set}}(\delta(M))$ and M $\mathbf{where}_{\mathsf{set}}$ N as $\delta(\iota(M)$ $\mathbf{where}_{\mathsf{bag}}$ $N)$, but we prefer to include these constructs as primitives for symmetry. Generally, we will allow ourselves to write M **where** N and **empty**(M) without subscripts if the collection kind of these operations is irrelevant or made clear by the context. We freely use syntax for unlabeled tuples $\langle\overrightarrow{M}\rangle, M.i$ and tuple types $\overrightarrow{\sigma}$ and consider them to be syntactic sugar for labeled records.

The typing rules for the calculus are standard and provided in the full version of this paper [44]. For the purposes of this discussion, we will highlight two features of the type system. The first is that the calculus used here differs from our previous work by using constants and table names, whose types are described by a fixed signature Σ:

$$
\frac{\Sigma(c)=\overrightarrow{b}\to b \qquad (\Gamma\vdash M_i:\sigma_i)_{i=1,\ldots,n}}{\Gamma\vdash c(\overrightarrow{M}):\tau}
\qquad\qquad
\frac{\Sigma(t)=\overrightarrow{\ell:b}}{\Gamma\vdash t:\Lbag\langle\overrightarrow{\ell:b}\rangle\Rbag}
$$

As usual, a typing judgment $\Gamma\vdash M:\sigma$ states that a term M is well-typed of type σ, assuming that its free variables have the types declared in the typing context $\Gamma = x_1:\sigma_1,\ldots,x_k:\sigma_k$. For the two rules above, note in particular that the primitive functions c can only take inputs of base type and produce results at base type, and table constants t are always multisets of records where the fields are of base type. We refer to a type of the form $\langle\overrightarrow{\ell : b}\rangle$ as *flat*; if σ is flat, we refer to $\{\sigma\}$ and $\wr\sigma\wr$ as *flat collection types.*

The second is that our type system uses an approach à la Church, meaning that variable abstractions (in lambdas/comprehensions), empty sets and empty bags are annotated with their type in order to ensure the uniqueness of typing.

Lemma 1. *In $\mathcal{NRC}_\lambda(Set, Bag)$, if $\Gamma \vdash M : \sigma$ and $\Gamma \vdash M : \tau$, then $\sigma = \tau$.*

In the context of a larger language implementation, most of these type annotations can be elided and inferred by type inference. We have chosen to dispense with these details in the main body of this paper to avoid unnecessary syntactic cluttering.

We will use a largely standard denotational semantics for $\mathcal{NRC}_\lambda(Set, Bag)$, in which sets and multisets are modeled as finitely-supported functions from their element types to Boolean values $\{0, 1\}$ or natural numbers respectively. This approach follows the so-called K-relation semantics for queries [23,18] as used for example in the HoTTSQL formalization [10]. The full typing rules and semantics are included in the full version of this paper [44].

$\mathcal{NRC}_\lambda(Set, Bag)$ subsumes previous systems including $\mathcal{NRC}$ [4,55], $\mathcal{BQL}$ [33] and $\mathcal{NRC}_\lambda$ [11,8]. In this paper, we restrict our attention to queries in which collection types taking part in δ, ι or bag difference contain only flat records. There are various reasons for excluding function types from these operators: for starters, any concrete implementation that used function types in these positions would need to decide the equality of functions; secondly, our rewrite system can ensure that a term whose type does not contain function types has a normal form without lambda abstractions and applications only if any δ, ι, or bag difference used in that term are applied to first-order collections. We thus want to exclude terms such as:

$$\biguplus \wr x\ \wr 1 \wr\ \wr 2 \wr | x \leftarrow \iota(\{\lambda yz.y\} \cup \{\lambda yz.z\})\wr$$

which do not have an SQL representation despite having a flat collection type.

In order to obtain simpler normal forms, in which comprehensions only reference generators with a flat collection type, we also disallow nested collections within δ, ι, and bag difference. We believe this is without loss of generality because of Libkin and Wong's results showing that allowing such operations at nested types does not add expressiveness to $\mathcal{BQL}$.

We have extended Wong's normalizing rewrite rule system, so as to simplify queries to a form that is close to SQL, with no intermediate nested collections. Since our calculus is more liberal than Wong's, allowing queries to be defined by mixing sets and bags and also using bag difference, we have added non-standard rules to take care of unwanted situations. In particular, we use the following constrained eta-expansions for comprehensions:

$$\bigcup\{\delta(M - N)|\Theta\} \rightsquigarrow \bigcup\{\{z\}|\Theta, z \leftarrow \delta(M - N)\}$$

$$\biguplus \wr \iota M|\Theta\wr \rightsquigarrow \biguplus \wr \wr z\wr|\Theta, z \leftarrow \iota M\wr$$

$$\biguplus \wr M - N|\Theta\wr \rightsquigarrow \biguplus \wr \wr z\wr|\Theta, z \leftarrow M - N\wr$$

$$
\begin{array}{lrl}
\textbf{General normal forms} & M & ::= X \mid \langle \overrightarrow{\ell = M} \rangle \mid Q \mid R \\
\textbf{Base type terms} & X & ::= x.\ell \mid c(\overrightarrow{X}) \mid \textbf{empty}_{\textsf{set}}(Q^*) \mid \textbf{empty}_{\textsf{bag}}(R^*) \\
\textbf{Set normal forms} & Q & ::= \bigcup \overrightarrow{C} \\
 & C & ::= \bigcup \{\{M\} \, \textbf{where}_{\textsf{set}} \, X | \overrightarrow{x \leftarrow F}\} \\
 & F & ::= \delta t \mid \delta(R_1^* - R_2^*) \\
\textbf{Bag normal forms} & R & ::= \biguplus \overrightarrow{D} \\
 & D & ::= \biguplus \wr \wr M \wr \, \textbf{where}_{\textsf{bag}} \, X | \overrightarrow{x \leftarrow G} \wr \\
 & G & ::= t \mid \iota Q^* \mid R_1^* - R_2^*
\end{array}
$$

Fig. 3. Nested relational normal forms.

The rationale of these rules is that in order to achieve, for comprehensions, a form that can be easily translated to an SQL select query, we need to move all the syntactic forms that are blocking to most normalization rules (i.e. promotion and bag difference) from the head of the comprehension to a generator. In order for this strategy to work out, we also need to know that the type of these subexpressions is flat, as we previously mentioned.

In Figure 3 we show the grammar for the normal forms for terms of *nested relational types*, i.e. types of the following form:

$$\sigma ::= b \mid \langle \overrightarrow{\ell : \sigma} \rangle \mid \{\sigma\} \mid \wr \sigma \wr$$

For ease of presentation, the grammar actually describes a "standardized" version of the normal forms in which:

- $\emptyset$ is represented as the trivial union $\bigcup \overrightarrow{C}$ where $\overrightarrow{C}$ is the empty sequence; $\mho$ has a similar representation using a trivial disjoint union;
- comprehensions without a guard are considered to be the same as those with a trivial true guard:
$$\bigcup\{\{M\}|\Theta\} = \bigcup\{\{M\} \textbf{ where true} \mid \Theta\}$$
- singletons that do not appear as the head of a comprehension are represented as trivial comprehensions:
$$\{M\} = \bigcup\{\{M\} \mid \ \}$$

Each normal form M can be either a term of base type X, a tuple $\langle \overrightarrow{\ell = M} \rangle$, a set Q, or a bag R. The normal forms of sets and bags are rather similar, both being defined as unions of comprehensions with a singleton head. The generators for set comprehensions F include deduplicated tables and deduplicated bag differences; the generators for bag comprehensions G must be either tables, promoted set queries, or bag differences.

The non-terminals used as the arguments of emptiness tests, promotion, and bag difference have been marked with a star to emphasize the fact that they

$$
\begin{array}{rlrl}
(\emptyset)^{\mathsf{sql}} &= \texttt{SELECT 42 WHERE } 0 = 1 & (\mho)^{\mathsf{sql}} &= \texttt{SELECT 42 WHERE } 0 = 1 \\
(x.\ell)^{\mathsf{sql}} &= x.\ell & (c(\overrightarrow{X}))^{\mathsf{sql}} &= (c)^{\mathsf{sql}}(\overrightarrow{(X)^{\mathsf{sql}}}) \\
(\langle\overrightarrow{\ell = X}\rangle)^{\mathsf{sql}} &= (X_1)^{\mathsf{sql}} \texttt{ AS } \ell_1, \ldots, (X_n)^{\mathsf{sql}} \texttt{ AS } \ell_n & & \\
(\mathbf{empty}_{\mathsf{set}}(Q^*))^{\mathsf{sql}} &= \texttt{NOT EXISTS } (Q^*)^{\mathsf{sql}} & (\mathbf{empty}_{\mathsf{bag}}(R^*))^{\mathsf{sql}} &= \texttt{NOT EXISTS } (R^*)^{\mathsf{sql}} \\
(Q_1^* \cup Q_2^*)^{\mathsf{sql}} &= (Q_1^*)^{\mathsf{sql}} \texttt{ UNION } (Q_2^*)^{\mathsf{sql}} & (R_1^* \uplus R_2^*)^{\mathsf{sql}} &= (R_1^*)^{\mathsf{sql}} \texttt{ UNION ALL } (R_2^*)^{\mathsf{sql}} \\
(t)^{\mathsf{sql}} &= \texttt{SELECT * FROM } t & (R_1^* - R_2^*)^{\mathsf{sql}} &= (R_1^*)^{\mathsf{sql}} \texttt{ EXCEPT ALL } (R_2^*)^{\mathsf{sql}} \\
(\delta t)^{\mathsf{sql}} &= \texttt{SELECT DISTINCT * FROM } t & (\iota(Q^*))^{\mathsf{sql}} &= (Q^*)^{\mathsf{sql}} \\
(\delta(R_1^* - R_2^*))^{\mathsf{sql}} &= \texttt{SELECT DISTINCT * FROM } ((R_1^*)^{\mathsf{sql}} \texttt{ EXCEPT ALL } (R_2^*)^{\mathsf{sql}} s)\ r & & \\
(x \leftarrow F)^{\mathsf{sql}} &= \begin{cases} ((F)^{\mathsf{sql}})\ x & (x \text{ closed}) \\ \texttt{LATERAL } ((F)^{\mathsf{sql}})\ x & (\text{otherwise}) \end{cases} & & \\
(x \leftarrow G)^{\mathsf{sql}} &= \begin{cases} ((G)^{\mathsf{sql}})\ x & (x \text{ closed}) \\ \texttt{LATERAL } ((G)^{\mathsf{sql}})\ x & (\text{otherwise}) \end{cases} & &
\end{array}
$$

$$(\bigcup\{\{M^*\}\ \mathbf{where}_{\mathsf{set}}\ X \mid \overrightarrow{x \leftarrow F}\})^{\mathsf{sql}} = \texttt{SELECT DISTINCT } (M^*)^{\mathsf{sql}} \texttt{ FROM } \overrightarrow{(x \leftarrow F)^{\mathsf{sql}}} \texttt{ WHERE } (X)^{\mathsf{sql}}$$

$$(\biguplus \{\!|M^*|\!\}\ \mathbf{where}_{\mathsf{bag}}\ X \mid \overrightarrow{x \leftarrow G}|\!\})^{\mathsf{sql}} = \texttt{SELECT } (M^*)^{\mathsf{sql}} \texttt{ FROM } \overrightarrow{(x \leftarrow G)^{\mathsf{sql}}} \texttt{ WHERE } (X)^{\mathsf{sql}}$$

Fig. 4. Translation to SQL

must have a flat collection type. The corresponding grammar can be obtained from the grammar for nested normal forms by replacing the rule for M with the following:

$$M^* ::= \langle\overrightarrow{\ell = X}\rangle$$

Normalized queries can be translated to SQL as shown in Figure 4 as long as they have a flat collection type. The translation uses `SELECT DISTINCT` and `UNION` where a set semantics is needed, and `SELECT`, `UNION ALL` and `EXCEPT ALL` in the case of bag semantics. Note that promotion expressions ιQ^* are translated simply by translating Q^*, because in SQL there is no type distinction between set and multiset queries: all query results are multisets, and sets are considered to be multisets having no duplicates.

The other main complication in this translation is in handling generators $x \leftarrow F$, $x \leftarrow G$ where F or G may be a non-closed expression $\iota(Q^*)$, $R_1^* - R_2^*$, or $\delta(R_1^* - R_2^*)$ containing references to other locally-bound variables. To deal with the resulting lateral variable references, we add the `LATERAL` keyword to such queries. As explained earlier, the use of `LATERAL` can be problematic and we will return to this issue in Section 5.

Remark 1 (Record flattening). The above translations handle queries that take flat tables as input and produce flat results (collections of flat records $\langle\overrightarrow{\ell : b}\rangle$). It is straightforward to support queries that return nested records (i.e. records containing other records, but not collections). For example, a query $M : \{\!|\langle b_1, \langle b_2, b_3\rangle\rangle|\!\}$ can be handled by defining both directions of the obvious isomorphism $N : \{\!|\langle b_1, \langle b_2, b_3\rangle\rangle|\!\} \cong \{\!|\langle b_1, b_2, b_3\rangle|\!\} : N^{-1}$, normalizing the flat query $N \circ M$, evaluating the corresponding SQL, and applying the inverse N^{-1} to the results. Such *record flattening* is described in detail by Cheney et al. [9] and is implemented in Links, so we will use it from now on without further discussion.

$$\frac{(\Gamma, \overrightarrow{x_{i-1} : \sigma_{i-1}} \vdash L_i : \{\sigma_i\})_{i=1,\dots,n} \quad \Gamma, \overrightarrow{x : \sigma} \vdash M : \{\tau\}}{\Gamma \vdash \mathcal{G}^{\mathsf{set}}(\overrightarrow{x \leftarrow L}; M) : \vec{\sigma} \dashv \{\tau\}}
\qquad
\frac{(\Gamma, \overrightarrow{x_{i-1} : \sigma_{i-1}} \vdash L_i : \{\sigma_i\})_{i=1,\dots,n} \quad \Gamma, \overrightarrow{x : \sigma} \vdash M : \wr\tau\wr}{\Gamma \vdash \mathcal{G}^{\mathsf{bag}}(\overrightarrow{x \leftarrow L}; M) : \vec{\sigma} \dashv \wr\tau\wr}$$

$$\frac{\Gamma \vdash M : \vec{\sigma} \dashv \tau \qquad (\Gamma \vdash N_i : \sigma_i)_i}{\Gamma \vdash M \circledast (\vec{N}) : \tau}
\qquad
\frac{\Gamma \vdash M : \vec{\sigma} \dashv \wr\tau\wr \quad \Gamma \vdash N : \vec{\sigma} \dashv \wr\tau\wr}{\Gamma \vdash M - N : \vec{\sigma} \dashv \wr\tau\wr}$$

$$\frac{\Gamma \vdash M : \vec{\sigma} \dashv \{\tau\} \quad \Gamma \vdash N : \vec{\sigma} \dashv \{\tau\}}{\Gamma \vdash M \cup N : \vec{\sigma} \dashv \{\tau\}}
\qquad
\frac{\Gamma \vdash M : \vec{\sigma} \dashv \wr\tau\wr \quad \Gamma \vdash N : \vec{\sigma} \dashv \wr\tau\wr}{\Gamma \vdash M \uplus N : \vec{\sigma} \dashv \wr\tau\wr}$$

$$\frac{\Gamma \vdash M : \vec{\sigma} \dashv \wr\tau\wr}{\Gamma \vdash \delta M : \vec{\sigma} \dashv \{\tau\}}
\qquad
\frac{\Gamma \vdash M : \vec{\sigma} \dashv \{\tau\}}{\Gamma \vdash \iota M : \vec{\sigma} \dashv \wr\tau\wr}$$

Fig. 5. $\mathcal{NRC}_{\mathcal{G}}$ additional typing rules.

4 A relational calculus of tabular functions

We now introduce $\mathcal{NRC}_{\mathcal{G}}$, an extension of the calculus $\mathcal{NRC}_{\lambda}(Set, Bag)$ providing a new type of finite tabular function graphs (in the remainder of this paper, also called simply "graphs"; they are similar to the finite maps and tables of Gibbons et al. [20]). The syntax of $\mathcal{NRC}_{\mathcal{G}}$ is defined as follows:

Types $\sigma, \tau ::= \cdots \mid \vec{\sigma} \dashv \tau$

Terms $M, N ::= \cdots \mid \mathcal{G}^{\mathsf{set}}(\Theta; N) \mid \mathcal{G}^{\mathsf{bag}}(\Theta; N) \mid M \circledast (\vec{N})$

Semantically, the type of graphs $\vec{\sigma} \dashv \tau$ will be interpreted as the set of finite functions from sequences of values of type $\vec{\sigma}$ to values in τ: such functions can return non-trivial values only for a finite subset of their input type. In our settings, we will require the output type of graphs to be a collection type (i.e. τ shall be either $\{\tau'\}$ or $\wr\tau'\wr$ for some τ'), and we will use $\emptyset$ or $\mho$ as the trivial value. The typing rules involving graphs are shown in Figure 5.

Graphs are created using the *graph abstraction* operations $\mathcal{G}^{\mathsf{set}}(\Theta; N)$ and $\mathcal{G}^{\mathsf{bag}}(\Theta; N)$, where Θ is a sequence of generators in the form $\overrightarrow{x \leftarrow M}$; the dual operation of *graph application* is denoted by $M \circledast (\vec{N})$. An expression of the form $\mathcal{G}^{\mathsf{set}}(\overrightarrow{x \leftarrow M}; N)$ is used to construct a (finite) tabular function mapping each sequence of values $R_1, \dots, R_n$ in the sets $M_1, \dots, M_n$ to the set $N\left[\vec{R}/\vec{x}\right]$. If each M_i has type $\{\sigma_i\}$ and N has type $\{\tau\}$, then the graph has type $\vec{\sigma} \dashv \{\tau\}$. Similarly, if N has type $\wr\tau\wr$, $\mathcal{G}^{\mathsf{bag}}(\overrightarrow{x \leftarrow M}; N)$ has type $\vec{\sigma} \dashv \wr\tau\wr$. The terms $M_1, \dots, M_n$ constitute the (finite) *domain* of this graph. When the kind of graph application (set-based or bag-based) is clear from the context or unimportant, we will allow ourselves to write $\mathcal{G}(-;-)$ instead of $\mathcal{G}^{\mathsf{set}}(-;-)$ or $\mathcal{G}^{\mathsf{bag}}(-;-)$.

A graph G of type $\overrightarrow{\sigma} \dashrightarrow \tau$ can be applied to a sequence of terms $N_1, \ldots, N_n$ of type $\sigma_1, \ldots, \sigma_n$ to obtain a term of type τ. If $G = \mathcal{G}(\overrightarrow{x \leftarrow L}; M)$, then we will want the semantics of $\mathcal{G}(\overrightarrow{x \leftarrow L}; M) \circledast (\overrightarrow{N})$ to be the same as that of $M\left[\overrightarrow{N}/\overrightarrow{x}\right]$, provided that each of the N_i is in the corresponding element of the domain of the graph. The typing rule does *not* enforce this requirement and if any of the N_i is not an element of L_i, the graph application will evaluate to an empty set or bag (depending on τ).

Graphs can also be merged by union, using $\cup$ or $\uplus$ depending on their output collection kind. Furthermore, graphs that return bags can be subtracted from one another using bag difference; the deduplication and promotion operations also extend to graphs in the obvious way.

Lemma 2. *In $\mathcal{NRC}_{\mathcal{G}}$, $\Gamma \vdash M : \sigma$ and $\Gamma \vdash M : \tau$, then $\sigma = \tau$.*

Whenever M is well typed and its typing environment is made clear by the context, we will allow ourselves to write $ty(M)$ for the type of M. Furthermore, given a sequence of generators $\Theta = x_1 \leftarrow L_1, \ldots x_n \leftarrow L_n$, such that for $i = 1, \ldots, n$ we have $x_1 : \sigma_1, \ldots, x_{i-1} : \sigma_{i-1} \vdash L_i : \sigma_i$, we will write $ty(\Theta)$ to denote the associated typing context:

$$ty(\Theta) := x_1 : \sigma_1, \ldots, x_n : \sigma_n$$

4.1 Semantics and translation to $\mathcal{NRC}_\lambda(Set, Bag)$

The semantics of $\mathcal{NRC}_\lambda(Set, Bag)$ is extended to $\mathcal{NRC}_{\mathcal{G}}$ as follows:

$$\begin{aligned}
&\left[\!\left[\mathcal{G}^{\mathsf{set}}(\overrightarrow{x \leftarrow L}; M)\right]\!\right] \rho(\overrightarrow{u}, v) \\
&\quad = (\textstyle\bigwedge_i [\![L_i]\!]\, \rho[x_1 \mapsto u_1, \ldots, x_{i-1} \mapsto u_{i-1}] u_i) \wedge [\![M]\!]\, \rho[\overrightarrow{x \mapsto u}] v \\
&\left[\!\left[\mathcal{G}^{\mathsf{bag}}(\overrightarrow{x \leftarrow L}; M)\right]\!\right] \rho(\overrightarrow{u}, v) \\
&\quad = (\textstyle\bigwedge_i [\![L_i]\!]\, \rho[x_1 \mapsto u_1, \ldots, x_{i-1} \mapsto u_{i-1}] u_i) \times [\![M]\!]\, \rho[\overrightarrow{x \mapsto u}] v \\
&\left[\!\left[M \circledast (\overrightarrow{N})\right]\!\right] \rho v = [\![M]\!]\, \rho\, (\overrightarrow{[\![N]\!]\, \rho}, v)
\end{aligned}$$

In this definition, graph abstractions are interpreted as collections of pairs of values $(\overrightarrow{u}, v)$ where the $\overrightarrow{u}$ represent the input and v the corresponding output of the graph; consequently, the semantics of a graph $\mathcal{G}^{\mathsf{set}}(\overrightarrow{x \leftarrow L}; M)$ states that the multiplicity of $(\overrightarrow{u}, v)$ is equal to the multiplicity of v in the semantics of M (where each x_i is mapped to u_i) if each u_i is in the semantics of L_i, and zero otherwise. The semantics of bag graph abstractions is similar, with $\times$ substituted for $\wedge$ to allow multiplicities greater than one in the graph output.

For graph applications $M \circledast (\overrightarrow{N})$, the multiplicity of v is obtained as the multiplicity of $(\overrightarrow{[\![N]\!]\, \rho}, v)$ in the semantics of M. The semantics of set and bag union, bag difference, bag deduplication, and set promotion, as defined in $\mathcal{NRC}_\lambda(Set, Bag)$, are extended to graphs and remain otherwise unchanged in $\mathcal{NRC}_{\mathcal{G}}$.

In fact (as noted for example by Gibbons et al. [20]), the graph constructs of $\mathcal{NRC}_{\mathcal{G}}$ are just a notational convenience: we can translate $\mathcal{NRC}_{\mathcal{G}}$ back to $\mathcal{NRC}_{\lambda}(Set, Bag)$ by translating types $\overrightarrow{\sigma} \dashv\!\!\!\rightarrow \{\tau\}$ and $\overrightarrow{\sigma} \dashv\!\!\!\rightarrow \wr\tau\wr$ to $\{\langle\overrightarrow{\sigma},\tau\rangle\}$ and $\wr\langle\overrightarrow{\sigma},\tau\rangle\wr$ respectively, and the term constructs are rewritten as follows:

$$\begin{aligned}
\mathcal{G}^{\mathsf{set}}(\overrightarrow{x \leftarrow L}; M) &\rightsquigarrow \bigcup\{\{\langle\overrightarrow{x},y\rangle\} \mid \overrightarrow{x \leftarrow L}, y \leftarrow M\}\\
\mathcal{G}^{\mathsf{bag}}(\overrightarrow{x \leftarrow L}; M) &\rightsquigarrow \biguplus\wr\wr\langle\overrightarrow{x},y\rangle\wr \mid \overrightarrow{x \leftarrow \iota(L)}, y \leftarrow M\wr\\
M \circledast \langle\overrightarrow{N}\rangle &\rightsquigarrow \bigcup\{\{y\}\ \mathbf{where}_{\mathsf{set}}\ \overrightarrow{x} = \overrightarrow{N} \mid \langle\overrightarrow{x},y\rangle \leftarrow M\} \quad (M : \overrightarrow{\sigma} \dashv\!\!\!\rightarrow \{\tau\})\\
M \circledast \langle\overrightarrow{N}\rangle &\rightsquigarrow \biguplus\wr\wr y\wr\ \mathbf{where}_{\mathsf{bag}}\ \overrightarrow{x} = \overrightarrow{N} \mid \langle\overrightarrow{x},y\rangle \leftarrow M\wr \quad (M : \overrightarrow{\sigma} \dashv\!\!\!\rightarrow \wr\tau\wr)
\end{aligned}$$

5 Delateralization

As explained at the end of section 3, if a subexpression of the form $\iota(N)$ or $N_1 - N_2$ contains free variables introduced by other generators in the query (i.e. not globally-scoped table variables), such queries cannot be translated directly to SQL, unless the SQL:1999 `LATERAL` keyword is used.

More precisely, we can give the following definition of lateral variable occurrence.

Definition 1. *Given a query containing a comprehension* $\bigcup\{M \mid \Theta, x \leftarrow N, \Theta'\}$ *or* $\biguplus\wr M \mid \Theta, x \leftarrow N, \Theta'\wr$ *as a subterm, we say that* x occurs laterally *in* Θ' *if, and only if, there is a binding* $y \leftarrow N'$ *in* Θ' *such that* $x \in \mathrm{FV}(N')$.

Since `LATERAL` is not implemented on all databases, and is sometimes implemented inefficiently, we would still like to avoid it. In this section we show how lateral occurrences can be eliminated even in the presence of bag promotion and bag difference, by means of a process we call *delateralization*.

Using the $\mathcal{NRC}_{\mathcal{G}}$ constructs, we can delateralize simple cases of deduplication or multiset difference as follows:

$$\begin{aligned}
&\biguplus\wr M \mid x \leftarrow N, y \leftarrow \iota(P)\wr \rightsquigarrow \biguplus\wr M \mid x \leftarrow N, y \leftarrow \iota(\mathcal{G}(x \leftarrow \delta N; P)) \circledast x\wr\\
&\biguplus\wr M \mid x \leftarrow N, y \leftarrow P_1 - P_2\wr \rightsquigarrow\\
&\qquad \biguplus\wr M \mid x \leftarrow N, y \leftarrow (\mathcal{G}(x \leftarrow \delta N; P_1) - \mathcal{G}(x \leftarrow \delta N; P_2)) \circledast x\wr\\
&\bigcup\{M \mid x \leftarrow N, y \leftarrow \delta(P_1 - P_2)\} \rightsquigarrow\\
&\qquad \bigcup\{M \mid x \leftarrow N, y \leftarrow \delta(\mathcal{G}(x \leftarrow N; P_1) - \mathcal{G}(x \leftarrow N; P_2)) \circledast x\}
\end{aligned}$$

It is necessary to deduplicate N in the first two rules to ensure that the results correctly represent finite maps from the distinct elements of N to multisets of corresponding elements of P. (In any case, N needs to be deduplicated in order to be used as a set in $\mathcal{G}(x \leftarrow \delta N; \_)$).

Given a query expression in normal form, the above rules together with standard equivalences (such as commutativity of independent generators) can be used to delateralize it: that is, remove all occurrences of free variables in subexpressions of the form $\iota(N)$, $M_1 - M_2$, or $\delta(M_1 - M_2)$.

Theorem 1. *If M is a flat query in normal form, then there exists M' equivalent to M with no lateral variable occurrences.*

The proof of correctness of the basic delateralization rules and the above correctness theorem are in the full version of this paper [44].

To illustrate some subtleties of the translation, here is a trickier example:

$$\biguplus \{\!\!\{ M \mid x \leftarrow N, y \leftarrow Q - \iota(P) \}\!\!\}$$

where Q, P both depend on x. We proceed from the outside in, first delateralizing the difference:

$$\biguplus \{\!\!\{ M \mid x \leftarrow N, y \leftarrow (\mathcal{G}(x \leftarrow \delta(N); Q) - \mathcal{G}(x \leftarrow \delta(N); \iota(P))) \circledast x \}\!\!\}$$

Note that this still contains a lateral subquery, namely $\iota(P)$ depends on x. After translating back to $\mathcal{NRC}_\lambda(\mathit{Set}, \mathit{Bag})$, and delateralizing $\iota(P)$, the query normalizes to:

$$\begin{array}{l} Q_1 = \bigcup \{(x, z) \mid x \in \delta(N), z \leftarrow P\} \\ Q_2 = (\biguplus \{\!\!\{(x, z) \mid x \in \iota\delta(N), z \leftarrow Q\}\!\!\}) - (\biguplus \{\!\!\{(x, z) \mid x \in \iota\delta(N), (x', z) \leftarrow \iota(Q_1), x = x'\}\!\!\}) \\ \quad \biguplus \{\!\!\{ M \mid x \leftarrow N, (x', y) \leftarrow Q_2, x = x' \}\!\!\} \end{array}$$

6 Query lifting and shredding

In the previous sections, we have discussed how to translate queries with flat collection input and output to SQL. The shredding technique, introduced in [8], can be used to convert queries with *nested* output (but flat input) to multiple flat queries that can be independently evaluated on an SQL database, then stitched together to obtain the required nested result. This section provides an improved version of shredding, extended to a more liberal setting mixing sets and bags and allowing bag difference operations, and described using the graph operations we have introduced, allowing an easier understanding of the shredding process.

We introduce, in Figure 6, a *shredding judgment* to denote the process by which, given a normalized $\mathcal{NRC}_\lambda(\mathit{Set}, \mathit{Bag})$ query, each of its subqueries having a nested collection type is lifted (in a manner analogous to lambda-lifting [30]) to an independent graph query: more specifically, shredding will produce a *shredding environment* (denoted by $\Phi, \Psi, \ldots$), which is a finite map associating special *graph variables* φ, ψ to $\mathcal{NRC}_\mathcal{G}$ terms:

$$\Phi, \Psi, \ldots ::= [\overrightarrow{\varphi \mapsto M}]$$

The shredding judgment has the following form:

$$\Phi; \Theta \vdash M \Rightarrow \check{M} \mid \Psi$$

where the $\Rightarrow$ symbol separates the input (to the left) from the output (to the right). The normalized $\mathcal{NRC}_\lambda(\mathit{Set}, \mathit{Bag})$ term M is the query that is being considered for shredding; M may contain free variables declared in Θ, which must be a sequence of $\mathcal{NRC}_\lambda(\mathit{Set}, \mathit{Bag})$ set comprehension bindings. Θ is initially empty,

$$\frac{X \text{ is a base term}}{\Phi; \Theta \vdash X \Mapsto X \mid \Phi} \qquad \frac{(\Phi_{i-1}; \Theta \vdash M_i \Mapsto \breve{M}_i \mid \Phi_i)_{i=1,\ldots,n}}{\Phi_0; \Theta \vdash \langle \overrightarrow{\ell = M} \rangle \Mapsto \langle \overrightarrow{\ell = \breve{M}} \rangle \mid \Phi_n}$$

$$\frac{\begin{array}{c}\varphi \notin \mathrm{dom}(\Phi_n) \\ (\Phi_{i-1}; \Theta \vdash C_i \Mapsto \psi_i \circledast \mathrm{dom}(\Theta) \mid \Phi_i)_{i=1,\ldots,n}\end{array}}{\begin{array}{c}\Phi_0; \Theta \vdash \bigcup \vec{C} \Mapsto \varphi \circledast \mathrm{dom}(\Theta) \\ \mid (\Phi_n \setminus \vec{\psi})[\varphi \mapsto \bigcup \overrightarrow{\Phi_n(\psi)}]\end{array}} \qquad \frac{\begin{array}{c}\varphi \notin \mathrm{dom}(\Phi_n) \\ (\Phi_{i-1}; \Theta \vdash D_i \Mapsto \psi_i \circledast \mathrm{dom}(\Theta) \mid \Phi_i)_{i=1,\ldots,n}\end{array}}{\begin{array}{c}\Phi_0; \Theta \vdash \biguplus \vec{D} \Mapsto \varphi \circledast \mathrm{dom}(\Theta) \\ \mid (\Phi_n \setminus \vec{\psi})[\varphi \mapsto \biguplus \overrightarrow{\Phi_n(\psi)}]\end{array}}$$

$$\frac{\begin{array}{c}\varphi \notin \mathrm{dom}(\Psi) \\ \Phi; \Theta, \overrightarrow{x \leftarrow F} \vdash M \Mapsto \breve{M} \mid \Psi\end{array}}{\begin{array}{c}\Phi; \Theta \vdash \bigcup \{\{M\} \mathbf{\ where\ } X | \overrightarrow{x \leftarrow F}\} \Mapsto \varphi \circledast \mathrm{dom}(\Theta) \\ \mid \Psi[\varphi \mapsto \mathcal{G}(\Theta; \bigcup \{\{\breve{M}\} \mathbf{\ where\ } X | \overrightarrow{x \leftarrow F}\})]\end{array}}$$

$$\frac{\begin{array}{c}\varphi \notin \mathrm{dom}(\Psi) \\ \Phi; \Theta, \overrightarrow{x \leftarrow G^\delta} \vdash M \Mapsto \breve{M} \mid \Psi\end{array}}{\begin{array}{c}\Phi_0; \Theta \vdash \biguplus \{\!\{ M \}\!\} \mathbf{\ where\ } X | \overrightarrow{x \leftarrow G} \} \Mapsto \varphi \circledast \mathrm{dom}(\Theta) \\ \mid \Psi[\varphi \mapsto \mathcal{G}(\Theta; \biguplus \{\!\{ \breve{M} \}\!\} \mathbf{\ where\ } X | \overrightarrow{x \leftarrow G} \})]\end{array}}$$

$$G^\delta \triangleq \begin{cases} Q^* & \text{if } G = \iota Q^* \\ \delta G & \text{otherwise} \end{cases} \qquad \Phi \setminus \vec{\psi} \triangleq [(\varphi \mapsto N) \in \Phi \mid \varphi \notin \vec{\psi}]$$

Fig. 6. Shredding rules.

but during shredding it is extended with parts of the input that have already been processed. Similarly, the input shredding environment Φ is initially empty, but will grow during shredding to collect shredded queries that have already been generated. It is crucial, for our algorithm to work, that M be in the form previously described in Figure 3, as this allows us to make assumptions on its shape: in describing the judgment rules, we will use the same metavariables as are used in that grammar.

The output of shredding consists of a shredded term $\breve{M}$ and an output shredding environment Ψ. Ψ extends Φ with the new queries obtained by shredding M; $\breve{M}$ is an output $\mathcal{NRC}_\mathcal{G}$ query obtained from M by lifting its collection typed subqueries to independent queries defined in Ψ.

The rules for the shredding judgment operate as follows: the first rule expresses the fact that a normalized base term X does not contain subexpressions with nested collection type, therefore it can be shredded to itself, leaving the shredding environment Φ unchanged; in the case of tuples, we perform shredding pointwise on each field, connecting the input and output shredding environments in a pipeline, and finally combining together the shredded subterms in the obvious way.

The shredding of collection terms (i.e. unions and comprehensions) is performed by means of *query lifting*: we turn the collection into a globally defined (graph) query, which will be associated to a fresh name φ and instantiated to the local comprehension context by graph application. This operation is reminiscent

$$\frac{}{\vdash \cdot : \cdot} \qquad \frac{\vdash \Phi : \Gamma \qquad \Gamma \vdash M : \overrightarrow{\sigma} \multimap \tau \qquad \varphi \notin \mathrm{dom}(\Gamma)}{\vdash \Phi[\varphi \mapsto M] : (\Gamma, \varphi : \overrightarrow{\sigma} \multimap \tau)}$$

Fig. 7. Typing rules for shredding environments.

of the lambda lifting and closure conversion techniques used in the implementation of functional languages to convert local function definitions into global ones. Thus, when shredding a collection, besides processing its subterms recursively, we will need to extend the output shredding environment with a definition for the new global graph φ. In the interesting case of comprehensions, φ is defined by graph-abstracting over the comprehension context Θ; notice that, since we are only shredding normalized terms, we know that they have a certain shape and, in particular, the judgment for bag comprehensions must ensure that generators $\overrightarrow{G}$ be converted into sets.

The shredding of set and bag unions is performed by recursion on the subterms, using the same plumbing technique we employed for tuples; additionally, we optimize the output shredding environment by removing the graph queries $\overrightarrow{\psi}$ resulting from recursion, since they are absorbed into the new graph φ.

Notice that since the comprehension generators of our normalized queries must have a flat collection type, they do not need to be processed recursively. Furthermore, since our normal forms ensure that promotion and bag difference terms can only appear as comprehension generators, we do not need to provide rules for these cases.

The shredding environments used by the shredding judgment must be well typed, in the sense described by the rules of Figure 7: the judgment $\vdash \Phi : \Gamma$ means that the graph variables of Φ are mapped to terms whose type is described by Γ. Whenever we add a mapping $[\varphi \mapsto M]$ to Φ, we must make sure that M is well typed (of graph type) in the typing environment Γ associated to Φ.

If $\vdash \Phi : \Gamma$, we will write $ty(\Phi)$ to refer to the typing environment Γ associated to Φ. The following result states that shredding preserves well-typedness:

Theorem 2. *Let Θ be well-typed and $ty(\Theta) \vdash M : \sigma$. If $\Theta \vdash M \Rightarrow \breve{M} \mid \Phi$, then:*

- *Φ is well-typed*
- *$ty(\Phi), ty(\Theta) \vdash \breve{M} : \sigma$*

We now intend to prove the correctness of shredding: first, we state a lemma which we can use to simplify certain expressions involving the semantics of graph application:

Definition 2. *Let Θ be a closed, well-typed sequence of generators. A substitution ρ is a model of Θ (notation: $\rho \vDash \Theta$) if, and only if, for all $x \in \mathrm{dom}(\Theta)$, we have $[\![\Theta(x))]\!]\, \rho(x) > 0$.*

Lemma 3. *1.* $\left[\!\left[(\bigcup \overrightarrow{G}) \circledast (\overrightarrow{N})\right]\!\right] \rho = \bigvee_i \left[\!\left[G_i \circledast (\overrightarrow{N})\right]\!\right] \rho$

2. If $\rho \vDash \Theta$, then for all M we have $[\![\mathcal{G}(\Theta; M) \circledast (\mathrm{dom}(\Theta))]\!]\,\rho = [\![M]\!]\,\rho$.

To state the correctness of shredding, we need the following notion of shredding environment substitution.

Definition 3. *For every well-typed shredding environment Φ, the substitution of Φ into an $\mathcal{NRC}_{\mathcal{G}}$ term M (notation: $M\Phi$) is defined as the operation replacing within M every free variable $\varphi \in \mathrm{dom}(\Phi)$ with $(\Phi(\varphi))\Phi$ (i.e.: the value assigned by Φ to φ, after recursively substituting Φ).*

We can easily show that the above definition is well posed for well-typed Φ.

We now show that shredding preserves the semantics of the input term, in the sense that the term obtained by substituting the output shredding environment into the output term is equivalent to the input.

Theorem 3 (Correctness of shredding). *Let Θ be well-typed and $ty(\Theta) \vdash M : \sigma$. If $\Phi; \Theta \vdash M \Rrightarrow \check{M} \mid \Psi$, then, for all $\rho \vDash \Theta$, we have $[\![M]\!]\,\rho = [\![\check{M}\Psi]\!]\,\rho$.*

Proof. By induction on the shredding judgment. We comment two representative cases:

- in the set comprehension case, we want to prove

$$[\![\bigcup\{\{M\} \textbf{ where } X | \overrightarrow{x \leftarrow F}\}]\!]\,\rho\, v =$$
$$[\![(\varphi \circledast (\mathrm{dom}(\Theta)))\Psi[\varphi \mapsto \bigcup\{\mathcal{G}(\Theta; \bigcup\{\{\check{M}\} \textbf{ where } X | \overrightarrow{x \leftarrow F}\})\}]]\!]\,\rho\, v$$

  where $\rho \vDash \Theta$. We rewrite the lhs as follows:

$$\begin{aligned}&[\![\bigcup\{\{M\} \textbf{ where } X | \overrightarrow{x \leftarrow F}\}]\!]\,\rho\, v\\ &= \bigvee_{\overrightarrow{u}}([\![M]\!]\,\rho_n = v) \wedge ([\![X]\!]\,\rho_n) \wedge ([\![F_i]\!]\,\rho_{i-1}\, u_i))_{i=1,\ldots,n}\end{aligned}$$

  where $\rho_i = \rho[x_1 \mapsto u_1, \ldots, x_i \mapsto u_i] \vDash \Theta, x_1 \leftarrow F_1, \ldots, x_i \leftarrow F_i$ for all $i = 1, \ldots, n$, and u_i s.t. $[\![F_i]\!]\,\rho_{i-1} u_i$. By the definition of substitution and by Lemma 3, we rewrite the rhs:

$$\begin{aligned}&[\![(\varphi \circledast (\mathrm{dom}(\Theta)))\Psi[\varphi \mapsto \mathcal{G}(\Theta; \bigcup\{\{\check{M}\} \textbf{ where } X | \overrightarrow{x \leftarrow F}\})]]\!]\,\rho\, v\\ &= [\![(\mathcal{G}(\Theta; \bigcup\{\{\check{M}\Psi\} \textbf{ where } X | \overrightarrow{x \leftarrow F}\})) \circledast (\mathrm{dom}(\Theta))]\!]\,\rho\, v\\ &= [\![\bigcup\{\{\check{M}\Psi\} \textbf{ where } X | \overrightarrow{x \leftarrow F}\}]\!]\,\rho\, v\\ &= \bigvee_{\overrightarrow{u}}([\![\check{M}\Psi]\!]\,\rho_n = v) \wedge ([\![F_i]\!]\,\rho_{i-1}\, u_i))_{i=1,\ldots,n} \wedge ([\![X]\!]\,\rho')\end{aligned}$$

  We can prove that for all $\overrightarrow{u}$ such that $\rho_n \nvDash \Theta, \overrightarrow{x \leftarrow F}$, $([\![F_i]\!]\,\rho_{i-1}\, u_i)_{i=1,\ldots,n} = 0$. Therefore, we only need to consider those $\overrightarrow{u}$ such that $\rho_n \vDash \Theta, \overrightarrow{x \leftarrow F}$. Then, to prove the thesis, we only need to show:

$$[\![M]\!]\,\rho_n = [\![\check{M}\Phi]\!]\,\rho_n$$

  which follows by induction hypothesis, for $\rho_n \vDash \Theta, \overrightarrow{x \leftarrow F}$.

– in the set union case, we want to prove

$$\left[\!\left[\bigcup \vec{C}\right]\!\right] \rho\, v = \left[\!\left[(\varphi \circledast (\mathrm{dom}(\Theta)))(\Psi \setminus \vec{\psi})[\varphi \mapsto \bigcup \overrightarrow{\Psi(\psi)}]\right]\!\right] \rho\, v$$

where $\rho \models \Theta$. We rewrite the lhs as follows:

$$\left[\!\left[\bigcup \vec{C}\right]\!\right] \rho\, v = \bigvee_i [\![C_i]\!]\, \rho\, v$$

By the definition of substitution and by Lemma 3, we rewrite the rhs:

$$\begin{aligned}&\left[\!\left[(\varphi \circledast (\mathrm{dom}(\Theta)))(\Psi \setminus \vec{\psi})[\varphi \mapsto \bigcup \overrightarrow{\Psi(\psi)}]\right]\!\right] \rho\, v\\ &= \left[\!\left[(\bigcup \overrightarrow{(\Psi(\psi))\Psi}) \circledast (\mathrm{dom}(\Theta))\right]\!\right] \rho\, v\\ &= \textstyle\bigvee_i [\![(\Psi(\psi_i))\Psi \circledast (\mathrm{dom}(\Theta))]\!]\, \rho\, v\end{aligned}$$

By induction hypothesis and unfolding of definitions, we know for all i:

$$[\![C_i]\!]\, \rho = \left[\!\left[(\psi_i \circledast \overrightarrow{(\mathrm{dom}(\Theta)))\Psi}\right]\!\right] \rho = \left[\!\left[\overrightarrow{(\Psi(\psi_i))\Psi \circledast (\mathrm{dom}(\Theta))}\right]\!\right] \rho$$

which proves the thesis. □

6.1 Reflecting shredded queries into $\mathcal{NRC}_\lambda(\mathit{Set}, \mathit{Bag})$

The output of the shredding judgment is a stratified version of the input term, where each element of the output shredding environment provides a layer of collection nesting; furthermore, the output is ordered so that each element of the shredding environment only references graph variables defined to its left, which is convenient for evaluation. Our goal is to evaluate each shredded item as an independent query: however, these items are not immediately convertible to flat queries, partly because their type is still nested, and also due to the presence of graph operations introduced during shredding. We thus need to provide a translation operation capable of converting the output of shredding into independent flat terms of $\mathcal{NRC}_\lambda(\mathit{Set}, \mathit{Bag})$. This translation uses two main ingredients:

– an *index* function to convert graph variable references to a flat type $\mathbb{I}$ of indices, such that $\phi, \vec{x}$ are recoverable from $\mathit{index}(\phi, \vec{x})$;
– a technique to express graphs as standard $\mathcal{NRC}_\lambda(\mathit{Set}, \mathit{Bag})$ relations.

The resulting translation, denoted by $\lfloor\cdot\rfloor$, is shown in in Figure 8. Let us remark that the translation need be defined only for term forms that can be produced as the output of shredding: this allows us, for instance, not to consider terms such as ιM or $M - N$, which can only appear as part of flat generators of comprehensions or graphs.

We discuss briefly the interesting cases of the definition of the flattening translation. Base expressions X are expressible in $\mathcal{NRC}_\lambda(\mathit{Set}, \mathit{Bag})$, therefore they can be mapped to themselves (this is also true for **empty**(M), since normalization ensures that the type of M be a flat collection). Graph applications

$$\lfloor X \rfloor = X \qquad \left\lfloor \overrightarrow{\langle \ell = M \rangle} \right\rfloor = \langle \overrightarrow{\ell = \lfloor M \rfloor} \rangle$$

$$\left\lfloor \bigcup \vec{C} \right\rfloor = \bigcup \overrightarrow{\lfloor C \rfloor} \qquad \left\lfloor \biguplus \vec{D} \right\rfloor = \biguplus \overrightarrow{\lfloor D \rfloor}$$

$$\lfloor \varphi \circledast (\vec{x}) \rfloor = index(\varphi, \vec{x})$$

$$\left\lfloor \bigcup \{\{M\} \text{ where } X | \overrightarrow{x \leftarrow F}\} \right\rfloor = \bigcup \{\{\lfloor M \rfloor\} \text{ where } X | \overrightarrow{x \leftarrow F}\}$$

$$\left\lfloor \biguplus \wr \wr M \wr \text{ where } X | \overrightarrow{x \leftarrow G} \wr \right\rfloor = \biguplus \wr \wr \lfloor M \rfloor \wr \text{ where } X | \overrightarrow{x \leftarrow G} \wr$$

$$\left\lfloor \mathcal{G}^{\mathsf{set}}(\overrightarrow{x \leftarrow F}; M) \right\rfloor = \bigcup \{\langle x, y \rangle | \overrightarrow{x \leftarrow F}, y \leftarrow \lfloor M \rfloor\}$$

$$\left\lfloor \mathcal{G}^{\mathsf{bag}}(\overrightarrow{x \leftarrow F}; M) \right\rfloor = \biguplus \wr \langle x, y \rangle | \overrightarrow{x \leftarrow \iota F}, y \leftarrow \lfloor M \rfloor \wr$$

Fig. 8. Flattening embedding of shredded queries into $\mathcal{NRC}_\lambda(Set, Bag)$.

$\varphi \circledast (\vec{x})$, as we said, are translated with the help of an *index* abstract operation: this is where the primary purpose of the translation is accomplished, by flattening a collection type to the flat type $\mathbb{I}$, making it possible for a shredded query to be converted to SQL; although we do not specify the concrete implementation of *index*, it is worth noting that it must store the arguments of the graph application along with the (quoted) *name* of the graph variable φ. Tuples, unions, and comprehensions only require a recursive translation of their subterms: however the generators of comprehensions must have a flat collection type, so no recursion is needed there. Finally, we translate graphs as collections of the pairs obtained by associating elements of the domain of the graph to the corresponding output; it is simple to come up with a comprehension term building such a collection: set-valued graphs are translated using set comprehension, while bag-valued ones use bag comprehension (this also means that in the latter case the generators for the domain of the graph, which are set-typed, must be wrapped in a ι).

We can prove that the flattening embedding produces flat-typed terms, as expected.

Definition 4. *A well-typed set comprehension generator Θ is flat-typed if, and only if, for all $x \in \mathrm{dom}(\Theta)$, there exists a flat type σ such that $ty(\Theta(x)) = \{\sigma\}$.*

A well-typed shredding environment Φ is flat-typed if, and only if, for all $\varphi \in \mathrm{dom}(\Phi)$, we have that $ty(\lfloor \Phi(\varphi) \rfloor)$ is a flat collection type.

Lemma 4. *Suppose $\Phi; \Theta \vdash M \Rrightarrow \breve{M} \mid \Psi$, where Φ and Θ are flat-typed. Then, $\breve{M}$ and Ψ are also flat-typed.*

It is important to note that the composition of shredding and $\lfloor \cdot \rfloor$ does not produce normalized $\mathcal{NRC}_\lambda(Set, Bag)$ terms: when we shred a comprehension, we add to the output shredding environment a graph returning a comprehension, and when we translate this to $\mathcal{NRC}_\lambda(Set, Bag)$ we get two nested comprehensions:

$$\left\lfloor \mathcal{G}(x \leftarrow \delta t; \biguplus \wr \wr \breve{M} \wr | y \leftarrow \iota Q^* \wr) \right\rfloor = \biguplus \wr \langle x, z \rangle | x \leftarrow \iota \delta t, z \leftarrow \biguplus \wr \wr \left\lfloor \breve{M} \right\rfloor \wr | y \leftarrow \iota Q^* \wr \wr$$

$$
\begin{aligned}
(\!|X : b|\!)\Xi &\triangleq X \quad \text{(if } X \text{ is not an index)} \\
(\!|\langle \overrightarrow{\ell = N} \rangle : \langle \overrightarrow{\ell : \tau} \rangle|\!)\Xi &\triangleq \langle \overrightarrow{\ell = (\!|N : \tau|\!)\Xi} \rangle \\
(\!|\langle \overrightarrow{\ell = N} \rangle.\ell_i : \tau|\!)\Xi &\triangleq (\!|N_i : \tau|\!)\Xi \\
(\!|index(\varphi, \vec{V}) : \{\tau\}|\!)\Xi &\triangleq \bigcup\{\{(\!|p.2 : \tau|\!)\Xi\} \mid p \leftarrow \Xi(\varphi), p.1 = \langle \vec{V} \rangle\} \\
(\!|index(\varphi, \vec{V}) : \wr\tau\wr|\!)\Xi &\triangleq \biguplus\wr\wr(\!|p.2 : \tau|\!)\Xi\wr \mid p \leftarrow \Xi(\varphi), p.1 = \langle \vec{V} \rangle\wr
\end{aligned}
$$

Fig. 9. The stitching function.

In fact, not only is this term not in normal form, but it may even contain, within Q^*, a lateral reference to x; thus, after a flattening translation, we will always require the resulting queries to be renormalized and, if needed, delateralized.

Let *norm* denote $\mathcal{NRC}_\lambda(Set, Bag)$ normalization, and $\mathcal{S}$ denote the evaluation of relational normal forms: we define the shredded value set Ξ corresponding to a shredding environment Φ as follows:

$$\Xi \triangleq \{\varphi \mapsto \mathcal{S}(norm(\lfloor M \rfloor)) | [\varphi \mapsto M] \in \Phi\}$$

The evaluation $\mathcal{S}$ is ordinarily performed by a DBMS after converting the $\mathcal{NRC}_\lambda(Set, Bag)$ query to SQL, as described in Section 5. The result of this evaluation is reflected in a programming language such as Links as a list of records.

6.2 The stitching function

Given a $\mathcal{NRC}_\lambda(Set, Bag)$ term with nested collections, we have first shredded it, obtaining a shredded $\mathcal{NRC}_\mathcal{G}$ term $\breve{M}$ and a shredding environment Φ containing $\mathcal{NRC}_\mathcal{G}$ graphs; then we have used a flattening embedding to reflect both $\breve{M}$ and Φ back into the flat fragment of $\mathcal{NRC}_\lambda(Set, Bag)$; next we used normalization and DBMS evaluation to convert the shredding environment into a shredded value set Ξ. As the last step to evaluate $M : \tau$, we need to combine $\lfloor \breve{M} \rfloor$ and Ξ together to reconstruct the correct nested value $(\!|\lfloor \breve{M} \rfloor : \tau|\!)\Xi$ by *stitching* together partial flat values.

The stitching function is shown in Figure 9: its job is to visit all the components of tuples and collections, ignoring atomic values other than indices along the way. The real work is performed when an $index(\varphi, \vec{V})$ is found: conceptually, the index should be replaced by the result of the evaluation of $\varphi \circledast (\vec{V})$. Remember that Ξ contains the result of the evaluation of the graph function φ after translation to $\mathcal{NRC}_\lambda(Set, Bag)$, i.e. a collection of pairs associating each input of φ to the corresponding output: then, to obtain the desired result, we can take $\Xi(\varphi)$, filter all the pairs p whose first component is $\langle \vec{V} \rangle$, and return the second component of p after a recursive stitching. Finally, observe that we track the result type argument in order to disambiguate whether to construct a set or multiset when we encounter an index.

Theorem 4 (Correctness of stitching). *Let Θ be well-typed and $ty(\Theta) \vdash M : \sigma$. Let Φ be well-typed, and suppose $\Phi; \Theta \vdash M \Rightarrow \breve{M} \mid \Psi$. Let Ξ be the result of evaluating the flattened queries in Ψ as above. Then $\left[\!\left[\breve{M}\Psi \right]\!\right] \rho = \left[\!\left[(\!\left| \left\lfloor \breve{M} \right\rfloor : \tau \right|\!) \Xi \right]\!\right] \rho$.*

The full correctness result follows by combining the Theorems 3 and 4.

Corollary 1. *For all M such that $\vdash M : \tau$, suppose $\vdash M \Rightarrow \breve{M}' \mid \Psi$, and let Ξ be the shredded value set obtained by evaluating the flattened queries in Ψ. Then $[\![M]\!] = \left[\!\left[(\!\left| \left\lfloor \breve{M} \right\rfloor : \tau \right|\!) \Xi \right]\!\right]$.*

7 Related work

Work on language-integrated query and comprehension syntax has taken place over several decades in both the database and programming language communities. We discuss the most closely related work below.

Comprehensions, normalization and language integration The database community had already begun in the late 1980s to explore proposals for so-called *non-first-normal-form* relations in which collections could be nested inside other collections [46], but following Trinder and Wadler's initial work connecting database queries with monadic comprehensions [50], query languages based on these foundations were studied extensively, particularly by Buneman et al. [4,3]. For our purposes, Wong's work on query normalization and translation to SQL [55] is the most important landmark; this work provided the basis for practical implementations such as Kleisli and later Links. Almost as important is the later work by Libkin and Wong [33], studying the questions of expressiveness of bag query languages via a language $\mathcal{BQL}$ that extended basic $\mathcal{NRC}$ with deduplication and bag difference operators. They related this language to $\mathcal{NRC}$ with set semantics extended with aggregation (count/sum) operations, but did not directly address the question of normalizing and translating $\mathcal{BQL}$ queries to SQL. Grust and Scholl [28] were early advocates of the use of comprehensions mixing set, bag and other monadic collections for query rewriting and optimization, but did not study normalization or translatability properties.

Although comprehension-based queries began to be used in general-purpose programming languages with the advent of Microsoft LINQ [36] and Links [12], Cooper [11] made the next important foundational contribution by extending Wong's normalization result to queries containing higher-order functions and showing that an effect system could be used to safely compose queries using higher-order functions even in an ambient language with side-effects and recursive functions that cannot be used in queries. This work provided the basis for subsequent development of language-integrated query in Links [34] and was later adapted for use in F# [7], Scala [41], and by Kiselyov et al. [48] in the OCaml library QUEΛ. However, on revisiting Cooper's proof to extend it to heterogeneous queries, we found a subtle gap in the proof, which was corrected in a recent paper [43]; the original result was correct. As a result, in this paper we focus on first-order fragments of these languages without loss of generality.

Giorgidze et al. [22] have shown how to support non-recursive datatypes (i.e. sums) and Grust and Ulrich [29] built on this to show how to support function types in query results using defunctionalization [29]. We considered using sums to support a defunctionalization-style strategy for query lifting, but Giorgidze et al. [22] map sum types to nested collections, which makes their approach unsuitable to our setting. Wong's original normalization result also considered sum types, but to the best of our knowledge normalization for $\mathcal{NRC}_\lambda(Set, Bag)$ extended with sum types has not yet been proved.

Recent work by Suzuki et al. [48] have outlined further extensions to language-integrated query in the QUEΛ system, which is based on finally-tagless syntax [6] and employs Wong's and Cooper's rewrite rules; Katsushima and Kiselyov's subsequent short paper [31] outlined extensions to handling ordering and grouping. Kiselyov and Katsushima [32] present an extension to QUEΛ called SQUR to handle ordering based on effect typing, and they provide an elegant translation from SQUR queries to SQL based on normalization-by-evaluation. Okura and Kameyama [39] outline an extension to handle SQL-style grouping and aggregation operators in QUEΛ_G; however, their approach potentially generates lateral variable occurrences inside grouping queries. These systems QUEΛ, SQUR and QUEΛ_G consider neither heterogeneity nor nested results.

Our adoption of tabulated functions (*graphs*) is inspired in part by Gibbons et al. [20], who provided an elegant rational reconstruction of relational algebra showing how standard principles for reasoning about queries arise from adjunctions. They employed types for (finite) maps and tables to show how joins can be implemented efficiently, and observed that such structures form a *graded monad.* We are interested in further exploring these structures and extending our work to cover ordering, grouping and aggregation.

Query decorrelation and delateralization There is a large literature on *query decorrelation*, for example to remove aggregation operations from `SELECT` or `WHERE` clauses (see e.g. [38,5] for further discussion). Delateralization appears related to decorrelation, but we are aware of only a few works on this problem, perhaps because most DBMSs only started to support `LATERAL` in the last few years. (Microsoft SQL Server has supported similar functionality for much longer through a keyword `APPLY`.) Our delateralization technique appears most closely related to Neumann and Kemper's work on query unnesting [38]. In this context, unnesting refers to removal of "dependent join" expressions in a relational algebraic query language; such joins appear to correspond to lateral subqueries. This approach is implemented in the HyPER database system, but is not accompanied by a proof of correctness, nor does it handle nested query results. It would be interesting to formalize this approach (or others from the decorrelation literature) and relate it to delateralization.

Querying nested collections Our approach to querying nested heterogeneous collections clearly specializes to the homogeneous cases for sets and multisets respectively, which have been studied separately. Van den Bussche's work on simulating queries on nested sets using flat ones [54] has also inspired subsequent work on query shredding, flattening and (in this paper) lifting, though the simulation technique itself does not appear practical (as discussed in the extended version of Cheney et al. [9]). More recently, Benedikt and Pradic [1] presented results on representing queries on nested collections using a bounded number of *interpretations* (first-order logic formulas corresponding to definable flat query expressions) in the context of their work on *synthesizing* $\mathcal{NRC}$ queries from proofs. This approach considers set-valued $\mathcal{NRC}$ only, and its relationship to our approach should be investigated further.

Cheney et al.'s previous work on query shredding for multiset queries [8] is different in several important respects. In that work we did not consider deduplication and bag difference operations from $\mathcal{BQL}$, which Libkin and Wong showed cannot be expressed in terms of other $\mathcal{NRC}$ operations. The shredding translation was given in several stages, and while each stage is individually comprehensible, the overall approach is not easy to understand. Finally, the last stages of the translation relied on SQL features not present (or expressible) in the source language, such as ordering and the SQL:1999 `ROW_NUMBER` construct, to synthesize uniform integer keys. Our approach, in contrast, handles set, bag, and mixed queries, and does not rely on any SQL:1999 features.

In a parallel line of work, Grust et al. [26,21,51,53,52] have developed a number of approaches to querying nested *list* data structures, first in the context of XML processing [24] and subsequently for $\mathcal{NRC}$-like languages over lists. The earlier approach [26], named *loop-lifting* (not to be confused with *query lifting*!) made heavy use of SQL:1999 capabilities for numbering and indexing to decouple nested collections from their context, and was implemented in both Links [51] and earlier versions of the Database Supported Haskell library [21], both of which relied on an advanced query optimizer called *Pathfinder* [27] to optimize these queries. The more recent approach, implemented by Ulrich in the current version of DSH and described in detail in his thesis [52], is called *query flattening* and is instead based on techniques from *nested data parallelism* [2]. Both loop-lifting and query flattening are very powerful, and do not rely on an initial normalization stage, while supporting a rich source language with list semantics, ordering, grouping, aggregation, and deduplication which can in principle emulate set or multiset semantics. However, to the best of our knowledge no correctness proofs exist for either technique. We view finding correctness results for richer query languages as an important challenge for future work.

Another parallel line of work started by Fegaras and Maier [15,14] considers heterogeneous query languages based on *monoid* comprehensions, with set, list, and bag collections as well as grouping, aggregation and ordering operations, in the setting of object-oriented databases, and forms the basis for complex object database systems such as λDB [16] and Apache MRQL [14]. However, Wong-style normalization results or translations from flat or nested queries to SQL are not known for these calculi.

Lambda-lifting and closure conversion Since Johnsson's original work [30], lambda-lifting and closure conversion have been studied extensively for functional languages, with Minamide et al.'s *typed closure conversion* [37] of particular interest in compilers employing typed intermediate languages. We plan to study whether known optimizations in the lambda-lifting and closure conversion literature offer advantages for query lifting. The immediate important next step is to implement our approach and compare it empirically with previous techniques such as query shredding and query flattening. By analogy with lambda-lifting and closure conversion, we expect additional optimizations to be possible by a deeper analysis of how variables/fields are used in lifted subqueries. Another problem we have not resolved is how to deal with deduplication or bag difference at nested collection types in practice. Libkin and Wong [33] showed that such nesting can be eliminated from $\mathcal{BQL}$ queries, but their results do not provide a constructive algorithm for eliminating the nesting.

8 Conclusions

Monadic comprehensions have proved to be a remarkably durable foundation for database programming and language-integrated query, and has led to language support (LINQ for .NET, Quill for Scala) with widespread adoption. Recent work has demonstrated that techniques for evaluating queries over nested collections, such as query shredding or query flattening, can offer order-of-magnitude speedups in database applications [19] without sacrificing declarativity or readability. However, query shredding lacks the ability to express common operations such as deduplication, while query flattening is more expressive but lacks a detailed proof of correctness, and both techniques are challenging to understand, implement, or extend. We provide the first provably correct approach to querying nested heterogeneous collections involving both sets and multisets.

Our most important insight is that working in a heterogeneous language, with both set and multiset collection types, actually makes the problem easier, by making it possible to calculate finite maps representing the behavior of nested query subexpressions under all of the possible environments encountered at run time. Thus, instead of having to maintain or synthesize keys linking inner and outer collections, as is done in all previous approaches, we can instead use the values of variables in the closures of nested query expressions themselves as the keys. The same approach can be used to eliminate sideways information-passing. This is analogous to lambda-lifting or closure conversion in compilation of functional languages, but differs in that we lift local queries to (queries that compute) finite maps rather than ordinary function abstractions. We believe this idea may have broader applications and will next investigate its behavior in practice and applications to other query language features.

Acknowledgments This work was supported by ERC Consolidator Grant Skye (grant number 682315), and by an ISCF Metrology Fellowship grant provided by the UK government's Department for Business, Energy and Industrial Strategy (BEIS). We are grateful to Simon Fowler for feedback and to anonymous reviewers for constructive comments.

References

1. Benedikt, M., Pradic, P.: Generating collection transformations from proofs. Proc. ACM Program. Lang. **5**(POPL) (Jan 2021), https://doi.org/10.1145/3434295
2. Blelloch, G.E.: Vector Models for Data-Parallel Computing. MIT Press (1990)
3. Buneman, P., Libkin, L., Suciu, D., Tannen, V., Wong, L.: Comprehension syntax. SIGMOD Record **23** (1994)
4. Buneman, P., Naqvi, S., Tannen, V., Wong, L.: Principles of programming with complex objects and collection types. Theor. Comput. Sci. **149**(1) (1995). https://doi.org/10.1016/0304-3975(95)00024-Q
5. Cao, B., Badia, A.: SQL query optimization through nested relational algebra. ACM Trans. Database Syst. **32**(3), 18–es (Aug 2007). https://doi.org/10.1145/1272743.1272748
6. Carette, J., Kiselyov, O., Shan, C.: Finally tagless, partially evaluated: Tagless staged interpreters for simpler typed languages. J. Funct. Program. **19**(5), 509–543 (2009). https://doi.org/10.1017/S0956796809007205
7. Cheney, J., Lindley, S., Wadler, P.: A practical theory of language-integrated query. In: ICFP (2013). https://doi.org/10.1145/2500365.2500586
8. Cheney, J., Lindley, S., Wadler, P.: Query shredding: efficient relational evaluation of queries over nested multisets. In: SIGMOD. pp. 1027–1038. ACM (2014). https://doi.org/10.1145/2588555.2612186
9. Cheney, J., Lindley, S., Wadler, P.: Query shredding: Efficient relational evaluation of queries over nested multisets (extended version). CoRR **abs/1404.7078** (2014), http://arxiv.org/abs/1404.7078
10. Chu, S., Weitz, K., Cheung, A., Suciu, D.: HoTTSQL: Proving query rewrites with univalent SQL semantics. In: PLDI. pp. 510–524. ACM (2017). https://doi.org/10.1145/3062341.3062348
11. Cooper, E.: The script-writer's dream: How to write great SQL in your own language, and be sure it will succeed. In: DBPL (2009). https://doi.org/10.1007/978-3-642-03793-1_3
12. Cooper, E., Lindley, S., Wadler, P., Yallop, J.: Links: web programming without tiers. In: FMCO (2007). https://doi.org/10.1007/978-3-540-74792-5_12
13. Copeland, G., Maier, D.: Making Smalltalk a database system. SIGMOD Rec. **14**(2) (1984)
14. Fegaras, L.: An algebra for distributed big data analytics. J. Funct. Program. **27**, e27 (2017). https://doi.org/10.1017/S0956796817000193
15. Fegaras, L., Maier, D.: Optimizing object queries using an effective calculus. ACM Trans. Database Syst. **25**(4), 457–516 (2000)
16. Fegaras, L., Srinivasan, C., Rajendran, A., Maier, D.: lambda-DB: An ODMG-based object-oriented DBMS. In: Chen, W., Naughton, J.F., Bernstein, P.A. (eds.) SIGMOD. p. 583. ACM (2000). https://doi.org/10.1145/342009.335494
17. Fehrenbach, S., Cheney, J.: Language-integrated provenance. Science of Computer Programming **155**, 103–145 (2018)
18. Foster, J.N., Green, T.J., Tannen, V.: Annotated XML: queries and provenance. In: PODS. pp. 271–280 (2008)
19. Fowler, S., Harding, S., Sharman, J., Cheney, J.: Cross-tier web programming for curated databases: a case study. International Journal of Digital Curation **15**(1) (2020). https://doi.org/10.2218/ijdc.v15i1.717, pre-print presented at IDCC 2020
20. Gibbons, J., Henglein, F., Hinze, R., Wu, N.: Relational algebra by way of adjunctions. Proc. ACM Program. Lang. **2**(ICFP) (Jul 2018). https://doi.org/10.1145/3236781

21. Giorgidze, G., Grust, T., Schreiber, T., Weijers, J.: Haskell boards the Ferry - database-supported program execution for Haskell. In: IFL. pp. 1–18. No. 6647 in LNCS, Springer-Verlag (2010)
22. Giorgidze, G., Grust, T., Ulrich, A., Weijers, J.: Algebraic data types for language-integrated queries. In: DDFP. pp. 5–10 (2013)
23. Green, T.J., Karvounarakis, G., Tannen, V.: Provenance semirings. In: PODS (2007)
24. Grust, T., Mayr, M., Rittinger, J.: Let SQL drive the XQuery workhorse (XQuery join graph isolation). In: EDBT. pp. 147–158 (2010). https://doi.org/10.1145/1739041.1739062
25. Grust, T., Mayr, M., Rittinger, J., Schreiber, T.: Ferry: Database-supported program execution. In: SIGMOD (June 2009)
26. Grust, T., Rittinger, J., Schreiber, T.: Avalanche-safe LINQ compilation. PVLDB **3**(1) (2010)
27. Grust, T., Rittinger, J., Teubner, J.: Pathfinder: XQuery off the relational shelf. IEEE Data Eng. Bull. **31**(4) (2008)
28. Grust, T., Scholl, M.H.: How to comprehend queries functionally. J. Intell. Inf. Syst. **12**(2-3), 191–218 (1999). https://doi.org/10.1023/A:1008705026446
29. Grust, T., Ulrich, A.: First-class functions for first-order database engines. In: DBPL (2013), `http://arxiv.org/abs/1308.0158`
30. Johnsson, T.: Lambda lifting: Treansforming programs to recursive equations. In: FPCA. pp. 190–203 (1985). https://doi.org/10.1007/3-540-15975-4_37
31. Katsushima, T., Kiselyov, O.: Language-integrated query with ordering, grouping and outer joins (poster paper). In: PEPM. pp. 123–124 (2017)
32. Kiselyov, O., Katsushima, T.: Sound and efficient language-integrated query - maintaining the ORDER. In: APLAS 2017. pp. 364–383 (2017). https://doi.org/10.1007/978-3-319-71237-6_18
33. Libkin, L., Wong, L.: Query languages for bags and aggregate functions. J. Comput. Syst. Sci. **55**(2) (1997). https://doi.org/10.1006/jcss.1997.1523
34. Lindley, S., Cheney, J.: Row-based effect types for database integration. In: TLDI (2012). https://doi.org/10.1145/2103786.2103798
35. Lindley, S., Wadler, P.: The audacity of hope: Thoughts on reclaiming the database dream. In: ESOP (2010)
36. Meijer, E., Beckman, B., Bierman, G.M.: LINQ: reconciling object, relations and XML in the .NET framework. In: SIGMOD (2006). https://doi.org/10.1145/1142473.1142552
37. Minamide, Y., Morrisett, J.G., Harper, R.: Typed closure conversion. In: POPL. pp. 271–283 (1996). https://doi.org/10.1145/237721.237791
38. Neumann, T., Kemper, A.: Unnesting arbitrary queries. In: Datenbanksysteme für Business, Technologie und Web (BTW). pp. 383–402 (2015)
39. Okura, R., Kameyama, Y.: Language-integrated query with nested data structures and grouping. In: FLOPS. pp. 139–158 (2020). https://doi.org/10.1007/978-3-030-59025-3_9
40. Paredaens, J., Van Gucht, D.: Converting nested algebra expressions into flat algebra expressions. ACM Trans. Database Syst. **17**(1) (1992). https://doi.org/10.1145/128765.128768
41. Quill: Compile-time language integrated queries for Scala. Open source project, https://github.com/getquill/quill
42. Ricciotti, W., Cheney, J.: Mixing set and bag semantics. In: DBPL. pp. 70–73 (2019). https://doi.org/10.1145/3315507.3330202

43. Ricciotti, W., Cheney, J.: Strongly normalizing higher-order relational queries. In: FSCD. pp. 28:1–28:22 (2020). https://doi.org/10.4230/LIPIcs.FSCD.2020.28
44. Ricciotti, W., Cheney, J.: Query lifting: Language-integrated query for heterogeneous nested collections. ArXiv e-prints (2021), https://arxiv.org/abs/2101.04102
45. Russell, C.: Bridging the object-relational divide. Queue **6** (May 2008). https://doi.org/10.1145/1394127.1394139
46. Schek, H., Scholl, M.H.: The relational model with relation-valued attributes. Inf. Syst. **11**(2), 137–147 (1986). https://doi.org/10.1016/0306-4379(86)90003-7
47. Stolarek, J., Cheney, J.: Language-integrated provenance in Haskell. The Art, Science, and Engineering of Programming **2**(3), A11 (2018)
48. Suzuki, K., Kiselyov, O., Kameyama, Y.: Finally, safely-extensible and efficient language-integrated query. In: PEPM. pp. 37–48 (2016). https://doi.org/10.1145/2847538.2847542
49. Syme, D.: Leveraging .NET meta-programming components from F#: integrated queries and interoperable heterogeneous execution. In: ML Workshop (2006)
50. Trinder, P., Wadler, P.: Improving list comprehension database queries. In: TENCON '89. (1989). https://doi.org/10.1109/TENCON.1989.176921
51. Ulrich, A.: A Ferry-based query backend for the Links programming language. Master's thesis, University of Tübingen (2011)
52. Ulrich, A.: Query Flattening and the Nested Data Parallelism Paradigm. Ph.D. thesis, University of Tübingen, Germany (2019)
53. Ulrich, A., Grust, T.: The flatter, the better: Query compilation based on the flattening transformation. In: SIGMOD. pp. 1421–1426. ACM (2015). https://doi.org/10.1145/2723372.2735359
54. Van den Bussche, J.: Simulation of the nested relational algebra by the flat relational algebra, with an application to the complexity of evaluating powerset algebra expressions. Theor. Comput. Sci. **254**(1-2) (2001)
55. Wong, L.: Normal forms and conservative extension properties for query languages over collection types. J. Comput. Syst. Sci. **52**(3) (1996). https://doi.org/10.1006/jcss.1996.0037
56. Wong, L.: Kleisli, a functional query system. J. Funct. Program. **10**(1) (2000). https://doi.org/10.1017/S0956796899003585

Reverse AD at Higher Types: Pure, Principled and Denotationally Correct

Matthijs Vákár(✉)

Utrecht University, Utrecht, Netherlands m.i.l.vakar@uu.nl

Abstract. We show how to define forward- and reverse-mode automatic differentiation source-code transformations or on a standard higher-order functional language. The transformations generate purely functional code, and they are principled in the sense that their definition arises from a categorical universal property. We give a semantic proof of correctness of the transformations. In their most elegant formulation, the transformations generate code with linear types. However, we demonstrate how the transformations can be implemented in a standard functional language without sacrificing correctness. To do so, we make use of abstract data types to represent the required linear types, e.g. through the use of a basic module system.

Keywords: automatic differentiation · program correctness · semantics.

1 Introduction

Automatic differentiation (AD) is a technique for transforming code that implements a function f into code that computes f's derivative, essentially by using the chain rule for derivatives. Due to its efficiency and numerical stability, AD is the technique of choice whenever derivatives need to be computed of functions that are implemented as programs, particularly in high dimensional settings. Optimization and Monte-Carlo integration algorithms, such as gradient descent and Hamiltonian Monte-Carlo methods, rely crucially on the calculation of derivatives. These algorithms are used in virtually every machine learning and computational statistics application, and the calculation of derivatives is usually the computational bottleneck. These applications explain the recent surge of interest in AD, which has resulted in the proliferation of popular AD systems such as TensorFlow [1], PyTorch [30], and Stan Math [9].

AD, roughly speaking, comes in two modes: forward-mode and reverse-mode. When differentiating a function $\mathbb{R}^n \to \mathbb{R}^m$, forward-mode tends to be more efficient if $m \gg n$, while reverse-mode generally is more performant if $n \gg m$. As most applications reduce to optimization or Monte-Carlo integration of an objective function $\mathbb{R}^n \to \mathbb{R}$ with n very large (today, in the order of $10^4 - 10^7$), reverse-mode AD is in many ways the more interesting algorithm.

However, reverse AD is also more complicated to understand and implement than forward AD. Forward AD can be implemented as a structure-preserving program transformation, even on languages with complex features [32]. As such,

N. Yoshida (Ed.): ESOP 2021, LNCS 12648, pp. 607–634, 2021.
https://doi.org/10.1007/978-3-030-72019-3_22

it admits an elegant proof of correctness [20]. By contrast, reverse-AD is only well-understood as a source-code transformation (also called *define-then-run* style AD) on limited programming languages. Typically, its implementations on more expressive languages that have features such as higher-order functions make use of *define-by-run* approaches. These approaches first build a computation graph during runtime, effectively evaluating the program until a straight-line first-order program is left, and then they evaluate this new program [30,9]. Such approaches have the severe downside that the differentiated code cannot benefit from existing optimizing compiler architectures. As such, these AD libraries need to be implemented using carefully, manually optimized code, that for example does not contain any common subexpressions. This implementation process is precarious and labour intensive. Further, some whole-program optimizations that a compiler would detect go entirely unused in such systems.

Similarly, correctness proofs of reverse AD have taken a define-by-run approach and have relied on non-standard operational semantics, using forms of symbolic execution [2,28,8]. Most work that treats reverse-AD as a source-code transformation does so by making use of complex transformations which introduce mutable state and/or non-local control flow [31,38]. As a result, we are not sure whether and why such techniques are correct. Another approach has been to compile high-level languages to a low-level imperative representation first, and then to perform AD at that level [22], using mutation and jumps. This approach has the downside that we might lose important opportunities for compiler optimizations, such as map-fusion and embarrassingly parallel maps, which we can exploit if we perform define-then-run AD on a high-level representation.

A notable exception to these define-by-run and non-functional approaches to AD is [16], which presents an elegant, purely functional, define-then-run version of reverse AD. Unfortunately, their techniques are limited to first-order programs over tuples of real numbers. This paper extends the work of [16] to apply to higher-order programs over (primitive) arrays of reals:

- It defines purely functional define-then-run reverse-mode AD on a higher-order language.
- It shows how the resulting, mysterious looking program transformation arises from a universal property if we phrase the problem in a suitable categorical language. Consequently, the transformations automatically respect equational reasoning principles.
- It explains, from this categorical setting, precisely in what sense reverse AD is the "mirror image" of forward AD.
- It presents an elegant proof of semantic correctness of the AD transformations, based on a semantic logical relations argument, demonstrating that the transformations calculate the derivatives of the program in the usual mathematical sense.
- It shows that the AD definitions and correctness proof are extensible to higher-order primitives such as a **map**-operation over our primitive arrays.
- It discusses how our techniques are readily implementable in standard functional languages to give purely functional, principled, semantically correct, define-then-run reverse-mode AD.

2 Key Ideas

Consider a simple programming language. Types are statically sized arrays $\mathbf{real}^n$ for some n, and programs are obtained from a collection of (unary) primitive operations $x : \mathbf{real}^n \vdash \mathsf{op}(x) : \mathbf{real}^m$ (intended to implement differentiable functions like linear algebra operations and sigmoid functions) by sequencing.

We can implement both forward mode $\overrightarrow{\mathcal{D}}$ and reverse mode AD $\overleftarrow{\mathcal{D}}$ on this language as source-code translations to the larger language of a simply typed λ-calculus over the ground types $\mathbf{real}^n$ that includes at least the same operations. Forward (resp. reverse) AD translates a type τ to a pair of types $\overrightarrow{\mathcal{D}}(\tau) = (\overrightarrow{\mathcal{D}}(\tau)_1, \overrightarrow{\mathcal{D}}(\tau)_2)$ (resp. $\overleftarrow{\mathcal{D}}(\tau) = (\overleftarrow{\mathcal{D}}(\tau)_1, \overleftarrow{\mathcal{D}}(\tau)_2)$) – the first component for holding function values, also called *primals* in the AD literature; the second component for holding derivative values, also called *tangents* (resp. *adjoints* or *cotangents*):

$$\overrightarrow{\mathcal{D}}(\mathbf{real}^n) \stackrel{\text{def}}{=} \overleftarrow{\mathcal{D}}(\mathbf{real}^n) = (\mathbf{real}^n, \mathbf{real}^n).$$

We translate terms $x : \tau \vdash t : \sigma$ to pairs of terms $\overrightarrow{\mathcal{D}}(t) = (\overrightarrow{\mathcal{D}}(t)_1, \overrightarrow{\mathcal{D}}(t)_2)$ for forward AD and $\overleftarrow{\mathcal{D}}(t) = (\overleftarrow{\mathcal{D}}(t)_1, \overleftarrow{\mathcal{D}}(t)_2)$ for reverse AD, which have types

$$\begin{array}{lll} x : \overrightarrow{\mathcal{D}}(\tau)_1 \vdash \overrightarrow{\mathcal{D}}(t)_1 : \overrightarrow{\mathcal{D}}(\sigma)_1 & \text{and} & x : \overleftarrow{\mathcal{D}}(\tau)_1 \vdash \overleftarrow{\mathcal{D}}(t)_1 : \overleftarrow{\mathcal{D}}(\sigma)_1 \\ x : \overrightarrow{\mathcal{D}}(\tau)_1 \vdash \overrightarrow{\mathcal{D}}(t)_2 : \overrightarrow{\mathcal{D}}(\tau)_2 \to \overrightarrow{\mathcal{D}}(\sigma)_2 & & x : \overleftarrow{\mathcal{D}}(\tau)_1 \vdash \overleftarrow{\mathcal{D}}(t)_2 : \overleftarrow{\mathcal{D}}(\sigma)_2 \to \overleftarrow{\mathcal{D}}(\tau)_2. \end{array}$$

$\overrightarrow{\mathcal{D}}(t)_1$ and $\overleftarrow{\mathcal{D}}(t)_1$ perform the primal computations for the program t, while $\overrightarrow{\mathcal{D}}(t)_2$ and $\overleftarrow{\mathcal{D}}(t)_2$ compute the derivatives, resp., for forward and reverse AD.

Indeed, we define, by induction on the syntax:

$$\overrightarrow{\mathcal{D}}(x) \stackrel{\text{def}}{=} \overleftarrow{\mathcal{D}}(x) \stackrel{\text{def}}{=} (x, \lambda y.y) \quad \overrightarrow{\mathcal{D}}(\mathsf{op}(t))_1 \stackrel{\text{def}}{=} \mathsf{op}(\overrightarrow{\mathcal{D}}(t)_1) \quad \overleftarrow{\mathcal{D}}(\mathsf{op}(t))_1 \stackrel{\text{def}}{=} \mathsf{op}(\overleftarrow{\mathcal{D}}(t)_1)$$

$$\overrightarrow{\mathcal{D}}(\mathsf{op}(t))_2 \stackrel{\text{def}}{=} \lambda y.(D\mathsf{op})(\overrightarrow{\mathcal{D}}(t)_1)\,(\overrightarrow{\mathcal{D}}(t)_2\, y) \quad \overleftarrow{\mathcal{D}}(\mathsf{op}(t))_2 \stackrel{\text{def}}{=} \lambda y.\overleftarrow{\mathcal{D}}(t)_2\,((D\mathsf{op})^t(\overleftarrow{\mathcal{D}}(t)_1)\, y),$$

where we assume that we have chosen suitable terms $x : \mathbf{real}^n \vdash (D\mathsf{op})(x) : \mathbf{real}^n \to \mathbf{real}^m$ and $x : \mathbf{real}^n \vdash (D\mathsf{op})^t(x) : \mathbf{real}^m \to \mathbf{real}^n$ to represent the (multivariate) derivative and transposed (multivariate) derivative, respectively, of the primitive operation $\mathsf{op} : \mathbf{real}^n \to \mathbf{real}^m$.

For example, in case of multiplication $x : \mathbf{real}^n \vdash \mathsf{op}(x) = (*)(x) : \mathbf{real}$, we can choose $D(*)(x) = \lambda y : \mathbf{real}^2.\mathbf{swap}(x) \bullet y$ and $(D(*))^t(x) = \lambda y : \mathbf{real}.y \cdot \mathbf{swap}(x)$, where $\mathbf{swap}$ is a unary operation on $\mathbf{real}^2$ that swaps both components, $(\bullet)$ is a binary inner product operation on $\mathbf{real}^2$ and $(\cdot)$ is a binary scalar product operation for rescaling a vector in $\mathbf{real}^2$ by a real number .

To illustrate the difference between $\overrightarrow{\mathcal{D}}$ and $\overleftarrow{\mathcal{D}}$, consider the program $t = \mathsf{op}_2(\mathsf{op}_1(x))$ performing two operations in sequence. Then, $\overrightarrow{\mathcal{D}}(t)_1 = \mathsf{op}_2(\mathsf{op}_1(x)) = \overleftarrow{\mathcal{D}}(t)_1$ and (after β-reducing, for legibility)

$$\overrightarrow{\mathcal{D}}(t)_2 = \lambda y.(D\mathsf{op}_2)(\mathsf{op}_1(x))((D\mathsf{op}_1)(x)(y))$$
$$\overleftarrow{\mathcal{D}}(t)_2 = \lambda y.(D\mathsf{op}_1)^t(x)((D\mathsf{op}_2)^t(\mathsf{op}_1(x))(y)).$$

In general, $\overrightarrow{\mathcal{D}}$ computes the derivative of a program that is a composition of operations $\mathsf{op}_1, \ldots, \mathsf{op}_n$ as the composition $(D\mathsf{op}_1), \ldots, (D\mathsf{op}_n)$ of the (multivariate) derivatives, in the same order as the original computation. By constrast, $\overleftarrow{\mathcal{D}}$ computes the *transposed* derivative of such a composition of $\mathsf{op}_1, \ldots, \mathsf{op}_n$ as the composition of the transposed derivatives $(D\mathsf{op}_n)^t, \ldots, (D\mathsf{op}_1)^t$. Observe the *reversed order* compared to the original composition!

While this AD technique works on the limited first-order language we described, it is far from satisfying. Notably, it has the following two shortcomings:

1. it does not tell us how to perform AD on programs that involve tuples or operations of multiple arguments;
2. it does not tell us how to perform AD on higher-order programs, that is, programs involving λ-abstractions and applications.

The key contributions of this paper are its extension of this transformation (see §7) to apply to a full simply typed λ-calculus (of §3), and its proof that this transformation is correct (see §8).

Shortcoming 1 seems easy to address, at first sight. Indeed, as the (co)tangent vectors to a product of spaces are simply tuples of (co)tangent vectors, one would expect to define, for a product type $\tau * \sigma$,

$$\overrightarrow{\mathcal{D}}(\tau*\sigma) \stackrel{\text{def}}{=} (\overrightarrow{\mathcal{D}}(\tau)_1 * \overrightarrow{\mathcal{D}}(\sigma)_1, \overrightarrow{\mathcal{D}}(\tau)_2 * \overrightarrow{\mathcal{D}}(\sigma)_2) \qquad \overleftarrow{\mathcal{D}}(\tau*\sigma) \stackrel{\text{def}}{=} (\overleftarrow{\mathcal{D}}(\tau)_1 * \overleftarrow{\mathcal{D}}(\sigma)_1, \overleftarrow{\mathcal{D}}(\tau)_2 * \overleftarrow{\mathcal{D}}(\sigma)_2).$$

Indeed, this technique straightforwardly applies to forward mode AD:

$$\overrightarrow{\mathcal{D}}(\langle t, s\rangle) \stackrel{\text{def}}{=} (\langle \overrightarrow{\mathcal{D}}(t)_1, \overrightarrow{\mathcal{D}}(s)_1\rangle, \lambda y.\langle \overrightarrow{\mathcal{D}}(t)_2(y), \overrightarrow{\mathcal{D}}(s)_2(y)\rangle)$$

$$\overrightarrow{\mathcal{D}}(\mathbf{fst}\, t) \stackrel{\text{def}}{=} (\mathbf{fst}\, \overrightarrow{\mathcal{D}}(t)_1, \lambda y.\mathbf{fst}\, \overrightarrow{\mathcal{D}}(t)_2(y)) \qquad \overrightarrow{\mathcal{D}}(\mathbf{snd}\, t) \stackrel{\text{def}}{=} (\mathbf{snd}\, \overrightarrow{\mathcal{D}}(t)_1, \lambda y.\mathbf{snd}\, \overrightarrow{\mathcal{D}}(t)_2(y)).$$

For reverse mode AD, however, tuples already present challenges. Indeed, we would like to use the definitions below, but they require terms $\vdash \underline{0} : \tau$ and $t + s : \tau$ for any two $t, s : \tau$ for each type τ:

$$\overleftarrow{\mathcal{D}}(\langle t, s\rangle) \stackrel{\text{def}}{=} (\langle \overleftarrow{\mathcal{D}}(t)_1, \overleftarrow{\mathcal{D}}(s)_1\rangle, \lambda y.\overleftarrow{\mathcal{D}}(t)_2\,(\mathbf{fst}\, y) + \overleftarrow{\mathcal{D}}(s)_2\,(\mathbf{snd}\, y))$$

$$\overleftarrow{\mathcal{D}}(\mathbf{fst}\, t) \stackrel{\text{def}}{=} (\mathbf{fst}\, \overleftarrow{\mathcal{D}}(t)_1, \lambda y.\langle \overleftarrow{\mathcal{D}}(t)_2(y), \underline{0}\rangle) \qquad \overleftarrow{\mathcal{D}}(\mathbf{snd}\, t) \stackrel{\text{def}}{=} (\mathbf{snd}\, \overleftarrow{\mathcal{D}}(t)_1, \lambda y.\langle \underline{0}, \overleftarrow{\mathcal{D}}(t)_2(y)\rangle).$$

These formulae capture the well-known issue of fanout translating to addition in reverse AD, caused by the contravariance of its second component [31]. Such $\underline{0}$ and $+$ could indeed be defined by induction on the structure of types, using $\underline{0}$ and $+$ at $\mathbf{real}^n$. However, more problematically, $\langle -, -\rangle$, $\mathbf{fst}\, -$ and $\mathbf{snd}\, -$ represent explicit uses of structural rules of contraction and weakening at types τ, which, in a λ-calculus, can also be used *implicitly* in the typing context Γ. Thus, we should also make these implicit uses *explicit* to account for their presence in the code. Then, we can appropriately translate them into their "mirror image": we map the contraction-weakening comonoids to the monoid structures $(+, \underline{0})$.

Insight 1. *In functional define-then-run reverse AD, we need to make use of explicit structural rules and "mirror them", which we can do by first translating our language into combinators. This translation allows us to avoid the usual practice (e.g. [38]) of accumulating adjoints at run-time with mutable state: instead, we detect all adjoints to accumulate at compile-time.*

Put differently: we define AD on the syntactic category **Syn** with types τ as objects and $(\alpha)\beta\eta$-equivalence classes of programs $x : \tau \vdash t : \sigma$ as morphisms $\tau \to \sigma$.

Yet the question remains: why should this translation for tuples be correct? What is even less clear is how to address shortcoming 2. What should the spaces of tangents $\overrightarrow{\mathcal{D}}(\tau \to \sigma)_2$ and adjoints $\overleftarrow{\mathcal{D}}(\tau \to \sigma)_2$ look like? This is not something we are taught in Calculus 1.01. Instead, we again employ category theory:

Insight 2. *Follow where the categorical structure of the syntax leads you, as doing so produces principled definitions that are easy to prove correct.*

With the aim of categorical compositionality in mind, we note that our translations compose according to a sort of "syntactic chain-rule", which says that

$$\overrightarrow{\mathcal{D}}(t[^s/_x]) \stackrel{\text{def}}{=} (\overrightarrow{\mathcal{D}}(t)_1[^{\overrightarrow{\mathcal{D}}(s)_1}/_x], \lambda y.\overrightarrow{\mathcal{D}}(t)_2[^{\overrightarrow{\mathcal{D}}(s)_1}/_x](\overrightarrow{\mathcal{D}}(s)_2(y)))$$
$$\overleftarrow{\mathcal{D}}(t[^s/_x]) \stackrel{\text{def}}{=} (\overleftarrow{\mathcal{D}}(t)_1[^{\overleftarrow{\mathcal{D}}(s)_1}/_x], \lambda y.\overleftarrow{\mathcal{D}}(s)_2(\overleftarrow{\mathcal{D}}(t)_2(y)[^{\overleftarrow{\mathcal{D}}(s)_1}/_x])).$$

By the following trick, these equations are functoriality laws. Given a Cartesian closed category $(\mathcal{C}, \mathbb{1}, \times, \Rightarrow)$, define categories $\overrightarrow{\mathfrak{D}}[\mathcal{C}]$ and $\overleftarrow{\mathfrak{D}}[\mathcal{C}]$ as having objects pairs (A_1, A_2) of objects A_1, A_2 of $\mathcal{C}$ and morphisms

$$\overrightarrow{\mathfrak{D}}[\mathcal{C}]((A_1, A_2), (B_1, B_2)) \stackrel{\text{def}}{=} \mathcal{C}(A_1, B_1) \times \mathcal{C}(A_1, A_2 \Rightarrow B_2)$$
$$\overleftarrow{\mathfrak{D}}[\mathcal{C}]((A_1, A_2), (B_1, B_2)) \stackrel{\text{def}}{=} \mathcal{C}(A_1, B_1) \times \mathcal{C}(A_1, B_2 \Rightarrow A_2).$$

Both have identities $\mathrm{id}_{(A_1,A_2)} \stackrel{\text{def}}{=} (\mathrm{id}_{A_1}, \Lambda(\pi_2))$, where we write Λ for categorical currying and π_2 for the second projection. Composition in $\overrightarrow{\mathfrak{D}}[\mathcal{C}]$ and $\overleftarrow{\mathfrak{D}}[\mathcal{C}]$, respectively, of $(A_1, A_2) \xrightarrow{(k_1,k_2)} (B_1, B_2) \xrightarrow{(l_1,l_2)} (C_1, C_2)$ are

$$(k_1, k_2); (l_1, l_2) \stackrel{\text{def}}{=} (k_1; l_1, \lambda a_1 : A_1.\lambda a_2 : A_2.l_2(k_1(a_1))(k_2(a_1, a_2)))$$
$$(k_1, k_2); (l_1, l_2) \stackrel{\text{def}}{=} (k_1; l_1, \lambda a_1 : A_1.\lambda c_2 : C_2.k_2(a_1)(l_2(k_1(a_1), c_2))),$$

where we work in the internal language of $\mathcal{C}$. Then, we have defined two functors:

$$\overrightarrow{\mathcal{D}} : \mathbf{Syn}_1 \to \overrightarrow{\mathfrak{D}}[\mathbf{Syn}] \qquad\qquad \overleftarrow{\mathcal{D}} : \mathbf{Syn}_1 \to \overleftarrow{\mathfrak{D}}[\mathbf{Syn}],$$

where we write $\mathbf{Syn}_1$ for the syntactic category of our restrictive first-order language, and we write **Syn** for that of the full λ-calculus. We would like to extend these to functors

$$\mathbf{Syn} \to \overrightarrow{\mathfrak{D}}[\mathbf{Syn}] \qquad\qquad \mathbf{Syn} \to \overleftarrow{\mathfrak{D}}[\mathbf{Syn}].$$

$\overrightarrow{\mathfrak{D}}[\mathcal{C}]$ turns out to be a category with finite products, given by $(A_1, A_2) \times (B_1, B_2) = (A_1 \times B_1, A_2 \times B_2)$. Thus, we can easily extend $\overrightarrow{\mathcal{D}}$ to apply to an extension of $\mathbf{Syn}_1$ with tuples by extending the functor in the unique structure-preserving way. However, $\overleftarrow{\mathfrak{D}}[\mathbf{Syn}]$ does not have products and neither $\overrightarrow{\mathfrak{D}}[\mathbf{Syn}]$ nor $\overleftarrow{\mathfrak{D}}[\mathbf{Syn}]$ supports function types. (The reason turns out to be that not all functions are linear in the sense of respecting $\underline{0}$ and $+$.) Therefore, the categorical structure does not give us guidance on how to extend our translation to all of **Syn**.

Insight 3. *Linear types can help. By using a more fine-grained type system, we can capture the linearity of the derivative. As a result, we can phrase AD on our full language simply as the unique structure-preserving functor that extends the uncontroversial definitions given so far.*

To implement this insight, we extend our λ-calculus to a language **LSyn** with limited linear types (in §4): linear function types $\multimap$ and a kind of multiplicative conjunction $!(-) \otimes (-)$, in the sense of the enriched effect calculus [14]. The algebraic effect giving rise to these linear types, in this instance, is that of the theory of commutative monoids. As we have seen, such monoids are intimately related to reverse AD. Consequently, we demand that every f with a linear function type $\tau \multimap \sigma$ is indeed linear, in the sense that $f\,\underline{0} = \underline{0}$ and $f\,(t + s) = (f\,t) + (f\,s)$. For the categorically inclined reader: that is, we enrich **LSyn** over the category of commutative monoids.

Now, we can give more precise types to our derivatives, as we know they are linear functions: for $x : \tau \vdash t : \sigma$, we have $x : \overrightarrow{\mathcal{D}}(\tau)_1 \vdash \overrightarrow{\mathcal{D}}(t)_2 : \overrightarrow{\mathcal{D}}(\tau)_2 \multimap \overrightarrow{\mathcal{D}}(\sigma)_2$ and $x : \overleftarrow{\mathcal{D}}(\tau)_1 \vdash \overleftarrow{\mathcal{D}}(t)_2 : \overleftarrow{\mathcal{D}}(\sigma)_2 \multimap \overleftarrow{\mathcal{D}}(\tau)_2$. Therefore, given any model $\mathcal{L}$ of our linear type theory, we generalise our previous construction of the categories $\overrightarrow{\mathfrak{D}}[\mathcal{L}]$ and $\overleftarrow{\mathfrak{D}}[\mathcal{L}]$, but now we work with linear functions in the second component. Unlike before, both $\overrightarrow{\mathfrak{D}}[\mathcal{L}]$ and $\overleftarrow{\mathfrak{D}}[\mathcal{L}]$ are now Cartesian closed (by §6)!

Thus, we find the following corollary, by the universal property of **Syn**. This property states that any well-typed choice of interpretations $F(\mathsf{op})$ of the primitive operations in a Cartesian closed category $\mathcal{C}$ extends to a unique Cartesian closed functor $F : \mathbf{Syn} \to \mathcal{C}$. It gives a principled definition of AD and explains in what sense reverse AD is the "mirror image" of forward AD.

Corollary (Definition of AD, §7). *Once we fix the interpretation of the primitives operations* op *to their respective derivatives and transposed derivatives, we obtain unique structure-preserving forward and reverse AD functors* $\overrightarrow{\mathcal{D}} : \mathbf{Syn} \to \overrightarrow{\mathfrak{D}}[\mathbf{LSyn}]$ *and* $\overleftarrow{\mathcal{D}} : \mathbf{Syn} \to \overleftarrow{\mathfrak{D}}[\mathbf{LSyn}]$.

In particular, the following definitions are forced on us by the theory:

Insight 4. *For reverse AD, an adjoint at function type* $\tau \to \sigma$*, needs to keep track of the incoming adjoints* v *of type* $\overleftarrow{\mathcal{D}}(\sigma)_2$ *for each a primal* x *of type* $\overleftarrow{\mathcal{D}}(\tau)_1$ *on which we call the function. We store these pairs* (x, v) *in the type* $!\overleftarrow{\mathcal{D}}(\tau)_1 \otimes \overleftarrow{\mathcal{D}}(\sigma)_2$ *(which we will see is essentially a quotient of a list of pairs of type* $\overleftarrow{\mathcal{D}}(\tau)_1 * \overleftarrow{\mathcal{D}}(\sigma)_2$*). Less surprisingly, for forward AD, a tangent at function type* $\tau \to \sigma$ *consists of a function sending each argument primal of type* $\overrightarrow{\mathcal{D}}(\tau)_1$ *to the outgoing tangent of type* $\overrightarrow{\mathcal{D}}(\sigma)_2$.

$$\overrightarrow{\mathcal{D}}(\tau \to \sigma) \stackrel{\text{def}}{=} (\overrightarrow{\mathcal{D}}(\tau)_1 \to (\overrightarrow{\mathcal{D}}(\sigma)_1 * (\overrightarrow{\mathcal{D}}(\tau)_2 \multimap \overrightarrow{\mathcal{D}}(\sigma)_2)), \overrightarrow{\mathcal{D}}(\tau)_1 \to \overrightarrow{\mathcal{D}}(\sigma)_2)$$
$$\overleftarrow{\mathcal{D}}(\tau \to \sigma) \stackrel{\text{def}}{=} (\overleftarrow{\mathcal{D}}(\tau)_1 \to (\overleftarrow{\mathcal{D}}(\sigma)_1 * (\overleftarrow{\mathcal{D}}(\sigma)_2 \multimap \overleftarrow{\mathcal{D}}(\tau)_2)), !\overleftarrow{\mathcal{D}}(\tau)_1 \otimes \overleftarrow{\mathcal{D}}(\sigma)_2)$$

With these definitions in place, we turn to the correctness of the source-code transformations. To phrase correctness, we first need to construct a suitable denotational semantics with an uncontroversial notion of semantic differentiation. A technical challenge arises, as the usual calculus setting of Euclidean spaces (or manifolds) and smooth functions cannot interpret higher-order functions. To solve this problem, we work with a conservative extension of this standard calculus setting (see §5): the category **Diff** of diffeological spaces. We model our types as diffeological spaces, and programs as smooth functions. By keeping track of a commutative monoid structure on these spaces, we are also able to interpret the required linear types. We write $\mathbf{Diff}_{\mathbf{CM}}$ for this "linear" category of commutative diffeological monoids and smooth monoid homomorphisms.

By the universal properties of the syntax, we obtain canonical, structure-preserving functors $[\![-]\!] : \mathbf{LSyn} \to \mathbf{Diff_{CM}}$ and $[\![-]\!] : \mathbf{Syn} \to \mathbf{Diff}$ once we fix interpretations $\mathbb{R}^n$ of $\mathbf{real}^n$ and well-typed interpretations $[\![\mathsf{op}]\!]$ for each operation op. These functors define a semantics for our language.

Having constructed the semantics, we can turn to the correctness proof (of §8). Because calculus does not provide an unambiguous notion of derivative at function spaces, we cannot prove that the AD transformations correctly implement mathematical derivatives by plain induction on the syntax. Instead, we use a logical relations argument over the semantics, which we phrase categorically:

Insight 5. *Once we show that the derivatives of primitive operations* op *are correctly implemented, correctness of derivatives of other programs follows from a standard logical relations construction over the semantics that relates a curve to its (co)tangent curve. By the chain-rule, all programs respect the logical relations.*

To show correctness of forward AD, we construct a category $\overrightarrow{\mathbf{SScone}}$ whose objects are triples $((X,(Y_1,Y_2)),P)$ of an object X of $\mathbf{Diff}$, an object (Y_1,Y_2) of $\overrightarrow{\mathfrak{D}}[\mathbf{Diff_{CM}}]$ and a predicate P on $\mathbf{Diff}(\mathbb{R},X) \times \overrightarrow{\mathfrak{D}}[\mathbf{Diff_{CM}}]((\mathbb{R},\mathbb{R}),(Y_1,Y_2))$. It has morphisms $((X,(Y_1,Y_2)),P) \xrightarrow{(f,(g,h))} ((X',(Y_1',Y_2')),P')$, which are a pair of morphisms $X \xrightarrow{f} X'$ and $(Y_1,Y_2) \xrightarrow{(g,h)} (Y_1',Y_2')$ such that for any $(\gamma,(\delta_1,\delta_2)) \in P$, we have that $(\gamma;f,(\delta_1,\delta_2);(g,h)) \in P'$. $\overrightarrow{\mathbf{SScone}}$ is a standard category of logical relations, or subscone, and it is widely known to inherit the Cartesian closure of $\mathbf{Diff} \times \overrightarrow{\mathfrak{D}}[\mathbf{Diff_{CM}}]$ (see §§8.1). It also comes equipped with a Cartesian closed functor $\overrightarrow{\mathbf{SScone}} \to \mathbf{Diff} \times \overrightarrow{\mathfrak{D}}[\mathbf{Diff_{CM}}]$. Therefore, once we fix predicates $P^f_{\mathbf{real}^n}$ on $([\![-]\!],\overrightarrow{\mathfrak{D}}[[\![-]\!]])(\mathbf{real}^n)$ and show that all operations op respect these predicates, it follows that our denotational semantics lifts to give a unique structure-preserving functor $\mathbf{Syn} \xrightarrow{(\!|-|\!)^f} \overrightarrow{\mathbf{SScone}}$, such that the left diagram below commutes (by the universal property of $\mathbf{Syn}$).

$$\begin{array}{ccc} \mathbf{Syn} & \xrightarrow{(\mathrm{id},\overrightarrow{\mathcal{D}})} & \mathbf{Syn} \times \overrightarrow{\mathfrak{D}}[\mathbf{LSyn}] \\ {\scriptstyle (\!|-|\!)^f}\downarrow & & \downarrow{\scriptstyle [\![-]\!]\times\overrightarrow{\mathfrak{D}}[[\![-]\!]]} \\ \overrightarrow{\mathbf{SScone}} & \longrightarrow & \mathbf{Diff} \times \overrightarrow{\mathfrak{D}}[\mathbf{Diff_{CM}}] \end{array} \qquad \begin{array}{ccc} \mathbf{Syn} & \xrightarrow{(\mathrm{id},\overleftarrow{\mathcal{D}})} & \mathbf{Syn} \times \overleftarrow{\mathfrak{D}}[\mathbf{LSyn}] \\ {\scriptstyle (\!|-|\!)^r}\downarrow & & \downarrow{\scriptstyle [\![-]\!]\times\overleftarrow{\mathfrak{D}}[[\![-]\!]]} \\ \overleftarrow{\mathbf{SScone}} & \longrightarrow & \mathbf{Diff} \times \overleftarrow{\mathfrak{D}}[\mathbf{Diff_{CM}}] \end{array}$$

Consequently, we can work with $P^f_{\mathbf{real}^n} \stackrel{\mathrm{def}}{=} \{(f,(g,h)) \mid g = f \text{ and } h = Df\}$, where we write $Df(x)(v)$ for the multivariate calculus derivative of f at a point x evaluated at a tangent vector v. By an application of the chain rule for differentiation, we see that every op respects this predicate, as long as $[\![D\mathsf{op}]\!] = D[\![\mathsf{op}]\!]$. The commuting of our diagram then virtually establishes the correctness of forward AD. The only remaining step in the argument is to note that any tangent vector at $[\![\tau]\!] \cong \mathbb{R}^N$, for first-order τ, can be represented by a curve $\mathbb{R} \to [\![\tau]\!]$. For reverse AD, the same construction works, if $[\![D\mathsf{op}^t]\!] = D[\![\mathsf{op}]\!]^t$, by replacing $\overrightarrow{\mathfrak{D}}[-]$ with $\overleftarrow{\mathfrak{D}}[-]$ and $\overrightarrow{\mathcal{D}}$ with $\overleftarrow{\mathcal{D}}$. We can then choose $P^r_{\mathbf{real}^n} \stackrel{\mathrm{def}}{=} \left\{(f,(g,h)) \mid g = f \text{ and } h = x \mapsto (Df(x))^t\right\}$, as the predicates for constructing $(\!|\mathbf{real}^n|\!)^r$, where we write A^t for the matrix transpose of A. We obtain our main theorem, which crucially holds even for t that involve higher-order subprograms.

Theorem (Correctness of AD, Thm. 1). *For any typed term $x : \tau \vdash t : \sigma$ in* **Syn** *between first-order types τ, σ, we have that*

$$[\![\overrightarrow{\mathcal{D}}(t)_2]\!](x) = D[\![t]\!](x) \quad \text{and} \quad [\![\overleftarrow{\mathcal{D}}(t)_2]\!](x) = D[\![t]\!](x)^t.$$

Next, we address the practicality of our method (in §9). The code transformations we employ are not too daunting to implement. It is well-known how to mechanically translate λ-calculus and functional languages into a (categorical) combinatory form [12]. However, the implementation of the required linear types presents a challenge. Indeed, types like $!(-) \otimes (-)$ and $(-) \multimap (-)$ are absent from languages such as Haskell and O'Caml. Luckily, in this instance, we can implement them using abstract data types by using a (basic) module system:

Insight 6. *Under the hood, $!\tau \otimes \sigma$ can consist of a list of values of type $\tau * \sigma$. Its API ensures that the list order and the difference between $xs +\!\!+ [(t, s), (t, s')] +\!\!+ ys$ and $xs +\!\!+ [(t, s + s')] +\!\!+ ys$ cannot be observed: as such, it is a quotient type. Meanwhile, $\tau \multimap \sigma$ can be implemented as a standard function type $\tau \to \sigma$ with a limited API that enforces that we can only ever construct linear functions: as such, it is a subtype.*

We phrase the correctness proof of the AD transformations in elementary terms, such that it holds in the applied setting where we use abstract types to implement linear types. We show that our correctness results are meaningful, as they make use of a denotational semantics that is adequate with respect to the standard operational semantics. Finally, to stress the applicability of our method, we show that it extends to higher-order (primitive) operations, such as **map**.

3 λ-Calculus as a Source Language for AD

As a source language for our AD translations, we can begin with a standard, simply typed λ-calculus which has ground types $\mathbf{real}^n$ of statically sized arrays of n real numbers, for all $n \in \mathbb{N}$, and sets $\mathsf{Op}^m_{n_1,\ldots,n_k}$ of primitive operations op for all $k, m, n_1, \ldots, n_k \in \mathbb{N}$. These operations will be interpreted as smooth functions $(\mathbb{R}^{n_1} \times \ldots \times \mathbb{R}^{n_k}) \to \mathbb{R}^m$. Examples to keep in mind for op include

- constants $\underline{c} \in \mathsf{Op}^n$ for each $c \in \mathbb{R}^n$, for which we slightly abuse notation and write $\underline{c}(\langle\rangle)$ as $\underline{c}$;
- elementwise addition and product $(+), (*) \in \mathsf{Op}^n_{n,n}$ and matrix-vector product $(\star) \in \mathsf{Op}^n_{n\cdot m,m}$;
- operations for summing all the elements in an array: $\mathrm{sum} \in \mathsf{Op}^1_n$;
- some non-linear functions like the sigmoid function $\varsigma \in \mathsf{Op}^1_1$.

We intentionally present operations in a schematic way, as primitive operations tend to form a collection that is added to in a by-need fashion, as an AD library develops. The precise operations needed will depend on the applications, but, in statistics and machine learning applications, Op tends to include a mix of multi-dimensional linear algebra operations and mostly one-dimensional non-linear functions. A typical library for use in machine learning would work with multi-dimensional arrays (sometimes called "tensors"). We focus here on one-dimensional arrays as the issues of how precisely to represent the arrays are orthogonal to the concerns of our development.

The types τ, σ, ρ and terms t, s, r of our AD source language are as follows:

τ, σ, ρ ::=		types	$\mid\ \tau_1 {*} \tau_2$	binary product
	$\mid$ $\mathbf{real}^n$	real arrays	$\mid\ \tau \to \sigma$	function
	$\mid$ $\mathbf{1}$	nullary product		

t, s, r ::=		terms	$\mid\ \mathbf{fst}\, t \mid \mathbf{snd}\, t$	product projections
	x	variable	$\mid\ \lambda x.t$	function abstraction
	$\mid$ $\mathsf{op}(t)$	operations	$\mid\ t\, s$	function application
	$\mid$ $\langle\rangle \mid \langle t, s\rangle$	product tuples		

The typing rules are in Fig. 1, where we write $\mathbf{Dom}(\mathsf{op}) \stackrel{\text{def}}{=} \mathbf{real}^{n_1} {*} \ldots {*} \mathbf{real}^{n_k}$ for an operation $\mathsf{op} \in \mathsf{Op}^m_{n_1,\ldots,n_k}$. We employ the usual syntactic sugar $\mathbf{let}\, x = t\, \mathbf{in}\, s \stackrel{\text{def}}{=} (\lambda x.s)\, t$ and write $\mathbf{real}$ for $\mathbf{real}^1$. As Fig. 2 displays, we consider the terms of our language up to the standard $\beta\eta$-theory. We could consider further equations for our operations, but we do not as we will not need them.

This standard λ-calculus is widely known to be equivalent to the free Cartesian closed category **Syn** generated by the objects $\mathbf{real}^n$ and the morphisms op. **Syn** effectively represents programs as (categorical) combinators, also known as "point-free style" in the functional programming community. Indeed, there are well-studied mechanical translations from the λ-calculus to the free Cartesian closed category (and back) [26,13]. The translation from **Syn** to λ-calculus is self-evident, while the translation in the opposite direction is straightforward after we first convert our λ-terms to de Bruijn indexed form. Concretely,

- **Syn** has types τ, σ, ρ objects;
- **Syn** has morphisms $t \in \mathbf{Syn}(\tau, \sigma)$ which are in 1-1 correspondence with terms $x : \tau \vdash t : \sigma$ up to $\beta\eta$-equivalence (which includes α-equivalence); explicitly, they can be represented by
  - identities: $\mathrm{id}_\tau \in \mathbf{Syn}(\tau, \tau)$ (cf., variables up to α-equivalence);
  - composition: $t; s \in \mathbf{Syn}(\tau, \rho)$ for any $t \in \mathbf{Syn}(\tau, \sigma)$ and $s \in \mathbf{Syn}(\sigma, \rho)$ (corresponding to the capture avoiding substitution $s[^t/_y]$ if we represent $x : \tau \vdash t : \sigma$ and $y : \sigma \vdash s : \rho$);
  - terminal morphisms: $\langle\rangle_\tau \in \mathbf{Syn}(\tau, \mathbf{1})$;
  - product pairing: $\langle t, s\rangle \in \mathbf{Syn}(\tau, \sigma {*} \rho)$ for any $t \in \mathbf{Syn}(\tau, \sigma)$ and $s \in \mathbf{Syn}(\tau, \rho)$;
  - product projections: $\mathbf{fst}_{\tau,\sigma} \in \mathbf{Syn}(\tau {*} \sigma, \tau)$ and $\mathbf{snd}_{\tau,\sigma} \in \mathbf{Syn}(\tau {*} \sigma, \sigma)$;

$$\frac{((x:\tau) \in \Gamma)}{\Gamma \vdash x : \tau} \qquad \frac{\Gamma \vdash t : \mathbf{Dom}(\mathsf{op}) \quad (\mathsf{op} \in \mathsf{Op}^m_{n_1,\ldots,n_k})}{\Gamma \vdash \mathsf{op}(t) : \mathbf{real}^m} \qquad \frac{}{\Gamma \vdash \langle\rangle : \mathbf{1}} \qquad \frac{\Gamma \vdash t : \tau \quad \Gamma \vdash s : \sigma}{\Gamma \vdash \langle t, s\rangle : \tau {*} \sigma}$$

$$\frac{\Gamma \vdash t : \tau {*} \sigma}{\Gamma \vdash \mathbf{fst}\, t : \tau} \qquad \frac{\Gamma \vdash t : \tau {*} \sigma}{\Gamma \vdash \mathbf{snd}\, t : \sigma} \qquad \frac{\Gamma, x : \tau \vdash t : \sigma}{\Gamma \vdash \lambda x.t : \tau \to \sigma} \qquad \frac{\Gamma \vdash t : \sigma \to \tau \quad \Gamma \vdash s : \sigma}{\Gamma \vdash t\, s : \tau}$$

Fig. 1. Typing rules for the AD source language.

$$t = \langle\rangle \qquad \mathbf{fst}\,\langle t, s\rangle = t \quad \mathbf{snd}\,\langle t, s\rangle = s \quad t = \langle \mathbf{fst}\, t, \mathbf{snd}\, t\rangle \quad (\lambda x.t)\, s = t[^s/_x] \quad t \overset{\# x}{=} \lambda x.t\, x$$

Fig. 2. Standard $\beta\eta$-laws for products and functions. We write $\overset{\# x_1,\ldots,x_n}{=}$ to indicate that the variables $x_1, \ldots, x_n$ need to be fresh in the left hand side. Equations hold on pairs of terms of the same type. As usual, we only distinguish terms up to α-renaming of bound variables.

- function evaluation: $\mathrm{ev}_{\tau,\sigma} \in \mathbf{Syn}((\tau \to \sigma)*\tau, \sigma)$;
- currying: $\Lambda_{\tau,\sigma,\rho}(t) \in \mathbf{Syn}(\tau, \sigma \to \rho)$ for any $t \in \mathbf{Syn}(\tau*\sigma, \rho)$;
- operations: $\mathsf{op} \in \mathbf{Syn}(\mathbf{real}^{n_1}*..*\mathbf{real}^{n_k}, \mathbf{real}^m)$ for any $\mathsf{op} \in \mathsf{Op}^m_{n_1,..,n_k}$.

– all subject to the usual equations of a Cartesian closed category [26].

$\mathbf{1}$ and $*$ give finite products in $\mathbf{Syn}$, while $\to$ gives categorical exponentials.

$\mathbf{Syn}$ has the following universal property: for any Cartesian closed category $(\mathcal{C}, \mathbb{1}, \times, \Rightarrow)$, we obtain a unique Cartesian closed functor $F : \mathbf{Syn} \to \mathcal{C}$, once we choose objects $F\mathbf{real}^n$ of $\mathcal{C}$ as well as, for each $\mathsf{op} \in \mathsf{Op}^m_{n_1,\ldots,n_k}$, make well-typed choices of $\mathcal{C}$-morphisms $\quad F\mathsf{op} : (F\mathbf{real}^{n_1} \times \ldots \times F\mathbf{real}^{n_k}) \to F\mathbf{real}^m$.

4 Linear λ-Calculus as an Idealised AD Target Language

As a target language for our AD source code transformations, we consider a language that extends the language of §3 with limited linear types. We could opt to work with a full linear logic as in [6] or [4]. Instead, however, we will only include the bare minimum of linear type formers that we actually need to phrase the AD transformations. The resulting language is closely related to, but more minimal than, the Enriched Effect Calculus of [14]. We limit our language in this way because we want to stress that the resulting code transformations can easily be implemented in existing functional languages such as Haskell or O'Caml. As we discuss in §9, the idea will be to make use of a module system to implement the required linear types as abstract data types.

In our idealised target language, we consider *linear types* (aka computation types) $\underline{\tau}$, $\underline{\sigma}$, $\underline{\rho}$, in addition to the *Cartesian types* (aka value types) τ, σ, ρ that we have considered so far. We think of Cartesian types as denoting spaces and linear types as denoting spaces equipped with an algebraic structure. As we are interested in studying differentiation, the relevant space structure in this instance is a geometric structure that suffices to define differentiability. Meanwhile, the relevant algebraic structure on linear types turns out to be that of a commutative monoid, as this algebraic structure is needed to phrase automatic differentiation algorithms. Indeed, we will use the linear types to denote spaces of (co)tangent vectors to the spaces of primals denoted by Cartesian types. These spaces of (co)tangents form a commutative monoid under addition.

Concretely, we extend the types and terms of our language as follows:

$\underline{\tau}, \underline{\sigma}, \underline{\rho}$ ::=		linear types	|	$\underline{\tau}*\underline{\sigma}$	binary product
|	$\underline{\mathbf{real}}^n$	real array	|	$\tau \to \underline{\sigma}$	function
|	$\underline{\mathbf{1}}$	unit type	|	$!\tau \otimes \underline{\sigma}$	tensor product
τ, σ, ρ ::=		Cartesian types	|	$\underline{\tau} \multimap \underline{\sigma}$	linear function
|	...	as in §3			

$$\frac{}{\Gamma;x:\underline{\tau}\vdash x:\underline{\tau}} \qquad \frac{\Gamma\vdash t:\mathbf{Dom}(\mathsf{lop}) \quad \Gamma;x:\underline{\tau}\vdash s:\mathbf{LDom}(\mathsf{lop}) \quad (\mathsf{lop}\in\mathsf{LOp}^m_{n_1,\ldots,n_k;n'_1,\ldots,n'_l})}{\Gamma;x:\underline{\tau}\vdash \mathsf{lop}(t;s):\underline{\mathbf{real}}^m}$$

$$\frac{}{\Gamma;x:\underline{\tau}\vdash\langle\rangle:\underline{\mathbf{1}}} \qquad \frac{\Gamma;x:\underline{\tau}\vdash t:\underline{\sigma} \quad \Gamma;x:\underline{\tau}\vdash s:\underline{\rho}}{\Gamma;x:\underline{\tau}\vdash\langle t,s\rangle:\underline{\sigma}*\underline{\rho}} \qquad \frac{\Gamma;x:\underline{\tau}\vdash t:\underline{\sigma}*\underline{\rho}}{\Gamma;x:\underline{\tau}\vdash\mathbf{fst}\,t:\underline{\sigma}} \qquad \frac{\Gamma;x:\underline{\tau}\vdash t:\underline{\sigma}*\underline{\rho}}{\Gamma;x:\underline{\tau}\vdash\mathbf{snd}\,t:\underline{\rho}}$$

$$\frac{\Gamma,y:\sigma;x:\underline{\tau}\vdash t:\underline{\rho}}{\Gamma;x:\underline{\tau}\vdash\lambda y.t:\sigma\to\underline{\rho}} \qquad \frac{\Gamma;x:\underline{\tau}\vdash t:\sigma\to\underline{\rho} \quad \Gamma\vdash s:\sigma}{\Gamma;x:\underline{\tau}\vdash t\,s:\underline{\rho}} \qquad \frac{\Gamma\vdash t:\sigma \quad \Gamma;x:\underline{\tau}\vdash s:\underline{\rho}}{\Gamma;x:\underline{\tau}\vdash !t\otimes s:!\sigma\otimes\underline{\rho}}$$

$$\frac{\Gamma;x:\underline{\tau}\vdash t:!\sigma\otimes\underline{\rho} \quad \Gamma,y:\sigma;z:\underline{\rho}\vdash s:\underline{\rho}'}{\Gamma;x:\underline{\tau}\vdash\mathbf{case}\,t\,\mathbf{of}\,!y\otimes z\to s:\underline{\rho}'} \qquad \frac{\Gamma;x:\underline{\tau}\vdash t:\underline{\sigma}}{\Gamma\vdash\underline{\lambda}x.t:\underline{\tau}\multimap\underline{\sigma}}$$

$$\frac{\Gamma\vdash t:\underline{\rho}\multimap\underline{\sigma} \quad \Gamma;x:\underline{\tau}\vdash s:\underline{\rho}}{\Gamma;x:\underline{\tau}\vdash t\{s\}:\underline{\sigma}} \qquad \frac{}{\Gamma;x:\underline{\tau}\vdash\underline{0}:\underline{\sigma}} \qquad \frac{\Gamma;x:\underline{\tau}\vdash t:\underline{\sigma} \quad \Gamma;x:\underline{\tau}\vdash s:\underline{\sigma}}{\Gamma;x:\underline{\tau}\vdash t+s:\underline{\sigma}}$$

Fig. 3. Typing rules for the idealised AD target language with linear types.

$$\begin{array}{llll}
t,s,r ::= & \text{terms} & \mid\ !t\otimes s \mid \mathbf{case}\,t\,\mathbf{of}\,!y\otimes z\to s & \text{tensor product}\\
\quad\mid \ \ldots & \text{as in §3} & \mid\ \underline{\lambda}x.t \mid t\{s\} & \text{abstraction/appl.}\\
\quad\mid \ \mathsf{lop}(t;s) & \text{linear op.} & \mid\ \underline{0} \mid t+s & \text{monoid structure.}
\end{array}$$

We work with linear operations $\mathsf{lop}\in\mathsf{LOp}^m_{n_1,\ldots,n_k;n'_1,\ldots,n'_l}$, which are intended to represent functions which are linear (in the sense of respecting $\underline{0}$ and $+$) in the last l arguments but not in the first k. We write $\mathbf{Dom}(\mathsf{lop})\stackrel{\text{def}}{=}\mathbf{real}^{n_1}*\ldots*\mathbf{real}^{n_k}$ and $\mathbf{LDom}(\mathsf{lop})\stackrel{\text{def}}{=}\underline{\mathbf{real}}^{n'_1}*\ldots*\underline{\mathbf{real}}^{n'_l}$ for $\mathsf{lop}\in\mathsf{LOp}^m_{n_1,\ldots,n_k;n'_1,\ldots,n'_l}$. These operations can include e.g. dense and sparse matrix-vector multiplications. Their purpose is to serve as primitives to implement derivatives $D\mathsf{op}(x;y)$ and $(D\mathsf{op})^t(x;y)$ of the operations op from the source language as terms that are linear in y.

In addition to the judgement $\Gamma\vdash t:\tau$, which we encountered in §3, we now consider an additional judgement $\Gamma;x:\underline{\tau}\vdash t:\underline{\sigma}$. While we think of the former as denoting a (structure-preserving) function between spaces, we think of the latter as a (structure-preserving) function from the space which Γ denotes to the space of (structure-preserving) monoid homomorphisms from the denotation of $\underline{\tau}$ to that of $\underline{\sigma}$. In this instance, "structure-preserving" will mean differentiable.

Fig. 3 displays the typing rules of our language. We consider the terms of this language up to the $\beta\eta+$-equational theory of Fig. 4. It includes $\beta\eta$-rules as well as commutative monoid and homomorphism laws.

$$\begin{array}{ll}
\mathbf{case}\,!t\otimes s\,\mathbf{of}\,!x\otimes y\to r = r[^t/_x,{}^s/_y] & t[^s/_x]\stackrel{\#y,z}{=}\mathbf{case}\,s\,\mathbf{of}\,!y\otimes z\to t[^{!y\otimes z}/_x]\\
(\underline{\lambda}x.t)\{s\}=t[^s/_x] & t\stackrel{\#x}{=}\underline{\lambda}x.t\{x\}\\
t+\underline{0}=t \qquad \underline{0}+t=t & (t+s)+r=t+(s+r) \qquad t+s=s+t\\
(\Gamma;x:\underline{\tau}\vdash t:\underline{\sigma})\Rightarrow t[^{\underline{0}}/_x]=\underline{0} & (\Gamma;x:\underline{\tau}\vdash t:\underline{\sigma})\Rightarrow t[^{s+r}/_x]=t[^s/_x]+t[^r/_x]
\end{array}$$

Fig. 4. Equational rules for the idealised, linear AD language, which we use on top of the rules of Fig. 2. In addition to standard $\beta\eta$-rules for $!(-)\otimes(-)$- and $\multimap$-types, we add rules making $(\underline{0},+)$ into a commutative monoid on the terms of each linear type as well as rules which say that terms of linear types are homomorphisms in their linear variable. Equations hold on pairs of terms of the same type.

5 Semantics of the Source and Target Languages

5.1 Preliminaries

Category theory We assume familiarity with categories, functors, natural transformations, and their theory of (co)limits and adjunctions. We write:

- unary, binary, and I-ary products as $\mathbb{1}$, $X_1 \times X_2$, and $\prod_{i\in I} X_i$, writing π_i for the projections and $()$, (x_1, x_2), and $(x_i)_{i\in I}$ for the tupling maps;
- unary, binary, and I-ary coproducts as $\mathbb{0}$, $X_1 + X_2$, and $\sum_{i\in I} X_i$, writing ι_i for the injections and $[]$, $[x_1, x_2]$, and $[x_i]_{i\in I}$ for the cotupling maps;
- exponentials as $Y \Rightarrow X$, writing Λ and ev for currying and evaluation.

Monoids We assume familiarity with the category **CMon** of commutative monoids $X = (|X|, 0_X, +_X)$, such as $\underline{\mathbb{R}}^n \stackrel{\text{def}}{=} (\mathbb{R}^n, 0, +)$, their cartesian product $X\times Y$, tensor product $X \otimes Y$, and the free monoid $!S$ on a set S (write δ for the inclusion $S \hookrightarrow |!S|$). We will sometimes write $\sum_{i=1}^n x_i$ for $((x_1+x_2)+\ldots)\ldots+x_n$.

Recall that a category $\mathcal{C}$ is called **CMon**-enriched if we have a commutative monoid structure on each homset $\mathcal{C}(C, C')$ and function composition gives monoid homomorphisms $\mathcal{C}(C, C') \otimes \mathcal{C}(C', C'') \to \mathcal{C}(C, C'')$. Finite products in a category $\mathcal{C}$ are well-known to be biproducts (i.e. simultaneously products and coproducts) if and only if $\mathcal{C}$ is **CMon**-enriched (see e.g. [17]): define $[] \stackrel{\text{def}}{=} 0$ and $[f, g] \stackrel{\text{def}}{=} \pi_1; f + \pi_2; g$ and, conversely, $0 \stackrel{\text{def}}{=} []$ and $f + g \stackrel{\text{def}}{=} (\mathrm{id}, \mathrm{id}); [f, g]$.

5.2 Abstract Semantics

The language of §3 has a canonical interpretation in any Cartesian closed category $(\mathcal{C}, \mathbb{1}, \times, \Rightarrow)$, once we fix $\mathcal{C}$-objects $[\![\mathbf{real}^n]\!]$ to interpret $\mathbf{real}^n$ and $\mathcal{C}$-morphisms $[\![\mathsf{op}]\!] \in \mathcal{C}([\![\mathbf{Dom}(\mathsf{op})]\!], [\![\mathbf{real}^m]\!])$ to interpret $\mathsf{op} \in \mathsf{Op}^m_{n_1,\ldots,n_k}$. We interpret types τ and contexts Γ as $\mathcal{C}$-objects $[\![\tau]\!]$ and $[\![\Gamma]\!]$: $[\![x_1 : \tau_1, \ldots, x_n : \tau_n]\!] \stackrel{\text{def}}{=} [\![\tau_1]\!] \times \ldots \times [\![\tau_n]\!]$ $\quad [\![\mathbf{1}]\!] \stackrel{\text{def}}{=} \mathbb{1}$ $\quad [\![\tau * \sigma]\!] \stackrel{\text{def}}{=} [\![\tau]\!] \times [\![\sigma]\!]$ $\quad [\![\tau \to \sigma]\!] \stackrel{\text{def}}{=} [\![\tau]\!] \Rightarrow [\![\sigma]\!]$.

We interpret terms $\Gamma \vdash t : \tau$ as morphisms $[\![t]\!]$ in $\mathcal{C}([\![\Gamma]\!], [\![\tau]\!])$:

$$[\![x_1 : \tau_1, \ldots, x_n : \tau_n \vdash x_k : \tau_k]\!] \stackrel{\text{def}}{=} \pi_k \qquad [\![\langle\rangle]\!] \stackrel{\text{def}}{=} () \qquad [\![\langle t, s\rangle]\!] \stackrel{\text{def}}{=} ([\![t]\!], [\![s]\!])$$

$$[\![\mathbf{fst}\,]\!] \stackrel{\text{def}}{=} \pi_1 \quad [\![\mathbf{snd}\,]\!] \stackrel{\text{def}}{=} \pi_2 \qquad [\![\lambda x.t]\!] \stackrel{\text{def}}{=} \Lambda([\![t]\!]) \qquad [\![t\, s]\!] \stackrel{\text{def}}{=} ([\![t]\!], [\![s]\!]); \mathrm{ev}.$$

This is an instance of the universal property of **Syn** mentioned in §3.

We discuss how to extend $[\![-]\!]$ to apply to the full target language of §4. Suppose that $\mathcal{L} : \mathcal{C}^{op} \to \mathbf{Cat}$ is a locally indexed category (see e.g. [27, §§§9.3.4]), i.e. a (strict) contravariant functor from $\mathcal{C}$ to the category **Cat** of categories, such that $\mathrm{ob}\,\mathcal{L}(C) = \mathrm{ob}\,\mathcal{L}(C')$ and $\mathcal{L}(f)(L) = L$ for any object L of $\mathrm{ob}\,\mathcal{L}(C)$ and any $f : C' \to C$ in $\mathcal{C}$. We say that $\mathcal{L}$ is *biadditive* if each category $\mathcal{L}(C)$ has (chosen) finite biproducts $(\mathbb{1}, \times)$ and $\mathcal{L}(f)$ preserves them, for any $f : C' \to C$ in $\mathcal{C}$, in the sense that $\mathcal{L}(f)(\mathbb{1}) = \mathbb{1}$ and $\mathcal{L}(f)(L \times L') = \mathcal{L}(f)(L) \times \mathcal{L}(f)(L')$. We say that it *supports* $!(-) \otimes (-)$*-types and* $\Rightarrow$*-types*, if $\mathcal{L}(\pi_1)$ has a left adjoint $!C' \otimes_C -$ and a right adjoint functor $C' \Rightarrow_C -$, for each product projection $\pi_1 : C \times C' \to C$ in $\mathcal{C}$, satisfying a Beck-Chevalley condition: $!C' \otimes_C L = !C' \otimes_{C''} L$ and $C' \Rightarrow_C L = C' \Rightarrow_{C''} L$ for any $C, C'' \in \mathrm{ob}\,\mathcal{C}$. We simply write $!C' \otimes L$ and $C' \Rightarrow L$. Let us write

Φ and Ψ for the natural isomorphisms $\mathcal{L}(C)(!C' \otimes L, L') \xrightarrow{\cong} \mathcal{L}(C \times C')(L, L')$ and $\mathcal{L}(C \times C)(L, L') \xrightarrow{\cong} \mathcal{L}(C)(L, C' \Rightarrow L')$. We say that $\mathcal{L}$ *supports Cartesian* $\multimap$*-types* if the functor $\mathcal{C}^{op} \to \mathbf{Set}$; $C \mapsto \mathcal{L}(C)(L, L')$ is representable for any objects L, L' of $\mathcal{L}$. That is, we have objects $L \multimap L'$ of $\mathcal{C}$ with isomorphisms $\underline{\Lambda} : \mathcal{L}(C)(L, L') \xrightarrow{\cong} \mathcal{C}(C, L \multimap L')$, natural in C. We call an $\mathcal{L}$ satisfying all these conditions a *categorical model* of the language of §4. In particular, any biadditive model of intuitionistic linear logic [29,17] is such a categorical model.

If we choose $[\![\mathbf{\underline{real}}^n]\!] \in \mathrm{ob}\,\mathcal{L}$ to interpret $\mathbf{\underline{real}}^n$ and compatible $\mathcal{L}$-morphisms $[\![\mathsf{lop}]\!]$ in $\mathcal{L}([\![\mathbf{Dom}(\mathsf{lop})]\!])([\![\mathbf{LDom}(\mathsf{lop})]\!], [\![\mathbf{\underline{real}}^k]\!])$ for each $\mathsf{LOp}^m_{n_1,\ldots,n_k;n'_1,\ldots,n'_l}$, then we can interpret linear types $\underline{\tau}$ as objects $[\![\underline{\tau}]\!]$ of $\mathcal{L}$:

$$[\![\underline{\mathbf{1}}]\!] \stackrel{\mathrm{def}}{=} \mathbb{1} \quad [\![\underline{\tau} * \underline{\sigma}]\!] \stackrel{\mathrm{def}}{=} [\![\underline{\tau}]\!] \times [\![\underline{\sigma}]\!] \quad [\![\tau \to \underline{\sigma}]\!] \stackrel{\mathrm{def}}{=} [\![\tau]\!] \Rightarrow [\![\underline{\sigma}]\!] \quad [\![!\tau \otimes \underline{\sigma}]\!] \stackrel{\mathrm{def}}{=} ![\![\tau]\!] \otimes [\![\underline{\sigma}]\!].$$

We can interpret $\underline{\tau} \multimap \underline{\sigma}$ as the $\mathcal{C}$-object $[\![\underline{\tau} \multimap \underline{\sigma}]\!] \stackrel{\mathrm{def}}{=} [\![\underline{\tau}]\!] \multimap [\![\underline{\sigma}]\!]$. Finally, we can interpret terms $\Gamma \vdash t : \tau$ as morphisms $[\![t]\!]$ in $\mathcal{C}([\![\Gamma]\!], [\![\tau]\!])$ and terms $\Gamma; x : \underline{\tau} \vdash t : \underline{\sigma}$ as $[\![t]\!]$ in $\mathcal{L}([\![\Gamma]\!])([\![\underline{\tau}]\!], [\![\underline{\sigma}]\!])$:

$$[\![\Gamma; x : \underline{\tau} \vdash x : \underline{\tau}]\!] \stackrel{\mathrm{def}}{=} \mathrm{id}_{[\![\underline{\tau}]\!]} \quad [\![\langle\rangle]\!] \stackrel{\mathrm{def}}{=} () \quad [\![\langle t, s\rangle]\!] \stackrel{\mathrm{def}}{=} ([\![t]\!], [\![s]\!]) \quad [\![\mathbf{fst}\,]\!] \stackrel{\mathrm{def}}{=} \pi_1 \quad [\![\mathbf{snd}\,]\!] \stackrel{\mathrm{def}}{=} \pi_2$$

$$[\![\lambda x.t]\!] \stackrel{\mathrm{def}}{=} \Psi([\![t]\!]) \quad [\![t\, s]\!] \stackrel{\mathrm{def}}{=} \mathcal{L}((\mathrm{id}, [\![s]\!]))(\Psi^{-1}([\![t]\!]))$$

$$[\![!t \otimes s]\!] \stackrel{\mathrm{def}}{=} \mathcal{L}((\mathrm{id}, [\![t]\!]))(\Phi(\mathrm{id})); (![\![\sigma]\!] \otimes [\![s]\!]) \quad [\![\mathbf{case}\, t\, \mathbf{of}\, !y \otimes x \to s]\!] \stackrel{\mathrm{def}}{=} [\![t]\!]; \Phi^{-1}([\![s]\!])$$

$$[\![\underline{\lambda} x.t]\!] \stackrel{\mathrm{def}}{=} \underline{\Lambda}([\![t]\!]) \quad [\![t\{s\}]\!] \stackrel{\mathrm{def}}{=} \underline{\Lambda}^{-1}([\![t]\!]); [\![s]\!] \quad [\![\underline{0}]\!] \stackrel{\mathrm{def}}{=} [\,] \quad [\![t + s]\!] \stackrel{\mathrm{def}}{=} (\mathrm{id}, \mathrm{id}); [[\![t]\!], [\![s]\!]].$$

Observe that we interpret $\underline{0}$ and $+$ using the biproduct structure of $\mathcal{L}$.

Proposition 1. *The interpretation* $[\![-]\!]$ *of the language of §4 in categorical models is both sound and complete with respect to the* $\beta\eta+$*-equational theory:* $t \stackrel{\beta\eta+}{=} s$ *iff* $[\![t]\!] = [\![s]\!]$ *in each such model.*

Soundness follows by case analysis on the $\beta\eta+$-rules. Completeness follows by the construction of the syntactic model $\mathbf{LSyn} : \mathbf{CSyn}^{op} \to \mathbf{Cat}$:

- $\mathbf{CSyn}$ extends its full subcategory $\mathbf{Syn}$ with Cartesian $\multimap$-types;
- Objects of $\mathbf{LSyn}(\tau)$ are linear types $\underline{\sigma}$ of our target language.
- Morphisms in $\mathbf{LSyn}(\tau)(\underline{\sigma}, \underline{\rho})$ are terms $x : \tau; y : \underline{\sigma} \vdash t : \underline{\rho}$ modulo $(\alpha)\beta\eta+$-equivalence.
- Identities in $\mathbf{LSyn}(\tau)$ are represented by the terms $x : \tau; y : \underline{\sigma} \vdash y : \underline{\sigma}$.
- Composition of $x : \tau; y_1 : \underline{\sigma}_1 \vdash t : \underline{\sigma}_2$ and $x : \tau; y_2 : \underline{\sigma}_2 \vdash t : \underline{\sigma}_3$ in $\mathbf{LSyn}(\tau)$ is defined by the capture avoiding substitution $x : \tau; y_1 : \underline{\sigma}_1 \vdash s[{}^t/_{y_2}] : \underline{\sigma}_3$.
- Change of base $\mathbf{LSyn}(t) : \mathbf{LSyn}(\tau) \to \mathbf{LSyn}(\tau')$ along $(x' : \tau' \vdash t : \tau) \in \mathbf{CSyn}(\tau', \tau)$ is defined $\mathbf{LSyn}(t)(x : \tau; y : \underline{\sigma} \vdash s : \underline{\rho}) \stackrel{\mathrm{def}}{=} x' : \tau'; y : \underline{\sigma} \vdash s[{}^t/_x] : \underline{\rho}$.
- All type formers are interpreted as one expects based on their notation, using introduction and elimination rules for the required structural isomorphisms.

5.3 Concrete Semantics

Diffeological Spaces Throughout this paper, we have an instance of the abstract semantics of our languages in mind, as we intend to interpret $\mathbf{real}^n$ as the usual Euclidean space $\mathbb{R}^n$ and to interpret each program $x_1 : \mathbf{real}^{n_1}, \ldots, x_k : \mathbf{real}^{n_k} \vdash t : \mathbf{real}^m$ as a smooth (C^∞-) function $\mathbb{R}^{n_1} \times \ldots \times \mathbb{R}^{n_k} \to \mathbb{R}^m$. A challenge is that the usual settings for multivariate calculus and differential geometry do not form Cartesian closed categories, obstructing the interpretation of higher types (see [20, Appx. A]). A solution, recently employed by [20], is to work with *diffeological spaces* [33,21], which generalise the usual notions of differentiability from Euclidean spaces and smooth manifolds to apply to higher types (as well as a range of other types such a sum and inductive types). We will also follow this route and use such spaces to construct our concrete semantics. Other valid options for a concrete semantics exist: convenient vector spaces [19,7], Frölicher spaces [18], or synthetic differential geometry [25], to name a few. We choose to work with diffeological spaces mostly because they seem to us to provide simplest way to define and analyse the semantics of a rich class of language features.

Diffeological spaces formalise the intuition that a higher-order function is smooth if it sends smooth functions to smooth functions, meaning that we can never use it to build non-smooth first-order functions. This intuition is reminiscent of a logical relation, and it is realised by *directly axiomatising smooth maps into the space*, rather than treating smoothness as a derived property.

Definition 1. *A* diffeological space $X = (|X|, \mathcal{P}_X)$ *consists of a set* $|X|$ *together with, for each* $n \in \mathbb{N}$ *and each open subset* U *of* $\mathbb{R}^n$, *a set* $\mathcal{P}_X^U$ *of functions* $U \to |X|$ *called* plots, *such that*
- ***(constant)*** *all constant functions are plots;*
- ***(rearrangement)*** *if* $f : V \to U$ *is smooth and* $p \in \mathcal{P}_X^U$, *then* $f; p \in \mathcal{P}_X^V$;
- ***(gluing)*** *if* $\left(p_i \in \mathcal{P}_X^{U_i}\right)_{i \in I}$ *is a compatible family of plots* ($x \in U_i \cap U_j \Rightarrow p_i(x) = p_j(x)$) *and* $(U_i)_{i \in I}$ *covers* U, *then the gluing* $p : U \to |X| : x \in U_i \mapsto p_i(x)$ *is a plot.*

We think of plots as the maps that are axiomatically deemed "smooth". We call a function $f : X \to Y$ between diffeological spaces *smooth* if, for all plots $p \in \mathcal{P}_X^U$, we have that $p; f \in \mathcal{P}_Y^U$. We write $\mathbf{Diff}(X, Y)$ for the set of smooth maps from X to Y. Smooth functions compose, and so we have a category **Diff** of diffeological spaces and smooth functions. We give some examples of such spaces.

Example 1 (Manifold diffeology). Given any open subset X of a Euclidean space $\mathbb{R}^n$ (or, more generally, a smooth manifold X), we can take the set of smooth (C^∞) functions $U \to X$ in the traditional sense as $\mathcal{P}_X^U$. Given another such space X', then $\mathbf{Diff}(X, X')$ coincides precisely with the set of smooth functions $X \to X'$ in the traditional sense of calculus and differential geometry.

Put differently, the categories **CartSp** of Euclidean spaces and **Man** of smooth manifolds with smooth functions form full subcategories of **Diff**.

Example 2 (Product diffeology). Given diffeological spaces $(X_i)_{i \in I}$, we can equip $\prod_{i \in I} |X_i|$ with the *product diffeology*: $\mathcal{P}^U_{\prod_{i \in I} X_i} \stackrel{\text{def}}{=} \{(\alpha_i)_{i \in I} \mid \alpha_i \in \mathcal{P}^U_{X_i}\}$.

Example 3 (Functional diffeology). Given diffeological spaces X, Y, we can equip $\mathbf{Diff}(X, Y)$ with the *functional diffeology* $\mathcal{P}^U_{Y^X} \stackrel{\text{def}}{=} \{\Lambda(\alpha) \mid \alpha \in \mathbf{Diff}(U \times X, Y)\}$.

Examples 2 and 3 give us the categorical product and exponential objects, respectively, in **Diff**. The embeddings of **CartSp** and **Man** into **Diff** preserve products (and coproducts).

We work with the concrete semantics, where we fix $\mathcal{C} = \mathbf{Diff}$ as the target for interpreting Cartesian types and their terms. That is, by choosing the interpretation $[\![\mathbf{real}^n]\!] \stackrel{\text{def}}{=} \mathbb{R}^n$, and by interpreting each $\mathsf{op} \in \mathsf{Op}^m_{n_1,\ldots,n_k}$ as the smooth function $[\![\mathsf{op}]\!] : \mathbb{R}^{n_1} \times \ldots \times \mathbb{R}^{n_k} \to \mathbb{R}^m$ that it is intended to represent, we obtain a unique interpretation $[\![-]\!] : \mathbf{CSyn} \to \mathbf{Diff}$.

Diffeological Monoids To interpret linear types and their terms, we need a semantic setting $\mathcal{L}$ that is both compatible with **Diff** and enriched over the category of commutative monoids. We choose to work with *commutative diffeological monoids*. That is, commutative monoids internal to the category **Diff**.

Definition 2. *A* diffeological monoid $X = (|X|, \mathcal{P}_X, 0_X, +_X)$ *consists of a diffeological space* $(|X|, \mathcal{P}_X)$ *with a monoid structure* $(0_X \in |X|, (+_X) : |X| \times |X| \to |X|)$*, such that* $+_X$ *is smooth. We call a diffeological monoid* commutative *if the underlying monoid structure on* $|X|$ *is commutative.*

We write $\mathbf{Diff_{CM}}$ for the category whose objects are commutative diffeological monoids and whose morphisms $(|X|, \mathcal{P}_X, 0_X, +_X) \to (|Y|, \mathcal{P}_Y, 0_Y, +_Y)$ are functions $f : |X| \to |Y|$ that are both smooth $(|X|, \mathcal{P}_X) \to (|Y|, \mathcal{P}_Y)$ and monoid homomorphisms $(|X|, 0_X, +_X) \to (|Y|, 0_Y, +_Y)$. Given that $\mathbf{Diff_{CM}}$ is **CMon**-enriched, finite products are biproducts.

Example 4. The real numbers $\mathbb{R}$ form a commutative diffeological monoid $\underline{\mathbb{R}}$ by combining its standard diffeology with its usual commutative monoid structure $(0, +)$. Similarly, $\underline{\mathbb{N}} \in \mathbf{Diff_{CM}}$ by equipping $\mathbb{N}$ with $(0, +)$ and the discrete diffeology, in which plots are locally constant functions.

Example 5. We form the (categorical) product in $\mathbf{Diff_{CM}}$ of $(X_i)_{i \in I}$ by equipping $\prod_{i \in I} |X_i|$ with the product diffeology and product monoid structure.

Example 6. For a commutative diffeological monoid X, we can equip the monoid $!(|X|, 0_X, +_X)$ with the diffeology $\mathcal{P}^U_{!X} \stackrel{\text{def}}{=} \{\sum_{i=1}^n \alpha_i; \delta \mid n \in \mathbb{N} \text{ and } \alpha_i \in \mathcal{P}^U_X\}$.

Example 7. Given commutative diffeological monoids X and Y, we can equip the tensor product monoid $(|X|, 0_X, +_X) \otimes (|Y|, 0_Y, +_Y)$ with the *tensor product diffeology*: $\mathcal{P}^U_{X \otimes Y} \stackrel{\text{def}}{=} \{\sum_{i=1}^n \alpha_i \otimes \beta_i \mid n \in \mathbb{N} \text{ and } \alpha_i \in \mathcal{P}^U_X, \beta_i \in \mathcal{P}^U_Y\}$.

In this paper, we only use the combined operation $!X \otimes Y$ (read: $(!X) \otimes Y$).

Example 8. Given commutative diffeological monoids X and Y, we can define a commutative diffeological monoid $X \multimap Y$ with underlying set $\mathbf{Diff_{CM}}(X, Y)$, $0_{X \multimap Y}(x) \stackrel{\text{def}}{=} 0_Y$, $(f +_{X \multimap Y} g)(x) \stackrel{\text{def}}{=} f(x) +_Y g(x)$ and
$\mathcal{P}^U_{X \multimap Y} \stackrel{\text{def}}{=} \left\{\alpha : U \to |X \multimap Y| \mid \alpha \in \mathcal{P}^U_{(|X|, \mathcal{P}_X) \Rightarrow (|Y|, \mathcal{P}_Y)}\right\}$.

In this paper, we will primarily be interested in $X \multimap Y$ as a diffeological space, and we will mostly disregard its monoid structure for now.

Example 9. Given a diffeological space X and a commutative diffeological monoid Y, we can define a commutative diffeological monoid structure $X \Rightarrow Y$ on $X \Rightarrow (|Y|, \mathcal{P}_Y)$ by using the pointwise monoid structure: $0_{X\Rightarrow Y}(x) \stackrel{\text{def}}{=} 0_Y$ and $(f +_{X\Rightarrow Y} g)(x) \stackrel{\text{def}}{=} f(x) +_Y g(x)$.

Given $f \in \mathbf{Diff}(X, Y)$, we can define $!f \in \mathbf{Diff}_{\mathbf{CM}}(!X, !Y)$ by $!f(\sum_{i=1}^n x) = \sum_{i=1}^n f(x)$. ! is a left adjoint to the obvious forgetful functor $\mathbf{Diff}_{\mathbf{CM}} \to \mathbf{Diff}$, while $!(X \times Y) \cong !X \otimes !Y$ and $!\mathbb{1} \cong \mathbb{N}$. Seeing that $(\mathbb{N}, \otimes, \multimap)$ defines a symmetric monoidal closed structure on $\mathbf{Diff}_{\mathbf{CM}}$, cognoscenti will recognise that $(\mathbf{Diff}, \mathbb{1}, \times, \Rightarrow) \leftrightarrows (\mathbf{Diff}_{\mathbf{CM}}, \mathbb{N}, \mathbb{1}, \times, \otimes, \multimap)$ is a model of intuitionistic linear logic [29]. In fact, seeing that $\mathbf{Diff}_{\mathbf{CM}}$ is **CMon**-enriched, the model is biadditive [17].

However, we do not need such a rich type system. For us, the following suffices. Define $\mathbf{Diff}_{\mathbf{CM}}(X)$, for $X \in \text{ob}\,\mathbf{Diff}$, to have the objects of $\mathbf{Diff}_{\mathbf{CM}}$ and homsets $\mathbf{Diff}_{\mathbf{CM}}(X)(Y, Z) \stackrel{\text{def}}{=} \mathbf{Diff}(X, Y \multimap Z)$. Identities and composition are defined as $x \mapsto (y \mapsto y)$ and $f;_{\mathbf{Diff}_{\mathbf{CM}}(X)} g$ is defined by $x \mapsto (f(x);_{\mathbf{Diff}_{\mathbf{CM}}} g(x))$. Given $f \in \mathbf{Diff}(X, X')$, we define change-of-base $\mathbf{Diff}_{\mathbf{CM}}(X') \to \mathbf{Diff}_{\mathbf{CM}}(X)$ as $\mathbf{Diff}_{\mathbf{CM}}(f)(g) \stackrel{\text{def}}{=} f;_{\mathbf{Diff}} g$. $\mathbf{Diff}_{\mathbf{CM}}(-)$ defines a locally indexed category. By taking $\mathcal{C} = \mathbf{Diff}$ and $\mathcal{L}(-) = \mathbf{Diff}_{\mathbf{CM}}(-)$, we obtain a concrete instance of our abstract semantics. Indeed, we have natural isomorphisms

$$\mathbf{Diff}_{\mathbf{CM}}(X)(!X' \otimes Y, Z) \xrightarrow{\Phi} \mathbf{Diff}_{\mathbf{CM}}(X \times X')(Y, Z)$$

$$\mathbf{Diff}_{\mathbf{CM}}(X \times X')(Y, Z) \xrightarrow{\Psi} \mathbf{Diff}_{\mathbf{CM}}(X)(Y, X' \Rightarrow Z)$$

$$\Phi(f)(x, x')(y) \stackrel{\text{def}}{=} f(x)(\delta(x') \otimes y) \qquad \Phi^{-1}(f)(x)(\sum_{i=1}^n (\delta(x'_i) \otimes y_i)) \stackrel{\text{def}}{=} \sum_{i=1}^n f(x, x'_i)(y_i)$$

$$\Psi(f)(x)(y)(x') \stackrel{\text{def}}{=} f(x, x')(y) \qquad \Psi^{-1}(f)(x, x')(y) \stackrel{\text{def}}{=} f(x)(y)(x').$$

The prime motivating examples of morphisms in this category are derivatives. Recall that the *derivative at* x, $Df(x)$, and *transposed derivative at* x, $(Df)^t(x)$, of a smooth function $f : \mathbb{R}^n \to \mathbb{R}^m$ are defined as the unique functions $Df(x) : \mathbb{R}^n \to \mathbb{R}^m$ and $(Df)^t(x) : \mathbb{R}^m \to \mathbb{R}^n$ satisfying

$$Df(x)(v) = \lim_{\delta \to 0} \frac{f(x + \delta \cdot v) - f(x)}{\delta} \qquad (Df)^t(x)(w) \bullet v = w \bullet Df(x)(v),$$

where we write $v \bullet v'$ for the inner product $\sum_{i=1}^n (\pi_i v) \cdot (\pi_i v')$ of vectors $v, v' \in \mathbb{R}^n$. Now, for $f \in \mathbf{Diff}(\mathbb{R}^n, \mathbb{R}^m)$, Df and $(Df)^t$ give maps in $\mathbf{Diff}_{\mathbf{CM}}(\mathbb{R}^n)(\underline{\mathbb{R}}^n, \underline{\mathbb{R}}^m)$ and $\mathbf{Diff}_{\mathbf{CM}}(\mathbb{R}^n)(\underline{\mathbb{R}}^m, \underline{\mathbb{R}}^n)$, respectively. Indeed, derivatives $Df(x)$ of f at x are linear functions, as are transposed derivatives $(Df)^t(x)$. Both depend smoothly on x in case f is C^∞-smooth. Note that the derivatives are not merely linear in the sense of preserving 0 and +. They are also multiplicative in the sense that $(Df)(x)(c \cdot v) = c \cdot (Df)(x)(v)$. *We could have captured this property by working with vector spaces internal to* **Diff**. *However, we will not need this property to* *phrase or establish correctness of AD.* Therefore, we restrict our attention to the more straightforward structure of commutative monoids.

Defining $[\![\mathbf{real}^n]\!] \stackrel{\text{def}}{=} \mathbb{R}^n$ and interpreting each $\mathsf{lop} \in \mathsf{LOp}$ as the smooth function $[\![\mathsf{lop}]\!] : (\mathbb{R}^{n_1} \times \ldots \times \mathbb{R}^{n_k}) \to (\underline{\mathbb{R}}^{n'_1} \times \ldots \times \underline{\mathbb{R}}^{n'_l}) \multimap \underline{\mathbb{R}}^m$ it is intended to represent, we obtain a canonical interpretation of our target language in $\mathbf{Diff}_{\mathbf{CM}}$.

6 Pairing Primals with Tangents/Adjoints, Categorically

In this section, we show that any categorical model $\mathcal{L} : \mathcal{C}^{op} \to \mathbf{Cat}$ of our target language gives rise to two Cartesian closed categories $\Sigma_{\mathcal{C}}\mathcal{L}$ and $\Sigma_{\mathcal{C}}\mathcal{L}^{op}$ (which we wrote $\overrightarrow{\mathfrak{D}}[\mathcal{L}]$ and $\overleftarrow{\mathfrak{D}}[\mathcal{L}]$ in §2). We believe these observations of Cartesian closure are novel. Surprisingly, they are highly relevant for obtaining a principled understanding of AD on a higher-order language: the former for forward AD, and the latter for reverse AD. Applying these constructions to the syntactic category $\mathbf{LSyn} : \mathbf{CSyn}^{op} \to \mathbf{Cat}$ of our language, we produce a canonical definition of the AD macros, as the canonical interpretation of the λ-calculus in the Cartesian closed categories $\Sigma_{\mathbf{CSyn}}\mathbf{LSyn}$ and $\Sigma_{\mathbf{CSyn}}\mathbf{LSyn}^{op}$. In addition, when we apply this construction to the denotational semantics $\mathbf{Diff}_{\mathbf{CM}} : \mathbf{Diff}^{op} \to \mathbf{Cat}$ and invoke a categorical logical relations technique, known as *subsconing*, we find an elegant correctness proof of the source code transformations. The abstract construction delineated in this section is in many ways the theoretical crux of this paper.

6.1 Grothendieck Constructions on Strictly Indexed Categories

Recall that for any strictly indexed category, i.e. a (strict) functor $\mathcal{L} : \mathcal{C}^{op} \to \mathbf{Cat}$, we can consider its total category (or Grothendieck construction) $\Sigma_{\mathcal{C}}\mathcal{L}$, which is a fibred category over $\mathcal{C}$ (see [23, sections A1.1.7, B1.3.1]). We can view it as a Σ-type of categories, which generalizes the Cartesian product. Concretely, its objects are pairs (A_1, A_2) of objects A_1 of $\mathcal{C}$ and A_2 of $\mathcal{L}(A_1)$. Its morphisms $(A_1, A_2) \to (B_1, B_2)$ are pairs (f_1, f_2) of a morphism $f_1 : A_1 \to B_1$ in $\mathcal{C}$ and a morphism $f_2 : A_2 \to \mathcal{L}(f_1)(B_2)$ in $\mathcal{L}(A_1)$. Identities are $\mathrm{id}_{(A_1,A_2)} \stackrel{\text{def}}{=} (\mathrm{id}_{A_1}, \mathrm{id}_{A_2})$ and composition is $(f_1, f_2); (g_1, g_2) \stackrel{\text{def}}{=} (f_1; g_1, f_2; \mathcal{L}(f_1)(g_2))$. Further, given a strictly indexed category $\mathcal{L} : \mathcal{C}^{op} \to \mathbf{Cat}$, we can consider its fibrewise dual category $\mathcal{L}^{op} : \mathcal{C}^{op} \to \mathbf{Cat}$, which is defined as the composition $\mathcal{C}^{op} \xrightarrow{\mathcal{L}} \mathbf{Cat} \xrightarrow{op} \mathbf{Cat}$. Thus, we can apply the same construction to $\mathcal{L}^{op}$ to obtain a category $\Sigma_{\mathcal{C}}\mathcal{L}^{op}$.

6.2 Structure of $\Sigma_{\mathcal{C}}\mathcal{L}$ and $\Sigma_{\mathcal{C}}\mathcal{L}^{op}$ for Locally Indexed Categories

§§6.1 applies, in particular, to the locally indexed categories of §5. In this case, we will analyze the categorical structure of $\Sigma_{\mathcal{C}}\mathcal{L}$ and $\Sigma_{\mathcal{C}}\mathcal{L}^{op}$. For reference, we first give a concrete description.

$\Sigma_{\mathcal{C}}\mathcal{L}$ is the following category:

– objects are pairs (A_1, A_2) of objects A_1 of $\mathcal{C}$ and A_2 of $\mathcal{L}$;

- morphisms $(A_1, A_2) \to (B_1, B_2)$ are pairs (f_1, f_2) with $f_1 : A_1 \to B_1 \in \mathcal{C}$ and $f_2 : A_2 \to B_2 \in \mathcal{L}(A_1)$;
- composition of $(A_1, A_2) \xrightarrow{(f_1,f_2)} (B_1, B_2)$ and $(B_1, B_2) \xrightarrow{(g_1,g_2)} (C_1, C_2)$ is given by $(f_1; g_1, f_2; \mathcal{L}(f_1)(g_2))$ and identities $\mathrm{id}_{(A_1,A_2)}$ are $(\mathrm{id}_{A_1}, \mathrm{id}_{A_2})$.

$\Sigma_{\mathcal{C}}\mathcal{L}^{op}$ is the following category:

- objects are pairs (A_1, A_2) of objects A_1 of $\mathcal{C}$ and A_2 of $\mathcal{L}$;
- morphisms $(A_1, A_2) \to (B_1, B_2)$ are pairs (f_1, f_2) with $f_1 : A_1 \to B_1 \in \mathcal{C}$ and $f_2 : B_2 \to A_2 \in \mathcal{L}(A_1)$;
- composition of $(A_1, A_2) \xrightarrow{(f_1,f_2)} (B_1, B_2)$ and $(B_1, B_2) \xrightarrow{(g_1,g_2)} (C_1, C_2)$ is given by $(f_1; g_1, \mathcal{L}(f_1)(g_2); f_2)$ and identities $\mathrm{id}_{(A_1,A_2)}$ are $(\mathrm{id}_{A_1}, \mathrm{id}_{A_2})$.

We examine the categorical structure present in $\Sigma_{\mathcal{C}}\mathcal{L}$ and $\Sigma_{\mathcal{C}}\mathcal{L}^{op}$ for categorical models $\mathcal{L}$ in the sense of §5 (i.e., in case $\mathcal{L}$ has biproducts and supports $\Rightarrow$-, $!(-) \otimes (-)$-, and Cartesian $\multimap$-types). We believe this is a novel observation. We will make heavy use of it to define our AD algorithms and to prove them correct.

Proposition 2. *$\Sigma_{\mathcal{C}}\mathcal{L}$ has terminal object $\mathbb{1} = (\mathbb{1}, \mathbb{1})$, binary product $(A_1, A_2) \times (B_1, B_2) = (A_1 \times B_1, A_2 \times B_2)$, and exponential $(A_1, A_2) \Rightarrow (B_1, B_2) = (A_1 \Rightarrow (B_1 \times (A_2 \multimap B_2)), A_1 \Rightarrow B_2)$.*

Proof. We have (natural) bijections

$$\Sigma_{\mathcal{C}}\mathcal{L}((A_1, A_2), (\mathbb{1}, \mathbb{1})) = \mathcal{C}(A_1, \mathbb{1}) \times \mathcal{L}(A_1)(A_2, \mathbb{1}) \cong \mathbb{1} \times \mathbb{1} \cong \mathbb{1} \qquad \{\ \mathbb{1} \text{ terminal in } \mathcal{C} \text{ and } \mathcal{L}(A_1)\ \}$$

$$\begin{aligned}
&\Sigma_{\mathcal{C}}\mathcal{L}((A_1, A_2), (B_1 \times C_1, B_2 \times C_2)) = \mathcal{C}(A_1, B_1 \times C_1) \times \mathcal{L}(A_1)(A_2, B_2 \times C_2) \\
&\cong \mathcal{C}(A_1, B_1) \times \mathcal{C}(A_1, C_1) \times \mathcal{L}(A_1)(A_2, B_2) \times \mathcal{L}(A_1)(A_2, C_2) && \{\ \times \text{ product in } \mathcal{C} \text{ and } \mathcal{L}(A_1)\ \} \\
&\cong \Sigma_{\mathcal{C}}\mathcal{L}((A_1, A_2), (B_1, B_2)) \times \Sigma_{\mathcal{C}}\mathcal{L}((A_1, A_2), (C_1, C_2))
\end{aligned}$$

$$\begin{aligned}
&\Sigma_{\mathcal{C}}\mathcal{L}((A_1, A_2) \times (B_1, B_2), (C_1, C_2)) = \Sigma_{\mathcal{C}}\mathcal{L}((A_1 \times B_1, A_2 \times B_2), (C_1, C_2)) \\
&= \mathcal{C}(A_1 \times B_1, C_1) \times \mathcal{L}(A_1 \times B_1)(A_2 \times B_2, C_2) \\
&\cong \mathcal{C}(A_1 \times B_1, C_1) \times \mathcal{L}(A_1 \times B_1)(A_2, C_2) \times \mathcal{L}(A_1 \times B_1)(B_2, C_2) && \{\ \times \text{ coproducts in } \mathcal{L}(A_1 \times B_1)\ \} \\
&\cong \mathcal{C}(A_1 \times B_1, C_1) \times \mathcal{L}(A_1)(A_2, B_1 \Rightarrow C_2) \times \mathcal{L}(A_1 \times B_1)(B_2, C_2) && \{\ \Rightarrow\text{-types in } \mathcal{L}\ \} \\
&\cong \mathcal{C}(A_1 \times B_1, C_1) \times \mathcal{L}(A_1)(A_2, B_1 \Rightarrow C_2) \times \mathcal{C}(A_1 \times B_1, B_2 \multimap C_2) && \{\ \text{Cartesian } \multimap\text{-types}\ \} \\
&\cong \mathcal{C}(A_1 \times B_1, C_1 \times (B_2 \multimap C_2)) \times \mathcal{L}(A_1)(A_2, B_1 \Rightarrow C_2) && \{\ \times \text{ is product in } \mathcal{C}\ \} \\
&\cong \mathcal{C}(A_1, B_1 \Rightarrow (C_1 \times (B_2 \multimap C_2))) \times \mathcal{L}(A_1)(A_2, B_1 \Rightarrow C_2) && \{\ \Rightarrow \text{ is exponential in } \mathcal{C}\ \} \\
&= \Sigma_{\mathcal{C}}\mathcal{L}((A_1, A_2), (B_1 \Rightarrow (C_1 \times (B_2 \multimap C_2)), B_1 \Rightarrow C_2)) \\
&= \Sigma_{\mathcal{C}}\mathcal{L}((A_1, A_2), (B_1, B_2) \Rightarrow (C_1, C_2)).
\end{aligned}$$

□

We observe that we need $\mathcal{L}$ to have biproducts (equivalently: to be **CMon** enriched) in order to show Cartesian closure. Further, we need linear $\Rightarrow$-types and Cartesian $\multimap$-types to construct exponentials.

Proposition 3. *$\Sigma_{\mathcal{C}}\mathcal{L}^{op}$ has terminal object $\mathbb{1} = (\mathbb{1}, \mathbb{1})$, binary product $(A_1, A_2) \times (B_1, B_2) = (A_1 \times B_1, A_2 \times B_2)$, and exponential $(A_1, A_2) \Rightarrow (B_1, B_2) = (A_1 \Rightarrow (B_1 \times (B_2 \multimap A_2)), !A_1 \otimes B_2)$.*

Proof. We have (natural) bijections

$$\Sigma_{\mathcal{C}}\mathcal{L}^{op}((A_1,A_2),(\mathbb{1},\mathbb{1})) = \mathcal{C}(A_1,\mathbb{1}) \times \mathcal{L}(A_1)(\mathbb{1},A_2) \cong \mathbb{1}\times\mathbb{1}\cong\mathbb{1} \quad \{ \mathbb{1} \text{ terminal in } \mathcal{C}, \text{ initial in } \mathcal{L}(A_1) \}$$

$$\begin{aligned}
&\Sigma_{\mathcal{C}}\mathcal{L}^{op}((A_1,A_2),(B_1\times C_1, B_2\times C_2)) = \mathcal{C}(A_1, B_1\times C_1)\times\mathcal{L}(A_1)(B_2\times C_2, A_2)\\
&\cong \mathcal{C}(A_1,B_1)\times\mathcal{C}(A_1,C_1)\times\mathcal{L}(A_1)(B_2,A_2)\times\mathcal{L}(A_1)(C_2,A_2) && \{ \times \text{ product in } \mathcal{C}, \text{ coproduct in } \mathcal{L}(A_1) \}\\
&= \Sigma_{\mathcal{C}}\mathcal{L}^{op}((A_1,A_2),(B_1,B_2))\times\Sigma_{\mathcal{C}}\mathcal{L}^{op}((A_1,A_2),(C_1,C_2))
\end{aligned}$$

$$\begin{aligned}
&\Sigma_{\mathcal{C}}\mathcal{L}^{op}((A_1,A_2)\times(B_1,B_2),(C_1,C_2)) = \Sigma_{\mathcal{C}}\mathcal{L}^{op}((A_1\times B_1, A_2\times B_2),(C_1,C_2))\\
&= \mathcal{C}(A_1\times B_1, C_1)\times\mathcal{L}(A_1\times B_1)(C_2, A_2\times B_2)\\
&\cong \mathcal{C}(A_1\times B_1, C_1)\times\mathcal{L}(A_1\times B_1)(C_2,A_2)\times\mathcal{L}(A_1\times B_1)(C_2,B_2) && \{ \times \text{ is product in } \mathcal{L}(A_1\times B_1) \}\\
&\cong \mathcal{C}(A_1\times B_1, C_1)\times\mathcal{C}(A_1\times B_1, C_2\multimap B_2)\times\mathcal{L}(A_1\times B_1)(C_2,A_2) && \{ \text{Cartesian } \multimap\text{-types} \}\\
&\cong \mathcal{C}(A_1\times B_1, C_1\times(C_2\multimap B_2))\times\mathcal{L}(A_1\times B_1)(C_2,A_2) && \{ \times \text{ is product in } \mathcal{C} \}\\
&\cong \mathcal{C}(A_1, B_1\Rightarrow(C_1\times(C_2\multimap B_2)))\times\mathcal{L}(A_1\times B_1)(C_2,A_2) && \{ \Rightarrow \text{ is exponential in } \mathcal{C} \}\\
&\cong \mathcal{C}(A_1, B_1\Rightarrow(C_1\times(C_2\multimap B_2)))\times\mathcal{L}(A_1)(!B_1\otimes C_2,A_2) && \{ !(-)\otimes(-)\text{-types} \}\\
&= \Sigma_{\mathcal{C}}\mathcal{L}^{op}((A_1,A_2),(B_1\Rightarrow(C_1\times(C_2\multimap B_2)), !B_1\otimes C_2))\\
&= \Sigma_{\mathcal{C}}\mathcal{L}^{op}((A_1,A_2),(B_1,B_2)\Rightarrow(C_1,C_2)).
\end{aligned}$$

□

Observe that we need the biproduct structure of $\mathcal{L}$ to construct finite products in $\Sigma_{\mathcal{C}}\mathcal{L}^{op}$. Further, we need Cartesian $\multimap$-types and $!(-)\otimes(-)$-types, but not biproducts, to construct exponentials.

7 Novel AD Algorithms as Source-Code Transformations

As $\Sigma_{\mathbf{CSyn}}\mathbf{LSyn}$ and $\Sigma_{\mathbf{CSyn}}\mathbf{LSyn}^{op}$ are both Cartesian closed categories by §6, the universal property of **Syn** yields unique structure-preserving macros, $\overrightarrow{\mathcal{D}}(-) : \mathbf{Syn}\to\Sigma_{\mathbf{CSyn}}\mathbf{LSyn}$ (forward AD) and $\overleftarrow{\mathcal{D}}(-) : \mathbf{Syn}\to\Sigma_{\mathbf{CSyn}}\mathbf{LSyn}^{op}$ (reverse AD), once we fix a compatible definition for the macros on $\mathbf{real}^n$ and basic operations op. By definition of equality in **Syn**, $\Sigma_{\mathbf{CSyn}}\mathbf{LSyn}$ and $\Sigma_{\mathbf{CSyn}}\mathbf{LSyn}^{op}$, *these macros automatically respect equational reasoning principles*, in the sense that $t \overset{\beta\eta}{=} s$ implies that $\overrightarrow{\mathcal{D}}(t) \overset{\beta\eta+}{=} \overrightarrow{\mathcal{D}}(s)$ and $\overleftarrow{\mathcal{D}}(t) \overset{\beta\eta+}{=} \overleftarrow{\mathcal{D}}(s)$.

We need to choose suitable terms $D\mathsf{op}(x;y)$ and $D\mathsf{op}^t(x;y)$ to represent the forward- and reverse-mode derivatives of the basic operations $\mathsf{op}\in\mathsf{Op}^m_{n_1,\ldots,n_k}$. For example, for elementwise multiplication $(*)\in\mathsf{Op}^n_{n,n}$, we can define $D(*)(x;y) = (\mathbf{fst}\,x)*(\mathbf{snd}\,y)+(\mathbf{snd}\,x)*(\mathbf{fst}\,y)$ and $D(*)^t(x;y) = \langle(\mathbf{snd}\,x)*y, (\mathbf{fst}\,x)*y\rangle$, where we use (linear) elementwise multiplication $(*)\in\mathsf{LOp}^n_{n;n}$. We represent derivatives as linear functions. This representation allows for efficient Jacobian-vector/adjoint product implementations, which avoid first calculating a full Jacobian and next taking a product. Such implementations are known to be important to achieve performant AD systems.

$$\overrightarrow{\mathcal{D}}(\mathbf{real}^n)_1 \overset{\text{def}}{=} \mathbf{real}^n \quad \overrightarrow{\mathcal{D}}(\mathbf{real}^n)_2 \overset{\text{def}}{=} \underline{\mathbf{real}}^n \quad \overleftarrow{\mathcal{D}}(\mathbf{real}^n)_1 \overset{\text{def}}{=} \mathbf{real}^n \quad \overrightarrow{\mathcal{D}}(\mathbf{real}^n)_2 \overset{\text{def}}{=} \underline{\mathbf{real}}^n$$

$$\overrightarrow{\mathcal{D}}(\mathsf{op})_1 \overset{\text{def}}{=} \mathsf{op} \quad \overrightarrow{\mathcal{D}}(\mathsf{op})_2 \overset{\text{def}}{=} x:\mathbf{real}^{n_1}*..*\mathbf{real}^{n_k}; y:\underline{\mathbf{real}}^{n_1}*..*\underline{\mathbf{real}}^{n_k}\vdash D\mathsf{op}(x;y):\underline{\mathbf{real}}^m$$

$$\overleftarrow{\mathcal{D}}(\mathsf{op})_1 \overset{\text{def}}{=} \mathsf{op} \quad \overleftarrow{\mathcal{D}}(\mathsf{op})_2 \overset{\text{def}}{=} x:\mathbf{real}^{n_1}*..*\mathbf{real}^{n_k}; y:\underline{\mathbf{real}}^{m}\vdash D\mathsf{op}^t(x;y):\underline{\mathbf{real}}^{n_1}*..*\underline{\mathbf{real}}^{n_k}$$

For the AD transformations to be correct, it is important that these derivatives of language primitives are implemented correctly in the sense that

$$[\![x; y \vdash D\mathsf{op}(x; y)]\!] = D[\![\mathsf{op}]\!] \qquad [\![x; y \vdash D\mathsf{op}^t(x; y)]\!] = D[\![\mathsf{op}]\!]^t.$$

In practice, AD library developers tend to assume the subtle task of correctly implementing such derivatives $D\mathsf{op}(x; y)$ and $D\mathsf{op}^t(x; y)$ whenever a new primitive operation op is added to the library.

The extension of the AD macros $\overrightarrow{\mathcal{D}}$ and $\overleftarrow{\mathcal{D}}$ to the full source language are now canonically determined, as the unique Cartesian closed functors that extend the previous definitions, following the categorical structure described in §6. Because of the counter-intuitive nature of the Cartesian closed structures on $\Sigma_{\mathbf{CSyn}}\mathbf{LSyn}$ and $\Sigma_{\mathbf{CSyn}}\mathbf{LSyn}^{op}$, we list the full macros explicitly in [36, Appx. A].

8 Proving Reverse and Forward AD Semantically Correct

In this section, we will show that the source code transformations described in §7 correctly implement mathematical derivatives. We make correctness precise as the statement that for programs $x : \tau \vdash t : \sigma$ between first-order types τ and σ, i.e. types not containing any function type constructors, we have that $[\![\overrightarrow{\mathcal{D}}(t)_2]\!] = D[\![t]\!]$ and $[\![\overleftarrow{\mathcal{D}}(t)_2]\!] = (D[\![t]\!])^t$, where $[\![-]\!]$ is the semantics of §5. The proof mainly consists of logical relations arguments over the semantics in $\Sigma_{\mathbf{Diff}}\mathbf{Diff_{CM}}$ and $\Sigma_{\mathbf{Diff}}\mathbf{Diff_{CM}}^{op}$. This logical relations proof can be phrased in elementary terms, but the resulting argument is technical and would be hard to discover. Instead, we prefer to phrase it in terms of a categorical subsconing construction, a more abstract and elegant perspective on logical relations. We discovered the proof by taking this categorical perspective, and, while we have verified the elementary argument (see [36, Appx. D]), we would not otherwise have come up with it.

8.1 Preliminaries

Subsconing Logical relations arguments provide a powerful proof technique for demonstrating properties of typed programs. The arguments proceed by induction on the structure of types. Here, we briefly review the basics of categorical logical relations arguments, or *subsconing constructions*. We restrict to the level of generality that we need here, but we would like to point out that the theory applies much more generally.

Consider a Cartesian closed category $(\mathcal{C}, \mathbb{1}, \times, \Rightarrow)$. Suppose that we are given a functor $F : \mathcal{C} \to \mathbf{Set}$ to the category $\mathbf{Set}$ of sets and functions which preserves finite products in the sense that $F(\mathbb{1}) \cong \mathbb{1}$ and $F(C \times C') \cong F(C) \times F(C')$. Then, we can form the *subscone* of F, or category of logical relations over F, which is Cartesian closed, with a faithful Cartesian closed functor π_1 to $\mathcal{C}$ which forgets about the predicates [24]:

- objects are pairs (C, P) of an object C of $\mathcal{C}$ and a predicate $P \subseteq FC$;
- morphisms $(C, P) \to (C', P')$ are $\mathcal{C}$ morphisms $f : C \to C'$ which respect the predicates in the sense that $F(f)(P) \subseteq P'$;

- identities and composition are as in $\mathcal{C}$;
- $(\mathbb{1}, F\mathbb{1})$ is the terminal object, and products and exponentials are given by $(C,P)\times(C',P') = (C\times C', \{\alpha \in F(C\times C') \mid F(\pi_1)(\alpha)\in P, F(\pi_2)(\alpha)\in P'\})$ $(C,P)\Rightarrow(C',P') = (C\Rightarrow C', \{F(\pi_1)(\gamma) \mid \gamma \in F((C\Rightarrow C')\times C)$ s.t. $F(\pi_2)(\gamma)\in P$ implies $F(\mathrm{ev})(\gamma)\in P'\})$.

In typical applications, $\mathcal{C}$ can be the syntactic category of a language (like **Syn**), the codomain of a denotational semantics $[\![-]\!]$ (like **Diff**), or a product of the above, if we want to consider n-ary logical relations. Typically, F tends to be a hom-functor (which always preserves products), like $\mathcal{C}(\mathbb{1},-)$ or $\mathcal{C}(C_0,-)$, for some important object C_0. When applied to the syntactic category **Syn** and $F = \mathbf{Syn}(1,-)$, the formulae for products and exponentials in the subscone clearly reproduce the usual recipes in traditional, syntactic logical relations arguments. As such, subsconing generalises standard logical relations methods.

8.2 Subsconing for Correctness of AD

We will apply the subsconing construction above to

$$\mathcal{C} = \mathbf{Diff}\times\Sigma_{\mathbf{Diff}}\mathbf{Diff}_{\mathbf{CM}} \quad F = \mathbf{Diff}\times\Sigma_{\mathbf{Diff}}\mathbf{Diff}_{\mathbf{CM}}((\mathbb{R},(\mathbb{R},\underline{\mathbb{R}})),-) \quad \text{(forward AD)}$$
$$\mathcal{C} = \mathbf{Diff}\times\Sigma_{\mathbf{Diff}}\mathbf{Diff}_{\mathbf{CM}}{}^{op} \quad F = \mathbf{Diff}\times\Sigma_{\mathbf{Diff}}\mathbf{Diff}_{\mathbf{CM}}{}^{op}((\mathbb{R},(\mathbb{R},\underline{\mathbb{R}})),-) \quad \text{(reverse AD)},$$

where we note that **Diff**, $\Sigma_{\mathbf{Diff}}\mathbf{Diff}_{\mathbf{CM}}$, and $\Sigma_{\mathbf{Diff}}\mathbf{Diff}_{\mathbf{CM}}{}^{op}$ are Cartesian closed (given the arguments of §5 and §6) and that the product of Cartesian closed categories is again Cartesian closed. Let us write $\overrightarrow{\mathbf{SScone}}$ and $\overleftarrow{\mathbf{SScone}}$, respectively, for the resulting categories of logical relations.

Seeing that $\overrightarrow{\mathbf{SScone}}$ and $\overleftarrow{\mathbf{SScone}}$ are Cartesian closed, we obtain unique Cartesian closed functors $(\!|-|\!)^f : \mathbf{Syn}\to\overrightarrow{\mathbf{SScone}}$ and $(\!|-|\!)^r : \mathbf{Syn}\to\overleftarrow{\mathbf{SScone}}$ once we fix an interpretation of $\mathbf{real}^n$ and all operations op. We write P^f_τ and P^r_τ, respectively, for the relations $\pi_2(\!|\tau|\!)^f$ and $\pi_2(\!|\tau|\!)^r$. Let us interpret

$$(\!|\mathbf{real}^n|\!)^f \stackrel{\text{def}}{=} (((\mathbb{R}^n,(\mathbb{R}^n,\underline{\mathbb{R}}^n)),\{(f,(g,h)) \mid f = g \text{ and } h = Df\}))$$
$$(\!|\mathbf{real}^n|\!)^r \stackrel{\text{def}}{=} (((\mathbb{R}^n,(\mathbb{R}^n,\underline{\mathbb{R}}^n)),\{(f,(g,h)) \mid f = g \text{ and } h = (Df)^t\}))$$
$$(\!|\mathsf{op}|\!)^f \stackrel{\text{def}}{=} ([\![\mathsf{op}]\!],([\![\overrightarrow{\mathcal{D}}(\mathsf{op})_1]\!],[\![\overrightarrow{\mathcal{D}}(\mathsf{op})_2]\!])) \qquad (\!|\mathsf{op}|\!)^r \stackrel{\text{def}}{=} ([\![\mathsf{op}]\!],([\![\overleftarrow{\mathcal{D}}(\mathsf{op})_1]\!],[\![\overleftarrow{\mathcal{D}}(\mathsf{op})_2]\!])),$$

where we write Df for the semantic derivative of f (see §5). We need to verify, respectively, that $([\![\mathsf{op}]\!],([\![\overrightarrow{\mathcal{D}}(\mathsf{op})_1]\!],[\![\overrightarrow{\mathcal{D}}(\mathsf{op})_2]\!]))$ and $([\![\mathsf{op}]\!],([\![\overleftarrow{\mathcal{D}}(\mathsf{op})_1]\!],[\![\overleftarrow{\mathcal{D}}(\mathsf{op})_2]\!]))$ respect the logical relations P^f and P^r. This respecting of relations follows immediately from the chain rule for multivariate differentiation, as long as we have implemented our derivatives correctly for the basic operations op:

$$[\![x;y\vdash D\mathsf{op}(x;y)]\!] = D[\![\mathsf{op}]\!] \qquad \text{and} \qquad [\![x;y\vdash (D\mathsf{op})^t(x;y)]\!] = (D[\![\mathsf{op}]\!])^t.$$

Writing $\mathbf{real}^{n_1,..,n_k} \stackrel{\text{def}}{=} \mathbf{real}^{n_1}*..*\mathbf{real}^{n_k}$ and $\mathbb{R}^{n_1,..,n_k} \stackrel{\text{def}}{=} \mathbb{R}^{n_1}\times..\times\mathbb{R}^{n_k}$, we compute

$$(\!|\mathbf{real}^{n_1,..,n_k}|\!)^f = ((\mathbb{R}^{n_1,..,n_k},(\mathbb{R}^{n_1,..,n_k},\underline{\mathbb{R}}^{n_1,..,n_k})),\{(f,(g,h)) \mid f = g, h = Df\})$$
$$(\!|\mathbf{real}^{n_1,..,n_k}|\!)^r = ((\mathbb{R}^{n_1,..,n_k},(\mathbb{R}^{n_1,..,n_k},\underline{\mathbb{R}}^{n_1,..,n_k})),\{(f,(g,h)) \mid f = g, h = (Df)^t\})$$

since derivatives of tuple-valued functions are computed component-wise. (In fact, the corresponding facts hold more generally for any first-order type, as an iterated product of $\mathbf{real}^n$.) Suppose that $(f,(g,h)) \in P^f_{\mathbf{real}^{n_1,\ldots,n_k}}$, i.e. $g = f$ and $h = Df$. Then, using the chain rule in the last step, we have

$$\begin{aligned}
&(f,(g,h)); (\llbracket \mathsf{op} \rrbracket, (\llbracket \overrightarrow{\mathcal{D}}(\mathsf{op})_1 \rrbracket, \llbracket \overrightarrow{\mathcal{D}}(\mathsf{op})_2 \rrbracket)) = (f,(f,Df)); (\llbracket \mathsf{op} \rrbracket, (\llbracket \mathsf{op} \rrbracket, \llbracket x; y \vdash D\mathsf{op}(x;y) \rrbracket))\\
&= (f,(f,Df)); (\llbracket \mathsf{op} \rrbracket, (\llbracket \mathsf{op} \rrbracket, D\llbracket \mathsf{op} \rrbracket)) = (f; \llbracket \mathsf{op} \rrbracket, (f; \llbracket \mathsf{op} \rrbracket, x \mapsto r \mapsto D\llbracket \mathsf{op} \rrbracket(f(x))(Df(x)(r))))\\
&= (f; \llbracket \mathsf{op} \rrbracket, (f; \llbracket \mathsf{op} \rrbracket, D(f; \llbracket \mathsf{op} \rrbracket))) \in P^f_{\mathbf{real}^m}.
\end{aligned}$$

Similarly, if $(f,(g,h)) \in P^r_{\mathbf{real}^{n_1,\ldots,n_k}}$, then by the chain rule and linear algebra

$$\begin{aligned}
&(f,(g,h)); (\llbracket \mathsf{op} \rrbracket, (\llbracket \overleftarrow{\mathcal{D}}(\mathsf{op})_1 \rrbracket, \llbracket \overleftarrow{\mathcal{D}}(\mathsf{op})_2 \rrbracket)) = (f,(f,(Df)^t)); (\llbracket \mathsf{op} \rrbracket, (\llbracket \mathsf{op} \rrbracket, \llbracket x; y \vdash (D\mathsf{op})^t(x;y) \rrbracket)) =\\
&(f,(f,Df^t)); (\llbracket \mathsf{op} \rrbracket, (\llbracket \mathsf{op} \rrbracket, (D\llbracket \mathsf{op} \rrbracket)^t)) = (f; \llbracket \mathsf{op} \rrbracket, (f; \llbracket \mathsf{op} \rrbracket, x \mapsto v \mapsto Df^t(x)(D\llbracket \mathsf{op} \rrbracket^t(f(x))(v)))) =\\
&(f; \llbracket \mathsf{op} \rrbracket, (f; \llbracket \mathsf{op} \rrbracket, x \mapsto v \mapsto (Df(x); D\llbracket \mathsf{op} \rrbracket(f(x)))^t(v))) = (f; \llbracket \mathsf{op} \rrbracket, (f; \llbracket \mathsf{op} \rrbracket, (D(f; \llbracket \mathsf{op} \rrbracket))^t)) \in P^r_{\mathbf{real}^m}.
\end{aligned}$$

Consequently, we obtain our Cartesian closed functors $(\!|-|\!)^f$ and $(\!|-|\!)^r$.

Further, observe that $\Sigma_{\llbracket - \rrbracket} \llbracket - \rrbracket(t_1, t_2) \overset{\mathrm{def}}{=} (\llbracket t_1 \rrbracket, \llbracket t_2 \rrbracket)$ defines a Cartesian closed functor $\Sigma_{\llbracket - \rrbracket} \llbracket - \rrbracket : \Sigma_{\mathbf{CSyn}} \mathbf{LSyn} \to \Sigma_{\mathbf{Diff}} \mathbf{Diff_{CM}}$. Similarly, we get a Cartesian closed functor $\Sigma_{\llbracket - \rrbracket} \llbracket - \rrbracket^{op} : \Sigma_{\mathbf{CSyn}} \mathbf{LSyn}^{op} \to \Sigma_{\mathbf{Diff}} \mathbf{Diff_{CM}}^{op}$. As a consequence, the two squares below commute.

$$\begin{array}{ccc}
\mathbf{Syn} & \xrightarrow{(\mathrm{id}, \overrightarrow{\mathcal{D}})} & \mathbf{Syn} \times \Sigma_{\mathbf{CSyn}} \mathbf{LSyn}\\
{\scriptstyle (\!|-|\!)^f} \downarrow & & \downarrow {\scriptstyle \llbracket - \rrbracket \times \Sigma_{\llbracket - \rrbracket} \llbracket - \rrbracket}\\
\overrightarrow{\mathbf{SScone}} & \xrightarrow[\pi_1]{} & \mathbf{Diff} \times \Sigma_{\mathbf{Diff}} \mathbf{Diff_{CM}}
\end{array}
\qquad
\begin{array}{ccc}
\mathbf{Syn} & \xrightarrow{(\mathrm{id}, \overleftarrow{\mathcal{D}})} & \mathbf{Syn} \times \Sigma_{\mathbf{CSyn}} \mathbf{LSyn}^{op}\\
{\scriptstyle (\!|-|\!)^r} \downarrow & & \downarrow {\scriptstyle \llbracket - \rrbracket \times \Sigma_{\llbracket - \rrbracket} \llbracket - \rrbracket^{op}}\\
\overleftarrow{\mathbf{SScone}} & \xrightarrow[\pi_1]{} & \mathbf{Diff} \times \Sigma_{\mathbf{Diff}} \mathbf{Diff_{CM}}^{op}.
\end{array}$$

Indeed, going around the squares in both directions define Cartesian closed functors that agree on their action on $\mathbf{real}^n$ and all operations op. So, by the universal property of $\mathbf{Syn}$, they must coincide. In particular, $(\llbracket t \rrbracket, (\llbracket \overrightarrow{\mathcal{D}}(t)_1 \rrbracket, \llbracket \overrightarrow{\mathcal{D}}(t)_2 \rrbracket))$ is a morphism in $\overrightarrow{\mathbf{SScone}}$ and therefore respects the logical relations P^f for any well-typed term t of the source language of §3. Similarly, $(\llbracket t \rrbracket, (\llbracket \overleftarrow{\mathcal{D}}(t)_1 \rrbracket, \llbracket \overleftarrow{\mathcal{D}}(t)_2 \rrbracket))$ is a morphism in $\overleftarrow{\mathbf{SScone}}$ and therefore respects the logical relations P^r.

Most of the work is now in place to show correctness of AD. We finish the proof below. To ease notation, we work with terms in a context with a single type. Doing so is not a restriction as our language has products, and the theorem holds for arbitrary terms between first-order types.

Theorem 1 (Correctness of AD). *For programs $x : \tau \vdash t : \sigma$ between first-order types τ and σ,*

$$\llbracket \overrightarrow{\mathcal{D}}(t)_1 \rrbracket = \llbracket t \rrbracket \qquad \llbracket \overrightarrow{\mathcal{D}}(t)_2 \rrbracket = D\llbracket t \rrbracket \qquad \llbracket \overleftarrow{\mathcal{D}}(t)_1 \rrbracket = \llbracket t \rrbracket \qquad \llbracket \overleftarrow{\mathcal{D}}(t)_2 \rrbracket = D\llbracket t \rrbracket^t,$$

where we write D and $(-)^t$ for the usual calculus derivative and matrix transpose.

Proof (sketch, see [36, Appx. B] for details). To show that $\llbracket \overrightarrow{\mathcal{D}}(t)_1 \rrbracket(x) = \llbracket t \rrbracket(x)$ and $\llbracket \overrightarrow{\mathcal{D}}(t)_2 \rrbracket(x)(v) = D\llbracket t \rrbracket(x)(v)$, we choose a smooth curve $\gamma : \mathbb{R} \to \llbracket \tau \rrbracket$ such that $\gamma(0) = 0$ and $D\gamma(0)(1) = v$ and use that t respects the logical relations P^f.

To show that $\llbracket \overleftarrow{\mathcal{D}}(t)_1 \rrbracket(x) = \llbracket t \rrbracket(x)$ and $\llbracket \overleftarrow{\mathcal{D}}(t)_2 \rrbracket(x)(v) = D\llbracket t \rrbracket(x)^t(v)$, we choose smooth curves $\gamma_i : \mathbb{R} \to \llbracket \tau \rrbracket$ such that $\gamma_i(0) = x$ and $\gamma_i(0)(1) = e_i$, for all standard basis vectors e_i of $\llbracket \overleftarrow{\mathcal{D}}(\tau)_2 \rrbracket \cong \mathbb{R}^N$. It now follows that $\llbracket \overleftarrow{\mathcal{D}}(t)_1 \rrbracket(x) = \llbracket t \rrbracket(x)$ and $e_i \bullet \llbracket \overleftarrow{\mathcal{D}}(t)_2 \rrbracket(x)(v) = e_i \bullet D\llbracket t \rrbracket(x)^t(v)$ as t respects the logical relations P^r. □

$$\frac{\Gamma \vdash t : \mathbf{Dom}(\mathsf{lop}) \quad (\mathsf{lop} \in \mathsf{LOp}^m_{n_1,\ldots,n_k;n'_1,\ldots,n'_l})}{\Gamma \vdash \mathsf{lop}(t) : \mathbf{LFun}(\mathbf{LDom}(\mathsf{lop}), \mathbf{real}^m)} \quad \frac{}{\Gamma \vdash \underline{0}_\tau : \tau} \quad \frac{\Gamma \vdash t : \tau \quad \Gamma \vdash s : \tau}{\Gamma \vdash t +_\tau s : \tau}$$

$$\frac{}{\Gamma \vdash \mathbf{lid} : \mathbf{LFun}(\tau, \tau)} \quad \frac{\Gamma \vdash t : \mathbf{LFun}(\tau, \sigma) \quad \Gamma \vdash s : \mathbf{LFun}(\sigma, \rho)}{\Gamma \vdash t ; s : \mathbf{LFun}(\tau, \rho)} \quad \frac{\Gamma \vdash t : \mathbf{LFun}(\tau, \sigma) \quad \Gamma \vdash s : \tau}{\Gamma \vdash \mathbf{lapp}(t, s) : \sigma}$$

$$\frac{\Gamma \vdash t : \tau \to \mathbf{LFun}(\sigma, \rho)}{\Gamma \vdash \mathbf{lswap}\, t : \mathbf{LFun}(\sigma, \tau \to \rho)} \quad \frac{\Gamma \vdash t : \tau}{\Gamma \vdash \mathbf{leval}_t : \mathbf{LFun}(\tau \to \sigma, \sigma)}$$

$$\frac{\Gamma \vdash t : \tau}{\Gamma \vdash \{(t, -)\} : \mathbf{LFun}(\sigma, \mathbf{Tens}(\tau, \sigma))} \quad \frac{\Gamma \vdash t : \tau \to \mathbf{LFun}(\sigma, \rho)}{\Gamma \vdash \mathbf{lcur}^{-1} t : \mathbf{LFun}(\mathbf{Tens}(\tau, \sigma), \rho)} \quad \frac{}{\Gamma \vdash \mathbf{lfst} : \mathbf{LFun}(\tau * \sigma, \tau)}$$

$$\frac{}{\Gamma \vdash \mathbf{lsnd} : \mathbf{LFun}(\tau * \sigma, \sigma)} \quad \frac{\Gamma \vdash t : \mathbf{LFun}(\tau, \sigma) \quad \Gamma \vdash s : \mathbf{LFun}(\tau, \rho)}{\Gamma \vdash \mathbf{lpair}(t, s) : \mathbf{LFun}(\tau, \sigma * \rho)}$$

Fig. 5. Typing rules for the applied target language, to extend the source language.

9 Practical Relevance and Implementation

Popular functional languages, such as Haskell and O'Caml, do not natively support linear types. As such, the transformations described in this paper may seem hard to implement. However, as we summarize in this section (and detail in [36, Appx. C]), we can easily implement the limited linear types needed for the transformations as abstract data types by using merely a basic module system.

Specifically, we consider, as an alternative, applied target language for our transformations, the extension of the source language of §3 with the terms and types of Fig. 5. We can define a faithful translation $(-)^\dagger$ from our linear target language of §4 to this language: define $(!\tau \otimes \underline{\sigma})^\dagger \stackrel{\text{def}}{=} \mathbf{Tens}(\tau^\dagger, \underline{\sigma}^\dagger)$, $(\underline{\tau} \multimap \underline{\sigma})^\dagger \stackrel{\text{def}}{=} \mathbf{LFun}(\underline{\tau}^\dagger, \underline{\sigma}^\dagger)$, $(\underline{\mathbf{real}}^n)^\dagger \stackrel{\text{def}}{=} \mathbf{real}^n$ and extend $(-)^\dagger$ structurally recursively, letting it preserve all other type formers. We then translate $(x_1 : \tau, \ldots, x_n : \tau; y : \underline{\sigma} \vdash t : \underline{\rho})^\dagger \stackrel{\text{def}}{=} x_1 : \tau^\dagger, \ldots, x_n : \tau^\dagger \vdash t^\dagger : (\underline{\sigma} \multimap \underline{\rho})^\dagger$ and $(x_1 : \tau, \ldots, x_n : \tau \vdash t : \sigma)^\dagger \stackrel{\text{def}}{=} x_1 : \tau^\dagger, \ldots, x_n : \tau^\dagger \vdash t^\dagger : \sigma^\dagger$. We believe an interested reader can fill in the details. This exhibits the linear target language as a sublanguage of the applied target language. The applied target language merely collapses the distinction between linear and Cartesian types and it adds the constructs $\mathbf{lapp}(t, s)$ for practical usability and to ensure that our adequacy result below is meaningful.

We can implement the API of Fig. 5 as a module that defines the abstract types $\mathbf{LFun}(\tau, \sigma)$, under the hood implemented as a plain function type $\tau \to \sigma$, and $\mathbf{Tens}(\tau, \sigma)$, which is implemented as lists of pairs $\mathbf{List}(\tau * \sigma)$. Then, the required terms of Fig. 5 can be implemented as follows, using standard idiom $[\,]$, $t :: s$, $\mathbf{fold}\, op\, \mathbf{over}\, x\, \mathbf{in}\, t\, \mathbf{from}\, acc = init$ for empty lists, cons-ing, and folding:

$$\underline{0}_1 = \langle\rangle \quad t +_1 s = \langle\rangle \quad \underline{0}_{\underline{\tau} * \underline{\sigma}} = \langle \underline{0}_{\underline{\tau}}, \underline{0}_{\underline{\sigma}} \rangle \quad t +_{\underline{\tau} * \underline{\sigma}} s = \langle \mathbf{fst}\, t +_{\underline{\tau}} \mathbf{fst}\, s, \mathbf{snd}\, t +_{\underline{\sigma}} \mathbf{snd}\, s \rangle$$

$$\underline{0}_{\tau \to \underline{\sigma}} = \lambda\_.\underline{0}_{\underline{\sigma}} \quad t +_{\tau \to \underline{\sigma}} s = \lambda x. t\, x +_{\underline{\sigma}} s\, x \quad \underline{0}_{\mathbf{LFun}(\tau, \underline{\sigma})} = \lambda\_.\underline{0}_{\underline{\sigma}} \quad t +_{\mathbf{LFun}(\tau, \underline{\sigma})} s = \lambda x. t\, x +_{\underline{\sigma}} s\, x$$

$$\underline{0}_{\mathbf{Tens}(\tau, \sigma)} \stackrel{\text{def}}{=} [\,] \quad t +_{\mathbf{Tens}(\tau, \sigma)} s \stackrel{\text{def}}{=} \mathbf{fold}\, x :: acc\, \mathbf{over}\, x\, \mathbf{in}\, t\, \mathbf{from}\, acc = s$$

$$\mathbf{lid} \stackrel{\text{def}}{=} \lambda x. x \quad t ; s \stackrel{\text{def}}{=} \lambda x. s\, (t\, x) \quad \mathbf{lapp}(t, s) \stackrel{\text{def}}{=} t\, s \quad \mathbf{lswap}\, t \stackrel{\text{def}}{=} \lambda x. \lambda y. t\, y\, x \quad \mathbf{leval}_t \stackrel{\text{def}}{=} \lambda x. x\, t$$

$$\{(t,-)\} \stackrel{\text{def}}{=} \lambda x.\langle t, x\rangle :: [\,] \quad \mathbf{lcur}^{-1} t \stackrel{\text{def}}{=} \lambda z.\mathbf{fold}\, t\, (\mathbf{fst}\, x)\, (\mathbf{snd}\, x) + acc\, \mathbf{over}\, x\, \mathbf{in}\, z\, \mathbf{from}\, acc = \underline{0}$$

$$\mathbf{lfst} \stackrel{\text{def}}{=} \lambda x.\mathbf{fst}\, x \quad \mathbf{lsnd} \stackrel{\text{def}}{=} \lambda x.\mathbf{snd}\, x \quad \mathbf{lpair}(t,s) \stackrel{\text{def}}{=} \lambda x.\langle t\, x, s\, x\rangle$$

Our denotational semantics extends to this applied target language and is adequate with respect to the operational semantics induced by the suggested implementation. Further, our correctness proofs of the induced source-code translations also transfer to this applied setting, and they can be usefully phrased as manual, extensible logical relations proofs. As an application, we can extend our source language with higher-order primitives, like $\mathbf{map} \in \mathbf{Syn}((\mathbf{real} \to \mathbf{real}) {*} \mathbf{real}^n, \mathbf{real}^n)$ to "map" functions over the black-box arrays $\mathbf{real}^n$. Then, our proofs extend to show that their correct forward and reverse derivatives are

$$\overrightarrow{\mathcal{D}}(\mathbf{map})_1(f,v) \stackrel{\text{def}}{=} \mathbf{map}(f;\mathbf{fst}\,, v) \quad \overrightarrow{\mathcal{D}}(\mathbf{map})_2(f,v)(g,w) \stackrel{\text{def}}{=} \mathbf{map}\, g\, v + \mathbf{zipWith}(f;\mathbf{snd}\,)\, v\, w$$
$$\overleftarrow{\mathcal{D}}(\mathbf{map})_1(f,v) \stackrel{\text{def}}{=} \mathbf{map}(f;\mathbf{fst}\,, v) \quad \overleftarrow{\mathcal{D}}(\mathbf{map})_2(f,v)(w) \quad \stackrel{\text{def}}{=} \langle \mathbf{zip}\, v\, w, \mathbf{zipWith}\,(f;\mathbf{snd}\,)\, v\, w\rangle,$$

where we use the standard functional programming idiom **zip** and **zipWith**. Here, we can operate directly on the internal representations of $\mathbf{LFun}(\tau,\sigma)$ and $\mathbf{Tens}(\tau,\sigma)$, as the definitions of derivatives of primitives live inside our module.

10 Related and Future Work

Related work This work is closely related to [20], which introduced a similar semantic correctness proof for a version of forward-mode AD, using a subsconing construction. A major difference is that this paper also phrases and proves correctness of reverse-mode AD on a λ-calculus and relates reverse-mode to forward-mode AD. Using a syntactic logical relations proof instead, [5] also proves correctness of forward-mode AD. Again, it does not address reverse AD.

[11] proposes a similar construction to that of §6, and it relates it to the differential λ-calculus. This paper develops sophisticated axiomatics for semantic reverse differentiation. However, it neither relates the semantics to a source-code transformation, nor discusses differentiation of higher-order functions. Our construction of differentiation with a (biadditive) linear target language might remind the reader of differential linear logic [15]. In differential linear logic, (forward) differentiation is a first-class operation in a (biadditive) linear language. By contrast, in our treatment, differentiation is a meta-operation.

Importantly, [16] describes and implements what are essentially our source-code transformations, though they were restricted to first-order functions and scalars. [37] sketches an extension of the reverse-mode transformation to higher-order functions in essentially the same way as proposed in this paper. It does not motivate or derive the algorithm or show its correctness. Nevertheless, this short paper discusses important practical considerations for implementing the algorithm, and it discusses a dependently typed variant of the algorithm.

Next, there are various lines of work relating to correctness of reverse-mode AD that we consider less similar to our work. For example, [28] define and prove correct a formulation of reverse-mode AD on a higher-order language that depends on a non-standard operational semantics, essentially a form of symbolic execution. [2] does something similar for reverse-mode AD on a first-order language extended with conditionals and iteration. [8] defines an AD algorithm in a simply typed λ-calculus with linear negation (essentially, the continuation-based AD of [20]) and proves it correct using operational techniques. Further, they show that this algorithm corresponds to reverse-mode AD under a non-standard operational semantics (with the "linear factoring rule"). These formulations of reverse-mode AD all depend on non-standard run-times and fall into the category of "define-by-run" formulations of reverse-mode AD. Meanwhile, we are concerned with "define-then-run" formulations: source-code transformations producing differentiated code at compile-time, which can then be optimized during compilation with existing compiler tool-chains.

Finally, there is a long history of work on reverse-mode AD, though almost none of it applies the technique to higher-order functions. A notable exception is [31], which gives an impressive source-code transformation implementation of reverse AD in Scheme. While very efficient, this implementation crucially uses mutation. Moreover, the transformation is complex and correctness is not considered. More recently, [38] describes a much simpler implementation of a reverse AD code transformation, again very performant. However, the transformation is quite different from the one considered in this paper as it relies on a combination of delimited continuations and mutable state. Correctness is not considered, perhaps because of the semantic complexities introduced by impurity.

Our work adds to the existing literature by presenting (to our knowledge) the first principled and pure define-then-run reverse AD algorithm for a higher-order language, by arguing its practical applicability, and by proving semantic correctness of the algorithm.

Future work We plan to build a practical, verified AD library based on the methods introduced in this paper. This will involve calculating the derivative of many first- and higher-order primitives according to our method.

Next, we aim to extend our method to other expressive language features. We conjecture that the method extends to source languages with variant and inductive types as long as one makes the target language a linear dependent type theory [10,34]. Indeed, the dimension of (co)tangent spaces to a disjoint union of spaces depends on the choice of base point. The required colimits to interpret such types in $\Sigma_{\mathcal{C}}\mathcal{L}$ and $\Sigma_{\mathcal{C}}\mathcal{L}^{op}$ should exist by standard results about arrow and container categories [3]. We are hopeful that the method can also be made to apply to source languages with general recursion by calculating the derivative of fixpoint combinators similarly to our calculation for **map**. The correctness proof will then rely on a domain theoretic generalisation of our techniques [35].

Acknowledgements This project has received funding from the European Union's Horizon 2020 research and innovation programme under the Marie Skłodowska-Curie grant agreement No. 895827. We thank Michael Betancourt, Philip de Bruin, Bob Carpenter, Mathieu Huot, Danny de Jong, Ohad Kammar, Gabriele Keller, Pieter Knops, Curtis Chin Jen Sem, Amir Shaikhha, Tom Smeding, and Sam Staton for helpful discussions about automatic differentiation.

References

1. Abadi, M., Barham, P., Chen, J., Chen, Z., Davis, A., Dean, J., Devin, M., Ghemawat, S., Irving, G., Isard, M., et al.: Tensorflow: A system for large-scale machine learning. In: 12th USENIX Symposium on Operating Systems Design and Implementation (OSDI 16). pp. 265–283 (2016)
2. Abadi, M., Plotkin, G.D.: A simple differentiable programming language. In: Proc. POPL 2020. ACM (2020)
3. Abbott, M., Altenkirch, T., Ghani, N.: Categories of containers. In: International Conference on Foundations of Software Science and Computation Structures. pp. 23–38. Springer (2003)
4. Barber, A., Plotkin, G.: Dual intuitionistic linear logic. University of Edinburgh, Department of Computer Science, Laboratory for Foundations of Computer Science (1996)
5. Barthe, G., Crubillé, R., Lago, U.D., Gavazzo, F.: On the versatility of open logical relations: Continuity, automatic differentiation, and a containment theorem. In: Proc. ESOP 2020. Springer (2020), to appear
6. Benton, P.N.: A mixed linear and non-linear logic: Proofs, terms and models. In: International Workshop on Computer Science Logic. pp. 121–135. Springer (1994)
7. Blute, R., Ehrhard, T., Tasson, C.: A convenient differential category. Cahiers de topologie et géométrie différentielle catégoriques **53**(3), 211–232 (2012)
8. Brunel, A., Mazza, D., Pagani, M.: Backpropagation in the simply typed lambda-calculus with linear negation. In: Proc. POPL 2020 (2020)
9. Carpenter, B., Hoffman, M.D., Brubaker, M., Lee, D., Li, P., Betancourt, M.: The Stan math library: Reverse-mode automatic differentiation in C++. arXiv preprint arXiv:1509.07164 (2015)
10. Cervesato, I., Pfenning, F.: A linear logical framework. Information and Computation **179**(1), 19–75 (2002)
11. Cockett, J.R.B., Cruttwell, G.S.H., Gallagher, J., Lemay, J.S.P., MacAdam, B., Plotkin, G.D., Pronk, D.: Reverse derivative categories. In: Proc. CSL 2020 (2020)
12. Curien, P.L.: Categorical combinators. Information and Control **69**(1-3), 188–254 (1986)
13. Curien, P.L.: Typed categorical combinatory logic. In: Colloquium on Trees in Algebra and Programming. pp. 157–172. Springer (1985)
14. Egger, J., Møgelberg, R.E., Simpson, A.: Enriching an effect calculus with linear types. In: International Workshop on Computer Science Logic. pp. 240–254. Springer (2009)
15. Ehrhard, T.: An introduction to differential linear logic: proof-nets, models and antiderivatives. Mathematical Structures in Computer Science **28**(7), 995–1060 (2018)
16. Elliott, C.: The simple essence of automatic differentiation. Proceedings of the ACM on Programming Languages **2**(ICFP), 70 (2018)
17. Fiore, M.P.: Differential structure in models of multiplicative biadditive intuitionistic linear logic. In: International Conference on Typed Lambda Calculi and Applications. pp. 163–177. Springer (2007)
18. Frölicher, A.: Smooth structures. In: Category theory. pp. 69–81. Springer (1982)
19. Frölicher, A.: Linear spaces and differentiation theory. Pure and Applied Mathematics (1988)
20. Huot, M., Staton, S., Vákár, M.: Correctness of automatic differentiation via diffeologies and categorical gluing. In: Proc. FoSSaCS (2020)

21. Iglesias-Zemmour, P.: Diffeology. American Mathematical Soc. (2013)
22. Innes, M.: Don't unroll adjoint: differentiating SSA-Form programs. arXiv preprint arXiv:1810.07951 (2018)
23. Johnstone, P.T.: Sketches of an elephant: A topos theory compendium, vol. 2. Oxford University Press (2002)
24. Johnstone, P.T., Lack, S., Sobocinski, P.: Quasitoposes, quasiadhesive categories and Artin glueing. In: Proc. CALCO 2007 (2007)
25. Kock, A.: Synthetic differential geometry, vol. 333. Cambridge University Press (2006)
26. Lambek, J., Scott, P.J.: Introduction to higher-order categorical logic, vol. 7. Cambridge University Press (1988)
27. Levy, P.B.: Call-by-push-value: A Functional/imperative Synthesis, vol. 2. Springer Science & Business Media (2012)
28. Mak, C., Ong, L.: A differential-form pullback programming language for higher-order reverse-mode automatic differentiation (2020), arxiv:2002.08241
29. Mellies, P.A.: Categorical semantics of linear logic. Panoramas et syntheses **27**, 15–215 (2009)
30. Paszke, A., Gross, S., Chintala, S., Chanan, G., Yang, E., DeVito, Z., Lin, Z., Desmaison, A., Antiga, L., Lerer, A.: Automatic differentiation in pytorch (2017)
31. Pearlmutter, B.A., Siskind, J.M.: Reverse-mode AD in a functional framework: Lambda the ultimate backpropagator. ACM Transactions on Programming Languages and Systems (TOPLAS) **30**(2), 7 (2008)
32. Shaikhha, A., Fitzgibbon, A., Vytiniotis, D., Peyton Jones, S.: Efficient differentiable programming in a functional array-processing language. Proceedings of the ACM on Programming Languages **3**(ICFP), 97 (2019)
33. Souriau, J.M.: Groupes différentiels. In: Differential geometrical methods in mathematical physics, pp. 91–128. Springer (1980)
34. Vákár, M.: A categorical semantics for linear logical frameworks. In: International Conference on Foundations of Software Science and Computation Structures. pp. 102–116. Springer (2015)
35. Vákár, M.: Denotational correctness of forward-mode automatic differentiation for iteration and recursion. arXiv preprint arXiv:2007.05282 (2020)
36. Vákár, M.: Reverse ad at higher types: Pure, principled and denotationally correct (full version). arXiv preprint arXiv:2007.05283 (2020)
37. Vytiniotis, D., Belov, D., Wei, R., Plotkin, G., Abadi, M.: The differentiable curry (2019)
38. Wang, F., Wu, X., Essertel, G., Decker, J., Rompf, T.: Demystifying differentiable programming: Shift/reset the penultimate backpropagator. Proceedings of the ACM on Programming Languages **3**(ICFP) (2019)

Sound and Complete Concolic Testing for Higher-order Functions

Shu-Hung You[✉], Robert Bruce Findler, and Christos Dimoulas

Northwestern University, Evanston, IL, USA
shu-hung.you@eecs.northwestern.edu, robby@cs.northwestern.edu, chrdimo@northwestern.edu

Abstract. Higher-order functions have become a staple of modern programming languages. However, such values stymie concolic testers, as the SMT solvers at their hearts are inherently first-order.
This paper lays a formal foundations for concolic testing higher-order functional programs. Three ideas enable our results: (i) our tester considers only program inputs in a canonical form; (ii) it collects novel constraints from the evaluation of the canonical inputs to search the space of inputs with partial help from an SMT solver and (iii) it collects constraints from canonical inputs even when they are arguments to concretized calls. We prove that (i) concolic evaluation is sound with respect to concrete evaluation; (ii) modulo concretization and SMT solver incompleteness, the search for a counter-example succeeds if a user program has a bug and (iii) this search amounts to directed evolution of inputs targeting hard-to-reach corners of the program.

1 Introduction

Concolic testing [8, 20] allows symbolic evaluation to leverage concrete inputs as it attempts to uncover bugs. The role of concrete inputs is twofold. First, they help symbolic evaluation focus on one control-flow path at a time, thus allowing the exploration of the behavior of a user program in an incremental and directed fashion. Second, they enable concretization, permitting symbolic evaluation to seamlessly switch to concrete evaluation and back, thus facilitating interoperability with external libraries. Testament to the success of concolic testing is adaptations to a gamut of linguistic, platform and application settings [3, 6, 7, 12, 14, 15, 17, 21, 22, 23, 25, 29, 30, 35, 37, 38, 39, 41, 43].

However, concolic testers' generation of inputs hinges on the power of SMT solvers. That is, at the end of a run of a user program, the concolic tester constructs a formula whose solution determines the next input. Alas, SMT solvers largely deal with first-order formulas that cannot capture higher-order properties of inputs. As a result, existing concolic testers struggle with JavaScript, Python or Racket components whose inputs are often higher-order functions and fall back to incomplete approximations [17, 28, 31, 36].

The **goal of this paper** is to introduce provably correct foundations that lift concolic testing to the world of higher-order functions.

N. Yoshida (Ed.): ESOP 2021, LNCS 12648, pp. 635-663, 2021.
https://doi.org/10.1007/978-3-030-72019-3_23

```
call-twice = λf. let i = f (equals 2) in          error-trigger =
                 let j = f (equals 30) in           λg. (cond [(g 2) 12]
                 let k = f (equals 7) in                      [(g 30) 5]
                 (cond [!(i = 12) 1]                          [else -2])
                       [!(j = 5) 2]
                       [!(k = -2) 3]
                       [else error])
```

Figure 1: One Argument Call Is Not Enough; Example & Error-Triggering Input

There are three interdependent challenges for the design of a correct higher-order concolic tester. First, a higher-order concolic tester needs to be able to generate sufficiently complex function inputs to explore the behavior of a user program. Even in simple higher-order programs, this set of inputs includes functions with sophisticated structure. The left-hand side of figure 1 displays one such program, `call-twice`. It consumes a higher-order function **f** that when given a predicate on numbers returns a number. It calls **f** with three different predicates that return true if their input is `2`, `30` and `7` respectively. If the result of any of these calls is different than a specific number, `call-twice` terminates successfully; otherwise `call-twice` errors. Hence, only a fine-tuned input can make `call-twice` error. In particular, it has to be a function that calls its argument at least twice with different numbers and returns the right result in each case, like the counterexample on the right-hand side of the figure.

The second challenge is that a higher-order concolic tester needs to be able to generate structurally complex function inputs in a directed manner. Specifically, to preserve the character of first-order concolic testing, a higher-order concolic tester must start with a default input that evolves, with each run of the user program and the help of an SMT solver, to a new input that aims to exercise a previously unexplored region of the program. Returning to the example from figure 1, a higher-order concolic tester should start from a simple **f** such as a constant function and then use hints from the evaluation of the example to add appropriate calls inside **f** that call **f**'s argument, targeting the last branch of `call-twice`'s `cond` expression.

```
date< = λd1. λd2. (or ((date-year d1) < (date-year d2))
                      ((date-month d1) < (date-month d2))
                      ((date-day d1) < (date-day d2)))
main = λdates. (let sorted-dates = (sort dates date<) in ···)
```

Figure 2: Broken Argument for a Library Function.

The third challenge is that, in a higher-order setting, concretization demands that the concolic tester is ready to concretize any call to a higher-order function. For example the `main` function in figure 2 takes as input a list of dates, calls `sort` with the comparison function `date<` and expects the results to be lexicographically sorted (as there are many reasons why sorting is necessary we leave the details to the imagination of the reader). If `sort` is a library function whose implementation is inaccessible, then the concolic tester has to concretize the call to `sort` and disable symbolic evaluation for the extent of that call. Unfortunately, `date<` does not implement the lexicographical order and discovering this requires the concolic tester to track symbolically the flow of values in and out of `date<` in order to generate a list of dates that exhibits the bug. In other words, the concolic tester should be able to perform "partial" concretization so that `date<` interacts with `sort` in a concrete manner while the the evaluation of `date<` still produces the symbolic information the tester needs.

Our paper contributes the first formal model for a concolic tester for higher-order functions that meets all three challenges:

1. Inspired by the function application rules of unknown symbolic values in higher-order symbolic evaluation [32, 33], we construct a novel set of canonical functions that the concolic tester uses to generate inputs. We prove that if a higher-order program under test errors for some input, there is a canonical input that triggers an error too (representation completeness).
2. We devise input constraints to record at runtime facts about the structure of the generated function inputs separately from the first-order control flow path formulas from the symbolic evaluation of the user program. We specify an input evolution process that captures how the concolic tester can use input constraints to iteratively search through the space of canonical functions with the help of an SMT solver. We establish that, relative to the completeness of the solver, the concolic tester can always start with a default input and, through evolution, generate a counter-example, if one exists (search completeness). Furthermore the input evolution is directed by the input constraints that the concolic tester collects (directness).
3. Building on top of higher-order contracts [16], we develop concretization that employs wrappers around higher-order functions that are consumed by library and other inaccessible code. The wrappers allow the concolic tester to maintain control of function inputs and evaluate their bodies symbolically while producing concrete values when they interact with code that the concolic tester does not control. We prove that, in the presence of concretization, the search for the bug is not complete but the concolic tester still evaluates user programs consistently with respect to concrete evaluation (soundness).

The remainder of the paper is organized as follows. Section 2 gives an in depth by-example presentation of our approach to higher-order concolic testing. Section 3 presents our formal model and section 4 establishes its correctness properties. Section 5 describes a proof-of-concept implementation of our model that provides evidence that the model is a reasonable basis for the development of effective higher-order testers. Finally, section 6 places our results in the context of related work and section 7 offers some concluding thoughts.

2 Higher-order Concolic Testing by Example

The linguistic setting of our exposition of concolic testing is a small call-by-value dynamically-typed functional language without mutable state. Furthermore, we represent bugs explicitly as the term `error` and assume that user programs come with type-like input specifications.

2.1 First-Order Concolic Execution in a Nutshell

The goal of a concolic tester is to find a value for the inputs to a user program that cause the execution to reach `error`. To do so, the tester runs the user program in a *concolic loop* with a different input for each loop iteration. There are two differences between concolic evaluation and concrete evaluation. To explain them, consider the user program in the left-hand column of figure 3, where **X** represents the numeric input.

(cond
  [(**X**×**X** - **X** - 992 = 0)
   (cond
    [(**X** < 0) error]
    [else 12])]
  [else 11])
	Input:
	X ↦ 0
	Log:
	• cond: (false)
	  ‹**X**×**X** - **X** - 992 = 0›
		Input:
		X ↦ 32
		Log:
		• cond: (true)
		  ‹**X**×**X** - **X** - 992 = 0›
		• cond: (false)
		  ‹**X** < 0›

Figure 3: A First, First-order Concolic Example

The first difference is that, instead of concrete values, concolic evaluation utilizes values of the form ‹**t**›, where **t** is a first-order formula over the input variables that codifies the provenance of the value. Concretely, assume that in the first run of our example program the concolic tester picks the concrete input `0`. Instead of just starting the evaluation of the program by replacing **X** with `0`, the concolic machine keeps an environment that maps **X** to `0` and runs the program with the concolic value ‹**X**› as the input. The concrete counterpart of a concolic value can be computed from the concrete values in the environment and the (first-order) formula **t** at any point during concolic evaluation.

To kick-off concolic evaluation, the concolic machine evaluates the test expression of the outer `cond` of the example. Specifically the primitive operation × detects that its input is ‹**X**› and returns ‹**X**×**X**›. Even though the concrete counterparts of both of these concolic values are `0`, they bear a different relation to the input **X**. The concolic machine proceeds with the rest of the evaluation of the test expression, yielding ‹**X**×**X** - **X** - 992 = 0›. At this point, the concolic machine uses the concrete counterpart of the concolic value and thus decides to follow the "else" branch of the outer `cond`. Hence, the first run does not trigger `error`.

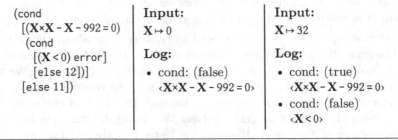

The second characteristic of concolic evaluation are the connections it creates between the inputs and the evaluation of a user program. Specifically, the concolic machine logs the concolic value of the test expressions of cond expressions in the user program in the order they are evaluated; we refer to these entries of the log as *path constraints*. The middle column of figure 3 shows the log (and the inputs) for the run of our example when **X** is 0. Since only one cond expression is evaluated, the log contains a single path constraint that the concrete counterpart of the concolic value ‹**X**×**X** - **X** - 992 = 0› is false, that is the first branch of the cond was not taken. Intuitively, the path constraint connects the evaluation of a cond expression with the input to the program via concolic values. After the first run, the concolic tester asks the SMT solver for an input where **X**×**X** - **X** - 992 = 0 holds, forcing the branch to go the other way. The SMT solver may respond with 32, leading to the run represented in the right-hand column of figure 3. That run again fails to trigger the error, but has a log showing that the first branch of the outer cond was taken this time because **X**×**X** - **X** - 992 = 0 is true. It also has another constraint that indicates that the first branch of the inner cond was not taken because **X** < 0 is false. At this point, the concolic tester can formulate a new SMT problem that requires both **X**×**X** - **X** - 992 = 0 and **X** < 0 to be true. The problem is satisfiable and the SMT solver replies that the new concrete value for **X** should be -31, which uncovers the error.

2.2 From Numbers to Function Inputs

As described so far, concolic testing cannot handle inputs that are not numbers or other data types that SMT solvers understand. The concolic tester relies solely on a solver to generate new inputs and for that it needs to prepare a first-order problem that the solver can solve. Our first insight to surpass this restriction is to split the generation of function inputs into two subproblems:

1. testing programs with first-order function inputs and;
2. testing programs with higher-order function inputs.

As with many problems that involve higher-order functions, the first subproblem is the hard one. The solution for the second subproblem falls out of that for the first one, exploiting the natural co- and contravariance of higher-order functions. So, we first focus on first-order function inputs and we return to higher-order inputs in section 2.5.

The left-hand column in figure 4 shows a program whose input **F** is a first-order function from numbers to numbers. One of the many functions that can trigger error in this example is λ**x**. 2-**x**. However, a key aspect of our approach is recognizing that we care only about the behavior of the input when given 1 and 2. Since the program calls **F** with only those arguments, other arguments are irrelevant. In general, any program that terminates calls its input a finite number times so the concolic tester can model first-order function inputs as functions that look up values from a table, which we represent with a case expression.

As with non-function inputs, the concolic tester starts with the simplest possible function input: λ**x**. (case **x**), as shown in the middle column of figure 4.

(cond [((**F** 1) × 3 = (**F** 2) + 3) error] [else 11])	**Input:** **F** ↦ λ**x**. (case **x**) **Log:** • call: (**F** 1) • call: (**F** 2) • cond: (false) ‹0×3 = 0+3›	**Input:** **F** ↦ λ**x**.(case **x** [1 ‹**Y**›] [2 ‹**Z**›]) **Y** ↦ 0 **Z** ↦ 0 **Log:** • call: (**F** 1) • call: (**F** 2) • cond: (false) ‹**Y**×3 = **Z**+3›

Figure 4: First-order Input

This function looks up its argument in an empty table and returns always 0. If the concolic machine treated this function as a first-order input, it would record that the first branch of cond was not taken because ‹(**F** 1) × 3 = (**F** 2) + 3› is false. This formula, however, involves function symbols which SMT solvers cannot handle when higher-order functions come into play. Thus the concolic machine does not record the constraint and instead simply reduces all applications of **F** en route to the concolic value of the test expression. Unfortunately, this first function input does not help the concolic tester make progress. Since the input returns the constant 0 for any argument, the concolic value of the test loses any connection to **F** and the concolic tester does not have much leverage to adjust **F**'s behavior and affect the evaluation of the program.

To rectify the situation our concolic tester aims to generate a new input with a shape that gives to the tester increased control over **F**'s behavior. The pivotal idea that enables the input evolution process is that the concolic machine logs so called *input constraints*. That is, in addition to the path constraints of the user program, it also records the values that the user program provides to **F**, or any other function input. Back to the example, the evaluation records two input constraints: one for argument 1 and one for 2. The middle column of figure 4 shows the new log entries along with the path constraint from the evaluation of the cond expression.

With the input constraint from the log, the concolic tester can construct a second function input as shown in the right-hand column of figure 4. This new function input has a case expression with two clauses: one for when the argument is 1 and one for when it is 2. Furthermore the concolic tester introduces two fresh input variables **Y** and **Z** as the actions of the two clauses. The initial values for these two new inputs are both 0. However, exactly because the results of the function are input variables rather than mere constants, the concolic tester can configure the values for these inputs to trigger the error with the help of an SMT solver. Specifically, the concolic value of the test of the first branch of the cond expression in the example becomes ‹**Y**×3 = **Z**+3›, as shown in the log. This problem has solutions and the SMT solver discovers that **Y**=1 and **Z**=0 are sufficient to "switch" the evaluation of the conditional, which triggers the error.

In sum, to handle first-order function inputs, the concolic tester starts with the simplest possible function, records input constraints that describe the arguments that the function consumes, uses the constraints to generate a new function that, in turn, introduces fresh inputs, and finally employs the SMT solver to fine-tune the values for these inputs.

As a final remark in this section, function inputs are regular functions that behave like a concrete input would behave. For the concolic machine though, the evaluation of their bodies is a source of new information that powers the subsequent iterations of the concolic loop. This is a key observation for concretization in the our setting. A concolic tester concretizes calls to functions when it cannot evaluate their bodies in a concolic manner. This situation arises when the function comes from an external library, such as `sort` from section 1, and the function's code is not under the control of the concolic machine. In the context of this section, this translates to the situation where the function's body cannot interact with any concolic values nor can its evaluation record path constraints in the log of the machine. A naive solution to the issue is that the concolic machine computes the concrete counterpart of the argument, delegates the call of the function to a concrete machine and then uses the result of the concrete call to proceed. This means, however, that the concolic machine loses any constraints from the evaluation of the body of the argument if the argument is a function itself. Instead, our concolic machine uses a proxy argument for the concrete call that wraps the actual argument. Thus calls to the argument go back to the concolic machine that records all the usual constraints and only concretizes any first-order results the argument produces. We return to our approach to concretization in section 3.3.

2.3 Input Interactions

The previous example supplies a constant number to **F**. However, programs can also supply other, first-order inputs to their function inputs, as in the example in the left-hand column of figure 5.

(cond [((**F X**) × 3 = (**F** (**X**×2)) + 3) error] [else 11])	**Input:** **F** ↦ λ**x**. (case **x**) **X** ↦ 0 **Log:** • call: (**F** ‹**X**›) • call: (**F** ‹**X**×2›) • cond: (false) ‹0×3 = 0+3›	**Input:** **F** ↦ λ**x**.(case **x** [‹**X**› ‹**Y**›] [‹**X**×2› ‹**Z**›]) **X** ↦ 1 **Y** ↦ 0 **Z** ↦ 0 **Log:** • call: (**F** ‹**X**›) • call: (**F** ‹**X**×2›) • cond: (false) ‹**Y**×3 = **Z**+3›

Figure 5: Interacting Inputs

In order to trigger the error in this example, **F** must be able to return different results from its two different calls. However, if the initial concrete value for **X** is 0, the concrete counterparts of the arguments to the calls to **F** are the same for both calls. Thus, if the concolic machine logs only the concrete counterparts of the arguments as part of input constraints, the concolic tester loses the connection between **X** and the values that the user program passes to **F**. Instead, the concolic machine uses the concolic values when logging input constraints. As shown in the log in the middle column of figure 5, the concolic values of the arguments to the two calls to **F** are ‹**X**› and ‹**X**×2›. Thus, the concolic tester can extend the case of **F** with two clauses, one for when the concrete counterpart of the argument of **F** matches that of ‹**X**› and one when it matches that of ‹**X**×2›. The effect of this extension is that any problems the concolic tester sends to the SMT solver contain the additional constraint that **X** and **X**×2 are different. Consequently, in a manner similar to the previous example, the concolic tester eventually uses 1 as the concrete value for **X** and discovers the error. The right-hand column of figure 5 displays this counter-example.

2.4 Blind Extensions Are Not Enough

So far we have seen how the concolic tester uses input constraints and concolic values to extend the case expression of a first-order function input. However, the extension may lead the concolic tester to a dead-end. This is a subtle point that, unfortunately, requires a complex example to illustrate. Figure 6 contains the simplest one we know.

This example is complex enough that it deserves a brief walkthrough. To start, note that it has two inputs, **F**, a function from numbers to numbers, and **X**, a number, and that reaching the error requires that the tests of all of the branches of the cond expression of the example fail. In effect, the condition for triggering error is the conjunction of the four formulas that follow the negations in the example. To confirm that this example does have a error-triggering input, take **X** to be -10 and **F** to be λ**x**. 11 × (**x**+11).

If the concolic tester follows the process described so far in this section, it manages to generate an input that makes the tests of the first three branches of cond to fail. But then, it seems impossible for the concolic tester to extend the input further to make the test of the fourth branch cond succeed. To see how this plays out, the middle column in figure 6 shows the state of the concolic machine after a few iterations of the concolic loop. The concolic tester first runs the example with the default constant zero function as the input, which results in 11 and logs the argument **X** for **F**; the concolic tester then extends the case of **F** with a clause that returns a fresh concolic variable **Y**. It then discovers **Y** must be set to 11 to skip the first branch in the cond expression. For this input, the example produces result 7, failing to also skip the second branch of the cond expression. After another iteration, the concolic tester manages to skip the second branch of cond and generates the input shown in the middle column of figure 6.

```
(cond
  [!(F X=11) 1]
  [!(F 0=121) 7]
  [!(F (X+10)=121) 2]
  [!(X=-10) 9]
  [else error])
```

```
Input:
F ↦                      X↦1
λx.(case x               Z↦121
  [‹X› ‹Y›]              Y↦11
  [0 ‹Z›])

Log:
• call: (F ‹X›)
• cond: (false)
  ‹!(Y=11)›
• call: (F 0)
• cond: (false)
  ‹!(Z=121)›
• call: (F ‹X+10›)
• cond: (true)
  ‹!(0=121)›
```

```
Input:
F ↦                      X↦1
λx.(case x               W↦121
  [‹X› ‹Y›]              Z↦121
  [0 ‹Z›]                Y↦11
  [‹X+10› ‹W›])

Log:
• call: (F ‹X›)
• cond: (false)
  ‹!(Y=11)›
• call: (F 0)
• cond: (false)
  ‹!(Z=121)›
• call: (F ‹X+10›)
• cond: (false)
  ‹!(W=121)›
• cond: (true)
  ‹!(X=-10)›
```

Figure 6: A Complex, Subtle Example

Let us analyze the middle section of the figure to understand the concolic tester's state at this point in the process. The input consists of a function **F** that returns ‹**Y**› when it sees the input ‹**X**›, where **Y** is 11 and returns ‹**Z**› when it sees 0, where **Z** is 121. When we feed this input to the program in the left-hand column, we skip the first and second branches of the cond, because **F** has been tuned to get through them. This part of the execution produces the first four entries in the log. Next the concolic machine arrives at the third branch of the cond and the call (**F** (**X**+10)), which produces the fifth entry in the log. The concrete value of the argument is 11, which has no matching clause in the case of **F** so **F** returns 0, and the program terminates with 2, following the fourth branch as recorded in the last entry in the log.

The straightforward next step is to insist that this third call has its own distinct clause in **F**, meaning the concolic engine asks the solver for a solution to the equations !(**X**=0) and !(0=**X**+10). An input based on the solution to these equations is shown in the third column of figure 6, and it too deserves a careful look. The log is identical up to the last "call" entry so the program evaluates the same to that point. The next entry in the log (second to last) reveals the concolic machine skips the third branch of the cond and thus proceeds with the evaluation of the test **X**=-10 of the fourth branch. Since the value for the input **X** is 1, the machine follows the branch and the program returns 9.

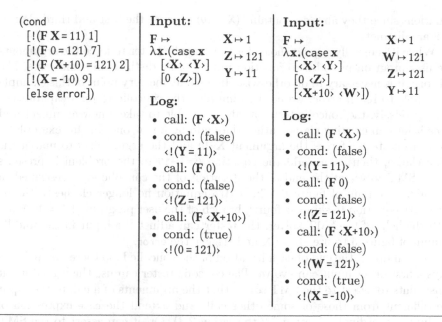

Clearly, since we want the machine to skip the fourth branch too, the tester should present to the solver the same set of equations that lead to the latest input and assert in addition **X**=-10. Unfortunately, there is no solution to these equations since they already contain !(**X** = -10) because the first and third clauses of **F** are distinct.

While it is usually a good choice for the concolic tester to force the arguments the user program provides to function inputs to be distinct, in some cases, like this one, it is necessary to do otherwise. Indeed, at the very point of this example to be able to reach `error`, we need to improve the concolic tester's capabilities. More precisely, the concolic tester needs to be able to take a new argument and force it into an existing clause rather than adding a new one. In this example, if the concolic tester forces the argument **X**+10 and the argument 0 to match the same clause, then it can add the equation 0 = **X**+10 to the problem it presents to the SMT solver at the end of the iteration of the concolic loop described in the middle column of figure 6. This extra equation no longer clashes with the necessary equation to skip the fourth branch of the user program (!(**X** = -10)) and with the help of the SMT solver, the tester can adjust the input in the middle column of figure 6 to use -10 as **X** and trigger the `error`.

To sum up, at the end of each iteration of the concolic loop there are multiple ways a first-order input can evolve. The concolic tester can use the logged input constraints to assert to the SMT solver that the arguments of a call to the input are different from those of some other calls and extend the `case` expression of the input accordingly (section 2.2 to section 2.3). Or, it can assert to the SMT solver that the arguments of two calls to the input are equal (section 2.4). In either case, the concolic tester asks the SMT solver to determine the values of first-order inputs. We revisit formally the evolution of inputs in section 3.2. As a concluding note, we underline that the concolic tester may have to try any number of the possible ways an input can evolve. The strategy the concolic tester uses to prioritize and search the space of these possibilities is out of the scope of this paper. Herein, we focus instead on what the concolic tester can do at each point in the concolic loop and whether a sequence of its choices is guaranteed to reveal a possible `error` in a user program.

2.5 Higher-order Inputs

Handling higher-order inputs, that is functions that consume and/or return other functions, not just numbers, requires a generalization of the ideas in the previous section. However, the seed of the key insight is already there in the way our concolic tester handles first-order function inputs. Intuitively, the tester treats a first-order function input as a source of new, latent inputs that the concolic tester provides to the user program. As we discuss above this is exactly the rationale for the fresh input variables that appear in the actions of the `case` expressions of first-order function inputs.

Contravariantly, when an input consumes a function argument, the tester can simply treat the function argument as a source of further, latent arguments that the user program provides. The input can decide how and when to call its function argument in order to obtain these latent arguments. These function calls, in turn, open up new points where the concolic tester supplies additional inputs to the user program.

```
(cond
  [(G (λx. x+1) + G (λx. x+2) = 9)
   error]
  [else 11])
```

Input:

```
G ↦ λf. ‹X›
```

Input:

```
G ↦ λf. let fY = f ‹Y› in
          (case fY [‹Y+1› ‹X›]
                   [‹Y+2› ‹Z›])
```

Figure 7: Co- & Contravariance at Work

Concretely, consider the left-hand program in figure 7. It has one input, **G**, which consumes a function **f** on numbers and returns a number. As before, the concolic tester starts out by generating the constant zero function. Of course, this does not uncover the `error` so, same as for first-order function inputs, the concolic tester turns to the input constraints in its log. However, the log simply shows that the user program provides **G** with two procedures. Therefore the `case`-expression approach does not apply in a straightforward manner. The concolic tester can change the input **G** to return a fresh input variable **X** as in the middle column of figure 7. Unfortunately, this still does not help trigger the `error`.

While many programming languages offer a certain notion of physical equality for procedures, our approach is for the concolic tester to generate a function **G** that calls its argument **f** and then inspects the result **fY** with a `case` expression as if it was yet another argument to **G**. In this case, **G** calls **f** with a fresh input variable **Y** then binds the result to **fY** which acts as a latent argument that the user program provides to **G**. To account for latent arguments, we generalize input constraints to keep track of variables such as **fY** together with the results of calls to function arguments.

The overall effect is that the concolic tester acquires the vantage point it needs to follow the same process as for first-order function inputs. In particular, the input constraints for **fY** contain the results from calling **f** that in turn are tied to input variable **Y** and thus under the control of the concolic tester. Furthermore, just like for first-order functions, they provide guidance for filling in the clauses of the `case` expression of **G**. Concretely in our example, the input constraints for **fY** record that it is equal to either ‹**Y+1**› or ‹**Y+2**›, which the concolic tester can consider as distinct and, with the help of the SMT solver, generate the **G** on the right-hand side of figure 7 that triggers the `error`, where **X** and **Z** are fresh input variables mapped to `4` and `5` respectively.

Overall, the concolic tester handles function inputs by decomposing them one layer at a time until it ends up with first-order functions. At each point of decomposition, that is when an input calls one of its arguments, the concolic tester introduces fresh input variables and logs input constraints that connect the fresh input variables and the calls' results. Then it keeps track of these connections with input constraints and uses the constraints to fill in the `case` expressions in the bodies of higher-order function inputs. Effectively, this approach entails that the concolic tester considers inputs in a so called canonical form only. Informally, canonical inputs nest `let`-expressions and `case`-expressions. The precise definition of canonical functions and their evolution are the subject of Section 3 along with the rest of the model for higher-order concolic testing.

3 Formalizing Higher-order Concolic Testing

The core of our formal model of higher-order concolic testing is a concolic (abstract) machine that loads and runs user programs, and the input evolution metafunction that generates inputs for the next run.

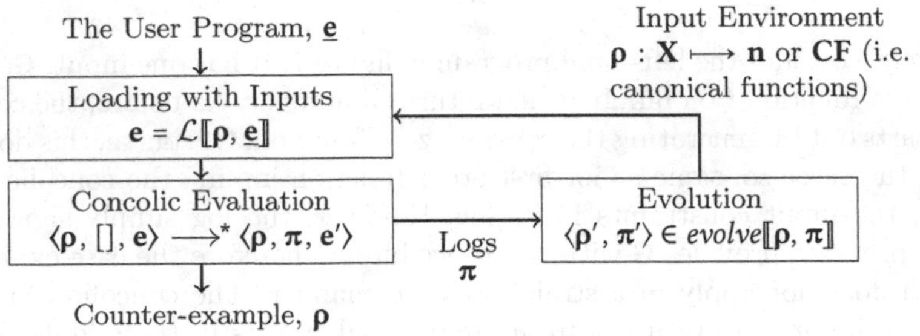

Figure 8: The Full Input Evolution Cycle

Figure 8 depicts how the concolic machine and the input evolution metafunction work together to form the concolic loop. At the beginning of each iteration of the loop, the load metafunction $\mathcal{L}$ consumes the environment $\boldsymbol{\rho}$ that maps each input variable **X** in the user program $\underline{\mathbf{e}}$ to a value and prepares the user program for the concolic machine. The concolic machine evaluates the loaded program, **e**, with the help of two registers: the environment of inputs $\boldsymbol{\rho}$ and the log $\boldsymbol{\pi}$ (that is initially empty). If the result of the evaluation is not an error, the final content of log $\boldsymbol{\pi}$ together with the environment $\boldsymbol{\rho}$ determine how the input evolves. Specifically, the *evolve* metafunction uses them to compute a list of pairs that each contains a new environment of inputs $\boldsymbol{\rho}'$ and a prediction of the contents of the log $\boldsymbol{\pi}'$ of the concolic machine after evaluating the program with $\boldsymbol{\rho}'$. The concolic loop repeats and, with each iteration, explores one more input. When it discovers an error in the user program, the loop terminates and the environment of the error-generating input turns into a concrete counter-example.

Section 3.1 details the concolic machine, section 3.2 formalizes the evolution function and section 3.3 extends the model with concretization.

3.1 From User Programs to Concolic Evaluation

op ::= `!` | `+` | `-` | `×` | `<` | `=` | `integer?` | `procedure?`

$\underline{\mathbf{e}}$ ::= **n** | `error` | **x** | **X** | (λ**x**. $\underline{\mathbf{e}}$) | **op** $\underline{\mathbf{e}}$ | **op** $\underline{\mathbf{e}}$ $\underline{\mathbf{e}}$ | $\underline{\mathbf{e}}$ $\underline{\mathbf{e}}$ | (`cond` [$\underline{\mathbf{e}}$ $\underline{\mathbf{e}}$] ... [`else` $\underline{\mathbf{e}}$])

X, **Y**, **Z**, **F**, **G**, etc., are concolic variables.

Figure 9: The Syntax of User Programs

$$\begin{aligned}
\mathbf{CF} &::= (\lambda \mathbf{x}.\ \mathbf{case_x}) \\
\mathbf{case_x} &::= (\mathsf{case}^{\ell}\ \mathbf{x}) \mid (\mathsf{case}^{\ell}\ \mathbf{x}\ [\mathsf{procedure?}\ \mathbf{e}^{\circ}]^{\ell}\ [\langle \mathbf{t}\rangle\ \mathbf{e}^{\circ}]^{\ell} \ldots) \\
\mathbf{e}^{\circ} &::= \mathbf{v}^{\circ} \mid (\mathsf{let}\ \mathbf{z} = \mathbf{f}\ \mathbf{v}^{\circ}\ \mathsf{in}\ \mathbf{case_z}) \\
\mathbf{v}^{\circ} &::= \mathbf{x} \mid \langle \mathbf{X}\rangle \mid \mathbf{CF}
\end{aligned}$$

Figure 10: Canonical Functions

Figure 9 collects the constructs of the language of user programs, including numbers **n**, error, primitive operators **op** $\underline{\mathbf{e}}$ ..., multi-way conditional expressions cond, and uppercase variables **X**, **Y**, **F**, etc., for the inputs of a user program. These inputs are either numbers or, as we discuss briefly in section 2.5, functions in canonical form. The error construct represents actual bugs in user programs; dynamic type errors manifest themselves as stuck terms.

Figure 10 provides the formal definition of canonical functions. The body of a canonical function with argument **x** is a $\mathbf{case_x}$ expression with zero or more clauses. As we mention in section 2, a $\mathbf{case_x}$ that has no clauses is equivalent to the constant 0. Different than the presentation in section 2 and due to the dynamically-typed nature of our model, the very first clause of every non-empty $\mathbf{case_x}$ always checks whether **x** is a function. If **x** is a function **f**, similar to the discussion in section 2.5, the action $\mathbf{e}^{\circ}$ of the procedure? clause is typically a let expression that applies **f** and inspects the result of the application **z** with yet another case expression.[1] If **x** is a number then the $\mathbf{case_x}$ compares **x** with each of the concolic values ‹**t**› and delegates to the corresponding action $\mathbf{e}^{\circ}$. Similar to the examples of section 2, the argument $\mathbf{v}^{\circ}$ for **f** in a let expression is an input, i.e., a concolic value ‹**X**› where **X** is a fresh concolic variable, or a canonical function. Some goes for the actions $\mathbf{e}^{\circ}$ of a non-procedure? clause of a case expression. However, in these positions the model can also use variables in scope in an attempt to identify a counter-example for a user program with fewer concolic loop iterations, which is helpful when proving the metatheoretical properties of the model. In general, despite their restricted shape, canonical functions can simulate any function input that triggers an error in a user program. We return to this point in section 4.

As a final remark on canonical functions, one important difference from the discussion of function inputs in section 2.5 is that, herein, each case expression comes with labels ℓ. There are two kinds of labels: labels that uniquely identify a case expression and labels that uniquely identify a clause of a case. As we explain further on, their purpose is to allow the concolic tester to analyze the log of the concolic machine after each iteration of the concolic loop to direct the evolution of a canonical function.

Figure 11 shows the complete definition of the concolic machine. As we mention at the beginning of this section, the machine has three registers: the input environment $\boldsymbol{\rho}$ that maps concolic variables **X** to either numbers or canonical functions; the log of constraints $\boldsymbol{\pi}$; and the term **e** the machine evaluates.

[1] We use let $\mathbf{x} = \mathbf{e}_1$ in $\mathbf{e}_2$ as shorthand for $(\lambda \mathbf{x}.\ \mathbf{e}_2)\ \mathbf{e}_1$.

M ::= ⟨**ρ**, **π**, **e**⟩

ρ : **X** ⟼ **n** or **CF**

π ::= [**p**, ...]
p ::= ⟨"R-COND", "FALSE", ‹**t**›⟩ | ⟨"R-COND", "TRUE", ‹**t**›⟩
| ⟨"R-CASE", **ℓ**, **v**, "MISS"⟩ | ⟨"R-CASE", **ℓ**, **v**, "HIT": **ℓ**⟩

t ::= **X** | **n** | !**t** | **op t t**
e ::= ‹**t**› | error | **x** | (λ**x. e**) | **op e** | **op e e** | **e e** | (cond [**e e**] ... [else **e**])
| (case$^{\ell}$ **e**) | (case$^{\ell}$ **e** [procedure? **e**]$^{\ell}$ [‹**t**› **e**]$^{\ell}$ ...)
v ::= (λ**x. e**) | ‹**t**›
E ::= []
| **op E** | **op E e** | **op v E** | **E e** | **v E** | (cond [**E e**] [**e e**] ... [else **e**])
| (case$^{\ell}$ **E**) | (case$^{\ell}$ **E** [procedure? **e**]$^{\ell}$ [‹**t**› **e**]$^{\ell}$ ...)

$\mathcal{L}$: **ρ** $\underline{\mathbf{e}}$ ⟶ **e** (interesting cases)
$\mathcal{L}$⟦**ρ**, **n**⟧ = ‹**n**›
$\mathcal{L}$⟦**ρ**, **X**⟧ = ‹**X**›
where **ρ**(**X**) = **n**
$\mathcal{L}$⟦**ρ**, **F**⟧ = λ**x. case$_{\mathbf{x}}$**
where **ρ**(**F**) = (λ**x. case$_{\mathbf{x}}$**)

$\mathcal{E}$: **ρ t** ⟶ **n**
$\mathcal{E}$⟦**ρ**, **n**⟧ = **n**
$\mathcal{E}$⟦**ρ**, **X**⟧ = **n**
where **ρ**(**X**) = **n**
$\mathcal{E}$⟦**ρ**, **op t$_1$** ...⟧ = **n**
where **op** ∈ {!, +, −, ×, <, =},
δ⟦**op**, $\mathcal{E}$⟦**ρ**, **t$_1$**⟧, ...⟧ = **n**

Figure 11: The Concolic Machine and the Evaluation Language

Evaluation terms **e** are user program terms extended with canonical functions and concolic values ‹**t**›. Recall from section 2 that the latter keep track of the provenance of a value as a symbolic first-order formula **t** that an SMT solver can handle. The concrete counterpart of a concolic value can be computed at any point in the evaluation from **t** and the input environment **ρ** of the concolic machine with the simple $\mathcal{E}$ metafunction.

The log, **π**, of the concolic machine collects two kinds of constraints, **p**. Path constraints are either ⟨"R-COND", "FALSE", ‹**t**›⟩ or ⟨"R-COND", "TRUE", ‹**t**›⟩ and are logged by evaluating cond expressions. The first indicates that the test of a branch failed during concolic evaluation; the second that the test succeeded. In either case, the concolic value of the test is ‹**t**› where the symbolic first-order formula **t** codifies the necessary and sufficient condition for the test to succeed.

Input constraints, ⟨"R-CASE", **ℓ**, **v**, "HIT": **ℓ$_i$**⟩ and ⟨"R-CASE", **ℓ**, **v**, "MISS"⟩, are logged by evaluating case expressions in canonical functions. The label **ℓ** associates each input constraint with a case expression in the input environment **ρ**. A ⟨"R-CASE", **ℓ**, **v**, "HIT": **ℓ$_i$**⟩ constraint indicates that the case expression with label **ℓ** given value **v** followed the action of its clause with label **ℓ$_i$**. A ⟨"R-CASE", **ℓ**, **v**, "MISS"⟩ indicates that the case with label **ℓ** given value **v** followed the implicit in our model "else" clause, whose action is the constant 0. Since the first thing a canonical function does when it interacts with the user program is to inspect the value it receives with case, some of the values **v** in input constraints are exactly the values that the user program provides to function inputs and consequently the concolic tester. Others are the results of calls to functions of the user program that higher-order function inputs perform with their `let` expressions, which are also values that the user program provides to the concolic tester as we discuss in section 2.5. Hence the input constraints here supersede the simplified input constraints from section 2.

Since concolic evaluation handles concolic rather than concrete values, the $\mathcal{L}[\![\boldsymbol{\rho}, \underline{\mathbf{e}}]\!]$ metafunction prepares a user program $\underline{\mathbf{e}}$ accordingly for the concolic machine. It traverses $\underline{\mathbf{e}}$ and replaces every integer **n** with ‹**n**›, concolic variables **X** with ‹**X**› if **ρ** maps **X** to an integer and **F** with the actual function if **ρ** maps **F** to a canonical function. Note that $\mathcal{L}$ does not introduce any ‹**F**› since **ρ**(**F**) can be a higher-order function which, in general, SMT solvers have no theory for.

Given a loaded program, the concolic machine operates in accordance with the reduction rules from figure 12. The rules can be divided into four groups. Group SYM implements base-value provenance tracking for primitive operators. For primitive operators that have straightforward SMT formula counterparts, rule [R-TRACE1] produces a concolic value whose formula is formed by the operator and the symbolic provenance of the operands. Otherwise, [R-TRACE2] discards the provenance information of the operands and simply returns the concolic value ‹**n**› where **n** is the concrete result of the operation.

The next group, COND, includes the rules for cond expressions. In general, the concolic machine inspects the concrete counterpart of the value of the test expression in the first clause of a cond determine whether to take or skip a branch. When $\mathcal{E}[\![\boldsymbol{\rho}, \mathbf{t}]\!]$ is non-zero, [R-CONDTRUE] proceeds with the action expression $\mathbf{e}_1$ of the first clause and logs the path constraint ⟨“R-COND”, “TRUE”, ‹**t**›⟩. When $\mathcal{E}[\![\boldsymbol{\rho}, \mathbf{t}]\!]$ is zero, rule [R-CONDFALSE] drops the first clause of the cond and appends the path constraint ⟨“R-COND”, “FALSE”, ‹**t**›⟩ to the list of path constraints. If cond has no other clauses but the `else` one, [R-CONDELSE] replaces the conditional expression with the action expression e of its `else` clause.

The third group, CASE, describe the evaluation of case expressions from canonical functions. When evaluating a case expression, the concolic machine searches the clauses for a match. If the case expression is empty or if the input (**v**) is a concolic value whose concrete counterpart is a number that is different from tests of all clauses, [R-CASEMISS1] and [R-CASEMISS2] (respectively) reduce the case expression to the default action expression ‹0›. They also append the input constraint ⟨“R-CASE”, ℓ, **v**, “MISS”⟩ to the log. Otherwise, the last two rules of the group handle successful matches. For cases where the input **v** is a function λ**x**. **e**, [R-CASEHIT1] reduces case to the action expression of its first clause e. For cases where the input **v** is a concolic value ‹**t**›, rule [R-CASEHIT2] selects the matching clause with label ℓ_i and reduces case to the corresponding action $\mathbf{e}_i$. Both rules log the input constraint ⟨“R-CASE”, ℓ, **v**, “HIT”: ℓ_i⟩ with the label ℓ of the case expression, the input **v** and the label ℓ_i of the matching clause.

The last group, OTHER, completes the definition of the reduction rules. Rule [R-APP] is the standard call-by-value β-reduction while rule [R-ERROR] and [R-CTXT] close the rules over evaluation contexts.

Group Sym

$$\frac{\mathbf{op} \in \{!, +, -, \times, <, =\}}{\langle \rho, \pi, \mathbf{op}\ \langle t_1 \rangle \ldots \rangle \longrightarrow \langle \rho, \pi, \langle \mathbf{op}\ \mathbf{t}_1 \ldots \rangle \rangle}\ [\text{R-Trace1}]$$

$$\frac{\mathbf{op} \in \{\texttt{integer?}, \texttt{procedure?}\}}{\langle \rho, \pi, \mathbf{op}\ \mathbf{v} \rangle \longrightarrow \langle \rho, \pi, \langle tag\llbracket \mathbf{op}, \mathbf{v} \rrbracket \rangle \rangle}\ [\text{R-Trace2}]$$

$$\begin{array}{ll}
tag : \mathbf{op}\ \mathbf{v} \longrightarrow 0 \text{ or } 1 & \\
tag\llbracket \texttt{integer?}, \langle \mathbf{t} \rangle \rrbracket & = 1 \\
tag\llbracket \texttt{integer?}, (\lambda \mathbf{x}.\ \mathbf{e}) \rrbracket & = 0 \\
tag\llbracket \texttt{procedure?}, \langle \mathbf{t} \rangle \rrbracket & = 0 \\
tag\llbracket \texttt{procedure?}, (\lambda \mathbf{x}.\ \mathbf{e}) \rrbracket & = 1
\end{array}$$

Group Cond

$$\frac{\mathcal{E}\llbracket \rho, \mathbf{t} \rrbracket \neq 0 \qquad \pi' = \pi \mathbin{+\!\!+} [\langle \text{“R-Cond”}, \text{“True”}, \langle \mathbf{t} \rangle \rangle]}{\langle \rho, \pi, (\texttt{cond}\ [\langle \mathbf{t} \rangle\ \mathbf{e}_1']\ [\mathbf{e}_2\ \mathbf{e}_2']\ \ldots\ [\texttt{else}\ \mathbf{e}_k']) \rangle \longrightarrow \langle \rho, \pi', \mathbf{e}_1' \rangle}\ [\text{R-CondTrue}]$$

$$\frac{\mathcal{E}\llbracket \rho, \mathbf{t} \rrbracket = 0 \qquad \pi' = \pi \mathbin{+\!\!+} [\langle \text{“R-Cond”}, \text{“False”}, \langle \mathbf{t} \rangle \rangle]}{\begin{array}{l}\langle \rho, \pi, (\texttt{cond}\ [\langle \mathbf{t} \rangle\ \mathbf{e}_1']\ [\mathbf{e}_2\ \mathbf{e}_2']\ \ldots\ [\texttt{else}\ \mathbf{e}_k']) \rangle \longrightarrow \\ \langle \rho, \pi', (\texttt{cond}\ [\mathbf{e}_2\ \mathbf{e}_2']\ \ldots\ [\texttt{else}\ \mathbf{e}_k']) \rangle\end{array}}\ [\text{R-CondFalse}]$$

$$\frac{}{\langle \rho, \pi, (\texttt{cond}\ [\texttt{else}\ \mathbf{e}]) \rangle \longrightarrow \langle \rho, \pi, \mathbf{e} \rangle}\ [\text{R-CondElse}]$$

Group Case

$$\frac{\pi' = \pi \mathbin{+\!\!+} [\langle \text{“R-Case”}, \ell, \mathbf{v}, \text{“Miss”} \rangle]}{\langle \rho, \pi, (\texttt{case}^{\ell}\ \mathbf{v}) \rangle \longrightarrow \langle \rho, \pi', \langle 0 \rangle \rangle}\ [\text{R-CaseMiss1}]$$

$$\frac{\mathcal{E}\llbracket \rho, \mathbf{t} \rrbracket \notin \{\mathcal{E}\llbracket \rho, \mathbf{t}_2 \rrbracket, \ldots\} \qquad \pi' = \pi \mathbin{+\!\!+} [\langle \text{“R-Case”}, \ell, \langle \mathbf{t} \rangle, \text{“Miss”} \rangle]}{\langle \rho, \pi, (\texttt{case}^{\ell}\ \langle \mathbf{t} \rangle\ [\texttt{procedure?}\ \mathbf{e}_1]^{\ell_1}\ [\langle \mathbf{t}_2 \rangle\ \mathbf{e}_2]^{\ell_2} \ldots) \rangle \longrightarrow \langle \rho, \pi', \langle 0 \rangle \rangle}\ [\text{R-CaseMiss2}]$$

$$\frac{\pi' = \pi \mathbin{+\!\!+} [\langle \text{“R-Case”}, \ell, (\lambda \mathbf{x}.\ \mathbf{e}), \text{“Hit”}: \ell_1 \rangle]}{\langle \rho, \pi, (\texttt{case}^{\ell}\ (\lambda \mathbf{x}.\ \mathbf{e})\ [\texttt{procedure?}\ \mathbf{e}_1]^{\ell_1}\ [\langle \mathbf{t}_2 \rangle\ \mathbf{e}_2]^{\ell_2} \ldots) \rangle \longrightarrow \langle \rho, \pi', \mathbf{e}_1 \rangle}\ [\text{R-CaseHit1}]$$

$$\frac{\begin{array}{c}[\langle \ell_2, \mathbf{t}_2, \mathbf{e}_2 \rangle, \ldots] = [\langle \ell_p, \mathbf{t}_p, \mathbf{e}_p \rangle, \ldots] \mathbin{+\!\!+} [\langle \ell_i, \mathbf{t}_i, \mathbf{e}_i \rangle] \mathbin{+\!\!+} [\langle \ell_s, \mathbf{t}_s, \mathbf{e}_s \rangle, \ldots] \\ \mathcal{E}\llbracket \rho, \mathbf{t} \rrbracket \notin \{\mathcal{E}\llbracket \rho, \mathbf{t}_p \rrbracket, \ldots\} \qquad \mathcal{E}\llbracket \rho, \mathbf{t} \rrbracket = \mathcal{E}\llbracket \rho, \mathbf{t}_i \rrbracket \\ \pi' = \pi \mathbin{+\!\!+} [\langle \text{“R-Case”}, \ell, \langle \mathbf{t} \rangle, \text{“Hit”}: \ell_i \rangle]\end{array}}{\langle \rho, \pi, (\texttt{case}^{\ell}\ \langle \mathbf{t} \rangle\ [\texttt{procedure?}\ \mathbf{e}_1]^{\ell_1}\ [\langle \mathbf{t}_2 \rangle\ \mathbf{e}_2]^{\ell_2} \ldots) \rangle \longrightarrow \langle \rho, \pi', \mathbf{e}_i \rangle}\ [\text{R-CaseHit2}]$$

Group Other

$$\frac{}{\langle \rho, \pi, (\lambda \mathbf{x}.\ \mathbf{e})\ \mathbf{v} \rangle \longrightarrow \langle \rho, \pi, \mathbf{e}\{\mathbf{x} \mapsto \mathbf{v}\} \rangle}\ [\text{R-App}]$$

$$\frac{\langle \rho, \pi_1, \mathbf{e}_1 \rangle \longrightarrow \langle \rho, \pi_2, \mathbf{e}_2 \rangle}{\begin{array}{l}\langle \rho, \pi_1, \mathbf{E}[\mathbf{e}_1] \rangle \longrightarrow \\ \langle \rho, \pi_2, \mathbf{E}[\mathbf{e}_2] \rangle\end{array}}\ [\text{R-Ctxt}] \qquad \frac{\mathbf{E} \neq [\,]}{\begin{array}{l}\langle \rho, \pi, \mathbf{E}[\texttt{error}] \rangle \longrightarrow \\ \langle \rho, \pi, \texttt{error} \rangle\end{array}}\ [\text{R-Error}]$$

Figure 12: The Reduction Relation of Concolic Evaluation

Before concluding, it is worth mentioning that if the concolic evaluation of a user program raises `error`, it is straightforward for the concolic tester to produce a counter-example in the language of user programs. All the necessary information is in the latest input environment of the concolic machine.

3.2 Evolution of Higher-order Inputs

If the concolic machine evaluates a user program without raising an error, the metafunction *evolve*⟦ρ, π⟧ analyzes the log of the machine and compiles a list of new input environments. Specifically, for each constraint from π, *evolve*⟦ρ, π⟧ "switches" its truthfulness and computes all new input environments ρ′ that are compatible with the switched constraint. Here, a new input environment ρ′ is compatible with π if running the user program with ρ′ produces a log π′ that has the same prefix as π plus the constraint that *evolve* has switched to obtain ρ′. Put differently, *evolve* returns all possible evolutions of the current input that direct the concolic tester to explore a new aspect of the behavior of the user program. Theorem 3 from section 4 states this property formally.

$$\frac{\langle \rho', \pi' \rangle \in \mathit{evolve}[\![\rho, \pi]\!]}{\langle \rho', \pi' \rangle \in \mathit{evolve}[\![\rho, \pi \mathbin{+\!\!+} [\mathbf{p}]]\!]}\ [\text{M-PREFIX}]$$

$$\frac{\begin{array}{l}\pi = \pi_1 \mathbin{+\!\!+} [\langle\text{"R-COND"}, \text{"FALSE"}, \mathbf{v}\rangle] \\ \pi' = \pi_1 \mathbin{+\!\!+} [\langle\text{"R-COND"}, \text{"TRUE"}, \mathbf{v}\rangle] \\ \rho' = \mathit{update}[\![\rho, \pi']\!]\end{array}}{\langle \rho', \pi' \rangle \in \mathit{evolve}[\![\rho, \pi]\!]}\ [\text{M-TRUE}] \qquad \frac{\begin{array}{l}\pi = \pi_1 \mathbin{+\!\!+} [\langle\text{"R-COND"}, \text{"TRUE"}, \mathbf{v}\rangle] \\ \pi' = \pi_1 \mathbin{+\!\!+} [\langle\text{"R-COND"}, \text{"FALSE"}, \mathbf{v}\rangle] \\ \rho' = \mathit{update}[\![\rho, \pi']\!]\end{array}}{\langle \rho', \pi' \rangle \in \mathit{evolve}[\![\rho, \pi]\!]}\ [\text{M-FALSE}]$$

Figure 13: Negating Conditional Branches in User Programs

Figure 13 collects the three most basic rules of the definition of *evolve*. The first rule, [M-PREFIX], is an administrative one; it allows the removal of an arbitrary suffix from the log π so that the rest of the rules can focus on the last entry of the remaining log.

The next two rules, [M-FALSE] and [M-TRUE], form the first-order aspect of *evolve* that we discuss in section 2.1. They fire when the last entry of the log is a path constraint from a branch of a `cond` expression of the user program. Their purpose is to guide *evolve* to generate an input that forces concolic evaluation to change the outcome of the branch. To do so, the two rules replace the constraint with its "negation" and then, with metafunction *update*, they present the modified list of constraints as a problem to an SMT solver and use the solution to obtain a new input environment ρ′.

Figure 14 presents the higher-order rules and figure 15 contains the auxiliary definitions they need. The higher-order rules switch an input constraint of form ⟨"R-CASE", ℓ, **v**, _⟩. Recall that such constraints result from the evaluation of a `case` expression with label ℓ in the body of a canonical function. Thus an input

$$\frac{\begin{array}{l}\mathbf{F} \in \mathrm{dom}(\boldsymbol{\rho}),\ \boldsymbol{\rho}(\mathbf{F}) = \mathbf{C}^{\circ}[(\mathtt{case}^{\ell}\ \mathbf{y})] \qquad \boldsymbol{\pi} = \boldsymbol{\pi}_1 +\!\!+ [\langle\text{“R-CASE”}, \ell, (\lambda\mathbf{x}.\ \mathbf{e}), \text{“MISS”}\rangle] \\ \langle\boldsymbol{\rho}_1, \mathbf{e}^{\circ}\rangle \in \mathit{action}_b[\![\boldsymbol{\rho}, \mathit{locals}[\![\mathbf{C}^{\circ}]\!], \{\mathbf{y}\} \cup \mathit{locals}_p[\![\mathbf{C}^{\circ}]\!]]\!] \\ \text{fresh } \ell_1 \notin \mathrm{labels}(\boldsymbol{\rho}_1, \mathbf{e}^{\circ}) \qquad \boldsymbol{\pi}' = \boldsymbol{\pi}_1 +\!\!+ [\langle\text{“R-CASE”}, \ell, (\lambda\mathbf{x}.\ \mathbf{e}), \text{“HIT”: } \ell_1\rangle] \\ \boldsymbol{\rho}' = \boldsymbol{\rho}_1[\mathbf{F} \mapsto \mathbf{C}^{\circ}[(\mathtt{case}^{\ell}\ \mathbf{y}\ [\mathtt{procedure?}\ \mathbf{e}^{\circ}]^{\ell_1})]]\end{array}}{\langle\boldsymbol{\rho}', \boldsymbol{\pi}'\rangle \in \mathit{evolve}[\![\boldsymbol{\rho}, \boldsymbol{\pi}]\!]}\ [\text{M-NEWPROC1}]$$

$$\frac{\begin{array}{l}\mathbf{F} \in \mathrm{dom}(\boldsymbol{\rho}),\ \boldsymbol{\rho}(\mathbf{F}) = \mathbf{C}^{\circ}[(\mathtt{case}^{\ell}\ \mathbf{y})] \qquad \boldsymbol{\pi} = \boldsymbol{\pi}_1 +\!\!+ [\langle\text{“R-CASE”}, \ell, \langle\mathbf{t}\rangle, \text{“MISS”}\rangle] \\ \langle\boldsymbol{\rho}_1, \mathbf{e}^{\circ}\rangle \in \mathit{action}_b[\![\boldsymbol{\rho}, \mathit{locals}[\![\mathbf{C}^{\circ}]\!], \{\mathbf{y}\} \cup \mathit{locals}_p[\![\mathbf{C}^{\circ}]\!]]\!] \\ \text{fresh } \ell_1 \notin \mathrm{labels}(\boldsymbol{\rho}_1, \mathbf{e}^{\circ}) \qquad \boldsymbol{\pi}' = \boldsymbol{\pi}_1 +\!\!+ [\langle\text{“R-CASE”}, \ell, \langle\mathbf{t}\rangle, \text{“MISS”}\rangle] \\ \boldsymbol{\rho}' = \boldsymbol{\rho}_1[\mathbf{F} \mapsto \mathbf{C}^{\circ}[(\mathtt{case}^{\ell}\ \mathbf{y}\ [\mathtt{procedure?}\ \mathbf{e}^{\circ}]^{\ell_1})]]\end{array}}{\langle\boldsymbol{\rho}', \boldsymbol{\pi}'\rangle \in \mathit{evolve}[\![\boldsymbol{\rho}, \boldsymbol{\pi}]\!]}\ [\text{M-NEWPROC2}]$$

$$\frac{\begin{array}{l}\mathbf{F} \in \mathrm{dom}(\boldsymbol{\rho}),\ \boldsymbol{\rho}(\mathbf{F}) = \mathbf{C}^{\circ}[(\mathtt{case}^{\ell}\ \mathbf{y}\ [\mathtt{procedure?}\ \mathbf{e}^{\circ}_1]^{\ell_1}\ [\langle\mathbf{t}_2\rangle\ \mathbf{e}^{\circ}_2]^{\ell_2} \ldots)] \\ \boldsymbol{\pi} = \boldsymbol{\pi}_1 +\!\!+ [\langle\text{“R-CASE”}, \ell, \langle\mathbf{t}\rangle, \_\rangle] \\ \langle\boldsymbol{\rho}_1, \mathbf{e}^{\circ}\rangle \in \mathit{action}_b[\![\boldsymbol{\rho}, \mathit{locals}[\![\mathbf{C}^{\circ}]\!], \mathit{locals}_p[\![\mathbf{C}^{\circ}]\!]]\!] \\ \text{fresh } \ell_{n+1} \notin \mathrm{labels}(\boldsymbol{\rho}_1, \mathbf{e}^{\circ}) \qquad \boldsymbol{\pi}' = \boldsymbol{\pi}_1 +\!\!+ [\langle\text{“R-CASE”}, \ell, \langle\mathbf{t}\rangle, \text{“HIT”: } \ell_{n+1}\rangle] \\ \boldsymbol{\rho}_2 = \boldsymbol{\rho}_1[\mathbf{F} \mapsto \mathbf{C}^{\circ}[(\mathtt{case}^{\ell}\ \mathbf{y}\ [\mathtt{procedure?}\ \mathbf{e}^{\circ}_1]^{\ell_1}\ [\langle\mathbf{t}_2\rangle\ \mathbf{e}^{\circ}_2]^{\ell_2} \ldots [\langle\mathbf{t}\rangle\ \mathbf{e}^{\circ}]^{\ell_{n+1}})]] \\ \boldsymbol{\rho}' = \mathit{update}[\![\boldsymbol{\rho}_2, \boldsymbol{\pi}']\!]\end{array}}{\langle\boldsymbol{\rho}', \boldsymbol{\pi}'\rangle \in \mathit{evolve}[\![\boldsymbol{\rho}, \boldsymbol{\pi}]\!]}\ [\text{M-NEWINT}]$$

$$\frac{\begin{array}{l}\boldsymbol{\pi} = \boldsymbol{\pi}_1 +\!\!+ [\langle\text{“R-CASE”}, \ell, \langle\mathbf{t}\rangle, \_\rangle] \\ \mathbf{F} \in \mathrm{dom}(\boldsymbol{\rho}),\ \boldsymbol{\rho}(\mathbf{F}) = \mathbf{C}^{\circ}[(\mathtt{case}^{\ell}\ \mathbf{y}\ [\mathtt{procedure?}\ \mathbf{e}^{\circ}_1]^{\ell_1}\ [\langle\mathbf{t}_2\rangle\ \mathbf{e}^{\circ}_2]^{\ell_2} \ldots)] \\ [\langle\mathbf{t}_2, \ell_2\rangle, \ldots] = [\langle\mathbf{t}_p, \ell_p\rangle, \ldots] +\!\!+ [\langle\mathbf{t}_i, \ell_i\rangle] +\!\!+ [\langle\mathbf{t}_s, \ell_s\rangle, \ldots] \\ \boldsymbol{\pi}' = \boldsymbol{\pi}_1 +\!\!+ [\langle\text{“R-CASE”}, \ell, \langle\mathbf{t}\rangle, \text{“HIT”: } \ell_i\rangle] \qquad \boldsymbol{\rho}' = \mathit{update}[\![\boldsymbol{\rho}, \boldsymbol{\pi}']\!]\end{array}}{\langle\boldsymbol{\rho}', \boldsymbol{\pi}'\rangle \in \mathit{evolve}[\![\boldsymbol{\rho}, \boldsymbol{\pi}]\!]}\ [\text{M-CHANGE}]$$

Figure 14: Directed Evolution of Higher-order Inputs

constraint is sufficient for *evolve* to identify the case expression in the input environment it concerns.

Rules [M-NEWPROC1] and [M-NEWPROC2] apply when the case expression with label $\boldsymbol{\ell}$ is empty. They modify $\boldsymbol{\rho}$ to extend the case expression with a procedure? clause, the default first clause for recognizing function arguments. Rule [M-NEWPROC1] handles the situation where $\mathbf{v}$, the value case examines, is a function. To create a new clause, [M-NEWPROC1] calls action_b to compute new actions — we return to this metafunction towards the end of the section. Rule [M-NEWPROC2] handles the situation where $\mathbf{v}$ is a first-order concolic value $\langle\mathbf{t}\rangle$. It is the same as [M-NEWPROC1] except that the new list of constraints still ends with $\langle$“R-CASE”, $\boldsymbol{\ell}$, $\mathbf{v}$, “MISS”$\rangle$ as $\langle\mathbf{t}\rangle$ cannot match the new procedure? clause of the case expression.

If the case expression with label $\boldsymbol{\ell}$ is non-empty, the concolic tester can change its evaluation only when $\mathbf{v}$ is not a function. After all, if $\mathbf{v}$ is a function, the evaluation of a non-empty case always follows the first clause of the case. As

$\mathbf{C}^\circ$ is the compatible context of $\mathbf{e}^\circ$.

$\Delta \subset \{\mathbf{x}, \mathbf{y}, \mathbf{z}, \dots\}$ stands for any finite subset of non-concolic variables.

$locals : \mathbf{C}^\circ \longrightarrow \Delta$

Given a compatible context of canonical functions, computes the set of all variables in scope in the hole.

$locals_p : \mathbf{C}^\circ \longrightarrow \Delta$

Given a compatible context of canonical functions, compute the set of all variables in scope in the hole that are bound to functions.

$\boxed{action_b : \rho\ \Delta\ \Delta \longrightarrow [\langle \rho, \mathbf{e}^\circ \rangle, \dots]}$

$$\frac{\langle \rho', \mathbf{v}^\circ \rangle \in action_c[\![\rho, \Delta]\!] \quad \mathbf{f} \in \Delta_p \quad \text{fresh } \mathbf{x} \notin \Delta \quad \text{fresh } \ell \notin \text{labels}(\rho, \mathbf{v}^\circ)}{\langle \rho', \texttt{let } \mathbf{x} = \mathbf{f}\ \mathbf{v}^\circ \texttt{ in } (\texttt{case}^\ell\ \mathbf{x}) \rangle \in action_b[\![\rho, \Delta, \Delta_p]\!]} \text{[E-Havoc]}$$

$$\frac{\langle \rho', \mathbf{v}^\circ \rangle \in action_c[\![\rho, \Delta]\!]}{\langle \rho', \mathbf{v}^\circ \rangle \in action_b[\![\rho, \Delta, \Delta_p]\!]} \text{[E-Const]}$$

$\boxed{action_c : \rho\ \Delta \longrightarrow [\langle \rho, \mathbf{v}^\circ \rangle, \dots]}$

$$\frac{\text{fresh } \mathbf{X} \notin \text{dom}(\rho)}{\langle \rho[\mathbf{X} \mapsto 0], \mathbf{X} \rangle \in action_c[\![\rho, \Delta]\!]} \text{[C-Int1]} \qquad \frac{\mathbf{x} \in \Delta}{\langle \rho, \mathbf{x} \rangle \in action_c[\![\rho, \Delta]\!]} \text{[C-Bound]}$$

$$\frac{\mathbf{X} \in \text{dom}(\rho),\ \rho(\mathbf{X}) = \mathbf{n}}{\langle \rho, \mathbf{X} \rangle \in action_c[\![\rho, \Delta]\!]} \text{[C-Int2]} \qquad \frac{\text{fresh } \mathbf{x} \notin \Delta \quad \text{fresh } \ell \notin \text{labels}(\rho)}{\langle \rho, \lambda \mathbf{x}.\ (\texttt{case}^\ell\ \mathbf{x}) \rangle \in action_c[\![\rho, \Delta]\!]} \text{[C-Proc]}$$

Figure 15: Computation of New Actions & Local Variables

we discuss in section 2.3 and section 2.4, if **v** is a first-order concolic value ‹**t**›, the tester has two options: either to extend the case expression with a new clause, or to assert that ‹**t**› matches an existing clause. Rules [M-NewInt] and [M-Change] handle these two cases, respectively. There are two subcases for [M-NewInt]: ‹**t**› matches an existing clause but the tester opts to create a dedicated clause for it in the next iteration of the concolic loop, or ‹**t**› does not match any existing clause and the tester extends the case to accommodate it. In either case, rule [M-NewInt] computes the new actions for the additional clause in the same manner as in [M-NewProc1] and the new clause is inserted into the case expression. As a last step, rule [M-NewInt] queries the SMT solver to adjust the values of first-order inputs in the environment, ensuring that all the clauses of the extended case are distinct. Rule [M-Change] corresponds to the discussion in section 2.4 and its goal is to assert that ‹**t**› matches an existing clause ℓ_i of the case expression. Hence *evolve* replaces the last entry of the log with ⟨"R-Case", ℓ, ‹**t**›, "Hit": ℓ_i⟩. Similar to the previous rule, as a last step rule [M-Change] consults the SMT solver to adjust the input environment given the new constraint about ‹**t**›.

As a final remark, metafunction $action_b$ computes the set of actions for the new case clauses that *evolve* introduces. It largely follows the grammar of $\mathbf{e}^\circ$ discussed in section 3.1. When it introduces a new function or a let-expression as a new action, $action_b$ constructs an empty case for their corresponding body expressions. Moreover, $action_b$ delegates to *locals* and $locals_p$ to compute the set of variables that new actions can refer to. The metafunction *locals* takes a context $\mathbf{C}^{\circ}$ and extracts the set of all local variables visible in the hole. The metafunction $locals_p$ is similar to *locals* but only extracts variables that are bound to functions.

3.3 Adding Concretization

$$\underline{\mathbf{e}} ::= \ldots \mid \texttt{concretize}(\underline{\mathbf{e}}) \qquad \mathbf{e} ::= \ldots \mid \texttt{concretize}(\mathbf{e})$$

$$\frac{\mathbf{n} = \mathcal{E}[\![\boldsymbol{\rho}, \mathbf{t}]\!]}{\langle \boldsymbol{\rho}, \boldsymbol{\pi}, \texttt{concretize}(\langle \mathbf{t} \rangle) \rangle \longrightarrow \langle \boldsymbol{\rho}, \boldsymbol{\pi}, \langle \mathbf{n} \rangle \rangle} \text{[R-CONCRETIZE]}$$

Figure 16: Adding Concretization to Concolic Evaluation

Figure 16 shows the extensions for concretization. For simplicity, we identify concrete values with ‹**n**› and consider such terms as feasible to interoperate with external functions. We do not introduce any specific concrete evaluation rules. Instead, we augment the reduction rules of the concolic machine with the [R-CONCRETIZE] that reduces the new form, concretize(‹**t**›), to its concrete counterpart with the help of $\mathcal{E}$. Recall that the latter metafunction uses the current input $\boldsymbol{\rho}$ to compute the value of the formula **t** of a concolic value.

```
date<     = λd1. λd2. (or ((date-year d1) < (date-year d2)) ⋯)
main-bad  = λdates. (let sorted-dates = (sort dates date<) in ⋯)
sort/wrap = λlst. λcmp. (sort lst (λx. λy. concretize(cmp x y)))
main-ok   = λdates. (let sorted-dates = (sort/wrap dates date<) in ⋯)
```

Figure 17: sort With Concretization Wrapper

The astute reader will have noticed that the concretization extension handles only first-order values. In the remainder of the section, by revisiting the example from section 1 in figure 17, we argue informally that in fact this is sufficient, even for functions. In the example, `date<` is a buggy comparison function and `sort` is a library function that is polymorphic in its list argument. Since `sort` is external to the concolic tester, the evaluation of its body is delegated to a concrete machine which does not record constraints nor handles concolic values. This quickly becomes an issue for testing `main-bad`. To discover the bug, the concolic machine needs to log constraints from the evaluation of `date<` and `main-bad`. However, this implies that `date<` produces concolic values which flow to `sort` and disrupt the concrete evaluation of its body.

A straightforward non-solution is to fully concretize the list of dates and miss recording the critical path constraints from the evaluation of `date<`'s body. In contrast, our approach enables both the seamless interoperation of the concolic tester with external libraries and the collection of constraints. The key insight is to create wrappers that strategically `concretize` concolic values. By assumption, `sort` is parametric to its input list. Thus `sort` can consume a list of concolic values as long as the comparison function produces concrete results. This leads to the `sort/wrap` function that behaves like `sort`, except that its `cmp` argument is wrapped in a function that concretizes `cmp`'s return value.

The mechanism for creating correct wrappers for higher-order constructs from user annotations is well-studied [13, 16, 40], thus we do not formalize it. However, we note that our proof-of-concept implementation, discussed in section 5, supports all the necessary features to run the example of this section including lists, external functions, concretization annotations and interoperability between a concrete and a concolic machine.

4 Correctness of Higher-order Concolic Testing

This section establishes three facts about our concolic tester that together entail its correctness. First, given an input, if concolic evaluation of a user program triggers an `error` so does the concrete evaluation of the program (soundness). Second, relative to the completeness of SMT solvers, the concolic tester always manages to produce an input in canonical form that triggers `error` in the user program, if a counter-example for the program exists (completeness). Third, for each iteration of the concolic loop, the concolic tester produces a new input that explores a specific and selected-in-advance aspect of the behavior of the user program (directness). Here we discuss the necessary bits for the formal statements of the three facts. The complete formal development with all the proofs are at **`https://github.com/shhyou/chop-esop-supplementary`**.

Soundness guarantees that the concolic machine respects the semantics of user programs. Thus, the information that the concolic machine logs or its use of concolic values do not affect the evaluation of programs. Specifically, the soundness theorem states that if the concolic evaluation of user program $\underline{\mathbf{e}}$ with proper input environment $\boldsymbol{\rho}$ reduces to `error`,[2] the concrete evaluation of $\underline{\mathbf{e}}$ with $\boldsymbol{\rho}$ also reduces to `error`. Since `error` represents bugs in the user program, soundness effectively reassures that concolic evaluation does not discover spurious bugs.

For the formal statement of the theorem, we first introduce a few technical devices. For closed user programs, i.e., those without input or other free variables, we define a standard call-by-value reduction semantics with reduction relation $\longrightarrow_{\lambda}$. Let $\mathcal{C}[\![\boldsymbol{\rho}, \underline{\mathbf{e}}]\!]$ be the metafunction that constructs concrete inputs from the input environment $\boldsymbol{\rho}$ and substitutes them in $\underline{\mathbf{e}}$. That is, $\mathcal{C}$ traverses the user program $\underline{\mathbf{e}}$, dropping any `concretize` forms and, for each $\mathbf{X}$ in $\underline{\mathbf{e}}$, if $\boldsymbol{\rho}$ maps $\mathbf{X}$ to a number, $\mathcal{C}$ replaces $\mathbf{X}$ with the number. Otherwise if $\boldsymbol{\rho}$ maps $\mathbf{X}$ to a function, $\mathcal{C}$ compiles the canonical function into an equivalent concrete function and replaces $\mathbf{X}$ with the result.

[2] An environment $\boldsymbol{\rho}$ is *proper* if (i) it maps all concolic variables occurring free in canonical functions in $\boldsymbol{\rho}$ to numbers, (ii) all labels in $\boldsymbol{\rho}$ are unique and (iii) the concrete counterparts of the tests of the clauses in `case` expressions are numbers. In this section, we only consider proper environments.

Theorem 1 (Soundness). *Let* $\underline{\mathbf{e}}$ *be any user program written in the extended language from section 3.3, i.e.* $\underline{\mathbf{e}}$ *with* concretize *forms. Let* ρ *be any input environment closing* $\underline{\mathbf{e}}$. *If* $\langle \rho, [], \mathcal{L}[\![\rho, \underline{\mathbf{e}}]\!]\rangle \longrightarrow^* \langle \rho, \pi, \mathsf{error}\rangle$ *then* $C[\![\rho, \underline{\mathbf{e}}]\!] \longrightarrow_\lambda^* \mathsf{error}$.

Completeness captures that if the concrete evaluation of a user program with some input raises error, our concolic tester can find the input through the iterative evolution of initially default inputs. More precisely, Theorem 2 formalizes the iterative evolution process as a sequence of pairs of inputs and logs $\langle \rho_1, \pi_1\rangle, \ldots, \langle \rho_m, \pi_m\rangle$ such that (i) the sequence starts with an input environment that contains numbers and default canonical functions and ends with an input environment that triggers error; (ii) each π_i is the log produced by the concolic evaluation of the user program with input environment ρ_i, and (iii) most importantly, each and every adjacent pairs in the sequence is connected by *evolve*: $\langle \rho_{i+1}, \pi'\rangle \in evolve[\![\rho_i, \pi_i]\!]$ and π' is equivalent to a prefix of π_{i+1}. In particular, conclusion (iii) says that using the logs from each iteration, *evolve* predicts the logs for the next iteration.

Theorem 2 (Completeness). *For any* $\underline{\mathbf{e}}$ *written in the user language in section 3.1 with concolic variables* $\mathbf{X}_1, \ldots, \mathbf{X}_n$, *if there exists closed values* $\underline{\mathbf{v}}_1, \ldots, \underline{\mathbf{v}}_n$ *in the language of user programs such that none of the values contain* error *and* $\underline{\mathbf{e}}\{\mathbf{X}_1 \mapsto \underline{\mathbf{v}}_1, \ldots\} \longrightarrow_\lambda^* \mathsf{error}$ *then there exists a sequence of environments and logs* $\langle \rho_1, \pi_1\rangle, \ldots, \langle \rho_m, \pi_m\rangle$ *such that* $dom(\rho_1) = \{\mathbf{X}_1, \ldots, \mathbf{X}_n\}$ *and*

1. *For all* $\mathbf{X} \in dom(\rho_1)$, *either* $\rho_1(\mathbf{X}) = 0$ *or* $\rho_1(\mathbf{X}) = \lambda\mathbf{x}.\ (\mathsf{case}^\ell\ \mathbf{x})$.
2. *For all* $1 \leqslant i < m$, $\langle \rho_i, [], \mathcal{L}[\![\rho_i, \underline{\mathbf{e}}]\!]\rangle \longrightarrow^* \langle \rho_i, \pi_i, \mathbf{e}_i\rangle$.
3. *For all* $1 \leqslant i < m$, *there exists a pair* $\langle \rho_{i+1}, \pi'_{i+1}\rangle \in evolve[\![\rho_i, \pi_i]\!]$ *such that* π'_{i+1} *is equivalent to a prefix of* π_{i+1}.
4. $\langle \rho_m, [], \mathcal{L}[\![\rho_m, \underline{\mathbf{e}}]\!]\rangle \longrightarrow^* \langle \rho_m, \pi_m, \mathsf{error}\rangle$.

There are two points worth unpacking here. First, conclusion 1 assumes an appropriate choice between numbers and default canonical functions in the initial environment ρ_1. In an implementation, either the user supplies an input specification or the tester employs some sophisticated search strategy over all combinations. Second, since the user program may diverge, in conclusion 2 the concolic machine may need to end the evaluation early. As the maximum number of steps needed is finite, an implementation can overcome this by setting a time limit.

We prove Theorem 2 in two steps. First, we show that if there is an input for which the concrete evaluation of a user program raises error, then there exists an input environment ρ that contains numbers and canonical functions that also causes the concolic machine to triggers an error. Thus this step validates the definition of canonical functions.

Lemma 1 (Representation Completeness). *We say that* $\langle \rho, \pi\rangle$ *is a* proper counterexample *for a user program* $\underline{\mathbf{e}}$ *if (i)* ρ *closes* $\underline{\mathbf{e}}$, *i.e.* $FV(\underline{\mathbf{e}}) \subset dom(\rho)$, *(ii)* $\langle \rho, [], \mathcal{L}[\![\rho, \underline{\mathbf{e}}]\!]\rangle \longrightarrow^* \langle \rho, \pi, \mathsf{error}\rangle$ *and (iii)* π *does not contain input constraints of the form* ⟨"R-CASE", ℓ, $\mathbf{v}$, "MISS"⟩.

For any user program $\underline{\mathbf{e}}$ *with inputs* $\mathbf{X}_1, \ldots, \mathbf{X}_n$. *if there exists closed values* $\underline{\mathbf{v}}_1, \ldots, \underline{\mathbf{v}}_n$ *such that no value contains* `error` *and* $\underline{\mathbf{e}}\{\mathbf{X}_1 \mapsto \underline{\mathbf{v}}_1, \ldots\} \longrightarrow_{\lambda}^{*}$ `error` *then there exists a proper counterexample of* $\underline{\mathbf{e}}$.

In the second step of the proof of Theorem 2, we show that the evolution of inputs during the concolic loop results in an environment input that can trigger an `error` if such an input exists. As a consequence, the concolic tester only needs to explore inputs it generates with *evolve*.

Lemma 2 (Search Completeness). *For any* $\underline{\mathbf{e}}$ *with inputs* $\mathbf{X}_1, \ldots, \mathbf{X}_n$, *if* $\underline{\mathbf{e}}$ *has a proper counterexample then there exists a sequence of environments and logs satisfying Theorem 2 (1)–(4).*

The last fact we establish for our concolic tester is necessary for the proof of Lemma 2, but also has value on its own. It entails that, at each iteration of the concolic loop, the concolic tester aims to explore a specific aspect of the behavior of the user program and indeed produces new inputs that achieve this goal. We call this the *concolic property*. Formally, Theorem 3 shows that after the concolic machine evaluates a user program with an input environment produced by *evolve*, the machine's log is a prefix of the log *evolve* predicts.

Theorem 3 (Concolic). *For any* $\underline{\mathbf{e}}$ *and* $\boldsymbol{\rho}_1$, *if*

1. $\langle \boldsymbol{\rho}_1, [], \mathcal{L}[\![\boldsymbol{\rho}_1, \underline{\mathbf{e}}]\!]\rangle \longrightarrow^{*} \langle \boldsymbol{\rho}_1, \boldsymbol{\pi}_1 +\!\!+ [\mathbf{p}_1], \mathbf{e}_1\rangle$.
2. $\boldsymbol{\pi}_1$ *has no "miss" input constraints (of the form* $\langle$"R-CASE", $\boldsymbol{\ell}$, $\mathbf{v}$, "MISS"$\rangle$*).*
3. $\langle \boldsymbol{\rho}_2, \boldsymbol{\pi}_1 +\!\!+ [\mathbf{p}]\rangle \in evolve[\![\boldsymbol{\rho}_1, \boldsymbol{\pi}_1 +\!\!+ [\mathbf{p}_1]]\!]$.

then $\langle \boldsymbol{\rho}_2, [], \mathcal{L}[\![\boldsymbol{\rho}_2, \underline{\mathbf{e}}]\!]\rangle \longrightarrow^{*} \langle \boldsymbol{\rho}_2, \boldsymbol{\pi}_2 +\!\!+ [\mathbf{p}_2], \mathbf{e}_2\rangle$ *such that* $\boldsymbol{\pi}_1 +\!\!+ [\mathbf{p}]$ *is equivalent to* $\boldsymbol{\pi}_2 +\!\!+ [\mathbf{p}_2]$.

5 From the Model to a Proof-of-Concept Implementation

A question about our model is whether it can serve as a guide for an effective higher-order concolic tester. To provide some positive evidence, we have implemented a prototype that closely follows the model. The prototype plays the role of a sanity check that our theoretically-correct model is not inherently impractical; performance was not a serious concern. Notably, the prototype's input generation strategy is naive. To ensure progress, the prototype sets a configurable timeout for each run and avoids duplicating work with a log from trying each input it generates. We leave the details to `https://github.com/shhyou/chop-esop-supplementary` and only summarize our experimental results here.

We compiled a benchmark suite from three sources. The primary source is Nguyễn et al. [33]'s work, specifically from the `jfp` branch of `https://github.com/philnguyen/soft-contract`. These programs ultimately come from other papers; see figure 18. The second source is CutEr [18], the Erlang concolic tester. We collected all of the test cases in CutEr's test suite that use higher-order functions and translated them to our prototype's language. Finally, we contribute three small examples as as part of this work that have proven out of reach for

Name	Failures	Source
games	3/3	Nguyễn et al. [32, 33]
hors	0/23	Kobayashi et al. [27]
mochi-new	0/11	Kobayashi et al. [27]
octy	0/13	Tobin-Hochstadt and Felleisen [44]
others	1/26	Nguyễn et al. [32, 33], Tobin-Hochstadt and Van Horn [45]
softy	0/12	Cartwright and Fagan [10], Wright and Cartwright [46]
terauchi	0/7	Terauchi [42]
cuter	0/20	Giantsios et al. [18]
c-hop	0/3	Interesting examples we discovered
total	**4/118**	

Figure 18: Benchmark Results

both Nguyễn et al. [33]'s tool and CutEr. Overall, the benchmark programs use the Scheme numeric tower, booleans, lists, objects encoded as functions [1], strings, symbols, and higher-order functions.

Out of 118 benchmarks, our prototype fails to discover bugs in 4 of the programs. These programs can be grouped based on two limitations of our prototype. First, our search strategy is naive and as a result two benchmarks time out after an hour. Second, our prototype does not handle Racket's `struct` declaration and a few other complex syntactic features of Racket that two of Nguyễn et al. [33]'s benchmarks use.

6 Related Work

Concolic Testing. CutEr [17, 18] is a concolic testing tool for Erlang [4]. Although CutEr generates functions, it does not generate inputs that contain calls in their bodies.[3] Palacios and Vidal [34] offer an instrumentation approach for concolic testers of functional languages but do not address the generation of higher-order inputs.

Li et al. [31] extend the design of path constraints with symbolic subtype expressions to handle polymorphism in object-oriented languages. However, their input generation uses only already defined classes.

Path explosion remains a central challenge for concolic testing techniques [5, 9], and it is a challenge that has lead to approaches that rely on the correct handling of function inputs. Godefroid [19] compute function summaries on-the-fly to tame the combinatorial explosion of the search space of control-flow paths. Similarly, Anand et al. [2] performs symbolic execution compositionally using function summaries. FOCAL [24] breaks programs down into small units to reduce the search space; it tests each units individual and constructs a system-level tests by using summaries. In all three cases, the summaries are first-order and do not include higher-order interactions between functions.

[3] Personal communication with Kostis Sagonas.

Higher-order Symbolic Execution. Nguyễn et al. [33] and Tobin-Hochstadt and Van Horn [45] propose the idea of refining symbolic unknown values into canonical shapes to generate higher-order counterexamples. We adapt their refinement rules into the grammar of canonical functions in figure 10. Unfortunately, despite opposite claims, their rules are not complete and fail to generate a counter-example for our buggy `call-twice` from section 1.[4] Our work provably fixes this issue. Moreover, we introduce the notion of input constraints to support the directed search of the higher-order input space.

Random Testing. QuickCheck [11] supports random testing of higher-order functions by using user-provided maps from the input type to integers and from integers to the output type. Koopman and Plasmeijer [28] improves upon QuickCheck by using a predefined datatype to represent the syntax of higher-order functions. LambdaTester [36] focuses on testing and generating higher-order functions that mutate an object's state in order to affect control-flow paths that depend on this state. Klein et al. [26] random-generate higher-order inputs that call their arguments to trigger bugs in stateful programs with opaque types.

7 Conclusion

This work offers a theoretical roadmap for generalizing concolic testing to programs with higher-order inputs. The central innovation is that our concolic tester records salient information about the interactions between a user program and its (canonical) inputs. The information induces an SMT problem that describes a new canonical input that exercises a yet unexplored aspect of the user program.

For this paper, we focus on the quintessential higher-order linguistic feature, higher-order functions. That said, much remains to be done to build this theory into a production tool by, for example, using the insights of this paper to support other features such as objects and mutable state. Specifically for state, our model can be easily and soundly extended to imperative user programs. However, completeness and the generation of stateful function inputs requires further study. Finally, another important direction is improving the implementation, notably exploring search optimizations and strategies. Our prototype uses a naive strategy and this hampers its performance. Nevertheless, we view this paper an essential first step towards sophisticated testing strategies for modern programming languages.

Acknowledgments We appreciate Phúc C. Nguyễn, Sam Tobin-Hochstadt, David Van Horn, Aggelos Giantsios, Nikolaos Papaspyrou and Konstantinos Sagonas for explaining the details of their work and being an inspiration for ours. We thank Spencer P. Florence, Lukas Lazarek, Wung Jae Lee, Alex Owens, Peter Zhong, and the anonymous reviewers of their thoughtful feedback on earlier versions of this paper. This material is based upon work supported by the National Science Foundation under Grant No. CNS-1823244.

[4] Personal communication with Phúc Nguyễn.

References

[1] Harold Abelson, Gerald Jay Sussman, and Julie Sussman. *Structure and Interpretation of Computer Programs.* MIT Press, 1985.

[2] Saswat Anand, Patrice Godefroid, and Nikolai Tillmann. Demand-driven Compositional Symbolic Execution. In *Proc. International Conference on Tools and Algorithms for the Construction and Analysis of Systems*, pp. 367–3831, 2008.

[3] Saswat Anand, Mayur Naik, Mary Jean Harrold, and Hongseok Yang. Automated Concolic Testing of Smartphone Apps. In *Proc. International Symposium on on the Foundations of Software Engineering*, pp. 59:1–59:11, 2012.

[4] Joe Armstrong, Robert Virding, Claes Wikström, and Mike Williams. *Programming Erlang: Software for a Concurrent World.* Prentice Hall, 2007.

[5] Roberto Baldoni, Emilio Coppa, Daniele Cono D'Elia, Camil Demetrescu, and Irene Finocchi. A Survey of Symbolic Execution Techniques. *ACM Comput. Surv.* 51(3), 2018.

[6] Jacob Burnim and Koushik Sen. Heuristics for Scalable Dynamic Test Generation. In *Proc. ACM/IEEE International Conference on Automated Software Engineering*, pp. 443–446, 2008.

[7] Cristian Cadar, Daniel Dunbar, and Dawson Engler. KLEE: Unassisted and Automatic Generation of High-coverage Tests for Complex Systems Programs. In *Proc. USENIX Symposium on Operating Systems Design and Implementation*, pp. 209–224, 2008.

[8] Cristian Cadar and Dawson Engler. Execution Generated Test Cases: How to Make Systems Code Crash Itself. In *Proc. International SPINConference on Model Cheching Software*, pp. 2–23, 2005.

[9] Cristian Cadar and Koushik Sen. Symbolic Execution for Software Testing: Three Decades Later. *Communications of the ACM*, pp. 82–90, 2013.

[10] Robert Cartwright and Mike Fagan. Soft Typing. In *Proc. ACM Conference on Programming Language Design and Implementation*, pp. 278–292, 1991.

[11] Koen Claessen and John Hughes. QuickCheck: A Lightweight Tool for Random Testing of Haskell Programs. In *Proc. ACM International Conference on Functional Programming*, pp. 268–279, 2000.

[12] Marko Dimjašević, Dimitra Giannakopoulou, Falk Howar, Falk Howar, Falk Howar, and Falk Howar. The Dart, the Psyco, and the Doop: Concolic Execution in Java. *ACM SIGSOFT Software Engineering Notes* 40(1), pp. 1–5, 2015.

[13] Christos Dimoulas, Sam Tobin-Hochstadt, and Matthias Felleisen. Complete Monitors for Behavioral Contracts. In *Proc. European Symposium on on Programming*, pp. 214–233, 2012.

[14] Michael Emmi, Rupak Majumdar, and Koushik Sen. Dynamic Test Input Generation for Database Applications. In *Proc. International Symposium on Software Testing and Analysis*, pp. 151–162, 2007.

[15] Azadeh Farzan, Andreas Holzer, Niloofar Razavi, and Helmut Veith. Con2Colic Testing. In *Proc. International Symposium on on the Foundations of Software Engineering*, pp. 37–47, 2013.

[16] Robert B. Findler and Matthias Felleisen. Contracts for Higher-Order Functions. In *Proc. ACM International Conference on Functional Programming*, pp. 48–59, 2002.

[17] Aggelos Giantsios, Nikolaos Papaspyrou, and Konstantinos Sagonas. Concolic Testing for Functional Languages. In *Proc. ACM International Conference on Principles and Practice of Declarative Programming*, pp. 137–148, 2015.

[18] Aggelos Giantsios, Nikolaos Papaspyrou, and Konstantinos Sagonas. Concolic Testing for Functional Languages. *Science of Computer Programming*, pp. 109–134, 2017.

[19] Patrice Godefroid. Compositional Dynamic Test Generation. In *Proc. ACM Symposium on Principles of Programming Languages*, pp. 47–54, 2007.

[20] Patrice Godefroid, Nils Klarlund, and Koushik Sen. DART: Directed Automated Random Testing. In *Proc. ACM Conference on Programming Language Design and Implementation*, pp. 213–223, 2005.

[21] Patrice Godefroid, Michael Y. Levin, and David Molnar. Automated Whitebox Fuzz Testing. In *Proc. Network and Distributed System Security Symposium*, 2008.

[22] Patrice Godefroid, Michael Y. Levin, and David Molnar. SAGE: Whitebox Fuzzing for Security Testing. *ACM Queue* 10(1), pp. 20:20–20:27, 2012.

[23] Li Guodong, Esben Andreasen, and Indradeep Ghosh. SymJS: Automatic Symbolic Testing of JavaScript Web Applications. In *Proc. International Symposium on on the Foundations of Software Engineering*, pp. 449–459, 2014.

[24] Yunho Kim, Shin Hong, and Moonzo Kim. Target-Driven Compositional Concolic Testing with Function Summary Refinement for Effective Bug Detection. In *Proc. International Symposium on on the Foundations of Software Engineering*, pp. 16–26, 2019.

[25] Yunho Kim and Moonzoo Kim. SCORE: A Scalable Concolic Testing Tool for Reliable Embedded Software. In *Proc. International Symposium on on the Foundations of Software Engineering*, pp. 420–423, 2011.

[26] Casey Klein, Matthew Flatt, and Robert Bruce Findler. Random Testing for Higher-order, Stateful Programs. In *Proc. ACM Conference on Object-Oriented Programming, Systems, Languages and Applications*, pp. 555–566, 2010.

[27] Naoki Kobayashi, Ryosuke Sato, and Hiroshi Unno. Predicate Abstraction and CEGAR for Higher-Order Model Checking. In *Proc. ACM Conference on Programming Language Design and Implementation*, pp. 222–233, 2011.

[28] Pieter Koopman and Rinus Plasmeijer. Automatic Testing of Higher Order Functions. In *Proc. Asian Symposium on Programming Languages and Systems*, pp. 148–164, 2006.

[29] Guodong Li, Indradeep Ghosh, and Sreeranga P. Rajan. KLOVER: A Symbolic Execution and Automatic Test Generation Tool for C++ Programs. In *Proc. International Conference on Computer Aided Verification*, pp. 609–615, 2011.

[30] Guodong Li, Peng Li, Geof Sawaya, Ganesh Gopalakrishnan, Indradeep Ghosh, and Sreeranga P. Rajan. GKLEE: Concolic Verification and Test Generation for GPUs. In *Proc. Symposium on Principles and Practice of Parallel Programming*, pp. 215–224, 2012.

[31] Lian Li, Yi Lu, and Jingling Xue. Dynamic Symbolic Execution for Polymorphism. In *Proc. International Conference on Compiler Construction*, pp. 120–130, 2017.

[32] Phúc Nguyễn, Sam Tobin-Hochstadt, and David Van Horn. Relatively complete counterexamples for higher-order programs. In *Proc. ACM Conference on Programming Language Design and Implementation*, pp. 446–456, 2015.

[33] Phúc Nguyễn, Sam Tobin-Hochstadt, and David Van Horn. Higher order symbolic execution for contract verification and refutation. *Journal of Functional Programming*(27), pp. e3:1–e3:54, 2017.

[34] Adrián Palacios and Germán Vidal. Concolic Execution in Functional Programming by Program Instrumentation. In *Proc. International Symposium on Logic-Based Program Synthesis and TRansformation*, pp. 277–292, 2015.

[35] Niloofar Razavi, Franjo Ivančić, Vineet Kahlon, and Aarti Gupta. Concurrent Test Generation Using Concolic Multi-trace Analysis. In *Proc. Asian Symposium on Programming Languages and Systems*, pp. 239–255, 2012.

[36] Marija Selakovic, Michael Pradel, Rezwana Karim, and Frank Tip. Test Generation for Higher-order Functions in Dynamic Languages. *Proceedings of the ACM on Programming Languages (OOPSLA)* 2, pp. 161:1–161:27, 2018.

[37] Koushik Sen and Gul Agha. CUTE and jCUTE: Concolic Unit Testing and Explicit Path Model-checking Tools. In *Proc. International Conference on Computer Aided Verification*, pp. 419–423, 2006.

[38] Koushik Sen, Swaroop Kalasapur, Brutch Tasneem, and Simon Gibbs. Jalangi: A Selective Record-replay and Dynamic Analysis Framework for JavaScript. In *Proc. International Symposium on on the Foundations of Software Engineering*, pp. 488–498, 2013.

[39] Koushik Sen, Darko Marinov, and Gul Agha. CUTE: A Concolic Unit Testing Engine for C. In *Proc. International Symposium on on the Foundations of Software Engineering*, pp. 263–272, 2005.

[40] T. Stephen Strickland, Sam Tobin-Hochstadt, Robert B. Findler, and Matthew Flatt. Chaperones and Impersonators: Run-time Support for Reasonable Interposition. In *Proc. ACM Conference on Object-Oriented Programming, Systems, Languages and Applications*, pp. 943–962, 2012.

[41] Youcheng Sun, Min Wu, Wenjie Ruan, Xiaowei Huang, Marta Kwiatkowska, and Daniel Kroening. Concolic Testing for Deep Neural Networks. In *Proc. ACM/IEEE International Conference on Automated Software Engineering*, pp. 109–119, 2018.

[42] Tachio Terauchi. Dependent Types from Counterexamples. In *Proc. ACM Symposium on Principles of Programming Languages*, pp. 119–130, 2010.

[43] Nikolai Tillmann and Jonathan de Halleux. Pex: White Box Test Generation for .NET. In *Proc. International Conference on Tests and Proofs*, pp. 134–153, 2008.

[44] Sam Tobin-Hochstadt and Matthias Felleisen. Logical Types for Untyped Languages. In *Proc. ACM International Conference on Functional Programming*, pp. 117–128, 2010.

[45] Sam Tobin-Hochstadt and David Van Horn. Higher-Order Symbolic Execution via Contracts. In *Proc. ACM Conference on Object-Oriented Programming, Systems, Languages and Applications*, pp. 537–554, 2012.

[46] Andrew K. Wright and Robert Cartwright. A Practical Soft Type System for Scheme. *ACM Transactions on Programming Languages and Systems* 19(1), pp. 87–152, 1997.

Strong-Separation Logic

Jens Pagel and Florian Zuleger (✉)

TU Wien, Vienna, Austria
{pagel,zuleger}@forsyte.at

Abstract. Most automated verifiers for separation logic are based on the symbolic-heap fragment, which disallows both the magic-wand operator and the application of classical Boolean operators to spatial formulas. This is not surprising, as support for the magic wand quickly leads to undecidability, especially when combined with inductive predicates for reasoning about data structures. To circumvent these undecidability results, we propose assigning a more restrictive semantics to the separating conjunction. We argue that the resulting logic, strong-separation logic, can be used for symbolic execution and abductive reasoning just like "standard" separation logic, while remaining decidable even in the presence of both the magic wand and the list-segment predicate—a combination of features that leads to undecidability for the standard semantics.

1 Introduction

Separation logic [40] is one of the most successful formalisms for the analysis and verification of programs making use of dynamic resources such as heap memory and access permissions [7,30,10,5,17,24,9]. At the heart of the success of separation logic (SL) is the *separating conjunction*, $*$, which supports concise statements about the disjointness of resources. In this article, we will focus on separation logic for describing the heap in single-threaded heap-manipulating programs. In this setting, the formula $\varphi * \psi$ can be read as "the heap can be split into two disjoint parts, such that φ holds for one part and ψ for the other."

Our article starts from the following observation: The standard semantics of $*$ allows splitting a heap into two arbitrary sub-heaps. The magic-wand operator $-\!\!*$, which is the adjoint of $*$, then allows adding arbitrary heaps. This arbitrary splitting and adding of heaps makes reasoning about SL formulas difficult, and quickly renders separation logic undecidable when inductive predicates for data structures are considered. For example, Demri et al. recently showed that adding only the singly-linked list-segment predicate to propositional separation logic (i.e., with $*$, $-\!\!*$ and classical connectives $\wedge, \vee, \neg$) leads to undecidability [16].

Most SL specifications used in automated verification do not, however, make use of arbitrary heap compositions. For example, the widely used symbolic-heap fragments of separation logic considered, e.g., in [3,4,13,21,22], have the following property: a symbolic heap satisfies a separating conjunction, if and only if one can split the model at locations that are the values of some program variables.

Motivated by this observation, we propose a more restrictive separating conjunction that allows splitting the heap only at location that are the values of some

N. Yoshida (Ed.): ESOP 2021, LNCS 12648, pp. 664–692, 2021.
https://doi.org/10.1007/978-3-030-72019-3_24

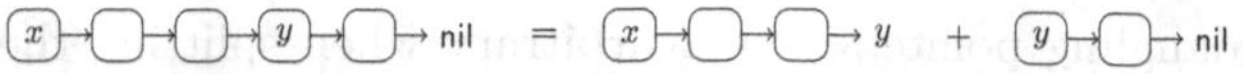

(a) A model of $\mathtt{ls}(x,y) * \mathtt{ls}(y,\mathsf{nil})$ in both the standard semantics and our semantics.

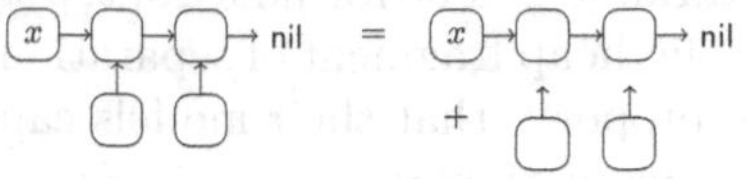

(b) A model of $\mathtt{ls}(x,\mathsf{nil}) * \mathtt{t}$ in the standard semantics.

Fig. 1: Two models and their decomposition into disjoint submodels. Dangling arrows represent dangling pointers.

program variables. We call the resulting logic *strong-separation logic*. Strong-separation logic (SSL) shares many properties with standard separation-logic semantics; for example, the models of our logic form a separation algebra. Because the *frame rule* and other standard SL inference rules continue to hold for SSL, SSL is suitable for deductive Hoare-style verification à la [23,40], symbolic execution [4], as well as abductive reasoning [10,9]. At the same time, SSL has much better computational properties than standard SL—especially when formulas contain expressive features such as the *magic wand*, $-\!\!*$, or negation.

We now give a more detailed introduction to the contributions of this article.

The standard semantics of the separating conjunction. To be able to justify our changed semantics of $*$, we need to introduce a bit of terminology. As standard in separation logic, we interpret SL formulas over *stack–heap pairs*. A *stack* is a mapping of the program variables to memory locations. A *heap* is a finite partial function between memory locations; if a memory location l is mapped to location l', we say the heap contains a *pointer* from l to l'. A memory location l is *allocated* if there is a pointer of the heap from l to some location l'. We call a location *dangling* if it is the target of a pointer but not allocated; a pointer is dangling if its target location is dangling.

Dangling pointers arise naturally in compositional specifications, i.e., in formulas that employ the separating conjunction $*$: In the standard semantics of separation logic, a stack–heap pair (s,h) satisfies a formula $\varphi * \psi$, if it is possible to split the heap h into two disjoint parts h_1 and h_2 such that (s,h_1) satisfies φ and (s,h_2) satisfies ψ. Here, disjoint means that the allocated locations of h_1 and h_2 are disjoint; however, the targets of the pointers of h_1 and h_2 do not have to be disjoint.

We illustrate this in Fig. 1a, where we show a graphical representation of a stack–heap pair (s,h) that satisfies the formula $\mathtt{ls}(x,y) * \mathtt{ls}(y,\mathsf{nil})$. Here, $\mathtt{ls}$ denotes the list-segment predicate. As shown in Fig. 1a, h can be split into two disjoint parts h_1 and h_2 such that (s,h_1) is a model of $\mathtt{ls}(x,y)$ and (s,h_2) is a model of $\mathtt{ls}(y,\mathsf{nil})$. Now, h_1 has a dangling pointer with target $s(y)$ (displayed with an orange background), while no pointer is dangling in the heap h.

In what sense is the standard semantics too permissive? The standard semantics of $*$ allows splitting a heap into two arbitrary sub-heaps, which may result in the introduction of arbitrary dangling pointers into the sub-heaps. We note, however, that the introduction of dangling pointers is *not* arbitrary when splitting the models of $\mathtt{ls}(x, y) * \mathtt{ls}(y, \mathsf{nil})$; there is only one way of splitting the models of this formula, namely at the location of program variable y. The formula $\mathtt{ls}(x, y) * \mathtt{ls}(y, \mathsf{nil})$ belongs to a certain variant of the symbolic-heap fragment of separation logic, and all formulas of this fragment have the property that their models can only be split at locations that are the values of some variables.

Standard SL semantics also allows the introduction of dangling pointers without the use of variables. Fig. 1b shows a model of $\mathtt{ls}(x, \mathsf{nil}) * \mathtt{t}$—assuming the standard semantics. Here, the formula $\mathtt{t}$ (for *true*) stands for any arbitrary heap. In particular, this includes heaps with arbitrary dangling pointers into the list segment $\mathtt{ls}(x, \mathsf{nil})$. This power of introducing arbitrary dangling pointers is what is used by Demri et al. for their undecidability proof of propositional separation logic with the singly-linked list-segment predicate [16].

Strong-separation logic. In this article, we want to explicitly *disallow* the *implicit* sharing of dangling locations when composing heaps. We propose to parameterize the separating conjunction by the stack and exclusively allow the union of heaps that only share locations that are pointed to by the stack. For example, the model in Fig. 1b is *not* a model of $\mathtt{ls}(x, \mathsf{nil}) * \mathtt{t}$ in our semantics because of the dangling pointers in the sub-heap that satisfies $\mathtt{t}$. *Strong-separation logic* (SSL) is the logic resulting from this restricted definition of the separating conjunction.

Why should I care? We argue that SSL is a promising proposal for automated program verification:

1) We show that the memory models of strong-separation logic form a *separation algebra* [11], which guarantees the soundness of the standard *frame rule* of SL [40]. Consequently, SSL can be potentially be used instead of standard SL in a wide variety of (semi-)automated analyzers and verifiers, including Hoare-style verification [40], symbolic execution [4], and bi-abductive shape analysis [10].

2) To date, most automated reasoners for separation logic have been developed for *symbolic-heap separation logic* [3,4,10,21,22,26,32,27]. In these fragments of separation logic, assertions about the heap can exclusively be combined via $*$; neither the magic wand $-\!\!*$ nor classical Boolean connectives are permitted. We show that the strong semantics agrees with the standard semantics on symbolic heaps. For this reason, symbolic-heap SL specifications remain unchanged when switching to strong-separation logic.

3) We establish that the satisfiability and entailment problem for full propositional separation logic with the singly-linked list-segment predicate is decidable in our semantics (in PSPACE)—in stark contrast to the aforementioned undecidability result obtained by Demri et al. [16] assuming the standard semantics.

4) The standard Hoare-style approach to verification requires discharging verification conditions (VCs), which amounts to proving for loop-free pieces of code that a pre-condition implies some post-condition. Discharging VCs can be automated by calculi that symbolically execute the pre-condition forward resp. the post-condition backward, and then using an entailment checker for proving the implication. For SL, symbolic execution calculi can be formulated using the magic wand resp. the septraction operator. However, these operators have

proven to be difficult for automated procedures: "VC-generators do not work especially well with separation logic, as they introduce magic-wand $-\!\!*$ operators which are difficult to eliminate." [2, p. 131] In contrast, we demonstrate that SSL can overcome the described difficulties. We formulate a forward symbolic execution calculus for a simple heap-manipulating programming language using SSL. In conjunction with our entailment checker, see 3), our calculus gives rise to a fully-automated procedure for discharging VCs of loop-free code segments.

5) Computing solutions to the *abduction problem* is an integral building block of Facebook's Infer analyzer [9], required for a scalable and fully-automated shape analysis [10]. We show how to compute explicit representations of optimal, i.e., *logically weakest* and *spatially minimal*, solutions to the abduction problem for the separation logic considered in this paper. The result is of theoretical interest, as explicit representations for optimal solutions to the abduction problem are hard to obtain [10,19].

Contributions. Our main contributions are as follows:

1. We propose and motivate *strong-separation logic* (SSL), a new semantics for separation logic.
2. We present a PSPACE decision procedure for strong-separation logic with points-to assertions, the list-segment predicate $\mathtt{ls}(x, y)$, and spatial and classical operators, i.e., $*$, $-\!\!*$, $\wedge$, $\vee$, $\neg$[1]—a logic that is undecidable when assuming the standard semantics [16].
3. We present symbolic execution rules for SSL, which allow us to discharge verification conditions fully automatically.
4. We show how to compute explicit representations of optimal solutions to the abduction problem for the SSL considered in (2).

We strongly believe that these results motivate further research on SSL (e.g., going beyond the singly-linked list-segment predicate, implementing our decision procedure and integrating it into fully-automated analyzers).

Related work. The undecidability of separation logic was established already in [12]. Since then, decision problems for a large number of fragments and variants of separation logic have been studied. Most of this work has been on symbolic-heap separation logic or other variants of the logic that neither support the magic wand nor the use of negation below the $*$ operator. While entailment in the symbolic-heap fragment with inductive definitions is undecidable in general [1], there are decision procedures for variants with built-in lists and/or trees [3,13,34,35,36], support for defining variants of linear structures [20] or tree structures [42,22] or graphs of bounded tree width [21,26]. The expressive heap logics STRAND [29] and DRYAD [37] also have decidable fragments, as have some other separation logics that allow combining shape and data constraints. Besides the already mentioned work [35,36], these include [28,25].

[1] An extension of this result to a separation logic that also supports trees can be found in the dissertation of the first author [31]

Among the aforementioned works, the graph-based decision procedures of [13] and [25] are most closely related to our approach. Note however, that neither of these works supports reasoning about magic wands or negation below the separating conjunction.

In contrast to symbolic-heap SL, separation logics with the *magic wand* quickly become undecidable. Propositional separation logic with the magic wand, but without inductive data structures, was shown to be decidable in PSPACE in the early days of SL research [12]. Support for this fragment was added to CVC4 a few years ago [39]. Some tools have "lightweight" support for the magic wand involving heuristics and user annotations, in part motivated by the lack of decision procedures [6,41].

There is a significant body of work studying first-order SL with the magic wand and unary points-to assertions, but without a list predicate. This logic was first shown to be undecidable in [8]; a result that has since been refined, showing e.g. that while satisfiability is still in PSPACE if we allow one quantified variable [15], two variables already lead to undecidability, even without the separating conjunction [14]. Echenim et al. [18] have recently addressed the satisfiability problem of SL with $\exists^*\forall^*$ quantifier prefix, separating conjunction, magic wand, and full Boolean closure, but no inductive definitions. The logic was shown to be undecidable in general (contradicting an earlier claim [38]), but decidable in PSPACE under certain restrictions.

Outline. In Section 2, we introduce two semantics of propositional separation logic, the standard semantics and our new *strong-separation* semantics. We show the decidability of the satisfiability and entailment problems of SSL with lists in Section 3. We present symbolic execution rules for SSL in Section 4. We show how to compute explicit representations of optimal solutions to the abduction problem in Section 5. We conclude in Section 6. All missing proofs are given in the extended version [33] for space reasons.

2 Strong- and Weak-Separation Logic

2.1 Preliminaries

We denote by $|X|$ the cardinality of the set X. Let f be a (partial) function. Then $\mathrm{dom}(f)$ and $\mathrm{img}(f)$ denote the domain and image of f, respectively. We write $|f| := |\mathrm{dom}(f)|$ and $f(x) = \bot$ for $x \notin \mathrm{dom}(f)$. We frequently use set notation to define and reason about partial functions: $f := \{x_1 \mapsto y_1, \ldots, x_k \mapsto y_k\}$ is the partial function that maps x_i to y_i, $1 \leq i \leq k$, and is undefined on all other values; $f^{-1}(b)$ is the set of all elements a with $f(a) = b$; we write $f \cup g$ resp. $f \cap g$ for the union resp. intersection of partial functions f and g, provided that $f(a) = g(a)$ for all $a \in \mathrm{dom}(f) \cap \mathrm{dom}(g)$; similarly, $f \subseteq g$ holds if $\mathrm{dom}(f) \subseteq \mathrm{dom}(g)$. Sets and ordered sequences are denoted in boldface, e.g., $\mathbf{x}$. To list the elements of a sequence, we write $\langle x_1, \ldots, x_k \rangle$.

We assume a linearly-ordered infinite set of variables $\mathbf{Var}$ with $\mathsf{nil} \in \mathbf{Var}$ and denote by $\max(\mathbf{v})$ the maximal variable among a set of variables $\mathbf{v}$ according

$$\tau ::= \mathbf{emp} \mid x \mapsto y \mid \mathtt{ls}(x,y) \mid x = y \mid x \neq y$$
$$\varphi ::= \tau \mid \varphi * \varphi \mid \varphi \text{-}\circledast \varphi \mid \varphi \wedge \varphi \mid \varphi \vee \varphi \mid \neg\varphi$$

Fig. 2: The syntax of separation logic with list segments.

$(s,h) \models \mathbf{emp}$ iff $\mathrm{dom}(h) = \emptyset$
$(s,h) \models x = y$ iff $\mathrm{dom}(h) = \emptyset$ and $s(x) = s(y)$
$(s,h) \models x \neq y$ iff $\mathrm{dom}(h) = \emptyset$ and $s(x) \neq s(y)$
$(s,h) \models x \mapsto y$ iff $h = \{s(x) \mapsto s(y)\}$
$(s,h) \models \mathtt{ls}(x,y)$ iff $\mathrm{dom}(h) = \emptyset$ and $s(x) = s(y)$ or there exist $n \geq 1, \ell_0, \dots, \ell_n$ with $h = \{\ell_0 \mapsto \ell_1, \dots, \ell_{n-1} \mapsto \ell_n\}, s(x) = \ell_0$ and $s(y) = \ell_n$
$(s,h) \models \varphi_1 \wedge \varphi_2$ iff $(s,h) \models \varphi_1$ and $(s,h) \models \varphi_2$
$(s,h) \models \neg\varphi$ iff $(s,h) \not\models \varphi$
$(s,h) \models^{\mathsf{wk}} \varphi_1 * \varphi_2$ iff there exist h_1, h_2 with $h = h_1 + h_2, (s,h_1) \models^{\mathsf{wk}} \varphi_1, (s,h_2) \models^{\mathsf{wk}} \varphi_2$
$(s,h) \models^{\mathsf{wk}} \varphi_1 \text{-}\circledast \varphi_2$ iff exist h_1 with $(s,h_1) \models^{\mathsf{wk}} \varphi_1, h + h_1 \neq \bot$ and $(s, h+h_1) \models^{\mathsf{wk}} \varphi_2$
$(s,h) \models^{\mathsf{st}} \varphi_1 * \varphi_2$ iff there exists h_1, h_2 with $h = h_1 \uplus^s h_2, (s,h_1) \models^{\mathsf{st}} \varphi_1, (s,h_2) \models^{\mathsf{st}} \varphi_2$
$(s,h) \models^{\mathsf{st}} \varphi_1 \text{-}\circledast \varphi_2$ iff exists h_1 with $(s,h_1) \models^{\mathsf{st}} \varphi_1, h \uplus^s h_1 \neq \bot$ and $(s, h \uplus^s h_1) \models^{\mathsf{st}} \varphi_2$

Fig. 3: The standard, "weak" semantics of separation logic, $\models^{\mathsf{wk}}$, and the "strong" semantics, $\models^{\mathsf{st}}$. We write $\models$ when there is no difference between $\models^{\mathsf{wk}}$ and $\models^{\mathsf{st}}$.

to this order. In Fig. 2, we define the syntax of the separation-logic fragment we study in this article. The atomic formulas of our logic are the *empty-heap predicate* **emp**, *points-to assertions* $x \mapsto y$, the *list-segment predicate* $\mathtt{ls}(x,y)$, equalities $x = y$ and disequalities $x \neq y$[2] ; in all these cases, $x, y \in \mathbf{Var}$. Formulas are closed under the classical Boolean operators $\wedge, \vee, \neg$ as well as under the *separating conjunction* $*$ and the existential magic wand, also called the *septraction*, $\text{-}\circledast$ (see e.g. [8]). We collect the set of all SL formulas in **SL**. We also consider derived operators and formulas, in particular the *separating implication* (or *magic wand*), $\text{-}\!*$, defined by $\varphi \text{-}\!* \psi := \neg(\varphi \text{-}\circledast \neg\psi)$.[3] We also use *true*, defined as $\mathsf{t} := \mathbf{emp} \vee \neg\mathbf{emp}$. Finally, for $\Phi = \{\varphi_1, \dots, \varphi_n\}$, we define $\ast\Phi := \varphi_1 * \varphi_2 * \cdots * \varphi_n$ if $n > 1$ and $\ast\Phi := \mathbf{emp}$ if $n = 0$. By $\mathsf{fvs}(\varphi)$ we denote the set of (free) variables of φ. We define the *size* of the formula φ as $|\varphi| = 1$ for atomic formulas φ, $|\varphi_1 \times \varphi_2| := |\varphi_1| + |\varphi_2| + 1$ for $\times \in \{\wedge, \vee, *, \text{-}\circledast\}$ and $|\neg\varphi_1| := |\varphi_1| + 1$.

2.2 Two Semantics of Separation Logic

Memory model. **Loc** is an infinite set of *heap locations*. A *stack* is a partial function $s\colon \mathbf{Var} \rightharpoonup \mathbf{Loc}$. A *heap* is a partial function $h\colon \mathbf{Loc} \rightharpoonup \mathbf{Loc}$. A *model* is a stack–heap pair (s,h) with $\mathsf{nil} \in \mathrm{dom}(s)$ and $s(\mathsf{nil}) \notin \mathrm{dom}(h)$. We let $\mathsf{locs}(h) :=$

[2] As our logic contains negation, $x \neq y$ can be expressed as $\neg(x = y)$. However, we treat disequalities as atomic to be able to use them in the positive fragment of our logic, defined later, which precludes the use of negation.

[3] As $\text{-}\!*$ can be defined via $\text{-}\circledast$ and $\neg$ and vice-versa, the expressivity of our logic does not depend on which operator we choose. We have chosen $\text{-}\circledast$ because we can include this operator in the positive fragment considered later on.

$\text{dom}(h) \cup \text{img}(h)$. A location ℓ is *dangling* if $\ell \in \text{img}(h) \setminus \text{dom}(h)$. We write $\mathbf{S}$ for the set of all stacks and $\mathbf{H}$ for the set of all heaps.

Two notions of disjoint union of heaps. We write $h_1 + h_2$ for the union of disjoint heaps, i.e.,

$$h_1 + h_2 := \begin{cases} h_1 \cup h_2, & \text{if } \text{dom}(h_1) \cap \text{dom}(h_2) = \emptyset \\ \bot, & \text{otherwise.} \end{cases}$$

This standard notion of disjoint union is commonly used to assign semantics to the separating conjunction and magic wand. It requires that h_1 and h_2 are domain-disjoint, but does not impose any restrictions on the *images* of the heaps. In particular, the dangling pointers of h_1 may alias arbitrarily with the domain and image of h_2 and vice-versa.

Let s be a stack. We write $h_1 \uplus^s h_2$ for the disjoint union of h_1 and h_2 that restricts aliasing of dangling pointers to the locations in stack s. This yields an infinite family of union operators: one for each stack. Formally,

$$h_1 \uplus^s h_2 := \begin{cases} h_1 + h_2, & \text{if } \mathsf{locs}(h_1) \cap \mathsf{locs}(h_2) \subseteq \text{img}(s) \\ \bot, & \text{otherwise.} \end{cases}$$

Intuitively, $h_1 \uplus^s h_2$ is the (disjoint) union of heaps that share only locations that are in the image of the stack s. Note that if $h_1 \uplus^s h_2$ is defined then $h_1 + h_2$ is defined, but not vice-versa.

Just like the standard disjoint union $+$, the operator $\uplus^s$ gives rise to a separation algebra, i.e., a cancellative, commutative partial monoid [11]:

Lemma 1. *Let s be a stack and let u be the empty heap (i.e., $\text{dom}(u) = \emptyset$). The triple $(\mathbf{H}, \uplus^s, u)$ is a separation algebra.*

Weak- and strong-separation logic. Both $+$ and $\uplus^s$ can be used to give a semantics to the separating conjunction and septraction. We denote the corresponding model relations $\overset{\mathsf{wk}}{\models}$ and $\overset{\mathsf{st}}{\models}$ and define them in Fig. 3. Where the two semantics agree, we simply write $\models$.

In both semantics, **emp** only holds for the empty heap, and $x = y$ holds for the empty heap when x and y are interpreted by the same location[4]. Points-to assertions $x \mapsto y$ are precise, i.e., only hold in singleton heaps. (It is, of course, possible to express intuitionistic points-to assertions by $x \mapsto y * \mathsf{t}$.) The list segment predicate $\mathtt{ls}(x, y)$ holds in possibly-empty lists of pointers from $s(x)$ to $s(y)$. The semantics of Boolean connectives are standard. The semantics of the separating conjunction, $*$, and septraction, $-\circledast$, differ based on the choice of $+$ vs. $\uplus^s$ for combining disjoint heaps. In the former case, denoted $\overset{\mathsf{wk}}{\models}$, we get the standard semantics of separation logic (cf. [40]). In the latter case, denoted $\overset{\mathsf{st}}{\models}$, we get a semantics that imposes stronger requirements on sub-heap composition: Sub-heaps may only overlap at locations that are stored in the stack.

[4] Usually $x = y$ is defined to hold for *all* heaps, not just the empty heap, when x and y are interpreted by the same location; however, this choice does not change the expressivity of the logic: the formula $(x = y) * \mathsf{t}$ expresses the standard semantics. Our choice is needed for the results on the positive fragment considered in Section 2.3

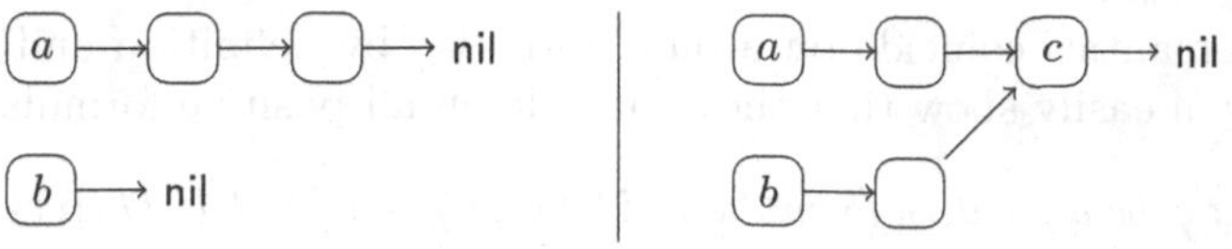

Fig. 4: Two models of $(\mathtt{ls}(a, \mathsf{nil}) * \mathsf{t}) \wedge (\mathtt{ls}(b, \mathsf{nil}) * \mathsf{t})$ for a stack with domain a, b and a stack with domain a, b, c.

Because the semantics $\overset{\mathsf{st}}{\models}$ imposes stronger constraints, we will refer to the standard semantics $\overset{\mathsf{wk}}{\models}$ as the *weak* semantics of separation logic and to the semantics $\overset{\mathsf{st}}{\models}$ as the *strong* semantics of separation logic. Moreover, we use the terms *weak-separation logic* (WSL) and *strong-separation logic* (SSL) to distinguish between SL with the semantics $\overset{\mathsf{wk}}{\models}$ and $\overset{\mathsf{st}}{\models}$.

Example 1. Let $\varphi := a \neq b * (\mathtt{ls}(a, \mathsf{nil}) * \mathsf{t}) \wedge (\mathtt{ls}(b, \mathsf{nil}) * \mathsf{t})$. In Fig. 4, we show two models of φ. On the left, we assume that a, b are the only program variables, whereas on the right, we assume that there is a third program variable c.

Note that the latter model, where the two lists overlap, is possible in SSL *only* because the lists come together at the location labeled by c. If we removed variable c from the stack, the model would no longer satisfy φ according to the strong semantics, because $\uplus^s$ would no longer allow splitting the heap at that location. Conversely, the model would still satisfy φ with standard semantics.

This is a feature rather than a bug of SSL: By demanding that the user of SSL specify aliasing explicitly—for example by using the specification $\mathtt{ls}(a, c) * \mathtt{ls}(b, c) * \mathtt{ls}(c, \mathsf{nil}) \wedge c \neq \mathsf{nil}$—we rule out unintended aliasing effects. △

Satisfiability and Semantic Consequence. We define the notions of satisfiability and semantic consequence parameterized by a finite set of variables $\mathbf{x} \subseteq \mathbf{Var}$. For a formula φ with $\mathsf{fvs}(\varphi) \subseteq \mathbf{x}$, we say that φ is *satisfiable* w.r.t. $\mathbf{x}$ if there is a model (s, h) with $\mathrm{dom}(s) = \mathbf{x}$ such that $(s, h) \overset{\mathsf{st}}{\models} \varphi$. We say that φ *entails* ψ w.r.t. $\mathbf{x}$, in signs $\varphi \overset{\mathsf{st}}{\models}_{\mathbf{x}} \psi$, if $(s, h) \overset{\mathsf{st}}{\models} \varphi$ then also $(s, h) \overset{\mathsf{st}}{\models} \psi$ for all models (s, h) with $\mathrm{dom}(s) = \mathbf{x}$.

2.3 Correspondence of Strong and Weak Semantics on Positive Formulas

We call an SL formula φ *positive* if it does not contain $\neg$. Note that, in particular, this implies that φ does *not* contain the magic wand $-\!\!*$ or the atom t.

In models of positive formulas, all dangling locations are labeled by variables:

Lemma 2. *Let φ be positive and $(s, h) \overset{\mathsf{wk}}{\models} \varphi$. Then,* $(\mathrm{img}(h) \setminus \mathrm{dom}(h)) \subseteq \mathrm{img}(s)$.

As every location shared by heaps h_1 h_2 in $h_1 + h_2$ is dangling either in h_1 or in h_2 (or both), the operations $+$ and $\uplus^s$ coincide on models of positive formulas:

Lemma 3. *Let $(s, h_1) \overset{\mathsf{wk}}{\models} \varphi_1$ and $(s, h_2) \overset{\mathsf{wk}}{\models} \varphi_2$ for positive formulas φ_1, φ_2. Then $h_1 + h_2 \neq \bot$ iff $h_1 \uplus^s h_2 \neq \bot$.*

Since the semantics coincide on atomic formulas by definition and on $*$ by Lemma 2, we can easily show that they coincide on all positive formulas:

Lemma 4. *Let* φ *be a positive formula and let* (s,h) *be a model. Then* $(s,h) \models^{\mathsf{wk}} \varphi$ *iff* $(s,h) \models^{\mathsf{st}} \varphi$.

By negating Lemma 4, we have that $\{(s,h) \mid (s,h) \models^{\mathsf{wk}} \varphi\} \neq \left\{(s,h) \mid (s,h) \models^{\mathsf{st}} \varphi\right\}$ implies that φ contains negation, either explicitly or in the form of a magic wand or $\mathtt{t}$. In particular, Lemma 4 implies that the two semantics coincide on the popular *symbolic-heap fragment* of separation logic.[5]

We remark that formula φ in Example 1 only employs $\mathtt{t}$ but not $\neg$, $\mathrel{-\!\!*}$. Hence, even if only $\mathtt{t}$ would be added to the positive fragment, Lemma 4 would no longer hold. Likewise, Lemma 4 does not hold under intuitionistic semantics: as the intuitionistic semantics of a predicate p is equivalent to $p * \mathtt{t}$ under classic semantics, if is sufficient to consider $\varphi := a \neq b * (\mathtt{ls}(a, \mathsf{nil}) \wedge (\mathtt{ls}(b, \mathsf{nil}))$.

3 Deciding the SSL Satisfiability Problem

The goal of this section is to develop a decision procedure for SSL:

Theorem 1. *Let* $\varphi \in \mathbf{SL}$ *and let* $\mathbf{x} \subseteq \mathbf{Var}$ *be a finite set of variables with* $\mathsf{fvs}(\varphi) \subseteq \mathbf{x}$. *It is decidable in* PSPACE *(in* $|\varphi|$ *and* $|\mathbf{x}|$*) whether there exists a model* (s,h) *with* $\mathrm{dom}(s) = \mathbf{x}$ *and* $(s,h) \models^{\mathsf{st}} \varphi$.

Our approach is based on abstracting stack–heap models by *abstract memory states* (AMS), which have two key properties, which together imply Theorem 1:

Refinement (Theorem 2). If (s_1,h_1) and (s_2,h_2) abstract to the same AMS, then they satisfy the same formulas. That is, the AMS abstraction *refines* the satisfaction relation of SSL.

Computability (Theorem 5, Lemmas 20 and 22). For each formula φ, we can compute (in PSPACE) the set of all AMSs of all models of φ; then, φ is satisfiable if this set is nonempty.

The AMS abstraction is motivated by the following insights.

1. The operator $\uplus^s$ induces a unique decomposition of the heap into at most $|s|$ minimal *chunks* of memory that cannot be further decomposed.
2. To decide whether $(s,h) \models^{\mathsf{st}} \varphi$ holds, it is sufficient to know for each chunk of (s,h) a) which atomic formulas the chunk satisfies and b) which variables (if any) are allocated in the chunk.

[5] Strictly speaking, Lemma 4 implies this only for the symbolic-heap fragment of the separation logic studied in this paper, i.e., with the list predicate but no other data structures. The result can, however, be generalized to symbolic heaps with trees (see the dissertation of the first author [31]). Symbolic heaps of bounded treewidth as proposed in [21] are an interesting direction for future work.

We proceed as follows. In Sec 3.1, we make precise the notion of memory chunks. In Sec. 3.2, we define *abstract memory states* (AMS), an abstraction of models that retains for every chunk precisely the information from point (2) above. We will prove the *refinement theorem* in 3.3. We will show in Sections 3.4–3.6 that we can compute the AMS of the models of a given formula φ, which allows us to decide satisfiability and entailment problems for SSL. Finally, we prove the PSPACE-completeness result in Sec. 3.7.

3.1 Memory Chunks

We will abstract a model (s, h) by abstracting every *chunk* of h, which is a *minimal* nonempty sub-heap of (s, h) that can be split off of h according to the strong-separation semantics.

Definition 1 (Sub-heap). *Let* (s, h) *be a model. We say that* h_1 *is a* sub-heap *of* h*, in signs* $h_1 \sqsubseteq h$*, if there is some heap* h_2 *such that* $h = h_1 \uplus^s h_2$*. We collect all sub-heaps in the set* $\mathsf{subHeaps}(s, h)$*.* △

The following proposition is an immediate consequence of the above definition:

Proposition 1. *Let* (s, h) *be a model. Then,* $(\mathsf{subHeaps}(s, h), \sqsubseteq, \sqcup, \sqcap, \neg)$ *is a Boolean algebra with greatest element* h *and smallest element* $\emptyset$*, where*

- $(s, h_1) \sqcup (s, h_2) := (s, h_1 \cup h_2)$,
- $(s, h_1) \sqcap (s, h_2) := (s, h_1 \cap h_2)$*, and*
- $\neg(s, h_1) := (s, h_1')$*, where* $h_1' \in \mathsf{subHeaps}(s, h)$ *is the unique sub-heap with* $h = h_1 \uplus^s h_1'$*.*

The fact that the sub-models form a Boolean algebra allows us to make the following definition[6]:

Definition 2 (Chunk). *Let* (s, h) *be a model. A* chunk *of* (s, h) *is an atom of the Boolean algebra* $(\mathsf{subHeaps}(s, h), \sqsubseteq, \sqcup, \sqcap, \neg)$*. We collect all chunks of* (s, h) *in the set* $\mathsf{chunks}(s, h)$*.* △

Because every element of a Boolean algebra can be uniquely decomposed into atoms, we obtain that every heap can be fully decomposed into its chunks:

Proposition 2. *Let* (s, h) *be a model and let* $\mathsf{chunks}(s, h) = \{h_1, \ldots, h_n\}$ *be its chunks. Then,* $h = h_1 \uplus^s h_2 \uplus^s \cdots \uplus^s h_n$*.*

Example 2. Let $s = \{x \mapsto 1, y \mapsto 3, u \mapsto 5, z \mapsto 3, w \mapsto 7, v \mapsto 9\}$ and $h = \{1 \mapsto 2, 2 \mapsto 3, 3 \mapsto 8, 4 \mapsto 6, 5 \mapsto 6, 6 \mapsto 3, 7 \mapsto 6, 9 \mapsto 9, 10 \mapsto 11, 11 \mapsto 10\}$. The model (s, h) is illustrated in Fig. 5. This time, we include the identities of

[6] It is an interesting question for future work to relate the chunks considered in this paper to the atomic building blocks used in SL symbolic executions engines. Likewise, it would be interesting to build a symbolic execution engine based on the chunks resp. on the AMS abstraction proposed in this paper.

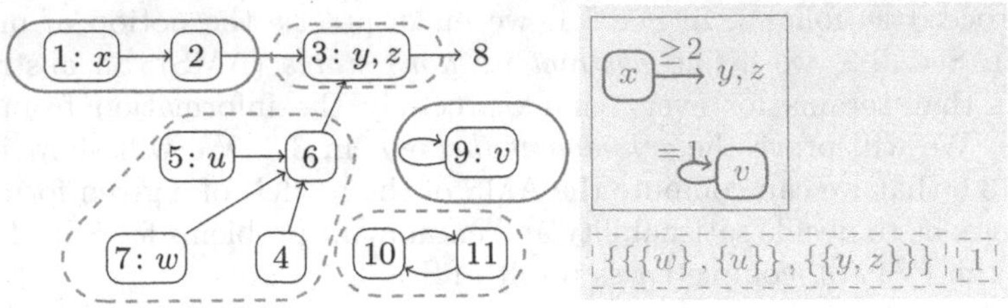

Fig. 5: Graphical representation of a model consisting of five chunks (left, see Ex. 2) and its induced AMS (right, see Ex. 5).

the locations in the graphical representation; e.g., $3\colon y, z$ represents location 3, $s(y) = 3$, $s(z) = 3$. The model consists of five chunks, $h_1 := \{1 \mapsto 2, 2 \mapsto 3\}$, $h_2 := \{9 \mapsto 9\}$, $h_3 := \{4 \mapsto 6, 5 \mapsto 6, 6 \mapsto 3, 7 \mapsto 6\}$, $h_4 := \{3 \mapsto 8\}$, and $h_5 := \{10 \mapsto 11, 11 \mapsto 10\}$. △

We distinguish two types of chunks: those that satisfy SSL atoms and those that don't.

Definition 3 (Positive and Negative chunk). *Let $h_c \subseteq h$ be a chunk of (s, h). h_c is a* positive chunk *if there exists an atomic formula τ such that $(s, h_c) \overset{\text{st}}{\models} \tau$. Otherwise, h_c is a* negative chunk. *We collect the respective chunks in* $\mathsf{chunks}^+(s, h)$ *and* $\mathsf{chunks}^-(s, h)$.

Example 3. Recall the chunks h_1 through h_5 from Ex. 2. h_1 and h_2 are positive chunks (blue in Fig. 5), h_3 to h_5 are negative chunks (orange). △

Negative chunks fall into three (not mutually-exclusive) categories:

Garbage. Chunks with locations that are inaccessible via stack variables.

Unlabeled dangling pointers. Chunks with an unlabeled sink, i.e., a dangling location that is not in $\mathrm{img}(s)$ and thus *cannot* be "made non-dangling" via composition using $\uplus^s$.

Overlaid list segments. Overlaid list segments that cannot be separated via $\uplus^s$ because they are joined at locations that are not in $\mathrm{img}(s)$.

Example 4 (Negative chunks). The chunk h_3 from Example 2 contains garbage, namely the location 4 that cannot be reached via stack variables, *and* two overlaid list segments (from 5 to 3 and 7 to 3). The chunk h_4 has an unlabeled dangling pointer. The chunk h_5 contains only garbage.

3.2 Abstract Memory States

In *abstract memory states* (AMSs), we retain for every chunk enough information to (1) determine which atomic formulas the chunk satisfies, and (2) keep track of which variables are allocated within each chunk.

Definition 4. *A quadruple $\mathcal{A} = \langle V, E, \rho, \gamma \rangle$ is an* abstract memory state, *if*

1. *V is a* partition *of some finite set of variables, i.e., $V = \{\mathbf{v}_1, \ldots, \mathbf{v}_n\}$ for some non-empty disjoint finite sets $\mathbf{v}_i \subseteq \mathbf{Var}$,*
2. *$E\colon V \rightharpoonup V \times \{=1, \geq 2\}$ is a partial function such that there is no $\mathbf{v} \in \mathrm{dom}(E)$ with $\mathsf{nil} \in \mathbf{v}$*[7]*,*
3. *ρ consists of disjoint subsets of V such that every $R \in \rho$ is disjoint from* $\mathrm{dom}(E)$ *and there is no $\mathbf{v} \in R$ with $\mathsf{nil} \in \mathbf{v}$,*
4. *γ is a natural number, i.e., $\gamma \in \mathbb{N}$.*

We call V the nodes, *E the* edges, *ρ the* negative-allocation constraint *and γ the* garbage-chunk count *of $\mathcal{A}$. We call the AMS $\mathcal{A} = \langle V, E, \rho, \gamma \rangle$* garbage-free *if $\rho = \emptyset$ and $\gamma = \emptyset$.*

We collect the set of all AMSs in **AMS**. *The* size *of $\mathcal{A}$ is given by $|\mathcal{A}| := |V| + \gamma$. Finally, the* allocated variables *of an AMS are given by* $\mathbf{alloc}(\mathcal{A}) := \mathrm{dom}(E) \cup \bigcup \rho$. △

Every model induces an AMS, defined in terms of the following auxiliary definitions. The equivalence class of variable x with regard to stack s is $[x]^s_= := \{y \mid s(y) = s(x)\}$; the set of all equivalence classes of a given stack s is $\mathsf{cls}_=(s) := \{[x]^s_= \mid x \in \mathrm{dom}(s)\}$. We now define the edges induced by a model (s, h). For every equivalence class $[x]^s_= \in \mathsf{cls}_=(s)$, we set

$$\mathsf{edges}(s,h)([x]^s_=) := \begin{cases} \langle [y]^s_=, =1 \rangle & \text{there are } y \in \mathrm{dom}(s) \text{ and } h_c \in \mathsf{chunks}^+(s,h) \\ & \text{with } (s,h_c) \models^{\mathsf{st}} x \mapsto y \\ \langle [y]^s_=, \geq 2 \rangle & \text{there are } y \in \mathrm{dom}(s) \text{ and } h_c \in \mathsf{chunks}^+(s,h) \\ & \text{with } (s,h_c) \models^{\mathsf{st}} \mathtt{ls}(x,y) \land \neg x \mapsto y \\ \bot, & \text{otherwise.} \end{cases}$$

Finally, we denote the sets of variables allocated in negative chunks by

$$\mathsf{alloc}^-(s,h) := \{\{[x]^s_= \mid s(x) \in \mathrm{dom}(h_c)\} \mid h_c \in \mathsf{chunks}^-(s,h)\} \setminus \{\emptyset\},$$

where (equivalence classes of) variables that are allocated in the same negative chunk are grouped together in a set.

Now we are ready to define the *induced AMS* of a model.

Definition 5. *Let (s, h) be a model. Let $V := \mathsf{cls}_=(s)$, $E := \mathsf{edges}(s,h)$, $\rho := \mathsf{alloc}^-(s,h)$ and $\gamma := \left|\mathsf{chunks}^-(s,h)\right| - \left|\mathsf{alloc}^-(s,h)\right|$.*

Then, we say that $\mathsf{ams}(s,h) := \langle V, E, \rho, \gamma \rangle$ is the induced AMS *of (s, h).* △

Example 5. The induced AMS of the model (s, h) from Ex. 2 is illustrated on the right-hand side of Fig. 5. The blue box depicts the graph (V, E) induced by the positive chunks h_1, h_2; the negative chunks that allocate variables are abstracted to the set $\rho = \{\{\{w\}, \{u\}\}, \{\{y, z\}\}\}$ (note that the variables w and u are allocated in the chunk h_3 and the aliasing variables y, z are allocated in h_4); and the garbage-chunk count is 1, because h_5 is the only negative chunk that does not allocate stack variables. △

[7] The edges of an AMS represent either a single pointer (case "$=1$") or a list segment of at least length (case "≥ 2").

Observe that the induced AMS is indeed an AMS:

Proposition 3. *Let* (s, h) *be a model. Then* $\mathsf{ams}(s, h) \in \mathbf{AMS}$.

The reverse also holds: Every AMS is the induced AMS of at least one model; in fact, even of a model of linear size.

Lemma 5 (Realizability of AMS). *Let* $\mathcal{A} = \langle V, E, \rho, \gamma \rangle$ *be an AMS. There exists a model* (s, h) *with* $\mathsf{ams}(s, h) = \mathcal{A}$ *whose size is linear in the size of* $\mathcal{A}$.

The following lemma demonstrates that we only need the ρ and γ components in order to be able to deal with negation and/or the magic wand:

Lemma 6 (Models of Positive Formulas have Garbage-free Abstractions). *Let* (s, h) *be a model. If* $(s, h) \models \varphi$ *for a positive formula* φ, *then* $\mathsf{ams}(s, h)$ *is garbage-free.*

We abstract SL formulas by the set of AMS of their models:

Definition 6. *Let* s *be a stack. The* **SL** abstraction *w.r.t.* s, $\alpha_s \colon \mathbf{SL} \to 2^{\mathbf{AMS}}$, *is given by*

$$\alpha_s(\varphi) := \{\mathsf{ams}(s, h) \mid h \in \mathbf{H},\ \text{and } (s, h) \overset{\mathsf{st}}{\models} \varphi\}. \qquad \triangle$$

Because AMSs do not retain any information about heap locations, just about aliasing, abstractions do not differ for stacks with the same equivalence classes:

Lemma 7. *Let* s, s' *be stacks with* $\mathsf{cls}_=(s) = \mathsf{cls}_=(s')$. *Then* $\alpha_s(\varphi) = \alpha_{s'}(\varphi)$ *for all formulas* φ.

3.3 The Refinement Theorem for SSL

The main goal of this section is to show the following *refinement theorem*:

Theorem 2 (Refinement Theorem). *Let* φ *be a formula and let* (s, h_1), (s, h_2) *be models with* $\mathsf{ams}(s, h_1) = \mathsf{ams}(s, h_2)$. *Then* $(s, h_1) \overset{\mathsf{st}}{\models} \varphi$ *iff* $(s, h_2) \overset{\mathsf{st}}{\models} \varphi$.

We will prove this theorem step by step, characterizing the AMS abstraction of all atomic formulas and of the composed models before proving the refinement theorem. In the remainder of this section, we fix some model (s, h).

Abstract Memory States of Atomic Formulas The empty-heap predicate **emp** is only satisfied by the empty heap, i.e., by a heap that consists of zero chunks:

Lemma 8. $(s, h) \models \mathbf{emp}$ *iff* $\mathsf{ams}(s, h) = \langle \mathsf{cls}_=(s), \emptyset, \emptyset, 0 \rangle$

Lemma 9. *1.* $(s, h) \models x = y$ *iff* $\mathsf{ams}(s, h) = \langle \mathsf{cls}_=(s), \emptyset, \emptyset, 0 \rangle$ *and* $[x]^s_= = [y]^s_=$.
2. $(s, h) \models x \neq y$ *iff* $\mathsf{ams}(s, h) = \langle \mathsf{cls}_=(s), \emptyset, \emptyset, 0 \rangle$ *and* $[x]^s_= \neq [y]^s_=$.

Models of points-to assertions consist of a single positive chunk of size 1:

Lemma 10. *Let* $E = \{[x]^s_= \mapsto \langle [y]^s_=, =1\rangle\}$. $(s,h) \models x \mapsto y$ *iff* $\mathsf{ams}(s,h) = \langle \mathsf{cls}_=(s), E, \emptyset, 0\rangle$.

Intuitively, the list segment $\mathtt{ls}(x,y)$ is satisfied by models (s,h) that consist of zero or more positive chunks, corresponding to a (possibly empty) list from some equivalence class $[x]^s_=$ to $[y]^s_=$ via (zero or more) intermediate equivalence classes $[x_1]^s_=, \ldots, [x_n]^s_=$. We will use this intuition to define abstract lists; this notion allows us to characterize the AMSs arising from abstracting lists.

Definition 7. *Let* $\mathcal{A} = \langle V, E, \rho, \gamma\rangle \in \mathbf{AMS}$, *s be a stack and* $x, y \in \mathbf{Var}$. *We say* A *is an* abstract list *w.r.t.* x *and* y, *in signs* $\mathcal{A} \in \mathbf{AbstLists}(x,y)$, *iff*

1. $V = \mathsf{cls}_=(s)$,
2. $\rho = \emptyset$ *and* $\gamma = 0$, *and*
3. *we can pick nodes* $\mathbf{v}_1, \ldots, \mathbf{v}_n \in V$ *and labels* $\iota_1, \ldots, \iota_{n-1} \in \{=1, \geq 2\}$ *such that* $x \in \mathbf{v}_1$, $y \in \mathbf{v}_n$ *and* $E = \{\mathbf{v}_i \mapsto \langle \mathbf{v}_{i+1}, \iota_i\rangle \mid 1 \leq i < n\}$. △

Lemma 11. $(s,h) \models \mathtt{ls}(x,y)$ *iff* $\mathsf{ams}(s,h) \in \mathbf{AbstLists}(x,y)$.

Abstract Memory States of Models composed by the Union Operator Our next goal is to lift the union operator $\uplus^s$ to the abstract domain **AMS**. We will define an operator $\bullet$ with the following property:

$$\text{if } h_1 \uplus^s h_2 \neq \bot \text{ then } \mathsf{ams}(s, h_1 \uplus^s h_2) = \mathsf{ams}(s,h_1) \bullet (s,h_2).$$

AMS composition is a partial operation defined only on *compatible* AMS. Compatibility enforces (1) that the AMSs were obtained for equivalent stacks (i.e., for stacks s, s' with $\mathsf{cls}_=(s) = \mathsf{cls}_=(s')$), and (2) that there is no double allocation.

Definition 8 (Compatibility of AMSs). *AMSs* $\mathcal{A}_1 = \langle V_1, E_1, \rho_1, \gamma_1\rangle$ *and* $\mathcal{A}_2 = \langle V_2, E_2, \rho_2, \gamma_2\rangle$ *are* compatible *iff (1)* $V_1 = V_2$ *and (2)* $\mathbf{alloc}(\mathcal{A}_1) \cap \mathbf{alloc}(\mathcal{A}_2) = \emptyset$.

Note that if $h_1 \uplus^s h_2$ is defined, then $\mathsf{ams}(s,h_1)$ and $\mathsf{ams}(s,h_2)$ are compatible. The converse is not true, because $\mathsf{ams}(s,h_1)$ and $\mathsf{ams}(s,h_2)$ may be compatible even if $\mathrm{dom}(h_1) \cap \mathrm{dom}(h_2) \neq \emptyset$.

AMS composition is defined in a point-wise manner on compatible AMSs and undefined otherwise.

Definition 9 (AMS composition). *Let* $\mathcal{A}_i = \langle V_i, E_i, \rho_i, \gamma_i\rangle$ *for* $i = 1, 2$ *be two AMS. The* composition *of* $\mathcal{A}_1, \mathcal{A}_2$ *is then given by*

$$\mathcal{A}_1 \bullet \mathcal{A}_2 := \begin{cases} \langle V_1, E_1 \cup E_2, \rho_1 \cup \rho_2, \gamma_1 + \gamma_2\rangle, & \text{if } \mathcal{A}_1, \mathcal{A}_2 \text{ compatible} \\ \bot, & \text{otherwise.} \end{cases}$$

Lemma 12. *Let s be a stack and let* h_1, h_2 *be heaps. If* $h_1 \uplus^s h_2 \neq \bot$ *then* $\mathsf{ams}(s,h_1) \bullet \mathsf{ams}(s,h_2) \neq \bot$.

We next show that $\mathsf{ams}(s, h_1 \uplus^s h_2) = \mathsf{ams}(s, h_1) \bullet \mathsf{ams}(s, h_2)$ whenever $h_1 \uplus^s h_2$ is defined:

Lemma 13 (Homomorphism of composition). *Let* $(s, h_1), (s, h_2)$ *be models with* $h_1 \uplus^s h_2 \neq \bot$. *Then,* $\mathsf{ams}(s, h_1 \uplus^s h_2) = \mathsf{ams}(s, h_1) \bullet \mathsf{ams}(s, h_2)$.

To show the refinement theorem, we need one additional property of AMS composition. If an AMS $\mathcal{A}$ of a model (s, h) can be decomposed into two smaller AMS $\mathcal{A} = \mathcal{A}_1 \bullet \mathcal{A}_2$, it is also possible to decompose the heap h into smaller heaps h_1, h_2 with $\mathsf{ams}(s, h_i) = \mathcal{A}_i$:

Lemma 14 (Decomposability of AMS). *Let* $\mathsf{ams}(s, h) = \mathcal{A}_1 \bullet \mathcal{A}_2$. *There exist* h_1, h_2 *with* $h = h_1 \uplus^s h_2$, $\mathsf{ams}(s, h_1) = \mathcal{A}_1$ *and* $\mathsf{ams}(s, h_2) = \mathcal{A}_2$.

These results suffice to prove the Refinement Theorem stated at the beginning of this section (see the extended version [33] for a proof).

Corollary 1. *Let* (s, h) *be a model and* φ *be a formula.* $(s, h) \models^{\mathsf{st}} \varphi$ *iff* $\mathsf{ams}(s, h) \in \alpha_s(\varphi)$.

3.4 Recursive Equations for Abstract Memory States

In this section, we derive recursive equations that reduce the set of AMS $\alpha_s(\varphi)$ for arbitrary compound formulas to the set of AMS of the constituent formulas of φ. In the next sections, we will show that we can actually evaluate these equations, thus obtaining an algorithm for computing the abstraction of arbitrary formulas.

Lemma 15. $\alpha_s(\varphi_1 \wedge \varphi_2) = \alpha_s(\varphi_1) \cap \alpha_s(\varphi_2)$.

Lemma 16. $\alpha_s(\varphi_1 \vee \varphi_2) = \alpha_s(\varphi_1) \cup \alpha_s(\varphi_2)$.

Lemma 17. $\alpha_s(\neg\varphi_1) = \{\mathsf{ams}(s, h) \mid h \in \mathbf{H}\} \setminus \alpha_s(\varphi_1)$.

The Separating Conjunction In Section 3.3, we defined the composition operation, $\bullet$, on pairs of AMS. We now lift this operation to sets of AMS $\mathbf{A}_1, \mathbf{A}_2$:

$$\mathbf{A}_1 \bullet \mathbf{A}_2 := \{\mathcal{A}_1 \bullet \mathcal{A}_2 \mid \mathcal{A}_1 \in \mathbf{A}_1, \mathcal{A}_2 \in \mathbf{A}_2, \mathcal{A}_1 \bullet \mathcal{A}_2 \neq \bot\}.$$

Lemma 13 implies that α_s is a homomorphism from formulas and $*$ to sets of AMS and $\bullet$:

Lemma 18. *For all* φ_1, φ_2, $\alpha_s(\varphi_1 * \varphi_2) = \alpha_s(\varphi_1) \bullet \alpha_s(\varphi_2)$.

The septraction operator. We next define an *abstract septraction operator* $-\!\bullet$ that relates to $\bullet$ in the same way that $-\!\circledast$ relates to $*$. For two sets of AMS $\mathbf{A}_1, \mathbf{A}_2$ we set:

$$\mathbf{A}_1 -\!\bullet\, \mathbf{A}_2 := \{\mathcal{A} \in \mathbf{AMS} \mid \text{ there exists } \mathcal{A}_1 \in \mathbf{A}_1 \text{ s.t. } \mathcal{A} \bullet \mathcal{A}_1 \in \mathbf{A}_2\}$$

Then, α_s is a homomorphism from formulas and $-\!\circledast$ to sets of AMS and $-\!\bullet$:

Lemma 19. *For all* φ_1, φ_2, $\alpha_s(\varphi_1 -\!\circledast\, \varphi_2) = \alpha_s(\varphi_1) -\!\bullet\, \alpha_s(\varphi_2)$.

3.5 Refining the Refinement Theorem: Bounding Garbage

Even though we have now characterized the set $\alpha_s(\varphi)$ for every formula φ, we do not yet have a way to implement AMS computation: While $\alpha_s(\varphi)$ is finite if φ is a spatial atom, the set is infinite in general; see the cases $\alpha_s(\neg\varphi)$ and $\alpha_s(\varphi_1 \text{-}\circledast \varphi_2)$. However, we note that for a fixed stack s only the garbage-chunk count γ of an AMS $\langle V, E, \rho, \gamma\rangle \in \alpha_s(\varphi)$ can be of arbitrary size, while the size of the nodes V, the edges E and the negative-allocation constraint ρ is bounded by $|s|$. Fortunately, to decide the satisfiability of any fixed formula φ, it is *not* necessary to keep track of arbitrarily large garbage-chunk counts.

We introduce the *chunk size* $\lceil\varphi\rceil$ of a formula φ, which provides an upper bound on the number of chunks that may be necessary to satisfy and/or falsify the formula; $\lceil\varphi\rceil$ is defined as follows:

- $\lceil \mathbf{emp} \rceil = \lceil x \mapsto y \rceil = \lceil \mathtt{ls}(x,y) \rceil = \lceil x = y \rceil = \lceil x \neq y \rceil := 1$
- $\lceil \varphi * \psi \rceil := \lceil\varphi\rceil + \lceil\psi\rceil$
- $\lceil \varphi \text{-}\circledast \psi \rceil := \lceil\psi\rceil$
- $\lceil \varphi \wedge \psi \rceil = \lceil \varphi \vee \psi \rceil := \max(\lceil\varphi\rceil, \lceil\psi\rceil)$
- $\lceil \neg\varphi \rceil := \lceil\varphi\rceil$.

Observe that $\lceil\varphi\rceil \leq |\varphi|$ for all φ. Intuitively, $\lceil\varphi\rceil - 1$ is an upper bound on the number of times the operation $\uplus^s$ needs to be applied when checking whether $(s,h) \overset{\text{st}}{\models} \varphi$. For example, let $\psi := x \mapsto y * ((b \mapsto c) \text{-}\circledast (\mathtt{ls}(a,c))$. Then $\lceil\psi\rceil = 2$, and to verify that ψ holds in a model that consists of a pointer from x to y and a list segment from a to b, it suffices to split this model $\lceil\varphi\rceil - 1 = 1$ many times using $\uplus^s$ (into the pointer and the list segment).

We generalize the refinement theorem, Theorem 2, to models whose AMS differ in their garbage-chunk count, provided both garbage-chunk counts exceed the chunk size of the formula:

Theorem 3 (Refined Refinement Theorem). *Let φ be a formula with $\lceil\varphi\rceil = k$. Let $m \geq k$, $n \geq k$ and let (s,h_1) and (s,h_2) be models such that* $\mathsf{ams}(s,h_1) = \langle V, E, \rho, m\rangle$, $\mathsf{ams}(s,h_2) = \langle V, E, \rho, n\rangle$. *Then, $(s,h_1) \overset{\text{st}}{\models} \varphi$ iff $(s,h_2) \overset{\text{st}}{\models} \varphi$.*

This implies that φ is satisfiable over stack s iff φ is satisfiable by a heap that contains at most $\lceil\varphi\rceil$ garbage chunks:

Corollary 2. *Let φ be an formula with $\lceil\varphi\rceil = k$. Then φ is satisfiable over stack s iff there exists a heap h such that (1)* $\mathsf{ams}(s,h) = (V, E, \rho, \gamma)$ *for some $\gamma \leq k$ and (2) $(s,h) \overset{\text{st}}{\models} \varphi$.*

3.6 Deciding SSL by AMS Computation

Due to Cor. 2, we can decide the SSL satisfiability problem by means of a function $\mathsf{abst}_s(\varphi)$ that computes the (finite) intersection of the (possibly infinite) set $\alpha_s(\varphi)$ and the (finite) set $\mathbf{AMS}_{k,s} := \{\langle V, E, \rho, \gamma\rangle \in \mathbf{AMS} \mid V = \mathsf{cls}_{=}(s) \text{ and } \gamma \leq k\}$ for $k = \lceil\varphi\rceil$. We define $\mathsf{abst}_s(\varphi)$ in Fig. 6. For atomic predicates we only need to consider garbage-chunk-count 0, whereas the cases $*$, $\text{-}\circledast$, $\wedge$ and $\vee$ require *lifting* the bound on the garbage-chunk count from m to $n \geq m$.

$$\begin{aligned}
\mathsf{abst}_s(\mathbf{emp}) &:= \{\langle \mathsf{cls}_=(s), \emptyset, \emptyset, 0\rangle\} \\
\mathsf{abst}_s(x = y) &:= \text{if } s(x) = s(y) \text{ then } \{\langle \mathsf{cls}_=(s), \emptyset, \emptyset, 0\rangle\} \text{ else } \emptyset \\
\mathsf{abst}_s(x \neq y) &:= \text{if } s(x) \neq s(y) \text{ then } \{\langle \mathsf{cls}_=(s), \emptyset, \emptyset, 0\rangle\} \text{ else } \emptyset \\
\mathsf{abst}_s(x \mapsto y) &:= \{\langle \mathsf{cls}_=(s), \{[x]^s_= \mapsto [y]^s_=\}, \emptyset, 0\rangle\} \\
\mathsf{abst}_s(\mathtt{ls}(x,y)) &:= \mathbf{AbstLists}(x,y) \cap \mathbf{AMS}_{0,s} \\
\mathsf{abst}_s(\varphi_1 * \varphi_2) &:= \mathbf{AMS}_{\lceil \varphi_1 * \varphi_2 \rceil, s} \cap \\
&\qquad (\mathsf{lift}_{\lceil \varphi_1 \rceil \nearrow \lceil \varphi_1 * \varphi_2 \rceil}(\mathsf{abst}_s(\varphi_1)) \bullet \mathsf{lift}_{\lceil \varphi_2 \rceil \nearrow \lceil \varphi_1 * \varphi_2 \rceil}(\mathsf{abst}_s(\varphi_2))) \\
\mathsf{abst}_s(\varphi_1 -\!\circledast \varphi_2) &:= \mathbf{AMS}_{\lceil \varphi_1 -\circledast \varphi_2 \rceil, s} \cap (\mathsf{abst}_s(\varphi_1) -\!\bullet \mathsf{lift}_{\lceil \varphi_2 \rceil \nearrow \lceil \varphi_1 \rceil + \lceil \varphi_2 \rceil}(\mathsf{abst}_s(\varphi_2))) \\
\mathsf{abst}_s(\varphi_1 \wedge \varphi_2) &:= \mathsf{lift}_{\lceil \varphi_1 \rceil \nearrow \lceil \varphi_1 \wedge \varphi_2 \rceil}(\mathsf{abst}_s(\varphi_1)) \cap \mathsf{lift}_{\lceil \varphi_2 \rceil \nearrow \lceil \varphi_1 \wedge \varphi_2 \rceil}(\mathsf{abst}_s(\varphi_2)) \\
\mathsf{abst}_s(\varphi_1 \vee \varphi_2) &:= \mathsf{lift}_{\lceil \varphi_1 \rceil \nearrow \lceil \varphi_1 \vee \varphi_2 \rceil}(\mathsf{abst}_s(\varphi_1)) \cup \mathsf{lift}_{\lceil \varphi_2 \rceil \nearrow \lceil \varphi_1 \vee \varphi_2 \rceil}(\mathsf{abst}_s(\varphi_2)) \\
\mathsf{abst}_s(\neg \varphi_1) &:= \mathbf{AMS}_{\lceil \varphi_1 \rceil, s} \setminus \mathsf{abst}_s(\varphi_1)
\end{aligned}$$

Fig. 6: Computing the abstract memory states of the models of φ with stack s.

Definition 10. *Let $m, n \in \mathbb{N}$ with $m \leq n$ and let $\mathcal{A} = \langle V, E, \rho, \gamma \rangle \in \mathbf{AMS}$. The* bound-lifting *of $\mathcal{A}$ from m to n is*

$$\mathsf{lift}_{m \nearrow n}(\mathcal{A}) := \begin{cases} \{\mathcal{A}\} & \text{if } \gamma < m \\ \{\langle V, E, \rho, k \rangle \mid m \leq k \leq n\} & \text{if } \gamma = m. \end{cases}$$

We generalize bound-lifting to sets of AMS: $\mathsf{lift}_{m \nearrow n}(\mathbf{A}) := \bigcup_{\mathcal{A} \in \mathbf{A}} \mathsf{lift}_{m \nearrow n}(\mathcal{A})$. △

As a consequence of Theorem 3 bound-lifting is sound for all $n \geq \lceil \varphi \rceil$, i.e.,

$$\mathsf{lift}_{\lceil \varphi \rceil \nearrow n}(\alpha_s(\varphi) \cap \mathbf{AMS}_{\lceil \varphi \rceil}) = \alpha_s(\varphi) \cap \mathbf{AMS}_n.$$

By combining this observation with the lemmas characterizing α_s, that is Lemmas 8,9,10, 11,15, 16,17, 18 and 19, we obtain the correctness of $\mathsf{abst}_s(\varphi)$:

Theorem 4. *Let s be a stack and φ be a formula. Then,* $\mathsf{abst}_s(\varphi) = \alpha_s(\varphi) \cap \mathbf{AMS}_{\lceil \varphi \rceil, s}$.

Computability of $\mathsf{abst}_s(\varphi)$. We note that the operators $\bullet, -\!\bullet, \cap, \cup$ and $\setminus$ are all computable as the sets that occur in the definition of $\mathsf{abst}_s(\varphi)$ are all finite. It remains to argue that we can compute the set of AMS for all atomic formulas. This is trivial for **emp**, (dis-)equalities, and points-to assertions. For the list-segment predicate, we note that the set $\mathsf{abst}_s(\mathtt{ls}(x,y)) = \mathbf{AbstLists}(x,y) \cap \mathbf{AMS}_{\lceil 0 \rceil, s}$ can be easily computed as there are only finitely many abstract lists w.r.t. the set of nodes $V = \mathsf{cls}_=(s)$. We obtain the following results:

Corollary 3. *Let s be a (finite) stack. Then $\mathsf{abst}_s(\varphi)$ is computable for all formulas φ.*

Theorem 5. *Let $\varphi \in$ **SL** and let $\mathbf{x} \subseteq$ **Var** be a finite set of variables with $\mathsf{fvs}(\varphi) \subseteq \mathbf{x}$. It is decidable whether there exists a model (s,h) with $\mathrm{dom}(s) = \mathbf{x}$ and $(s,h) \models^{\mathsf{st}} \varphi$.*

Corollary 4. *$\varphi \models^{\mathsf{st}}_{\mathbf{x}} \psi$ is decidable for all finite sets of variables $\mathbf{x} \subseteq$ **Var** and $\varphi, \psi \in$ **SL**.*

$$\mathsf{qbf\_to\_sl}(F) := \mathbf{emp} \wedge \bigwedge_{\text{pairwise different QBF variables } x,y} x \neq y \wedge \mathsf{aux}(F)$$

$$\mathsf{aux}(x) := (x \mapsto \mathsf{nil}) * \mathsf{t} \qquad \mathsf{aux}(\neg x) := \neg \mathsf{aux}(x)$$
$$\mathsf{aux}(F \wedge G) := \mathsf{aux}(F) \wedge \mathsf{aux}(G) \qquad \mathsf{aux}(F \vee G) := \mathsf{aux}(F) \vee \mathsf{aux}(G)$$
$$\mathsf{aux}(\exists x.\, F) := (x \mapsto \mathsf{nil} \vee \mathbf{emp}) -\!\circledast \mathsf{aux}(F) \qquad \mathsf{aux}(\forall x.\, F) := (x \mapsto \mathsf{nil} \vee \mathbf{emp}) -\!\!* \mathsf{aux}(F)$$

Fig. 7: Translation $\mathsf{qbf\_to\_sl}(F)$ from closed QBF formula F (in negation normal form) to a formula that is satisfiable iff F is true.

3.7 Complexity of the SSL Satisfiability Problem

It is easy to see that the algorithm $\mathsf{abst}_s(\varphi)$ runs in exponential time. We conclude this section with a proof that SSL satisfiability and entailment are actually PSPACE-complete.

PSPACE-*hardness.* An easy reduction from quantified Boolean formulas (QBF) shows that the SSL satisfiability problem is PSPACE-hard. The reduction is presented in Fig. 7. We encode positive literals x by $(x \mapsto \mathsf{nil}) * \mathsf{t}$ (the heap contains the pointer $x \mapsto \mathsf{nil}$) and negative literals by $\neg((x \mapsto \mathsf{nil}) * \mathsf{t})$ (the heap does not contain the pointer $x \mapsto \mathsf{nil}$). The magic wand is used to simulate universals (i.e., to enforce that we consider both the case $x \mapsto \mathsf{nil}$ and the case **emp**, setting x both to true and to false). Analogously, septraction is used to simulate existentials. Similar reductions can be found (for standard SL) in [12].

Lemma 20. *The SSL satisfiability problem is* PSPACE*-hard (even without the* `ls` *predicate).*

Note that this reduction simultaneously proves the PSPACE-hardness of SSL model checking: If F is a QBF formula over variables $x_1, \ldots, x_k$, then $\mathsf{qbf\_to\_sl}(F)$ is satisfiable iff $(\{x_i \mapsto l_i \mid 1 \leq i \leq n\}, \emptyset) \overset{\text{st}}{\models} \mathsf{qbf\_to\_sl}(F)$ for some locations ℓ_i with $\ell_i \neq \ell_j$ for $i \neq j$.

PSPACE-*membership.* For every stack s and every bound on the garbage-chunk count of the AMS we consider, it is possible to encode every AMS by a string of polynomial length.

Lemma 21. *Let $k \in \mathbb{N}$, let s be a stack and $n := k+|s|$. There exists an injective function* $\mathsf{encode}\colon \mathbf{AMS}_{k,s} \to \{0,1\}^*$ *such that*

$$|\mathsf{encode}(\mathcal{A})| \in \mathcal{O}(n \log(n)) \quad \textit{for all } \mathcal{A} \in \mathbf{AMS}_{k,s}.$$

An enumeration-based implementation of the algorithm in Fig. 6 (that has to keep in memory at most one AMS per subformula at any point in the computation) therefore runs in PSPACE:

Lemma 22. *Let $\varphi \in \mathbf{SL}$ and let $\mathbf{x} \subseteq \mathbf{Var}$ be a finite set of variables with $\mathsf{fvs}(\varphi) \subseteq \mathbf{x}$. It is decidable in* PSPACE *(in $|\varphi|$ and $|\mathbf{x}|$) whether there exists a model (s,h) with $\mathrm{dom}(s) = \mathbf{x}$ and $(s,h) \overset{\text{st}}{\models} \varphi$.*

The PSPACE-completeness result, Theorem 1, follows by combining Lemmas 20 and 22.

$$\frac{}{\{x \mapsto z\}\, x.\mathsf{next} := y\, \{x \mapsto y\}} \qquad \frac{}{\{\mathbf{emp}\}\, \mathsf{malloc}(x)\, \{x \mapsto m\}}$$

$$\frac{}{\{x \mapsto z\}\, \mathsf{free}(x)\, \{\mathbf{emp}\}} \qquad \frac{}{\{\mathbf{emp}\}\, x := y\, \{x = y\}}$$

$$\frac{}{\{y \mapsto z\}\, x := y.\mathsf{next}\, \{y \mapsto z * x = z\}}\; x \text{ different from } y$$

$$\frac{}{\{\mathbf{emp}\}\, \mathsf{assume}(\varphi)\, \{\varphi\}}\; \varphi \text{ is } x = y \text{ or } x \neq y$$

Fig. 8: Local proof rules of program statements for forward symbolic execution.

$$\text{Frame rule}\; \frac{\{P\}\, c\, \{Q\}}{\{A * P\}\, c\, \{A[\mathbf{x}'/\mathbf{x}] * Q\}}\; \mathbf{x} = \mathsf{modifiedVars}(c),\ \mathbf{x}' \text{ fresh}$$

$$\text{Materialization}\; \frac{\{P\}\, c\, \{Q\}}{\{P\}\, c\, \{x \mapsto z * ((x \mapsto z) \text{-}\!\circledast Q)\}}\; Q \not\models^{\mathsf{st}} \neg((x \mapsto \mathsf{nil}) \text{-}\!\circledast \mathsf{t}),\ z \text{ fresh}$$

Fig. 9: The frame and the materialization rule for forward symbolic execution.

4 Program Verification with Strong-Separation Logic

Our main practical motivation behind SSL is to obtain a decidable logic that can be used for fully automatically discharging verification conditions in a Hoare-style verification proof. Discharging VCs can be automated by calculi that symbolically execute pre-conditions forward resp. post-conditions backward, and then invoking an entailment checker. Symbolic execution calculi typically either introduce first-order quantifiers or fresh variables in order to deal with updates to the program variables. We leave the extension of SSL to support for quantifiers for future work and in this paper develop a forward symbolic execution calculus based on fresh variables.

We target the usual Hoare-style setting where a verification engineer annotates the pre- and post-condition of a function and provides loop invariants. We exemplify two annotated functions in Fig. 10; the left function reverses a list and the right function copies a list. In addition to the program variables, our annotations may contain logical variables (also known as ghost variables); for example, the annotations of list reverse only contain program variables, while the annotations of list copy also contain the logical variable u (which is assumed to be equal to x in the pre-condition)[8].

Forward Symbolic Execution Rules. We state local proof rules for a simple heap-manipulating programming language in Fig. 8. We remark that we do not include a rule for the statement x := x.next for ease of exposition; however, this is w.l.o.g. because x := x.next can be simulated by the statements y := x.next; x := y at the expense of introducing an additional program variable y. Our only non-standard choice is the modelling of the malloc statement: we assume a special program variable m, which is never referenced by any program statement and only used

[8] m is a special program variable introduced for modelling malloc.

in the modelling; the malloc statement updates the value of the variable m to the target of the newly allocated memory cell; this modelling justifies the proof rule for malloc stated in Fig. 8. For a small-step operational semantics of our program statements we refer the reader to the extended version [33]. The rules for the program statements in Fig. 8 are local in the sense that they only deal with a single pointer or the empty heap. The rules in Fig. 9 are the main rules of our forward symbolic execution calculus. The frame rule is essential for lifting the local proof rules to larger heaps. The materialization rule ensures that the frame rule can be applied whenever the pre-condition of a local proof rule can be met. We now give more details. For a sequence of program statements $\mathbf{c} = c_1 \cdots c_k$ and a pre-condition P_{start} the symbolic execution calculus derives triples $\{P_{start}\}\, c_1 \cdots c_i \,\{Q_i\}$ for all $1 \leq i \leq k$. In order to proceed from i to $i+1$, either 1) only the frame rule is applied or 2) the materialization rule is applied first followed by an application of the frame rule. The frame rule can be applied if the formula Q_i has the shape $Q_i = A * P$, where A is suitably chosen and P is the pre-condition of the local proof rule for statement c_i. Then, Q_{i+1} is given by $Q_{i+1} = A[\mathbf{x}'/\mathbf{x}] * Q$, where $\mathbf{x} = \mathsf{modifiedVars}(c)$, $\mathbf{x}'$ are fresh copies of the variables $\mathbf{x}$ and Q is the right hand side of the local proof rule for statement c_i, i.e., we have $\{P\}\, c_i \,\{Q\}$. Note that the frame rule requires substituting the modified program variables with fresh copies: We set $\mathsf{modifiedVars}(c) := \{x, m\}$ for $c = \mathsf{malloc}(x)$, $\mathsf{modifiedVars}(c) := \{x\}$ for $c = \mathsf{x} := \mathsf{y.next}$ and $c = \mathsf{x} := \mathsf{y}$, and $\mathsf{modifiedVars}(c) := \emptyset$, otherwise. The materialization rule may be applied in order to ensure that Q_i has the shape $Q_i = A * P$. This is not needed in case $P = \mathbf{emp}$ but may be necessary for $P = x \mapsto y$. We note that Q_i guarantees that a pointer x is allocated iff $Q_i \models^{\mathsf{st}} \neg((x \mapsto \mathsf{nil}) \circledast \mathsf{t})$. Under this condition, the rule allows introducing a name z for the target of the pointer x. We remark that while backward-symbolic execution calculi typically employ the magic wand, our forward calculus makes use of the dual septraction operator; we were able to design a general rule that guarantees a predicate of shape $Q_i = A * P$ without the need of coming up with dedicated rules for, e.g., unfolding list predicates.

Applying the forward symbolic execution calculus for verification. We now explain how the proof rules presented in Fig. 8 and 9 can be used for program verification. Our goal is to verify that the pre-condition P of a loop-free piece of code c (in our case, a sequence of program statements) implies the post-condition Q. For this, we apply the symbolic execution calculus and derive a triple $\{P\}\, c \,\{Q'\}$. It then remains to verify that the final state of the symbolic execution Q' implies the post-condition Q. Here, we face the difficulty that the symbolic execution introduces additional variables: Let us assume that all annotations are over a set of variables $\mathbf{x}$, which includes the program variables and the logical variables. Further assume that the symbolic execution $\{P\}\, c \{Q'\}$ introduced the fresh variables $\mathbf{y}$. With the results of Section 3 we can then verify the entailment $Q' \models^{\mathsf{st}}_{\mathbf{x} \cup \mathbf{y}} Q$. However, we need to guarantee that all models (s, h) of Q with $\mathrm{dom}(s) = \mathbf{x} \cup \mathbf{y}$ are also models when we restrict $\mathrm{dom}(s)$ to $\mathbf{x}$ (note that we can think of the variables $\mathbf{y}$ as implicitly existentially quantified). In order to deal with this issue, we require annotations to be robust:

```
{ls(x, nil)} % list reverse
  a := nil;
  while(x ≠ nil)
   {ls(x, nil) * ls(a, nil)}
   { b := x.next;
     x.next := a;
     a := x;
     w := b;    }
  x := w;
{ls(x, nil)}
```

```
{ls(x, nil) * u = x} % list copy
  malloc(s);
  r := s;
  while(x ≠ nil)
  {ls(u, x) * ls(x, nil) * ls(r, s) * s ↦ m}
  {  malloc(t);
     % t.data := x.data; not modelled
     s.next := t;
     s := t;
     y := x.next;
     x := y;    }
  s.next := nil;
{ls(u, nil) * ls(r, nil)}
```

Fig. 10: List reverse (left) and list copy (right) annotated pre- and post-condition and loop invariants.

Definition 11 (Robust Formula). *We call a formula* $\varphi \in \mathbf{SL}$ robust, *if for all models* (s_1, h) *and* (s_2, h) *with* $\mathsf{fvs}(\varphi) \subseteq \mathrm{dom}(s_1)$ *and* $\mathsf{fvs}(\varphi) \subseteq \mathrm{dom}(s_2)$ *and* $s_1(x) = s_2(x)$ *for all* $x \in \mathsf{fvs}(\varphi)$*, we have that* $(s_1, h) \overset{\mathsf{st}}{\models} \varphi$ *iff* $(s_2, h) \overset{\mathsf{st}}{\models} \varphi$.

Lemma 23. *Let* $\varphi \in \mathbf{SL}$ *be a positive formula. Then,* φ *is robust.*

Lemma 4 states that all formulas from the positive fragment are robust. In particular, the annotations in Fig. 10 are robust. As an example for a non-robust formula consider φ in Example 1. We note that Lemma 4 does not cover all robust formulas, e.g., t is robust. We leave the identification of further robust formulas for future work.

We now state the soundness of our symbolic execution calculus:

Lemma 24 (Soundness of Forward Symbolic Execution). *Let* **c** *be a sequence of program statements, let* P *be a robust formula, let* $\{P\}\,\mathbf{c}\,\{Q\}$ *be the triple obtained from symbolic execution, and let* V *be the fresh variables introduced during symbolic execution. Then,* Q *is robust and for all stack-heap pairs* $(s, h), (s', h')$ *such that* $(s, h) \overset{\mathsf{st}}{\models} P$ *and* (s', h') *can be obtained from* (s, h) *by executing* **c***, there is a stack* s'' *with* $s' \subseteq s''$*,* $V \subseteq \mathrm{dom}(s'')$ *and* $(s'', h') \overset{\mathsf{st}}{\models} Q$.

Automation. We note that the presented approach can fully-automatically verify that the pre-condition of a loop-free piece of code guarantees its post-condition: For every program statement, we apply its local proof rule using the frame rule (and in addition the materialization rule in case the existence of a pointer target must be guaranteed). We then discharge the entailment query using our decision procedure from Section 3. We now illustrate this approach on the programs from Fig. 10. For both programs we verify that the loop invariant is inductive (in both cases the loop-invariant P is propagated forward through the loop body; it is then checked that the obtained formula Q again implies the loop invariant P; for verifying the implication we apply our decision procedure from Corollary 4):

Example 6. Verifying the loop invariant of list reverse:

$\{\mathtt{ls}(x, \mathsf{nil}) * \mathtt{ls}(a, \mathsf{nil})\}\ (=: P)$

`assume(x ≠ nil)`

$\{\mathtt{ls}(x, \mathsf{nil}) * \mathtt{ls}(a, \mathsf{nil}) * x \neq \mathsf{nil}\}$

`# materialization`

$\{x \mapsto z \mathbin{-\circledast} (\mathtt{ls}(x, \mathsf{nil}) * \mathtt{ls}(a, \mathsf{nil}) * x \neq \mathsf{nil}) * x \mapsto z\}$

`b := x.next`

$\{x \mapsto z \mathbin{-\circledast} (\mathtt{ls}(x, \mathsf{nil}) * \mathtt{ls}(a, \mathsf{nil}) * x \neq \mathsf{nil}) * x \mapsto z * b = z\}$

`x.next := a`

$\{x \mapsto z \mathbin{-\circledast} (\mathtt{ls}(x, \mathsf{nil}) * \mathtt{ls}(a, \mathsf{nil}) * x \neq \mathsf{nil}) * x \mapsto a * b = z\}$

`a := x`

$\{x \mapsto z \mathbin{-\circledast} (\mathtt{ls}(x, \mathsf{nil}) * \mathtt{ls}(a', \mathsf{nil}) * x \neq \mathsf{nil}) * x \mapsto a' * b = z * a = x\}$

`x := b`

$$\{x' \mapsto z \mathbin{-\circledast} (\mathtt{ls}(x', \mathsf{nil}) * \mathtt{ls}(a', \mathsf{nil}) * x' \neq \mathsf{nil}) * x' \mapsto a' * b = z * a = x' * x = b\}\ (=: Q)$$

$\{\mathtt{ls}(x, \mathsf{nil}) * \mathtt{ls}(a, \mathsf{nil})\}\ (=: P)$

Example 7. Verifying the loop invariant of list copy:

$\{\mathtt{ls}(u, x) * \mathtt{ls}(x, \mathsf{nil}) * \mathtt{ls}(r, s) * s \mapsto m\}\ (=: P)$

`assume(x ≠ nil)`

$\{\mathtt{ls}(u, x) * \mathtt{ls}(x, \mathsf{nil}) * \mathtt{ls}(r, s) * s \mapsto m * x \neq \mathsf{nil}\}$

`malloc(t)`

$\{\mathtt{ls}(u, x) * \mathtt{ls}(x, \mathsf{nil}) * \mathtt{ls}(r, s) * s \mapsto m' * x \neq \mathsf{nil} * t \mapsto m\}$

`s.next := t`

$\{\mathtt{ls}(u, x) * \mathtt{ls}(x, \mathsf{nil}) * \mathtt{ls}(r, s) * s \mapsto t * x \neq \mathsf{nil} * t \mapsto m\}$

`s := t`

$\{\mathtt{ls}(u, x) * \mathtt{ls}(x, \mathsf{nil}) * \mathtt{ls}(r, s') * s' \mapsto t * x \neq \mathsf{nil} * t \mapsto m * s = t\}$

`# materialization`

$$\{x \mapsto z \mathbin{-\circledast} (\mathtt{ls}(u, x) * \mathtt{ls}(x, \mathsf{nil}) * \mathtt{ls}(r, s') * s' \mapsto t * x \neq \mathsf{nil} * t \mapsto m * s = t) * x \mapsto z\}$$

`y := x.next`

$$\{x \mapsto z \mathbin{-\circledast} (\mathtt{ls}(u, x) * \mathtt{ls}(x, \mathsf{nil}) * \mathtt{ls}(r, s') * s' \mapsto t * x \neq \mathsf{nil} * t \mapsto m * s = t) * x \mapsto z * y = z\}$$

`x := y`

$$\{x' \mapsto z \mathbin{-\circledast} (\mathtt{ls}(u, x') * \mathtt{ls}(x', \mathsf{nil}) * \mathtt{ls}(r, s') * s' \mapsto t * x' \neq \mathsf{nil} * t \mapsto m * s = t) * x' \mapsto z * y = z * x = y\}\ (=: Q)$$

$\{\mathtt{ls}(u, x) * \mathtt{ls}(x, \mathsf{nil}) * \mathtt{ls}(r, s) * s \mapsto m\}\ (=: P)$

While our decision procedure can automatically discharge the entailments in both of the above examples, we give a short direct argument for the benefit of the reader for the entailment check of Example 6 (a direct argument could similarly be worked out for Example 7): We note that Q' simplifies to $Q'' = \{a \mapsto x \text{-}\circledast (\mathtt{ls}(a, \mathsf{nil}) * \mathtt{ls}(a', \mathsf{nil})) * a \mapsto a'\}$. Every model (s, h) of Q'' must consist of a pointer $a \mapsto a'$, a list segment $\mathtt{ls}(a', \mathsf{nil})$ and a heap h' to which the pointer $a \mapsto x$ can be added in order to obtain the list segment $\mathtt{ls}(a, \mathsf{nil})$; by looking at the semantics of the list segment predicate we see that h' in fact must be the list segment $\mathtt{ls}(x, \mathsf{nil})$. Further, the pointer $a \mapsto a'$ can be composed with the list segment $\mathtt{ls}(a', \mathsf{nil})$ in order to obtain $\mathtt{ls}(a, \mathsf{nil})$.

5 Normal Forms and the Abduction Problem

In this section, we discuss how every AMS can be expressed by a formula, which in turn makes it possible to compute a normal form for every formula. We then discuss how the normal form transformation has applications to the abduction problem.

Normal Form. We lift the abstraction functions from stacks to sets of variables: Let $\mathbf{x} \subseteq \mathbf{Var}$ be a finite set of variables and $\varphi \in \mathbf{SL}$ be a formula with $\mathsf{fvs}(\varphi) \subseteq \mathbf{x}$. We set $\alpha_{\mathbf{x}}(\varphi) := \{\alpha_{\mathbf{s}}(\varphi) \mid \mathrm{dom}(s) = \mathbf{x}\}$ and $\mathsf{abst}_{\mathbf{x}}(\varphi) := \alpha_{\mathbf{x}}(\varphi) \cap \mathbf{AMS}_{\lceil\varphi\rceil,\mathbf{x}}$, where $\mathbf{AMS}_{k,\mathbf{x}} := \{\langle V, E, \rho, \gamma\rangle \in \mathbf{AMS} \mid \bigcup V = \mathbf{x} \text{ and } \gamma \leq k\}$. (We note that $\alpha_{\mathbf{x}}(\varphi)$ is computable by the same argument as in the proof of Theorem 5.)

Definition 12 (Normal Form). *Let* $\mathsf{NF}_{\mathbf{x}}(\varphi) := \bigvee_{\mathcal{A}\in\alpha_{\mathbf{x}}(\varphi)} \mathsf{AMS2SL}^{\lceil\varphi\rceil}(\mathcal{A})$ *the* normal form *of* φ*, where* $\mathsf{AMS2SL}^{m}(\mathcal{A})$ *is defined as in Fig. 11.* △

The definition of $\mathsf{AMS2SL}^{m}(\mathcal{A})$ represents a straightforward encoding of the AMS $\mathcal{A}$: *aliasing* encodes the aliasing between the stack variables as implied by V; *graph* encodes the points-to assertions and lists of length at least two corresponding to the edges E; *negalloc* encodes that the negative chunks $R \in \rho$ precisely allocate the variables $\mathbf{v} \in R$; *garbage* ensures that there are either exactly γ additional non-empty memory chunks that do not allocate any stack variable (if $\gamma < m$) or at least γ such chunks (if $\gamma = m$); *negalloc* and *garbage* use the formula *negchunk* which precisely encodes the definition of a negative chunk. We have the following result about normal forms:

Theorem 6. $\mathsf{NF}_{\mathbf{x}}(\varphi) \models^{\mathsf{st}}_{\mathbf{x}} \varphi$ *and* $\varphi \models^{\mathsf{st}}_{\mathbf{x}} \mathsf{NF}_{\mathbf{x}}(\varphi)$.

The abduction problem. We consider the following relaxation of the entailment problem: The *abduction problem* is to replace the question mark in the entailment $\varphi * [?] \models^{\mathsf{st}}_{\mathbf{x}} \psi$ by a formula such that the entailment becomes true. This problem

$$
\begin{aligned}
\mathsf{AMS2SL}^m(\mathcal{A}) &:= \mathsf{aliasing}(\mathcal{A}) * \mathsf{graph}(\mathcal{A}) * \mathsf{negalloc}(\mathcal{A}) * \mathsf{garbage}^m(\mathcal{A}) \\
\mathsf{aliasing}(\mathcal{A}) &:= \left(\mathop{\ast}_{\mathbf{v}\in V, x,y\in\mathbf{v}} x = y \right) * \left(\mathop{\ast}_{\mathbf{v},\mathbf{w}\in V, \mathbf{v}\neq\mathbf{w}} \max(\mathbf{v}) \neq \max(\mathbf{w}) \right) \\
\mathsf{graph}(\mathcal{A}) &:= \left(\mathop{\ast}_{E(\mathbf{v})=\langle\mathbf{v}',=1\rangle} \max(\mathbf{v}) \mapsto \max(\mathbf{v}') \right) * \\
&\qquad \left(\mathop{\ast}_{E(\mathbf{v})=\langle\mathbf{v}',\geq 2\rangle} \mathtt{ls}_{\geq 2}(\max(\mathbf{v}), \max(\mathbf{v}')) \right) \\
\mathsf{negalloc}(\mathcal{A}) &:= \mathop{\ast}_{R\in\rho} \mathsf{negchunk}(\mathcal{A}) \wedge \bigwedge_{\mathbf{v}\in R} \mathsf{alloc}(\max(\mathbf{v})) \wedge \bigwedge_{\mathbf{v}\in V\setminus R} \neg\mathsf{alloc}(\max(\mathbf{v})) \\
\mathsf{garbage}^m(\mathcal{A}) &:= \begin{cases} \mathsf{garbage}(\mathcal{A},\gamma) & \text{if } \gamma < m \\ \mathsf{garbage}(\mathcal{A}, m\text{-}1) * \neg\mathbf{emp} \bigwedge_{\mathbf{v}\in V} \neg\mathsf{alloc}(\max(\mathbf{v})) & \text{otherwise} \end{cases} \\
\mathsf{garbage}(\mathcal{A},k) &:= \begin{cases} \mathbf{emp} & \text{if } k = 0 \\ \mathsf{garbage}(\mathcal{A}, k\text{-}1) * \mathsf{negchunk}(\mathcal{A}) \wedge \bigwedge_{\mathbf{v}\in V} \neg\mathsf{alloc}(\max(\mathbf{v})) & \text{otherwise} \end{cases} \\
\mathsf{negchunk}(\mathcal{A}) &:= \neg\mathbf{emp} \wedge \neg(\neg\mathbf{emp} * \neg\mathbf{emp}) \wedge \\
&\qquad \bigwedge_{\mathbf{v},\mathbf{w}\in V, \varphi\in\{\max(\mathbf{v})\mapsto\max(\mathbf{w}), \mathtt{ls}(\max(\mathbf{v}),\max(\mathbf{w}))\}} \neg\varphi \\
\mathsf{alloc}(x) &:= \neg((x \mapsto \mathsf{nil}) \mathrel{-\circledast} \mathsf{t}) \\
\mathtt{ls}_{\geq 2}(x,y) &:= \mathtt{ls}(x,y) \wedge \neg(x \mapsto y)
\end{aligned}
$$

Fig. 11: The induced formula $\mathsf{AMS2SL}^m(\mathcal{A})$ of AMS $\mathcal{A} = \langle V, E, \rho, \gamma\rangle$ with $\gamma \leq m$.

is central for obtaining a scalable program analyzer as discussed in [10] [9]. The abduction problem does in general not have a unique solution. Following [10], we thus consider optimization versions of the abduction problem, looking for *logically weakest* and *spatially minimal* solutions:

Definition 13. *Let* $\varphi, \psi \in \mathbf{SL}$ *and* $\mathbf{x} \subseteq \mathbf{Var}$ *be a finite set of variables. A formula* ζ *is the* weakest *solution to the abduction problem* $\varphi * [?] \models^{st}_{\mathbf{x}} \psi$ *if it holds for all abduction solutions* ζ' *that* $\zeta' \models^{st}_{\mathbf{x}} \zeta$*. An abduction solution is* ζ minimal, *if there is no abduction solution* ζ' *with* $\zeta \models^{st}_{\mathbf{x}} \zeta' * (\neg\mathbf{emp})$.

Lemma 25. *Let* φ, ψ *be formulas and let* $\mathbf{x} \subseteq \mathbf{Var}$ *be a finite set of variables. Then, 1) the weakest solution to the abduction problem* $\varphi * [?] \models^{st}_{\mathbf{x}} \psi$ *is given by the formula* $\varphi \mathrel{-\!\!*} \psi$*, and the 2) weakest minimal solution is given by the formula* $\varphi \mathrel{-\!\!*} \psi \wedge \neg((\varphi \mathrel{-\!\!*} \psi) * \neg\mathbf{emp})$.

[9] While the program analyzer proposed in [10] employs *bi-abductive* reasoning, the bi-abduction procedure in fact proceeds in two separate abduction and frame-inference steps, where the main technical challenge is the abduction step, as frame inference can be incorporated into entailment checking. We believe that the situation for SSL is similar, i.e., solving abduction is the key to implementing a bi-abductive prover for SSL; hence, our focus on the abduction problem.

We now explain how the normal form has applications to the abduction problem. According to Lemma 25, the best solutions to the abduction problem are given by the formulas $\zeta := \varphi \mathrel{-\!\!*} \psi$ and $\zeta' := \varphi \mathrel{-\!\!*} \psi \wedge \neg((\varphi \mathrel{-\!\!*} \psi) * \neg \mathbf{emp})$. While it is great that the existence of these solutions is guaranteed, we a-priori do not have a means to *compute* an explicit representation of these solutions nor to further analyze their structure. However, the normal form operator allows us to obtain the explicit representations $\mathsf{NF}_{\mathbf{x}}(\zeta)$ and $\mathsf{NF}_{\mathbf{x}}(\zeta')$. We believe that using these explicit representations in a program analyzer or studying their properties is an interesting topic for further research. Here, we establish one concrete result on solutions to the abduction problem based on normal forms:

We can compute the weakest resp. the weakest minimal solution to the abduction problem from the positive fragment. Observe that among the sub-formulas of $\mathsf{aliasing}$ and graph, only the formula $\mathtt{ls}_{\geq 2}$ is negative. To be able to use $\mathtt{ls}_{\geq 2}(x, y)$ in a positive formula, we first need to add a new spatial atom $\mathtt{ls}_{\geq 2}(x, y)$ to SSL with the following semantics: $\mathtt{ls}_{\geq 2}(x, y)$ holds in a model iff the model is a list segment of length at least 2 from x to y. (The whole development in Sections 2 and 3 can be extended by this predicate.) We can then simplify the formula $\mathsf{graph}(\mathcal{A})$ in $\mathsf{AMS2SL}^m(\mathcal{A})$ by directly translating edges $E(\mathbf{v}) = \langle \mathbf{v}', \geq 2 \rangle$ to the atom $\mathtt{ls}_{\geq 2}(\max(\mathbf{v}), \max(\mathbf{v}'))$. Then, $\bigvee_{\langle V,E,\rho,\gamma \rangle \in \alpha_{\mathbf{x}}(\zeta) \text{ with } \rho=\emptyset,\gamma=0} \mathsf{AMS2SL}^{\lceil \varphi \rceil}(\mathcal{A})$ for $\zeta = \varphi \mathrel{-\!\!*} \psi$ or $\zeta = \varphi \mathrel{-\!\!*} \psi \wedge \neg((\varphi \mathrel{-\!\!*} \psi) * \neg \mathbf{emp})$ is the weakest resp. the weakest minimal solution to the abduction problem from the positive fragment.

6 Conclusion

We have shown that the satisfiability problem for "strong" separation logic with lists is in the same complexity class as the satisfiability problem for standard "weak" separation logic without any data structures: PSPACE-complete. This is in stark contrast to the undecidability result for standard (weak) SL semantics, as shown in [16].

We have demonstrated the potential of SSL for program verification: 1) We have provided symbolic execution rules that, in conjunction with our result on the decidability of entailment, can be used for fully-automatically discharging verification conditions. 2) We have discussed how to compute explicit representations to optimal solutions of the abduction problem. This constitutes the first work that addresses the abduction problem for a separation logic closed under Boolean operators and the magic wand.

We consider our results just the first steps in examining strong-separation logic, motivated by the desire to circumvent the undecidability result of [16]. Future work is concerned with the practical evaluation of our decision procedures, with extending the symbolic execution calculus to a full Hoare logic as well as extending the results of this paper to richer separation logics (SL) such as SL with nested data structures or SL with limited support for arithmetic reasoning.

References

1. T. Antonopoulos, N. Gorogiannis, C. Haase, M. I. Kanovich, and J. Ouaknine. Foundations for decision problems in separation logic with general inductive predicates. In *Foundations of Software Science and Computation Structures - 17th International Conference, FOSSACS 2014, Held as Part of the European Joint Conferences on Theory and Practice of Software, ETAPS 2014, Grenoble, France, April 5-13, 2014, Proceedings*, pages 411–425. Springer Berlin Heidelberg, 2014.
2. A. W. Appel. *Program Logics - for Certified Compilers.* Cambridge University Press, 2014.
3. J. Berdine, C. Calcagno, and P. W. O'Hearn. A decidable fragment of separation logic. In *FSTTCS 2004: Foundations of Software Technology and Theoretical Computer Science, 24th International Conference, Chennai, India, December 16-18, 2004, Proceedings*, pages 97–109. Springer, 2004.
4. J. Berdine, C. Calcagno, and P. W. O'Hearn. Symbolic execution with separation logic. In *Programming Languages and Systems, Third Asian Symposium, APLAS 2005, Tsukuba, Japan, November 2-5, 2005, Proceedings*, pages 52–68. 2005.
5. J. Berdine, B. Cook, and S. Ishtiaq. Slayer: Memory safety for systems-level code. In *Computer Aided Verification - 23rd International Conference, CAV 2011, Snowbird, UT, USA, July 14-20, 2011. Proceedings*, pages 178–183, 2011.
6. S. Blom and M. Huisman. Witnessing the elimination of magic wands. *International Journal on Software Tools for Technology Transfer*, 17(6):757–781, 2015.
7. R. Bornat, C. Calcagno, P. W. O'Hearn, and M. J. Parkinson. Permission accounting in separation logic. In *Proceedings of the 32nd ACM SIGPLAN-SIGACT Symposium on Principles of Programming Languages, POPL 2005, Long Beach, California, USA, January 12-14, 2005*, pages 259–270, 2005.
8. R. Brochenin, S. Demri, and E. Lozes. On the almighty wand. *Information and Computation*, 211:106 – 137, 2012.
9. C. Calcagno, D. Distefano, J. Dubreil, D. Gabi, P. Hooimeijer, M. Luca, P. O'Hearn, I. Papakonstantinou, J. Purbrick, and D. Rodriguez. Moving fast with software verification. In K. Havelund, G. Holzmann, and R. Joshi, editors, *NASA Formal Methods: 7th International Symposium, NFM 2015, Pasadena, CA, USA, April 27-29, 2015, Proceedings*, pages 3–11, Cham, 2015. Springer International Publishing.
10. C. Calcagno, D. Distefano, P. W. O'Hearn, and H. Yang. Compositional shape analysis by means of bi-abduction. *J. ACM*, 58(6):26:1–26:66, Dec. 2011.
11. C. Calcagno, P. O'Hearn, and H. Yang. Local action and abstract separation logic. In *Logic in Computer Science, 2007. LICS 2007. 22nd Annual IEEE Symposium on*, pages 366–378, July 2007.
12. C. Calcagno, H. Yang, and P. O'Hearn. Computability and complexity results for a spatial assertion language for data structures. In R. Hariharan, V. Vinay, and M. Mukund, editors, *FST TCS 2001: Foundations of Software Technology and Theoretical Computer Science*, volume 2245 of *Lecture Notes in Computer Science*, pages 108–119. Springer Berlin Heidelberg, 2001.
13. B. Cook, C. Haase, J. Ouaknine, M. J. Parkinson, and J. Worrell. Tractable reasoning in a fragment of separation logic. In *CONCUR 2011 - Concurrency Theory - 22nd International Conference, CONCUR 2011, Aachen, Germany, September 6-9, 2011. Proceedings*, pages 235–249, 2011.
14. S. Demri and M. Deters. Expressive completeness of separation logic with two variables and no separating conjunction. In *Proceedings of the Joint Meeting of the*

Twenty-Third EACSL Annual Conference on Computer Science Logic (CSL) and the Twenty-Ninth Annual ACM/IEEE Symposium on Logic in Computer Science (LICS), CSL-LICS '14, pages 37:1–37:10, New York, NY, USA, 2014. ACM.
15. S. Demri, D. Galmiche, D. Larchey-Wendling, and D. Méry. Separation logic with one quantified variable. In E. Hirsch, S. Kuznetsov, J.-É. Pin, and N. Vereshchagin, editors, *Computer Science - Theory and Applications*, volume 8476 of *Lecture Notes in Computer Science*, pages 125–138. Springer International Publishing, 2014.
16. S. Demri, É. Lozes, and A. Mansutti. The effects of adding reachability predicates in propositional separation logic. In C. Baier and U. Dal Lago, editors, *Foundations of Software Science and Computation Structures*, pages 476–493, Cham, 2018. Springer International Publishing.
17. K. Dudka, P. Peringer, and T. Vojnar. Predator: A practical tool for checking manipulation of dynamic data structures using separation logic. In *Computer Aided Verification - 23rd International Conference, CAV 2011, Snowbird, UT, USA, July 14-20, 2011. Proceedings*, pages 372–378, 2011.
18. M. Echenim, R. Iosif, and N. Peltier. The bernays-schönfinkel-ramsey class of separation logic on arbitrary domains. In M. Bojańczyk and A. Simpson, editors, *Foundations of Software Science and Computation Structures*, pages 242–259, Cham, 2019. Springer International Publishing.
19. N. Gorogiannis, M. Kanovich, and P. W. O'Hearn. The complexity of abduction for separated heap abstractions. In E. Yahav, editor, *Static Analysis: 18th International Symposium, SAS 2011, Venice, Italy, September 14-16, 2011. Proceedings*, pages 25–42, Berlin, Heidelberg, 2011. Springer Berlin Heidelberg.
20. X. Gu, T. Chen, and Z. Wu. A complete decision procedure for linearly compositional separation logic with data constraints. In *Automated Reasoning - 8th International Joint Conference, IJCAR 2016, Coimbra, Portugal, June 27 - July 2, 2016, Proceedings*, pages 532–549, 2016.
21. R. Iosif, A. Rogalewicz, and J. Simácek. The tree width of separation logic with recursive definitions. In *Automated Deduction - CADE-24 - 24th International Conference on Automated Deduction, Lake Placid, NY, USA, June 9-14, 2013. Proceedings*, pages 21–38, 2013.
22. R. Iosif, A. Rogalewicz, and T. Vojnar. Deciding entailments in inductive separation logic with tree automata. In *Automated Technology for Verification and Analysis - 12th International Symposium, ATVA 2014, Sydney, NSW, Australia, November 3-7, 2014, Proceedings*, pages 201–218, 2014.
23. S. S. Ishtiaq and P. W. O'Hearn. BI as an assertion language for mutable data structures. In *Conference Record of POPL 2001: The 28th ACM SIGPLAN-SIGACT Symposium on Principles of Programming Languages, London, UK, January 17-19, 2001*, pages 14–26, 2001.
24. B. Jacobs, J. Smans, P. Philippaerts, F. Vogels, W. Penninckx, and F. Piessens. Verifast: A powerful, sound, predictable, fast verifier for C and java. In *NASA Formal Methods - Third International Symposium, NFM 2011, Pasadena, CA, USA, April 18-20, 2011. Proceedings*, pages 41–55, 2011.
25. J. Katelaan, D. Jovanović, and G. Weissenbacher. A separation logic with data: Small models and automation. In D. Galmiche, S. Schulz, and R. Sebastiani, editors, *Automated Reasoning*, pages 455–471, Cham, 2018. Springer International Publishing.
26. J. Katelaan, C. Matheja, and F. Zuleger. Effective entailment checking for separation logic with inductive definitions. In *Tools and Algorithms for the Construction and Analysis of Systems - 25th International Conference, TACAS 2019,*

Held as Part of the European Joint Conferences on Theory and Practice of Software, ETAPS 2019, Prague, Czech Republic, April 6-11, 2019, Proceedings, Part II, pages 319–336, 2019.

27. J. Katelaan and F. Zuleger. Beyond symbolic heaps: Deciding separation logic with inductive definitions. In E. Albert and L. Kovács, editors, *LPAR 2020: 23rd International Conference on Logic for Programming, Artificial Intelligence and Reasoning, Alicante, Spain, May 22-27, 2020*, volume 73 of *EPiC Series in Computing*, pages 390–408. EasyChair, 2020.
28. Q. L. Le, M. Tatsuta, J. Sun, and W. Chin. A decidable fragment in separation logic with inductive predicates and arithmetic. In *Computer Aided Verification - 29th International Conference, CAV 2017, Heidelberg, Germany, July 24-28, 2017, Proceedings, Part II*, pages 495–517, 2017.
29. P. Madhusudan, G. Parlato, and X. Qiu. Decidable logics combining heap structures and data. In *Proceedings of the 38th Annual ACM SIGPLAN-SIGACT Symposium on Principles of Programming Languages*, POPL '11, pages 611–622, New York, NY, USA, 2011. ACM.
30. P. W. O'Hearn. Resources, concurrency, and local reasoning. *Theor. Comput. Sci.*, 375(1-3):271–307, 2007.
31. J. Pagel. *Decision Procedures for Separation Logic: Beyond Symbolic Heaps.* PhD thesis, TU Wien, 2020. `https://repositum.tuwien.at/handle/20.500.12708/16333`.
32. J. Pagel, C. Matheja, and F. Zuleger. Complete entailment checking for separation logic with inductive definitions. *CoRR*, abs/2002.01202, 2020.
33. J. Pagel and F. Zuleger. Strong-separation logic. *CoRR*, abs/2001.06235, 2020.
34. J. A. N. Pérez and A. Rybalchenko. Separation logic modulo theories. In *Programming Languages and Systems - 11th Asian Symposium, APLAS 2013, Melbourne, VIC, Australia, December 9-11, 2013. Proceedings*, pages 90–106. 2013.
35. R. Piskac, T. Wies, and D. Zufferey. Automating separation logic using SMT. In N. Sharygina and H. Veith, editors, *Computer Aided Verification*, volume 8044 of *Lecture Notes in Computer Science*, pages 773–789. Springer Berlin Heidelberg, 2013.
36. R. Piskac, T. Wies, and D. Zufferey. Automating separation logic with trees and data. In *Computer Aided Verification - 26th International Conference, CAV 2014, Held as Part of the Vienna Summer of Logic, VSL 2014, Vienna, Austria, July 18-22, 2014. Proceedings*, pages 711–728, 2014.
37. X. Qiu, P. Garg, A. Stefanescu, and P. Madhusudan. Natural proofs for structure, data, and separation. In *ACM SIGPLAN Conference on Programming Language Design and Implementation, PLDI '13, Seattle, WA, USA, June 16-19, 2013*, pages 231–242, 2013.
38. A. Reynolds, R. Iosif, and C. Serban. Reasoning in the bernays-schönfinkel-ramsey fragment of separation logic. In *Verification, Model Checking, and Abstract Interpretation - 18th International Conference, VMCAI 2017, Paris, France, January 15-17, 2017, Proceedings*, pages 462–482, 2017.
39. A. Reynolds, R. Iosif, C. Serban, and T. King. A decision procedure for separation logic in smt. In C. Artho, A. Legay, and D. Peled, editors, *Automated Technology for Verification and Analysis*, pages 244–261, Cham, 2016. Springer International Publishing.
40. J. C. Reynolds. Separation logic: A logic for shared mutable data structures. In *17th IEEE Symposium on Logic in Computer Science (LICS 2002), 22-25 July 2002, Copenhagen, Denmark, Proceedings*, pages 55–74, 2002.

41. M. Schwerhoff and A. J. Summers. Lightweight support for magic wands in an automatic verifier. In *29th European Conference on Object-Oriented Programming, ECOOP 2015, July 5-10, 2015, Prague, Czech Republic*, pages 614–638, 2015.
42. M. Tatsuta and D. Kimura. Separation logic with monadic inductive definitions and implicit existentials. In *Programming Languages and Systems - 13th Asian Symposium, APLAS 2015, Pohang, South Korea, November 30 - December 2, 2015, Proceedings*, pages 69–89, 2015.

Author Index

Printed in the United States
by Baker & Taylor Publisher Services

Printed in the United States
by Baker & Taylor Publisher Services